ADVANCED TOPICS IN FORENSIC DNA TYPING

This work was funded in part by the National Institute of Justice (NIJ) through interagency agreement 2008-DN-R-121 with the NIST Office of Law Enforcement Standards. Points of view in this document are those of the author and do not necessarily represent the official position or policies of the U.S. Department of Justice. Certain commercial equipment, instruments, and materials are identified in order to specify experimental procedures as completely as possible. In no case does such identification imply a recommendation or endorsement by the National Institute of Standards and Technology nor does it imply that any of the materials, instruments, or equipment identified are necessarily the best available for the purpose.

Completed February 2011

ADVANCED TOPICS IN FORENSIC DNA TYPING: METHODOLOGY

John M. Butler

National Institute of Standards and Technology
Gaithersburg, Maryland, USA

ELSEVIER

AMSTERDAM • BOSTON • HEIDELBERG • LONDON • NEW YORK
OXFORD • PARIS • SAN DIEGO • SAN FRANCISCO
SINGAPORE • SYDNEY • TOKYO
Academic Press is an imprint of Elsevier

Contribution of the National Institute of Standards and Technology, 2011

Academic Press is an imprint of Elsevier
225 Wyman Street, Waltham, MA 02451, USA
525 B Street, Suite 1800, San Diego, California 92101-4495, USA
84 Theobald's Road, London WC1X 8RR, UK

Notices

Knowledge and best practice in this field are constantly changing. As new research and experience broaden our understanding, changes in research methods, professional practices, or medical treatment may become necessary.

Practitioners and researchers must always rely on their own experience and knowledge in evaluating and using any information, methods, compounds, or experiments described herein. In using such information or methods they should be mindful of their own safety and the safety of others, including parties for whom they have a professional responsibility.

To the fullest extent of the law, neither the Publisher nor the authors, contributors, or editors, assume any liability for any injury and/or damage to persons or property as a matter of products liability, negligence or otherwise, or from any use or operation of any methods, products, instructions, or ideas contained in the material herein.

Library of Congress Cataloging-in-Publication Data
Butler, John M. (John Marshall), 1969-
Advanced topics in forensic DNA typing : methodology / John M. Butler.
p. cm.
ISBN 978-0-12-374513-2
1. DNA fingerprinting. 2. Forensic genetics. I. Title.
RA1057.55.B87 2012
614'.1–dc22

2011010514

British Library Cataloguing-in-Publication Data
A catalogue record for this book is available from the British Library

For information on all Academic Press publications
visit our Web site at www.elsevierdirect.com

Dedication

To the hardworking professionals
throughout the forensic DNA community
and the individuals and families
impacted by your service
– your work makes a difference!

Contents

Foreword

Once again, John Butler has provided the forensic community with a much needed definitive text. Several editions of the original book have appeared since 2000. It has now evolved into a project, as the original will no longer fit easily into a single volume. This is now the second book in the series—*Advanced Topics in Forensic DNA Typing: Methodology*.

The information provided is easily amenable to a wide audience, from scientists and lawyers to the interested public. The comprehensive referencing makes it a handy document to refer to when "giving evidence" in court, as a definitive authority on the "state of the science."

The new volume is organized in the same order as the work flow, beginning with "sample collection and storage." The second and subsequent chapters provide comprehensive reviews of extraction methods, quantitation, amplification, and separation. One important topic considered for the first time is the importance of manufacturing controls to prevent potential contamination of plasticware and other reagents, a problem first highlighted by the "German phantom." The STR marker section is completely up to date, describing the European Standard Set (ESS) of markers and referring to a discussion on the proposed expansion of US core loci. Each locus is described in turn, with details of their molecular structures and listing of aberrant alleles such as a point mutation in D16S539. There is a very useful comparison of all STR typing kits along with their respective dye colors and sizes mapped for individual loci.

There are comprehensive reviews of non-autosomal DNA: mitochondrial DNA, Y-chromosomal DNA, and a brand new chapter on X-chromosomal DNA.

The chapter on degraded DNA leads into a discussion on the development of mini-STRs and their incorporation into the new multiplexes. John provides a timeline that stretches back 17 years to 1994, where the first STR multiplex was used in the Waco disaster. The subsequent chapter is a discussion on low-copy-number (or low template) DNA analysis. A balanced review is provided of this sometimes contentious area.

The appendices are particularly interesting. They provide an updated compilation of all the rare, and common, alleles currently observed and sequenced in the systems. The final appendix contains interviews with highly experienced expert witnesses and attorneys, providing valuable perspectives on how to be a good witness. John's books have become an essential adjunct to this objective.

I look forward to the third volume in the series, and marvel that John can physically find the time to do so much good work. I wonder what his secret is?

Peter Gill, Ph.D.
University of Oslo, Norway

Introduction

Since the second edition of *Forensic DNA Typing* was written in 2004, a great deal has happened in the field of forensic DNA analysis. Hence, the need to update the information contained in the book in as comprehensive a manner as possible. In forensic science review articles published in 2005, 2007, and 2009 in the journal *Analytical Chemistry*, I briefly described topics from hundreds of articles published during the time frame of 2003–2008. In my own laboratory at the National Institute of Standards and Technology (NIST), we have published over 75 articles since 2004 on a variety of subjects including miniSTRs, Y-STRs, mtDNA, SNPs, validation, and DNA quantitation (see http://www.cstl.nist.gov/biotech/strbase/NISTpub.htm).

Since 2004, I have also had the privilege of teaching more than three dozen workshops (see http://www.cstl.nist.gov/biotech/strbase/training.htm) to thousands of scientists and lawyers either at conferences or individual laboratories. In addition, I have responded to hundreds of email requests for more information on various topics. These interactions with forensic scientists, lawyers, and the general public have provided me with a valuable perspective on topics that need further clarification and questions that have not been answered with the information in the first or second edition of *Forensic DNA Typing*.

I have divided what is essentially the third edition of *Forensic DNA Typing* up into three volumes: a basic volume for students and beginners in the field and two advanced volumes for professionals/practitioners who may be interested in more detail. The basic volume was released in September 2009 (with a publication date of 2010) and is entitled *Fundamentals of Forensic DNA Typing*. The present book, *Advanced Topics in Forensic DNA Typing: Methodology*, is volume 2. A forthcoming book, to be titled *Advanced Topics in Forensic DNA Typing: Interpretation*, will be volume 3.

Several reasons exist for dividing the material. First and foremost, people use books more frequently if they are less bulky. I have heard from more than one colleague at conferences that they prefer to carry the smaller first edition with them to court or other teaching situations. Second, by having multiple books, each volume can be focused on its intended audience rather than trying to be all things to all readers. Third, the books will enable both undergraduate and graduate studies with each building upon the previous volumes.

With a vast majority of the topics, there is only minor overlap in subject matter between the various volumes. The basic *Fundamentals* volume contains the simpler "starter" information while most of the "updates" to the field are found in the *Advanced Topics* volumes. It is my intention that the three volumes together provide a comprehensive view of the current state of forensic DNA analysis.

NEW MATERIAL IN THIS VOLUME

In many ways, this is a completely new book. Those familiar with the previous editions of my book will find that *Advanced Topics in Forensic DNA Typing: Methodology* is substantially enhanced with additional information. Since the first edition was written in the winter months of 2000, the published literature on STR typing and its use in forensic DNA testing has grown dramatically. With more than 3,500 papers now available describing STR markers, technology for typing these STRs, and allele frequencies in various populations around the world, the scientific basis for forensic DNA typing is sound. The foundational material in the previous editions is still relevant and thus has remained essentially unchanged. However, as with every scientific field, advances are being made and thus new information needs to be shared to bring the book up-to-date.

In addition to updating information on essentially every topic in the second edition of *Forensic DNA Typing*, I have included new chapters on X-chromosome markers (Chapter 15) and legal aspects of serving as an expert witness in a U.S. court of law (Chapter 18). The chapter on DNA databases (Chapter 8) is significantly expanded and new information on familial DNA searches is included (Appendix 2).

At the end of each chapter throughout the book, I have included a fairly comprehensive list of references that serve as a foundation for citations found throughout the chapter as well as a launching point where interested readers can go for additional information. More than 2800 references are provided enabling readers to expand their study beyond the information contained between the covers of this book. References to journal articles include titles to enhance value.

In this edition, I again utilize **D**ata, **N**otes, and **A**pplications (D.N.A.) Boxes to cover specific topics of general interest, to review example calculations, or to cover a topic that serves to highlight information needed by a DNA analyst.

OVERVIEW OF BOOK CHAPTERS

Many times information within chapters and even the order of the chapters themselves have been changed from the second edition. These structural changes reflect changes in my way of thinking about how to present the information to the intended audience. Note that new topics are being added and old ones phased out. A brief "cross-walk" of major topics covered across the various editions of *Forensic DNA Typing* is shown below with chapters (Ch.) and appendices (App.) indicated.

Topic	1st Edition (2001)	2nd Edition (2005)	Fundamentals (2010)	Advanced Topics: Methodology (2012)	Advanced Topics: Interpretation (2013)
History of DNA	Ch. 1	Ch. 1	Ch. 1 & 3	–	–
DNA basics	Ch. 2	Ch. 2	Ch. 2	–	–
Sample collection	Ch. 3	Ch. 3	Ch. 4	Ch. 1	–

(Continued)

(Cont'd)

Topic	1st Edition (2001)	2nd Edition (2005)	Fundamentals (2010)	Advanced Topics: Methodology (2012)	Advanced Topics: Interpretation (2013)
DNA extraction	Ch. 3	Ch. 3	Ch. 5	Ch. 2	–
DNA quantitation	Ch. 3	Ch. 3	Ch. 6	Ch. 3	–
PCR	Ch. 4	Ch. 4	Ch. 7	Ch. 4	–
STR markers	Ch. 5	Ch. 5	Ch. 8	Ch. 5	–
Data interpretation	Ch. 6 & 13	Ch. 6 & 15	Ch. 10	–	Ch 1-8
DNA databases	Ch. 16	Ch. 18	Ch. 12	Ch. 8	–
Capillary electrophoresis	Ch. 9 & 11	Ch. 12 & 14	Ch. 9	Ch. 6	Ch. 8
FMBIO gel imaging system	Ch. 12	Ch. 14	DNA Box 9.2	–	–
Random match probability calculations	–	Ch. 21	Ch. 11	–	Ch. 11
Statistics & probability basics	–	Ch. 19	App. 3	–	Ch. 9
Familial searching	–	–	Ch. 12 (p. 282)	App. 2	–
DNA mixtures	Ch. 7	Ch. 7	Ch. 14	–	Ch. 6
Low copy number DNA testing	–	Ch. 7	Ch. 14	Ch. 9	Ch. 7 & 13
Validation	Ch. 14	Ch. 16	Ch. 13	Ch. 7	–
SNPs	Ch. 8	Ch. 8	Ch. 15	Ch. 12	–
Y-STRs	Ch. 8	Ch. 9	Ch. 16	Ch. 13	–
mtDNA	Ch. 8	Ch. 10	Ch. 16	Ch. 14	–
X-STRs	–	–	–	Ch. 15	–
Non-human DNA	Ch. 8	Ch. 11	Ch. 15	Ch. 16	–
New technologies	Ch. 15	Ch. 17	Ch. 18	Ch. 17	–
Disaster victim identification	Ch. 17	Ch. 24	Ch. 17	Ch. 9	–
Expert witness testimony	–	–	–	Ch. 18, App. 4	–
Reported STR alleles	App. 1	App. 1	–	App. 1	–
FBI QAS	App. 3 (1998/99)	App. 4 (1998/99)	–	–	App. 2 (2011)
Glossary	–	–	App. 1	–	App. 6

Appendices

There are four appendices at the back of the book that provide supplemental material.

- Appendix 1 describes all reported alleles for the 13 CODIS and other commonly used STR loci as of December 2010. Sequence information, where available, has been included along with the reference that first described the noted allele. As most laboratories now use either a Promega or an Applied Biosystems STR typing kit for PCR amplification, we have listed the expected size for each allele based on the sequence information.
- Appendix 2 discusses familial DNA searching and the potential, pitfalls, and privacy concerns surrounding this controversial technique.
- Appendix 3 is a compilation of companies and organizations that are suppliers of DNA analysis equipment, products, and services. Over 80 companies are listed along with their addresses, phone numbers, Internet web pages, and a brief description of their products and/or services.
- Appendix 4 is a compilation of responses to interview questions asked of several scientists and lawyers relating to issues faced when serving as an expert witness.

Acknowledgments

I express a special thanks to colleagues and fellow researchers who kindly provided important information and supplied some of the figures for this book or previous editions of *Forensic DNA Typing*. These individuals include Michael Baird, Susan Ballou, Brad Bannon, Martin Bill, Theresa Caragine, George Carmody, Mike Coble, Robin Cotton, David Duewer, Dan Ehrlich, Nicky Fildes, Lisa Forman, Ron Fourney, Lee Fraser, Richard Guerrieri, Chip Harding, Doug Hares, Bruce Heidebrecht, Debbie Hobson, Bill Hudlow, Ted Hunt, Dennis Kilcoyne, Margaret Kline, Ken Konzak, Carll Ladd, Steve Lee, Dina Mattes, Bruce McCord, Ruth Montgomery, Steven Myers, Steve Niezgoda, Thomas Schnibbe, Richard Schoske, Jim Schumm, Scott Scoville (and the Orange County DA's DNA Unit), Bob Shaler, Michelle Shepherd, Gary Sims, Melissa Smrz, Amanda Sozer, Jill Spriggs, Mark Stolorow, Kevin Sullivan, Lois Tully, and Charlotte Word.

I am indebted to the dedicated Human Identity Project team members, past and present, who work with me at the U.S. National Institute of Standards and Technology: Jill Appleby, Erica Butts, Mike Coble, Amy Decker, David Duewer, Becky Hill, Margaret Kline, Kristen Lewis O'Connor, Jan Redman, Dennis Reeder, Patti Rohmiller, Christian Ruitberg, Richard Schoske, and Pete Vallone. It is a pleasure to work with such supportive and hard-working scientists.

Several other people deserve specific recognition for their support of this endeavor. The information reported in this book was in large measure made possible by a comprehensive collection of references on the STR markers used in forensic DNA typing. For this collection now numbering more than 3000 references, I am indebted to the initial work of Christian Ruitberg for tirelessly collecting and cataloging these papers and the steady efforts of Jan Redman to monthly update this STR reference database. A complete listing of these references may be found at http://www.cstl.nist.gov/biotech/strbase.

My wife Terilynne, who carefully reviewed the manuscript and made helpful suggestions, was always a constant support in the many hours that this project took away from our family. As the initial editor of all my written materials, Terilynne helped make the book more coherent and readable. In addition, David Duewer and Katherine Sharpless provided a fine technical review of the *Fundamentals* book as well as this one. Review of materials and input from Mary Satterfield and several members of my research group was also very helpful. The support of NIST management especially Laurie Locascio and Willie May made completion of this book possible.

I was first exposed to forensic DNA typing in 1990 when a friend gave me a copy of Joseph Wambaugh's *The Blooding* to read, and since then I have watched with wonder as the forensic DNA community has rapidly evolved. DNA testing that once took weeks can now be performed in a matter of hours. I enjoy being a part of the developments in this field and hope that this book will help many others come to better understand the fundamental principles behind the biology, technology, and genetics of STR markers.

About the Author

John Marshall Butler grew up in the U.S. midwest and, enjoying science and law, decided to pursue a career in forensic science at an early age. After completing an undergraduate education at Brigham Young University in chemistry, he moved east to pursue graduate studies at the University of Virginia. While a graduate student, he enjoyed the unique opportunity of serving as an FBI Honors Intern and guest researcher for more than two years in the FBI Laboratory's Forensic Science Research Unit. His Ph.D. dissertation research, which was conducted at the FBI Academy in Quantico, Virginia, involved pioneering work in applying capillary electrophoresis to STR typing. After completing his Ph.D. in 1995, Dr. Butler obtained a prestigious National Research Council postdoctoral fellowship to the National Institute of Standards and Technology (NIST). While a postdoc at NIST, he designed and built STRBase, the widely used Short Tandem Repeat Internet Database (http://www.cstl.nist.gov/biotech/strbase) that contains a wealth of standardized information on STRs used in human identity applications. He worked for several years as a staff scientist and project leader at a California startup company named GeneTrace System developing rapid DNA analysis technologies involving time-of-flight mass spectrometry. In the fall of 1999, he returned to NIST to lead their efforts in human identity testing with funding from the National Institute of Justice.

Dr. Butler is currently a NIST Fellow and Group Leader of Applied Genetics in the Biochemical Science Division at the National Institute of Standards and Technology. He is a regular invited guest of the FBI's Scientific Working Group on DNA Analysis Methods (SWGDAM) and a member of the Department of Defense Quality Assurance Oversight Committee for DNA Analysis. Following the terrorist attacks of September 11, 2001, he aided the DNA identification efforts and served as part of the distinguished World Trade Center Kinship and Data Analysis Panel (WTC KADAP). He is a member of the International Society of Forensic Genetics and serves as an Associate Editor for *Forensic Science International: Genetics*.

Dr. Butler has received numerous awards including the Presidential Early Career Award for Scientists and Engineers (2002), the Department of Commerce Silver Medal (2002) and Gold Medal (2008), the Arthur S. Flemming Award (2007), the Edward Uhler Condon Award (2010), Brigham Young University's College of Physical and Mathematical Sciences Honored Alumnus (2005), and the Scientific Prize of the International Society of Forensic Genetics (2003).

He has more than 100 publications describing aspects of forensic DNA testing and is one of the most prolific active authors in the field with articles appearing regularly in every major forensic science journal. Dr. Butler has been an invited speaker to numerous national and international forensic DNA meetings and in the past few years has spoken in Germany, France, England, Canada, Mexico, Denmark, Belgium, Poland, Portugal, Cyprus, The Netherlands, Argentina, Japan, and Australia. Much of the content in this book has come from his Group's research efforts over the past two decades. In addition to his busy scientific career, he and his wife serve in their community and church and are the proud parents of six children, all of whom have been proven to be theirs through the power of DNA typing.

C H A P T E R

1

Sample Collection, Storage, and Characterization

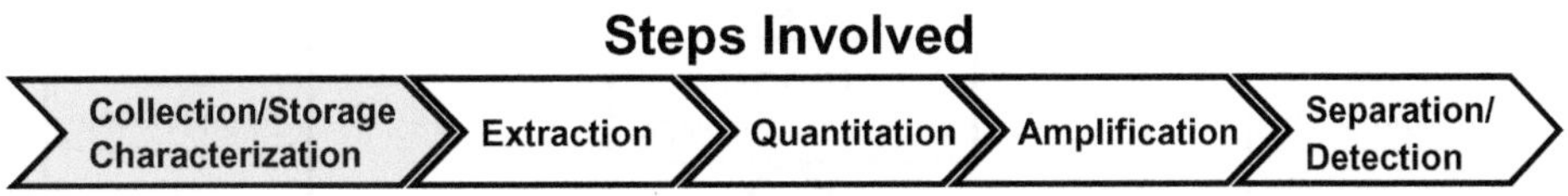

DNA typing, since it was introduced in the mid-1980s, has revolutionized forensic science and the ability of law enforcement to match perpetrators with crime scenes. Each year, thousands of cases around the world are closed with guilty suspects punished and innocent ones freed because of the power of a silent biological witness at the crime scene. This book explores the science behind DNA typing and the biology, technology, and genetics that make DNA typing the most useful investigative tool to law enforcement since the development of fingerprinting over 100 years ago. As noted in the Introduction, this volume is intended primarily for DNA analysts or advanced students with a more in-depth look into subjects than its companion volume *Fundamentals of Forensic DNA Typing*.

STEPS IN DNA TESTING PROCESS

A summary of the steps involved in processing forensic DNA samples is illustrated in Figure 1.1. Following collection of biological material (Chapter 1) from a crime scene or paternity investigation, DNA is extracted from its biological source material (Chapter 2) and then measured to evaluate the quantity of DNA recovered (Chapter 3). Specific regions of the DNA are targeted and copied with the polymerase chain reaction, or PCR (Chapter 4). Commercial kits are commonly used to enable simultaneous PCR of 13 to 15 short tandem repeat (STR) markers (Chapter 5). STR alleles are interpreted relative to PCR amplification artifacts following separation by size using capillary electrophoresis (Chapter 6) and data analysis software. A statistical interpretation assesses the rarity of the alleles from the resulting DNA profile, which can be single-source or a mixture depending on the sample origin.

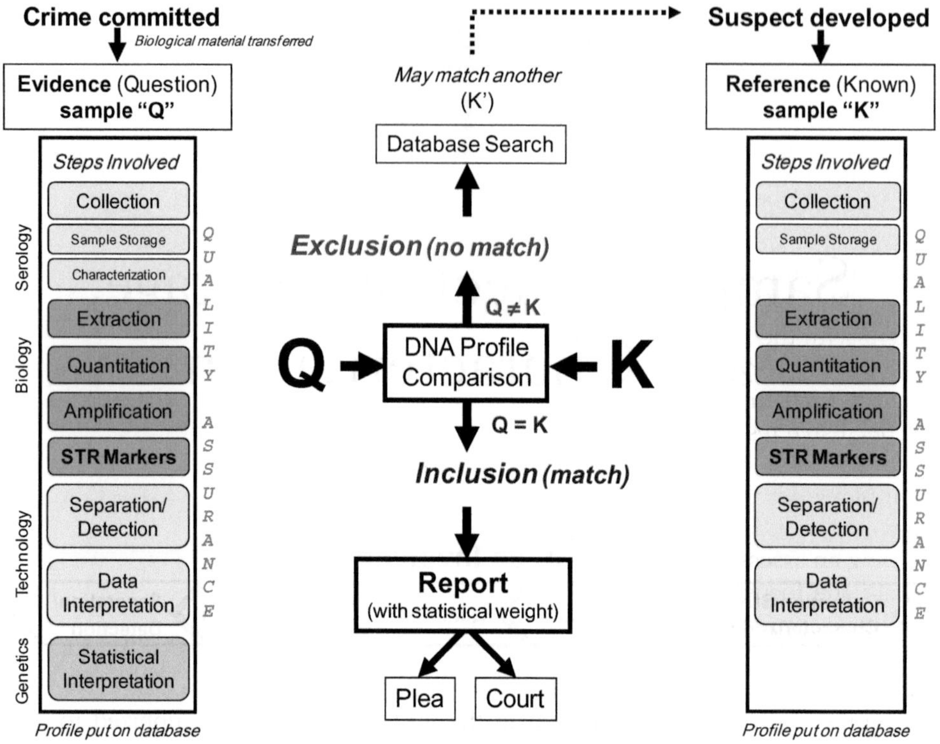

FIGURE 1.1 Overview of steps involved in DNA testing.

Ideally, the parameters and protocols for each step in this process are established through laboratory validation with quality assurance measures in place to aid in obtaining the highest quality data (Chapter 7). Following the DNA testing, a written report is created summarizing the work conducted and results obtained. If the case goes to court, expert witness testimony may be required of the laboratory report's author (Chapter 18).

DNA analysis always requires that a comparison be made between two samples: (1) a questioned sample, commonly referred to as a "Q", and (2) a known sample, referred to as a "K" (Figure 1.1). In forensic cases, crime scene evidence (Q) is always compared to a single suspect (K) or multiple suspects (K_1, K_2, K_3, etc.). In a case without a suspect, the evidence DNA profile may be compared to a computer database (Chapter 8) containing DNA profiles from previous offenders ($K_1 \ldots K_n$).

Note that in Figure 1.1 under the reference sample steps, no characterization of the sample is performed nor is there a statistical interpretation given of the rarity of the DNA profile. Since sample K is from a known source, there is no need to determine its origin (e.g., bloodstain vs. saliva stain) or to calculate a random match probability because through accurate chain-of-custody records the DNA analyst should truly know the source of the sample.

Other applications of DNA testing involve direct or biological kinship comparisons. With paternity testing, an alleged father (Q) or fathers (Q_1, Q_2, ...) are compared to a child (K). The victim's remains (Q) in missing persons or mass disaster cases (Chapter 9) are identified through use of biological relatives (K). Likewise, a soldier's remains (Q) may be identified through comparison to the direct reference blood stain (K) that was collected for each soldier prior to combat and is maintained by a country's military. In each situation, the known sample K is used to assess or determine the identity of the unknown or questioned sample Q. A simple way to think about this comparison is that a K sample has a name of an individual associated with it while a Q sample does not.

The results of this Q-K comparison are either (a) an inclusion, (b) an exclusion, or (c) an inconclusive result. Sometimes different language is used to describe these results. An inclusion may also be referred to as a "match" or as "failure to exclude" or "is consistent with." Another way that lab reports often state this information is "the DNA profile from sample Q is consistent with the DNA profile of sample K—therefore sample K cannot be eliminated as a possible contributor of the genetic material isolated from sample Q." An exclusion may be denoted as "no-match" or "is not consistent with."

An inconclusive result may be reported with some evidentiary samples that produce partial or complex DNA profiles due to damaged DNA (Chapter 10), too little DNA (Chapter 11), or complex mixtures. As illustrated in Figure 1.1, if a comparison finds the Q and K samples equivalent or indistinguishable, then a statistical evaluation is performed and a report is issued stating an assessment of the rarity of the match.

Although the focus of modern forensic DNA testing involves autosomal STR markers, this same Q-K approach applies to other genetic marker systems: single nucleotide polymorphisms (SNPs, Chapter 12), Y-chromosome markers (Chapter 13), mitochondrial DNA (mtDNA, Chapter 14), X-chromosome markers (Chapter 15), and non-human DNA (Chapter 16). However, some statistical calculations may be different in assessing match probabilities due to different genetic inheritance patterns. More on interpretation issues will be covered in the forthcoming volume, *Advanced Topics in Forensic DNA Typing: Interpretation*.

SAMPLE COLLECTION

Before a DNA test can be performed on a sample, it must be collected and the DNA isolated and put in the proper format for further characterization. This chapter covers the important topics of sample collection, characterization, and preservation. These steps are vital to obtaining a successful result regardless of the DNA typing procedure used. If the samples are not handled properly in the initial stages of an investigation, then no amount of hard work in the final analytical or data interpretation steps can compensate.

DNA Sample Sources

DNA is present in every nucleated cell and is therefore present in biological materials left at crime scenes. DNA has been successfully isolated and analyzed from a variety of biological materials. Introduction of the polymerase chain reaction (PCR), which is described in Chapter 4, has extended the range of possible DNA samples that can be successfully analyzed because PCR enables many copies to be made of the DNA markers to be examined. While the most common materials tested in forensic laboratories are typically bloodstains and semen stains, Table 1.1 includes a listing from one laboratory of over 100

TABLE 1.1 Some Sources of Biological Materials Used for PCR-Based DNA Typing. This Listing of Exhibits Produced Successful DNA Profiles in the Canadian RCMP Forensic Biology Laboratories. Adapted from Kuperus et al. (2003).

DNA SOURCE: HANDS		
Arm-rest (automobile)	Electrical cord	Paper (hand-folded)
Baseball cap (brim)	Envelope (self-adhesive)	Pen (bank robbery – roped pen owned by bank)
Binder twine	Expended .22 caliber cartridge	Plastic bag handles
Bottle cap	Fingerprint (single)	Pry bar with shoulder straps
Chocolate bar (handled end)	Gauze and tape (to cover fingertips)	Remote car starter
Cigarette ligher	Gloves (interior and exterior)	Rope
Cigarette paper	Hammer (head and handle)	Screwdriver handle
Signal light control lever (automobile)	Handcuffs	Seatbelt buckle (automobile)
Credit card (ATM card)	Hash-like ball (1 cm & hand-rolled)	Shoe laces
Detachable box magazine (pistol)	Hold-up note	Steering wheel
Dime	Ignition switch	Tape on club handle (exposed surface and initial start under layers)
Door bell	Keys	Toy gun
Door pull	Knife handle	Wiener (hot dog)
Drug syringe barrel exterior	Magazine (from handgun)	
DNA SOURCE: MOUTH AND NOSE		
Air bag (vehicle)	Envelope	Salami (bite mark)
Apple core – bite marks	Glass rim	Stamps (including self-adhesive)
Balaclava (knitted cap)	Gum	Straw (from drinking glass)
Bile on sidewalk	Ham (bite mark)	Telephone receiver
Bite marks	Inhaler (inside mouth piece)	Thermos (cup attached)
Bottle top	Lipstick (top surface and outside surface of lipstick case)	Tooth
Buccal stick only (swab cut off)	Nasal secretions (tissue)	Toothbrush
Cake (bite mark)	Peach strudel	Toothpick
Cheesecake (bite mark)	Pop cans/bottles	Utensils (fork, spoon, etc.)
Chicken wing	Popsicle stick	Vomit (bile-like sputum/liquid)
Chocolate bar (bite mark)	Ski coat collar	Welding goggles (rim of eye/nose)
Cigarette butt		

(*Continued*)

TABLE 1.1 Some Sources of Biological Materials Used for PCR-Based DNA Typing. This Listing of Exhibits Produced Successful DNA Profiles in the Canadian RCMP Forensic Biology Laboratories. Adapted from Kuperus et al. (2003). (*Continued*)

DNA SOURCE: GENERAL BODY		
Baseball cap/cowboy hat (swab of inside rim)	Eyeglasses (ear and nose pieces)	Tears (on tissue)
Bullet hole in wall and bullet	Hair	Tissue paper wiping of underarms of shirt (sweat)
Buried remains	Hair comb (for head hair)	Socks
Burned remains	Head-rest (automobile)	Toilet—knife found in "toilet trap"
Contact lens fragments (from vacuum cleaner bag)	Hood (attached to back of jacket)	Urine in snow
Dandruff (and cellular debris) from balaclava/toque	Paraffin-embedded tissue	Water—"S" trap of shower
Embryonic (umbilical) cord embedded in paraffin	Razor (disposable type/blade and plastic cap)	

unusual casework exhibit materials that yielded successful DNA profiles (Kuperus et al. 2003). Even a few cells left with latent fingerprint residue can serve as effective sources of DNA (Schulz & Reichert 2002, Balogh et al. 2003). DNA molecules are amazingly durable and in many cases can yield DNA typing results even when subjected to extreme conditions such as irradiation (Castle et al. 2003, Withrow et al. 2003) or explosive blasts (Esslinger et al. 2004).

Biological Evidence at Crime Scenes

Different types of biological evidence collected at a crime scene can be used to associate or to exclude an individual from involvement with a crime. In particular, the direct transfer of DNA from one individual to another individual or to an object can be used to link a suspect to a crime scene. As noted by Dr. Henry Lee, formerly of the Connecticut State Forensic Laboratory, this direct transfer could involve (Lee 1996):

1. The suspect's DNA deposited on the victim's body or clothing;
2. The suspect's DNA deposited on an object;
3. The suspect's DNA deposited at a location;
4. The victim's DNA deposited on the suspect's body or clothing;
5. The victim's DNA deposited on an object;
6. The victim's DNA deposited at a location;
7. The witness's DNA deposited on victim or suspect; or
8. The witness's DNA deposited on an object or at a location.

As Dr. Paul Kirk noted in his 1953 book *Crime Investigation*: "The blood or semen that [the perpetrator of a crime] deposits or collects—all these and more bear mute witness against him. This is evidence that does not forget... Physical evidence cannot be wrong; it cannot perjure itself; it cannot be wholly absent... Only human failure to find, study and understand it can diminish its value" (Kirk 1953).

DNA evidence collection from a crime scene must be performed carefully and a chain of custody established in order to produce DNA profiles that are meaningful and legally accepted in court. DNA testing techniques have become so sensitive that biological evidence too small to be easily seen with the naked eye can be used to link suspects to crime scenes. The evidence must be carefully collected, preserved, stored, and transported prior to any analysis conducted in a forensic DNA laboratory. The National Institute of Justice has produced a brochure entitled "What Every Law Enforcement Officer Should Know About DNA Evidence" (now available as online training as well, see http://www.dna.gov) that contains helpful hints for law enforcement personnel who are the first to arrive at a crime scene.

One crime scene investigator (Blozis 2010) categorized three types of DNA samples: (1) unknown samples recovered from crime scenes, (2) elimination samples from individuals such as the victim(s) or family members who had prior legitimate access to the crime scene, and (3) biological material abandoned by an individual known to law enforcement. The last category might include a cigarette butt discarded in a public place.

It can be pointless to collect samples for DNA testing in many cases. For example, swabbing a car steering wheel to pick up touch DNA will likely reveal the owner(s) or legitimate drivers of the car rather than the perpetrator in a car theft situation. In many situations, an uninformative, complicated mixture may be created from the legitimate drivers rather than a clean, clear-cut DNA profile that can unambiguously be linked to a suspect. Likewise, just because human DNA was successfully isolated from a mosquito and helped solve a crime (Spitaleri et al. 2006) does not mean that mosquitoes are optimal evidence to collect for every case! Thus, thought and judgment are required by the crime scene investigators to collect optimal samples for DNA testing.

Unfortunately, the "CSI effect" (see Chapter 18) in some situations has spread to detectives and crime scene investigators who try to collect and submit as many samples as possible to the crime laboratory. The watching of "forensic" television shows has created unrealistic expectations in the general public and even some law enforcement officials in terms of both the speed and probability of success with DNA results obtained. The submission of excessive numbers and sometimes unnecessary samples can bog down the laboratory, which then limits the ability to process legitimate samples in a timely manner.

Evidence Collection and Preservation

The importance of proper DNA evidence collection cannot be overemphasized. If the DNA sample is contaminated from the start, obtaining unambiguous information becomes a challenge at best.

Samples for collection should be carefully chosen as well to prevent needless redundancy in the evidence for a case. The following suggestions are helpful during evidence collection to preserve it properly:

- Avoid contaminating the area where DNA might be present by not touching it with your bare hands, or sneezing or coughing over the evidence.
- Use clean latex gloves for collecting each item of evidence. Gloves and/or tweezers should be changed between handling of different items of evidence.

- Package each item of evidence separately to prevent potential transfer and cross-contamination between different items.
- Air-dry bloodstains, semen stains, and other types of liquid stain prior to sealing the package.
- Package samples in paper envelopes or paper bags after drying. Plastic bags should be avoided because water condenses in them, especially in areas of high humidity, and moisture can speed the degradation of DNA molecules. Packages should be clearly marked with case number, item number, collection date, and initialed across the package seal in order to maintain a proper chain of custody.
- Transfer stains on unmovable surfaces (such as a table or floor) with sterile cotton swabs and distilled water. Rub the stained area with the moist swab until the stain is transferred to the swab. Allow the swab to air dry without touching any others. Store each swab in a separate paper envelope.

One of the most common methods for optimally collecting cellular material is the so-called "double swab technique" where a moist swab is followed by a dry one (Sweet et al. 1997, Pang & Cheung 2007). The wet swab, which has been moistened by dipping it in sterile, distilled water, is first brushed over a surface to loosen any cells present and to rehydrate them. The second swab, which is initially dry, then helps collect additional cells from the surface. It is thought that the rehydrated cells adhere more easily to the second swab. Since both swabs are collected from the same sample, they are usually combined to maximize the yield of collected cellular material. Unfortunately, as will be discussed briefly in Chapter 2, poor extraction efficiencies from the swab can sometimes limit the amount of recovered DNA.

One of the challenges with collecting sexual assault evidence from vaginal samples using cotton swabs is that the sperm cells can stick to the cotton fibers and not be easily released during DNA extraction. Digestion of the cotton swab with cellulase, an enzyme that breaks down the cellulose fibers in cotton, was found to improve DNA recovery (Voorhees et al. 2006, Norris et al. 2007). In another approach, a nylon flocked swab was found to promote cell release during the extraction steps and produce a higher yield of DNA when compared with cotton swabs (Benschop et al. 2010).

Another effective technique for recovering cellular material from clothing or other evidentiary items is the use of an adhesive tape attached to a plastic or acetate support (Hall & Fairley 2004, Hansson et al. 2009, Barash et al. 2010). The tape is pressed multiple times over the area where cellular material may be present. The tape is then placed directly into the DNA extraction tube and dissolved to enable optimal recovery (May & Thomson 2009). Tape lifting enables samples to be examined for gunshot residue or other trace evidence prior to being extracted for DNA.

Collection of Reference DNA Samples

To perform comparative DNA testing with evidence collected from a crime scene, biological samples must also be obtained from suspects or evidentiary DNA profiles searched against a database of potential suspects (Chapter 8). Family reference samples may be used in paternity testing, missing persons investigations, and mass disaster victim identifications (Chapter 9).

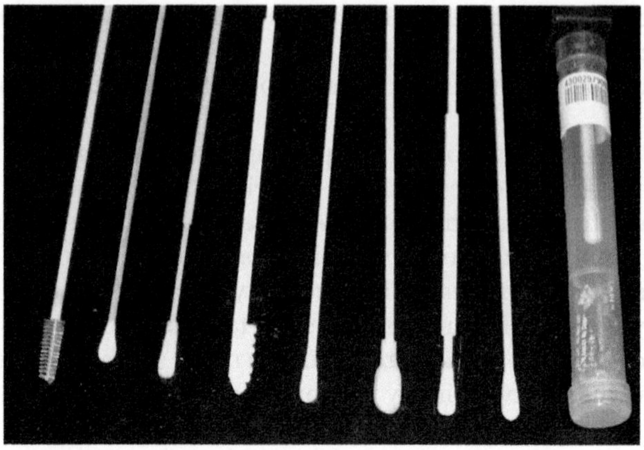

FIGURE 1.2 Photograph of several different buccal swab collectors.

It is advantageous to obtain these reference DNA samples as rapidly and painlessly as possible. Thus, many laboratories often use buccal cell collection rather than drawing blood. Buccal cell collection involves wiping a cotton swab similar to a Q-tip against the inside cheek of an individual's mouth to collect some skin cells. The swab is then dried or can be pressed against a treated collection card to transfer epithelial cells for storage purposes. Adhesive tapes may also be used for collecting reference DNA samples (Zamir et al. 2004).

Bode Technology Group (Lorton, VA) has produced a simple Buccal DNA Collector (Fox et al. 2002, Schumm et al. 2004, Burger et al. 2005) that is widely used for direct collection of buccal cell samples. This collection system also comes with a transport pouch containing a desiccant to keep the sample dry and has a unique bar code on each DNA collector to enable automated sample tracking. Several types of buccal collectors are shown in Figure 1.2.

A disposable toothbrush can be used for collecting buccal cells in a non-threatening manner (Burgoyne 1997, Tanaka et al. 2000). This method can be very helpful when samples need to be collected from children. After the buccal cells have been collected by gently rubbing a wet toothbrush across the inner cheek, the brush can be tapped onto the surface of treated collection paper for sample storage and preservation. Saliva collection also works and can be a useful method to obtain reference samples for human population genetic studies (Quinque et al. 2006).

If a liquid blood sample is collected, then typically a few drops of blood are spotted onto a piece of treated or untreated filter paper. Blood samples are advantageous in that it is easy to see that a sample has been collected (as opposed to a colorless swab from a saliva sample).

Regardless of the method of collecting a DNA sample from a reference or crime scene source, it is imperative that the collection material be DNA-free prior to use. For over 15 years investigators in Europe chased what was popularly referred to as the "German phantom," a supposed serial offender whose DNA profile was continually appearing in a variety of crimes (Himmelreich 2009, Neuhuber et al. 2009). In 2008, the "offender" was discovered to be an elderly lady who worked for a manufacturer packaging DNA collection swabs. In placing the swabs in their packages, she had inadvertantly contaminated some of them with her own DNA, which when used for the purpose of crime scene investigation revealed her DNA profile rather than biological material from the crime scene. The important issue of potential reagent and consumable contamination will be covered in greater detail in Chapter 4.

SAMPLE STORAGE AND TRANSPORT OF DNA EVIDENCE

Carelessness or ignorance of proper handling procedures during storage and transport of DNA from the crime scene to the laboratory can result in a specimen unfit for analysis. For example, bloodstains should be thoroughly dried prior to transport and storage to prevent mold growth. A recovered bloodstain on a cotton swab should be air-dried in an open envelope before being sealed for transport. DNA can be stored long-term as non-extracted tissue or as fully extracted DNA. DNA samples are, however, not normally extracted until they reach the laboratory.

Most biological evidence is best preserved when stored dry and cold (Baust 2008). These conditions reduce the rate of bacterial growth and degradation of DNA. Samples should be packaged carefully and hand-carried or shipped using overnight delivery to the forensic laboratory conducting the DNA testing. Evidence collection cardboard boxes have been designed for shipping and handling bloodstains and other crime scene evidence (Hochmeister et al. 1998). Inside the laboratory, DNA samples are either stored in a refrigerator at 4°C or a freezer at −20°C. For long periods of time, extracted DNA samples may be stored at −80°C.

DNA molecules survive best if they are dry (to prevent base hydrolysis) and protected from DNA digesting enzymes called DNases. A common method of storing DNA reference samples is on bloodstain cards (Kline et al. 2002, Sjöholm et al. 2007, Coble et al. 2008). This method involves adding a few drops of liquid blood to a cellulose-based filter paper and then air-drying the bloodstain before storing it. Some bloodstain cards have been treated with chemicals to enhance DNA longevity. Buccal (cheek) cells can also be transferred to treated paper for storage (Sigurdson et al. 2006). The dried bloodstain card can also be vacuum sealed with a desiccant to prevent humidity from breaking the stored DNA molecules into smaller pieces and destroying the ability to recover a full DNA profile.

Many police evidence lockers and storage vaults that hold crime scene evidence have freezers to enable storage of rape kits or other material containing biological evidence. Storage and availability of this evidence after many years, in some cases, has enabled post-conviction DNA testing of individuals incarcerated prior to the availability of DNA testing (see Butler 2010, *Fundamentals* D.N.A. Box 1.1). Large-scale DNA reference sample collection has been performed by the U.S. military since the early 1990s in an effort to be able to identify all recovered remains of military casualties and thus prevent there ever being another "unknown soldier" (see Butler 2010, *Fundamentals* D.N.A. Box 4.3).

While large freezers work well for preserving evidence by keeping it cold, these freezers are expensive to power and to maintain. Freezers generate a lot of heat and take up considerable space. Recent room temperature storage approaches through chemically treating DNA samples to protect them from degradation have been developed by several companies including Biomatrica (San Diego, CA) and GenVault (Carlsbad, CA).

In the summer and autumn months of 2007, a set of DNA samples stored at ambient temperatures in Biomatrica's SampleMatrix were shipped back and forth across the United States with no insulation or refrigeration (Lee et al. 2010). These samples, which were dried down aliquots of 1 ng/μL, 0.25 ng/μL, and 0.05 ng/μL pristine genomic DNA, were compared at various time points over a 208-day window against equivalent samples stored in the laboratory. While the shipped samples experienced extreme temperature ranges of almost 45°C and relative humidity differences of almost 60%, full Identifiler DNA profiles were obtained with all of the tested samples (Lee et al. 2010). These data suggest that the SampleMatrix material, now marketed by QIAGEN (Valencia, CA) as QiaSafe, will help preserve DNA outside of a stable, cold environment enabling cost savings for storing biological samples.

Studies have shown that bloodstain samples which are stored dry (through vacuum sealing with a desiccant) can be successfully stored for over 20 years at ambient temperatures and still yield full DNA profiles (Coble et al. 2008, Kline 2010). Furthermore, an examination of bloodstains on four different filter papers found that keeping the sample dry through desiccation was more important than the type of paper (treated or untreated) that the sample was stored on (Kline et al. 2002). Likewise, appropriate room temperature storage of soft tissue samples, which may be recovered during disaster victim identification (Chapter 9) has been successful (Graham et al. 2008).

Every effort should be made to avoid completely consuming or destroying evidence so that a portion is available for future testing if needed. As the 1996 National Research Council's *The Evaluation of Forensic DNA Evidence* states: "The ultimate safeguard against error due to sample mixup is to provide an opportunity for retesting" (NRCII, p. 81).

SAMPLE CHARACTERIZATION

When crime scene evidence is first received into a laboratory, it is usually evaluated to see if any biological material is present. Some laboratories perform both *preliminary tests* and *confirmatory tests* prior to sending a cutting or swab for DNA testing in an effort to develop a DNA profile. A presumptive test, which really serves as a preliminary evaluation or examination, may be followed by a confirmatory test to verify the results of the first test.

In a 2007 survey of 42 laboratories from 10 different countries, Ron Fourney and colleagues at the Royal Canadian Mounted Police found that most of the surveyed laboratories perform some form of either presumptive or confirmatory tests for biological screening (Fourney et al. 2007). A summary of their results is found in Table 1.2.

Forensic Serology: Presumptive and Confirmatory Tests

Forensic evidence from crime scenes comes in many forms. For example, a bed sheet may be collected from the scene of a sexual assault. This sheet will have to be carefully examined in the forensic laboratory before selecting the area to sample for further testing. Prior to making the effort to extract DNA from a sample, *presumptive tests* are often performed to indicate whether or not biological fluids such as blood or semen are present on an item of evidence (e.g., a pair of pants). Locating a blood or semen stain on a soiled undergarment can be a trying task. Primary stains of forensic interest come from blood, semen, and saliva. Identification of vaginal secretions, urine, and feces can also be important to an investigation.

TABLE 1.2 Summary of Results from a 2007 Survey Examining Types of Presumptive and Confirmatory Tests Performed in 42 Laboratories (Fourney et al. 2007).

Test	Numbers	Most Prevelant Methods
Blood Presumptive	42/42	Phenolphthalein, Luminol, Hemastix
Blood Confirmatory	17/42	Takayama & HemaTrace
Blood Species Identification	36/42	HemaTrace
Semen Presumptive	42/42	Fast Blue, Alternate light sources
Semen Confirmatory	42/42	Microscopic examination with Christmas Tree staining, ABACard for p30
Saliva Presumptive	35/42	Alternate Light Sources, Phadebas
Saliva Confirmatory	7/35	High levels of amylase
Vaginal Fluid Presumptive	21/42	Alternate Light Sources
Vaginal Fluid Confirmatory	1/42	Fast Blue coupled with PSA and microscopic examination
Urine Presumptive	25/42	Alternate Light Sources
Urine Confirmatory	1/42	BFID-Urine kit
Feces Presumptive	20/42	Urobilinogen (Edelman's test)
Feces Confirmatory	0/42	
Hair	40/42	Microscopic examination for suitability/species

Serology is the term used to describe a broad range of laboratory tests that utilize antigen and serum antibody reactions (Ballantyne 2000). For example, the ABO blood group types are determined using anti-A and anti-B serums and examining agglutination when mixed with a blood sample (Li 2008). One of the principle tools of forensic science in the past, serology still plays an important role in modern forensic biology but has taken a backseat to DNA since presumptive tests do not have the ability to individualize a sample like a DNA profile can.

Presumptive tests should be simple, inexpensive, safe, and easy to perform (Shaler 2002). They should use only a small amount of material and have no adverse effect on any downstream DNA testing that might be conducted on the evidentiary material (Tobe et al. 2007, Virkler & Lednev 2009). Besides helping to locate the appropriate material for DNA analysis, stain characterization can in some cases provide probative value to a case (e.g., semen in a victim's mouth as evidence of an oral sexual assault).

Primary providers for presumptive forensic serology tests have been Abacus Diagnostics (West Hills, CA) and Seratec (Goettingen, Germany). Their *in-vitro* diagnostic tests, which appear very similar to home pregnancy tests, involve applying a small aliquot of a sample to a cartridge with a membrane containing specific antibodies. The presence of the appropriate molecules (e.g., hemoglobin with a blood test) on this immuno-chromatographic strip test will be detected as a colored line. Internal standards are run to verify that the test is working properly.

Independent Forensics (Hillside, IL) has released lateral flow strip tests for detecting the presence of blood, saliva, semen, and urine from forensic evidence. The RSID (Rapid Stain Identification) tests are confirmatory for blood (Schweers et al. 2008) and semen and presumptive for saliva and urine. These tests use different markers from the commonly used lateral flow strip tests (i.e., they do not use hemoglobin, PSA/p30, urea, or enzymatic activity for the detection of blood, semen, urine, or saliva, respectively) and are therefore more specific with fewer false positives and false negatives.

Independent Forensics also has developed a forensic-specific fluorescence kit for staining microscope slides used to scan sexual assault evidence for sperm called "SPERM HY-LITER." This test is confirmatory for human sperm heads. The RSID Blood and RSID Semen tests are confirmatory and designed to not cross-react with other human body fluids or body fluids of other animals like some of the presumptive tests do. Information on the RSID products is available at http://www.ifi-test.com/rsid.php.

Edwin Jones in his review of methods for identification of semen and other body fluids points out that the fastest way to locate a body fluid stain is by visual examination (Jones 2004). Dried semen stains as well as saliva, urine, and vaginal fluid stains contain substances that when irradiated with a handheld UV lamp or argon laser can fluoresce, or emit light, in the visible-light region. A high-intensity light source with appropriate excitation and emission filters is known as an *alternate light source*, or ALS. ALS is an effective screening tool in the initial examination of forensic evidence (Vandenberg & van Oorschot 2006).

Bloodstains

Blood is composed of liquid plasma and serum with solid components consisting of red blood cells (erythrocytes), white blood cells (leukocytes), and platelets (thrombocytes). Most presumptive tests for blood focus on detecting the presence of hemoglobin molecules, which are found in the red blood cells and used for transport of oxygen and carbon dioxide.

A simple immuno-chromatographic test for identification of human blood is available from Abacus Diagnostics (West Hills, CA) as the ABAcard HemaTrace kit. This test has a hemoglobin limit of detection of 0.07 μg/mL and shows specificity for human blood along with higher primate and ferret blood (Johnston et al. 2003). On the other hand, the RSID Blood test from Independent Forensics utilizes monoclonal antibodies to the red blood cell membrane specific protein glycophorin A rather than hemoglobin and does not cross-react with ferret, skunk, or primate blood (Schweers et al. 2008).

Luminol is another presumptive test for identification of blood that has been popularized by the TV series *CSI: Crime Scene Investigation*. The luminol reagent is prepared by mixing 0.1 g 3-amino-phthalhydrazide and 5.0 g sodium carbonate in 100 mL of distilled water. Before use, 0.7 g of sodium perborate is added to the solution (Saferstein 2001). Large areas can be rapidly evaluated for the presence of bloodstains by spraying the luminol reagent onto the item under investigation. Objects that have been sprayed need to be located in a darkened area so that the luminescence can be more easily viewed. Luminol can be used to locate traces of blood that have been diluted up to 10 million times (Saferstein 2001). The use of luminol has been shown to not inhibit DNA testing of STRs that may need to be performed on evidence recovered from a crime scene (Gross et al. 1999).

Demonstration that presumptive tests do not interfere with subsequent DNA testing can be important when making decisions on how biological evidence is processed in a forensic laboratory (Hochmeister et al. 1991, Budowle et al. 2000). Unfortunately the use of Hemastix, a screening test for bloodstains, has been shown to introduce problems with downstream processing involving magnetic-bead DNA extraction (Poon et al. 2009). This problem was solved by first transferring a portion of the bloodstain under investigation to a separate piece of filter paper for the presumptive test. The remaining portion of the original sample could then be processed for DNA extraction without coming in contact with the interferring chemicals.

Saliva Stains

A presumptive test for amylase is used for indicating the presence of saliva (Whitehead & Kipps 1975, Auvdel 1986), which is especially difficult to see since saliva stains are nearly invisible to the naked eye. Two common methods for estimating amylase levels in forensic samples include the Phadebas test and the starch iodine radial diffusion test (Shaler 2002, Myers & Adkins 2008). The presence of saliva in a stain has also been verified through detecting oral bacterial DNA (Nakanishi et al. 2009, Donaldson et al. 2010).

Saliva stains may be found on bite-marks, cigarette butts, and drinking vessels (Abaz et al. 2002, Shaler 2002). As will be described later in this chapter, a molecular biology approach using messenger RNA profiling is being developed to enable sensitive and specific tests for various body fluids including saliva (Juusola & Ballantyne 2003, Hanson & Ballantyne 2010). This approach holds promise to permit simultaneous tests for blood, semen, and saliva with great specificity and sensitivity.

Semen Stains

Prior to the expanded use of DNA testing for high-volume crimes such as burglary, roughly two-thirds of cases pursued with DNA analysis involved sexual assault evidence. Hundreds of millions of sperm are typically ejaculated in several milliliters of seminal fluid. Semen stains can be characterized with visualization of sperm cells, or acid phosphatase (AP) or prostate specific antigen (PSA or p30) tests (Jones 2004).

A microscopic examination to look for the presence of spermatozoa is performed in some laboratories on sexual assault evidence. However, aspermic or oligospermic males have either no sperm or a low sperm count in their seminal fluid ejaculate. In addition, vasectomized males will not release sperm. Therefore tests that can identify semen-specific enzymes are helpful in verifying the presence of semen in sexual assault cases.

Acid phosphatase (AP) is an enzyme secreted by the prostate gland into seminal fluid and is found in concentrations up to 400 times greater in semen than in other body fluids (Sensabaugh 1979, Saferstein 2001). A purple color with the addition of a few drops of sodium alpha naphthylphosphate and Fast Blue B solution or the fluorescence of 4-methyl umbelliferyl phosphate under a UV light indicates the presence of AP. Large areas of fabric can be screened by pressing the garment or bed sheet against an equal sized piece of moistened filter paper and then subjecting the filter paper to the presumptive tests. Systematic searches may also be performed by carefully examining sections of the garment or bed sheet. Each successive test can then help narrow the precise location of the semen stain (Saferstein 2001).

Prostate specific antigen (PSA) was discovered in the 1970s and shown to have forensic value with the identity of a protein named p30 due to its apparent 30 000 molecular weight (Sensabaugh 1978). p30 was initially thought to be unique to seminal fluid although it has been reported at lower levels in breast milk (Yu & Diamandis 1995) and other fluids (Diamandis & Yu 1995). PSA varies in concentration from approximately 300 ng/mL to 4200 ng/mL in semen (Shaler 2002). Seratec (Goettingen, Germany) and Abacus Diagnostics (West Hills, CA) market PSA/p30 test kits that are similar to home-pregnancy tests and which may be used for the forensic identification of semen stains (Hochmeister et al. 1999, Simich et al. 1999).

Laboratory reports where presumptive tests for semen were performed may indicate that an item was found to be "AP positive" or "p30 positive"—in other words, semen was detected implying some form of sexual contact on the evidentiary item.

Direct Observation of Sperm

Most forensic laboratories like to observe spermatozoa as part of confirming the presence of semen in an evidentiary sample (note that in Table 1.2, 42 out of 42 labs confirm semen). A common method of doing this is to recover dried semen evidence from fabric or on human skin with a deionized water-moistened swab. A portion of the recovered cells are then placed onto a microscope slide and fixed to the slide with heat. The immobilized cells are stained with a "Christmas Tree" stain consisting of aluminum sulfate, nuclear Fast Red, picric acid, and indigo carmine (Shaler 2002). The stained slide is then examined under a light microscope for sperm cells with their characteristic head and long tail. The Christmas Tree stain marks the anterior sperm heads light red or pink, the posterior heads dark red, the spermatozoa's mid-piece blue, and the tails stain yellowish green (Shaler 2002).

Professor John Herr at the University of Virginia developed several "sperm paints" to fluorescently label the head and tail portions of spermatozoa with antibodies specific to sperm and thus make it easier to observe sperm cells in the presence of excess female epithelial cells (Herr 2007).

Independent Forensics' SPERM HY-LITER PLUS kit enables detection of even a single human sperm head in the presence of an overwhelming amount of epithelial cells. Development of sample characterization tools that utilize fluorescently tagged monoclonal antibodies, such as the SPERM HY-LITER kit, represents a major advancement and should enable much faster and accurate processing of sexual assault evidence.

Body Fluid Identification with RNA Testing

Another method for body fluid identification that has seen recent research activity is the monitoring of cell-specific gene expression through the analysis of ribonucleic acid (RNA). Erin Hanson and Jack Ballantyne from the University of Central Florida published a thorough review of RNA profiling efforts for body fluid identification (Hanson & Ballantyne

2010). They note that conventional methods for body fluid identification often involve labor-intensive, diverse approaches that are performed sequentially rather than simultaneously. Both time and sample are lost when many of these older characterization assays are performed.

As can be seen by reviewing the previous sections and Table 1.2, there are different presumptive and confirmatory tests for each type of body fluid. Some of the current tests have cross-reactivity with other species and most are not specific to a tissue or fluid. In addition, because these traditional tests can only be performed one at a time, precious evidentiary sample is often consumed and time expended in trying to identify a stain. A method that was both sensitive and specific to multiple body fluids would be a major advance over the conventional approaches now in use.

Different types of cells in our body, such as skin versus semen, contain different collections of mRNA (messenger ribonucleic acid) that are unique to that cell type. Therefore, mRNA profiling offers an opportunity to develop fluid- or tissue-specific assays provided that unique target genes can be found.

Research on RNA techniques has shown that, although less stable than DNA (due to its single-stranded structure and often rapid destruction from digesting enzymes), RNA is useful for stain identification (Juusola & Ballantyne 2003). Work with RNA requires modified extraction protocols in order to co-extract RNA and DNA (Alvarez et al. 2004). The RNA can then be used for body fluid ID while the DNA can be PCR-amplified for DNA typing purposes (Figure 1.3).

Multiple RNA transcripts have been detected with reverse-transcriptase-PCR followed by gel or capillary electrophoresis (Juusola & Ballantyne 2007, Haas et al. 2009, Fleming & Harbison 2010) or real-time PCR (Noreault-Conti & Buel 2007, Haas et al. 2009). Blood, semen, saliva, menstrual blood, and vaginal secretions have been simultaneously identified with some of these assays (Haas et al. 2009, Fleming & Harbison 2010). mRNA markers for blood and saliva have provided successful results on 16-year-old stains (Zubakov et al.

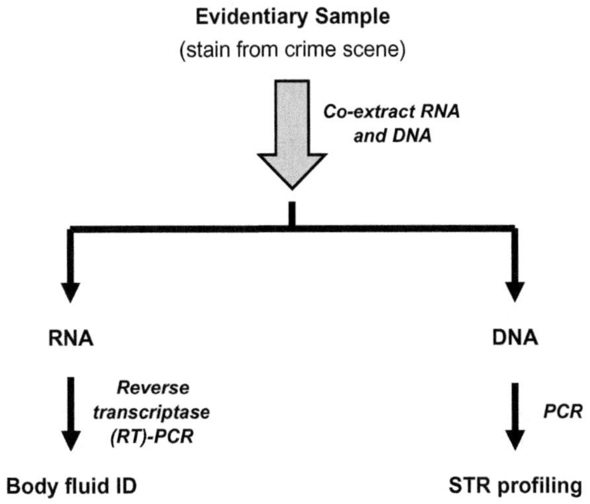

FIGURE 1.3 RNA and DNA co-extraction enables both body fluid identification and STR profiling.

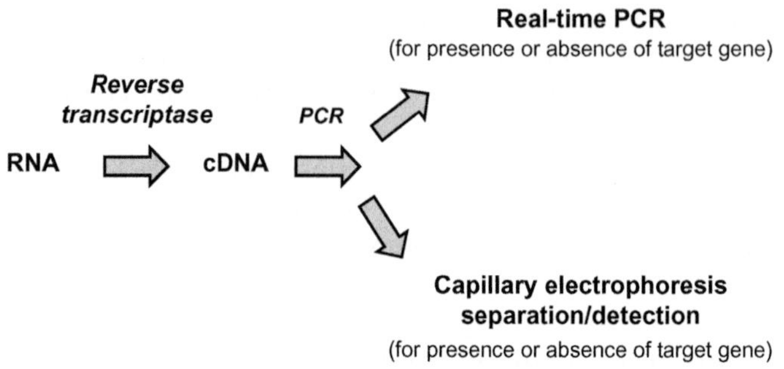

FIGURE 1.4 RNA profiling approaches. The reverse transcriptase step uses gene-specific primers to convert RNA into a double-stranded form (complementary DNA, cDNA) for stability. The PCR step performs exponential amplification of the cDNA targets and can be detected with either real-time PCR (see Chapter 3) or capillary electrophoresis (see Chapter 6).

2008, Zubakov et al. 2009). Figure 1.4 illustrates the approaches taken for RNA profiling to identify body fluids.

At least nine different research groups have identified candidate gene targets for the various body fluids of forensic interest (Table 1.3) and developed tissue-specific mRNA assays in order to create a comprehensive approach to body fluid identification. These groups include efforts at the University of Central Florida (Orlando, Florida), Erasmus University (Rotterdam, Holland), the University of Bonn (Bonn, Germany), the Institute of Environmental Science and Research (ESR, Auckland, New Zealand), the University of Zurich (Zurich, Switzerland), the Vermont Forensic Laboratory (Waterbury, Vermont), Applied Biosystems (Foster City, CA), Ingenetix Ltd. (Vienna, Austria), and the Japanese National Research Institute of Police Science (Chiba, Japan).

A number of so-called "housekeeping" genes which should be present in every sample, have been included in various assays to act as an RNA postive control. These include β-actin, glyceraldehyde-3-phosphate dehydrogenase (GAPDH), ubiquitin conjugating enzyme (UCE), glucose-6-phosphate dehydrogenase (GGPDH), and transcription elongation factor 1α (TEF).

The European DNA Profiling Group (EDNAP) conducted a collaborative exercise with 16 labs examining HBB, SPTB, and PBGD target genes for the identification of blood (Haas et al. 2011). Despite most of the laboratories not having prior RNA experience, 15 of the 16 participating labs produced successful RNA profiles even with 6 different kits for RNA extraction, 7 different reverse transcription kits, 5 different PCR mixes, 7 different thermal cyclers, and 6 different Genetic Analyzers (Haas et al. 2011).

In an effort to find reliable tissue-specific signatures from potentially degraded stains, microRNA (miRNA) targets, which are typically less than 25 nucleotides in length, are being examined (Hanson et al. 2009, Zubakov et al. 2010). Only time will tell how successful research efforts are for identifying and applying RNA or miRNA targets to body fluid identification.

TABLE 1.3 List of Abbreviations for mRNA Gene Markers Used in Body Fluid Identification. For More Information, See Hanson & Ballantyne (2010) and Associated References.

Blood	Semen	Saliva	Vaginal Secretions	Menstrual Blood	Housekeeping
HBB	PRM1	HTN3	MUC4	MMP7	S15
HBA	PRM2	STATH	HBD1	MMP10	β-actin
ALAS2	SEGM1	PRB4	ESR1	MMP11	GAPDH
HMBS	SEGM2	SPRR3		CK19	TEF
GYPA	TGM4	SPRR1A		PR	UCE
ANK1	PSA	KRT4			G6PDH
SPTB		KRT6A			
C1QR1		KRT13			
AMICA1					
AQP9					
NCF2					
CASP2					
C5R1					
ALOX5AP					
MNDA					
ARGHAP26					

Attempts to Determine Bloodstain Age

Many times in crime scene reconstruction it would be helpful to know how long a bloodstain has been on a surface. The quantitation of RNA degradation has been used in an effort to determine post-mortem intervals and to determine the age of blood stains (Anderson et al. 2005, Bauer et al. 2003a, Bauer et al. 2003b). A group from The Netherlands has shown that targeting T-cell rearrangements can be used to predict human age from blood with an accuracy of ±9 years (Zubakov et al. 2010). Application of this approach could enable the classification of a sample's source to an appropriate generation (child vs. adult vs. elderly individual).

Species Identification

Samples being processed as biological evidence may come from non-human sources. For example, in some missing person or disaster victim identification situations, human bones may need to be sorted from non-human bones. As part of sample characterization, species identification may be performed or outsourced to a laboratory that specializes in animal DNA testing (Chapter 16).

CONTAMINATION CONCERNS

Modern DNA testing methods are very sensitive and can be capable of generating DNA profiles from as little as a single cell (see D.N.A. Box 11.3). It is imperative that every precaution be taken to collect samples carefully with appropriate personal protective equipment (Blozis 2010). While a sample may be collected properly from a crime scene, there may be other opportunities for contamination either at the crime scene before the evidence was collected, while the evidentiary item (e.g., a gun) is being handled by examiners in other forensic disciplines—such as fingerprint or firearms examiners—as part of routine casework, or while the sample is being processed in the DNA lab. More on the issues surrounding potential consumable contamination in the DNA lab are covered in Chapter 4.

In the final part of this chapter, we briefly explore two potential concerns with "contamination" before the evidence is collected. The first is commonly referred to as secondary transfer, which is the possibility of individual #1 handling an item and transferring his/her DNA to the item that is then transferred to individual #2 upon their touching the item at a later time. The second concern is the potential for "fake DNA" to be planted at a crime scene to possibly implicate someone else or to confuse investigators.

Impacts of Other Forensic Examinations

Brushes used to dust for fingerprints can cross-contaminate samples if precautions are not taken by the crime scene investigator (van Oorschot et al. 2005). One study found that out of 51 used latent fingerprint brushes tested a full or partial DNA profile was obtained 86% of the time (Proff et al. 2006). Some secondary transfer with contaminated fingerprint brushes was also demonstrated. Thus, changing brushes after investigating crime scenes or a thorough decontamination procedure for brushes after use is recommended (Proff et al. 2006).

Another illustration of potential contamination during other forensic examinations is with firearms examinations, which should be conducted after DNA collection if possible. Alternatively, the firearm examiners need to wear gloves, masks, and other personal protective equipment in order to protect the evidence from contamination. In all cases, it is beneficial to have DNA profiles from latent print and firearms examiners on file as part of the staff elimination database (see Chapter 4). In addition, prior to utilizing chemicals for presumptive testing, it is best to evaluate potential impact on obtaining successful results with downstream DNA testing.

Secondary Transfer Studies

Since DNA results can be successfully obtained from only a few cells (Chapter 11), concerns exist regarding the potential for transfer of cells between an individual and an object or another person, which is commonly referred to as *primary transfer*. When DNA that has been deposited on an item or a person is, in turn, transferred to another item or person or onto a different place on the same item or person, this is referred to as *secondary transfer* (Goray et al. 2010a). In other words, can a DNA profile be obtained from collected cells that were transferred through a second contact rather than the primary contact from the original source? As noted by Mariya Goray and colleagues, a biological sample that has been transferred multiple times, if it can even be detected, will most often appear as a component in a DNA mixture (Goray et al. 2010a).

Studies have shown that the amount of secondary transfer is highly dependent on the surface texture and sample moisture. Porous substances and/or dry samples provided on average less than 0.36% of the original biological material being transferred (Goray et al. 2010a). In this same study, moist samples and non-absorbent surfaces, such as plastic, produced transfer rates of 50% to 95% while moist samples with absorbent surfaces, such as cotton or wool, transferred on average 2%—and only 5% when friction was applied (Goray et al. 2010a). While it has been demonstrated that secondary transfer of DNA can occur, whether or not it is plausible in a particular case will be dependent on a variety of factors including the surface texture and sample moisture (e.g., a fresh bloodstain versus an older bloodstain).

Fake DNA and Sample Authentication

In August 2009, the *New York Times* and several other news sources ran a story on the potential of DNA evidence being manufactured and planted at crime scenes (Pollack 2009). This story arose because scientists at a company named Nucleix (Tel Aviv, Israel) published an article in *Forensic Science International: Genetics* where they artificially created a biological sample with a manufactured DNA profile (Frumkin et al. 2010). This work was done under the guise of trying to create a unique service for authenticating natural versus artificial DNA samples via a methylation detection test. Several letters to the editor following this article expressed concern over why this work was performed (Morling et al. 2011, Barash 2011).

As the International Society of Forensic Genetics board members note in their letter to the editor: "In itself, the problem of possible manipulation and questioning the integrity of any forensic evidence is not new, and has always been a consideration both during the investigation and the trial phase" (Morling et al. 2011). They go on to note: "Forensic experts and perpetrators committing crimes are in what could be considered an evolutionary race where criminal minds react to advances in forensic science with remediation such as gloves to not leave fingerprints, condoms to prevent semen evidence, and putting on their victims' clothes as to not deposit any fibers. Fortunately for all law abiding citizens, not all perpetrators are that organized and of course impulse crimes are not planned at all, so that standard forensic techniques are still a useful tool for processing a crime scene. Scientists need to stay ahead in this race" (Morling et al. 2011). A primary purpose in writing this book is to help forensic DNA scientists do their best in staying ahead of criminals with the new technologies available.

READING LIST AND INTERNET RESOURCES

Overall DNA Testing Process

Butler, J. M. (2010). *Fundamentals of forensic DNA typing*. San Diego: Elsevier Academic Press.

National Research Council (NRCII) Committee on DNA Forensic Science (1996). *The evaluation of forensic DNA evidence*. Washington, DC: National Academy Press.

Sample Collection

Benecke, M. (2005). Forensic DNA samples—collection and handling. In J. Fuchs & M. Podda (Eds.), *Encyclopedia of diagnostic genomics and proteomics* (Vol. 1, pp. 500–504). New York: Marcel Dekker. Available at <http://www.benecke.com/dnacollection.html>.

Bond, J. W. (2007). Value of DNA evidence in detecting crime. *Journal of Forensic Sciences, 52*, 128–136.

Bond, J. W., & Hammond, C. (2008). The value of DNA material recovered from crime scenes. *Journal of Forensic Sciences, 53*, 797–801.

Himmelreich, C. (2009, March 27). Germany's phantom serial killer: A DNA blunder. *Time Magazine* Available at <http://www.time.com/time/world/article/0,8599,1888126,00.html>.

Kirk, P. (1953). *Crime investigation: Physical evidence and the police*. New York: Laboratory Interscience Publishers, Inc.

Neuhuber, F., et al. (2009). Female criminals—it's not always the offender! *Forensic Science International: Genetics Supplement Series, 2*, 145–146.

DNA Sample Sources

Adams, D. E., et al. (1991). Deoxyribonucleic acid (DNA) analysis by restriction fragment length polymorphisms of blood and other body fluid stains subjected to contamination and environmental insults. *Journal of Forensic Sciences, 36*, 1284–1298.

Balogh, M. K., et al. (2003). STR genotyping and mtDNA sequencing of latent fingerprint on paper. *Forensic Science International, 137*, 188–195.

Bär, W., et al. (1988). Postmortem stability of DNA. *Forensic Science International, 39*, 59–70.

Castle, P. E., et al. (2003). Effects of electron-beam irradiation on buccal-cell DNA. *American Journal of Human Genetics, 73*, 646–651.

Cina, S. J., et al. (2000). Isolation and identification of female DNA on postcoital penile swabs. *American Journal of Forensic Medicine and Pathology, 21*, 97–100.

Crowe, G., et al. (2000). The effect of laundering on the detection of acid phosphatase and spermatozoa on cotton t-shirts. *Canadian Society of Forensic Sciences Journal, 33*, 1–5.

Esslinger, K. J., et al. (2004). Using STR analysis to detect human DNA from exploded pipe bomb devices. *Journal of Forensic Sciences, 49*, 481–484.

Hillier, E., et al. (2005). Recovery of DNA from shoes. *Canadian Society of Forensic Sciences Journal, 38*, 143–150.

Kuperus, W. R., et al. (2003). Crime scene links through DNA evidence: The practical experience from Saskatchewan casework. *Canadian Society of Forensic Science Journal, 36*, 19–28.

Lee, H. C., et al. (1998). Forensic applications of DNA typing: Part 2: Collection and preservation of DNA evidence. *American Journal of Forensic Medicine and Pathology, 19*, 10–18.

Lee, H. C., & Ladd, C. (2001). Preservation and collection of biological evidence. *Croatian Medical Journal, 42*, 225–228.

Schulz, M. M., & Reichert, W. (2002). Archived or directly swabbed latent fingerprints as a DNA source for STR typing. *Forensic Science International, 127*, 128–130.

Withrow, A. G., et al. (2003). Extraction and analysis of human nuclear and mitochondrial DNA from electron beam irradiated envelopes. *Journal of Forensic Sciences, 48*, 1302–1308.

Biological Evidence at Crime Scenes

Blozis, J. (2010). Forensic DNA evidence collection at a crime scene: an investigator's commentary. *Forensic Science Review, 22*, 121–130.

Bozzo, W. R., et al. (2009). DNA recovery from different evidences in 300 cases of sexual assault. *Forensic Science International: Genetics Supplement Series, 2*, 141–142.

Colussi, A., et al. (2009). Sexual assault cases related to unknown perpetrator: almost 50% of the analyzed cases corresponded to serial offenders. *Forensic Science International: Genetics Supplement Series, 2*, 143–144.

Crime scene and DNA basics. <http://dna.gov/training/evidence>.

Gingras, F., et al. (2009). Biological and DNA evidence in 1000 sexual assault cases. *Forensic Science International: Genetics Supplement Series, 2*, 138–140.

Lee, H. C. (1996). Collection and preservation of DNA evidence. In *Proceedings of the seventh international symposium on human identification* (pp. 39–45). Available at <http://www.promega.com/geneticidproc>.

McNally, L., et al. (1989). Evaluation of deoxyribonucleic acid (DNA) isolated from human bloodstains exposed to ultraviolet light, heat, humidity, and soil contaminations. *Journal of Forensic Sciences, 34*, 1059–1069.

Raymond, J. J., et al. (2009). Trace DNA success rates relating to volume crime offences. *Forensic Science International: Genetics Supplement Series, 2*, 136–137.

Spitaleri, S., et al. (2006). Genotyping of human DNA recovered from mosquitoes found on a crime scene. *Progress in Forensic Genetics 11, ICS 1288*, 574–576.

What every law enforcement officer should know about DNA evidence: First responding officers and investigators and evidence technicians. <http://dna.gov/training/letraining>.

Evidence Collection

Barash, M., et al. (2010). The use of adhesive tape for recovery of DNA from crime scene items. *Journal of Forensic Sciences, 55*, 1058–1064.

Benschop, C. C. G., et al. (2010). Post-coital vaginal sampling with nylon flocked swabs improves DNA typing. *Forensic Science International: Genetics, 4*, 115–121.

Copan nylon flocked swabs. <http://www.copanswabs.com/products/forensics/>.

Grassberger, M., et al. (2005). Evaluation of a novel tagging and tissue preservation system for potential use in forensic sample collection. *Forensic Science International, 151*, 233–237.

Hall, D., & Fairley, M. (2004). A single approach to the recovery of DNA and firearm discharge residue evidence. *Science & Justice, 44*, 15–19.

Hansson, O., et al. (2009). Trace DNA collection – performance of minitape and three different swabs. *Forensic Science International: Genetics Supplement Series, 2*, 189–190.

Hochmeister, M., et al. (1997). A foldable cardboard box for drying and storage of by cotton swab collected biological samples. *Archiv fur Kriminologie, 200*, 113–120.

Lee, H. C., et al. (1998). Forensic applications of DNA typing: Part 2: Collection and preservation of DNA evidence. *American Journal of Forensic Medicine and Pathology, 19*, 10–18.

Lee, H. C., & Ladd, C. (2001). Preservation and collection of biological evidence. *Croatian Medical Journal, 42*, 225–228.

May, R., & Thomson, J. (2009). Optimisation of cellular DNA recovery from tape-lifts. *Forensic Science International: Genetics Supplement Series, 2*, 191–192.

Norris, J. V., et al. (2007). Expedited, chemically enhanced sperm cell recovery from cotton swabs for rape kit analysis. *Journal of Forensic Sciences, 52*, 800–805.

Pang, B. C., & Cheung, B. K. (2007). Double swab technique for collecting touched evidence. *Legal Medicine (Tokyo), 9*, 181–184.

Sweet, D., et al. (1997). An improved method to recover saliva from human skin: The double swab technique. *Journal of Forensic Sciences, 42*, 320–322.

Voorhees, J. C., et al. (2006). Enhanced elution of sperm from cotton swabs via enzymatic digestion for rape kit analysis. *Journal of Forensic Sciences, 51*, 574–579.

Reference Sample Collection

Bode Technology Buccal DNA Collector. <http://www.bodetech.com/solutions/collection-products>.

Burgoyne, L. A. (1997). Convenient DNA collection and processing: disposable toothbrushes and FTA paper as a non-threatening buccal-cell collection kit compatible with automatable DNA processing. In *Proceedings of the eighth international symposium on human identification*. Available at <http://www.promega.com/geneticidproc/>.

Burger, M. F., et al. (2005). Buccal DNA samples for DNA typing: New collection and processing methods. *BioTechniques, 39*, 257–261.

Fox, J. C., et al. (2002). New device and method for buccal cell collection and processing. In *Proceedings of the thirteenth international symposium on human identification*. Available online at <http://www.promega.com/geneticidproc/ussymp13proc/contents/>.

Martinez-Gonzalez, L. J., et al. (2007). Intentional mixed buccal cell reference sample in a paternity case. *Journal of Forensic Sciences, 52*, 397–399.

Quinque, D., et al. (2006). Evaluation of saliva as a source of human DNA for population and association studies. *Analytical Biochemistry, 353*, 272–277.

Schumm, J. W., et al. (2004). Collecting and processing buccal cell samples. *Progress in Forensic Genetics 10, ICS 1261*, 550–552.

Tanaka, M., et al. (2000). Usefulness of a toothbrush as a source of evidential DNA for typing. *Journal of Forensic Sciences, 45*, 674–676.

Zamir, A., et al. (2004). A possible source of reference DNA from archived treated adhesive lifters. *Journal of Forensic Sciences, 49*, 68–70.

Sample Storage

Armed Forces Repository of Specimen Samples for the Identification of Remains (AFRSSIR). <http://www.afip.org/consultation/AFMES/AFDIL/AFRSSIR/index.html>.

Baust, J. G. (2008). Strategies for the storage of DNA. *Biopreservation and Biobanking, 6*, 251–252.

Biomatrica. <http://www.biomatrica.com/>.

Bonnet, J., et al. (2010). Chain and conformation stability of solid-state DNA: implications for room temperature storage. *Nucleic Acids Research, 38*, 1531–1546.

Coble, M. D., et al. (2008). A ten year study of DNA blood references collected on untreated filter paper and stored at room temperature. *Proceedings of the American Academy of Forensic Sciences, 14*, 90–91.

DNA bank network: Long term DNA storage workshop proceedings. <http://www.dnabank-network.org/publications/Workshop_Long-term_DNA_storage-Summary_and_Abstracts.pdf>.

Gaillard, C., & Strauss, F. (2000). Eliminating DNA loss and denaturation during storage in plastic microtubes. *International Biotechnology Laboratory, 18*(13), 6. Available at <http://frstrauss.free.fr/reprints/gaillard_IBL00.pdf>.

GenVault. <http://www.genvault.com/>.

Graham, E. A. M., et al. (2008). Room temperature DNA preservation of soft tissue for rapid DNA extraction: An addition to the disaster victim identification investigators toolkit? *Forensic Science International: Genetics, 2*, 29–34.

Hochmeister, M. N., et al. (1998). A simple foldable "swab box" for the drying and storage of biological material recovered on cotton swabs. *Progress in Forensic Genetics, 7*, 24.

Kansagara, A. G., et al. (2008). Dry-state, room-temperature storage of DNA and RNA. *Nature Methods, 5*(9), iv–v.

Kilpatrick, C. W. (2002). Non-cryogenic preservation of mammalian tissue for DNA extraction: an assessment of storage methods. *Biochemical Genetics, 40*, 53–62.

Kline, M. C., et al. (2002). Polymerase chain reaction amplification of DNA from aged blood stains: Quantitative evaluation of the "suitability for purpose" of four filter papers as archival media. *Analytical Chemistry, 74*, 1863–1869.

Kline, M. C. (2010). DNA Stability Studies. Presentation at the Forensics@NIST Symposium on December 8, 2010. Available at <http://www.cstl.nist.gov/biotech/strbase/NISTpub.htm>.

Lee, S. B., et al. (2010). Optimizing storage and handling of DNA extracts. *Forensic Science Review, 22*, 131–144.

Marrone, A., & Ballantyne, J. (2010). Hydrolysis of DNA and its molecular components in the dry state. *Forensic Science International: Genetics, 4*, 168–177.

Seah, L. H., et al. (2001). Photosensitizer initiated attacks on DNA under dry conditions and their inhibition: a DNA archiving issue. *Journal of Photochemistry and Photobiology B, 61*, 10–20.

Shikama, K. (1965). Effect of freezing and thawing on the stability of double helix of DNA. *Nature, 207*, 529–530.

Sjöholm, M. I., et al. (2007). Assessing quality and functionality of DNA from fresh and archival dried blood spots and recommendations for quality control guidelines. *Clinical Chemistry, 53*(8), 1401–1407.

Sigurdson, A. J., et al. (2006). Long-term storage and recovery of buccal cell DNA from treated cards. *Cancer Epidemiology Biomarkers & Prevention, 15*, 385–388.

Smith, S., & Morin, P. A. (2005). Optimal storage conditions for highly dilute DNA samples: A role for trehalose as a preserving agent. *Journal of Forensic Sciences, 50*, 1101–1108.

Swinfield, C. E., et al. (2009). The use of DNA stabilizing solution to enable room temperature storage and transportation of buccal and trace sample swabs. *Forensic Science International: Genetics Supplement Series, 2*, 183–184.

Zhu, B., et al. (2007). Natural DNA mixed with trehalose persists in B-form double-stranding even in the dry state. *Journal of Physical Chemistry B, 111*, 5542–5544.

Sample Characterization

Ballantyne, J. (2000). Serology. In J. A. Siegel, et al. (Ed.), *Encyclopedia of forensic sciences* (pp. 1322–1331). San Diego: Academic Press.

Fourney, R. M., et al. (2007). Recent progress in processing biological evidence and forensic DNA profiling: A review 2004 to 2007. In *Interpol 15th international forensic science symposium* (pp. 635–719). Available at <http://www.cstl.nist.gov/biotech/strbase/tools/IFSS07-BioReview.pdf>.

Independent Forensics Rapid Stain Identification Series. <http://www.ifi-test.com/rsid.php>.

Jones, E. L. (2004). The identification of semen and other body fluids (2nd ed.). In R. Saferstein (Ed.), *Forensic science handbook* (Vol. II, pp. 329–399). Upper Saddle River, NJ: Pearson Prentice Hall.

Testing of body fluids and tissues. <http://dna.gov/training/forensicbiology>.

Li, R. (2008). *Forensic biology*. Boca Raton, FL: CRC Press.

Saferstein, R. (2001). *Criminalistics: An introduction to forensic science* (7th ed.). (Chapters 12 and 13, pp. 320–394). Upper Saddle River, NJ: Prentice Hall.

Shaler, R. C. (2002). Modern forensic biology (2nd ed.). In R. Saferstein (Ed.), *Forensic science handbook* (Vol. I, pp. 525–613). Upper Saddle River, NJ: Prentice Hall.

Vandenberg, N., & van Oorschot, R. A. (2006). The use of Polilight in the detection of seminal fluid, saliva, and bloodstains and comparison with conventional chemical based screening tests. *Journal of Forensic Sciences, 51*, 361–370.

Virkler, K., & Lednev, I. K. (2009). Analysis of body fluids for forensic purposes: from laboratory testing to non-destructive rapid confirmatory identification at a crime scene. *Forensic Science International, 188*, 1–17.

Bloodstains

Abacus Diagnostics ABAcard HemaTrace kit. <http://www.abacusdiagnostics.com/blood.htm>.

Budowle, B., et al. (2000). The presumptive reagent fluorescein for detection of dilute bloodstains and subsequent STR typing of recovered DNA. *Journal of Forensic Sciences, 45*, 1090–1092.

Gross, A. M., et al. (1999). The effect of luminol on presumptive tests and DNA analysis using the polymerase chain reaction. *Journal of Forensic Sciences, 44*, 837–840.

Hochmeister, M. N., et al. (1991). Effects of presumptive test reagents on the ability to obtain restriction fragment length polymorphism (RFLP) patterns from human blood and semen stains. *Journal of Forensic Sciences, 36*, 656–661.

Hochmeister, M. N., et al. (1999). Validation studies of an immunochromatographic 1-step test for the forensic identification of human blood. *Journal of Forensic Sciences, 44*, 597–602.

Independent Forensics Rapid Stain Identification-Blood. <http://www.ifi-test.com/rsid_blood.php>.

Johnson, S., et al. (2003). Validation study of the Abacus Diagnostics ABAcard HemaTrace membrane test for the forensic identification of human blood. *Canadian Society of Forensic Science Journal, 36*(3), 173–183.

Ponce, A. C., & Pascual, F. A. V. (1999). Critical revision of presumptive tests for bloodstains. *Forensic Science Communications, 1*(2), 1–15.

Poon, H., et al. (2009). The use of Hemastix and the subsequent lack of DNA recovery using the Promega DNA IQ system. *Journal of Forensic Sciences, 54*, 1278–1286.

Schweers, B. A., et al. (2008). Developmental validation of a novel lateral flow strip test for rapid identification of human blood (Rapid Stain Identification ™ -Blood). *Forensic Science International: Genetics, 2*, 243–247.

Tobe, S. S., et al. (2007). Evaluation of six presumptive tests for blood, their specificity, sensitivity, and effect on high molecular-weight DNA. *Journal of Forensic Sciences, 52*, 102–109.

Webb, J. L., et al. (2006). A comparison of the presumptive luminol test for blood with four non-chemiluminescent forensic techniques. *Luminescence, 21*, 214–220.

Saliva Stains

Abacus Diagnostics SALIgAE saliva identification kit. <http://www.abacusdiagnostics.com/saliva.htm>.

Abaz, J., et al. (2002). Comparison of the variables affecting the recovery of DNA from common drinking containers. *Forensic Science International, 126*, 233–240.

Auvdel, M. J. (1986). Amylase levels in semen and saliva stains. *Journal of Forensic Sciences, 31*, 426–431.

Donaldson, A. E., et al. (2010). Using oral microbial DNA analysis to identify expirated bloodspatter. *International Journal of Legal Medicine, 124*, 569–576.

Hochmeister, M. N., et al. (1998). PCR analysis from cigarette butts, postage stamps, envelope sealing flaps, and other saliva-stained material. *Methods in Molecular Biology, 98*, 27–32.

Independent Forensics Rapid Skin Identification-Saliva. <http://www.ifi-test.com/rsid_saliva.php>.

Myers, J. R., & Adkins, W. K. (2008). Comparison of modern techniques for saliva screening. *Journal of Forensic Sciences, 53*, 862–867.

Nakanishi, H., et al. (2009). A novel method for the identification of saliva by detecting oral streptococci using PCR. *Forensic Science International, 183*, 20–23.

Phadebas amylase products. <http://www.phadebas.com/applications/forensic>.

Whitehead, P. H., & Kipps, A. E. (1975). The significance of amylase in forensic investigations of body fluids. *Journal of Forensic Sciences, 6*, 137–144.

Semen Stains

Abacus Diagnostics ABAcard p30 kit. <http://www.abacusdiagnostics.com/semen.htm>.

Apostolov, A., et al. (2009). DNA identification of biological traces and interpretation in a sexual assault case. *American Journal of Forensic Medicine and Pathology, 30*, 57–60.

Diamandis, E. P., & Yu, H. (1995). Prostate-specific antigen and lack of specificity for prostate cells. *Lancet, 345*, 1186.

Hochmeister, M. N., et al. (1997). High levels of alpha-amylase in seminal fluid may represent a simple artifact in the collection process. *Journal of Forensic Sciences, 42*, 535–536.

Hochmeister, M. N., et al. (1999). Evaluation of prostate-specific antigen (PSA) membrane test assays for the forensic identification of seminal fluid. *Journal of Forensic Sciences, 44*, 1057–1060.

Independent Forensics Rapid Stain Identification-Semen. <http://www.ifi-test.com/rsid_semen.php>.

Jobin, R. M., & De Gouffe, M. (2003). The persistence of seminal constituents on panties after laundering: significance to investigations of sexual assault. *Canadian Society of Forensic Sciences Journal, 36*, 1–10.

Sato, I., et al. (2002). Use of the 'SMITEST' PSA card to identify the presence of prostate-specific antigen in semen and male urine. *Forensic Science International, 127*, 71–74.

Sato, I., et al. (2007). Applicability of Nanotrap Sg as a semen detection kit before male-specific DNA profiling in sexual assaults. *International Journal of Legal Medicine, 121*, 315–319.

Sensabaugh, G. F. (1978). Isolation and characterization of a semen-specific protein from human seminal plasma: A potential new marker for semen identification. *Journal of Forensic Sciences, 23*, 106–115.

Sensabaugh, G. F. (1979). The quantitative acid phosphatase test: a statistical analysis of endogenous and postcoital acid phosphatase levels in the vagina. *Journal of Forensic Sciences, 24*, 346–365.

Seratec PSA Semiquant kit. <http://www.seratec.com>.

Simich, J. P., et al. (1999). Validation of the use of a commercially available kit for the identification of prostate specific antigen (PSA) in semen stains. *Journal of Forensic Sciences, 44*, 1229–1231.

Yu, H., & Diamandis, E. P. (1995). Prostate-specific antigen in milk of lactating women. *Clinical Chemistry, 41*, 54–58.

Sperm and Sperm Detection

Herr, J. (2007). *SpermPaint optimization and validation*. NIJ Grant 2000-IJ-CX-K013 Report. Available at <http://www.ncjrs.gov/pdffi les1/nij/grants/220289.pdf>.

Independent Forensics SPERM HY-LITER PLUS kit. <http://www.spermhy-liter.com>.

Willot, G. M., & Allard, J. E. (1982). Spermatozoa—their persistence after sexual intercourse. *Forensic Science International, 19*, 135–154.

Body Fluid Identification with RNA Testing

Alvarez, M., et al. (2004). An mRNA and DNA co-isolation method for forensic casework samples. *Analytical Biochemistry, 335*, 289–298.

Bauer, M., et al. (1999). Detection of epithelial cells in dried blood stains by reverse transcriptase-polymerase chain reaction. *Journal of Forensic Sciences, 44*, 1232–1236.

Bauer, M., & Patzelt, D. (2002). Evaluation of mRNA markers for the identification of menstrual blood. *Journal of Forensic Sciences, 47*, 1278–1282.

Bauer, M., & Patzelt, D. (2003). Protamine mRNA as molecular marker for spermatozoa in semen stains. *International Journal of Legal Medicine, 117*, 175–179.

Bauer, M., & Patzelt, D. (2003). A method for simultaneous RNA and DNA isolation from dried blood and semen stains. *Forensic Science International, 136*, 76–78.

Bauer, M. (2007). RNA in forensic science. *Forensic Science International: Genetics, 1*, 69–74.

Bauer, M., & Patzelt, D. (2008). Identification of menstrual blood by real time RT-PCR: technical improvements and the practical value of negative test results. *Forensic Science International, 174*, 55–59.

Cossu, C., et al. (2009). How specific are the vaginal secretion mRNA-markers HBD1 and MUC4? *Forensic Science International: Genetics Supplement Series, 2*, 536–537.
Fang, R., et al. (2006). Realtime PCR assays for the detection of tissues and body fluid specific mRNAs. *Progress in Forensic Genetics 11, ICS 1288*, 685–687.
Ferri, G., et al. (2004). Successful identification of two years old menstrual bloodstain by using MMP11 shorter amplicons. *Journal of Forensic Sciences, 49*(6), 1387.
Fleming, R. I., & Harbison, S. (2010). The development of a mRNA multiplex RT-PCR assay for the definitive identification of body fluids. *Forensic Science International: Genetics, 4*, 244–256.
Hanson, E. K., & Ballantyne, J. (2010). RNA profiling for the identification of the tissue origin of dried stains in forensic biology. *Forensic Science Review, 22*, 145–157.
Haas, C., et al. (2009). mRNA profiling for body fluid identification by reverse transcription endpoint PCR and real-time PCR. *Forensic Science International: Genetics, 3*, 80–88.
Haas, C., et al. (2011). mRNA profiling for the identification of blood—results of a collaborative EDNAP exercise. *Forensic Science International: Genetics, 5*, 21–26.
Heinrich, M., et al. (2007). Successful RNA extraction from various human postmortem tissues. *International Journal of Legal Medicine, 121*, 136–142.
Juusola, J., & Ballantyne, J. (2003). Messenger RNA profiling: a prototype method to supplant conventional methods for body fluid identification. *Forensic Science International, 135*, 85–96.
Juusola, J., & Ballantyne, J. (2005). Multiplex mRNA profiling for the identification of body fluids. *Forensic Science International, 152*, 1–12.
Juusola, J., & Ballantyne, J. (2007). mRNA profiling for body fluid identification by multiplex quantitative RT-PCR. *Journal of Forensic Sciences, 52*, 1252–1262.
Karlsson, H., et al. (2003). Extraction of RNA from dried blood on filter papers after long-term storage. *Clinical Chemistry, 49*, 979–981.
Noreault-Conti, T. L., & Buel, E. (2007). The use of real-time PCR for forensic stain identification. *Profiles in DNA, 10*, 3–5.
Noreault-Conti, T. L., & Buel, E. (2008). Development of an RNA-based screening assay for forensic stain identification. In *Proceedings of the 19th international symposium on human identification*. Available at <http://www.promega.com/geneticidproc/ussymp19proc/oralpresentations/Buel.pdf>.
Nussbaumer, C., et al. (2006). Messenger RNA profiling: A novel method for body fluid identification by real-time PCR. *Forensic Science International, 157*, 181–186.
Park, N. J., et al. (2006). Characterization of RNA in saliva. *Clinical Chemistry, 52*, 988–994.
Sakurada, K., et al. (2009). Evaluation of mRNA-based approach for identification of saliva and semen. *Legal Medicine, 11*, 125–128.
Setzer, M., et al. (2008). Recovery and stability of RNA in vaginal swabs and blood, semen, and saliva stains. *Journal of Forensic Sciences, 53*, 296–305.
Van Hoof, A., & Parker, R. (2002). Messenger RNA degradation: beginning at the end. *Current Biology, 12*, 285–287.
Zubakov, D., et al. (2008). Stable RNA markers for identification of blood and saliva stains revealed from whole genome expression analysis of time-wise degraded samples. *International Journal of Legal Medicine, 122*, 135–142.
Zubakov, D., et al. (2009). New markers for old stains: stable mRNA markers for blood and saliva identification from up to 16-year-old stains. *International Journal of Legal Medicine, 123*, 71–74.

miRNA

Beuvink, I., et al. (2007). A novel microarray approach reveals new tissue-specific signatures of known and predicted mammalian microRNAs. *Nucleic Acids Research, 35*(7), e52.
Carthew, R. W., & Sontheimer, E. J. (2009). Origins and mechanisms of miRNAs and siRNAs. *Cell, 136*, 642–655.
Hanson, E., et al. (2009). Identification of forensically relevant body fluids using a panel of differentially expressed microRNAs. *Forensic Science International: Genetics Supplement Series, 2*, 503–504.
Zubakov, D., et al. (2010). MicroRNA markers for forensic body fluid identification obtained from microarray screening and quantitative RT-PCR confirmation. *International Journal of Legal Medicine, 124*, 217–226.

Attempts to Determine Bloodstain Age

Anderson, S., et al. (2005). A method for determining the age of a bloodstain. *Forensic Science International, 148*, 37–45.

Bauer, M., et al. (2003a). Quantification of RNA degradation by semi-quantitative duplex and competitive RT-PCR: a possible indicator of the age of bloodstains? *Forensic Science International, 138*, 94–103.

Bauer, M., et al. (2003b). Quantification of mRNA degradation as possible indicator of postmortem interval–a pilot study. *Legal Medicine, 5*, 220–227.

Zubakov, D., et al. (2010). Estimating human age from T-cell DNA rearrangements. *Current Biology, 20*, R970–R971.

Potential Impact of Other Forensic Tests

Andersen, J., & Bramble, S. (1997). The effects of finger mark enhancement light sources on subsequent PCR-STR DNA analysis of fresh bloodstains. *Journal of Forensic Sciences, 42*, 303–306.

Budowle, B., et al. (2000). The presumptive reagent fluorescein for detection of dilute bloodstains and subsequent STR typing of recovered DNA. *Journal of Forensic Sciences, 45*, 1090–1092.

Della Manna, A., & Montpetit, S. (2000). A novel approach to obtaining reliable PCR results from luminol-treated bloodstains. *Journal of Forensic Sciences, 45*, 886–890.

Fregeau, C. J., et al. (2000). Fingerprint enhancement revisited and the effects of blood enhancement chemicals on subsequent Profiler Plus fluorescent short tandem repeat DNA analysis of fresh and aged bloody fingerprints. *Journal of Forensic Sciences, 45*, 354–380.

Hochmeister, M. N., et al. (1997). Effects of toluidine blue and destaining reagents used in sexual assault examinations on the ability to obtain DNA profiles from postcoital vaginal swabs. *Journal of Forensic Sciences, 42*, 316–319.

Proff, C., et al. (2006). Experiments on the DNA contamination risk via latent fingerprint brushes. *Progress in Forensic Genetics 11, ICS 1288*, 601–603.

van Oorschot, R. A., et al. (2005). Beware of the possibility of fingerprinting techniques transferring DNA. *Journal of Forensic Sciences, 50*, 1417–1422.

Transfer Studies

Aitken, C., et al. (2003). A graphical model for recovery of cross-transfer evidence in DNA profile. *Theoretical Population Biology, 63*, 179–190.

Goray, M., et al. (2010a). Secondary DNA transfer of biological substances under varying test conditions. *Forensic Science International: Genetics, 4*, 62–67.

Goray, M., et al. (2010b). Investigation of secondary DNA transfer of skin cells under controlled test conditions. *Legal Medicine, 12*, 117–120.

Ladd, C., et al. (1999). A systematic analysis of secondary DNA transfer. *Journal of Forensic Sciences, 44*, 1270–1272.

Lowe, A., et al. (2002). The propensity of individuals to deposit DNA and secondary transfer of low level DNA from individuals to inert surfaces. *Forensic Science International, 129*, 25–34.

Phipps, M., & Petricevic, S. (2007). The tendency of individuals to transfer DNA to handled items. *Forensic Science International, 168*, 162–168.

Poy, A. L., & van Oorschot, R. A. H. (2006). Trace DNA presence, origin, and transfer within a forensic biology laboratory and its potential effect on casework. *Journal of Forensic Identification, 56*, 558–576.

Rudin, N., & Inman, K. (2007). The urban myths & conventional wisdom of transfer: DNA as trace evidence. *The CACNews, 3rd quarter*, 26–29. Available at <http://www.cacnews.org/news/3rdq07a.pdf>.

Rutty, G. N. (2002). An investigation into the transference and survivability of human DNA following simulated manual strangulation with consideration of the problem of third party contamination. *International Journal of Legal Medicine, 116*, 170–173.

van Oorschot, R. A. H., et al. (2009). Impact of relevant variables on the transfer of biological substances. *Forensic Science International: Genetics Supplement Series, 2*, 547–548.

Fake DNA and Sample Authentication

Barash, M. (2011). Letter to the editor: Authentication of forensic DNA samples. *Forensic Science International: Genetics*, 5, 253–254.

Frumkin, D., et al. (2011). Authentication of forensic DNA samples. *Forensic Science International: Genetics, 4*, 95–103.

Frumkin, D., & Wasserstrom, A. (2011). Response to letter to the editor by Mr. Mark Barash. *Forensic Science International: Genetics*, 5, 255–256.

Frumkin, D., & Wasserstrom, A. (2011). Response to letter to the editor by Prinz et al. *Forensic Science International: Genetics*, 5, 251–252.
Morling, N., et al. (2011). Letter to the editor: Authentication of forensic DNA samples. *Forensic Science International: Genetics*, 5, 249–250.
Pollack, A. (2009, August 18). DNA evidence can be fabricated, scientists show. *New York Times*. Available at <http://www.nytimes.com/2009/08/18/science/18dna.html>.

CHAPTER

2

DNA Extraction Methods

Steps Involved

PURPOSE OF DNA EXTRACTION

A biological sample obtained from a crime scene in the form of a blood or semen stain or a tissue (blood or buccal swab) sample from a known individual contains a number of substances besides DNA. Cellular proteins that package and protect DNA in the environment of the cell can inhibit the ability to analyze the DNA. Therefore, extraction methods have been developed to separate proteins and other cellular materials from the DNA molecules. Ideally, the DNA extraction process removes inhibitors that reduce or prevent polymerase chain reaction (PCR) amplification. The extraction process should also produce a stable solution containing high-quality DNA that will not degrade over time during sample storage.

The goals of the DNA extraction process are typically to (1) lyse cells to release the DNA molecules, (2) separate the DNA molecules from other cellular material, and (3) isolate the DNA into a format compatible with downstream applications including PCR amplification. The quantity and quality of DNA often need to be measured prior to proceeding further with analytical procedures to ensure optimal results. This chapter will focus on the DNA extraction process while the following chapter will cover assessment of DNA quantity and quality prior to further sample processing.

All samples must be carefully handled regardless of the DNA extraction method to avoid sample-to-sample contamination or introduction of extraneous DNA. The extraction process is probably where the DNA sample is more susceptible to contamination in the laboratory than at any other time in the forensic DNA analysis process. For this reason, laboratories usually process the evidence samples at separate times and sometimes even different locations from the reference samples.

TABLE 2.1 Typical DNA Amounts That May Be Extracted from Biological Materials (Lee & Ladd 2001). Both Quality and Quantity of DNA Recovered from Evidentiary Samples Can Be Significantly Affected by Environmental Factors.

Type of Sample	Amount of DNA
Liquid blood	20000 ng/mL to 40000 ng/mL
Blood stain	250 ng/cm^2 to 500 ng/cm^2
Liquid semen	150000 ng/mL to 300000 ng/mL
Post-coital vaginal swab	10 ng/swab to 3000 ng/swab
Plucked hair (with root)	1 ng/root to 750 ng/root
Shed hair (with root)	1 ng/root to 10 ng/root
Liquid saliva	1000 ng/mL to 10000 ng/mL
Oral swab	100 ng/swab to 1500 ng/swab
Urine	1 ng/mL to 20 ng/mL
Bone	3 ng/mg to 10 ng/mg
Tissue	50 ng/mg to 500 ng/mg

For many years, a popular method for preparation of reference samples was to make a blood stain by applying a drop of blood to a cotton cloth, referred to as a swatch, to produce a spot about 1 cm^2 in area. Ten microliters of whole blood, about the size of a drop, contains approximately 70,000 to 80,000 white blood cells and should yield approximately 500 ng of genomic DNA. The actual yield will vary with the number of white blood cells present in the sample and the efficiency of the DNA extraction process. The typical amounts of DNA extracted from various biological materials are shown in Table 2.1.

Extracted DNA is typically stored at −20°C, or even −80°C for long-term storage, to prevent nuclease activity. Nucleases are protein enzymes found in cells that degrade DNA to allow the cells to recycle nucleotide components. Nucleases need magnesium to work properly so one of the measures to prevent them from digesting DNA in blood is the use of purple-topped tubes containing a blood preservative known as EDTA. The EDTA chelates, or binds up, most of the free magnesium and thus helps prevent the nucleases from destroying the DNA in the collected blood sample.

PCR Inhibitors and DNA Degradation

When extracting biological materials for the purpose of forensic DNA typing, it is important to try to avoid further degradation of the DNA template as well as to remove inhibitors of PCR where possible. The presence of inhibitors or degraded DNA can lead to complete PCR amplification failure or a reduced sensitivity of detection usually for the larger PCR products.

Two PCR inhibitors commonly found in forensic cases are hemoglobin and indigo dyes from denim. Melanin found in hair samples can be a source of PCR inhibition when trying to amplify mitochondrial DNA. These inhibitors likely bind in the active site of the *Taq* DNA polymerase and prevent its proper functioning during PCR amplification.

DNA degrades through a variety of mechanisms including both enzymatic and chemical processes. Once an organism dies its DNA molecules face cellular nucleases followed by bacterial, fungal, and insect onslaughts depending on the environmental conditions. In addition, hydrolytic cleavage and oxidative base damage can limit successful retrieval and amplification of DNA. The main target for hydrolytic cleavage is the glycosidic base sugar bond. Breakage here leads to nucleobase loss and then a single-stranded "nick" at the abasic site.

If a sufficient number of DNA molecules in the biological sample break in a region where primers anneal or between the forward and reverse primers, then PCR amplification (Chapter 4) efficiency will be reduced or the target region may fail to be amplified at all. Thus, heat and humidity, which speed up hydrolytic cleavage, are enemies of intact DNA molecules. Furthermore, UV irradiation (e.g., direct sunlight) can lead to cross-linking of adjacent thymine nucleotides on the DNA molecule which will prevent passage of the polymerase during PCR. The problems and potential solutions for samples possessing degraded or damaged DNA will be covered further in Chapter 10. In addition, methods for overcoming the effects of PCR inhibitors will be touched upon in Chapter 4.

EARLY TECHNIQUES USED FOR DNA EXTRACTION

There are several primary techniques for DNA extraction used in today's forensic DNA laboratory: organic extraction, Chelex extraction, and FTA or solid-phase extraction (Figure 2.1). The exact extraction or DNA isolation procedure varies depending on the type of biological evidence being examined. For example, whole blood must be treated differently from a bloodstain or a bone fragment. James Stray and colleagues at Applied Biosystems/Life Technologies have reviewed different DNA extraction methods (Stray et al. 2010, Stray & Shewale 2010).

Organic (Phenol-Chloroform) Extraction

Organic extraction, sometimes referred to as phenol chloroform extraction, has been in use for the longest period of time and for many years was the most widely used method for DNA extraction. High molecular weight DNA, which was essential for early RFLP methods, may be obtained most effectively with organic extraction. In the past decade, new extraction methods have been developed that use chemicals that are far less toxic than phenol.

Organic extraction involves the serial addition of several chemicals. First sodium dodecylsulfate (SDS) and proteinase K are added to break open the cell membranes and to break down the proteins that protect the DNA molecules while they are in chromosomes. Next a phenol/chloroform mixture is added to separate the proteins from the DNA. The DNA is more soluble in the aqueous portion of the organic–aqueous mixture. When centrifuged, the unwanted proteins and cellular debris are separated away from the aqueous phase and double-stranded DNA molecules can be cleanly transferred for analysis.

Some initial protocols involved a Centricon 100 (Millipore, Billerica, MA) dialysis and concentration step in place of the ethanol precipitation to remove heme inhibitors (Comey

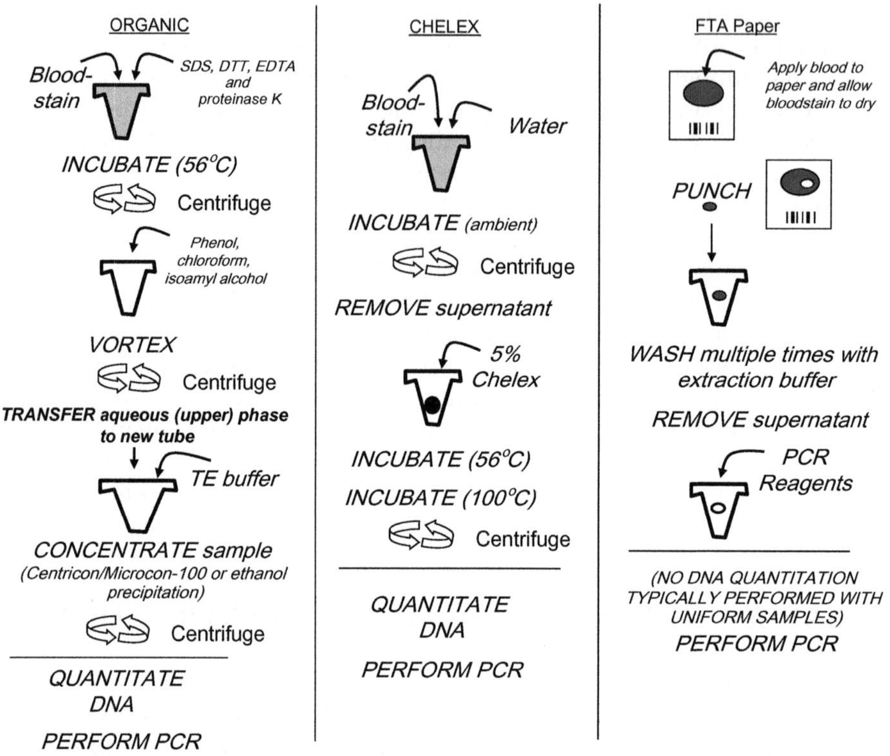

FIGURE 2.1 Schematic of commonly used DNA extraction processes.

et al. 1994). While the organic extraction method works well for recovery of high molecular weight DNA, it is time-consuming, involves the use of hazardous chemicals, and requires the sample to be transferred between multiple tubes, which increases the risk of error or contamination. When Millipore stopped selling Centricon 100 concentrators a few years ago, forensic DNA labs changed to Vivacon (Sartorius-Stedim, Concord, CA) or Microcon 100 (Millipore) ultrafiltration devices for sample concentration.

Chelex Extraction

An alternative and inexpensive procedure for DNA extraction that has become popular among forensic scientists is the use of a chelating-resin suspension that can be added directly to the sample (e.g., blood, bloodstain, or semen). Introduced in 1991 to the forensic DNA community, Chelex 100 (Bio-Rad Laboratories, Hercules, CA) is an ion-exchange resin that is added as a suspension to the samples (Walsh et al. 1991). The Chelex method of DNA extraction is more rapid than the organic extraction method. In addition, Chelex extraction involves fewer steps and thus fewer opportunities for sample contamination.

Chelex is composed of styrene divinylbenzene copolymers containing paired iminodiacetate ions that act as chelating groups in binding polyvalent metal ions such as magnesium.

Like iron filings to a magnet, the magnesium ions are drawn in and bound by the resin. By removing the magnesium from the reaction, DNA-destroying nuclease enzymes are inactivated and the DNA molecules are protected.

In most protocols, biological samples such as bloodstains are added to a 5% Chelex suspension and boiled for several minutes to break open the cells and release the DNA. An initial, prior wash step is helpful to remove possible contaminants and inhibitors such as heme and other proteins. The exposure to 100°C temperatures denatures the DNA as well as disrupting the cell membranes and destroying the cell proteins. After a quick spin in a centrifuge to pull the Chelex resin and cellular debris to the bottom of the tube, the supernatant is removed and can be added directly to the PCR amplification reaction.

Chelex denatures double-stranded DNA and yields single-stranded DNA from the extraction process. Thus, it can only be followed by PCR-based analyses. However, Chelex extraction is an advantage for PCR-based typing methods because it removes inhibitors of PCR and uses only a single tube for the DNA extraction, which reduces the potential for laboratory-induced contamination.

The addition of too much whole blood or too large a bloodstain to the Chelex extraction solution can result in some PCR inhibition. The AmpFlSTR kit manuals recommend 3 μL whole blood or a bloodstain approximately 3 mm × 3 mm (Applied Biosystems 1998).

FTA Paper

Another approach to DNA extraction involves the use of FTA paper. In the late 1980s, FTA paper was developed by Lee Burgoyne at Flinders University in Australia as a method for storage of DNA (Burgoyne et al. 1994). FTA originally stood for "Fitzco/Flinder Technology Agreement." FTA paper is an absorbent cellulose-based paper that contains four chemical substances to protect DNA molecules from nuclease degradation and preserve the paper from bacterial growth (Burgoyne 1996). As a result, DNA on FTA paper is stable at room temperature over a period of several years. However, a 2002 study evaluating FTA and three other commercial papers as DNA storage media found little difference in their ability to obtain typeable STR results after 19 months of storage (Kline et al. 2002).

Use of FTA paper simply involves adding a spot of blood to the paper and allowing the stain to dry. The cells are lysed upon contact with the paper and DNA from the white blood cells is immobilized within the matrix of the paper. A small punch of the paper is removed from the FTA card bloodstain and placed into a tube for washing. The bound DNA can then be purified by washing it with FTA Purification Reagent (Whatman, Clifton, NJ) to remove heme and other inhibitors of the PCR reaction. This purification of the paper punch can be seen visually because as the paper is washed, the hemoglobin red color is removed with the supernatant. The clean punch is then added directly to the PCR reaction. Alternatively, some groups have performed a Chelex extraction on the FTA paper punch and used the supernatant in the PCR reaction (Lorente et al. 1998, Kline et al. 2002).

Devices have also been developed for collection of saliva or buccal cells using a spongy swab that is then pressed against an FTA card to transfer the collected cells for sample preservation. Indicator paper that changes color with liquid contact is typically used to enable visualization of sample transfer to the FTA card.

A major advantage of FTA paper is that consistent results may be obtained without quantification because a uniform amount of cells are typically being sampled. Furthermore the procedure may be automated on a robotic workstation (Belgrader et al. 1995, Belgrader & Marino 1997, Tack et al. 1997). For situations where multiple assays need to be run on the same sample, a bloodstained punch may be reused for sequential DNA amplifications and typing (Del Rio et al. 1996). Unfortunately, due to static electricity, dry paper punches do not like to stay in their assigned tubes and can "jump" between wells in a sample tray. Thus, this method is not as widely used today as was once envisioned. However, due to its preservation and storage capabilities, efforts have been made to use FTA cards for more widespread collection of crime scene evidence (Lorente et al. 2004).

Other Methods

A few other methods have been used for DNA extraction from biological samples including "salting out" the DNA with sodium acetate (Miller et al. 1988), use of sodium hydroxide (Klintschar & Neuhuber 2000), and digestion of cellular proteins with a thermostable proteinase (Moss et al. 2003). A liquid extraction method using the thermostable proteinase approach has been developed by ZyGEM (Hamilton, New Zealand).

SOLID-PHASE DNA EXTRACTION METHODS

With the desire to automate more steps in DNA analysis, many laboratories have moved to various forms of solid-phase extraction where DNA is selectively bound to a substrate such as silica particles. The DNA is retained while proteins and other cellular components are washed away. Then the DNA is released in a purified form. Chapter 17 will discuss more on specific robotic platforms for automated sample processing. The bind-wash-elute format is illustrated in Figure 2.2.

The most widely used solid-phase extraction methods are QIAGEN columns, DNA IQ, and PrepFiler. The primary characteristics of each method are featured in Table 2.2.

QIAGEN Extraction Chemistry and Kits

Solid-phase extraction methods for DNA have been developed in recent years in formats that enable high-throughput DNA extractions. One of the most active efforts in this area is with silica-based extraction methods and products from QIAGEN, Inc. (Valencia, CA). For more than a decade, QIAamp spin columns have proven effective as a means of DNA isolation (Greenspoon et al. 1998).

In this approach, nucleic acids selectively absorb to silica on a support, such as small glass beads, in the presence of high concentrations of chaotropic salts such as guanidine hydrochloride, guanidine isothiocyanate, sodium iodide, and sodium perchlorate (Vogelstein & Gillespie 1979, Boom et al. 1990, Duncan et al. 2003). These chaotropic salts disrupt hydrogen-bonding networks in liquid water and thereby make denatured proteins and nucleic acids more thermodynamically stable than their native folded or structured counterparts (Tereba et al. 2004).

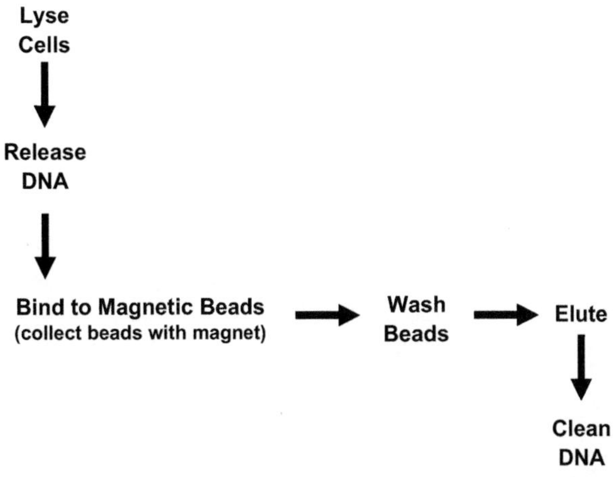

FIGURE 2.2 Bind-wash-elute method utilized in DNA IQ and PrepFiler DNA extraction and purification chemistries.

TABLE 2.2 Comparison of DNA Extraction Methods.

	QIAGEN	Promega	Applied Biosystems
Products	QIAamp	DNA IQ	PrepFiler
Solid-phase	Silica beads	Magnetic silica beads	Magnetic silica beads
Wash performed	Centrifugation or vacuum manifold	Magnet	Magnet
Robotic platform	EZ1, M48, QIACube	Maxwell 16, Tecan	AutoMate Express, Tecan

If the solution is more acidic than pH 7.5, DNA adsorption to the silica is typically around 95% and unwanted impurities can be washed away. Under alkaline conditions and low salt concentrations, the DNA will efficiently elute from the silica material. This solid-phase extraction approach can be performed with centrifugation or vacuum manifolds in single tube or 96-well plate formats (Hanselle et al. 2003, Yasuda et al. 2003) and is even being developed into formats that will work on a microchip (Wolfe et al. 2002, Bienvenue & Landers 2010). Several robotic platforms have been developed to enable automated processing of QIAGEN DNA extractions including the EZ1, M48, and QIAcube. The EZ1 liquid-handling robot (Figure 2.3) can process either 6 or 14 samples (depending on the model) in about 20 minutes following a previous incubation/cell lysis step.

DNA IQ

Another solid-phase extraction approach is the DNA IQ system marketed by Promega Corporation (Madison, WI). The DNA IQ system, which stands for "isolation" and

FIGURE 2.3 QIAGEN EZ1 DNA extraction robot.

"quantitation," utilizes the same silica-based DNA binding and elution chemistries as QIAGEN kits but with silica-coated paramagnetic resin (Tereba et al. 2004). With this approach, DNA isolation can be performed in a single tube by simply adding and removing solutions.

First, the DNA molecules are reversibly bound to the magnetic beads in solution with a pH more acidic than pH 7.5 (the same as noted previously for the QIAGEN chemistry). A magnet is used to draw the silica-coated magnetic beads to the bottom or side of the tube leaving any impurities in solution. These solution impurities (proteins, cell debris, etc.) are easily removed by drawing the liquid off of the beads. The magnetic particles with DNA attached can be washed multiple times to more thoroughly clean the DNA. Finally, a defined amount of DNA can be released into solution via heating for a few minutes.

The quantity of DNA isolated with this approach is based on the number and capacity of the magnetic particles used. Since flow-through vacuum filtration or centrifugation steps are not used, magnetic bead procedures enable simple, rapid, and automated methods. This extraction method has been automated on the Beckman 2000 robot workstation and implemented into forensic casework by the Virginia Department of Forensic Science and a growing number of other crime labs (Greenspoon et al. 2004).

A Maxwell 16 robot (Promega Corporation) is often used to automate the DNA IQ extraction sample processing. The Maxwell 16 can extract 16 samples simultaneously at a price of about $6 per sample in less than 30 minutes following off-instrument incubation. For laboratories needing higher throughput, Tecan liquid-handling robots have been used (Frégeau et al. 2010). Methods are also being developed to simultaneously extract both DNA and RNA using the DNA IQ chemistry (Bowden et al. 2010).

The magnetic bead approach is dependent on DNA binding to the beads. If anything interferes with this binding, the DNA sample can be lost in the washes. During part of a large criminal investigation involving processing of tens of thousands of samples, the Royal

Canadian Mounted Police (RCMP) DNA lab found that chemicals present in a presumptive test for blood known as Hemastix prevented the expected DNA extraction results with DNA IQ (Poon et al. 2009). Additional studies by the RCMP found that chemical warfare agents such as sulfur mustard, sarin, sodium 2-fluoroacetate, and diazinon were removed to below detectable limits as part of the DNA IQ extraction process (Wilkinson et al. 2007a, 2007b). Thus, the DNA IQ process can remove these dangerous chemicals and render samples safe to handle following DNA extraction.

PrepFiler

In 2008 Applied Biosystems released a magnetic particle based DNA extraction technology named PrepFiler that is similar to DNA IQ (Applied Biosystems 2008). PrepFiler has been validated (Barbaro et al. 2009, Brevnov et al. 2009) and enables isolation of high-quality DNA from forensic samples in high yields primarily because a small bead size is used to provide a higher surface area (compared to larger magnetic bead systems) for capturing DNA molecules during the extraction process.

Up to 96 samples can be processed at a time in under 2.5 hours using the Tecan Freedom EVO automated liquid-handling workstation. A small liquid-handling robot similar to the QIAGEN EZ1 has also been released by Applied Biosystems called the AutoMate Express Forensic DNA Extraction System (Applied Biosystems 2010). To improve extraction efficiencies with calcified tissues including bone and teeth as well as adhesives, Applied Biosystems has developed a BTA (bone, teeth, adhesive) lysis buffer protocol (Stray et al. 2009).

Protocols for Various Tissue Types

Optimal DNA extraction may come from slightly different procedures depending on the source of the biological sample. The reference lists at the back of this chapter include citations to methods developed for DNA extraction from a variety of tissue types including bloodstains, bone, formalin-fixed paraffin embedded (FFPE) tissues, hair, teeth, urine, and saliva from stamps and envelopes.

DIFFERENTIAL EXTRACTION

Differential extraction is a modified version of the organic extraction method that separates epithelial and sperm cells (Figure 2.4). Differential extraction was first described in 1985 by Peter Gill and coworkers (Gill et al. 1985). This method is commonly used today by the FBI Laboratory and other forensic crime laboratories to isolate the female and male fractions in sexual assault cases that contain a mixture of male and female DNA. By separating the male fraction away from the victim's DNA profile, it is much easier to interpret the perpetrator's DNA profile in a rape case.

The differential extraction procedure involves preferentially breaking open the female epithelial cells with incubation in an SDS/proteinase K mixture. Sperm nuclei are subsequently lysed by treatment with an SDS/proteinase K/dithiothreitol (DTT) mixture. The DTT breaks down the protein disulfide bridges that make up sperm nuclear membranes. Differential

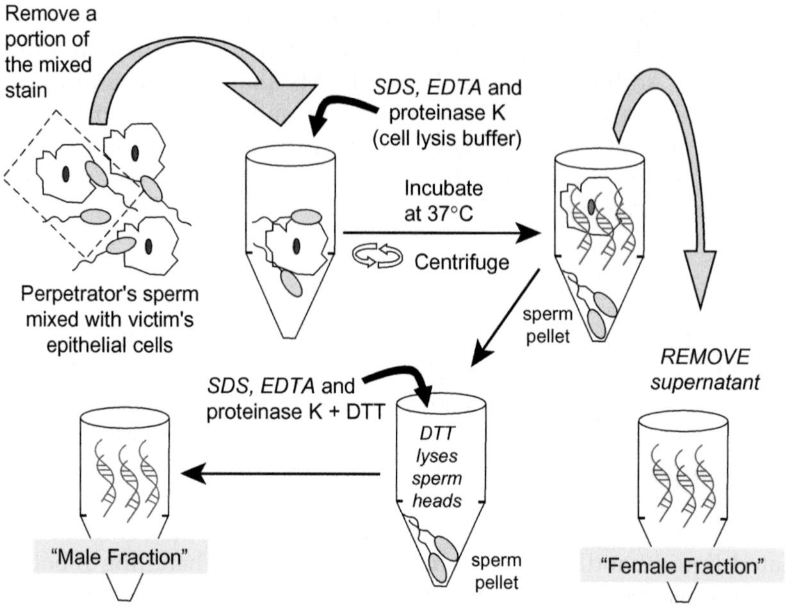

FIGURE 2.4 Schematic of differential extraction process used to separate male sperm cells from female epithelial cells.

extraction works because sperm nuclei are impervious to digestion without DTT. The major difference between the regular version of organic extraction described earlier and differential extraction is the initial incubation in SDS/proteinase K without DTT present.

Promega Corporation (Madison, WI) has developed an automated Differex method that involves using DNA IQ magnetic beads to hold the sperm pellet in place while a separation solution keeps the digestion buffer and epithelial DNA away from the sperm pellet during the wash steps (Knox & Olsen 2008). Up to 40 samples can be processed in a 96-well plate in less than 5 hours using Differex.

Differential extraction works well in most sexual assault cases to separate female and male fractions from one another (Figure 2.5). However, some perpetrators of sexual assaults have had a vasectomy in which case there is an absence of spermatozoa. Azoospermic semen, i.e., without sperm cells, cannot be separated from the female fraction with differential extraction. In the case of azoospermic perpetrators, the use of Y chromosome specific markers permit male DNA profiles to be deduced in the presence of excess female DNA. Failure to separate the male and female portions of a sexual assault sample results in a mixture of both the perpetrator's and the victim's DNA profiles. DNA mixtures can sometimes be challenging to interpret.

Other Approaches

Figure 2.6 compares several other approaches for separating victim and perpetrator cells and/or DNA in sexual assault evidence. Methods for directly capturing sperm cells have

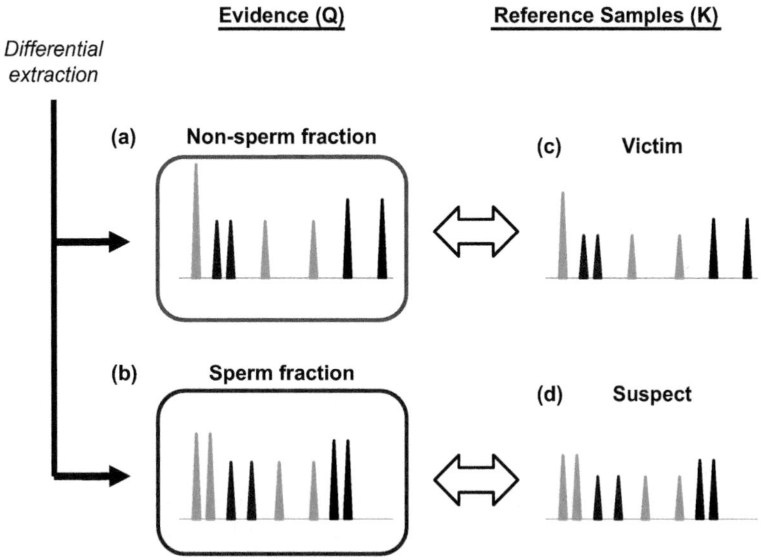

FIGURE 2.5 Illustration of results from the four samples typically associated with a sexual assault case. During differential extraction, the evidence sample is divided into two fractions: (a) non-sperm or epithelial fraction and (b) the sperm fraction (see Figure 2.4). The suspect result (d) is compared to the sperm fraction (b) to see if they match. The victim's DNA profile (c) provides confirmation of sample integrity with the non-sperm fraction (a).

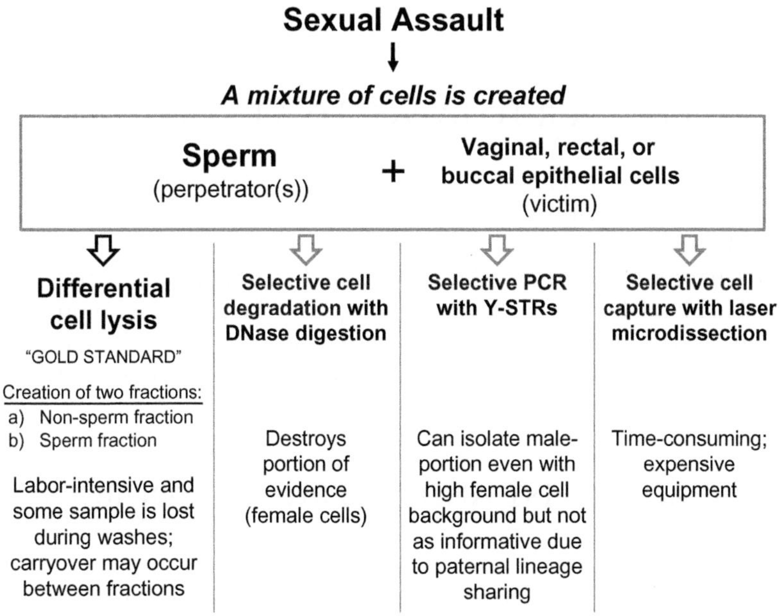

FIGURE 2.6 Different methods for separating perpetrator(s)'s sperm and victim's epithelial cells created in sexual assault DNA samples.

been developed including laser-capture microdissection (see below). By physically separating the perpetrator's sperm cells from the victim's epithelial cells, the perpetrator's DNA can be enriched and isolated from even a vast preponderance of victim's cells. Digestion of victim's epithelial cells to try to increase yield from the perpetrator's DNA has also been successful (Gavin et al. 2009).

Laser-Capture Microdissection

Sperm cells can be selectively captured using a clinical procedure known as *laser-capture microdissection* (LCM), which is commonly used to select tumor cells from surrounding tissue on microscope slides. Sperm cells from sexual assault evidence spread on microscope slides can be collected with laser-capture microdissection to perform reliable STR testing (Elliott et al. 2003, Sanders et al. 2006). When sperm cells are observed in the field of view of the microscope, a tiny laser is activated and a thin plastic film placed over the slide melts at the specific point of laser light contact to capture or enclose the cell of interest. By moving the microscope slide around, dozens of sperm cells are collected onto this thin film that sits directly above the sample. The collection film is then transferred to a tube where DNA from the isolated sperm can be extracted and amplified using the polymerase chain reaction. Other LCM methods catapult identified cells directly into a collection tube.

Non-sperm male cells may also be detected with *fluorescent in-situ hybridization* (FISH) techniques enabling selective capture of male versus female cells from a mixed cell population (Anslinger et al. 2007). While the use of FISH and LCM add to the expense of forensic casework, these clinical techniques can enable speciality cases to be solved that would not otherwise be possible.

DIRECT PCR TO BYPASS DNA EXTRACTION

One of the latest developments in forensic DNA typing is the application of direct PCR with no DNA extraction. Improved reaction components and engineered DNA polymerases permit PCR amplification without DNA extraction and purification steps to remove inhibitors (see Chapter 4). The PowerPlex 16 HS and Identifiler Direct STR typing kits (see Chapter 5) enable bloodstains from reference samples to be processed more rapidly without DNA extraction. An advantage of this approach is that samples are effectively concentrated as DNA material is not lost during wash steps that typically occur with DNA extraction methods.

READING LIST AND INTERNET RESOURCES

General Information

Allard, J. E., et al. (2007). A comparison of methods used in the UK and Ireland for the extraction and detection of semen on swabs and cloth samples. *Science & Justice*, *47*, 160–167.

Bienvenue, J. M., & Landers, J. P. (2010). DNA extraction on microfluidic devices. *Forensic Science Review*, *22*, 187–197.

DNA extraction and quantitation. <http://dna.gov/training/extraction/>.

Hoff-Olson, P., et al. (1999). Extraction of DNA from decomposed human tissue: an evaluation of five extraction methods for short tandem repeat typing. *Forensic Science International, 105*, 171–183.

Kobilinsky, L. (1992). Recovery and stability of DNA in samples of forensic significance. *Forensic Science Review, 4*, 68–87.

Lee, H. C., & Ladd, C. (2001). Preservation and collection of biological evidence. *Croatian Medical Journal, 42*, 225–228.

Lindahl, T. (1993). Instability and decay of the primary structure of DNA. *Nature, 362*, 709–715.

Stray, J. E., et al. (2010). Extraction of DNA from forensic biological samples for genotyping. *Forensic Science Review, 22*, 159–175.

Stray, J. E., & Shewale, J. G. (2010). Extraction of DNA from human remains. *Forensic Science Review, 22*, 177–185.

Organic Extraction

Comey, C. T., et al. (1994). DNA extraction strategies for amplified fragment length polymorphism analysis. *Journal of Forensic Sciences, 39*, 1254–1269.

Vandenberg, N., et al. (1997). An evaluation of selected DNA extraction strategies for short tandem repeat typing. *Electrophoresis, 18*, 1624–1626.

Chelex Extraction

Crouse, C. A., et al. (1993). Extraction of DNA from forensic-type sexual assault specimens using simple, rapid sonication procedures. *Biotechniques, 15*, 641–648.

Walsh, P. S., et al. (1991). Chelex 100 as a medium for simple extraction of DNA for PCR-based typing from forensic material. *BioTechniques, 10*, 506–513.

Willard, J. M., et al. (1998). Recovery of DNA for PCR amplification from blood and forensic samples using a chelating resin. *Methods in Molecular Biology, 98*, 9–18.

FTA Paper

Belgrader, P., et al. (1995). Automated DNA purification and amplification from blood-stained cards using a robotic workstation. *BioTechniques, 19*, 427–432.

Belgrader, P., & Marino, M. A. (1997). Automated sample processing using robotics for short tandem repeat polymorphisms by capillary electrophoresis. *Laboratory Robotics and Automation, 9*, 3–7.

Burgoyne, L., et al. (1994). Safe collection, storage and analysis of DNA from blood. In *Proceedings of the fifth international symposium on human identification*. (p. 163) Madison, Wisconsin: Promega Corporation.

Burgoyne, L. A. (1996). Solid medium and method for DNA storage. U.S. Patent 5,496,562.

Del Rio, S. A., et al. (1996). Reusing the same blood-stained punch for sequential DNA amplifications and typing. *Biotechniques, 20*, 970–974.

Kline, M. C., et al. (2002). Polymerase chain reaction amplification of DNA from aged blood stains: quantitative evaluation of the "suitability for purpose" of four filter papers as archival media. *Analytical Chemistry, 74*, 1863–1869.

Lorente, J. A., et al. (1998). Newborn genetic identification: Expanding the fields of forensic haemogenetics. *Progress in Forensic Genetics, 7*, 114–116.

Lorente, J.A., et al. (2004). Recovering biological samples from crime scene using FTA paper. In *Proceedings of the American Academy of Forensic Sciences* (Vol. X, p. 103). Meeting held in Dallas, Texas.

Tack, L. C., et al. (2007). Automated forensic DNA purification optimized for FTA card punches and Identifiler STR-based PCR analysis. *Clinical Laboratory Medicine, 27*, 183–191.

Other Extraction Methods

Klintschar, M., & Neuhuber, F. (2000). Evaluation of an alkaline lysis method for the extraction of DNA from whole blood and forensic stains for STR analysis. *Journal of Forensic Sciences, 45*, 669–673.

Miller, S. A., et al. (1988). A simple salting out procedure for extracting DNA from human nucleated cells. *Nucleic Acids Research, 16*, 1215.

Moss, D., et al. (2003). An easily automated, closed-tube forensic DNA extraction procedure using a thermostable proteinase. *International Journal of Legal Medicine, 117*, 340–349.

Solid-Phase Extraction

QIAGEN

Anslinger, K., et al. (2005). Application of the BioRobot EZ1 in a forensic laboratory. *Legal Medicine, 7*, 164–168.

Boom, R., et al. (1990). Rapid and simple method for purification of nucleic acids. *Journal of Clinical Microbiology, 28*, 495–503.

Castella, V., et al. (2006). Forensic evaluation of the QIAshredder/QIAamp DNA extraction procedure. *Forensic Science International, 156*, 70–73.

Duncan, E., et al. (2003). Isolation of genomic DNA. In B. Bowien & P. Dürre (Eds.), *Nucleic acids isolation methods* (pp. 7–19). Stevenson Ranch, California: American Scientific Publishers.

Greenspoon, S. A., et al. (1998). QIAamp spin columns as a method of DNA isolation for forensic casework. *Journal of Forensic Sciences, 43*, 1024–1030.

Hanselle, T., et al. (2003). Isolation of genomic DNA from buccal swabs for forensic analysis using fully automated silica-membrane purification technology. *Legal Medicine, 5*, S145–S149.

Holland, M. M., et al. (2003). Development of a quality, high throughput DNA analysis procedure for skeletal samples to assist with the identification of victims from the World Trade Center attacks. *Croatian Medical Journal, 44*, 264–272.

Johnson, D. J., et al. (2005). STR-typing of human DNA from human fecal matter using the QIAGEN QIAamp stool mini kit. *Journal of Forensic Sciences, 50*, 802–808.

Kishore, R., et al. (2006). Optimization of DNA extraction from low-yield and degraded samples using the BioRobot EZ1 and BioRobot M48. *Journal of Forensic Sciences, 51*, 1055–1061.

Montpetit, S. A., et al. (2005). A simple automated instrument for DNA extraction in forensic casework. *Journal of Forensic Sciences, 50*, 555–563.

Nagy, M., et al. (2005). Optimization and validation of a fully automated silica-coated magnetic beads purification technology in forensics. *Forensic Science International, 152*, 13–22.

Nakazono, T., et al. (2005). Successful DNA typing of urine stains using a DNA purification kit following dialfiltration. *Journal of Forensic Sciences, 50*, 860–864.

Vogelstein, B., & Gillespie, D. (1979). Preparative and analytical purification of DNA from agarose. *Proceedings of the National Academy of Sciences of the United States of America, 76*, 615–619.

Wolfe, K. A., et al. (2002). Toward a microchip-based solid-phase extraction method for isolation of nucleic acids. *Electrophoresis, 23*, 727–733.

Yasuda, T., et al. (2003). A simple method of DNA extraction and STR typing from urine samples using a commercially available DNA/RNA extraction kit. *Journal of Forensic Sciences, 48*, 108–110.

DNA IQ

Bowden, A., et al. (2010). A method for DNA and RNA co-extraction for use on forensic samples using the Promega DNA IQ system. *Forensic Science International: Genetics, 5*, 64–68.

Duval, K., et al. (2010). Optimized manual and automated recovery of amplifiable DNA from tissues preserved in buffered formalin and alcohol-based fixative. *Forensic Science International: Genetics, 4*, 80–88.

Frégeau, C., et al. (2010). Validation of a DNA IQ-based extraction method for TECAN robotic liquid handling workstations for processing casework. *Forensic Science International: Genetics, 4*, 292–304.

Greenspoon, S. A., et al. (2004). Application of the BioMek 2000 Laboratory Automation Workstation and the DNA IQ System to the extraction of forensic casework samples. *Journal of Forensic Sciences, 49*, 29–39.

Grubb, J. C., et al. (2010). Implementation and validation of the Teleshake unit for DNA IQ robotic extraction and development of a large volume DNA IQ method. *Journal of Forensic Sciences, 55*, 706–714.

Ng, L.-K., et al. (2007). Optimization of recovery of human DNA from envelope flaps using DNA IQ System for STR genotyping. *Forensic Science International: Genetics, 1*, 283–286.

Poon, H., et al. (2009). The use of Hemastix and the subsequent lack of DNA recovery using the Promega DNA IQ system. *Journal of Forensic Sciences, 54*, 1278–1286.

Promega Corporation (2009). *DNA IQ system – small sample casework protocol.* Available at <http://www.promega.com/tbs/tb296/tb296.pdf>.

Promega Maxwell 16. <http://www.promega.com/maxwell16/>.

Tereba, A. M., et al. (2004). Simultaneous isolation and quantitation of DNA. U.S. Patent 6,673,631.

Wilkinson, D. A., et al. (2007a). The fate of the chemical warfare agent during DNA extraction. *Journal of Forensic Sciences, 52*, 1272–1283.

Wilkinson, D. A., et al. (2007b). Recovery of DNA from exhibits contaminated with chemical warfare agents: a preliminary study of the effect of decontamination agents and chemical warfare agents on DNA. *Canadian Society of Forensic Sciences Journal, 40*, 15–22.

Ye, J., et al. (2004). A simple and efficient method for extracting DNA from old and burned bone. *Journal of Forensic Sciences, 49*, 754–759.

PrepFiler

Applied Biosystems. (2008). *PrepFiler Forensic DNA Extraction Kit user guide.* P/N 4390932 Rev. B. Available from <http://www.appliedbiosystems.com>.

Applied Biosystems. (2010). *AutoMate Express Forensic DNA Extraction System.* Product bulletin available: <http://www3.appliedbiosystems.com/cms/groups/applied_markets_marketing/documents/generaldocuments/cms_086047.pdf>.

Barbaro, A., et al. (2009). Validation of PrepFiler Forensic DNA Extraction Kit (Applied Biosystems). *Forensic Science International: Genetics Supplement Series, 2*, 176–177.

Brevnov, M. G., et al. (2009). Validation of the PrepFiler Forensic DNA Extraction Kit for extraction of genomic DNA from biological samples. *Journal of Forensic Sciences, 54*, 599–607.

Hashiyada, M., et al. (2009). Utility validation of extraction of genomic DNA from hard tissues, bone and nail, using PrepFiler Forensic DNA Extraction Kit. *Forensic Science International: Genetics Supplement Series, 2*, 172–173.

Stray, J., et al. (2009). Extraction of high quality DNA from biological materials and calcified tissues. *Forensic Science International: Genetics Supplement Series, 2*, 159–160.

DNA Extraction Methods

Malyusz, V., et al. (2006). Enzyrim: a new additive to increase the DNA yield from different materials such as teeth, blood or saliva. *Progress in Forensic Genetics 11, ICS 1288*, 562–564.

Schiffner, L. A., et al. (2005). Optimization of a simple, automatable extraction method to recover sufficient DNA from low copy number DNA samples for generation of short tandem repeat profiles. *Croatian Medical Journal, 46*, 578–586.

Wurmb-Schwark, N., et al. (2006). Fast and simple DNA extraction from saliva and sperm cells obtained from the skin or isolated from swabs. *Legal Medicine, 8*, 177–181.

Bloodstains

Jung, J. M., et al. (1991). Extraction strategy for obtaining DNA from bloodstains for PCR amplification and typing of the HLA-DQ alpha gene. *International Journal of Legal Medicine, 104*, 145–148.

Bone

Arismendi, J. L., et al. (2004). Effects of processing techniques on the forensic DNA analysis of human skeletal remains. *Journal of Forensic Sciences, 49*, 930–934.

Davoren, J., et al. (2007). Highly effective DNA extraction method for nuclear short tandem repeat testing of skeletal remains from mass graves. *Croatian Medical Journal, 48*, 478–485.

Hagelberg, E., & Clegg, J. B. (1991). Isolation and characterization of DNA from archaeological bone. *Proceedings of the Royal Society of London B, 36*, 45–50.

Hochmeister, M. N., et al. (1991). Typing of deoxyribonucleic acid (DNA) extracted from compact bone from human remains. *Journal of Forensic Sciences, 36*, 1649–1661.

Hochmeister, M. N. (1998). PCR analysis of DNA from fresh and decomposed bodies and skeletal remains in medicolegal death investigations. *Methods in Molecular Biology, 98*, 19–26.

Kitayama, T., et al. (2010). Evaluation of a new experimental kit for the extraction of DNA from bones and teeth using a non-powder method. *Legal Medicine, 12*, 84–89.

Loreille, O., et al. (2007). High efficiency DNA extraction from bone by total demineralization. *Forensic Science International: Genetics, 1*, 191–195.

Milos, A., et al. (2007). Success rates of nuclear short tandem repeat typing from different skeletal elements. *Croatian Medical Journal, 48*, 486–493.

Salamon, N., et al. (2005). Relatively well preserved DNA is present in the crystal aggregates of fossil bones. *Proceedings of the National Academy of Sciences of the United States of America, 102*, 13783–13788.

Ye, J., et al. (2004). A simple and efficient method for extracting DNA from old and burned bone. *Journal of Forensic Sciences, 49*, 754–759.

Formalin-Fixed Paraffin Embedded (FFPE) Tissues

Chaw, Y. F. M., et al. (1980). Isolation and identification of cross-links from formaldehyde-treated nucleic acids. *Biochemistry, 19*, 5525–5531.

Gilbert, M. T. P., et al. (2007). The isolation of nucleic acids from fixed, paraffin embedded tissues-Which methods are useful when? *PLoS ONE, 2*(6), e537.

Goelz, S. E., et al. (1985). Purification of DNA from formaldehyde-fixed and paraffin-embedded human tissue. *Biochemical and Biophysical Research Communication, 130*, 118–126.

Metz, B., et al. (2004). Identification of formaldehyde-induced modifications in proteins. *Journal of Biological Chemistry, 279*, 6235–6243.

Romero, R. L., et al. (1997). The applicability of formalin-fixed and formalin fixed paraffin embedded tissues in forensic DNA analysis. *Journal of Forensic Sciences, 42*, 708–714.

Sepp, R., et al. (1994). Rapid techniques for DNA extraction from routinely processed archival tissue for use in PCR. *Journal of Clinical Pathology, 47*, 318–323.

Hair

Amory, S., et al. (2007). STR typing of ancient DNA extracted from hair shafts of Siberian mummies. *Forensic Science International, 166*, 218–229.

Graffy, E. A., & Foran, D. R. (2005). A simplified method for mitochondrial DNA extraction from head hair shafts. *Journal of Forensic Sciences, 50*, 1119–1122.

Hellmann, A., et al. (2001). STR typing of human telogen hairs–a new approach. *International Journal of Legal Medicine, 114*, 269–273.

Kolowski, J. C., et al. (2004). A comparison study of hair examination methodologies. *Journal of Forensic Sciences, 49*, 1253–1255.

McNevin, D., et al. (2005). Short tandem repeat (STR) genotyping of keratinised hair. Part 1. Review of current status and knowledge gaps. *Forensic Science International, 153*, 237–246.

McNevin, D., et al. (2005). Short tandem repeat (STR) genotyping of keratinised hair. Part 2. An optimised genomic DNA extraction procedure reveals donor dependence of STR profiles. *Forensic Science International, 153*, 247–259.

Muller, K., et al. (2007). Improved STR typing of telogen hair root and hair shaft DNA. *Electrophoresis, 28*, 2835–2842.

Opel, K. L., et al. (2008). Evaluation and quantification of nuclear DNA from human telogen hairs. *Journal of Forensic Sciences, 53*, 853–857.

Wilson, M. R., et al. (1995). Extraction, PCR amplification, and sequencing of mitochondrial DNA from human hair shafts. *BioTechniques, 18*, 662–669.

Saliva from Stamps and Envelopes

Allen, M., et al. (1994). PCR-based DNA typing of saliva on stamps and envelopes. *Biotechniques, 17*, 546–552.

Fridez, F., & Coquoz, R. (1996). PCR DNA typing of stamps: Evaluation of the DNA extraction. *Forensic Science International, 78*, 103–110.

Hochmeister, M. N. (1996). A discussion of 'PCR DNA typing of stamps: Evaluation of the DNA extraction'. *Forensic Science International, 83*, 75–79.

Sinclair, K., & McKechnie, V. M. (2000). DNA extraction from stamps and envelope flaps using QIAamp and QIAshredder. *Journal of Forensic Sciences, 45*, 229–230.

Teeth

Alakoc, Y. D., & Aka, P. S. (2009). "Orthograde entrance technique" to recover DNA from ancient teeth preserving the physical structure. *Forensic Science International, 188*, 96–98.

Gaytmenn, R., & Sweet, D. (2003). Quantification of forensic DNA from various regions of human teeth. *Journal of Forensic Sciences, 48*, 622–625.

Ginther, C., et al. (1992). Identifying individuals by sequencing mitochondrial DNA from teeth. *Nature Genetics, 2*, 135–138.

Kemp, B. M., & Smith, D. G. (2005). Use of bleach to eliminate contaminating DNA from the surfaces of bones and teeth. *Forensic Science International, 154*, 53–61.

Malaver, P. C., & Yunis, J. J. (2003). Different dental tissues as source of DNA from human identification in forensic cases. *Croatian Medical Journal, 44*, 306–309.

Pinchi, V., et al. (2010). Techniques of dental DNA extraction: Some operative experiences. *Forensic Science International, 204*, 111–114.

Schwartz, T., et al. (1991). Characterization of deoxyribonucleic acid (DNA) obtained from teeth subjected to various environmental conditions. *Journal of Forensic Sciences, 36*, 979–990.

Smith, B. C., et al. (1993). A systematic approach to the sampling of dental DNA. *Journal of Forensic Sciences, 38*, 1194–1209.

Trivedi, R., et al. (2002). A new improved method for extraction of DNA from teeth for analysis of hypervariable loci. *American Journal of Forensic Medicine and Pathology, 23*, 191–196.

Urine

Castella, V., et al. (2006). Forensic identification of urine samples: a comparison between nuclear and mitochondrial DNA markers. *International Journal of Legal Medicine, 120*, 67–72.

Castella, V., et al. (2007). Successful DNA typing of ultrafiltered urines used to detect EPO doping. *Forensic Science International: Genetics, 1*, 281–282.

Junge, A., et al. (2002). Successful DNA typing of a urine sample in a doping control case using human mitochondrial DNA analysis. *Journal of Forensic Sciences, 47*, 1022–1024.

Other Sources

Abrams, S., et al. (2008). A simulated arson experiment and its effect on the recovery of DNA. *Canadian Society of Forensic Sciences Journal, 41*, 53–60.

Chiou, F. S., et al. (2001). Extraction of human DNA for PCR from chewed residues of betel quid using a novel "PVP/CTAB" method. *Journal of Forensic Sciences, 46*, 1174–1179.

Graham, E. A. M., et al. (2007). Investigation into the usefulness of DNA profiling of earprints. *Science & Justice, 47*, 155–159.

Graham, E. A. M., & Rutty, G. N. (2008). Investigation into "normal" background DNA on adult necks: implications for DNA profiling of manual strangulation victims. *Journal of Forensic Sciences, 53*, 1074–1082.

Kreike, J., et al. (1999). Isolation and characterization of human DNA from mosquitoes (*Culicidae*). *International Journal of Legal Medicine, 112*, 380–382.

Maguire, S., et al. (2008). Retrieval of DNA from the faces of children aged 0–5 years: a technical note. *Journal of Forensic Nursing, 4*, 40–44.

Motani, H., et al. (2006). Usefulness of dura mater in providing DNA samples for identifying cadavers. *Journal of Forensic Sciences, 51*, 888–892.

Niemcunowicz-Janica, A., et al. (2007a). Typeability of AmpFlSTR SGM Plus loci in kidney, liver, spleen and pancreas tissue samples incubated in different environments. *Advances in Medical Science, 52*, 135–138.

Niemcunowicz-Janica, A., et al. (2007b). Typeability of AmpFlSTR SGM Plus loci in brain and thyroid gland tissue samples incubated in different environments. *Journal of Forensic Sciences, 52*, 867–869.

Niemcunowicz-Janica, A., et al. (2008). Detectability of SGM Plus profiles in heart and lungs tissue samples incubated in different environments. *Legal Medicine, 10*, 35–38.

Ravard-Goulvestre, C., et al. (2004). Successful extraction of human genomic DNA from serum and its application to forensic identification. *Journal of Forensic Sciences, 49*, 60–63.

Zamir, A., et al. (2007). DNA profiling from heroin street dose packages. *Journal of Forensic Sciences, 52*, 389–392.

Differential Extraction

Bienvenue, J. M., et al. (2006). Microchip-based cell lysis and DNA extraction from sperm cells for application to forensic analysis. *Journal of Forensic Sciences*, *51*, 266–273.

Garvin, A. M. (2003). Filtration based DNA preparation for sexual assault cases. *Journal of Forensic Sciences*, *48*, 1084–1087.

Garvin, A. M., et al. (2009). DNA preparation from sexual assault cases by selective degradation of contaminating DNA from the victim. *Journal of Forensic Sciences*, *54*, 1297–1303.

Gill, P., et al. (1985). Forensic application of DNA 'fingerprints'. *Nature*, *318*, 577–579.

Horsman, K. M., et al. (2005). Separation of sperm and epithelial cells in a microfabricated device: potential application to forensic analysis of sexual assault evidence. *Analytical Chemistry*, *77*, 742–749.

Knox, C., & Olson, R. (2008). Tackling the backlog using automated differential extraction. *Forensic Magazine*, *5*(2), 22–25.

Wiegand, P., et al. (1992). DNA extraction from mixtures of body fluid using mild preferential lysis. *International Journal of Legal Medicine*, *104*, 359–360.

Yoshida, K., et al. (1995). The modified method of two-step differential extraction of sperm and vaginal epithelial cell DNA from vaginal fluid mixed with semen. *Forensic Science International*, *72*, 25–33.

Laser Capture Microdissection

Vandewoestyne, M., & Deforce, D. (2010). Laser capture microdissection in forensic research: A review. *International Journal of Legal Medicine*, *124*, 513–521.

Technology

Bonner, R. F., et al. (1997). Laser capture microdissection: Molecular analysis of tissue. *Science*, *278*, 1481–1483.

Burgemeister, R. (2005). New aspects of laser microdissection in research and routine. *Journal of Histochemistry and Cytochemistry*, *53*, 409–412.

Emmert-Buck, M. R., et al. (1996). Laser capture microdissection. *Science*, *274*, 998–1001.

Espina, V., et al. (2006). Laser-capture microdissection. *Nature Protocols*, *1*, 586–603.

Kolble, K. (2000). The LEICA microdissection system: design and applications. *Journal of Molecular Medicine*, *78*, B24–B25.

Micke, P., et al. (2005). Laser-assisted cell microdissection using the PALM system. *Methods in Molecular Biology*, *293*, 151–166.

Murray, G. I., & Curran, S. (2005). *Laser capture microdissection – methods and protocols*. Totowa, NJ: Humana Press.

Murray, G. I. (2007). An overview of laser microdissection technologies. *Acta Histochemistry*, *109*, 171–176.

Forensic Applications

Anslinger, K., et al. (2005). Digoxigenin labelling and laser capture microdissection of male cells. *International Journal of Legal Medicine*, *119*, 374–377.

Anslinger, K., et al. (2007). Sex-specific fluorescent labeling and laser capture microdissection of male cells. *International Journal of Legal Medicine*, *121*, 54–56.

Anoruo, B., et al. (2007). Isolating cells from non-sperm cellular mixtures using the PALM microlaser micro dissection system. *Forensic Science International*, *173*, 93–96.

Bauer, M., et al. (2002). Paternity testing after pregnancy termination using laser microdissection of chorionic villi. *International Journal of Legal Medicine*, *116*, 39–42.

Budimlija, Z. M., et al. (2005). Forensic applications of laser capture microdissection: use in DNA-based parentage testing and platform validation. *Croatian Medical Journal*, *46*, 549–555.

Di Martino, D., et al. (2004). Single sperm cell isolation by laser microdissection. *Forensic Science International*, *146*(Suppl.), S151–S153.

Di Martino, D., et al. (2004). Laser microdissection and DNA typing of cells from single hair follicles. *Forensic Science International*, *146*(Suppl.), 155–157.

Di Martino, D., et al. (2006). LMD as a forensic tool in a sexual assault casework: LCN DNA typing to identify the responsible. *Progress in Forensic Genetics 11*, *ICS 1288*, 571–573.

Elliott, K., et al. (2003). Use of laser microdissection greatly improves the recovery of DNA from sperm on microscope slides. *Forensic Science International, 137*, 28–36.

Giuffrè, G., et al. (2004). Analyses of genomic low copy number DNA from cells harvested by laser microdissection. *Pathologica, 96*, 396.

Lambie-Anoruo, B., et al. (2006). Laser microdissection and pressure catapulting with PALM to assist typing of target DNA in dirt samples. *Progress in Forensic Genetics 11, ICS 1288*, 559–561.

Miyazaki, T., et al. (2008). An efficient novel method for analyzing STR loci from a single sperm captured by laser microdissection. *Forensic Science International: Genetics Supplement Series, 1*, 437–438.

Murray, C., et al. (2006). Use of fluorescence in situ hybridization and laser microdissection to isolate male non-sperm cells in cases of sexual assault. *Progress in Forensic Genetics 11, ICS 1288*, 622–624.

Murray, C., et al. (2007). Identification and isolation of male cells using fluorescence in situ hybridization and laser microdissection, for use in the investigation of sexual assault. *Forensic Science International: Genetics, 1*, 247–252.

Robino, C., et al. (2006). Incestuous paternity detected by STR-typing of chorionic villi isolated from archival formalin-fixed paraffin-embedded abortion material using laser microdissection. *Journal of Forensic Sciences, 51*, 90–92.

Sanders, C. T., et al. (2006). Laser microdissection separation of pure spermatozoa from epithelial cells for short tandem repeat analysis. *Journal of Forensic Sciences, 51*, 748–757.

Saravo, L., et al. (2007). Laser microdissection in forensic analysis. In R. Rapley & D. Whitehouse (Eds.), *Molecular forensics* (Chapter 10, pp. 163–170). Hoboken, NJ: John Wiley & Sons.

Seidl, S. (2005). Contact-free isolation of sperm and epithelial cells by laser microdissection and pressure catapulting. *Forensic Science, Medicine, and Pathology, 1*, 153–158.

Staiti, N., et al. (2006). Molecular analysis of genomic low copy number DNA extracted from laser-microdissected cells. *Progress in Forensic Genetics 11, ICS 1288*, 568–570.

Vandewoestyne, M., et al. (2009). Automatic detection of spermatozoa for laser capture microdissection. *International Journal of Legal Medicine, 123*, 169–175.

Vandewoestyne, M., et al. (2009). Suspension fluorescence in situ hybridization (S-FISH) combined with automatic detection and laser microdissection for STR profiling of male cells in male/female mixtures. *International Journal of Legal Medicine, 123*, 441–447.

Single Cell Manipulation and Low Volume PCR

Li, C., et al. (2009). The combination of single cell micromanipulation with LV-PCR system and its application in forensic science. *Forensic Science International: Genetics Supplement Series, 2*, 516–517.

Novotný, J., & Hadrys, T. (2008). Bringing laser microdissection and on-chip PCR together. *Profiles in DNA (Promega), 11*(2), 6–7. Available at <http://www.promega.com/profiles/1102/ProfilesInDNA_1102_06.pdf>.

Direct PCR

Identifiler Direct kit. <http://marketing.appliedbiosystems.com/mk/get/IDENTIFILER_DIRECT_ LANDING?CID=FL-86541_godirect>.

PowerPlex 16 HS kit. <http://www.promega.com/powerplex16hs/>.

CHAPTER

3

DNA Quantitation

PURPOSE OF DNA QUANTITATION

When biological evidence from a crime scene is processed to isolate the DNA present, all sources of DNA are extracted and are present in the samples to be examined. Thus, non-human DNA, such as bacterial, fungal, plant, or animal material, may also be present in the total DNA recovered from the sample along with the human DNA of interest.

To ensure that DNA recovered from an extraction is human rather than from another source such as bacteria, the FBI's Quality Assurance Standards (Standard 9.4, QAS 2009) requires human-specific DNA quantitation. Only after DNA in a sample has been isolated can its quantity and quality be reliably assessed. The primary purpose of DNA quantitation in forensic casework is to determine the appropriate amount of DNA template to include in PCR amplification of short tandem repeat loci in order to avoid off-scale data and associated artifacts.

Determination of the amount of DNA in a sample is essential for most PCR-based assays because a narrow concentration range works best with multiplex short tandem repeat (STR) typing. Typically 0.5 ng to 2.0 ng of input human DNA is optimal with current commercial STR kits. With direct PCR (see Chapter 4), the number of PCR cycles can be adjusted so that a uniform spot of blood or buccal cells provides an equivalent amount of DNA and results in on-scale data.

PCR amplification of too much DNA results in overblown electropherograms that make interpretation of results more challenging and time-consuming to review. Too little DNA can result in loss of alleles due to stochastic amplification and failure to equally sample the STR alleles present in the sample. Figure 3.1 illustrates the "Goldilocks" principle of not wanting too much or too little DNA in a PCR reaction to produce an STR profile.

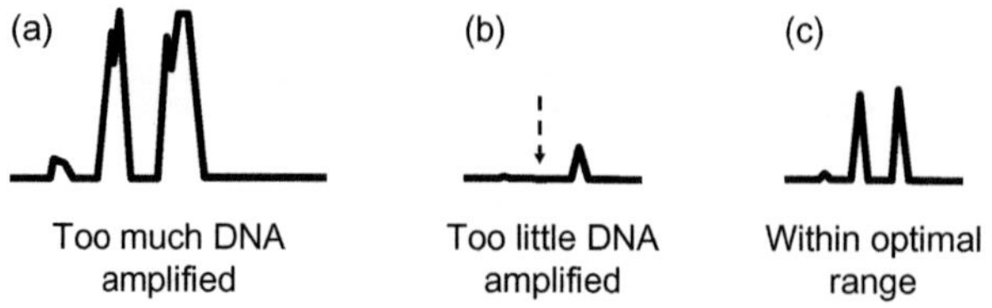

FIGURE 3.1 Illustration of STR typing results at a single heterozygous locus for a single source sample with (a) too much DNA template showing off-scale, split peaks, (b) too little DNA template where the arrow points to allele dropout due to stochastic effects, or (c) just the right amount so that two allele peaks are balanced and on-scale.

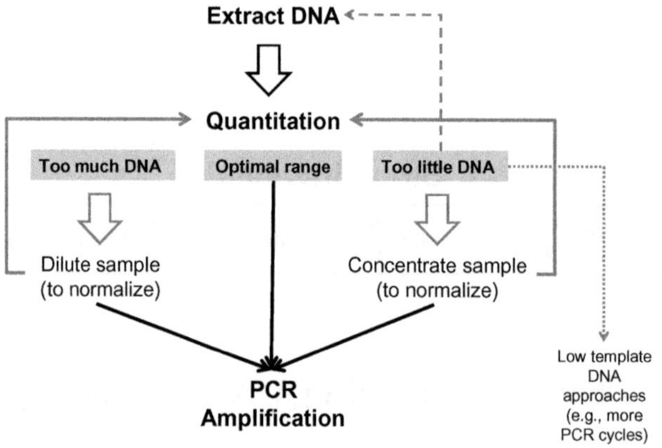

FIGURE 3.2 Flow chart illustrating role of DNA quantitation following DNA extraction. If the sample contains a DNA quantity within the optimal range, then an analyst would proceed with PCR amplification. With too much DNA, a sample could be diluted and either re-checked for DNA quantity or sent directly to the PCR amplification step. When DNA results below the optimal range are observed, the sample could be concentrated, re-extracted or treated with low template DNA approaches depending on laboratory policy and amount of available sample.

If the amount of DNA in a sample is outside of the target range for creating a "just right" DNA profile, then the DNA amount must be adjusted prior to putting it into the PCR reaction. The process of achieving a DNA concentration that fits the optimal window for analysis is called *normalization*. This involves diluting the sample down to the desired range or concentrating it by removing excess fluid. Figure 3.2 illustrates that if too little DNA is detected during the quantitation step then re-extraction or increased PCR cycles (provided the laboratory has a validated protocol, see Chapter 11) may be attempted.

Evaluation of human DNA quantity in a sample can be used to screen for samples that should be sent forward through the DNA testing process. When having to wade through a large number of samples, a sample screening process based on the amount of human DNA present can be very helpful and cost-effective. DNA quantitation that is performed well can save time during the data review process as data signal will be on-scale. By not having to repeat the testing process for an off-scale DNA result, the often-limited biological evidence will not have to be further consumed to try and obtain a better quality result.

TABLE 3.1 Quality Assessments Possible with Appropriate Quantitative PCR (qPCR) Assays.

Quality Assessment	How Assessed	Possible PCR Solutions
PCR inhibitor	IPC cycle threshold	PCR kit with improved buffer (Ch. 5)
Male-to-total DNA ratio is low	Dual Y and human qPCR	Y-STRs (Ch. 13)
Very low human genomic DNA	Multi-copy probe target can help; mtDNA can help	Increased cycles (Ch. 11); mtDNA (Ch. 14)
Degraded DNA	Different size qPCR targets	miniSTRs (Ch. 10); mtDNA (Ch. 14)
Non-human DNA	Species test (e.g., cyt b)	Use appropriate non-human DNA primers (Ch. 16)

In addition, DNA quantitation can serve as a gateway to potential DNA testing options. For example, if an assay can assess the relative levels of total genomic DNA compared to male DNA, then depending on the DNA quantitation results either autosomal STRs or Y-STRs may be attempted as a the first course of action with the evidentiary sample (Table 3.1).

DNA Quantities Used

PCR amplification is dependent on the quantity of template DNA molecules added to the reaction. Based on the amount of DNA determined to be in a sample with a quantitation method, the extracted DNA for each sample is adjusted to a level that will work optimally in the PCR amplification reaction. As mentioned above, commercial STR typing kits work best with an input DNA template of around 1 ng.

A quantity of 1 ng of human genomic DNA corresponds to approximately 303 copies of each locus that will be amplified (D.N.A. Box 3.1). There are approximately 6 pg (one millionth of one millionth of a gram or 10^{-12} grams) of genomic DNA in each cell containing a single diploid copy of the human genome. Thus, a range of typical DNA quantities from 0.1 ng to 25 ng would involve approximately 30 to 8330 copies of every nuclear DNA sequence to be examined.

Attempts to correlate the measured DNA quantity to PCR performance are complicated by the fact that target regions for the qPCR and STR assays are not the same. As more human genomes are being sequenced, we are learning that the differences between people can be greater than previously thought (e.g., copy number variation for large chromosomal regions).

DNA QUANTITATION METHODS

A number of DNA quantitation tests have been used over the years to estimate the amount of total DNA or human DNA present in a sample (Nicklas & Buel 2003, Barbisin & Shewale 2010). These DNA quantitation tests, which will be discussed briefly below, include UV absorbance, yield gels, slot blot, PicoGreen, end-point PCR, and real-time quantitative PCR. Early assays were "home-brew" (i.e., prepared by the laboratory performing the test)

D.N.A. BOX 3.1

CALCULATION OF DNA QUANTITIES IN GENOMIC DNA

1. Relative molecular mass of a DNA base pair = 618 g/mol
   A = 313 g/mol; T = 304 g/mol; A-T base pairs = 617 g/mol
   G = 329 g/mol; C = 289 g/mol; G-C base pairs = 618 g/mol

2. Relative molecular mass of DNA = 1.98×10^{12} g/mol
   There are 3.2 billion base pairs in a haploid cell ($\approx 3.2 \times 10^{9}$ bp).
   ($\approx 3.2 \times 10^{9}$ bp) $\times$ (618 g/mol/bp) = 1.98×10^{12} g/mol

3. Quantity of DNA in a haploid cell = 3 picograms
   1 mole = 6.02×10^{23} molecules
   (1.98×10^{12} g/mol) $\times$ (1 mole/6.02×10^{23} molecules)
   $= 3.3 \times 10^{-12}$ g = 3.3 picograms (pg)
   A diploid human cell contains $\approx$6.6 pg genomic DNA.

4. One ng of human DNA comes from $\approx$152 diploid cells.
   1 ng genomic DNA (1000 pg)/6.6 pg/cell = $\approx$303 copies of each locus
   (2 per 152 diploid genomes)

while most forensic DNA quantitation is now performed using commercial kits from suppliers like Applied Biosystems or Promega Corporation.

UV Absorbance and Yield Gels

Early methods for DNA quantitation typically involved either measurement of absorbance at a wavelength of 260 nm or fluorescence after staining a yield gel with ethidium bromide. Unfortunately, because these approaches are not very sensitive, they consume valuable and often irreplaceable forensic specimens. In addition, absorbance measurements are not specific for DNA, and contaminating proteins or phenol left over from the extraction procedure can give falsely high signals. To overcome these problems, several methods have been developed for DNA quantitation purposes. These include the slot blot procedure and fluorescence-based microtiter plate assays as well as so-called "real-time" or "quantitative PCR" approaches.

Slot Blot

The most commonly used method in forensic labs during the late 1990s and beginning years of the twenty-first century for genomic DNA quantitation was the so-called "slot blot" procedure. This test was specific for human and other primate DNA due to a 40 base pair probe that bound to a region on chromosome 17 called D17Z1. The slot blot assay was

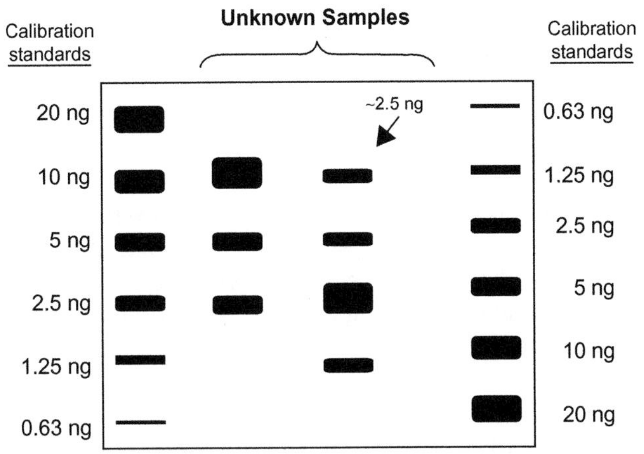

FIGURE 3.3 Illustration of a human DNA quantitation result with the slot blot procedure. A serial dilution of a human DNA standard is run on either side of the slot blot membrane for comparison purposes. The quantity of each of the unknown samples is estimated by visual comparison to the calibration standards. For example, the sample indicated by the arrow is closest in appearance to the 2.5ng standard.

first described with radioactive probes (Waye et al. 1989), but was later modified and commercialized with chemiluminescent or colorimetric detection formats (Walsh et al. 1992, Budowle et al. 1995).

Slot blots involved the capture of genomic DNA on a nylon membrane followed by addition of a human-specific probe. Chemiluminescent or colorimetric signal intensities were then compared between a set of standards and the samples (Figure 3.3).

As with almost all DNA quantitation methods, the slot blot procedure involved a relative measurement that compared unknown samples to a set of standards. These standard samples were prepared via a serial dilution from a DNA sample of known concentration. The comparison between the standards and unknowns was usually performed visually—and therefore influenced by subjectivity of the analyst. However, digital capture and quantification of slot blot images was also an option using a charge-coupled device (CCD) camera imaging system (Budowle et al. 2001).

Up to 30 samples could be tested on a slot blot membrane with six to eight standard samples run on each side of the membrane for comparison purposes. For example, the standards might be a serial dilution of human DNA starting with 20ng, 10ng, 5ng, 2.5ng, etc. Typically about 5 μL of DNA extract from each sample was consumed in order to perform this DNA quantitation test.

The slot blot assay took several hours to perform and could detect both single-stranded and double-stranded DNA down to levels of approximately 150pg (Walsh et al. 1992). Even when no results were seen with this hybridization assay, some forensic scientists still went forward with DNA testing and often obtained a successful STR profile. Thus, the slot blot assay was not as sensitive as desired. In addition, as with most "human-specific" tests, primate samples, such as chimpanzees and gorillas, also produced signal due to similarities in human and other primate DNA sequences.

In 2006, Applied Biosystems (Foster City, CA), the final commercial source for slot blot assay reagents, stopped selling the QuantiBlot Human DNA Quantitation Kit. Thus, this assay is now a thing of the past.

PicoGreen Microtiter Plate Assay

As higher throughput methods for DNA determination are being developed, more automated procedures are needed for rapid assessment of extracted DNA quantity prior to DNA amplification. To this end, in the mid-1990s, the Forensic Science Service (UK) developed a PicoGreen assay that is capable of detecting as little as 250 pg of double-stranded DNA in a 96-well microtiter plate format (Hopwood et al. 1997). PicoGreen is a fluorescent interchelating dye whose fluorescence is greatly enhanced when bound to double-stranded DNA (Ahn et al. 1996).

To perform this microtiter plate assay, 5 μL of sample are added to 195 μL of a solution containing the PicoGreen dye. Each sample is placed into an individual well on a 96-well plate and then examined with a fluorometer. A 96-well plate containing 80 individual samples and 16 calibration samples can be analyzed in less than 30 minutes (Hopwood et al. 1997). The DNA samples are quantified through comparison to a standard curve. This assay has been demonstrated to be useful for the adjustment of input DNA into the amplification reaction of STR multiplexes (Hopwood et al. 1997). It has been automated on a robotic workstation as well. Unfortunately, this assay quantifies total DNA in a sample and is not specific for human DNA.

AluQuant Human DNA Quantitation System

Around 2000, the Promega Corporation developed a human DNA quantitation system, known as AluQuant, that enabled fairly sensitive detection of DNA using *Alu* repeats that are in high abundance in the human genome (Mandrekar et al. 2001). Probe-target hybridization initiated a series of enzymatic reactions that ended in oxidation of luciferin with production of light. The light intensity was then read by a luminometer with the signal being proportional to the amount of DNA present in the sample. Sample quantities were determined by comparison to a standard curve. The AluQuant assay possesses a range of 0.1 ng to 50 ng for human DNA and can be automated on a robotic liquid-handling workstation (Hayn et al. 2004). While this assay was used for several years by laboratories such as the Virginia Department of Forensic Sciences (Greenspoon et al. 2006), it has been made obsolete with the introduction of real-time quantitative PCR (qPCR) assays.

End-Point PCR

A less elegant (and less expensive than qPCR, see below) approach for testing the "amplifiability" of a DNA sample is to perform an end-point PCR test. In this approach a single STR locus (Kihlgren et al. 1998, Fox et al. 2003) or other region of the human genome, such as an *Alu* repeat (Sifis et al. 2002, Nicklas & Buel 2003), is amplified along with DNA samples of known concentrations. A standard curve can be generated from the samples with known amounts to which samples of unknown concentration are compared.

A fluorescent intercalating dye such as SYBR Green (Zipper et al. 2004) can be used to detect the generated PCR products. Based on the signal intensities resulting from amplification of the single STR marker or *Alu* repeat region, the level of DNA can be adjusted prior to amplifying the multiplex set of DNA markers in order to obtain the optimal results. This method is a functional test because it also monitors the level of PCR inhibitors present in the sample. The amelogenin locus has also been used in conjunction with capillary electrophoresis separation and detection to provide gender and relative quantity assessment when compared to a standard curve of known DNA amounts (Allen & Fuller 2006).

In the end, each of the DNA quantitation methods described here has advantages and disadvantages and could be used depending on the equipment available and the needs of the laboratory.

REAL-TIME QUANTITATIVE PCR (QPCR)

The primary purpose in performing a DNA quantification test is to determine the amount of "amplifiable" DNA. A PCR amplification reaction may fail due to the presence of co-extracted inhibitors, highly degraded DNA, insufficient DNA quantity, or a combination of all of these factors. Thus, a test that can accurately reflect both the quality and the quantity of the DNA template present in an extracted sample is beneficial to making decisions about how to proceed. "Real-time" PCR assays provide such an assessment of both DNA yield and purity for amplification purposes.

Instruments and assays are now available that can monitor the PCR process as it is happening, enabling "real-time" data collection. Real-time quantitative PCR (qPCR), which was first described by Higuchi and co-workers at the Cetus Corporation in the early 1990s (Higuchi et al. 1992, 1993), is sometimes referred to as quantitative PCR or "kinetic analysis" because it analyzes the cycle-to-cycle change in fluorescence signal resulting from amplification of a target sequence during PCR. This analysis is performed without opening the PCR tube and therefore can be referred to as a closed-tube or homogeneous detection assay.

Several approaches to performing qPCR homogeneous detection assays have been published. The most common approaches utilize either the fluorogenic 5′ nuclease assay—better known as Taqman—or use of an intercalating dye, such as SYBR Green, that is highly specific for double-stranded DNA molecules. The TaqMan approach monitors change in fluorescence due to displacement of a dual dye-labeled probe from a specific sequence within the target region while the SYBR Green assay detects formation of any PCR product.

Instruments Used For qPCR

A number of different instruments have been used for qPCR assays and commercial kits include the ABI 7000 (Applied Biosystems, Foster City, CA), ABI 7500, ABI 7700, ABI 7900, the Corbett Rotogene 3000 (now sold as the QIAGEN Roto-Gene Q by QIAGEN, Valencia, CA), the iCycler (Bio-Rad, Hercules, CA), and the Roche LightCycler (Roche Applied Science, Indianapolis, IN). Currently, the most widely used qPCR instrument in forensic DNA laboratories is probably the ABI 7500.

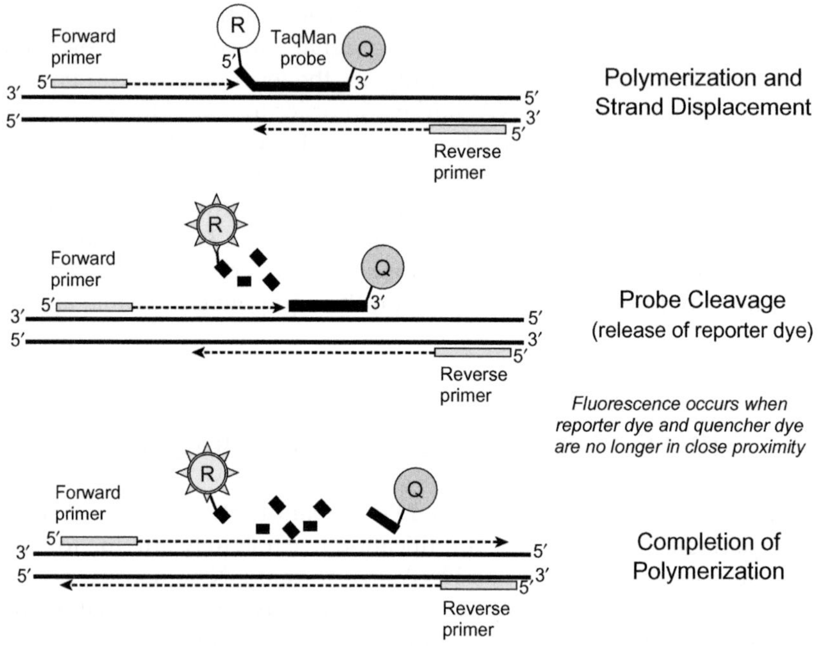

FIGURE 3.4 Schematic of TaqMan (5′ nuclease) assay.

The 5′ Nuclease Assay (TaqMan)

TaqMan probes are labeled with two fluorescent dyes that emit at different wavelengths (Figure 3.4). The probe sequence is intended to hybridize specifically in the DNA target region of interest between the two PCR primers. Typically the probe is designed to have a slightly higher annealing temperature compared to the PCR primers so that the probe will be hybridized when extension (polymerization) of the primers begins. A minor groove binder is sometimes used near the 3′-end of TaqMan probes to enable the use of shorter sequences that have higher annealing temperatures than would be expected for sequences of equivalent length.

The "reporter" (R) dye is attached at the 5′-end of the probe sequence while the "quencher" (Q) dye is synthesized on the 3′-end. A popular combination of dyes is FAM or VIC for the reporter dye and TAMRA for the quencher dye. When the probe is intact and the reporter dye is in close proximity to the quencher dye, little to no fluorescence will result because of suppression of the reporter fluorescence due to an energy transfer between the two dyes.

During polymerization, strand synthesis will begin to displace any TaqMan probes that have hybridized to the target sequence. The Taq DNA polymerase used has a 5′-exonuclease activity and therefore will begin to chew away at any sequences in its path (i.e., those probes that have annealed to the target sequence). When the reporter dye molecule is released from the probe and is no longer in close proximity to the quencher dye, it can begin to fluoresce (Figure 3.4). Increase in the fluorescent signal results if the target sequence is

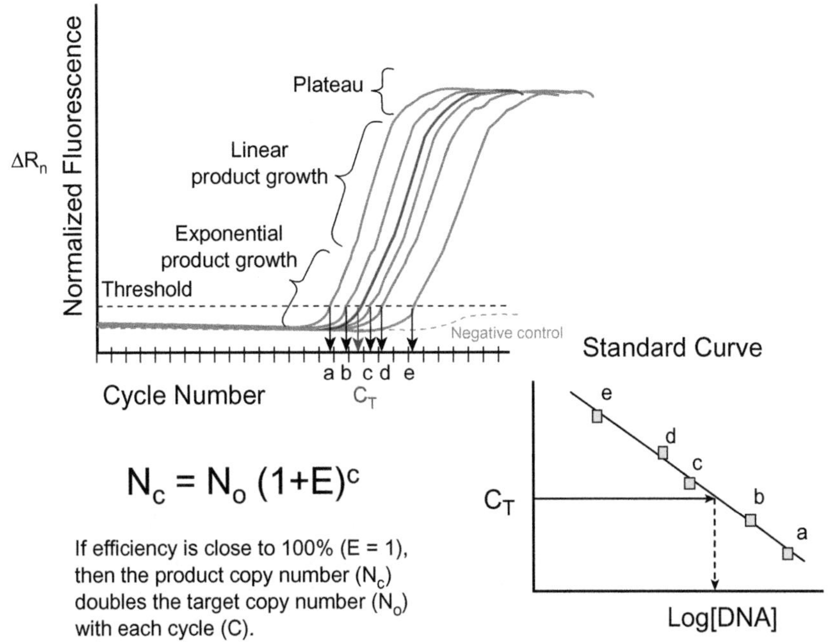

FIGURE 3.5 Real-time PCR output and example standard curve used to determine quantity of input DNA.

complementary to the TaqMan probe. It is important to note that mismatches between the DNA template sequence and the TaqMan probe can cause failure to detect the DNA template appropriately (Smith et al. 2002).

Some assays, such as the Quantifiler kit, include an internal PCR control (IPC) that enables verification that the polymerase, the assay, and the detection instrumentation are working correctly. In this case, the IPC is labeled with a VIC (green) reporter dye and hybridizes to a synthetic template added to each reaction. The TaqMan probe for detecting the target region of interest is labeled with a FAM (blue) reporter dye and is therefore spectrally resolvable from the green VIC dye. Instruments such as the ABI Prism 7000 or 7500 Real Time PCR System enable another dye like ROX (red dye) to be placed in each well to adjust for well-to-well differences across a plate through background subtraction.

Real-Time PCR Analysis

There are three distinct phases that define the PCR process: geometric or exponential amplification, linear amplification, and the plateau region. These regions can be seen in a plot of fluorescence versus PCR cycle number (Figure 3.5). During exponential amplification, there is a high degree of precision surrounding the production of new PCR products. When the reaction is performing at close to 100% efficiency, then a doubling of amplicons occurs with each cycle. A plot of cycle number versus a log scale of the DNA concentration should result in a linear relationship during the exponential phase of PCR amplification.

A linear phase of amplification follows the exponential phase as one or more components fall below a critical concentration and amplification efficiency slows down to an arithmetic increase rather than the geometric one in the exponential phase. Since components such as deoxynucleotide triphosphates (dNTPs) or primers may be used up at slightly different rates between reactions, the linear phase is not as consistent from sample-to-sample and therefore is not as useful for comparison purposes.

The final phase of PCR is the plateau region where accumulation of PCR product slows to a halt as multiple components have reached the end of their effectiveness in the assay. The fluorescent signal observed in the plateau phase levels out. The accumulation of PCR product generally ceases when its concentration reaches approximately 10^{-7} mol/L.

The optimal place to measure fluorescence versus cycle number is in the exponential phase of PCR where the relationship between the amount of product and input DNA is more likely to be consistent. Real-time PCR instruments use what is termed the cycle threshold (C_T) for calculations. The C_T value is the point in terms of PCR amplification cycles when the level of fluorescence exceeds some arbitrary threshold, such as 0.2, that is set by the real-time PCR software to be above the baseline noise observed in the early stages of PCR. The fewer cycles it takes to get to a detectable level of fluorescence (i.e., to cross the threshold set by the software), the greater the initial number of DNA molecules put into the PCR reaction. Thus a plot of the log of DNA concentrations versus the C_T value for each sample results in a linear relationship with a negative slope (Figure 3.5).

The cleavage of TaqMan probes or binding of SYBR Green intercalating dye to double-stranded DNA molecules results in an increase in fluorescence signal. This rise in fluorescence can be correlated to the initial DNA template amounts when compared with samples of known DNA concentration. For example in Figure 3.5, five samples (a,b,c,d,e) are used to generate a standard curve based on their measured C_T values. Provided that the PCR amplification conditions are consistent from sample-to-sample, a sample with an unknown DNA quantity can be compared to this standard curve to calculate its initial DNA template concentration.

In October 2007, the U.S. National Institute of Standards and Technology (NIST) released a reference material for human DNA quantitation. Standard Reference Material (SRM) 2372 contains three DNA samples that can be used to calibrate human DNA quantity measurements (D.N.A. Box 3.2).

Several real-time PCR assays have been developed with the human identity testing market in mind. Commercial kits for detecting human DNA as well as a real-time PCR assay for determining the amount of human Y-chromosome DNA present in a sample are now available. These kits include Quantifiler, Quantifiler Y, and Quantifiler Duo from Applied Biosystems and Plexor HY from Promega Corporation (Table 3.2).

Interlaboratory Studies

Several interlaboratory tests to evaluate DNA quantification methods have been conducted by NIST to better understand the measurement variability seen with various techniques (Duewer et al. 2001, Kline et al. 2003). A ten-fold range of reported concentrations was observed in one study (Figure 3.6). Most DNA quantitation measurements are precise to within a factor of two if performed properly (Kline et al. 2003, Kline et al. 2005). While

D.N.A. BOX 3.2

NIST SRM 2372: HUMAN DNA QUANTITATION STANDARD

In October 2007, after many years of research, the U.S. National Institute of Standards and Technology (NIST) released Standard Reference Material (SRM) 2372 for quantitation of human genomic DNA (Kline et al. 2009, Vallone et al. 2008). SRM 2372 contains three components labeled A, B, and C. All components are human genomic DNA. Component A was prepared at NIST from Buffy coat white blood cells from a single source anonymous male. Component B was prepared at NIST from Buffy coat cells from multiple anonymous female donors. Component C was obtained as a commercial lyophilized human genomic extract and has both male and female donors.

The DNA materials were characterized based on their absorbance properties at 260nm. Under the assumption that an absorbance of 1.0 at 260nm equals 50ng/μL of double-stranded DNA, nominal DNA concentrations of 52.5, 53.6, and 54.3ng/μL are present in the SRM 2372 components. These materials were initially characterized with Quantifiler and Quantifiler Y kits (Green et al. 2005), the "Vermont's *Alu*" assay (Nicklas & Buel 2003), and the CFS-HumRT assay (Richard et al. 2003). Subsequent studies of the three SRM 2372 components (LaSalle et al. 2011) with Quantifiler Duo (Barbisin et al. 2009) and Plexor HY (Krenke et al. 2008), which became available after the release of SRM 2372, have shown that there are some apparent copy number effects with these kits. Thus, it is important to remember that reference materials can only be held to their certified values and may not be fully computable to future assays or commercial kits.

SRM 2372 is not intended for use as a daily calibrant with qPCR assays. Rather,

DNA standard calibration using SRM 2372

	Commercial standard							
	1		2		3		4	
	[DNA]	S.D.	[DNA]	S.D.	[DNA]	S.D.	[DNA]	S.D.
Dilution								
10×	105	3.2	122	1.0	126	5.8	256	10.1
50×	105	3.3	122	7.3	145	0.8	272	7.8
100×	99	6.2	113	11.6	138	0.5	270	10.5
200×	100	1.7	137	18.5	137	3.9	311	3.7
Assigned	102		123		136		277	
Stated	200		200		200		260	
Deviation (%)	−49		−38		−32		6	

D.N.A. BOX 3.2 (*cont'd*)

laboratories can value assign their individual kit/assay calibrant materials based on comparison to SRM 2372. This may be done by diluting a kit calibrant or commercial DNA standard multiple times and testing it using dilutions of an SRM 2372 component for the standard curve. As noted in Vallone et al. (2008) Table 2 (which is reproduced at the bottom of the previous page), different lots of a commercial calibrant (samples 1, 2, and 3 in the Vallone et al. 2008 Table 2 example) may differ by more than 30% from their stated value of 200 ng/μL (e.g., 102, 123, and 136 ng/μL). Assigning these samples their appropriate values (e.g., 102 ng/μL instead of 200 ng/μL) will enable consistency over time and better correlation of DNA quantitation values with STR typing results.

TABLE 3.2 Real-Time Quantitative PCR Assays for DNA Quantitation and Assessment. For a More Complete List, See Barbisin & Shewale (2010).

Assay/Kit	Chemistry	Application	Target Gene	Amplicon Size	Standard Curve Range
Quantifiler	TaqMan	Total human DNA	Human: telomerase reverse transcriptase (hTERT) IPC: synthetic oligo	62 bp 79 bp	46 pg to 100 ng
Quantifiler Y	TaqMan	Human male DNA	Male: sex-determining region Y chromosome (SRY) IPC: synthetic oligo	64 bp 79 bp	46 pg to 100 ng
Quantifiler Duo	TaqMan	Total human & male DNA	Human: ribonuclease P RNA component 1 (RPPH1) Male: SRY	140 bp 130 bp	46 pg to 100 ng
Plexor HY	Plexor	Total human & male DNA	Human: RNU2 (multi-copy) Male: TSPY (multi-copy)	99 bp 133 bp	6.4 pg to 100 ng
"Vermont's" *Alu* (Nicklas & Buel 2003)	SYBR	Total human DNA	Human: Ya5 subfamily *Alu* repeat (multi-copy)	124 bp	1 pg to 16 ng
"CFS" HumRT (Richard et al. 2003)	TaqMan	Total human DNA	Human: flanking region of TH01 STR locus	62 bp	25 pg to 25 ng
CA DOJ quadruplex (Hudlow et al. 2008)	TaqMan	Total human, degradation, & male DNA	Human: TH01 STR allele Male: SRY Degradation: CSF1PO flanking IPC: synthetic oligo	≈170–190 bp 137 bp 67 bp 77 bp	7.2 pg to 100 ng

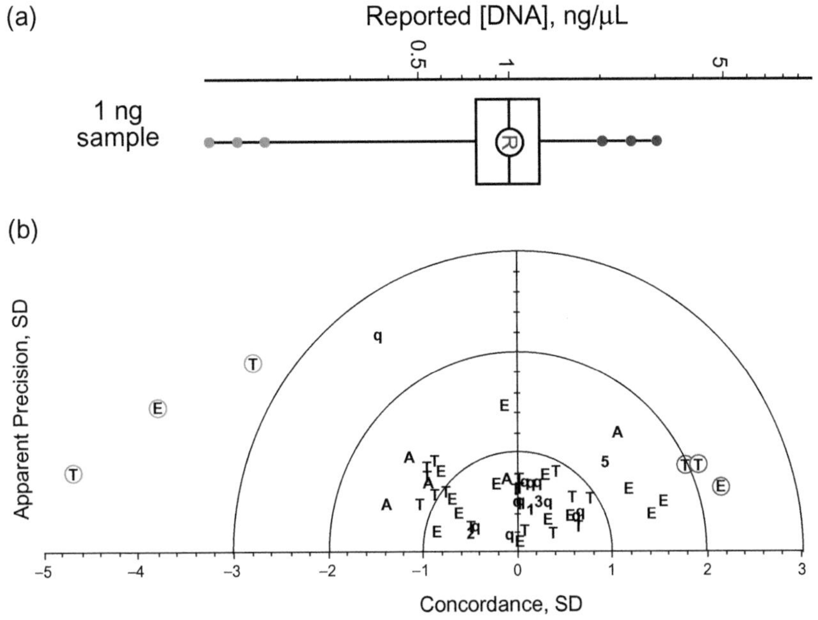

FIGURE 3.6 (a) Range of DNA concentrations reported for a 1 ng DNA sample supplied to 74 laboratories in an interlaboratory study (Kline et al. 2003). Overall the median value was very close to the expected 1 ng level with 50% falling in the boxed region. However, laboratories returned values ranging from 0.1 ng to 3 ng. (b) A target plot examining concordance and apparent precision for the various laboratory methods used. Legend: A = ACES kit; q = Quantiblot with unreported visualization method; E = Quantiblot with chemiluminescent detection; T = Quantiblot with colorimetric detection; 1, 2, 3, 4, and 5 represent methods used by only one lab.

this degree of imprecision may seem large, recall that a factor of two corresponds to one exponential-phase PCR amplification cycle; quantitation results are usually sufficiently valid to estimate DNA template amounts that will enable optimal PCR amplification.

In the NIST Quantitation Study 2004 (QS04), a total of 60 data sets from 287 submitted involved qPCR (Kline et al. 2005). Of the 60 qPCR data sets, 37 came from Quantifiler (Figure 3.7). Overall the Quantifiler assay performed well with the median value from participants coming close to the expected value (center of the target plot in Figure 3.7). However, outliers did exist emphasizing the need for care in pipetting and conducting qPCR assays.

Correlation of DNA Quantity and STR Amplification

In spite of the sensitivity of qPCR, some studies have shown that STR typing results can be obtained even when a "zero" quantitative value is observed (Cupples et al. 2009). Stochastic variation with low amounts of DNA is the reason for such observations (see Chapter 4). While there is DNA present in such samples, the qPCR result is very low or zero due to the PCR primers failing to find sufficient target to amplify. How then can qPCR

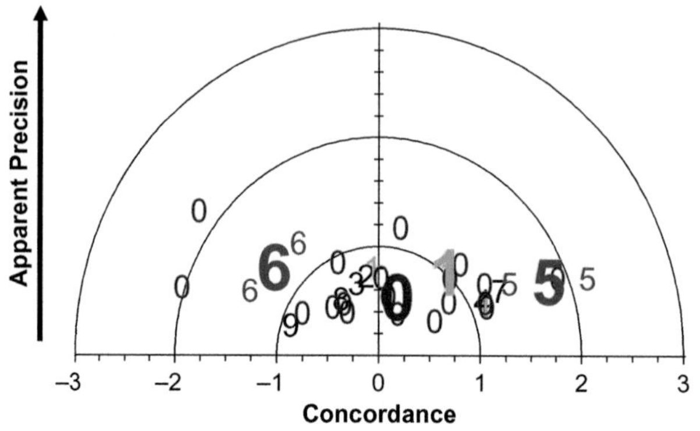

FIGURE 3.7 Target plot comparing interlaboratory results from 60 data sets involving 8 different samples using 10 different qPCR methods (Kline et al. 2005). Larger characters in bold font represent the median performance for all results submitted for a particular method. Note that specific methods may exhibit a bias relative to other assays. 0 = Quantifiler, which represented 37 of the 60 data sets (see Table 1 in Kline et al. 2005 for full description of qPCR assay codes).

results be an appropriate gatekeeper about whether or not a DNA sample should be processed further?

It is important that several things be kept in mind. First, just as with STR typing results from low amounts of DNA, stochastic variation can limit the reliability of qPCR results due to allele dropout. And, as with low template DNA testing (see Chapter 11), replicate qPCR testing is a possible solution to strengthen confidence in the result (D.N.A. Box 3.3).

Second, remember that there are different volumes of input DNA being used. Many qPCR assays require 2 μL of input DNA while STR typing PCR reactions can take 10 μL or more of input DNA. Thus, because five times as much DNA extraction volume can be included in the STR amplification reaction, more input DNA can be included giving rise to a result when the qPCR value was "zero."

Third, the PCR buffers between the qPCR and STR reactions may be different. If the STR amplification buffer contains a different polymerase or materials to enable overcoming PCR inhibition, then results may not be equivalent and the qPCR assay may not provide a true measure of STR typing performance. Furthermore, the different input volumes going into the qPCR versus STR amplification reactions could lead to different concentrations for PCR inhibitors coming from casework samples so that the qPCR or STR amplifications fail at a different rate.

Fourth, pipetting accuracy may be a factor. Pipetting 2 μL is generally less accurate than is pipetting 10 μL. A mis-pipetting of the DNA sample going into the qPCR assay could make a result appear lower than it really is. Reduction of volume to save money with qPCR assays (Westring et al. 2007) could exacerbate pipetting accuracy issues as well as effectively concentrate PCR inhibitors.

Finally, it is important that the qPCR result is appropriately correlated with STR typing performance. Internal validation (see Chapter 7) is crucial in developing appropriate interpretation of results. Variation in different lots of qPCR kit calibrants have led to problems in

D.N.A. BOX 3.3

REPLICATE TESTING AIDS CONFIDENCE IN DNA QUANTITATION VALUES OF "ZERO"

A study by the Institute of Legal Medicine in Munich, Germany attempted to correlate the DNA quantitation values with STR performance (Kremser et al. 2009). A set of 3,068 casework samples that had been extracted using the QIAGEN EZ1 robot was tested twice with the Quantifiler qPCR kit and the results averaged. Based on the internal positive control (IPC) during qPCR showing no increase in cycle threshold values, it was assumed that potential PCR inhibitors had been removed during DNA extraction. STR amplification was then performed with the Nanoplex^{QS} kit from Biotype (Dresden, Germany) followed by the SEfiler kit (Applied Biosystems) to confirm allele calls on all positive results. Based on the average of the two Quantifiler results, samples were divided into four groups: Group 1 (0 pg/µL to 5 pg/µL), Group 2 (5 pg/µL to 10 pg/µL), Group 3 (10 pg/µL to 30 pg/µL), and Group 4 (>30 pg/µL).

Generally, STR typing results correlated with the amount of DNA. Full profiles were observed 96% of the time when >30 pg/µL were reported. Likewise, no STR results were obtained 96% of the time when DNA quantities in the range of 0 pg/µL to 5 pg/uL were reported. However, full or partial DNA profiles were observed 4% of the time when essentially the DNA quantity was zero (Group 1, 0 pg/µL to 5 pg/uL obtained). The 1564 samples in Group 1 were explored further by examining the individual Quantifiler results.

When both Quantifiler replicate results were zero, then 100% of the time subsequent STR typing failed to obtain results (from 750 tested samples). Thus, when using DNA quantitation in a gatekeeper function for whether or not to proceed with further

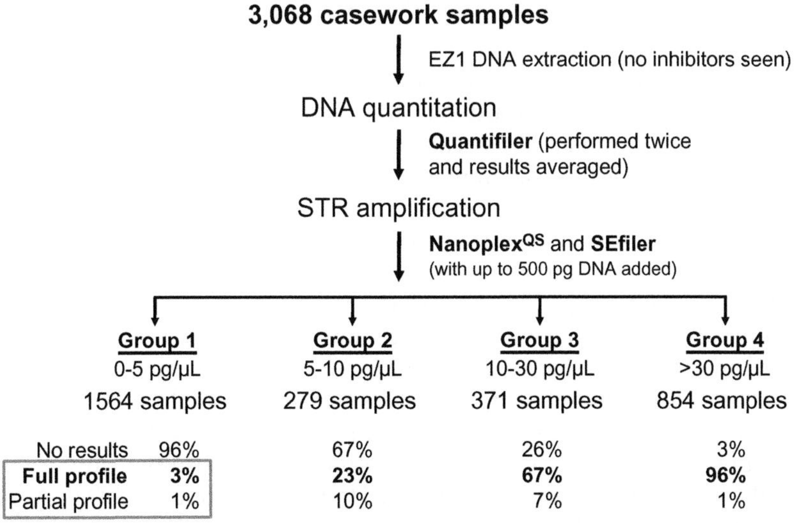

D.N.A. BOX 3.3 (*cont'd*)

1564 Samples with "Zero" Quantifiler Results (pg/μL)

	0,0	0,>0	>0,>0
Number of Samples	750	478	336
Positive results	0%	7%	27%
Negative results	100%	93%	63%

testing, replicate zero values were important to guarantee no DNA was present. This same concept of replicate testing aids reliability with low template DNA (see Chapter 11).

Source:

Kremser, A., et al. (2009). Quantifiler Human DNA Quantification Kit (Applied Biosystems) as a screening kit for DNA profiling. Forensic Science International: Genetics Supplement Series, 2, *106–107.*

correlating DNA quantitation values with expected STR typing performance (Nielsen et al. 2008). Thus, calibration to a certified reference material such as NIST SRM 2372 (D.N.A. Box 3.2) is valuable in adjusting qPCR kit calibrant material amounts in order to maintain consistency in DNA quantitation results over time.

DNA QUANTITATION AS A GATEKEEPER

While DNA quantitation is not mandatory (except for casework samples as described under FBI Quality Assurance Standard 9.4), it is a good idea and aids adjustment of DNA input amounts into PCR to enable on-scale STR allele peaks for improved data interpretation. However, DNA quantity measurements are usually not perfect and represent a "ballpark figure." Internal validation to correlate qPCR values to expected STR results is crucial.

Moreover, if new STR kits with improved buffer formulations to overcome PCR inhibitors are used (e.g., PP16 HS and Identifiler Plus, see Chapter 5), then many qPCR assays (e.g., Quantifiler) may no longer be an appropriate gatekeeper. Thus, qPCR DNA quantitation systems must be compatible with new and improved STR systems.

A properly tuned and applied DNA quantity/quality assay can save time and expense in terms of halting downstream sample processing when little-to-no DNA is present. Too avoid problems associated with low-level DNA testing (see Chapter 11), a laboratory may opt to halt testing for a specific sample when quantitation results below a specified validated threshold are observed for that sample. However, as noted in D.N.A. Box 3.3, replicate qPCR testing is advisable to strengthen reliability in correlating DNA quantitation results with expected STR typing performance.

READING LIST AND INTERNET RESOURCES

General Information

Barbisin, M., & Shewale, J. G. (2010). Assessment of DNA extracted from forensic samples prior to genotyping. *Forensic Science Review, 22*, 199–214.

DNA extraction and quantitation. <http://dna.gov/training/extraction/> .

Nicklas, J. A., & Buel, E. (2003). Quantification of DNA in forensic samples. *Analytical and Bioanalytical Chemistry, 376*, 1160–1167.

Quality Assurance Standards (QAS) for Forensic DNA Testing Laboratories. (2009). Available at <http://www2.fbi.gov/hq/lab/html/testinglab.htm> or <http://www.fbi.gov/about-us/lab/codis/qas_testlabs> .

PicoGreen Assay

Ahn, S. J., et al. (1996). PicoGreen quantitation of DNA: Effective evaluation of samples pre- or post-PCR. *Nucleic Acids Research, 24*, 2623–2625.

Hopwood, A., et al. (1997). Rapid quantification of DNA samples extracted from buccal scrapes prior to DNA profiling. *BioTechniques, 23*, 18–20.

Slot Blot

Budowle, B., et al. (1995). DNA protocols for typing forensic biological evidence: Chemiluminescent detection for human DNA quantitation and restriction fragment length polymorphism (RFLP) analyses and manual typing of polymerase chain reaction (PCR) amplified polymorphisms. *Electrophoresis, 16*, 1559–1567.

Budowle, B., et al. (2001). Using a CCD camera imaging system as a recording device to quantify human DNA by slot blot hybridization. *BioTechniques, 30*, 680–685.

Waye, J. S., et al. (1989). A simple and sensitive method for quantifying human genomic DNA in forensic specimen extracts. *BioTechniques, 7*, 852–855.

Walsh, P. S., et al. (1992). A rapid chemiluminescent method for quantitation of human DNA. *Nucleic Acids Research, 20*, 5061–5065.

AluQuant Kit

Greenspoon, S. A., et al. (2006). Automated PCR setup for forensic casework samples using the Normalization Wizard and PCR Setup robotic methods. *Forensic Science International, 164*, 240–248.

Hayn, S., et al. (2004). Evaluation of an automated liquid hybridization method for DNA quantitation. *Journal of Forensic Sciences, 49*, 87–91.

Mandrekar, M. N., et al. (2001). Development of a human DNA quantitation system. *Croatian Medical Journal, 42*, 336–339.

End Point PCR

Allen, R. W., & Fuller, V. M. (2006). Quantitation of human genomic DNA through amplification of the amelogenin locus. *Journal of Forensic Sciences, 51*, 76–81.

Fox, J. C., et al. (2003). Development, characterization, and validation of a sensitive primate-specific quantification assay for forensic analysis. *BioTechniques, 34*, 314–322.

Kihlgren, A., et al. (1998). Using D3S1358 for quantification of DNA amenable to PCR and for genotype screening. In B. Olaisen, B. Brinkmann & P. J. Lincoln (Eds.), *Progress in forensic genetics 7* (pp. 31–33). New York: Elsevier.

Nicklas, J. A., & Buel, E. (2003). Development of an *Alu*-based, QSY 7-labeled primer PCR method for quantitation of human DNA in forensic samples. *Journal of Forensic Sciences, 48*, 282–291.

Sifis, M. E., et al. (2002). A more sensitive method for the quantitation of genomic DNA by *Alu* amplification. *Journal of Forensic Sciences, 47*, 589–592.

Zipper, H., et al. (2004). Investigations on DNA intercalation and surface binding by SYBR Green I: Its structure determination and methodological implications. *Nucleic Acids Research, 32*, e103.

Real-Time Quantitative PCR (qPCR)

AAFS 2008 qPCR workshop. <http://www.cstl.nist.gov/biotech/strbase/training/AAFS2008_qPCRworkshop.htm>.

Higuchi, R., et al. (1992). Simultaneous amplification and detection of specific DNA sequences. *Biotechnology, 10,* 413–417.

Higuchi, R., et al. (1993). Kinetic PCR analysis: Real-time monitoring of DNA amplification reactions. *Biotechnology, 11,* 1026–1030.

Katz, D. E. (2007). The hidden benefits of real-time PCR: Assessing and addressing qualitative challenges. *Profiles in DNA, 10*(1), 6–8.

LaSalle, H. E., et al. (2011). An analysis of single and multi-copy methods for DNA quantitation by real-time polymerase chain reaction. *Forensic Science International: Genetics,* 5, 185–193.

NFSTC 2006 qPCR workshop. <http://www.cstl.nist.gov/biotech/strbase/qPCRworkshop.htm>.

Smith, S., et al. (2002). The effects of sequence length and oligonucleotide mismatches on 5′ exonuclease assay efficiency. *Nucleic Acids Research, 30,* e111.

Singleplex qPCR Assays

Nicklas, J. A., & Buel, E. (2003). Development of an Alu-based, real-time PCR method for quantitation of human DNA in forensic samples. *Journal of Forensic Sciences, 48,* 936–944.

Nicklas, J. A., & Buel, E. (2005). An Alu-based, MGB Eclipse real-time PCR method for quantitation of human DNA in forensic samples. *Journal of Forensic Sciences, 50,* 1081–1090.

Walker, J. A., et al. (2003). Human DNA quantitation using Alu element-based polymerase chain reaction. *Analytical Biochemistry, 315,* 122–128.

Multiplex qPCR Assays

Alonso, A., et al. (2004). Real-time PCR designs to estimate nuclear and mitochondrial DNA copy number in forensic and ancient DNA studies. *Forensic Science International, 139,* 141–149.

Andreasson, H., et al. (2002). Real-time DNA quantification of nuclear and mitochondrial DNA in forensic analysis. *BioTechniques, 33,* 402–411.

Andreasson, H., et al. (2003). Rapid quantification and sex determination of forensic evidence materials. *Journal of Forensic Sciences, 48,* 1280–1287.

Andreasson, H., et al. (2006). Nuclear and mitochondrial DNA quantification of various forensic materials. *Forensic Science International, 164,* 56–64.

Horsman, K. M., et al. (2006). Development of a human-specific real-time PCR assay for the simultaneous quantitation of total genomic and male DNA. *Journal of Forensic Sciences, 51,* 758–765.

Hudlow, W. R., et al. (2008). A quadruplex real-time qPCR assay for the simultaneous assessment of total human DNA, human male DNA, DNA degradation and the presence of PCR inhibitors in forensic samples: A diagnostic tool for STR typing. *Forensic Science International: Genetics, 2,* 108–125.

Nicklas, J. A., & Buel, E. (2006). Simultaneous determination of total human and male DNA using a duplex real-time PCR assay. *Journal of Forensic Sciences, 51,* 1005–1015.

Niederstätter, H., et al. (2007). A modular real-time PCR concept for determining the quantity and quality of human nuclear and mitochondrial DNA. *Forensic Science International: Genetics, 1,* 29–34.

Richard, M., et al. (2003). Developmental validation of a real-time quantitative PCR assay for automated quantification of human DNA. *Journal of Forensic Sciences, 48,* 1041–1045.

Shewale, J. G., et al. (2007). Human genomic DNA quantitation system, h-quant: Development and validation for use in forensic casework. *Journal of Forensic Sciences, 52,* 364–370.

Swango, K. L., et al. (2007). Developmental validation of a multiplex qPCR assay for assessing the quantity and quality of nuclear DNA in forensic samples. *Forensic Science International, 170,* 35–45.

Timken, M. D., et al. (2005). A duplex real-time qPCR assay for the quantification of human nuclear and mitochondrial DNA in forensic samples: implications for quantifying DNA in degraded samples. *Journal of Forensic Sciences, 50,* 1044–1060.

Walker, J. A., et al. (2005). Multiplex polymerase chain reaction for simultaneous quantitation of human nuclear, mitochondrial, and male Y-chromosome DNA: application in human identification. *Analytical Biochemistry, 337,* 89–97.

Quantifiler Kit

Green, R. L., et al. (2005). Developmental validation of the Quantifiler real-time PCR kits for the quantification of human nuclear DNA samples. *Journal of Forensic Sciences, 50,* 809–825.

Westring, C. G., et al. (2007). Validation of reduced-scale reactions for the Quantifiler human DNA kit. *Journal of Forensic Sciences, 52*, 1035–1043.

Quantifiler Duo Kit

Barbisin, M., et al. (2009). Development validation of the Quantifiler Duo DNA quantification kit for simultaneous quantification of total human and human male DNA and detection of PCR inhibitors in biological samples. *Journal of Forensic Sciences, 54*, 305–319.

O'Donnell, P., et al. (2008). An integrated sexual assault solution. *Forensic Magazine, 5*(2), 28–33.

Quantifiler Duo. <http://duo.appliedbiosystems.com>.

Plexor HY Kit

Krenke, B. E., et al. (2008). Developmental validation of a real-time PCR assay for the simultaneous quantification of total human and male DNA. *Forensic Science International: Genetics, 3*, 14–21.

Plexor HY. <http://www.promega.com/plexorhy/>.

Interlaboratory Studies

Bulander, N., & Rolf, B. (2009). Comparison of the Plexor HY system, Quantifiler, Quantifiler Duo kits using the roche LightCycler 480 system and the ABI 7900 real time PCR instrument. *Forensic Science International: Genetics Supplement Series, 2*, 104–105.

Duewer, D. L., et al. (2001). NIST Mixed Stain Studies #1 and #2: interlaboratory comparison of DNA quantification practice and short tandem repeat multiplex performance with multiple-source samples. *Journal of Forensic Sciences, 46*, 1199–1210.

Kline, M. C., et al. (2003). NIST mixed stain study 3: DNA quantitation accuracy and its influence on short tandem repeat multiplex signal intensity. *Analytical Chemistry, 75*, 2463–2469.

Kline, M. C., et al. (2005). Results from the NIST 2004 DNA quantitation study. *Journal of Forensic Sciences, 50*, 571–578.

Nielsen, K., et al. (2008). Comparison of five DNA quantification methods. *Forensic Science International: Genetics, 2*, 226–230.

NIST SRM 2372

Kline, M. C., et al. (2009). Production and certification of NIST standard reference material 2372 human DNA quantitation standard. *Analytical & Bioanalytical Chemistry, 394*, 1183–1192.

NIST SRM 2372 certificate. <https://www-s.nist.gov/srmors/view_detail.cfm?srm=2372>.

NIST SRM 2372 STRBase page. <http://www.cstl.nist.gov/strbase/srm2372.htm>.

Vallone, P. M., et al. (2008). Development and usage of a NIST standard reference material for real-time PCR quantitation of human DNA. *Forensic Science International: Genetics Supplement Series, 1*, 80–82.

Correlation of qPCR Observations to STR Results

Cupples, C. M., et al. (2009). STR profiles from DNA samples with "undetected" or low Quantifiler results. *Journal of Forensic Sciences, 54*, 103–107.

Grgicak, C. M., et al. (2010). Investigation of reproducibility and error associated with qPCR methods using Quantifiler Duo DNA quantification kit. *Journal of Forensic Sciences, 55*, 1331–1339.

Kontanis, E. J., & Reed, F. A. (2006). Evaluation of real-time PCR amplification efficiencies to detect PCR inhibitors. *Journal of Forensic Sciences, 51*, 795–804.

Koukoulas, I., et al. (2008). Quantifiler observations of relevance to forensic casework. *Journal of Forensic Sciences, 53*, 135–141.

Kremser, A., et al. (2009). Quantifiler Human DNA Quantification Kit (Applied Biosystems) as a screening kit for DNA profiling. *Forensic Science International: Genetics Supplement Series, 2*, 106–107.

Swango, K. L., et al. (2006). A quantitative PCR assay for the assessment of DNA degradation in forensic samples. *Forensic Science International, 158*, 14–26.

CHAPTER

4

PCR Amplification: Capabilities and Cautions

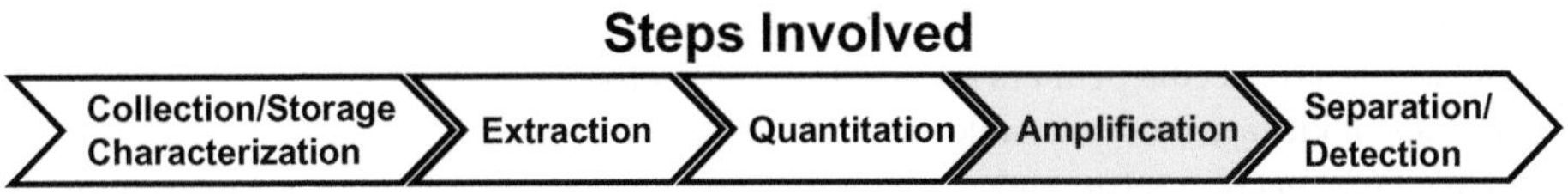

Forensic science and DNA-typing laboratories have greatly benefited from the discovery of a technique known as the polymerase chain reaction or PCR. First described in 1985 by Kary Mullis and members of the Human Genetics group at the Cetus Corporation (now Roche Molecular Systems), PCR has revolutionized molecular biology through the ability to make hundreds of millions of copies of a specific sequence of DNA in a matter of only a few hours. The impact of PCR has been such that its inventor, Kary Mullis, received the Nobel Prize in Chemistry in 1993—less than 10 years after it was first described.

Without the ability to make copies of DNA molecules, many forensic samples would be impossible to analyze. DNA from crime scenes is often limited in both quantity and quality and obtaining a cleaner, more concentrated sample is normally out of the question (most perpetrators of crimes are, not surprisingly, unwilling to donate more evidence material to aid their prosecution). The PCR DNA amplification technology is well suited to analysis of forensic DNA samples because it is sensitive, rapid, and not as limited by the quality of the DNA as the original restriction fragment length polymorphism (RFLP) methods were when they were used (see Butler 2010, *Fundamentals*, Chapter 3). Some advantages and disadvantages of PCR are summarized in D.N.A. Box 4.1.

PCR BACKGROUND AND BASICS

PCR is an enzymatic process in which a specific region of DNA is replicated over and over again to yield many copies of a particular sequence. This molecular "xeroxing" process involves heating and cooling samples in a precise thermal cycling pattern over ≈30 cycles

D.N.A. BOX 4.1

ADVANTAGES AND DISADVANTAGES OF PCR

The advantages of PCR amplification for biological evidence include the following:

- Very small amounts of DNA template may be used from as little as a single cell (see Chapter 11).
- DNA degraded to fragments only a few hundred base pairs in length can serve as effective templates for amplification.
- Large numbers of copies of specific DNA sequences can be amplified simultaneously with multiplex PCR reactions.
- Contaminant DNA, such as fungal and bacterial sources, will not amplify because human-specific primers are used.
- Commercial kits are now available for easy PCR reaction setup and amplification.

There are three potential pitfalls that could be considered disadvantages of PCR:

- The target DNA template may not amplify due to the presence of PCR inhibitors in the extracted DNA.
- Amplification may fail due to sequence changes in the primer-binding region of the genomic DNA template.
- Contamination from other human DNA sources besides the forensic evidence at hand or previously amplified DNA samples is possible without careful laboratory technique and validated protocols.

(Figure 4.1). During each cycle, a copy of the target DNA sequence is generated for every molecule containing the target sequence (Figure 4.2). The boundaries of the amplified product are defined by oligonucleotide primers that are complementary to the 3′-ends of the sequence of interest.

In the ideal reaction with 100% amplification efficiency, approximately a billion copies of the target region on the DNA template have been generated after 32 cycles (Table 4.1). However, a reduction in amplification efficiency through PCR inhibition or poor primer annealing leads to lower quantities of PCR product being produced.

The equation for the number of target molecules produced, which incorporates the amplification efficiency, is

$$X_n = X_o(1 + E)^{(N-2)}$$

where X_n is the predicted number of target molecules created, X_o is the number of starting molecules, E is the efficiency of the reaction (between 0% and 100% or 0 to 1), and N is the number of cycles. The N-2 takes into account that for the first two cycles the specific double-stranded target is not yet created. At 100% efficiency, there is a doubling of target molecules with each cycle after the third cycle, where the ends of the PCR product are fully defined by the forward and reverse primers (Table 4.1).

If one of the PCR primers is labeled with a fluorescent dye, then the total number of single-stranded dye-labeled products at the end of each PCR cycle is actually slightly larger

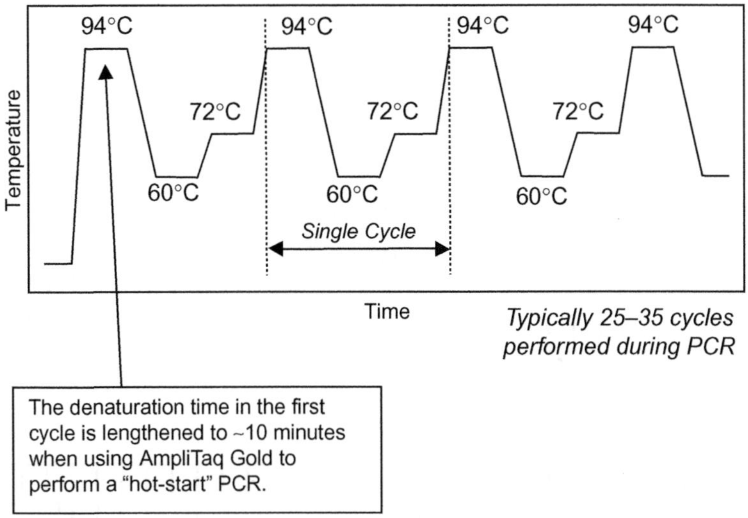

FIGURE 4.1 Thermal cycling temperature profile for PCR. Thermal cycling typically involves 3 different temperatures that are repeated over and over again 25 to 35 times. At 94°C, the DNA strands separate, or 'denature'. At 60°C, primers bind or 'anneal' to the DNA template and target the region to be amplified. At 72°C, the DNA polymerase extends the primers by copying the target region using the deoxynucleotide triphosphate building blocks. The entire PCR process is about 3 hours in duration with each cycle taking ≈5 minutes on conventional thermal cyclers: 1 minute each at 94°C, 60°C, and 72°C and about 2 minutes ramping between the 3 temperatures.

than shown in Table 4.1 because an additional linear amplification occurs after the second cycle off of an extra labeled product.

Following amplification, the PCR product, sometimes referred to as an "amplicon," is then in sufficient quantity that it can be easily measured by a variety of techniques, the most common of which is fluorescence detection (Chapter 6). For this reason, commercial short tandem repeat (STR) typing assays (Chapter 5) label one primer in every primer pair with a fluorescent dye (Figure 4.3). In this way, the amplicon becomes fluorescently labeled and can be detected when the dye label is excited by light of the appropriate wavelength. By using dye labels that can be distinguished from one another in terms of their color (fluorescent emission characteristics), the number of DNA regions that can be analyzed simultaneously is increased. Thus, the primer positions within a sequence and their spacing from one another define the overall PCR product length while the fluorescent dye establishes the amplicon's detection characteristics (e.g., what color if visible dyes are used).

The PCR amplification process, therefore, has a dual purpose: (1) to increase the number of molecules representing a specific target site, and (2) to attach a label, most often a fluorescent dye, that enables detection of the amplicons produced. Both the amplification and labeling elements of the PCR process enhance detection sensitivity and specificity.

PCR is commonly performed with a sample volume in the range of 5μL to 100μL. At such low volumes, evaporation can be a problem and accurate pipetting of the reaction components can become a challenge. On the other hand, larger solution volumes lead to thermal equilibrium issues for the reaction mixture because it takes longer for an external

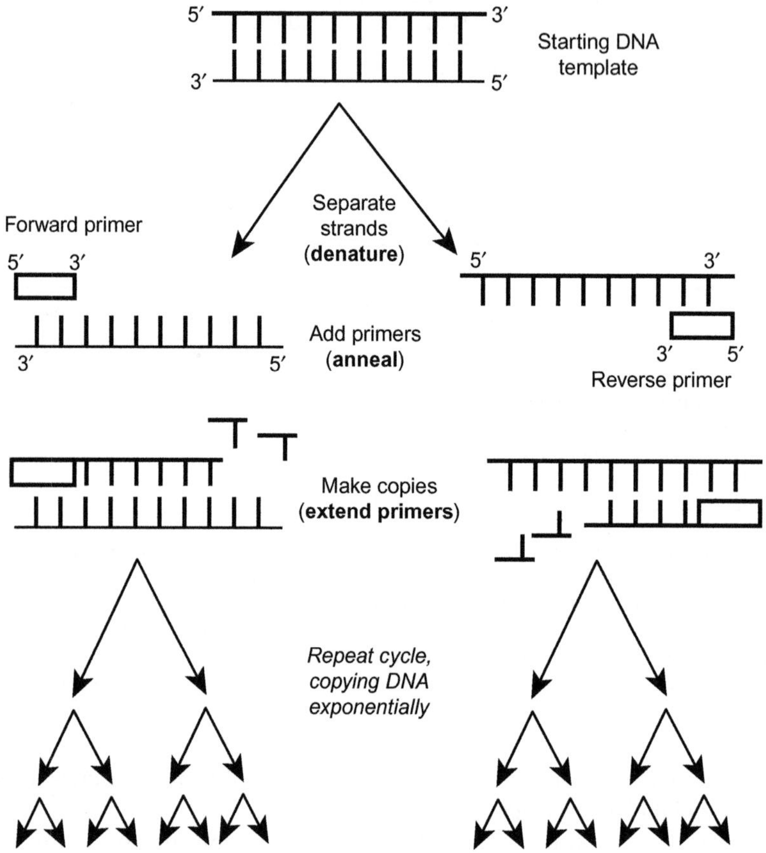

FIGURE 4.2 DNA amplification process with the polymerase chain reaction. In each cycle, the two DNA template strands are first separated (denatured) by heat. The sample is then cooled to an appropriate temperature to bind (anneal) the oligonucleotide primers. Finally the temperature of the sample is raised to the optimal temperature for the DNA polymerase and it extends the primers to produce a copy of each DNA template strand. For each cycle, the number of DNA molecules (with the sequence between the two PCR primers) doubles.

temperature change to be transmitted to the center of a larger solution than a smaller one. Therefore, longer hold times are needed at each temperature, which leads to longer overall thermal cycling times. Most molecular biology protocols for PCR are thus in the 20 μL to 50 μL range.

The sample is pipetted into a variety of reaction tubes designed for use in PCR thermal cyclers. The most common tube in use with 20 μL to 50 μL PCR reactions is a thin-walled 0.2 mL tube. These 0.2 mL tubes can be purchased as individual tubes with and without attached caps or as "strip-tubes" with 8 or 12 tubes connected together in a row. In high-throughput labs, 96-well or 384-well plates are routinely used for PCR amplification. Some work has also been performed with PCR amplification from sample spots on microscope slides that have been overlaid with mineral oil (Schmidt et al. 2006).

TABLE 4.1 Number of Target DNA Molecules Created by PCR with Various Levels of Efficiency. Only at 100% Efficiency Is There a Doubling with Each Cycle. The Sharp Drop-off in the Amount of PCR Product with Lower Efficiencies Shows Why PCR Inhibitors Can Have Such an Impact. The Target DNA Sequence Is Not Completely Defined by the Forward and Reverse Primers Until the Third Cycle.

	Number of Double-Stranded Target Molecules (Specific PCR Product)				
Cycle Number	**100% Efficiency**	**95% Efficiency**	**90% Efficiency**	**50% Efficiency**	**30% Efficiency**
1	0	0	0	0	0
2	0	0	0	0	0
3	2	2	2	2	1
4	4	4	4	2	2
5	8	7	7	3	2
6	16	14	13	5	3
7	32	28	25	8	4
8	64	55	47	11	5
9	128	107	89	17	6
10	256	209	170	26	8
11	512	408	323	38	11
12	1,024	795	613	58	14
13	2,048	1,550	1,165	86	18
14	4,096	3,023	2,213	130	23
15	8,192	5,895	4,205	195	30
16	16,384	11,494	7,990	292	39
17	32,768	22,414	15,181	438	51
18	65,536	43,707	28,844	657	67
19	131,072	85,229	54,804	985	87
20	262,144	166,197	104,127	1,478	112
21	524,288	324,084	197,842	2,217	146
22	1,048,576	631,964	375,900	3,325	190
23	2,097,152	1,232,329	714,209	4,988	247
24	4,194,304	2,403,042	1,356,998	7,482	321
25	8,388,608	4,685,933	2,578,296	11,223	418
26	16,777,216	9,137,569	4,898,763	16,834	543
27	33,554,432	17,818,260	9,307,650	25,251	706
28	67,108,864	34,745,606	17,684,534	37,877	917

(Continued)

TABLE 4.1 Number of Target DNA Molecules Created by PCR with Various Levels of Efficiency. Only at 100% Efficiency Is There a Doubling with Each Cycle. The Sharp Drop-off in the Amount of PCR Product with Lower Efficiencies Shows Why PCR Inhibitors Can Have Such an Impact. The Target DNA Sequence Is Not Completely Defined by the Forward and Reverse Primers Until the Third Cycle. (*Continued*)

	Number of Double-Stranded Target Molecules (Specific PCR Product)				
Cycle Number	**100% Efficiency**	**95% Efficiency**	**90% Efficiency**	**50% Efficiency**	**30% Efficiency**
29	134,217,728	67,753,932	33,600,615	56,815	1,193
30	268,435,456	132,120,168	63,841,168	85,223	1,550
31	536,870,912	257,634,328	121,298,220	127,834	2,015
32	1,073,741,824	502,386,940	230,466,618	191,751	2,620
33	2,147,483,648	979,654,533	437,886,574	287,627	3,406
34	4,294,967,296	1,910,326,339	831,984,491	431,440	4,428

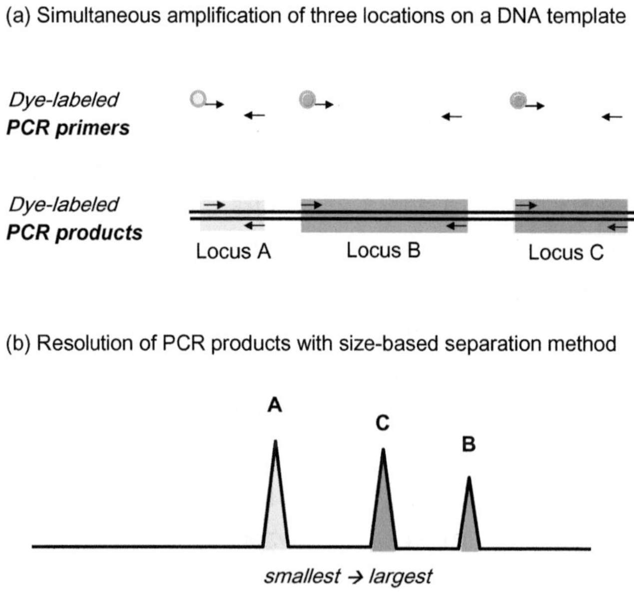

FIGURE 4.3 Schematic of multiplex PCR and how labeled PCR primers create labeled PCR products. (a) Three sets of primers, represented by arrows, are shown here to amplify three different loci on a DNA template. The primers were designed so that the PCR products for locus A, locus B, and locus C would be different sizes and therefore resolvable with a size-based separation system (b).

PCR has been simplified in recent years by the availability of reagent kits that allow a forensic DNA laboratory to simply add a DNA template to a pre-made PCR mix containing all the necessary components for the amplification reaction. These kits are optimized through extensive research efforts on the part of commercial manufacturers. The kits are typically prepared so that a user adds an aliquot of the kit solution to a particular amount of genomic DNA. The best results with these commercial kits are obtained if the DNA template is added in an amount that corresponds to the concentration range designed for the kit; hence, the need for DNA quantitation and sample quantity normalization described in Chapter 3.

Thermal Cyclers

The instrument that heats and cools a DNA sample in order to perform the PCR reaction is known as a thermal cycler. Accurate and consistent sample heating and cooling is crucial to PCR in order to guarantee consistent results. There are a wide variety of thermal cycler options available from multiple manufacturers. A few of these options are contained in the chapter reference list. These instruments vary in the number of samples that can be handled at a time, the size of the sample tube and volume of reagents that can be handled, and the speed at which the temperature can be changed. Prices for thermal cycling devices range from a few thousand dollars to over 10,000 dollars.

The most prevalent thermal cycler in forensic DNA laboratories today is the GeneAmp 9700 from Applied Biosystems (Foster City, CA). The "9700" is typically used to heat and cool 96 samples in an 8×12-well microplate format at a rate of approximately 1°C per second, although its maximum ramp rate is 4°C per second.

Thermal Cycling Parameters

A wide range of PCR cycling protocols have been used for various molecular biology applications. The primary reason that PCR protocols vary is that different primer sequences have different hybridization properties and thus anneal to the DNA template strands at different rates. Annealing time and temperature are some of the most critical parameters to optimize with multiplex PCR. Alternatively, primer sequences may be altered during development to fit a defined PCR thermal cycling protocol.

Most forensic protocols utilize 28 to 30 cycles of PCR with fluorescence detection. To improve detection with low-template DNA samples some laboratories have opted to increase the number of PCR cycles to 31 or even 34 cycles (see Chapter 11). It is important to recognize that increasing sensitivity through additional cycles needs to be carefully validated as additional artifacts may arise.

PCR COMPONENTS & CONTROLS

A PCR sample is prepared by mixing several individual components and then adding deionized water to achieve the desired volume and concentration of each of the components. Commercial kits with pre-mixed components may also be used for PCR. These kits have greatly simplified the use of PCR in forensic DNA laboratories.

The most important components of a PCR sample are the two primers, which are short DNA sequences that precede or "flank" the region to be copied. A primer acts to identify or "target" the portion of the DNA template to be copied. It is a chemically synthesized

TABLE 4.2 Typical Components for PCR Amplification.

Reagent	Optimal Concentration
Tris-HCl, pH 8.3 (25°C)	10–50 mM
Magnesium chloride	1.2–2.5 mM
Potassium chloride	50 mM
Deoxynucleotide triphosphates (dNTPs)	200 μM each dATP, dTTP, dCTP, dGTP
DNA polymerase, thermal stable[a]	0.5–5U
Bovine serum albumin (BSA)	100 μg/mL
Primers	0.1–1.0 μM
Template DNA	1–10 ng genomic DNA

[a]*__Taq__ and __Taq__Gold are the two most common thermal stable polymerases used for PCR.*

oligonucleotide that is added in a high concentration relative to the DNA template to drive the PCR sample. Considerable knowledge of the DNA sequence to be copied is required in order to select appropriate primer sequences.

The other components of a PCR sample consist of template DNA that will be copied, deoxynucleotide triphosphate (dNTP) building blocks that supply each of the four nucleotides, and a DNA polymerase that adds the building blocks in the proper order based on the template DNA sequence. The various components and their optimal concentrations are listed in Table 4.2. Thermally stable polymerases that do not fall apart during the near-boiling denaturation temperature steps have been important to the success of PCR. The most commonly used thermally stable polymerase is *Taq*, which comes from a bacterium named *Thermus aquaticus* that inhabits hot springs.

When setting up a set of samples that contain the same primers and reaction components, it is common to prepare a "master mix" that can then be dispensed in equal quantities to each PCR tube. This procedure helps to insure relative homogeneity among samples. Also by setting up a larger number of reactions at once, small pipetting volumes can be avoided, which improves the accuracy of adding each component (and thus the reproducibility of your method). When performing a common test on a number of different samples, the goal should be to examine the variation in the DNA samples not variability in the reaction components used and the sample preparation method.

Controls Used to Monitor PCR

Controls are used to monitor the effectiveness of the chosen experimental conditions and/or the technique of the experimenter. These controls typically include a "negative control," which is the entire PCR reaction mixture without any DNA template. The negative control usually contains water or buffer of the same volume as the DNA template and is useful to assess whether or not any of the PCR components have been contaminated by DNA (e.g., you or someone else in your lab). An extraction "blank" is also useful to verify that the reagents used for DNA extraction are free from any extraneous DNA templates.

A "positive control" is a valuable indicator of whether or not any of the PCR components have failed or were not added during the reaction setup phase of experiments conducted. A standard DNA template of known sequence with good-quality DNA should be used for the positive control. This DNA template should be amplified with the same PCR primers as used on the rest of the samples in the batch that is being amplified. The purpose of a positive control is to ensure confidence that the reaction components and thermal cycling parameters are working for amplifying a specific region of DNA.

The challenge with a negative control is that a single PCR tube (or other plasticware that the DNA samples pass through during sample processing) may contain contaminating DNA. If the contaminant DNA is present in only the negative control PCR tube, then the testing analyst may get a false impression that other samples in the batch are contaminated when in fact they are clean. If the contaminant DNA is present in one of the casework DNA samples, then a mixture may result between the contaminant DNA and the original casework sample—and the clean negative control would not be helpful in assessing that a contaminant is present in one of the tested samples.

Peter Gill and Amanda Kirkham from the UK Forensic Science Service (Gill & Kirkham 2004) advocate maintaining a record of profiles that appear in negative controls in order to establish a level of predicted lab contamination from exogenous DNA in contaminated plasticware. An example of a prominent profile from consumable contamination is shown in D.N.A. Box 4.2.

DNA Template Source

Typically following DNA extraction and quantitation, an appropriate amount of genomic DNA would be added to the PCR sample (see Chapter 3). It has been demonstrated that old PCR samples (from DQ alpha or a CTT triplex) contain enough genomic DNA that a subsequent amplification with an STR kit can recover a full STR profile (Patchett et al. 2002). Likewise, STR results have been obtained from old RFLP membranes (Steadman et al. 2008). Hence, storage of old evidence has proven useful when needing to obtain STR typing results for comparison purposes.

Hot-Start PCR

Regular DNA polymerases exhibit some activity below their optimal temperature, which for *Taq* polymerase is 72°C. Thus, primers can anneal non-specifically to the template DNA at room temperature when PCR reactions are being set-up and non-specific products may result. It is also possible at a low temperature for the primers to bind to each other creating products called "primer dimers." These are a particular problem because their small size relative to the PCR products means that they will be preferentially amplified.

Once low-temperature non-specific priming occurs, these undesirable products will be efficiently amplified throughout the remaining PCR cycles. Because the polymerase is busy amplifying these competing products, the target DNA region will be amplified less efficiently. If this happens, you will get less of what you are looking for and you may not have enough specific DNA to run your other tests.

D.N.A. BOX 4.2

CONTAMINANT DNA PROFILE FOUND IN SOME MICROCON DEVICES USED FOR DNA CONCENTRATION

Similar to the German phantom swab contamination discussed in Chapter 1, a number of U.S. forensic DNA laboratories have observed a contaminating DNA profile in Microcon (Millipore, Billerica, MA) centrifugal filter devices used for DNA concentration. Presumably this DNA profile is from an employee of Millipore who works with the Microcon product line as it has appeared in multiple Microcon production lots. The full Identifiler STR profile is included to raise awareness among laboratories who may have observed this full profile or portions of it (due to stochastic PCR amplification from low amounts of DNA) in a reagent blank or PCR negative control.

It is hoped that future lots of Microcon devices will be contaminant-free as more manufacturing control processes are put into place as advocated by leading forensic DNA groups (see D.N.A. Box 4.3).

Locus	DNA Type
amelogenin	X,X
D8S1179	13,15
D21S11	29,30
D7S820	10,10
CSF1PO	10,11
D3S1358	16,17
TH01	7,9
D13S317	8,9
D16S539	13,13
D2S1338	20,25
D19S433	14,14
vWA	17,18
TPOX	8,11
D18S51	14,16
D5S818	11,11
FGA	20,23

Low-temperature mispriming can be avoided by initiating PCR at an elevated temperature, a process usually referred to as "hot-start" PCR. Hot-start PCR may be performed by introducing a critical reaction component, such as the polymerase, after the temperature of the sample has been raised above the desired annealing temperature (e.g., 60°C). This minimizes the possibility of mispriming and misextension events by not having the polymerase present during reaction setup. However, this approach is cumbersome and time-consuming when working with large numbers of samples. Perhaps a more important disadvantage is the fact that the sample tubes must be opened at the thermal cycler to introduce the essential component, which gives rise to a greater opportunity for cross-contamination between samples. As will be discussed in the next section, a modified form of *Taq* DNA polymerase has been developed that requires thermal activation and thus enables a closed-tube hot-start

D.N.A. BOX 4.3

ENFSI-SWGDAM-BSAG STATEMENT TO MANUFACTURERS

In the July 2010 issue of *Forensic Science International: Genetics*, the European Network of Forensic Science Institutes (ENFSI), the FBI Laboratory's Scientific Working Group on DNA Analysis Methods (SWGDAM) composed of U.S. and Canadian members, and the Australian Biology Specialist Advisory Group (BSAG) published a joint statement to commercial manufacturers of disposable plasticware and other reagents used by forensic DNA laboratories worldwide (Gill et al. 2010). Recognizing that consumable products have been observed with detectable DNA in the past (see Chapter 1 for discussion on the "German phantom" from contaminated buccal swabs), these groups proposed that a new product grade be made available for forensic applications that would include:

(a) Automation of manufacturing lines
(b) Minimizing interaction of staff with manufacturing lines
(c) Ensuring that products which come into contact with staff are adequately protected (i.e., staff gowned and masked, with feet and hair covered)
(d) Use of positive pressure airflow through HEPA filters, i.e., Class 10,000 clean room standard or equivalent
(e) Continual quality control (QC) checks, using PCR analysis, of a number of consumable items—preferably sensitive enough to detect a single cell with all profiles observed being recorded for future comparison
(f) Once the consumables have been manufactured, an additional stage may be used to physically destroy any DNA contaminant that may have been inadvertently introduced.
(g) QC checks and use of process controls to ensure the post-production treatment(s) have been effective.

The ENFSI-SWGDAM-BSAG joint position statement also advocates that forensic DNA laboratories maintain an elimination database for screening DNA results as appropriate (Gill et al. 2010). The elimination database should contain (1) forensic laboratory staff (including DNA laboratory, evidence recovery, and other support staff DNA profiles along with former staff members), (2) regular visitors to laboratory areas, (3) contractors such as service engineers and cleaning staff that have access to the laboratory, (4) manufacturing staff of forensic kits and consumables (where possible), (5) unexplained profiles observed in negative controls (see D.N.A. Box 4.2), and (6) police personnel, forensic medical examiners, mortuary staff and pathologists who would potentially have contact with biological samples provided to the forensic DNA laboratory.

Regarding the manufacturing staff profiles, the statement goes on to propose that DNA profiles are either held anonymously on a central database or held by individual suppliers with access available to their customers (Gill et al. 2010). Part of the concern within the United States is that the Genetic Information Nondiscrimination Act of 2008 (GINA) prevents employers from retaining genetic information on their employees (see http://www.genome.gov/24519851). There is an exception for forensic DNA laboratories in creating staff elimination databases

D.N.A. BOX 4.3 (*cont'd*)

for detecting potential sample contamination but it is unclear how this clause impacts manufacturers of reagents used in forensic DNA testing. The forensic DNA exception clause within GINA, Section 202(b)(6), states: "where the employer conducts DNA analysis for law enforcement purposes as a forensic laboratory or for purposes of human remains identification, and requests or requires genetic information of such employer's employees, but only to the extent that such genetic information is used for analysis of DNA identification markers for quality control to detect sample contamination."

Promega Corporation (Madison, WI), which supplies STR kits and other reagents for human identity testing, has responded that they meet or exceed all of the ENFSI-SWGDAM-BSAG recommendations to reduce the chance of human-to-product contamination (Pearson et al. 2010). It is hoped that other manufacturers will respond in a similar fashion.

Sources:

Gill, P., et al. (2010). Manufacturer contamination of disposable plastic-ware and other reagents—an agreed position statement by ENFSI, SWGDAM and BSAG. Forensic Science International: Genetics, *4, 269–270.*

Pearson, K., et al. (2010). Manufacturing high-quality forensic tools—Promega quality standards. Profiles in DNA, 13(2). *Available at http://www.promega.com/profiles/1302/1302_08.html.*

PCR. This enzyme, named AmpliTaq Gold, has greatly benefited the specificity of PCR amplifications.

AmpliTaq Gold DNA Polymerase

AmpliTaq Gold DNA polymerase is a chemically modified enzyme that is rendered inactive until heated. An extended pre-incubation of 95°C, usually for 10 or 11 minutes, is used to activate the AmpliTaq Gold. The chemical modification involves a derivatization of the epsilon-amino groups of the lysine residues. At a pH below 7.0 the chemical modification moieties fall off and the activity of the polymerase is restored (Birch et al. 1998).

The pH of the Tris buffer in the PCR reaction varies with temperature; higher temperatures cause the solution pH to go down by approximately 0.02 pH units with every 1°C. A Tris buffer with pH 8.3 at 25°C will go down to pH $\approx$6.9 at 95°C. Thus, not only is the template DNA well denatured but the polymerase is activated just when it is needed, and not in a situation where primer dimers and mispriming can occur as easily.

Other DNA polymerases have been developed recently that are rendered active for hot-start PCR with shorter times (e.g., 1 to 2 minutes instead of 10 to 11 minutes). These enzymes can help reduce the overall time for PCR amplification and enable rapid PCR efforts.

MULTIPLEX PCR

The polymerase chain reaction permits more than one region to be copied simultaneously by simply adding more than one primer set to the reaction mixture (Edwards & Gibbs 1994). The simultaneous amplification of two or more regions of DNA is commonly known as multiplexing or multiplex PCR (Figure 4.3).

For a multiplex reaction to work properly the primer pairs need to be compatible. In other words, (1) the primer annealing temperatures should be similar and (2) excessive regions of complementarity between the primers should be avoided to prevent the formation of primer dimers that will cause the primers to bind to one another instead of the template DNA. The addition of each new primer in a multiplex PCR reaction exponentially increases the complexity of possible primer interactions (Butler et al. 2001).

Each new PCR application is likely to require some degree of optimization in either the reagent components or thermal cycling conditions. Multiplex PCR is no exception. In fact, multiplex PCR optimization is more of a challenge than singleplex reactions because so many primer-annealing events must occur simultaneously without interfering with each other. Extensive optimization is normally required to obtain a good balance between the amplicons of the various loci being amplified (Kimpton et al. 1996, Markoulatos et al. 2002).

The variables that are examined when trying to obtain optimal results for a multiplex PCR amplification include concentrations for many of the reagents listed in Table 4.2 as well as the thermal cycling temperature profile. Primer sequences and concentrations along with magnesium concentrations are usually the most crucial for multiplex PCR. Extension times during thermal cycling are often increased for multiplex reactions in order to give the polymerase time to fully copy all of the DNA targets. Obtaining successful co-amplification with well-balanced PCR product yields sometimes requires redesign of primers and tedious experiments with adjusting primer concentrations.

Primer design for the STR DNA markers discussed in Chapter 5 includes some additional challenges. Primers need to be adjusted on the STR markers to achieve good size separation between loci labeled with the same fluorescent dye. In addition, the primers must produce robust amplifications with good peak height balance between loci as well as specific amplification with no non-specific products that might interfere with proper interpretation of a sample's DNA profile. Finally, primers should produce a maximal non-template-dependent "A" addition to all PCR products to ease data interpretation.

PCR Primer Design

Well-designed primers are probably the most important components of a good PCR reaction. The target region on the DNA template is defined by the position of the primers. PCR yield is directly affected by the annealing characteristics of the primers. For the PCR to work efficiently, the two primers must be specific to the target region, possess similar annealing temperatures, not interact significantly with each other or themselves to form "primer dimers," and be structurally compatible. Likewise, the sequence region to which the primers bind must be fairly well conserved because if the sequence changes from one DNA template to the next then the primers will not bind appropriately. Some general guidelines to optimal PCR primer design are listed in Table 4.3 (see also Dieffenbach et al. 1993, Butler 2005).

TABLE 4.3 General Guidelines for PCR Primer Design.

Parameter	Optimal Values
Primer length	18–30 bases
Primer T_m (melting temperature)	55–72°C
Percentage GC content	40–60%
No self-complementarity (hairpin structure)	≤3 contiguous bases
No complementarity to other primer (primer dimer)	≤3 contiguous bases (especially at the 3′-ends)
Distance between two primers on target sequence	<2000 bases apart
Unique oligonucleotide sequence	Best match in BLAST[a] search
T_m difference between forward and reverse primers in pair	≤5°C
No long runs with the same base	<4 contiguous bases

[a]*BLAST search examines similarity of the primer to other known sequences that may result in multiple binding sites for the primer and thus reduce the efficiency of the PCR amplification reaction. BLAST searches may be conducted via the Internet: http://www.ncbi.nlm.nih.gov/ BLAST.*

A number of primer design software packages are commercially available including Primer Express (Applied Biosystems, Foster City, CA) and Oligo (Rychlik & Rhoads 1989; Molecular Biology Insights, Cascade, CO). These programs use thermodynamic "nearest neighbor" calculations to predict annealing temperatures and primer interactions with themselves or other possible primers (Mitsuhashi 1996, SantaLucia 1998).

The Internet has become a valuable resource for tools that aid primer selection. For example, a primer design program called Primer 3 (Rozen & Skaletsky 2000) is available on the World Wide Web through the Whitehead Institute (http://frodo.wi.mit.edu/). With Primer 3, the user inputs a DNA sequence and specifies the target region within that sequence to be amplified. Parameters such as PCR product size, primer length, and desired annealing temperature may also be specified by the user. The program then ranks the best PCR primer pairs and passes them back to the user over the Internet. Primer 3 works well for quickly designing singleplex primer pairs that amplify just one region of DNA at a time. The National Center of Biotechnology Information recently released a combined Primer-BLAST tool that enables finding specific PCR primers through combining the features of Primer3 and BLAST (see http://www.ncbi.nlm.nih.gov).

Multiplex PCR Optimization

The development of an efficient multiplex PCR reaction requires careful planning and numerous tests and efforts in the area of primer design and balancing reaction components (Shuber et al. 1995, Henegariu et al. 1997, Markoulatos et al. 2002). A range of thermal cycling parameters including annealing temperatures and extension times are often examined in developing the final protocol.

Obtaining a nicely balanced multiplex PCR reaction with each PCR product having a similar yield is a challenging task. With the widespread availability of commercial kits, individual forensic laboratories rarely perform PCR optimization experiments anymore. Rather, internal validation studies focus on performance of the multiplex with varying conditions around the optimal parameters supplied with the kit protocol. For example, PCR product yields in the form of STR peak heights produced by a commercial kit might be evaluated at the optimal annealing temperature (e.g., 59°C) and 2°C and 4°C higher and lower (e.g., 55°C, 57°C, 61°C, and 63°C). Differences, if any, would then be noted relative to the optimal annealing temperature supplied in the kit protocol.

Primer concentrations are one of the largest factors in a multiplex PCR reaction determining the overall yield of each amplicon (Schoske et al. 2003). Repeated experiments and primer titrations are usually performed to achieve an optimal balance. Concentrations of magnesium chloride and dNTPs are typically increased slightly relative to singleplex reactions. A thorough evaluation of performance for a multiplex will also involve addition and removal of primer sets to see if overall balance in other amplification targets is affected.

The availability of 5-dye detection systems has enabled development of multiplexes capable of amplifying and analyzing in excess of 20 short tandem repeat loci (Butler et al. 2002, Hanson & Ballantyne 2004, Hill et al. 2009) and 52 single nucleotide polymorphism markers (Sanchez et al. 2006).

The basic principles of STR assay development have been described in several publications from the Human Identity Project Team at the National Institute of Standards and Technology (NIST) (Schoske et al. 2003, Butler 2005, Hill et al. 2009). NIST also provides a downloadable software program called *AutoDimer* to check hairpin structures (intra-primer comparisons) and primer dimers (inter-primer comparisons) when developing multiplex assays (Vallone & Butler 2004). A recent software tool called *Multiplex Manager* enables PCR primer and assay design (Holleley & Geerts 2009; http://www.multiplexmanager.com/).

PCR INHIBITION

As mentioned in Chapter 2, the PCR amplification process can be affected by substances known as "inhibitors," which interfere or prevent the DNA amplification process from occurring properly (Bessetti 2007). These inhibitors can be present in DNA samples collected from crime scenes. Outdoor crimes may leave body fluid such as blood and semen on soil, sand, wood, or leaf litter that contain substances which may co-extract with the perpetrator's DNA and prevent PCR amplification. Textile dyes, leather, and wood surfaces from interior crime scenes may also contain DNA polymerase inhibitors.

Inhibitors can (1) interfere with the cell lysis necessary for DNA extraction, (2) interfere by nucleic acid degradation or capture, and (3) inhibit polymerase activity thus preventing enzymatic amplification of the target DNA (Wilson 1997). Occasionally substances such as textile dyes from clothing or hemoglobin from red blood cells can remain with the DNA throughout the sample preparation process and interfere with the polymerase to prevent successful PCR amplification (Akane et al. 1994, DeFanchis et al. 1988, Rådström et al. 2004).

The result of amplifying a DNA sample containing an inhibitor, such as hematin, is a loss of the alleles from the larger-sized STR loci or even complete failure of all loci. Some examples of PCR inhibitors and their sources are found in Table 4.4.

TABLE 4.4 Some PCR Inhibitors and Their Sources.

PCR Inhibitor	Possible Source
Heme (hematin)	Blood
Melanin	Tissue and hair
Polysaccharides	Feces, plant material
Bile salts	Feces
Humic compounds	Soil
Urea	Urine
Indigo dye (denim)	Clothing (blue jeans)
Collagen	Tissue
Myoglobin	Muscle tissue
Calcium ions	Bone

Samples containing PCR inhibitors often produce partial profile results that look similar to a degraded DNA sample (see Chapter 10). Thus, failure to amplify the larger STR loci for a sample can be either due to degraded DNA where there are not enough intact copies of the DNA template or due to the presence of a sufficient level of PCR inhibitor that reduces the activity of the polymerase. Reduced-size STR amplicons can aid in recovery of information from a sample that is inhibited since smaller PCR products may be amplified more efficiently than larger ones.

Solutions to PCR Inhibition

A nice review of strategies to generate PCR-compatible samples has been published (Rådström et al. 2004, see also Wilson 1997). PCR inhibitors may be removed or their effects reduced by one or more of the following solutions. The genomic DNA template may be diluted, which also dilutes the PCR inhibitor, and re-amplified in the presence of less inhibitor. Alternatively, more DNA polymerase can be added to overcome the inhibitor. With this approach some fraction of the *Taq* polymerase binds to the inhibiting molecule(s) and removes them from the reaction so that the rest of the *Taq* can do its job and amplify the DNA template. In addition, polymerases other than *Taq* have been shown to work well with blood and feces, which typically inhibit PCR when performed with *Taq* DNA polymerase (Al-Soud & Rådström 1998). A recent effort mixed multiple DNA polymerases to improve PCR performance in the presence of various types of inhibitors (Hedman et al. 2010).

Additives to the PCR reaction, such as bovine serum albumin (BSA) (Comey et al. 1994, Kreader 1996) or betaine (Al-Soud & Rådström 2000), have been shown to prevent or minimize the inhibition of PCR. For this reason, BSA is a common ingredient in most STR typing kits. It should be noted though that BSA quality can vary between sources and that acetylated BSA is actually inhibitory to PCR.

A sodium hydroxide treatment of DNA has also been shown to neutralize inhibitors of *Taq* polymerase (Bourke et al. 1999). The addition of aluminum ammonium sulfate proved helpful to prevent the co-purification of inhibitors with DNA from soil samples (Braid et al. 2003). Finally, a separation step may be performed prior to PCR to separate the extracted DNA from the inhibiting compound. Centricon-100 and Microcon-100 filters have been used for this purpose (Comey et al. 1994) as have low-melt agarose gel plugs (Moreira 1998).

Where possible, sample collection should avoid adding inhibitors. For example, swabbing of surfaces containing inhibitors such as denim instead of processing cuttings of sample can help. Ideally, as noted in Chapter 2, the process of DNA extraction purifies the desired DNA away from inhibitors. If not, then monitoring an internal positive control (IPC) in qPCR assays used for DNA quantitation can at least make an analyst aware that PCR inhibitors are present (Kontanis & Reed 2006).

MODIFICATIONS TO IMPROVE PCR

A number of modifications to PCR buffer, primers, and DNA polymerases have enabled improvements in PCR performance in recent years. These modifications have also enabled direct PCR amplification from bloodstains as well as more rapid PCR amplification as will be discussed later in the chapter.

PCR Primer Improvements

Another source of potential improvement in PCR reactions is the oligonucleotide primer itself. Figure 4.4 illustrates some of the potential modifications that have been made in PCR primers used in STR typing assays. These modifications include use of fluorescent dye tags (including energy transfer primers), non-nucleotide linkers to alter the electrophoretic mobility of the PCR product, extra forward or reverse primers to cover multiple primer binding site possibilities, and high-stability analogs such as locked nucleic acids (Table 4.5).

Work with Other DNA Polymerases

In an effort to improve success with forensic DNA samples, alternative polymerases have been explored. Johannes Hedman and colleagues at the Swedish National Laboratory of Forensic Science investigated Bio-X-Act Short (Bioline, London, UK), Ex*Taq* Hot Start (Takara Bio Inc., Shiga, Japan), KAPA2G Robust (KAPA Biosystems, Cape Town, South Africa), Omni*Taq* (DNA Polymerase Technologies, St. Louis, MO, USA), PicoMaxx High Fidelity (Stratagene, La Jolla, CA, USA), r*Tth* (Applied Biosystems), *Taq*, and *Tth* (Roche Diagnostics, Mannheim, Germany) compared to AmpliTaq Gold (Applied Biosystems) (Hedman et al. 2009). They found that use of Bio-X-Act Short, Ex*Taq* Hot Start, or PicoMaxx High Fidelity provided significant improvement in amplification success from AmpliTaq Gold-inhibited PCR samples.

Furthermore, a blend of *ExTaq* Hot Start and PicoMaxx High Fidelity enabled 34 of 42 "inhibited" crime scene samples to yield better DNA profiles than could be obtained with standard

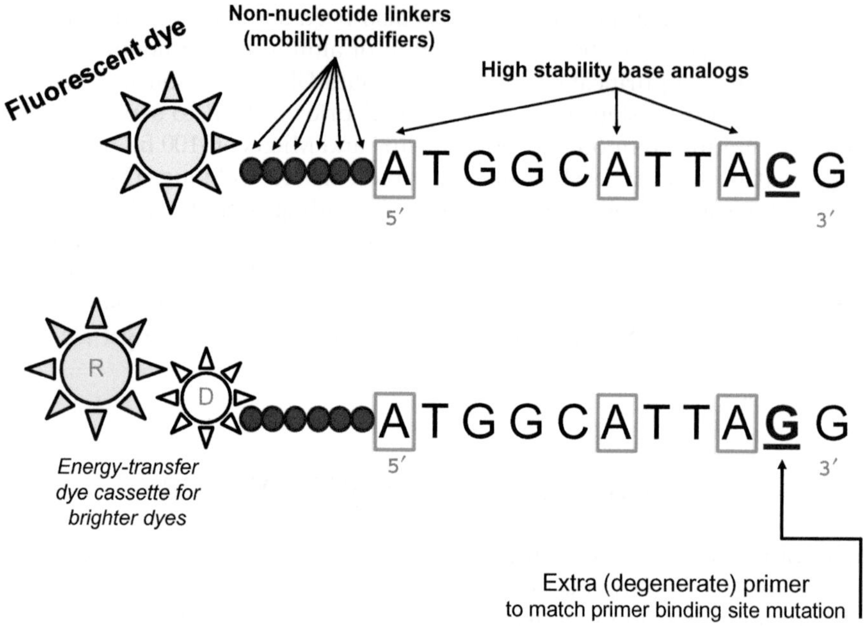

FIGURE 4.4 Representation of a portion of a PCR primer sequence with potential modifications (for more information on the purpose of each modification, see Table 4.5).

TABLE 4.5 PCR Primer (Oligonucleotide) Labels and Possible Modifications as Illustrated in Figure 4.4.

Modification	Purpose
Fluorescent dye tag	Enables laser-induced fluorescence detection of single-stranded DNA and with multiple dyes, spectral resolution enables detection of PCR products that possess overlapping size ranges
Mobility modifiers (non-nucleotide linkers)	Enables an apparent size shift during electrophoresis such that STR allele size ranges may be altered while retaining original primer sequences to avoid "discovering" primer binding site mutations
High stability nucleic acid analogs	Increases primer annealing stability to aid with DNA amplification in the presence of potential PCR inhibitors
Degenerate (extra) primer	Provides for amplification of a DNA sample containing a primer binding site mutation that would normally result in the primer not annealing and allele dropout occurring
Location along the target DNA sequence	Alters the overall PCR product size—if closer to the STR repeat region, then a "miniSTR" amplicons may improve amplification success with degraded or inhibited DNA samples—if either closer or further away from the STR repeat region, then amplicon size ranges may fit more optimally into another STR kit or "in-house" assay

AmpliTaq Gold amplifications (Hedman et al. 2010). Polymerase blends have also successfully aided rapid PCR efforts (Vallone et al. 2008).

STOCHASTIC EFFECTS

Forensic DNA specimens often possess low levels of DNA. When amplifying very low levels of DNA template, a phenomenon known as stochastic fluctuation can occur. Stochastic effects, which are an unequal sampling of the two alleles present from a heterozygous individual, result when only a few DNA molecules are used to initiate PCR. Under conditions of limited template, the PCR primers used to amplify a specific region may not consistently find and hybridize to the entire set of DNA molecules present in the PCR amplification reaction. With a heterozygous locus, where two alleles are present, the unequal sampling of the alleles can result in failure to detect one or both of the alleles. Loss of a single allele is referred to as "allele drop-out" while loss of both alleles is termed "locus drop-out."

PCR reactions involving DNA template levels below approximately 100pg of DNA, or about 15 diploid copies of genomic DNA, have been shown to exhibit allele dropout. False homozygosity results if one of the alleles fails to be detected (Figure 4.5).

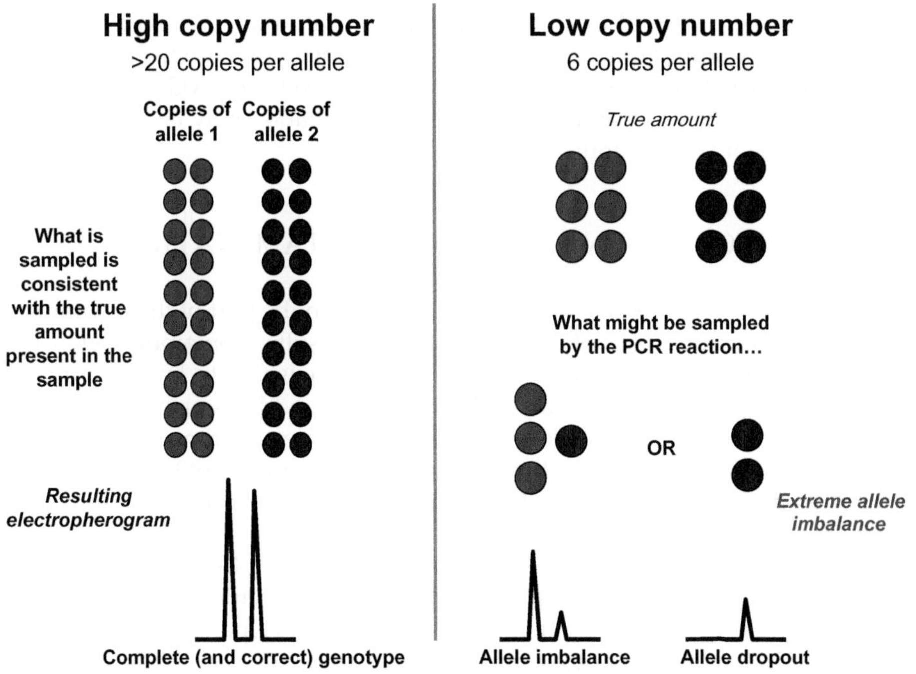

FIGURE 4.5 An illustration of stochastic statistical sampling that may occur with low template amounts where the two alleles sampled at a genetic locus during PCR are represented as red and blue circles. Allele imbalance, allele dropout, or even locus dropout may occur resulting in an electropherogram that does not accurately reflect the original DNA sample.

Stochastic (random) variation is a fundamental physical law of the PCR amplification process when examining low amounts of DNA (Butler & Hill 2010). Stochastic effects are manifest as a fluctuation of results between replicate analyses. In other words, PCR amplifying the same DNA extract twice can result in different alleles being detected at a locus.

Stochastic artifacts can be avoided by adjusting the cycle number of the PCR reaction such that approximately 20 or more copies of target DNA are required to yield a successful typing result (Walsh et al. 1992). However, efforts have been made to obtain results with low-copy number (LCN) or low template DNA (LT-DNA) testing (Gill et al. 2000). The challenges of LCN work and trying to interpret data obtained with less than 100 pg of DNA template will be addressed in Chapter 11.

Since stochastic effects cannot be avoided when testing small quantities of DNA, there are essentially two schools of thought on how to handle these types of samples: (1) stop testing or interpreting data before you go low enough to be in the stochastic realm, or (2) try to limit the impact of the stochastic variation by additional testing and careful interpretation guidelines based on validation studies (Butler & Hill 2010).

Those who advocate the second approach usually enhance their method sensitivity, such as increasing the number of PCR cycles, in order to get as much out of the limited sample as possible. The "enhanced interrogation" approach typically involves replicate testing and the development of consensus profiles (see Chapter 11).

Some scientists have insisted that whole genome amplification (WGA) techniques can be used to increase the number of target molecules and limit or reduce stochastic effects when working with low-level DNA. Unfortunately, the early cycles of WGA are also subject to stochastic effects and therefore an uneven allelic representation may be created with WGA. Chapter 11 covers more on this topic.

PRECAUTIONS AGAINST CONTAMINATION

The sensitivity of PCR necessitates constant vigilance on the part of the laboratory staff to ensure that contamination does not affect DNA typing results. Contamination of PCR reactions is always a concern because the technique is very sensitive to low amounts of DNA. A scientist setting up the PCR reaction can inadvertently add his or her own DNA to the reaction if he or she is not careful. Likewise, the police officer or crime scene technician collecting the evidence can contaminate the sample if proper care is not taken. For this reason, each piece of evidence should be collected with clean tweezers or handled with disposable gloves that are changed frequently.

To aid discovery of laboratory contamination, everyone in a forensic DNA laboratory is typically genotyped in order to have a record of possible contaminating DNA profiles. This is often referred to as a staff elimination database. Laboratory personnel should be appropriately gowned during interactions with samples prior to PCR amplification (Rutty et al. 2003). The appropriate covering includes lab coats and gloves as well as facial masks and hairnets to prevent skin cells or hair from falling into the amplification tubes. These precautions are especially critical when working with miniscule amounts of sample or sample that has been degraded.

Some tips for avoiding contamination with PCR reactions in a laboratory setting include:

- Pre- and post-PCR sample processing areas should be physically separated. Usually a separate room or a containment cabinet is used for setting up the PCR amplification reactions.
- Equipment, such as pipettors, and reagents for setting up PCR should be kept separate from other laboratory supplies, especially those used for analysis of PCR products.
- Disposable gloves should be worn and changed frequently.
- Reactions may also be set up in a laminar flow hood, if available.
- Aerosol-resistant pipette tips should be used and changed on every new sample to prevent cross-contamination during liquid transfers. Pipette tips should never be reused. Even a tiny droplet of PCR product left in a pipette tip may contain millions of copies of the amplifiable sequence. By comparison, a nanogram of human genomic DNA contains only about 300 copies of single-copy DNA markers (see D.N.A. Box 3.1).
- Reagents should be carefully prepared to avoid the presence of any contaminating DNA or nucleases.
- Ultraviolet irradiation of laboratory PCR setup space when the area is not in use and cleaning workspaces and instruments with isopropanol and/or 10% bleach solutions help ensure that extraneous DNA molecules are destroyed prior to DNA extraction or PCR setup (Kwok & Higuchi 1989, Prince & Andrus 1992).

PCR product carryover results from amplified DNA contaminating a sample that has not yet been amplified. Because the amplified DNA is many times more concentrated than the unamplified DNA template, it will be preferentially copied during PCR and the unamplified sample will be masked. The inadvertent transfer of even a very small volume of a completed PCR amplification to an unamplified DNA sample can result in the amplification and detection of the "contaminating" sequence. For this reason, the evidence samples are typically processed through a forensic DNA laboratory prior to the suspect reference samples to avoid any possibility of contaminating the evidence with the suspect's amplified DNA.

Reagent and Consumable Contamination

As was noted in Chapter 1, it is important that collection swabs be DNA-free prior to sample collection. Likewise, other DNA extraction reagents and consumables such as tubes and tips need to be clean prior to use so that the DNA profile being processed accurately reflects the individual collected and not a consumable contaminant.

Unfortunately with a highly sensitive technique like PCR, contamination does occur in some instances. The DNA results from a contaminant DNA profile observed in multiple U.S. forensic DNA laboratories is shown in D.N.A. Box 4.2. In order to significantly reduce the potential for contaminant DNA profiles being put on national DNA databases, efforts need to be taken to have DNA-free products. Recommendations from several prominent forensic DNA organizations regarding improved manufacturing protocols to produce DNA-free products are listed in D.N.A. Box 4.3.

Consumable Sterilization Efforts

Research has found that ethylene oxide treatment, which is routinely used in hospital equipment sterilization, is an effective method to remove background DNA (Archer et al. 2010, Shaw et al. 2008). In fact, dual ethylene oxide treatment effectively removed DNA molecules such that profiles were not obtained from items intentionally contaminated with 10 μL of blood or saliva while gamma irradiation and electron beam methods of sterilization were not as successful at removing the contaminating DNA (Archer et al. 2010). Unfortunately, ethylene oxide is a highly toxic gas and so consumables and reagents to be used in a forensic DNA laboratory would need to either come pretreated with ethylene oxide by the original manufacturer or be sent out to a treatment facility (and risk contamination with the additional handling).

Another study found that treating consumables with a 2 h autoclave treatment could eliminate nanogram quantities of DNA (Gefrides et al. 2010). Still others prefer ultraviolet irradiation to eliminate exogenous DNA from plasticware and water used in preparing reagents (Tamariz et al. 2006).

NEW CAPABILITIES WITH IMPROVEMENTS IN PCR

Improvements in various components and aspects of the PCR process have led to some new capabilities including direct PCR, which enables bypassing DNA extraction and quantitation, and rapid PCR, which permits obtaining results in a fraction of the time traditionally needed to perform multiplex PCR amplification.

Direct PCR

Amplification directly from a blood stain can save DNA extraction time and reagents and may enable greater sensitivity from small samples as the wash steps involved in DNA extraction often reduce the overall extraction efficiency and sample recovery.

The creation of new DNA polymerases (Wang et al. 2004), such as the Phusion High-Fidelity DNA polymerase (Finnzymes Espoo, Finland), enables increased affinity for double-stranded DNA to help overcome PCR inhibitors, incorporation of more nucleotides per binding event, and a decrease in the number of binding events for DNA strand elongation (see http://www.finnzymes.com/directpcr/).

Next-generation STR kits, such as Identifiler Direct and PowerPlex 16 HS, have been engineered to enable PCR amplification in the presence of heme and other PCR inhibitors so that biological samples may be directly amplified without prior purification (Wang et al. 2009, Chang et al. 2010).

Rapid PCR

The current forensic DNA typing process takes about 8 to 10 hours. The longest single step in this process is multiplex PCR amplification, which requires approximately three hours using manufacturer-supplied protocols for commercial STR typing kits. There is great interest in developing portable, rapid DNA-typing devices for a number of applications. For example, the ability to perform multiplex PCR amplification with commonly used STR markers in a few minutes rather than hours could open new potential biometric applications for DNA testing including analysis of individuals while they wait at a country border or an airport.

STR kit manufacturers have validated their kits with 1°C/s temperature ramp rates and dwell times of around one minute per temperature step. The time required is for 28 to 32 cycles is typically two-and-a-half to three hours. Part of this time is a 10 minute front-end hot-start to active the AmpliTaq Gold DNA polymerase. A 30 to 60 minute 60°C soak is used at the end of thermal cycling to enable full adenylation of the PCR products produced.

Using different DNA polymerases and a faster temperature ramp rate with shorter dwell times at each temperature, PCR amplifications of STR typing kits have been reduced to approximately 35 minutes on a conventional GeneAmp 9700 thermal cycler, which can change temperatures at a maximum rate of 4°C/s (Vallone et al. 2008). With faster ramp rate cyclers, STR typing results have been obtained in as low as 15 minutes (Giese et al. 2009, Vallone et al. 2009).

The improved capabilities in terms of both direct PCR and rapid PCR will open new avenues and applications for DNA testing. Only time will tell how far and fast we can go in terms of PCR amplification.

READING LIST AND INTERNET RESOURCES

Butler, J. M. (2010). *Fundamentals of forensic DNA typing*. San Diego: Elsevier Academic Press.

PCR Background & Basics

Bloch, W. (1991). A biochemical perspective of the polymerase chain reaction. *Biochemistry, 30*, 2735–2747.

Mullis, K., et al. (1986). Specific enzymatic amplification of DNA *in vitro*: The polymerase chain reaction. *Cold Spring Harbor Symposium on Quantitative Biology, 51*, 263–273.

Mullis, K. (1987). Process for amplifying nucleic acid sequences. Cetus Corporation. U.S. Patent 4,683,202.

Mullis, K. B., & Faloona, F. A. (1987). Specific synthesis of DNA *in vitro* via a polymerase-catalyzed chain reaction. *Methods in Enzymology, 155*, 335–350.

Mullis, K. B. (1990). The unusual origin of the polymerase chain reaction. *Scientific American, 262*, 56–65.

Mullis, K. B., Ferré, F., & Gibbs, R. A. (Eds.), (1994). *The polymerase chain reaction*. Boston: Birkhäuser.

Saiki, R. K., et al. (1985). Enzymatic amplification of beta-globin genomic sequences and restriction site analysis for diagnosis of sickle cell anemia. *Science, 230*, 1350–1354.

Saiki, R. K., et al. (1988). Primer-directed enzymatic amplification of DNA with a thermostable DNA polymerase. *Science, 239*, 487–491.

Schmidt, U., et al. (2006). Low-volume amplification on chemically structured chips using the PowerPlex 16 DNA amplification kit. *International Journal of Legal Medicine, 120*, 42–48.

Weissensteiner, T., Griffin, H. G., & Griffin, A. M. (Eds.), (2004). *PCR technology: Current innovations* (2nd ed.). Boca Raton: CRC Press.

Thermal cyclers

Applied Biosystems GeneAmp 9700. <https://products.appliedbiosystems.com/>.

Applied Biosystems veriti 96-well cycler. <https://products.appliedbiosystems.com/>.

Cepheid SmartCycler. <http://www.cepheid.com/systems-and-software/smartcycler-system/>.

Eppendorf Mastercycler pro. <http://www.eppendorf.com/>.

QIAGEN Rotor-Gene Q. <http://www.qiagen.com/products/rotor-geneq.aspx>.

Schoder, D., et al. (2005). Novel approach for assessing performance of PCR cyclers used for diagnostic testing. *Journal of Clinical Microbiology, 43*, 2724–2728.

PCR Components, Controls, and Improvements

Hot-Start PCR & Taq Gold

Birch, D. E., et al. (1996). Simplified hot start PCR. *Nature, 381*, 445–446.

Birch, D. E., et al. (1998). Nucleic acid amplification using a reversibly inactivated thermostable enzyme. U.S. Patent 5,773,258.

D'Aquila, R. T., et al. (1991). Maximizing sensitivity and specificity of PCR by preamplification heating. *Nucleic Acids Research, 19*, 3749.

Innis, M. A., Gelfand, D. H., & Sninsky, J. J. (Eds.), (1999). *PCR applications: protocols for functional genomics*. San Diego: Academic Press.

Moretti, T., et al. (1998). Enhancement of PCR amplification yield and specificity using AmpliTaq Gold™ DNA polymerase. *BioTechniques, 25*, 716–722.

DNA TEMPLATE SOURCES

Hochmeister, M. N., et al. (1995). A method for the purification and recovery of genomic DNA from an HLA DQA1 amplification product and its subsequent amplification and typing using the Amplitype PM PCR amplification and typing kit. *Journal of Forensic Sciences, 40*, 649–653.

Lorente, M., et al. (1997). Sequential multiplex amplification: Utility in forensic casework with minimal amounts of DNA and partially degraded samples. *Journal of Forensic Sciences, 42*, 923–925.

Patchett, K. L., et al. (2002). Recovery of genomic DNA from archived PCR product mixes for subsequent multiplex amplification and typing of additional loci: Forensic significance for older unsolved criminal cases. *Journal of Forensic Sciences, 47*, 786–796.

Steadman, S. A., et al. (2008). Recovery and STR amplification of DNA from RFLP membranes. *Journal of Forensic Sciences, 53*, 349–358.

Multiplex PCR

Butler, J. M., et al. (2001). Capillary electrophoresis as a tool for optimization of multiplex PCR reactions. *Fresenius Journal of Analytical Chemistry, 369*, 200–205.

Chamberlain, J. S., et al. (1988). Deletion screening of the Duchenne muscular dystrophy locus via multiplex DNA amplification. *Nucleic Acids Research, 16*, 11141–11156.

Edwards, M. C., & Gibbs, R. A. (1994). Multiplex PCR: Advantages, development, and applications. *PCR Methods and Applications, 3*, S65–S75.

Henegariu, O., et al. (1997). Multiplex PCR: Critical parameters and step-by-step protocol. *BioTechniques, 23*, 504–511.

Assay Design

Butler, J. M., et al. (2002). A novel multiplex for simultaneous amplification of 20 Y chromosome STR markers. *Forensic Science International, 129*, 10–24.

Butler, J. M. (2005). Constructing multiplex STR assays. *Methods in Molecular Biology, 297*, 53–66.

Hanson, E. K., & Ballantyne, J. (2004). A highly discriminating 21 locus Y-STR "megaplex" system designed to augment the minimal haplotype loci for forensic casework. *Journal of Forensic Sciences, 49*, 40–51.

Hill, C. R., et al. (2009). A new 26plex assay for use in human identity testing. *Journal of Forensic Sciences, 54*, 1008–1015.

Holleley, C. E., & Geerts, P. G. (2009). Multiplex Manager 1.0: A cross-platform computer program that plans and optimizes multiplex PCR. *BioTechniques, 46*, 511–517. Program available at <http://www.multiplexmanager.com/>.

Kimpton, C. P., et al. (1994). Evaluation of an automated DNA profiling system employing multiplex amplification of four tetrameric STR loci. *International Journal of Legal Medicine, 106*, 302–311.

Kimpton, C. P., et al. (1996). Validation of highly discriminating multiplex short tandem repeat amplification systems for individual identification. *Electrophoresis, 17*, 1283–1293.

Markoulatos, P., et al. (2002). Multiplex polymerase chain reaction: A practical approach. *Journal of Clinical Laboratory Analysis, 16*, 47–51.

Sanchez, J. J., et al. (2006). A multiplex assay with 52 single nucleotide polymorphisms for human identification. *Electrophoresis, 27*, 1713–1724.

Schoske, R., et al. (2003). Multiplex PCR design strategy used for the simultaneous amplification of 10 Y chromosome short tandem repeat (STR) loci. *Analytical and Bioanalytical Chemistry, 375*, 333–343.

Shuber, A. P., et al. (1995). A simplified procedure for developing multiplex PCRs. *Genome Research, 5*, 488–493.

PCR Primer Design

Dieffenbach, C. W., et al. (1993). General concepts of PCR primer design. *PCR Methods and Applications, 3*, S30–S37.

Mitsuhashi, M. (1996). Technical report: Part 2. Basic requirements for designing optimal PCR primers. *Journal of Clinical Laboratory Analysis, 10*, 285–293.

Robertson, J. M., & Walsh-Weller, J. (1998). An introduction to PCR primer design and optimization of amplification reactions. *Methods in Molecular Biology, 98*, 121–154.

Rozen, S., & Skaletsky, H. J. (2000). Primer3 on the WWW for general users and for biologist programmers. In S. Krawetz & S. Misener (Eds.), *Bioinformatics methods and protocols: methods in molecular biology* (pp. 365–386). Humana Press.

Rychlik, W., & Rhoads, R. E. (1989). A computer program for choosing optimal oligonucleotides for filter hybridization, sequencing and in-vitro amplification of DNA. *Nucleic Acids Research, 17*, 8543–8551.

SantaLucia, J. (1998). A unified view of polymer, dumbbell, and oligonucleotide DNA nearest-neighbor thermodynamics. *Proceedings of the National Academy of Sciences of the United States of America, 95*, 1460–1465.

Vallone, P. M., & Butler, J. M. (2004). AutoDimer: A screening tool for primer-dimer and hairpin structures. *Biotechniques, 37*, 226–231. Program available at <http://www.cstl.nist.gov/biotech/strbase/software.htm>.

PCR Volume Reduction

Gaines, M. L., et al. (2002). Reduced volume PCR amplification reactions using the AmpFlSTR Profiler Plus kit. *Journal of Forensic Sciences, 47*, 1224–1237.

Leclair, B., et al. (2003). STR DNA typing: Increased sensitivity and efficient sample consumption using reduced PCR reaction volumes. *Journal of Forensic Sciences, 48*, 1001–1013.

Spathis, R., & Lum, J. K. (2008). An updated validation of Promega's PowerPlex 16 System: High throughput databasing under reduced PCR volume conditions on Applied Biosystem's 96 capillary 3730xl DNA Analyzer. *Journal of Forensic Sciences, 53*, 1353–1357.

DNA Polymerase Improvements

Finnzymes PHUSION enzyme. <http://www.finnzymes.com/pcr/phusion_products.html>.

Hedman, J., et al. (2009). Improved forensic DNA analysis through the use of alternative DNA polymerases and statistical modeling of DNA profiles. *Biotechniques, 47*, 951–958.

Hedman, J., et al. (2010). Synergy between DNA polymerases increases polymerase chain reaction inhibitor tolerance in forensic DNA analysis. *Analytical Biochemistry, 405*, 192–200.

Kermekchiev, M. B., et al. (2003). Cold-sensitive mutants of Taq DNA polymerase provide a hot start for PCR. *Nucleic Acids Research, 31*, 6139–6147.

Kermekchiev, M. B., et al. (2009). Mutants of Taq DNA polymerase resistant to PCR inhibitors allow DNA amplification from whole blood and crude soil samples. *Nucleic Acids Research, 37*(5), e40.

Wang, Y., et al. (2004). A novel strategy to engineer DNA polymerases for enhanced processivity and improved performance *in vitro*. *Nucleic Acids Research, 32*(3), 1197–1207.

Zhang, Z., et al. (2010). Direct DNA amplification from crude clinical samples using a PCR enhancer cocktail and novel mutants of Taq. *Journal of Molecular Diagnostics, 12*, 152–161.

PCR Buffer Improvements

Chakrabarti, R., & Schutt, C. E. (2001a). The enhancement of PCR amplification by low molecular weight amides. *Nucleic Acids Research, 29*, 2377–2381.

Chakrabarti, R., & Schutt, C. E. (2001b). The enhancement of PCR amplification by low molecular weight sulfones. *Gene, 274*, 293–298.

Information on PCR additives. <http://www.staff.uni-mainz.de/lieb/additiva.html>.

PCRboost (Biomatrica). <http://www.biomatrica.com/product/pcrBoostOverview.html>.

Ralser, M., et al. (2006). An efficient and economic enhancer mix for PCR. *Biochemical and Biophysical Research Communications, 347,* 747–751.

Spiess, A. N., et al. (2004). Trehalose is a potent PCR enhancer: Lowering of DNA melting temperature and thermal stabilization of Taq polymerase by the disaccharide trehalose. *Clinical Chemistry, 50,* 1256–1259.

PCR Primer Improvements

Ballantyne, K. N., et al. (2008). Locked nucleic acids in PCR primers increase sensitivity and performance. *Genomics, 91,* 301–305.

Ballantyne, K. N., et al. (2010). Increased amplification success from forensic samples with locked nucleic acids. *Forensic Science International: Genetics.* (in press) (doi:10.1016/j.fsigen.2010.04.001).

Mulero, J. J., & Hennessy, L. K. (2009, January 1). Method and composition for nucleic acid amplification. U.S. Patent Application. US 2009/0004662 A1.

PCR Inhibition and Solutions

Al-Soud, W. A., & Rådström, P. (1998). Capacity of nine thermostable DNA polymerases to mediate DNA amplification in the presence of PCR-inhibiting samples. *Applied and Environmental Microbiology, 64,* 3748–3753.

Al-Soud, W. A., et al. (2000). Identification and characterization of immunoglobin G in blood as a major inhibitor of diagnostic PCR. *Journal of Clinical Microbiology, 38,* 345–350.

Al-Soud, W. A., & Rådström, P. (2000). Effects of amplification facilitators on diagnostic PCR in the presence of blood, feces, and meat. *Journal of Clinical Microbiology, 38,* 4463–4470.

Al-Soud, W. A., & Rådström, P. (2001). Purification and characterization of PCR-inhibitory components in blood cells. *Journal of Clinical Microbiology, 39,* 485–493.

Akane, A., et al. (1994). Identification of the heme compound copurified with deoxyribonucleic acid (DNA) from bloodstains, a major inhibitor of polymerase chain reaction. *Journal of Forensic Sciences, 39,* 362–372.

Akane, A. (1996). Hydrogen peroxide decomposes the heme compound in forensic specimens and improves the efficiency of PCR. *BioTechniques, 21,* 392–394.

Belec, L., et al. (1998). Myoglobin as a polymerase chain reaction (PCR) inhibitor: A limitation of PCR from skeletal muscle tissue avoided by the use of *Thermus thermophilus* polymerase. *Muscle and Nerve, 21,* 1064–1067.

Bessetti, J. (2007). An introduction to PCR inhibitors. *Profiles in DNA, 10*(1), 9–10. Available at <http://www.promega.com/profiles>.

Bourke, M. T., et al. (1999). NaOH treatment to neutralize inhibitors of Taq polymerase. *Journal of Forensic Sciences, 44,* 1046–1050.

Comey, C. T., et al. (1994). DNA extraction strategies for amplified fragment length polymorphism analysis. *Journal of Forensic Sciences, 39,* 1254–1269.

Demeke, T., & Adams, R. P. (1992). The effects of plant polysaccharides and buffer additives on PCR. *Biotechniques, 12,* 332–334.

DNA polymerase technology. <http://www.klentaq.com/products/inhibition_resistant>.

Eckhart, L., et al. (2000). Melanin binds reversibly to thermostable DNA polymerase and inhibits its activity. *Biochemical & Biophysical Research Communication, 271,* 726–730.

Hedman, J., et al. (2010). Synergy between DNA polymerases increases polymerase chain reaction inhibitor tolerance in forensic DNA analysis. *Analytical Biochemistry, 405,* 192–200.

Katcher, H. L., & Schwartz, I. (1994). A distinctive property of *Tth* DNA polymerase: Enzymatic amplification in the presence of phenol. *Biotechniques, 16,* 84–92.

Khan, G., et al. (1991). Inhibitory effects of urine on the polymerase chain reaction for cytomegalovirus DNA. *Journal of Clinical Pathology, 44,* 360–365.

Kontanis, E. J., & Reed, F. A. (2006). Evaluation of real-time PCR amplification efficiencies to detect PCR inhibitors. *Journal of Forensic Sciences, 51,* 795–804.

Kreader, C. A. (1996). Relief of amplification inhibition in PCR with bovine serum albumin or T4 gene 32 protein. *Applied and Environmental Microbiology, 62,* 1102–1106.

Lantz, P. G., et al. (1997). Removal of PCR inhibitors from human faecal samples through the use of an aqueous two-phase system for sample preparation prior to PCR. *Journal of Microbiology Methods, 28,* 159–167.

Monteiro, L., et al. (1997). Complex polysaccharides as PCR inhibitors in feces: *Helicobacter pylori* model. *Journal of Clinical Microbiology, 35*, 995–998.

Moreira, D., et al. (1998). Efficient removal of PCR inhibitors using agarose-embedded DNA preparations. *Nucleic Acids Research, 26*(13), 3309–3310.

MO BIO Inhibitor Removal Technology. <http://www.mobio.com/samples-high-in-pcr-inhibitors/what-is-irt.html>.

Opel, K. L., et al. (2010). A study of PCR inhibition mechanisms using real time PCR. *Journal of Forensic Sciences, 55*, 25–33.

Rådström, P., et al. (2004). Pre-PCR processing: Strategies to generate PCR-compatible samples. *Molecular Biotechnology, 26*, 133–146.

Shutler, G. G., et al. (1999). Removal of a PCR inhibitor and resolution of DNA STR types in mixed human-canine stains from a five year old case. *Journal of Forensic Sciences, 44*, 623–626.

Tsai, Y. L., & Olson, B. H. (1992). Rapid method for separation of bacterial DNA from humic substances in sediments for polymerase chain reaction. *Applied and Environmental Microbiology, 58*, 2292–2295.

Watson, R. J., & Blackwell, B. (2000). Purification and characterization of a common soil component which inhibits the polymerase chain reaction. *Canadian Journal of Microbiology, 46*, 633–642.

Weyant, R. S., et al. (1990). Effect of ionic and nonionic detergents on the *Taq* polymerase. *Biotechniques, 9*, 308–309.

Wiedbrauk, D. L., et al. (1995). Inhibition of PCR by aqueous and vitreous fluids. *Journal of Clinical Microbiology, 33*, 2643–2646.

Wilson, I. G. (1997). Inhibition and facilitation of nucleic acid amplification. *Applied and Environmental Microbiology, 63*, 3741–3751.

Yoshii, T., et al. (1993). Water-soluble eumelanin as a PCR inhibitor and a simple method for its removal. *Nihon Hoigaku Zasshi, 47*, 323–329.

Stochastic Effects

Butler, J. M., & Hill, C. R. (2010). Scientific issues with analysis of low amounts of DNA. *Profiles in DNA, 13*(1) [Internet]. Available at <http://www.promega.com/profiles>.

Gill, P., et al. (2000). An investigation of the rigor of interpretation rules for STRs derived from less than 100 pg of DNA. *Forensic Science International, 112*, 17–40.

Walsh, P. S., et al. (1992). Preferential PCR amplification of alleles: Mechanisms and solutions. *PCR Methods and Applications, 1*, 241–250.

Contamination Concerns

Gill, P. (1997). The utility of 'substrate controls' in relation to 'contamination'. *Forensic Science International, 85*, 105–111.

Gill, P., & Kirkham, A. (2004). Development of a simulation model to assess the impact of contamination in casework using STRs. *Journal of Forensic Sciences, 49*(3), 485–491.

Gill, P., et al. (2005). A graphical simulation model of the entire DNA process associated with the analysis of short tandem repeat loci. *Nucleic Acids Research, 33*, 632–643.

Howitt, T. (2003). Ensuring the integrity of results: A continuing challenge in forensic DNA analysis. In *Proceedings of the 14th international symposium on human identification*. Available at <http://www.promega.com/geneticidproc/ussymp14proc/oralpresentations/Howitt.pdf>.

Schmidt, T., et al. (1995). Evidence of contamination in PCR laboratory disposables. *Naturwissenschaften, 82*, 423–431.

Precautions to Prevent Contamination

Frégeau, C. J., et al. (2008). Automated processing of forensic casework samples using robotic workstations equipped with nondisposable tips: Contamination prevention. *Journal of Forensic Sciences, 53*, 632–651.

Kemp, B. M., & Smith, D. G. (2005). Use of bleach to eliminate contaminating DNA from the surface of bones and teeth. *Forensic Science International, 154*, 53–61.

Kwok, S., & Higuchi, R. (1989). Avoiding false positives with PCR. *Nature, 339*, 237–238.

Lowe, A., et al. (2002). The propensity of individuals to deposit DNA and secondary transfer of low level DNA from individuals to inert surfaces. *Forensic Science International, 129*(1), 25–34.

Pearson, K., et al. (2010). Manufacturing high-quality forensic tools—Promega quality standards. *Profiles in DNA, 13*(2). Available at <http://www.promega.com/profiles/1302/1302_08.html>.

Port, N. J., et al. (2006). How long does it take a static speaking individual to contaminate the immediate environment? *Forensic Science, Medicine, and Pathology, 2*, 157–163.

Preusse-Prange, A., et al. (2009). The problem of DNA contamination in forensic case work—how to get rid of unwanted DNA? *Forensic Science International: Genetics Supplement Series, 2*, 185–186.

Prince, A. M., & Andrus, L. (1992). PCR: How to kill unwanted DNA. *Biotechniques, 12*, 358–360.

Rutty, G. N., et al. (2003). The effectiveness of protective clothing in the reduction of potential DNA contamination of the scene of crime. *International Journal of Legal Medicine, 117*, 170–174.

Sarkar, G., & Sommer, S. S. (1990). Shedding light on PCR contamination. *Nature, 343*, 27.

Toothman, M. H., et al. (2008). Characterization of human DNA in environmental samples. *Forensic Science International, 178*, 7–15.

Sterilization to Eliminate Contaminating DNA

Archer, E., et al. (2010). Validation of a dual cycle ethylene oxide treatment technique to remove DNA from consumables used in forensic laboratories. *Forensic Science International: Genetics, 4*, 239–243.

Gefrides, L. A., et al. (2010). UV irradiation and autoclave treatment for elimination of contaminating DNA from laboratory consumables. *Forensic Science International: Genetics, 4*, 89–94.

Gill, P., et al. (2010). Manufacturer contamination of disposable plastic-ware and other reagents—an agreed position statement by ENFSI, SWGDAM and BSAG. *Forensic Science International: Genetics, 4*, 269–270.

Shaw, K., et al. (2008). Comparison of the effects of sterilization techniques on subsequent DNA profiling. *International Journal of Legal Medicine, 122*, 29–33.

Sarkar, G., & Sommer, S. S. (1993). Removal of DNA contamination in polymerase chain reaction reagents by ultraviolet irradiation. *Methods in Enzymology, 218*, 381–388.

Tamariz, J., et al. (2006). The application of ultraviolet irradiation to exogenous sources of DNA in plasticware and water for the amplification of low copy number DNA. *Journal of Forensic Sciences, 51*, 790–794.

Direct PCR

Bu, Y., et al. (2008). Direct polymerase chain reaction (PCR) from human whole blood and filter-paper-dried blood by using a PCR buffer with a higher pH. *Analytical Biochemistry, 375*, 370–372.

Burckhardt, J. (1994). Amplification of DNA from whole blood. *PCR Methods and Applications, 3*, 239–243.

Chang, C.-W., et al. (2010, January 21). Method for direct amplification from crude nucleic acid samples. U.S. Patent Application US 2010/0015621 A1.

Finnzymes. <http://www.finnzymes.com/directpcr/>.

Identifiler Direct kit. <http://marketing.appliedbiosystems.com/mk/get/IDENTIFILER_DIRECT_LANDING?CID=FL-86541_godirect>.

Identifiler Direct user manual. <http://www3.appliedbiosystems.com/cms/groups/applied_markets_support/documents/generaldocuments/cms_065522.pdf>.

Nishimura, N., et al. (2000). Direct polymerase chain reaction from whole blood without DNA isolation. *Annals of Clinical Biochemistry, 37*, 674–680.

Park, S. J., et al. (2008). Direct STR amplification from whole blood and blood- or saliva-spotted FTA without DNA purification. *Journal of Forensic Sciences, 53*, 335–341.

PowerPlex 16 HS kit. <http://www.promega.com/powerplex16hs/>. <http://www.promega.com/powerplex16hs/docs/Interactive_Brochure.pdf>.

Wang, D. Y., et al. (2009). Direct amplification of STRs from blood or buccal cell samples. *Forensic Science International: Genetics Supplement Series, 2*, 113–114.

Yang, Y. G., et al. (2007). A novel buffer system, AnyDirect, can improve polymerase chain reaction from whole blood without DNA isolation. *Clinica Chimica Acta, 380*, 112–117.

Zhang, Z., et al. (2010). Direct DNA amplification from crude clinical samples using a PCR enhancer cocktail and novel mutants of Taq. *Journal of Molecular Diagnostics, 12*, 152–161.

Rapid PCR

Giese, H., et al. (2009). Fast multiplexed polymerase chain reaction for conventional and microfluidic short tandem repeat analysis. *Journal of Forensic Sciences*, *54*, 1287–1296.

Laurin, N., & Frégeau, C. (2011). Optimization and validation of a fast amplification protocol for AmpFlSTR Profiler Plus for rapid forensic human identification. *Forensic Science International: Genetics* (in press) (doi: 10.1016/j.fsigen.2011.01.011).

Tsukada, K., et al. (2008). Fast PCR amplification of AmpFlSTR Identifiler. *Forensic Science International: Genetics Supplement Series*, *1*, 130–131.

Tsukada, K., et al. (2009). Fast PCR amplification using AmpFlSTR Identifiler: Second report. *Forensic Science International: Genetics Supplement Series*, *2*, 108–110.

Vallone, P. M., et al. (2008). Demonstration of rapid multiplex PCR amplification involving 16 genetic loci. *Forensic Science International: Genetics*, *3*, 42–45.

Vallone, P. M., et al. (2009). Rapid amplification of commercial STR typing kits. *Forensic Science International: Genetics Supplement Series*, *2*, 111–112.

Verheij, S., et al. (2011). A protocol for direct and rapid multiplex PCR amplification on forensically relevant samples. *Forensic Science International: Genetics* (in press) (doi: 10.1016/j.fsigen.2011.03.014).

Wang, D. Y., et al. (2009). Rapid STR analysis of single source DNA samples in 2h. *Forensic Science International: Genetics Supplement Series*, *2*, 115–116.

CHAPTER

5

Short Tandem Repeat (STR) Loci and Kits

GENETIC MARKERS AND REPEATED DNA SEQUENCES

Since it has been estimated that over 99.7% of the human genome is the same from individual to individual, regions that differ need to be found in the remaining 0.3% in order to tell people apart at the genetic level. There are many repeated DNA sequences scattered throughout the human genome. As these repeat sequences are typically located between genes, they can vary in size from person to person without impacting the genetic health of the individual.

Eukaryotic genomes are full of repeated DNA sequences (Ellegren 2004). These repeated DNA sequences come in all sizes and are typically designated by the length of the core repeat unit and the number of contiguous repeat units or the overall length of the repeat region. Long repeat units may contain several hundred to several thousand bases in the core repeat.

These regions are often referred to as *satellite* DNA and may be found surrounding the chromosomal centromere. The term satellite arose due to the fact that frequently one or more minor "satellite bands" were seen in early experiments involving equilibrium density gradient centrifugation (Britten & Kohne 1968, Primrose 1998).

The core repeat unit for a medium-length repeat, sometimes referred to as a *minisatellite* or a VNTR (variable number of tandem repeats), is in the range of approximately 8 base pairs (bp) to 100 bp in length (Tautz 1993, Chambers & MacAvoy 2000). The most commonly used minisatellite marker in the 1990s was D1S80, which has a 16 bp repeat unit and contains alleles spanning the range of 14 to 41 repeat units (Kasai et al. 1990, Butler 2010, *Fundamentals*, Chapter 3).

DNA regions with repeat units that are 2 bp to 7 bp in length are called *microsatellites, simple sequence repeats* (SSRs), or most usually *short tandem repeats* (STRs). STRs have become popular DNA repeat markers because they are easily amplified by the polymerase chain reaction (PCR) without the problems of differential amplification. This is because both alleles from a heterozygous individual are similar in size since the repeat size is small.

The number of repeats in STR markers can be highly variable among individuals, which makes these STRs effective for human identification purposes.

Literally thousands of polymorphic microsatellites have been characterized in human DNA and there may be more than a million microsatellite loci present depending on how they are counted (Ellegren 2004). Regardless, microsatellites account for approximately 3% of the total human genome (International Human Genome Sequencing Consortium 2001). STR markers are scattered throughout the genome and occur on average every 10,000 nucleotides (Edwards et al. 1991, Collins et al. 2003, Subramanian et al. 2003). However, not all STR loci exhibit variability between individuals.

Computer searches of the recently available human genome reference sequence have cataloged the number and nature of STR markers in the genome (see Collins et al. 2003, Subramanian et al. 2003). A large number of STR markers have been characterized by academic and commercial laboratories for use in disease gene location studies. For example, the Marshfield Medical Research Foundation in Marshfield, Wisconsin (http://research.marshfieldclinic.org/genetics/) has gathered genotype data on over 8000 STRs that are scattered across the 23 pairs of human chromosomes for the purpose of developing human genetic maps (Broman et al. 1998, Ghebranious et al. 2003).

To perform analysis on STR markers, the invariant flanking regions surrounding the repeats must be determined. Once the flanking sequences are known then PCR primers can be designed and the repeat region amplified for analysis. New STR markers are usually identified in one of two ways: (1) searching DNA sequence databases such as GenBank for regions with more than six or so contiguous repeat units (Weber & May 1989, Collins et al. 2003, Subramanian et al. 2003); or (2) performing molecular biology isolation methods (Edwards et al. 1991, Chambers & MacAvoy 2000).

Types of STR Markers

STR repeat sequences are named by the length of the repeat unit. Dinucleotide repeats have two nucleotides repeated next to each other over and over again. Trinucleotides have three nucleotides in the repeat unit, tetranucleotides have four, pentanucleotides have five, and hexanucleotides have six nucleotides in the core repeat. Theoretically, there are 4, 16, 64, 256, 1024, and 4096 possible motifs for mono-, di-, tri-, tetra-, penta-, and hexanucleotide repeats, respectively (Jin et al. 1994). However, because microsatellites are tandemly repeated, some motifs are actually equivalent to others. For reasons that will be discussed below, tetranucleotide repeats have become the most popular STR markers for human identification.

STR sequences not only vary in the length of the repeat unit and the number of repeats but also in the rigor with which they conform to an incremental repeat pattern. STRs are often divided into several categories based on the repeat pattern. *Simple repeats* contain units of identical length and sequence, *compound repeats* comprise two or more adjacent simple repeats, and *complex repeats* may contain several repeat blocks of variable unit length as well as variable intervening sequences (Urquhart et al. 1994). *Complex hypervariable repeats* also exist with numerous non-consensus alleles that differ in both size and sequence and are therefore challenging to genotype reproducibly (Urquhart et al. 1993, Gill et al. 1994). This last category of STR markers is not as commonly used in forensic DNA typing due to difficulties with allele nomenclature and measurement variability between laboratories, although several commercial kits now include the complex hypervariable STR locus SE33, sometimes called ACTBP2 (Urquhart et al. 1993).

Not all alleles for an STR locus contain complete repeat units. Even simple repeats can contain non-consensus alleles that fall in between alleles with full repeat units. *Microvariants* are alleles that contain incomplete repeat units. Perhaps the most common example of a microvariant is the allele 9.3 at the TH01 locus, which contains nine tetranucleotide repeats and one incomplete repeat of three nucleotides because the seventh repeat is missing a single adenine out of the normal AATG repeat unit (Puers et al. 1993)—or a single thymine out of the TCAT repeat if the other strand is considered for nomenclature purposes.

STRs Used in Forensic DNA Typing

For human identification purposes it is important to have DNA markers that exhibit the highest possible variation or a number of less polymorphic markers that can be combined in order to obtain the ability to discriminate between samples. Forensic specimens are often challenging to PCR amplify because the DNA in the samples may be severely degraded (i.e., broken up into small pieces). Mixtures are prevalent as well in some forensic samples, such as those obtained from sexual assault cases containing biological material from both the perpetrator and victim.

The small size of STR alleles (≈100bp to 400bp) compared to minisatellite VNTR alleles (≈400bp to 1000bp) make the STR markers better candidates for use in forensic applications where degraded DNA is common. PCR amplification of degraded DNA samples can be better accomplished with smaller product sizes (see Chapter 10). These reduced-size STR amplicons are often referred to as *miniSTRs*. Allelic dropout of larger alleles in minisatellite markers caused by preferential amplification of the smaller allele is also a significant problem with minisatellites (Tully et al. 1993). Furthermore, single-base resolution of DNA fragments can be obtained more easily with sizes below 500bp using high-resolution capillary electrophoresis (see Chapter 6). Thus, for both biology and technology reasons the smaller STRs are advantageous compared to the larger minisatellite VNTRs.

Among the various types of STR systems, tetranucleotide repeats have become more popular than di- or trinucleotides. Penta- and hexanucleotide repeats are less common in the human genome but are being examined by some laboratories (Bacher et al. 1999). A biological phenomenon known as "stutter" results when STR alleles are PCR amplified. *Stutter products* are amplicons that are typically one or more repeat units less in size than the true allele and arise during PCR because of strand slippage (Walsh et al. 1996).

Stutter product amounts vary depending on the STR locus and even the length of the allele within the locus but are usually less than 15% of the allele product quantity with tetranucleotide repeats. With di- and trinucleotides, the stutter percentage can be much greater (30% or more) making it difficult to interpret sample mixtures. In addition, the four-base spread in alleles with tetranucleotides makes closely spaced heterozygotes easier to resolve with size-based electrophoretic separations compared to alleles that could be two or three bases different in size with dinucleotide and trinucleotide markers, respectively.

```
GGAGGATGACTGTGTTCCCACTCTCAGTCCTGCCGAGGTGCCTGACAGCCCTG
CACCCAGGAGCTGGGGGGTCTAAGAGCTTGTAAAAAGTGTACAAGTGCCAGAT
GCTCGTTGTGCACAAATCTAAATGCAGAAAAGCACTGAAAGAAGAATCCCGAA
AACCACAGTTCCCATTTTTATATGGGAGCAAACAAAGCAGATCCCAAGCTCTT
CCTCTTCCCTAGATCAATACAGACAGACAGACAGGTG/gata/gata/gata/
gata/gata/gata/gata/gata/gata/gata/gata/TCATTGAAAGACA
AAACAGAGATGGATGATAGATACATGCTTACAGATGCACACACAAACGCTAAA
TGGTATAAAAATGGAATCACTCTGTAGGCTGTTTTACCACCTACTTTACTAAA
TTAATGAGTTATTGAGTATAATTTAATTTTATATACTAATTTGAAACTGTGTC
ATTAGGTTTTTAAGT
```

FIGURE 5.1 DNA sequence of a D16S539 allele containing 11 GATA repeats (shown in blue font). The STR repeat sequence is included in lowercase font with breaks between each repeat unit for emphasis. Underlined regions in green font indicate PowerPlex 16 primer binding sites (Krenke et al. 2002) with the shaded portion showing the PCR product, which is 288 bp (see Appendix 1). This top strand of the reference sequence is the reverse complement of GenBank entry AC024591 available from http://www.cstl.nist.gov/biotech/strbase/seq_ref.htm. The "T" shown in red font indicates a point mutation that resulted in a null allele with a previous primer (Nelson et al. 2002).

Thus, to summarize, the advantages of using tetranucleotide STR loci in forensic DNA typing over VNTR minisatellites or di- and trinucleotide repeat STRs include:

- A narrow allele size range that permits multiplexing;
- A narrow allele size range that reduces allelic dropout from preferential amplification of smaller alleles;
- The capability of generating small PCR product sizes that benefit the recovery of information from degraded DNA specimens; and
- Reduced stutter product formation compared to dinucleotide repeats that benefit the interpretation of sample mixtures.

A portion of the DNA sequence around the STR locus D16S539 is shown in Figure 5.1. This particular allele contains 11 GATA repeats and is 288 bp in length with the PCR primers highlighted (Krenke et al. 2002). PCR primers anneal to portions of the sequence on either side of the repeat region. In this manner, the variation that occurs between different alleles (e.g., 9 GATA repeats or 13 GATA repeats instead of the 11 GATA repeat units shown) will be captured by the overall size of the PCR product. Alleles differing by a single GATA repeat unit will be approximately 4 bp apart when separated by size using capillary electrophoresis (see Chapter 6). With these primers and 11 repeat units, there are 288 bp copied from the D16S539 locus. Thus, because allele 11 is 288 bp with the Promega primers, allele 10 will be 284 bp (4 bp smaller), allele 12 will be 292 bp (4 bp larger), and so forth. See Appendix 1 for a comprehensive listing of alleles and their sizes for each STR typing kit.

Using a different set of primers that are closer to the STR repeat region (Butler et al. 2003), the PCR product size for this same 11 GATA repeat allele is 105 bp in length (Figure 5.2).

In the past two decades, a number of tetranucleotide STRs have been explored for application to human identification. The types of STR markers that have been sought have

GGAGGATGACTGTGTTCCCACTCTCAGTCCTGCCGAGGTGCCTGACAGCCCTG
CACCCAGGAGCTGGGGGGTCTAAGAGCTTGTAAAAAGTGTACAAGTGCCAGAT
GCTCGTTGTGCACAAATCTAAATGCAGAAAAGCACTGAAAGAAGAATCCCGAA
AACCACAGTTCCCATTTTTATATGGGAGCAAACAAAGCAGATCCCAAGCTCTT
CCTCTTCCCTAGATCA**ATACAGACAGACAGACAGGTG**/gata/gata/gata/
gata/gata/gata/gata/gata/gata/gata/gata/TCATTGAAAGACA
AAAC**AGAGATGGATGATAGATACATGC**TTACAGATGCACACACAAACGCTAAA
TGGTATAAAAATGGAATCACTCTGTAGGCTGTTTTACCACCTACTTTACTAAA
TTAATGAGTTATTGAGTATAATTTAATTTTATATACTAATTTGAAACTGTGTC
ATTAGGTTTTTAAGT

FIGURE 5.2 DNA sequence of a D16S539 allele containing 11 GATA repeats. Underlined regions indicate miniSTR primer binding sites (Butler et al. 2003) with the shaded portion showing the PCR product, which is 105 bp, or a 183 bp size reduction over a PowerPlex 16 PCR product (see Figure 5.1).

included short STRs for typing degraded DNA materials (Coble & Butler 2005), STRs with low stuttering characteristics for analyzing mixtures (Bacher et al. 1999), and male-specific Y chromosome STRs for analyzing male-female mixtures from sexual crimes (Carracedo & Lareu 1998, Kayser et al. 2004). The selection criteria for candidate STR loci in human identification applications include the following characteristics (Gill et al. 1996, Carracedo and Lareu 1998):

- High discriminating power with observed heterozygosity 70%;
- Separate (or widely spaced) chromosomal locations to ensure that closely linked loci are not chosen;
- Robustness and reproducibility of results when multiplexed with other markers;
- Low stutter characteristics;
- Low mutation rate; and
- Predicted length of alleles that fall in the range of 90 bp to 500 bp with smaller sizes better suited for analysis of degraded DNA samples.

In order to take advantage of the product rule and be able to combine the genetic information across multiple loci, STR markers used in forensic DNA typing are typically chosen from separate chromosomes or are widely spaced on the same chromosome to avoid any problems with linkage between the markers.

CORE AND COMMON STR MARKERS

For DNA typing markers to be effective across a wide number of jurisdictions, a common set of standardized markers must be used. The STR loci that are commonly used today were initially characterized and developed either in the laboratory of Dr. Thomas Caskey at the Baylor College of Medicine (Edwards et al. 1991, Hammond et al. 1994) or at the Forensic Science Service (FSS) in England (Kimpton et al. 1993, Urquhart et al. 1994). The Promega Corporation (Madison, Wisconsin) initially commercialized many of the Caskey markers while Applied Biosystems (Foster City, California) incorporated the FSS STR loci and also developed some new markers.

Today both Applied Biosystems and the Promega Corporation have STR kits that address the needs of the DNA typing community and cover a common set of STR loci. The availability of STR kits that permit robust multiplex amplification of eight or more STR markers has truly revolutionized forensic DNA. Matching probabilities that exceed one in a billion are possible in a single amplification with 1 ng (or less) of DNA sample. Just as impressive is the fact that results can be obtained today in only a few hours compared to the weeks that restriction fragment length polymorphism (RFLP) methods took just a few years ago.

Early Developments

One of the first STR multiplexes to be developed was a quadruplex created by the Forensic Science Service that comprised the four loci TH01, FES/FPS, vWA, and F13A1 (Kimpton et al. 1994). This so-called "first-generation multiplex" had a matching probability of approximately 1 in 10,000. The FSS followed with a second-generation multiplex (SGM) made up of six polymorphic STRs and a gender identification marker (Kimpton et al. 1996, Sparkes et al. 1996). The six STRs in SGM were TH01, vWA, FGA, D8S1179, D18S51, and D21S11 and provided a matching probability of approximately 1 in 50 million. The gender identification marker amelogenin (Sullivan et al. 1993) will be described in more detail later in this chapter.

The first commercial STR kit capable of multiplex amplification for silver stain analysis became available from the Promega Corporation in 1994. This kit consisted of the STR loci CSF1PO, TPOX, and TH01 and is often referred to as the "CTT" triplex using the first letter in each locus. The CTT triplex only had a matching probability of ~1 in 500 but was still widely used in the United States in the mid-1990s as it was the first available STR multiplex kit and could be performed with a fairly low start-up cost. More information on early silver-stain and fluorescent STR multiplex assays is available in Chapter 3 of the *Fundamentals of Forensic DNA Typing* volume (Butler 2010).

The 13 CODIS STR Loci

In the United States, utilization of STRs initially lagged behind that of Europe, especially the efforts of the Forensic Science Service in the United Kingdom. However, beginning in 1996, the FBI Laboratory sponsored a community-wide forensic science effort to establish core STR loci for inclusion within the national DNA database known as CODIS (Combined DNA Index System).

Chapter 8 covers CODIS and DNA databases in more detail. This STR Project beginning in April 1996 and concluding in November 1997 involved 22 DNA typing laboratories and the evaluation of just 17 candidate STR loci: CSF1PO, F13A01, F13B, FES/FPS, FGA, LPL, TH01, TPOX, vWA, D3S1358, D5S818, D7S820, D8S1179, D13S317, D16S539, D18S51, and D21S11. Remember that the Human Genome Project was still ongoing and relatively few population studies had been conducted at that time.

At the STR Project meeting on November 13–14, 1997, 13 core STR loci were chosen to be the basis of the future CODIS national DNA database (Budowle et al. 1998). The 13 CODIS core loci are CSF1PO, FGA, TH01, TPOX, vWA, D3S1358, D5S818, D7S820, D8S1179, D13S317, D16S539, D18S51, and D21S11 (see Butler 2006). Table 5.1 lists the original references in the literature for

TABLE 5.1 Original Reference Describing Each of the 23 Common STR Loci and the Gender Identification Marker Amelogenin. Cooperative Human Linkage Center Information is Available via the Internet: http://www.chlc.org.

Locus Name	Reference
CSF1PO	Hammond, H.A., et al. (1994). Evaluation of 13 short tandem repeat loci for use in personal identification applications. *American Journal of Human Genetics, 55*, 175–189.
FGA	Mills, K.A., et al. (1992). Tetranucleotide repeat polymorphism at the human alpha fibrinogen locus (FGA). *Human Molecular Genetics, 1*, 779.
TH01	Polymeropoulos, M.H., et al. (1991). Tetranucleotide repeat polymorphism at the human tyrosine hydroxylase gene (TH). *Nucleic Acids Research, 19*, 3753.
SE33 (ACTBP2)	Polymeropoulos, M.H., et al. (1992). Tetranucleotide repeat polymorphism at the human beta-actin related pseudogene H-beta-Ac-psi-2 (ACTBP2). *Nucleic Acids Research, 20*, 1432.
TPOX	Anker, R., et al. (1992). Tetranucleotide repeat polymorphism at the human thyroid peroxidase (hTPO) locus. *Human Molecular Genetics, 1*, 137.
vWA	Kimpton, C.P., et al. (1992). A further tetranucleotide repeat polymorphism in the vWF gene. *Human Molecular Genetics, 1*, 287.
D1S1656	Cooperative Human Linkage Center GATA44E05.40831
D2S441	Cooperative Human Linkage Center GATA8F03.505
D2S1338	Cooperative Human Linkage Center GGAA3A09.31762
D3S1358	Li, H., et al. (1993). Three tetranucleotide polymorphisms for loci: D3S1352, D3S1358, D3S1359. *Human Molecular Genetics, 2*, 1327.
D5S818	Cooperative Human Linkage Center GATA3F03.512
D7S820	Cooperative Human Linkage Center GATA3F01.511
D8S1179	Cooperative Human Linkage Center GATA7G07.37564
D10S1248	Cooperative Human Linkage Center G00-366-431
D12S391	Cooperative Human Linkage Center GATA11H08.731
D13S317	Cooperative Human Linkage Center GATA7G10.415
D16S539	Cooperative Human Linkage Center GATA11C06.715
D18S51	Staub, R.E., et al. (1993). A microsatellite genetic linkage map of human chromosome 18. *Genomics, 15*, 48–56.
D19S433	Cooperative Human Linkage Center GGAA2A03.135
D21S11	Sharma, V., & Litt, M. (1992). Tetranucleotide repeat polymorphism at the D21S11 locus. *Human Molecular Genetics, 1*, 67.
D22S1045	Cooperative Human Linkage Center ATA37D06.40596
Penta D	Bacher, J., & Schumm, J.W. (1998). Development of highly polymorphic pentanucleotide tandem repeat loci with low stutter. *Profiles in DNA, 2(2)*, 3–6.
Penta E	Bacher, J., & Schumm, J.W. (1998). Development of highly polymorphic pentanucleotide tandem repeat loci with low stutter. *Profiles in DNA, 2(2)*, 3–6.
Amelogenin	Sullivan, K.M., et al. (1993). A rapid and quantitative DNA sex test: fluorescence-based PCR analysis of X-Y homologous gene amelogenin. *BioTechniques, 15*, 637–641.

these 13 STRs. When all 13 CODIS core loci are tested, the average random match probability is rarer than one in a trillion among unrelated individuals (Chakraborty et al. 1999).

Of the original 13 CODIS STR loci, the three most polymorphic markers are FGA, D18S51, and D21S11. TPOX, CSF1PO, and TH01 typically exhibit the least amount of variation between individuals. A summary of information on the 13 CODIS STRs (and 10 other commonly used loci) is contained in Table 5.2, which describes the chromosomal location and physical location on the human genome reference sequence, the repeat motif, the allele range, and the GenBank accession number where the DNA sequence for a reference allele may be found. The chromosomal locations for these STRs have been updated on the completed human genome reference sequence. Detailed allele sequence information and PCR product sizes with commercially available STR kits may be found in Appendix 1.

For those who wonder why poor-performing loci such as CSF1PO and TPOX were selected, we can go back to a presentation made at the October 1995 Promega meeting. The state of Alabama was an early adopter of STR typing technology, which at that time only had silver-stain triplexes available. By October 1995, Alabama had tested 13,610 offenders with CSF1PO, TPOX, and TH01 (Hicks 1995). At that point in time, this would probably have been the largest set of DNA samples containing STR data in the United States.

The Deputy Director of the Alabama Department of Forensic Sciences in 1995 was the former FBI Laboratory director, John W. Hicks. Director Hicks actually writes that these offender samples had been examined "under the assumption that STR systems will soon be embraced by CODIS *which will include the TH01, TPOX and CSF1PO loci*" (Hicks 1995, emphasis added). This statement was recorded more than two years before the original 13 CODIS STR loci were officially selected. While these loci are perhaps not optimal for human identity testing, we may be stuck with them now that almost 10 million profiles have been run in the United States.

Using the previously described classification scheme for categorizing STR repeat motifs (Urquhart et al. 1994), the 13 CODIS core STR loci may be divided up into four categories:

1. Simple repeats consisting of one repeating sequence: TPOX, CSF1PO, D5S818, D13S317, D16S539;
2. Simple repeats with non-consensus alleles (e.g., 9.3): TH01, D18S51, D7S820;
3. Compound repeats with non-consensus alleles: vWA, FGA, D3S1358, D8S1179; and
4. Complex repeats: D21S11.

The European Standard Set

European forensic DNA laboratories utilize many of the same STR loci as used in the United States. Originally building on the initial FSS work, a European Standard Set (ESS) of STR loci were selected in 1999 (Schneider 2009). The original ESS included FGA, TH01, vWA, D3S1358. D8S1179, D18S51, and D21S11. These seven STR loci are the six SGM markers plus D3S1358. When D16S539, which is part of the CODIS core loci and present in many STR typing kits, is analyzed, there are eight STR loci that overlap between European and U.S. DNA tests.

The Interpol international DNA database requires testing at least the ESS so that seven STR loci will be in common when comparisons are made. Thus, the ESS are the same as the

TABLE 5.2 Information on Commonly Used Autosomal STR Loci. The 13 CODIS Core Loci Are Highlighted in Bold Font.

Locus (UniSTS)*	Chromosomal Location	Physical Position GRCh37 Assembly	GenBank Accession (allele repeat #)	Category and Repeat Motif	Allele Range (Appendix 1)
D1S1656 (58809)	1q42	Chr 1 230.905 Mb	G07820 (15.3)	compound TAGA	8 to 20.3
TPOX (240638)	2p25.3 thyroid peroxidase, 10th intron	Chr 2 1.493 Mb	M68651 (11)	simple AATG	4 to 16
D2S441 (71306)	2p14	Chr 2 68.239 Mb	AC079112 (12)	compound TCTA/TCAA	8 to 17
D2S1338 (30509)	2q35	Chr 2 218.879 Mb	AC010136 (23)	compound TGCC/TTCC	10 to 31
D3S1358 (148226)	3p21.31	Chr 3 45.582 Mb	AC099539 (16)	compound TCTA/TCTG	6 to 26
FGA (240635)	4q31.3 alpha fibrinogen, 3rd intron	Chr 4 155.509 Mb	M64982 (21)	compound CTTT/TTCC	12.2 to 51.2
D5S818 (54700)	5q23.2	Chr 5 123.111 Mb	AC008512 (11)	simple AGAT	4 to 29
CSF1PO (156169)	5q33.1 c-fms proto-oncogene, 6th intron	Chr 5 149.455 Mb	X14720 (12)	simple AGAT	5 to 17
SE33 (ACTBP2) (none reported)	6q14 beta-actin related pseudogene	Chr 6 88.987 Mb	V00481 (26.2)	complex AAAG	3 to 49
D7S820 (74895)	7q21.11	Chr 7 83.789 Mb	AC004848 (13)	simple GATA	5 to 16
D8S1179 (83408)	8q24.13	Chr 8 125.907 Mb	AF216671 (13)	compound TCTA/TCTG	6 to 20
D10S1248 (51457)	10q26.3	Chr 10 131.093 Mb	AL391869 (13)	simple GGAA	7 to 19
TH01 (240639)	11p15.5 tyrosine hydroxylase, 1st intron	Chr 11 2.192 Mb	D00269 (9)	simple TCAT	3 to 14
vWA (240640)	12p13.31 von Willebrand Factor, 40th intron	Chr 12 6.093 Mb	M25858 (18)	compound TCTA/TCTG	10 to 25
D12S391 (2703)	12p13.2	Chr 12 12.450 Mb	G08921(20)	compound AGAT/AGAC	13 to 27.2
D13S317 (7734)	13q31.1	Chr 13 82.692 Mb	AL353628 (11)	simple TATC	5 to 17
Penta E (none reported)	15q26.2	Chr 15 97.374 Mb	AC027004 (5)	simple AAAGA	5 to 32
D16S539 (45590)	16q24.1	Chr 16 86.386 Mb	AC024591 (11)	simple GATA	4 to 17
D18S51 (44409)	18q21.33	Chr 18 60.949 Mb	AP001534 (18)	simple AGAA	5.3 to 40
D19S433 (33588)	19q12	Chr 19 30.416 Mb	AC008507 (14)	compound AAGG/TAGG	5.2 to 20
D21S11 (240642)	21q21.1	Chr 21 20.554 Mb	AP000433 (29.1)	complex TCTA/TCTG	12 to 43.2
Penta D (none reported)	21q22.3	Chr 21 45.056 Mb	AP001752 (13)	simple AAAGA	1.1 to 19
D22S1045 (49680)	22q12.3	Chr 22 37.536 Mb	AL022314 (17)	simple ATT	7 to 20

Adapted from Butler (2006). Physical positions are from Thanakiatkrai & Welch (2010).
**UniSTS is a comprehensive database of sequence tagged sites (STSs) available on the NCBI website: http://www.ncbi.nlm.nih.gov/entrez/query.fcgi?db=unists.*

Interpol Standard Set of Loci (ISSOL). However, as described in Chapter 8, when DNA databases grow in numbers, more loci are required to avoid adventitious matches. In Germany, the highly polymorphic locus SE33 was adopted as part of their national DNA database.

At the European Network of Forensic Science Institutes (ENFSI) meeting in April 2005, several new European STR loci were recommended for inclusion in future European STR typing kits. These include D2S441, D10S1248, D22S1045, D1S1656, and D12S391 (Gill et al. 2006a, Gill et al. 2006b). In April 2009, ENFSI voted to extend the ESS to 12 loci—the original ESS seven plus the five recommended loci. The extended ESS loci were formally adopted by the European Union in November 2009 to enable DNA data exchange across Europe.

The Expanded U.S. Core Loci

With the U.S. national DNA database surpassing nine million profiles by the end of 2010, the FBI Laboratory began exploring possible loci to expand the U.S. core set. In order to permit more international comparisons when needed, the expanded ESS loci are being considered to extend the U.S. core beyond the original 13 STRs to 18 or more STRs. The STR loci under consideration are part of the 23 markers described in Table 5.2 and utilized in various commercially available kits. At the time this book was completed in early 2011, the final set of expanded U.S. core loci had not yet been selected. More information on the U.S. core loci can be found at http://www.fbi.gov/about-us/lab/codis.

COMMERCIAL STR KITS

A typical STR typing kit consists of the following five components: (1) a **PCR primer mixture** containing oligonucleotides designed to amplify a set of STR loci (one of each pair of primers is labeled with a fluorescent dye), (2) a **PCR buffer** containing deoxynucleotide triphosphates, $MgCl_2$, and other reagents necessary to perform PCR, (3) a **DNA polymerase**, which is sometimes premixed with the PCR buffer, (4) an **allelic ladder** with common alleles for the STR loci being amplified to enable calibration of allele repeat size, and (5) a **positive control DNA** sample to verify that the kit reagents are working properly.

A number of kits are available for single or multiplex PCR amplification of STR markers used in DNA typing. Two primary vendors for STR kits used by the forensic DNA community exist: the Promega Corporation located in Madison, Wisconsin, and Applied Biosystems located in Foster City, California. These companies have expended a great deal of effort over the past 15 years to bring STR markers to forensic scientists in kit form. More recently in Europe, companies such as Serac (Bad Homburg, Germany) and Biotype (Dresden, Germany) have begun offering commercial STR kits, but due to patent and licensing issues some of these kits have limited distribution. For example, QIAGEN (Hilden, Germany) sells their Investigator Human Identification PCR kits, which were originally developed by Biotype, in Europe but not in the United States. A list of commercially available STR multiplexes and when they were released as products is shown in Table 5.3.

The adoption of the 13 core loci for CODIS in the United States has led to development of STR multiplexes that cover these markers. At the turn of the century, two PCR reactions were required to obtain information from all 13 STRs: either PowerPlex 1.1 and PowerPlex

TABLE 5.3 Commercially Available Autosomal STR Multiplexes (Fluorescently-Labeled). Kits with Improved Buffers That Overcome PCR Inhibitors Are Listed in Bold Font.

Name	Source	Release Date
AmpFlSTR Blue *(no longer available)*	Applied Biosystems	Oct 1996
AmpFlSTR Green I *(no longer available)*	Applied Biosystems	Jan 1997
CTTv	Promega	Jan 1997
FFFL	Promega	Jan 1997
GammaSTR	Promega	Jan 1997
PowerPlex 1.1, PowerPlex 1.2	Promega	Jan 1997, Sept 1998
AmpFlSTR Profiler	Applied Biosystems	May 1997
AmpFlSTR Profiler Plus	Applied Biosystems	Dec 1997
AmpFlSTR COfiler	Applied Biosystems	May 1998
AmpFlSTR SGM Plus	Applied Biosystems	Feb 1999
PowerPlex 2.1 (for Hitachi FMBIO users)	Promega	June 1999
PowerPlex 16	Promega	May 2000
PowerPlex 16 BIO (for Hitachi FMBIO users)	Promega	May 2001
AmpFlSTR Identifiler	Applied Biosystems	July 2001
AmpFlSTR Profiler Plus ID (extra unlabeled D8-R primer)	Applied Biosystems	Sept 2001
PowerPlex ES	Promega	Mar 2002
AmpFlSTR SEfiler *(no longer available)*	Applied Biosystems	Sept 2002
AmpFlSTR MiniFiler	Applied Biosystems	Mar 2007
AmpFlSTR SEfiler Plus *(improved buffer)*	Applied Biosystems	Nov 2007
AmpFlSTR Sinofiler *(labeling & documentation only available in Chinese)*	Applied Biosystems	Mar 2008
PowerPlex 16 HS *(same primers, improved reagents)*	Promega	Mar 2009
PowerPlex ESX 16 & ESX 17	Promega	Sept 2009
PowerPlex ESI 16 & ESI 17	Promega	Sept 2009
AmpFlSTR Identifiler Direct *(same primers, improved reagents)*	Applied Biosystems	Nov 2009
AmpFlSTR Identifiler Plus *(same primers, improved reagents)*	Applied Biosystems	Jan 2010
AmpFlSTR NGM	Applied Biosystems	Jan 2010
Investigator ESSplex	QIAGEN	April 2010
Investigator Decaplex SE	QIAGEN	April 2010
Investigator Triplex AFS QS	QIAGEN	April 2010
Investigator Triplex DSF	QIAGEN	April 2010

(Continued)

TABLE 5.3 Commercially Available Autosomal STR Multiplexes (Fluorescently-Labeled). Kits with Improved Buffers That Overcome PCR Inhibitors Are Listed in Bold Font. (*Continued*)

Name	Source	Release Date
Investigator IDplex	QIAGEN	Aug 2010
Investigator HDplex	QIAGEN	Sept 2010
Investigator Hexaplex ESS	QIAGEN	Sept 2010
Investigator Nonaplex ESS	QIAGEN	Sept 2010
Investigator ESSplex SE	QIAGEN	Oct 2010
AmpFlSTR NGM SElect	Applied Biosystems	Dec 2010
PowerPlex 18D	Promega	Feb 2011

2.1 or Profiler Plus and COfiler. As an internal check to reduce the possibility of mixing up samples, both manufacturers included overlapping loci in their kits that should produce concordant data between samples amplified from the same biological material. The Profiler Plus and COfiler kits have the loci D3S1358 and D7S820 (and the sex-typing marker amelogenin) in common while the PowerPlex 1.1 and PowerPlex 2.1 Systems have the loci TH01, TPOX, and vWA in common.

Since 2000, both Promega and Applied Biosystems have marketed multiplex PCR reactions that permit co-amplification of all 13 STRs in a single reaction along with the amelogenin sex-typing marker and two additional STR loci.

For the first decade or so of STR use, two primary methods were applied to separate and detect fluorescently labeled STR alleles: gel electrophoresis and capillary electrophoresis (see Butler 2010, *Fundamentals*, Chapter 9). Several of the PowerPlex kits were balanced to work with the Hitachi FMBIO scanner following polyacrylamide gel electrophoresis while PowerPlex 16, Identifiler, Profiler Plus, and COfiler reactions are typically analyzed on an ABI Prism 310 or 3100 Genetic Analyzer capillary electrophoresis system (see Chapter 6). Today capillary electrophoresis is exclusively used for routine STR testing.

Commercial manufacturers of STR kits have spent a great deal of research effort defining which markers would be included in each kit as well as verifying if primer pairs are compatible and will work well in combination with each other during multiplex PCR conditions (Wallin et al. 2002, Krenke et al. 2002). Promega has published and patented their PCR primer sequences (Masibay et al. 2000, Krenke et al. 2002) whereas Applied Biosystems have kept their primer sequences proprietary although some information has been revealed regarding the use of degenerate primers (Leibelt et al. 2003). The issue over failure to disclose kit primer sequences impacted several court cases early on in the legal acceptance of STR technology but appears to have been resolved now (see Butler 2010, *Fundamentals* D.N.A. Box 8.2).

Most laboratories do not have the time or resources to design primers, optimize PCR multiplexes, and monitor the quality control of primer synthesis. The convenience of using ready-made kits is also augmented by the fact that widely used primer sets and conditions allow improved opportunities for sharing data between laboratories without fear of possible null alleles. Available STR multiplex sets vary based on which STR loci are included, the fluorescent dye combinations, the DNA strand that is labeled, allelic ladders present in kits, and most importantly, the primer sequences utilized for PCR amplification. It is important to keep in mind that commercially available kits quickly dictate which STRs will be used by the vast majority of forensic laboratories.

Allelic Ladders

An allelic ladder is an artificial mixture of the common alleles present in the human population for a particular STR marker (Sajantila et al. 1992). They are generated with the same primers as tested samples and thus provide a reference DNA size for each allele included in the ladder. Allelic ladders have been shown to be important for accurate genotype determinations (Smith 1995, Kline et al. 1997). These allelic ladders serve as a standard like a ruler for each STR locus. They are necessary to adjust for different sizing measurements obtained from different instruments and conditions used by various laboratories.

Allelic ladders are constructed by combining genomic DNA or locus-specific PCR products from multiple individuals in a population, which possess alleles that are representative of the variation for the particular STR marker (Sajantila et al. 1992, Baechtel et al. 1993). The samples are then co-amplified to produce an artificial sample containing the common alleles for the STR marker. Allele quantities are balanced by adjusting the input amount of each component so that the alleles are fairly equally represented in the ladder. For example, to produce a ladder containing five alleles with 6, 7, 8, 9, and 10 repeats, individual samples with genotypes of (6,8), (7,10), and (9,9) could be combined. Alternatively, the combination of genotypes could be (6,9), (7,8), and (10,10) or (6,6), (7,7), (8,8), (9,9), and (10,10).

Additional quantities of the same allelic ladder (second- and third-generation ladders) may be produced by simply diluting the original ladder 1/1000 to 1/1000000 parts with deionized water and then re-amplifying it using the same PCR primers (Baechtel et al. 1993). It is imperative that allelic ladders be generated with the same PCR primers as used to amplify unknown samples so that the allele "rung" on the ladder will accurately line up with that of the repeat number of the unknown sample when the unknown is compared to the ladder.

Commercial manufacturers provide allelic ladders in their STR typing kits so that individual laboratories do not have to produce their own allelic ladders. Manufacturing processes have improved so that well-balanced allelic ladders can be consistently provided to the forensic DNA community. Kits from Applied Biosystems, Promega Corporation, or QIAGEN for comparable STR markers often contain different alleles in their allelic ladders. For example, the Promega PowerPlex ESI 17 allelic ladder for D16S539 contains consecutive alleles ranging from 4 to 16 repeats while the QIAGEN ESSplex D16S539 allelic ladder contains 8 to 16 repeats (Figure 5.3). Presumably QIAGEN did not have access to D16S539 samples with 4, 5, 6, or 7 repeats when their allelic ladders were developed.

AmpFlSTR Identifiler Kit Innovations

Applied Biosystems introduced two new technologies with their AmpFlSTR Identifiler kit when it was released in 2001 (Applied Biosystems 2001, Collins et al. 2004). The first, and most obvious, involved the use of five-dye detection systems where four different dyes (6FAM,

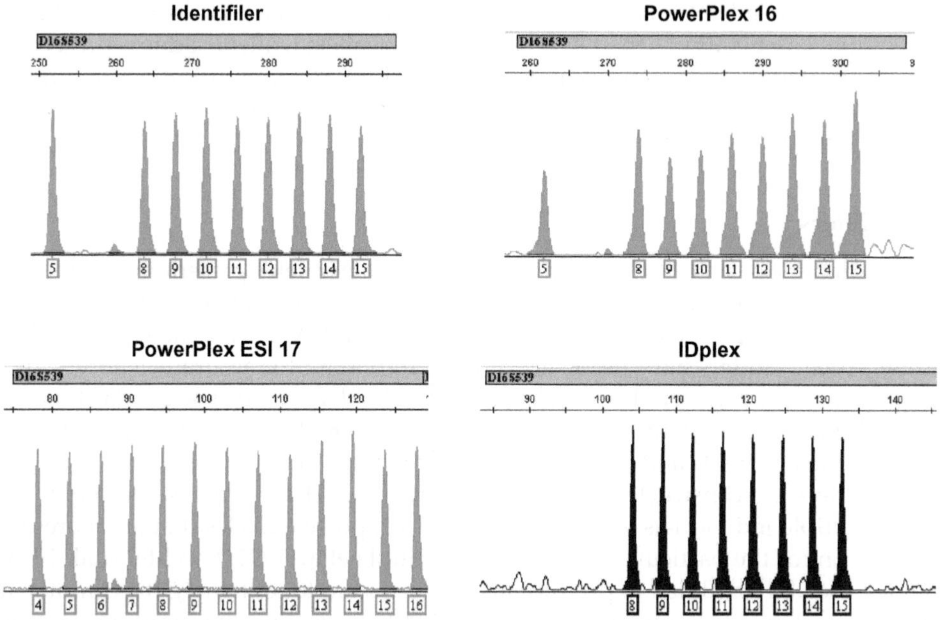

FIGURE 5.3 D16S539 allelic ladders for Identifiler (ABI), PowerPlex 16 (Promega), PowerPlex ESI 17 (Promega), and IDplex (QIAGEN). Figure courtesy of Becky Hill, NIST.

VIC, NED, and PET) are used to label the PCR products rather than the traditional three dyes (5FAM, JOE, NED or FL, JOE, TMR) as used with the previous AmpFlSTR or PowerPlex kits. One dye detection channel is always used for an internal size standard to correlate electrophoretic mobilities to an apparent PCR product size. Thus, the fifth dye (LIZ) in 5-dye detection and the fourth dye (ROX or CXR) in 4-dye detection are used for labeling the internal size standard. The extra dye channel for labeling PCR products enables smaller PCR products to be generated and placed in a separate dye channel rather than extending the size range for amplicons within the three previously available dye channels.

The second technology introduced with the Identifiler kit involves mobility-modifying non-nucleotide linkers (Applied Biosystems 2001). The mobility modifier is composed of hexaethyleneoxide (HEO) that imparts a shift of approximately 2.5 nucleotides with each additional HEO unit (Grossman et al. 1994). This non-nucleotide linker is synthesized into the 5′-end of the PCR primer so that when the PCR product is created it contains these extra molecules on one end (see Figure 4.4). By incorporating non-nucleotide linkers, mobilities for amplified alleles from one member of a pair of closely spaced STR loci can be shifted relative to the other. Thus, overlapping size ranges can be prevented.

The primary reason for introducing mobility modifiers is to permit continued use of the same PCR primers for amplifying STR loci and still have optimal inter-locus spacing within the various color channels. For example, if the loci D7S820 and CSF1PO, which are labeled with two different fluorophores in the COfiler kit and therefore do not interfere with one another, were labeled with the same colored fluorescent label (e.g., 6FAM) as they are in

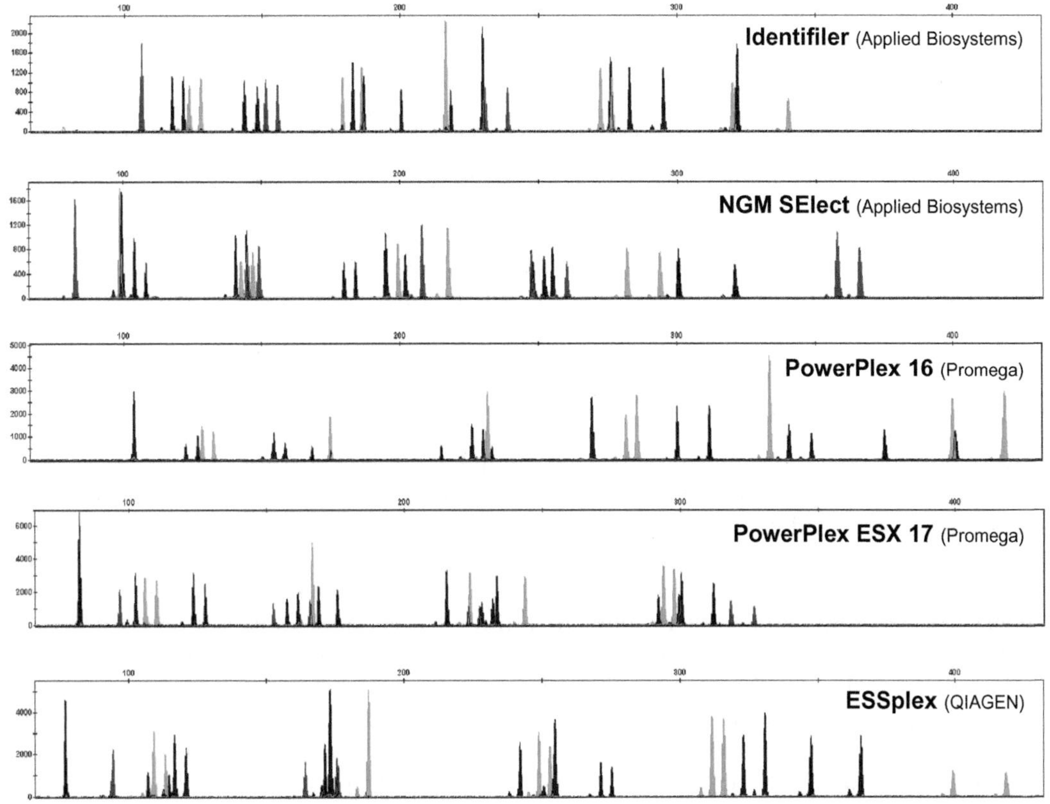

FIGURE 5.4 The same female DNA sample amplified with five different STR typing kits. Internal size standards are not shown. The PowerPlex 16 kit uses three fluorescent dye colors to label its PCR products while all of the other kits utilize four dyes. Figure courtesy of Becky Hill, NIST.

the Identifiler STR kit, the allelic ladder products would have overlapped by approximately 13bp. To prevent this overlap in allele size ranges, either PCR primer binding sites must be altered to change the overall size of the PCR product or mobility modifiers can be introduced to shift the apparent molecular weight of the larger PCR product to an even larger size. In the case of the Identifiler kit, the locus CSF1PO was shifted by approximately 25bp—through the addition of 10 HEO non-nucleotide linkers to the 5′-end of the labeled PCR primer. Non-nucleotide linkers are also present on four other loci in the Identifiler kit: D2S1338, D13S317, D16S539, and TPOX.

Promega has changed primer sequences for a few of the loci between PowerPlex versions (see Masibay et al. 2000, Butler et al. 2001, Krenke et al. 2002). For example, between the PowerPlex 1.1 and PowerPlex 16 kits, the CSF1PO primer positions were drastically altered in order to achieve a 30bp shift in PCR product size between the two kits. This primer change and subsequent PCR product shift was instituted so that CSF1PO and D16S539 loci could be labeled with the same dye in the PowerPlex 16 kit. Note that if the original CSF1PO primers had been kept, there would have been a 13bp overlap between D16S539 allele 15 (304bp) and

CSF1PO allele 6 (291 bp) making these systems incompatible in the same dye color without altering the PCR product size (i.e., primer positions) for one of them.

Different primer positions have the potential to lead to allele dropout if a primer binding site mutation impacts one of the primer pairs. Hence concordance studies are needed between various STR kits to assess the level of potential allele dropout (Budowle et al. 2001, Hill et al. 2010). Applied Biosystems has maintained the same primers over time and through their various AmpFlSTR kits (Holt et al. 2002) by introducing five-dye chemistry and mobility modifiers for products that would normally overlap with one another. With very few exceptions (e.g., MiniFiler primers and SE33 in NGM SElect), Applied Biosystems has maintained its primer sequences between kits helping to ensure consistency of results across kits (see Hill et al. 2010).

Next-Generation STR Kits

Although the contents of newer and what might be termed "next-generation" STR typing kits have not been fully disclosed by their manufacturers, they perform like turbo-charged engines with increased capabilities for improved performance particularly in the presence of PCR inhibitors. As discussed in Chapter 4, these improvements may include the presence of new DNA polymerases, additives to the PCR reaction, substitution of high-stability nucleic acid analogs along the primers to improve their annealing stability (Mulero & Hennessy 2009, Ballantyne et al. 2010), and energy-transfer dye-labeled primers to improve PCR product sensitivity (Yeung et al. 2008).

The next-generation kits containing improved buffer formulations are listed in bold font in Table 5.3. They include (in order of release date): MiniFiler, SEfiler Plus, PowerPlex 16 HS, PowerPlex ESX 16/17, PowerPlex ESI 16/17, Identifiler Direct, Identifiler Plus, NGM, and NGM SElect. These next-generation kits have shown the capability of producing STR profiles in the presence of PCR inhibitors such as heme, humic acid, and tanic acid. In addition, because of their increased tolerance of PCR inhibitors these kits have enabled direct PCR from bloodstains without DNA extraction and purification (see Chapter 4). New STR loci have also been introduced with these new kits. Figure 5.4 compares electropherograms for the same source DNA for five of these systems.

In 2010, QIAGEN began selling STR typing kits in Europe. However, due to patent restrictions (e.g., in the U.S. and Japan), these kits are not sold worldwide. In the U.S., Identifiler and PowerPlex 16 are most commonly used while in Europe SGM Plus and SEfiler Plus were used prior to the more recently released NGM and PowerPlex ESI/ESX kits (Table 5.4).

Figure 5.5 contains a summary of STR loci (including dye label and relative size position) in 25 STR kits available from Applied Biosystems, Promega Corporation, and QIAGEN. The next section describes each of the 23 commonly used STR loci in more detail.

INFORMATION ON 23 CORE AND COMMONLY USED STR LOCI

Each of the 23 commonly used STR loci has unique characteristics, either in terms of the number of alleles present, the type of repeat sequence, or the kinds of microvariants that

TABLE 5.4 Comparison of STR Loci Present in Kits Used in the U.S. and Europe. The Eight Shaded Loci Overlap.

U.S.			Europe				
PP16	**Identifiler**	**MiniFiler**	**ESX/ESI17**	**NGM (SElect)**	**SEfiler Plus**	**SGM Plus**	**ESSplex**
TPOX	TPOX						
CSF1PO	CSF1PO	CSF1PO					
D5S818	D5S818						
D7S820	D7S820	D7S820					
D13S317	D13S317	D13S317					
FGA	FGA	FGA	FGA	FGA	FGA	FGA	FGA
vWA	vWA		vWA	vWA	vWA	vWA	vWA
D3S1358	D3S1358		D3S1358	D3S1358	D3S1358	D3S1358	D3S1358
D8S1179	D8S1179		D8S1179	D8S1179	D8S1179	D8S1179	D8S1179
D18S51	D18S51	D18S51	D18S51	D18S51	D18S51	D18S51	D18S51
D21S11	D21S11	D21S11	D21S11	D21S11	D21S11	D21S11	D21S11
TH01	TH01		TH01	TH01	TH01	TH01	TH01
D16S539	D16S539	D16S539	D16S539	D16S539	D16S539	D16S539	D16S539
	D2S1338	D2S1338	D2S1338	D2S1338	D2S1338	D2S1338	D2S1338
	D19S433		D19S433	D19S433	D19S433	D19S433	D19S433
			D12S391	D12S391			D12S391
			D1S1656	D1S1656			D1S1656
			D2S441	D2S441			D2S441
			D10S1248	D10S1248			D10S1248
			D22S1045	D22S1045			D22S1045
			SE33	(SE33)	SE33		
Penta D							
Penta E							

Loci	Amelogenin	CSF1PO	FGA	TH01	TPOX	vWA	D3S1358	D5S818	D7S820	D8S1179	D13S317	D16S539	D18S51	D21S11	D2S1338	D19S433	Penta D	Penta E	D1S1656	D2S441	D10S1248	D12S391	D22S1045	SE33
Autosomal STR Typing Kits																								
Applied Biosystems AmpFISTR kits																								
Profiler	1	4	3	2	3	2	1	1	3		2													
Profiler Plus (ID)	1		3			2	1	1	3	2	2		4	3										
COfiler	1	4		2	3		1		1			2												
SGM Plus	1		3	2		2	1			2		3	4	3	4	1								
Identifiler (Direct, Plus)	1	4	3	2	3	2	1	2	3	1	3	4	4	2	5	1								
SEfiler Plus	1		3	2		2	1			2		3	2	1	4	1								3
MiniFiler	1	1	2						2		1	1	2	3	2									
NGM	1		4	3		2	2			2		3	4	3	4	2			3	1	1	4	1	
NGM SElect	1		4	3		2	2			2		3	4	3	4	2			3	1	1	4	1	5
Promega PowerPlex kits																								
PowerPlex 1.1 (1.2)	3	5		2	4	1		1	3		2	4												
PowerPlex 2.1			4	2	3	1	1			2			4	3				5						
PowerPlex 16 (BIO, HS)	1	5	5	2	4	2	1	1	3	3	2	4	4	3			6	5						
PowerPlex S5	1		2	1						2			3											
PowerPlex ES	1		4	2		2	1			3			4	3										1
PowerPlex ESX 16	1		4	3		2	2			3		4	5	4	3	3			2	1	1	2	1	
PowerPlex ESX 17	1		4	3		2	2			3		4	5	4	3	3			2	1	1	2	1	4
PowerPlex ESI 16	1		2	1		2	2			1		1	2	3	4	3			3	5	4	4	5	
PowerPlex ESI 17	1		2	1		2	2			1		1	2	3	4	3			3	5	4	4	5	3
PowerPlex 18D	1	5	5	2	4	2	1	1	3	3	2	4	4	3	2	1	6	5						
QIAGEN Investigator kits																								
ESSplex	1		4	2		4	3			4		1	2	5	5	3			2	1	1	3	2	
ESSplex SE	1		3	2		4	3			4		1	2	5	5	3			2	1	1	3	2	4
Hexaplex ESS	1			1															3	1	2	2	2	
Nonaplex ESS	1		4	2		4	3			2			1	5					2	1	1	3	2	3
Decaplex SE	1		2	2		4	3			3		1	1	5	4	2								1
IDplex	1	2	4	2	1	4	3	4	2	2	3	1	1	5	5	3								

FIGURE 5.5 Commercially available STR typing kits with dye labels and size positions for loci present in the kit.

have been observed. This section reviews some of the basic details on each of the core and commonly used STR loci that are present in commercial STR kits.

Appendix 1 contains a detailed summary of the alleles that have been reported as of late 2010 for the 13 CODIS and other commonly used STR loci along with their expected sizes using various kits that are available from Promega or Applied Biosystems. The size difference in the PCR products produced by the different STR kits is important because a large difference is more likely to lead to null alleles when comparing results between two kits.

The 13 CODIS STR Loci

CSF1PO is a simple tetranucleotide repeat found in the sixth intron of the c-fms proto-oncogene for the CSF-1 receptor on the long arm of chromosome 5. Common alleles contain an AGAT core repeat and range in size from 6 to 15 repeats. An allele 16 has also been reported (Margolis-Nunno et al. 2001) as have several x.1 and x.3 variant alleles (see Appendix 1). PCR products from Promega's PowerPlex 1.1 STR kit are 11 bp larger than those generated with Applied Biosystems kits for equivalent alleles. Since PowerPlex 16 adds 30bp to the size of CSF1PO relative to PowerPlex 1.1, the PowerPlex 16 PCR products for CSF1PO are 41bp larger than those generated with AmpFlSTR kits. Mobility modifiers are included with CSF1PO in the Identifiler kit to increase the apparent PCR product size by around 25bp (see Applied Biosystems 2001).

FGA is a compound tetranucleotide repeat found in the third intron of the human alpha fibrinogen locus on the long arm of chromosome 4. FGA has also been referred to in the literature as FIBRA or HUMFIBRA. The locus contains a CTTT repeat flanked on either side by degenerate repeats. The spread in allele sizes is larger for FGA than for any of the other core STR loci. Reported alleles range in size from 12.2 repeats to 51.2 repeats, spanning over 35 repeats! A 2bp deletion, from the loss of a CT, in the region just prior to the core repeat motif is responsible for the x.2 microvariant alleles that are very prevalent in this STR system. PCR products from Promega's PowerPlex 2.1 and 16 STR kits are 112bp larger than those generated with Applied Biosystems AmpFlSTR kits for equivalent alleles. This size difference between these two primer sets is the largest of any of the 13 core loci. So far a total of 95 different FGA alleles have been reported (see Appendix 1) making it one of the most polymorphic loci used in human identity testing.

TH01 is a simple tetranucleotide repeat found in intron 1 of the tyrosine hydroxylase gene on the short arm of chromosome 11. The locus name arises from the initials for tyrosine hydroxylase and intron 1 (i.e., 01). The locus is sometimes incorrectly referred to as "THO1" with a letter "O" instead of a "zero." In the literature, TH01 has also been referred to as TC11 and HUMTH01.

TH01 has a simple tetranucleotide sequence with a repeat motif of TCAT on the upper strand in the GenBank reference sequence. The repeat motif is commonly referenced as AATG, which is correct for the complementary (bottom) strand to the GenBank reference sequence. A common microvariant allele that exists in Caucasians contains a single base deletion from allele 10 and is designated allele 9.3. Other x.3 alleles have been reported such as 8.3, 10.3, and 13.3 (Griffiths et al. 1998). TH01 has probably been the most studied of the 13 core loci with over 1000 population studies reported in the literature using this DNA marker. PCR products from Promega's PowerPlex 1.1 STR kit are 11bp larger than those generated with Applied Biosystems AmpFlSTR kits for equivalent alleles. PowerPlex 2.1 STR kits produce amplicons that are 19bp smaller than PowerPlex 1.1. The PowerPlex 2.1 and PowerPlex 16 STR kits contain the same PCR primers for TH01 (Butler et al. 2001, Krenke et al. 2002).

TPOX is a simple tetranucleotide repeat found in intron 10 of the human thyroid peroxidase gene near the very end of the short arm of chromosome 2. TPOX has also been referred to in the literature as hTPO. This STR locus possesses a simple AATG repeat and is the least polymorphic of the 13 core loci. PCR products from Promega's PowerPlex 1.1 STR kit are 7bp larger than those generated with Applied Biosystems AmpFlSTR kits for equivalent alleles. PowerPlex 2.1 STR kits produce amplicons that are 38bp larger in size relative to PowerPlex 1.1. The PowerPlex 2.1 and PowerPlex 16 STR kits contain the same PCR primers for TPOX (Masibay et al. 2000, Krenke et al. 2002). Tri-allelic (three banded) patterns are more prevalent in TPOX than in any other forensic STR marker.

vWA is a compound tetranucleotide repeat found in intron 40 of the von Willebrand Factor gene on the short arm of chromosome 12. vWA has also been referred to in the literature as vWF and vWA. It possesses a TCTA repeat interspersed with a TCTG repeat. The vWA marker targeted by STR multiplex kits is only one of three repeats present in that region of the von Willebrand Factor. The other two have not been found to be as polymorphic (Kimpton et al. 1992). PCR products from Promega's PowerPlex 1.1 STR kit are 29bp smaller than those generated with Applied Biosystems AmpFlSTR kits for equivalent alleles. The PowerPlex 1.1 and PowerPlex 2.1 STR kits overlap at three STRs including vWA. Both kits produce amplicons that are equivalent in size for vWA alleles. The PowerPlex 2.1 and PowerPlex 16 STR kits contain the same PCR primers for vWA (Butler et al. 2001, Krenke et al. 2002).

D3S1358 is a compound tetranucleotide repeat found on the short arm of chromosome 3. This locus possesses both AGAT and AGAC repeat units (Mornhinweg et al. 1998). The D3 marker is common to Applied Biosystems' AmpFlSTR multiplexes Blue, Profiler, Profiler Plus, COfiler, SGM Plus, SEfiler, Identifiler, and NGM. PCR products from Promega's PowerPlex 2.1 STR kit are 2bp larger than those generated with Applied Biosystems kits for equivalent alleles. The PowerPlex 2.1 and PowerPlex 16 STR kits contain the same PCR primers for D3S1358 (Butler et al. 2001, Krenke et al. 2002).

D5S818 is a simple tetranucleotide repeat found on the long arm of chromosome 5. The locus possesses AGAT repeat units with alleles ranging in size from 7 to 16 repeats. In both Promega and Applied Biosystems STR kits, D5S818 is one of the smaller sized loci and as such should appear more often than some of the other loci in degraded DNA samples. Only a few rare microvariants have been reported at this STR marker. PCR products from Promega's PowerPlex 1.1 STR kit are 15bp smaller than those generated with Applied Biosystems kits for equivalent alleles and PowerPlex 16 retains the original PowerPlex 1.1 primers (Masibay et al. 2000, Krenke et al. 2002).

D7S820 is a simple tetranucleotide repeat found on the long arm of chromosome 7. The locus possesses primarily a GATA repeat. However, a number of new D7 microvariant alleles have been reported recently (see Appendix 1). These x.1 and x.3 alleles likely result due to a variation in the number of T nucleotides found in a poly(T) stretch that occurs 13 bases downstream of the core GATA repeat. Sequencing has revealed that "on-ladder" alleles contain nine tandem T's while x.3 alleles contain eight T's and x.1 alleles contain 10 T's (Egyed et al. 2000). PCR products from Promega's PowerPlex 1.1 STR kit are 42bp smaller than those generated with Applied Biosystems kits for equivalent alleles.

D8S1179 is a compound tetranucleotide repeat found on chromosome 8. In early publications by the Forensic Science Service, D8S1179 is listed as D6S502 because of a labeling error in the Cooperative Human Linkage Center database from which this STR was chosen (Oldroyd et al. 1995, Barber & Parkin 1996). The locus consists primarily of alleles containing TCTA although a TCTG repeat unit enters the motif for all alleles larger than 13 repeats, usually at the second or third position from the 5′-end of the repeat region (Barber & Parkin 1996). PCR products from Promega's PowerPlex 2.1 and PowerPlex 16 STR kits are 80bp larger than those generated with Applied Biosystems kits for equivalent alleles. AmpFlSTR Identifiler and Profiler Plus ID kits possess an extra, unlabeled D8S1179 reverse primer to prevent allele drop-out in a small portion of Asian populations due to a mutation in the middle of the primer-binding site (Leibelt et al. 2003).

D13S317 is a simple TATC tetranucleotide repeat found on the long arm of chromosome 13. Common alleles contain between 7 to 15 repeat units although alleles 5, 6, and 16 have been reported (see Appendix 1). PCR products from Promega's PowerPlex 1.1 STR kit are 36bp smaller than those generated with Applied Biosystems AmpFlSTR kits for equivalent alleles.

A 4bp deletion has been reported 24 bases downstream from the core TATC repeat that can impact allele calls with different primer sets (Butler et al. 2003, Drábek et al. 2004). PowerPlex 16 primers (Krenke et al. 2002), while generating the same size amplicons as the original PowerPlex 1.1 primers (Masibay et al. 2000), have been shifted to avoid this 4bp deletion that is present in some African-American samples (Krenke et al. 2002).

D16S539 is one of the core U.S. loci and present in most commercial STR kits. It is a simple tetranucleotide repeat found on the long arm of chromosome 16. Nine common alleles exist that possess a core repeat unit of GATA. These include an allele with five repeats and consecutive alleles ranging from 4 to 17 repeat units in length. PCR products from Promega STR kits are 31bp larger than those generated with Applied Biosystems kits for equivalent alleles.

A point mutation (T→A) 38bp downstream of the STR repeat impacts the reverse primers for both the Applied Biosystems and Promega primer sets (see Figure 5.1). Applied Biosystems added an extra or "degenerate" unlabeled primer in their COfiler, SGM Plus, and Identifiler kits so that both possible alleles could be amplified (Wallin et al. 2002). On the other hand, Promega altered their D16S539 reverse primer sequence between kits but kept the overall amplicon size the same (Butler et al. 2001, Masibay et al. 2000, Krenke et al. 2002). The 3′-end of the PowerPlex 1.1 reverse primer was lengthened by five nucleotides to create the PowerPlex 16 reverse primer and thus move the primer mismatch caused by this mutation further into the primer to prevent allele dropout (Nelson et al. 2002, Krenke et al. 2002).

D18S51 is a simple tetranucleotide repeat found on the long arm of chromosome 18. It has a repeat motif of AGAA. A number of x.2 allele variants exist due to a 2bp deletion from a loss of AG in the 3′-flanking region (Barber & Parkin 1996). More than 70 alleles have been reported for D18S51 making it one of the more polymorphic of the 13 core loci. PCR products from Promega's PowerPlex 2.1 STR kit are 22bp larger than those generated with Applied Biosystems AmpFlSTR kits for equivalent alleles. The PowerPlex 2.1 and PowerPlex 16 STR kits contain the same PCR primers for D18S51 (Butler et al. 2001, Krenke et al. 2002).

D21S11 is a complex tetranucleotide repeat found on the long arm of chromosome 21. A variable number of TCTA and TCTG repeat blocks surround a constant 43bp section made up of the sequence {$[TCTA]_3$ TA $[TCTA]_3$ TCA $[TCTA]_2$ TCCA TA}. The x.2 microvariant alleles arise primarily from a 2bp (TA) insertion on the 3′-end of the repeat region (Brinkmann et al. 1996). PCR products from Promega's PowerPlex 2.1 STR kit are 17bp larger than those generated with Applied Biosystems AmpFlSTR kits for equivalent alleles. The PowerPlex 2.1 and PowerPlex 16 STR kits contain the same PCR primers for D21S11.

Early papers in the literature by the Forensic Science Service had alleles named based on the dinucleotide subunit CV, where the V represents either an A, T, or G (Urquhart et al. 1994), while other authors adopted a different allele naming scheme based on the primary tetranucleotide repeat (Möller et al. 1994). As outlined in the European DNA Profiling Group interlaboratory study on D21S11 (Gill et al. 1997), a simple formula can be used to convert the Urquhart (U) designation into the Möller (M) equivalent:

$$M = \frac{1}{2} \times (U - 5)$$

Today most laboratories use the Moller allele notation since it fits the ISFG allele designation recommendation (Bär et al. 1997) format that is described later in this chapter.

D21S11 is far more polymorphic than can be easily detected with sized-based length separations. A careful search of the literature has revealed 90 reported alleles, many of which are the same length (see Appendix I). Fine differences in the D21S11 allele structures can only be determined by DNA sequencing since so many of the alleles have the same length but different internal sequence structure because some of the repeat units are switched around. For example, there are four different alleles designated as 30 repeats, which are indistinguishable by size-based methods alone (Appendix 1).

Additional Core and Common Loci Present in STR Kits

The STR markers described in this section are present in commercial STR typing kits and thus analyzed in conjunction with the core (required) loci covered in the previous section. Because these markers are included in the STR multiplexes co-amplified with core loci used for developing DNA databases, potentially millions of DNA samples will be run with these loci as DNA databases grow worldwide.

In 1999, Applied Biosystems released the AmpFlSTR SGM Plus kit that co-amplifies 10 STR loci including two additional STRs: D19S433 and D2S1338. With the adoption of the SGM Plus kit by the Forensic Science Service and much of Europe, the number of population data on the STR loci D19S433 and D2S1338 is now in the millions of profiles. These two loci are also part of the Identifiler and NGM 16plex STR kits as well as the PowerPlex ESX 17, PowerPlex ESI 17, and PowerPlex 18D.

Likewise, the Promega Corporation included two pentanucleotide STR loci, Penta E and Penta D, in their PowerPlex 2.1 and PowerPlex 16 kits that were released at the turn of the century. Since the German national DNA database requires analysis of the complex hypervariable STR locus SE33, commercial kits are available with SE33 including PowerPlex ES, PowerPlex ESX 17, PowerPlex ESI 17, SEfiler Plus, and NGM SElect.

D2S1338 is a compound tetranucleotide repeat found on the long arm of chromosome 2. Alleles ranging from 10 to 31 repeats have been observed. D2S1338 has a high heterozygosity and is present in the SGM Plus, Identifiler, SEfiler Plus, MiniFiler, NGM, and NGM SElect kits from Applied Biosystems and the PowerPlex ESI 16/17, PowerPlex ESX 16/17, and PowerPlex 18D kits from Promega.

D19S433 is a compound tetranucleotide repeat located on chromosome 19 with observed alleles ranging from 5.2 to 20 repeats. The x.2 alleles are due to an "AG" deletion prior to the core AAGG repeat (Heinrich et al. 2005). D19S433 is present in the SGM Plus, Identifiler, SEfiler Plus, NGM, and NGM SElect kits from Applied Biosystems and the PowerPlex ESI 16/17, PowerPlex ESX 16/17, and PowerPlex 18D kits from Promega.

Penta D is a pentanucleotide repeat found on chromosome 21 about 25 Mb from D21S11. It is present in the PowerPlex 16 and PowerPlex 18D kits from Promega.

Penta E is a pentanucleotide repeat with very low stutter product formation that is located on the long arm of chromosome 15 with alleles ranging from 5 to 32 repeats. It is present in the PowerPlex 2.1, PowerPlex 16, and PowerPlex 18D kits from Promega.

D1S1656 is a tetranucleotide repeat found on the long arm of chromosome 1 with alleles ranging from 8 to 20.3 repeats. The x.3 alleles arise from a TGA insertion typically after four full TAGA repeats. It is part of the extended European Standard Set and possesses a high heterozygosity.

D2S441 is a tetranucleotide repeat located on the short arm of chromosome 2 more than 60Mb from TPOX. It can be amplified as a miniSTR and works well on degraded DNA samples (Coble & Butler 2005). Some x.3 alleles have been observed as well as same-size, different-sequence alleles (Phillips et al. 2011). D2S441 is part of the extended European Standard Set and is present in NGM and NGM SElect kits from Applied Biosystems and the PowerPlex ESI and ESX Systems from Promega.

D10S1248 is a simple tetranucleotide repeat found on the long arm of chromosome 10 and possesses 7 to 19 GGAA repeats. It can be amplified as a miniSTR and works well on degraded DNA samples (Coble & Butler 2005). It is part of the extended European Standard Set and is present in NGM and NGM SElect kits from Applied Biosystems and the PowerPlex ESI and ESX Systems from Promega.

D12S391 is a highly polymorphic compound tetranucleotide found on the short arm of chromosome 12 only 6.3 megabases from vWA. It possesses over 50 different alleles ranging from 13 to 27.2 repeats in length. A number of same-size, different-sequence alleles have been identified through sequence analysis (Lareu et al. 1996, Phillips et al. 2011). It is part of the extended European Standard Set and is present in NGM and NGM SElect kits from Applied Biosystems and the PowerPlex ESI and ESX Systems from Promega.

D22S1045 is a simple trinucleotide repeat found on chromosome 22 with alleles ranging from 7 to 20 ATT repeats. While it is not as polymorphic as most of the other 23 core and common STR loci, it can be amplified as a miniSTR and works well on degraded DNA samples (Coble & Butler 2005). D22S1045 is part of the extended European Standard Set and is present in NGM and NGM SElect kits from Applied Biosystems and the PowerPlex ESI and ESX Systems from Promega.

SE33 is the most variable STR locus studied to date. It is located on the long arm of chromosome 6 and contains a core AAAG repeat structure. Appendix 1 describes 178 observed alleles ranging from 3 to 49 repeats. Sequence analysis has revealed 15 different 29.2 alleles possessing a variety of internal sequence combinations. SE33 is a core locus for the German national DNA database and with its renewed availability in the NGM SElect and PowerPlex ESI 17 and ESX 17 Systems is being adopted by other laboratories around Europe.

Other Non-Kit Based Common STR Loci

The 13 core loci used within the United States for CODIS and the additional STRs present in the STR kits (particularly the extended ESS loci) are effective DNA markers for human identification and will most likely continue to be used for some time especially due to the existence now of large DNA databases containing information from these autosomal STR loci (see Chapter 8). However, these 23 markers are by no means the only STRs that have been evaluated or used by forensic labs around the world. Dozens of other markers have been used, some quite extensively (Grubwieser et al. 2007).

For example, a 26plex assay developed by researchers at the National Institute of Standards and Technology (Hill et al. 2009) enables collection of information from 15 chromosomes with 25 STR markers (and amelogenin for sex-typing) that are sufficiently spaced from current core STR loci to be considered unlinked and thus enable the use of the product rule when combining information across the various loci (see Table 10.3). This 26plex assay has been used in conjunction with Identifiler to provide 40 STRs in order to strengthen relationship comparisons (O'Connor et al. 2010).

In addition to the autosomal STR loci described in this chapter, both kit and non-kit Y-chromosome STR markers (Chapter 13) and X-chromosome STR loci (Chapter 15) are covered in this book along with their applications in forensic investigations and relationship testing. Cat and dog STR loci are also described in Chapter 16 (see Table 16.1 and Table 16.2).

STR ALLELE NOMENCLATURE

To aid in interlaboratory reproducibility and comparisons of data, a common nomenclature has been developed in the forensic DNA community. DNA results cannot be effectively shared unless all parties are speaking the same language and referring to the same conditions. (It would do little good to describe the recipe for baking a cake in a language that is not understood by both the recipe giver and the chef. For example, if the recipe says to turn the oven on to 450 degrees Fahrenheit and the chef uses 450 Kelvin [≈250°F], the results would be vastly different.)

If one laboratory calls a sample 15 repeats at a particular STR locus and the same sample is designated 16 repeats by another laboratory, a match would not be considered, and the samples would be assumed to come from separate sources. As discussed in Chapter 8, the advent of national DNA databases with many laboratories contributing information to those databases has made it crucial to have internationally accepted nomenclature for designating STR alleles.

A repeat sequence is named by the structure (base composition) of the core repeat unit and the number of repeat units. However, because DNA has two strands, which may be used to designate the repeat unit for a particular STR marker, more than one choice is available and confusion can arise without a standard format. Also, where an individual starts counting the number of repeats can also make a difference. With double-stranded DNA sequences being read in the 5′ to 3′ direction, the choice of the strand impacts the sequence designation. For example, the "top" strand for an STR marker may be 5′-…$(GATA)_n$…-3′

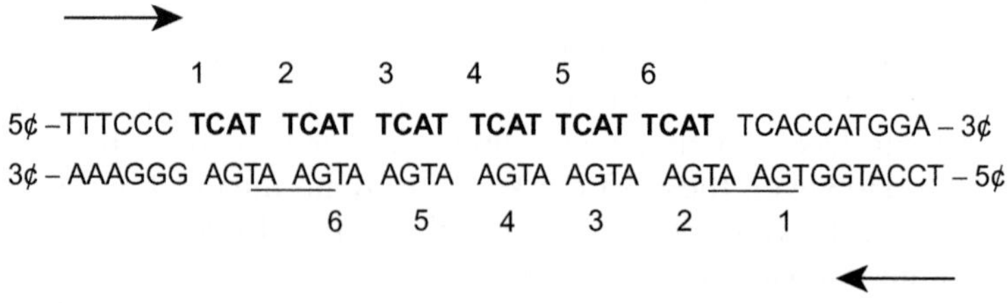

FIGURE 5.6 Example of the DNA sequence in a STR repeat region. Note that using the top strand versus the bottom strand results in different repeat motifs and starting positions. In this example, the top strand has 6 TCTA repeat units while the bottom strand has 6 TGAA repeat units. Under ISFG recommendations, the top strand from GenBank should be used. Thus, this example would be described as having [TCAT] as the repeat motif. Repeat numbering, indicated above and below the sequence, proceeds in the 5′-to-3′ direction as illustrated by the arrows.

while the "bottom" strand for the same sequence would be 5′-...(TATC)$_n$ ...-3′. Depending on the sequence surrounding the repeat region, the core repeat could be shifted relative to the other strand (Figure 5.6).

ISFG DNA Commission Recommendations

The International Society of Forensic Genetics (ISFG), which was founded in 1968 and formerly known as the International Society of Forensic Haemogenetics (ISFH), today represents a group of approximately 1100 scientists from more than 60 countries (see http://www.isfg.org/). Meetings are held biannually to discuss the latest topics in forensic genetics. Every few years, as a specific need arises, a DNA Commission of the ISFG is formed and makes recommendations on the use of genetic markers. These publications are available at http://www.isfg.org/Publications/DNA+Commission and include guidelines for designating STR allele nomenclature:

- Naming variant alleles (Bär et al. 1994)
- Repeat nomenclature (Bär et al. 1997)
- Y-STR use in forensic analysis (Gill et al. 2001)
- Additional Y-STRs—nomenclature (Gusmão et al. 2006)

The ISFG 1994 recommendations focused on allelic ladders and designation of alleles that contain partial repeat sequences. The ISFG 1997 guidelines discussed the sequence and repeat designation of STRs. Further comments on STR allele nomenclature with specific interest in Y-chromosome markers were published in 2001 (Gill et al. 2001) and 2006 (Gusmão et al. 2006). A more recent detailed description of STR allele nomenclature rules with specific examples from Y-chromosome loci was released by scientists from the U.S. National Institute of Standards and Technology (NIST) primarily to help the genetic genealogy community (Butler et al. 2008).

The 1994 ISFG DNA Commission publication addressed designations of alleles containing partial repeat sequences: "When an allele does not conform to the standard repeat motif of the system in question it should be designated by the number of complete repeat units and the number of base pairs of the partial repeat. These two values should be separated by a decimal point" (Bär et al. 1994). For example, an allele with [AATG]$_5$ ATG [AATG]$_4$ is designated as a "9.3" since it contains nine full AATG repeats plus three additional nucleotides. Thus, tetranucleotide repeats (i.e., those containing four nucleotides in the repeat motif) could have x.1, x.2, and x.3 variant alleles that exhibit one, two, or three additional nucleotides beyond the number of complete repeat units found in the allele.

The 1997 ISFG recommendations are reviewed below (Bär et al. 1997):

Choice of the Strand

- For STRs within protein coding regions (as well as in the intron of the genes), the coding strand should be used. This would apply to STRs such as vWA (GenBank: M25716), TPOX (GenBank: M68651), and CSF1PO (GenBank: X14720).
- For repetitive sequences without any connection to protein coding genes like many of the D#S### loci, the sequence originally described in the literature of the first public database

entry shall become the standard reference (and strand) for nomenclature. Examples here include D18S51 (GenBank: L18333) and D21S11 (GenBank: M84567).
- If the nomenclature is already established in the forensic field but not in accordance with the aforementioned guideline, the nomenclature shall be maintained to avoid unnecessary confusion. This recommendation applies to the continued use by some laboratories of the "AATG repeat" strand for the STR marker TH01. The GenBank sequence for TH01 uses the coding strand and therefore contains the complementary "TCAT repeat" instead.

Choice of the Motif and Allele Designation

- **The repeat sequence motif should be defined so that the first 5′-nucleotides that can define a repeat motif are used.** For example, 5′-GG TCA TCA TCA TGG-3′ could be seen as having 3 × TCA repeats or 3 × CAT repeats. However, under the recommendations of the ISFH committee only the first one (3 × TCA) is correct because it defines the first possible repeat motif.
- Designation of incomplete repeat motifs should include the number of complete repeats and, separated by a decimal point, the number of base pairs in the incomplete repeat. Examples of "microvariants" with incomplete repeat units include allele 9.3 at the TH01 locus. TH01 allele 9.3 contains nine tetranucleotide AATG repeats and one incomplete ATG repeat of three nucleotides (Puers et al. 1993). Another microvariant example is allele 22.2 at the FGA locus, which contains 22 tetranucleotide repeats and one incomplete repeat with two nucleotides (Barber et al. 1996).
- Allelic ladders containing sequenced alleles that are named according to the recommendations listed above should be used as a reference for allele designation in unknown samples. Allelic ladders may be commercially obtained or prepared in house and should contain all common alleles.

This article further notes: "For those situations where two or more nomenclatures already exist, priority should be given to the nomenclature that more closely adheres to the [1997 ISFG] guidelines. If this is not possible, priority shall be given to the nomenclature that was documented first" (Bär et al. 1997). When reviewing the STR literature prior to 1997, an individual should keep in mind that repeat nomenclatures often differ from the ISFG 1997 guidelines. This fact can lead to some confusion if one is not careful. For example, early descriptions of the STR locus TH01 by the Forensic Science Service label the repeat TCAT (Kimpton et al. 1993) while Caskey and co-workers described the TH01 repeat as AATG (Edwards et al. 1991).

The 2006 ISFG DNA Commission made the following eight nomenclature recommendations (Gusmão et al. 2006):

1. Alleles should be named according to the total number of contiguous variant and non-variant repeats determined from sequence data. Single repeat units located adjacent to the main repeat array and consisting of the same sequence as the main variable repeat should be considered as part of the repeat motif. For example, a hypothetical STR allele with the sequence …$(GATA)_n(GACA)_2(GATA)$… should be considered to have $n + 2 + 1$ repeats.

2. Repetitive motifs that are not adjacent to the variable stretch and have three or less units and show no size variation within humans or between humans and chimpanzees should not be included in the allele nomenclature. For example, a hypothetical STR with the sequence … … $(GATA)_n(GACA)_2N_8(GATA)_3$…, where N contains nucleotides that are not part of the repeat motif, should be called $n + 2$, excluding the non-adjacent $(GATA)_3$ repetitive stretch from the allele nomenclature. If the number of interrupting nucleotides (N) is similar to or less than the number of nucleotides in the repeat motif, then the region is considered one repeat unit with a length corresponding to the total number of nucleotides. Thus, …$(GATA)_n(GACA)_2N_4(G ATA)_3$… is considered as one complex locus with $n + 2 + 1 + 3$ units, while …$(GATA)_n(GA CA)_2N_5(GATA)_3$… is considered to be two loci with $n + 2$ and 3 units, respectively, of which $n + 2$ would be included in the primary STR allele nomenclature.
3. Intermediate alleles (e.g., 11.1) fall into two classes: an insertion/deletion either (a) within the repeat motif or (b) in the flanking region encompassed by the PCR primer positions. If the partial repeat is found within the repeat motif, such as …$(GATA)_nT(GATA)_m$, alleles should be called as noted in the 1994 ISFG recommendations: "…by the number of complete repeat units and the number of base pairs of the partial repeat separated by a decimal point" (Bär et al. 1994).
4. Intermediate alleles arising due to mutations in the flanking sequences that alter the length or electrophoretic migration of a PCR product should be designated by additional information indicated after the number of complete STR repeat units. For example, an allele with 11 repeats and a T insertion at nucleotides 40 upstream from the repeat is not named "11.1" but rather "11(U40Tins)" where 11 stands for the number of complete repeats, U40 indicates the direction and position of the mutation relative to the STR repeat block (i.e., the mutation is located 40 bases upstream of the repeat), and "Tins" indicates that a T nucleotide has been inserted. If the exact position of the deletion or insertion cannot be determined because it is part of a homopolymeric tract (i.e., a stretch of the same nucleotides such as TTTTT), then the deletion or insertion should be assigned to the highest numbered end of the homopolymeric stretch. Using Gusmão et al. 2006 Figure 2 as an example, the deletion that gives rise to the "16.3" allele should more appropriately be referred to as a "17D80Tdel" allele since the single T deletion occurs at the end of a polymeric T stretch that is 80 nucleotides downstream of the repeat region.
5. Point mutations in a PCR primer binding region may prevent sufficient annealing of this primer and result in a "null" or "silent" allele due to failure to generate a detectable amount of PCR product. It is recommended that point mutations which impact primer annealing be verified by DNA sequence analysis and published using a designation as in recommendation #4. For example, DYS438 (D7A→C) would indicate that the "A" nucleotide 7 bases downstream of the DYS438 repeat has changed into a "C" nucleotide in the tested STR allele.
6. If no additional sequence variation is found in the 166 Y-STR markers described by Kayser et al. 2004, then these authors' locus delimitation criteria should be adopted.
7. Journal editors, reviewers, and organizers of quality assurance schemes should focus on the use of standardized nomenclatures in order to obtain uniformity and avoid the spread of confusing nomenclatures.
8. Commercial Y-STR kits should follow the nomenclature recommendations so that direct comparisons between results obtained with different kits are possible.

While these guidelines provide a framework for STR allele nomenclature designation, they do not capture every possible permutation that exists, particularly with complex repeats. Following recommendations #1 and #2 described above, scientists at NIST devised what they termed the "one-change-rule" in that a single change to the repeat motif can be allowed in deciding what to include or not in an STR repeat block (Butler et al. 2008). However, when the single change in the repeat motif creates an adjacent homopolymeric stretch, it was decided not to include this portion in the repeat count. For example, with the repeat motif of CTT, if an adjacent sequence of TTT occurs (e.g., DYS481), then this approach only counts the number of CTT repeats. On the other hand, with a repeat structure of $(GATA)_n(GACA)$, the repeat count would be $n + 1$.

Today most forensic DNA scientists do not worry about STR allele nomenclature because STR typing is almost universally performed with commerically available kits containing allelic ladders prepared with alleles designated according to the ISFG rules by the manufacturer. However, occasionally there are differences in nomenclature that need to be spelled out to avoid confusion, such as with the Y-STR locus GATA-H4 contained in the Yfiler kit (Mulero et al. 2006). The use of certified reference materials and common positive controls with known genotypes also further promotes consistency across laboratories in terms of STR allele designation.

Most of the time measured alleles will correlate to the alleles present in the STR kit allelic ladders and be appropriately designated as "on-ladder" alleles using genotyping software. However, there are exceptions, and new alleles are being discovered as more DNA samples are examined around the world. In addition, sometimes more than two alleles can be inherited or exhibited as is the case with the so-called triallelic patterns. Finally, due to variation in the STR flanking regions, some PCR primers may fail to amplify a particular allele—a situation known as allele dropout due to a silent or "null" allele. These topics are discussed in the following sections.

NULL (SILENT) ALLELES

When amplifying DNA fragments that contain STR repeat regions, it is possible to have a phenomenon known as *allele drop-out*. Sequence polymorphisms are known to occur within or around STR repeat regions. These variations can occur in three locations (relative to the primer binding sites): within the repeat region, in the flanking region, or in the primer-binding region.

If a base pair change occurs in the DNA template at the PCR primer binding region, the hybridization of the primer can be disrupted resulting in a failure to amplify, and therefore failure to detect an allele that exists in the template DNA. More simply, the DNA template exists for a particular allele but fails to amplify during PCR due to primer hybridization problems. This phenomenon results in what is known as a *null allele*. Fortunately null alleles are rather rare because the flanking sequence around STR repeats is fairly stable and consistent between samples.

Concordance Studies Aid Discovery of Null Alleles

Null alleles have been "discovered" by the observation of different typing results when utilizing independent STR primer sets. During a comparison of STR typing results on

600 population samples at the vWA locus, one sample typed 16,19 with Promega's PowerPlex kit and 16,16 with Applied Biosystem's AmpFlSTR Blue kit (Kline et al. 1998). In this case, the vWA allele 19 dropped out with the AmpFlSTR vWA primer set due to a sequence polymorphism near the 3′-end of the forward primer (Walsh 1998).

Allele dropout may occur due to mutations (variants) at or near the 3′-end of a primer. If a primer binding site mutation exists, then little or no primer extension will occur during PCR. Of course, this failure to amplify depends on the PCR conditions including the annealing temperature used. In the situation described above, the vWA allele 19 was present in the sample but failed to be amplified by one of the primer sets. It was later reported that the null allele resulted from a rare A→T nucleotide change in the DNA template that occurred at the second base from the 3′-end of the AmpFlSTR vWA forward primer (Walsh 1998).

Potential null alleles resulting from allele dropout can be predicted by statistical analysis of the STR typing data. The observed number of homozygotes can be compared to the expected number of homozygotes based on Hardy-Weinberg equilibrium (Chakraborty et al. 1992). An abnormally high level of homozygotes would indicate the possible presence of null alleles. Thus, each set of population data should be carefully examined when new STR markers are being tested in a forensic DNA laboratory.

A number of primer concordance studies have been conducted in the past few years as use of various STR kits has become more prevalent. An examination of over 2000 samples comparing the PowerPlex 16 kit to the Profiler Plus and COfiler kit results found 22 examples of allele dropout due to a primer mismatch at 7 of the 13 core STR loci: CSF1PO, D8S1179, D16S539, D21S11, FGA, TH01, and vWA (Budowle et al. 2001, Budowle & Sprecher 2001).

Use of Degenerate Primers in Commercial Kits

In some cases, STR kit manufacturers have added an additional PCR primer to the assay that can hybridize properly to the alternative allele when it exists in a sample. This has been the preferred solution for Applied Biosystems (e.g., Wallin et al. 2002) while Promega has moved their primers to overcome allele dropout problems (e.g., Nelson et al. 2002). According to their publications, Applied Biosystems has added an additional primer to correct for single point mutations in AmpFlSTR primer binding sites for D16S539 (Wallin et al. 2002), vWA (Lazaruk et al. 2001), and D8S1179 (Leibelt et al. 2003).

STR TYPING

As described in the next chapter, STR alleles are separated and sized using capillary electrophoresis. Data interpretation software is used to size PCR products amplified using STR primers and to convert the DNA sizes to STR alleles through use of allelic ladders (Figure 5.7). As noted earlier in this chapter, allelic ladders are provided by the commercial kit providers (although a laboratory could prepare its own ladder by gathering alleles from a diverse set of samples). The ladders are prepared with commonly observed STR alleles usually spaced a single repeat unit apart from one another. The ladder alleles are PCR-amplified with the same primers as provided in the STR typing kit for testing unknown samples. Thus, samples amplified with a kit will produce alleles that are the same size as an allele in the allelic ladder.

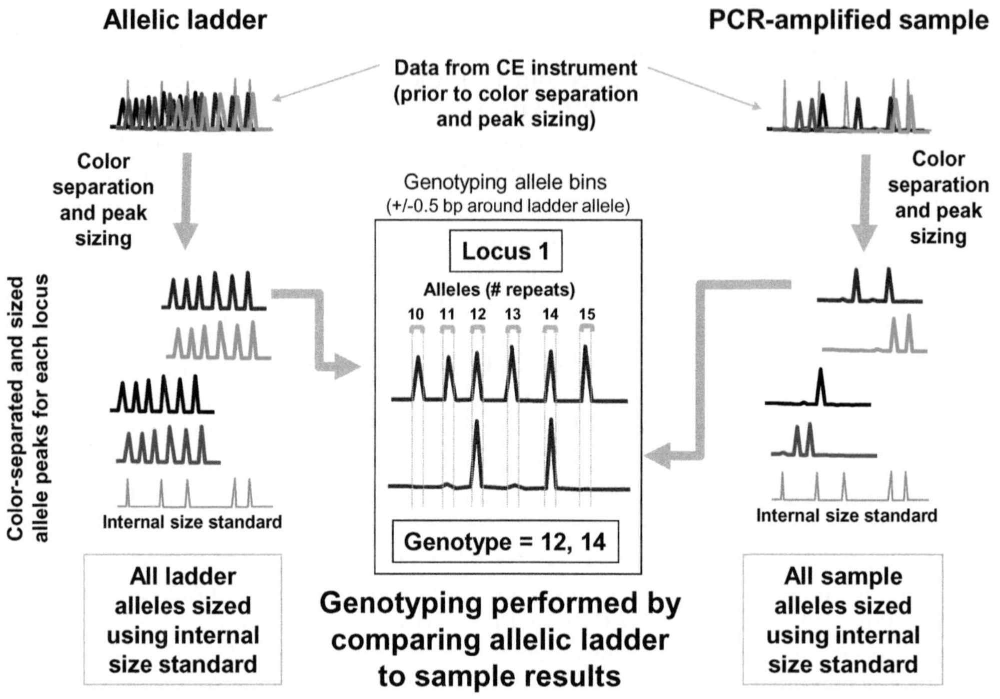

FIGURE 5.7 Genotyping is performed through a comparison of sized peaks from PCR-amplified samples to allele size bins. These allele bins are defined with the genotyping software using size information from an allelic ladder run with each batch of samples. Any peak falling in a particular dye color and allele bin size range is designated as an allele for that locus. Peaks in both the allelic ladder and the PCR-amplified samples are sized using the same internal size standard so that they may be compared to one another.

Each allele or "rung" of an allelic ladder has been characterized in terms of the number of repeats it contains through DNA sequencing. The STR kit manufacturer supplies information to the users regarding the allele nomenclature and number of repeats present in each allele in the ladder. The data analysis software enables a conversion of all peaks in samples being processed from DNA size (relative to a common internal size standard) to repeat number. The DNA sizes of the allelic ladder alleles are used to calibrate size ranges for allele classification. A common size range for the genotyping allele bins is ±0.5bp around each allele. This size range enables PCR products that are 1bp different from one another to be differentiated. Due to slight changes in instrument environmental conditions over time, allelic ladders are run regularly (typically with every batch of samples) in order to keep the size-to-allele conversion process well calibrated.

Any peak with the same dye-color label that is sized within half a base pair of an allelic ladder is designated by the STR genotyping software as being that allele. An analyst while performing DNA profile review assesses whether or not the labeled peak is truly an allele or an artifact, such as a stutter product or pull-up of signal from another dye color. Further information on artifacts and data interpretation will be covered in the forthcoming *Advanced Topics in Forensic DNA Typing: Interpretation.*

Same Length but Different Sequence Alleles

Complex repeat sequences, such as those found in D21S11, can contain variable repeat blocks in which the order is switched around for alleles that are the same length. For example, the STR locus D21S11 has four alleles that are all 210bp when amplified with the Identifiler kit (Appendix 1). While these alleles would be sized based on overall length to be "allele 30," they contain repeat blocks of 4-6-CR-12, 5-6-CR-11, 6-5-CR-11, and 6-6-CR-10 for the pattern [TCTA]-[TCTG]-constant region (CR)-[TCTA]. In such cases, variant alleles would only be detectable with complete sequence analysis.

It is important to realize that from an operational point of view internal allele variation is not significant. In the end a match is being made against many loci not just one, such as D21S11, with possible internal sequence variation. Most of the STR loci used in human identity testing have not exhibited internal sequence variation, particularly the simple repeat loci TPOX, CSF1PO, D5S818, D16S539, TH01, D18S51, and D7S820. Alleles are binned based on measured size with STR typing since sequence analysis of individual alleles is too time consuming and, because STR variation is primarily size-based, would rarely reveal additional information.

Over the past several years, work with mass spectrometry has demonstrated that same-size STR alleles with different internal sequences or alleles with sequence variation in the flanking region can be resolved from one another using a base composition approach (Oberacher et al. 2008, Pitterl et al. 2008, Planz et al. 2009, Pitterl et al. 2010). This sequence variation is sometimes refered to as a SNPSTR, where single nucleotide variation is coupled with STR allele identification. As seen in Appendix 1, certain STR loci, such as SE33, are more prone to internal sequence variation.

A comparison of the variation observed in 11 STRs—the 10 SGM Plus loci and SE33—in DNA samples from 94 Yakut and 108 Khoisan individuals was performed using conventional STR analysis, mass spectrometric STR analysis, and direct sequencing (Pitterl et al. 2010). The mass spectrometry approach that enabled both sequence and length variation to be detected clearly expanded the number of detectable alleles.

These same length but different internal sequence alleles can be used in research to track mutations if the sequences can be differentiated from one another. A C→T polymorphism was discovered 13 nucleotides upstream of the D5S818 repeat region (Edwards & Allen 2004). A restriction enzyme cutting site is created when the T is present that enables differentiation of samples with and without the polymorphism. Use of this SNPSTR assay permitted evaluation of mutations that were observed of which 34 out of 40 were paternal in origin and 23 of 26 (where the repeat change could be determined) were single repeat unit shifts. This study also found that while alleles 13 and 14 were prone to mutation, allele 11 was not—suggesting that not all alleles have equal frequencies of mutation (Edwards & Allen 2004). In fact, the American Association of Blood Banks (AABB) annual report on relationship testing laboratories is now seeking to quantify these allele-specific mutation events (AABB 2008).

GENDER IDENTIFICATION WITH AMELOGENIN

The ability to designate whether a sample originated from a male or a female source is useful in sexual assault cases, where distinguishing between the victim and the perpetrator's evidence is important. Likewise, missing persons and mass disaster investigations can benefit from gender identification of the remains. Over the years a number of gender identification assays have been demonstrated using PCR methods (Sullivan et al. 1993, Eng et al. 1994, Reynolds & Varlaro 1996). By far the most popular method for sex-typing today is the amelogenin system as it can be performed in conjunction with STR analysis.

Amelogenin is a gene that codes for proteins found in tooth enamel. The British Forensic Science Service was the first to describe the particular PCR primer sets that are used so prevalently in forensic DNA laboratories today (Sullivan et al. 1993). These primers flank a 6bp deletion within intron 1 of the amelogenin gene on the X homologue (Figure 5.8). PCR amplification of this area with their primers results in 106bp and 112bp amplicons from the X and Y chromosomes, respectively. Primers, which yield a 212bp X-specific amplicon and a 218bp Y-specific product by bracketing the same 6bp deletion, were also described in the original amelogenin paper (Sullivan et al. 1993) and have been used in conjunction with the D1S80 VNTR system (Budowle et al. 1996).

An advantage with the above approach, i.e., using a single primer set to amplify both chromosomes, is that the X chromosome product itself plays a role as a positive control. This PCR-based assay is extremely sensitive. Mannucci and co-workers were able to detect as little as 20 pg ($\approx$3 diploid copies) as well as sample mixtures where female DNA was in 100-fold excess of male DNA (Mannucci et al. 1994).

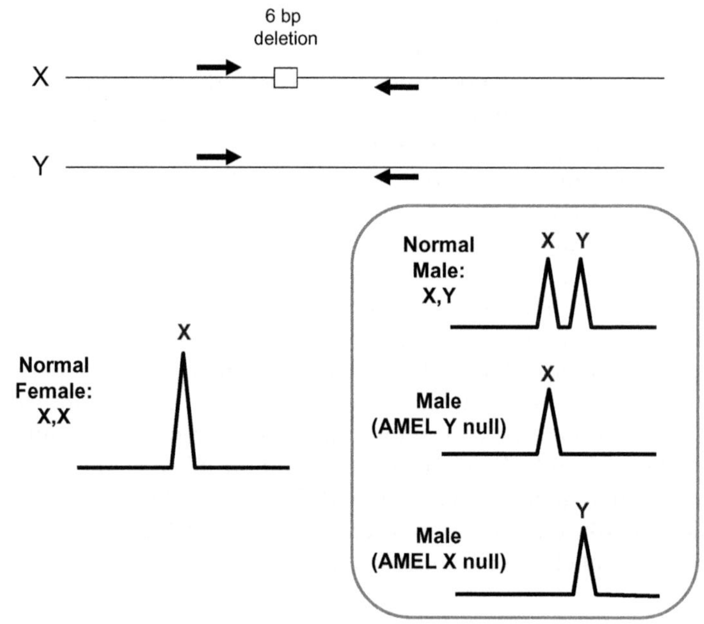

FIGURE 5.8 Schematic of the amelogenin sex-typing assay. The X and Y chromosomes contain a high degree of sequence homology at the amelogenin (AMEL) locus and primers, as depicted by the arrows, can target a 6bp deletion that is present only on the X chromosome (Sullivan et al. 1993). In most circumstances, the presence of a single X peak indicates that the sample comes from a female while two peaks identifies the sample's source as male. Both AMEL Y and AMEL X null alleles have been reported.

Other regions of the amelogenin gene have size differences between the X and Y homologues and may be exploited for sex-typing purposes. For example, Eng and co-workers (1994) used a single set of primers that generated a 977bp product for the X-chromosome and a 788bp fragment for the Y-chromosome. In this case, a 189bp deletion in the Y relative to the X-chromosome was used to differentiate the two chromosomes.

A careful study found that 19 regions of absolute homology, ranging in size from 22bp to 80bp, exist between the human amelogenin X and Y genes that can be used to design a variety of primer sets (Haas-Rochholz & Weiler 1997). Thus, by spanning various deletions of the X and/or Y chromosome, it is possible to generate PCR products from the X and Y homologues that differ in size and contain size ranges that can be integrated into future multiplex STR amplifications.

While amelogenin is an effective method for sex-typing biological samples in most cases, the results are not foolproof either due to primer binding sites that lead to null alleles or chromosomal deletions. Amelogenin Y allele dropouts have been observed due to loss of portions of the Y chromosome in some population groups. Amelogenin X allele dropouts have been seen primarily due to primer binding site mutations.

Amelogenin Y Allele Dropout

A rare deletion of the amelogenin gene on the Y chromosome can cause the Y chromosome amplicon to be absent (Santos et al. 1998). In such a case, a male sample would falsely appear as a female with only the amelogenin X allele being amplified. It appears that this deletion of the Y chromosome amelogenin region is more common in Indian populations (Thangaraj et al. 2002) than those of European or African origins. A study of almost 30,000 males in the Austrian National DNA database revealed that only six individuals lacked the amelogenin Y-amplicon (Steinlechner et al. 2002). These individuals were verified to be male with Y-STRs and amplification of the SRY region (see Chapter 13).

More recent studies have attempted to map the Y deletions in detail and to track the specific biogeographic ancestry of these interesting variants (Cadenas et al. 2007, Jobling et al. 2007). Through examining adjacent STR markers and sequence-specific tag sites, the extent of the Y chromosome deletion can be mapped (Takayama et al. 2009). When amplifying Y-STR loci, the locus DYS458 in Yfiler (see Chapter 13) is the most likely one to be lost with amelogenin Y deletions due to its close proximity to the AMEL Y (see Figure 13.6).

Amelogenin X Allele Dropout

Amelogenin X allele dropout has also been observed in males. In this case only the amelogenin Y-amplicon is present (Shewale et al. 2000, Alves et al. 2006, Maciejewska & Pawłowski 2009). In one study, this phenomenon was observed only three times out of almost 7000 males examined (Shewale et al. 2000). The authors of this study felt that the AMEL X null was most likely a result of a rare polymorphism in the primer binding sites for the amelogenin primers used in commercial STR kits. A different set of amelogenin primers targeting the same 6bp deletion on the X chromosome amplified both the X and Y alleles of amelogenin (Shewale et al. 2000). However, in some populations, this loss of the AMEL X allele is more common. In a study of 503 individuals from São Tomé Island (West Africa),

10 male individuals displayed only the Y allele from amelogenin amplification due to a primer binding site mutation in the AMEL X allele (Alves et al. 2006). A different mutation caused one male out of 5534 Polish males tested to display only the AMEL Y allele (Maciejewska & Pawłowski 2009).

A report of males examined in paternity testing labs using Applied Biosystems STR typing kits found that there were a higher number of African American males showing only the AMEL Y allele (i.e., the AMEL X allele dropped out). Still, this AMEL X null is fairly rare being seen only 48 times in 144,391 males tested or 0.03% of the time (AABB 2008).

STRBASE: AN INTERNET RESOURCE

The rapid growth of the human identification applications for STR loci ensures that static written materials, such as this book, will quickly become out-of-date. New alleles are constantly being discovered (including "off-ladder" microvariant alleles), additional STR markers are being developed, and population data increases with each month of published journals. Indeed, a growing list of publications describing the application of STR loci to forensic DNA typing has exceeded 3500 references.

The World Wide Web enables dynamic sources of information to be widely available. More than a decade ago a website was created to enable forensic scientists to keep abreast of the rapidly evolving field of DNA typing. STRBase was officially launched in July 1997 and is maintained by the Applied Genetics Group of the National Institute of Standards and Technology (Butler & Reeder 1997, Ruitberg et al. 2001, Butler et al. 2008). STRBase may be reached via the World Wide Web using the following URL: http://www.cstl.nist.gov/biotech/strbase.

STRBase contains a number of useful sections. Continually updated information includes the listing of references related to STRs and DNA typing (over 3500 references), addresses for scientists working in the field, and new microvariant or "off-ladder" STR alleles. Other information that is updated less frequently includes STR fact sheets (with allele information similar to Appendix 1), links to other web pages, a review of technology used for DNA typing as well as published primer sequence information, population data for STR markers, and summaries of NIST forensic DNA reference materials. Sections with information on Y-STR markers and low template DNA testing are also available.

STR markers have become important tools for human identity testing. Commercially available STR kits are now widely used in forensic and paternity testing laboratories. The adoption of the 13 CODIS core loci for the U.S. national DNA database ensures that these STR markers will be used for many years to come.

READING LIST AND INTERNET RESOURCES

Butler, J. M. (2010). *Fundamentals of forensic DNA typing*. San Diego: Elsevier Academic Press.

Repeated DNA and Genetic Markers

Biemont, C., & Vieira, C. (2006). Junk DNA as an evolutionary force. *Nature*, *443*, 521–524.

Britten, R. J., & Kohne, D. E. (1968). Repeated sequences in DNA. Hundreds of thousands of copies of DNA sequences have been incorporated into the genomes of higher organisms. *Science*, *161*, 529–540.

Broman, K. W., et al. (1998). Comprehensive human genetic maps: individual and sex-specific variation in recombination. *American Journal of Human Genetics, 63*, 861–869.

Butler, J. M. (2007). Short tandem repeat typing technologies used in human identity testing. *BioTechniques, 43*(4), Sii–Sv.

Chambers, G. K., & MacAvoy, E. S. (2000). Microsatellines: consensus and controversy. *Comparative Biochemistry and Physiology, Part B, Biochemistry and Molecular Biology, 126*, 455–476.

Collins, J. R., et al. (2003). An exhaustive DNA micro-satellite map of the human genome using high performance computing. *Genomics, 82*, 10–19.

Edwards, A., et al. (1991). DNA typing and genetic mapping with trimeric and tetrameric tandem repeats. *American Journal of Human Genetics, 49*, 746–756.

Ellegren, H. (2004). Microsatellites: simple sequences with complex evolution. *Nature Reviews Genetics, 5*, 435–445.

Gemayel, R., et al. (2010). Variable tandem repeats accelerate evolution of coding and regulatory sequences. *Annual Review of Genetics, 44*, 445–477.

Gill, P. (2002). Role of short tandem repeat DNA in forensic casework in the UK–past, present, and future perspectives. *BioTechniques, 32*, 366–372.

Ghebranious, N., et al. (2003). STRP screening sets for the human genome at 5 cM density. *BMC Genomics, 4*, 6.

International Human Genome Sequencing Consortium, Initial sequencing and analysis of the human genome. *Nature, 409*, 860–921.

Kasai, K., et al. (1990). Amplification of a variable number of tandem repeats (VNTR) locus (pMCT118) by the polymerase chain reaction (PCR) and its application in forensic science. *Journal of Forensic Sciences, 35*, 1196–1200.

Primrose, S. B. (1998). *Principles of genome analysis: A guide to mapping and sequencing DNA from different organisms* (2nd ed.). Malden, MA: Blackwell Science.

Subramanian, S., et al. (2003). Genome-wide analysis of microsatellite repeats in humans: their abundance and density in specific genomic regions. *Genome Biology, 4*, R13. Available at <http://genomebiology.com/2003/4/2/R13>.

Tautz, D. (1993). Notes on definitions and nomenclature of tandemly repetitive DNA sequences. In D. J. Pena (Ed.), *DNA fingerprinting: State of the science* (pp. 21–28). Basel: Birkhauser Verlag.

Weber, J. L., & May, P. E. (1989). Abundant class of human DNA polymorphisms which can be typed using the polymerase chain reaction. *American Journal of Human Genetics, 44*, 388–396.

Types of STR Markers

Applied Biosystems. (2002). AmpFlSTR SEfiler PCR Amplification Kit User's Manual. Foster City, CA.

Applied Biosystems (2011). AmpFlSTR NGM SElect PCR Amplification Kit User Guide. Foster City, CA.

Gill, P., et al. (1994). Report of the European DNA profiling group (EDNAP)—towards standardisation of short tandem repeat (STR) loci. *Forensic Science International, 65*, 51–59.

Jin, L., et al. (1994). The exact numbers of possible microsatellite motifs [letter]. *American Journal of Human Genetics, 55*, 582–583.

Promega Corporation. (2002). PowerPlex ES System Technical Manual. Madison, WI.

Promega Corporation. (2009). PowerPlex ESI 17 System Technical Manual. Madison, WI.

Promega Corporation. (2009). PowerPlex ESX 17 System Technical Manual. Madison, WI.

Puers, C., et al. (1993). Identification of repeat sequence heterogeneity at the polymorphic short tandem repeat locus HUMTH01[AATG]n and reassignment of alleles in population analysis by using a locus-specific allelic ladder. *American Journal of Human Genetics, 53*, 953–958.

Urquhart, A., et al. (1993). Sequence variability of the tetranucleotide repeat of the human beta-actin related pseudogene H-beta-Ac-psi-2 (ACTBP2) locus. *Human Genetics, 92*, 637–638.

Urquhart, A., et al. (1994). Variation in short tandem repeat sequences–a survey of twelve microsatellite loci for use as forensic identification markers. *International Journal of Legal Medicine, 107*, 13–20.

STR Markers Used in Forensic DNA Testing

Butler, J. M., et al. (2003). The development of reduced size STR amplicons as tools for analysis of degraded DNA. *Journal of Forensic Sciences, 48*(5), 1054–1064.

Kayser, M., et al. (2004). A comprehensive survey of human Y-chromosomal microsatellites. *American Journal of Human Genetics, 74*, 1183–1197.

Tully, G., et al. (1993). Analysis of 6 VNTR loci by 'multiplex' PCR and automated fluorescent detection. *Human Genetics, 92*, 554–562.

Walsh, P. S., et al. (1996). Sequence analysis and characterization of stutter products at the tetranucleotide repeat locus vWA. *Nucleic Acids Research, 24*, 2807–2812.

Core and Common STR Markers

Bacher, J. W., et al. (1999). Pentanucleotide repeats: highly polymorphic genetic markers displaying minimal stutter artifact. *Proceedings of the ninth international symposium on human identification* (pp. 24–37). Madison, Wisconsin: Promega Corporation. Available at <http://www.promega.com/geneticidproc/ussymp9proc/content/08.pdf>.

Budowle, B., et al. (1998). CODIS and PCR-based short tandem repeat loci: law enforcement tools. *Proceedings of the second European symposium on human identification* (pp. 73–88). Madison, Wisconsin: Promega Corporation. Available at <http://www.promega.com/geneticidproc/eusymp2proc/17.pdf>.

Butler, J. M. (2006). Genetics and genomics of core short tandem repeat loci used in human identity testing. *Journal of Forensic Sciences, 51*, 253–265.

Carracedo, A., & Lareu, M. V. (1998). Development of new STRs for forensic casework: criteria for selection, sequencing and population data and forensic validation. *Proceedings of the ninth international symposium on human identification* (pp. 89–107). Madison, Wisconsin: Promega Corporation. Available at <http://www.promega.com/geneticidproc/>.

Chakraborty, R., et al. (1999). The utility of short tandem repeat loci beyond human identification: Implications for development of new DNA typing systems. *Electrophoresis, 20*, 1682–1696.

Coble, M. D., & Butler, J. M. (2005). Characterization of new miniSTR loci to aid analysis of degraded DNA. *Journal of Forensic Sciences, 50*, 43–53.

Cruz, C., et al. (2004). vWA STR locus structure and variability. *Progress in Forensic Genetics, 10, ICS 1261*, 248–250.

Gill, P., et al. (1996). A new method of STR interpretation using inferential logic–development of a criminal intelligence database. *International Journal of Legal Medicine, 109*, 14–22.

Gill, P., et al. (2006). The evolution of DNA databases-Recommendations for new European STR loci. *Forensic Science International, 156*, 242–244.

Gill, P., et al. (2006). New multiplexes for Europe-amendments and clarification of strategic development. *Forensic Science International, 163*, 155–157.

Hammond, H. A., et al. (1994). Evaluation of 13 short tandem repeat loci for use in personal identification applications. *American Journal of Human Genetics, 55*, 175–189.

Hicks, J. W. (1995). The Alabama DNA database system. *Proceedings of the 6th international symposium on human identification.* Available at <http://www.promega.com/geneticidproc/ussymp6proc/hicks.htm>.

Kimpton, C. P., et al. (1993). Automated DNA profiling employing multiplex amplification of short tandem repeat loci. *PCR Methods and Applications, 3*, 13–22.

Kimpton, C. P., et al. (1994). Evaluation of an automated DNA profiling system employing multiplex amplification of four tetrameric STR loci. *International Journal of Legal Medicine, 106*, 302–311.

Kimpton, C. P., et al. (1996). Validation of highly discriminating multiplex short tandem repeat amplification systems for individual identification. *Electrophoresis, 17*, 1283–1293.

Möller, A., et al. (1994). Different types of structural variation in STRs: HumFES/FPS, HumVWA and HumD21S11. *International Journal of Legal Medicine, 106*, 319–323.

Möller, A., & Brinkmann, B. (1994). Locus ACTBP2 (SE33). Sequencing data reveal considerable polymorphism. *International Journal of Legal Medicine, 106*, 262–267.

Phillips, C., et al. (2011). Analysis of global variability in 15 established and 5 new European Standard Set (ESS) STRs using the CEPH human genome diversity panel. *Forensic Science International: Genetics, 5*, 155–169.

Schneider, P. M. (2009). Expansion of the European Standard Set of DNA database loci—the current situation. *Profiles in DNA, 12*(1), 6–7. Available at <http://www.promega.com/profiles/1201/ProfilesInDNA_1201_06.pdf>.

Sparkes, R., et al. (1996). The validation of a 7-locus multiplex STR test for use in forensic casework. (II), artefacts, casework studies and success rates. *International Journal of Legal Medicine, 109*, 195–204.

Sullivan, K. M., et al. (1993). A rapid and quantitative DNA sex test: fluorescence-based PCR analysis of X-Y homologous gene amelogenin. *BioTechniques, 15*, 637–641.

Thanakiatkrai, P., & Welch, L. (2010). Evaluation of nucleosome forming potentials (NFPs) of forensically important STRs. *Forensic Science International: Genetics* (in press). (doi: 10.1016/j.fsigen.2010.05.002)

Commercial STR Kits

Budowle, B., et al. (2001). STR primer concordance study. *Forensic Science International, 124*, 47–54.

Buse, E. L., et al. (2003). Performance evaluation of two multiplexes used in fluorescent short tandem repeat DNA analysis. *Journal of Forensic Sciences, 48*, 348–357.

Butler, J. M., et al. (2001). Comparison of primer sequences used in commercial STR kits. *Proceedings of the 53th American academy of forensic sciences*. Seattle, Washington. Available at <http://www.cstl.nist.gov/biotech/strbase/pub_pres/AAFS_Feb2001.pdf>.

Collins, P. J., et al. (2004). Developmental validation of a single-tube amplification of the 13 CODIS STR loci, D2S1338, D19S433, and amelogenin: the AmpFlSTR Identifiler PCR Amplification Kit. *Journal of Forensic Sciences, 49*, 1265–1277.

Hill, C. R., et al. (2010). Strategies for concordance testing. *Profiles in DNA (Promega), 13*(1) Available at <http://www.promega.com/profiles/>.

Holt, C. L., et al. (2002). TWGDAM validation of AmpFlSTR PCR amplification kits for forensic DNA casework. *Journal of Forensic Sciences, 47*, 66–96.

Krenke, B. E., et al. (2002). Validation of a 16-locus fluorescent multiplex system. *Journal of Forensic Sciences, 47*, 773–785.

LaFountain, M. J., et al. (2001). TWGDAM validation of the AmpFlSTR Profiler Plus and AmpFlSTR COfiler STR multiplex systems using capillary electrophoresis. *Journal of Forensic Sciences, 46*, 1191–1198.

Leibelt, C., et al. (2003). Identification of a D8S1179 primer binding site mutation and the validation of a primer designed to recover null alleles. *Forensic Science International, 133*, 220–227.

Masibay, A., et al. (2000). Promega Corporation reveals primer sequences in its testing kits [letter]. *Journal of Forensic Sciences, 45*, 1360–1362.

Wallin, J. M., et al. (2002). Constructing universal multiplex PCR systems for comparative genotyping. *Journal of Forensic Sciences, 47*, 52–65.

Allelic Ladders

Baechtel, F. S., et al. (1993). Multigenerational amplification of a reference ladder for alleles at locus D1S80. *Journal of Forensic Sciences, 38*, 1176–1182.

Griffiths, R. A., et al. (1998). New reference allelic ladders to improve allelic designation in a multiplex STR system. *International Journal of Legal Medicine, 111*, 267–272.

Kline, M. C., et al. (1997). Interlaboratory evaluation of short tandem repeat triplex CTT. *Journal of Forensic Sciences, 42*, 897–906.

Puers, C., et al. (1993). Identification of repeat sequence heterogeneity at the polymorphic short tandem repeat locus HUMTH01 [AATG]n and reassignment of alleles in population analysis by using a locus-specific allelic ladder. *American Journal of Human Genetics, 53*, 953–958.

Sajantila, A., et al. (1992). Amplification of reproducible allele markers for amplified fragment length polymorphism analysis. *Biotechniques, 12*, 16–22.

Smith, R. N. (1995). Accurate size comparison of short tandem repeat alleles amplified by PCR. *Biotechniques, 18*, 122–128.

Mobility Modifiers

Applied Biosystems (2001). AmpFlSTR Identifiler PCR Amplification Kit User's Manual. Foster City, CA.

Grossman, P. D., et al. (1994). High-density multiplex detection of nucleic acid sequences: oligonucleotide ligation assay and sequence-coded separation. *Nucleic Acids Research, 22*, 4527–4534.

Next-Generation STR Kits

Applied Biosystems (2009). AmpFlSTR Identifiler Direct PCR Amplification Kit User's Guide. Foster City, CA.

Applied Biosystems (2010). AmpFlSTR Identifiler Plus PCR Amplification Kit User's Guide. Foster City, CA.

Chang, C.-W., et al. (January 21, 2010). Method for direct amplification from crude nucleic acid samples. U.S. Patent Application 20100015621. Available at <http://www.pat2pdf.org/>.

Ensenberger, M. G., et al. (2010). Developmental validation of the PowerPlex 16 HS System: an improved 16-locus fluorescent STR multiplex. *Forensic Science International: Genetics, 4*, 257–264.

Hill, C. R., et al. (2010). Concordance and population studies along with stutter and peak height ratio analysis for the PowerPlex ESX 17 and ESI 17 Systems. *Forensic Science International: Genetics* (in press) (doi: 10/1016/j.fsigen.2010.03.014).

Mulero, J. J., & Hennessy, L. K. (January 1, 2009). Method and composition for nucleic acid amplification. U.S. Patent Application 20090004662. Available at <http://www.pat2pdf.org/>.

Oldroyd, N., et al. (January 2011). Development of the AmpFlSTR NGM SElect kit: new sequence discoveries and implications for genotype concordance. *Forensic News (Applied Biosystems)*. Available at <http://marketing.appliedbiosystems.com/mk/get/FORENSICNEWS_PAST_ISSUES>.

Sprecher, C. J., et al. (2009). PowerPlex ESX and ESI Systems: a suite of new STR systems designed to meet the changing needs of the DNA-typing community. *Forensic Science International: Genetics Supplement Series, 2*, 2–4.

Tucker, V. C., et al. (2010). Developmental validation of the PowerPlex ESI 16 and PowerPlex ESI 17 Systems: STR multiplexes for the new European standard. *Forensic Science International: Genetics* (in press) (doi: 10.1016/j.fsigen.2010.09.004).

Yeung, S. H., et al. (2008). Fluorescence energy transfer-labeled primers for high-performance forensic DNA profiling. *Electrophoresis, 29*, 2251–2259.

Information on 23 Common STR Loci

Barber, M. D., et al. (1996). Structural variation in the alleles of a short tandem repeat system at the human alpha fibrinogen locus. *International Journal of Legal Medicine, 108*, 180–185.

Barber, M. D., & Parkin, B. H. (1996). Sequence analysis and allelic designation of the two short tandem repeat loci D18S51 and D8S1179. *International Journal of Legal Medicine, 109*, 62–65.

Brinkmann, B., et al. (1996). Complex mutational events at the HumD21S11 locus. *Human Genetics, 98*, 60–64.

Drábek, J., et al. (2004). Concordance study between miniplex STR assays and a commercial STR typing kit. *Journal of Forensic Sciences, 49*(4), 859–860.

Dupuy, B. M., & Olaisen, B. (1997). A dedicated internal standard in fragment length analysis of hyperpolymorphic short tandem repeats. *Forensic Science International, 86*, 207–227.

Egyed, B., et al. (2000). Analysis of eight STR loci in two Hungarian populations. *Forensic Science International, 113*, 25–27.

Kimpton, C., et al. (1992). A further tetranucleotide repeat polymorphism in the vWF gene. *Human Molecular Genetics, 1*, 287.

Lareu, M. V., et al. (1996). A highly variable STR at the D12S391 locus. *International Journal of Legal Medicine, 109*, 134–138.

Lareu, M. V., et al. (1998). Sequence variation of a hypervariable short tandem repeat at the D1S1656 locus. *International Journal of Legal Medicine, 111*, 244–247.

Margolis-Nunno, H., et al. (2001). A new allele of the short tandem repeat (STR) locus, CSF1PO. *Journal of Forensic Sciences, 46*, 1480–1483.

Masibay, A., et al. (2000). Promega Corporation reveals primer sequences in its testing kits. *Journal of Forensic Sciences, 45*, 1360–1362.

Mornhinweg, E., et al. (1998). D3S1358: sequence analysis and gene frequency in a German population. *Forensic Science International, 95*, 173–178.

Nelson, M. S., et al. (2002). Detection of a primer-binding site polymorphism for the STR locus D16S539 using the PowerPlex 1.1 system and validation of a degenerate primer to correct for the polymorphism. *Journal of Forensic Sciences, 47*, 345–349.

Oldroyd, N. J., et al. (1995). A highly discriminating octoplex short tandem repeat polymerase chain reaction system suitable for human individual identification. *Electrophoresis, 16*, 334–337.

Wiegand, P., et al. (1999). D18S535, D1S1656 and D10S2325: three efficient short tandem repeats for forensic genetics. *International Journal of Legal Medicine, 112*, 360–363.

Additional STR Loci

Becker, D., et al. (2007). New alleles and mutational events at 14 STR loci from different German populations. *Forensic Science International: Genetics, 1*, 232–237.

Betz, T., et al. (2007). "Paterniplex", a highly discriminative decaplex STR multiplex tailored for investigating special problems in paternity testing. *Electrophoresis, 28*, 3868–3874.

Butler, J. M., et al. (2007). New autosomal and Y-chromosome STR loci: characterization and potential uses. *Proceedings of the eighteenth international symposium on human identification*. Available at <http://www.promega.com/geneticidproc/>.

Chung, U., et al. (2007). Population data of nine miniSTR loci in Koreans. *Forensic Science International, 168*, e51–e53.

Egeland, T., & Sheehan, N. (2008). On identification problems requiring linked autosomal markers. *Forensic Science International: Genetics, 2*, 219–225.

Grubwieser, P., et al. (2007). Evaluation of an extended set of 15 candidate STR loci for paternity and kinship analysis in an Austrian population sample. *International Journal of Legal Medicine, 121*, 85–89.

Henke, J., & Henke, L. (2005). Which short tandem repeat polymorphisms are required for identification? Lessons from complicated kinship cases. *Croatian Medical Journal, 46*, 593–597.

Henke, L., et al. (2007). Validation of a "new" short tandem repeat (STR) fluorescent multiplex system and report of population genetic data. *Clinical Laboratory, 53*, 477–482.

Hill, C. R., et al. (2008). Characterization of 26 miniSTR loci for improved analysis of degraded DNA samples. *Journal of Forensic Sciences, 53*, 73–80.

Hill, C. R., et al. (2009). A new 26plex for use in human identity testing. *Journal of Forensic Sciences, 54*, 1008–1015.

O'Connor, K. L., et al. (2010). Evaluation the effect of additional forensic loci on likelihood ratio values for complex kinship analysis. *Proceedings of the 21st international symposium on human identification*. Available at <http://www.promega.com/geneticidproc/ussymp21proc/oralpresentations/OConnor.pdf>.

STR Allele Nomenclature

Bär, W., et al. (1994). DNA recommendations – 1994 report concerning further recommendations of the DNA Commission of the ISFH regarding PCR-based polymorphisms in STR (short tandem repeat) systems. *International Journal of Legal Medicine, 107*, 159–160.

Bär, W., et al. (1997). DNA recommendations – further report of the DNA Commission of the ISFH regarding the use of short tandem repeat systems. *International Journal of Legal Medicine, 110*, 175–176.

Butler, J. M., et al. (2008). Addressing Y-chromosome short tandem repeat (Y-STR) allele nomenclature. *Journal of Genetic Genealogy, 4*(2), 125–148.

Gill, P., et al. (1997). Considerations from the European DNA profiling group (EDNAP) concerning STR nomenclature. *Forensic Science International, 87*, 185–192.

Gill, P., et al. (1997). Development of guidelines to designate alleles using an STR multiplex system. *Forensic Science International, 89*, 185–197.

Gill, P., et al. (2001). DNA Commission of the International Society of Forensic Genetics: Recommendations on forensic analysis using Y-chromosome STRs. *Forensic Science International, 124*, 5–10.

Gusmão, L., et al. (2006). DNA Commission of the International Society of Forensic Genetics (ISFG): an update of the recommendations on the use of Y-STRs in forensic analysis. *Forensic Science International, 157*, 187–197.

Kayser, M., et al. (2004). A comprehensive survey of human Y-chromosomal microsatellites. *American Journal of Human Genetics, 74*, 1183–1197.

Mulero, J. J., et al. (2006). Letter to the Editor—Nomenclature and allele repeat structure update for the Y-STR locus GATA-H4. *Journal of Forensic Sciences, 51*, 694.

Tautz, D. (1993). Notes on definition and nomenclature of tandemly repetitive DNA sequences. In D. J. Pena, R. Chakraborty, J. T. Epplen & A. J. Jeffreys (Eds.), *DNA fingerprinting: State of the science* (pp. 21–28). Basel: Birkhauser Verlag.

Same-Length, Different-Sequence Alleles

Edwards, M., & Allen, R. W. (2004). Characteristics of mutations at the D5S818 locus studied with a tightly linked marker. *Transfusion, 44*, 83–90.

Hofstadler, S. A., et al. (2009). Analysis of DNA forensic markers using high throughput mass spectrometry. *Forensic Science International: Genetics Supplement Series, 2*, 524–526.

Oberacher, H., et al. (2008). Increased forensic efficiency of DNA fingerprints through simultaneous resolution of length and nucleotide variability by high-performance mass spectrometry. *Human Mutation, 29*(3), 427–432.

Oberacher, H., & Parson, W. (2007). Forensic DNA fingerprinting by liquid chromatography-electrospray ionization mass spectrometry. *Biotechniques, 43*(4), vii–xiii.

Pitterl, F., et al. (2008). The next generation of DNA profiling—STR typing by multiplexed PCR-ion-pair RP LC-ESI time-of-flight MS. *Electrophoresis, 29*, 4739–4750.

Pitterl, F., et al. (2010). Increasing the discrimination power of forensic STR testing by employing high-performance mass spectrometry, as illustrated in indigenous South African and Central Asian populations. *International Journal of Legal Medicine, 124*, 551–558.

Planz, J. V., et al. (2009). Enhancing resolution and statistical power by utilizing mass spectrometry for detection of SNPs within the short tandem repeats. *Forensic Science International: Genetics Supplement Series, 2*, 529–531.

Gender Identification with Amelogenin

Budowle, B., et al. (1996). Multiplex amplification and typing procedure for the loci D1S80 and amelogenin. *Journal of Forensic Sciences, 41*, 660–663.

Eng, B., et al. (1994). Anomalous migration of PCR products using nondenaturing polyacrylamide gel electrophoresis: the amelogenin sex-typing system. *Journal of Forensic Sciences, 39*, 1356–1359.

Francès, F., et al. (2007). Amelogenin test: From forensics to quality control in clinical and biochemical genomics. *Clinica Chimica Acta, 386*, 53–56.

Haas-Rochholz, H., & Weiler, G. (1997). Additional primer sets for an amelogenin gene PCR-based DNA-sex test. *International Journal of Legal Medicine, 110*, 312–315.

Mannucci, A., et al. (1994). Forensic application of a rapid and quantitative DNA sex test by amplification of the X-Y homologous gene amelogenin. *International Journal of Legal Medicine, 106*, 190–193.

Reynolds, R., & Varlaro, J. (1996). Gender determination of forensic samples using PCR amplification of ZFX/ZFY gene sequences. *Journal of Forensic Sciences, 41*, 279–286.

Sullivan, K. M., et al. (1993). A rapid and quantitative DNA sex test: fluorescence-based PCR analysis of X-Y homologous gene amelogenin. *BioTechniques, 15*, 637–641.

Tschentscher, F., et al. (2008). Amelogenin sex determination by pyrosequencing of short PCR products. *International Journal of Legal Medicine, 122*, 333–335.

Amelogenin Anomalies

AABB (2008). Annual report summary for testing in 2008. Available at <http://www.aabb.org/sa/facilities/Documents/rtannrpt08.pdf>.

Alves, C., et al. (2006). The amelogenin locus displays a high frequency of X homologue failures in Sao Tome Island (West Africa). *Progress in Forensic Genetics, 11, ICS 1288*, 271–273.

Cadenas, A. M., et al. (2007). Male amelogenin dropouts: phylogenetic context, origins and implications. *Forensic Science International, 166*, 155–163.

Chang, Y. M., et al. (2007). A distinct Y-STR haplotype for Amelogenin negative males characterized by a large Y(p)11.2 (DYS458-MSY1-AMEL-Y) deletion. *Forensic Science International, 166*, 115–120.

Jobling, M. A., et al. (2007). Structural variation on the short arm of the human Y chromosome: recurrent multigene deletions encompassing Amelogenin Y. *Human Molecular Genetics, 16*(3), 307–316.

Kumagai, R., et al. (2008). DNA analysis of family members with deletion in Yp11.2 region containing amelogenin locus. *Legal Medicine, 10*, 39–42.

Lattanzi, W., et al. (2005). A large interstitial deletion encompassing the *amelogenin* gene on the short arm of the Y chromosome. *Human Genetics, 116*, 395–401.

Maciejewsha, A., & Pawlowski, R. (2009). A rare mutation in the primer binding region of the Amelogenin X homologue gene. *Forensic Science International: Genetics, 3*, 265–267.

Mitchell, R. J., et al. (2006). Amelogenin Y negative males: multiple origins. *Progress in Forensic Genetics, 11, ICS 1288*, 274–276.

Murphy, K. M., et al. (2007). Constitutional duplication of a region of chromosome Yp encoding AMELY, PRKY, and TBL1Y: implications for sex chromosome analysis and bone marrow engraftment analysis. *Journal of Molecular Diagnostics, 9*, 408–413.

Oz, C., et al. (2008). A Y-chromosome STR marker should be added to commercial multiplex STR kits. *Journal of Forensic Sciences, 53*, 858–861.

Raina, A., et al. (2010). Misinterpretation of results in medico-legal cases due to microdeletion in the Y-chromosome. *Molecular and Cellular Probes, 24*, 418–420.

Santos, F. R., et al. (1998). Reliability of DNA-based sex tests. *Nature Genetics, 18*(2) 103–103.

Shadrach, B., et al. (2004). A rare mutation in the primer binding region of the Amelogenin gene can interfere with gender identification. *Journal of Molecular Diagnostics, 6*(4), 401–405.

Shewale, J. G., et al. (2000). Anomalous amplification of the amelogenin locus typed by AmpFlSTR Profiler Plus amplification kit. *Forensic Science Communications*, 2(4) Available at <http://www.fbi.gov/hq/lab/fsc/backissu/oct2000/shewale.htm>.

Steinlechner, M., et al. (2002). Rare failures in the amelogenin sex test. *International Journal of Legal Medicine, 116*(2), 117–120.

Takayama, T., et al. (2009). Determination of deletion regions from Yp11.2 of an amelogenin negative male. *Legal Medicine, 11*, S578–S580.

Thangaraj, K., et al. (2002). Is the amelogenin gene reliable for gender identification in forensic casework and prenatal diagnosis? *International Journal of Legal Medicine, 116*(2), 121–123.

STRBase

Butler, J. M., et al. (1997). STRBase: a short tandem repeat DNA internet-accessible database. *Proceedings of the eighth international symposium on human identification 1997* (pp. 38–47). Promega Corporation. Available at <http://www.promega.com/geneticidproc/ussymp8proc/>.

Butler, J. M. (October 2-3, 2007). STRBase: 10 years and beyond—new internet resources for the human identity testing community. *Poster at eighteenth international symposium on human identification*. Hollywood, CA: Available at <http://www.cstl.nist.gov/biotech/strbase/NISTpub.htm>.

Butler, J. M. (2008). New resources for the forensic genetics community available on the NIST STRBase website. *Forensic Science International: Genetics Supplement Series (Progress in Forensic Genetics 12), 1*(1), 97–99.

Ruitberg, C. M., et al. (2001). STRBase: a short tandem repeat DNA database for the human identity testing community. *Nucleic Acids Res, 29*, 320–322.

STRBase. <http://www.cstl.nist.gov/biotech/strbase>.

CHAPTER

6

Capillary Electrophoresis: Principles and Instrumentation

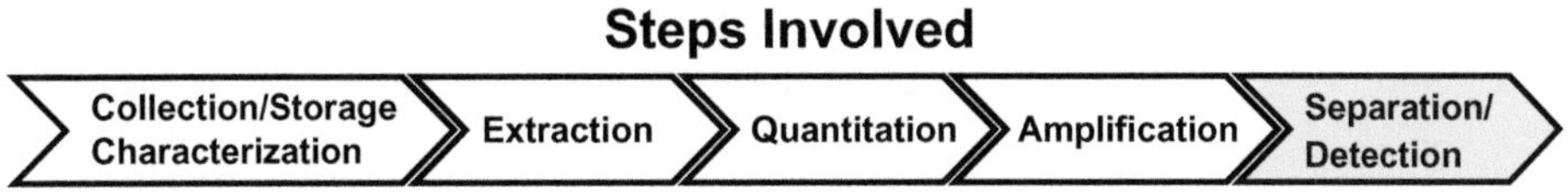

Capillary electrophoresis (CE) is the primary methodology used for separating and detecting short tandem repeat (STR) alleles in forensic DNA laboratories worldwide. This chapter will examine the general principles and components of injection, separation, and detection of STR alleles using CE (Butler et al. 2004). The various Applied Biosystems (ABI) Genetic Analyzers, which are the instruments used worldwide for STR typing, will be discussed. Additional information on CE instruments including troubleshooting tips will be available in the forthcoming volume *Advanced Topics in Forensic DNA Typing: Interpretation*. Readers needing a more basic understanding of DNA separation and detection are encouraged to review Chapter 9 in *Fundamentals of Forensic DNA Typing* (Butler 2010).

REQUIREMENTS FOR STR TYPING

To achieve reliable STR typing, three conditions must be met. First, ***spatial resolution*** is needed to separate STR alleles that may differ in size by a single nucleotide (see Appendix 1). Second, ***spectral resolution*** is needed to separate fluorescent dye colors from one another so that PCR products from loci labeled with different dyes can be resolved. Third, *DNA sizing precision* from run to run must be consistent enough so that samples can be related to allelic ladders that are run for calibration purposes (see Figure 5.7).

These requirements have been met with a variety of CE systems. Since its introduction in July 1995 by Applied Biosystems, the single-capillary ABI Prism 310 Genetic Analyzer has been a popular method for STR typing in forensic DNA laboratories. More recently a variety

TABLE 6.1 Information on Genetic Analyzer (Capillary Electrophoresis) Instrumentation Available from Applied Biosystems (Foster City, CA). Until the 3500 Series, All Systems Used Argon Ion (Ar^+) Lasers with 488/514 nm Wavelengths for Fluorescence Excitation. Information Courtesy of Michelle S. Shepherd, Applied Biosystems, LIFE Technologies.

ABI Genetic Analyzer	Years Released for Human ID	Number of Capillaries	Laser	Polymer Delivery	Other Features
373 (gel system)	1992–2003	–	40 mW Ar+ (488/514 nm)	–	PMTs and color filter wheel for detection
377 (gel system)	1995–2006	–	40 mW Ar+ (488/514 nm)	–	CCD camera
310	1995	1	10 mW Ar+ (488/514 nm)	syringe	Mac operating system & Windows NT (later)
3100	2000–2005	16	25 mW Ar+ (488/514 nm)	syringe	
3100-Avant	2002–2007	4	25 mW Ar+ (488/514 nm)	syringe	
3130	2003–2011	4	25 mW Ar+ (488/514 nm)	pump	
3130xl	2003–2011	16	25 mW Ar+ (488/514 nm)	pump	
3500	2010	8	10–25 mW diode (505 nm)	new pump	110 V power; RFID-tagged reagents; normalization & 6-dye detection possible
3500xl	2010	24			
3700	2002–2003	96	25 mW Ar+ (488/514 nm)	cuvette-based	Split beam technology
3730	2005	48	25 mW Ar+ (488/514 nm)	pump	
3730xl	2005	96	25 mW Ar+ (488/514 nm)	pump	

of capillary array instruments have become available and forensic laboratories have used the 3100, 3130, 3700, 3730, and 3500 series instruments. Table 6.1 reviews features of the various models of ABI Genetic Analyzers along with the number of capillaries used, which relates to the instrument's throughput capabilities.

PRINCIPLES AND COMPONENTS OF CAPILLARY ELECTROPHORESIS

The primary elements of a basic CE instrument include a narrow glass capillary, two buffer vials, and two electrodes connected to a high-voltage power supply. CE systems also contain a laser excitation source, a fluorescence detector, an autosampler to hold the sample tubes or tray, and a computer to control the sample injection and detection (Figure 6.1). CE capillaries are made of glass and typically have an internal diameter of 50 μm (similar to the thickness of a human hair). ABI Genetic Analyzers typically use capillaries with 36cm or 50cm injection-to-detection distances. For some higher-resolution work, such as long-read DNA sequencing, 80cm capillaries may be used.

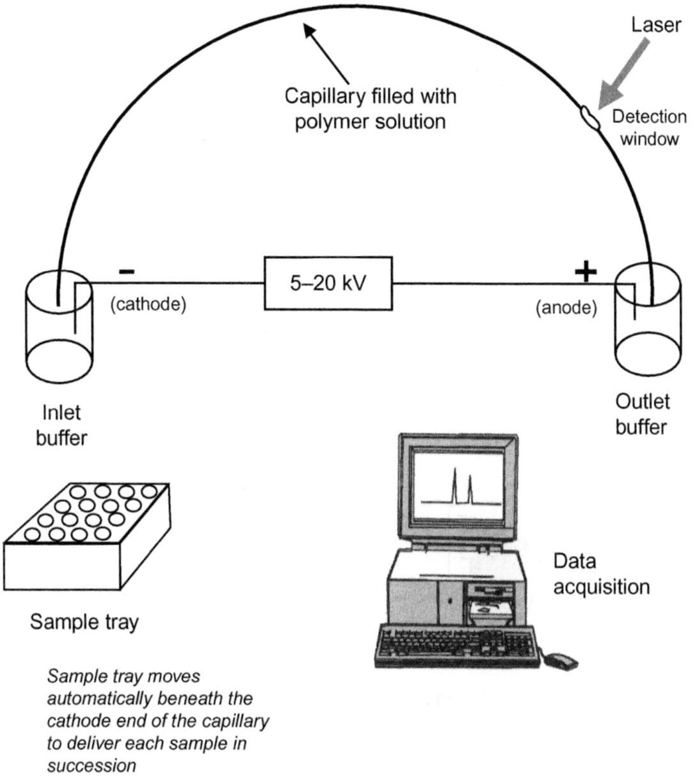

FIGURE 6.1 Schematic of capillary electrophoresis instruments used for DNA analysis. The capillary is a narrow glass tube approximately 50 cm long and 50 μm in diameter. It is filled with a viscous polymer solution that acts much like a gel in creating a sieving environment for DNA molecules. Samples are placed into a tray and injected onto the capillary by applying a voltage to each sample sequentially. A high voltage (e.g., 15,000 volts) is applied across the capillary after the injection in order to separate the DNA fragments in a matter of minutes. Fluorescent dye-labeled products are analyzed as they pass by the detection window and are excited by a laser beam. Computerized data acquisition enables rapid analysis and digital storage of separation results.

The same buffers that are used in gel electrophoresis may also be used with CE. However, instead of a gel matrix through which the DNA molecules pass, a viscous polymer solution serves as the sieving medium. The linear, flexible polymer chains act as obstacles that must be navigated by the negatively-charged DNA fragments on their way to the positive electrode. The larger DNA molecules move more slowly through the capillary than the smaller, more agile DNA fragments, which allows the molecules to be separated based on their size.

Prior to injecting each sample, a new gel is "poured" by filling the capillary with a fresh aliquot of the polymer solution. The CE capillary can be thought of as one lane in a gel that is only wide enough for one sample at a time. Different DNA samples are mixed with a constant set of DNA fragments of known size that serve as internal size standards in order to correlate results from run-to-run. An important difference between CE and gels is that the

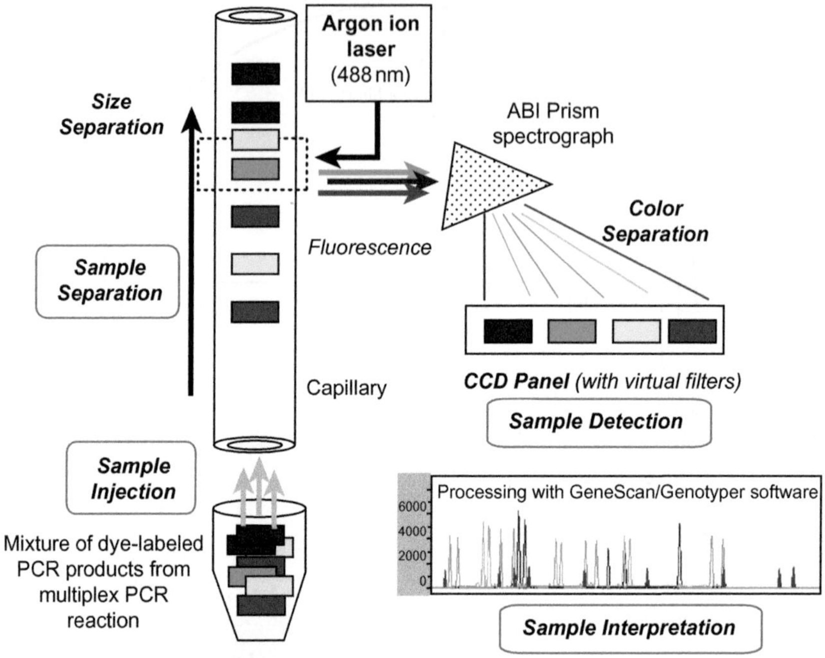

FIGURE 6.2 Schematic illustration of the separation and detection of STR alleles with an ABI Prism 310 Genetic Analyzer or a single capillary in an ABI 3100 or other multi-capillary instrument.

electric fields are on the order of 10 to 100 times stronger with CE (i.e., 300 V/cm instead of 10 V/cm), which results in much faster run times for CE.

Detection of the sample is performed automatically by the CE instrument by measuring the time span from sample injection to sample detection with a laser placed near the end of the capillary. Laser light is shined on to the capillary at a fixed position where a window has been burned into the coating of the capillary. DNA fragments are illuminated as they pass by this window. The smaller DNA molecules arrive at the detection point first followed by the larger molecules in order of their migration speed, which correlates with length or the number of base pairs. Data from CE separations are plotted as a function of the relative fluorescence intensity observed from fluorescence emission of dyes passing the detector. The fluorescent emission signals from dyes attached to the DNA molecules can then be used to detect and quantify the DNA molecules passing the detector (Figure 6.2).

ELECTROKINETIC INJECTION

The most common method used to introduce DNA samples into a capillary is a process known as *electrokinetic injection*, where a voltage is applied to a liquid sample immersed in one end of a capillary for a defined time. As DNA molecules are negatively charged in a neutral pH environment, a positive voltage draws the DNA molecules into the capillary.

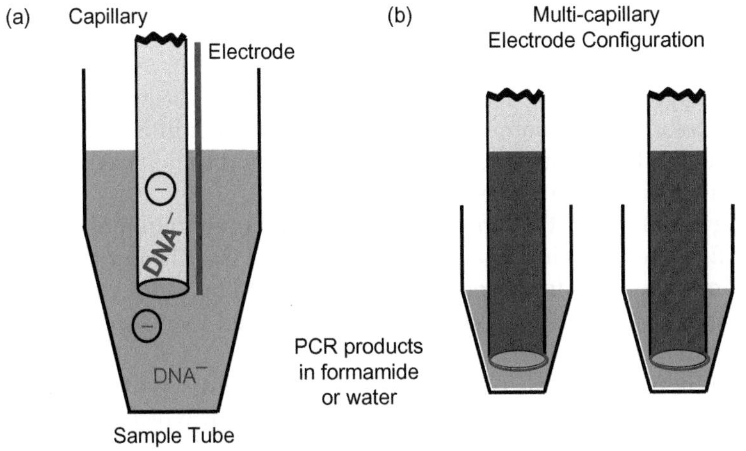

FIGURE 6.3 Comparison of capillary and electrode configurations with (a) single capillary ABI 310 and (b) multi-capillary systems. In (a) the electrode is adjacent to the capillary and in (b) the electrode surrounds the capillary.

Electrokinetic injections produce narrow injection zones that permit high-resolution DNA separations to occur in a relatively short separation distance.

In order to get DNA molecules onto the CE capillary, an electric voltage is applied while the end of the capillary is immersed into the liquid DNA sample. An electrode (cathode) is adjacent to the single capillary in the ABI 310 instrument while each capillary in capillary array instruments is enclosed in a platinum electrode (Figure 6.3). The flow of current generated by the voltage applied and the resistance experienced pulls the negatively-charged DNA molecules into the end of the capillary. However, CE injections of DNA are highly sensitive to the sample matrix—specifically the ionic strength of small negative ions, such as chloride from the PCR solution, provide competition for larger, slower DNA molecules in entering the end of the capillary.

The quantity of DNA injected into a CE column ($[DNA_{injected}]$) is a function of the voltage or electric field applied (E), the injection time (t), the concentration of DNA in the sample ($[DNA_{sample}]$), the area of the capillary opening (πr^2), and the ionic strength of the sample (λ_{sample}) versus the buffer (λ_{buffer}). The electrophoretic mobility (μ_{ep}), or how quickly a charged molecule moves when experiencing an electric field, also impacts the quantity of the DNA loaded into a capillary as does the electroosmotic flow (μ_{eof}), which will be explained further in the next section. The equation for amount of DNA injected—and hence detected—in a CE system is (Rose et al. 1988, Butler et al. 2004):

$$[DNA_{injected}] = \frac{Et(\pi r^2)(\mu_{ep} + \mu_{eof})[DNA_{sample}](\lambda_{buffer})}{\lambda_{sample}}$$

This equation reveals how a high sample ionic strength can impact the amount of DNA injected. Chloride (Cl^-) ions and other buffer ions present in PCR samples contribute to the sample conductivity and thus will compete with DNA for injection onto the capillary. This inverse relationship between sample conductivity (caused by its salt content) and amount of DNA injected into the capillary is the reason that post-PCR purification can increase the CE signal (see Chapter 11).

Sample Preparation

Sample preparation can impact electrokinetic injection. The PCR products created from amplifying a genomic DNA sample with an STR typing kit are typically diluted to levels of approximately 1 in 10 with deionized formamide (e.g., 1 μL PCR product into 9 μL of formamide) both to help denature the double-stranded DNA molecules and to help reduce the salt levels and aid the electrokinetic injection process.

Since formamide is a strong denaturant, it is commonly used in the preparation of single-stranded DNA samples for CE. Merely placing a sample in formamide is sufficient to denature it. However, heating a sample to 95°C for several minutes followed by rapid cooling to around 4°C (commonly referred to as "snap-cooling") is often performed to ensure that the two complementary DNA strands are separated or denatured.

Use of high-quality formamide with low conductivity is important. As formamide degrades it produces ionic decomposition products including formic acid, which are negatively charged at a neutral pH and will be preferentially injected into the capillary. The formamide by-products can cause problems in both sensitivity and resolution (Buel et al. 1998). The quality of formamide can be easily measured using a portable conductivity meter and should be approximately 100 μS/cm (the SI unit of conductivity is Siemens/meter) or lower to obtain the best results. The Hi-Di formamide (Applied Biosystems, Foster City, CA) used by most forensic DNA laboratories has a conductivity of <25 μS/cm and generally works well.

Many laboratories purchase ultrapure formamide and freeze aliquots immediately to ensure sample quality. Water has also been successfully used in the preparation of STR samples for CE analysis instead of formamide (Butler et al. 1995, Biega & Duceman 1999). Use of deionized water can eliminate the health hazard and the cost of formamide as well as problems associated with disposal. While studies have shown that water gives fully concordant results with formamide, long-term sample stability suffers because DNA molecules will renature (complementary strands will reanneal or come back together) in water after a few days.

The injection process moves the DNA molecules from their position in the sample tray onto the end of the capillary—essentially the starting line of a race where mixtures of different length molecules (amplified STR alleles) are separated.

DNA SEPARATION

Like marathon runners with different abilities, DNA molecules separate out along the race course of a capillary once a voltage is applied. Although the different length molecules begin the "race" together, the smaller ones move more quickly and are detected earlier at the "finish line." The time at which the DNA molecules cross the finish line is converted to base pair size through the use of internal size standards—analogous to runners with known abilities that move through the race course enabling a calibration of finish time with a runner's ability (DNA size).

There are several components that impact DNA separations within CE systems: the polymer used for enabling the separation, the capillary, the electrophoresis buffer, and the voltage applied or electric field strength (Butler 1995, Buel et al. 2003). STR allelic ladders, which contain multiple PCR products that are 4bp (or less) different in size, are useful tools for monitoring system resolution.

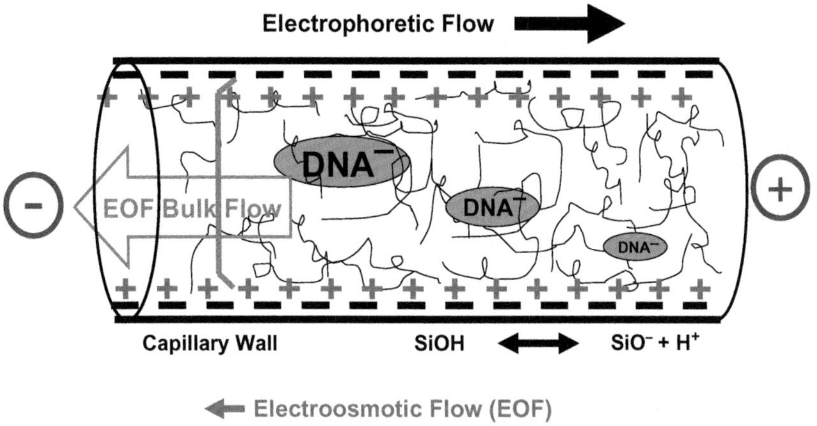

FIGURE 6.4 Illustration of internal capillary environment and forces at play with moving DNA molecules through a sieving polymer buffer.

Figure 6.4 illustrates the inner environment of a CE capillary. DNA moves with the electrophoretic flow from the negative electrode (cathode) shown on the left towards the positive electrode (anode) shown on the right. Strands of entangled polymer form transient pores that serve as obstacles to inhibit progress of DNA molecules based on their size. Smaller DNA molecules are able to move more easily through the obstructions.

As illustrated in Figure 6.4, another force is at play inside the capillary. The capillaries are made of glass or fused silica (silicon dioxide, SiO_2) but have hydroxyl groups (silanol, SiOH) along the inner walls and are negatively charged above approximately pH 5. Since the electrophoresis buffer used is typically around pH 8, positive ions from the buffer solution will line up with the negative siloxy (SiO^-) ions along the walls creating what is known as a double-layer. Under the electric field applied during CE separation (e.g., 15,000 volts), the positive ions will migrate toward the negative electrode. The movement of these positive ions will create a bulk flow of the solution within the capillary with what is known as *electroosmotic flow* or EOF. EOF can be reduced or eliminated by coating the inner capillary wall to prevent exposure of negative charges along the wall and buildup of positive ions from solution.

Polymer Solution

Applied Biosystems sells two primary polymer formulations for use with the ABI Prism 310 and other Genetic Analyzers: POP-4 and POP-6, where "POP" stands for Performance Optimized Polymer. These polymer solutions are 4% and 6% concentrations of linear, uncross-linked dimethyl polyacrylamide, respectively (Madabhushi et al. 1996, Madabhushi 1998). A high concentration of urea is also present in the polymer solution to help create an environment in the capillary that will keep the DNA molecules denatured.

POP-4 is commonly used for DNA fragment analysis including STR typing while the POP-6 polymer, which is the same polydimethylacrylamide polymer present at a higher concentration, is capable of higher resolution to meet the single-base resolution needs of DNA sequencing. More recently, POP-7 polymer has been introduced for both STR typing and DNA sequencing applications.

Entangled polymers are characterized by a rapid increase in viscosity as the polymer concentration reaches a certain threshold value. The viscosity of these materials is also dependent on the polymer's relative molecular mass. The ideal polymer should have at least the same separation properties as classical polyacrylamide gels, combined with a low viscosity that allows easy replacement before each run is conducted on the CE instrument.

Buffer

The buffer that is used to dissolve the polymer in CE systems is important as it stabilizes and solubilizes the DNA and provides charge carriers for the electrophoretic current. If the buffer concentration and concomitant conductivity are too high, then the column will overheat resulting in a loss of resolution. In the process of electrophoresis, the composition of the anode and the cathode buffers may change due to electrolysis and migration of buffer ions. Thus, to avoid problems with poor size calibration of the system over time, it is a good policy to regularly replace the CE buffers with fresh solution.

The Genetic Analyzer buffer commonly used with the ABI 310 is 100 mmol/L TAPS and 1 mmol/L EDTA, adjusted to pH 8.0 with NaOH (Rosenblum et al. 1997). TAPS is short for *N*-tris-(hydroxymethyl)-methyl-3-aminopropane-sulfonic acid. TAPS is used instead of Tris-borate-EDTA (TBE) since TBE is temperature and pH-sensitive. As analysis temperature is increased with TBE, the pH decreases at a rate of 0.02 pH units with every 1°C. As pH decreases so does the fluorescence emission of many dyes (Singer & Johnson 1997).

Under the analysis parameters typically employed for STR analysis, the amplified DNA fragments must remain denatured. To accomplish this DNA denaturation, the CE run temperature is set to higher than room temperature, and buffer additives such as formamide, urea, and 2-pyrrolidinone are added to keep the DNA from reannealing. Even under strong denaturing conditions, DNA molecules can sometimes assume various conformations due to intramolecular attractions. Therefore, capillary run temperatures of 60°C are commonly employed to help reduce secondary structure in DNA (Rosenblum et al. 1997). In addition, high concentrations of urea and elevated temperatures are used to keep the various STR alleles uniformly denatured, since the mobility of DNA fragments can be affected by its conformation. Even with these measures, CE instruments need a stable ambient temperature, as temperature variations can have profound effects on allele migration (D.N.A. Box 6.1).

Many laboratories assess an internal standard peak (such as the 250 peak in the ABI GS500 internal standard), which is particularly sensitive to temperature variation to demonstrate that their CE systems are stable and well-calibrated (Klein et al. 2003). CE analysis of DNA fragments at elevated pH conditions, where the DNA molecule is predominately denatured, suggests that DNA secondary structure is responsible for the variations observed in DNA size determinations with fluctuating temperatures (Nock et al. 2001). By carefully controlling the run conditions, i.e., pH, buffer, denaturants, and temperature, variations within and between runs can be minimized and overall run precision improved. Run-to-run precision can also be enhanced using a global Southern sizing algorithm rather than the traditional local Southern sizing (Klein et al. 2003, Hartzell et al. 2003).

D.N.A. BOX 6.1

UNDERSTANDING CE INSTRUMENT SENSITIVITY TO ROOM TEMPERATURE CHANGES

Swings in room temperature of more than ≈2°C have been shown to adversely impact sizing precision when DNA separations are occurring in an ABI 310 or other Genetic Analyzer. This imprecision can lead to improperly calling "off-ladder" alleles when comparisons are made to sequentially-run allelic ladders. The reasons why temperature variation leads to imprecise measurements and inaccurate allele calls are enumerated below.

Voltage is determined by current times resistance (V = I × R), which is also known as Ohm's law after Georg Ohm who discovered this relationship in 1827. Rearranging this equation, current is equal to voltage divided by resistance. Voltage is the energy put into the system by the power supply. In the case of an ABI 310 or 3100 Genetic Analyzer, the voltage delivered for the separation step is typically 15,000 or 15kV. For the injection step, a lower voltage and hence lower current is often used to coax the DNA molecules into the end of the capillary. While thousands of volts may seem like a lot of energy, it is the current, or the flow of electrons or charged particles, that matters with electricity and electrophoresis. The speed at which the DNA molecules move is directly related to the current flow—not the voltage delivered. Resistance is high inside of a narrow glass capillary filled with a viscous polymer solution so current flow is typically in the 10 to 100 microampere region.

Excessive room temperature changes (swings of more than several degrees Celsius) can lead to temperature variation inside the capillary electrophoresis (CE) instrument and inside the capillary itself. Temperature changes that occur inside the capillary change the viscosity of the polymer which in turn alters the resistance experienced by the DNA molecules and other ions flowing during electrophoresis. As the polymer concentration inside the capillary effectively changes due to this temperature change, the mobility, or speed of movement, of DNA molecules shifts. If the temperature goes up, the polymer network of transient pores inside the capillary (see Figure 6.4) becomes more flexible (essentially less concentrated) and the DNA molecules move more quickly. Thus, while the voltage may be constant between runs, the resistance can change—leading to shifting in the current experienced by the DNA molecules undergoing electrophoresis.

Different length DNA sequences have different electrophoretic mobilities because they tumble or gyrate through a capillary or gel environment at different rates. Longer DNA molecules have a larger radius of gyration, which means that they will interact more frequently with polymer strands that effectively slow the DNA molecules and their movement through the capillary. Sequence differences in DNA molecules impact their 3-dimensional structure (their radius of gyration). Thus, in some cases, it is possible to separate two DNA molecules with the same length but different internal sequence (or to see a shift in the apparent size between them). This is the reason that allelic ladders are necessary in order to accurately genotype STR alleles separated and sized by electrophoresis. The allelic ladder alleles have the same DNA sequence as the STR allele being measured and thus possess the same radius of gyration

D.N.A. BOX 6.1 (*cont'd*)

when exposed to the same electrophoresis conditions.

How does this information relate to loss of precision in CE systems when room temperature varies? DNA sizes measured in CE are determined relative to an internal size standard, which contains a series of DNA fragments. These fragments have a different internal sequence compared to STR alleles. When the electrophoresis conditions change between two runs of the CE instrument (e.g., due to a room temperature shift that ultimately alters the polymer concentration in the capillary), the differential movement of the size standard peaks compared to the STR alleles may be sufficiently different between sequential runs to alter the apparent size of the STR alleles. If this happens, then the allelic ladder allele corresponding to the sample allele being measured may appear slightly different in size. If it falls outside of the ± 0.5 bp genotyping bin, then the sample allele is incorrectly labeled as "off-ladder." Thus, precise temperature control either within the instrument itself (or the room where the instrument is housed or both) is absolutely critical to obtaining quality STR typing results.

The Capillary

The capillary column is central to the separation capabilities of CE. As mentioned above, in uncoated capillary columns, residual charges on the silica surface induce a flow of the bulk solution toward the negative electrode. This EOF creates problems for reproducible DNA separations because the velocity of the DNA molecules can change from run to run. Capillary and microchip channel walls, which contain the charged siloxy groups, can be chemically modified (Hjertén 1985) or dynamically coated (Rosenblum et al. 1997) to prevent EOF in DNA separations. The charged sites on the wall can be masked by adsorption of neutral linear polymers that provide a viscous layer on the capillary surface.

The commercially available poly-dimethylacrylamide POP-4 and POP-6 polymers are successfully used in DNA genotyping by CE because they provide a sieving matrix for the separation of single-stranded DNA and, at the same time, suppress the EOF (Rosenblum et al. 1997). POP-4 consists of 4% linear dimethylacrylamide, 8 mol/L urea, 5% 2-pyrrolidinone (Rosenblum et al. 1997, Wenz et al. 1998).

Manufacturers of capillaries often suggest replacing a capillary at around 100 or 150 injections to avoid problems with resolution failure. Capillary lifetimes can be improved by rinsing the capillary with consecutive washes of water, tetrahydrofuran, hydrochloric acid, and polymer solution (Madabhushi 1998). Unfortunately, ABI CE systems do not permit an on-the-instrument wash so the capillary must first be removed to conduct the rinsing procedure. With good sample preparation, many forensic laboratories see capillary lifetimes extend far past the 100 injections recommended by the manufacturer. Through effective monitoring of sample resolution, capillaries can be replaced when resolution declines (Buel et al. 2003).

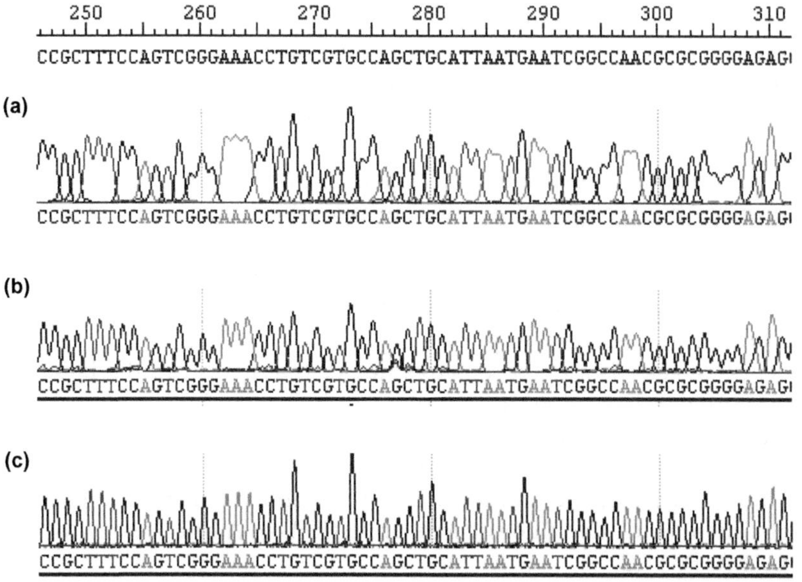

FIGURE 6.5 Impact of capillary length and polymer concentration on obtaining single base resolution in DNA sequencing. (a) POP-4 with 36 cm ABI 310 capillary (20 minute run time); (b) POP-6 with 50 cm ABI 310 capillary (120 minute run time); (c) POP-7 with 80 cm ABI 3130xl array (120 minute run time). Data courtesy of Tomohiro Takayama, NIST guest researcher.

Factors Impacting Resolution

A number of factors influence resolution in a CE system include capillary length, separation voltage, and polymer concentration. Separation of similarly-sized DNA molecules is achieved with an increased number of interactions with the entangled polymer strands while passing through the capillary. Thus, longer capillaries, lower separation voltages, and higher polymer concentrations improve resolution—but at the expense of longer separation times.

Figure 6.5 illustrates the benefit of a longer capillary and higher polymer concentration on the separation of DNA sequencing products that differ by a single nucleotide. A 36cm capillary with POP-4 polymer was barely able to subdivide the three "A" peaks at positions 262 to 264 (Figure 6.5a). These same three "A" peaks exhibited better resolution with a 50cm capillary and the more concentrated POP-6 polymer (Figure 6.5b). The best results, where baseline resolution was achieved, were seen with an 80cm capillary and POP-7 (Figure 6.5c). However, the better resolutions from the longer capillaries came at the expense of longer run times.

FLUORESCENCE DETECTION

Fluorescence-based detection assays are widely used in forensic laboratories due to their capabilities for multi-color analysis as well as rapid and easy-to-use formats. In the application to DNA typing with STR markers, a fluorescent dye is attached to a PCR primer that is incorporated into the amplified target region of DNA. Amplified STR alleles are represented by peaks on an electropherogram as the labeled DNA molecules pass the detector (Figure 6.2). In this section, fluorescence detection is discussed in the context of the chemistry and instruments used to label and detect the PCR products produced from STR markers.

A significant advantage of fluorescent labeling over other methods is the ability to record two or more fluorophores separately using optical filters. The signal produced has to be spectrally resolved. This is accomplished using a fluorophore color separation algorithm known as a matrix, which is sometimes referred to as a "spectral calibration." With this multi-color capability, components of complex mixtures can be labeled individually and identified separately in the same sample.

A fluorescence detector is a photosensitive device that measures the light intensity emitted from a fluorophore. Detection of low-intensity light may be accomplished with a photomultiplier tube (PMT) or a charge-coupled device (CCD). The action of a photon striking the detector is converted to an electric signal. The strength of the resultant current is proportional to the intensity of the emitted light. This light intensity is typically reported in arbitrary units, such as relative fluorescence units (RFUs). A brief review of fluorescence is included in D.N.A. Box 6.2.

Optics for Genetic Analyzers

Multi-wavelength detection has expanded the capabilities of DNA analysis beyond a single dye color and permitted greater multiplexing for STR markers. The key to the utilization of this technology is to covalently bind a different dye onto the 5′ (nonreactive)-end of each primer or set of primers. These dyes have a number of interesting properties. They are all excited by a single argon ion laser tuned to 488 nm, yet fluoresce in different regions of the spectra.

Lasers are an effective excitation source because the light they emit is very intense and mostly at one or a few wavelengths. The argon ion gas laser (Ar^+) produces a blue light with dominant wavelengths of 488 nm and 514.5 nm. This laser is by far the most popular for applications involving fluorescent DNA labeling because a number of dyes are available that closely match its excitation capabilities. The ABI 3500 instrument utilizes a 505 nm diode laser.

The intensity of the light emitted by a fluorophore is directly dependent on the amount of light that the dye has absorbed. Thus, the excitation source is very important in the behavior of a fluorophore. Other important instrument parameters to be considered include optical filters used for signal discrimination and the sensitivity and spectral response of the detector.

A multi-wavelength analyzer, such as a CCD camera, can be used to determine which dye is present, based on the emission of each fragment as it passes the detector window. This technique permits the analysis of fragments of DNA that overlap in size as long as they are labeled with different dyes, which fluoresce at different wavelengths.

The ABI 310 Genetic Analyzer uses virtual filters to collect the light striking the CCD camera at particular wavelength intervals after the emitted light has gone through the optical path illustrated in Figure 6.6.

D.N.A. BOX 6.2

FLUORESCENCE

Fluorescence measurements involve exciting a dye molecule and then detecting the light that is emitted from the excited dye. A molecule that is capable of fluorescence is called a *fluorophore*. Fluorophores come in a variety of shapes, sizes, and abilities. The ones that are primarily used in DNA labeling are dyes that fluoresce in the visible region of the spectrum, which consists of light emitted in the range of approximately 400 nm to 600 nm.

The fluorescence process is shown in the figure to the right. In the first step, a photon ($h\nu_{ex}$) from a laser source excites a fluorophore electron from its ground energy state (S_0) to an excited transition state (S'_1). This electron then undergoes conformational changes and interacts with its environment resulting in the relaxed singlet excitation state (S_1). During the final step of the process, a photon ($h\nu_{em}$) is emitted at a lower energy when the excited electron falls back to its ground state. Because energy and wavelength are inversely related to one another, the emission photon has a longer wavelength than the excitation photon.

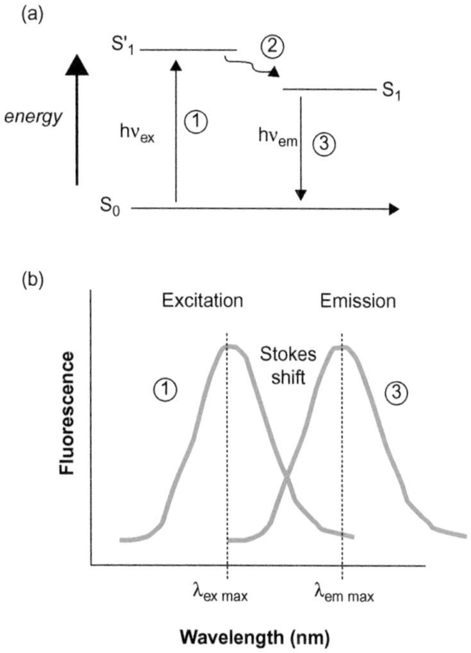

The difference between the apex of the absorption and emission spectra is called the *Stokes shift*. This shift permits the use of optical filters to separate excitation light from emission light. Fluorophores have characteristic light absorption and emission patterns that are based upon their chemical structure and the environmental conditions. With careful selection and optical filters, fluorophores may be chosen with emission spectra that are resolvable from one another. This capability permits the use of multiple fluorophores to measure several different DNA molecules simultaneously. The rate at which samples can be processed is much greater with multiple fluorophores than measurements involving a single fluorophore.

There are a number of factors that affect how well a fluorophore will emit light, or fluoresce. These factors include the following:

- Molar extinction coefficient: the ability of a dye to absorb light;
- Quantum yield: the efficiency with which the excited fluorophore converts absorbed light to emitted light;
- Photo stability: the ability of a dye to undergo repeated cycles of excitation and emission without being destroyed in the excited state, or experiencing "photobleaching,' and;

D.N.A. BOX 6.2 (*cont'd*)

- Dye environment: factors that affect fluorescent yield include pH, temperature, solvent, and the presence of quenchers, such as hemoglobin.

The overall fluorescence efficiency of a dye molecule depends on a combination of these four factors.

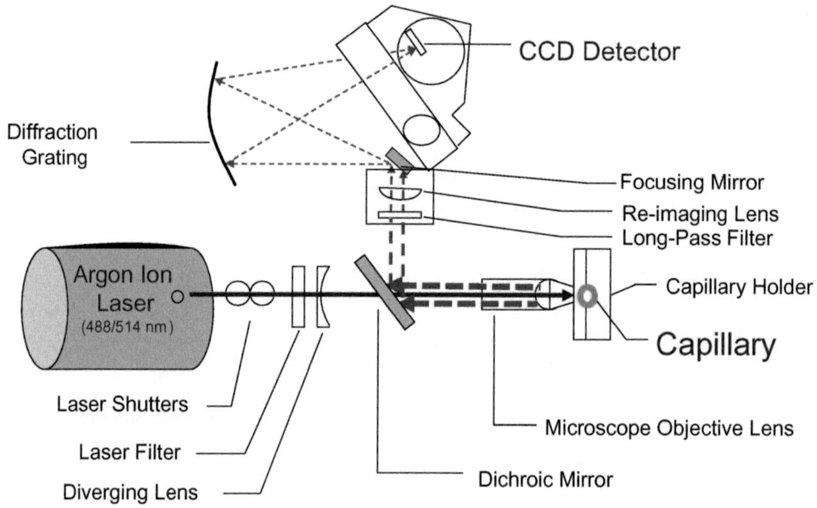

FIGURE 6.6 Optics in an ABI 310 Genetic Analyzer. Argon ion laser with 488 nm and 514.5 nm light (blue line) excites fluorophores passing through the capillary (green circle). Emitted light is projected through lenses, mirrors, and filters to a diffraction grating that spreads the wavelengths of light and then to a charged-coupled device (CCD) detector that simultaneously detects all wavelengths from 525 nm to 680 nm. Image adapted from Watts (1998). Figure courtesy of Bruce McCord, Florida International University.

Light from the argon ion laser passes through the laser filter, which removes low-intensity sidebands and other broadband spontaneous emission. Light is then focused by the diverging lens onto the dichroic mirror. The dichroic mirror is used to separate excitation and emission light paths. The beam then passes through the microscope objective to the sample. The emitted light is then reflected by the dichroic mirror onto a re-imaging lens after it passes through a long-pass filter.

The long-pass filter prevents light from the argon ion laser from interfering with the detection of the dye signals. Light is then directed onto a spectrograph where a diffraction grating disperses the light by wavelength and focuses the resulting spectrum onto a CCD array (Figure 6.6).

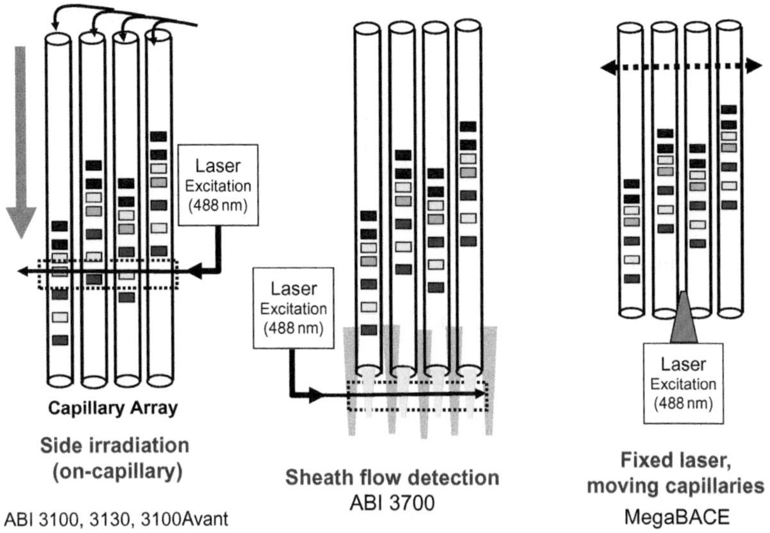

FIGURE 6.7 Different strategies for fluorescence excitation and detection with capillary array systems. The excitation beam is actually split and brought into both sides of the array with the 3100 and other ABI Genetic Analyzers.

With a single-capillary system like the ABI 310, the laser light can be trained continuously on the capillary enabling fluorescence excitation for any fluorophore passing the detector. However, with capillary array systems the laser light must illuminate multiple capillaries. Three approaches with capillary arrays have been utilized (Figure 6.7): on-capillary side irradiation, off-capillary sheath flow, and moving capillaries. The on-capillary side irradiation is used by the ABI 3100 and more recent capillary array systems from Applied Biosystems.

Fluorescent Dyes and Emission Filter Sets

Dye-labeled PCR primers label only a single strand of a PCR product. This simplifies data interpretation because the complementary DNA strand is not visible to the detector. In addition, dye-labeled primers enable multiple PCR products to be labeled simultaneously in an independent fashion thus increasing throughput capabilities because amplicons of overlapping size can be distinguished from one another by their dye label.

Figure 6.8a illustrates the range of fluorescence emission spectra for the different dyes commonly used to label PCR products in STR typing kits. The positions of light collected using several common virtual filters in the ABI 310 are noted in Figure 6.8b. The correct filter needs to be selected to match the fluorescent dye combinations in use in order to maximize sensitivity.

Spectral Calibration

In order for the computer software that is used for data analysis to know with what dye color a detected DNA fragment is labeled, the instrument detector and data collection

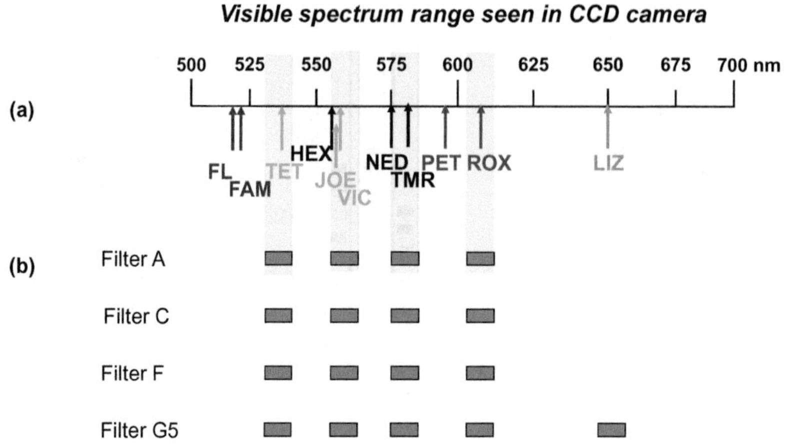

FIGURE 6.8 (a) Commonly used fluorescent dyes in STR typing kits shown by color with their spectral emission maxima (arrows). (b) Virtual filter sets used in the ABI 310 determine from which regions of the CCD camera visible light is collected for data interpretation.

software need to be calibrated. A multi-component spectral calibration is performed by testing a standard set of DNA fragments labeled with each individual dye, known as matrix standard samples. The term "matrix" comes from the use of multiple equations (e.g., samples labeled with a single dye) being used to solve multiple unknowns (e.g., the amount of fluorescent signal contribution from each dye color in other dye color channels) in the form of a mathematical matrix (e.g., 4×4 with four dye colors).

Computer software provided with the CE instrument then analyzes the data from each of the dyes and creates a matrix or spectral calibration file to reflect the color overlap between the various fluorescent dyes. These matrix files are a summary or template of how much overlap one should expect to see just by virtue of the dyes themselves given a particular instrument and environmental conditions. The difference between these matrix values and what is actually observed in the raw data becomes part of the data set.

Spectral calibration is unique to each instrument due to small variations in the laser and detector employed and other environmental conditions. This calibration needs to be performed on a regular basis as instrument and environmental conditions, such as laser excitation power, temperature, and solution pH, can drift over time and impact the fluorescence intensity of the dyes. A spectral calibration should be performed anytime a new laser or detector is installed. As long as the electrophoresis conditions are constant from run to run, then the emission spectra of the dyes should be reproducible and spectral overlap can be accurately deciphered.

If the matrix color deconvolution does not work properly to separate spectral overlap of the dyes used for STR allele detection, then the baseline analytical signal from the instrument can be uneven or a phenomenon known as "pull-up" can occur. *Pull-up* is the result of a color bleeding from one spectral channel into another, usually because of off-scale peaks.

The most common occurrence of pull-up involves small green peaks showing up under blue peaks when the blue peaks are several thousand RFUs (relative fluorescence units)

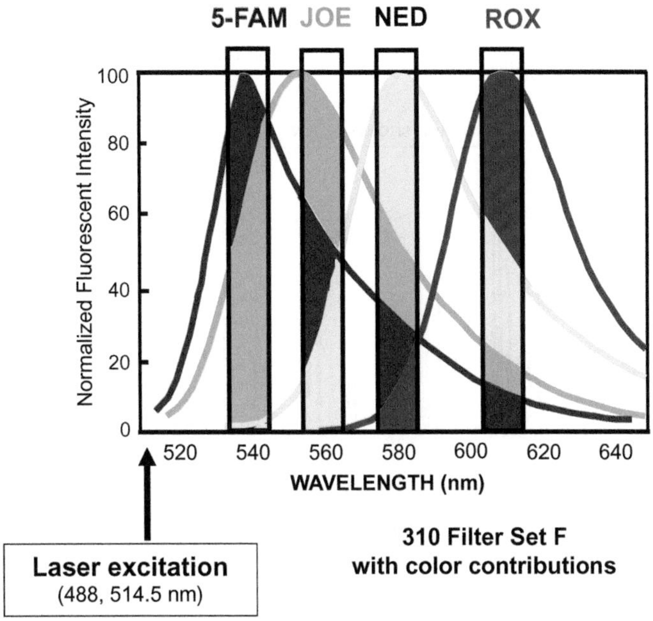

FIGURE 6.9 Fluorescent emission spectra of ABI dyes used with AmpFlSTR kits. ABI 310 Filter Set F is represented by the 4 boxes centered on each of the 4 dye spectra. Each dye filter contains color contributions from adjacent overlapping dyes that must be removed by a matrix deconvolution. The dyes are excited by an argon ion laser, which emits light at 488 and 514.5 nm.

in signal or off-scale. This occurs because of the significant overlap of the blue and green dyes seen in Figure 6.9. Samples can be diluted and analyzed again to reduce or eliminate the offending pull-up peak(s). Pull-up, also known as "bleed-through," is discussed in more detail the forthcoming *Advanced Topics in Forensic DNA: Interpretation* as it relates to data interpretation.

Raw data from a fluorescently labeled DNA sample is compared to the color-separated processed data in Figure 6.10. DNA fragments labeled with the yellow dye are commonly shown in black to make the display more visible.

The multi-capillary ABI 3100 series instruments automatically apply a spectral calibration to the CE separated fluorescence data as it is being collected so that there is no "raw data" generated by these instruments. Thus, if the color separation is not working properly, then new spectral calibration standards will have to be run and the previously poor performing samples (i.e., those exhibiting excessive pull-up) will have to be re-injected in order to obtain higher quality data.

Adjusting Dye Sensitivities with Variable Binning

Since not all of the dyes are equally sensitive when excited with a single laser wavelength, electronic signal enhancement has been used with newer versions of software to strengthen the weaker signals. ABI 3100 Data Collection software following the original v1.0.1 release

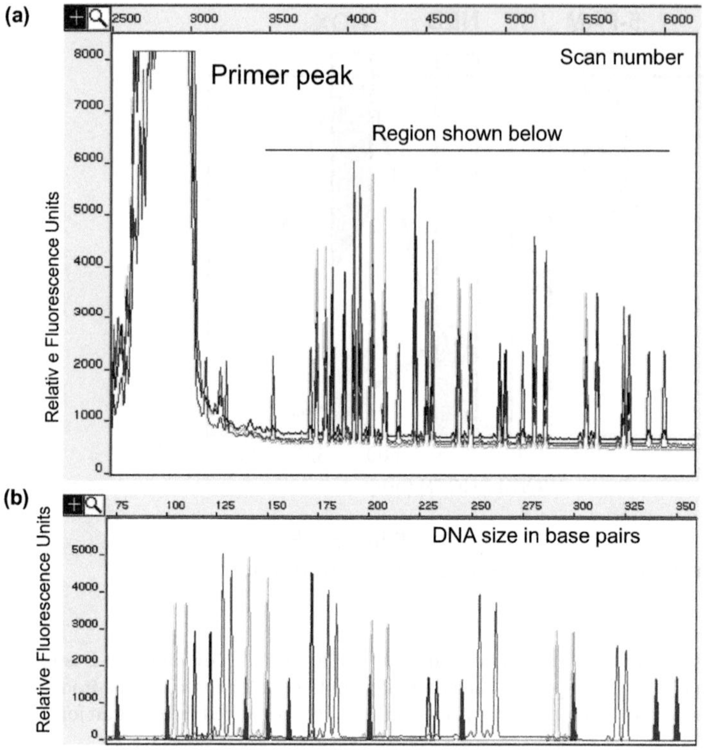

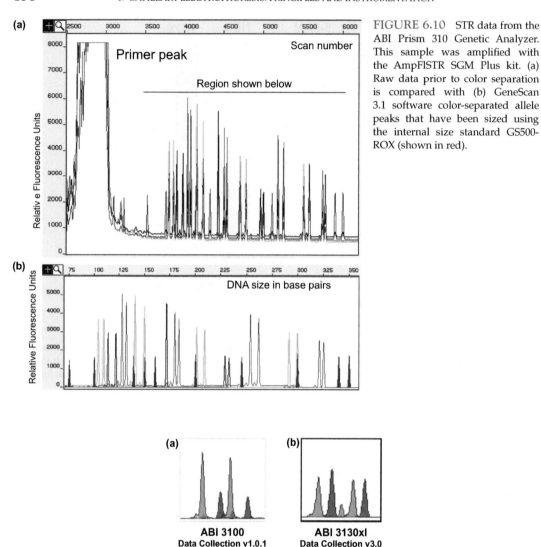

FIGURE 6.10 STR data from the ABI Prism 310 Genetic Analyzer. This sample was amplified with the AmpFlSTR SGM Plus kit. (a) Raw data prior to color separation is compared with (b) GeneScan 3.1 software color-separated allele peaks that have been sized using the internal size standard GS500-ROX (shown in red).

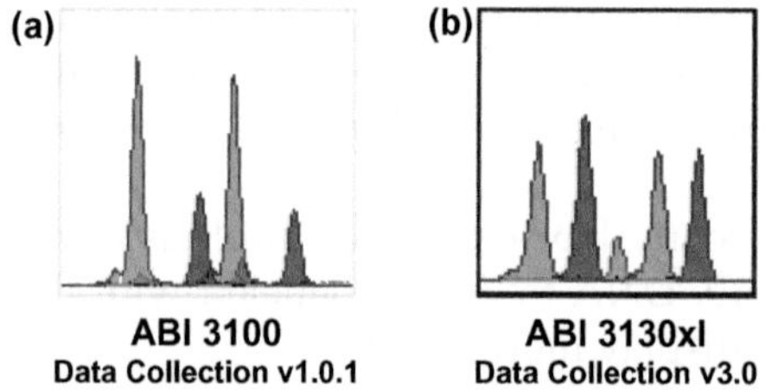

FIGURE 6.11 The same PCR products examined with different data collection versions. In (a) there is an equal number of pixels of light collected from the CCD camera for the blue-labeled and red-labeled peaks. In (b) the signal increase in the red dye-labeled PCR products is accomplished with "variable binning" where more pixels of light are collected from the CCD camera in the red channel to help balance the less sensitive red dye with blue dye-labeled amplicons.

(including versions 1.1, 2.0, and 3.0) tweak the red-color channels to balance the signal for 5-dye chemistry kits such as Identifiler (Figure 6.11). The technique is referred to as "variable binning" and involves collecting more light from the CCD camera with weaker dyes to help balance the overall signal output.

INSTRUMENTATION

A number of DNA separation and fluorescence detection platforms exist and have been used for STR allele determination (see Table 9.1 from the *Fundamentals* volume, Butler 2010). In the mid-to-late 1990s when STR typing first started, the gel-based ABI 373 and 377 instruments were the instrumental workhorses for both DNA typing and DNA sequencing (see Table 6.1).

Since the introduction of the single capillary ABI 310 in 1995 and a subsequent series of capillary array instruments including the ABI 3130xl, CE has now replaced slab gel systems throughout the forensic DNA community. CE systems are easy to use, automate data collection, and reduce labor compared to the early gel electrophoresis systems. With CE a set of samples are loaded into an instrument along with other reagents and the operator can walk away after starting the computerized data collection. There is no more need to clean gel plates, prepare polyacrylamide gels, or carefully load samples onto a gel with millimeter tolerances.

Overview of Sample Processing Steps

As has been described throughout this chapter, the single-capillary ABI 310 and multi-capillary CE systems perform DNA separations with multiple-color fluorescence detection and provide the capability of unattended operation. An operator prepares a batch of samples and then loads them in the instrument "autosampler," enters the name and well position in the autosampler tray for each sample into the data collection software, places a capillary and a syringe full of polymer solution in the instrument (or capillary array and bottle of polymer solution in the case of the ABI 3130xl), and starts the "run."

For the ABI 310, the data are serially processed at the rate of approximately one sample every 30 minutes of operation. Run times are usually slightly longer with the ABI 3100 or 3130 instruments (e.g., 35 to 45 minutes) but with the advantage of being able to collect information on either 4 or 16 samples simultaneously, depending on the number of capillaries present in the array. A major advantage of the technique for forensic laboratories is that the DNA sample is not fully consumed and may be retested if need be. In many cases, retesting is as simple as reinjecting the already prepared DNA samples.

The ABI Prism 310 Genetic Analyzer

Figure 6.12 shows the inside of an ABI 310 Genetic Analyzer. A single capillary is located between the gel block and the inlet electrode. The capillary is filled with polymer solution through the gel block. A heat plate is used to raise the temperature of the capillary to a specified temperature. Samples are placed in an autosampler tray that moves up and down to insert the sample onto the capillary and electrode for the injection process.

ABI 3100 and ABI 3130xl Instruments

The multi-capillary ABI 3100 Genetic Analyzer became available in 2000 and enabled higher throughputs compared to the single-capillary ABI 310 instrument. The 3130xl

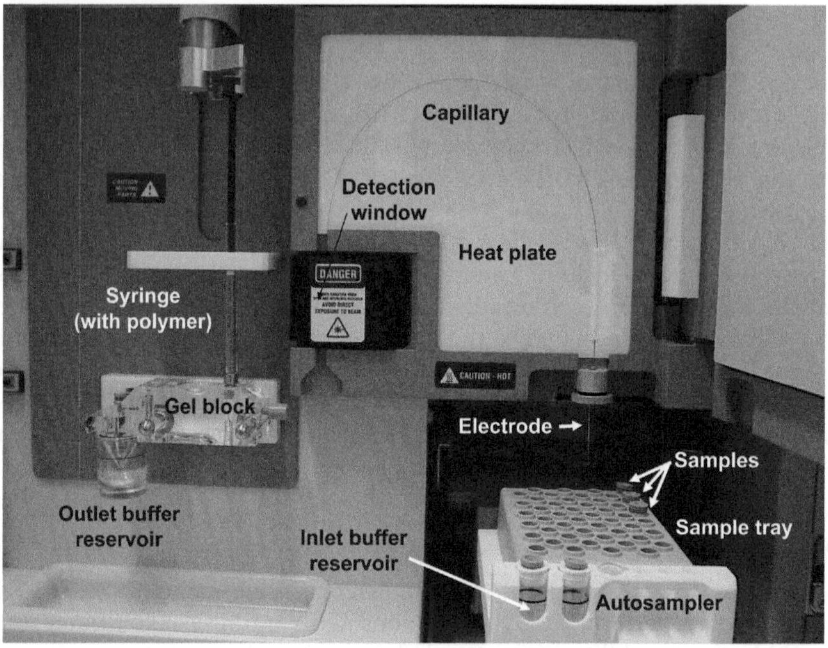

FIGURE 6.12 Photograph of ABI Prism 310 Genetic Analyzer with a single capillary.

16-capillary instrument became available in 2003 (Table 6.1). A photo of a capillary array as it appears inside the ABI 3130xl instrument is shown in Figure 6.13. The primary difference between the 3100 and 3130xl instruments is the use of a mechanical pump to fill the capillaries with polymer rather than a syringe as in the ABI 3100 (Figure 6.14).

Both 96-well and 384-well plates of samples may be processed in an ABI 3100 or 3130xl. With each run taking roughly 45 minutes, a 96-well plate can be analyzed in approximately five hours with six injections containing 16 samples each. Injections occur onto all 16 capillaries at once so if a user does not have 16 samples (2 columns of 8 samples in a 96-well plate), then formamide is put in the empty wells to prevent "dry" injections that can shorten the life of the capillaries.

An important difference between the ABI 310 and 3100 is that spatial and spectral calibrations are required prior to collecting data on the ABI 3100. The spatial calibration enables the CCD detector to know the location of each capillary while spectral calibration enables the dye colors to be resolved from one another.

Precision studies conducted on the ABI 3100 (Sgueglia et al. 2003, Butler et al. 2004) and the ABI 3700 (Gill et al. 2001) have demonstrated that reliable results can be obtained with multi-capillary CE systems.

ABI PRISM 3500 and 3500xl Genetic Analyzers

The ABI 3500 instrument (Figure 6.15) is available in 8 capillary (3500) or 24 capillary (3500xl) formats. This latest generation of CE instruments has several new features

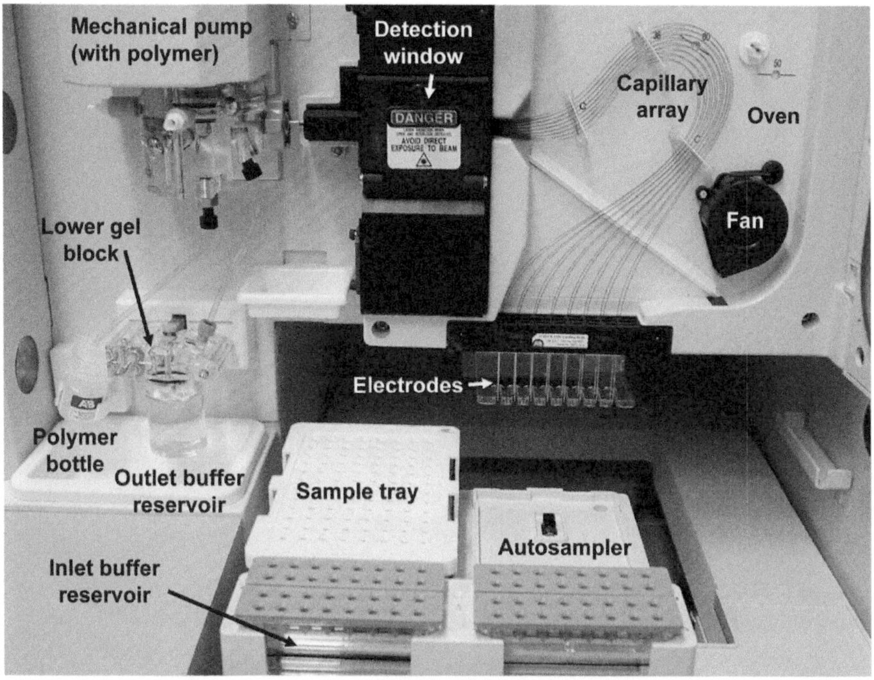

FIGURE 6.13 Photograph of ABI 3130xl Genetic Analyzer with a 16-capillary array.

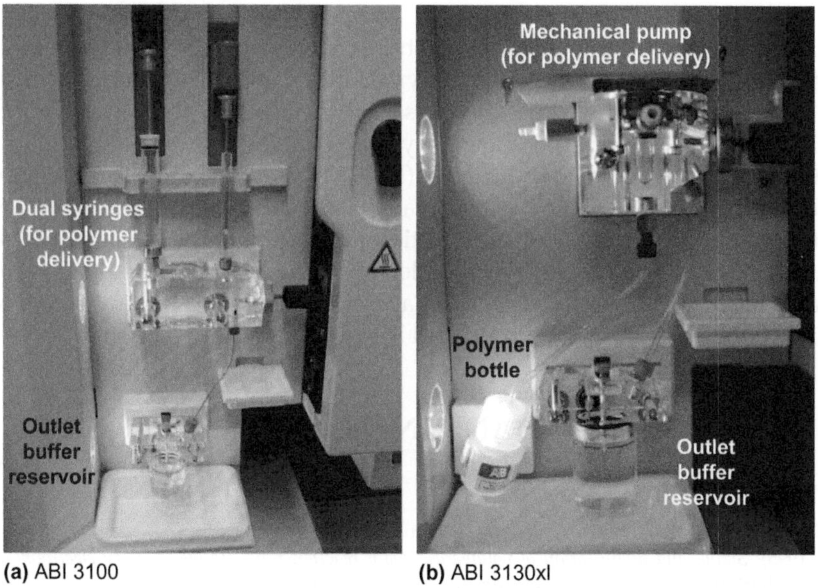

FIGURE 6.14 (a) ABI 3100 syringe used to fill 16-capillary array. (b) ABI 3130xl mechanical pump used for polymer delivery from bottle.

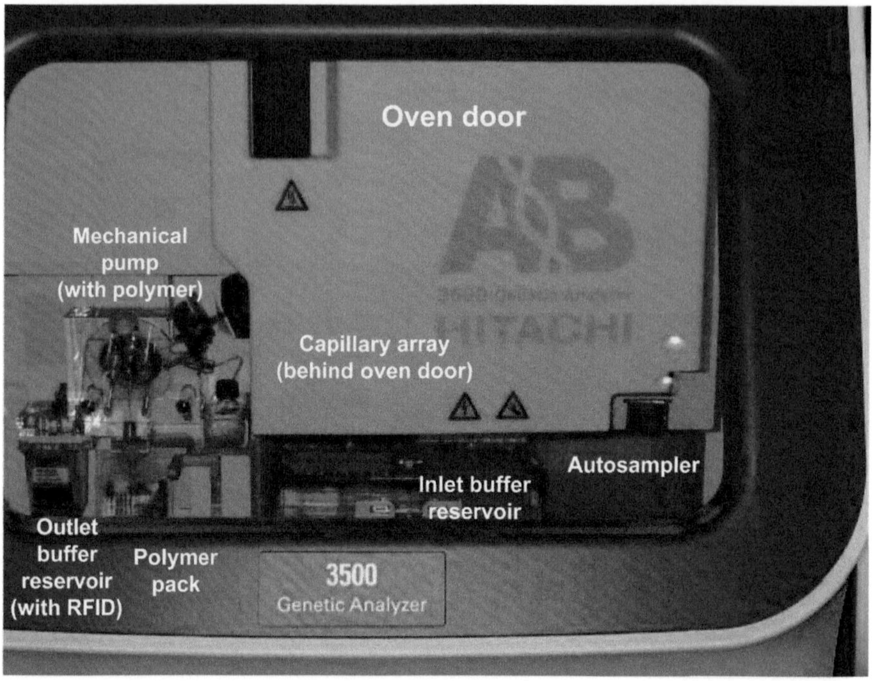

FIGURE 6.15 Photograph of ABI 3500 Genetic Analyzer (8-capillary array not shown).

including a smaller area for the array with better seals for more consistent temperature control, an improved mechanical pump for polymer filling of the capillaries with less waste, new laser technology (a solid state laser instead of an argon ion laser), reduced power requirements (110 V instead of 220 V), and 6-dye detection capability.

In addition, radio frequency identification (RFID) tags are used for tracking consumables (polymer, buffer, and capillaries) which are made available in ready-to-use formats to enable easier switching of reagents. The data collection software includes quality control features for rapid identification and re-injection of failed samples. With the use of a specific internal size standard (LIZ-600 v2), peak height normalization is possible leading to improved peak height uniformity across capillaries, runs, and instruments within a laboratory.

READING LIST AND INTERNET RESOURCES

Capillary Electrophoresis

Amplified DNA product separation. <http://dna.gov/training/separation/>.

Butler, J. M. (1995). *Sizing and quantitation of polymerase chain reaction products by capillary electrophoresis for use in DNA typing*. Charlottesville: University of Virginia. PhD dissertation.

Butler, J. M., et al. (2004). Forensic DNA typing by capillary electrophoresis using the ABI Prism 310 and 3100 genetic analyzers for STR analysis. *Electrophoresis, 25*, 1397–1412.

Butler, J. M. (2010). *Fundamentals of forensic DNA typing*. San Diego: Elsevier Academic Press. (See Chapter 9, Fundamentals of DNA separation and detection, pp. 175–203.)

McCord, B. R. (2003). Troubleshooting capillary electrophoresis systems. *Profiles in DNA, 6*(2), 10–12. Available at: <http://www.promega.com/profiles/>.

Rosenblum, B. B., et al. (1997). Improved single-strand DNA sizing accuracy in capillary electrophoresis. *Nucleic Acids Research, 25*, 3925–3929.

Wenz, H. M., et al. (1998). High-precision genotyping by denaturing capillary electrophoresis. *Genome Research, 8*, 69–80.

Electrokinetic Injection

Butler, J. M. (1997). Effects of sample matrix and injection on DNA separations. In C. Heller (Ed.), *Analysis of nucleic acids by capillary electrophoresis* (Chapter 5, pp. 125–134). Germany: Viewig.

Rose, D. J., & Jorgenson, J. W. (1988). Characterization and automation of sample introduction methods for capillary zone electrophoresis. *Analytical Chemistry, 60*, 642–648.

Sample Preparation

Amresco formamide. <http://www.amresco-inc.com/>.

Biega, L. A., & Duceman, B. W. (1999). Substitution of H_2O for formamide in the sample preparation protocol for STR analysis using the capillary electrophoresis system: the effects on precision, resolution, and capillary life. *Journal of Forensic Sciences, 44*, 1029–1031.

Hi-Di formamide. <http://www.appliedbiosystems.com>.

Janssen, L., et al. (2009). Increased sensitivity for amplified STR alleles on capillary sequencers with BigDye XTerminator. *Forensic Science International: Genetics Supplement Series, 2*, 123–124.

DNA Separation

Buel, E., et al. (2003). Using resolution calculations to assess changes in capillary electrophoresis run parameters. *Journal of Forensic Sciences, 48*, 77–79.

Hartzell, B., et al. (2003). Response of short tandem repeat systems to temperature and sizing methods. *Forensic Science International, 133*, 228–234.

Hjertén, S. (1985). High-performance electrophoresis: Elimination of electroendosmosis and solute adsorption. *Journal of Chromatography, 347*, 191–198.

Klein, S. B., et al. (2003). Addressing ambient temperature variant effects on sizing precision of AmpFlSTR Profiler Plus alleles detected on the ABI Prism 310 Genetic Analyzer. *Forensic Science Communications, 5*(1). Available at <http://www.fbi.gov/about-us/lab/forensic-science-communications/>.

Nock, T., et al. (2001). Temperature and pH studies of short tandem repeat systems using capillary electrophoresis at elevated pH. *Electrophoresis, 22*, 755–762.

DNA Separation Mechanisms

Barron, A. E., & Blanch, H. W. (1995). DNA separations by slab gel and capillary electrophoresis. *Separation and Purification Methods, 24*, 1–118.

Grossman, P. D. (1992). Capillary electrophoresis in entangled polymer solutions. In P. D. Grossman & J. C. Colburn (Eds.), *Capillary electrophoresis: Theory and practice* (pp. 215–233). San Diego: Academic Press.

Ogston, A. G. (1958). The spaces in a uniform random suspension of fibres. *Transactions of the Faraday Society, 54*, 1754–1757.

Slater, G. W., et al. (2000). Theory of DNA electrophoresis: A look at some current challenges. *Electrophoresis, 21*, 3873–3887.

Viovy, J.-L., & Duke, T. (1993). DNA electrophoresis in polymer solutions: Ogston sieving, reptation and constraint release. *Electrophoresis, 14*, 322–329.

Polymer

Bienvenue, J. M., et al. (2005). Evaluation of sieving polymers for fast, reproducible electrophoretic analysis of short tandem repeats (STR) in capillaries. *Journal of Forensic Sciences, 50*(4), 842–848.

Boulos, S., et al. (2008). Development of an entangled polymer solution for improved resolution in DNA typing by CE. *Electrophoresis, 29*, 4695–4703.

Madabhushi, R. S., et al. (1996). Polymers for separation of biomolecules by capillary electrophoresis. U.S. Patent 5,552,028.

Madabhushi, R. S. (1998). Separation of 4-color DNA sequencing extension products in noncovalently coated capillaries using low viscosity polymer solutions. *Electrophoresis, 19*, 224–230.

Madabhushi, R. (2001). DNA sequencing in noncovalently coated capillaries using low viscosity polymer solutions. *Methods in Molecular Biology, 163*, 309–315.

Fluorescence Detection

Mansfield, E. S., & Kronick, M. N. (1993). Alternative labeling techniques for automated fluorescence based analysis of PCR products. *BioTechniques, 15*, 274–279.

Singer, V. L., & Johnson, I. D. (1997). Fluorophore characteristics: Making intelligent choices in application-specific dye selection: *Proceedings of the eighth international symposium on human identification* (pp. 70–77). Madison, Wisconsin: Promega Corporation.

Watts, D. (1998). Genotyping STR loci using an automated DNA sequencer. In P. J. Lincoln & J. Thomson (Eds.), *Forensic DNA profiling protocols* (pp. 193–208). Totowa, NJ: Humana Press.

Zipper, H., et al. (2004). Investigations on DNA intercalation and surface binding by SYBR Green I: Its structure determination and methodological implications. *Nucleic Acids Research, 32*, e103.

Energy Transfer Dyes

Ju, J., et al. (1995). Design and synthesis of fluorescence energy transfer dye-labeled primers and their application for DNA sequencing and analysis. *Analytical Biochemistry, 231*, 131–140.

Ju, J. Y., et al. (1996). Energy transfer primers: A new fluorescence labeling paradigm for DNA sequencing and analysis. *Nature Medicine, 2*, 246–249.

Rosenblum, B. B., et al. (1997). New dye-labeled terminators for improved DNA sequencing patterns. *Nucleic Acids Research, 25*, 4500–4504.

Yeung, S. H. I., et al. (2008). Fluorescence energy transfer-labeled primers for high-performance forensic DNA profiling. *Electrophoresis, 29*, 2251–2259.

Instrumentation

Early CE Work with STR Typing

Butler, J. M., et al. (1994). Rapid analysis of the short tandem repeat HUMTH01 by capillary electrophoresis. *BioTechniques, 17*, 1062–1070.

Butler, J. M., et al. (1995). Application of dual internal standards for precise sizing of polymerase chain reaction products using capillary electrophoresis. *Electrophoresis, 16*, 974–980.

Early Capillary Array Systems

Gill, P., et al. (2001). Sizing short tandem repeat alleles in capillary array gel electrophoresis instruments. *Electrophoresis, 22*, 2670–2678.

Mansfield, E. S., et al. (1996). Sensitivity, reproducibility, and accuracy in short tandem repeat genotyping using capillary array electrophoresis. *Genome Research, 6*, 893–903.

Wang, Y., et al. (1995). Rapid sizing of short tandem repeat alleles using capillary array electrophoresis and energy-transfer fluorescent primers. *Analytical Chemistry, 67*, 1197–1203.

ABI 373 and 377

Frazier, R. R. E., et al. (1996). Validation of the Applied Biosystems Prism™ 377 automated sequencer for forensic short tandem repeat analysis. *Electrophoresis, 17*, 1550–1552.

Frégeau, C. J., et al. (1999). Validation of highly polymorphic fluorescent multiplex short tandem repeat systems using two generations of DNA sequencers. *Journal of Forensic Sciences, 44*, 133–166.

ABI Prism 310 Genetic Analyzer

Buel, E., et al. (1998). Capillary electrophoresis STR analysis: Comparison to gel-based systems. *Journal of Forensic Sciences, 43*, 164–170.

Isenberg, A. R., et al. (1998). Analysis of two multiplexed short tandem repeat systems using capillary electrophoresis with multiwavelength florescence detection. *Electrophoresis, 19*, 94–100.

Lazaruk, K., et al. (1998). Genotyping of forensic short tandem repeat (STR) systems based on sizing precision in a capillary electrophoresis instrument. *Electrophoresis, 19*, 86–93.

Moretti, T. R., et al. (2001). Validation of short tandem repeats (STRs) for forensic usage: Performance testing of fluorescent multiplex STR systems and analysis of authentic and simulated forensic samples. *Journal of Forensic Sciences, 46*, 647–660.

Moretti, T. R., et al. (2001). Validation of STR typing by capillary electrophoresis. *Journal of Forensic Sciences, 46*, 661–676.

Shewale, J. G., et al. (2000). Detection and correction of a migration anomaly on a 310 genetic analyzer. *Journal of Forensic Sciences, 45*, 1339–1342.

ABI 3100

Bardill, S. C., et al. (2006). Validation and evaluation of the ABI 3100 genetic analyser for use with STR analysis of buccal swabs—report of erroneous SGM Plus profiles caused by poor spectral calibration. *Progress in Forensic Genetics 11, ICS 1288*, 507–509.

Koumi, P., et al. (2004). Evaluation and validation of the ABI 3700, ABI 3100, and the MegaBACE 1000 capillary array electrophoresis instruments for use with short tandem repeat microsatellite typing in a forensic environment. *Electrophoresis, 25*, 2227–2241.

Sgueglia, J. B., et al. (2003). Precision studies using the ABI prism 3100 genetic analyzer for forensic DNA analysis. *Analytical and Bioanalytical Chemistry, 376*, 1247–1254.

Stewart, J. E., et al. (2003). Evaluation of a multicapillary electrophoresis instrument for mitochondrial DNA typing. *Journal of Forensic Sciences, 48*, 571–580.

ABI 3500

Applied Biosystems (2009). *Applied Biosystems 3500/3500xL Genetic Analyzer User Guide*. Foster City, CA: Life Technologies.

Hill, C. R., & Butler, J. M. (2010). *ABI 3500 studies*. Presentation given December 7, 2010. Available at <http://www.cstl.nist.gov/strbase/pub_pres/ForensicsNIST-ABI3500.pdf>.

CHAPTER

7

Quality Assurance and Validation

IMPORTANCE OF QUALITY ASSURANCE

Any scientific test that results in information that may lead to the loss of liberty of an individual accused of a crime needs to be performed with utmost care. DNA typing is no exception. It is a multi-step, technical process that needs to be performed by qualified and effectively trained personnel to ensure that accurate results are obtained and interpreted correctly. When the process is conducted properly, DNA testing is an effective investigative tool for the law enforcement community with results that stand up to legal scrutiny in court. When laboratories have not followed validated protocols or have not had adequately trained personnel, problems have arisen in the past.

Two topics are commonly referred to when discussing the importance of maintaining good laboratory practices to obtain accurate scientific results: quality assurance and quality control. *Quality assurance* (QA) refers to those planned or systematic actions necessary to provide adequate confidence that a product or service will satisfy given requirements for quality. *Quality control* (QC), on the other hand, usually refers to the day-to-day operational techniques and the activities used to fulfill requirements of quality.

Thus, an organization plans QA measures and performs QC activities in the laboratory. The forensic DNA community has long recognized the importance of quality results and, since early in the development of forensic DNA technology, has established organizations to recommend and oversee quality assurance guidelines and quality control measures.

Organizations Involved

A number of organizations exist around the world that work on a local, national, or international level to aid in quality assurance work and to ensure that DNA testing is performed properly. The organizations are made up primarily of working scientists who want to coordinate their efforts to benefit the DNA typing community as a whole.

The *International Society of Forensic Genetics* (ISFG), which was founded in 1968 and formerly known as the International Society of Forensic Haemogenetics (ISFH), today represents a group of approximately 1100 scientists from more than 60 countries. Meetings are held biannually to discuss the latest topics in forensic genetics. Conference volumes were originally published under the title "Advances in Forensic Haemogenetics" and are now titled "Progress in Forensic Genetics." The 2007 ISFG meeting proceedings (*Progress in Forensic Genetics 12*) and 2009 ISFG meeting proceedings (*Progress in Forensic Genetics 13*) were published online as part of the *Forensic Science International: Genetics Supplement Series* (http://www.fsigeneticssup.com/).

Every few years, as a specific need arises, a *DNA Commission of the ISFG* is formed and makes recommendations on the use of genetic markers. These publications are available at http://www.isfg.org/Publications/DNA+Commission and include the following topics (with their publication year): DNA polymorphisms (1989), PCR-based polymorphisms (1992), naming variant STR alleles (1994), STR repeat nomenclature (1997), mitochondrial DNA (2000), Y-STR use in forensic analysis (2001), additional information on Y-STRs including nomenclature (2006), mixture interpretation (2006), disaster victim identification (2007), biostatistics for paternity testing (2008), and non-human (animal) DNA testing (2011). For additional information on ISFG, visit its website: http://www.isfg.org.

The *International Organization for Standardization* (ISO) issues guidance documents on a variety of topics. ISO 17025:2005 entitled "General requirements for the competence of testing and calibration laboratories" is the standard to which many DNA testing laboratories seek to be accredited by accrediting organizations, such as ASCLD/LAB or FQS-I (see below). For more information on ISO, see http://www.iso.org.

The *Technical Working Group on DNA Analysis Methods* (TWGDAM) was established in November 1988 under FBI Laboratory sponsorship to aid forensic DNA scientists throughout North America. Since 1998, TWGDAM has been known as SWGDAM, which stands for the *Scientific Working Group on DNA Analysis Methods*. SWGDAM is a group of approximately 50 scientists representing federal, state, and local forensic DNA laboratories in the United States and Canada. Meetings are held twice a year, usually in January and July. Public meetings have also been held in conjunction with scientific meetings such as the International Symposium on Human Identification, sponsored each fall by the Promega Corporation. Since 2006 a public SWGDAM meeting has been held as part of the FBI-sponsored National CODIS Conference.

Over the past two decades, five individuals have served as TWGDAM or SWGDAM chairmen: James Kearney (FBI), Bruce Budowle (FBI), Richard Guerrieri (FBI), David Coffman (Florida Department of Law Enforcement), and Ted Staples (Georgia Bureau of Investigation). In January 2011, Tony Onorato (FBI) was appointed by the FBI Laboratory Director to be the chair of SWGDAM.

Over the years, a number of TWGDAM or SWGDAM subcommittees have operated to bring recommendations before the entire group. These subcommittees have included (at different times): restriction fragment length polymorphism (RFLP), polymerase chain reaction (PCR), Combined DNA Index System (CODIS), mitochondrial DNA, short tandem repeat (STR) interpretation, training, validation, Y-chromosome, expert systems, quality assurance, missing persons/mass disasters, mixture interpretation, mass spectrometry, enhanced method detection and interpretation, and rapid DNA analysis. TWGDAM issued guidelines for quality assurance in DNA analysis in 1989, 1991, and 1995. Revised SWGDAM validation guidelines were published in 2004 (these will be discussed in more detail later in the chapter). Several ad hoc subcommittees have produced recommendations on such topics as review of outsourced data and handling partial matches. The reference list contains all published SWGDAM guidelines as of early 2011.

The *DNA Advisory Board* (DAB) was a congressionally mandated organization that was created and funded by the United States Congress DNA Identification Act of 1994. The first meeting of the DAB was held on May 12, 1995 and chaired by Nobel laureate Dr. Joshua Lederberg. The DAB consisted of 13 voting members that included scientists from state, local, and private forensic laboratories; molecular geneticists and population geneticists not affiliated with a forensic laboratory; a representative from the National Institute of Standards and Technology (NIST); the chair of TWGDAM; and a judge.

The original members of the DAB included Joshua Lederberg (Rockefeller University), Arthur Eisenberg (University of North Texas Health Science Center), Shirley Abrahamson (Wisconsin State Supreme Court), Jack Ballantyne (Suffolk County Crime Lab), Bruce Budowle (FBI Laboratory), Ranajit Chakraborty (University of Texas Health Science Center), Bernard Devlin (Carnegie Mellon University), Marcia Eisenberg (Laboratory Corporation of America), Paul Ferrara (Virginia Division of Forensic Science), John Hicks (Alabama Department of Forensic Sciences), Margaret Kuo (Orange County Sheriff's Office), Terry Laber (Minnesota Bureau of Criminal Apprehension), and Dennis Reeder (NIST). A number of other individuals attended and participated in various DAB meetings over the five years that the group met.

The DAB was created for a five-year period to issue standards for the forensic DNA community. When the DAB's responsibilities ended in 2000, SWGDAM was designated as the group responsible for offering recommendations to the forensic community within the United States. In 2007 SWGDAM revised the Quality Assurance Standards for Forensic Caseworking Laboratories and the Quality Assurance Standards for DNA Databasing Laboratories. These revised standards went into effect July 1, 2009 after being approved by the FBI Laboratory Director. Further revisions regarding data review were made at the January 2011 SWGDAM meeting.

The *American Society of Crime Laboratory Directors* (ASCLD) and its Laboratory Accreditation Board (ASCLD/LAB) play an important role in the United States as well as internationally for laboratory accreditation programs. The ASCLD/LAB motto is "quality assurance through inspection." The Crime Laboratory Accreditation Program is a voluntary program in which any crime laboratory may participate to demonstrate that its management, operations, personnel, procedures, and instruments meet stringent standards. The goal of accreditation is to improve the overall service of forensic laboratories to the criminal justice system. If a forensic laboratory is interested in becoming accredited, an ASCLD/LAB Accreditation Manual is available from the Executive Secretary for a fee. Laboratories becoming accredited in forensic biology are audited against the FBI's Quality Assurance Standards for the laboratory operations pertaining to DNA testing. ASCLD/LAB accreditation may be under the Legacy Program or the International Program. However, no new Legacy Program applications have been processed since April 2009. Laboratories are being supported under the Legacy Program until they can transition to ASCLD/LAB-*International*, which accredits to ISO/IEC 17025 requirements. As of December 2010, a total of 388 crime laboratories were accredited by ASCLD/LAB although not all of them are doing DNA testing. For additional information on ASCLD/LAB, visit its website: http://www.ascld-lab.org.

Forensic Quality Services (FQS) and *Forensic Quality Services – International* (FQS-I) are not-for-profit organizations established in 2003 by the National Forensic Science Technology Center (NFSTC), which is located in Largo, FL. FQS-I accredits forensic laboratories to ISO 17025. As of December 2010, a total of 52 labs were accredited by FQS-I. For additional information on FQS and FQS-I, visit their website: http://www.forquality.org.

The *American Association of Blood Banks* (AABB) sets standards for laboratories performing DNA parentage or relationship testing. AABB provides accreditation for paternity testing laboratories. As of December 2010, there were 39 accredited paternity testing laboratories in the United States. For more information on AABB, visit its website: http://www.aabb.org.

The *American Board of Criminalistics* (ABC) offers voluntary levels of certification for forensic scientists. Exams are given on a regular basis to test general understanding or specific knowledge in an area of forensic science such as molecular biology or drug analysis. Two levels of certification can be achieved: Diplomat (D-ABC) and Fellow (F-ABC). For more information on ABC, visit its website: http://www.criminalistics.com.

The *European Network of Forensic Science Institutes* (ENFSI) was started in 1995 to set standards for exchange of data between European member states and to be an accrediting body through conducting laboratory audits. Within the ENFSI, there is a DNA working group that meets twice a year to discuss forensic DNA protocols and research in much the same fashion as SWGDAM does within North America. For additional information on ENFSI, visit its website: http://www.enfsi.eu.

The European forensic DNA community has another organization similar to SWGDAM named *European DNA Profiling Group* (EDNAP), that first began meeting in October 1988. EDNAP is effectively a working group of the International Society of Forensic Genetics and consists of representatives from more than a dozen European nations. EDNAP has conducted a series of interlaboratory studies on various STR markers to investigate the reproducibility of multiple laboratories in testing the same samples. These studies have demonstrated that with the proper quality control measures excellent reproducibility can be achieved between forensic laboratories. EDNAP typically meets twice a year in conjunction with the ENFSI DNA working group meetings. For additional information on EDNAP, visit its website: http://www.isfg.org/EDNAP.

A *Forensic Science Regulator* works with organizations and practioners who provide forensic science services to the criminal justice system in England and Wales. Following concerns in data quality raised by the Omagh bombing trial (see D.N.A. Box 11.1), the office of a Forensic Science Regulator was established in the UK. Andrew Rennison was appointed in February 2008 to a three-year term, which was renewed in early 2011. The Regulator oversees efforts to maintain or improve quality in UK forensic laboratories. For further information, see http://www.homeoffice.gov.uk/police/forensic-science-regulator/.

The *College of American Pathologists* (CAP) offers external proficiency testing to forensic and paternity testing labs as well as clinical laboratories. For further information on CAP, visit their website: www.cap.org.

Cellmark Diagnostics, now *Orchid Cellmark*, a forensic DNA testing laboratory, provides a proficiency test program to help ensure ongoing laboratory quality. Their International Quality Assessment Scheme (IQAS) DNA Proficiency Test Program is designed for all laboratories conducting forensic DNA analysis. The proficiency tests consist of simulated forensic evidence case samples that are distributed four times a year. The Cellmark tests include questioned bloodstain and semen stain evidence along with known samples of blood. For more information on Orchid Cellmark, visit their website: www.orchidcellmark.com/forensicdna/iqasproficiency.html.

Collaborative Testing Services, Inc. (CTS) is an ASCLD/LAB proficiency test provider offering six different tests in its forensic biology program. For more information on CTS, visit their website: www.collaborativetesting.com.

The *Human Identity Trade Association* (HITA) is a non-profit organization that represents the interests of DNA companies and suppliers within the human identity market. HITA generally meets in conjunction with the International Symposium on Human Identification each fall. For additional information on HITA, visit the organization's website: www.humanidentity.org.

The *National Institute of Standards and Technology* (NIST) develops Standard Reference Materials (SRMs) that may be used by forensic laboratories to calibrate and verify their analytical procedures. Under the DAB standards, a laboratory is required to check its DNA procedures annually or whenever substantial changes are made to the protocol(s) against an appropriate and available NIST Standard Reference Material or a standard traceable to a NIST standard (QAS Standard 9.5.5). The various SRMs available from NIST are described below in the section on DNA standards. For additional information regarding NIST, visit its website: www.nist.gov.

The *Serological Research Institute* (SERI) is an ASCLD/LAB proficiency test provider with body fluid identification and mock case proficiencies offered to forensic laboratories. For more information on SERI, visit their website: www.serological.com.

The *Grupo Iberoamericano de Trabajo en Analisis de DNA* (GITAD) was organized in 1998 to serve the needs of forensic DNA laboratories and institutions in Latin America and the two countries of the Iberian Peninsula, Spain and Portugal. Much like SWGDAM and ENSFI, the primary objectives of GITAD include standardizing techniques, implementing a quality assurance/quality control system, and facilitating communication and training of laboratory personnel. For additional information regarding GITAD, visit their website: gitad.ugr.es/principal.htm.

The *Senior Managers of Australian and New Zealand Forensic Laboratories* (SMANZFL) was formed in 1986 to operate in a similar fashion as ASCLD does in the U.S. SMANZFL is supported by Specialist Advisory Groups, of which there are eight. The *Biology Specialist Advisory Group* (BSAG) oversees DNA efforts and is essentially equivalent to the U.S. SWGDAM group. For more information on SMANZFL, visit their website: www.nifs.com.au/SMANZFL/index.asp.

The *Asian Forensic Sciences Network* (AFSN) was formed in 2008. The group has a quality assurance and standards committee and workgroups for DNA, illicit drugs, toxicology, and trace evidence. As of early 2011, member institutes include representatives from Brunei Darussalam, Indonesia, Korea, Malaysia, Mongolia, People's Republic of China, Philippines, Singapore, Thailand, and Vietnam. For more information on AFSN, visit their website: www.asianforensic.net.

LEVELS OF QA/QC

Table 7.1 summarizes the overall quality assurance measures utilized within the United States, from the community level down to the individual case, that are in place to help provide confidence in the results produced by laboratories. Each of these levels will be covered in more depth in subsequent sections.

At the broadest level of the entire U.S. forensic DNA typing community, *quality assurance standards* have been established that require laboratories to carefully conduct their work. Guidelines and recommendations from organizations like SWGDAM and the ISFG DNA Commission play an important role in community-wide standardization. *Exploratory interlaboratory studies*, although not required, are also occasionally conducted to demonstrate that laboratories are obtaining comparable results.

At the individual laboratory level, *audits* are conducted regularly and *accreditation* granted when minimum standards are met. *Proficiency testing* and continuing education are required to help the individual analyst stay current in his or her work. Individual instruments and methods are validated and performance verified on a regular basis—often with traceability to a certified reference material. Each laboratory has *standard operating procedures* to describe the steps of the process to be followed to help ensure consistency over time and across cases within that laboratory.

At the sample batch level, positive and negative PCR amplification controls help demonstrate that sample reagents are working properly. Allelic ladders verify that all detectable STR alleles can be resolved from one another. Internal size standards are included with each sample processed for capillary electrophoresis STR allele separation and detection. Technical and administrative case review is performed to confirm the results obtained and conclusions reached. Finally, within the U.S. legal system, defendants have a right to counsel. Defense discovery requests and review of case information on evidence going to court provides an additional quality check on the DNA results (see Chapter 18).

TABLE 7.1 Quality Assurance/Quality Control (QA/QC) Measures in Place at Each Level Within the Forensic DNA Community.

Level	QA/QC Measure
Community	Quality assurance standards
Laboratory	Accreditation and audits
Analyst	Proficiency tests and continuing education
Method/instrument	Validation of performance *(along with use of traceable standard samples)*
Protocol	Standard operating procedure written and followed
Data sets	Positive and negative amplification controls
Individual sample	Internal size standard present in every sample
Interpretation of result	Case review by a second qualified analyst or supervisor
Court presentation of evidence	Defense attorneys and experts (discovery requests)

Quality Assurance Standards

Forensic DNA laboratories in the United States are mandated by Congress to follow strict quality assurance standards. In October 1998, the FBI Laboratory's DNA Advisory Board issued *Quality Assurance Standards* (QAS) that define how forensic laboratories are required to conduct business. These QAS were revised a decade later and went into effect July 1, 2009 (QAS 2009). Some minor revisions were introduced in 2011 regarding data review. U.S. forensic DNA laboratories are governed by the QAS and regularly audited for their compliance to these standards.

There are 17 topics covered in the revised (and original) QAS: (1) scope, (2) definitions, (3) quality assurance program, (4) laboratory organization and management, (5) personnel, (6) facilities, (7) evidence/sample control, (8) validation, (9) analytical procedures, (10) equipment calibration and maintenance, (11) reports/documentation, (12) review, (13) proficiency testing, (14) corrective action, (15) audits, (16) safety, and (17) outsourcing.

Audits

A *laboratory audit* evaluates the entire operation of a laboratory. It is a systematic examination that may be conducted by the laboratory management or by an independent organization according to pre-established guidelines. A laboratory must possess *standard operating procedures* (SOPs) and adhere to these protocols. Likewise, instruments and other equipment vital to the successful completion of a forensic DNA case must be maintained properly, and personnel must be appropriately trained to perform their jobs.

An audit team, typically consisting of scientists from other forensic DNA laboratories, visits the lab being audited and evaluates this lab according to criteria spelled out in an audit/assessment document. Audit documents for forensic DNA testing and DNA databasing laboratories are available on the FBI website at http://www.fbi.gov/about-us/lab/codis/audit_testlabs and http://www.fbi.gov/about-us/lab/codis/audit-document-for-dna-databasing-labs, respectively.

Records of an audit are maintained and serve to describe the findings of the audit team and a course of action that may be taken to resolve any existing problems. If any negative findings are noted, then the lab has to take corrective action or lose accreditation.

Laboratory Accreditation

Laboratory accreditation results from a successful completion of an inspection or audit by an accrediting body. The two primary accrediting organizations within the United States that are recognized by the forensic DNA community are ASCLD-LAB and FQS (and FQS-I). Accreditation requires that the laboratory demonstrate and maintain good lab practices including chain-of-custody and evidence-handling procedures.

The accreditation process generally involves several steps such as a laboratory self-evaluation, filing application and supporting documents to initiate the accreditation process, on-site inspection by a team of trained auditors, an inspection report, and an annual accreditation review report. The inspection evaluates the facilities and equipment, the training of the technical staff, the written operating and technical procedures, and the casework reports and supporting documentation of the applicant laboratory.

Proficiency Tests

A *proficiency test*, as it relates to the DNA typing field, is an evaluation of a laboratory analyst's performance in conducting DNA analysis procedures. These tests are performed periodically, usually on a semiannual basis, for each DNA analyst or examiner. In fact, the Quality Assurance Standards (Standard 13.1) require that each DNA analyst undergo an external proficiency test at least twice a year. Biological specimens with a previously determined DNA profile are submitted to the laboratory personnel being tested. The purpose of the test is to evaluate the analyst's ability to obtain a concordant result using the laboratory's approved SOPs.

These proficiency tests may be administered by someone else in the laboratory (*internal proficiency test*) or by an external organization (*external proficiency test*). If the test administered by an external organization is performed such that the laboratory personnel do not know that a test is being conducted, then it is termed a *blind external proficiency test*. A blind external proficiency test is generally considered the most effective at monitoring a laboratory's abilities but can be rather expensive and time-consuming to arrange and conduct.

Participation in a proficiency-testing program is an essential part of a successful laboratory's quality assurance effort. Forensic laboratories develop their own proficiency-testing programs or establish one in cooperation with other laboratories. The German DNA profiling group (GEDNAP) has established a successful blind proficiency-testing program (Rand et al. 2002, Rand et al. 2004).

The purpose of proficiency testing is to evaluate the performance of an analyst using a sample or set of samples that is unknown to the analyst but known to the test provider. Recommendation 3.2 of 1996 National Research Council report *The Evaluation of Forensic DNA Evidence* states that: "Laboratories should participate regularly in proficiency tests, and the results should be available for court proceedings." Successful completion of this examination permits a degree of confidence to exist in how an analyst might perform on a real forensic case sample. Unfortunately, if analysts are aware that they are being tested, they might be more careful than they would when normally processing routine samples on a daily basis. Thus, the concept of blind proficiency has often been discussed in order to have a true test of the entire system because the analyst would not know that he or she was being tested. However, a number of challenges and costs are associated with blind proficiency tests (Peterson et al. 2003a, 2003b).

Validation

While work quality of analysts can be confirmed through proficiency tests, instruments used and methods performed are verified through validation. *Validation* refers to the process of demonstrating that a laboratory procedure is robust, reliable, and reproducible in the hands of the personnel performing the test in that laboratory.

A *robust method* is one in which successful results are obtained a high percentage of the time and few, if any, samples need to be repeated. A *reliable method* refers to one in which the obtained results are accurate and correctly reflect the sample being tested. A *reproducible method* means that the same or very similar results are obtained each time a sample is tested. All three qualities are important for methods performed in forensic laboratories.

There are generally considered to be two stages of validation: developmental validation and internal validation. *Developmental validation* involves the testing of new STR loci or STR kits, new primer sets, and new technologies for detecting STR alleles. *Internal validation*, on the other hand, involves verifying that established procedures, previously developmentally validated will work effectively in one's own laboratory. Developmental validation is typically performed by commercial STR kit manufacturers and large laboratories such as the FBI Laboratory while internal validation is the primary form of validation performed in smaller local and state forensic DNA laboratories. Further details on developmental and internal validation will be covered later in this chapter.

Standard Operating Procedures and Interpretation Guidelines

Each forensic laboratory develops or adopts standard operating procedures (SOPs) that give a detailed listing of all the materials required to perform an assay as well as the exact steps required to successfully complete the experiment. In addition, SOPs list critical aspects of the assay that must be monitored carefully. SOPs are followed exactly when performing forensic DNA casework.

SOPs also include interpretation guidelines to aid analysts in making decisions in evaluating data. For example, should a peak observed in an electropherogram be called an allele or be removed from consideration in the DNA profile because it is an instrumental artifact (e.g., a spike) or a biological artifact (e.g., a stutter product)? These interpretation guidelines are based on internal validation studies performed by the laboratory. Usually, the more specific the interpretation guidelines are written, the more consistent data review will be between analysts within a laboratory and across cases examined by the same analyst over time.

Case Review

As with patients who request a second opionion when faced with a medical procedure, DNA results are reviewed by a second analyst and/or supervisor to confirm allele calls and case conclusions. Forensic DNA laboratories conduct administrative and technical reviews of case files and reports prior to releasing this information to ensure that conclusions reached are reasonable based on the data collected.

Controls for Data Sets and Individual Samples

Multiple levels of quality control are available for DNA samples being processed. Biological samples are quantified to determine the amount of human DNA present prior to PCR amplification. Reagent blanks, which are analytical control samples containing no template DNA, are carried through the DNA typing process from extraction onward to monitor potential contamination. PCR amplification positive and negative controls are amplified alongside the casework evidence or reference samples to demonstrate that the PCR reagents are working properly and are not contaminated (see Chapter 4).

Allelic ladder samples permit an evaluation of DNA separation, resolution, and sizing precision over time—particularly because multiple allelic ladders are often associated with each set of data collected. Each sample is also mixed with an internal size standard prior to being analyzed with capillary electrophoresis. These controls enable troubleshooting of the process should something go wrong during PCR amplification or data collection on the CE instrument (see Chapter 6). Proper performance of each control also provides confidence in the results obtained.

Court Proceedings

A case report prepared based on the laboratory results obtained may be entered into evidence as part of court proceedings. In the United States' legal system, defense attorneys and defense experts have the power to make *discovery requests* (see Chapter 18). Under a discovery request, the forensic laboratory is required to turn over the items requested so that they can be reviewed in the interest of the defendant. Thus, lab results may be scrutinized before and during a trial. This provides another level of review to ensure that quality results have been obtained in the case under consideration. In addition, an analyst may be called upon to testify in court to the DNA results obtained. Cross-examination by the defense team then provides the final level of review in order to confirm the DNA testing results.

LEVELS OF VALIDATION

Validation is an important part of forensic DNA typing and provides confidence in results obtained. Judges and defense lawyers today rarely challenge the science behind DNA typing—rather they challenge the process by which the laboratory and the analyst performs the DNA analysis. Thus, the scientific community must carefully document the validity of new techniques and technologies to ensure that procedures performed in the laboratory accurately reflect the examined samples. In addition, a laboratory must carefully document their technical procedures and policies for interpretation of data and follow them to guarantee that each sample is handled and processed appropriately.

ISO 17025 Section 5.4.5.1 states: "Validation is the confirmation by examination and the provision of objective evidence that the particular requirements for a specific intended use are fulfilled" (ISO/IEC 17025:2005). Furthermore, the FBI QAS define validation as "a process by which a procedure is evaluated to determine its efficacy and reliability for forensic casework analysis" (QAS 2009). Thus, a primary purpose of validation is to demonstrate that a method is suitable for its intended purpose.

With the adoption of ISO 17025 by many forensic laboratories, analysts have to face the concept of *measurement uncertainty* (D.N.A. Box 7.1). One of the purposes of validation is to gain a better understanding of the measurement uncertainty associated with specific steps in the analytical process used to perform forensic DNA testing.

General levels of validation include the following:

- **Developmental Validation**—commonly performed by the commercial manufacturer of a novel method or technology (more extensive than internal validation)
- **Internal Validation**—performed by an individual lab when a new method is introduced
- **Performance Checks**—performed after instrument repair or receipt of new reagents to verify that the instrument or reagents are working properly; monitoring and assessment of control samples and the internal size standard run with each test or set of samples can be considered a performance check.

D.N.A. BOX 7.1

MEASUREMENT UNCERTAINTY

Limitations exist in our ability to measure anything. We can never be 100% certain in science. As Jeff Salyards notes in his article *Estimating the Uncertainty*: "Remembering the limitations of our measurements will keep us intellectually honest, and distinguishing opinions and interpretations will clarify our reports for the investigative and legal communities" (Salyards 2008). An important purpose of validation experiments is to better understand the limitations of measurements (e.g., sensitivity and reproducibility) being made in the laboratory with a specific method.

International Standards Organization (ISO) 17025 document Section 5.4.6 discusses "measurement uncertainty." This term can be confused with the term "error." While in measurement science the term "error" is the difference between the measured value and the true value of the thing being measured, "uncertainty" can best be summed up as a quantification of the doubt about the measurement result (Bell 1999). Uncertainty addresses the question of "Just how sure are you?" about a result produced when measuring something (Salyards 2008).

To measure uncertainty, the sources of uncertainty need to be known and quantified. Replicate analyses are typically performed and these measurements then statistically evaluated (Wallace 2010). The results may then be summarized with an average value plus or minus the standard deviation. Just including the average value does not reflect the level of variation being observed in a data set, which is why a standard deviation is appropriately included when listing an average value. Detailed guidance on measurement uncertainty has been published (EURACHEM 2000, GUM 2008).

A recent article summarizes ten methods for estimating this measurement uncertainty: (1) proficiency tests; (2) readability limits; (3) independent reference materials; (4) operational limits applied during calibration; (5) expert judgment; (6) precision control samples without (6) and with (7) contributions from extramural sources of error; (8) error budgets; (9) historical performance; and (10) ruggedness tests (Wallace 2010).

Measurement uncertainty exists with DNA testing particularly during the DNA quantitation and STR allele sizing steps. With appropriate validation studies, variation that does exist can be understood so that experiments performed may yield reliable results.

Sources:

EURACHEM/CITAC. (2000). Quantifying Uncertainty in Analytical Measurement. Available at http://www.citac.cc/QUAM2000-1.pdf.

ISO/IEC 17025:2005 (2005). General requirements for the competence of testing and calibration laboratories. Available from http://www.iso.org.

Joint Committee for Guides in Metrology (2008). Evaluation of Measurement Data – Guide to the Expression of Uncertainty in Measurement *(GUM). Available at http://www.bipm.org/en/publications/guides/gum.html.*

NIST Reference on Constants, Units, and Uncertainty: http://www.physics.nist.gov/cuu/Uncertainty/index.html.

Salyards, J. (2008). Estimating the uncertainty. Forensic Magazine (Feb/Mar 2008), *42–44. Available at http://www.forensicmag.com/article/estimating-uncertainty.*

Taylor, B.N., & Kuyatt, C.E. (1994). Guidelines for evaluating and expressing the uncertainty of NIST measurement results. NIST Technical Note 1297. *Available at http://physics.nist.gov/Pubs/guidelines/TN1297/tn1297s.pdf.*

Wallace, J. (2010). Ten methods for calculating the uncertainty of measurement. Science & Justice, 50, *182–186.*

History of Guidance Documents on Forensic DNA Validation

The primary purpose in forming TWGDAM and maintaining SWGDAM over the past two decades is to provide guidance on validation and other aspects of quality measurements and data interpretation in forensic DNA typing laboratories. As mentioned previously, TWGDAM issued guidelines for quality assurance in DNA analysis in 1989, 1991, and 1995. Revised SWGDAM validation guidelines were published in 2004. The original DAB quality assurance standards released in 1998 and 1999 have been superceded by the FBI revised QAS of 2009. (The validation section did not change for the revised 2011 QAS.) The ENFSI DNA Working Group issued guidance on validation in November 2010 (ENFSI 2010).

The topics covered in the 1991/1995 TWGDAM, 2004 SWGDAM, 1998/1999 QAS, and 2009/2011 QAS are compared for developmental validation studies (Table 7.2) and internal validation studies (Table 7.3). The 1989 TWGDAM guidelines are not included in these comparisons as the early guidelines focused on the now obsolete restriction fragment length polymorphism methodologies. Evolving technology and laboratory practices make it necessary to periodically issue revisions in quality assurance standards for DNA testing. While only the current guidelines or standards may be applicable to laboratories today, it is helpful to keep a historical perspective.

Developmental Validation Studies

Standard 8.2 in the 2009/2011 revised FBI Quality Assurance Standards requires that developmental validation precede the use of a novel methodology for forensic DNA analysis (QAS 2009). Over the years, different topics have been emphasized as part of developmental validation studies in different guidance documents (Table 7.2).

QAS Standard 8.2.1 incorporates the studies listed in the SWGDAM Revised Validation Guidelines (SWGDAM 2004). These "include, where applicable, characterization of the genetic marker, species specificity, sensitivity studies, stability studies, reproducibility, case-type samples, population studies, mixture studies, precision and accuracy studies, and PCR-based studies" (QAS 2009). PCR-based studies are defined to "include reaction conditions, assessment of differential and preferential amplification, effects of multiplexing, assessment of appropriate controls, and product detection studies." Each of these topics is explored further in the next section.

Validation Studies and Their Purposes

While the 1995 TWGDAM guidelines were the basis for most early validation studies on STR typing kits, more recent validation studies use information from a set of revised validation guidelines that were approved by SWGDAM in July 2003 and finally published and made publicly available in July 2004 (SWGDAM 2004). The 2004 SWGDAM Revised Validation Guidelines have been incorporated into the revised QAS (QAS 2009). The standard developmental validation studies that are conducted to become "SWGDAM Validated" are listed below with either the original 1995 TWGDAM Validation Guideline (Budowle et al. 1995) or 2004 SWGDAM Revised Validation Guideline (SWGDAM 2004) numerical headings shown in parentheses. The purpose of each study is also enumerated. As noted in the

TABLE 7.2 Comparison of Developmental Validation Topics in Current and Previous TWGDAM/SWGDAM Validation Guidelines and DNA Advisory Board (DAB)/FBI Quality Assurance Standards (QAS).

TWGDAM (1991/1995)	DAB QAS (1998/1999)	SWGDAM (2004)	FBI QAS (2009/2011)
Guidelines 4.1 to 4.4	*Standards 8.1.1 &8.1.2*	*Guidelines 2.1 to 2.10*	*Standards 8.2*
Locus characteristics determined & documented: inheritance, chromosomal location, detection, polymorphism (4.2)	Documentation exists & available which defines & characterizes the locus (8.1.2.1)	Genetic marker characterization (2.1): inheritance (2.1.1), chromosomal location (2.1.2), detection (2.1.3), polymorphism (2.1.4)	Genetic marker characterization
Standard specimens (4.1.5.1)			
Different tissues, same type (4.1.5.1)	Precision & accuracy (8.1.2)	Precision & accuracy (2.9)	Precision & accuracy studies
Consistency within & between labs (4.1.5.2)			
Minimum sample (4.1.5.10)	Sensitivity studies (8.1.2.2)	Sensitivity studies (2.3)	Sensitivity studies
Population studies (4.1.5.3)	Population distribution data (8.1.2.3)	Population studies (2.7)	Population studies
Reproducibility (4.1.5.4)	Reproducibility (8.1.2)	Reproducibility (2.5)	Reproducibility
Environmental studies (4.1.5.6)	Stability studies (8.1.2.2)	Stability studies (2.4)	Stability studies
Matrix studies (4.1.5.7)			
Non-probative evidence (4.1.5.8)	Non-probative evidence (8.1.3.1)	Case-type samples (2.6)	Case-type samples
Non-human studies (4.1.5.9)	Species specificity (8.1.2.2)	Species specificity (2.2)	Species specificity
Mixed specimen studies (4.1.5.5)	Mixture studies (8.1.2.2)	Mixture studies (2.8)	Mixture studies
On-site evaluation (4.1.5.11)			
PCR-based procedures (4.4)		PCR-based procedures (2.10)	PCR-based studies
Reaction conditions: thermocycling parameters & critical reagent concentrations (primers, polymerase and salts) needed for required specificity (4.4.1.3)		Reaction conditions: thermocycling parameters, primer concentrations, $MgCl_2$, DNA polymerase, & other critical reagents (2.10.1)	Reaction conditions
Number(s) of cycles to produce reliable results (4.4.1.4)			
Assessment of differential amplification (4.4.1.5)		Amplification assessment: differential, preferential, stochastic (2.10.2)	Amplification assessment: differential & preferential

(*Continued*)

TABLE 7.2 Comparison of Developmental Validation Topics in Current and Previous TWGDAM/SWGDAM Validation Guidelines and DNA Advisory Board (DAB)/FBI Quality Assurance Standards (QAS). (*Continued*)

TWGDAM (1991/1995)	DAB QAS (1998/1999)	SWGDAM (2004)	FBI QAS (2009/2011)
Multiplex amplification effects documented (4.4.1.6)		Multiplex effects & artifacts (2.10.3)	Multiplexing effects
		Positive & negative controls validated (2.10.4)	Appropriate controls
Establish appropriate standards for assessing alleles (e.g., size markers) (4.4.2.1)		Measurement standards for allele (2.10.5.1.1) or sequence data (2.10.5.1.2) characterization	Product detection studies
Characterization with hybridization (4.4.2.2)		Detection by hybridization (2.10.5.2)	
PCR primers of known sequence (4.1.1.1)		Publication of primer sequences not required (2.10)	
Validation results shared & available (4.1.5.12)	Developmental validation appropriately documented (8.1.1)	Peer-reviewed publication encouraged (1.2.1.2)	Required peer-reviewed publication of underlying principles (8.2.2)

SWGDAM 2004 Revised Validation Guidelines, some studies may not be necessary for a particular method.

Developmental validation is performed and often published by the manufacturer of a new DNA test, instrument, or software (see Table 7.5). If a forensic laboratory decides to use a DNA test, instrument, or software in a way not previously explored by the manufacturer, then a full scale developmental validation may be in order. For example, if an STR typing kit is designed and tested by the manufacturer to work down to approximately 125 pg with 28 cycles, then increasing the cycle number to 31 cycles to improve the kit sensitivity would warrant additional validation studies (Caragine et al. 2009) in order to characterize amplification reliability and the stochastic effects likely to arise with low-level DNA analysis (see Chapter 11).

Major points regarding developmental validation in the *2004 SWGDAM guidelines* or *1995 TWGDAM guidelines* are emphasized below with their corresponding section:

- ***Characterization of genetic markers*** (2.1) or *locus characteristics* (4.2). It is important to understand what is being measured and how a specific genetic marker is expected to perform when tested. The inheritance, chromosomal location, method of detection, and polymorphism should be known and documented. Examination of two- or three-generation family samples is commonly performed to measure genetic marker inheritance. The Human Genome Project has aided determination of genetic marker locations throughout the human genome. Genome information on other species is often available as well due to extensive genomic studies in recent years. Numerous population studies

TABLE 7.3 Comparison of Internal Validation Topics in Current and Previous TWGDAM/SWGDAM Validation Guidelines and DNA Advisory Board (DAB)/FBI Quality Assurance Standards (QAS).

TWGDAM (1991/1995)	DAB/QAS (1998)	SWGDAM (2004)	QAS (2009/2011)
Guideline 4.5	*Standard 8.1.3*	*Guidelines 3.1 to 3.7*	*Standards 8.3 to 8.5*
Known samples (4.5.1)	Known and non-probative evidence samples (8.1.3.1)	Known and non-probative evidence samples (3.1)	Known and non-probative evidence or mock evidence samples (8.3.1)
	Monitor and document reproducibility and precision (8.1.3.1)	Reproducibility and precision (3.2)	Reproducibility and precision (8.3.1)
Precision to establish match criteria (4.5.3)	Establish & document match criteria (8.1.3.2)	Match criteria (3.3)	
		Sensitivity and stochastic studies (3.4)	Sensitivity and stochastic studies (8.3.1)
		Mixture studies (3.5)	Mixture studies (8.3.1)
Contamination assessment (4.5.4)		Contamination & controls (3.6)	Contamination assessment (8.3.1)
Proficieny test samples (4.5.5)	Qualifying test (8.1.3.3)	Qualifying test (3.7)	Competency test (8.4)
			Documented and summarized (8.3.1)
			Approved by technical leader (8.3.1)
			Summary available at each site in a multi-laboratory system (8.3.1.1)
			Studies to define QA parameters and interpretation guidelines (8.3.2)
			Change in detection platform or test kit shall require internal validation studies (8.3.3)
New procedures must be compared to original procedures with identical samples when modified (4.5.2)			Modified procedure compared to original procedure using similar DNA samples (8.5)

enable characterization of the alleles and polymorphism present at the genetic markers of interest. Information resources such as the NIST STRBase website (http://www.cstl.nist.gov/biotech/strbase) have documented locus characteristics for commonly used STR loci (see Chapter 5).

- ***Species specificity*** (2.2) or *non-human studies* (4.1.5.9). The DNA typing system being evaluated is subjected to non-human DNA to see if other biological sources could interfere with the ability to obtain reliable results on samples recovered from crime scenes. Primates, such as gorillas and chimpanzees, are typically tested along with domestic animals, such as horses, cattle, dogs, and cats. Bacteria and yeast, which can be prevalent in sexual assault evidence, are also tested. Most STR loci used for human identity testing are primate-specific, that is, they amplify in gorillas and chimps but not dogs or cats. Bacteria, yeast, and most non-primates typically do not yield any detectable products with the STR kits currently available. The sex-typing marker amelogenin does amplify in a number of other species but with DNA fragments that are slightly smaller in size than the standard 106 and 112bp for human X and Y alleles (Buel et al. 1995).
- ***Sensitivity studies*** (2.3) or *minimum sample* (4.1.5.10). The minimum quantity of genomic DNA needed to obtain a reliable result is typically determined by examining a dilution series of a sample with a known genotype. For example, 10ng, 5ng, 2ng, 1ng, 0.5ng, 0.25ng and 0.1ng might be evaluated. Most protocols call for using at least 0.25ng to 0.5ng genomic DNA for PCR amplification to avoid allele dropout from stochastic effects during the PCR step or poor sensitivity during the detection phase of the analysis. Laboratories wanting to perform low-level DNA work should perform additional validation studies to assess the impact of stochastic effects (see Chapter 11).
- ***Stability studies*** (2.4). If environmental insults, chemical insults, or substrates could potentially impact results, then they should be evaluated using known samples to determine the effects of these factors. Past studies have shown that a correct full or partial profile may be obtained in most instances and thus these studies are not performed as commonly today as in the early days of DNA testing.
- ***Environmental studies*** (4.1.5.6). Samples of known genotype are environmentally stressed and examined to verify that the correct genotype is obtained. The environmental studies reflect the situations typical of a forensic case (i.e., exposure to sunlight, humidity, and temperature fluctuations).
- ***Matrix studies*** (4.1.5.7). Samples of known genotype are examined after contact with a variety of substrates commonly encountered in forensic cases. For example, blood and semen may be deposited on leather, denim, glass, metal, wool, or cotton as well as mixed with dyes and soil. DNA profiles from samples exposed to these substrates are carefully examined for non-specific artifacts and amplification failure at any of the loci studied.
- ***Reproducibility*** (2.5) or *consistency* (4.1.5.2). The measurement technique is evaluated repeatedly to assess the reproducibility of the method within and sometimes between laboratories. The power of DNA testing is only fully realized when results can be compared between laboratories in different areas or when offender samples present in DNA databases can be accurately matched with crime scene samples originating from that offender. Thus, results must be comparable across both distance and time. The use of internal sizing standards and allelic ladders has greatly improved the consistency of STR typing across laboratories.

- ***Case-type samples*** (2.6) or *non-probative evidence* (4.1.5.8). DNA profiles are obtained from existing samples that are part of forensic cases that have already been closed. These samples demonstrate that the DNA typing system being examined can handle real casework situations. In some situations, mock evidentiary samples may be created to simulate PCR inhibitors, DNA degradation, or other challenges commonly found in forensic specimens.
- ***Population studies*** (2.7). A set of anonymous samples that have been grouped by ethnicity is analyzed to determine allele frequencies for each major population group that exists in a forensic laboratory's vicinity. These allele frequencies are then used in reporting population statistics and calculating the probability of a random match.
- ***Mixture studies*** (2.8) or *mixed specimen studies* (4.1.5.5). The ability of the DNA typing system to detect the various components of mixed specimens is investigated. Evidence samples in forensic cases often originate from more than one individual and thus it is essential that typing systems can detect mixtures. Several studies are typically conducted to define the limitations of the DNA typing system. Genomic DNA from two samples of known genotype is often mixed in various ratios ranging from 20:1 to 1:20. The limit of detection for the minor component is determined by examining the profiles of the mock mixtures. Studies are also performed to examine the peak height ratios of heterozygote alleles within a locus and to determine the range of stutter percentages for each allele of each locus. The results of these relative peak height measurements can then be used to establish guidelines for separating a minor component of a mixture from the stutter product of a single-source sample.
- ***Precision and accuracy*** (2.9). The calculated base pair sizes for STR allele amplification products are measured. All measured alleles should fall within a 0.5 bp window around the measured size for the corresponding allele in the allelic ladder.
- ***PCR reaction conditions*** (2.10.1). Reaction conditions need to provide the required degree of specificity and robustness. Manufacturer developmental validation studies typically involve varying the amount or concentration of primers, DNA polymerase, magnesium chloride, and thermal cycling conditions.
  - *Annealing temperature studies.* These studies are commonly conducted by running the amplification protocol with the annealing temperature either two degrees above or two degrees below the optimal temperature. Annealing temperature studies are important because thermal cyclers might not always be calibrated accurately and can drift over time if not maintained properly. Thus, an operator might think that the annealing temperature during each cycle is 59 °C when in fact the thermal cycler is running hotter at 61 °C. If any primers in the multiplex mix are not capable of withstanding slight temperature variation (i.e., they do not hybridize as well), then a locus could drop out or non-specific amplification products could arise. While severe thermal cycler temperature drift is unlikely, understanding the limits of an assay or kit can help with troubleshooting.
  - *Cycle number studies.* The optimal PCR conditions (i.e., denaturing, annealing, and extension temperatures and times) are examined with a reduced number of cycles as well as a higher number of cycles than those called for by the standard protocol to evaluate the performance of the STR multiplex system. The sensitivity of detection of alleles for each locus is dependent of course on the quality of input DNA template.

The cycle number studies permit a laboratory to determine the tolerance levels of an STR multiplex system with various amounts of DNA template. While a higher number of PCR cycles (e.g., 34 instead of 28) might be able to better amplify very low levels of genomic DNA, the likelihood of non-specific amplification products arising increases with higher numbers of PCR cycles (see Chapter 11).

- ***PCR product characterization*** (2.10.5.1.1). Measurement standards for characterizing alleles need to be established. Common studies include examining peak height ratio variation in heterozygous samples and characterizing observed stutter percentages.
  - *Stutter studies.* The percentage of observed stutter at each STR locus is examined by calculating the ratio of the stutter peak area and/or peak height compared to the corresponding allele peak area and height. Stutter values are derived from homozygotes and heterozygotes with alleles separated by at least two repeat units. The upper levels of stutter observed for each locus are then used to develop interpretation guidelines. Because the levels of stutter for each of the commonly used tetranucleotide STR loci have been described and usually fall below 10% of the allele peak area and height, some labs just use a standard 15% cutoff for interpreting stutter products. If the stutter peak is below 15% of the allele peak, it is ignored as a biological artifact of the sample. However, if it is above 15% then a possible mixture could be present in the sample (Gill et al. 2006).
  - *Heterozygous peak height balance.* The peak heights of the smaller and the larger allele are compared typically by dividing the peak height of the smaller-sized allele height by the peak height of the larger-sized allele. In other words, the height of the lower peak in relative fluorescence units (RFU) is divided by the height of the higher peak (in RFU). This peak height ratio is expressed as a percentage. The average heterozygote peak height ratio is usually greater than 90% meaning that a heterozygous individual generally possesses well-balanced peaks. Ratios below 60% or 70% are rare in normal, unmixed samples (although sequence variation in the PCR primer binding region can cause one of the alleles to not amplify well).

The following studies are not commonly performed anymore because they have been shown to be true and thus repeating them would likely have little value:

- *Standard specimens* (4.1.5.1). DNA is isolated from different tissues and body fluids coming from the same individual and tested to make sure that the same type is observed. These studies were initially important to verify that blood samples or buccal swabs from a suspect could be used to match semen found at a crime scene.
- *Reproducibility* (4.1.5.4). Dried blood and semen stains are typed and compared to DNA profiles obtained from liquid samples. Samples from the same source should match. Obviously, this fact is important since a crime scene stain should match the reference blood sample of a suspect if he or she is the perpetrator of the crime.

As noted in QAS Standards 8.2.1 and 8.3.1 (QAS 2009), all validation studies should be documented. This documentation permits others to understand what studies have been performed in order to assess the extent of the validation work conducted. In some cases, hundreds or even thousands of samples may be tested as part of a developmental validation. These developmental validation experiments may also be coordinated across multiple laboratories to spread the load as well as to demonstrate consistency between laboratories.

Table 7.4 contains a summary of the validation studies performed in the developmental validation of the PowerPlex Y kit (Krenke et al. 2004). This particular study involved 1269 samples examined as part of 17 different studies conducted by 8 laboratories.

TABLE 7.4 PowerPlex Y Developmental Validation Experiments (Distilled from Krenke et al. 2005).

Study Completed (17 studies performed)	**Description of Samples Tested (performed in 7 labs and Promega)**	**Number of Samples Analyzed**
Single source (Concordance)	5 samples × 8 labs	40
Mixture ratio (male:female)	6 labs × 2 M/F mixture series × 11 ratios (1:0, 1:1, 1:10, 1:100, 1:300, 1:1000, 0.5:300, 0.25:300, 0.125:300, 0.0625:300, 0.03:300 ng M:F)	132
Mixture ratio (male:male)	6 labs × 2 M/M mixtures series × 11 ratios (1:0, 19:1, 9:1, 5:1, 2:1, 1:1, 1:2, 1:5, 1:9, 1:19, 0:1)	132
Sensitivity	7 labs × 2 series × 6 amounts (1/0.5/0.25/0.125/0.06/0.03)	84
Non-human	24 animals	24
NIST SRM	6 components of SRM 2395	6
Precision(ABI 3100 and ABI 377)	10 ladder replicates + 10 samples replicated + [8 ladders + 8 samples for 377]	36
Non-probative Cases	65 cases with 102 samples	102
Stutter	412 males used	412
Peak Height Ratio	*N/A (except for DYS385 but no studies were noted)*	–
Cycling parameters	5 cycles (28/27/26/25/24) × 8 punch sizes × 2 samples	80
Annealing temperature	5 labs × 5 temperatures (54/58/60/62/64) × 1 sample	25
Reaction volume	5 volumes (50/25/15/12.5/6.25) × [5 amounts + 5 concentrations]	50
Thermal cycler test	4 models (480/2400/9600/9700) × 1 sample + [3 models × 3 sets × 12 samples]	76
Male-specificity	2 females × 1 titration series (0-500 ng female DNA) × 5 amounts each	10
TaqGold DNA polymerase titration	5 amounts (1.38/2.06/2.75/3.44/4.13 U) × 4 quantities (1/0.5/0.25/0.13 ng DNA)	20
Primer pair titration	5 amounts (0.5x/0.75x/1x/1.5x/2x) × 4 quantities (1/0.5/0.25/0.13 ng DNA)	20
Magnesium titration	5 amounts (1/1.25/1.5/1.75/2 mM Mg) × 4 quantities (1/0.5/0.25/0.13 ng DNA)	20
	TOTAL SAMPLES EXAMINED	1269

Internal Validation of Established Procedures

In order to meet QAS requirements and to perform good science, forensic DNA laboratories conduct internal validation studies as part of becoming "validated." These studies demonstrate that DNA typing results can be consistently and accurately obtained *in the specific laboratory environment where the testing is performed*. Developmental validation demonstrates that the overall technology (i.e., STR kit or instrument) is reliable while internal validation demonstrates that a specific instrument or kit works properly in a specific laboratory environment. Internal validation anchors efforts within a laboratory to the previously performed developmental validation conducted by manufacturers or other laboratories.

Validation studies are performed with each new DNA typing system that is developed and used. For example, a lab may be validated with the Profiler Plus kit but it would need to perform additional validation studies when expanding its capabilities to amplifying the STR loci included in the Identifiler kit. The addition of a new instrument platform, such as the ABI 3500 (see Chapter 6), requires internal validation experiments to set detection and interpretation thresholds.

Typical studies for an internal validation include reproducibility, precision measurements for sizing alleles, and sensitivity (e.g., 50ng down to 20pg) along with mixture analysis and non-probative casework samples. In sizing precision studies, the calculated allele sizes in base pairs are plotted against the size deviation from the corresponding allele in the allelic ladder with which the genotype was determined. If a high degree of precision cannot be maintained due to laboratory conditions such as temperature fluctuations (see Chapter 6), then samples may not be able to be genotyped accurately.

In discussing internal validation, the 2004 SWGDAM Revised Validation Guidelines state: "The internal validation process should include the studies detailed below encompassing **a total of at least 50 samples**. Some studies may not be necessary due to the method itself" (SWGDAM 2004).

The seven sections from the 2004 SWGDAM guidelines that cover internal validation studies are listed below with some commentary and suggestions:

- ***Known and non-probative evidence samples*** (3.1). A method should first be evaluated using known samples where the quality and quantity of the sample itself is well-characterized and not a concern. In other words, the method being tested should be the variable not the sample being tested. Positive controls provided with STR typing kits, appropriate NIST Standard Reference Materials (see Table 7.7), or other well-characterized samples maintained in a laboratory can be used for the initial studies. Following the examination of known samples and demonstrating that the method is working properly, authentic or simulated case samples should be examined. The purpose of these samples is to explore the limits of a method in terms of handling typical case samples that may be degraded, contain PCR inhibitors, be limited in quantity, or contain a mixture of two or more individuals. The method must not only work on pristine DNA samples, but should also be able to cope with challenges present in forensic specimens. Non-probative evidence samples, such as biological material from a previously completed case, may be used if sufficient quantities are available. Alternatively, artificial case-similar samples may be created (e.g., artificial mixtures as described in the mixture studies section below).

- ***Reproducibility and precision*** (3.2). The laboratory needs to document a method's reproducibility and precision using appropriate control samples that are repeatedly tested. Replicate injections of an allelic ladder enables sizing precision to be determined for each allele spanning the size range of the STR typing kit. Typically, 5 to 10 injections (see Figure 7.1) of an allelic ladder will provide adequate information on STR allele sizing reproducibility.
- ***Match criteria*** (3.3). For procedures that entail separation of DNA molecules based on size, precision of sizing should be determined by repetitive analyses of appropriate samples to establish criteria for matching or allele designation. Typically genotyping software utilizes a ± 0.5 bp window so that alleles that are 1 bp apart can be appropriately designated. Match criteria depend on results from the precision experiments. A simple way to test match criteria when validating STR typing kits is to run more than one allelic ladder with a batch of samples—but only designate the first allelic ladder in the analysis software as a "ladder" for calibration purposes. If all of the alleles present in the other ladders, which are treated as "samples" rather than "ladders," are designated correctly, then the match criteria used by the analysis software is working appropriately. If on the other hand, some of the ladder alleles are designated "off-ladder," then room temperature may be shifting during the course of the sample batch processing time (see Chapter 6). Environmental conditions would have to be changed to restore run-to-run precision. Alternatively, procedural changes may be required to ensure reliable results, such as running an allelic ladder for calibration purposes on a more frequent basis.
- ***Sensitivity and stochastic studies*** (3.4). Reliability and integrity of sample results are important. PCR-based methods are very sensitive but can be subject to stochastic sampling variation when low amounts of DNA are being amplified (see Chapter 11). Limits of sensitivity are typically characterized through testing a dilution series of one or more samples. Upper limits of performance with a method should also be studied and understood. Observing the impact of adding both too much and too little DNA to a PCR amplification can be instructive in defining the optimal range and limits of the method being validated. Thus, a sensitivity study for validating a new STR typing kit may include amounts of 5 ng, 2 ng, 1 ng, 0.5 ng, 0.25 ng, 0.1 ng, 0.05 ng, 0.03 ng, and 0.01 ng from one or more DNA samples when the optimital template target range is 0.5 ng to 1 ng.
- ***Mixture studies*** (3.5). Forensic casework laboratories should define and mimic the range of detectable mixture ratios. The ability to reliably distinguish between major and minor components in a mixture should also be examined as part of mixture studies. For example, artificial mixtures may be created by combining one part female DNA with a serial dilution of male DNA and vice versa. Mixture ratios studied may include 1:1, 1:2, 1:3, etc., in increments down to 1:10 or more. Samples that mimic casework are also valuable to use in these studies such as postcoital vaginal swabs that contain a mixture of male and female cells.
- ***Contamination*** (3.6). The laboratory needs to demonstrate that the method under investigation, as well as its general procedures, minimizes contamination that would compromise the integrity of results obtained. Negative PCR amplification controls and extraction blanks are typically used to assess the purity of the reagents used. For example, if fluorescent dye artifacts are present in a specific batch of PCR primers, then they will be observed in the negative control.

- ***Qualifying test*** (3.7). Analysts who are becoming qualified to perform a specific method need to demonstrate that they are proficient with the method. This qualifying test may involve using previous proficiency samples or other types of samples routinely examined by the laboratory. For example, a previously characterized bone sample could be used by a mitochondrial DNA laboratory as a qualifying test for a new analyst. Once the analyst becomes qualified then he or she enters the cycle of proficiency testing required by the laboratory to demonstrate that competenancy is being maintained over time.

Additional Efforts with Bringing a Method "Online"

Besides the actual internal validation experiments that are performed, there is additional effort typically required to bring a new method "online" before it can be used in forensic casework. Some of this effort takes place before the validation experiments and some after. There is pre-validation learning and preparation and post-validation training.

In their 2006 "Validation and Implementation of (New) Methods" guidance document, ENFSI notes that the level of validation required depends on the type of method being validated (ENFSI 2006). ENFSI establishes categories of (1) an existing standard method, (2) a changed method, and (3) a new method, which is often called an "in-house" method.

Bringing a procedure (assay, instrument, or software) "online" in a forensic lab setting typically includes (1) learning about the technique and how to perform it properly through studying the literature and talking to others who have previously implemented the technique, (2) installing the instrumentation or software and purchasing the assay reagents, (3) designing a validation plan with appropriate experiments to assess reliability and range (limitations) of the procedure, (4) assembling a set of samples for testing based on the validation plan, (5) examining the analytical procedure through conducting predetermined validation studies and maintaining documentation on results, (6) summarizing the studies and getting approval of the laboratory's technical leader, (7) creating standard operating procedures for the laboratory (including controls and critical reagents to be used for quality assurance purposes) with interpretation guidelines based on the validation studies, and (8) training other personnel on the procedure. Each trained analyst will then need to pass a qualifying test before he or she can use the procedure in forensic casework.

After a procedure has been successfully implemented for use with forensic casework, proficiency tests are performed on a regular basis (usually twice a year) to demonstrate successful application of the technique over time by qualified analysts. In addition, new materials and instruments need to be evaluated over time through a quality control process involving a performance check on the validated procedure.

Designing an Internal Validation Study

While the 2004 SWGDAM guidelines provide helpful information, they do not include specific recommendations in terms of the minimum number of samples to be tested for each internal validation study. The only concrete figure provided in the SWGDAM guidelines is that a minimum of at least 50 samples should be run for internal validation purposes by a forensic laboratory.

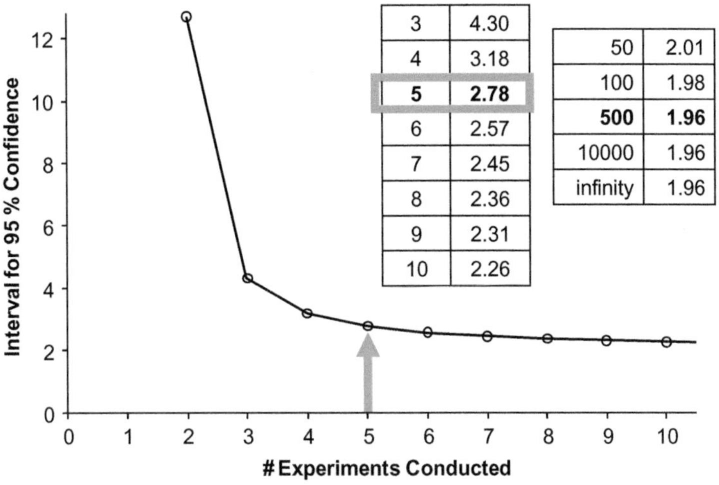

FIGURE 7.1 Student's *t* distribution showing the impact of the number of experiments on capturing variability in a population of data. Five replicate experiments works well as a minimum sample number because there are diminishing returns with each successive experiment.

While everyone may have different comfort levels and absolute numbers for defined studies will not likely be widely accepted, it is worth noting that each study does not require an excessive number of samples to be run and that not all validation studies are essential for every procedure under consideration. Validation should not be an attempt to mimic every potential situation that may be seen in future casework within a laboratory. Rather, data collected during validation should relate to how well potential data to be collected during future work using a specific method should perform.

The Student's *t* distribution is a statistical approach to associate how well a sample (or set of data) can estimate the characteristics of a population of data (or larger set of data). With each additional repeated experiment, greater confidence is typically gained in the measured result. Figure 7.1 shows a Student's *t* curve with the 95% confidence interval decreasing as the number of replicate experiments conducted increases. Note that there are diminishing returns from repeating more than 5 to 10 replicates in terms of the confidence around a set of data (Figure 7.1). This figure illustrates why five replicate experiments are often selected as a minimum sample number.

There is no requirement for how long a validation study should take and thus the "at least 50 samples" recommended by SWGDAM could be run in a matter of days rather than weeks or months. Not all studies may be necessary due to the method involved (D.N.A. Box 7.2). Experimental design can also be implemented in many studies to aid in examining the variables under investigation. Some suggested approaches involving experimental design are available at http://www.haag.com/Seminars_files/How%20Many%20Data%20Handout.pdf.

Companies supplying commercial STR kits have created validation guides to aid laboratories in developing and conducting internal validation studies. Validation services are also available where a company will for a fee come into a forensic laboratory, set up a new

D.N.A. BOX 7.2

REVIEW OF URBAN LEGENDS

In September 2006 I published an article reviewing eight 'urban legends' surrounding validation (Butler 2006). The urban legends discussed in this article included the following:

1. Hundreds or thousands of samples are required to fully validate an instrument or method.
2. Validation is uniformly performed throughout the community.
3. Each component of a DNA test or process must be validated separately.
4. Validation should seek to understand everything that could potentially go wrong with an instrument or technique.
5. Learning the technique and training other analysts are part of validation.
6. Validation is boring and should be performed by summer interns since it is beneath the dignity of a qualified analyst.
7. Documenting validation is difficult and should be extensive.
8. Once a validation study is completed you never have to revisit it.

As technology advances and new methods are developed, there will always be something to validate in a laboratory. A primary purpose is writing the *Urban Legends* article was to help analysts appreciate that validation requires common sense and is best performed (where possible) with well-characterized samples through concordance to results produced from previous methods. Some aspects of validation can be achieved with a minimal amount of DNA samples while other aspects will require more extensive studies. In November 2010, the European Network of Forensic Science Institutes (ENFSI) DNA Working Group QA/QC subcommittee released a document building on the *Urban Legends* article and provided more detail on various aspects of the DNA typing process (ENFSI 2010).

Treating validation as a one-time event that is performed by a single individual (perhaps a summer intern who leaves the lab after performing the measurements) can lead to problems. Every analyst that is interpreting DNA typing data should be familiar with and understand the validation studies that hopefully underpin the laboratory's standard operating procedures. Validation defines the scope of a technique and thus its limitations. Making measurements around the edges of what works well will help better define the reliable boundaries of the technique. While developmental validation may be broadly applicable, internal validation is not transferable in the same way. The performance characteristics and limitations of an instrument, a software program, and a DNA typing assay are important to understand in order to effectively interpret forensic DNA data.

Sources:

Butler, J.M. (2006). Debunking some urban legends surrounding validation within the forensic DNA community. Profiles in DNA, 9(2), 3-6. *Available at http://www.promega.com/profiles/.*

ENFSI DNA Working Group (2010). Recommended minimum criteria for the validation of various aspects of the DNA profiling process. Available at http://www.enfsi.eu.

instrument or assay, perform validation experiments, produce validation documentation, and train analysts on the new instrument or assay.

Publication and Presentation of Validation Results

Results of developmental validation studies are shared as soon as possible with the scientific community either through presentations at professional meetings or publication in peer-reviewed journals. Rapid dissemination of information about these studies is important to the legal system that forensic science serves because the courts must decide whether or not the DNA evidence is admissible (see Chapter 18). Publication of a technology or methodology in a peer-reviewed journal is one method of showing that it is generally accepted in the scientific field. Thus, revised QAS Standard 8.2.2 requires peer-reviewed publication of the underlying scientific principle(s) of a technology (QAS 2009). Table 7.5 contains a listing of some published developmental and internal validation studies.

The most commonly used scientific journals for publishing validation studies and population data results are the *Journal of Forensic Sciences (JFS)*, the *International Journal of Legal Medicine*, *Legal Medicine*, and *Forensic Science International (FSI)* (and since 2007 its daughter journal *FSI Genetics*). Other forensic journals include *Science and Justice*, *Canadian Society of Forensic Science Journal*, *American Journal of Forensic Medicine and Pathology*, *Forensic Science Review*, and *Forensic Science, Medicine, and Pathology*. Forensic DNA studies have also been published in *Analytical Chemistry*, *Electrophoresis*, *Human Mutation*, *Genome Research*, and other scientific journals. The FBI Laboratory maintains an online journal entitled *Forensic Science Communications* that is published quarterly and is available at http://www2.fbi.gov/hq/lab/fsc/current/index.htm. Prior to 1999, this journal was known as *Crime Laboratory Digest*.

Scientific meetings where DNA typing research and validation studies are presented include the *International Symposium on Human Identification* (ISHI, sponsored each fall by the Promega Corporation), the *American Academy of Forensic Sciences* (AAFS, held each February), the *Congress of the International Society of Forensic Genetics* (ISFG, held in late summer biannually), and the *International Association of Forensic Sciences* (IAFS, held every three years in the summer months). An examination of the first 14 years of the ISHI meeting abstracts found greater than 10% of the 1220 presentations covered validation studies based on the title of the talk or poster (Butler et al. 2004).

Within the United States, there are several additional meetings sponsored by private companies involved in the forensic DNA community. Each spring Bode Technology Group sponsors an East Coast conference and a West Coast conference. During the summer months, Applied Biosystems and Promega Corporation often conduct traveling road shows to discuss their latest products.

Several regional U.S. forensic organizations hold annual meetings including the Northeastern Association of Forensic Scientists (NEAFS), the Mid-Atlantic Association of Forensic Scientists (MAAFS), the Midwestern Association of Forensic Scientists (MAFS), the Northwestern Association of Forensic Scientists (NWAFS), the Southwestern Association of Forensic Scientists (SWAFS), the Southern Association of Forensic Scientists (SAFS), and the California Association of Criminalists (CAC). These meetings often have workshops associated with them where validation data are shared.

TABLE 7.5 Published Validation Studies Conducted Using Various STR Kits, Assays, Instruments, or Software.

Kit, Assay, or Instrument	Reference (D = developmental validation; I = internal validation)
AmpFlSTR Blue	**D** – Wallin et al. (1998)
AmpFlSTR Green I	**D** – Holt et al. (2002)
COfiler	**D** – Holt et al. (2002), Wallin et al. (2002); **I** – LaFountain et al. (2001), Moretti et al. (2001), Tomsey et al. (2001), Buse et al. (2003)
Identifiler	**D** – Collins et al. (2004)
Identifiler (low template)	**D** – Caragine et al. (2009)
MiniFiler	**D** – Mulero et al. (2008), **I** – Luce et al. (2009)
Profiler	**D** – Holt et al. (2002)
Profiler Plus	**D** – Holt et al. (2002), Wallin et al. (2002), Frégeau et al. (2003); **I** – Pawlowski & Maciejewska (2000), Frank et al. (2001), LaFountain et al. (2001), Moretti et al. (2001), Tomsey et al. (2001), Buse et al. (2003)
Profiler Plus (reduced volume)	**D** – Frégeau et al. (2003); **I** – Gaines et al. (2002)
Profiler Plus *ID*	**D** – Leibelt et al. (2003)
SEfiler	**D** – Coticone et al. (2004)
SGM Plus	**D** – Cotton et al. (2000)
Yfiler	**D** – Mulero et al. (2006); **I** – Gross et al. (2008)
CTT	**D** – Budowle et al. (1997)
PowerPlex 1.1	**D** – Micka et al. (1999); **I** – Tomsey et al. (2001), Greenspoon et al. (2001)
PowerPlex 1.1 + D16 primer	**I** – Nelson et al. (2002)
PowerPlex 2.1	**D** – Levedakou et al. (2002); **I** – Tomsey et al. (2001)
PowerPlex 16	**D** – Krenke et al. (2002); **I** – Tomsey et al. (2001)
PowerPlex 16 (reduced volume)	**I** – Spathis & Lum (2008)
PowerPlex 16 BIO	**D** – Greenspoon et al. (2004b)
PowerPlex 16 HS	**D** – Ensenberger et al. (2010)
PowerPlex Y	**D** – Krenke et al. (2005)
PowerPlex ESI 16 & ESI 17	**D** – Tucker et al. (2011)
Y-PLEX 6	**D** – Sinha et al. (2003a)
Y-PLEX 5	**D** – Sinha et al. (2003b)
Y-PLEX 12	**D** – Shewale et al. (2004)
genRES MPX-2	**D** – Junge et al. (2003)
Amelogenin	**I** – LaFountain et al. (1998)
D3S1358, D8S1179, D18S51	**I** – Potter (2003)

(Continued)

TABLE 7.5 Published Validation Studies Conducted Using Various STR Kits, Assays, Instruments, or Software. (*Continued*)

Kit, Assay, or Instrument	Reference (D = developmental validation; I = internal validation)
D12S391	**D** – Junge et al. (1999)
TH01	**D** – van Oorschot et al. (1996), Wiegand et al. (1993)
TH01, VWA, F13A1, FES, LPL	**D** – Pestoni et al. (1995)
TH01, VWA, F13A1, FES	**D** – Kimpton et al. (1994); **I** – Lygo et al. (1994), Clayton et al. (1995), Andersen et al. (1996)
SGM	**D** – Sparkes et al. (1996a), Sparkes et al. (1996b), Kimpton et al. (1996)
STR sets	**D** – Crouse & Schumm (1995), Micka et al. (1996)
Q8 (short amplicon multiplex)	**D** – Muller et al. (2009)
Miniplexes (short amplicons)	**D** – Opel et al. (2007)
Y-STR 4plex	**D** – Prinz et al. (2001)
Y-STR 10plex	**D** – Johnson et al. (2003)
Y-STR 19plex	**D** – Daniels et al. (2004)
X-STR 12plex	**D** – Turrina et al. (2007)
Eurasian badger STRs	**D** – Dawnay et al. (2008)
Canine STRs	**D** – Dayton et al. (2009)
Marijuana STRs	**D** – Howard et al. (2008)
RSID – blood	**D** – Schweers et al. (2008)
RSID – saliva	**D** – Old et al. (2009)
qPCR *Alu* DNA quant	**D** – Nicklas & Buel (2003)
qPCR CFS TH01 DNA quant	**D** – Richard et al. (2003)
qPCR CA DOJ quadruplex	**D** – Hudlow et al. (2008)
AluQuant DNA quant assay	**D** – Mandrekar et al. (2001)
BodeQuant	**D** – Fox et al. (2003)
Plexor HY	**D** – Krenke et al. (2008)
Quantifiler	**D** – Green et al. (2005)
Quantifiler (reduced volume)	**I** – Westring et al. (2007)
Quantifiler Duo	**D** – Barbisin et al. (2009)
Feline, bovine, equine, & cervid qPCR assays	**D** – Lindquist et al. (2011)
mtDNA sequencing	**D** – Wilson et al. (1995), Holland & Parsons (1999); **I** – Jarman et al. (2009)
mtDNA minisequencing	**D** – Morley et al. (1999)
Biomek 2000 with DNA IQ	**D** – Greenspoon et al. (2004a)

(*Continued*)

TABLE 7.5 Published Validation Studies Conducted Using Various STR Kits, Assays, Instruments, or Software. (*Continued*)

Kit, Assay, or Instrument	Reference (D = developmental validation; I = internal validation)
PrepFiler	**D** – Brevnov et al. (2009)
SNP autosomal 21plex	**D** – Dixon et al. (2005)
SNP*for*ID 52plex	**D** – Musgrave-Brown et al. (2007)
IrisPlex	**D** – Walsh et al. (2011)
ABI 377	**D** – Frazier et al. (1996), Fregeau et al. (1999)
ABI 310	**D** – Lazaruk et al. (1998); **I** – Isenberg et al. (1998), Moretti et al. (2001b)
ABI 3100	**D** – Koumi et al. (2004); **I** – Sgueglia et al. (2003)
ABI 3700	**D** – Gill et al. (2001), Koumi et al. (2004)
ABI 3730xl	**D** – Spathis & Lum (2008)
MegaBACE	**D** – Koumi et al. (2004)
TrueAllele software	**D** – Kadash et al. (2004)
CompareCalls software	**I** – Ryan et al. (2004)

Documenting and Applying Validation Information

Some journals view validation results as not sufficiently novel to warrant publication (Buckleton 2009). Yet information within the validation studies is important and should be shared with the community. Early adopters of a new technology or DNA testing kit should be able to share their experiences with future users. If utilized as a hub for sharing information, websites, such as the NIST STRBase validation section discussed below, could benefit the forensic DNA community around the world. Such posting of information from individual forensic laboratories' internal validation studies can help the community quickly gain a sense of the numbers of samples and types of samples run in other labs.

The NIST STRBase website has been widely used by the forensic DNA typing community since it was introduced in 1997. A validation section was created in 2004 that can serve as a repository of helpful information on kit, assay, software, and instrument validation studies performed in forensic DNA laboratories (see http://www.cstl.nist.gov/biotech/strbase/validation.htm). This site also contains links to the FBI Quality Assurance Standards and the SWGDAM Revised Validation Guidelines. Publications in the literature involving validation of forensic DNA tests are also listed and some are summarized with Validation Summary Sheets like the information shown in Table 7.4 for the developmental validation of PowerPlex Y (Krenke et al. 2005).

OTHER AIDS TO QUALITY ASSURANCE

There are several other aids to quality assurance that can strengthen confidence in results. These include interlaboratory tests, certified reference materials, and commercial STR kits.

Automation of data interpretation as well as sample handling and tracking (see Chapter 17) also help production of high-quality DNA typing results.

Exploratory Interlaboratory Tests

Exploratory interlaboratory tests are one way that the forensic community uses to demonstrate that multiple laboratories can generate comparable results with the same DNA samples. Since DNA databases (see Chapter 8) rely on information contributed from multiple laboratories, interlaboratory studies that demonstrate consistency in results across laboratories on the same DNA samples can increase confidence in work performed by these laboratories. The reference listing at the end of this chapter includes 53 interlaboratory publications in the past two decades.

Since 1994, the European DNA Profiling Group (EDNAP) has conducted a series of interlaboratory evaluations on various STR loci and methodologies used for analyzing them. Each study involved the examination of five to seven bloodstains that were distributed to multiple laboratories (usually a dozen or more) to test their abilities to obtain consistent results. In all cases where simple STR loci were tested, consistent results were obtained. However, in early studies, complex STR markers, such as ACTBP2 (SE33), often gave inconsistent results. Thus, at that time, STRs with complex repeat structures were not recommended for use in DNA databases in which results are submitted from multiple laboratories. The availability of commercial kits and allelic ladders that enable consistent amplification and typing of SE33 now means that obtaining reproducible results is more feasible.

In the United States several interlaboratory studies have been performed. The first large test with commercial STR typing kits was conducted by the National Institute of Standards and Technology (NIST) and involved 34 laboratories that evaluated the three STRs TH01, TPOX, and CSF1PO in a multiplex amplification format (Kline et al. 1997). This study concluded that as long as locus-specific allelic ladders were used, a variety of separation and detection methods could be used to obtain equivalent genotypes for the same samples.

NIST has also conducted several DNA quantitation and mixture interlaboratory studies (Duewer et al. 2001, Kline et al. 2003, Kline et al. 2005). While different instrument sensitivities have been observed between laboratories, these studies have generally demonstrated that consistent results can be obtained between participating laboratories, thus helping support the conclusion that forensic DNA typing methods are reliable and reproducible when performed properly.

Table 7.6 contains a summary of NIST and EDNAP interlaboratory studies conducted since the early 1990s. These studies have enabled laboratories to learn from one another, to improve their techniques, and to implement new methodologies with greater confidence. The reference list at the back of the chapter includes citations to publications involving 20 EDNAP and 15 Spanish and Portugese-Speaking Working Group of the ISFG (GEP-ISFG) collaborative exercises along with 13 publications describing NIST-coordinated interlaboratory studies.

Since 1991, the English-Speaking Working Group of the ISFG has conducted paternity testing workshops. Each year a paper challenge is provided to requesting laboratories in order to assess reporting results and calculations used in relationship testing. A series of publications

TABLE 7.6 Summary of NIST and EDNAP Interlaboratory Collaborative Studies.

Study/Purpose	# Labs	References
NIST		
RFLP studies	22	Mudd et al. (1994)
	20	Duewer et al. (1995)
	22	Stolorow et al. (1996)
	22	Duewer et al. (1997)
	36	Duewer et al. (1998)
	29/20	Duewer et al. (2000)
	51 (>1000 data sets)	Duewer et al. (2000)
Evaluation of CSF1PO, TPOX, and TH01	34	Kline et al. (1997)
Mixed Stain Studies #1 and #2 (Apr.–Nov 1997 & Jan–May 1999)	45	Duewer et al. (2001)
Mixed Stain Study #3 (Oct 2000-May 2001)	74	Kline et al. (2003) Duewer et al. (2004)
DNA Quantitation Study (Jan-Mar 2004)	80	Kline et al. (2005)
Mixture Interpretation Study (Jan-June 2005)	69	Kline & Butler (2005)
EDNAP		
RFLP studies: single locus VNTR probe (different protocols)	11	Schneider et al. (1991)
RFLP studies: uniformity obtainable (same protocol)	14	Gill et al. (1992)
Examination of TH01 and ACTBP2 (SE33)	14	Gill et al. (1994)
Examination of TH01, VWA, FES/FPS, F13A1	30	Kimpton et al. (1995)
Evaluation of TH01 and VWA	16	Andersen et al. (1996)
Evaluation of D21S11 and FGA	16	Gill et al. (1997)
Examination of ACTBP2, APAI1 and D11S554; Evaluation of D12S391 in 7 labs and D1S1656	7; 12	Gill et al. (1998)
Evaluation of mtDNA sequencing	12	Carracedo et al. (1998)
Use of DYS385	14	Schneider et al. (1999)
Evaluation of pentaplex for DYS19, DYS389I/II, DYS390, and DYS393	18	Carracedo et al. (2001)
Examination of artificially degraded DNA samples	38	Schneider et al. (2004)
Examination of mtDNA sequencing issues	21	Parson et al. (2004)
Evaluation of mtDNA heteroplasmy in hairs	10	Tully et al. (2004)

(Continued)

TABLE 7.6 Summary of NIST and EDNAP Interlaboratory Collaborative Studies. (*Continued*)

Study/Purpose	# Labs	References
Evaluation of 11 Y-SNP markers (SRY-1532, M40, M35, M213, M9, 92R7, M17, P25, M18, M153, M167)	8	Brion et al. (2005)
Evaluation of degraded DNA with low-copy number STR profiling, miniSTRs, and SNPs	9	Dixon et al. (2006)
West Eurasian mitochondrial haplogroups by mtDNA SNP screening	12	Parson et al. (2008)
Typing of autosomal SNPs with a 29 SNP-multiplex	12	Sanchez et al. (2008)
Comparison of miniSTRs (MiniFiler) versus standard STRs (SGM Plus)	4	Welch et al. (2011)
mRNA profiling for the identification of blood	16	Haas et al. (2011)
SNP typing with GenPlex HID 48plex	14	Tomas et al. (2011)

have described the results of these interlaboratory studies for 1991 to1994 (Syndercombe-Court & Lincoln 1995), 1995 and 1996 (Bjerre et al. 1997), 1997 to 1999 (Hallenberg & Morling 2001), 2000 and 2001 (Hallenberg & Morling 2002), and 2002 to 2008 (Thomsen et al. 2009).

Certified Reference Materials

One of the primary ways to support a consistent and calibrated STR allele nomenclature is for DNA testing laboratories to use common reference materials. The National Institute of Standards and Technology, which is a non-regulatory agency in the U.S. Department of Commerce, provides reference materials for a variety of fields to enable accurate and comparable measurements. NIST supplies over 1300 reference materials to industry, academia, and government laboratories to facilitate quality assurance and support measurement traceability. These Standard Reference Materials (SRMs) are certified through carefully characterizing the properties for which values are assigned. The term SRM is the NIST name for a certified reference material.

Reference DNA samples are crucial to the validation of any DNA testing procedure. Standard 9.5.5 in the revised Quality Assurance Standards states: "The laboratory shall check its DNA procedures annually or whenever substantial changes are made to the protocol(s) against an appropriate and available NIST standard reference material or standard traceable to a NIST standard."

NIST supplies several DNA SRMs to enable validation of a laboratory's measurement capabilities as well as calibration of instrumentation and methods (Table 7.7). Current SRMs used by the forensic DNA community include SRM 2391b PCR-Based DNA Profiling Standard for autosomal STR markers, SRM 2392-I Mitochondrial DNA Sequencing for mtDNA sequence information, SRM 2395 Human Y-Chromosome DNA Profiling Standard for Y-chromosome markers, and SRM 2372 Human DNA Quantitation Standard for human DNA quantitation.

TABLE 7.7 NIST SRMs for Use in Forensic DNA or Human Identity Testing Applications (as of 2010).

NIST Standard Reference Material	Release date and renewals	Purpose/contents
SRM 2390	1992	DNA profiling standard (RFLP)
SRM 2391b	1995, 1999, 2002, 2008	PCR-based DNA profiling standard (STRs)
SRM 2392-I	2003, 2009	Mitochondrial DNA sequencing (human HL-60 DNA)
SRM 2395	2003, 2008	Human Y-chromosome DNA profiling standard
SRM 2372	2007	Human genomic DNA quantitation standard

A review of the various SRM materials that are now or have been available to aid the forensic DNA typing community is given below.

RFLP Testing Standard: NIST SRM 2390

SRM 2390 DNA Profiling Standard (RFLP-based typing methods) was released in August 1992 and for many years was used in standardizing forensic and paternity testing quality assurance procedures for restriction fragment length polymorphism (RFLP) testing that used *Hae*III restriction enzymes as well as instructional law enforcement and non-clinical research purposes. It contained two well-characterized human DNA samples: a female cell line (K562) and a male source (TAW). Both samples were available in three forms: as a cell pellet (3×10^6 cells), an extracted genomic DNA (≈200ng/µL), and a *Hae*III restriction digest (pre-cut DNA; 25ng/µL). A relative molecular mass marker for DNA sizing purposes and six quantitation standards (250ng, 100ng, 50ng, 25ng, 12.5ng, and 6ng) were also included along with agarose for slab gel preparation. Certified values for the DNA band sizes were available for five commonly used RFLP markers. These markers (and variable number of tandem repeat probes) were D2S44 (YNH24), D4S139 (PH30), D10S28 (TBQ7), D1S7 (MS1), and D17S79 (V1). The certified values represented the pooled results from analyses performed at NIST and 28 collaborating laboratories and came with calculated uncertainties (see Duewer et al. 2000). With the change in technology from RFLP to PCR in the mid-1990s, SRM 2390 is no longer used.

Autosomal STR Testing Standard: NIST SRM 2391b

SRM 2391b PCR-Based DNA Profiling Standard was reissued in 2002. It is an update of the original SRM 2391 that became available in 1995 and includes certified values for new STR loci. SRM 2391b is intended for use in standardizing forensic and paternity testing quality assurance procedures involving polymerase chain reaction (PCR)-based genetic testing as well as instructional law enforcement and non-clinical research purposes.

It contains 12 components of well-characterized DNA in two forms: genomic DNA and DNA to be extracted from cells spotted on filter paper. There are 10 genomic DNA samples, all at a concentration of 1 ng/μL (20 μL volume). Cell lines 9947A and 9948 are included on a 6 mm Schleicher & Schuell 903 filter paper circle spotted with 5×10^4 cells. The cells permit a laboratory to test its ability to perform DNA extraction while the genomic DNA materials may be used to verify reliable PCR amplification and detection technologies.

Certified genotype values for the 12 SRM components are listed for the FBI's CODIS 13 STR loci (CSF1PO, D3S1358, D5S818, D7S820, D8S1179, D13S317, D16S539, D18S51, D21S11, FGA, TH01, TPOX, and VWA) as well as additional STR loci F13A01, F13B, FES/FPS, LPL, Penta D, Penta E, D2S1338, D19S433, and SE33. These STR markers are all available in commercial kits from either the Promega Corporation or Applied Biosystems. Certified values for the genetic loci HLA-DQA1, PolyMarker, D1S80, and amelogenin were removed for the 12 components in the last update as these kits are no longer commercially available or in use by the forensic community. In 2008, certified values were added for 26 miniSTR loci (see Chapter 10). When the supply of SRM 2391b runs out, it will be replaced by SRM 2391c.

Mitochondrial DNA Testing Standard: NIST SRM 2392-I

SRM 2392-I Mitochondrial DNA Sequencing (Human) Standard was released in June 2003. It was recertified in 2009. This SRM is intended to provide quality control when performing the polymerase chain reaction (PCR) and sequencing human mitochondrial DNA (mtDNA) for forensic investigations, medical diagnosis, or mutation detection as well as to serve as a control when PCR-amplifying and sequencing any DNA sample.

SRM 2392-I contains extracted DNA from the human cell line HL-60 (65 μL DNA at 1.4 ng/μL) that has been sequenced across the entire mtDNA genome (Levin et al. 2003). A list of 58 unique primer sets that were designed to amplify any portion or the entire human mtDNA genome is also included.

Human Y-Chromosome DNA Profiling Standard: NIST SRM 2395

SRM 2395 Human Y-Chromosome DNA Profiling Standard was released in July 2003 for use with verifying results involving Y-chromosome STR testing (see Chapter 13). SRM 2395 includes five male DNA samples (50 μL at 2 ng/μL) selected to exhibit a diverse set of alleles across 31 commonly used Y chromosome STRs and 42 single nucleotide polymorphism (SNP) markers. A female DNA sample is also included to serve as a negative control for male-specific DNA tests. In addition to the typing results from all commercially available Y-STR kits, the five male samples in SRM 2395 have been sequenced at 22 Y-STR loci to confirm allele calls (Kline et al. 2003b). SRM 2395 was recertified in 2008, and information was added on 20 additional Y-STRs useful for genetic genealogy testing.

Human DNA Quantitation Standard: NIST SRM 2372

SRM 2372 Human DNA Quantitation Standard was released in October 2007 to aid DNA quantitation (see Chapter 3). It contains three components: a single-source male DNA sample, a multiple-source female DNA sample, and a DNA sample containing a mixture of male and female sources. Each of these components was certified for decadic attenuance (absorbance) at 260 nm with informational values provided based on the conventional conversion that an optical density of 1.0 at 260 nm in a cuvette with a 1 cm pathlength has a DNA concentration of 50 ng/µL (Kline et al. 2009).

Commercial STR Kits and Concordance Studies

In the early days of STR typing, forensic laboratories put together their own PCR mixes, primer sets, and allelic ladders. This meant that variation existed in the materials used for various laboratories and sometimes in the interpretation of a sample's genotype. Laboratories often had to spend a significant amount of time preparing the allelic ladders and verifying that each lot of primer mix worked appropriately.

Today, commercially available STR typing kits (see Chapter 5) help to maintain a high level of confidence in results and to ensure consistency in nomenclature between laboratories. Use of commercial kits does increase the cost of DNA testing but aids in overall quality assurance due to compatibility and consistency of results (both in terms of loci examined and STR allele nomenclature used). These commercial kits come with company-supplied allelic ladders, which are composed of common alleles and used in sample data interpretation to make the specific STR allele designations.

Production of STR kits by commercial manufacturers requires extensive quality control. A fluorescent dye is attached to one primer for each locus amplified by the multiplex STR kit. Each primer must be purified and combined in the correct amount in order to produce a balanced amplification. Variation in this primer mix production can affect locus-to-locus balance in the multiplex amplification. In addition, allelic ladders must also be produced on a large scale and be well-characterized since they serve as the standard for performing the DNA typing experiments with unknown samples.

As discussed in Chapter 8, DNA databases may acquire DNA profiles from STR typing kits that utilize different PCR primers. Concordance studies, where the same DNA samples are tested with different STR kits, are important to locate potential primer binding site mutations that could lead to allele drop-out and discordance of results (Figure 7.2). Fortunately, concordance studies have shown that equivalent results can be obtained greater than 99.9% of the time (Hill et al. 2010). A null allele page is available on the NIST STRBase website to catalog observed differences between kits: http://www.cstl.nist.gov/biotech/strbase/NullAlleles.htm.

Summary and Final Thoughts

Quality assurance of the DNA typing process requires diligence and action at many levels to help maintain reliable scientific results. A number of organizations play crucial roles in standardizing efforts internationally so that DNA data can be shared among laboratories. Internal validation experiments need to be carefully performed and should serve as the basis for interpretation protocols, thresholds, and decisions. Much can be learned from interlaboratory studies or collaborative exercises where multiple laboratories run the same samples and compile results obtained.

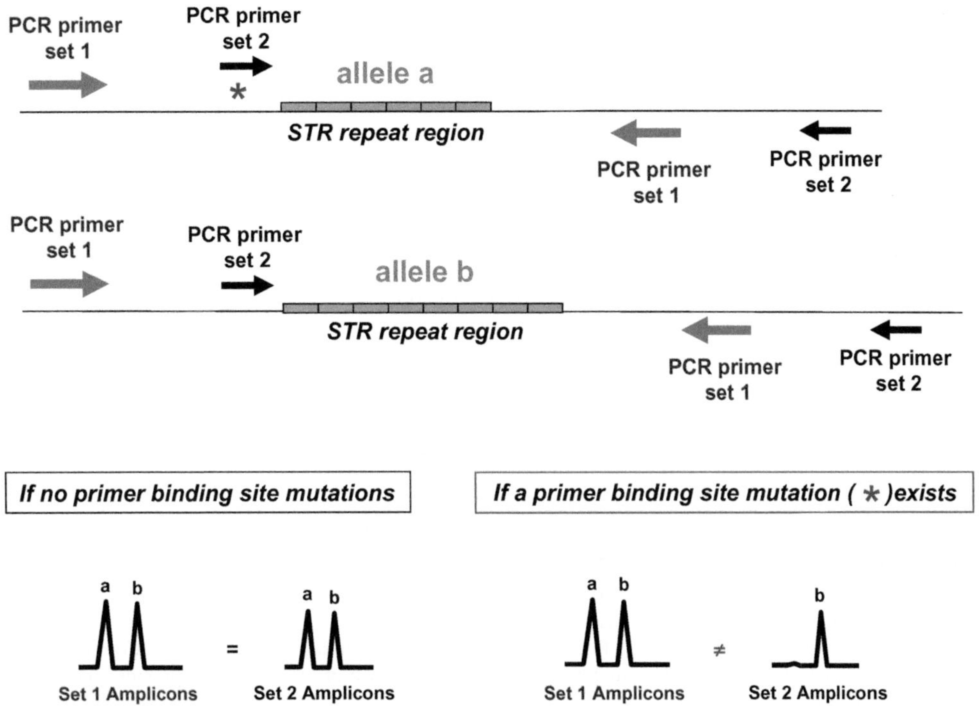

FIGURE 7.2 When different PCR primer sets are utilized to amplify the same genetic marker, sequence variability in the primer binding regions (represented as an asterisk upstream of the STR repeat region in allele a) could cause one of the primers to not fully anneal to the DNA template. In this case, PCR could fail to amplify this DNA target and result in allele drop-out that reproducibly impacts one set of primers but not another.

READING LIST AND INTERNET RESOURCES

Quality Assurance

Aboul-Enein, H. Y., et al. (2001). *Quality and reliability in analytical chemistry*. Washington, DC: CRC Press.

Cormier, K. L., et al. (2005). Evolution of the quality assurance documents for DNA laboratories. *Forensic Magazine, 2*(1), 16–19.

Christian, G. D. (2004). *Analytical chemistry* (6th ed.). New York: John Wiley & Sons.

ISO/IEC 17025:2005 (2005). *General requirements for the competence of testing and calibration laboratories*. Available from <http://www.iso.org>.

Malkoc, E., & Neuteboom, W. (2007). The current status of forensic science laboratory accreditation in Europe. *Forensic Science International, 167*, 121–126.

Presley, L. A. (1999). The evolution of quality assurance standards for forensic DNA analyses in the United States. *Profiles in DNA, 3*(2), 10–11.

Roper, P., et al. (2001). *Applications of reference materials in analytical chemistry*. Cambridge, UK: Royal Society of Chemistry.

Reeder, D. J. (1999). Impact of DNA typing on standards and practice in the forensic community. *Archives of Pathology & Laboratory Medicine, 123*, 1063–1065.

Schneider, P. M. (2007). Scientific standards for studies in forensic genetics. *Forensic Science International, 165*, 238–243.

Swartz, M. E., & Krull, I. S. (1997). *Analytical method development and validation*. New York: Marcel Dekker.
Taylor, J. K. (1981). Quality assurance of chemical measurements. *Analytical Chemistry, 53*, 1588A–1596A.
Taylor, J. K. (1983). Validation of analytical methods. *Analytical Chemistry, 55*, 600A–608A.
Taylor, J. K. (1987). *Quality assurance of chemical measurements*. Chelsea, Michigan: Lewis Publishers.
Taylor, J. K. (1990). *Statistical techniques for data analysis*. Chelsea, Michigan: Lewis Publishers.
VIM (2008). *International vocabulary of metrology—basic and general concepts and associated terms, VIM* (3rd ed.). JCGM 200:2008; also published as ISO Guide 99 (ISO/IEC Guide 99-12:2007). Available for download at <http://www.bipm.org/utils/common/documents/jcgm/JCGM_200_2008.pdf>.

Standards Organizations

American National Standards Institute (ANSI). <http://www.ansi.org/>.
American Society of Standards and Testing Materials (ASTM). <http://www.astm.org/>.
Bureau International des Poids et Mesures (BIPM). <http://www.bipm.org/>.
International Organization for Standardization <http://www.iso.org>.

Scientific Organizations

European Network of Forensic Science Institutes (ENFSI). <http://www.enfsi.eu>.
International Society of Forensic Genetics (ISFG). <http://www.isfg.org>.

ISFG Guidelines/Recommendations

Brinkmann, B., et al. (1989). Editorial: Recommendations of the Society for Forensic Haemogenetics Concerning DNA polymorphisms. *Forensic Science International, 43*, 109–111.
Brinkmann, B., et al. (1992). Editorial: 1991 Report concerning recommendations of the DNA Commission of the International Society for Forensic Haemogenetics relating to the use of DNA polymorphisms. *Forensic Science International, 52*, 125–130.
Bär, W., et al. (1992). Editorial: Recommendations of the DNA Commission of the International Society for Forensic Haemogenetics relating to the use of PCR-based polymorphisms. *Forensic Science International, 55*, 1–3.
Bär, W., et al. (1993). Editorial: Statement by DNA Commission of the International Society for Forensic Haemogenetics concerning the National Academy of Sciences report on DNA technology in forensic science in the USA. *Forensic Science International, 59*, 1–2.
Bär, W., et al. (1994). DNA recommendations—1994 report concerning further recommendations of the DNA Commission of the ISFH regarding PCR-based polymorphisms in STR (short tandem repeat) systems. *International Journal Legal Medicine, 107*, 159–160.
Bär, W., et al. (1997). DNA recommendations—further report of the DNA Commission of the ISFH regarding the use of short tandem repeat systems. *International Journal Legal Medicine, 110*, 175–176.
Carracedo, A., et al. (2000). DNA Commission of the International Society for Forensic Genetics: Guidelines for mitochondrial DNA typing. *Forensic Science International, 110*, 79–85.
Gill, P., et al. (2001). DNA Commission of the International Society of Forensic Genetics: Recommendations on forensic analysis using Y-chromosome STRs. *Forensic Science International, 124*, 5–10.
Gusmão, L., et al. (2006). DNA Commission of the International Society of Forensic Genetics (ISFG): An update of the recommendations on the use of Y-STRs in forensic analysis. *Forensic Science International, 157*, 187–197.
Gill, P., et al. (2006). DNA Commission of the International Society of Forensic Genetics: Recommendations on the interpretation of mixtures. *Forensic Science International, 160*, 90–101.
Gjertson, D. W., et al. (2007). ISFG: Recommendations on biostatistics in paternity testing. *Forensic Science International: Genetics, 1*(3–4), 223–231.
Linacre, A., et al. (2011). ISFG: Recommendations regarding the use of non-human (animal) DNA in forensic genetic investigations. *Forensic Science International: Genetics* (in press, doi:10.1016/j.fsigen.2010.10.017).
Morling, N., et al. (2002). Paternity Testing Commission of the International Society of Forensic Genetics: Recommendations on genetic investigations in paternity cases. *Forensic Science International, 129*, 148–157.
Prinz, M., et al. (2007). DNA Commission of the International Society for Forensic Genetics (ISFG): Recommendations regarding the role of forensic genetics for disaster victim identification (DVI). *Forensic Science International: Genetics, 1*(1), 3–12.

SWGDAM/TWGDAM/DAB Guidelines

Budowle, B., et al. (1995). Guidelines for a quality assurance program for DNA analysis. *Crime Laboratory Digest, 22*(2), 20–43.

DNA Advisory Board (2000). Statistical and population genetics issues affecting the evaluation of the frequency of occurrence of DNA profiles calculated from pertinent population database(s). *Forensic Science Communications, 2*(3). (Available at <http://www2.fbi.gov/hq/lab/fsc/backissu/july2000/dnastat.htm>.

Kearney, J., et al. (1989). Guidelines for a quality assurance program for DNA restriction fragment length polymorphism analysis. *Crime Laboratory Digest, 16*(2), 40–59.

Kearney, J., et al. (1991). Guidelines for a quality assurance program for DNA analysis. *Crime Laboratory Digest, 18*(2), 44–75.

SWGDAM (2000). Short tandem repeat (STR) interpretation guidelines. *Forensic Science Communications, 2*(3) Available at http://www2.fbi.gov/hq/lab/fsc/backissu/july2000/strig.htm>.

SWGDAM (2001). Training guidelines. *Forensic Science Communications, 3*(4). Available at <http://www2.fbi.gov/hq/lab/fsc/backissu/oct2001/kzinski.htm>

SWGDAM (2003). Bylaws of the scientific working group on DNA analysis methods. *Forensic Science Communications, 5*(2). Available at <http://www2.fbi.gov/hq/lab/fsc/backissu/april2003/swgdambylaws.htm>.

SWGDAM (2003). Guidelines for mitochondrial DNA (mtDNA) nucleotide sequence interpretation. *Forensic Science Communications, 5*(2). Available at <http://www2.fbi.gov/hq/lab/fsc/backissu/april2003/swgdammitodna.htm>.

SWGDAM (2003). Guidance document for implementing health and safety programs in DNA laboratories. *Forensic Science Communications, 5*(2). Available at <http://www2.fbi.gov/hq/lab/fsc/backissu/april2003/swgdam-safety.htm>.

SWGDAM (2004). Revised validation guidelines. *Forensic Science Communications, 6*(3). Available at <http://www2.fbi.gov/hq/lab/fsc/backissu/july2004/standards/2004_03_standards02.htm>.

SWGDAM (2004). Report on the current activities of the scientific working group on DNA analysis methods Y-STR subcommittee. *Forensic Science Communications, 6*(3). Available at <http://www2.fbi.gov/hq/lab/fsc/backissu/july2004/standards/2004_03_standards03.htm>.

SWGDAM (2009). Y-chromosome short tandem repeat (Y-STR) interpretation guidelines. *Forensic Science Communications, 11*(1). Available at <http://www2.fbi.gov/hq/lab/fsc/backissu/jan2009/standards/2009_01_standards01.htm>.

SWGDAM (2009). SWGDAM recommendations to the FBI director on the "Interim plan for the release of information in the event of a 'partial match' at NDIS". *Forensic Science Communications, 11*(4). Available at <http://www2.fbi.gov/hq/lab/fsc/backissu/oct2009/standard_guidlines/swgdam.html>.

SWGDAM. (2010). *SWGDAM interpretation guidelines for autosomal STR typing by forensic DNA testing laboratories.* Available at <http://www.fbi.gov/about-us/lab/codis/swgdam-interpretation-guidelines>.

Quality Assurance Standards

Federal Bureau of Investigation (2000). Quality assurance standards for forensic DNA testing laboratories. *Forensic Science Communications, 2*(3). Available at: <http://www2.fbi.gov/hq/lab/fsc/backissu/july2000/codispre.htm> or <http://www2.fbi.gov/hq/lab/fsc/backissu/july2000/codis2a.htm>.

Federal Bureau of Investigation (2000). Quality assurance standards for convicted offender DNA databasing laboratories. *Forensic Science Communications, 2*(3). Available at: <http://www2.fbi.gov/hq/lab/fsc/backissu/july2000/codispre.htm> or <http://www2.fbi.gov/hq/lab/fsc/backissu/july2000/codis1a.htm>.

Presley, L. A. (1999). The evolution of quality assurance standards for forensic DNA analyses in the United States. *Profiles in DNA, 3*(2), 10–11. Available at <http://www.promega.com/profiles>.

Quality Assurance Standards (QAS) for Forensic DNA Testing Laboratories. (2009). Available at <http://www2.fbi.gov/hq/lab/html/testinglab.htm> or <http://www.fbi.gov/about-us/lab/codis/qas_testlabs>.

Quality Assurance Standards (QAS) for DNA Databasing Laboratories. (2009). Available at <http://www.fbi.gov/about-us/lab/codis/qas_databaselabs>.

Laboratory Accreditation

American Society of Crime Laboratory Directors-Laboratory Accreditation Board (ASCLD-LAB). <http://www.ascld-lab.org/>.

Forensic Quality Services-International (FQS-I). <http://www.forquality.org>.

ISO/IEC 17025:2005 (2005) General requirements for the competence of testing and calibration laboratories. Available from <http://www.iso.org>.

Malkoc, E., & Neuteboom, W. (2007). The current status of forensic science laboratory accreditation in Europe. *Forensic Science International, 167*, 121–126.

Proficiency Testing

Collaborative Testing Services (CTS). <http://www.cts-interlab.com/>.

College of American Pathologists (CAP). <http://www.cap.org>.

GEDNAP. <http://www.gednap.org/>.

National Research Council (1996). *The evaluation of forensic DNA evidence.* Washington, DC: National Academy Press.

Peterson, J. L., et al. (2003). The feasibility of external blind DNA proficiency testing: I. Background and findings. *Journal of Forensic Sciences, 48*, 21–31.

Peterson, J. L., et al. (2003). The feasibility of external blind DNA proficiency testing: II. Experience with actual blind tests. *Journal of Forensic Sciences, 48*, 32–40.

Rand, S., et al. (2002). The GEDNAP (German DNA profiling group) blind trial concept. *International Journal of Legal Medicine, 116*, 199–206.

Rand, S., et al. (2004). The GEDNAP blind trial concept part II. Trends and developments. *International Journal of Legal Medicine, 118*, 83–89.

Serological Research Institute. <http://www.serological.com/>.

Validation

Buckleton, J. (2009). Validation issues around DNA typing of low level DNA. *Forensic Science International: Genetics, 3*, 255–260.

Budowle, B., et al. (2008). Criteria for validation of methods in microbial forensics. *Applied and Environmental Microbiology, 74*, 5599–5607.

Butler, J. M., et al. (2004). Can the validation process in forensic DNA typing be standardized? In *Proceedings of the 15th international symposium on human identification*. Available at <http://www.promega.com/geneticidproc/ussymp15proc/oralpresentations/butler.pdf>.

Butler, J. M. (2006). Debunking some urban legends surrounding validation within the forensic DNA community. *Profiles in DNA, 9*(2), 3–6. Available at <http://www.promega.com/profiles/>.

Butler, J. M. (2007). Validation: what is it, why does it matter, and how should it be done?. *Forensic News* (Applied Biosystems newsletter), January 2007 issue. Available at <http://marketing.appliedbiosystems.com/mk/get/FORENSICNEWS_PAST_ISSUES>; see also <http://www.cstl.nist.gov/biotech/strbase/pub_pres/Butler_ForensicNews_Jan2007.pdf>.

ENFSI (2006). *Validation and implementation of (New) methods.* Available at <www.enfsi.eu/get_doc.php?uid = 144>.

ENFSI DNA Working Group (2010). *Recommended minimum criteria for the validation of various aspects of the DNA profiling process.* Available at <http://www.enfsi.eu>.

EURACHEM Guide. (1998). *The fitness for purpose of analytical methods: a laboratory guide to method validation and related topics.* Available at <http://www.eurachem.org/guides/pdf/valid.pdf>.

Feinberg, M., et al. (2004). New advances in method validation and measurement uncertainty aimed at improving the quality of chemical data. *Analytical and Bioanalytical Chemistry, 380*, 502–514.

Green, J. M. (1996). A practical guide to analytical method validation. *Analytical Chemistry, 68*, 305A–309A.

Gunzler, H. (Ed.). (1996). *Accreditation and quality assurance in analytical chemistry.* New York: Springer.

Huber, L. (1999). *Validation and qualification in analytical laboratories.* Boca Raton: CRC Press.

Peters, F. T., et al. (2007). Validation of new methods. *Forensic Science International, 165*, 216–224.

Promega Corporation. (2006). Internal validation of STR systems reference manual. Available at <http://www.promega.com/techserv/apps/hmnid/referenceinformation/powerplex/ValidationManual.pdf>.

Validation information on STRBase. <http://www.cstl.nist.gov/biotech/strbase/validation.htm>.

Vincent, E. B., & Bessetti, J. (2003). Validation questions and answers. *Profiles in DNA, 6*(2), 13–14. Available at <http://www.promega.com/profiles>.

Measurement Uncertainty

Bell, S. (1999). A beginner's guide to uncertainty of measurement. *Measurement Good Practice Guide, 11*(2). National Physical Laboratory: Teddington, UK. Available at <http://www.wmo.int/pages/prog/gcos/documents/gruanmanuals/UK_NPL/mgpg11.pdf>.

NIST Reference on constants, units, and uncertainty. <http://www.physics.nist.gov/cuu/Uncertainty/index.html>.

Salyards, J. (2008, Feb/Mar). Estimating the uncertainty. *Forensic Magazine*, 42–44. Available at <http://www.forensicmag.com/article/estimating-uncertainty>.

Taylor, B. N., & Kuyatt, C. E. (1994). Guidelines for evaluating and expressing the uncertainty of NIST measurement results. *NIST Technical Note 1297*. Available at <http://physics.nist.gov/Pubs/guidelines/TN1297/tn1297s.pdf>.

VIM (2008). *International vocabulary of metrology—basic and general concepts and associated terms, VIM* (3rd ed.), JCGM 200:2008; also published as ISO Guide 99 (ISO/IEC Guide 99-12:2007). Available for download at: <http://www.bipm.org/utils/common/documents/jcgm/JCGM_200_2008.pdf>.

Developmental Validation Studies

Barbisin, M., et al. (2009). Developmental validation of the Quantifiler Duo DNA Quantification kit for simultaneous quantification of total human and human male DNA and detection of PCR inhibitors in biological samples. *Journal of Forensic Sciences, 54*, 305–319.

Brevnov, M. G., et al. (2009). Developmental validation of the PrepFiler Forensic DNA Extraction Kit for extraction of genomic DNA from biological samples. *Journal of Forensic Sciences, 54*, 599–607.

Budowle, B., et al. (1997). Validation studies of the CTT STR multiplex system. *Journal of Forensic Sciences, 42*(4), 701–707.

Buel, E., et al. (1995). PCR amplification of animal DNA with human X-Y amelogenin primers used in gender determination. *Journal of Forensic Sciences, 40*, 641–644.

Caragine, T., et al. (2009). Validation of testing and interpretation protocols for low template DNA samples using AmpFlSTR Identifiler. *Croatian Medical Journal, 50*, 250–267.

Collins, P. J., et al. (2004). Developmental validation of a single-tube amplification of the 13 CODIS STR loci, D2S1338, D19S433, and amelogenin: the AmpFlSTR Identifiler PCR amplification kit. *Journal of Forensic Sciences, 49*, 1265–1277.

Coticone, S. R., et al. (2004). Development of the AmpFlSTR SEfiler PCR amplification kit: A new multiplex containing the highly discriminating ACTBP2 (SE33) locus. *International Journal of Legal Medicine, 118*, 224–234.

Cotton, E. A., et al. (2000). Validation of the AMPFlSTR SGM Plus system for use in forensic casework. *Forensic Science International, 112*, 151–161.

Crouse, C., & Schumm, J. W. (1995). Investigation of species specificity using nine PCR-based human STR systems. *Journal of Forensic Sciences, 40*(6), 952–956.

Daniels, D. L., et al. (2004). SWGDAM developmental validation of a 19-locus Y-STR system for forensic casework. *Journal of Forensic Sciences, 49*, 668–683.

Dawnay, N., et al. (2008). A forensic STR profiling system for the Eurasian badger: A framework for developing profiling systems for wildlife species. *Forensic Science International: Genetics, 2*, 47–53.

Dayton, M., et al. (2009). Developmental validation of short tandem repeat reagent kit for forensic DNA profiling of canine biological material. *Croatian Medical Journal, 50*, 268–285.

Dixon, L. A., et al. (2005). Validation of a 21-locus autosomal SNP multiplex for forensic identification purposes. *Forensic Science International, 154*, 62–77.

Ensenberger, M. G., et al. (2010). Developmental validation of the PowerPlex 16 HS System: An improved 16-locus fluorescent STR multiplex. *Forensic Science International: Genetics, 4*, 257–264.

Fox, J. C., et al. (2003). Development, characterization, and validation of a sensitive primate-specific quantification assay for forensic analysis. *Biotechniques, 34*, 314–322.

Frazier, R. R., et al. (1996). Validation of the Applied Biosystems Prism™ 377 automated sequencer for forensic short tandem repeat analysis. *Electrophoresis, 17*, 1550–1552.

Frégeau, C. J., et al. (1999). Validation of highly polymorphic fluorescent multiplex short tandem repeat systems using two generations of DNA sequencers. *Journal of Forensic Sciences, 44*, 133–166.

Frégeau, C. J., et al. (2003). AmpFlSTR Profiler Plus short tandem repeat DNA analysis of casework samples, mixture samples, and nonhuman DNA samples amplified under reduced PCR volume conditions (25 microL). *Journal of Forensic Sciences, 48*(5), 1014–1034.

Gill, P., et al. (2001). Sizing short tandem repeat alleles in capillary array gel electrophoresis instruments. *Electrophoresis, 22*, 2670–2678.

Green, R. L., et al. (2005). Developmental validation of the Quantifiler real-time PCR kits for the quantification of human nuclear DNA samples. *Journal of Forensic Sciences, 50*, 809–825.

Greenspoon, S. A., et al. (2004). Application of the BioMek 2000 Laboratory Automation Workstation and the DNA IQ System to the extraction of forensic casework samples. *Journal of Forensic Sciences, 49*, 29–39.

Greenspoon, S. A., et al. (2004). Validation and implementation of the PowerPlex 16 BIO System STR multiplex for forensic casework. *Journal of Forensic Sciences, 49*, 71–80.

Holland, M. M., & Parsons, T. J. (1999). Mitochondrial DNA sequence analysis – validation and use for forensic casework. *Forensic Science Review, 11*(1), 22–50.

Holt, C. L., et al. (2002). TWGDAM validation of AmpFlSTR PCR amplification kits for forensic DNA casework. *Journal of Forensic Sciences, 47*, 66–96.

Howard, C., et al. (2008). Developmental validation of a Cannabis sativa STR multiplex system for forensic analysis. *Journal of Forensic Sciences, 53*, 1061–1067.

Hudlow, W. R., et al. (2008). A quadruplex real-time qPCR assay for the simultaneous assessment of total human DNA, human male DNA, DNA degradation and the presence of PCR inhibitors in forensic samples: a diagnostic tool for STR typing. *Forensic Science International: Genetics, 2*, 108–125.

Johnson, C. L., et al. (2003). Validation and uses of a Y-chromosome STR 10-plex for forensic and paternity laboratories. *Journal of Forensic Sciences, 48*(6), 1260–1268.

Junge, A., & Madea, B. (1999). Validation studies and characterization of variant alleles at the short tandem repeat locus D12S391. *International Journal of Legal Medicine, 112*, 67–69.

Junge, A., et al. (2003). Validation of the multiplex kit genRESMPX-2 for forensic casework analysis. *International Journal of Legal Medicine, 117*, 317–325.

Kadash, K., et al. (2004). Validation study of the TrueAllele automated data review system. *Journal of Forensic Sciences, 49*, 660–667.

Kimpton, C. P., et al. (1994). Evaluation of an automated DNA profiling system employing multiplex amplification of four tetrameric STR loci. *International Journal of Legal Medicine, 106*, 302–311.

Kimpton, C. P., et al. (1996). Validation of highly discriminating multiplex short tandem repeat amplification systems for individual identification. *Electrophoresis, 17*(8), 1283–1293.

Koumi, P., et al. (2004). Evaluation and validation of the ABI 3700, ABI 3100, and the MegaBACE 1000 capillary array electrophoresis instruments for use with short tandem repeat microsatellite typing in a forensic environment. *Electrophoresis, 25*, 2227–2241.

Krenke, B. E., et al. (2002). Validation of a 16-locus fluorescent multiplex system. *Journal of Forensic Sciences, 47*, 773–785.

Krenke, B. E., et al. (2005). Validation of a male-specific, 12-locus fluorescent short tandem repeat (STR) multiplex. *Forensic Science International, 148*, 1–14.

Krenke, B. E., et al. (2008). Developmental validation of a real-time PCR assay for the simultaneous quantification of total human and male DNA. *Forensic Science International Genetics, 3*, 14–21.

Lazaruk, K., et al. (1998). Genotyping of forensic short tandem repeat (STR) systems based on sizing precision in a capillary electrophoresis instrument. *Electrophoresis, 19*, 86–93.

Levedakou, E. N., et al. (2002). Characterization and validation studies of PowerPlex 2.1, a nine-locus short tandem repeat (STR) multiplex system and Penta D monoplex. *Journal of Forensic Sciences, 47*, 757–772.

Leibelt, C., et al. (2003). Identification of a D8S1179 primer binding site mutation and the validation of a primer designed to recover null alleles. *Forensic Science International, 133*, 220–227.

Lindquist, C. D., et al. (2011). Developmental validation of feline, bovine, equine, and cervid quantitative PCR assays. *Journal of Forensic Sciences, 56*(Suppl.), S29–S35.

Mandrekar, M. N., et al. (2001). Development of a human DNA quantitation system. *Croatian Medical Journal, 42*(3), 336–339.

Micka, K. A., et al. (1996). Validation of multiplex polymorphic STR amplification sets developed for personal identification applications. *Journal of Forensic Sciences, 41*(4), 582–590.

Micka, K. A., et al. (1999). TWGDAM validation of a nine-locus and a four-locus fluorescent STR multiplex system. *Journal of Forensic Sciences, 44*, 1243–1257.

Morley, J. M., et al. (1999). Validation of mitochondrial DNA mini-sequencing for forensic casework. *International Journal of Legal Medicine, 112*, 241–248.

Mulero, J. J., et al. (2006). Development and validation of the AmpFlSTR Yfiler PCR Amplification kit: A male specific, single amplification 17 Y-STR multiplex system. *Journal of Forensic Sciences, 51*, 64–75.

Mulero, J. J., et al. (2008). Development and validation of the AmpFlSTR MiniFiler PCR Amplification kit: A mini-STR multiplex for the analysis of degraded and/or PCR inhibited DNA. *Journal of Forensic Sciences, 53*, 838–852.

Muller, K., et al. (2009). Validation of the short amplicon multiplex Q8 including the German DNA database systems. *Journal of Forensic Sciences, 54*, 862–865.

Musgrave-Brown, E., et al. (2007). Forensic validation of the SNPforID 52-plex assay. *Forensic Science International: Genetics, 1*, 186–190.

Nicklas, J. A., & Buel, E. (2003). Development of an Alu-based, real-time PCR method for quantitation of human DNA in forensic samples. *Journal of Forensic Sciences, 48*(5), 936–944.

Old, J. B., et al. (2009). Developmental validation of RSID-saliva: A lateral flow immunochromatographic strip test for the forensic detection of saliva. *Journal of Forensic Sciences, 54*, 866–873.

Opel, K. L., et al. (2007). Developmental validation of reduced-size STR miniplex primer sets. *Journal of Forensic Sciences, 52*, 1263–1271.

Prinz, M., et al. (2001). Validation and casework application of a Y chromosome specific STR multiplex. *Forensic Science International, 120*, 177–188.

Richard, M. L., et al. (2003). Developmental validation of a real-time quantitative PCR assay for automated quantification of human DNA. *Journal of Forensic Sciences, 48*(5), 1041–1046.

Schweers, B. A., et al. (2008). Developmental validation of a novel lateral flow strip test for rapid identification of human blood (Rapid Stain Identification—Blood). *Forensic Science International: Genetics, 2*, 243–247.

Shewale, J. G., et al. (2004). Y-chromosome STR system, Y-PLEX 12, for forensic casework: Development and validation. *Journal of Forensic Sciences, 49*(6), 1278–1290.

Sinha, S. K., et al. (2003). Development and validation of a multiplexed Y-chromosome STR genotyping system, Y-PLEX 6, for forensic casework. *Journal of Forensic Sciences, 48*(1), 93–103.

Sinha, S. K., et al. (2003). Development and validation of the Y-PLEX 5, a Y-chromosome STR genotyping system, for forensic casework. *Journal of Forensic Sciences, 48*(5), 985–1000.

Spathis, R., & Lum, J. K. (2008). An updated validation of Promega's PowerPlex 16 System: High throughput databasing under reduced PCR volume conditions on Applied Biosystem's 96 capillary 3730xl DNA Analyzer. *Journal of Forensic Sciences, 53*, 1353–1357.

Tucker, V. C., et al. (2011). Developmental validation of the PowerPlex ESI 16 and PowerPlex ESI 17 Systems: STR multiplexes for the new European standard. *Forensic Science International: Genetics* (in press) (doi:10.1016/j.fsigen.2010.03.014).

Turrina, S., et al. (2007). Development and forensic validation of a new multiplex PCR assay with 12 X-chromosomal short tandem repeats. *Forensic Science International: Genetics, 1*, 201–204.

Wallin, J. M., et al. (1998). TWGDAM validation of the AmpFlSTR Blue PCR amplification kit for forensic casework analysis. *Journal of Forensic Sciences, 43*, 854–870.

Wallin, J. M., et al. (2002). Constructing universal multiplex PCR systems for comparative genotyping. *Journal of Forensic Sciences, 47*(1), 52–65.

Walsh, S., et al. (2011). Developmental validation of the IrisPlex system: Determination of blue and brown iris colour for forensic intelligence. *Forensic Science International: Genetics* (in press) (doi:10.1016/j.fsigen.2010.09.008).

Wilson, M. R., et al. (1995). Validation of mitochondrial DNA sequencing for forensic casework analysis. *International Journal of Legal Medicine, 108*, 68–74.

Internal Validation Studies

Andersen, J. F., et al. (1996). Further validation of a multiplex STR system for use in routine forensic identity testing. *Forensic Science International, 78*, 47–64.

Buse, E. L., et al. (2003). Performance evaluation of two multiplexes used in fluorescent short tandem repeat DNA analysis. *Journal of Forensic Sciences, 48*(2), 348–357.

Clayton, T. M., et al. (1995). Further validation of a quadruplex STR DNA typing system: a collaborative effort to identify victims of a mass disaster. *Forensic Science International, 76*, 17–25.

Crouse, C. A. (2001). Implementation of forensic DNA analysis on casework evidence at the Palm Beach County Sheriff's Office Crime Laboratory: Historical perspective. *Croatian Medical Journal, 42*(3), 247–251.

Drábek, J. (2009). Validation of software for calculating the likelihood ratio for parentage and kinship. *Forensic Science International: Genetics, 3*, 112–118.

Frank, W. E., et al. (2001). Validation of the AmpFlSTR Profiler Plus PCR amplification kit for use in forensic casework. *Journal of Forensic Sciences, 46*(3), 642–646.

Gaines, M. L., et al. (2002). Reduced volume PCR amplification reactions using the AmpFlSTR Profiler Plus kit. *Journal of Forensic Sciences, 47*(6), 1224–1237.

Greenspoon, S. A., et al. (2000). Validation of the PowerPlex 1.1 loci for use in human identification. *Journal of Forensic Sciences, 45*(3), 677–683.

Gross, A. M., et al. (2008). Internal validation of the AmpFlSTR Yfiler amplification kit for use in forensic casework. *Journal of Forensic Sciences, 53*, 125–134.

Isenberg, A. R., et al. (1998). Analysis of two multiplexed short tandem repeat systems using capillary electrophoresis with multiwavelength florescence detection. *Electrophoresis, 19*, 94–100.

Jarman, P. G., et al. (2009). Mitochondrial DNA validation in a state laboratory. *Journal of Forensic Sciences, 54*, 95–102.

LaFountain, M., et al. (1998). Validation of capillary electrophoresis for analysis of the X-Y homologous amelogenin gene. *Journal of Forensic Sciences, 43*(6), 1188–1194.

LaFountain, M. J., et al. (2001). TWGDAM validation of the AmpFlSTR Profiler Plus and AmpFlSTR COfiler STR multiplex systems using capillary electrophoresis. *Journal of Forensic Sciences, 46*(5), 1191–1198.

Luce, C., et al. (2009). Validation of the AMPFlSTR MiniFiler PCR amplification kit for use in forensic casework. *Journal of Forensic Sciences, 54*, 1046–1054.

Lygo, J. E., et al. (1994). The validation of short tandem repeat (STR) loci for use in forensic casework. *International Journal of Legal Medicine, 107*, 77–89.

Moretti, T. R., et al. (2001). Validation of short tandem repeats (STRs) for forensic usage: performance testing of fluorescent multiplex STR systems and analysis of authentic and simulated forensic samples. *Journal of Forensic Sciences, 46*(3), 647–660.

Moretti, T. R., et al. (2001). Validation of STR typing by capillary electrophoresis. *Journal of Forensic Sciences, 46*(3), 661–676.

Nelson, M. S., et al. (2002). Detection of a primer-binding site polymorphism for the STR locus D16S539 using the Powerplex 1.1 system and validation of a degenerate primer to correct for the polymorphism. *Journal of Forensic Sciences, 47*(2), 345–349.

Pawlowski, R., & Maciejewska, A. (2000). Forensic validation of a multiplex containing nine STRs—population genetics in northern Poland. *International Journal of Legal Medicine, 114*, 45–49.

Pestoni, C., et al. (1995). The use of the STRs HUMTH01, HUMVWA31/A, HUMF13A1, HUMFES/FPS, HUMLPL in forensic application: Validation studies and population data for Galicia (NW Spain). *International Journal of Legal Medicine, 107*, 283–290.

Potter, T. (2003). Co-amplification of ENFSI-loci D3S1358, D8S1179 and D18S51: Validation of new primer sequences and allelic distribution among 2874 individuals. *Forensic Science International, 138*, 104–110.

Ryan, J. H., et al. (2004). The application of an automated allele concordance analysis system (CompareCalls) to ensure the accuracy of single-source STR DNA profiles. *Journal of Forensic Sciences, 49*(3), 492–499.

Sgueglia, J. B., et al. (2003). Precision studies using the ABI Prism 3100 genetic analyzer for forensic DNA analysis. *Analytical and Bioanalytical Chemistry, 376*, 1247–1254.

Sparkes, R., et al. (1996). The validation of a 7-locus multiplex STR test for use in forensic casework. (I). Mixtures, ageing, degradation and species studies. *International Journal of Legal Medicine, 109*, 186–194.

Sparkes, R., et al. (1996). The validation of a 7-locus multiplex STR test for use in forensic casework. (II), Artefacts, casework studies and success rates. *International Journal of Legal Medicine, 109*, 195–204.

Tomsey, C. S., et al. (2001). Comparison of PowerPlex 16, PowerPlex 1.1/2.1, and ABI AmpFlSTR Profiler Plus/COfiler for forensic use. *Croatian Medical Journal, 42*(3), 239–243.

van Oorschot, R. A., et al. (1996). HUMTH01 validation studies: effect of substrate, environment, and mixtures. *Journal of Forensic Sciences, 41*(1), 142–145.

Westring, C. G., et al. (2007). Validation of reduced-scale reactions for the Quantifiler Human DNA kit. *Journal of Forensic Sciences, 52*, 1035–1043.

Wiegand, P., et al. (1993). Forensic validation of the STR systems SE 33 and TC 11. *International Journal of Legal Medicine, 105*, 315–320.

Interlaboratory Studies

Summary of interlab studies. <http://www.cstl.nist.gov/biotech/strbase/interlab.htm>.

EDNAP (20)

Andersen, J. F., et al. (1996). Report on the third EDNAP collaborative STR exercise. *Forensic Science International, 78*, 83–93.

Bjerre, A., et al. (1997). A report of the 1995 and 1996 paternity testing workshops of the english speaking working group of the International Society of Forensic Haemogenetics. *Forensic Science International, 90*, 41–55.

Brion, M., et al. (2005). A collaborative study of the EDNAP group regarding Y-chromosome binary polymorphism analysis. *Forensic Science International, 153*, 103–108.

Carracedo, A., et al. (1998). Reproducibility of mtDNA analysis between laboratories: A report of the European DNA Profiling group (EDNAP). *Forensic Science International, 97*, 165–170.

Carracedo, A., et al. (2001). Results of a collaborative study of the EDNAP group regarding the reproducibility and robustness of the Y-chromosome STRs DYS19, DYS389 I and II, DYS390 and DYS393 in a PCR pentaplex format. *Forensic Science International, 119*, 28–41.

Dixon, L. A., et al. (2006). Analysis of artificially degraded DNA using STRs and SNPs–results of a collaborative European (EDNAP) exercise. *Forensic Science International, 164*, 33–44.

Gill, P., et al. (1992). A report of an international collaborative experiment to demonstrate the uniformity obtainable using DNA profiling techniques. *Forensic Science International, 53*, 29–43.

Gill, P., et al. (1994). Report of the European DNA profiling group (EDNAP) – towards standardization of short tandem repeat (STR) loci. *Forensic Science International, 65*, 51–59.

Gill, P., et al. (1997). Report of the European DNA profiling group (EDNAP): An investigation of the complex STR loci D21S11 and HUMFIBRA (FGA). *Forensic Science International, 86*, 25–33.

Gill, P., et al. (1998). Report of the European DNA Profiling group (EDNAP) – an investigation of the hypervariable loci ACTBP2, APOA11 and D11S554 and the compound loci D12S391 and D1S1656. *Forensic Science International, 98*, 193–200.

Haas, C., et al. (2011). mRNA profiling for the identification of blood-Results of a collaborative EDNAP exercise. *Forensic Science International: Genetics, 5*, 21–26.

Kimpton, C. P., et al. (1995). Report on the second EDNAP collaborative STR exercise. *Forensic Science International, 71*, 137–152.

Parson, W., et al. (2004). The EDNAP mitochondrial DNA population database (EMPOP) collaborative exercises: Organisation, results and perspectives. *Forensic Science International, 139*, 215–226.

Parson, W., et al. (2008). Identification of West Eurasian mitochondrial haplogroups by mtDNA SNP screening: Results of the 2006-2007 EDNAP collaborative exercise. *Forensic Science International: Genetics, 2*, 61–68.

Sanchez, J. J., et al. (2008). Forensic typing of autosomal SNPs with a 29 SNP-multiplex–results of a collaborative EDNAP exercise. *Forensic Science International: Genetics, 2*, 176–183.

Schneider, P. M., et al. (1991). Report of a European collaborative exercise comparing DNA typing results using a single locus VNTR probe. *Forensic Science International, 49*, 1–15.

Schneider, P. M., et al. (1999). Results of a collaborative study regarding the standardization of the Y-linked STR system DYS385 by the European DNA Profiling (EDNAP) group. *Forensic Science International, 102*, 159–165.

Schneider, P. M., et al. (2004). STR analysis of artificially degraded DNA—results of a collaborative European exercise. *Forensic Science International, 139*, 123–134.

Tomas, C., et al. (2011). Autosomal SNP typing of forensic samples with the GenPlex HID System: Results of a collaborative study. *Forensic Science International: Genetics* (in press) (doi:10.1016/j.fsigen.2010.06.007).

Tully, G., et al. (2004). Results of a collaborative study of the EDNAP group regarding mitochondrial DNA heteroplasmy and segregation in hair shafts. *Forensic Science International, 140*, 1–11.

Welch, L., et al. (2011). A comparison of mini-STRs versus standard STRs-Results of a collaborative European (EDNAP) exercise. *Forensic Science International: Genetics, 5*, 257–258.

English Speaking Working Group-ISFG (5)

Bjerre, A., et al. (1997). A report of the 1995 and 1996 paternity testing workshops of the English Speaking Working Group of the International Society for Forensic Haemogenetics. *Forensic Science International, 90*, 41–55.

Hallenberg, C., & Morling, N. (2001). A report of the 1997, 1998 and 1999 paternity testing workshops of the English Speaking Working Group of the International Society for Forensic Genetics. *Forensic Science International, 116*, 23–33.

Hallenberg, C., & Morling, N. (2002). A report of the 2000 and 2001 paternity testing workshops of the English Speaking Working Group of the International Society for Forensic Genetics. *Forensic Science International, 129*, 43–50.

Syndercombe-Court, D., & Lincoln, P. (1995). A review of the 1991-1994 paternity testing workshops of the English-Speaking Working Group. In A. Carracedo, B. Brinkmann & W. Bär (Eds.), *Advances in forensic haemogenetics 6* (pp. 683–685). Berlin: Springer-Verlag.

Thomsen, A. R., et al. (2009). A report of the 2002-2008 paternity testing workshops of the English Speaking Working Group of the International Society for Forensic Genetics. *Forensic Science International: Genetics, 3,* 214–221.

GEP-ISFG (15)

Alonso, A., et al. (2002). Results of the 1999-2000 collaborative exercise and proficiency testing program on mitochondrial DNA of the GEP-ISFG: An inter-laboratory study of the observed variability in the heteroplasmy level of hair from the same donor. *Forensic Science International, 125,* 1–7.

Crespillo, M., et al. (2006). Results of the 2003-2004 GEP-ISFG collaborative study on mitochondrial DNA: Focus on the mtDNA profile of a mixed semen-saliva stain. *Forensic Science International, 160,* 157–167.

Gómez, J., et al. (1997). A review of the collaborative exercises on DNA typing of the Spanish and Portuguese ISFH Working Group. International Society for Forensic Haemogenetics. *International Journal of Legal Medicine, 110,* 273–277.

Gómez, J., & Carracedo, A. (2000). The 1998-1999 collaborative exercises and proficiency testing program on DNA typing of the Spanish and Portuguese Working Group of the International Society for Forensic Genetics (GEP-ISFG). *Forensic Science International, 114,* 21–30.

Gusmão, L., et al. (2003). Results of the GEP-ISFG collaborative study on the Y chromosome STRs GATA A10, GATA C4, GATA H4, DYS437, DYS438, DYS439, DYS460 and DYS461: Population data. *Forensic Science International, 135,* 150–157.

Gusmão, L., et al. (2005). Mutation rates at Y chromosome specific microsatellites. *Human Mutation, 26,* 520–528.

Gusmão, L., et al. (2009). A GEP-ISFG collaborative study on the optimization of an X-STR decaplex: Data on 15 Iberian and Latin American populations. *International Journal of Legal Medicine, 123,* 227–234.

Montesino, M., et al. (2007). Analysis of body fluid mixtures by mtDNA sequencing: An inter-laboratory study of the GEP-ISFG working group. *Forensic Science International, 168,* 42–56.

Prieto, L., et al. (2003). The 2000-2001 GEP-ISFG Collaborative Exercise on mtDNA: Assessing the cause of unsuccessful mtDNA PCR amplification of hair shaft samples. *Forensic Science International, 134,* 46–53.

Prieto, L., et al. (2008). 2006 GEP-ISFG collaborative exercise on mtDNA: Reflections about interpretation, artifacts, and DNA mixtures. *Forensic Science International: Genetics, 2,* 126–133.

Prieto, L., et al. (2010). The GHEP-EMPOP collaboration on mtDNA population data-A new resource for forensic casework. *Forensic Science International Genetics* (in press)

Salas, A., et al. (2005). Mitochondrial DNA error prophylaxis: Assessing the causes of errors in the GEP'02-03 proficiency testing trial. *Forensic Science International, 148,* 191–198.

Sánchez-Diz, P., et al. (2003). Results of the GEP-ISFG collaborative study on two Y-STRs tetraplexes: GEPY I (DYS461, GATA C4, DYS437 and DYS438) and GEPY II (DYS460, GATA A10, GATA H4 and DYS439). *Forensic Science International, 135,* 158–162.

Sánchez-Diz, P., et al. (2008). Population and segregation data on 17 Y-STRs: Results of a GEP-ISFG collaborative study. *International Journal of Legal Medicine, 122,* 529–533.

van Asch, B., et al. (2009). Forensic analysis of dog (Canis lupus familiaris) mitochondrial DNA sequences: an inter-laboratory study of the GEP-ISFG working group. *Forensic Science International: Genetics, 4,* 49–54.

NIST (13)

Butler, J. M., & Kline, M. C. (2005). NIST Mixture interpretation interlaboratory study 2005 (MIX05). In *Proceedings of the 16th international symposium on human identification*. Available at <http://www.cstl.nist.gov/biotech/strbase/interlab/MIX05/MIX05poster.pdf>.

Duewer, D. L., et al. (1995). Interlaboratory comparison of autoradiographic DNA profiling measurements. 2. Measurement uncertainty and its propagation. *Analytical Chemistry, 67,* 1220–1231.

Duewer, D. L., et al. (1997). Interlaboratory comparison of autoradiographic DNA profiling measurements. 4. Protocol effects. *Analytical Chemistry, 69,* 1882–1892.

Duewer, D. L., et al. (1998). Interlaboratory comparison of autoradiographic DNA profiling measurements: Precision and concordance. *Journal of Forensic Sciences, 43,* 465–471.

Duewer, D. L., et al. (2000). RFLP band size standards: NIST Standard Reference Material® 2390. *Journal of Forensic Sciences, 45*, 1093–1105.

Duewer, D. L., et al. (2000). RFLP band size standards: Cell line K562 values from 1991—1997 proficiency studies. *Journal of Forensic Sciences, 45*, 1106–1118.

Duewer, D. L., et al. (2001). NIST Mixed Stain Studies #1 and #2: interlaboratory comparison of DNA quantification practice and short tandem repeat multiplex performance with multiple-source samples. *Journal of Forensic Sciences, 46*, 1199–1210.

Duewer, D. L., et al. (2004). NIST Mixed Stain Study #3: Signal intensity balance in commercial short tandem repeat multiplexes. *Analytical Chemistry, 76*, 6928–6934.

Kline, M. C., et al. (1997). Interlaboratory evaluation of short tandem repeat triplex CTT. *Journal of Forensic Sciences, 42*(5), 897–906.

Kline, M. C., et al. (2003). NIST mixed stain study 3: DNA quantitation accuracy and its influence on short tandem repeat multiplex signal intensity. *Analytical Chemistry, 75*, 2463–2469.

Kline, M. C., et al. (2005). Results from the NIST 2004 DNA quantitation study. *Journal of Forensic Sciences, 50*(3), 571–578.

Mudd, J. L., et al. (1994). Interlaboratory comparison of autoradiographic DNA profiling measurements. 1. Data and summary statistics. *Analytical Chemistry, 66*, 3303–3317.

Stolorow, A. M., et al. (1996). Interlaboratory comparison of autoradiographic DNA profiling measurements. 3. Repeatability and reproducibility of RFLP band sizing, particularly bands of molecular size > 10 k base pairs. *Analytical Chemistry, 68*, 1941–1947.

Reference Materials

Institute for Reference Materials and Measurements (IRMM). <http://irmm.jrc.ec.europa.eu/html/homepage.htm>.

National Institute of Standards and Technology (NIST). <http://www.nist.gov>.

Fregeau, C. J., et al. (1995). Characterization of human lymphoid cell lines GM9947 and GM9948 as intra- and interlaboratory reference standards for DNA typing. *Genomics, 28*, 184–197.

Kline, M. C. (2006). NIST SRM Updates: Value-added to the current materials in SRM 2391b and SRM 2395. In *Poster at 17th international symposium on human identification*. Nashville, TN. (Available at <http://www.cstl.nist.gov/biotech/strbase/pub_pres/Promega2006_Kline.pdf>).

Kline, M. C., et al. (2009). Production and certification of NIST standard reference material 2372 human DNA quantitation standard. *Analytical & Bioanalytical Chemistry, 394*, 1183–1192.

May, W. E., et al. (1999). Definitions of terms and modes used at NIST for value-assignment of reference materials for chemical measurements: *NIST Special Publication 260-136*. Washington DC: US Government Printing Office. Available at <http://www.cstl.nist.gov/div839/special_pubs/SP260136.pdf>.

NIST SRMs. <http://www.nist.gov/srm>

NIST SRM 2372 STRBase page. <http://www.cstl.nist.gov/strbase/srm2372.htm>.

Szibor, R., et al. (2003). Cell line DNA typing in forensic genetics—the necessity of reliable standards. *Forensic Science International, 138*, 37–43.

Vallone, P. M., et al. (2008). Development and usage of a NIST standard reference material for real-time PCR quantitation of human DNA. *Forensic Science International Genetics Supplement Series, 1*, 80–82.

STR Typing Kits and Concordance Studies

Budowle, B., & Sprecher, C. J. (2001). Concordance study on population database samples using the PowerPlex 16 kit and AmpFlSTR Profiler Plus kit and AmpFlSTR COfiler kit. *Journal of Forensic Sciences, 46*, 637–641.

Budowle, B., et al. (2001). STR primer concordance study. *Forensic Science International, 124*, 47–54.

Clayton, T. M., et al. (2004). Primer binding site mutations affecting the typing of STR loci contained within the AMPFlSTR SGM Plus kit. *Forensic Science International, 139*, 255–259.

Hill, C. R., et al. (2010). Strategies for concordance testing. *Profiles in DNA (Promega), 13*(1). Available at <http://www.promega.com/profiles/>.

Kline, M. C., et al. (1998). Non-amplification of a vWA allele. *Journal of Forensic Sciences, 43*(1), 250.

STRBase Null Allele Report. <http://www.cstl.nist.gov/biotech/strbase/NullAlleles.htm>.

CHAPTER

8

DNA Databases: Uses and Issues

Of any aspect of forensic DNA typing, DNA databases have arguably had the most significant impact on the criminal justice system in recent years. Serial crimes have been connected and solved. Cases without initial suspects have been brought to resolution. The innocence of unjustly incarcerated individuals has been verified when post-conviction evidence has matched another offender.

On October 13, 1998, the Federal Bureau of Investigation (FBI) officially launched its nationwide DNA database for participating law enforcement agencies. The Combined DNA Index System or CODIS involves software and hardware systems used to connect laboratories housing DNA data at the local, state, and national level in LDIS (Local DNA Index System), SDIS (State DNA Index System), or NDIS (National DNA Index System), respectively. As this chapter is being written more than 12 years later, NDIS contains over 9 million short tandem repeat (STR) profiles and links all 50 states in the United States with the capability to search criminal DNA profiles. DNA databases around the world have revolutionized the ability to use DNA profile information to link crime scene evidence to perpetrators.

These databases are effective because a majority of crimes are committed by repeat offenders. Studies have shown that more than 60% of those individuals put in prison for violent offenses and subsequently released are re-arrested for a similar offense in less than three years (McEwen & Reilly 1994, Langan & Levin 2002, Langan et al. 2003). Serious serial crimes can be connected and their perpetrators stopped through matching biological evidence between crime scenes and offenders. This chapter discusses the DNA databases being used in the United States and throughout the world to stop criminals. Issues surrounding the use and potential expansion of DNA databases are also covered.

VALUE OF DNA DATABASES

Information sharing has always been crucial to successful law enforcement. Good information can solve crimes and ultimately save lives. DNA databases have demonstrated their ability to serve as valuable tools in aiding law enforcement investigations (Gabriel et al. 2010). Their effectiveness continues to grow as the databases get larger. These databases can be used to locate suspects in crime cases that would otherwise never have been solved. However, with the growth and success of DNA databases, privacy concerns have been raised regarding the use and potential expansion of DNA databases as discussed later in the chapter.

An important role that DNA databases can serve is to make associations between groups of unsolved cases. Criminals do not honor the same geographical boundaries that law enforcement personnel do. Crimes committed in Florida can be linked to those committed in Virginia through an effective national DNA database.

DNA profile information must be in the database for it to be of value. For many years, tremendous sample backlogs have existed in the United States (Lovirich et al. 2004, Nelson 2010)—meaning that samples have been collected from either crime scenes or qualifying offenders but are awaiting analysis and entry into the DNA database. In order to try to alleviate this sample backlog, hundreds of millions of dollars have been poured into U.S. forensic DNA laboratories since U.S. Attorney General John Ashcroft announced the President's DNA Initiative in March 2003.

The Debbie Smith Act of 2004 (42 U.S.C 13701), which was named for a sexual assault victim whose attacker was eventually identified through a DNA database match, provides federal funding to state and local governments to perform DNA testing of backlogged samples. This funding was initially approved by Congress in 2004 and renewed in 2008. From 2005 to 2009, the U.S. government committed over $150 million per year for backlog reduction. With the renewal of the Debbie Smith Act, this funding for increasing the numbers of samples in DNA databases should continue through 2014. For more information on this initiative and results, see http://www.dna.gov.

The result of this influx of substantial funding has been the rapid expansion of the DNA database size in the United States. Yet sample backlogs still exist because the success of DNA testing has encouraged more sample submissions (Nelson 2010). In addition, expanded laws enable a wider collection of qualified offenders that translates into larger numbers of DNA samples that must be processed. Many U.S. states now have laws requiring those arrested for any felony offense to have their DNA collected and submitted to a DNA database.

The establishment of an effective DNA database requires time and full cooperation between forensic DNA laboratories, the law enforcement community, and government policy makers. An analysis of the return on this investment illustrates the worth of this work to society and especially to victims of crime (Wickenheiser 2004; see Butler 2010, *Fundamentals*, D.N.A. Box 12.1).

Definitions: Database vs. Databank

It is helpful to define several terms as we will use them in the course of this book: database, databank, and population database. A *database* is a collection of computer files containing entries of DNA profiles that can be searched to look for potential matches. In the case of essentially all forensic laboratories today, a DNA profile consists of a listing of STR genotypes produced through the process described in the previous chapters.

However, because each country may choose to use a different set of core STR markers, not all data will be compatible between countries or laboratories if there was ever a desire to search someone else's database with your unknown crime scene profile. The need for a compatible currency of data exchange is the reason that the 13 CODIS core STR loci were selected in the United States in November 1997 (see Chapter 5) almost a year before launching NDIS in October 1998.

The samples from which STR profiles are generated are usually from forensic casework or a criminal offender who has been deemed to legally qualify for entry into the database. A *databank*, as the term will be used in this book, is a collection of the actual samples—usually in the form of a blood sample or buccal swab or their DNA extracts. Most jurisdictions permit the retention of the biological specimen even after the STR typing results have been obtained and the DNA profile entered into the database. This sample retention is for quality control purposes (including hit confirmation) and enables testing of additional STRs or other genetic loci should a new technology be developed in the future. However, as will be discussed later in the chapter, sample retention is one of the first points raised by critics as inappropriate due to their fear that other genetic information will be analyzed from these samples.

Finally, information on allele frequencies from a group or groups of representative samples is included in a *population database*. Again, as a database, this refers to a collection of DNA profiles. However, this population database is not used for any kind of sample matching purposes. Rather, it is used to estimate random match probabilities based on allele frequency measurements from a group of usually 100 or more individuals selected to represent a specific group of interest. The individuals from which DNA profiles are generated for use in a population database are completely anonymous and only classified and grouped by their self-identified ethnicity. Within the CODIS software, a computer program known as PopStats performs the match probability calculations using allele frequencies from a previously typed set of samples whose STR profiles comprise the various classifications of the population database (e.g., African American, Caucasian, etc.).

Aspects of a National DNA Database

Implementing an effective national DNA database is an enormous task. A number of components must be in place before the database can be established and actually be effective. These include:

- A commitment on the part of each state (and local) government to provide samples for the DNA database—both offender and crimescene samples;
- A common set of DNA markers or standard core set so that results can be compared between all samples entered into the database;
- Standard software and computer formats so that data can be transferred between laboratories and a secure computer network to connect the various sites involved in the database (if more than one laboratory is submitting data); and
- Quality standards so that everyone can rely on results from each laboratory.

The technology of forensic DNA databases basically involves three parts: (1) collecting specimens from known criminals or other qualifying individuals as defined by law,

(2) analyzing those specimens and placing their DNA profiles in a computer database, and (3) subsequently comparing unknown or "Q" profiles obtained from crime scene evidence with the known or "K" profiles in the database. This last part often requires laboratories to work cases without suspects in order to put the crime scene DNA profiles into the database. A DNA database then enables a massive forensic unknown to offender comparison. Using these DNA databases, law enforcement agencies have been successful in identifying suspects in cases that would likely be unsolvable by any other means.

All 50 states within the U.S. have enacted legislation to establish a DNA database containing profiles from individuals convicted of specific crimes. The laws vary widely across the states concerning the scope of crimes requiring sample collection for DNA databank entry. Almost all of the states now collect samples from all felons and a growing fraction are entering DNA profiles from those arrested and accused for certain felony offenses. The trend toward broader coverage of criminal DNA databases will likely continue as these resources demonstrate their value to the criminal justice system.

ENFSI DNA Working Group Recommendations

The European Network of Forensic Science Institutes (ENFSI) DNA Working Group has produced a nice set of recommendations on DNA database management. The full document, which is updated annually following the April ENFSI DNA Working Group meeting, is available on the ENFSI website: http://www.enfsi.eu/page.php?uid=98.

The 28 recommendations from the April 2010 document are listed below (ENFSI 2010):

1. Every EU/ENFSI-country should establish a forensic DNA-database and specific legislation for its implementation and management.
2. The type of crime-related stain DNA-profiles which can be included in a DNA-database should not be restricted.
3. To increase the chance of DNA-profiles of stains to match a person, the number of persons in a DNA-database who are likely to cause matches with those stains should be as high as legally (and financially) possible.
4. Managers of national DNA-databases should establish (together with other stakeholders) criteria for the inclusion of partial DNA-profiles to obtain an acceptable balance between the minimum allowable level of evidential value (maximum random match probability) of a DNA-profile and maximum number of adventitious matches a partial DNA-profile is expected to generate.
5. DNA-profiles produced by older commercial kits should be upgraded (if possible) after a match in the National DNA-database to increase the evidential value of the match and also to fulfill the criteria for international comparison if a country wants to include DNA-profiles produced by older commercial kits in international search actions.
6. The number of loci in reference samples should be the maximum of the number of loci present in the kit(s) used for the production of the DNA-profiles of the reference samples to enhance the chance of finding relevant matches with partial DNA-profiles.
7. Labs producing DNA-profiles for a DNA-database should, as a minimum, be ISO-17025 (and/or nationally equivalent) accredited and should participate in challenging proficiency tests.

8. When DNA-profiles produced from low levels of DNA are included in a DNA-database they should be recognizable and a dedicated (near) match strategy should be used for them.
9. When a new allele is observed in a DNA-profile, its presence should be confirmed by repeated DNA-isolation, PCR, capillary electrophoresis and allele calling of the DNA-profile. Only new alleles, of which the size can be accurately determined using the internal DNA-size-standard, should be included in the DNA database.
10. Alleles from loci with chromosomal anomalies should not be included in a DNA-database as they may be caused by somatic mutations which may only occur in certain tissues/body fluids.
11. Wild cards that do not represent a designated allele should not be part of the minimum number of loci/alleles required by the Prüm-matching rules.
12. The guidelines in the document of the ISFG-working group on the analysis of mixed profiles should be used for the analysis of mixed profiles.
13. A numerical match between a reference sample and a mixed profile must always be checked against the plot of the mixed profile.
14. Mixed profiles of more than 2 persons should not systematically be included in a DNA-database because they generally will produce too many adventitious matches.
15. If the removal of a DNA-profile from the DNA-database is dependent on external information, a process should be in place to give the custodian of the DNA-database access to this information preferably by means of an automated message after an event which influences the deletion date of a DNA-profile.
16. There should be a system that can be consulted by those responsible for sampling persons to see whether a person is already present in the DNA-database.
17. The system which can be consulted by those responsible for sampling persons to see whether a person is already present in the DNA-database should be combined with a rapid biometric identification system like fingerprints to verify whether a person is already present in the DNA-database.
18. Any DNA-database should have an associated elimination DNA-database (or databases). This should include laboratory staff of all categories as well as visiting maintenance personnel. Profiles from those with access to samples (e.g., police) should also be included in addition to unidentified DNA-profiles found in negative control samples which may originate in manufacturing disposables and/or chemicals. The latter category of DNA-profiles should be shared with other ENFSI-countries.
19. The occurrence of errors in DNA-databases as a result of human mistakes associated with data entry should be avoided as much as possible by automating the allele calling and the DNA-database import process. When DNA-profiles are entered manually into the DNA-database this should be done by a process which detects typing errors, for example by double (blind) entry of data.
20. As a national DNA-database regularly is subject to attention from the public, politicians and the media, a DNA-database manager should consider establishing performance parameters and making these publicly available.
21. DNA-database managers should be aware of the possibility of adventitious matches and be able to calculate their expected numbers for the matches they report. When reporting a DNA-database match, a warning should be included indicating the factors that

increase the possibility of finding an adventitious match (size of the database, number of searches, mixed and partial profiles/random match probability, presence of family members).

22. A DNA-database match report of a crime scene related DNA-profile with a person should be informative and apart from the usual indication of the evidential value of the match (RMP) it should also contain a warning indicating the possibility of finding adventitious matches (as mentioned in recommendation 21) and its implication that the match should be considered together with other information.
23. DNA-profiles should be entered into a database in a way that guarantees their correct import. Access to the DNA-database should be limited to those persons who need to have access, by physical and organizational measures. Regular back-ups should be made, stored in a safe place, and put back at regular intervals to simulate recovery from a disaster. When DNA-profiles and their associated information are present in different systems, these systems should be regularly compared to check whether they are still properly synchronized.
24. To detect false negative matches (e.g. matches which should be found but are not found because one of the DNA-profiles contains an error) regular full DNA database searches allowing one or more mismatches should be performed. When a match between two DNA-profiles contains a mismatch in one of the loci, the original data of both DNA-profiles should be checked to see if one of the DNA-profiles contains an error.
25. Information from a National DNA-database should be combined with other types of evidence to increase the number of crimes for which a lead can be identified.
26. As automated processes reduce the possibility of human errors, they should be introduced for those processes that are straight forward.
27. From a forensic point of view the cell material of reference samples should be stored as long as their corresponding DNA-profiles.
28. Because DNA-databases have a very important but also very delicate role in society, the custodian of a DNA-database should develop tools to make objective information about the DNA-database available to politicians, the public and the media.

NATIONAL DNA DATABASES AROUND THE WORLD

A number of countries around the world have started national DNA databases (Table 8.1). The first national DNA databank, and so far the most effective (and aggressive in its application), was created in the United Kingdom in April 1995. The tremendous success of DNA in aiding crime solving has spawned extensive growth of DNA testing and formation of DNA databases around the globe.

According to a 2008 Interpol survey of 186 countries around the world, 120 countries (65%) are performing DNA profiling and 54 countries (29%) have national DNA databases (Table 8.1). Over 16 million DNA profiles existed at the time of the survey with roughly 8% of the total (1.2 million) representing crime scene evidence and the rest being from known individuals such as convicted offenders, arrestees, or volunteers. As of this 2008 survey, less than 20,000 samples had been collected worldwide from missing persons or unidentified human remains (Table 8.1).

TABLE 8.1 Summary of Global DNA Profiling and Databases.

Interpol Region		Africa	Americas	Asia & South Pacific	Europe	North Africa & Middle East	Total
Number of Countries		48	37	35	49	17	186
DNA Profiling		14	27	20	46	13	120
DNA Database		2	5	7	31	9	54
Number of Samples	# countries contributing						
Crime Scene	71	66,941	279,475	257,947	667,738	4,281	1,276,382
Convicted Offenders	44	0	6,424,724	1,052,150	287,149	25,672	7,789,695
Suspects/Arrestees	48	33,781	136,296	309,326	726,171	1,322	1,206,896
Convict or Suspect	12	–	–	–	5,990,593	–	5,990,593
Victim/Volunteer	41	21,262	587	66,141	2,133	2,250	92,373
Other	27	0	6,700	31,501	36,210	72	74,483
Missing Person	34	0	519	30	2,955	1	3,505
Unidentified Human Remains	48	0	2,285	9,615	1,588	1,521	15,009
						TOTAL	**16,448,936**

Source: Interpol DNA Unit (Interpol Global DNA Profiling 2008 Survey, Table 6.3, p. 67).

The UK National DNA Database (NDNAD)

On April 10, 1995 the world's first national DNA database, often referred to as NDNAD, was launched by the United Kingdom's Home Office (Werrett 1997). This database originally stored data from only six STR loci from the Second Generation Multiplex (SGM) consisting of FGA, TH01, VWA, D8S1179, D18S51, and D21S11. In 1999, an expansion was made to 10 STR loci (the six SGM loci plus D3S1358, D16S539, D2S1338, and D19S433) using the SGM Plus kit from Applied Biosystems. In 2009, the European Union voted to require additional STR loci in order to enable greater DNA data sharing across European countries (see Chapter 5). Plans for a future Pan-European database will likely expand the number of core loci used in the UK to 15 STRs.

In its first five years (1995 to 2000), more than 500,000 DNA profiles were entered into the database and more than 50,000 criminal investigations were aided. As of 2010, the NDNAD contains more than four million profiles and regularly aids UK law enforcement personnel in resolving thousands of crimes each year. With around 50 million people in the UK, their DNA database of greater than four million profiles represents the highest proportion of its population.

A survey in 2004 (Asplen 2004) showed at the time that the NDNAD delivered over 1700 crime scene-to-crime scene or suspect-to-crime scene hits per week! The UK government invested more than £182 million into NDNAD in the first 10 years of its existence, which equates to approximately £3 ($5) per citizen invested in DNA databasing.

Since April 2007, the UK NDNAD has been the responsibility of the National Policing Improvement Agency (NPIA), whose role it is to run database operations and to maintain integrity of the data. A National DNA Database Strategy Board governs and provides oversight of the operation of the NDNAD.

The UK database has come under intense scrutiny since a December 2008 ruling by the European Court of Human Rights. In the case of *S. and Marper v. The United Kingdom*, it was decided that retaining DNA profiles of individuals who were arrested but not convicted was a violation of the right to privacy under the European Convention of Human Rights (see ruling at http://www.webcitation.org/5g6FzdBr4). In May 2009, the UK government responded that it would continue holding DNA profiles of convicted individuals for an indefinite period of time but that adults arrested but not convicted would have their DNA profiles deleted after a period of 6 or 12 years depending on the type of crime for which the individual was arrested. Arrested juveniles can have their profiles removed when they turn 18 if they are not convicted of a crime.

Despite the recent challenges and scrutiny, the NDNAD has been a model for many of the other DNA databases developed around the world. The success of this law enforcement tool has led to legislation in many other countries enabling the development and growth of national DNA databases.

Other National DNA Databases Around the World

National DNA databases are being used in many countries around the world, and a number of other nations are in the early stages of building their own DNA databases. The same STR markers are being used in many instances. For example, there are eight STR loci (FGA, TH01, VWA, D3S1358, D8S1179, D16S539, D18S51, and D21S11) that overlap between European and United States DNA database collection efforts. This fact will permit international collaborations on cases that warrant them although having more loci in common would be beneficial as the various DNA databases continue to grow in size. Some countries, such as Germany, use STR markers (e.g., the highly polymorphic STR locus SE33) that are not as widely applied in other national DNA databases. Therefore, information from additional genetic markers like SE33 cannot be used in linking potential cross-border crime since it would not be available in data sets from both countries.

A minimal standard set of loci known as the European Standard Set (ESS) have been adopted by the European community. The original ESS included the seven STR loci FGA, TH01, VWA, D3S1358, D8S1179, D18S51, and D21S11. As noted in Chapter 5, the European Union voted in November 2009 to adopt five additional STR loci bringing the required extended ESS to 12 STRs: FGA, TH01, VWA, D3S1358, D8S1179, D18S51, D21S11, D12S391, D1S1656, D2S441, D10S1248, and D22S1045. In addition, D16S539, D2S1338, and D19S433 are often present in commercial multiplex STR kits enabling 15 common STRs to be genotyped.

Canada, New Zealand, Australia, Japan, and a number of countries in Europe besides the United Kingdom have developed successful DNA databases. The European Network of Forensic Science Institutes (ENFSI) provides periodic surveys and information on DNA databases and database laws in Europe on their website (see http://www.enfsi.eu). Each country has different laws regarding reasons for obtaining a DNA profile, when a profile would be expunged from the database, whether or not a DNA sample will be stored following analysis, and which STR loci are included. Most countries within the European Union are standardizing on use of the 15 STRs mentioned above, which will enable fruitful collaboration of criminal DNA information in the future. China and India, the two nations with the largest populations, have also begun efforts to produce DNA databases. As of late 2010, China reportedly has over five million DNA profiles in their national DNA database being produced by a network of more than 200 laboratories.

For international cross-border DNA comparisons, Interpol has adopted the ESS along with the sex-typing marker amelogenin as additional optional information. For more information on core STR loci used by various countries, see http://www.cstl.nist.gov/biotech/strbase/coreSTRs.htm.

International Data Comparison

Several approaches have been taken to permit examination of data across international borders. These include (1) having a network of individual DNA databases that can be queried by all approved personnel, (2) sending a query profile (typically a crime scene profile from an unknown source) to another country's DNA database administrator and requesting a search against the country's index of crime scene profiles and/or index of offender profiles, and (3) some kind of combination of either #1 or #2. Differences in legislation between countries prevent DNA databases from being unified—instead data is exchanged between countries based on agreements made and legislation authorizing such communication.

Interpol has established a platform for exchange of data called the "Interpol Gateway." In May 2005, seven European countries signed what is known as the Prüm treaty to facilitate DNA profile, fingerprint, and vehicle data exchange. Two years later, the European Union adopted the Prüm treaty requiring all member countries to exchange DNA profile information. Many countries use the CODIS software (see next section), which could help unify and standardize data storage and exchange formats.

An ISO (International Standards Organization, see Chapter 7) documentary standard for DNA data exchange is in development to aid forensic and biometrics applications. "ISO/IEC 19794 Biometric Data Interchange Formats, Part 14 – DNA Data" is scheduled to be released in May 2012. The intent of this ISO standard is to establish minimum criteria for the structure of data generated by instruments and stored in DNA databases. With consistent inputs and outputs, information sharing is possible where and when desired. Thus, international DNA data exchange would be enabled with a universal language for information content and connectivity.

THE U.S. NATIONAL DNA DATABASE

The United States Congress authorized the FBI Laboratory to establish and oversee a U.S. national DNA database with the DNA Identification Act of 1994 (Public Law 103–322). However, the FBI had started a pilot project several years earlier with 14 state and local crime laboratories to see how effective a DNA database could be with the initial concepts of the CODIS system outlined at a meeting in 1990 (Baechtel et al. 1991). For the initial CODIS pilot project, DNA labs included the Arizona Department of Public Safety, the California Department of Justice, the Florida Department of Law Enforcement, the Minnesota Bureau of Criminal Apprehension, the Virginia Division of Forensic Science, the Washington State Patrol Crime Lab, Broward County Sheriff's Crime Lab (Ft. Lauderdale, Florida), Metro Dade Police Department Crime Lab (Miami, Florida), Orange County (California) Sheriff's Crime Lab, and Washoe County Sheriff's Office Crime Lab (Reno, Nevada).

It took several years to gather enough DNA profiles from convicted offenders to reach the critical mass necessary to obtain matches for crime scene evidence. During the 1990s, the number of samples in CODIS grew to several hundred thousand. In addition, the number of laboratories submitting data increased.

The original 1994 law also established a DNA Advisory Board, which served from 1995 to 2000, with the mandate to create quality assurance standards (see Chapter 7) to ensure the reliability of data going into the U.S. national DNA database. Since 2000, the DNA Advisory Board designated the Scientific Working Group on DNA Analysis Methods (SWGDAM) with the responsibility for recommending revisions of the Quality Assurance Standards (QAS) to the FBI Director. The most recent (as of the time this book was completed in early 2011) QAS versions for casework and database laboratories went into effect on July 1, 2009.

When NDIS was launched in October 1998, only nine states participated. The number of NDIS-participating states grew as state laws were passed that permitted DNA data collection. In addition, states had to receive the necessary computer hardware and sign an NDIS memorandum of understanding (MOU) in which they agreed to abide by NDIS Procedures before they could participate. Since July 2004, all 50 states within the U.S. participate in NDIS as do the FBI Laboratory, the U.S. Army Criminal Investigation Laboratory (USACIL), and the Bureau of Alcohol, Tobacco, and Firearms (ATF) Laboratory on the federal level.

The National DNA Index System (NDIS) manages nationwide information in a single repository maintained by the FBI Laboratory. Participating states submit their DNA profiles in order to have searches performed on a national level. The role of NDIS is to search casework and offender indices, manage candidate matches, and return results of matches to the local and/or state level.

Local, State, and National Levels

The U.S. national DNA database is composed of three tiers: local, state, and national (Figure 8.1). All three levels contain the convicted offender and casework indexes and the population data file. The original CODIS software was configurable to support any RFLP (restriction fragment length polymorphism) or PCR DNA markers although as of 2000 only STR data have been added. At the local level, or Local DNA Index System (LDIS), DNA analysts can input forensic DNA profiles and search for matches with local cases. Forensic DNA records that originate at the local level can be "uploaded" or transmitted to the state and national levels.

Each participating state within the U.S. has a single laboratory that functions as the State DNA Index System (SDIS) to manage information at the state level. SDIS enables the exchange and comparison of DNA profiles within a state and is usually operated by the agency responsible for maintaining a state's offender DNA database program.

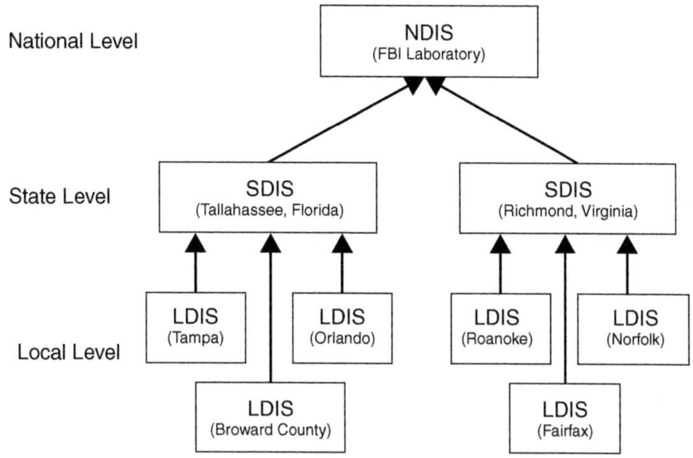

FIGURE 8.1 Schematic of the three tiers in the Combined DNA Index System (CODIS). DNA profile information begins at the local level, or Local DNA Index System (LDIS), and then can be uploaded to the state level, or State DNA Index System (SDIS), and finally to the national level, or National DNA Index System (NDIS). Each local or state laboratory maintains its portion of CODIS while the FBI Laboratory maintains the national portion (NDIS).

Combined DNA Index System (CODIS)

As noted previously, CODIS stands for the Combined DNA Index System and represents the software used to connect law enforcement laboratories housing U.S. DNA data at the local, state, and national level in LDIS, SDIS, and NDIS, respectively. These U.S. sites are all networked together on the CJIS WAN (Criminal Justice Information Systems Wide Area Network), a stand-alone law enforcement computer network that operates in a similar fashion to the Internet. The software is the same at all sites with various configurations that permit different levels of access (LDIS, SDIS, or NDIS). Software versions are updated periodically and provided to all CODIS laboratories by the FBI.

As of November 2010, CODIS software was installed in 190 U.S. laboratories representing all 50 states as well as the FBI Laboratory, USACIL, District of Columbia (Washington, DC), and Puerto Rico. This software enables NDIS-participating laboratories to submit DNA profiles for the 13 CODIS core STR loci to the U.S. national DNA database. Of the 190 sites where CODIS software is installed in the United States, 136 are LDIS and 54 are SDIS; the FBI is the only NDIS site.

The FBI has also provided a stand-alone version of the CODIS software to 68 government law enforcement laboratories in 34 different countries to aid their DNA database work. These countries include Argentina, Australia, Belgium, Bosnia, Botswana, Brazil, Canada, Cayman Islands, Chile, Columbia, Croatia, Czech Republic, Denmark, Estonia, Finland, France, Greece, Hong Kong, Hungary, Iceland, Israel, Italy, Latvia, Lithuania, Netherlands, Norway, Poland, Portugal, Singapore, Slovakia, South Korea, Spain, Sweden, and Switzerland. *It is important to note that the DNA databases in these countries use the CODIS software for their own DNA database initiatives and are not connected to the national, state, or local DNA databases in the United States.*

Each year, usually in October or November, the FBI Laboratory sponsors a National CODIS Conference to inform CODIS users of relevant issues and updates to the software and its use. Information on this conference is available at http://www.fbi.gov/about-us/lab/codis/.

CODIS Software

The CODIS software has been developed over the past two decades under multiple U.S. government contracts originally with SAIC (Scientific Applications International Corporation) and now with Unisys Corporation along with several subcontractors. A program manager within the FBI Laboratory manages the overall software development, which has cost tens of millions of dollars and taken many years to develop.

The CODIS software consists of four main subprograms: *Specimen Manager* handles the DNA profiles, *Match Manager* handles the candidate matches, *Autosearcher* conducts the database searches, and *PopStats* enables DNA profile probability calculations from population data.

CJIS WAN: The Computer Network of CODIS

Public crime laboratories in the United States are connected via the FBI's Criminal Justice Information Services Wide Area Network (CJIS WAN) through T1 lines capable of transmitting 1.5 megabytes of information per second. CJIS WAN provides Internet-like connectivity but without the security risk. This network is an intranet with access granted only to participating laboratories.

Each state pays for their end of the system. The computer equipment for a state system costs around $15,000 to $25,000. The FBI Laboratory provides the CODIS software and maintains the equipment for the national system. Each state (SDIS) laboratory signs an MOU with the FBI. LDIS labs must then adhere to the state signed MOU. CODIS users agree to adhere to FBI-issued quality assurance standards (and accreditation by a recognized accreditation source) and to submit to NDIS assessments.

Information Storage Categories or Indices

Data stored in the U.S. national DNA database are maintained in one of several categories, termed "indexes" (or "indices"). The convicted offender index and the forensic index are the two largest groups of sample data. The *convicted offender index* (sometimes shortened here to *offender index*) contains DNA profiles from individuals convicted of crimes such as sexual assault, murder, burglary, etc. On the other hand, the *forensic index* DNA profiles typically come from crime scene evidence without a suspect. However, forensic unknowns from solved crimes may be retained in the forensic index in order to help link serial crimes and aid the investigation of an unsolved case. In a sense, the forensic index provides "question" samples in the Q-K comparison while the offender index serves as the "known" sample.

With the passage of federal and state laws enabling DNA to be collected from individuals who are arrested for crimes (prior to conviction), an *arrestee index* was established a few years ago. When state laws permit collection of DNA samples at the point of arrest or probable cause determination, these DNA profiles are housed in the arrestee index. Only states authorized to collect and database DNA samples from arrestees may upload these DNA profiles to NDIS for searching at the national level.

A national missing persons program (see Chapter 9) is supported with several separate indices in NDIS. DNA profiles from missing persons, unidentified human remains, and biological relatives of missing persons can be stored and searched against one another to try to find a direct or kinship match.

Numbers of DNA Profiles Stored

When NDIS was first activated in October 1998, there were 119,000 offender profiles and 5000 forensic casework profiles from nine states. By December 1999, 21 states and the FBI had input 211,673 offender profiles and 11,112 forensic profiles. While many of the original DNA profiles were from RFLP markers, forensic DNA laboratories in the United States converted completely to the 13 core STR loci shortly after the turn of the century. Presumably all samples for the foreseeable future will be typed with these STRs or an expanded set of loci including all or most of the original 13 core loci. At the end of 2010, the total number of offender STR profiles stood at over 9.2 million with almost 352,000 forensic profiles present in NDIS. Table 8.2 shows the growth in the number of samples at NDIS in offender, forensic, and arrestee indices from 2000 to 2010. Arrestee data have only been allowed at NDIS since 2006.

TABLE 8.2 Growth in Numbers of DNA Profiles Present in Various NDIS Indices (Cumulative Totals by Year).

Year Ending Dec 31	Forensic	Convicted Offender	Arrestee	Total Offender*
2000	21,625	441,181	–	441,181
2001	27,897	750,929	–	750,929
2002	46,177	1,247,163	–	1,247,163
2003	70,931	1,493,536	–	1,493,536
2004	93,956	2,038,514	–	2,038,514
2005	126,315	2,826,505	–	2,826,505
2006	160,582	3,977,433	54,313	4,031,748
2007	203,401	5,287,505	85,072	5,372,773
2008	248,943	6,398,874	140,719	6,539,919
2009	298,369	7,389,917	351,926	7,743,329
2010	351,951	8,559,841	668,849	9,233,554

Source: CODIS brochure available at http://www.fbi.gov/about-us/lab/codis/codis_brochure and FBI Laboratory's CODIS Unit.

**The total offender column sums the convicted offender and arrestee data and also includes a relatively small number of profiles present in a Legal Index and a Detainee Index.*

An examination of the numbers of samples in these various categories over the past several years shows several trends. First, there has been tremendous growth in the number of DNA profiles submitted to NDIS. This is due to increased funding and expansion of DNA database laws. Second, there is a much smaller number of forensic samples being submitted. The primary reason for the smaller number of crime scene samples is that it is much harder to process crime scene samples than single-source DNA samples of high quality and quantity from offenders and arrestees. Convicted-offender and arrestee samples of high quality and quantity are also in the same format (i.e., liquid blood or DNA extracted from buccal swabs), which improves the ability to automate the DNA typing process. On the other hand, forensic cases can involve the examination of a dozen or more pieces of biological evidence from a variety of formats (e.g., semen stains, bloodstains, etc.), which makes them much more challenging to process, especially if DNA degradation is found or mixtures are present.

What Information is Stored

Since they were selected in November 1997, the 13 CODIS core STR loci (see Chapter 5) have been required for data entry into the national level of the U.S. DNA database. These 13 STR markers provide a random match probability (assuming unrelated individuals) of approximately 1 in 100 trillion.

While a complete DNA profile for the 13 core STR loci is required for the convicted offender index, a minimum of 10 of the 13 CODIS STR are needed for forensic casework index information before uploading to NDIS. Fewer core STR loci were originally acceptable at the state and local levels. The lower number of loci needed for casework DNA profiles comes from recognition that degraded DNA samples obtained from forensic cases may not yield results at every marker (see Chapter 10). Effort is also made to avoid putting mixtures into the database.

CODIS is not a criminal history information database but rather a system of pointers that provides only the information necessary for making Q-K comparisons and matches. CODIS information on each DNA sample includes four pieces of information: (1) an identifier of the submitting agency, (2) the specimen ID, (3) the STR profile itself, and (4) an identifier of the analyst responsible for the profile. As can be seen with the example in Table 8.3, there are no names associated with the STR profile stored in the CODIS software indices. No personal information, criminal history information, or case-related information is contained within CODIS.

As noted in Chapter 5, the 13 CODIS STR loci are not from gene coding regions (i.e., exons) nor are any of them trinucleotides, which can be prone to expansions that cause genetic defects. An STR profile is simply a string of numbers that provides a unique genetic identifier to a tested sample. While there has occasionally been some debate in the literature regarding potential linkage of human identity testing markers to genetic disease states, this is really a non-issue (D.N.A. Box 8.1).

Occasionally there may be a desire to require new loci as a DNA database grows (see below & Chapter 5). Because of the impact that this change may have on previous information in the database, time is typically required in order to make the change. Since the Justice for All Act of 2004, the U.S. Congress must be informed by the FBI at least six months prior

TABLE 8.3 Example of the STR Profile Information Stored in the CODIS DNA Database for a Single Sample. Note That There Is No Personal Information That Can Be Used to Link an Individual to Their DNA Profile. The Two Alleles for Each STR Marker Are Placed in Separate Columns Labeled Allele 1 and Allele 2. For Markers with Homozygous Results, Both Allele 1 and Allele 2 Are the Same (e.g., CSF1PO). The Information in the "Sample ID" Field Can Be Related to a Known Individual Only by the Originating Forensic DNA Laboratory. The Date and Time Stamp Are Included to Illustrate When the DNA Profile Was Uploaded to SDIS.

Agency ID	**Sample ID**	**Analyst ID**	**Category**	
VADFS-N	1999082605	JMB	Convicted Offender	
Marker	**Allele 1**	**Allele 2**	**Date**	**Time**
AMEL	X	Y	15-FEB-2000	17:38:30
CSF1PO	10	10	15-FEB-2000	17:38:30
D13S317	11	14	15-FEB-2000	17:38:30
D16S539	9	11	15-FEB-2000	17:38:30
D18S51	14	16	15-FEB-2000	17:38:30
D21S11	28	30	15-FEB-2000	17:38:30
D3S1358	16	17	15-FEB-2000	17:38:30
D5S818	12	13	15-FEB-2000	17:38:30
D7S820	9	9	15-FEB-2000	17:38:30
D8S1179	12	14	15-FEB-2000	17:38:30
FGA	21	22	15-FEB-2000	17:38:30
TH01	6	6	15-FEB-2000	17:38:30
TPOX	8	8	15-FEB-2000	17:38:30
VWA	17	18	15-FEB-2000	17:38:30

to any new loci being added to NDIS. One example of a recent change is that the sex-typing marker amelogenin is required for DNA profiles coming from missing persons samples, relatives of missing persons, and unidentified human remains.

How Data Quality is Maintained

The old adage of "garbage in, garbage out" applies with any database containing information that will be probed regularly. If the DNA profiles entered into a DNA database are not accurate, then they will be of little value for making a meaningful match. The high quality of data going into a DNA database is ensured by requiring laboratories to follow quality assurance standards, to submit to audits of their procedures, and by conducting regular proficiency tests of analysts (see Chapter 7).

Expert systems enable automated allele calling. When combined with laboratory information management systems (see Chapter 17), which provide electronic import of data into

D.N.A. BOX 8.1

STR MARKERS USED FOR HUMAN IDENTITY TESTING DO NOT PREDICT DISEASE

An STR profile is simply a string of numbers that provides a unique genetic identifier to a tested sample (see Table 8.3). Yet because this information ultimately may be linked back to an individual, privacy concerns have been raised as to whether or not predisposition to a genetic disease can be ascertained from the presence of a particular STR allele.

In the fall of 2007, there was a brief debate in the legal literature between Simon Cole (University of California-Irvine) and David Kaye (at that time from Arizona State University) over whether or not STR markers used in forensic DNA typing could be considered "junk DNA" and free of predicting disease or physical traits (Cole 2007, Kaye 2007). Portions of this debate arose because of a misunderstanding by Simon Cole over some of the things I had written in a review article on STR markers (Butler 2006).

As I stated in the 2006 review article, it is important to keep in mind that even though medical genetic researchers claim to have shown linkage between a particular disease gene and a core STR marker, these types of findings are often tentative and should not prevent the continued use of the STR locus in question (Butler 2006). In fact, many times these linkage "findings" can later be proven false with further studies. In the past, STR markers have been used by geneticists to follow genetic disease genes through specific alleles being passed within family pedigrees. However, this use of STRs for family linkage studies is different than associations of specific alleles in a general population with a disease state. Colin Kimpton and coworkers from the European DNA Profiling Group (EDNAP) recognized early on in the application of STRs for human identity testing that "it is likely that many or possibly most STRs will eventually be shown to be useful in following a genetic disease or other genetic trait *within a family* and therefore this possibility must be recognized at the outset of the use of such systems" (Kimpton et al. 1995; emphasis added). Family pedigree studies that track a few specific loci and alleles are different than equating a specific allele in the population with some kind of phenotypic correlation.

In 2005, an infrequently used X-chromosome STR marker named HumARA was removed from future consideration in human identity testing (Szibor et al. 2005) since it is located in an exon. Some of the longer CAG repeat alleles with HumARA have been shown to be the cause of a genetic disease, which is why this STR locus was removed from use. All of the 23 commonly used STR markers described throughout this book and present in current commercial STR kits are located in between genes ("junk DNA" regions) or in introns. Thus, by definition they are non-coding. Moreover, the relatively high mutation rate of STRs means that even if any linkage existed at one time between a specific allele and a genetic disease state, this linkage would likely not last beyond a few generations before mutation altered the allele length and effectively broke any linkage of an allele or genotype state to that specific phenotype state.

Sources:

Butler, J.M. (2006). Genetics and genomics of core STR loci used in human identity testing. Journal of Forensic Sciences, *51*, 253–265.

D.N.A. BOX 8.1 *(cont'd)*

Cole, S.A. (2007). Is the 'junk' DNA designation bunk? Northwestern University Law Review Colloquy, *102, 54–63. Available at http://www.law.northwestern.edu/lawreview/colloquy/2007/23/.*

Kaye, D.H. (2007). Please, let's bury the junk: the CODIS loci and the revelation of private information. Northwestern University Law Review Colloquy, *102, 70–81. Available at http://www.law.northwestern.edu/lawreview/colloquy/2007/25/.*

Kimpton, C.P., et al. (1995). Report on the second EDNAP collaborative STR exercise. Forensic Science International, *71, 137–152.*

Szibor, R., et al. (2005). Letter to the editor: the HumARA genotype is linked to spinal and bulbar muscular dystrophy and some further disease risks and should no longer be used as a DNA marker for forensic purposes. International Journal of Legal Medicine, *119, 179–180.*

the database, human intervention and error are reduced. When manual data entry is necessary, a "double-blind" approach is used, where the same DNA profile must be entered twice without being able to see the first entry (as in ENFSI 2010, recommendation #19). The software confirms that the two entries are the same before uploading the sample profile to the database.

In order for a state to have its DNA profiles included in the national DNA index system, a memorandum of understanding must be signed whereby the state DNA laboratories agree to adhere to the FBI-issued Quality Assurance Standards (QAS) and undergo regular audits and assessments to evaluate compliance of NDIS-participating laboratories to the forensic and databasing QAS in accordance with federal law. The original forensic QAS were adopted in October 1998 (April 1999 for convicted offender QAS). Revised QAS were implemented in July 2009 for both forensic and DNA databasing laboratories.

Audits are conducted annually for each NDIS-participating laboratory, and DNA analysts undergo semi-annual proficiency tests. Failure to pass this audit can result in a laboratory being disconnected from NDIS. Likewise, proficiency tests must be successfully completed in order for an analyst to continue to submit data to LDIS or SDIS for subsequent inclusion in NDIS.

Who Inputs Data

For a criminal DNA database to be successful, convicted offender DNA samples must be tested in addition to crimescene material from cases in which there is no suspect. Because the demand for DNA testing often surpasses the ability of public forensic laboratories to perform the tests, private contract laboratories have been used to reduce the sample backlogs for convicted offender as well as for some forensic casework samples. In the United States, much of this work is being performed with federal government financial assistance through grant programs administered by the National Institute of Justice (Nelson 2010).

Pursuant to federal law, as of 2011 only government law enforcement forensic DNA laboratories who comply with the QAS have access to CODIS. Therefore, while data may be generated by a private laboratory through outsourcing from a public forensic laboratory, the

TABLE 8.4 List of NDIS-Approved Expert Systems for Single-Source DNA Data Review (as of December 2010). Information Courtesy of Dr. Douglas Hares, FBI Laboratory CODIS Unit.

Expert System and Version(s) [Manufacturer]	Instrument Platform(s)	Kit(s)
GeneMapper*ID-X* v1.0 [Applied Biosystems]	AB 3100 (data collection v2.0)	Profiler Plus and COfiler
GeneMapper*ID-X* v1.0.1 [Applied Biosystems]	AB 3100 (data collection v2.0)	Profiler Plus and COfiler
GeneMapper*ID-X* v1.0.1 [Applied Biosystems]	AB 3130xl (data collection v3.0)	PowerPlex 16
GeneMapper*ID-X* v1.0.1 [Applied Biosystems]	AB 3130xl (data collection v3.0)	Identifiler
GeneMapper*ID-X* v1.0.1 [Applied Biosystems]	AB 3730 (data collection 3.0)	Identifiler
GeneMapper*ID-X* v1.1.1 [Applied Biosystems]	AB 3130xl (data collection v3.0)	Identifiler
GeneMapper*ID* v3.2.1* [Applied Biosystems]	AB 3130xl (data collection v3.0)	Identifiler
GeneMapper*ID* v3.2.1 [Applied Biosystems]	AB3130xl (data collection 3.0)	PowerPlex 16
i-Cubed v.4.0.2 using GeneMapper*ID* v3.2 [FSS/Promega and Applied Biosystems]	AB 3700 (data collection v3.1.1)	Identifiler
i-Cubed v.4.1.3 using GeneMapper*ID* v3.2 [FSS/Promega and Applied Biosystems]	AB 3130xl (data collection v3.0)	Identifiler
i-Cubed v.4.2.1 using GeneMapper*ID* v3.2 [FSS/Promega and Applied Biosystems]	AB 3130xl (data collection v3.0)	PowerPlex 16
i-Cubed v4.2.2 using GeneMapper*ID* v3.2.1 [FSS/Promega and Applied Biosystems]	AB 3130xl (data collection v3.0)	Identifiler
TrueAllele v2.7.348 [Cybergenetics]	AB 3100 (data collection v1.1)	Profiler Plus and COfiler
TrueAllele v2.9 [Cybergenetics]	AB 3100 (data collection v1.1)	Profiler Plus and COfiler
TrueAllele v2.9 [Cybergenetics]	AB 3130xl (data collection v3.0)	Identifiler
TrueAllele v2.9 [Cybergenetics]	AB 3130xl (data collection v3.0)	Profiler Plus and COfiler

**Originally approved as Genemapper ID-X 3.2, an update was provided by the vendor, retested by the submitting agency, and approved by the FBI.*

STR typing data must be evaluated by the public laboratory who assumes ownership of the data. Only then, after the quality of the STR typing data is confirmed, can it be uploaded by the public laboratory to LDIS, SDIS, and ultimately NDIS.

Over the past decade, contract laboratories have collectively generated millions of STR profiles and directly aided the rapid growth of the U.S. national DNA database. During this same time, with federal grant programs for capacity building, many government forensic laboratories have been working to build up their own capacity in order to be able to do all of their sample testing in-house. Improved automation through robotic sample handling and multi-capillary capillary electrophoresis (CE) systems have simplified the process of DNA typing and aided sample throughput. Several expert systems have been approved to review single-source DNA databasing profiles (Table 8.4).

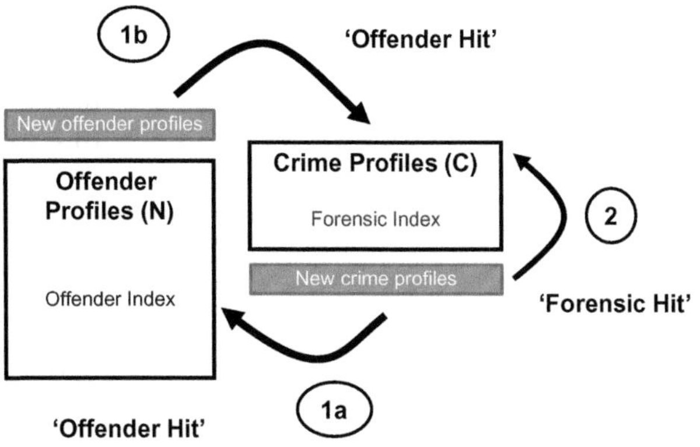

FIGURE 8.2 Primary searches conducted each week with the offender and forensic indices of the U.S. national DNA database. (1a) New crime profiles being added to the forensic index are searched against the entire offender index; (1b) new offender profiles are searched against the entire forensic index; and (2) new crime profiles are searched against the entire forensic index to help connect serial crimes. The arrestee index is treated like the offender index for these searches. A match between DNA profiles with searches 1a or 1b is termed an "offender hit" while a search 2 match results in a "forensic hit."

What Searches Are Conducted to Obtain Matches

Figure 8.2 illustrates the primary searches conducted with the two largest indices of the U.S. national DNA database and the types of "hits" or matches that can occur. An *offender hit* is produced when a match occurs between a DNA profile on the convicted-offender or arrestee index against the crime scene DNA profiles present in the forensic index during a search of offender or arrestee DNA profiles. This type of hit is sometimes referred to as a case-to-offender hit.

A *forensic hit* results from searching DNA profiles in the forensic index against other crime scene DNA profiles—essentially an effective method to look for crimes committed by a serial offender. This type of hit is sometimes referred to as a case-to-case hit.

How Success of the U.S. DNA Database Is Measured

The purpose of DNA databases is to solve crimes that would otherwise be unsolvable. While the material below is specific to the U.S. DNA database, similar concepts and metrics are used in other national DNA databases worldwide.

As mentioned in the previous section, a *hit* is a confirmed match between two or more DNA profiles discovered by the database search. Within CODIS, hits may occur at a local (LDIS), state (SDIS), or national (NDIS) level. Sometimes hits are distinguished as *"cold"* or *'warm"* depending on how much previous information is available when performing the search. A *cold hit* is one made without any prior investigative leads between the matching samples.

Both offender and forensic hits contribute to the bottom-line performance metric of a DNA database—the number of criminal *investigations aided*. The term "investigations aided" is defined as the number of criminal investigations to which CODIS has added value to the

TABLE 8.5 Hit Counting Statistics (Cumulative Totals by Year). Most Offender Hits (≈87%) Are Intrastate Rather than Interstate (National).

Year Ending Dec 31	Investigations Aided	Forensic Hits	Offender Hits	Within State Hits (≈87%)	National Offender Hits
2000	1573	507	731	705 (97%)	26
2001	3635	1031	2371	2204 (93%)	167
2002	6670	1832	5032	4394 (87%)	638
2003	11,220	3004	8269	7118 (86%)	1151
2004	20,788	5147	13,855	11,991 (87%)	1864
2005	31,485	7000	22,495	19,620 (87%)	2875
2006	45,364	9493	34,535	30,138 (87%)	4397
2007	62,725	11,890	50,244	43,688 (87%)	6556
2008	81,875	14,353	67,641	59,122 (87%)	8519
2009	105,918	17,935	89,798	78,581 (88%)	11,217
2010	129,514	21,790	112,742	97,190 (86%)	15,552

Source: CODIS brochure available at http://www.fbi.gov/about-us/lab/codis/codis_brochure and FBI Laboratory's CODIS Unit.

process (CODIS can only aid an investigation one time). In the first five years of operation (1998 to 2003), the CODIS system aided more than 11,000 investigations in the United States. Through the end of 2010, there have been more than 129,500 investigations aided using CODIS, allowing thousands of crimes to be linked and solved around the United States (Table 8.5).

Table 8.5 summarizes the growth of forensic and offender hits over the past few years. Note that almost 90% of the time, offender hits are occuring within states rather than between states, which emphasizes the value of DNA databases on a local level.

Because the number of hits is largely related to the size of the database, as the number of offender/arrestee profiles in NDIS continues to grow, there will be more investigations aided. The UK's NDNAD reportedly maintains close to a 40% chance of obtaining a match between a crime-scene profile and a "criminal justice" (arrestee or suspect) profile loaded into the database.

Number of DNA Profiles Compared with Different Searches

The number of DNA profiles being compared with different types of searches varies based on the number of DNA profiles contained in each index represented in Figure 8.2 and the types of searches performed (e.g., new forensic profile vs. entire offender index or new forensic profiles vs. entire forensic index).

Figure 8.3 illustrates the range of comparisons that may be made in forensic DNA analysis. The number of comparisons being made in each example is based on the number of crime scene samples in the forensic index (C) and the number of samples in the offender index (N).

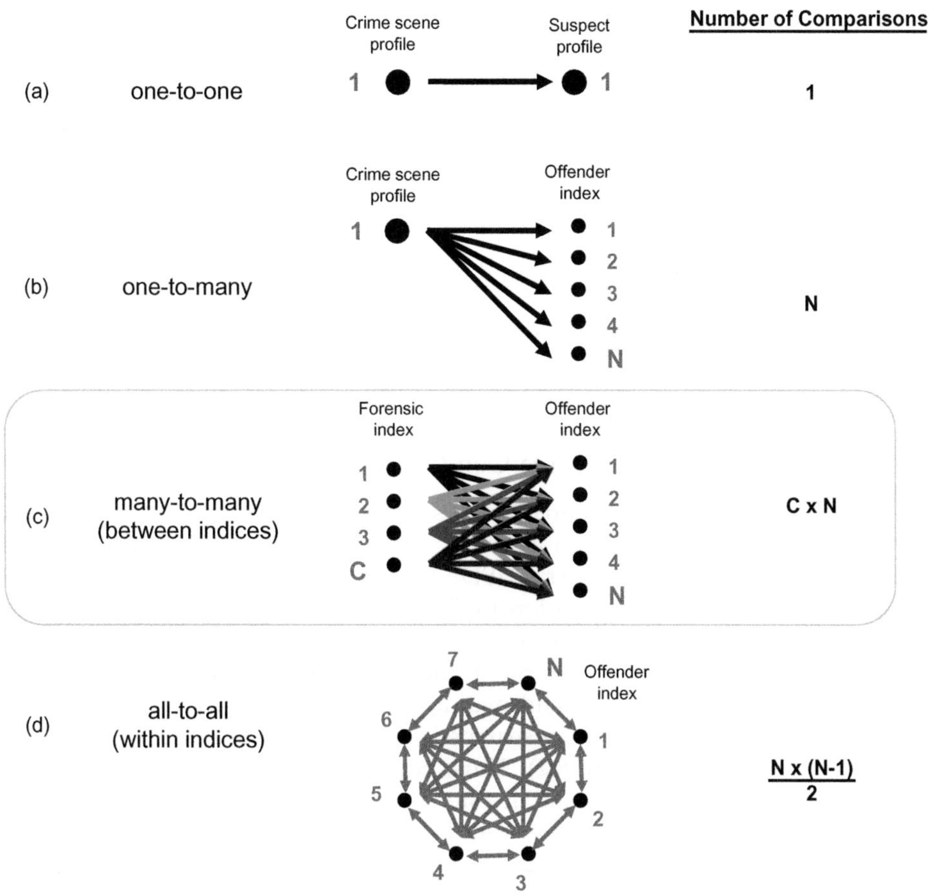

FIGURE 8.3 Illustration of various types and numbers of comparisons that may be performed in forensic DNA analysis with each dot representing a DNA profile: ranging from (a) a crime scene to suspect one-to-one comparison, (b) a "keyboard search" with one-to-many, (c) the typical database search between two indices containing C and N profiles, and (d) an all-to-all "Arizona search" within an index for quality control purposes.

Traditional forensic casework, in which a single-source profile is obtained, involves a one-to-one comparison of the question (Q) sample from the crime scene versus a single known suspect (K) sample (Figure 8.3a). Of course, if a mixture is obtained from the crime scene sample, then DNA profiles from multiple suspects or suspect(s) and victim may need to be evaluated.

If a single crime scene sample is compared to an offender index containing N individuals, then N comparisons are made (Figure 8.3b). This type of search is often called a "keyboard search." However, DNA databases contain many crime scene profiles that need to be compared to one another (requiring C × (C-1)/2 unique comparisons) to search for "forensic hits," or crime scene profiles that need to be compared to offender profiles (C × N comparisons) to search for possible "offender hits" (Figure 8.3c). In either case, the number of comparisons performed in the search is equal to the product of the number of samples in each index being compared (e.g., either C × C or C × N).

As mentioned above, an all-to-all search within an index (Figure 8.3d) can be useful for quality assurance purposes. Although these offender-to-offender searches can help maintain data quality and prevent unnecessary duplicates in the database, they can become expensive in terms of computer resources (software, hardware, and wall-clock time) due to the sheer volume of comparisons. With a million samples in a state DNA database, almost half a trillion (1 million × 1 million/2 = 500 billion) STR profile comparisons are required. This type of all-to-all search is commonly referred to as an "Arizona search" for reasons that will be explained later in the chapter.

As DNA databases grow in size, they become more valuable as an intelligence tool, but they also become more of a challenge to search rapidly.

When and How NDIS Searches Are Conducted

While state and local database uploads and searches are conducted as needed, the U.S. national database (NDIS) operates on a weekly schedule with searches performed once a week and data uploaded from each state (SDIS) on specific days for the remainder of the week. This schedule permits information to flow without clogging the system and gives time for candidate hits to be confirmed each week.

At the NDIS level, an AutoSearch is run at the beginning of each week. In actuality, the entire database is not searched over and over again each week. Rather, any DNA profiles received at NDIS in the past week are searched against the sample DNA profiles already present in the database (see Figure 8.2). Thus, new crime samples (≈1000 per week) are searched against the entire offender and arrestee indices. In addition, these new crime samples are searched against other specimens in the forensic index to look for potential case-to-case hits. New offender samples (≈25,000 per week) are likewise searched against the forensic index.

In a database of 9 million offender DNA profiles (N = 9,000,000) and 350 thousand crime samples (C = 350,000), there will be N × C comparisons made in searches between the offender and forensic indices (Figure 8.3c). Therefore, with 1000 new crime samples, nine billion comparisons are being made each week (N × C = 9,000,000 × 1000 = 9 billion). With the 25,000 new offender samples added to the database, another 8.8 billion comparisons are also being made (N × C = 25,000 × 350,000 = 8.8 billion).

Any candidate hits made during these searches are then communicated to the appropriate State or Local CODIS Administrator. By mid-week, most of the SDIS and LDIS labs have queued up hit confirmation samples. Verification of results can then be performed so that matching DNA profiles are connected to the offender's name so that local law enforcement in the appropriate jurisdiction can follow-up.

Search Stringency Used

To add to the complexity of a search, search algorithms have to take into account that DNA profiles in the forensic index, which often come from challenging evidentiary material, may be mixtures rather than single-source profiles or partial profiles due to degraded DNA (see Chapter 10) or PCR inhibition (see Chapter 4). With unresolved mixtures, multiple possibilities need to be permitted in profile matching algorithms. In addition, various LDIS or SDIS laboratories may be submitting samples to NDIS from different STR kits that amplify the same STR locus with different primers. Therefore, allele dropout could result with one STR kit being used versus another one (see Chapter 7).

In order to not miss the true connection between two DNA samples from the same source, search strategies must have the capability to permit two DNA profiles to "match" without 100% allele agreement. Lower stringency search algorithms may be used to address this issue. This type of lower stringency search takes longer than a perfect match search because more possibilities have to be considered during each comparison.

There are three levels of search stringency possible in the CODIS software: high, moderate, and low stringency. With *high stringency*, all available alleles match (i.e., are the same) in the two DNA profiles. A *moderate stringency* search requires all available alleles to match, but the two profiles can contain a different number of alleles. For example, the forensic index profile may include alleles 9,10,12 (from a mixture) while the candidate offender match has only alleles 9,12 (from a single source). Likewise, a 9,12 will match a 9,- where the 12 allele has dropped out either due to primer binding site mutation or degradation. Moderate stringency is the standard search configuration.

A *low-stringency* match occurs when one or more alleles match at a given STR locus when the two profiles are compared. Thus, a low-stringency match would exist between profiles containing alleles 8,11 and 11,14 at a given STR locus because the "11" is common to the two profiles. Low stringency searching is used in missing person related searches where a parent's DNA profile is being used to search for a child or vice versa.

Mixture Samples and Obligate Alleles

Forensic casework often results in DNA mixtures. Some of these mixtures cannot be separated into individual components (i.e., separate DNA profiles from the original people contributing to the sample). However, there may be some alleles in a mixture profile that have higher peak heights or are definitely not from the victim and have a high likelihood of being from the perpetrator. These alleles are termed "obligate" because they are required to be present in any DNA profile possibility returned from a database search. When these types of casework STR profiles are entered into the forensic index, obligate allele(s) may be designated to help reduce the pool of candidate genotypes that can be associated with the target profile being searched.

Entering a complex mixture containing many alleles into the forensic index can lead to many candidate matches, almost all of which will be spurious (see ENFSI 2010, recommendation #14). In order to reduce the chance of false positives or "adventitious matches" on a DNA database search, filters have been established to prevent inappropriate profiles from being entered. As will be discussed in the next section, the originating laboratory (i.e., the LDIS or SDIS lab submitting the mixture profile) has to follow up on any candidate hits to their casework unknown profile. Thus, the submitting lab needs to avoid putting "garbage" into a searching system that would generate mostly "garbage" in return.

Followup to Database "Cold Hits"

When a potential match is identified by the CODIS software, the laboratories responsible for the matching profiles are notified. They then contact each other to validate or refute the match. After the match has been confirmed by qualified DNA analysts, which may involve retesting of the matching convicted offender DNA sample, laboratories may exchange additional information, such as names and phone numbers of criminal investigators and case details. A hit is only counted once the candidate match is confirmed and it is determined that the match provided additional information to the case.

If a match is obtained with the convicted offender index, the identity and location of the convicted offender is determined and an arrest warrant procured. In many cases, the matching offender may already be behind bars.

PopStats: A Tool for Estimating the Rarity of DNA Profiles

As noted previously in the chapter, there is a population database provided to CODIS users with allele frequency information intended to represent major population groups found in the United States. These databases are used to estimate statistical frequencies of DNA profiles using the program *PopStats*. The PopStats estimates include random match probability, combined probability of exclusion/inclusion, and likelihood ratios.

In the U.S., Caucasians, African Americans, Southeast Hispanics, and Southwest Hispanics are the typical groups reported when estimating the rarity of a particular DNA profile. The STR allele frequencies used in PopStats were published in the May 2001 issue of the *Journal of Forensic Sciences* by Bruce Budowle and FBI colleagues in an article entitled "CODIS STR loci data from 41 sample populations" (Budowle et al. 2001).

Missing Persons

DNA databases can also play an important role in helping to identify missing individuals and aiding mass disaster reconstruction following a plane crash or terrorist activity (see Chapter 9). In these cases, DNA samples are often obtained from biological relatives that can be searched against DNA of remains recovered from a missing individual or a disaster site. Many states within the United States and nations around the world are beginning to establish missing persons databases to enable matching of recovered remains to their family members.

To aid missing persons investigations, CODIS has several indices that can store DNA profiles from both recovered remains and family samples that serve as references. Much of the data from missing persons investigations is in the form of mitochondrial DNA (mtDNA) sequences since this information can be successfully recovered from highly degraded samples. As noted in Chapter 14, use of mtDNA also enables access to a larger number of reference samples from maternal relatives of a victim.

CODIS 6.0 and future versions of the next generation CODIS software enable work with autosomal STR data, Y-STR, and mtDNA data to aid missing persons investigations and work with mass fatality samples (Bradford et al. 2010). As of early 2011, Y-STR data is only being databased and searched in connection with missing persons cases.

NDIS Procedures Board

Operational procedures are set by the NDIS Procedures Board that meets several times each year. The NDIS Procedures Board is currently composed of six state and local representatives, a representative elected by the state CODIS administrators, the Chair of the Scientific Working Group on DNA Analysis Methods (SWGDAM), and five FBI Laboratory representatives, of which four have voting privileges. The state and local representatives are selected based on region of the country, laboratory size, and the number of searchable DNA records contributed to NDIS.

The U.S. system works on the principle of shared governance with ownership of data at the local or state levels. An NDIS Custodian, who is part of the CODIS Unit within the FBI Laboratory, manages the entire system with input from an NDIS Board, which creates NDIS Procedures. State and local laboratories that are connected through the CODIS software sign memoranda of understanding (MOUs) with the FBI in order to get access to the software and to participate in data sharing.

Status as a public criminal justice agency and laboratory accreditation are requirements for connectivity to NDIS. State CODIS administrators (those running the state DNA databases) come together multiple times a year to provide input on the operations of the database. In addition, SWGDAM (see Chapter 7) has a CODIS subcommittee to provide additional guidance. Quality Assurance Standards audits and NDIS assessments are performed regularly to ensure quality and consistency in DNA operations and compliance with federal law and procedures for participation in the National DNA Index.

DNA DATABASE LAWS IN THE UNITED STATES

DNA databases work because most criminals are repeat offenders (McEwen & Reilly 1994, Langan & Levin 2002). If their DNA profiles can be entered into the system early in their criminal careers, then they can be identified when future crimes are committed. Serial crimes can also be linked effectively with a computerized DNA database. Ultimately, the value of the DNA database is in its ability to apprehend criminals who are not direct suspects in a case and to prevent further victims from crimes committed by those individuals. Within the United States, both federal and state laws impact the use of DNA databases.

Federal Laws

As mentioned earlier in the chapter, the FBI Laboratory received Congressional authority to establish NDIS with the DNA Identification Act of 1994. NDIS became operational in October 1998 with nine participating states. Table 8.6 summarizes several federal laws since 1994 that have expanded on what may be stored and searched at NDIS as well as expansions of the federal DNA database program or qualifying offenders/arrestees. The federal laws have expanded the authority for collection of DNA samples first from certain federal felony offenders, then to all federal felony offenders, and finally to all federal felony arrestees and federal detainees. Some of these laws described in Table 8.6 have also authorized an expansion of the scope of DNA profiles that may be uploaded to and searched at NDIS, to persons indicted for a crime and then to all samples legally collected, which would include arrestee profiles for states statutorily authorized to collect from arrestees.

TABLE 8.6 A Brief Review of the History of Federal U.S. Laws on DNA Databases.

Legislation	What Was Authorized
DNA Identification Act of 1994	FBI receives authority to establish a National DNA Index System (NDIS); NDIS becomes operational in Oct 1998 with 9 states participating
DNA Analysis Backlog Elimination Act of 2000	Authorizes collection of DNA samples from federal convicted offenders
USA Patriot Act of 2001	Amends the DNA Analysis Backlog Elimination Act of 2000 to include terrorism or crimes of violence in the list of qualifying federal offenses
Justice for All Act of 2004	DNA profiles from indicted persons permitted at NDIS, one-time "keyboard" search authorized; accreditation and audit for labs required; expansion to all felonies for federal convicted offenders; requires notification of Congress if new core loci are desired
DNA Fingerprint Act of 2005	Arrestee and legally collected samples permitted at NDIS; elimination of one-time "keyboard" search; expansion to arrestee and detainee samples for federal offenders
Adam Walsh Child Protection and Safety Act of 2006	Amends the DNA Analysis Backlog Elimination Act of 2000 to authorize the Attorney General to collect DNA samples from individuals who are facing charges or are convicted, in addition to individuals who are arrested.

In addition to enabling arrestees' and all other legally collected DNA samples to be stored and searched at NDIS, the DNA Fingerprinting Act of 2005 expanded collection of DNA at the federal level to all convicted offenders and non-U.S. citizens detained by the U.S. government. The FBI Laboratory restructured their DNA units in 2009 in order to accommodate the anticipated dramatic growth in the number of samples requiring analysis. By introducing automation and hiring additional staff, the FBI's Federal DNA Databasing Unit reached a capacity of 60,000 samples per month at the end of 2010 (see Chapter 17).

Crimes for Inclusion in a State DNA Database

By June 1998, all 50 states in the United States had passed legislation requiring convicted offenders to provide samples for DNA databasing. However, each state has different requirements as to what types of offenses are considered for DNA sample collection. In many states these requirements are changing over time to include more and more criminal offenses.

The requirements for having to provide a DNA sample range from strictly sex offenses to all felons to all arrestees. The trend has been to enact laws that require a DNA sample submission for any felony and is now expanding in many cases to arrested individuals. Table 8.7 includes a summary list of the qualifying offenses for entry into a state's DNA database and the number of states within the U.S. that fall into each category as of 1999, 2004, 2008, and 2010.

Some state DNA database statutes specify exactly how the sample will be collected while others simply require any biological sample containing DNA. A 1999 survey of state laws found that California required two specimens of blood, a saliva sample, and right thumb

TABLE 8.7 Summary of U.S. State DNA Database Laws and Qualifying Offenses for DNA Collection as of 1999, 2004, 2008, and 2010. For Up-to-Date Information, See http://www.dnaresource.com and http://www.ncsl.org.

	Number of States				Hit Rate Estimates*
Offenses	**1999**	**2004**	**2008**	**2010**	
Sex crimes	50	50	50	50	5%
All violent crimes	36	48	50	50	10%
Burglary	14	47	50	50	20%
All felons	5	37	47	49	45%
Juveniles	24	32	32	32	–
Arrestees	1	4	14	25	60%
Familial searching being actively used	–	–	2	2	–

**Hit rate estimates are from http://www.dnaresource.com and reflect the benefits of expanding the types of qualifying offenses and the DNA database size.*

and full palm print impressions to verify the identity of the submitting convicted offender, while South Carolina only asked for "a suitable sample" from which DNA may be obtained (Herkenham 1999).

The ability of state and local forensic DNA laboratories to improve their capabilities for DNA analysis, especially with the STR technology described in this book, has been greatly aided by federal funding. The DNA Identification Act of 1994 provided approximately $40 million in federal matching grants to aid states in DNA analysis activities. Additional Congressional allocations over the years have brought significant federal funding to state and local laboratories since the establishment of the U.S. national DNA database.

The Debbie Smith Act, part of the President's DNA Initiative, has brought hundreds of millions of dollars of funding to U.S. forensic DNA laboratories since 2004. This funding has been a great benefit to forensic DNA laboratories, which are often understaffed and underfunded. Progress on legislation regarding the use of DNA is available through the website http://www.dnaresource.com.

ISSUES AND CONCERNS WITH DNA DATABASES

There are a number of important issues for DNA databases. These issues include privacy and security of the information contained in the database, the ability to perform rapid searches and effective matching among large numbers of entries, and ensuring that high-quality data are submitted for both offender and forensic samples. In addition to maintaining the quality of the input data, database administrators must handle changes in technology. At the end of the chapter, further concerns commonly raised by DNA database critics will be addressed.

Privacy Concerns

One of the major challenges for maintaining a DNA database is the issue of privacy and security of the information stored since the database contains DNA profiles that correspond with a databank of biological samples. DNA samples contain genetic information that could be used against an individual or his or her family if not handled properly.

A conference held in Boston, Massachusetts on May 11–12, 2006 discussed many of the privacy and civil liberty concerns regarding DNA testing and DNA databases. The *Journal of Law, Medicine, & Ethics* published the proceedings of this "DNA Fingerprinting and Civil Liberties" conference in its summer 2006 issue. The titles and authors of the articles are included in Table 8.8.

The issue of privacy can be approached in multiple ways. First, the DNA markers, such as the 13 CODIS core STR loci, are in non-coding regions of the human genome and are not known to have any association with a genetic disease or any other genetic predisposition (Butler 2006, Kaye 2007). Thus, the information in the database is only useful for human identity testing (see D.N.A. Box 8.1).

Second, no names of individuals or other characterizing data are stored with the DNA profiles at the national level. The national level of CODIS only references the sources of the DNA profiles, such as Orange County Sheriff's Office or Palm Beach County Crime Laboratory. Specific case data are secured and controlled by the law enforcement agencies that submit the data. Thus, only the crime laboratory that submitted the DNA profile has the capability to link the DNA results with a known individual.

Third, data are encrypted and shared through a secure network only accessible to state and local CODIS administrators.

Fourth, federal and state penalties for improper use of criminal DNA samples include fines and possible imprisonment. Access to CODIS is solely for law enforcement purposes. There are strict penalties for anyone who uses the information or samples for any purpose other than for law enforcement. The penalties include a $250,000 fine for unauthorized disclosure of information on any sample (Herkenham 2006).

Handling Technology Changes and Legacy Data

Both computer and DNA technologies are evolving at a rapid rate. DNA databases have to be flexible enough to handle these changes. In particular, legacy data must be maintained, or the value of the database will be diminished. If different genetic markers are universally used at some time in the future, then previously collected data would be inaccessible unless there is an overlap or compatibility between the different marker systems (Gill et al. 2004). Typing potentially millions of previously tested samples with new genetic markers would be an expensive and time-consuming proposition. There are several possible ways forward to maintain core loci while adding auxillary information to established DNA databases.

As has been noted many times throughout this book, DNA testing is always a matter of comparing a question (Q) sample against a known (K) sample. This Q-K comparison requires that both samples be tested with the same genetic markers. Thus, if a new technology or set of genetic markers become available that enables improved recovery of information from crime scene samples, it would require retroactive analysis of all previously

TABLE 8.8 Authors and Titles of Articles Appearing in the Summer 2006 Issue of the *Journal of Law, Medicine, & Ethics*.

Author(s)	Page numbers	Article Title
Benjamin W. Moulton	147–148	DNA Fingerprinting and Civil Liberties
Alice A. Noble	149–152	DNA Fingerprinting and Civil Liberties
Mark A. Rothstein, Meghan K. Talbott	153–164	The Expanding Use of DNA in Law Enforcement: What Role for Privacy?
Tracey Maclin	165–187	Is Obtaining an Arrestee's DNA a Valid Special Needs Search Under the Fourth Amendment? What Should (and Will) the Supreme Court Do?
David H. Kaye	188–198	Who Needs Special Needs? On the Constitutionality of Collecting DNA and Other Biometric Data from Arrestees
Tania Simoncelli, Barry Steinhardt	199–213	California's Proposition 69: A Dangerous Precedent for Criminal DNA Databases
Amitai Etzioni	214–221	A Communitarian Approach: A Viewpoint on the Study of the Legal, Ethical and Policy Considerations Raised by DNA Tests and Databases
Frederick R. Bieber	222–233	Turning Base Hits into Earned Runs: Improving the Effectiveness of Forensic DNA Data Bank Programs
Robin Williams, Paul Johnson	234–247	Inclusiveness, Effectiveness and Intrusiveness: Issues in the Developing Uses of DNA Profiling in Support of Criminal Investigations
Henry T. Greely, Daniel P. Riordan, Nanibaa A. Garrison, Joanna L. Mountain	248–262	Family Ties: The Use of DNA Offender Databases to Catch Offenders' Kin
Erica Haimes	263–276	Social and Ethical Issues in the Use of Familial Searching in Forensic Investigations: Insights from Family and Kinship Studies
Pilar N. Ossorio	277–292	About Face: Forensic Genetic Testing for Race and Visible Traits
Troy Duster	293–300	Explaining Differential Trust of DNA Forensic Technology: Grounded Assessment or Inexplicable Paranoia?
Mervyn L. Tano	301–309	Interrelationships among Native Peoples, Genetic Research, and the Landscape: Need for Further Research into Ethical, Legal, and Social Issues
Paul C. Giannelli	310–319	Forensic Science
Margaret A. Berger	320–327	The Impact of DNA Exonerations on the Criminal Justice System
Sheila Jasanoff	328–341	Just Evidence: The Limits of Science in the Legal Process

(*Continued*)

TABLE 8.8 Authors and Titles of Articles Appearing in the Summer 2006 Issue of the *Journal of Law, Medicine, & Ethics*. (*Continued*)

Author(s)	Page numbers	Article Title
Gregory Carey, Irving I. Gottesman	342–351	Genes and Antisocial Behavior: Perceived versus Real Threats to Jurisprudence
Bartha Maria Knoppers, Madelaine Saginur, Howard Cash	352–365	Ethical Issues in Secondary Uses of Human Biological Materials from Mass Disasters
David Lazer, Viktor Mayer-Schönberger	366–374	Statutory Frameworks for Regulating Information Flows: Drawing Lessons for the DNA Data Banks from other Government Data Systems
R. E. Gaensslen	375–379	Should Biological Evidence or DNA be Retained by Forensic Science Laboratories After Profiling? No, Except Under Narrow Legislatively-Stipulated Conditions
M. Dawn Herkenham	380–384	Retention of Offender DNA Samples Necessary to Ensure and Monitor Quality of Forensic DNA Efforts: Appropriate Safeguards Exist to Protect the DNA Samples from Misuse
Michael E. Smith	385–389	Let's Make the DNA Identification Database as Inclusive as Possible
Tania Simoncelli	390–397	Dangerous Excursions: The Case Against Expanding Forensic DNA Databases to Innocent Persons
Lori Andrews	398–407	Who Owns Your Body? A Patient's Perspective on *Washington University v. Catalona*
Sharon F. Terry, Patrick F. Terry	408–414	A Consumer Perspective on Forensic DNA Banking

collected and typed forensic and offender samples (Gill et al. 2004, Gill et al. 2006a). Information not compatible with previously typed samples would render those existing DNA databases obsolete. Thus, what will likely happen in the future is to extend sample testing to additional loci but keep all or a portion of previously typed markers (Figure 8.4).

In many cases, the extension to additonal STR loci illustrated in Figure 8.4b is already happening with the analysis of STR kits like PowerPlex 16 or Identifiler, which include the 13 CODIS core STR loci plus two additional loci (e.g., Penta D and Penta E with PowerPlex 16 or D2S1338 and D19S433 with Identifiler). The ability to create large multiplex PCR assays is critical to being able to extend the reach of information collected on new loci while retaining original loci.

The scenario illustrated in Figure 8.4c is also possible because some of the original core STR loci are not very informative. For example, CSF1PO, TPOX, and TH01 are not as polymorphic as most of the other core STRs used in the U.S. They were originally selected for historical reasons as they were some of the first STRs analyzed (see Chapter 5). Now that many more STR loci have been characterized with higher powers of discrimination, replacing some of these early STRs with other loci is an option worth considering. Of course,

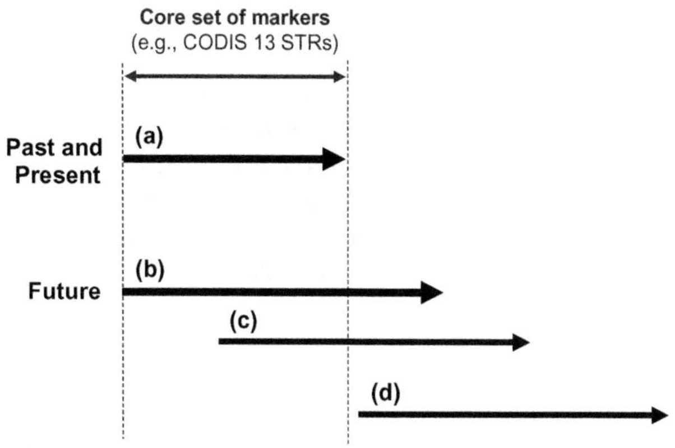

FIGURE 8.4 Possible scenarios for extending sets of genetic markers to be used in national DNA databases. (a) A core set of markers have been established for past and present DNA profiles now numbering in some cases in the millions of profiles (e.g., in the U.S., 13 CODIS core STR loci). Three future scenarios exist: (b) keep all of the current core loci and add some additional supplemental loci (e.g., Identifiler or PowerPlex 16 add two additional STRs), (c) only retain some of the current core loci and add more additional supplemental loci, or (d) abandon the previous genetic markers and have no overlap with current core loci.

the possibility of removing loci from future multiplex STR assays will have to be weighed against the value of retaining a connection to previous data from these markers.

What is unlikely, at least for applications involving criminal DNA databases in the foreseeable future, is the abandonment of previously typed genetic markers in favor of a whole new set (Figure 8.4d). However, new loci or assays could be used in other situations, such as parentage testing or disaster victim identification. For these applications, comparisons are made within a closed population data set. With a criminal DNA database, comparisons must be made across a much broader past, present, and future data set.

The expense of replacing previously typed samples from both offenders and crime scene evidence with new markers will likely mean that most countries will continue to work with legacy sets of genetic markers and will follow either of the Figure 8.4b or 8.4c scenarios. New STR typing kits will most likely become available to aid forensic DNA testing of the future with an overlap of old and new STR loci.

Working Unknown Suspect Cases

Crime laboratories must work cases that have no suspect in order to take full advantage of DNA databases. Convicted offender samples can be typed in large batches because large numbers come into the laboratory together and they are in the same format, such as liquid blood or buccal swabs.

Casework samples, on the other hand, present a different kind of challenge. Each case requires significant up-front work including evidence handling, locating a biological stain within the submitted evidence, and extraction of DNA from different types of substrates. Often sample mixtures must be dealt with and interpreted. Multiple pieces of evidence may also be involved in a case. In addition, significant work is required after analysis of the samples. For example, laboratory reports must be written and court testimony may be required once a suspect has been identified.

In spite of the time and effort required to obtain results on crime scene samples, it is these cases that make DNA databases effective. Law enforcement agencies must be encouraged to collect and submit evidence to the nation's crime laboratories especially if the statute of limitations is about to expire on a case (see information on "John Doe" warrants below). There have been reports of thousands of rape kits that are not submitted to crime laboratories but are sitting in police evidence rooms (Lovirich et al. 2004).

Backlogs

A National Institute of Justice-funded review of police evidence rooms published in 2004 found that over 540,000 cases with potential biological evidence were either still in the possession of local law enforcement or backlogged at forensic laboratories (Lovirich et al. 2004). Funding from the President's DNA Initiative (see http://www.dna.gov) has helped reduce these backlogs but new ones have arisen as the efforts to use DNA to solve crimes have expanded.

In a more recent report, the U.S. Department of Justice Office of Inspector General found that in March 2010, the FBI Laboratory had a backlog of 3211 forensic DNA cases (OIG 2010). Without taking on any new cases or adding new staff, the report estimated that it would take the FBI about two years to eliminate its existing forensic DNA case backlog. These backlogs are growing in many laboratories—by 757 cases for the FBI over an 18 month time period in 2009–2010 (OIG 2010). The existence of backlogged cases slows reporting of results to investigators—some case contributors have to wait more than 600 days for results from the FBI Laboratory (OIG 2010). Clearly, improving sample throughput is important if DNA cases are going to be handled in a timely manner. Capacity building through hiring additional personnel and making process improvements are crucial to reducing delays in completing cases.

NIJ published a special report in June 2010 entitled "Making sense of DNA backlogs—myths vs. reality" that addresses why DNA backlogs still exist despite the federal government investing hundreds of millions of dollars on this issue (Nelson 2010). This report concludes that "crime laboratories have increased their capacity to work cases significantly, but they are not able to eliminate their backlogs because the demand continues to exceed the increases made in capacity" (Nelson 2010).

The California Department of Justice Jan Bashinski DNA Laboratory publishes monthly statistics on its sample backlog and the progress made with adding new samples to the state DNA database (http://ag.ca.gov/bfs/pdf/Monthly.pdf). Data points from three months are included in Table 8.9 to illustrate the trends observed when trying to reduce backlogs.

Through a great deal of effort on the part of this DNA laboratory, the November 2006 starting backlog of 221,052 samples was reduced to 39,651 by November 2010. However, the ending backlog for November 2010 was 2028 samples larger (41,679 compared to 39,651) than the starting backlog for the same month because about 10% more samples were coming into the laboratory than could be processed that month. It is noteworthy that as the California SDIS database has grown in size so has the number of hits per month (e.g., 201 in November 2006 to 343 in November 2010).

TABLE 8.9 Three Time Points in the DNA Backlog Results from California's Jan Bashinski DNA Laboratory. For the Most Recent Data, See http://ag.ca.gov/bfs/pdf/Monthly.pdf.

Month	November 2006	July 2009	November 2010
Starting Backlog	221,052	61,611	39,651
Ending Backlog	197,227	60,815	41,679
Total Offender Profiles in SDIS	662,542	1,294,314	1,660,025
Total Forensic Unknowns in SDIS	14,813	26,887	35,800
Hits (that month)	201	317	343
Total Hits (cumulative)	3346	9701	14,925

Automation of sample processes—especially data review—helps speed analysis and increase sample throughput. Several expert systems have been approved to automatically review DNA profiles that are then uploaded to SDIS and NDIS (Table 8.4). These expert systems include the FSS-i^3 software available from Promega Corporation (Madison, WI), GeneMapper*ID* and GeneMapper*ID-X* available from Applied Biosystems (Foster City, CA), and TrueAllele from Cybergenetics (Pittsburgh, PA). At the National CODIS Conference in November 2010, the FBI's NDIS Custodian stated that, at that time, over one million of the almost nine million profiles in the national database had been reviewed with expert systems. Improved efficiency in data analysis is an important reason that the U.S. national database is growing more quickly in recent years.

Sample Collection from Convicted Offenders

One of the aspects of DNA databanks that is often overlooked is the sample collection process. Law enforcement personnel have to extract blood or obtain a saliva sample from incarcerated felons who are not always cooperative. In some cases, extraordinary efforts including force may be required to persuade felons to submit to sample collection (Spalding 1995). Collecting the actual samples can be a challenge considering the fact that the convicted offender likely knows his blood or saliva could be used to catch him committing another crime in the future or match him to a previous unsolved crime that he committed.

Unfortunately, there can be poor tracking of sample collection or incomplete communication between the prisons, probation officers, and DNA laboratory that result in failure to collect all of the appropriate DNA samples. In some situations, efforts are mounted to go back and get a DNA sample collected from *everyone* who qualifies. For example, the state of Wisconsin discovered that over a 16-year timeframe from August 1993 to September 2009, some 17,698 samples had not been collected from a total of 130,368 offenders who were required to provide a sample (DNA Task Force Report 2010). They are making every effort to recover the missing samples to make the database complete as required by the Wisconsin legal statutes and expected by the general public.

Duplicate Samples or Twins

Good communication is crucial between those agencies that collect offender and arrestee samples and the DNA laboratory that processes the samples. Due to the nature of recidivism among criminals and the fact that they are often given short stays in prison, a reference sample from the same individual may be submitted to a DNA database multiple times—particularly if multiple aliases are used when samples are collected at different points in time. Duplicates do occur in the offender index. Sometimes they are removed when further investigation reveals that the DNA profiles are from the same individual. For this reason, fingerprints are often used to verify that the DNA profile is from the same individual and not an identical twin. (Monozygotic or identical twins have the same DNA profile but different fingerprints.) Without an accompanying biometric like fingerprints to pre-screen the DNA samples, duplicate submissions may be inadvertently analyzed by the DNA database laboratory, thereby wasting scarce resources and time.

Matches to one member of a set of identical twins can cause problems for the prosecution, as in a 2009 case in Germany where authorities had to let two thieves go free after a DNA database hit matched both of them (Himmelreich 2009a). The court ruling stated in part: "From the evidence we have, we can deduce that at least one of the brothers took part in the crime, but it has not been possible to determine which one."

While there is no record kept on a national level for numbers of identical twins within the U.S. database (because no names or personal identifying information is kept on any of the NDIS samples), there have been a few reports from other national DNA databases. After its first four years of operation, the Swiss database contained 35 monozygotic twin pairs among a total of 61954 DNA profiles (Voegeli et al. 2006). As of March 31, 2007, the UK NDNAD reported 2914 sets of identical twins and 4 sets of identical triplets on their database of 3,874,500 individuals (NPIA 2007).

Sample Retention

Critics of DNA databases and databanks are concerned that DNA samples from offenders are retained after a DNA profile of STR markers has been generated from the sample (Gaensslen 2006, van Camp & Dierickx 2008). As has already been noted, the justification of retaining these samples is two-fold (Herkenham 2006). First and foremost, because samples are retested following an offender hit, it is necessary to have the original sample to confirm its STR profile. This hit confirmation is an important quality control measure and helps prevent any kind of potential error during laboratory processing that could cause a lead to be followed and a warrant to be issued for the wrong person.

As noted by the NRC II report, "the ultimate safeguard against error due to sample mixup is to provide an opportunity for retesting" (NRC 1996, p. 81). While we typically think of this statement in terms of evidentiary items from casework, it applies equally well to DNA database samples.

Another reason to retain sample specimens is to enable analyses using technology advancements in the future. If new genetic markers or assays are developed in the future (see Figure 8.4) to enable better recovery of information from forensic samples, then previously examined forensic evidence and offender samples would need to be retested with the new genetic markers/technology in order to permit a comparison between offender and forensic results.

Challenges with Sample/DNA Profile Expungement

If an arrested and/or convicted individual is later cleared of their charges, they may want their DNA profile removed from the database and their DNA sample destroyed or returned from the databank. However, from the laboratory's standpoint, the removal of electronic records and physical samples may not be trivial.

Forensic DNA laboratories generally do not have a link to any criminal justice or court databases. In most jurisdictions, procedures are not in place to track whether or not someone was acquitted during a trial or if charges were dropped during the judicial process. Automatic expungement is not really an option with the current system. Thus, the individual is typically asked to write the law enforcement agency, to request the removal of his/her DNA profile and the destruction of the DNA sample, and to provide appropriate documentation to support his/her request. For example, the FBI's CODIS expungement policy is available at http://www.fbi.gov/about-us/lab/codis/codis_expungement.

Measuring DNA Database Performance

Measuring success is important in any endeavor. A commonly used metric with DNA database searches is the "hit" that results from a match between an offender and an unknown DNA profile from a forensic case. As mentioned earlier, there are "cold" hits and "warm" hits that depend on whether or not prior information is available about a potential contributor. The growth of DNA databases has been driven by some spectacular success stories and data on the types of crime solved.

DNA databases are effective for identifying serial offenders. For example, in 2004 Fletcher Worrell (age 58 at the time) tried to purchase a shotgun in Atlanta, Georgia. His background check revealed two arrest warrants in New York City from 1978. After his DNA sample was collected and analyzed and his profile uploaded, it resulted in NDIS hits that matched 21 unsolved cases in Maryland (from the so-called "Silver Spring Rapist") and 8 unsolved cases from other states. Thus, the DNA database enabled 31 cases to be solved spanning more than 25 years! Some other success stories are available at http://www.dna.gov/case_studies/preventable/.

In 2006, the Swiss DNA database reported on their performance during the first four years of operation (Voegeli et al. 2006). A total of 61,954 DNA profiles had been collected using the SGM Plus kit, which contains 10 STR loci and amelogenin. Of these profiles, 53,400 were from suspects (89% male and 11% female) and 8,554 were from forensic stains (90.7% single-source, 9.3% mixtures). The qualifying offense for the suspects that resulted in the first 6,830 hits included 85% burglary, 4.2% homicide, 4% robbery, 2.4% sexual offenses, and 4.2% from other crimes such as arson, fraud, and illicit drug use. While most of the hits linked the offender to a single crime, in one case 62 different crime stains were linked to a single perpetrator through DNA testing.

In their report, the Swiss DNA laboratory noted that over this four-year period, 36 stains were matched to police or laboratory staff and appropriately detected as contamination that occurred during sample collection or analysis (Voegeli et al. 2006). They effectively avoided uploading these DNA profiles to the database because they searched their elimination database (see Chapter 4) regularly against all evidentiary results.

An analysis of the number of hits obtained over a particular time period can be instructive as to the types of offenses where DNA testing is making a difference. New York State found that its first 1,000 DNA database hits (see http://www.criminaljustice.state.ny.us/forensic/typesofcrimesfirst1000hits.htm) resulted in solving 730 sex offenses, 135 burglaries, 65 murders/attempted murders, 28 robberies, 17 assaults, and 25 "miscellaneous" crimes. Virginia estimates that 80% of their hits would have been missed if DNA collection was only limited to violent offenders. Their analysis also found that 40% of violent crimes are perpetrated by individuals who have previous property crime convictions (see http://www.dfs.virginia.gov/statistics/index.cfm).

In an effort to help normalize database output or efficiency and thereby gain a better idea of how input of information into a DNA databases impacts its output, Simon Walsh from the Australian Federal Police and colleagues from New Zealand have developed some models for measuring database output and efficiency (Walsh et al. 2010). The goal of their performance metrics is to see how well DNA databases perform with the idea that this information could be used to influence policy regarding the types of samples that should be collected and analyzed (D.N.A. Box 8.2).

Followup to Database Matches

On November 20, 2006 *USA Today* ran a story discussing the lack of follow-up to many DNA cold hits (Willing 2006). Even though a DNA hit has been observed and reported, police and prosecutors may not pursue the lead provided by a CODIS hit. Thus, the cold case stays cold in spite of the efforts of DNA scientists.

There are at least four general reasons that a DNA database hit does not result in a conviction of the individual matched to the evidentiary sample (Bieber 2006): (1) variable follow-up after the hit is reported to the police, (2) witness/suspect issues, (3) time, and (4) trial/evidentiary issues.

First, detectives and prosecutors may be overloaded with current cases and may not make an old/cold case a priority. Also, there may be a breakdown in reporting the hit to the appropriate law enforcement personnel.

Second, victims, police, and other witnesses involved in a cold case may have died, may be unable to be located, or may be unwilling to testify in an old case. Suspects may be dead, unable to be located, or already incarcerated. If a suspect is already in prison, then the investigators and prosecutors may not feel a need to attempt to convict the suspect for the crime connected with the DNA hit.

Third, statutes of limitations may have expired or victims may have put the crime behind them and moved on with their lives and are thus unwilling to open old wounds and revisit a difficult event from their past.

Finally, the DNA evidence may not necessarily be considered probative or otherwise admitted in trial. In this case, the jury may acquit if the prosecution is not able to make a strong enough case against the suspect without using the DNA evidence.

D.N.A. BOX 8.2

MODELING DNA DATABASE PERFORMANCE

With the rapid growth of DNA databases due to expanded legislation, the answers to several questions might be desired, such as (1) Are databases becoming more effective as they grow in size?, or (2) What is the impact of adding particular sets of individuals (such as arrestees)?

Simon Walsh of the Australian Federal Police, along with New Zealand statistician colleagues James Curran and John Buckleton, have developed a measure of DNA database performance in an effort to equate hit efficiency with the types of samples going into the database.

As was illustrated in Figure 8.2 and Figure 8.3c, hits are made as N offenders are compared against C crime stain profiles. The Walsh et al. (2010) model is that

$$H = \frac{\alpha N}{M} \times \omega C$$

where H is the number of DNA database hits (matches), N is the number of DNA profiles in the offender index, M is the active criminal population, C is the number of DNA profiles from crime scenes in the forensic index, α (alpha) is a quality factor related to person sampling, and ω (omega) is a quality factor related to crime scene sampling.

According to this model, the best return on a database (i.e., generating the highest number of possible hits) is (1) having an optimal ratio of N offender profiles to C forensic profiles, (2) having a low active criminal population, (3) having a high α value which relates to a sample collection strategy that effectively gathers the active criminals, and (4) having a high ω value which relates to a forensic sampling strategy that obtains the best samples associated with the crime and avoids irrelevant profiles.

Source:

Walsh, S.J., et al. (2010). Modeling forensic DNA database performance. Journal of Forensic Sciences, *55, 1174–1183.*

In one of the most thorough studies to-date, the San Francisco Police Department (SFPD) Criminalistics Laboratory reviewed case resolutions of 198 DNA database hits observed in their laboratory in order to evaluate the impact of their work on public safety (Gabriel et al. 2010). Their 198 LDIS hits came from 164 offender hits and 34 case-to-case hits with offenses involving 24 homicides, 110 sex crimes, 42 burglaries, and 22 other crimes. The SFPD scientists examined 12 felons in greater detail; collectively, these criminals had committed 199 offenses that led to arrests. Unfortunately, the criminal justice system was unable to successfully interrupt their criminal behavior patterns over time. For example, 46% of the sexual offenses in the cold hit cases reviewed had occurred while these 12 prolific felons were serving probation for prior convictions.

In some cases, the DNA hits helped strengthen the prosecution's case and increase the jail sentence. The SFPD scientists conclude that there need to be better tools for local jurisdictions to track cold hits and criminal case outcomes so that connecting DNA information does not slip through the cracks. They observed that 48% of cold cases were dismissed, typically because of victims declining to pursue prosecution. However, it was noted that not a single case that went to court resulted in aquittal by jury trial. In addition, 90% of property crime cases resulted in a CODIS-eligible profile with a 72% corresponding cold hit rate (Gabriel et al. 2010).

Potential of Adventitious Matches with Fewer Loci or Database Growth

An "adventitious" match is one that happens by chance instead of design. In the case of DNA testing, not having enough distinguishing characteristics (e.g., due to a partial profile) could lead to adventitious matches. As DNA databases grow in size and more comparisons are made, the potential exists for adventitious matches to occur unless additional loci are added to provide a finer resolution or increased ability to distinguish DNA profiles from one another. Examining additional loci in a sample will increase the random match probability. The ENFSI document on DNA database management relates the size of a DNA database to the potential for an adventitious match (D.N.A. Box 8.3).

The only published account of an adventitious (false positive) match from a DNA database came in 1999, when the UK database, then consisting of 660,000 profiles with only 6 STR loci (SGM assay), led to a "hit" between two individuals whose 6-locus random match probability was 1 in 37 million (Willing 2000). Further testing with four additional STRs (SGM Plus loci) showed that the samples were from different individuals. Around the same time, the UK expanded the number of core loci from 6 to 10 with the adoption of the SGM Plus kit to try to prevent another adventitious match.

The growth of DNA databases necessitates the inclusion of additional loci to avoid this problem. For this reason, in 2009, the European community expanded their core set of loci from 7 to 12 (see Chapter 5). As of late 2010, the U.S. is also considering expanding the number of required loci beyond the current 13 CODIS STRs to reduce the chance of future adventitious hits with database growth, to improve success with missing person investigations, and to make international data comparisons more feasible as needed.

Partial Matches and the "Arizona Search"

As mentioned previously, DNA profiles from relatives may be present in DNA databases. Therefore, adventitious hits could be observed from a portion of a DNA profile in the forensic index matching a relative of the true source of the sample found in the offender index. At the International Symposium on Human Identification (aka the Promega meeting) in 2000, a member of the Italian National Police noted an 8 STR locus match between two brothers in what was essentially an early familial search (Biondo 2000).

However, it was a poster presented the following year in October 2001, by a scientist from the Arizona Department of Public Safety that gained much greater attention. Kathryn Troyer's poster was entitled "A nine STR locus match between two apparently unrelated individuals using AmpFlSTR Profiler Plus and COfiler" (Troyer et al. 2001). Their abstract reads:

> *The Arizona Department of Public Safety Crime Laboratory is reporting a nine STR locus match between two apparently unrelated individuals at vWA, D21S11, D5S818, D13S317, D7S820, D16S539, TH01, TPOX, and CSF1PO. The samples were analyzed by Myriad Genetic Laboratories, using Applied Biosystem's AmpFlSTR Profiler Plus and COfiler kits. The nine STR locus match was discovered using a duplicate search by Myriad Genetic Laboratories. Further*

D.N.A. BOX 8.3

ESTIMATES OF ADVENTITIOUS MATCHES BASED ON DNA DATABASE SIZE AND MATCH PROBABILITY OF DNA PROFILES

As DNA databases add profiles and grow in size, there becomes a greater probability that two profiles will match by chance rather than because they originate from a common source. This false positive match is called an *adventitious match*. The best way to avoid an adventitious match when the size of the DNA database grows is to increase the overall "1 in X" average random match probability (RMP) for the profiles found within the database. Increasing this value is accomplished by adding more loci to the DNA profile. Alternatively, loci can be removed in simulation experiments to examine the impact of adventitious matches with partial profiles (Hicks et al. 2010).

For the past several years, the European Network of Forensic Science Institutes (ENFSI) DNA Working Group has annually prepared a document on DNA database management. Below is one of the tables from the 2010 document illustrating the expected number of adventitious matches when searching a DNA database of given size (horizontal axis) with a DNA profile having a certain RMP (vertical axis). Ideally, for the DNA profiles contained in the database, the "1 in X" RMP should be high enough that adventitious matches are avoided (i.e., much less than 1).

Sources:

ENFSI DNA Working Group (2010). DNA-Database Management: Review and Recommendations. Available at http://www.enfsi.eu/get_doc.php?uid=345.

Hicks, T., et al. (2010). Use of DNA profiles for investigation using a simulated national DNA database: Part I. Partial SGM Plus profiles. Forensic Science International: Genetics, *4*, 232–238.

Random *P* Match Probability (1:X)	Size of the DNA-database: 10,000	100,000	1,000,000	10,000,000
10,000	1	10	100	1,000
100,000	0.1	1	10	100
1,000,000	0.01	0.1	1	10
10,000,000	0.001	0.01	0.1	1
100,000,000	0.0001	0.001	0.01	0.1
1,000,000,000	0.00001	0.0001	0.001	0.01
10,000,000,000	0.000001	0.00001	0.0001	0.001

investigation by the Arizona Department of Public Safety revealed that the two offenders varied by age and race. In addition, it was noted that the two offenders shared one allele at three of the remaining four loci, D3S1358, D8S1179, and D18S51. The match is in the process of being confirmed with Applied Biosystem's AmpFlSTR Identifiler kit.

After comparing all offender profiles to all other profiles in the database, a partial match was identified between two different offender profiles in which 9 out of 13 loci had the same genotype. The type of search where *all samples* are compared to *all other samples* in a DNA database is commonly referred to now as an "Arizona search" (see Figure 8.3d). Often this type of search also includes looking for how many samples may match at 9, 10, 11, or 12 loci instead of the full 13 CODIS STRs.

In a 2004 *Journal of Forensic Sciences* article, Professor Bruce Weir noted that partial matches occur when examining profile comparisons in large data sets (Weir 2004). Not being aware of the Arizona search example, he states in his paper: "As offender databases grow…high degrees of matching are to be expected. It is very likely that there are already 9-locus matches within combined U.S. offender databases" (Weir 2004).

This partial match issues has been presented as being similar to the so-called "birthday problem" (Budowle et al. 2006, Budowle et al. 2009), which is described in D.N.A. Box 8.4. Keep in mind that the chance of a *specific* DNA profile matching to another DNA profile is a very different situation than the chance of *any* two DNA profiles matching.

Database Match Probabilities for Cold Hit Statistics

There is sometimes confusion between the *random match probability* (RMP) of a DNA profile and what is termed the *database match probability* (DMP). The 1996 National Research Council report (NRC II) recommendation 5.1 states that to determine the database match probability the random match probability should be multiplied by N, the number of persons in the database. The FBI's DNA Advisory Board endorsed the NRC II calculation in their February 2000 recommendations on statistical approaches.

While the DMP is easy to calculate once the RMP is determined, it is not usually put in case reports. Mentioning a DMP calculation during expert witness testimony may cause issues in court since having a DNA sample in a database would show prior conviction. This information could then possibly bias a jury against a defendant or lead to a mistrial.

Most of the confusion arises from the fact that these RMP and DMP values are answers to different questions (Chakraborty & Ge 2009). The RMP answers the question "What is the rarity of a specific DNA profile given the alleles observed?" The DMP answers the question "How often would a DNA profile match the relevant forensic sample in a database of size N?" The DMP relates to the types of searches illustrated in Figure 8.3c. The differences between RMP and DMP have been debated in several court cases—and several helpful articles have been written trying to make this topic clearer (Storvik & Egeland 2007, Kaye 2008, Chakraborty & Ge 2009).

Desire for Academic Research on NDIS Data

In December 2009, the journal *Science* published a letter to the editor from Dan Krane of Wright State University (Dayton, Ohio) and 40 (mostly) academic colleagues requesting that

D.N.A. BOX 8.4

THE "BIRTHDAY PROBLEM" AND THE IMPORTANCE OF HOW YOU FRAME THE QUESTION YOU WANT ANSWERED

The so-called "birthday problem" is related to the probability that, given a set of randomly chosen people some pair of them will share the same birth date. Although it does not seem immediately intuitive, after examining 23 pairs of individuals, there is a 50-50 chance of two people in the room sharing a birthday. And after only comparing 57 pairs of individuals, there is a 99% chance of a match between *any* two individuals. With a list of 23 people to compare, there are $23 \times (23\text{-}1)/2 = 253$ possible pairwise comparisons. The first individual is compared to the other 22, the second individual to 21 people (excluding the first individual who was already compared), and so forth until everyone has been compared to everyone else.

When the question is changed to how many people match a specific birthday, then the numbers of individuals that need to be available changes. In order to reach a greater than 50% probability that another people will share a *specific* birthday, such as April 1, at least 253 individuals will need to be queried.

The birthday problem asks whether *any* of the people in a given group has a birthday matching *any* of the others—not one in particular. Note that in the birthday problem, neither of the two people is chosen in advance. When a specific DNA profile is developed from crime scene evidence, the question has changed. Typically with a DNA profile comparision, the question is not whether *any* profiles match (e.g., 23 in the birthday example or Figure 8.3d) but whether another specific profile exists (e.g., 253 in the birthday example or Figure 8.3b).

Source:
http://en.wikipedia.org/wiki/Birthday_problem

the FBI Laboratory provide a copy of the U.S. national DNA database to them (and presumably other researchers) to study the STR allele frequencies contained within the database and to look at the occurrence of partial matches (Krane et al. 2009). The FBI has so far denied this request citing concerns about genetic privacy (Geddes 2010). According to the FBI, federal law prohibits sharing DNA profiles from the U.S. national database with non-criminal justice agencies.

While it would be interesting to examine allele frequencies and perform other potential research on the data within the U.S. national DNA database, it would be challenging to draw meaningful correlations to other sets of population-specific allele frequencies. As already previously noted in this chapter, twins and sample duplicates exist in the database. In addition, samples are not identified or categorized by ethnicity, preventing the ability to determine true Caucasian or African American allele frequencies. Perhaps in the future, a large data set with millions of DNA profiles can be examined, but it is doubtful that this information will dramatically change our understanding of DNA results or match statistics.

WHEN THERE ARE NO HITS AFTER A DATABASE SEARCH

If a perpetrator of a particular crime has not been arrested or convicted of another crime (and had a DNA sample previously collected and uploaded to a DNA database), then no amount of searching the database with a particular crime scene profile will help solve the case. Searching the database again at a future date may be helpful if the perpetrator has been included in the meantime for another crime.

Three approaches have been taken when no match was found following a DNA database search: (1) the issuance of a so-called "John Doe warrant" based on the evidence profile, (2) conducting a DNA dragnet or mass intelligence screen by collecting samples from "volunteers" in a focused area, or (3) expanding the effective size of the database by conducting familial searches where a partial match between the evidence DNA profile and an offender may help focus the investigation on a relative of the offender in the database. The challenges of each approach are discussed below. Efforts are also being made to predict phenotypic information (see Chapter 12) including appearance and age of an individual based on DNA information from the evidentiary sample—something that cannot be done with the STR loci in use for human identity testing.

With particularly heinous crimes, additional efforts or strategies are sometimes considered to help solve the case. These approaches can involve casting a wider net through collecting additional samples (DNA dragnets) or using currently available DNA profiles with expanded searching for possible relatives (familial searching).

John Doe Warrants

Many states have *statutes of limitations* meaning that, after a certain period of time, a crime cannot be prosecuted. In order to stop the clock on the statute of limitations for commencing a criminal case, "John Doe warrants" have been used in a number of cases (Gahn 2000). This action can then extend the timeframe for possibly solving a case. If DNA evidence exists from a crime scene yet no suspect has been located to be charged with the crime, a John Doe warrant may be issued based solely on the assailant's genetic code.

The capabilities of forensic DNA testing have generated new legal issues for prosecutors. The sensitivity of the polymerase chain reaction enables DNA profiles to be obtained from previously intractable evidence. Furthermore, the existence of DNA databases now permits matches between perpetrators of crimes spanning jurisdictions and cold hits on unsolved crimes many years after they occurred.

In September 1999, Norman Gahn, Assistant District Attorney from Milwaukee County, Wisconsin, filed the first warrant for the arrest of "John Doe," an unknown male who could be identified by his 13 locus STR profile (Gahn 2000). This approach has been successful in stopping the ticking clock of a crime's statute of limitations, making it possible to prosecute the crime when the assailant is identified through a DNA database cold hit in the future. Several of these John Doe's have been subsequently identified with DNA database cold hits and successfully prosecuted for the crimes they committed.

Wisconsin law governing the statute of limitations was amended in September 2001 to provide for the use of DNA profiles from individuals unknown to the prosecution at the time the warrant for arrest is issued. The new legislation creates an exception to the time limits for prosecuting sexual assault crimes if the state has DNA evidence related to the crime. John Doe warrants have also been issued in other states.

DNA Dragnets Through Mass Screens

In the past, there have been instances when a DNA dragnet was instituted if a DNA database search did not link any offenders on the database to a particular crime scene sample(s). Prior to the availability of national DNA databases, these DNA mass screens were more common.

The first use of forensic DNA testing involved a genetic dragnet of over 4,000 adult males in the Narborough, England area in 1986 and 1987. Samples that failed to be excluded from the crime scene sample with traditional blood typing were subjected to "DNA fingerprinting" or multi-locus RFLP testing. Colin Pitchfork was eventually apprehended based on this mass DNA intelligence screen and additional police work. However, challenges have been raised to the cost-effectiveness of this mass screening approach. For example, Colin Pitchfork was apparently the 4,583rd male tested for the mass screen described in Joseph Wambaugh's *The Blooding*.

DNA intelligence or mass screens to aid identification of a perpetrator and exclusion of innocent individuals in no-suspect cases have been successfully used many times by the UK's Forensic Science Service and other law enforcement agencies. In these mass screens, the police ask individuals within a predetermined group (e.g., males 18 to 35 years old within a defined location) to voluntarily provide DNA samples in an effort to identify the perpetrator of a crime or a series of crimes that have been linked by DNA evidence.

The largest mass screen conducted to date by the UK's Forensic Science Service was in conjunction with the investigation of the murder of Louise Smith, whose body was found near Chipping Sodbury, England in 1996. Over 4,500 samples from local volunteers were analyzed at an expense of over one million pounds. Eventually police realized that one of the potential suspects had since moved to South Africa. He was tracked down and his DNA sample taken, which was found to match a crime scene STR profile recovered from the scene. David Frost is now serving time for the crime he committed.

Of course, this type of effort and expense is not expended in every case but it has proven useful in some situations. However, collecting samples from every individual fitting a particular description or living in a particular geographic region is not always well received by the general public. Questions about genetic privacy and civil liberties are often raised, particularly in the United States, when mass screens are initiated. Within the United States, these types of DNA dragnets raise Constitutional concerns such as violation of Fourth Amendment rights that protect an individual's privacy until evidence is produced and a warrant obtained that would compel an invasive search.

In probably the largest genetic screening effort ever conducted within the United States, over 2100 individuals in the Dade County (Miami), Florida area were typed with AmpliType PM and HLA-DQA1 during the fall of 1994 (Kahn et al. 1996). Since six homicide victims had been prostitutes who were killed within a three mile radius between September 1994 and January 1995, tested individuals were primarily selected based on a prior arrest record for soliciting a prostitute. During the course of the investigation, three of the 2100 individuals tested matched with the PM + DQA1 screening assay, but subsequently were excluded by follow-up RFLP analysis, which has a higher power of discrimination (see Butler 2010, *Fundamentals*, Chapter 3). In the end, the serial rapist/murderer was caught when a potential victim freed herself and police were called. Thus, while the perpetrator's DNA was found to match DNA evidence from the previous six crime scenes (and this information was used in his prosecution), the mass screen was not responsible for his apprehension.

In April 2004, a DNA dragnet was conducted in Charlottesville, Virginia to try to stop a rapist who had attacked at least six women between 1997 and 2003. Community concerns that black men were being targeted led police in Charlottesville to eventually suspend the mass screen after only collecting and analyzing samples from about 200 men. The perception of being "guilty" before proven "innocent" through DNA testing is an issue often raised by critics of DNA dragnets—particularly in the United States where the criminal justice system attempts to treat individuals as "innocent until proven guilty."

A September 2004 report that surveyed DNA mass screens conducted in the United States over the previous two decades found these efforts to be "extremely unproductive" in identifying the true perpetrator (Walker 2004). This report recommended that police not conduct DNA mass screens based on general descriptions of criminal suspects. On the other hand, a study presented to the European Network of Forensic Science Institutes (ENFSI) DNA Working Group in April 2006 found that 315 out of 439 mass screens conducted in Europe were successful in identifying the perpetrator (Wenzel 2007). The 72% success rate in Europe illustrates that DNA intelligence-led screens can be helpful in solving crimes when other efforts have failed—although the approach may not be well accepted by the public in some areas. *It is hoped that the proper balance can be found in the future to fully utilize the power of DNA testing and yet preserve the privacy and civil liberties of innocent citizens.*

Partial Matches and Familial Searching

In a May 2006 *Science* article entitled "Finding criminals through DNA of their relatives," the authors propose that if a crime stain does not match anyone in the offender database that there is a chance that a relative might be in the database (Bieber et al. 2006). Since relatives will have similar DNA profiles, loosening the search stringency to permit partial matches rather than full high-stringency matches (where every allele in an STR profile must match) may return a list of results that could include a brother or other close relative. This list of potential relatives could be narrowed through further testing with Y-chromosome markers (for males only), which would require all of the potential relatives plus the crime scene sample to be examined with the additional genetic markers (Myers et al. 2010). In theory, with this approach, the use of offender profiles already on the DNA database enables close relatives of offenders to potentially be included in searches performed against DNA profiles coming from unsolved crime scenes.

The UK pioneered this partial matching technique, better known as "familial searching," and has used it to solve a number of cases—but not without controversy.

NDIS defines a "partial match" as a moderate stringency candidate match between two profiles having at each locus *all of the alleles* of one sample represented in the other sample. It is the result of a routine search at moderate stringency where the forensic scientist, when evaluating whether a candidate match is a viable match and should be processed through to confirmation, discovers that the candidate offender is, in fact, excluded as the possible perpetrator of the crime. However, because of a similarity in alleles between the target and candidate profiles, the analyst believes that a close biological relative of the offender could possibly be implicated in the crime. On the other hand, a familial search is a deliberate search looking for relatives.

A successful California familial search announced in July 2010 captured the attention of the world and brought a serial offender known as the Grim Sleeper to justice (D.N.A. Box 8.5, Miller 2010). This case certainly demonstrates the potential and power of familial searching when police have no other possible leads and the perpetrator poses a serious threat to public safety. However, the technique has technical pitfalls and privacy concerns that are discussed in Appendix 2.

D.N.A. BOX 8.5

THE "GRIM SLEEPER" CASE: A FAMILIAL SEARCH SUCCESS STORY

On the morning of July 7, 2010, officers from the Los Angeles Police Department (LAPD) waited quietly and impatiently outside the home of Lonnie Franklin, a 57-year-old mechanic. When he finally stepped outside, he was immediately surrounded and arrested on serial murder charges. His arrest brought closure to one of the most prolific perpetrators in L.A. history, but at the same time, opened the door nationwide to questions about the methods used to identify him. The police showed up on Mr. Franklin's doorstep because of DNA collected initially not from him but from his son. It was the typing of this DNA sample, combined with a specialized DNA search technique known as "familial searching" and the persistence of investigators who used the cutting edge capabilities of DNA testing that led to his arrest.

The investigation into a serial killer began with a DNA match—but one without a suspect. In June 2007, an LAPD task force was established to locate an active serial killer because of a case-to-case DNA hit identified by the LAPD Crime Lab a month earlier. The lab had found that DNA evidence recovered from a victim located in a South Los Angeles alley in January 2007 matched a previously analyzed 2003 case. Eventually, DNA matches would be made to a series of cases from the 1980s.

From 1985 through 1988, a killer had stalked the streets of Los Angeles murdering seven women and one man, who ranged in age from 18 to 36. A ninth victim was raped but survived in November 1988. A number of the victims were troubled women who

D.N.A. BOX 8.5 *(cont'd)*

were vulnerable and were out on the streets at night as prostitutes. These crimes were initially connected with forensic evidence involving bullet ballistics coming from a 0.25 caliber gun. However, no leads existed as to the person behind the crimes. Three more murders would be committed in March 2002, July 2003, and January 2007 (the last two were the first two connected by DNA testing).

In reviewing the cases, the LAPD found a 13-year gap in detected victims—leading an *LA Weekly* reporter in August 2008 to nickname the serial killer the "Grim Sleeper." The name stuck—and a media campaign was launched with billboards and a $500,000 reward for information leading to the killer's arrest. A common DNA profile, believed to be that of the perpetrator, was eventually developed from six of the 12 victims connected to this serial killer. Unfortunately, searches of state and national DNA databases yielded no result. The killer had somehow managed to keep out of reach from the long arm of the law for almost 25 years.

Meanwhile, the California Department of Justice (CA DOJ) DNA Laboratory (in Richmond, CA, northeast of San Francisco), which manages the offender DNA database in California, was developing software based on kinship analysis and performing validation studies on familial searching, a somewhat controversial technique that had seen some success in England. By reducing the stringency of a DNA search, the UK's Forensic Science Service (FSS) had shown that DNA profiles from unsolved crimes could be linked to relatives of the perpetrators who were present in their national DNA database. Used in 158 UK cases from 2003 to 2008, the FSS was able to close some 18 cases because of familial searching. In April 2008, the CA DOJ DNA laboratory, with the approval of the Office of the Attorney General, announced that it would perform familial searches of the state DNA database in cases of serious crime when all other methods had been exhausted. By October 2008, studies were complete and validated software was in place. They now had the tool to effectively widen their search net.

With the public and the victims' families clamoring for capture of the killer and closure to the serial murder cases, the LAPD sent a formal request to CA DOJ to perform a familial search of the state DNA database. In October 2008, this specialized search against the California state DNA database, which at that time contained over 1.1 million convicted offender profiles (1,102,659 to be exact), was performed looking for a possible relative of the "Grim Sleeper" evidence profile. No likely relatives were identified by this first search—leaving the LAPD empty-handed once again. "It was very discouraging," says Detective Dennis Kilcoyne, who led the LAPD task force, "[by June of 2010] we had spent three years essentially beating our heads against the wall and expending a lot of resources without any result."

Over the course of the 18 months following the initial search hundreds of thousands of new DNA profiles poured into the California state DNA database. In the spring of 2010 (after weekly direct searches of the database failed to locate a match), another formal request was made by the LAPD task force to search the offender database again using the familial searching approach. On June 30, 2010, Detective Kilcoyne received

D.N.A. BOX 8.5 (*cont'd*)

a call from Jill Spriggs, chief of the CA DOJ's Bureau of Forensic Services, asking him to quietly arrange a meeting later that week with the chief of police and the district attorney. Friday, July 2, Chief Spriggs and CA DOJ's Bureau of Investigation and Intelligence (BII) Chief Craig Buehler flew to LA and shared the results of their familial search.

Through a video conference with the CA DOJ scientists in Richmond, the LAPD learned that a two-part scientific screen, followed by careful investigative confirmation, had been used to locate a potential relative of the perpetrator. First, a ranked list of ≈150 individuals with the highest likelihood ratios, which indicated possible familial relationships with the Grim Sleeper DNA profile, had been developed from the state database, at that time containing 1,322,998 convicted offender profiles. Then these DNA samples were compared using Y-chromosome testing to eliminate all non-paternally related offenders who shared similar autosomal STR characteristics by chance. Most of these individuals had already been eliminated by Y-STR testing during the first familial search. Only a single individual remained on the list after the Y-STR testing—a man by the name of Christopher Franklin, who had alleles matching the Grim Sleeper DNA profile at all 15 tested autosomal STR loci.

Christopher Franklin's DNA profile had been added to the state database in early 2009 due to his conviction on a felony weapons possession charge. Thus, his DNA profile was not present during the initial October 2008 search. Further investigative footwork was performed by CA DOJ BII agents through public records searches to learn more about potential family members who may have lived in the LA area during the times of the crimes. All of this investigative work was performed *without talking to any member of the general public* and prior to giving the name of a potential suspect to the LAPD detectives. The 2010 familial searching results pointed to the biological father of Christopher Franklin, who lived in the vicinity of the Grim Sleeper crimes.

Within a few hours, Lonnie David Franklin, Jr. had over 20 detectives shadowing his every move and waiting for him to discard some biological sample in a public place so that the police would have a direct DNA reference sample to confirm their suspicions that he was the Grim Sleeper serial killer. It is important to note that Mr. Franklin had not previously been on the police radar as part of this investigation—and probably would not have been without the familial DNA association. Moreover, the police quickly discovered that he was not a litter bug and did not dispose of any useful items, such as cigarette butts or soda cans, within sight of their surveillance.

Finally, on Monday afternoon, July 5, Mr. Franklin went to a pizza restaurant to eat. An undercover officer became his waiter—and according to Detective Kilcoyne, Mr. Franklin probably received the best service he ever had in a restaurant. His dirty napkins were replaced with clean ones and his fork was removed if it was dropped. At the end of his meal, a piece of leftover pizza crust was also collected. In total, eight items were submitted to the LAPD DNA Lab for testing—and analysts worked quickly to generate results on the submitted items.

D.N.A. BOX 8.5 (*cont'd*)

On Wednesday morning, July 7, about 30 hours after submitting the samples, the LAPD Task Force received the laboratory reports. DNA on the napkin and the pizza crust eaten by Mr. Franklin was a direct match to the Grim Sleeper evidentiary DNA profile. With this DNA confirmation, the LAPD completed their preparations to perform the arrest. When Mr. Franklin came out of his house around 9:20 a.m. to do something in his yard, he was greeted by police officers with an arrest warrant. To further verify the results, the police immediately collected a buccal swab from Mr. Franklin to confirm the DNA match. Then, they proceeded to conduct a three-day search of his home to collect evidence. Lonnie David Franklin, Jr. was subsequently charged with 10 murders and is awaiting trial as of early 2011.

In many ways, this was a perfect success story for familial searching using DNA databases. A series of heinous crimes could not be solved any other way despite years of investigative effort. An initial search before the relative was in the database led to no further action. Y-STR testing for confirmation purposes on the second search yielded only one profile. Through public record searches—and without disturbing any potential family members—investigators learned that the individual in the database had a father who was the appropriate age and in the appropriate location to have committed the crimes.

In an opinion article a few days after Mr. Franklin was arrested, the *New York Times* praised the careful and conscientious efforts of the scientists and police investigators involved in this case. Even the American Civil Liberties Union (ACLU), typically a harsh critic of DNA databases, was complementary of the careful investigation in this case while protecting individual privacy and civil rights.

Detective Dennis Kilcoyne headed the task force, which was established in June 2007 to identify this serial killer who operated for at least 25 years without detection. Detective Kilcoyne believes that this case would not have been solved without the power of DNA testing and particularly familial searching. Both the CA DOJ scientists and LAPD investigators were aware that they were doing cutting edge work and were careful to preserve privacy at each stage of the investigation. In particular, a detailed protocol established by the CA DOJ laboratory was followed to protect privacy, while maximizing the reach of DNA testing, thus establishing an effective model for future familial searches. While familial searching currently has a success rate of 10% in California (as the nine previous searches failed to provide any leads), to a dedicated detective like Dennis Kilcoyne, this powerful technique provided closure on a critical case and brought a heinous killer to justice.

Sources (additional references are available at end of Chapter 8 and Appendix 2):

ACLU (2010). "Grim Sleeper" case doesn't justify expanding the reach of DNA databases, Available at http://www.aclu-sc.org/news_stories/view/102863/.

Editorial. (2010). A yellow light to DNA searches. New York Times, *July 13. Available at http://www.nytimes.com/2010/07/13/opinion/13tue1.html.*

Interviews with Detective Dennis Kilcoyne (LAPD) and Gary Sims & Steven Myers (CA DOJ).

Myers, S.P., et al. (2010). Searching for first-degree familial relationships in California's offender DNA database: validation of a likelihood ratio-based approach. Forensic Science International: Genetics, (in press). *doi:10.1016/j.fsigen.2010.10.010.*

CONCERNS OF DNA DATABASE CRITICS

The rapid expansion of DNA databases and their use to solve crimes has many privacy advocates concerned (Greeley et al. 2006, Krimsky & Simoncelli 2010). Within the United States, numerous legal challenges have tried unsuccessfully to claim that DNA collection violates Constitutional rights of American citizens. In any society, there are tradeoffs between public safety and individual privacy. In order to help readers better understand the concerns of DNA database critics, a few of the most common concerns are discussed below.

Constitutionality of Collection

During the time period of 1990 to 2010 in the United States, there have been over 200 reported cases brought to court relating to the constitutionality of federal and state DNA databank sample collection and DNA database searches (Dawn Herkenham, personal communication). Time after time the constitutionality of criminal DNA databases and databanks has been upheld.

Likewise, there is not any expectation of privacy for genetic material discarded at a crime scene (e.g., from a cigarette butt or from a semen stain). However, the more recent collection of DNA samples from arrestees has raised concerns that Fourth Amendment Constitutional rights against warrantless, suspicionless searches are being violated (Krimsky & Simoncelli 2010).

Arrestee Testing

As can be seen from Table 8.7, there are an increasing number of states moving to arrestee testing so that DNA profiles can be entered earlier in the criminal justice process. Currently, NDIS holds these records in a separate index from convicted offenders (see Table 8.2). Within the United States, as of late 2010, 25 states require individuals arrested for felony offenses to provide a DNA sample for inclusion in the state DNA database. Many countries around the world are also moving towards arrestee DNA testing.

If an arrested individual is not convicted, many of these laws require that the DNA profile be removed from the database and the DNA sample be destroyed. However, most laws call for the acquitted individual to request the profile expungement and sample destruction.

As the first state with experience implementing an arrestee index at SDIS, Virginia found that database hits for unsolved crimes could be made earlier and thus potentially prevent future crimes by the same individuals (Ferrara & Li 2004). In their first eight years of operation (2003 to 2010), Virginia observed over 625 hits to the arrestee index (see http://www.dfs.virginia.gov/statistics/index.cfm). Arrestee sample collection does result in connecting crimes through DNA, but more research would be helpful to see the real impact of making this connection earlier in the criminal justice process (i.e., at arrest instead of waiting for conviction).

Racial Distribution of the U.S. Database

A common argument of DNA database critics (e.g., see Chapter 15 in Krimsky & Simoncelli 2010) is that there is a higher representation of minorities (e.g., African

Americans and Hispanics) on the U.S. as well as other national DNA databases. Since LDIS, SDIS, and NDIS do not keep records as to the ethnicity or racial background of DNA profiles, this allegation cannot be confirmed. However, U.S. prison population statistics are available from which it may be possible to infer the potential racial composition of the NDIS offender index, which is composed of convicted offenders. This correlation of course is based on the assumption that all offender samples are being collected and placed into the DNA database.

Table 8.10 shows that a much higher number of African American (black) and Hispanic individuals are in U.S. prisons relative to the number of Caucasians (white). For example, there are 6.6 times as many African American versus Caucasian males ages 30 to 34 in prison and 2.2 times as many Hispanic versus Caucasian males of the same age range. If these prison population numbers correlate to the racial makeup of NDIS (or SDIS or LDIS), then as critics claim there is a higher number of non-Caucasian DNA profiles in the database.

However, it is important to note that the argument about minorities being over-represented on the DNA database has more to do with the criminal justice system as a whole and not the DNA database itself. The DNA samples that are put in the database are supposed to be collected at the local, state, or federal level from convicted offenders or those arrested for a legislated qualifying offense. *There is no pre-selection of certain population groups in terms of the DNA collection.* Whether or not individuals have their DNA collected has to do with whether or not they are convicted of or arrested for a crime that qualified them for DNA submission.

TABLE 8.10 Estimated Number of Inmates Held in Custody in State or Federal Prison, or in Local Jails per 100,000 U.S. Residents, by Sex, Race, and Age as of June 30, 2009.

	Male			Female		
Age	**White**	**Black**	**Hispanic**	**White**	**Black**	**Hispanic**
18–19	776	4403	1838	70	210	140
20–24	1389	8889	3937	194	595	329
25–29	1569	10,501	3954	222	733	314
30–34	1673	10,995	3650	260	896	302
35–39	1587	10,068	3090	263	895	300
40–44	1475	8668	2735	214	730	248
45–49	972	6387	2327	115	405	191
50–54	568	3914	1583	63	155	132
55–59	383	2203	1159	25	60	86
60–64	227	1134	758	9	49	36
65 or older	87	454	243	3	5	9

Source: http://bjs.ojp.usdoj.gov/content/pub/pdf/pim09st.pdf (Table 19 data).

A Universal Population-Wide Database?

As DNA database expansion has occurred, there have been calls by some for a universal database in which profiles of everyone in the population would be included on the database (Kaye & Smith 2003). The argument for doing so is typically two-fold. First, if more DNA profiles are in the database, then the advocates of this approach suggest that there will be an increase in the hit rate. This assumes that a probative biological sample will be left at most crime scenes from which a useful DNA profile can be obtained.

The second common argument for creating a universal database stems from the concern raised in the previous section, namely that there is a disproportionate level of minorities' samples in the DNA database. The reasoning of the universal database advocates is that if everyone is put in the database then there would be no racial inequality in terms of sampling.

A number of technical as well as ethical issues would exist with efforts to create a universal database. First, currently it would be expensive to generate a population-wide DNA database and would overwhelm a system that already has DNA backlogs (see Table 8.9). Moreover, if a DNA database contains a large number of innocent people who never commit crimes, the system would be bogged down by the expense of testing these individuals on the front end. Database searches would be clogged on the back end by having to sift through all of the extraneous data. Increasing the database size that dramatically (e.g., 300 million within the United States) would require more powerful search algorithms and much greater computer capacity. Additional loci would need to be tested to increase the profile random match probabilities to avoid adventitious matches (see D.N.A. Box 8.3).

The collection of samples would create both logistical and ethical issues. Among adults and juvenilles of crime-committing age, how do we go about collecting DNA from innocent people? What if someone is not willing to volunteer their sample for DNA testing? Would some form of coercion be used to collect the sample? Measures would have to be in place to avoid duplication of sample collection and processing if people move around. In other words, collection would not be a trivial task.

Would DNA be collected from children, for example, at birth or at a very young age? The benefit of collecting the children's DNA profiles at birth would not be seen until many years into the future as those who choose to commit crimes would not likely start until their late teenage years or older (and hopefully they would never start committing crimes). As a society, are we willing to collect DNA from innocent children as an investment for the future?

Predicting where we will be 20 years into the future is unrealistic in terms of the technology and genetic markers that will be in use. We might be typing genetic markers that may be obsolete 20 years from now. For the DNA profiles to be of value once the children grow old enough to commit crimes, the samples would have to be retained and tested or re-tested with new genetic markers of the future.

Would knowing that their DNA profile is on a database serve as a deterrent to bad behavior for people? Perhaps for some individuals. Unfortunately, as the SFPD study showed, serious repeat offenders keep offending even on probation (Gabriel et al. 2010)! DNA may be a deterrent to some criminals but certainly not to all potential offenders (see Prainsack & Kitzberger 2009).

Summary and Final Thoughts

As DNA databases continue to demonstrate their success in aiding law enforcement investigations, they will expand in size. New laws that effectively widen the search net by including offenders from an expanded list of crimes will bring in more DNA samples. The DNA testing community must cope with this growth and overcome sample backlogs. By the end of the first decade of the 21st century, the U.S. national DNA database is growing at a rate of more than one million new samples each year. Growth gives rise to operational challenges. Faster search algorithms are needed, additional core loci will need to be included to avoid adventitious matches, and safeguards on the application and use of the database need to be maintained.

DNA databases have shown their value in benefiting the criminal justice system. Database hits have linked serial crimes and located perpetrators who left biological evidence at crime scenes years earlier. Post-conviction exonerations of innocent people who have spent years behind bars have been made possible through DNA database connections to the true perpetrator. Any tool that is this powerful will be criticized and needs to be used responsibly in order to balance public safety with individual liberties.

READING LIST AND INTERNET RESOURCES

General Information

Bille, T. W. (1999). DNA analysis: A powerful investigative tool. *Profiles in DNA*, *3*(2), 8–9. Available at <http://www.promega.com/profiles/>.

Bradford, L., et al. (2010). Disaster victim investigation recommendations from two simulated mass disaster scenarios utilized for user acceptance testing CODIS 6.0. *Forensic Science International: Genetics* (in press). doi:10.1016/j.fsigen.2010.05.005.

Butler, J. M. (2006). Genetics and genomics of core short tandem repeat loci used in human identity testing. *Journal of Forensic Sciences*, *51*, 253–265.

Langan, P. A., & Levin, D. J. (2002). *Recidivism of prisoners released in 1994*. Washington, DC: Bureau of Justice Statistics, U.S. Department of Justice. Available at <http://www.ojp.usdoj.gov/bjs/abstract/rpr94.htm>.

Langan, P. A., et al. (2003). *Recidivism of sex offenders released from prison in 1994*. Washington, DC: Bureau of Justice Statistics, U.S. Department of Justice. Available at <http://www.ojp.usdoj.gov/bjs/abstract/rsorp94.htm>.

Lovirich, N. P., et al. (2004). National forensic DNA study report. Available at <http://www.ojp.usdoj.gov/nij/pdf/dna_studyreport_final.pdf>.

National Commission on the Future of DNA Evidence. *The future of forensic DNA testing: Predictions of the research and development working group*. Washington, D.C: National Institute of Justice. Available at <http://www.ojp.usdoj.gov/nij/pubs-sum/183697.htm>.

Wickenheiser, R. A. (2004). The business case for using forensic DNA technology to solve and prevent crime. *Journal of Biolaw and Business*, *7*, 34–50.

International DNA Efforts

DNA Resource. <http://www.dnaresource.com/>.

Asplen, C. H. (2004). International perspectives on forensic DNA databases. *Forensic Science International*, *146S*, S119–S121.

ENFSI DNA Working Group (2010). DNA-Database Management: Review and Recommendations. Available at <http://www.enfsi.eu/get_doc.php?uid=345>.

Harbison, S. A., et al. (2001). The New Zealand DNA databank: Its development and significance as a crime solving tool. *Science & Justice*, *41*, 33–37.

Interpol Handbook on DNA Data Exchange and Practice (2001). <http://www.interpol.int/Public/Forensic/dna/HandbookPublic.pdf>.

Interpol Handbook on DNA Data Exchange and Practice, 2nd edition (2009). <http://www.interpol.int/Public/ICPO/Publications/HandbookPublic2009.pdf>.
Martin, P. D., et al. (2001). A brief history of the formation of DNA databases in forensic science within Europe. *Forensic Science International, 119*, 225–231.
Martin, P. D. (2004). National DNA databases – practice and practicability. A forum for discussion. *Progress in Forensic Genetics 10. ICS 1261*, 1–8.
Oz, C., et al. (2011). The Israel Police DNA database: Recognizing the capability of databases in providing investigative leads. *Forensic Science International: Genetics* (in press) doi:10.1016/j.fsigen.2010.11.006.
Schneider, P. M., & Martin, P. D. (2001). Criminal DNA databases: The European situation. *Forensic Science International, 119*, 232–238.
Voegeli, P., et al. (2006). Evaluation of the 4-year test period of the Swiss DNA database. *Progress in Forensic Genetics 11, ICS 1288*, 731–733.
Walsh, S. J., et al. (2002). The collation of forensic DNA case data into a multi-dimensional intelligence database. *Science & Justice, 42*, 205–214.
Walsh, S. J. (2004). Recent advances in forensic genetics. *Expert Review in Molecular Diagnostics, 4*, 31–40.
Walsh, S. J. (2009). Evaluating the role and impact of forensic DNA profiling on key areas of the criminal justice system. PhD dissertation (443 pages). Sydney, Australia: University of Technology.

U.K. National Database (NDNAD)

Asplen, C. H. (2004). The application of DNA technology in England and Wales. Available at: <http://www.ojp.usdoj.gov/nij/pdf/uk_finaldraft.pdf>.
Association of Chief Police Officers of England, Wales and Northern Ireland. <http://www.acpo.police.uk/policies.asp>.
Forensic Science Service Annual Reports. <http://www.forensic.gov.uk/>.
Gill, P., et al. (1996). A new method of STR interpretation using inferential logic–development of a criminal intelligence database. *International Journal of Legal Medicine, 109*, 14–22.
Home Office. <http://www.homeoffice.gov.uk/> <http://www.homeoffice.gov.uk/science-research/using-science/dna-database/>.
LGC Forensics. <http://www.lgcforensics.com/>.
National DNA Database (2006). Parliament Office of Science and Technology, Postnote 258. <http://www.parliament.uk/documents/upload/postpn258.pdf>.
NPIA. (2007). National DNA Database Annual Report 2006–2007 Section 1. Available at <http://www.npia.police.uk/en/docs/NDNA_A4L_Section1-08.pdf>.
Werrett, D. J., & Sparkes, R. (1998). 300 matches per week – the effectiveness and future development of DNA intelligence databases – parts 1 and 2. *Proceedings of the ninth international symposium on human identification* (pp. 55–62). Available at <http://www.promega.com/geneticidproc/>.
Werrett, D. J. (1997). The National DNA Database. *Forensic Science International, 88*, 33–42.

Canadian DNA Database

Kuperus, W. R., et al. (2003). Crime scene links through DNA evidence: The practical experience from Saskatchewan casework. *Canadian Society of Forensic Sciences Journal, 36*, 19–28.
Lalonde, S. A. (2006). Canada's national DNA data bank: A success story. *Canadian Society of Forensic Sciences Journal, 39*, 39–46.
Royal Canadian Mounted Police (2007) National DNA Data Bank Advisory Committee 2006–2007 Annual Report. Available at <http://www.rcmp-grc.gc.ca/dna_ac/annualreport_e.htm>.

U.S. National Database

Baechtel, F. S., et al. (1991). Tracking the violent criminal offender through DNA typing profiles – a national database system concept. In T. Burke (Ed.), *DNA fingerprinting: Approaches and applications* (pp. 356–360). Basel, Switzerland: Birkhäuser Verlag.
Ban, J. D. (2001). Establishing a large DNA data bank using the PowerPlex 1.1 and 2.1 Systems. *Croatian Medical Journal, 42*, 256–259.
Ban, J. D. (2001). Operating and managing a statewide DNA program. *Croatian Medical Journal, 42*, 281–284.

Budowle, B., et al. (1998). CODIS and PCR-based short tandem repeat loci: Law enforcement tools. *Proceedings of the second european symposium on human identification* (pp. 73–88). Madison, Wisconsin: Promega Corporation. Available at <http://www.promega.com/geneticidproc/>.

Budowle, B., & Moretti, T. R. (1998). Examples of STR population databases for CODIS and for casework. *Proceedings of the ninth international symposium on human identification*. Available at <http://www.promega.com/geneticidproc/>.

Budowle, B., et al. (2001). CODIS STR loci data from 41 sample populations. *Journal of Forensic Sciences, 46*, 453–489.

FBI Laboratory's CODIS (Combined DNA Index System) Unit. <http://www.fbi.gov/hq/lab/html/codis1.htm>.

Ferrara, P. B., & Li, G. C. (2004). Creating and maintaining an arrestee database in Virginia—policy and practical aspects. *Profiles in DNA, 7*(1), 3–5. Available at <http://www.promega.com/profiles/>.

Hoyle, R. (1998). The FBI's national DNA database. *Nature Biotechnology, 16*, 987–987.

Niezgoda, S., & Brown, B. (1995). The FBI laboratory's combined DNA index system program. *Proceedings of the sixth international symposium on human identification*. Available at <http://www.promega.com/geneticidproc/>.

Niezgoda, S. (1997). CODIS program review. *Proceedings of the eighth international symposium on human identification*. Available at <http://www.promega.com/geneticidproc/>.

Pederson, J. (1999). DNA typing in action: Databasing in the Commonwealth of Virginia. *Profiles in DNA, 3*(1), 3–7. Available at <http://www.promega.com/profiles/>.

DNA Database Issues

DNA Task Force Report (2010). Report and recommendations of the Wisconsin DNA Task Force. Available at <http://www.wi-doc.com/PDF_Files/DNATaskForceReport.pdf>.

Geddes, L. (January 6, 2010). Unreliable evidence? Time to open up DNA databases. *New Scientist*. Available at <http://www.newscientist.com>.

Himmelreich, C. (March 23, 2009). Despite DNA evidence, twins charged in heist go free. *Time Magazine*. Available at <http://www.time.com/time/world/article/0,8599,1887111,00.html>.

Himmelreich, C. (March 27, 2009). Germany's phantom serial killer: A DNA blunder. *Time Magazine*. Available at <http://www.time.com/time/world/article/0,8599,1888126,00.html>.

Kaye, D. H. (2009). Trawling DNA databases for partial matches: What is the FBI afraid of? *Cornell Journal of Law and Public Policy, 19*, 145–171.

Krane, D. E., et al. (2009). Time for DNA disclosure. *Science, 326*, 1631–1632.

Prainsack, B., & Kitzberger, M. (2009). DNA behind bars: Other ways of knowing forensic DNA technologies. *Social Studies of Science, 39*, 51–79.

Sjerps, M., & Meester, R. (2009). Selection effects and database screening in forensic science. *Forensic Science International, 192*, 56–61.

Willing, R. (February 8, 2000). Mismatch calls DNA tests into question. *USA Today (February 8, 2000).*

DNA Database Performance

Buckleton, J., et al. (2009). Database crime to crime match rate calculation. *Forensic Science International: Genetics, 3*(3), 200–201.

Gabriel, M., et al. (2010). Beyond the cold hit: Measuring the impact of the national DNA data bank on public safety at the city and county level. *Journal of Law, Medicine, & Ethics, 38*, 396–411.

Walsh, S. J., et al. (2008). Comparing the growth and effectiveness of forensic DNA databases. *Forensic Science International: Genetics Supplement Series, 1*, 667–668.

Walsh, S. J., et al. (2010). Modeling forensic DNA database performance. *Journal of Forensic Sciences, 55*, 1174–1183.

Additional Loci

Gill, P., et al. (2004). An assessment of whether SNPs will replace STRs in national DNA databases–joint considerations of the DNA working group of the European Network of Forensic Science Institutes (ENFSI) and the Scientific Working Group on DNA Analysis Methods (SWGDAM). *Science & Justice, 44*, 51–53.

Gill, P., et al. (2006a). The evolution of DNA databases-Recommendations for new European STR loci. *Forensic Science International, 156*, 242–244.

Gill, P., et al. (2006b). New multiplexes for Europe-amendments and clarification of strategic development. *Forensic Science International, 163*, 155–157.

DNA Backlogs

Backlog Reduction Federal Funding Awards. <http://www.ojp.usdoj.gov/nij/topics/forensics/lab-operations/capacity/backlog-reduction-funding.htm>.

California Jan Bashinski DNA Laboratory Monthly Statistics. <http://ag.ca.gov/bfs/pdf/Monthly.pdf>.

Nelson, M. (2010). Making sense of DNA backlogs—myths vs. reality. *NIJ Journal, 266*, 20–25. For full special report, see <http://www.ncjrs.gov/pdffiles1/nij/230183.pdf>.

U.S. Department of Justice Office of the Inspector General (OIG) (2010). Review of the Federal Bureau of Investigation Laboratory's forensic DNA case backlog. Report 10–39 (August 2010). Available at <http://www.justice.gov/oig/reports/FBI/a1039.pdf>.

DNA Database Laws

DNA Resource.com (information on the latest developments in forensic DNA policy). <http://www.dnaresource.com/>.

Federal Legislation on Forensic DNA. <http://www.dna.gov/statutes-caselaw/federal-legislation/>.

Herkenham, M. D. (1999). *State DNA database statutes: Summary of provisions*. U.S. Department of Justice.

Herkenham, D. (2002). DNA database legislation and legal issues. *Profiles in DNA, 5*(1), 6–7. Madison, Wisconsin: Promega Corporation. Available at <http://www.promega.com/profiles>.

Kaye, D. H. (2002). Two fallacies about DNA databanks for law enforcement. *Brooklyn Law Review, 67*, 179–206.

Kaye, D. H., & Smith, M. E. (2003). DNA identification databases: Legality, legitimacy, and the case for population-wide coverage. *Wisconsin Law Review, 3*, 413–459.

McEwen, J. E., & Reilly, P. R. (1994). A review of state legislation on DNA forensic data banking. *American Journal of Human Genetics, 54*, 941–958.

McEwen, J. E. (1995). Forensic DNA data banking by state crime laboratories. *American Journal of Human Genetics, 56*, 1487–1492.

National Conference of State Legislatures (state laws on DNA data banks, qualifying offenses, others who must provide sample, summary as of July 2008). <http://www.ncsl.org/programs/cj/dnadatabanks.htm>.

Palmer, L. J. (2004). *Encyclopedia of DNA and the United States criminal justice system*. London: McFarland.

Spalding, V. B. (1995). DNA databanking laws: The North Carolina experience and a national review of laws and challenges. *Proceedings of the sixth international symposium on human identification*, Madison, Wisconsin: Promega Corporation (pp. 137–148). Available at <http://www.promega.com/geneticidproc/>.

Williams, R., & Johnson, P. (2005). Forensic DNA Databasing: A European Perspective (interim report). <http://www.dur.ac.uk/resources/sass/WilliamsandJohnsonInterimReport2005-1.pdf>.

Willing, R. (November 20, 2006). Many DNA matches aren't acted on. *USA Today*. Available at <http://www.usatoday.com/news/nation/2006-11-20-dna-matches_x.htm>.

Sample Retention

Gaensslen, R. E. (2006). Should biological evidence or DNA be retained by forensic science laboratories after profiling?. No, except under narrow legislatively-stipulated conditions. *Journal of Law, Medicine & Ethics, 34*, 375–379.

Herkenham, M. D. (2006). Retention of offender DNA samples necessary to ensure and monitor quality of forensic DNA efforts: Appropriate safeguards exist to protect the DNA samples from misuse. *Journal of Law, Medicine & Ethics, 34*, 380–384.

Van Camp, N., & Dierickx, K. (2008). The retention of forensic DNA samples: A socio-ethical evaluation of current practices in the EU. *Journal of Medical Ethics, 34*(8), 606–610.

Cold Hits and Database Match Probability

Balding, D. J., & Nichols, R. A. (1994). DNA profile match probability calculation: How to allow for population stratification, relatedness, database selection and single bands. *Forensic Science International, 64*, 125–140.

Balding, D. J., & Donnelly, P. (1996). Evaluating DNA profile evidence when the suspect is identified through a database search. *Journal of Forensic Sciences, 41*(4), 603–607.

Balding, D. J. (1997). Errors and misunderstandings in the second NRC report. *Jurimetrics Journal, 37*, 469–476.

Balding, D. J. (2002). The DNA database search controversy. *Biometrics, 58*, 214–244.

Budowle, B., et al. (2006). Clarification of statistical issues related to the operation of CODIS. *Proceedings of the seventeenth international symposium on human identification*. Promega Corporation. Available at <http://www.promega.com/geneticidproc/ussymp17proc/>.

Chakraborty, R., & Ge, J. (2009). Statistical weight of a DNA match in cold-hit cases. *Forensic Science Communications, 11*(3). Available at <http://www2.fbi.gov/hq/lab/fsc/backissu/july2009/index.htm>.

Devlin, B. (2000). The evidentiary value of a DNA database search. *Biometrics, 56*, 1276–1277.

DNA Advisory Board, Statistical and population genetic issues affecting the evaluation of the frequency of occurrence of DNA profiles calculated from pertinent population database(s). *Forensic Science Communications, 2*, 3. Available at <http://www2.fbi.gov/hq/lab/fsc/backissu/july2000/dnastat.htm>.

Kaye, D. H. (2008). People v. Nelson: A tale of two statistics. *Law, Probability, and Risk, 7*(4), 249–257.

Meester, R., & Sjerps, M. (2003). The evidentiary value in the DNA database search controversy and the two-stain problem. *Biometrics, 59*, 727–732.

Mueller, L. D. (2008). Can simple population genetic models reconcile partial match frequencies observed in large forensic databases? *Journal of Genetics, 87*, 101–108.

National Research Council, (1996). *The evaluation of forensic DNA evidence*. Washington, DC: National Academy Press.

Rudin, N., & Inman, K. (1st Quarter 2007). A frosty debate: The chilling effect of a "cold hit". *CAC News* (pp. 31–35). Available at <http://www.cacnews.org/> or <http://www.forensicdna.com/Articles.htm>.

Storvik, G., & Egeland, T. (2007). The DNA database search controversy revisited: Bridging the Bayesian-frequentist gap. *Biometrics, 63*, 922–925.

Taylor, C., & Colman, P. (2010). Forensics: experts disagree on statistics from DNA trawls. *Nature, 464*, 1266–1267.

Partial Matches Within Databases

Biondo, R. (2000). The impact of CODIS software in criminal investigations in the Italian national police. *Proceedings of the eleventh international symposium on human identification*. Available at <http://www.promega.com/geneticidproc/ussymp11proc/content/biondo.pdf>.

Brenner, C. (2007). Arizona DNA database matches. <http://www.dna-view.com/ArizonaMatch.htm>.

Budowle, B., et al. (2009). Partial matches in heterogeneous offender databases do not call into question the validity of random match probability calculations. *International Journal of Legal Medicine, 123*, 59–63.

CODIS Bulletin. (2006). Interim plan for the release of information in the event of a "partial match" at NDIS. Bulletin#: BT072006. Distributed 07/20/06 via the CJIS-WAN to U.S. NDIS participating labs.

Hicks, T., et al. (2010). Use of DNA profiles for investigation using a simulated national DNA database: Part I. Partial SGM Plus profiles. *Forensic Science International: Genetics, 4*, 232–238.

Troyer, K., et al. (2001). A nine STR locus match between two apparently unrelated individuals using AmpFlSTR Profiler Plus and COfiler. In *Proceedings of the twelfth international symposium on human identification*. Promega Corporation. Available at <http://www.promega.com/geneticidproc/ussymp12proc/abstracts.htm>.

Weir, B. S. (2004). Matching and partially-matching DNA profiles. *Journal of Forensic Sciences, 49*, 1009–1014.

John Doe Warrants

Denver DA John Doe Case Filings. <http://www.denverda.org/DNA/John_Doe_DNA_Warrants.htm>.

DNA.gov website information. <http://www.dna.gov/uses/solving-crimes/cold_cases/identifying_analyzing_prioritizing/johndoewarrant> <http://www.dna.gov/statutes-caselaw/caselaw/john-doe-caselaw>.

Gahn, N. interview (2000). John Doe: D1S7, D2S44, D5S110, D10S28, D17S79, Charged with Rape. *Profiles in DNA, 3*(3), 8–9. Available at <http://www.promega.com/profiles/303/ProfilesinDNA_303_08.pdf>.

DNA Dragnets Through Mass Screens

Forensic Science Service. <http://www.forensic.gov.uk> <http://www.washingtonpost.com> (April 14, 15, and 17, 2004).

Hansen, M. (2004). DNA dragnet. *American Bar Association Journal, 90*, 38–43. Available at <http://www.abajournal.com/magazine/dna_dragnet/>.

Kahn, R., et al. (1996). AmpliType PM testing of potential perpetrators on a massive scale. *Proceedings of the American academy of forensic sciences* (p. 52).

Kaye, D. H. (2009). Rounding up the usual suspects: A legal and logical analysis of DNA database trawls. *North Carolina Law Review, 87*(2), 425–503.

Szibor, R., et al. (2006). Forensic mass screening using mtDNA. *International Journal of Legal Medicine, 120*, 372–376.

Walker, S. (2004). Police DNA "sweeps" extremely unproductive: A national survey of police DNA "sweeps." A report by the Police Professionalism Initiative. Available at <http://www.unomaha.edu/criminaljustice/PDF/dnareport.pdf>.

Wambaugh, J. (1989). *The blooding*. New York: Bantam.

Wenzel, R. (2007). Report on criminal cases in Europe solved by ILS (DNA mass testing) for the European Network of Forensic Science Institutes DNA Working Group. Available at <http://www.enfsi.eu>.

Familial Searching (See also Appendix 2)

Bieber, F. R., et al. (2006). Finding criminals through DNA of their relatives. *Science, 312*, 1315–1316.

Miller, G. (2010). Familial DNA testing scores a win in serial killer case. *Science, 329*, 262.

Myers, S. P., et al. (2010). Searching for first-degree familial relationships in California's offender DNA database: Validation of a likelihood ratio-based approach. *Forensic Science International: Genetics (in press).* doi:10.1016/j.fsigen.2010.10.010.

Sims, G., et al. (2008). The DNA partial match and familial search policy of the California Department of Justice. *Proceedings of the ninteenth international symposium on human identification.* Available at <http://www.promega.com/geneticidproc/ussymp19proc/oralpresentations/Sims.pdf>.

Steinhauer, J. (July 8, 2010). "Grim Sleeper" arrest fans debate on DNA use. *New York Times*. Available at <http://www.nytimes.com/2010/07/09/us/09sleeper.html>.

Privacy Concerns

Cole, S. A. (2007). Is the "junk" DNA designation bunk? *Northwestern University Law Review Colloquy, 102*, 54–63. Available at <http://www.law.northwestern.edu/lawreview/colloquy/2007/23/>.

Gamero, J. J., et al. (2007). Spanish public awareness regarding DNA profile databases in forensic genetics: What type of DNA profiles should be included? *Journal of Medical Ethics, 33*, 598–604.

Gamero, J. -J., et al. (2008). A study of Spanish attitudes regarding the custody and use of forensic DNA databases. *Forensic Science International: Genetics, 2*, 138–149.

Greely, H. T. (2007). The uneasy ethical and legal underpinnings of large-scale genomic biobanks. *Annual Review of Genomics and Human Genetics, 8*, 343–364.

Guillén, M., et al. (2000). Ethical-legal problems of DNA databases in criminal investigation. *Journal of Medical Ethics, 26*, 266–271.

Hepple, B. (2009). Forensic databases: Implications of the cases of S and Marper. *Medicine, Science, and the Law, 49*, 77–87.

Kaye, D. H. (2006). Who needs special needs?: On the constitutionality of collecting DNA and other biometric data from arrestees. *Journal of Law, Medicine & Ethics, 34*, 188–198.

Kaye, J. (2006). Police collection and access to DNA samples. *Genomics, Society & Policy, 2*, 16–27. Available at <http://www.gspjournal.com/>.

Kaye, D. H. (2007). Please, let's bury the junk: The CODIS loci and the revelation of private information. *Northwestern University Law Review Colloquy, 102*, 70–81. Available at <http://www.law.northwestern.edu/lawreview/colloquy/2007/25/>.

Krimsky, S., & Simoncelli, T. (2010). *Genetic justice: DNA databanks, criminal investigations and civil liberties.* New York: Columbia University Press.

Levitt, M. (2007). Forensic databases: Benefits and ethical and social costs. *British Medical Bulletin, 83*, 235–248.

Murch, R. S., & Budowle, B. (1997). Are developments in forensic applications of DNA technology consistent with privacy protections? In M. A. Rothstein (Ed.), *Genetic secrets: Protecting privacy and confidentiality in the genetic era* (pp. 212–230). New Haven, CT: Yale University Press.

Nerko, C. J. (2008). Assessing Fourth Amendment challenges to DNA extraction statutes after Samson v. California. *Fordham Law Review, 77*(2), 917–949.

Nuffield Council on Bioethics (2007). The forensic use of bioinformation: Ethical issues. Available at <http://www.nuffieldbioethics.org>.

Patyn, A., & Dierckx, K. (2010). Forensic DNA databases: Genetic testing as a societal choice. *Journal of Medical Ethics, 36*, 319–320.

Privacy International. <http://www.privacyinternational.org>.

Rothstein, M. A., & Talbott, M. K. (2006). The expanding use of DNA in law enforcement: What role for privacy? *Journal of Law, Medicine & Ethics*, *34*, 153–164.

Sarkar, S. P., & Adshead, G. (2010). Whose DNA is it anyway? European court, junk DNA, and the problem with prediction. *Journal of American Academy of Psychiatry Law*, *38*, 247–250.

Simoncelli, T. (2006). Dangerous excursions: The case against expanding forensic DNA databases to innocent persons. *Journal of Law, Medicine & Ethics*, *34*, 390–397.

Simoncelli, T., & Krimsky, S. (2007). A new era of DNA collections: At what cost to civil liberties? An issue brief available at <http://www.acslaw.org/node/5338>.

Special issue of the *Journal of Law, Medicine, and Ethics* (summer 2006)—table of contents in Table 8.7.

Williams, R., & Johnson, P. (2006). Inclusiveness, effectiveness and intrusiveness: Issues in the developing uses of DNA profiling in support of criminal investigations. *Journal of Law, Medicine & Ethics*, *34*, 234–247.

CHAPTER

9

Missing Persons and Disaster Victim Identification Efforts

Kinship analysis and parentage testing typically involve one sample being compared to another sample or to a few samples with a specific relationship question in mind. This chapter will review efforts with missing persons investigations and disaster victim identification situations where a set of remains is being compared to many different samples, which introduces another level of complexity beyond the challenges of kinship analysis.

MISSING PERSONS INVESTIGATIONS

An estimated 40,000 unidentified human remains have been recovered and are currently located in medical examiner and coroners' offices around the United States (Ritter 2007). Every year in the United States, tens of thousands of people are reported "missing," often under suspious circumstances. While some of these missing persons are later located alive through law enforcement efforts, many become unidentified human remains that resulted from criminal activity, such as rape and murder. Knowledge of who the victim is can help solve these crimes and bring closure to families of the missing.

There are three categories of samples associated with missing persons cases: direct reference samples, family reference samples, and unidentified human remains (UHR) samples. The UHR samples are generally skeletal remains (bones), teeth, or tissue. Much of the data from missing person investigations is in the form of mitochondrial DNA sequences since this information can be successfully recovered from highly degraded samples. Mitochondrial DNA also enables access to a larger number of reference samples from maternal relatives of a victim (see Chapter 14).

Some possible direct reference samples include medical samples from the missing individual, such as a newborn screening bloodspot or a biopsy sample. Personal effects, such as a toothbrush or hairbrush, may also provide direct reference samples. Family reference samples can be buccal swabs from close biological relatives, such as parents, children, or siblings of the missing individual. More distant relatives, such as maternal aunts, maternal or paternal uncles, or maternal or paternal cousins, can also be useful if mitochondrial or Y-chromosome DNA testing are performed. The combined evaluation of samples from more than one close relative can help provide greater confidence in such kinship analyses.

DNA databases can play an important role in helping to identify missing individuals over time. When a family member goes missing, DNA samples can be obtained from direct reference samples or biological relatives. DNA profiles from these samples would then be uploaded to the database and searched against DNA profiles from unidentified human remains in an effort to make an association to a missing individual. Many states within the United States and nations around the world are beginning to establish missing persons databases to enable matching of recovered remains to their family members. The National DNA Index System (NDIS) discussed in Chapter 8 also contains indices to help with missing persons investigations. Figure 9.1 illustrates these indices and purposes of searches between them.

In an effort to help make connections between family members and their missing relatives, in 2007 the U.S. government established a National Missing and Unidentified Persons System (NamUs) website at http://www.namus.gov/. NamUs is composed of two sets of records—a missing persons database (http://www.findthemissing.org) and an unidentified persons database (https://identifyus.org/)—that are cross-matched against one another. The missing persons database contains information that can be entered by the general public regarding an individual who has gone missing. Only medical examiners and coroners can enter information in the unidentified persons database, which describes bodies found but not yet identified. However, as noted on the NamUs website, anyone can search the unidentified persons database using characteristics such as sex, race, distinct body features, and even dental information. The NamUs website provides the capability to print a missing persons poster with the missing individual's name, his or her photo, and contact information for investigators or family members.

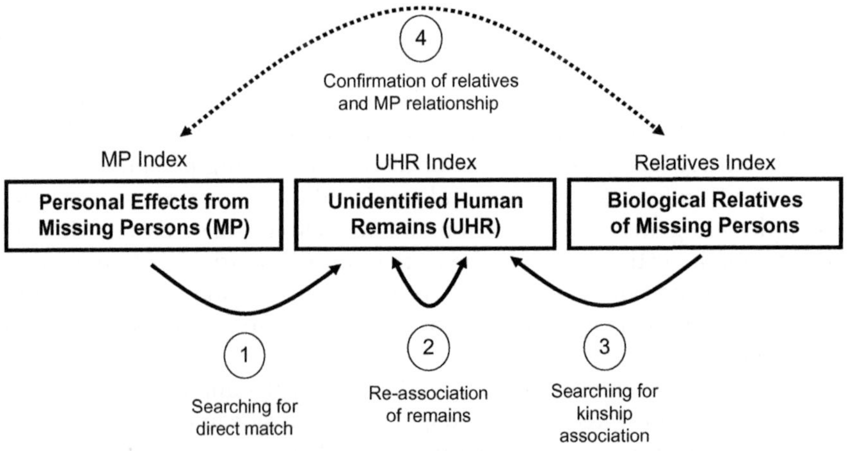

FIGURE 9.1 Searches conducted with missing persons DNA databases.

As of December 2010, NamUs listed 7538 unidentified human remains cases, of which 7214 (almost 96%) were still open. Of the 324 cases closed, 25 (or about 8%) had been aided by NamUs. At the same time, the missing persons database listed 5889 cases with 4912 (just over 83%) still open. Of the 977 cases closed, 44 (4.5%) had been aided by the NamUs website.

DISASTER VICTIM IDENTIFICATION (DVI)

Mass diasters, whether natural or man-made, can involve loss of life for many victims of the tragedy. Efforts to identify these victims are referred to as *disaster victim identification*, or DVI.

In the United States, DNA testing has now become routine and expected in disaster victim identification in the event of a plane crash, large fire, or terrorist attack. Military casualties are also identified through STR typing or mitochondrial DNA sequencing by the Armed Forces DNA Identification Laboratory (AFDIL). All airplane crashes within the United States are examined by the National Transportation Safety Board (http://www.ntsb.gov), which often contracts with AFDIL to identify the air crash victims through DNA testing as part of the investigation.

Often mass disasters leave human remains that are literally in pieces or burned beyond recognition. In some cases it is possible to visually identify a victim, but body parts can be separated from one another and the remains comingled making identification without DNA techniques virtually impossible. The use of fingerprints and dental records (odontology) still plays an important role in victim identification but these modalities obviously require a finger or an intact skull or jawbone along with previously archived fingerprint and dental records.

DNA testing has a major advantage in that it can be used to identify each and every portion of the remains recovered from the disaster site, provided (1) that there is sufficient intact DNA present to obtain a DNA type and (2) a reference sample is available for comparison purposes from a surviving family member or some verifiable personal item containing biological material. Personal items from the deceased including toothbrushes, combs, razors, or even dirty laundry can provide biological material to generate a reference DNA type for the victim. The direct comparison of DNA results from disaster victim remains to DNA recovered from personal items (Figure 9.2a) represents the easiest way to obtain a match—and hence an identification—provided it is possible to verify the source (e.g., the toothbrush was not used by some other household member). The use of DNA from biological relatives (Figure 9.2b) necessitates the added complexity of kinship analysis similar to that employed for paternity or reverse parentage testing.

DVI always involves comparison of post-mortem (PM) and ante-mortem (AM) data. PM data are generated from the recovered human remains, which may be highly fragmented depending on the type of disaster. AM data come from either direct reference samples (e.g., toothbrushes or razors known to belong to the victim) or kinship comparisons to biological relatives (e.g., parent, child, or sibling).

DVI is much more complicated than parentage testing because there are so many more comparisons that are being made depending on the number of victims involved. In addition, the quality of the recovered human remains may be compromised depending on the type of disaster and thus partial or mixed DNA profiles may result. DNA statistics for DVI work are usually best represented with likelihood ratios because this permits DNA results

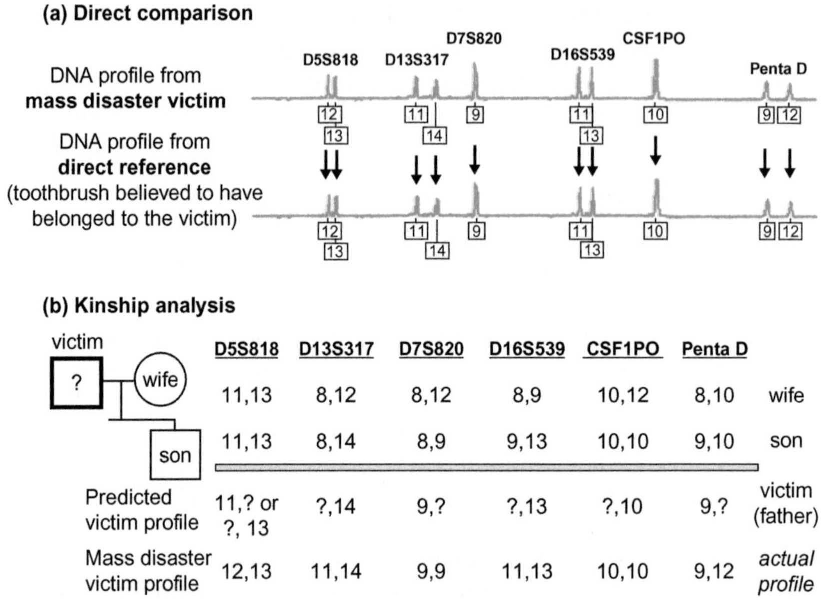

FIGURE 9.2 Example demonstrating the use of reference samples in mass disaster victim identification using DNA typing. (a) Direct comparison involves analysis of a direct reference sample from some kind of personal effect of the victim. (b) Kinship analysis utilizes close biological relatives, such as those illustrated in Figure 9.3, to reconstruct a victim's DNA profile.

to be combined between multiple genetic systems as well as other non-DNA evidence using Bayesian statistics.

DNA testing has been used to help identify victims of numerous airline crashes, the victims of terrorist attacks, recovered remains from mass graves, and in a more limited fashion in natural disasters like the Southeast Asia Tsunami in December 2004 and Hurricane Katrina that struck New Orleans in August 2005.

Several documents have been published with lessons learned from previous DVI work (AABB 2010, Budowle et al. 2005, Lessig et al. 2011, NIJ 2006). The International Society of Forensic Genetics (ISFG) published 12 recommendations for DVI work (Prinz et al. 2007) (D.N.A. Box 9.1).

ISSUES FACED DURING DISASTER VICTIM IDENTIFICATION EFFORTS

There are several important aspects of mass fatality incidents that will be discussed prior to moving into examples of victim identification efforts through DNA testing in recent mass disasters. The areas include collection of reference samples and federal assistance programs. The National Institute of Justice has published two documents to provide additional information on mass disaster investigations: *Mass Fatality Incidents: A Guide for Human Forensic*

D.N.A. BOX 9.1

ISFG RECOMMENDATIONS ON DISASTER VICTIM IDENTIFICATION

In the inaugural issue of the journal *Forensic Science International: Genetics*, the ISFG DNA Commission published 12 recommendations on disaster victim identification (DVI) using DNA (Prinz et al. 2007):

- **Recommendation #1:** Every forensic DNA laboratory should make an effort to contact the relevant authority dealing with emergency response and establish involvement in a possible mass fatality preparedness plan. Policy decisions about sample collection, scope and final goals of the effort will affect the victims' families and the work stream and should be decided as early as possible.
- **Recommendation #2:** The internal response plan needs to address throughput capacity, sample tracking, and must have names of supervisors responsible for different tasks that are updated as personnel changes.
- **Recommendation #3:** Several sample types (see Table 1 in Prinz et al. 2007) for DNA testing should be taken at the earliest possible stage of the investigation provided material traceability is guaranteed. Samples must be collected from each body or recognizable body part, even if identity is already established. Proper storage must be assured.
- **Recommendation #4:** Multiple direct references and samples from first-degree relatives should be collected for each missing person. Scientists with a background in genetics should be available for training or for consultations in the family liaison group.
- **Recommendation #5:** DVI DNA testing should only be performed by laboratories with demonstrated successful capabilities and continuous experience with these specified sample types.
- **Recommendation #6:** The set of loci to be analyzed has to be identified as soon as possible in concordance with the scientific community in the countries mostly involved. A minimum of 12 independent loci should be selected as standard set, but an even greater number of loci is preferred.
- **Recommendation #7:** All allele calls and all candidate matches have to be reviewed thoroughly. Composite DNA profiles can be generated if derived from the same specimen and consistent for overlapping loci. The duplication policy should consider the logistics and circumstances of the mass fatality incident.
- **Recommendation #8:** If the standard autosomal STR typing fails to give sufficient information, additional typing system such as mtDNA, Y-chromosomal STRs, or SNP markers may be used in selected cases.
- **Recommendation #9:** A centralized database is required for all data comparison. Electronic upload is recommended to avoid transcription errors.
- **Recommendation #10:** Especially if multiple family members are involved, DNA-based identification should whenever possible be anchored by anthropological and/or circumstantial data, a second identification modality, or multiple DNA references.

D.N.A. BOX 9.1 (*cont'd*)

- **Recommendation #11:** In DVI work, DNA statistics are best represented as likelihood ratios that permit DNA results to be combined among multiple genetic systems or with other non-DNA evidence. Likelihood ratio thresholds should be determined for when DNA data alone can suffice for an identification; this will be based on the size and circumstances (e.g. closed versus open) of the event. All evidence and/or circumstances should be checked in making an identification, even if DNA provides the primary or sole evidentiary factor.
- **Recommendation #12:** The preparedness plan of the laboratory needs to include policies for family notification, long-term sample disposition, and data archiving.

Source:

Prinz, M., et al. (2007). DNA Commission of the International Society of Forensic Genetics (ISFG): Recommendations regarding the role of forensic genetics for disaster victim identification (DVI). Forensic Science International: Genetics, *1*, 3–12.

Identification (prepared by the National Center for Forensic Science, NIJ 2005) and *Lessons Learned from 9/11: DNA Identification in Mass Fatality Incidents* (prepared by the World Trade Center Kinship and Data Analysis Panel, NIJ 2006).

Collection of Reference Samples

In order to be able to identify victims of mass fatality incidents, reference samples are needed in order to sort out DNA profiles obtained from recovered remains. If possible, it is preferable to obtain personal effects that enable a direct match to a victim (Figure 9.2a). These personal effects may be in the form of a used razor, hairbrush, toothbrush, dirty laundry, or other items that were handled solely by the victim and from which usable biological material may be recovered to generate a DNA profile.

Living biological relatives can also provide needed and valuable reference samples. Immediate relatives including siblings, parents, and children are the most effective indirect reference samples (Figure 9.3). More extended family members can provide helpful samples though if mitochondrial DNA or Y-chromosome testing is performed.

Kinship samples can also help confirm the validity of personal effects received for a missing individual. Often a lengthy and complicated administrative review of DNA results and reference sample chain-of-custody is needed to verify both direct reference samples from personal effects and indirect references from kinship samples to enable confidence in reporting DNA identifications (see Hennessey 2002).

Federal Assistance in Disaster Situations

The Disaster Mortuary Operational Response Team (DMORT) is a federally funded group of professionals with experience in disaster victim identification that becomes activated

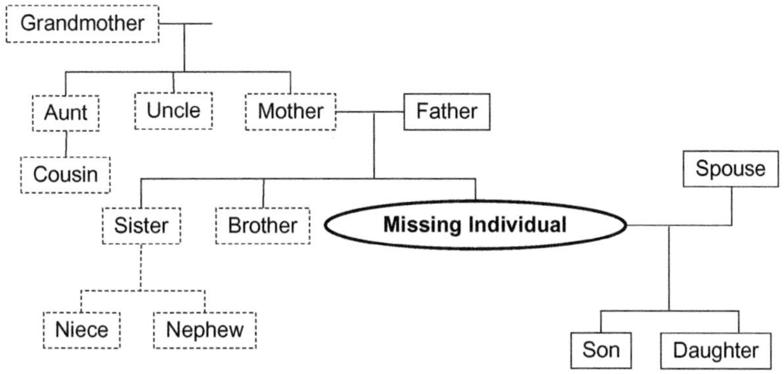

FIGURE 9.3 Direct biological relatives that can provide valuable reference samples for aiding identification of the missing individual. Ideally samples are available from multiple relatives to help establish robust kinship. A sample from a spouse is only valuable in connection with a child's sample in order to determine the expected alleles coming from the missing individual. Of course, more extended family members, with direct maternal or paternal linkage, can provide helpful samples when mitochondrial DNA or Y-chromosome testing is performed. Samples from extended family members that would be valuable for the maternally transmitted mitochondrial DNA are indicated in dashed boxes.

in response to a major disaster in the United States (see http://www.dmort.org). DMORT is part of the National Disaster Medical System, U.S. Department of Health and Human Services, and can be activated by one of four methods: (1) a request for assistance from a local official through the Federal Emergency Management Agency (FEMA) when a federal disaster has been declared, (2) a request for assistance from the National Transportation Safety Board when a passenger aircraft accident occurs, (3) under the U.S. Public Health Act to support a state or locality that cannot provide the necessary response to a disaster, and (4) when requested by a federal agency, such as the FBI, to provide disaster victim identification.

Usually within 24 to 48 hours after the disaster, the DMORT team is set up to provide professional personnel and technical support and assistance to the local medical examiner or coroner in forensic services and victim identification. The team is composed of forensic pathologists, forensic anthropologists, forensic dentists, medical investigators, funeral directors, and other technical support staff.

Dental records and X-rays along with fingerprints are normally the primary methods used in victim identification. DNA will be used as a last resort and only after all conventional means of identification are exhausted. DMORT does not perform DNA testing but rather gathers samples for future DNA testing, often by a laboratory such as AFDIL.

FEMA provides funding for the DNA identification effort along with other aspects of a disaster investigation after an official declaration of a major disaster or state of emergency has been declared by the President of the United States following a request for such a declaration from the governor of the affected state. This "state of emergency" declaration then activates a number of federal programs to assist in the response and recovery effort (see http://www.fema.gov).

Why Identify Remains of Victims?

Perhaps some wonder why the limited and precious resources of law enforcement and forensic laboratories are devoted to the challenging effort of identifying the remains of disaster victims. Although a variety of reasons can be cited, there are two primary reasons that impact living family members. First, in many jurisdictions, some form of identification is required before a death certificate can be issued that enables remaining family members to collect on life insurance policies. Second, the living family members may want the remains of their loved one returned to bring closure to the tragedy and to provide a proper burial and memorial service for their relative. As noted by Ballantyne (1997), there seems to be an overwhelming desire by many relatives to retrieve even the most miniscule tissue sample of a loved one.

Challenges with DNA Identification of Victims

Occasionally there are no known or living biological relatives or all immediate members of a family are among the victims making it difficult to associate the remains or to connect them to a valid reference sample. An additional challenge can come with simply locating surviving family members or communicating with them in the case of an international disaster.

Unfortunately, there can be challenges in dealing with family members of disaster victims such as family disputes (e.g., feuding family members fighting over who is entitled to the recovered remains) or discovery of illegitimate relationships when biological nonpaternity is demonstrated for someone who previously thought that they were the father or the child of a victim. Care must be taken by the laboratory director or other laboratory personnel who may interact directly with the families of victims to be sensitive to their grieving processes.

Collection of biological material from a disaster site is sometimes anything but trivial. For example, if a plane goes down at sea (e.g., Swissair Flight 111, see below), especially in deep water, then recovery of the remains can be quite challenging. By the very nature of the disaster, there is typically damage done to the biological samples and hence the DNA molecules contained therein. Extreme environmental conditions both during and after the disaster impact the quality of the recovered remains so that the DNA may be degraded, which can complicate DNA analysis and interpretation by the laboratory. As described in Chapter 10, degraded DNA gives rise to partial profiles, which then lower the statistics of a match because not all loci tested can be reported.

Trauma to Laboratory Personnel

Being exposed to large numbers of badly damaged human remains can have a psychological impact on laboratory personnel. In addition, loved ones may be among those who died making it difficult to cope with the rigors of careful laboratory work. Strain can be placed on the laboratory by political officials and the news media to produce results rapidly and to give regular updates of progress.

EARLY EXAMPLES OF DVI USING DNA

In the following pages, several mass disaster situations are highlighted where STR typing proved to be a valuable means for identifying human remains from burn victims, airplane crashes, terrorist acts, and mass grave sites. In these cases, STR typing was successfully performed in spite of heavy damage inflicted by a high-temperature fire (Branch Davidian compound in Waco, Texas, April 1993) or severe water damage (airplane crash of Swissair Flight 111 near Nova Scotia, September 1998). Identification of the victims of mass disasters, such as the terrorist attacks of September 11, 2001 on the World Trade Center Twin Towers, can require application of innovative biology, technology, and genetics.

Waco Branch Davidian Fire

On April 19, 1993, the Mount Carmel Branch Davidian compound in Waco, Texas burned during a raid by FBI agents. Over 80 individuals died and their remains were severely damaged following a high-temperature fire. While approximately half of these individuals could be identified by dental or fingerprint comparison and anthropological and pathological findings, the rest had to be identified based on information that could only be provided by DNA analysis. This was the first mass disaster investigation where DNA analysis with STR markers was used.

The Armed Forces DNA Identification Laboratory (AFDIL) and the Forensic Science Service (FSS) in England analyzed these samples by examining a variety of DNA markers including HLA DQ alpha, AmpliType PM, D1S80, amelogenin sex-typing, mitochondrial DNA sequencing, and four STR loci (TH01, F13A1, FES/FPS, VWA). Without the use of polymerase chain reaction (PCR)-based DNA typing procedures, specifically STR markers, approximately half of the individuals who perished in the Mount Carmel Compound of Branch Davidians would not have been identified.

AFDIL received 242 samples from the Mount Carmel Branch Davidian compound representing 82 sets of human remains (DiZinno et al. 1994). Blood-stain cards from living relatives provided reference samples for the unknowns. When usable tissue from the badly burned bodies was not available, portions of rib bones were removed and the DNA was extracted.

Body identifications were made by matching observed sample genotypes with predicted possible genotypes obtained from using results of relatives' reference blood samples and information gathered from family trees. This approach is basically a reverse parentage analysis where the parent genotypes are used to predict the child's genotype. A total of 26 positive identifications were made using the family tree matching approach (Clayton et al. 1995). A shortage of relatives prevented the identification of the other bodies. These results highlight the need for reference samples in order to take full advantage of DNA testing in mass disaster situations (Ballantyne 1997).

Spitsbergen and TWA Flight 800 Airplane Crashes

Two airplane crashes in 1996 helped demonstrate the value of DNA analysis in victim identification. On August 26, 1996, an airplane carrying 64 Russian and 77 Ukrainian individuals crashed into a mountain near Spitsbergen killing all 128 passengers and 13 crewmembers. The establishment of victim identity took only 20 days due to rapid analysis of samples in the University of Oslo (Norway) Institute of Forensic Medicine.

DNA profiles comprised of three STRs and five minisatellite loci enabled associating 257 body parts to 141 different individuals. Of these assortments, 139 were identified based on available reference samples submitted by 154 relatives (Olaisen et al. 1997). In this particular case, the rapid recovery of samples from a frigid environment (≈0°C) led to 100% success in producing DNA profiles from the remains. The cost of the DNA typing portion of the investigation was approximately 3% to 5% of the total cost of the entire operation.

Shortly after take-off on July 17, 1996, TWA Flight 800, a Boeing 747 en route to Paris, blew up in the sky above Long Island, New York, killing all 230 passengers and crew. Their fragmented remains were also identified with STR typing results (Ballantyne 1997). These early successes with DNA testing in aiding airline disaster victim identification paved the way for more recent uses.

Swissair Flight 111

On the evening of September 2, 1998, while en route to Geneva, Switzerland, from New York City, Swissair Flight 111 crashed into the Atlantic Ocean not far from Halifax, Nova Scotia. All 229 people on board (214 passengers and 15 crewmembers) were killed. The plane went down about 10 kilometers from land, requiring the wreckage to be raised from a depth of more than 60 meters (≈180 feet) of water.

Over the next few weeks, a large task force of investigators collected human remains from the crash scene. In addition to the proof-of-death and familial closure reasons discussed above, these remains were carefully collected and subsequently identified as an essential part of the crash investigation. Without a mechanical reason for the plane falling from the sky, criminal activity was a possibility. The plane's manifest listed 229 people on board. But were they all who they claimed to be? Any discrepancy from that number could be a sign of terrorist activity. A missing individual or an extra passenger who could not be accounted for might have been a terrorist with a bomb.

An important reason for identifying the victims of any mass disaster is to bring closure to the living relatives. If the remains of their loved ones can be identified, then something can be given back to the living relatives for burial and memorial purposes. However, one of the challenges for identifying the remains of airline crashes is that entire families often travel together. In this case, closely related individuals have to be distinguished from each other and sometimes without the benefit of a living relative to act as a reference sample.

A number of methods were used to identify the victims, including fingerprints, dental records, X-ray evaluation, and DNA testing. Only one body was intact enough for visual identification. A total of 147 victims could be identified by means other than DNA. For example, 1020 fingers were recovered from the crash site. However, these fingers allowed only 43 victims to be identified based on their fingerprints because only a small percentage of the victims had fingerprint records that could be located. Police visited the homes of the victims and tried to recover latent fingerprints from objects that they may have handled. These efforts led to the recovery of over 200 latent prints that were used to identify 33 of 43 victims mentioned above. An effective method of initial identification involved dental records, which were used to positively identify 102 of the victims and enable a certificate of death to be issued. Dental comparisons provided the fastest identification when reference samples were available.

Concurrent to other efforts to identify the crash victims, DNA testing was performed by the Royal Canadian Mounted Police (RCMP). DNA analysis was performed by four RCMP laboratories from across Canada and the Ontario Provincial Forensic Laboratory, each contributing a vital and specific subset of data. The DNA identification process was coordinated by the DNA Methods and Database section in Ottawa. This team of more than 50 DNA scientists consisted of members of the Biology sections of the RCMP Forensic Laboratories located in Halifax, Regina, Vancouver, and Ottawa and the Centre for Forensic Sciences in Toronto. DNA typing with the STR markers described in this book was used to help identify all 229 people on board Swissair Flight 111 (Leclair et al. 2004). In every case where other forms of identification were performed, DNA analysis helped confirm and support those results.

Two separate identification issues were addressed by DNA testing. First, recovered human remains showing identical STR genotypes were associated. Second, each passenger was identified through comparisons of human remains with the reference samples isolated from

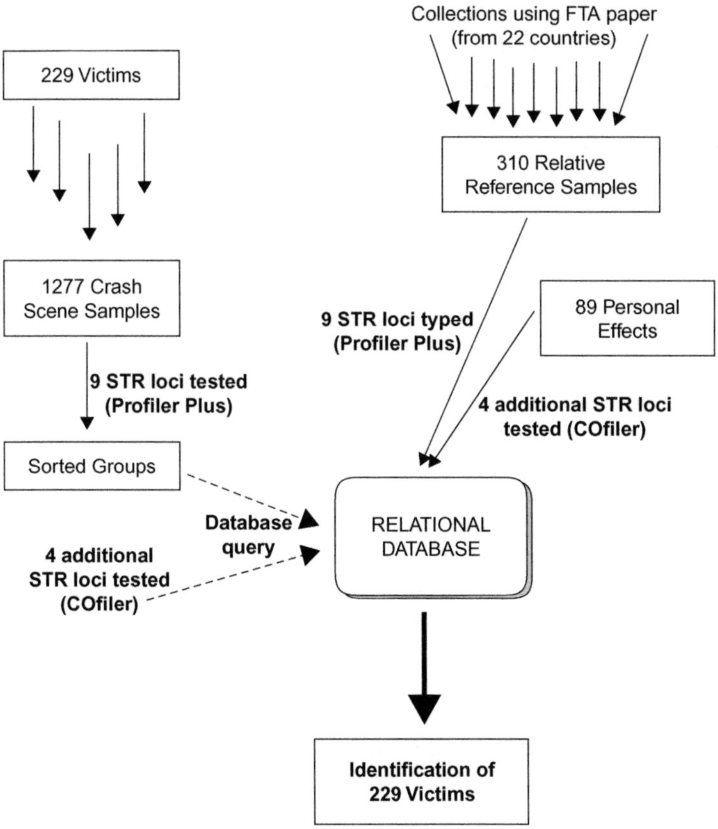

FIGURE 9.4 Strategy for disaster victim identification in the Swissair Flight 111 crash scene investigation. Most samples were tested with 9 STRs and amelogenin using the AmpFlSTR Profiler Plus kit and then 4 additional STRs were added with the COfiler kit as needed to obtain a higher power of discrimination between closely related individuals. The relational database compared genotypes of 1277 crash scene samples to genotypes of all 229 victims and family relatives, a total of 71,490 genotype comparisons (Leclair et al. 2004).

personal effects of the victims or reference blood samples submitted by relatives of the victims. In many cases, DNA analysis was the only means by which the samples could be positively identified.

Over 2400 human remains were recovered from the crash site of which 1277 were analyzed by DNA testing (Figure 9.4). These samples were analyzed along with 310 reference samples from relatives that were submitted on FTA paper blood cards (see Chapter 1) to be genotyped and used in a relational database. In addition, 89 personal effects, such as toothbrushes and hair from combs, were taken from the homes of 47 victims because no relatives were available to serve as a reference. One of the challenges of collecting the reference samples was the fact that the living relatives were from 21 different countries. The FTA kit enabled rapid blood collection and room temperature delivery of the reference samples and aided the successful completion of the investigation.

The AmpFlSTR Profiler Plus STR markers D3S1358, VWA, FGA, D8S1179, D21S11, D18S51, D5S818, D13S317, and D7S820 were the primary means of identifying the remains although additional STR loci TH01, TPOX, CSF1PO, and D16S539 from the AmpFlSTR COfiler kit were used to gain a higher power of discrimination (Frégeau et al. 2000). COfiler amplifications were performed on 118 crash scene remains and 129 "known" reference comparison samples. The crash scene samples were analyzed in approximately one week using either the nine STRs from Profiler Plus or all 13 STRs from Profiler Plus and COfiler. The challenge of making appropriate associations between the samples took a little longer. Genotypes of each of the 229 victims were compared to genotypes of all other victims and family relatives, which represented 71,490 genotype comparisons (Leclair et al. 2000, Leclair et al. 2004). The comparison of reference sample genotypes to profiles from the recovered remains involved over 180,000 comparisons because more known sample genotypes existed for cross-comparison purposes.

Traditional parentage trios with both living parents were encountered for only 25% of the 229 victims. Even more challenging was the fact that 43 families of 2 to 5 individuals were present among the victims. A pair of identical twins was also present on the plane and could not be individually identified with DNA testing. Nevertheless, the DNA testing led to confident kinship analysis in the case of 218 victims for whom reference samples from close relatives or personal effects were submitted (Leclair et al. 2000, Leclair et al. 2004).

The efforts of the RCMP demonstrated a successful model for how a mass disaster investigation should be conducted. Tremendous cooperation is required from forensic laboratories, law enforcement personnel, and family members of victims, often from a number of countries, in order to successfully identify the victims of mass fatality incidents.

The need for readily available reference samples was also highlighted by this investigation. In fact, a formal recommendation was made from the RCMP to the Canadian Transport Safety Board for all airline personnel and any private citizens who are frequent fliers to have fingerprints and DNA samples made available for identification purposes if ever the need arises. These records cannot be stored by the police but rather could be maintained by the airline or stored in an individual's safety deposit box.

Of the 229 victims of Swissair Flight 111, all 229 were positively identified, an astounding success compared to previously used conventional identification techniques and one that would not have been possible without the power of DNA typing with STR markers.

DNA IDENTIFICATION WORK WITH SEPTEMBER 11, 2001 VICTIMS

The terrorist attacks against the United States on September 11, 2001 left over 3000 victims in three different locations: the Pentagon in Washington, DC, a field near Shanksville (Somerset County), Pennsylvania, and the Twin Towers of the World Trade Center in New York City. Several teams of forensic scientists were involved in the DNA analysis of these mass disasters.

The Pentagon Site

Hijacked by five terrorists on the morning of September 11, 2001, American Airlines Flight 77 crashed into the Pentagon shortly after 9:40 a.m. killing all 59 passengers and crew on board, the 5 terrorists, and 124 Pentagon occupants. The remains, ranging in size from whole bodies to small fragments, were taken to Dover Air Force Base in Delaware where they were sampled for DNA testing. From the 2000 containers of evidence recovered, 938 samples were collected for DNA analysis. STR typing was then performed at the Armed Forces DNA Identification Laboratory in Rockville, Maryland using Profiler Plus. Reference samples included 49 direct reference bloodstain cards from the Armed Forces DNA Repository and 348 family references.

Over the course of the next two months (September 17, 2001 to November 15, 2001), 177 identifications were made using DNA only or a combination of DNA, dental records, and fingerprints. In addition, one victim was identified solely with dental records. Unfortunately, no biological material was recovered from the crash site for five of the missing individuals (Edson et al. 2004). In addition, there were five male STR profiles that did not match reference samples from any of the victims. These samples were classified as belonging to the terrorists who hijacked the plane and were further confirmed using mitochondrial DNA testing and comparison to Near Eastern mtDNA haplotypes (Edson et al. 2004).

The Somerset County (Shanksville, Pennsylvania) Site

Shortly after departing Newark, New Jersey on the morning of September 11, 2001 United Airlines Flight 93 was hijacked by four terrorists. The plane crashed near Shanksville, Pennsylvania at 10:10 a.m. killing all 40 passengers and crew along with the four terrorists. The 1319 total remains recovered from the Somerset County crash site were all highly fragmented because the plane went straight into the ground at a speed of more than 500 miles per hour. Scientists from the Armed Forces DNA Identification Laboratory collected 592 samples for DNA analysis including 423 bones, 141 tissues, 23 teeth, 2 hairs, and 3 fingernails. Reference samples used included 55 family references and 50 direct references.

All 40 passengers and crewmembers were able to be identified through DNA alone or a combination of DNA, dental records, and fingerprints. In addition, four male STR profiles that did not match family references were observed and ascribed to the four terrorists. These samples were tested with mtDNA and found to be associated with Near Eastern mtDNA haplotypes (Edson et al. 2004).

The World Trade Center DNA Identification Effort

The DNA identification efforts for the World Trade Center (WTC) victims have become arguably the world's largest forensic case to date (Biesecker et al. 2005, Brenner & Weir 2003, Budimlija et al. 2003, Leclair et al. 2007). In the first few months, almost 20,000 pieces of human remains were collected from a pile of rubble weighing over a million tons and reaching more than 70 feet in height following the crushing collapse of the Twin Towers. The initial removal and sorting of human remains took place between September 2001 and May 2002. However, the primary DNA identification efforts went on for more than three years—almost two-and-a-half years after the last piece of debris had been removed from the WTC site.

In the end, more than 1600 victims were identified of the 2749 present when the Twin Towers collapsed. Without the capabilities of DNA testing, there would have been only a fraction of the victims identified based on other modalities such as fingerprints and dental records (Table 9.1). As of June 4, 2010, a total of 12,769 remains (59%) from a total of 21,802 recovered at the World Trade Center site have been identified and associated with one of the 1626 victims identified so far (Mecki Prinz, NYC OCME, personal communication).

Biological samples recovered from the WTC site had been subjected to extreme environmental conditions with the building collapse and subterranean fires that continued to burn in the rubble pile for three months following the terrorist attack. The jet fuel from both planes that rammed the WTC towers ignited office furnishings leading to fires throughout the buildings. The buildings collapsed due to a synergy of the damage caused by the aircraft

TABLE 9.1 Summary of World Trade Center Victim and Remains Identification Efforts Completed as of June 2004. At That Time, the Number of Victims Stood at 2749 of Which 1558 Had Been Identified. Six Years Later (June 2010), with Some Additional Bone Fragments Located and Further DNA Testing, the Number Identified Had Climbed to 1626 Based on a Total of 21,802 Remains Recovered. Although DNA Far Outstrips Other Methods in Terms of Success at Recovering Information in This Disaster, Other Modalities Were Useful in Identifying Victims or Sets of Remains. Initial Information Courtesy of Dr. Robert Shaler and More Recent Information Courtesy of Dr. Mecki Prinz, New York City Office of Chief Medical Examiner.

Modality	Victims Identified			Remains Identified		
	Single Modality	Multiple Modalities	Total IDs	Single Modality	Multiple Modalities	Total IDs
DNA	817	465	1282	4231	3685	7916
Photo	11	14	25	11	14	25
Viewed	12	2	14	12	2	14
Body X-ray	0	3	3	0	4	4
Dental	102	424	526	117	497	614
Prints	53	215	268	56	240	296
Tattoos	0	6	6	0	6	6
Personal effects	16	59	75	18	61	79
Other	7	34	41	7	101	108

impact, the removal of fire-resistive insulation from the steel support structures, and fire-induced deformation of the remaining structure (see http://wtc.nist.gov). Thus, human remains were often comingled, very fragmented, and in many cases likely vaporized.

Dr. Robert Shaler, the director of Forensic Biology at the New York City's Office of Chief Medical Examiner (NYC OCME) stood at the helm of the WTC DNA efforts throughout the many months of this investigation (Shaler 2005). Dr. Shaler and his dedicated staff coordinated the efforts and assistance of outside companies and consultants. They worked tirelessly to collate every piece of possible information in the complex process of making a genetic match between a victim's DNA profile and that of a reference sample in the form of a personal effect or a victim's biological relative. A computer program named DNA-VIEW written by Dr. Charles Brenner played an important part in determining many of these kinship identifications.

Several innovations came out of the 9/11 attacks (Vastag 2002). These included new extraction methods from bone (Holland et al. 2003), reduced size amplicons or miniSTRs (Butler et al. 2003, Holland et al. 2003), panels of single nucleotide polymorphisms (SNPs), and high-throughput mitochondrial DNA sequencing. In addition, new software was developed to aid in matching reference samples and recovered remains as well as associating remains with the same DNA profile.

Three different software programs were used extensively in the WTC victim identification efforts: Mass Fatality Identification System (M-FISys), DNA-VIEW, and Mass Disaster Kinship Analysis Program (MDKAP). M-FISys was developed by Gene Codes Forensics (Ann Arbor, MI). It used a direct match algorithm and helped in collapsing and sorting data sets to obtain identifications (Hennessey 2002). DNA-VIEW deduced kinship by pedigree analyses (Brenner & Weir 2003), while MDKAP performed kinship analyses through pair-wise comparisons (Leclair et al. 2007). A variation of the MDKAP is now commercially available as the Bloodhound program (see http://www.ananomouse.com).

One of the largest challenges from this investigation was review of the massive amounts of data produced by contracting laboratories. The flow of DNA samples and data between the various laboratories involved in this tremendous effort is illustrated in Figure 9.5. In the initial 2001 to 2005 effort, more than 52,528 STR profiles, 16,938 SNP profiles, and 31,155 mtDNA sequences were generated in an effort to identify the 2749 victims of the World Trade Center collapse based on 19,917 recovered remains—truly a heroic effort. (Note that more remains have been recovered following the initial identification effort and a few more identifications made.)

Most of the data from the recovered remains contained only partial DNA profiles making it even more difficult to sort through and piece together sufficient information to make a reliable identification. The process for assigning identities to specific remains has three stages: collapsing, screening, and testing (Brenner & Weir 2003). Clustering algorithms can be used to help reconstruct likely pedigree information when multiple family members are part of the sample set being investigated (Cowell & Mostad 2003).

Kinship and Data Analysis Panel (KADAP)

The National Institute of Justice (NIJ) organized a panel of experts, referred to as the Kinship and Data Analysis Panel (KADAP), that convened almost every other month in the

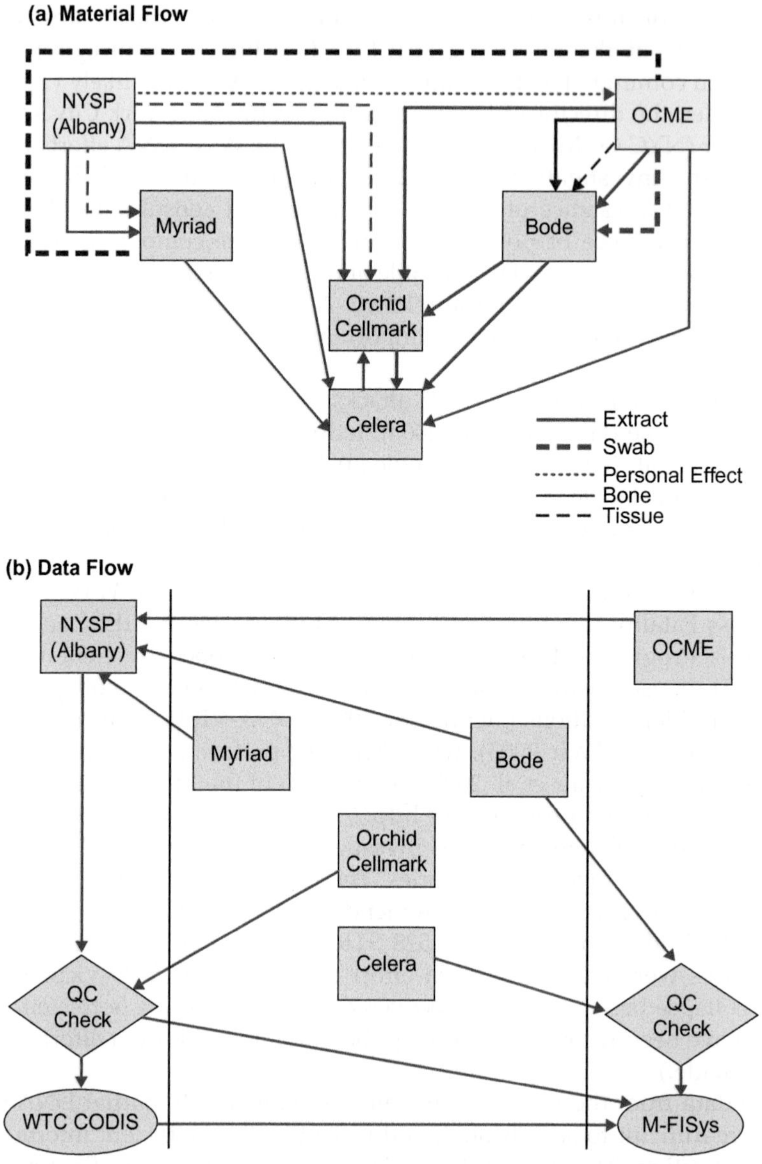

FIGURE 9.5 Illustration of (a) material and (b) data flow between laboratories involved in processing World Trade Center samples. Laboratories included Office of Chief Medical Examiner (OCME, New York City), New York State Police (NYSP, Albany, NY), Myriad Genetics (Salt Lake City, UT), Orchid Cellmark (Dallas, TX), Celera Genomics (Rockville, MD), and Bode Technology Group (Springfield, VA). Blue box colors represent the commercial labs and yellow boxes highlight the government labs. Physical materials shipped between laboratories included DNA extracts (solid red line), buccal swabs from biological relative reference samples (dashed red line), personal effects (dotted red line), recovered bones (solid blue line), and recovered tissue (dashed blue line). Note that most of the DNA samples were extracted at the NYSP and OCME laboratories although some tissue and bone were shipped directly to Myriad and Bode. All bones were extracted at Bode. Figure courtesy of National Institute of Justice World Trade Center Kinship and Data Analysis Panel and New York City Office of Chief Medical Examiner.

TABLE 9.2 World Trade Center Kinship and Data Analysis Panel (WTC KADAP) Members Convened to Aid New York City with WTC Identifications. National Institute of Justice Funded-Meetings Were Held Bimonthly from October 2001 to July 2003 in New York City, Albany, Baltimore, or Washington, DC (Not All Members Attended Every Meeting) to Discuss Progress with the Investigation and to Aid in Reviewing Technology Validation and Statistical Genetic Issues.

Member	Affiliation
Joan Bailey-Wilson, Ph.D.	National Institutes of Health-National Human Genome Research Institute
Jack Ballantyne, Ph.D.	University of Central Florida
Howard Baum, Ph.D.	New York City Office of Chief Medical Examiner
Fred Bieber, M.D, Ph.D.	Harvard Medical School
Erik Bieschke	New York City Office of Chief Medical Examiner
Les Biesecker, Ph.D.	National Institutes of Health-National Human Genome Research Institute
Charles Brenner, Ph.D.	DNA-View
Bruce Budowle, Ph.D.	Federal Bureau of Investigation Laboratory
John Butler, Ph.D.	National Institute of Standards and Technology
George Carmody, Ph.D.	Carleton University
Maureen Casey	New York City Police Department
Cheryl Conley	Orchid Genescreen Ohio
Michael Conneally, Ph.D.	Indiana University School of Medicine
Mark Dale	New York State Police; New York City Police Department Laboratory
Barry Duceman, Ph.D.	New York State Police
Art Eisenberg, Ph.D.	University of North Texas Health Science Center
Lisa Forman, Ph.D.	National Institute of Justice
Dennis Gaige	New York State Police
Mike Hennessy, MBA	Gene Codes Forensics
Steven Hogan, J.D.	New York State Police
Ken Kidd, Ph.D.	Yale University School of Medicine
Benoit Leclair, Ph.D.	Myriad Genetics
Elaine Mar	New York City Office of Chief Medical Examiner
Amy Mundorff	New York City Office of Chief Medical Examiner
Steve Niezgoda, MBA	National Institute of Justice Contractor
Judy Nolan, Ph.D.	Gene Codes Forensics
Tom Parsons, Ph.D.	Armed Forces DNA Identification Laboratory
Mecki Prinz, Ph.D.	New York City Office of Chief Medical Examiner
Elizabeth Pugh, Ph.D.	John Hopkins University/Center for Inherited Disease Research

(*Continued*)

TABLE 9.2 World Trade Center Kinship and Data Analysis Panel (WTC KADAP) Members Convened to Aid New York City with WTC Identifications. National Institute of Justice Funded-Meetings Were Held Bimonthly from October 2001 to July 2003 in New York City, Albany, Baltimore, or Washington, DC (Not All Members Attended Every Meeting) to Discuss Progress with the Investigation and to Aid in Reviewing Technology Validation and Statistical Genetic Issues. (*Continued*)

Member	Affiliation
Robert Shaler, Ph.D.	New York City Office of Chief Medical Examiner
Steve Sherry, Ph.D.	National Institutes of Health-National Center for Biotechnology Information
John Snyder	New York State Police Contractor
Amanda Sozer, Ph.D.	National Institute of Justice Contractor
Amy Sutton	Gene Codes Forensics
Steve Swinton	New York State Police
Lois Tully, Ph.D.	National Institute of Justice
Noelle Umback	New York City Office of Chief Medical Examiner
Anne Walsh, Ph.D.	New York State Department of Health
Peter Wistort	New York State Police

two years following September 11, 2001. The panel's mission was to aid in reviewing data and to provide guidance and recommendations to the NYC OCME regarding statistical thresholds for reporting DNA identifications based on direct matches and kinship associations (Biesecker et al. 2005). The names and affiliations of the advisory WTC KADAP are listed in Table 9.2. KADAP gathered in NYC, Albany, Baltimore, and Washington, DC for two-day meetings during Oct 2001, Dec 2001, Feb 2002, Apr 2002, July 2002, Sept 2002, Jan 2003, July 2003, and June 2005.

While we hope to never see the likes of another September 11, 2001 terrorist attack, forensic DNA typing laboratories should be prepared to aid in victim identification efforts in future mass fatality incidences. Lessons learned from the WTC DNA identification efforts by the KADAP were published in September 2006 by the National Institute of Justice (NIJ 2006). This report, entitled "Lessons Learned from 9/11: DNA Identification in Mass Fatality Incidents," provides information on project management, sample tracking and flow of information, suggestions on structuring communications between victim family members and the DNA laboratory, and vital issues to consider immediately after an incident occurs. It is safe to conclude that DNA analysis will continue to play a valuable support role in future mass fatality incidents, just as it does with law enforcement and the criminal justice system.

IDENTIFICATION OF HUMAN REMAINS IN MASS GRAVES USING DNA

DNA can play an important role in identifying remains in unmarked graves (Huffine 2001, Primorac 2004, Williams & Crew 2003). Unfortunately, there are regions of the world that have suffered severely under the hands of ruthless dictators who do not value human life. Mass graves are often the tragic trademark of such tyrants.

The former Yugoslavia contains an estimated 40,000 unidentified bodies in mass graves. The International Commission on Missing Persons (ICMP) was created in 1996 to help identify human remains in these mass graves. In effect, the ICMP is using DNA technology to map human genocide. More recently hundreds of individual remains have been recovered from mass graves found in Kuwait and Iraq. In the first five years of attempting DNA analysis on recovered remains from these mass graves, 233 victims were identified (Alenizi et al. 2009).

One of the major challenges to performing DNA identification from mass graves is obtaining biological reference samples from relatives. Family outreach centers take information and blood samples from living relatives such as parents or a spouse and a child of a missing loved one. These reference samples are then typed with STRs and mitochondrial DNA sequencing to perform kinship analysis using the DNA results obtained from the remains in mass graves.

In the past, mitochondrial DNA (see Chapter 14) has often been the only source of successful DNA recovery from bones that have been in the ground for many years. However, more recently improved DNA extraction methods have enabled successful STR typing results to be obtained (e.g., Davoren et al. 2007). DNA often provides the only way to confirm the death of a missing person, enable return of the remains to a living relative, and help bring justice to the criminals who initiated the massacres that led to the mass grave sites.

READING LIST AND INTERNET RESOURCES

Missing Persons Investigations

Baker, L. E., & Backer, E. J. (2008). Reuniting families: An online database to aid in the identification of undocumented immigrant remains. *Journal of Forensic Sciences*, *53*, 50–53.

FBI national missing persons program. <http://www.fbi.gov/wanted/kidnap/kidmiss.htm>.

Glod, M. (July 21, 2009). New path to restore identities of missing: Web site combines details of remains, disappearances. *Washington Post*. Available at <http://www.washingtonpost.com/>.

Holland, M. M., et al. (1993). Mitochondrial DNA sequence analysis of human skeletal remains: Identification of remains from the Vietnam War. *Journal of Forensic Sciences*, *38*, 542–553.

James, M., et al. (2008). Missing persons in Australia. *Trends and Issues in Crime and Criminal Justice*, *353*, 1–6. Available at <http://www.aic.gov.au>.

Lorente, J. A., et al. (2002). Social benefits of non-criminal genetic databases: Missing persons and human remains identification. *International Journal of Legal Medicine*, *116*, 187–190.

National Center for Missing & Exploited Children. <http://www.missingkids.com/>.

National Institute of Justice articles. <http://www.dna.gov/identifying-persons/missing-persons/>.

National Missing and Unidentified Persons System (NamUs). <http://www.namus.gov>.

National Crime Information Center (NCIC). <http://www.fbi.gov/hq/cjisd/ncic.htm>.

Pearsall, B., & Weiss, D. M. (2010). Solving missing persons cases. *NIJ Journal*, *264*, 4–8. Available at <http://www.ncjrs.gov/pdffiles1/nij/228382.pdf>.

Piccinini, A., et al. (2010). World War One Italian and Austrian soldier identification project: DNA results of the first case. *Forensic Science International: Genetics*, *4*, 329–333.

Ritter, N. (2007). Missing persons and unidentified remains: The nation's silent mass disaster. *NIJ Journal*, *256*, 2–7. Available at <http://www.ojp.usdoj.gov/nij/journals/256/missing-persons.html>.

Sweet, D., et al. (1999). Identification of a skeleton using DNA from teeth and a PAP smear. *Journal of Forensic Sciences*, *44*, 630–633.

Torwalt, C., et al. (2005). Cervical smears as an alternative source of DNA in the identification of human skeletal remains. *Canadian Society of Forensic Sciences Journal*, *38*, 165–169.

University of North Texas Center for Human Identification. <http://www.unthumanid.org>.

Wickenheiser, R. A., et al. (1999). Case of identification of severely burned human remains via paternity testing with PCR DNA typing. *Canadian Society of Forensic Sciences Journal, 32*, 15–24.

Disaster Victim Identification (DVI)

Alonso, A., et al. (2005). Challenges of DNA profiling in mass disaster investigations. *Croatian Medical Journal, 46*, 540–548.

Buckleton, J., et al. (2005). Disaster victim identification, identification of missing persons, and immigration cases. In J. Buckleton, C. M. Triggs, T. Clayton (Eds.), *Forensic DNA evidence interpretation* (Chapter 11, pp. 395–437). Boca Raton: CRC Press.

Corach, D., et al. (1995). Mass disasters: Rapid molecular screening of human remains by means of short tandem repeats typing. *Electrophoresis, 16*, 1617–1623.

De Valck, E. (2006). Major incident response: Collecting antemortem data. *Forensic Science International, 159*(Suppl.), S15–S19.

Graham, E. A. M. (2006). Disaster victim identification. *Forensic Science, Medicine, and Pathology, 2*, 203–207.

Li, T. H., et al. (2006). Interpreting anonymous DNA samples from mass disasters – probabilistic forensic inference using genetic markers. *Bioinformatics, 22*(14), e298–e306.

SNA International. <http://www.sna-intl.com/>.

Winskog, C., et al. (2010). The use of commercial alcohol products to sterilize bones prior to DNA sampling. *Forensic Science, Medicine, and Pathology, 6*, 127–129.

DVI Recommendations

AABB. (2010). *Guidelines for mass fatality DNA identification operations.* Available at <http://www.aabb.org/programs/disasterresponse/Documents/aabb>.

Bradford, L., et al. (2010). Disaster victim investigation recommendations from two simulated mass disaster scenarios utilized for user acceptance testing CODIS 6.0. *Forensic Science International: Genetics* (in press). doi:10.1016/j.fsigen.2010.05.005

Budowle, B., et al. (2005). Forensic aspects of mass disasters: Strategic considerations for DNA-based human identification. *Legal Medicine, 7*, 230–243.

International Criminal Police Organization. (2008). *Interpol disaster victim identification guide.* Available at <http://www.interpol.int/Public/DisasterVictim/default.asp>.

International Committee of the Red Cross. (2009). *Missing people, DNA analysis and identification of human remains: A guide to best practice in armed conflicts and other situations of armed violence.* 2nd ed. Available at <http://www.icrc.org/Web/Eng/siteeng0.nsf/htmlall/p4010/$File/ICRC_002_4010.PDF>.

Lee, J., et al. (2008). Recommendations for DNA laboratories supporting disaster victim identification (DVI) operations—Australian and New Zealand consensus on ISFG recommendations. *Forensic Science International: Genetics, 3*, 54–56.

Lessig, R., et al. (2011). German standards for forensic molecular genetics investigations in cases of mass disaster victim identification (DVI). *Forensic Science International: Genetics, 5*, 247–248.

National Institute of Justice. (2005). *Mass fatality incidents: A guide for human forensic identification.* <http://www.ojp.usdoj.gov/nij/pubs-sum/199758.htm>.

National Institute of Justice. (2006). *Lessons learned from 9/11: DNA identifications in mass fatality incidents.* <http://massfatality.dna.gov>.

Prinz, M., et al. (2007). DNA Commission of the International Society of Forensic Genetics (ISFG): Recommendations regarding the role of forensic genetics for disaster victim identification (DVI). *Forensic Science International: Genetics, 1*, 3–12.

Sweet, D. (2010). INTERPOL DVI best-practice standards—an overview. *Forensic Science International, 201*, 18–21.

Westen, A. A., et al. (2008). Femur, rib, and tooth sample collection for DNA analysis in disaster victim identification (DVI): A method to minimize contamination risk. *Forensic Science Medicine, and Pathology, 4*, 15–21.

Waco Branch Davidian Fire

Clayton, T. M., et al. (1995). Identification of bodies from the scene of a mass disaster using DNA amplification and short tandem repeat (STR) loci. *Forensic Science International, 76*, 7–15.

DiZinno, J., et al. (1994). The Waco, Texas incident: The use of DNA analysis to identify human remains. *Proceedings from the fifth international symposium on human identification* (pp. 129–135). Madison, Wisconsin: Promega.

Airplane Crashes

Ballantyne, J. (1997). Mass disaster genetics. *Nature Genetics, 15*, 329–331.

Goodwin, W., et al. (1999). The use of mitochondrial DNA and short tandem repeat typing in the identification of air crash victims. *Electrophoresis, 20*, 1707–1711.

Hsu, C. M., et al. (1999). Identification of victims of the 1998 Taoyuan Airbus crash accident using DNA analysis. *International Journal of Legal Medicine, 113*, 43–46.

Olaisen, B., et al. (1997). Identification by DNA analysis of the victims of the August 1996 Spitsbergen civil aircraft disaster. *Nature Genetics, 15*, 402–405.

Swissair Flight 111

Frégeau, C. J., et al. (2000). The Swissair Flight 111 disaster: Short tandem repeat mutations observed. *Progress in Forensic Genetics, 8*, 40–42.

Leclair, B., et al. (2000). Enhanced kinship analysis and STR-based DNA typing for human identification in mass disasters. *Progress in Forensic Genetics, 8*, 91–93.

Leclair, B., et al. (2004). Enhanced kinship analysis and STR-based DNA typing for human identification in mass fatality incidents: The Swissair flight 111 disaster. *Journal of Forensic Sciences, 49*, 939–953.

Southeast Asian Tsunami

Brenner, C. H. (2006). Some mathematical problems in the DNA identification of victims in the 2004 tsunami and similar mass fatalities. *Forensic Science International, 157*, 172–180.

Deng, Y. -J., et al. (2005). Preliminary DNA identification for the tsunami victims in Thailand. *Genomics, Proteomics, and Bioinfomatics, 3*, 143–157.

Lau, G., et al. (2005). After the Indian Ocean tsunami: Singapore's contribution to the international disaster victim identification effort in Thailand. *Annals of the Academy of Medicine Singapore, 34*(5), 341–351.

Morgan, O. W., et al. (2006). Mass fatality management following the South Asian tsunami disaster: Case studies in Thailand, Indonesia, and Sri Lanka. *PLoS Medicine, 3*(6), e195.

Zehner, R. (2007). "Foreign" DNA in tissue adherent to compact bone from tsunami victims. *Forensic Science International: Genetics, 1*, 218–222.

9/11/01: Pentagon and PA Sites

Edson, S. M., et al. (2004). Naming the dead—confronting the realities of rapid identification of degraded skeletal remains. *Forensic Science Review, 16*, 63–90.

9/11/01: World Trade Center DNA Identification Effort

Biesecker, L. G., et al. (2005). DNA identifications after the 9/11 World Trade Center attack. *Science, 310*, 1122–1123.

Brenner, C. H., & Weir, B. S. (2003). Issues and strategies in the identification of World Trade Center victims. *Theoretical and Population Biology, 63*, 173–178.

Budimlija, Z. M., et al. (2003). World Trade Center human identification project: Experiences with individual body indentification cases. *Croatian Medical Journal, 44*, 259–263.

Cowell, R. G., & Mostad, P. (2003). A clustering algorithm using DNA marker information for sub-pedigree reconstruction. *Journal of Forensic Sciences, 48*, 1239–1248.

Gill, J. R. (2006). 9/11 and the New York City Office of Chief Medical Examiner. *Forensic Science, Medicine, and Pathology, 2*, 29–32.

Hennessey, M.. (2002). World Trade Center DNA identifications: The administrative review process. *Proceedings of the Thirteenth International Symposium on Human Identification*. Available at <http://www.promega.com/geneticidproc/ussymp13proc/contents/hennesseyrev1.pdf>.

Holland, M. M., et al. (2003). Development of a quality, high throughput DNA analysis procedure for skeletal samples to assist with the identification of victims from the World Trade Center attacks. *Croatian Medical Journal, 44*, 264–272.

Leclair, B., et al. (2007). Bioinformatics and human identification in mass fatality incidents: The World Trade Center disaster. *Journal of Forensic Sciences, 52*, 806–819.

National Institute of Justice. (2006). *Lessons learned from 9/11: DNA identifications in mass fatality incidents*. Available at <http://massfatality.dna.gov>.

Ritter, N. (2007). Identifying remains: Lessons learned from 9/11. *NIJ Journal, 256*, 20–26. Available at <http://www.ojp.usdoj.gov/nij/journals/256/lessons-learned.html>.

Shaler, R. C. (2005). *Who they were—inside the world trade center DNA story: The unprecedented effort to identify the missing*. New York: Free Press.

Vastag, B. (2002). Out of tragedy, identification innovation. *JAMA: The Journal of the American Medical Association, 288*, 1221–1223.

Hurricane Katrina

Dolan, S. M., et al. (2009). The emerging role of genetics professionals in forensic kinship DNA identification following a mass fatality: Lessons learned from Hurricane Katrina volunteers. *Genetics in Medicine, 11*, 414–417.

Donkervoort, S., et al. (2008). Enhancing accurate data collection in mass fatality kinship identifications: Lessons learned from Hurricane Katrina. *Forensic Science International: Genetics, 2*, 354–362.

Other

Hartman, D., et al. (2011). The 2009 Victorian Bushfires Disaster: The importance of Guthrie cards and other medical samples for the direct matching of disaster victims using DNA profiling. *Forensic Science International, 205*, 59–63.

Lin, C. -Y., et al. (2010). The strategies to DVI challenges in Typhoon Morakot. *International Journal of Legal Medicine* (in press) (doi:10.1007/s00414-010-0479-8).

Sudoyo, H., et al. (2008). DNA analysis in perpetrator identification of terrorism-related disaster: Suicide bombing of the Australian Embassy in Jakarta 2004. *Forensic Science International: Genetics, 2*, 231–237.

Mass Graves

Alenizi, M. A., et al. (2009). Concordance between the AmpFlSTR MiniFiler and AmpFlSTR Identifiler PCR Amplification kits in the Kuwaiti population. *Journal of Forensic Sciences, 54*, 350–352.

Baraybar, J. P. (2008). When DNA is not available, can we still identify people? Recommendations for best practice. *Journal of Forensic Sciences, 53*, 533–540.

Biruš, I., et al. (2003). How high should paternity index be for reliable identification of war victims by DNA typing? *Croatian Medical Journal, 44*, 322–326.

Cox, M., et al. (2008). *The scientific investigation of mass graves: Towards protocols and standard operating procedures*. New York: Cambridge University Press.

Davoren, J., et al. (2007). Highly effective DNA extraction method for nuclear short tandem repeat testing of skeletal remains from mass graves. *Croatian Medical Journal, 48*, 478–485.

Gornik, I., et al. (2002). The identification of war victims by reverse paternity is associated with significant risks of false inclusion. *International Journal of Legal Medicine, 116*, 255–257.

Huffine, E., et al. (2001). Mass identification of persons missing from the break-up of the former Yugoslavia: Structure, function, and role of the International Commission on Missing Persons. *Croatian Medical Journal, 42*, 271–275.

Huffine, E., et al. (2007). Developing role of forensics in deterring violence and genocide. *Croatian Medical Journal, 48*, 431–436.

International Commission on Missing Persons (ICMP). <http://www.ic-mp.org>.

Kračun, S. K., et al. (2007). Population substructure can significantly affect reliability of a DNA-led process of identification of mass fatality victims. *Journal of Forensic Sciences, 52*, 874–878.

Primorac, D. (2004). The role of DNA technology in identification of skeletal remains discovered in mass graves. *Forensic Science International, 146S*, S163–S164.

Williams, E. D., & Crews, J. D. (2003). From dust to dust: Ethical and practical issues involved in the location, exhumation, and identification of bodies from mass graves. *Croatian Medical Journal, 44*, 251–258.

CHAPTER

10

Degraded DNA

DEGRADED DNA

DNA may be damaged or destroyed by adverse environmental conditions. Environmental exposure degrades DNA molecules by randomly breaking them into smaller pieces. Enemies to the survival of intact DNA molecules include water, oxygen, ultraviolent irradiation, and enzymes called nucleases that chew up DNA. These conditions are ubiquitous in nature and can result in fragmented DNA depending on the specific environmental situtation of a biological sample.

With older technologies such as restriction fragment length polymorphism (RFLP), severely degraded DNA samples would have been very difficult if not impossible to analyze as relative high molecular mass (aka molecular weight) DNA molecules needed to be intact in order to detect large VNTR (variable number of tandem repeat) alleles (Figure 10.1). The use of smaller short tandem repeat (STR) alleles enables better recovery of results with older, damaged DNA samples.

An ethidium-bromide stained agarose "yield gel" may be run to evaluate the quality of a DNA sample. Typically high molecular weight, high-quality genomic DNA runs as a relatively tight band of approximately 20,000 bp relative to an appropriate relative molecular mass marker. On the other hand, degraded DNA appears as a smear of DNA that is much less than 20,000 bp in size (Figure 10.2a).

Modern-day PCR methods, such as multiplex STR typing, are powerful because miniscule amounts of DNA can be measured by amplifying them to a level where they may be detected. Less than 1 ng of DNA can now be analyzed with multiplex PCR amplification of STR alleles compared to 100 ng or more that might have been required with RFLP only a few years ago. However, this sensitivity to low levels of DNA also brings the challenge of avoiding contamination from the police officer or crime scene technician who collects the biological evidence (see Chapter 4).

In order for PCR amplification to occur, the DNA template must be intact where the two primers bind as well as between the primers so that full extension can occur. Without an intact DNA strand that surrounds the STR repeat region to serve as a template strand, PCR will be unsuccessful because primer extension will halt at the break in the template.

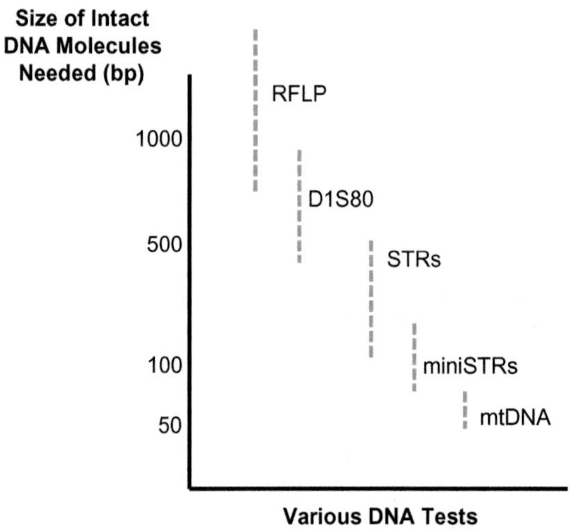

FIGURE 10.1 Illustration of required DNA fragment sizes for various DNA tests.

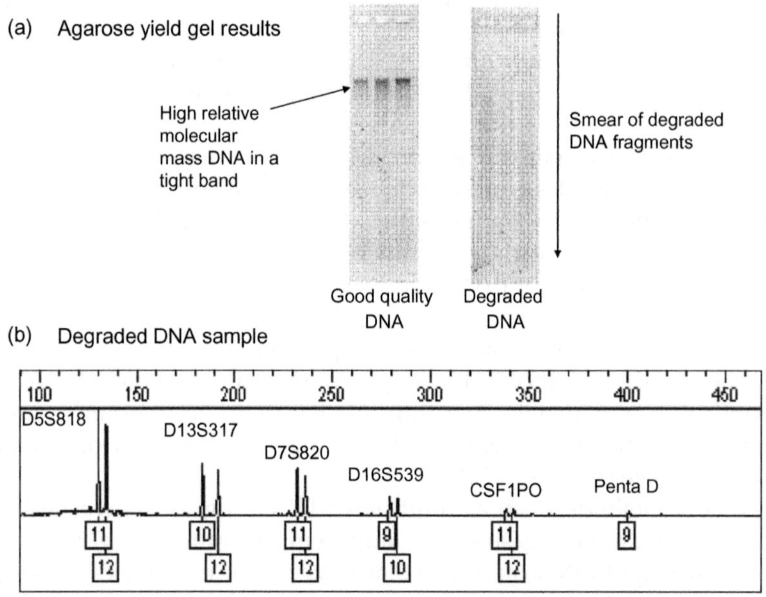

FIGURE 10.2 Impact of degraded DNA on (a) agarose yield gel results and (b) STR typing. (a) Degraded DNA is broken up into small pieces that appear as a smear on a scanned yield gel compared to good-quality DNA possessing intact high relative molecular mass DNA. (b) Signal strength is generally lost with larger-size PCR products when STR typing is performed on degraded DNA, such as is shown from the green dye-labeled loci in the PowerPlex 16 kit. Thus, 180bp D13S317 PCR products have a higher signal than 400bp Penta D amplicons because more DNA molecules are intact in the 200bp versus the 400bp size range.

The more degraded a DNA sample becomes, the more breaks occur in the template and fewer and fewer DNA molecules contain the full length needed for PCR amplification.

Benefits of STR Markers with Degraded DNA Samples

Fortunately, because STR loci can be amplified with fairly small product sizes, there is a greater chance for the STR primers to find some intact DNA strands for amplification. In addition, the narrow size range of STR alleles benefits analysis of degraded DNA samples because allele dropout via preferential amplification of the smaller allele is less likely to occur since both alleles in a heterozygous individual are similar in size.

A number of experiments have shown that there is an inverse relationship between the size of the locus and successful PCR amplification from degraded DNA samples, such as those obtained from a crime scene or a mass disaster (Whitaker et al. 1995, Sparkes et al. 1996, Takahashi et al. 1997, Schneider et al. 2004). The STR loci with larger-sized amplicons in a multiplex amplification, such as D18S51 and FGA or CSF1PO and Penta D, are the first to drop out of the DNA profile when amplifying extremely degraded DNA samples (Figure 10.2b).

In one of the first studies demonstrating the value of multiplex STR analysis with degraded DNA samples, the Forensic Science Service was able to successfully type a majority of 73 duplicate pathological samples obtained from the Waco Branch Davidian fire (see Chapter 9) with four STR markers (Whitaker et al. 1995). They observed no allele dropout and obtained concordant results on all samples where alleles were scored. A correlation was observed between successful typing at a locus and the average length of the alleles at that locus. The FES/FPS locus, which has alleles in the size range of 212 bp to 240 bp, only yielded 91 successful amplifications while the VWA locus with alleles ranging from 130 bp to 169 bp had 115 successful amplifications. Thus, loci with the larger alleles failed first. In addition, amelogenin amplicons (106 bp or 112 bp) were obtained on all 24 samples examined as part of the Waco identification program (Whitaker et al. 1995).

The potential for analysis of degraded DNA samples is an area where multiplex STR systems really shine over previously used DNA markers. STRs are more sensitive than single-locus probe RFLP methods, less prone to allelic dropout than VNTR systems (AmpFLPs) such as D1S80, and more discriminating than other PCR-based typing methods, such as HLA-DQA1 and AmpliType PolyMarker (see Butler 2010, *Fundamentals*, Chapter 3). Nevertheless, either due to degradation or inhibition, partial STR profiles still occur (Figure 10.3).

miniSTRs

The Use of Reduced Sized PCR Products (miniSTRs)

In an article entitled "Less is more – length reduction of STR amplicons using redesigned primers," Wiegand and Kleiber (2001) demonstrated that highly degraded DNA as well as very low amounts of DNA could be more successfully typed using some new redesigned PCR primers that were close to the STR repeat compared to the established sequences that generated longer amplicons for the same loci. This work built upon some previous work with creating smaller PCR products for mass spectrometry. Table 10.1 provides a timeline

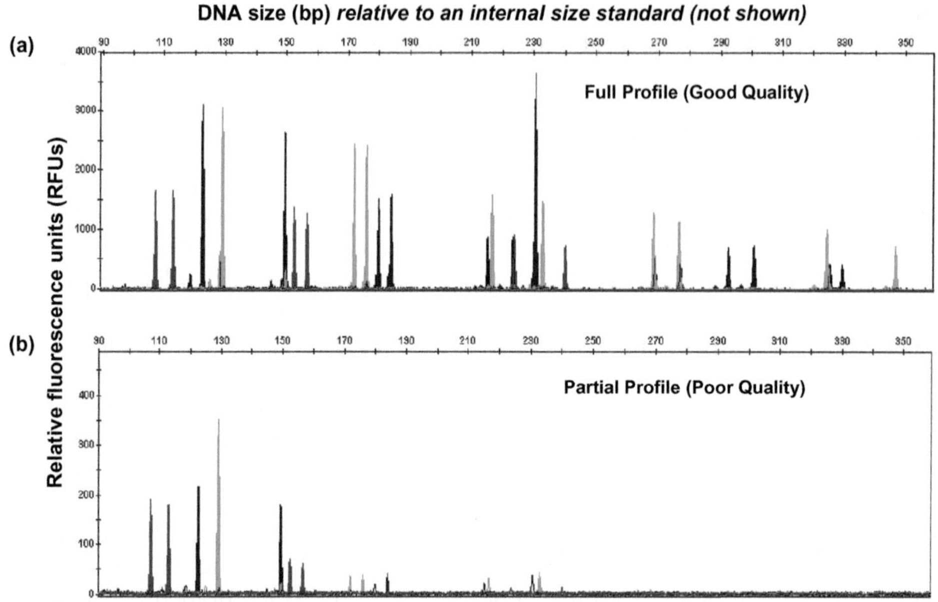

FIGURE 10.3 A comparison of DNA profiles originating from the same biological source but of different qualities. (a) Intact, good-quality DNA yields a full profile. (b) Degraded, poor-quality DNA yields a partial profile with only the lower-size PCR products producing detectable signal. With the degraded DNA sample shown in (b), information is lost at the larger-sized STR loci. Also note the lower relative fluorescence units with the poor-quality partial profile in (b). Figure courtesy of Margaret Kline, NIST.

of the history surrounding the development and implementation so-called "miniSTRs" or reduced-sized PCR products.

STR loci used in commercially available kits can extend past 400bp in size. Most of this length comes from the flanking sequences surrounding the STR repeat of interest. PCR primers for larger-sized STR markers have been moved away from the repeat region that imparts variability to the locus in order to fit into a desired size range for a particular multiplex assay (e.g., Krenke et al. 2002).

For example, the two PCR primers used for the PowerPlex 16 locus Penta D anneal 71bp upstream and 247bp downstream of the core AAAGA repeat. Amplification with these PCR primers generates amplicons in the size range of 376bp to 449bp with alleles ranging from 2.2 to 17 repeats (Krenke et al. 2002). When primers are brought to within 11bp upstream and 19bp downstream of the repeat region, the overall PCR product sizes drop by 282bp to a range of 94bp to 167bp for alleles 2.2bp to 17bp (Butler et al. 2003). Figure 10.4 illustrates this size reduction principle when creating reduced-size STR amplicons or "miniSTRs." It is important to keep in mind that some loci can be reduced in size more than others (Table 10.2).

Several disadvantages do exist for miniSTRs. A major disadvantage is that only a few loci can be simultaneously amplified in a multiplex because the size aspect has been removed. Large multiplex assays like PowerPlex 16 pack four or more loci into a single dye color by shifting primers away from the repeat region to make larger PCR products. The "miniplexes" created for amplifying miniSTRs have primers that are as close as possible to the

TABLE 10.1 Timeline of Events Surrounding Development and Use of miniSTR Loci for Forensic DNA Typing (see http://www.cstl.nist.gov/biotech/strbase/miniSTR/timeline.htm).

Date	Event*
1994	In running degraded DNA samples from remains of victims of the Branch Davidian fire in Waco, Texas, the Forensic Science Service find that smaller STRs in their 4plex work better than the larger loci (Lygo et al. 1994, Whitaker et al. 1995).
1996	GeneTrace Systems, a company in Menlo Park, California, begins work with shorter STR amplicons to perform rapid DNA typing using MALDI-TOF mass spectrometry; small PCR products are necessary to obtain successful results with MALDI-TOF.
Sept 1997	John Butler and coworkers from GeneTrace submit a patent on mass spec typing and multiplexing using small STR amplicons; U.S. patent 6,090,558 is granted July 18, 2000 (Butler et al. 2000).
1997–1999	Butler and coworkers from GeneTrace (funded by National Institute of Justice Grant 97-LB-VX-0003) give numerous talks on TOF-MS STR typing with smaller PCR products; some of their work is published (Butler et al. 1998a, Butler 1999); manuscripts are also published as part of the International Symposium on Human Identification in 1997 (Butler et al. 1998b) and 1998 (Butler & Becker 1999) as well as the Second European Symposium on Human Identification in 1998 (Butler et al. 1999).
June 1998	Hermann Schmitter of the German BKA hears Kathy Stephens from GeneTrace speak on small STRs and independently decides to try them on degraded DNA samples; the efforts of his laboratory lead to work with STR typing of telogen hair shafts (Hellmann et al. 2001).
Summer 2000	Butler (now back at NIST) puts fluorescent dyes on his GeneTrace mass spec primers and demonstrates reliable STR typing using the ABI 310; this work is presented as a poster at the 11th International Symposium on Human Identification (Ruitberg & Butler 2000).
Summer 2001	Bruce McCord (Ohio University) joins John Butler in an informal collaboration working on short STRs to aid analysis of degraded DNA samples.
October 2001	The National Institute of Justice publishes Butler's final report from his work at GeneTrace Systems including primer sequences for the short STR amplicons (see p. 24, Butler & Becker 2001).
November 2001	After discussions with the World Trade Center Kinship and Data Analysis Panel (WTC KADAP), Robert Shaler, of the New York City Office of the Chief Medical Examiner (OCME), who is leading the efforts to identify victims of the WTC attacks using DNA testing, contacts Butler at NIST and asks that efforts with short STRs be accelerated so that this technology may be used with aiding WTC victim identifications; the term "miniSTR" is coined at this time.
December 2001–January 2002	Butler, McCord, and postdoctoral student Yin Shen work to develop five miniplex assays that incorporate all of the CODIS STR loci as well as D2S1338, Penta D, and Penta E; some concordance studies and initial validation studies are performed but the primary focus is on primer development, generation of allelic ladders and creation of Genotyper macros rather than assay optimization in terms of sensitivity; a summary of this work is later published (Butler et al. 2003).
January 16, 2002	Butler speaks at SWGDAM (Quantico, VA) informing the attendees of research progress with miniSTRs; Mitch Holland of Bode Technology Group is present and learns of this effort; Butler meets with Shaler and Howard Baum of NYC OCME to make decisions about which miniplex would be tried by NYC OCME.
February 2002	"Big Mini" assay and protocols are supplied to NYC OCME and New York State Police in Albany for trial use; OCME work with Big Mini proves sensitive down to 0.5 ng of DNA template with the provided protocol of 28 cycle PCR and 1 U of TaqGold in 25 μL volumes.

(Continued)

TABLE 10.1 Timeline of Events Surrounding Development and Use of miniSTR Loci for Forensic DNA Typing (see http://www.cstl.nist.gov/biotech/strbase/miniSTR/timeline.htm). *(Continued)*

Date	Event*
February 22, 2002	Butler speaks to the WTC KADAP as part of their meeting in Albany, NY to inform the group of research progress with miniSTRs.
March 2002	McCord and Butler submit a proposal to the National Institute of Justice to further develop miniSTR assays; NIJ Grant 2002-IJ-CX-K007 is awarded and results in several publications (Chung et al. 2004, Drábek et al. 2004, Opel et al. 2006, Opel et al. 2007, Opel et al. 2008).
March 2002	Shaler meets with Jim Schumm of the Bode Technology Group and discusses the possibility of Bode performing miniSTR testing; Bode is already testing bones from the WTC investigation with conventional STR methods.
April 4, 2002	Schumm contacts Butler for primer sequences and information on miniplex work performed to date; an Excel file and PowerPoint presentation are emailed from NIST to Bode to aid their efforts.
Summer 2002	BodePlexes are developed by Schumm and coworkers at the Bode Technology Group using NIST supplied information as well as the NIJ-published GeneTrace report; a majority of the PCR primers are kept the same but dye labels are switched to provide different marker combinations; BodePlexes utilize 5X amount of TaqGold and 4–6 more PCR cycles to improve sensitivity over previous miniSTR work.
November 22, 2002	Schumm invites Shaler, Baum, and Butler to visit the Bode Technology Group (Springfield, VA) in order to review their validation studies for the BodePlex 1 and BodePlex 2 assays that were intended for use on WTC samples; while PCR primer sequences were not revealed, it was acknowledged that a majority of them came from the NIST and GeneTrace information.
Late 2002–Summer 2003	BodePlex 1 (D13S317, D21S11, D7S820, D16S539, and CSF1PO) and BodePlex 2 (TPOX, FGA, D7S820, and D18S51) are run by the Bode Technology Group on the bone and tissue samples that are part of the WTC investigation—the use of miniSTR BodePlexes has been described in several publications (Holland et al. 2003, Schumm et al. 2004).
September 2003	Butler, Shen, and McCord's publish miniSTR primer sequences (Butler et al. 2003) for 13 CODIS STRs and miniplex sets developed in late 2001 and early 2002.
December 2003	Mike Coble begins work at NIST as an NRC postdoctoral associate to develop miniSTRs for loci beyond the CODIS core.
February 2004	Coble speaks at the American Academy of Forensic Sciences meeting in Dallas, TX about efforts at NIST to develop new miniSTR assays. Denise Chung, a graduate student from Bruce McCord's lab at Ohio University, speaks on their progress with miniSTRs.
April 2004	Butler is invited to participate in the European DNA Profiling Group (EDNAP) and European Network of Forensic Science Institutes (ENFSI) meeting in Cyprus to help setup an interlaboratory test with Peter Gill on degraded DNA; this EDNAP/ENFSI study will involve conventional STR testing, miniSTR assays, and SNP assays on the same degraded DNA samples.
July 2004	Publication of McCord's lab work on miniSTRs (Chung et al. 2004, Drábek et al. 2004).
September 2004	EDNAP/ENFSI study involving miniSTRs and SNPs is initiated—materials for two miniSTR systems are provided by NIST to all participating laboratories: see http://www.cstl.nist.gov/biotech/strbase/miniSTR.htm#Protocols.
January 2005	Coble publishes his work with new miniSTR loci (Coble & Butler 2005).
September 2005	Coble outlines work with new miniSTR loci at the International Society of Forensic Genetics meeting (Coble et al. 2006).

(Continued)

TABLE 10.1 Timeline of Events Surrounding Development and Use of miniSTR Loci for Forensic DNA Typing (see http://www.cstl.nist.gov/biotech/strbase/miniSTR/timeline.htm). *(Continued)*

Date	Event*
October 2005	Applied Biosystems announces at the ENFSI meeting that they are working on a commercial kit involving miniSTR loci, which should be available in 2006.
January 2006	Gill, Lyn Fereday, Niels Morling, and Peter Schneider representing the EDNAP and ENFSI groups propose that miniSTRs be adopted as the way forward to increase both the robustness and sensitivity of forensic DNA analysis. Their recommendations are published (Gill et al. 2006). They also recommend that three new miniSTR loci be adopted by European laboratories: D10S1248, D14S1434 (now replaced by D2S441), and D22S1045—all loci described by Coble & Butler (2005).
February 2006	NIST staffer Becky Hill presents a poster at the AAFS meeting in Seattle, WA on allele frequencies in U.S. populations found with 27 new miniSTR loci under development at NIST (Hill et al. 2006a).
February 2006	Applied Biosystems announces at the AAFS meeting in Seattle, WA efforts to develop a 9plex miniSTR kit (using their 5-dye and mobility modifier technology); this miniSTR kit is designed to recover information from the larger loci in their Identifiler kit and will amplify the following loci: D13S317, D7S820, D2S1338, D21S11, D16S539, D18S51, CSF1PO, FGA, and amelogenin.
March 2006	McCord's group publishes their work using miniSTRs on skeletal remains (Opel et al. 2006).
October 2006	Hill presents a poster at the Promega meeting in Nashville, TN on characterization of 26 miniSTR loci under development at NIST (Hill et al. 2006b).
October 2006	Applied Biosystems publishes information about their new MiniFiler kit in their marketing newsletter Forensic News.
March 2007	Applied Biosystems releases their new MiniFiler kit.
July 2007	NIST and Applied Biosystems co-publish an article examining concordance of allele calls between the MiniFiler kit and other commercial STR kits (Hill et al. 2007).
July 2008	Applied Biosystems publishes their developmental validation work on MiniFiler (Mulero et al. 2008).

**Some additional work with small PCR products for STRs has been published that is not included on this timeline (see reference list at the back of the chapter).*

repeat region and therefore typically only have one locus per dye color because all of the loci have about the same size range of ≈100 bp (Butler et al. 2003). However, using mobility modifiers to adjust the electrophoretically observed PCR product sizes, Applied Biosystems was able to put eight miniSTRs and amelogenin into their single amplification MiniFiler kit (Mulero et al. 2008) (Figure 10.5).

Since different PCR primers are in use with miniSTRs compared to conventional STR megaplexes, it is important that concordance studies be performed to verify that allele dropout from primer binding site mutations is rare or non-existent (Hill et al. 2007). This is performed by examining the genotyping results to see if they are the same between the primer sets (see Chapter 6). Occasionally a point mutation or an insertion or deletion may occur in the flanking region outside of a miniSTR primer binding site which can lead to a problematic (and undetectable) difference in a heterozygous allele call (Butler et al. 2003, Drabek et al. 2004, Hill et al. 2007).

Regardless of these disadvantages, it is likely that miniSTRs will play a role in the future of degraded DNA analysis, helping recover information on larger loci that has been lost using conventional megaplex amplification.

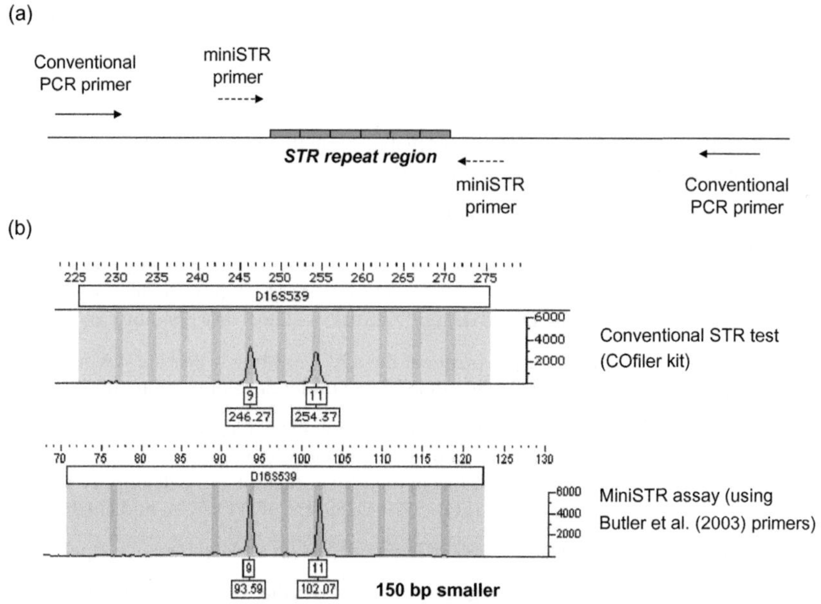

FIGURE 10.4 (a) MiniSTRs or reduced-sized amplicons for STR typing are created by designing PCR primers that anneal closer to the repeat region than conventional STR kit primers. (b) PCR product sizes, such as demonstrated here with D16S539, can be reduced by over 150bp relative to conventional tests. MiniSTR assays can produce the same typing result as those from larger STR amplicons produced by kits often with greater success on degraded DNA samples.

With enzyme-digested DNA, miniSTR loci performed better than loci from a commercial STR kit (Chung et al. 2004). As described in Chapter 9, reduced-size STR assays helped make possible some of the World Trade Center victim identifications from burned and damaged bone samples (Schumm et al. 2004). Even telogen hair shafts, which contain very little nuclear DNA, have been successfully typed using reduced-size STR amplicons (Hellman et al. 2001, Müller et al. 2007, Opel et al. 2008).

In 2006, the European DNA Profiling Group (EDNAP) published the results of a study with degraded DNA samples where miniSTR primer sets were compared to conventional STR multiplex kits and an experimental single nucleotide polymorphism (SNP) assay (Dixon et al. 2006). Overall, the miniSTR assays performed the best on the degraded DNA samples, which led leaders of the European community to advocate for miniSTR loci in future STR kits (Gill et al. 2006).

New miniSTR Loci

STR loci other than the CODIS markers and others that are currently used in forensic DNA typing have been developed as miniSTR systems with a focus on loci possessing small alleles and narrow size ranges (Ohtaki et al. 2002, Coble & Butler 2005, Hill et al. 2008).

TABLE 10.2 PCR Product Size Reduction Obtained with New Primers for Several miniSTR Loci (Butler et al. 2003).

Locus	miniSTR Size (bp)	Allele Range (repeat numbers)	Size Reduction*
TH01	51–98	3–14	−105 bp
TPOX	65–101	5–14	−148 bp
CSF1PO	89–129	6–16	−191 bp
VWA	88–148	10–15	−64 bp
FGA	125–281	12.2–51.2	−71 bp
D3S1358	72–120	8–20	−25 bp
D5S818	81–117	7–16	−53 bp
D7S820	136–176	5–15	−117 bp
D8S1179	86–134	7–19	−37 bp
D13S317	88–132	5–16	−105 bp
D16S539	81–121	5–15	−152 bp
D18S51	113–193	7–27	−151 bp
D21S11	153–211	24–38.2	−33 bp
Penta D	94–167	2.2–17	−282 bp
Penta E	80–175	5–24	−299 bp
D2S1338	90–142	15–28	−198 bp

**Compared to Applied Biosystems STR kits except for Penta D and Penta E, which are in Promega's PowerPlex 16 kit.*

A battery of additional assays has been made available to aid researchers and forensic practitioners in the future when working with degraded DNA specimens.

Scientists at the U.S. National Institute of Standards and Technology (NIST) selected a set of 26 new miniSTR loci from over 900 candidate STR loci based on expected allele ranges and the ability to design PCR primers close to the flanking region (Coble & Butler 2005, Coble et al. 2006). These 26 loci were characterized in U.S. population samples (Table 10.3). In addition, 25 of the loci were combined with amelogenin into a single 26plex assay for typing reference samples (Hill et al. 2009).

Nucleosome Protected Areas of the Genome

Another approach to enabling better recovery of results from potentially damaged DNA samples is to look for regions of the DNA that are better protected when DNA is chromosomally packaged inside the cell. In theory, when DNA is bound to histone proteins in its chromosome packaging, there will be less opportunity for degradative enzymes, such as

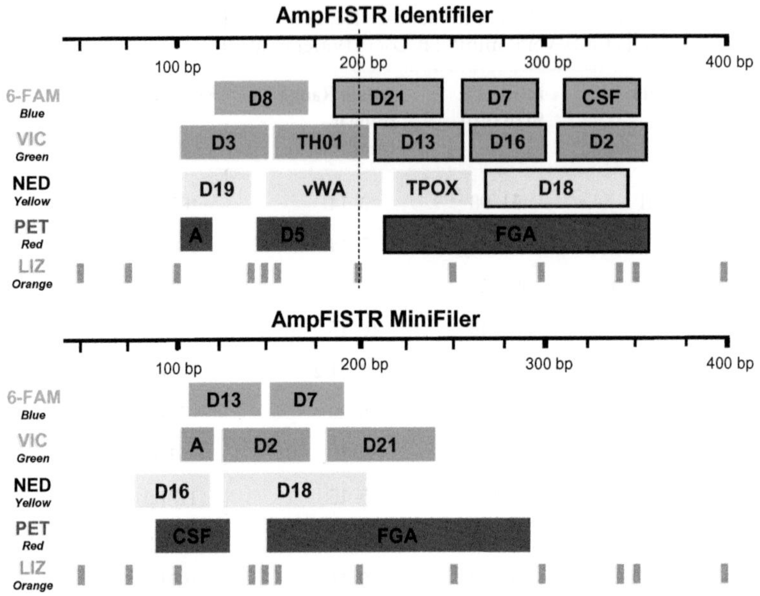

FIGURE 10.5 An illustration of the relative sizes and dye labels for PCR products generated with the Identifiler and MiniFiler STR kits. MiniFiler is designed to recover the larger sized Identifiler PCR products (those greater than 200 bp, with the exception of TPOX, as shown by the dotted line).

DNase I, to break the DNA into smaller fragments. The nucleosome core particle complex generally protects 147 bp regions of a DNA sequence (Richmond & Davey 2003). Efforts have been made to discover the predominant DNA sequences found within these nucleosome core particles in order to predict how well DNA sequences would be expected to survive DNA damage (Ioshikhes et al. 2006, Radwan et al. 2008).

Researchers at the University of Strathclyde in Glascow, Scotland have performed *in silico* studies on 60 forensic DNA markers, 58 STRs plus amelogenin X and Y sequences, in search of properties that promote or inhibit the DNA sequence from binding to histones (Thanakiatkrai & Welch 2010). They found that the majority of STR loci commonly used are likely to be bound as nucleosomes and thus better protected against DNA damage. They also propose that selection of markers, which appear to be protected best, might be used in the future to create an improved multiplex assay for degraded DNA samples.

The approach of finding optimal protected regions of DNA in order to design assays that will improve success rates on forensic casework samples is still in its infancy. It may be that different DNA sequence regions will work better than the STR loci in use today. However, the large national databases around the world containing millions of STR profiles (see Chapter 10) will probably discourage movement to other DNA markers unless success rates on casework samples with degraded DNA are significantly improved. Only time will tell if this approach plays a significant role in the future of forensic DNA typing.

TABLE 10.3 Information on 26 miniSTRs Characterized at NIST (Hill et al. 2008). Chromosomal Location and Base Pair (bp) Position of Each Marker Was Determined by Using BLAT (http://genome.ucsc.edu/cgi-bin/hgBlat) and the May 2004 Assembly of the Human Genome. The Observed Size Range (bp) Values Are Based on the miniSTR Amplicon Sizes That Were Observed in This Study Relative to the GS500 LIZ Size Standard. The Loci Are Listed in Order, Highest to Lowest, by the Overall Heterozygosity Values.

Locus	Repeat Motif	Chromosomal Location	Chromosome Position	Observed Size Range (bp)	N	Overall Heterozygosity
D9S2157	ATA	9q34.2	Chr 9 133.065 Mb	71–101	661	0.844
ATA63 (D12)	YAA	12q23.3	Chr 12 106.825 Mb	76–106	659	0.829
D10S1248 (NC01)	GGAA	10q26.3	Chr 10 130.567 Mb	83–123	663	0.792
D22S1045 (NC01)	ATT	22q12.3	Chr 22 35.779 Mb	76–109	663	0.784
D2S441 (NC02)	TCTA	2p14	Chr 2 68.214 Mb	78–110	660	0.774
D10S1435	TATC	10p15.3	Chr 10 2.233 Mb	82–139	663	0.766
D2S1776	AGAT	2q24.3	Chr 2 169.471 Mb	127–161	654	0.763
D3S4529	ATCT	3p12.1	Chr 3 85.935 Mb	111–139	660	0.761
D6S474	GATA	6q21	Chr 6 112.986 Mb	107–135	648	0.761
D5S2500	GRYW	5q11.2	Chr 5 58.735 Mb	85–125	664	0.747
D1S1627	ATT	1p21.1	Chr 1 106.676 Mb	81–100	660	0.746
D1S1677 (NC02)	TTCC	1q23.3	Chr 1 160.747 Mb	81–117	660	0.746
D6S1017	ATCC	6p21.1	Chr 6 41.785 Mb	81–109	664	0.740
D3S3053	TATC	3q26.31	Chr 3 173.234 Mb	84–108	648	0.739
D9S1122	TAGA	9q21.2	Chr 9 76.918 Mb	93–125	659	0.734
D17S974	CTAT	17p13.1	Chr 17 10.459 Mb	95–123	664	0.732
D11S4463	TATC	11q25	Chr 11 130.338 Mb	88–116	664	0.730
D4S2408	ATCT	4p15.1	Chr 4 30.981 Mb	85–109	654	0.722
D18S853	ATA	18p11.31	Chr 18 3.981 Mb	82–103	664	0.711
D20S1082	ATA	20q13.2	Chr 20 53.299 Mb	73–100	664	0.696
D14S1434 (NC01)	CTRT	14q32.13	Chr 14 93.298 Mb	70–98	663	0.696
D20S482	AGAT	20p13	Chr 20 4.454 Mb	86–126	648	0.691
GATA113 (D1)	GATA	1p36.23	Chr 1 7.377 Mb	81–105	654	0.668
D8S1115	ATT	8p11.21	Chr 8 42.656 Mb	63–96	664	0.663
D17S1301	AGAT	17q25.1	Chr 17 70.193 Mb	114–138	664	0.649
D4S2364 (NC02)	ATTC	4q22.3	Chr 4 93.976 Mb	67–83	660	0.511

ATTEMPTS WITH DNA REPAIR FOLLOWING DNA DAMAGE

New England Biolabs (Ipswich, MA) sells an enzyme cocktail to help repair DNA damage prior to performing PCR. While their "PreCR Repair Mix" cannot repair fragmented DNA, it contains a ligase and other enzymes capable of repairing nicks, thymine dimers caused by UV radiation, and abasic sites caused by hydrolysis. The effectiveness of the PreCR Repair Mix on artificially damaged DNA and on non-probative casework samples was examined by researchers at the Alcohol, Tobacco, and Firearms (ATF) and Armed Forces DNA Identification Laboratories (Bille et al. 2008), but unfortunately their experiments did not show any major advantages with the PreCR Repair Mix on the samples they tested.

The National Institute of Justice (NIJ) has funded several projects to work on repair of damaged DNA templates (Ballantyne 2006, Nelson 2009) and some promising results have been obtained. New DNA polymerases capable of PCR amplification from damaged or ancient DNA samples have been developed and studied (McDonald et al. 2006, d'Abbadie et al. 2007, Shapiro 2008).

John Nelson of the GE Global Research Center (Niskayuna, NY) in his NIJ final report (Nelson 2009) concludes that DNA may be damaged in a number of ways and not all of them can be repaired. He notes that "there is likely a 'window of opportunity' during exposure of DNA to sub-optimal conditions when the DNA molecular weight is large enough to still contain segments of DNA that encompass STR loci, but contain lesions that can be repaired" (Nelson 2009). He found that with the addition of enzymes such as Fpg (formamidopyrimidine [fapy]-DNA glycosylase), *E. coli* endonuclease IV, *E. coli* endonuclease VIII, and T4-PDG (pyrimidine dimer glycosylase) to a DNA polymerase/ligase enzyme cocktail there was an increase in the ability to repair DNA. Unfortunately, the use of additional enzymes means that there is a greater potential for introducing contaminating DNA in these reagents. Therefore, the enzyme cocktail reagents would have to be carefully screened by manufacturers to avoid contaminating forensic casework samples as well as being checked by forensic laboratories with additional reagent blanks to confirm that spurious DNA was not added (see D.N.A. Box 4.3).

Perhaps future DNA repair kits will enable laboratories to obtain results from forensic casework samples that currently fail to amplify or produce partial profiles.

READING LIST AND INTERNET RESOURCES

DNA Damage

David, D. L., et al. (2000). Analysis of the degradation of oligonucleotides strands during the freezing/thawing processes using MALDI-MS. *Analytical Chemistry, 72*, 5092–5096.

Englander, E. W., & Howard, B. H. (1997). Alu-mediated detection of DNA damage in the human genome. *Mutation Research, 385*, 31–39.

Greer, C. E., et al. (1991). PCR amplification from paraffin-embedded tissues: effects of fixative and fixation time. *American Journal of Clinical Pathology, 95*, 117–124.

Hall, A., & Ballantyne, J. (2004). Characterization of UVC-induced DNA damage in bloodstains: forensic implications. *Analytical and Bioanalytical Chemistry, 380*, 72–83.

Hofreiter, M., et al. (2001). DNA sequences from multiple amplifications reveal artifacts induced by cytosine deamination in ancient DNA. *Nucleic Acids Research, 29*, 4793–4799.

Hoss, M., et al. (1996). DNA damage and DNA sequence retrieval from ancient tissues. *Nucleic Acids Research, 24,* 1304–1307.

Johnson, L. A., & Ferris, J. A. (2002). Analysis of postmortem DNA degradation by single-cell gel electrophoresis. *Forensic Science International, 126,* 43–47.

Kaiser, C., et al. (2008). Molecular study of time dependent changes in DNA stability in soil buried skeletal residues. *Forensic Science International, 177,* 32–36.

Lindahl, T., & Karlstrom, O. (1973). Heat-induced depyrimidination of deoxyribonucleic acid in neutral solution. *Biochemistry, 12,* 5151–5154.

Marrone, A., & Ballantyne, J. (2010). Hydrolysis of DNA and its molecular components in the dry state. *Forensic Science International: Genetics, 4,* 168–177.

Misner, L. M., et al. (2009). The correlation between skeletal weathering and DNA quality and quantity. *Journal of Forensic Sciences, 54,* 822–828.

Paabo, S., et al. (1990). DNA damage promotes jumping between templates during enzymatic amplification. *Journal of Biological Chemistry, 265,* 4718–4721.

Pfeifer, G. P., et al. (2005). Mutations induced by ultraviolet light. *Mutation Research, 571,* 19–31.

Ravanat, J. L., et al. (2001). Direct and indirect effects of UV radiation on DNA and its components. *Journal of Photochemistry & Photobiology B, 63,* 88–102.

Romero, R. L., et al. (1997). The applicability of formalin-fixed and formalin fixed paraffin embedded tissues in forensic DNA analysis. *Journal of Forensic Sciences, 42,* 708–714.

Shapiro, R., & Danzig, M. (1972). Acidic hydrolysis of deoxycytidine and deoxyuridine derivatives: the general mechanism of deoxyribonucleoside hydrolysis. *Biochemistry, 11,* 23–29.

Shikama, K. (1985). Effect of freezing and thawing on the stability of double helix of DNA. *Nature, 207,* 529–530.

Yoon, J. H., et al. (2000). The DNA damage spectrum produced by simulated sunlight. *Journal of Molecular Biology, 299,* 681–693.

Degraded DNA

Alaeddini, R., et al. (2010). Forensic implications of genetic analyses from degraded DNA – a review. *Forensic Science International: Genetics, 4,* 148–157.

Alonso, A., et al. (2001). DNA typing from skeletal remains: evaluation of multiplex and megaplex STR systems on DNA isolated from bone and teeth samples. *Croatian Medical Journal, 42,* 260–266.

Asari, M., et al. (2009). Single nucleotide polymorphism genotyping by mini-primer allele-specific amplification with universal reporter primers for identification of degraded DNA. *Analytical Biochemistry, 386,* 85–90.

Barbaro, A., et al. (2008). Study about the effect of high temperatures on STR typing. *Forensic Science International: Genetics Supplement Series, 1,* 92–94.

Bender, K., et al. (2004). Preparation of degraded human DNA under controlled conditions. *Forensic Science International, 139,* 135–140.

Colotte, M., et al. (2009). Simultaneous assessment of average fragment size and amount in minute samples of degraded DNA. *Analytical Biochemistry, 388,* 345–347.

Dixon, L. A., et al. (2005). Validation of a 21-locus autosomal SNP multiplex for forensic identification purposes. *Forensic Science International, 154,* 62–77.

Dixon, L. A., et al. (2006). Analysis of artificially degraded DNA using STRs and SNPs – results of a collaborative European (EDNAP) exercise. *Forensic Science International, 164,* 33–44.

Fondevila, M., et al. (2008). Challenging DNA: assessment of a range of genotyping approaches for highly degraded forensic samples. *Forensic Science International: Genetics Supplement Series, 1,* 26–28.

Hughes-Stamm, S. R., et al. (2010). Assessment of DNA degradation and the genotyping success of highly degraded samples. *International Journal of Legal Medicine* (in press). (doi 10.1007/s00414-010-0455-3).

Irwin, J. A., et al. (2007). Application of low copy number STR typing to the identification of aged, degraded skeletal remains. *Journal of Forensic Sciences, 52,* 1322–1327.

Klevan, L., & Shade, L. L. (2007). Identifying degraded DNA. *Forensic Magazine, 4*(1), 24–28.

Kobilinsky, L. (1992). Recovery and stability of DNA in samples of forensic significance. *Forensic Science Review, 4,* 68–87.

Lindahl, T. (1993). Instability and decay of the primary structure of DNA. *Nature, 362,* 709–715.

Lygo, J. E., et al. (1994). The validation of short tandem repeat (STR) loci for use in forensic casework. *International Journal of Legal Medicine, 107,* 77–89.

Schmerer, W. M., et al. (1999). Optimized DNA extraction to improve reproducibility of short tandem repeat genotyping with highly degraded DNA as target. *Electrophoresis, 20*, 1712–1716.

Schneider, P. M., et al. (2004). STR analysis of artificially degraded DNA-results of a collaborative European exercise. *Forensic Science International, 139*, 123–134.

Takahashi, M., et al. (1997). Evaluation of five polymorphic microsatellite markers for typing DNA from decomposed human tissues – correlation between the size of the alleles and that of the template DNA. *Forensic Science International, 90*, 1–9.

Thacker, C. R., et al. (2006). An investigation into methods to produce artificially degraded DNA. *Progress in Forensic Genetics, 11, ICS 1288*, 592–594.

Tvedebrink, T., et al. (2011). Statistical model for degraded DNA samples and adjusted probabilities for allelic drop-out. *Forensic Science International: Genetics* (in press) (doi:10.1016/j.fsigen.2011.03.001).

Westen, A. A., et al. (2009). Tri-allelic SNP markers enable analysis of mixed and degraded DNA samples. *Forensic Science International: Genetics, 3*, 233–241.

Westen, A. A., & Sijen, T. (2009). Degraded DNA sample analysis using DNA repair enzymes, mini-STRs and (tri-allelic) SNPs. *Forensic Science International: Genetics Supplement Series, 2*, 505–507.

Whitaker, J. P., et al. (1995). Short tandem repeat typing of bodies from a mass disaster: high success rate and characteristic amplification patterns in highly degraded samples. *BioTechniques, 18*, 670–677.

Early Work with Reduced Size STR Amplicons

Butler, J. M., et al. (1998). Reliable genotyping of short tandem repeat loci without an allelic ladder using time-of-flight mass spectrometry. *International Journal of Legal Medicine, 112*, 45–49.

Butler, J. M., et al. (1998b). Rapid and automated analysis of short tandem repeat loci using time-of-flight mass spectrometry. *Proceedings of the eighth international symposium on human identification 1997* (pp. 94–101). Promega Corporation. Available at <http://www.promega.com/geneticidproc/ussymp8proc/28.html/>.

Butler, J. M., et al. (1999) High-throughput STR analysis by time-of-flight mass spectrometry. *Proceedings of the second European symposium on human identification 1998* (pp. 121–130). Promega Corporation. Available at <http://www.promega.com/geneticidproc/eusymp2proc/25.pdf/>.

Butler, J. M. (1999). STR analysis by time-of-flight mass spectrometry. *Profiles in DNA, 2*(3), 3–6. Available at <http://www.promega.com/profiles/203/ProfilesinDNA_203_03.pdf/>.

Butler, J. M., & Becker, C. H. (1999). High-throughput analysis of forensic STR and SNP markers using time-of-flight mass spectrometry. *Proceedings of the ninth international symposium on human identification 1998* (pp.43–51). Promega Corporation. Available at <http://www.promega.com/geneticidproc/ussymp9proc/content/10.pdf/>.

Butler, J. M., et al. (2000). DNA typing by mass spectrometry with polymorphic DNA repeat markers. U.S. Patent 6,090,558.

Butler, J. M., & Becker, C. H. (2001). Improved analysis of DNA short tandem repeats with time-of-flight mass spectrometry. Final Report for NIJ Grant 97-LB-VX-0003. Available at <http://www.ojp.usdoj.gov/nij/pubs-sum/188292.htm/>.

Ruitberg, C. R., & Butler, J. M. (2000). New primer sets for Y chromosome and CODIS STR loci. *Proceedings of the 11th international symposium on human identification.* Available at <http://www.promega.com/geneticidproc/ussymp11proc/abstracts/ruitberg.pdf/>.

miniSTRs

Asamura, H., et al. (2007). MiniY-STR quadruplex systems with short amplicon lengths for analysis of degraded DNA samples. *Forensic Science International: Genetics, 1*, 56–61.

Butler, J. M., et al. (2003). The development of reduced size STR amplicons as tools for analysis of degraded DNA. *Journal of Forensic Sciences, 48*(5), 1054–1064.

Butler, J. M. (2006). MiniSTRs: past, present, and future. *Forensic News* (Applied Biosystems), October 2006. Available at <http://marketing.appliedbiosystems.com/images/enews/ForensicNews_Vol7/PDF/02A_CustomerCorner_Butler.pdf/>.

Chung, D. T., et al. (2004). A study on the effects of degradation and template concentration on the efficiency of the STR miniplex primer sets. *Journal of Forensic Sciences, 49*(4), 733–740.

Drábek, J., et al. (2004). Concordance study between miniplex STR assays and a commercial STR typing kit. *Journal of Forensic Sciences, 49*(4), 859–860.

Fondevila, M., et al. (2008). Case report: identification of skeletal remains using short-amplicon marker analysis of severely degraded DNA extracted from a decomposed and charred femur. *Forensic Science International: Genetics, 2*, 212–218.

Gill, P., et al. (2006). The evolution of DNA databases – recommendations for new European STR loci. *Forensic Science International, 156*, 242–244.

Gill, P., et al. (2006). Letter to editor – New multiplexes for Europe-amendments and clarification of strategic development. *Forensic Science International, 163*, 155–157.

Grubwieser, P., et al. (2003). New sensitive amplification primers for the STR locus D2S1338 for degraded casework DNA. *International Journal of Legal Medicine, 117*, 185–188.

Grubwieser, P., et al. (2006). A new "miniSTR-multiplex" displaying reduced amplicon lengths for the analysis of degraded DNA. *International Journal of Legal Medicine, 120*, 115–120.

Hellmann, A., et al. (2001). STR typing of human telogen hairs – a new approach. *International Journal of Legal Medicine, 114*, 269–273.

Holland, M. M., et al. (2003). Development of a quality, high throughput DNA analysis procedure for skeletal samples to assist with the identification of victims from the World Trade Center attacks. *Croatian Medical Journal, 44*, 264–272.

Martin, P., et al. (2006). Application of mini-STR loci to severely degraded casework samples. *Progress in Forensic Genetics, 11, ICS 1288*, 522–525.

miniSTR timeline of events. <http://www.cstl.nist.gov/biotech/strbase/miniSTR/timeline.htm/>.

Müller, K., et al. (2007). Improved STR typing of telogen hair root and hair shaft DNA. *Electrophoresis, 28*, 2835–2842.

Opel, K. L., et al. (2006). The application of miniplex primer sets in the analysis of degraded DNA from human skeletal remains. *Journal of Forensic Sciences, 51*, 351–356.

Opel, K. L., et al. (2007). Developmental validation of reduced-size STR miniplex primer sets. *Journal of Forensic Sciences, 52*, 1263–1271.

Opel, K. L., et al. (2008). Evaluation and quantification of nuclear DNA from human telogen hairs. *Journal of Forensic Sciences, 53*, 853–857.

Parsons, T. J., et al. (2007). Application of novel "mini-amplicon" STR multiplexes to high volume casework on degraded skeletal remains. *Forensic Science International: Genetics, 1*, 175–179.

Ricci, U., et al. (1999). Modified primers for D12S391 and a modified silver staining technique. *International Journal of Legal Medicine, 112*, 342–344.

Schumm, J. W., et al. (2004). Robust STR multiplexes for challenging casework samples. *Progress in Forensic Genetics, 10, ICS 1261*, 547–549.

Szibor, R., et al. (2000). Identification of the human Y-chromosomal microsatellite locus DYS19 from degraded DNA. *American Journal of Forensic Medicine & Pathology, 21*, 252–254.

Tsukada, K., et al. (2002). Multiplex short tandem repeat typing in degraded samples using newly designed primers for the TH01, TPOX, CSF1PO and vWA loci. *Legal Medicine, 4*, 239–245.

Turrina, S., et al. (2008). STR typing of archival Bouin's fluid-fixed paraffin-embedded tissue using new sensitive redesigned primers for three STR loci (CSF1PO, D8S1179 and D13S317). *Journal of Forensic and Legal Medicine, 15*, 27–31.

Wiegand, P., & Kleiber, M. (2001). Less is more – length reduction of STR amplicons using redesigned primers. *International Journal of Legal Medicine, 114*, 285–287.

Wiegand, P., et al. (2006). Short amplicon STR multiplex for stain typing. *International Journal of Legal Medicine, 120*, 160–164.

Yoshida, K., et al. (1997). Evaluation of new primers for CSF1PO. *International Journal of Legal Medicine, 110*, 36–38.

MiniFiler kit

Alenizi, M. A., et al. (2009). Concordance between the AmpFlSTR MiniFiler and AmpFlSTR Identifiler PCR amplification kits in the Kuwaiti population. *Journal of Forensic Sciences, 54*, 350–352.

Hill, C. R., et al. (2007). Concordance study between the AmpFlSTR MiniFiler PCR Amplification Kit and conventional STR typing kits. *Journal of Forensic Sciences, 52*(4), 870–873.

Horsman-Hall, K. M., et al. (2009). Development of STR profiles from firearms and fired cartridge cases. *Forensic Science International: Genetics, 3*, 242–250.

Kline, M. C., et al. (2006). NIST SRM updates: value-added to the current Materials in SRM 2391b and SRM 2395. *Proceedings of the 17th international symposium on human identification*. Nashville, TN: Available at <http://www.cstl.nist.gov/biotech/strbase/pub_pres/Promega2006_Kline.pdf/>.

Luce, C., et al. (2009). Validation of the AmpFlSTR MiniFiler PCR amplification kit for use in forensic casework. *Journal of Forensic Sciences, 54,* 1046–1054.

Marjanovi , D., et al. (2009). Identification of skeletal remains of Communist Armed Forces victims during and after World War II: combined Y-chromosome (STR) and miniSTR approach. *Croatian Medical Journal, 50,* 296–304.

MiniFiler product information. <http://minifiler.appliedbiosystems.com/>.

Mulero, J. J., et al. (2008). Development and validation of the AmpFℓSTR MiniFiler PCR Amplification Kit: a miniSTR multiplex for the analysis of degraded and/or PCR inhibited DNA. *Journal of Forensic Sciences, 53,* 838–852.

Müller, K., et al. (2010). Casework testing of the multiplex kits AmpFlSTR SEfiler Plus PCR amplification kit (AB), PowerPlex S5 system (Promega) and AmpFlSTR MiniFiler PCR amplification kit (AB). *Forensic Science International: Genetics, 4,* 200–205.

Pinchi, V., et al. (2011). Techniques of dental DNA extraction: some operative experiences. *Forensic Science International, 204,* 111–114.

Vanek, D., et al. (2009). Kinship and Y-chromosome analysis of 7th century human remains: novel DNA extraction and typing procedure for ancient material. *Croatian Medical Journal, 50,* 286–295.

New miniSTR Loci

Aranda, X. G., et al. (2010). Genetic data for D1S1677, D2S441, D4S2364, D10S1248, D14S1434 and D22S1045 miniSTR loci from Libya. *Forensic Science International: Genetics, 4,* 267–268.

Asamura, H., et al. (2007). MiniSTR multiplex systems based on non-CODIS loci for analysis of degraded DNA samples. *Forensic Science International, 173,* 7–15.

Bai, R., et al. (2007). Allele frequencies for six miniSTR loci of two ethnic populations in China. *Forensic Science International, 168,* e25–e28.

Chung, U., et al. (2007). Population data of nine miniSTR loci in Koreans. *Forensic Science International, 168,* e51–e53.

Coble, M. D., & Butler, J. M. (2005). Characterization of new miniSTR loci to aid analysis of degraded DNA. *Journal of Forensic Sciences, 50*(1), 43–53.

Coble, M. D., et al. (2006) Characterization and performance of new miniSTR loci for typing degraded samples. *Progress in Forensic Genetics 11,* Elsevier Science: Amsterdam, The Netherlands, International Congress Series 1288, 504–506.

Decorte, R., et al. (2008). Development of a novel miniSTR multiplex assay for typing degraded DNA samples. *Forensic Science International: Genetics Supplement Series, 1,* 112–114.

Han, M. S., et al. (2009). Forensic genetic analysis of nine miniSTR loci in the Korean population. *Legal Medicine, 11,* 209–212.

Hill, C. R., et al. (2006a). Development of 27 new miniSTR loci for improved analysis of degraded DNA samples. *Poster at the 58th annual meeting of the American academy of forensic sciences.* Seattle, WA. Available at <http://www.cstl.nist.gov/biotech/strbase/pub_pres/Hill_AAFS2006_miniSTR.pdf/>.

Hill, C. R., et al. (2006b). Characterization of 26 new miniSTR loci. *Poster at the 17th international symposium on human identification.* Nashville, TN. Available at <http://www.cstl.nist.gov/biotech/strbase/pub_pres/Promega2006_Hill.pdf/>.

Hill, C. R., et al. (2008). Characterization of 26 miniSTR loci for improved analysis of degraded DNA samples. *Journal of Forensic Sciences, 53*(1), 73–80.

Hill, C. R., et al. (2009). A 26plex autosomal STR assay to aid human identity testing. *Journal of Forensic Sciences, 54,* 1008–1015.

Parys-Proszek, A., et al. (2010). Genetic variation of 15 autosomal STR loci in a population sample from Poland. *Legal Medicine, 12,* 246–248.

Ohtaki, H., et al. (2002). A powerful, novel, multiplex typing system for six short tandem repeat loci and the allele frequency distributions in two Japanese regional populations. *Electrophoresis, 23,* 3332–3340.

Reichert, M., & Pawlowski, R. (2009). Population genetics of six miniSTR loci (D1S1677, D2S441, D4S2364, D10S1248, D14S1434, D22S1045) in a Polish population. *Legal Medicine, 11,* 147–148.

Santos, L. L., et al. (2011). Allele distribution of six STR/miniSTR loci (CD4, FABP2, D12S391, D14S1434, D22S1045 and D10S1248) for forensic purposes in Southeastern Brazil. *Annals of Human Biology, 38,* 110–113.

Seider, T., et al. (2010). Allele frequencies of the five miniSTR loci D1S1656, D2S441, D10S1248, D12S391 and D22S1045 in a German population sample. *Forensic Science International: Genetics, 4,* e159–160.

Vullo, C., et al. (2010). Frequency data for 12 miniSTR loci in Argentina. *Forensic Science International: Genetics, 4,* e79–e81.

Yong, R. Y. Y., et al. (2007). Allele frequencies of six miniSTR loci of three ethnic populations in Singapore. *Forensic Science International, 166,* 240–243.

Zhu, B. F., et al. (2010). Genetic diversities of 21 non-CODIS autosomal STRs of a Chinese Tibetan ethnic minority group in Lhasa. *International Journal of Legal Medicine* (in press). (doi 10.1007/s00414-010-0519-4).

DNA Protection from Nucleosome Complex

Ioshikhes, I. P., et al. (2006). Nucleosome positions predicted through comparative genomics. *Nature Genetics, 38,* 1210–1215.

Koval, O. A., et al. (2003). New reagent for protein-DNA contacts footprinting. *Nucleosides, Nucleotides, and Nucleic Acids, 22,* 1587–1589.

Radwan, A., et al. (2008). Prediction and analysis of nucleosome exclusion regions in the human genome. *BMC Genomics, 9,* 186.

Richmond, T. J., & Davey, C. A. (2003). The structure of DNA in the nucleosome core. *Nature, 423,* 145–150.

Thanakiatkrai, P., & Welch, L. (2010). Evaluation of nucleosome forming potentials (NFPs) of forensically important STRs. *Forensic Science International: Genetics* (in press). (doi:10.1016/j.fsigen.2010.05.002).

DNA Repair

Ballantyne, J. (2006). Assessment and *in vitro* repair of damaged DNA templates. Final Report on NIJ Grant 2002-IJ-CX-K001. Available at <http://www.ncjrs.gov/pdffiles1/nij/grants/214166.pdf/>.

Bille, T., et al. (2008). Examination and optimization of the PreCR DNA Repair Mix on damaged DNA for short tandem repeat and mitochondrial DNA analysis. *Proceedings of the 19th international symposium on human identification.* Available at <http://www.promega.com/geneticidproc/ussymp19proc/oralpresentations/Farr.pdf/>.

Briggs, A. W., et al. (2010). Removal of deaminated cytosines and detection of *in vivo* methylation in ancient DNA. *Nucleic Acids Research, 38,* e87.

Brotherton, P., et al. (2007). Novel high-resolution characterization of ancient DNA reveals C → U-type base modification events as the sole cause of post mortem miscoding lesions. *Nucleic Acids Research, 35,* 5717–5728.

d'Abbadie, M., et al. (2007). Molecular breeding of polymerases for amplification of ancient DNA. *Nature Biotechnology, 25,* 939–943.

Di Bernardo, G., et al. (2002). Enzymatic repair of selected cross-linked homoduplex molecules enhances nuclear gene rescue from Pompeii and Herculaneum remains. *Nucleic Acids Research, 30,* 16–21.

Kovatsi, L., et al. (2009). DNA repair enables sex identification in genetic material from human teeth. *Hippokratia, 13,* 165–168.

McDonald, J. P., et al. (2006). Novel thermostable Y-family polymerases: applications for the PCR amplification of damaged or ancient DNAs. *Nucleic Acids Research, 34,* 1102–1111.

Mitchell, D., et al. (2005). Damage and repair of ancient DNA. *Mutation Research, 571,* 265–276.

Nelson, J. (2009). Repair of damaged DNA for forensic analysis. Final Report on NIJ Grant 2006-DN-BX-K018. Available at <http://www.ncjrs.gov/pdffiles1/nij/grants/227498.pdf/>.

preCR Repair Mix. <http://www.neb.com/nebecomm/products/productM0309.asp/>.

Pusch, C. M., et al. (1998). Repair of degraded duplex DNA from prehistoric samples using *Escherichia coli* DNA polymerase I and T4 DNA ligase. *Nucleic Acids Research, 26,* 857–859.

Shapiro, B. (2008). Engineered polymerases amplify the potential of ancient DNA. *Trends in Biotechnology, 26,* 285–287.

CHAPTER

11

Low-Level DNA Testing: Issues, Concerns, and Solutions

INTRODUCTION TO ISSUES AND HISTORICAL OVERVIEW

The polymerase chain reaction (PCR) is very sensitive and STR typing results have been demonstrated from as little DNA as that contained in a single collected cell (Findlay et al. 1997). This capability has encouraged attempts to try to recover DNA profiles from touch evidence that might be helpful in a case. However, this low-level DNA analysis can sometimes push the envelope of what constitutes reliable results unless measures are taken to demonstrate reproducibility of allele calls. This chapter will address approaches to improve DNA sensitivity and efforts made to strengthen reliability with low-level DNA testing.

Terms and Definitions

First, it is worth discussing a few terms that are commonly used to describe low-level DNA testing. The most common is probably *low copy number*—often shortened to the abbreviation LCN. More recently, some labs have begun referring to LCN as *low template DNA* (LT-DNA or LTDNA) to reflect the fact that very small amounts of DNA are being examined. The term LCN typically relates to using a higher sensitivity techique while the term LTDNA is meant to focus on the sample. Others have called this technique the analysis of DNA of low quality and quantity (DNALQQ). Throughout this chapter this topic is primarily called "low-level DNA" but these other terms are interchangeable in most instances.

Although there is not really a rigid line dividing low-level DNA from conventional STR typing (Gill & Buckleton 2010), a number of different definitions have been debated. The definitions can be divided into several groups: (1) those that refer to the amount of DNA tested in the PCR reaction (e.g., <100 pg or <200 pg) based on some form of quantitation assay, (2) a methodology usually involving increasing the number of PCR cycles (e.g., 34 cycles instead of 28 cycles) to improve assay sensitivity, and (3) DNA profile appearance that exhibits an increased imbalance of observed alleles (e.g., heterozygote peak height ratios below 60%). In all these definitional approaches, it is recognized that data reliability is inferior when lower amounts of DNA are tested and thus additional measures must be taken to improve the chance of obtaining results that accurately reflect the sample being examined.

LTDNA has been defined as "an ultra sensitive technique that has the potential to yield a DNA profile from sub-optimal biological samples" (Caddy et al. 2008). Another definition prepared by a U.S.-based committee in January 2009 is more explicit: "Based upon a laboratory's internal validation, any DNA typing results generated from limited quantity and/or quality DNA template using conditions that have demonstrated increased stochastic effects are defined as LCN or Low Level DNA analyses. The stochastic effects which may be observed in DNA samples subjected to these conditions include allelic drop-in or drop-out, increased stutter and increased intra-locus peak height imbalance. When used to analyze limited quantity and/or quality DNA template below the stochastic thresholds, LCN conditions may include the following: additional amplification cycles, post-amplification purification, reduced reaction volume, injection enhancement by increased voltage or time, and nested PCR" (SWGDAM Ad Hoc LCN Committee 2009, personal notes). Here the focus is more on performance issues rather than specifying a particular amount of DNA under which less reliable results may be obtained.

Many laboratories have demonstrated the ability to obtain DNA profiles from very small amounts of sample. Low-level DNA testing typically refers to examination of less than 100 pg of input DNA, or about 15 diploid cells (Gill et al. 2000). Others have raised their definitional LCN threshold to 200 pg or about 30 diploid cells (Caddy et al. 2008, Budowle et al. 2009).

Uses with Touch DNA and Potential Transfer Issues

The capability of obtaining a useful DNA profile is often only limited by the ability of the forensic investigator to find and collect the appropriate evidence. Remarkably, DNA profiles may be obtained from fingerprint residues due to cells that are left on the objects that are touched (van Oorschot & Jones 1997). DNA technology may permit the handles of tools used in crimes, such as knives or guns, to be effectively evaluated and used to link a perpetrator to his crime. A December 2010 review article on forensic trace DNA cites over 200 articles on this topic (van Oorschot et al. 2010).

It is important to realize that when trying to work with extremely low levels of DNA template, recovered DNA profiles may not be associated with the crime event itself but rather have been left innocently before the crime occurred (Gill 2001). Secondary transfer of skin cells due to casual contact such as hand shaking has been demonstrated to occur in controlled laboratory settings (Farmen et al. 2008). This phenomenon occurs to a variable degree depending on what kind of a "shedder" the individuals are (Lowe et al. 2002). A more recent study found no good shedders out of 60 volunteers tested (Phipps & Petricevic 2007). As noted in Chapter 1, potential transfer of DNA is highly variable depending on surface texture and sample moisture.

LT-DNA Labs and Published Studies

While many laboratories may be performing testing with low amounts of DNA, currently only a few laboratories are formally conducting LT-DNA casework with specific enhanced detection protocols. These LT-DNA laboratories include the Forensic Science

Service (Birmingham, UK), LGC Forensics (Middlesex, UK), Orchid Cellmark (Abingdon, UK), the Netherlands Forensic Institute (NFI, The Hague, The Netherlands), Institute for Environmental Science & Research (ESR, Auckland, New Zealand), the Swedish National Laboratory of Forensic Science (Linköping, Sweden), the German Bundeskriminalamt (BKA, Wiesbaden, Germany), the International Commission on Missing Persons DNA Laboratory (ICMP, Sarajevo, Bosnia and Herzegovina), the Armed Forces DNA Identification Laboratory (Rockville, Maryland), the University of North Texas Center for Human Identification (Ft. Worth, Texas), and the New York City Office of Chief Medical Examiner (NYC OCME) Forensic Biology Laboratory. The applications of LT-DNA testing range from missing persons investigations to forensic casework.

In addition to the early work by the FSS (Gill et al. 2000, Whitaker et al. 2001), validation studies on LT-DNA techniques have been published by scientists from NFI (Kloosterman et al. 2003, Western et al. 2009, Benschop et al. 2010), LGC (Forster et al. 2008, Gross et al. 2009), Orchid Cellmark (Roeder et al. 2009), NYC OCME (Caragine et al. 2009) and ESR (Petricevic et al. 2010). John Buckleton speculates that more LT-DNA validation articles have not been published because journals may not consider the techniques sufficiently novel (Buckleton 2009).

Historical Overview of Low-Level DNA Testing

Since the late 1990s, there have been numerous efforts with low-level DNA testing (Table 11.1). Single-cell analysis for clinical applications were being performed in 1995 (Findlay et al. 1995) and demonstrated with STR typing by 1997 (Findlay et al. 1997). Pierre Taberlet and colleagues at the French Laboratoire de Biologie des Populations d'Altitude first published the concept of performing replicate PCR amplifications to improve reliability with low quantities of DNA and only recording an allele if it was observed at least twice (Taberlet et al. 1996). As will be seen later in the chapter, this replicate amplification strategy has become the core feature of reliable low-level DNA testing.

Beginning in 1999, the FSS led the way with application of LCN to forensic DNA testing (Gill et al. 2000, Whitaker et al. 2001). The FSS also studied secondary transfer (Lowe et al. 2002) and eventually developed software to probabilistically model stochastic effects (Gill et al. 2007). In December 2007, the Omagh bombing case outcome (D.N.A. Box 11.1) led to a temporary suspension of LCN testing in the UK and the formation of a Forensic Regulator to oversee quality assurance efforts.

Within the U.S., the FBI urged caution and discouraged efforts towards LCN DNA analysis for criminal casework (Budowle et al. 2001). However, the NYC OCME began research with low-level DNA testing in 2001 and casework in 2006 after approval from the New York Forensic Science Commission. Over the past decade, they have published improvements to DNA extraction (Schiffner et al. 2005), procedures for decontaminating plasticware and water used in PCR reactions (Tamariz et al. 2006), and a description of their extensive validation studies (Caragine et al. 2009).

LCN Critics and the Omagh Trial

As with any technique that is subjected to scrutiny in court proceedings, there are often individuals with opposing points of view testifying for the defense. Critics of low-level DNA

TABLE 11.1 Timeline for Low-Level DNA Work.

Year	Events
1995	Single cell analysis for clinical applications (Findlay et al.)
1996	Reliable results from pg quantities using replicate amplifications (Taberlet et al.)
1997	DNA results from single cells (Findlay et al.); DNA results from touched objects (van Oorschot & Jones)
1998	Nested PCR approach (Strom & Rechitsky)
1999	SGM Plus kit released; FSS begins LCN casework with 34-cycle SGM Plus
2000	FSS LCN paper published (Gill et al.)
2001	FSS SGM Plus LCN paper published (Whitaker et al.); NYC OCME begins research; FBI urges caution (Budowle et al.)
2002	Secondary transfer studied (Lowe et al.); LCN data accepted on UK NDNAD
2003	Dutch publications on advantages & limitations of LCN (Kloosterman & Kersbergen)
2004	Whole genome amplification ineffective with low-level DNA (Schneider et al.)
2005	Modeling experiments (Gill et al.); NYC OCME receives approval from New York Forensic Science Commission for LT-DNA testing
2006	NYC OCME goes online with LT-DNA testing; ISFG DNA Commission publication on mixtures (recommendation #9 discusses LT-DNA)
2007	LoComationN software described (Gill et al.); Judgment in the Omagh bombing case (*R v Hoey*); interim suspension of FSS LCN
2008	Caddy report issued; Forensic Regulator response; LGC publication (Forster et al.)
2009	Critical review (Budowle et al.) and OCME validation (Caragine et al.) published; ISFG and ISHI conference debates; UK appeal (*R v Reed & Anor*) ruling in favor of FSS LCN
2010	SWGDAM committee established; NYC *Frye* ruling (*NY v Megnath*) allows OCME LT-DNA results; Wallace case in New Zealand finds LCN not inherently unreliable
2011	*Forensic Science International: Genetics* publishes several Letters to the Editor with an accompanying editorial requesting more science and less quarrelling on the topic

testing have included Professor Allan Jamieson of the Forensic Institute in Glascow, Scotland (http://www.theforensicinstitute.com/), Professor Dan Krane of Wright State University in Dayton, Ohio and founder of Forensic Bioinformatics (http://www.bioforensics.com/), and Professor Bruce Budowle of the University of North Texas Institute of Investigative Genetics in Fort Worth, Texas, who for many years was a senior scientist at the FBI Laboratory. At many of the trials involving LT-DNA, one or more of these three critics have voiced their concerns regarding low-level DNA analysis.

By early 2010, the UK's Forensic Science Service, which pioneered the approach more than a decade ago (Gill et al. 2000), reportedly had used LCN analysis on over 21,000 criminal cases (Gilbert 2010). However, the FSS efforts with LCN are most often connected to the 2007 Omagh bombing trial (D.N.A. Box 11.1) and the subsequent fallout that lead to

D.N.A. BOX 11.1

THE OMAGH BOMBING TRIAL

On the afternoon of Saturday, August 15, 1998, a car bomb exploded in the middle of a busy shopping center in the Northern Ireland town of Omagh. The powerful explosion destroyed the downtown area, killed 29 people, and injured over 200 others. It is considered by the media as Northern Ireland's worst terrorist attack. Pictures and information regarding those killed at Omagh are available at http://www.wesleyjohnston.com/users/ireland/past/omagh/dead.html.

Within a few weeks, the police arrested 12 men in connection with the crime, but all were subsequently released without charges due to lack of evidence against them. In February 1999, the police arrested Colm Murphy, a local building contractor, for questioning in connection with the Omagh bombing. Murphy was later charged and subsequently convicted in 2002 to 14 years in prison for conspiring to cause the Omagh bombing. However, in 2005, his conviction was overturned on appeal and in February 2010, Murphy was acquitted in a retrial in spite of being found liable for the bombing along with three others in a 2009 civil court ruling.

In September 2006, Murphy's nephew—an electrician named Sean Hoey—was placed on trial with 29 counts of murder as well as terrorism and explosive charges. A key part of the trial involved low-level DNA analysis by the Forensic Science Service on pieces of tape from the bomb timer and explosive wiring. When the controversial trial concluded on December 20, 2007, Mr. Hoey was found not guilty of all 58 charges brought against him.

But perhaps even more significantly the judge—Justice Weir—lashed out against the handling of the DNA evidence. Court records state: "The evidence establishes that the arrangements within the police in 1998 and 1999 for the recording and storage of items were thoroughly disorganized" (*R v Hoey*, paragraph 51). As noted in Chapter 1 of this book, if the evidence handling and chain-of-custody (bagging, labeling, packaging, storage, tracking, and transmission of evidence) is in doubt, then a case may be in jeopardy regardless of the DNA test results. In addition, because evidence in this case was handled prior to the development and implementation of the FSS LCN procedures, there were no programs in place by the crime scene investigators for special handling of evidentiary items that would later be scrutinized by the FSS with their highly sensitive 34-cycle LCN technique.

Justice Weir also expressed "concern about the present state of the validation of the science and methodology associated with LCN DNA and, in consequence, its reliability as an evidential tool." In particular, his ruling stated, "I am not satisfied that the publishing of two journal articles [(Gill et al. 2000, Whitaker et al. 2001)] describing a process invented by the authors can be regarded without more as having 'validated' that process for the purpose of its being confidently used for evidential purposes."

Media around the world picked up on the purported problems with LCN and suddenly the *The Queen v Sean Hoey* (*R v Hoey*) case became synonymous with poor DNA test results.

Sources:

R v Hoey (2007). Available at http://www.denverda.org/DNA_Documents/Hoey.pdf.
http://en.wikipedia.org/wiki/Omagh_bombing
http://en.wikipedia.org/wiki/Colm_Murphy
http://news.bbc.co.uk/2/hi/uk_news/northern_ireland/7154221.stm
http://news.bbc.co.uk/2/hi/uk_news/northern_ireland/7149505.stm

a review of the FSS efforts, the "Caddy Report" recommendations (D.N.A. Box 11.2), and establishment of a Forensic Science Regulator in the United Kingdom.

The Caddy Report and the Forensic Science Regulator

The Omagh bombing case (*R v Hoey*) judgment against LCN DNA testing in December 2007 sent shockwaves through forensic service providers in the United Kingdom, particularly the Forensic Science Service. An interim suspension was put on all LCN DNA analysis in criminal investigations in England and Wales while an internal review of on-going cases involving the FSS and LCN DNA was performed between December 21, 2007 and January 14, 2008.

The Crown Prosecution Service (CPS) that conducted this internal review concluded "that LCN DNA analysis provided by the FSS should remain available as potentially admissible evidence" (CPS Press Release, January 14, 2008). The CPS press release went on to state that "at present, there is no reason to believe that there is any inherent unreliability in the LCN DNA analysis process provided that it is carried out according to the prescribed processes, and that the results are properly interpreted. In its work so far, the review has found nothing that would indicate any serious flaws in the scientific principles."

A Forensic Science Regulator was established to help strengthen quality assurance processes in the UK. In addition, an expert review of LT-DNA was conducted from November 2007 to April 2008. Because this review was led by Professor Brian Caddy of Strathclyde University (Glasgow, Scotland), it is typically referred to as the "Caddy Report". Also serving with Professor Caddy were Dr. Graham Taylor of Cancer Research UK (Leeds, England) and Dr. Adrian Linacre, who was from Strathclyde University at the time.

The authors of the Caddy Report state that "it is our opinion that LCN and LTD[NA] are extensions of the internationally accepted process of standard DNA profiling" (Caddy et al. 2008, section 7.2). They further conclude that "reservations [with regard to the LCN technique] have been allayed from a study of the raw data produced by the FSS, recent experimental work conducted by the FSS and also from detailed information submitted by the other [UK] forensic science providers which clearly demonstrate the soundness of LTDNA analysis (including LCN) *providing all the appropriate conditions are met*" (emphasis added).

The Caddy Report emphasizes that "any LTDNA profile should always be reported to the jury with the caveats: that the nature of the original starting material is unknown; that the time at which the DNA was transferred cannot be inferred; and that the opportunity for secondary transfer is increased in comparison to standard DNA profiling" (Caddy et al. 2008, section 7.4). The report concluded with 21 recommendations (D.N.A. Box 11.2).

In May 2008, about a month after the Caddy Report was issued, the Forensic Science Regulator Andrew Rennison responded. Mr. Rennison concluded that after having considered the Caddy Report: "I am content that the science underpinning the LTDNA analytical services, as provided to the [criminal justice system], is sound and that the three forensic science suppliers [FSS, LGC Forensics, Orchid Cellmark Ltd] offering such services have properly validated their processes. There is no flaw inherent in the process which prevents its use with the [criminal justice system]" (Forensic Science Regulator 2008).

D.N.A. BOX 11.2

CADDY REPORT RECOMMENDATIONS

The Caddy Report, named for Professor Brian Caddy who led the investigation, was an expert panel review of low template DNA (LTDNA) work conducted from November 2007 to April 2008 as a follow-up to the concerns raised duing the Omagh bombing trial (D.N.A. Box 11.1). The Caddy report concluded with 21 recommendations provided primarily to the UK Forensic Science Regulator, which are summarized below. These 21 recommendations can be grouped into broad areas of training, quality standards, and research.

1. Institute a national education program teaching the advantages and limitations of LTDNA for crime scene investigators
2. Come to an agreement on what constitutes LTDNA success
3. Institute appropriate training programs and set standards to enable police forces to have a full grasp of what constitutes LTDNA analysis, and how such samples are to be collected and stored especially in relation to issues of contamination and the likelihood of success
4. Monitor the use of DNA quantification procedures
5. Ensure collection of DNA profiles from all serving operational police officers and crime scene personnel as a means of eliminating irrelevant DNA profiles
6. Establish a national standard for "DNA clean" consumables, especially in relation to crime scene recovery kits; only kits that meet such a standard should be used by police forces
7. Ensure the batch testing of all DNA reagents to verify that they are DNA free prior to their use
8. Oversee compliance with standards of competence for LTDNA laboratory specialists and suggest modifications where needed to training programs and record keeping
9. Police forensic science laboratories need to be accredited and comply with ISO 17025
10. Quantification of the material extracted for analysis from LTDNA samples must be undertaken
11. Develop a consensus from all the forensic science providers on how profiles and mixed profiles are to be interpreted—and then monitor their implementation and encourage openness in the availability of information that may have an impact on the way DNA profiles are interpreted in the context of a case; there needs to be a national agreement on how LTDNA profiles are to be interpreted especially in relation to "allele drop in and out," stochastic effects, inhibition, and mixtures
12. Institute a regular program of inspections of documentation associated with all validations
13. State appropriate caveats in witness statements/court reports when LTDNA analyses have been undertaken
14. Gather an independent internationally recognized expert panel to review validation data on a regular basis; copies of raw validation data should be lodged with the Regulator before the method is introduced into service
15. Assess the advantages and disadvantages of different approaches

D.N.A. BOX 11.2 (*cont'd*)

to LTDNA analysis; mention of a forthcoming paper that is now published (Forster et al. 2008)

16. Improve existing guidelines and standards with an advisory group; develop documentation that would guide the courts in the interpretation of evidence
17. Consider alternative technologies, such as the use of next generation sequencers; tap into the expertise of the Wellcome Trust Sanger Institute and look into mechanisms for improving funding
18. Seek funding for independent research and validation that is open to national competition
19. Establish national minimum technical standards for extraction, quantification/dilution and interpretation criteria that will be agreed upon by all forensic science providers
20. Quantify the problem of financing forensic science and explore mechanisms to correct any problems the inquiries reveal
21. Explore the means of establishing a professional forensic science provider's organization in order to develop mutually agreed standards

***Source*:**

Caddy, B. et al. (2008) Review of the science of low template DNA analysis. Available at http://police.homeoffice.gov.uk/publications/operational-policing/Review_of_Low_Template_DNA_1.pdf.

Scientific Conference Debates in 2009 & 2010

The debate of how to handle LT-DNA samples reached a boiling point at two large international scientific conferences in the fall of 2009. The International Society for Forensic Genetics (ISFG) concluded its September 15–18, 2009 conference in Buenos Aires, Argentina with presentations by Adrian Linacre, Bruce Budowle, and Peter Gill. Short articles describing the presenter's positions have been published in volume 2 of the *Forensic Science International: Genetics Supplement Series* (*Progress in Forensic Genetics 13*) available at http://www.fsigeneticssup.com/.

A month later the International Symposium on Human Identification (ISHI) sponsored by Promega Corporation held an LCN panel on October 15, 2009 in Las Vegas, Nevada. This LCN panel consisted of Charlotte Word, Bruce Budowle, Theresa Caragine, Angela van Daal, Gillian Tully, Brad Leventhal, and John Butler. Information on most of the presenter's positions is available in the March 2010 and September 2010 issues of Promega's *Profiles in DNA* available at http://www.promega.com/profiles/. Some of the presentations are also available on the NIST STRBase website at http://www.cstl.nist.gov/biotech/strbase/LTDNA.htm.

In September 2010, a follow-up debate occurred at the Australian-New Zealand Forensic Science Society (ANZFSS) meeting in Sydney, Australia with Peter Gill and John Buckleton supporting properly performed LT-DNA work and Bruce Budowle and Angela van Daal sharing their concerns regarding LCN in general. Adding to the drama of this debate was a series of Letters to the Editor that appeared throughout 2010 on the http://www.fsigenetics.com/inpress website.

These Letters to the Editor were published in the January 2011 issue of *Forensic Science International: Genetics* along with an editorial effectively calling for a "cease fire" and encouraging more scientific data to improve the field rather than revisiting the same arguments over and over (Schneider et al. 2011).

Admissibility within UK, U.S., and New Zealand Courts

In December 2009, the England and Wales Court of Appeals Crown Court ruled that LCN testing was reliable in an important UK appeals case in spite of concerns raised by Allan Jamieson and Bruce Budowle (*R v Reed & Anor 2009*). Within the United States, an important *Frye* hearing in February 2010 ruled in favor of admissibility of LCN DNA typing. This New York Supreme Court case, *The People of the State of New York v. Hemant Megnath*, involved extensive testimony by scientists from the NYC OCME, the FSS, and the DNA subcommittee chair of the New York Forensic Science Commission as well as defense expert testimony from Dan Krane and Bruce Budowle. The court found "that LCN DNA profiling as conducted by the OCME is *not a novel* scientific technique" and "that LCN DNA testing as conducted by the OCME is generally accepted as reliable in the forensic scientific community" (NYC LCN *Frye* hearing, Feb 2010; emphasis in the original).

As of early 2011 there have not been a lot of rulings for or against low template DNA testing because the technique has so far been used extensively in only a relatively few jurisdictions. Most of the court decisions have focused on the big-picture view of the method. For example, a March 2010 New Zealand appeals court ruling, *Michael Scott Wallace v. The Queen*, found "that LCN DNA evidence is not inherently unreliable" (Wallace v. Queen 2010). Although court judgments have ruled in favor of the admissibility and the capability of low-level DNA testing, the specifics of a laboratory's protocol or performance in an individual case may come under scrutiny. Thus, scientists need to be able to demonstrate that their methods have been validated so that the limits of the technique are known, understood, and applied.

STRATEGIES FOR IMPROVING SENSITIVITY

Improved sensitivity in a detection technique is usually a valuable asset to enable results to be obtained from limited biological evidence. Not satisfied with failure to obtain a result with low amounts of DNA template, some laboratories have decided to push the envelope and apply what could be termed "enhanced interrogation techniques" (Butler & Hill 2010). In fact, DNA testing has been successfully applied down to the single-cell level (D.N.A. Box 11.3).

The advantages and disadvantages of various strategies for improving sensitivity with low-level DNA samples are shown in Table 11.2. Each of these strategies will be briefly discussed in the following section.

Increasing detection sensitivity is like turning up the volume on a radio. This action results in improved ability to hear sound at a greater distance. However, increasing the volume may distort the quality of the sound as it becomes louder. Contamination of low amounts of DNA from exogenous sources and the possibility of picking up cells from secondary transfer (see Chapter 1) represent noise that can interfere with detecting the true signal when sensitivity of PCR is heightened.

D.N.A. BOX 11.3

SINGLE CELL STR TYPING SUCCESS RATES OBSERVED IN A 1997 STUDY

The first demonstration of single-cell analysis with short tandem repeat (STR) loci is instructive (Findlay et al. 1997). This work involved collaboration between the Department of Molecular Oncology at the University of Leeds and the Forensic Science Service (FSS), both in the UK. A total of 226 buccal cells from four different individuals were isolated using micromanipulation techniques. These individual cells were then amplified with the FSS Second Generation Multiplex (SGM) assay using AmpliTaq Gold and 34 cycles to improve sensitivity. The SGM assay amplified six STR markers (FGA, TH01, vWA, D8S1179, D18S51, and D21S11) as well as amelogenin for sex-typing purposes (see Chapter 5). Single-cell results were compared with known DNA profiles from the four donors. While a full (and correct) DNA profile was observed in 50% of the single-cell tests, some kind of result was obtained in 91% of the tests. Some of these single-test results did not accurately represent the original donor DNA profile due to allele drop-out or drop-in.

A summary of the Findlay et al. (1997) results are shown below:

Number of single cells analyzed	226
Results obtained	206 (91%)
Full STR profile (amelogenin, 6 STRs)	114 (50%)
Acceptable profile (amelogenin, 5 to 6 STRs)	144 (64%)
Partial profile (1 to 4 STRs)	62 (27%)
Amplification failure	20 (9%)
Allele drop-out	88 (39%)
Surplus alleles (apparent mixture)	28 (12%)
False alleles (allele drop-in)	11 (5%)

The enhanced sensitivity that brought 91% amplification success also resulted in allele drop-out and drop-in due to stochastic effects (see Chapter 4). Allele drop-in (noted as "surplus alleles" and "false alleles" in the original article) occurred in approximately 17% of the PCR amplifications. With the "surplus alleles" situation, additional alleles were present in combination with the true donor alleles creating an apparent mixture. In the "false alleles" situation, the extra alleles replaced the true alleles, which had dropped out. This study found that with the 39% allele drop-out observed, each allele had about a 10% probability of being missing. Thus, wild-card designations permitting any allele to be considered in statistical calculations are important to properly assess evidence analyzed from low-level DNA. This work laid the groundwork for the future FSS developments in low-copy-number DNA analysis.

Source:

Findlay, I., et al. (1997). DNA fingerprinting from single cells. Nature, *389, 555–556.*

TABLE 11.2 Advantages and Limitations of Different Sensitivity Improvement Strategies. Most Strategies Involve Either Creating More PCR Product during DNA Amplification or Injecting More PCR Product into the Capillary Electrophoresis (CE) to Improve Detection.

Strategy	Advantage	Limitation	Example Reference
Increased number of PCR cycles	Creates more PCR product	Allele drop-in possible	Gill et al. (2000)
Post-PCR sample desalting	Improves injection of PCR product into CE capillary	Extra expense to sample processing; stochastic threshold needs to be raised to avoid false homozygote designations	Smith & Ballantyne (2007)
Increased CE injection	Improves amount of PCR product injected into CE capillary	Stochastic threshold needs to be raised to avoid false homozygote designations	Westen et al. (2009)
Reduced volume PCR	Concentrates PCR product relative to amount subjected to CE analysis	PCR inhibitors may be concentrated causing amplification failure; pipetting precision can be more challenging	Leclair et al. (2003)
Nested PCR	Creates more PCR product	Prone to contamination because tubes are opened to add second round of primers and reagents	Strom & Rechitsky (1998)
PCR enhancements (primer positions, polymerase concentration, etc.)	Creates more PCR product	Stochastic threshold needs to be raised to avoid false homozygote designations	MiniFiler kit (see Chapter 10)
mtDNA	Higher starting copy number per cell	Lower power of discrimination; cannot resolve individuals from same maternal lineage	Holland & Parsons (1999)

Increased Number of PCR Cycles

In the late 1990s, the United Kingdom's Forensic Science Service pioneered the application of LCN analysis through increasing the number of PCR cycles in order to improve DNA detection sensitivity (Gill et al. 2000, Whitaker et al. 2001). Instead of using their STR kit manufacturer's recommended 28 cycles, which has a theoretical yield of 67 million copies for each target DNA sequence, an additional six cycles (34 total) are run to provide a theoretical yield of 4.3 billion copies or a 64-fold improvement in sensitivity (see Table 4.1). A more recent approach to high-sensitivity DNA testing uses a three-cycle signal enhancement to provide a theoretical 16-fold improvement in sensitivity (Caragine et al. 2009).

This increase in PCR amplification cycles enables STR typing to routinely obtain results with samples containing less than 100 pg of DNA template (Figure 11.1). However, application of low level DNA results should be approached with caution due to the possibilities of

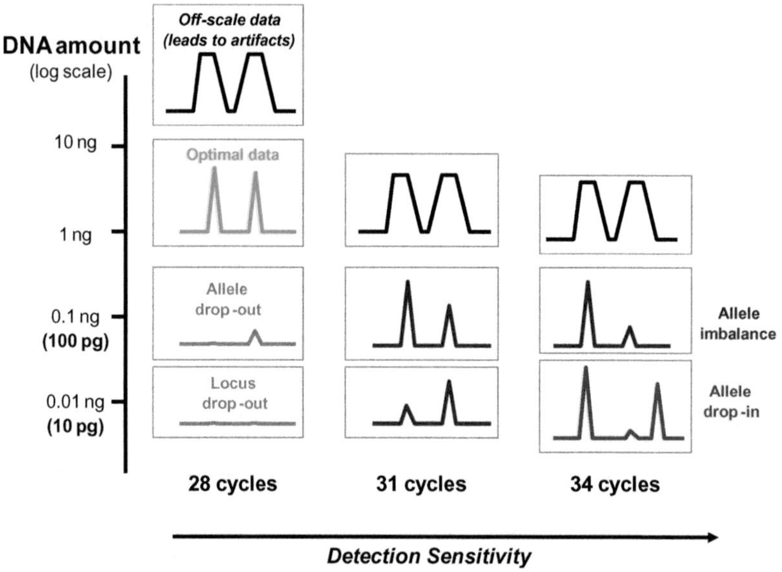

FIGURE 11.1 Illustration of hypothetical results at a heterozygous locus (two alleles expected in each box) with various levels of input DNA and detection sensitivity that is modulated through increasing the number of PCR cycles. Note that off-scale data occurs with lower amounts of DNA as the detection sensitivity is increased.

allele drop-out, allele drop-in, and increased risks of collection-based and laboratory-based contamination.

The original FSS approach was to run 34 PCR cycles with the SGM Plus kit without performing prior DNA quantitation. Thus, some "LCN" samples could be a nanogram or more in amount and generate off-scale data (Figure 11.1). The NFI developed a 28-cycle protocol with an extra six-cycle option (28 + 6) after the addition of fresh DNA polymerase (Kloosterman & Kersbergen 2003). The 28 + 6 approach permits screening samples at the 28-cycle level to prevent high amounts of DNA from being tested with the full 34-cycle enhanced method.

In 2001, Bruce Budowle and colleagues from the FBI Laboratory proposed several alternative strategies to boost STR profile signals without increasing PCR cycle number and experiencing the concomitant increased risk of contamination (Budowle et al. 2001). These strategies include: (1) increasing the injection time on the capillary electrophoresis (CE) instrument, (2) sample salt reduction through filtration of the PCR product to remove ions that compete with the STR amplicons when being injected into the capillary or use of a formamide with lower conductivity, and (3) reducing the PCR volume to get a more concentrated PCR product.

While these signal enhancement techniques can be helpful in some situations, none are as powerful in terms of boosting sensitivity as increasing the PCR cycle number.

Increased CE Injection

Detection sensitivity may also be improved through increasing the amount of PCR product added to the CE capillary by raising the voltage of the electrokinetic injection, lengthening the time of injection, or both. Higher levels of PCR product passing the detector in the CE instrument lead to increased peak intensities. The standard injection for an ABI 3100 or 3130xl Genetic Analyzer is 10 s at 3 kV or 30 kV-s (see Chapter 6). The LGC Forensics DNA SenCE technique (Forster et al. 2008) involves increased CE injections (30 s at 4 kV or 120 kV-s) as well as sample desalting (see next section) while the Orchid Cellmark EnhanCE (Roeder et al. 2009) approach adds nine times the amount of purified PCR product to the sample subjected to the electrokinetic injection. ESR uses 15 s at 5 kV or 75 kV-s for their enhanced injection (Petricevic et al. 2010) while NFI utilizes 15 s at 9 kV or 135 kV-s (Westen et al. 2009).

Post-PCR Purification

As discussed in Chapter 6, the quantity of DNA injected into a CE capillary using electrokinetic injection is inversely proportional to the amount of salt present in the sample. An easy way for improving signal is to lower the salt levels in the sample. Salts such as potassium chloride and magnesium chloride are a necessary part of the buffers used with DNA polymerase to perform PCR. Thus, post-PCR purification is performed to remove salts when they are no longer needed.

This purification process requires an extra step and additional expense but works well. Several products have been used including QIAGEN's MinElute (Smith & Ballantyne 2007, Forster et al. 2008), Millipore's Montage (Roeder et al. 2009), and Edge BioSystems' Performa DTR gel filtration columns (Westen et al. 2009). PCR products can also be diluted into low-conductivity formamide to aid sample injections. With all of these salt-level reduction techniques, CE signal will improve. Internal validation is necessary to verify performance and to set stochastic thresholds (see Chapter 7).

Reduced PCR Volume

Reducing PCR volume effectively concentrates the reagents and sample being amplified. Slight improvements in PCR amplification can be seen when using a smaller volume (Leclair et al. 2003). A disadvantage is that PCR inhibitors are also concentrated with a smaller volume PCR reaction, which may lead to amplification failure or reduced efficiency.

Nested PCR

Although not widely used anymore due to the possibility of contaminating a laboratory with PCR product, nested PCR has demonstrated the ability to improve detection sensitivity with low levels of DNA template (Strom & Rechitsky 1998). Nested PCR typically involves two separate PCR reactions on the same DNA template with a transfer step in between. The first round acts as a booster for the second round, which often utilizes different primers that bind internally and create smaller PCR products than the first-round target amplicon. A major problem with this approach is that amplification tubes must be opened to introduce new reagents for the second round or to transfer a portion of the first round amplicons to the second round PCR tube. Once a laboratory is contaminated with PCR product it is very difficult to get rid of it. This, of course, is why pre- and post-PCR areas are separated physically in forensic DNA laboratories (see Chapter 4).

Altering PCR Parameters besides Cycle Number

Since 2007 commercial suppliers of STR typing kits have released next-generation kits with improved buffers and possibly an increased amount of DNA polymerase (the user does not know the amount because it is added by the manufacturer). These new buffer-polymerase master mixes have a greater ability to cope with PCR inhibitors, which improves PCR efficiency.

In addition, some kits contain miniSTR primers (see Chapter 10). Moving PCR primers closer to the repeat region can improve PCR amplification success with degraded DNA but also improves PCR yield slightly because smaller PCR products are being generated.

Mitochondrial DNA Testing

When nuclear DNA levels are very low in a sample, such as a telogen hair shaft, mitochondrial DNA (mtDNA) testing may be employed due to a higher number of mtDNA molecules per cell (see Chapter 14). The higher initial copy number improves the chances of obtaining a result in many cases. A major disadvantage with the use of mtDNA testing is the loss of specificity due to maternal relatives having identical mtDNA sequences. However, mtDNA can be very effective in aiding missing persons investigations (see Chapter 9).

CONCERNS AND CHALLENGES WITH LOW-LEVEL DNA SAMPLES

While fluorescent multiplexes have been used to obtain STR typing results from as little as a single buccal cell, a number of challenges exist when trying to obtain results from low amounts of template DNA. Attempts to generate results with low levels of DNA come up against a fundamental scientific barrier of stochastic amplification (see Chapter 4). The stochastic effects exist due to random selection of alleles when a diluted DNA template-to-primer-to-polymerase ratio exists. Even sample enrichment techniques such as whole genome amplification have not successfully overcome this problem (Schneider et al. 2004).

Stochastic Effects during PCR Amplification of Low-Level DNA

As forensic DNA analysts attempt to recover information from low amounts of DNA present in evidentiary samples, they will encounter stochastic or random sampling effects that occur in the early cycles of PCR amplification. When a limited number of DNA template target molecules exist in a sample, the PCR primers used to amplify a specific region may not consistently find and hybridize to the entire set of DNA molecules present in the PCR amplification reaction.

When enhanced detection methods are employed at least four artifacts typically arise: (1) *allele drop-in*, where additional alleles are often observed in the DNA profile from sporadic contamination, (2) *allele drop-out*, where an allele that is present in the original sample fails to amplify due to stochastic effects, (3) *increased stutter product formation*, where stutter products are often higher than the typical 5% to 10% of the nominal allele, and (4) *heterozygote peak imbalance* is often exacerbated due to stochastic PCR amplification. If one of the alleles is amplified preferentially by chance during the early rounds of PCR, then a peak

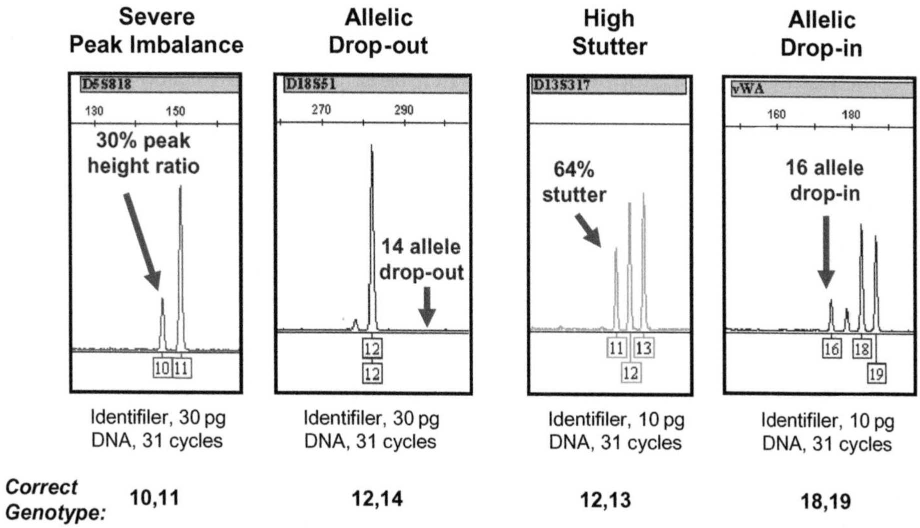

FIGURE 11.2 Stochastic effects that randomly occur when PCR amplifying low amounts of DNA using an increased number of PCR cycles. The STR typing kit, amount of DNA, and number of PCR cycles along with the correct genotype for each example are listed at the bottom. For further information on these samples, see http://www.cstl.nist.gov/biotech/strbase/LTDNA.htm.

height imbalance of greater than 60% can be observed between heterozygous alleles that should be equal or very similar in amount.

With a heterozygous locus, where two alleles are present, the unequal sampling of the alleles can result in failure to detect one or both of the alleles. Loss of a single allele is referred to as *allele drop-out* while loss of both alleles is termed *locus drop-out*. Allele drop-out can be thought of as an extreme form of heterozygote peak imbalance where one of the alleles has a peak height of zero.

Stochastic (random) variation is a fundamental physical law of the PCR amplification process when examining low amounts of DNA. Stochastic effects are manifest as a fluctuation of results between replicate analyses. In extreme stochastic sampling events, PCR amplifying the same DNA extract twice can result in different alleles being detected at a locus.

When pushing assay sensitivity through an increased number of PCR cycles, stochastic effects can become more evident. Figure 11.2 illustrates results possessing the different types of stochastic effects that may be observed when performing PCR amplification from low amounts of DNA: allele drop-out, allele drop-in, elevated stutter, and heterozygote peak imbalance.

The stochastic variation observed with the test results shown in Figure 11.2 would produce an incorrect result if no further information was available. Loss of signal, such as in the D18S51 allelic drop-out example, would make a true "12,14" heterozygote appear as a "12,12" homozygote. Likewise, the gain of signal with the high stutter or allelic drop-in could make a true single-source sample appear to be a mixture. Thus, when using enhanced interrogation techniques, such as a higher number of PCR cycles, further testing measures are required to avoid reporting incorrect results.

Since stochastic effects cannot be avoided when testing small quantities of DNA, there are essentially two schools of thought on how to handle these types of samples: (1) stop testing or interpreting data before you go low enough to be in the stochastic realm, or (2) try to limit the impact of the stochastic variation by additional testing and careful interpretation guidelines based on validation studies (Butler & Hill 2010). Those who advocate the second approach usually enhance their method sensitivity, such as increasing the number of PCR cycles, in order to get as much out of the limited sample as possible. The "enhanced interrogation" approach typically involves replicate testing and the development of consensus profiles.

APPROACHES TO IMPROVING RELIABILITY OF RESULTS

When working with low amounts of DNA, there are three primary areas in which to potentially improve the reliability of results obtained: (1) improving DNA recovery at the collection and extraction stages so that there is more starting material, (2) improving recovery of correct profiles at the analysis stage through replicate PCR amplifications, and (3) accounting for potential allele drop-out and other stochastic effects during statistical interpretation of data acquired.

Improving DNA Recovery

DNA recovery can potentially be improved at several stages in the sampling process. Some of the cells collected on a swab during evidence sampling may not be fully released from the swab during DNA extraction. In addition, the DNA found within recovered cells may not be fully released upon DNA extraction or may bind to the tube walls during sample storage. When DNA extraction requires multiple washes or steps involving fluid transfer, a portion of the sample may be lost at each step along the way. Direct PCR (see Chapter 4) has the potential to greatly improve success rates with low amounts of starting material because no transfer steps are involved.

Researchers at the NFI found that a nylon flocked swab provided a six-fold improvement in cellular elution compared to standard cotton swabs that appear to retain sperm cells (Benschop et al. 2010). The NYC OCME showed that the addition of 1 ng carrier RNA to the Microcon filter used to concentrate the DNA aided sample recovery (Schiffner et al. 2005). While progress has been made in this area, there is probably still room for improving DNA recovery efficiencies.

Replicate Testing and Consensus Profiles

The area that has gotten the most attention for trying to improve the reliability of low-level DNA testing is replicate testing. In order to avoid or limit the possibility of getting the wrong answer when testing low amounts of DNA, replicate PCR amplifications are performed and a consensus profile developed (Taberlet et al. 1996). The standard practice is to PCR amplify either two or three aliquots of a DNA extract (Gill et al. 2000, Caragine et al. 2009).

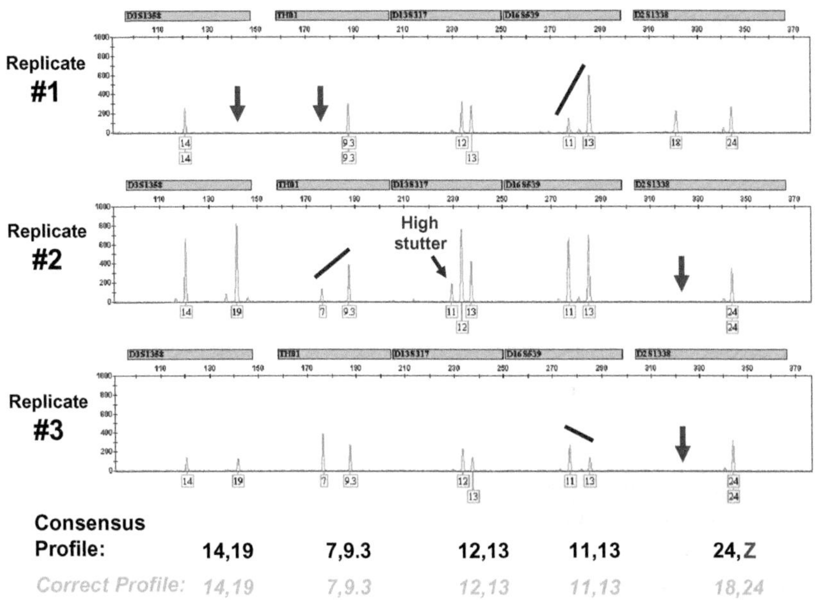

FIGURE 11.3 Three replicate PCR amplifications of a 10 pg single-source DNA template using the Identifiler kit (only green loci shown) and 31 cycles. The consensus profile, produced by recording all alleles that occurred at least two out of three times, matched the correct profile (note that the consensus wildcard "Z" for D2S1338 appropriately covers the allele 18 that has dropped out twice). The red arrows indicate positions of allele drop-out and the blue lines where severe peak height imbalance was observed.

Alleles that occur more than once (i.e., repeat) in the obtained profiles are deemed "reliable" as they have been reproduced in separate DNA tests. Based on observations during validation studies, another layer of interpretation may be applied as well before the final consensus profile is reported. For example, specific loci, such as those larger in size, may exhibit a higher rate of allelic drop-out. When reporting results from these loci, a wild card designation may be used in conjunction with a repeated single allele in order to account for potential allelic drop-out (e.g., "12,F" or "12,Z" instead of "12,12").

Three separate PCR amplifications of a 10 pg fully heterozygous DNA template using the Identifiler STR kit with 31 cycles are shown in Figure 11.3. The first locus in this figure, D3S1358, has a "14" in the first replicate, a "14,19" in the second replicate, and a "14,19" in the third replicate. The arrow indicates where the "19" allele should be in the first replicate. It has failed to amplify (i.e., allele drop-out) due to stochastic sampling effects present when only approximately two cells are available for testing. If the first replicate was the only one examined, then the D3S1358 genotype for this sample would incorrectly be designated "14,14". However, by looking for repeating alleles across the three replicates, the correct type of "14,19" can be determined as the "14" occurs in all three replicates and the "19" occurs in two out of the three.

While stochastic effects exist whenever low amounts of DNA are being examined with PCR, a replicate amplification approach with development of a consensus profile from the repeated alleles can produce reliable results (Figure 11.4). However, amplification results

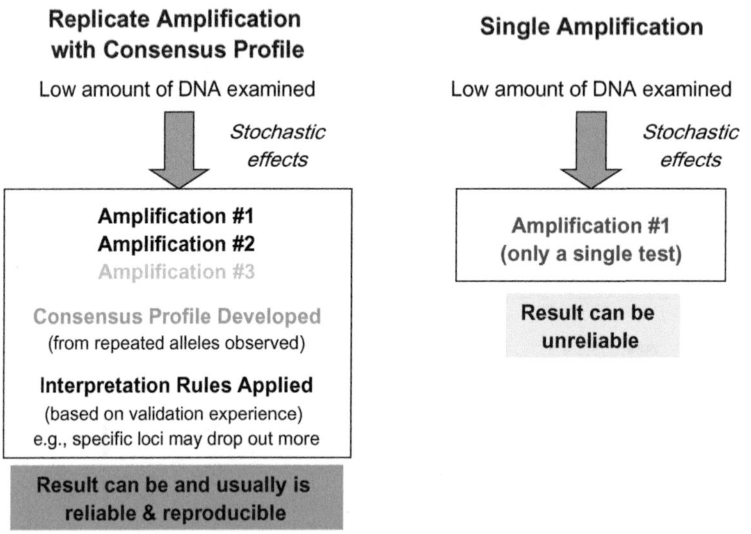

FIGURE 11.4 Comparison of approaches when examining low amounts of DNA. Replicate amplification with development of consensus profiles and application of interpretation rules based on validation experience can lead to reliable results.

from a single test can be unreliable due to allelic drop-out or allelic drop-in as noted earlier. As seen in Figure 11.3, individual results from replicate tests may vary but a combined consensus profile can generate an accurate answer when repeated alleles are recorded.

Researchers at the Netherlands Forensic Institute have studied the role of replicate number and the requested level of reproducibility through examining various combinations of six independent amplifications of known donor samples (D.N.A. Box 11.4).

NIST Data on Replicate Amplifications with Low-Level DNA

In order to evaluate reliability of results with low levels of DNA template separate from the effects of DNA degradation or PCR inhibition that might be present in forensic specimens, validation experiments were conducted at the National Institute of Standards and Technology (NIST) with pristine DNA samples (Butler & Hill 2010). Two single-source DNA samples, which were fully heterozygous at all of the tested loci, were quantified using the Quantifiler kit (Applied Biosystems, Foster City, CA) with a calibration curve created by Standard Reference Material (SRM) 2372 Component A (NIST, Gaithersburg, MD).

Following DNA quantification, dilutions were made to enable testing of 100pg, 30pg, and 10pg of DNA template in each PCR reaction. A total of 10 separate PCR reactions were performed for each sample in order to study the impact and value of replicate amplifications. While 10 replicates would not be practical to perform in a casework setting with limited forensic evidence, the extra studies are valuable in a validation context to examine if more than three replicates are helpful. Both the AmpFlSTR Identifiler kit (Applied Biosystems) and PowerPlex 16 HS kit (Promega Corporation, Madison, WI) were examined using half

D.N.A. BOX 11.4

REPLICATE NUMBERS, CONSENSUS PROFILES, AND GENOTYPING RELIABILITY

In the most thorough study of low template DNA conducted to date, researchers at the Netherlands Forensic Institute (NFI) performed six separate amplifications of low-level DNA samples from known donors. They then assembled consensus profiles using between two and six of the replicates and studied the impact of allele accuracy when requiring one of four possibilities: (a) that all alleles matched between each replicate, (b) that all but one replicate matched, (c) that at least half of the replicates matched, or (d) that the allele was observed twice. Each of these samples was studied with three different methods: (a) 28-cycle PCR with standard capillary electrophoresis (CE) injection, (b) 28-cycle PCR with sample desalting and higher CE injection (9 kV), and (c) 28 + 6 cycles (i.e., for a total of 34 PCR cycles) with standard CE injection. Stochastic effects were examined and the rate of allele drop-out and drop-in measured in 414 Identifiler single-donor profiles (obtained from 23 individual samples amplified six times and analyzed with the three different methods), 90 Identifiler mixed-donor profiles (five samples amplified six fold and analyzed with three methods), and 120 MiniFiler single-donor profiles (four DNA concentrations amplified 30 times and analyzed with one setting).

A computer program was written to examine all of the combinations of the DNA profiles generated with a variable level of requested reproducibility. For example, in a sample with three replicate amplifications there are 20 different combinations possible to consider with the four different types of consensus profiles studied. In total, the NFI researchers evaluated 6578 consensus profiles for the 23 single-donor samples and 1430 consensus profiles for the five two-person mixtures. The consensus profiles obtained from DNA extracts of five single-donors were also compared to an anonymized copy of the Dutch DNA database containing 86,277 offender profiles and 40,065 forensic profiles using a "moderate" stringency search to account for potential allele drop-out (see Chapter 8). Some of the findings of this study include:

- Allele drop-in was observed in 258 instances across the 414 Identifiler single-donor profiles of which about two-thirds came from the 34-cycle PCR method and one-third from the 9 kV CE injection method. About 74% of the time (192 out of 258), the drop-in allele occurred at a stutter position (104 at N + 4 and 88 at N − 4).
- Allele drop-out was found to be largely dependent on the amount of DNA tested. Only 41 of the 414 Identifiler single-donor profiles (10%) resulted in a profile without any allele drop-out across the 16 loci amplified (19 of the 41 came from the 9 kV method and 22 from the 34-cycle method). Aliquots involving DNA input levels of 10 pg, 15 pg, 20 pg, and 40 pg were amplified eight-fold with MiniFiler. Allele drop-out decreased as DNA input levels increased such that 10 pg observed a 44% drop-out, 15 pg observed a 27% drop-out, 20 pg observed a 21% drop-out, and 40 pg observed only a 3% drop-out rate.
- The locus drop-out rate corresponded well to expected values based on

D.N.A. BOX 11.4 (*cont'd*)

allele drop-out rates. In addition, STR allele peak heights can provide some information regarding how likely it is for allele drop-out of a true heterozygote sister allele to have occurred.

- The percentage of detected alleles observed in the standard STR typing method (28 cycles) is informative to decide on which low template method (9 kV or 6 additional PCR cycles) will be most effective. When >50% of the alleles are detected in the standard method, then increased CE injection is preferred. Whereas when <10% of the alleles are detected with 28 cycles, then the increased PCR cycle number approach works best.
- Consensus method studies found that three replicates with a requirement for allele duplication work well when the standard method (28 cycles) detects >25% of alleles. For profiles with <25% of alleles detected, then a fourth replicate is helpful. Increasing the replication number to six does not yield significant gains in reliability.
- Database search studies found that wrongful homozygote designations (due to allele drop-out of a true heterozygote sister allele) can lead to a large number of adventitious matches.

Source:

Benschop, C.C.G., et al. (2010). Low template STR typing: effect of replicate number and consensus method on genotyping reliability and DNA database search results. Forensic Science International: Genetics (in press) *(doi:10.1016/j.fsigen.2010.06.00).*

reactions to conserve costs and improve sensitivity. Identifiler was tested at both 28 (standard) and 31 (enhanced) cycles. PowerPlex 16 HS was tested at 31 (standard) and 34 (enhanced) cycles.

The resulting 240 electropherograms were examined to assess stochastic effects such as allelic drop-out and allelic drop-in. These electropherograms are all available for review (as PDF files) at http://www.cstl.nist.gov/biotech/strbase/LTDNA.htm. With 16 loci for each result, a total of 3840 loci (7680 alleles) could potentially be scored. In this analysis, all peaks above 50 relative fluorescence units (RFUs) were called without an attempt to filter genotypes based on heterozygote peak height ratios.

Figure 11.5 illustrates the results for one of the tested samples with the Identifiler kit using 28 and 31 cycles. Note that use of a higher number of cycles (31 cycles) resulted in more correct genotypes as denoted by the green squares. The three extra PCR cycles improved the success rate for a correct heterozygous call from 60% (290/480 possible) to 88% (423/480 possible). The improvement from locus drop-out to correct genotype (Figure 11.5, red-to-green squares) was most dramatic at the 10 pg level where full genotype recovery improved from 4% (7/160) to 68% (108/160). With 31 cycles, allelic drop-out across the three DNA amounts tested fell from 14% (65/480) to 9% (43/480). Locus drop-out was reduced from 26% (125/480) to 2% (10/480). Thus, boosting the cycle number did improve the sensitivity and the overall success rate.

However, there were four instances of allele drop-in (Figure 11.5, black squares) when a higher number of PCR cycles were used while none existed with the lower number of cycles.

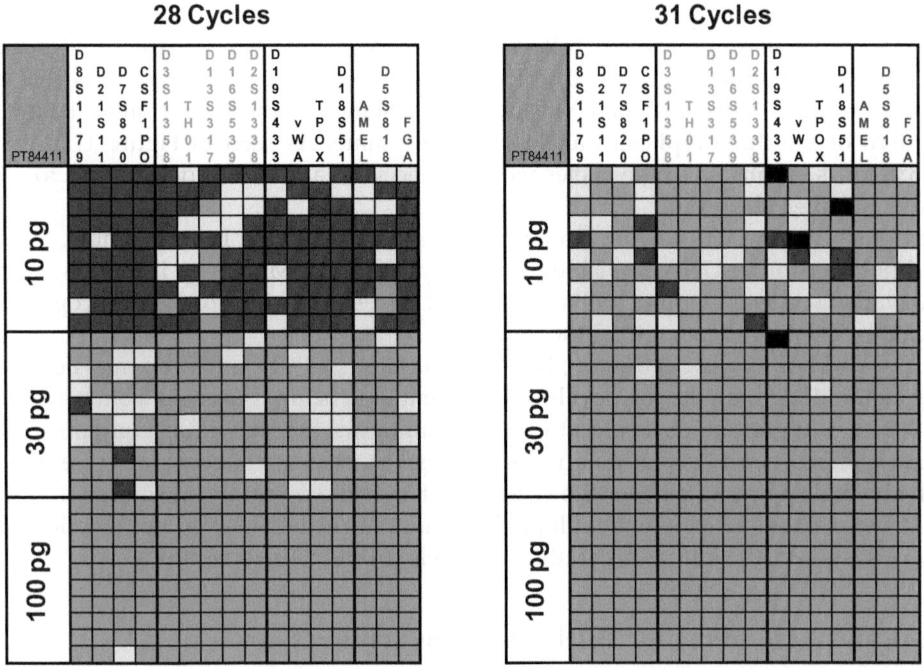

FIGURE 11.5 Sensitivity and performance summaries for Identifiler replicates with 28-cycle (standard) and 31-cycle (enhanced) data. A horizontal slice represents information from a single sample whereas a vertical slice represents the results from each of 10 replicates with the three different DNA template amounts. Green squares indicate that the full correct type was observed for that locus and PCR replicate. Yellow squares denote allele drop-out where one of the expected alleles is missing. Red squares highlight locus drop-out where both expected alleles are missing. Black squares indicate allele drop-in where an incorrect allele is observed above a 50 RFU (relative fluorescence unit) analytical threshold.

The potential occurrence of allele drop-in shows the importance of replicate amplifications and development of consensus profiles to avoid miscalls when utilizing enhanced interrogation techniques. Two of the allele drop-ins noted in Figure 11.5 are in D19S433 where the correct genotype is "13,15" yet a "13,14,15" was called with the "14" likely coming from elevated stutter of the "15" allele. The D18S51 drop-in event also appears to have arisen from high stutter. The vWA drop-in occurred at the allele "16" position when the correct type was "18,19" (see Figure 11.2).

The other sample tested with Identifiler at 31 cycles had two instances of allelic drop-in—both as a result of higher than expected stutter product formation (see http://www.cstl.nist.gov/biotech/strbase/LTDNA/ID31-summary.pdf and Figure 11.2). For the two PowerPlex 16 HS samples, one had a single observed incidence of allele drop-in at a stutter position in D3S1358 and the other sample exhibited four instances of allele drop-in at stutter positions (see http://www.cstl.nist.gov/biotech/strbase/LTDNA/PP34-summary.pdf). Since each STR typing kit will perform differently, the specific conditions and kit being examined in a forensic DNA laboratory need to be internally validated (see Chapter 7). If it is discovered that certain loci are more prone to allele and locus drop-out, then appropriate interpretation guidelines can be put in place to compensate.

In all cases with the pristine single-source DNA samples examined at NIST, replicate testing of *sequential* amplifications followed by development of consensus profiles successfully excluded any incorrect calls due to allelic drop-in. Equally important is that across *any* group of three replicates, there was never an instance of an incorrect allele being called when two of the three replicates alleles were the same. As seen in Figure 11.3, with the D2S1338 locus, duplicate single alleles were labeled with a wildcard designation to account for potential allele drop-out.

Obviously, if a limited starting amount of DNA was recovered from a sample, then there would not be enough DNA available for 10 amplifications. Moreover, if there was enough DNA available, then it would probably be used in a single high (or higher) copy number DNA analysis rather than splitting the sample.

In the world of forensic casework, DNA degradation or PCR inhibition may be a complicating factor along with the low levels of DNA template being recovered from a evidentiary item. When mixtures are observed at low DNA amounts, the individual components to the mixture will be even lower in amount and the stochastic effects become worse making it extremely challenging to recover the correct profile of the original contributors to the mixture. In these situations where the full profile cannot be recovered even with replication and consensus, statistical methods accounting for allele drop-out are an option.

Statistically Accounting for Allele Drop-out and Drop-in

In the seminal 2000 article on applying low copy number DNA techniques to forensic samples, Peter Gill, John Buckleton, and colleagues at the Forensic Science Service suggested a statistical approach that modeled the incidence of allele drop-out, laboratory contamination, and stutter (Gill et al. 2000). They envisioned that an expert system would be developed to apply their model so that the probabilities of allele drop-out and drop-in could be incorporated into the strength of evidence calculation for a crime scene profile.

While this statistical approach underpins the concepts behind replicate testing and consensus profile development (sometimes referred to as the "biological model"), the probability of drop-out is not routinely used by forensic laboratories as of early 2011. However, an approach for estimating the probability of allelic drop-out has been reported (Tvederbrink et al. 2009), and David Balding has written some free software that computes single-locus likelihood ratios allowing for drop-out of one or both alleles and drop-in of up to two alleles (Balding & Buckleton 2010). This topic will be covered more extensively in the forthcoming volume *Advanced Topics in Forensic DNA Typing: Interpretation*.

ASSORTED TOPICS

Features and Requirements of a High-Sensitivity Laboratory

Creating and maintaining a high-sensitivity laboratory that can perform LTDNA testing requires a lot of effort. Dr. Theresa Caragine from the NYC OCME DNA Laboratory spoke at a technical leaders meeting held in conjunction with the 21st International Symposium on Human Identification in October 2010. From her experience running a high-sensitivity laboratory that examines evidence in hundreds of low-level DNA cases each year, she offers five tips to preventing exogenous DNA contamination in forensic casework. These same tips are valuable for laboratories performing mitochondrial DNA testing as well.

First, utilize dedicated and protected workspaces such that each step in the DNA process has a different hood space. Always process the known reference samples separate from the unknowns. Conduct the evidence examination, pre-PCR, and post-PCR testing in separate rooms.

Second, wear proper personal protective equipment (PPE). This includes a laboratory coat, head covering, a mask or face shield, booties, eye protection, and double gloves. The primary reason for such extensive PPE is to protect the DNA samples from the staff working on them. The double gloves prevent skin contact. Only the outer gloves are changed in the laboratory between each item of evidence and after touching refrigerator handles or other items that could potentially cross-transfer any cellular material. Lab coats are single-use within the evidence exam area. Lab coats remain in the pre-PCR or post-PCR areas and each one is used by a single analyst for typically only a few days.

Third, perform regular cleaning of *everything*. Careful cleaning of the entire lab is conducted weekly and documented with a checklist. All surfaces are cleaned with 10% bleach, which is typically made daily to keep it fresh. Surfaces are then scrubbed with water and 70% ethanol after the bleach treatment. Hoods, pipets, and instruments are cleaned between each assay and piece of evidence. Aerosol-resistant pipet tips are used and changed with each new sample to prevent cross-contamination during liquid transfers. Scissors, tube openers, tweezers, and pens are all dedicated to the room where they are used (i.e., they do not leave the room) to prevent inadvertent transfer of any DNA material. A UV light is applied in each hood for 15 minutes before and after use. Tissue culture techniques are employed meaning that the pipet and the hands of the scientist never cross over open tubes or reagents when setting up assays. Only one sample tube is opened at a time to prevent cross-contamination. Sample tubes are also opened with a cap opener or a clean tissue.

Increased sensitivity with LTDNA or mtDNA techniques means that minute levels of contaminant DNA in labware or reagents may be detected from the manufacturer that would not be seen with conventional STR typing. Thus, all labware and reagents are UV-irradiated prior to use in PCR to try to inhibit the replication of exogenous DNA. All plasticware, instrumentation, extraction reagents, and even the water used is irradiated (Tamariz et al. 2006). If the item cannot be irradiated, then it is bleached.

Fourth, perform quality control testing on all reagents prior to use on evidentiary items. NYC OCME utilizes a multi-copy Alu qPCR assay for high-sensitivity DNA detection (see Chapter 3). Each batch of reagents must be cleared for use by showing no result with the qPCR assay as well as no detectable alleles with the enhanced detection LTDNA STR analysis. To ensure appropriate sensitivity for the STR typing kits, 100 pg, 25 pg, and 6 pg of a postive control DNA template are tested to determine if each amount yields an expected number of alleles as previously seen in their validation studies.

Fifth, evaluate controls with every batch of samples. The positive control tests whether the assay is robust and working properly. The negative control highlights any contamination that might be present in the PCR reagents. Negative controls are treated in as sensitive a manner as the tested samples and are amplified in triplicate as are the LTDNA samples in order to develop a consensus profile. Some stray alleles are occasionally detected in negative controls. During their validation studies, NYC OCME found that 89% of the time the negative controls were clean. However, most of the detected alleles in the remaining 11% of the samples were typically random and not due to gross contamination. If a labeled allele was found to repeat in two of three replications for the negative control, then any sample having that labeled allele at that locus is declared inconclusive for that locus. If there are more than two repeating alleles over the three replicates for a negative control, then the batch fails and testing would have to be repeated if sufficient sample remains.

Another important measure to detect potential contamination when using enhanced detection methods is an elimination database for comparison purposes. All lab staff, all cleaning and facilities staff, and all members of the local crime scene unit are DNA tested. Their DNA profiles are placed on the elimination database and compared to evidentiary profiles prior to completing a forensic case report. These profiles are never uploaded to the DNA database. Rather anyone who may have come in contact with the laboratory space or the original biological sample is eliminated first as a possible contaminant.

Minor Components in Mixtures May Be Low-Level DNA

Many DNA analysts may think that low-level DNA analysis does not apply to them because they are running 28-cycle PCR and not examining DNA down at a level of 100 pg or less. However, PCR amplification involving 1 ng total DNA with a two-person mixture and a 9:1 major-to-minor component ratio leaves the minor contributor in the low template range of approximately 100 pg or 15 cells (Table 11.3). Thus, minor contributor alleles in this situation could be experiencing stochastic sampling (allele drop-out, etc.) as well as allele masking by the taller major contributor alleles. This fact is important to keep in mind when working with DNA mixtures.

Validation Experiments

The low-level DNA characteristics of allele drop-out, allele drop-in, higher stutter, and greater heterozygote peak height ratio imbalance mean that internal validation experiments need to be performed in order to understand the limits of the specific technique being applied. Table 11.4 summarizes some of the published validation work performed by LCN DNA laboratories around the world. Note that each lab has selected different PCR conditions or CE injection parameters as optimal.

When performing validation studies, it is best to utilize samples that are heterozygous at all tested loci if possible so that allele drop-out can be monitored. The height of the surviving sister allele from the heterozygote is useful in determining where (or whether) a stochastic threshold can be set. The ESR validation paper (Petricevic et al. 2010) may serve as a useful model for plotting data obtained from validation experiments.

Examination of multiple samples is equally important as DNA quantitation values on the tested samples (that are then diluted to low levels for testing) may not be exact. Observing PCR performance in a range of samples, which may have slightly different true amounts of DNA, is valuable in setting interpretation guidelines based on the validation data obtained.

TABLE 11.3 Correlation of DNA Amount with the Approximate Number of Diploid Cells Used in Single-Source and Mixture Samples. Calculations for 1 ng Being Equivalent to 152 Diploid Cells May Be Found in D.N.A. Box 3.1. Shaded Boxes Contain Less than 20 Cells and Therefore May Exhibit Stochastic Effects (Walsh et al. 1992). Adapted from a 2003 Presentation by Robin Cotton (Then of Orchid Cellmark) at the American Academy of Forensic Sciences Low Copy Number DNA Workshop.

Single-Source *Amount of DNA*	*Total Cells in Sample*	*Approximate Number of Copies of Each Allele if Heterozygous*
1 ng	152	152
0.5 ng	76	76
0.25 ng	38	38
0.125 ng	19	19
0.0625 ng	10	10

1:1 Mixture *Amount of DNA*	*Total Cells in Sample*	*Approximate Number of Cells from Each Component*
1 ng	152	76
0.5 ng	76	38
0.25 ng	38	19
0.125 ng	19	10
0.0625 ng	10	5

1:3 Mixture *Amount of DNA*	*Approximate Number of Cells from* **Major Component**	*Approximate Number of Cells from* **Minor Component**
1 ng	114	38
0.5 ng	57	19
0.25 ng	28	10
0.125 ng	14	5
0.0625 ng	7	2

1:9 Mixture *Amount of DNA*	*Approximate Number of Cells from* **Major Component**	*Approximate Number of Cells from* **Minor Component**
1 ng	137	15
0.5 ng	68	8
0.25 ng	34	4
0.125 ng	17	2
0.0625 ng	9	1

TABLE 11.4 Examples of Some Validation Efforts with Low-Level DNA.

Laboratory	STR kit	Summary of Approach & Results	Reference
Forensic Science Service (UK)	SGM Plus	Gill: 21 of 31 negative controls showed minor levels of STR contamination; pair-wise comparisons performed on replicate amplifications found that 4 of 1225 (0.3%) showed a spurious allele being duplicated. Whitaker: Of 577 heterozygote loci tested, 37 showed locus drop-out and 58 showed allelic drop-out.	Gill et al. (2000), Whitaker et al. (2001)
Armed Forces DNA Identification Laboratory (U.S.)	PowerPlex 16 & Yfiler	Added twice the amount of Taq polymerase and added six PCR cycles (up to 36 total) to improve human remains identification; used triplicate amplifications with allele duplication required for reporting; ~30% allele drop-in observed; obtained results from 90-year-old specimen.	Irwin et al. (2007), Sturk et al. (2009)
LGC Forensics (UK)	SGM Plus	Forster: Compares use of 34-cycle PCR run in duplicate with DNA SenCE (Sensitive Capillary Electrophoresis), which is 28-cycle PCR with MinElute post-PCR clean-up and enhanced injection (30 s @ 4 kV compared to standard 10 s @ 3 kV), on 36 mock evidential items; observed a 0.7% drop-in rate per locus. Gross: Reviewed 1398 control samples processed alongside casework samples run over a five-month period; 12% (170/1398) had one or more drop-in peaks with a total of 255 extra alleles in 7040 loci for a drop-in probability of 3.6% per locus.	Forster et al. (2008), Gross et al. (2009)
Orchid Cellmark (UK)	SGM Plus & Identifiler	Examined 42 samples with various combinations of 28, 30, and 34 PCR cycles and Montage post-PCR clean-up with either 1 μL of PCR product added to 9 μL Hi-Di formamide (Phase 1 enhancement) or 9 μL of purified PCR product with 11 μL of Hi-Di formamide (Phase 2).	Roeder et al. (2009)
New York City Office of Chief Medical Examiner	Identifiler	Used 0.01% SDS to limit PCR inhibition and carrier RNA to improve recovery during DNA extraction; PCR reaction volume of 13 μL with 31 cycles (instead of 28 cycles); increased CE injection time and voltage (30 s @ 6 kV); samples were amplified in triplicate and all alleles above 75 RFU were scored with consensus profiles being developed when alleles were labeled in at least two of the three replicates; generated accurate allele calls on 319 forensic casework samples; developed a flow chart to aid in LT-DNA interpretation.	Caragine et al. (2009)
Institute of Environmental Science and Research (ESR) (New Zealand)	SGM Plus	Compared 1 ng DNA template results run at 28 cycles with 12.5 pg and 25 pg (amplified in duplicate) run at 34 cycles; normal CE injection (10 s @ 3 kV) compared with enhanced injection (15 s @ 5 kV); examined 20 samples that were fully heterozygous at the 10 SGM Plus STR loci; 28-cycle data was composed of 422 heterozygous loci; 34 cycle data contained 1688 heterozygous loci; average drop-in rate was 1.3% per locus; 99% of stutter products were less than 25% of the associated allele peak height; stochastic threshold set at 3000 RFU for normal CE injection and 7000 RFU for enhanced injection; encouraged use of models that place less emphasis on peak height differences with mixture interpretation.	Petricevic et al. (2010)
Netherlands Forensic Institute (NFI)	Identifiler	See D.N.A. Box 11.4.	Benschop et al. (2010)

Sampling Limitations with Sperm Cells

New sampling techniques such as laser capture microdissection (see Chapter 2) enable collection of specific cells. Keep in mind that individual sperm cells contain only half of the genomic material from the donor. Therefore, multiple sperm cells will need to be collected in order to represent the complete DNA profile (D.N.A. Box 11.5).

Whole Genome Amplification

A DNA enrichment technology known as whole genome amplification (WGA) has been explored as a possible method for recovery of limited quantities of DNA from evidentiary samples (Bergen et al. 2005, Hanson & Ballantyne 2005, Ballantyne et al. 2007). WGA involves a different DNA polymerase (phi29) than the TaqGold enzyme commonly used in forensic DNA analysis and amplifies the entire genome using random hexamers as priming points. The WGA enzymes work by multiple displacement amplification (MDA), which is sometimes referred to as rolling circle amplification. MDA is isothermal with an incubation temperature of 30°C and requires no heating and cooling like PCR.

QIAGEN (Valencia, CA) and Sigma-Aldrich (St. Louis, MO) both offer phi29 DNA polymerase cocktails for performing WGA. The kit sold by QIAGEN is called REPLI-g while Sigma-Aldrich's kit is GenomePlex. Yields of 4 μg to 7 μg of amplified genomic DNA are possible from as little as 1 ng of starting material. The phi29 enzyme has a high processivity and can amplify fragments of up to 100 kb because it displaces downstream product strands enabling multiple concurrent and overlapping rounds of amplification. In addition, phi29 has a higher replication fidelity compared to Taq polymerase due to 3′–5′ proofreading activity.

While all of these characteristics make WGA seem like a possible solution to the forensic problem of limited DNA starting material, studies have found that stochastic effects at low levels of DNA template prevent WGA from working reliably (Schneider et al. 2004). Allele drop-outs from STR loci were observed at 50 pg and 5 pg levels of starting material (Schneider et al. 2004) just as are seen with current LT-DNA testing. Work with "molecular crowding" materials such as polyethylene glycol, where the amount of DNA is enriched in localized areas of a sample, has shown improved success with STR typing from low amounts of DNA (Ballantyne et al. 2006).

It is possible that WGA may play a limited role in enriching samples for archiving purposes that are in the low ng range (Lasken & Egholm 2003), but it will probably not be the end-all solution to LT-DNA samples in the low picogram range. Thus, it appears, as with regular PCR techniques, stochastic selection of alleles present in low-level DNA samples limits the effectiveness of WGA to several hundred picograms in order to recover a full profile with a single amplification attempt.

Caution in Relying on DNA Quantitation Values

Is it possible to ascertain that sufficient DNA material exists to obtain reliable results where the DNA profile obtained is expected to accurately reflect the source of the biological sample? There are two primary points in the DNA testing process where potential DNA reliability may be assessed: (1) at the DNA quantitation stage prior to performing PCR

D.N.A. BOX 11.5

PROBABILITY OF ACHIEVING FULL ALLELIC REPRESENTATION FOR LOW NUMBERS OF HAPLOID CELLS

Sexual assault evidence is composed of sperm cells, which contain only half of the full complement of genomic DNA from the donor male because of meiosis. Thus, to obtain a representative *diploid* DNA profile containing both possible alleles from the original sample source, multiple sperm will need to be analyzed. Techniques such as laser capture microdissection enable collection of individual sperm cells (Elliott et al. 2003, see Chapter 2). When working with limited amounts of evidentiary material, the question becomes how many individual sperm cells are needed to obtain a fully representative DNA profile when multiple loci are being examined.

In a 2007 paper published in the journal *Science & Justice*, David Lucy and colleagues found that 19 haploid cells would be theoretically required to obtain a full 15-locus DNA profile with a 99.99% probability (Lucy et al. 2007). Since each sperm cell contains just over 3pg of DNA (see D.N.A. Box 3.1), approximately 60pg of sperm DNA extract would therefore be required to obtain a full profile containing both alleles at all 15 tested loci.

The number of haploid cells required to obtain complete representation of a full profile at a specified number of heterozygous loci with a given probability (ranging from 90% to 99.99%) is provided in the table to the right (Lucy et al. 2007).

Number of Loci	0.90	0.95	0.99	0.999	0.9999
1	5	6	8	11	15
2	6	7	9	12	16
3	6	7	10	13	16
6	7	8	11	14	17
10	8	9	11	15	18
15	9	10	12	15	19

This information is theoretical in nature and may not necessarily reflect the probabilities of what is observed after DNA extraction, PCR amplification, and capillary electrophoresis injection. The efficiency of these processes will govern the actual numbers of cells required. Research scientists from the Forensic Science Service found that several hundred sperm cells can be required in order to have a high probability of obtaining a complete STR profile (Elliott et al. 2003). Poor extraction efficiency and less than 100% amplification efficiency due to DNA degradation or PCR inhibition play a role in this discrepancy between the theoretical predictions and empirical observations.

Sources:

Elliott, K., et al. (2003). Use of laser microdissection greatly improves the recovery of DNA from sperm on microscope slides. Forensic Science International, *137, 28–36.*

Lucy, D., et al. (2007). The probability of achieving full allelic representation for LCN-STR profiling of haploid cells. Science & Justice, *47, 168–171.*

amplification of the STR markers of interest or (2) by examining the peak heights—and peak height ratios in heterozygous loci—in the STR profile obtained.

An empirically determined threshold (usually termed a "stochastic threshold") may be used at either the DNA quantitation or data interpretation stage to assess samples in the potential danger zone of unreliable results. For example, if the total amount of measured DNA is below 150pg, a laboratory may decide not to proceed with PCR amplification assuming that allelic drop-out due to stochastic effects is a very real possibility. Alternatively, a laboratory may proceed with testing a low-level DNA sample and then evaluate the peak height signals and peak ratios at heterozygous loci. When peak height ratios for heterozygous loci in single-source samples dip below 60%, there is an indication that stochastic effects are significant which would make it challenging to reliably pair alleles into major and minor genotypes with mixtures. This topic will be covered more extensively in the forthcoming volume *Advanced Topics in Forensic DNA Typing: Interpretation.*

Since the advent of quantitative PCR (qPCR) assays, DNA quantitation tests have become more sensitive—enabling quantities as small as a few genomic copies to be detected (see Chapter 3). However, it is important to keep in mind that qPCR is also subject to stochastic variation especially on the low end of DNA quantity measurement. Thus, numbers in the low picogram range may not be reliable and results with little or no "detectable" DNA may still amplify with STR kits (Cupples et al. 2009; see also D.N.A. Box 3.3).

In an early paper discussing stochastic effects and the limitations of PCR assays, Walsh et al. (1992) proposed avoiding stochastic effects by adjusting the number of PCR cycles in an assay so that the sensitivity limit is around 20 or more copies of target DNA. In other words, their goal was to enable a full DNA profile to be reliably obtained with approximately 125pg of DNA. Below roughly that amount, allele and locus drop-out would be expected and partial DNA profiles would result (Walsh et al. 1992). Obtaining a partial DNA profile is an indication that a low-level DNA amplification has occurred.

Depending on the STR typing kit primer and DNA polymerase concentrations and the fluorescent dye sensitivities, the number of PCR cycles is typically set by manufacturers in the range of 28 cycles to 32 cycles. However, as noted previously, STR kits certainly work beyond manufacturer recommended cycle numbers. If laboratories choose to increase cycle numbers beyond what is recommended by manufacturers, validation studies are needed to help set appropriate interpretation guidelines.

Thresholds Are Difficult to Set with Enhanced Detection Methods

Stochastic thresholds, such as 150 RFU or even 500 RFU, may not apply for enhanced detection methods that include increasing the number of PCR cycles. Instead, independent replicate amplifications and concensus profile development are necessary to compensate for allele drop-out and drop-in. Computer software that involves probabilistic modeling to data, such as LoComatioN (Gill et al. 2007), will be important to future advances with low-level DNA analysis.

STRBase Website on Low Template DNA

A low template DNA section of the NIST STRBase website was launched in October 2009 following the International Symposium on Human Identification LCN Panel. This website, which is available at http://www.cstl.nist.gov/biotech/strbase/LTDNA.htm, contains three primary sections: (1) presentations, (2) NIST data from sensitivity studies, and (3) a listing of literature on the topic.

With the LTDNA website launch, four presentations given by John Butler (NIST), Becky Hill (NIST), Theresa Caragine (NYC), and Charlotte Word (consultant) at the ISHI 2009 meeting were included. As previously mentioned, data from low-level DNA experiments using Identifiler and PowerPlex 16 HS kits with 100 pg, 30 pg, and 10 pg and different numbers of PCR cycles are available to be viewed as PDF files. The two DNA samples examined in these studies were fully heterozygous at all STR loci providing an opportunity to monitor peak imbalance and allelic drop-out under different conditions. Laboratories are encouraged to submit their validation data for inclusion on this community resource as suggested previously (Buckleton 2009, Buckleton & Gill 2011).

A literature listing of pertinent articles to help explain the issues involved with low-template DNA testing is provided on the STRBase LTDNA website and will continue to be updated over time. The articles are listed according to four categories in order to reflect their relative reliability in scientific terms: (1) peer-reviewed literature, (2) reports, (3) reviews, and (4) non-peer-reviewed literature. In science, as in other fields, not all information is equally authoritative or helpful. Thus, the literature on low-template DNA analysis is broken into several categories on the STRBase website in order to reflect the variation in scrutiny and support.

Summary and Final Thoughts

Every lab faces samples with low amounts of DNA. The choice becomes whether or not to attempt an "enhanced interrogation technique" such as increasing the cycle number, desalting samples, or injecting more sample onto the CE. If so, are there sufficient validation studies to underpin this work and to develop appropriate interpretation guidelines? Generating STR data with an increased number of PCR cycles and invoking an LCN philosophy can provide a useful lead in many instances for an investigation but it is unlikely to provide definitive probative evidence of a crime in every instance.

At what point does a laboratory draw a line and not attempt to analyze DNA data below this line (i.e., to declare a result inconclusive)? Is this line based on a certain amount of input DNA? If so, what validation data underpins this quantitation threshold? Does the laboratory have a predetermined stochastic threshold used during data interpretation? Again, on what validation data is this value based?

If a laboratory chooses to perform low-level DNA analysis with enhanced detection methods, interpretation guidelines need to reflect the potential artifacts of this high sensitivity environment. Laboratories should not report out a single result with LCN STR analysis (see Figure 11.4). Allele duplication with multiple replicates and formation of a consensus profile is currently the recommended best overall approach. However, this is not a license to report any and all replicated data. Caution is needed when interpreting data and drawing conclusions from low-level data due to stochastic effects that can and will exist in the results obtained.

When working with low amounts of DNA template, success rates are often poor. Dedicated "clean" facilities and extreme care are required to avoid or at least limit contamination. Often mixtures result from touch DNA or other low-level DNA analyses that may not yield meaningful results. Finally, in the end, results may not be probative if the sample could have been deposited innocently at the crime scene before the crime even occurred. Thus, low-level DNA recovered from a crime scene may not be relevant to the crime under investigation.

Nevertheless, research and validation experiments have demonstrated successful low-template DNA analyses that track appropriately back to the sample donor (e.g., D.N.A. Box 11.4). Thus, low-level DNA results can be reliable. When appropriate controls are in place and replicated results are repeatable, DNA interpretation should proceed—but cautiously.

The next-generation STR kits, such as the PowerPlex 16 HS, PowerPlex ESI 17 and ESX 17 Systems and AmpFlSTR Identifiler Plus and NGM kits, with their greater sensitivity and ability to overcome PCR inhibition, have the potential to make the current qPCR DNA quantitation kits obsolete as an appropriate gatekeeper to whether or not to continue with a low-level, compromised DNA sample. *With greater power to obtain results comes greater responsibility to report reliable results.* Careful validation studies and development of appropriate interpretation guidelines will continue to be essential as laboratories move forward with caution and care in analysis of low amounts of DNA.

READING LIST AND INTERNET RESOURCES

Issues and Historical Overview

Bajda, E., et al. (2004). Modification of amplification and STR detection conditions to enhance sensitivity of the Identifiler (ABI) and PowerPlex 16 (Promega) kits for low copy number DNA samples. *Proceedings of the fifteenth international symposium on human identification.* Available at <http://www.promega.com/geneticidproc/ussymp15proc/posterpresentations/25Bajda.pdf>.

Budowle, B. et al. (2001). Low copy number – consideration and caution. *Proceedings of the twelfth international symposium on human identification.* Madison, WI: Promega Corporation. Available at <http://www.promega.com/geneticidproc/ussymp12proc/contents/budowle.pdf>.

Budowle, B., et al. (2009). Validity of low copy number typing and applications to forensic science. *Croatian Medical Journal, 50,* 207–217.

Buckleton, J., & Gill, P. (2005). Low copy number. In J. Buckleton, C. M. Triggs & S. J. Walsh (Eds.), *Forensic DNA Evidence Interpretation* Chapter 8. (pp. 275–297). Boca Raton, FL: CRC Press.

Capelli, C., et al. (2003). "Ancient" protocols for the crime scene? Similarities and differences between forensic genetics and ancient DNA analysis. *Forensic Science International, 131,* 59–64.

Ellison, S. L. R., et al. (2006). Routes to improving the reliability of low level DNA analysis using real-time PCR. *BMC Biotechnology, 6,* 33.

Farmen, R. K., et al. (2008). Assessment of individual shedder status and implication for secondary DNA transfer. *Forensic Science International: Genetics Supplement Series, 1,* 415–417.

Findlay, I., et al. (1995). Allelic drop-out and preferential amplification in single cells and human blastomeres: Implications for preimplantation diagnosis of sex and cystic fibrosis. *Human Reproduction, 10,* 1609–1618.

Findlay, I., et al. (1997). DNA fingerprinting from single cells. *Nature, 389,* 555–556.

FSS Fact Sheet. <http://www.forensic.gov.uk/pdf/company/foi/publication-scheme/communications/DNA_Low_Copy_Number_000.pdf>.

Gilbert, N. (2010). DNA's identity crisis. *Nature, 464,* 347–348.

Gill, P. (2001). Application of low copy number DNA profiling. *Croatian Medical Journal, 42,* 229–232.

Gill, P., et al. (2000). An investigation of the rigor of interpretation rules for STRs derived from less than 100 pg of DNA. *Forensic Science International, 112,* 17–40.

Gill, P. (2002). Role of short tandem repeat DNA in forensic casework in the UK–past, present, and future perspectives. *BioTechniques, 32,* 366–385.

Jobling, M. A., & Gill, P. (2004). Encoded evidence: DNA in forensic analysis. *Nature Reviews Genetics, 5*, 739–751.

Kloosterman, A. D., & Kersbergen, P. (2003a). Efficacy and limits of genotyping low copy number (LCN) DNA samples by multiplex PCR of STR loci. *Journal de la Société de Biologie, 197*, 351–359.

Kloosterman, A. D., & Kersbergen, P. (2003b). Efficacy and limits of genotyping low copy number DNA samples by multiplex PCR of STR loci. *Progress in Forensic Genetics 9, ICS1239*, 795–798.

Lowe, A., et al. (2002). The propensity of individuals to deposit DNA and secondary transfer of low level DNA from individuals to inert surfaces. *Forensic Science International, 129*, 25–34.

Lowe, A., et al. (2003). Use of low copy number DNA in forensic inference. *Progress in Forensic Genetics 9, ICS 1239*, 799–801.

Lucy, D., et al. (2007). The probability of achieving full allelic representation for LCN-STR profiling of haploid cells. *Science & Justice, 47*, 168–171.

Murray, C., et al. (2001). Use of low copy number (LCN) DNA in forensic inference. *Proceedings of the twelfth international symposium on human identification*. Madison, WI: Promega Corporation. Available at <http://www.promega.com/geneticidproc/ussymp12proc/contents/murray.pdf>.

Raymond, J. J., et al. (2008). Trace DNA analysis: Do you know what your neighbour is doing? A multi-jurisdictional survey. *Forensic Science International: Genetics, 2*, 19–28.

Shaffer, S., et al. (2004). An investigation on the efficacy and limitations of STR multiplex systems in low copy number (LCN) DNA analysis. *Proceedings of the fifteenth international symposium on human identification.* Available at <http://www.promega.com/geneticidproc/ussymp15proc/posterpresentations/49Shaffer.pdf>.

Stouder, S. L., et al. (2001). Trace evidence scrapings: A valuable source of DNA? *Forensic Science Communications, 3*(4). Available at <http://www.fbi.gov/hq/lab/fsc/backissu/oct2001/stouder.htm>.

van Oorschot, R. A., & Jones, M. (1997). DNA fingerprints from fingerprints. *Nature, 387*, 767.

van Oorschot, R. A. H., et al. (2010). Forensic trace DNA: A review. *Investigative Genetics, 1*, 14. Available at <http://www.investigativegenetics.com/content/1/1/14>.

Wickenheiser, R. A. (2002). Trace DNA: A review, discussion of theory, and application of the transfer of trace quantities of DNA through skin contact. *Journal of Forensic Sciences, 47*, 442–450.

Caddy Report and the UK Forensic Science Regulator

CPS Press Release, (Jan. 14, 2008). <http://www.cps.gov.uk/news/press_releases/101_08/>.

Caddy, B. et al. (2008) Review of the science of low template DNA analysis. Available at <http://police.homeoffice.gov.uk/publications/operational-policing/Review_of_Low_Template_DNA_1.pdf>.

Forensic Science Regulator (2008) Response to Professor Brian Caddy's review of the science of low template DNA analysis. Available at <http://police.homeoffice.gov.uk/publications/operational-policing/response-caddy-dna-review>.

ISFG and ISHI 2009 Scientific Discussions and Follow-up

Buckleton, J., & Gill, P. (2011). Further Comment on "Low copy number typing has yet to achieve 'general acceptance'" by Budowle, B., et al., 2009. *Forensic Sci. Int. Genetics*: Supplement Series 2, 551–552. *Forensic Science International: Genetics, 5*, 7–11.

Budowle, B., et al. (2009). Low copy number has yet to achieve "general acceptance." *Forensic Science International: Genetics Supplement Series, 2*, 551–552. Available at <http://www.fsigeneticssup.com/>.

Budowle, B. (2010). Low copy number typing still lacks robustness and reliability. *Profiles in DNA, 13*(2). Available at <http://www.promega.com/profiles/1302/1302_02.html>.

Budowle, B., et al. (2011). Response to Comment on "Low copy number typing has yet to achieve 'general acceptance'" (Budowle et al., 2009. *Forensic Sci. Int. Genetics*: Supplement Series 2, 551–552) by Theresa Caragine, Mechthild Prinz. *Forensic Science International: Genetics, 5*, 5–7.

Budowle, B., & van Daal, A. (2011). Reply to Comments by Buckleton and Gill on "Low copy number typing has yet to achieve 'general acceptance'" by Budowle, B., et al., 2009. *Forensic Sci. Int.*: Genet. Suppl. Series 2, 551–552. *Forensic Science International: Genetics, 5*, 12–14.

Butler, J. M., & Hill, C. R. (2010). Scientific issues with analysis of low amounts of DNA. *Profiles in DNA, 13*(1) Available at <http://www.promega.com/profiles/1301/1301_02.html>.

Caragine, T., & Prinz, M. (2011). Comment on 'Low copy number typing has yet to achieve "general acceptance"' by Budowle et al., 2009, *Forensic Sci. Int. Genetics*: Supplement Series 2, 551–552. *Forensic Science International: Genetics, 5*, 3–4.

Gill, P., & Buckleton, J. (2009). Low copy number typing – where next? *Forensic Science International: Genetics Supplement Series, 2*, 553–555. Available at <http://www.fsigeneticssup.com/>.

Linacre, A. (2009). Review of low template DNA typing. *Forensic Science International: Genetics Supplement Series, 2*, 549–550. Available at <http://www.fsigeneticssup.com/>.

Leventhal, B. (2010). Low copy number analysis from a legal perspective. *Profiles in DNA, 13*(1). Available at <http://www.promega.com/profiles/1301/1301_03.html>.

Schneider, P. M., et al. (2011). Publications and letters related to the forensic genetic analysis of low amounts of DNA. *Forensic Science International: Genetics, 5*, 1–2.

van Daal, A. (2010). LCN DNA analysis: Limitations prevent 'general acceptance'. *Profiles in DNA, 13*(2). Available at <http://www.promega.com/profiles/1302/1302_01.html>.

Word, C. (2010). What is LCN?–definitions and challenges. *Profiles in DNA, 13*(1). Available at <http://www .promega.com/profiles/1301/1301_01.html>.

Court Judgments on LCN Cases

Denver DA Resource. <http://www.denverda.org/DNA/Low%20Copy%20DNA%20Profiling%20Cases.htm>.

NY v Megnath (2010). Available at <http://www.denverda.org/DNA_Documents/Megnath.pdf>.

R v Hoey (2007). Available at <http://www.denverda.org/DNA_Documents/Hoey.pdf>.

R v Reed & Anor (2009). Available at <http://www.bailii.org/ew/cases/EWCA/Crim/2009/2698.html>.

Wallace v. Queen (2010). Available at <http://www.courtsofnz.govt.nz/from/decisions/judgments/html>. (CA590/2007; judgment 3/3/10); see also media release at <http://www.courtsofnz.govt.nz/cases/wallace-v-r-2/at_download/fileMediaNotes>.

Omagh Bombing Case: Critics and Responses

<http://en.wikipedia.org/wiki/Omagh_bombing>.

<http://en.wikipedia.org/wiki/Colm_Murphy>.

<http://news.bbc.co.uk/2/hi/uk_news/northern_ireland/7154221.stm>.

<http://news.bbc.co.uk/2/hi/uk_news/northern_ireland/7149505.stm>.

The Forensic Institute. <http://www.theforensicinstitute.com/news/low-copy-number-dna-and-the-forensic-institute.html>.

Gilder, J., et al. (2009). Comments on the review of low copy number testing. *International Journal of Legal Medicine, 123*, 535–536.

Gill, P. (2008). LCN DNA: Proof beyond reasonable doubt? – a response. *Nature Reviews Genetics, 9*, 326.

Graham, E. A. M. (2008). DNA reviews: Low level DNA profiling. *Forensic Science, Medicine, and Pathology, 4*, 129–131.

McCartney, C. (2008). LCN DNA: Proof beyond reasonable doubt? *Nature Reviews Genetics, 9*, 726.

Whitaker, J., et al. (2009). Response to low level DNA profiling. *Forensic Science, Medicine, and Pathology, 5*, 102–103.

Methods for Improving Sensitivity

Benschop, C. C. G., et al. (2010). Post-coital vaginal sampling with nylon flocked swabs improves DNA typing. *Forensic Science International: Genetics, 4*, 115–121.

Forster, L., et al. (2008). Direct comparison of post-28-cycle PCR purification and modified capillary electrophoresis methods with the 34-cycle "low copy number" (LCN) method for analysis of trace forensic DNA samples. *Forensic Science International: Genetics, 2*, 318–328.

Gross, T., et al. (2009). A review of low template STR analysis in casework using the DNA SenCE post-PCR purification technique. *Forensic Science International: Genetics Supplement Series, 2*, 5–7.

Holland, M. M., & Parsons, T. J. (1999). Mitochondrial DNA sequence analysis – validation and use for forensic casework. *Forensic Science Review, 11*, 21–50.

Leclair, B., et al. (2003). STR DNA typing: Increased sensitivity and efficient sample consumption using reduced PCR reaction volumes. *Journal of Forensic Sciences, 48*, 1001–1013.

Lederer, T., et al. (2002). Purification of STR-multiplex-amplified micro samples can enhance signal intensity in capillary electrophoresis. *International Journal of Legal Medicine, 116*, 165–169.

Michel, S., et al. (2009). Interpretation of low-copy-number DNA profile after post-PCR purification. *Forensic Science International: Genetics Supplement Series, 2*, 542–543.

Roeder, A. D., et al. (2009). Maximizing DNA profiling success from sub-optimal quantities of DNA: A staged approach. *Forensic Science International: Genetics, 3*, 128–137.

Smith, P. J., & Ballantyne, J. (2007). Simplified low-copy-number DNA analysis by post-PCR purification. *Journal of Forensic Sciences*, *52*, 820–829.

Strom, C. M., & Rechitsky, S. (1998). Use of nested PCR to identify charred human remains and minute amounts of blood. *Journal of Forensic Sciences*, *43*, 696–700.

Westen, A. A., et al. (2009). Higher capillary electrophoresis injection settings as an efficient approach to increase the sensitivity of STR typing. *Journal of Forensic Sciences*, *54*, 591–598.

Yeung, S. H., et al. (2008). Fluorescence energy transfer-labeled primers for high-performance forensic DNA profiling. *Electrophoresis*, *29*, 2251–2259.

Approaches to Handle Potential Allele Drop-out

Gill, P., et al. (2005). A graphical simulation model of the entire DNA process associated with the analysis of short tandem repeat loci. *Nucleic Acids Research*, *33*, 632–643.

Taberlet, P., et al. (1996). Reliable genotyping of samples with very low DNA quantities using PCR. *Nucleic Acids Research*, *24*, 3189–3194.

Tvedebrink, T., et al. (2009). Estimating the probability of allelic drop-out of STR alleles in forensic genetics. *Forensic Science International: Genetics*, *3*, 222–226.

Walsh, P. S., et al. (1992). Preferential PCR amplification of alleles: Mechanisms and solutions. *PCR Methods and Applications*, *1*, 241–250.

Interpretation Issues

Anjos, M. J., et al. (2006). Low copy number: Interpretation of evidence results. *Progress in Forensic Genetics 10, ICS 1288*, 616–618.

Balding, D. J., & Buckleton, J. (2009). Interpreting low template DNA profiles. *Forensic Science International: Genetics*, *4*, 1–10.

Buckleton, J., & Triggs, C. (2006). Is the 2p rule always conservative? *Forensic Science International*, *159*, 206–209.

Cook, R., et al. (1998). A hierarchy of propositions: Deciding which level to address in casework. *Science & Justice*, *38*, 231–239.

Cowen, S., et al. (2010). An investigation of the robustness of the consensus method of interpreting low-template DNA profiles. *Forensic Science International: Genetics* (in press) (doi:10.1016/j.fsigen.2010.08.010).

Evett, I. W. (1993). Establishing the evidential value of a small quantity of material found at a crime scene. *Journal of Forensic Science Society*, *33*, 83–86.

Evett, I. W., et al. (2002). Interpreting small quantities of DNA: The hierarchy of propositions and the use of Bayesian networks. *Journal of Forensic Sciences*, *47*, 520–530.

Gill, P., et al. (2000). An investigation of the rigor of interpretation rules for STRs derived from less than 100 pg of DNA. *Forensic Science International*, *112*, 17–40.

Gill, P., et al. (2006). DNA commission of the International Society of Forensic Genetics: Recommendations on the interpretation of mixtures. *Forensic Science International*, *160*, 90–101.

Gill, P., et al. (2007). LoComatioN: A software tool for the analysis of low copy number DNA profiles. *Forensic Science International*, *166*, 128–138.

Gill, P., & Buckleton, J. (2010). A universal strategy to interpret DNA profiles that does not require a definition of *low-copy-number*. *Forensic Science International: Genetics*, *4*, 221–227.

Validation

Benschop, C. C. G., et al. (2010). Low template STR typing: Effect of replicate number and consensus method on genotyping reliability and DNA database search results. *Forensic Science International: Genetics* (in press). doi:10.1016/j.fsigen.2010.06.006.

Buckleton, J. (2009). Validation issues around DNA typing of low level DNA. *Forensic Science International: Genetics*, *3*, 255–260.

Caragine, T., et al. (2009). Validation of testing and interpretation protocols for low template DNA samples using AmpFlSTR Identifiler. *Croatian Medical Journal*, *50*, 250–267.

Petricevic, S., et al. (2010). Validation and development of interpretation guidelines for low copy number (LCN) DNA profiling in New Zealand using the AmpFlSTR SGM Plus multiplex. *Forensic Science International: Genetics*, *4*, 305–310.

Whitaker, J. P., et al. (2001). A comparison of the characteristics of profiles produced with the AMPFlSTR SGM Plus multiplex system for both standard and low copy number (LCN) STR DNA analysis. *Forensic Science International, 123*, 215–223.

High Sensitivity Laboratory

Caragine, T. (2010). Presentation at the technical leaders meeting held in conjunction with the 21st International Symposium on Human Identification.

Prinz, M., et al. (2006). Maximization of STR DNA typing success for touched objects. *Progress in Forensic Genetics 11, ICS 1288*, 651–653.

Schiffner, L. A., et al. (2005). Optimization of a simple, automatable extraction method to recover sufficient DNA from low copy number DNA samples for generation of short tandem repeat profiles. *Croatian Medical Journal, 46*, 578–586.

Tamariz, J., et al. (2006). The application of ultraviolent irradiation to exogenous sources of DNA in plasticware and water for the amplification of low copy number DNA. *Journal of Forensic Sciences, 51*, 790–794.

Whole Genome Amplification

Ballantyne, K. N., et al. (2006). Molecular crowding increases the amplification success of multiple displacement amplification and short tandem repeat genotyping. *Analytical Biochemistry, 355*, 298–303.

Ballantyne, K. N., et al. (2007). Decreasing amplification bias associated with multiple displacement amplification and short tandem repeat genotyping. *Analytical Biochemistry, 368*, 222–229.

Ballantyne, K. N., et al. (2007). Comparison of two whole genome amplification methods for STR genotyping of LCN and degraded DNA samples. *Forensic Science International, 166*, 35–41.

Barber, A. L., & Foran, D. R. (2006). The utility of whole genome amplification for typing compromised forensic samples. *Journal of Forensic Sciences, 51*, 1344–1349.

Bergen, A. W., et al. (2005). Effects of DNA mass on multiple displacement whole genome amplification and genotyping performance. *BMC Biotechnology, 5*, 24.

Bergen, A. W., et al. (2005). Comparison of yield and genotyping performance of multiple displacement amplification and OmniPlex whole genome amplified DNA generated from multiple DNA sources. *Human Mutation, 26*, 262–270.

Bonnette, M. D., et al. (2009). dcDegenerate oligonucleotide primed-PCR for multilocus, genome-wide analysis from limited quantities of DNA. *Diagnostic Molecular Pathology, 18*, 165–175.

Dean, F. B., et al. (2002). Comprehensive human genome amplification using multiple displacement amplification. *Proceedings of the National Academy of Sciences U.S.A, 99*, 5261–5266.

Giardina, E., et al. (2009). Whole genome amplification and real-time PCR in forensic casework. *BMC Genomics, 10*(159), 1–9.

Hanson, E. K., & Ballantyne, J. (2005). Whole genome amplification strategy for forensic genetic analysis using single or few cell equivalents of genomic DNA. *Analytical Biochemistry, 346*, 246–257.

Holbrook, J. F., et al. (2005). Exploring whole genome amplification as a DNA recovery tool for molecular genetic studies. *Journal of Biomolecular Technology, 16*, 125–133.

Hosono, S., et al. (2003). Unbiased whole-genome amplification directly from clinical samples. *Genome Research, 13*, 954–964.

Jiang, Z., et al. (2005). Genome amplification of single sperm using multiple displacement amplification. *Nucleic Acids Research, 33*, e91.

Lasken, R. S., & Egholm, M. (2003). Whole genome amplification: Abundant supplies of DNA from precious samples or clinical specimens. *Trends in Biotechnology, 21*, 531–535.

Lovmar, L., et al. (2003). Quantitative evaluation by minisequencing and microarrays reveals accurate multiplexed SNP genotyping of whole genome amplified DNA. *Nucleic Acids Research, 31*, e129.

Nagy, M., et al. (2006). Evaluation of whole-genome amplification of low-copy-number DNA in chimerism analysis after allogeneic stem cell transplantation using STR marker typing. *Electrophoresis, 27*, 3028–3037.

Schneider, P. M., et al. (2004). Whole genome amplification—the solution for a common problem in forensic casework? *Progress in Forensic Genetics 10, ICS 1261*, 24–26.

Sun, G., et al. (2005). Whole-genome amplification: Relative efficiencies of the current methods. *Legal Medicine, 7*, 279–286.

Zhang, L., et al. (1992). Whole genome amplification from a single cell: Implications for genetic analysis. *Proceedings of the National Academy of Sciences U.S.A, 89*, 5847–5851.
<http://www1.qiagen.com/Products/WholeGenomeAmplification/>.
<http://www.sigmaaldrich.com/life-science/molecular-biology/automation/whole-genome-amplification.html>.

Thresholds

Gill, P., et al. (2009). The *low-template-DNA* (stochastic) threshold – its determination relative to risk analysis for national DNA databases. *Forensic Science International: Genetics, 3*, 104–111.
Puch-Solis, R., et al. (2010). Practical determination of the low template DNA threshold. *Forensic Science International: Genetics* (in press) (doi:10.1016/j.fsigen.2010.09.001).
Tvederbrink, T., et al. (2009). Estimating the probability of allelic drop-out of STR alleles in forensic genetics. *Forensic Science International: Genetics, 3*, 222–226.

Low-Level Y-STR Testing

Hall, A., & Ballantyne, J. (2003). Novel Y-STR typing strategies reveal the genetic profile of the semen donor in extended interval post-coital cervicovaginal samples. *Forensic Science International, 136*, 58–72.
Mayntz-Press, K. A., & Ballantyne, J. (2007). Performance characteristics of commercial Y-STR multiplex systems. *Journal of Forensic Sciences, 52*, 1025–1034.
Sturk, K. A., et al. (2009). Evaluation of modified Yfiler amplification strategy for compromised samples. *Croatian Medical Journal, 50*, 228–238.

Cases Solved with Low-Level DNA

Dieltjes, P., et al. (2010). A sensitive method to extract DNA from biological traces present on ammunition for the purpose of genetic profiling. *International Journal of Legal Medicine* (in press) (doi:10.1007/s00414-010-0454-4).
Irwin, J. A., et al. (2007). Application of low copy number STR typing to the identification of aged, degraded skeletal remains. *Journal of Forensic Sciences, 52*, 1322–1327.
Pizzamiglio, M., et al. (2004). Forensic identification of a murderer by LCN DNA collected from the inside of the victim's car. *Progress in Forensic Genetics 10, ICS 1261*, 437–439.

CHAPTER

12

Single Nucleotide Polymorphisms and Applications

Core short tandem repeat (STR) loci are being used extensively today and will probably continue to be used for many years in the future because they are part of the DNA databases that are growing around the world. Yet forensic DNA scientists often use additional markers as the need arises to obtain further information about a particular sample. This chapter will focus on efforts with single nucleotide polymorphisms (SNPs) and insertion-deletion (indel) biallelic polymorphisms and their applications including ancestry estimation and phenotype prediction.

SINGLE NUCLEOTIDE POLYMORPHISMS (SNPs)

A single-base sequence variation between individuals at a particular point in the genome is often referred to as a *single nucleotide polymorphism*, or SNP (pronounced "snip"). SNPs are abundant in the human genome and, as such, are being used for linkage studies to track genetic diseases (Brookes 1999). Millions of SNPs exist per individual and thus the abundance of SNPs means that they could be used to help differentiate individuals from one another. Table 12.1 compares and contrasts SNP and STR markers.

A number of technologies have been developed to minaturize and automate the procedure for SNP analysis. Millions of SNPs can be processed simultaneously using next-generation sequencing technologies (Ku et al. 2010) from companies such as Illumina (San Diego, CA).

Pros and Cons of SNPs

SNPs have been considered as potential genetic markers by the forensic DNA community for several reasons. First and foremost, the polymerase chain reaction (PCR) products from

TABLE 12.1 Comparison of STR and SNP Markers. SNPs Are More Common in the Human Genome Than STRs But Are Not as Polymorphic.

Characteristics	Short Tandem Repeats (STRs)	Single Nucleotide Polymorphisms (SNPs)
Occurrence in human genome	≈1 in every 15 kb	≈1 in every 1 kb
General informativeness	High	Low; only 20% to 30% as informative as STRs
Mutation rate	≈1 in 1000	≈1 in 100 000 000
Marker type	Di-, tri-, tetra-, penta-nucleotide repeat markers with many alleles	Mostly bi-allelic markers with six possibilities: A/G, C/T, A/T, C/G, T/G, A/C
Number of alleles per marker	Usually 5 to 20	Typically 2 (some tri-allelic SNPs exist)
Detection methods	Gel/capillary electrophoresis	Sequence analysis; microchip hybridization
Multiplex capability	> 10 markers with multiple fluorescent dyes	Difficult to amplify more than 50 SNPs well (detection of 1000s with microchips)
Amplicon size	≈75 to 400 bp	Can be less than 100 bp
Ability to predict ethnicity (biogeographical ancestry)	Limited	Some SNPs associated with ethnicity
Phenotypic information	No	Possible to predict some hair colors, etc.
Major advantages for forensic application	Many alleles enabling higher success rates for detecting and deciphering mixtures	PCR products can be made small potentially enabling higher success rates with degraded DNA samples; low mutation rate may aid kinship analysis; phenotype prediction
Limitations for forensic application	Data interpretation must account for artifacts such as dye blobs, stutter, spikes, etc.	No widely established core loci; large multiplexing assays required; mixture resolution issues/interpretation; multiple typing platforms make universal SNP selection difficult; population substructure due to low mutation rate

SNPs can be less than 100 bp in size, which means that these markers are able to recover information from degraded DNA samples better than STRs that have amplicons as large as 300 bp to 400 bp. Second, they in principle can be multiplexed to a higher level than STRs because some detection methods (e.g., array hybridization) are not constrainted by electrophoretic space (e.g., 4 fluorescent dye labels and a size range of 75 bp to 450 bp). Third, the sample processing and data analysis can be more fully automated because a size-based separation is not needed. Fourth, there is no stutter artifact associated with each allele, which should help simplify interpretation of the allele call. Finally, the ability to predict ethnic origin and certain physical traits may be possible with careful selection of SNP markers. SNPs are most likely to impact forensic applications with this last reason—the ability to estimate ethnicity and to predict phenotypes (Butler et al. 2007).

The vast majority of SNPs are bi-allelic meaning that they have two possible alleles and therefore three possible genotypes. For example, if the alleles for a SNP locus are A and B (where "A" could represent a C, T, A, or G nucleotide and "B" could also be a C, T, A, or G), then the three possible genotypes would be AA, BB, or AB. Mixture interpretation can present a challenge with SNPs because it may be difficult to tell the difference between a true heterozygote and a mixture containing two homozygotes or a heterozygote and a homozygote (Butler et al. 2007). The ability to obtain quantitative information from SNP allele calls is important when attempting to decipher mixtures.

At this time, one of the biggest challenges to using SNPs in forensic DNA typing applications is the inability to simultaneously amplify enough SNPs in robust multiplexes from small amounts of DNA. Because a single bi-allelic SNP by itself yields less information than a multi-allelic STR marker, it is necessary to analyze a larger number of SNPs in order to obtain a reasonable power of discrimination to define a unique profile. Progress is being made in the area of multiplex PCR amplification and assays capable of amplifying and analyzing more than 50 SNPs simultaneously have been demonstrated (Sanchez et al. 2006).

Since each SNP locus typically possesses only two possible alleles, more markers are needed to obtain a high discriminatory power than for STR loci that possess multiple alleles. Computational analyses have shown that on average 25 to 45 SNP loci are needed to yield equivalent random match probabilities as the 13 core STR loci (Chakraborty et al. 1999). Another study predicted that 50 SNPs possessing frequencies in the range of 20% to 50% for the minor allele can theoretically result in likelihood ratios similar to approximately 12 STR loci (Gill 2001).

The number of SNPs needed may fluctuate in practice because some SNP loci have variable allele frequencies in different population groups. Most likely a battery of 50 to 100 SNPs will be required to match the same powers of discrimination and mixture resolution capabilities now achieved with 10 to 16 STR loci (Gill et al. 2004).

SNP Marker Categories and Applications

At the 2007 Congress of the International Society for Forensic Genetics held in Copenhagen, Denmark, an international panel of experts discussed SNP markers, technologies, and applications (Butler et al. 2008). The panel was moderated by Niels Morling (University of Copenhagen, Denmark) and John Butler (NIST, USA) and consisted of Bruce Budowle (FBI, USA), Peter Gill (Forensic Science Service, UK), Ken Kidd (Yale University, USA), Chris Phillips (University of Santiago de Compostela, Spain), Peter Schneider (University of Cologne, Germany), and Peter Vallone (NIST, USA). At this meeting, SNP markers were categorized based on application.

SNP markers may be classified into four general uses (Budowle & van Daal 2008, Butler et al. 2008): (1) individual identification or identity testing SNPs, (2) lineage-informative SNPs, (3) ancestry-informative SNPs, and (4) phenotype-informative SNPs. Table 12.2 defines these classifications and lists references to several examples for each. Most of the work to date has been performed with the identity testing SNPs using autosomal loci. Some SNP detection assays have also been used for pathology and toxicology purposes (Kiehne & Kauferstein 2007). Work with lineage informative SNPs will also be covered in Chapters 13, 14, and 15 on Y-chromosome, mitochondrial DNA, and X-chromosome, respectively.

TABLE 12.2 Categories of SNP Markers (See Budowle & van Daal 2008, Butler et al. 2008).

Category	Characteristics	Examples
Identity SNPs Individual Identification SNPs (IISNPs)	SNPs that collectively give very low probabilities of two individuals having the same multi-locus genotype	FSS 21plex (Dixon et al. 2005) SNPforID 52plex (Sanchez et al. 2006) Kidd group SNPs (Pakstis et al. 2010)
Lineage SNPs Lineage Informative SNPs (LISNPs)	Sets of tightly linked SNPs that function as multi-allelic markers that can serve to identify relatives with higher probabilities than simple bi-allelic SNPs	mtDNA coding region SNPs (Coble et al. 2004) Japanese Y-SNPs (Mizuno et al. 2010) Haplotype blocks (Ge et al. 2010)
Ancestry SNPs Ancestry Informative SNPs (AISNPs)	SNPs that collectively give a high probability of an individual's ancestry being from one part of the world or being derived from two or more areas of the world	SNPforID 34plex (Phillips et al. 2007b) 24 SNPs (Lao et al. 2010) FSS YSNPs (Wetton et al. 2005)
Phenotype SNPs Phenotype Informative SNPs (PISNPs)	SNPs that provide a high probability that the individual has particular phenotypes, such as a particular skin color, hair color, eye color, etc.	Red hair (Grimes et al. 2001) "Golden" gene pigmentation (Lamason et al. 2005) IrisPlex eye color (Walsh et al. 2010)

SNP Markers and Multiplexes

SNPs occur in noncoding regions of the genome as well as in genes (both exons and introns). Depending on the potential application, SNP markers might be selected outside of exons or the direct cause of a genetic mutation. From a forensic historical perspective, the first work with SNP typing was with the HLA-DQA1 and AmpliType PM kits (Butler 2010, *Fundamentals*, Chapter 3). These early PCR assays were sensitive but not very informative because collectively DQA1 and PolyMarker only examined six loci. In recent years, a great deal of work has been performed to characterize a number of new SNP loci and to develop useful SNP multiplex assays.

Several members of the European forensic DNA typing community launched a project in 2003 known as SNP*for*ID that worked to develop SNP assays to directly aid forensic DNA analysis. This group selected several sets of potential forensic SNP markers and developed highly multiplexed SNP assays. Population data was also gathered to measure SNP allele frequencies in various groups of interest. The SNP*for*ID website (http://www.snpforid.org) contains links to their publications and population data. The SNP*for*ID consortium has published a 52plex PCR and SNaPshot assay (Sanchez et al. 2006) as well as collaborated with Applied Biosystems to develop a 48 autosomal SNP + amelogenin sex-typing assay based on the GenPlex genotyping system (Tomas et al. 2008). The SNP*for*ID group has also developed a 34plex with ancestry informative SNPs (Phillips et al. 2007b).

Ken Kidd's group at Yale University has characterized allele frequencies for more than 100 SNPs in roughly 40 different global human populations in an effort to find optimal human identity SNP markers. This group has also published criteria for selecting what they term a "universal individual identification panel" of SNPs (Kidd et al. 2006, Pakstis et al. 2007, Pakstis et al. 2010).

SNP Information Databases

Large national and international efforts have been underway over the past few years to catalog human variation found in the form of SNP markers. The SNP Consortium (TSC) was established in the spring of 1999 to create a high-density SNP map of the human genome. The TSC effort (http://snp.cshl.org/) produced several million mapped and characterized human SNP markers that have been entered into public databases including dbSNP housed at the National Institutes of Health's National Center for Biotechnology Information (http://www.ncbi.nlm.nih.gov/SNP).

The original TSC work became the foundation for the International HapMap project that was a follow-on to the Human Genome Project. The HapMap work involved typing 270 individuals from African, European, and Asian populations with several million SNPs (http://www.hapmap.org/). With these large ventures ongoing around the world, there is no shortage of available SNP markers and accompanying population data.

The University of Santiago de Compostela in Spain has developed a web interface called SPSmart (SNPs for Population Studies-smart engine) to evaluate SNP population data (Amigo et al. 2008). This website also has a browser for examining SNP allele frequencies from the SNP*for*ID 52plex and 34plex assays (http://spsmart.cesga.es/snpforid.php).

SNP ANALYSIS TECHNIQUES

A number of SNP typing methods are available, each with its own strengths and weaknesses. Several reviews of SNP typing technologies have been published and can be consulted for a more in-depth view of methodologies (Gut 2001, Kwok 2001, Syvanen 2001, Sobrino et al. 2005, Perkel 2008). A few SNP analysis techniques are summarized in Table 12.3.

One of the important characteristics of a SNP assay is its ability to examine multiple markers simultaneously since SNPs are not as variable as STRs and typically a limited amount of DNA template is available in forensic casework. While pyrosequencing and TaqMan assays are limited in their multiplexing capabilities, Luminex and minisequencing (SNaPshot) assays enable multiplexed analysis of a dozen or more SNP markers simultaneously. A number of SNP assays for detecting mtDNA, Y-chromosome, and autosomal markers have been described in the literature using the SNaPshot approach, which can be run on ABI 310 and 3100 instruments already in use in most forensic DNA laboratories.

SNaPshot: A Primer Extension Assay Capable of Multiplex Analysis

Minisequencing, sometimes referred to as SNaPshot, involves allele-specific primer extension with fluorescent dye-labeled dideoxynucleotide triphosphates (ddNTPs) to help visualize the results. There are three primary steps in performing minisequencing: amplification, primer extension, and analysis (Figure 12.1). First, the region around each SNP locus is amplified using PCR. Amplicons can be pooled following singleplex PCR or simultaneously generated using multiplex PCR. The remaining dNTPs and primers following PCR are destroyed by simply adding two different enzymes to the initial reaction tube or well. Exonuclease (Exo) chews up the single-stranded primers while shrimp alkaline phosphatase

TABLE 12.3 SNP Analysis Techniques (See Perkel 2008 for Additional Technologies).

Method	Description	References
Reverse dot blot or linear arrays	A series of allele-specific probes are attached to a nylon test strip at separate sites; biotinylated PCR products hybridize to their complementary probes and are then detected with a colorimetric reaction and evaluated visually.	Saiki et al. (1989), Reynolds et al. (2000)
Genetic bit analysis	Primer extension with ddNTPs is detected with a colorimetric assay in a 96-well format.	Nikiforov et al. (1994)
Direct sequencing	PCR products are sequenced and compared to reveal SNP sites.	Kwok et al. (1994)
Denaturing HPLC	Two PCR products are mixed and injected on an ion-paired reversed-phase HPLC; single base differences in the two amplicons will be revealed by extra heteroduplex peaks.	Hecker et al. (1999)
TaqMan 5′ nuclease assay	A fluorescent probe consisting of reporter and quencher dyes is added to a PCR reaction; amplification of a probe-specific product causes cleavage of the probe and generates an increase in fluorescence.	Livak (1999)
Fluorescence polarization	Primer extension across the SNP site with dye-labeled ddNTPs; monitoring changes in fluorescence polarization reveals which dye is bound to the primer.	Chen et al. (1999)
Mass spectrometry	Primer extension across the SNP site with ddNTPs; mass difference between the primer and extension product is measured to reveal nucleotide(s) present.	Haff & Smirnov (1997), Li et al. (1999)
High-density arrays (Affymetrix chip)	Thousands of oligonucleotide probes are represented at specific locations on a microchip array; fluorescently labeled PCR products hybridize to complementary probes to reveal SNPs.	Wang et al. (1998), Sapolsky et al. (1999)
Electronic dot blot (Nanogen chip)	Potential SNP alleles are placed at discrete locations on a microchip array; an electric field at each point in the array is used to control hybridization stringency.	Sosnowski et al. (1997), Gilles et al. (1999)
Molecular beacons	Hairpin stem on oligonucleotide probe keeps fluorophore and its quencher in contact until hybridization to DNA target, which results in fluorescence.	Giesendorf et al. (1998)
Oligonucleotide ligation assay (OLA)	Colorimetric assay in microtiter 96-well format involving ligation of two probes if the complementary base is present.	Delahunty et al. (1996)
T_m-shift genotyping	Allelic-specific PCR is performed with a GC-tail attached to one of the forward allele-specific primers; amplified allele with GC-tailed primer will exhibit a melting curve at a higher temperature.	Germer & Higuchi (1999)
Pyrosequencing	Sequencing by synthesis of 20–30 nucleotides beyond primer site; dNTPs are added in a specific order and those incorporated result in release of pyrophosphate and light through an enzyme cascade.	Ahmadian et al. (2000), Andreasson et al. (2002)
Allele-specific hybridization (Luminex 100)	Dye-labeled PCR products hybridize to oligonucleotide probes (representing the various SNP types) attached to as many as 100 different colored beads; each bead is interrogated to determine its color and whether or not a PCR product is attached as the beads pass two lasers in a flow cytometer.	Armstrong et al. (2000), Budowle et al. (2004)

(Continued)

TABLE 12.3 SNP Analysis Techniques (See Perkel 2008 for Additional Technologies). *(Continued)*

Method	Description	References
Minisequencing (SNaPshot assay)	Allele-specific primer extension across the SNP site with fluorescently labeled ddNTPs; mobility modifying tails can be added to the 5′-end of each primer in order to spatially separate them during electrophoresis.	Tully et al. (1996)
SNPstream UHT	High-tech version of genetic bit analysis with a 384-well tag array and 12plex PCR.	Bell et al. (2002)

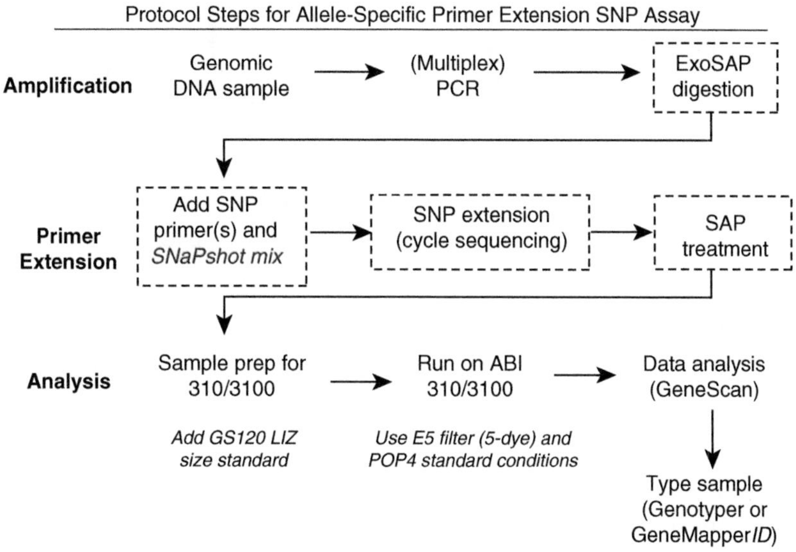

FIGURE 12.1 Steps in allele-specific primer extension SNP detection (e.g., minisequencing or SNaPshot) assay. The boxed portions illustrate additional steps performed in this assay relative to STR typing.

(SAP) destroys the dNTP building blocks. These enzymes are often sold together as "ExoSAP." It is necessary to remove the primers and dNTPs so they do not interfere with the subsequent primer extension reaction.

Primer extension is performed by adding SNP extension primers, a mixture of the four possible ddNTPs each with a unique fluorescent dye label, and a polymerase to the ExoSAP-treated PCR products. The SNaPshot "kit" from Applied Biosystems only supplies the fluorescently labeled ddNTPs, buffer, and polymerase making it generic to any primer set. The SNP extension primers are designed to anneal immediately adjacent to a SNP site so that the addition of a single ddNTP will interrogate the nucleotide present at the SNP site in the PCR product. The SNP extension reaction is heated and cooled, usually through 25 cycles on a thermal cycler, to permit a linear amplification of the fluorescent ddNTP addition to the SNP primer by the polymerase. If any dNTPs remain from the preceding PCR reaction, then extension can go beyond the single base. Likewise, the presence of remaining

(a)

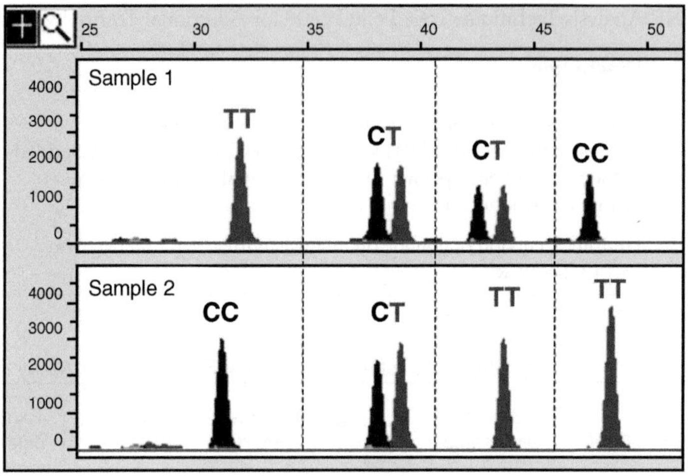

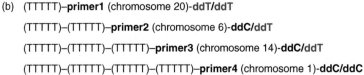

(b) (TTTTT)–**primer1** (chromosome 20)-**ddT/ddT**

(TTTTT)–(TTTTT)–**primer2** (chromosome 6)-**ddC/ddT**

(TTTTT)–(TTTTT)–(TTTTT)–**primer3** (chromosome 14)-**ddC/ddT**

(TTTTT)–(TTTTT)–(TTTTT)–(TTTTT)–**primer4** (chromosome 1)-**ddC/ddC**

FIGURE 12.2 Allele-specific primer extension results using four autosomal SNP markers on two different samples (a). SNP loci are from separate chromosomes (1, 6, 14, and 20) and therefore unlinked. Electrophoretic resolution of the SNP primer extension products occurs due to poly(T) tails that are 5 nucleotides different from one another (b).

PCR primers could mean that competing side reactions occur and thus interfere with the desired primer extension of the SNP primer.

Following the SNP extension reaction, the products are treated with SAP to remove unincorporated fluorescent ddNTPs. If the SAP treatment is incomplete, then dye artifacts (a.k.a. dye blobs) may occur in the electropherogram and obscure the SNP allele peaks being measured.

The availability of five-dye detection with electrophoretic platforms (see Chapter 6) enables an internal size standard to be added in the fifth dye channel to correct for run-to-run migration differences. Each of the four nucleotides has their own dye color: A (green), G (blue), C (yellow; usually displayed as black for better visual contrast), and T (red). Thus, the presence of a blue peak in the electropherogram would indicate that a G (ddGTP) had been incorporated by the polymerase at the SNP site.

Multiple primers can be analyzed simultaneously by linking a variable number of additional nucleotides to the 5′-end of the primers so that each primer differs by several nucleotides from its neighbor. Typically a poly(T) tail is used with a 3 to 5 base spread between primers (Tully et al. 1996, Vallone et al. 2004) although a mixed sequence that is not complementary to any human sequences has been used successfully (Sanchez et al. 2003). Thus, primer1 may contain a 5T 5′-tail, primer2 a 10T tail, primer3 a 15T tail, and primer4 a 20T tail in order to adequately resolve each locus during an electrophoretic separation (Figure 12.2).

The color of a peak in a minisequencing assay conveys the nucleotide present at the SNP site of interest while the size position of a peak correlates back to its locus based on the 5′-tailing used to differentiate the SNP marker from its neighbors. Homozygous alleles appear as single peaks and heterozygous alleles as two adjacent peaks (see upper middle section in Figure 12.2). Automated allele designation can be performed with computer programs such as Genotyper or GeneMapper designed to look for peaks in a particular color and size range.

A major advantage of allele-specific primer extension is that samples can be run on multi-color fluorescence detection electrophoresis instrumentation already available in most forensic DNA typing laboratories such as the ABI 310 or 3100 (see Chapter 6). The technique is sensitive, has the ability to be multiplexed, and has proven to be fairly robust with casework samples.

High-Density SNP Arrays

The genomics community has graduated to next-generation sequencing technologies and high-throughput SNP typing to feed their appetite for more genetic information. Will the forensic community follow? Perhaps—if prices per sample drop and the vast amounts of data generated with these technologies become more manageable.

High-density SNP arrays permit hundreds of thousands or even millions of SNPs to be analyzed in parallel. However, these arrays typically require hundreds of nanograms of DNA, which is often not available from casework samples arising from minute biological stains. These SNP arrays are being used to perform genome-wide association studies (GWAS) to associate genetic variants with physical traits and disease markers. One of the side benefits of these studies in the identification of SNPs that could aid forensic phenotyping.

Direct-to-consumer companies, such as 23andMe (https://www.23andme.com/), are using high-density SNP arrays to provide genetic testing for biogeographical ancestry assessment and disease prediction using GWAS information collected from the growing scientific literature. These companies are claiming that kinship associations can be extended to second or even third degree relatives with a large number of SNPs—something that cannot be done with STR markers. In May 2009, Casework Genetics LLC (http://www.caseworkgen.com/) was founded with the goal of bringing the power of high-density SNP array technology to the forensic community. Using deconvolution algorithms (Homer et al. 2008), Casework Genetics hopes that massively parallel SNP results can help solve the mixture resolution issue previously mentioned for bi-allelic SNP markers.

APPLICATIONS

In the following sections, each of the primary SNP applications will be briefly explored. References are provided at the back of the chapter to give interested readers further information on each topic.

Identity SNPs—Supplementing Human Identity Testing

While SNPs will likely not replace STRs for DNA databasing and casework anytime soon (see Butler et al. 2007), researchers have identified a number of useful candidate loci for human identity testing (Lee et al. 2005, Fang et al. 2009, Pakstis et al. 2010). Multiplex SNP assays have been constructed and population samples analyzed to measure allele frequencies (Vallone et al. 2005, Krjutskov et al. 2009, Nakahara et al. 2009, Pietrangeli et al. 2010).

As mentioned earlier, the SNP*for*ID project produced a 52plex PCR and SNP assay examining 52 autosomal SNP loci (Table 12.4). This assay, or minor variations of it, has been extensively studied in various population groups (Drobnic et al. 2010) and validated for forensic applications (Musgrave-Brown et al. 2007, Børsting et al. 2009) and paternity testing purposes (Børsting et al. 2008). These loci have also been tested for the NIST Standard Reference Material 2391b PCR-based DNA Profiling Standard (Børsting et al. 2011).

SNPs can serve as supplemental markers when STR results are not definitive enough in complex relationship tests (Phillips et al. 2008, Børsting & Morling 2011). The low mutation rate of SNPs relative to STRs means that the SNPs can help address multi-generational questions where STR mutations can produce an ambigous result. The Netherlands Forensic Institute has also developed tri-allelic SNPs to aid mixture interpretation and analysis of degraded DNA (Westen et al. 2009).

Lineage SNPs—Aiding Kinship Analyses

Closely spaced autosomal SNPs are genetically linked (i.e., recombination does not occur between them to shuffle the alleles being passed on to the next generation). These linked SNPs can move as a haplotype block through generational transmission. In this form, these blocks of information provide more allelic states than do single loci and as such can be helpful for kinship analyses (Ge et al. 2010). Haplotype blocks also occur on the X-chromosome, the Y-chromosome, and mtDNA.

As will be discussed in the next three chapters, Y-chromosome, X-chromosome, and mitochondrial DNA markers can serve a variety of purposes in human identity testing. They are lineage markers because they are uniparentally transmitted. While STR markers are most commonly used for X and Y chromosome analysis, SNP loci can be beneficial in some circumstances due to their low mutation rate. For mtDNA, coding region SNPs can improve the ability to resolve common haplotypes (Coble et al. 2004). The forensic usefulness of a 25 X-SNP marker set has been explored (Tomas et al. 2010). Y-SNPs are routinely used to define haplogroups (Sanchez et al. 2003, Vallone & Butler 2004) and in some situations can aid biogeographical ancestry prediction (Brion et al. 2005, Wetton et al. 2005).

Ancestry SNPs—Estimating Ethnicity

While many more SNPs than STRs are required to obtain similar random match probabilities, SNPs have the potential to be used in other ways to aid investigations, such as predicting a perpetrator's ancestral background. SNPs change on the order of once every 10^8 generations while STR mutation rates are approximately one in a thousand. Because of this much lower mutation rate, SNPs are more likely to become "fixed" in a population than are STRs. SNPs are thus usually the better predictors of ethnicity (Barnholtz-Sloan et al. 2005). SNPs and *Alu* insertions (Batzer et al. 1993) are often found to be population-specific (Cordaux et al. 2007).

TABLE 12.4 SNP*for*ID Loci Used in 52plex Assay (Sanchez et al. 2006). The Last Three Columns Show Allele Frequencies for the Various SNP Alleles in the Population Groups.

No.	NCBI dbSNP ID	Chr.	Nucleotide Position	Amplicon Size (bp)	SNP Allele	African-American	Asian	European
1	rs1490413	1	4,037,521	68	A/**G**	0.59/0.41	0.46/0.54	0.47/0.53
2	rs876724	2	104,974	83	**C**/T	0.72/0.28	0.46/0.54	0.69/0.31
3	rs1357617	3	936,782	90	**A**/T	0.85/0.15	0.80/0.20	0.65/0.35
4	rs2046361	4	10,719,942	79	**A**/T	0.65/0.35	0.70/0.30	0.80/0.20
5	rs717302	5	2,932,133	86	A/**G**	0.92/0.08	0.83/0.17	0.45/0.55
6	rs1029047	6	1,080,939	100	A/T	0.61/0.39	0.27/0.73	0.37/0.63
7	rs917118	7	4,201,341	87	C/**T**	0.10/0.90	0.50/0.50	0.50/0.51
8	rs763869	8	1,363,017	100	C/**T**	0.48/0.52	–	0.56/0.44
9	rs1015250	9	1,813,774	95	**C**/G	0.55/0.45	0.40/0.60	0.15/0.85
10	rs735155	10	3,328,178	100	A/**G**	0.38/0.62	0.82/0.18	0.41/0.59
11	rs901398	11	11,060,530	70	C/**T**	0.39/0.61	0.29/0.71	0.34/0.66
12	rs2107612	12	741,262	93	**A**/G	0.64/0.36	0.75/0.25	0.70/0.30
13	rs1886510	13	20,172,700	86	C/**T**	0.85/0.15	–	0.50/0.50
14	rs1454361	14	23,840,960	73	**A**/T	0.57/0.43	0.62/0.38	0.47/0.53
15	rs2016276	15	22,119,157	90	A/G	0.91/0.09	0.59/0.41	0.79/0.21
16	rs729172	16	5,606,490	60	A/C	0.23/0.77	0.06/0.94	0.38/0.62
17	rs740910	17	5,907,188	87	**A**/G	0.92/0.08	0.92/0.09	0.57/0.43
18	rs1493232	18	1,117,986	59	A/**C**	0.44/0.56	0.39/0.61	0.56/0.44
19	rs719366	19	33,155,177	105	C/**T**	0.24/0.76	0.15/0.85	0.38/0.62
20	rs1031825	20	4,442,483	98	A/**C**	0.60/0.40	0.41/0.59	0.30/0.70
21	rs722098	21	15,607,469	81	A/**G**	0.17/0.83	0.50/0.50	0.86/0.14
22	rs733164	22	26,141,338	68	A/**G**	0.26/0.74	0.16/0.84	0.34/0.66
23	rs826472	10	2,360,631	85	**C**/T	0.70/0.30	0.66/0.34	0.44/0.56
24	rs2831700	21	28,601,558	62	A/G	0.42/0.58	0.50/0.50	0.62/0.38
25	rs873196	14	96,835,572	63	**C**/T	0.30/0.70	0.19/0.81	0.37/0.63
26	rs1382387	16	79,885,888	69	**G**/T	0.55/0.45	0.40/0.60	0.25/0.75
27	rs2111980	12	104,830,721	72	**A**/G	0.69/0.31	0.60/0.40	0.56/0.44
28	rs2056277	8	139,370,172	73	C/**T**	0.70/0.30	0.75/0.25	0.55/0.45
29	rs1024116	18	73,559,363	76	A/**G**	0.37/0.63	0.12/0.88	0.50/0.50
30	rs727811	6	164,954,622	78	A/**C**	0.30/0.70	0.66/0.34	0.61/0.39

(Continued)

TABLE 12.4 SNP*for*ID Loci Used in 52plex Assay (Sanchez et al. 2006). The Last Three Columns Show Allele Frequencies for the Various SNP Alleles in the Population Groups. *(Continued)*

No.	NCBI dbSNP ID	Chr.	Nucleotide Position	Amplicon Size (bp)	SNP Allele	African-American	Asian	European
31	rs1413212	1	239,753,521	84	**A**/G	0.61/0.39	0.47/0.53	0.41/0.59
32	rs938283	17	78,065,617	85	**C**/T	0.09/0.91	0.17/0.83	0.30/0.70
33	rs1979255	4	191,013,970	86	C/**G**	0.38/0.62	0.33/0.67	0.35/0.65
34	rs1463729	9	122,257,493	87	**A**/G	0.79/0.21	0.48/0.52	0.56/0.44
35	rs2076848	11	134,205,198	89	A/**T**	0.38/0.62	0.58/0.42	0.49/0.51
36	rs1355366	3	192,127,021	90	A/**G**	0.40/0.60	0.95/0.05	0.70/0.30
37	rs907100	2	239,850,329	91	C/G	0.74/0.26	–	0.48/0.52
38	rs354439	13	104,636,412	93	**A**/T	0.50/0.50	0.58/0.42	0.64/0.36
39	rs2040411	22	46,048,653	94	**A**/G	0.75/0.25	0.08/0.92	0.71/0.29
40	rs737681	7	154,850,085	96	C/**T**	0.56/0.44	0.80/0.20	0.58/0.42
41	rs2830795	21	27,530,034	97	**A**/G	0.88/0.12	0.45/0.55	0.67/0.33
42	rs251934	5	174,759,601	98	**C**/T	0.26/0.74	0.16/0.84	0.42/0.58
43	rs914165	21	41,336,325	100	A/**G**	0.66/0.34	0.27/0.73	0.49/0.51
44	rs10495407	1	235,480,457	102	A/**G**	0.11/0.89	0.42/0.58	0.29/0.71
45	rs1360288	9	124,344,108	103	**C**/T	0.70/0.30	0.50/0.50	0.50/0.50
46	rs964681	10	132,172,819	106	**C**/T	0.37/0.63	0.23/0.77	0.41/0.59
47	rs1005533	20	40,172,539	107	**A**/G	0.55/0.45	0.60/0.40	0.45/0.55
48	rs8037429	15	51,332,965	108	**C**/T	0.58/0.42	0.42/0.58	0.62/0.38
49	rs891700	1	236,923,075	109	A/**G**	0.53/0.47	0.53/0.47	0.57/0.43
50	rs1335873	13	18,699,724	110	**A**/T	0.91/0.09	0.28/0.72	0.36/0.64
51	rs1028528	22	46,574,531	113	A/**G**	0.35/0.65	0.65/0.35	0.74/0.26
52	rs1528460	15	52,926,761	115	C/T	0.65/0.35	0.36/0.64	0.29/0.71

Individuals with mixed ancestral backgrounds may not possess the expected phenotypic characteristics (e.g., dark colored skin for African-Americans). Thus, results from genetic tests attempting to predict ethnic origin or ancestry should always be interpreted with caution and only in the context of other reliable evidence. For several years before it went out of business in 2008, a company named DNAPrint (Sarasota, Florida) provided a DNA test for estimating an individual's ethnic/racial background with a panel of SNPs (Frudakis 2008). DNAPrint targeted pigmentation and xenobiotic metabolism genes in their search for ancestrally informative SNPs (Frudakis et al. 2003a). Much of their work was based on the research efforts of Dr. Mark Shriver from Penn State University (State College, PA) who looks for ancestry informative markers (AIMs) that possess alleles with large frequency differences between populations (Shriver & Kittles 2004).

Population-specific alleles have been found in both STR and SNP markers. The DNAPrint SNP typing approach was used to aid the investigation of an important Louisianna serial rapist case in 2003 demonstrating the forensic value of this type of approach (Frudakis 2008, pp. 599-603). While presently used, AIMs are not 100% accurate for predicting ancestral background of samples (and perhaps never will be).

Several studies have shown that by analyzing many, many SNP markers it is possible to correlate genetic results with geographic location within Europe (Lao et al. 2008, Novembre et al. 2008). Mapping the country of origin may work for some places in Europe where language differences can discourage significant population movement. However, in countries like the United States where movement of the population is more fluid, greater levels of admixture are expected—and thus genetic testing results would not be as likely to correlate strongly with geographic location. Moreover, Myles and coworkers (2009) found that portability of ancestry informative markers was limited. In other words, identification of the optimal SNPs to differentiate populations in one group of samples does not necessarily mean that those same SNPs will work well in another set of samples.

While research results in this area are interesting, they are probably not ready for prime-time use in forensic investigations. It is important to keep in mind that investigators and juries may have a hard time understanding probabilities from ancestry or phenotyping predictions using DNA results. Telling a detective that the individual who left a biological sample at a crime scene has an 80% chance of having blue eyes is unfamiliar territory when he or she typically associates a DNA result as being irrefutable evidence (in their minds essentially 100% probability of being from a specific individual). If ancestry prediction and forensic phenotyping are pursued, then expectations of individuals using the information will need to be managed.

Phenotype SNPs—Predicting External Visible Traits

When the DNA profile obtained from an evidentiary sample does not match a known individual—from either a tested suspect or a search of offender or arrestee indices in a DNA database—then the case currently cannot be solved through a DNA result. Under these circumstances, investigators may try to collect more potential references as part of mass screens or expand the reach of the database with familial searching (see Appendix 2). If these efforts fail, a John Doe warrant may be issued based on the evidentiary DNA profile to stop the statute of limitations, if one exists, from expiring. However, this requires waiting for the perpetrator to be caught committing another crime and then having his DNA profile submitted to the DNA database for the connection to the first crime to be made.

Another potential approach when no matching individual can be found to an evidentiary DNA profile is to try to gain more information from the evidentiary sample itself. Efforts have been made over the years to predict appearance of an individual using information from the evidentiary DNA sample (Sundquist 2010). For example, the so-called "golden" gene within exon 3 of melanin index-associated gene SLC24A5 on chromosome 15 (dbSNP accession number rs1426654) impacts pigmentation (Lamason et al. 2005). Results from this single SNP are also very useful in ancestry estimation studies as fair skin typically correlates well with European ancestry.

In the earliest example of forensic phenotyping to predict a physical trait from examining a sample's DNA, the Forensic Science Service developed a simple test of the melanocortin 1 receptor (MC1R) gene that correlated well with red hair color (Grimes et al. 2001). More recently, an IrisPlex has been developed to help predict blue versus brown eye color (Walsh et al. 2010a). The IrisPlex assay uses 6 SNPs and has been extensively studied in terms of sensitivity and specificity as part of forensic validation (Walsh et al. 2010b).

As more and more information is uncovered about the nature and content of the human genome, genetic variants that code for additional phenotypic characteristics will be discovered. Perhaps SNP sites can be identified in the future that will correlate to facial features thus aiding investigators with information about the possible appearance of a perpetrator. However, due to the complexity of multigenic traits and outside factors such as aging and environment, it is unlikely that a few carefully chosen SNPs will present a foolproof picture of a sample's source. Prominent researchers in this field conclude that "predicting a complete facial image from a biological sample as would be desirable for police investigations will remain forensic science fiction for at least the near future" (Kayser & Schneider 2009). Research is continuing in the area of forensic phenotyping; it is hoped that it will provide beneficial information to investigations in the future.

ETHICAL CONSIDERATIONS

The expanded capabilities with ancestry and phenotypic SNPs to learn more about a biological sample than just simple identifying information available with STR typing raises potential ethical concerns. Should the capabilities and vast space of DNA information beyond the present STR profile be permitted for use in forensic casework?

In 2010, the University of Pennsylvania launched a forensic DNA ethics website (http://www.forensicdnaethics.org/) to explore the interplay between the advances being made in genetic information and appropriate privacy concerns. News stories on the topic of forensic phenotyping are available as is information on laws and scientific research efforts in this area.

Manfred Kayser's research group at the Erasmus University Medical Center in Rotterdam, The Netherlands, is probably the most active in an effort to bring phenotypic prediction to forensic science. Professor Kayser and Peter Schneider from the Unversity of Cologne (Cologne, Germany) published a landmark 2009 review covering the motivations, scientific challenges, and ethical considerations of DNA-based prediction for externally visible characteristics, such as hair color, eye color, facial features, etc. (Kayser & Schneider 2009). As discussed in Chapter 1, the Erasmus University phenotyping effort has also led to an approach to estimating human age based on T-cell DNA rearrangements, which provided an age estimate to within ± 9 years (Zubakov et al. 2010).

Professors Kayser and Schneider argue that traits such as hair color and eye color cannot be considered private information as they are known to everyone who has ever seen the individual. They further note that since forensic phenotyping—or what they term "external visible characteristics (EVCs) prediction"—is only performed on crime scene samples of unknown persons that no violation of privacy rights has to be considered (Kayser & Schneider 2009).

In a law review, Koops and Schellenkens argue that the sensitivity of the information revealed should dictate the level of phenotyping permitted in a forensic context. Terri Sundquist, in her *Promega Connections* article on the topic, notes that "The Netherlands is the only country that explicitly allows forensic phenotyping, within defined guidelines" (Sundquist 2010). Only EVCs can be used and only when the trait, such as hair color or eye color, contributes to the criminal investigation. Looking for genetic susceptibility to disease or a tendency for aggressive behavior is not permitted under Dutch law. However, in other parts of the world including the UK, forensic phenotyping is implicity allowed. Scientific research in this area continues to go forward—and so public discussion and perhaps legislative limits should be considered.

INSERTION-DELETION POLYMORPHISMS

Another form of a bi-allelic (or di-allelic) polymorphism is an insertion-deletion or indel. An indel can be the insertion or deletion of a segment of DNA ranging from one nucleotide to hundreds of nucleotides, which is seen with an *Alu* insertion (see Butler 2010, *Fundamentals*, D.N.A. Box 15.2). The two alleles for di-allelic indels can simply be classified as "short" and "long." From a certain perspective, STR markers can be thought of as multi-allelic indels since the different alleles are typically insertions or deletions of a tandem repeat unit.

Most di-allelic indels exhibit allele-length differences of only a few nucleotides. James Weber and colleagues at the Marshfield Medical Research Foundation have characterized over 2000 bi-allelic indels in the human genome (Weber et al. 2002). A total of 71% of these indels possessed 2-, 3-, or 4-nucleotide length differences with only 4% having greater than a 16-nucleotide length difference. Allele frequencies for the short and long alleles have been measured in African, European, Japanese, and Native American populations.

Rui Pereira and colleagues in Portugal and Spain have developed a multiplex assay with 38 bi-allelic autosomal indel markers that can be detected on standard capillary electrophoresis platforms (Pereira et al. 2009a, 2009b). The PCR amplicons were all designed to be less than 160 bp to accommodate degraded DNA. With this assay, complete profiles could be obtained down to approximately 300 pg of DNA template. All of the indel markers were found to be polymorphic in 306 individuals from Angola, Mozambique, Portugal, Macau, and Taiwan and produced random match probabilities on the order of 10^{-14}, which is similar to about 13 STRs (Pereira et al. 2009a). In some countries, QIAGEN (Hilden, Germany) offers the Investigator DIPlex kit that examines 30 insertion/deletion polymorphisms using the ABI Genetic Analyzer platforms.

SUMMARY AND FINAL THOUGHTS

It is unlikely that SNPs (or even other STR markers) will completely replace core STRs in the near- or even medium-term future as the primary source of information used in criminal investigations. Rather than replacing the millions of profiles that exist in large national DNA databases (see Chapter 8) through re-typing convicted offender and casework samples with new SNP markers, it is more likely that new STRs or SNPs will be slowly added to national DNA databases as technologies are proven and costs come down.

The primary selling point of SNPs in the forensic arena has been the ability to make small PCR products that can overcome challenges of strong PCR inhibitors or samples containing highly degraded material. Smaller PCR products should result in greater recovery of information from badly damaged samples. PCR products for SNP markers can be small because the target region is only a single nucleotide rather than an expandable array of 20 to 60 nucleotides as is present in tetra-nucleotide STRs with 5 to 15 repeats.

While the promise of SNPs in this area has been promoted for many years, studies comparing miniSTRs (see Chapter 10) with SNPs have shown no clear advantage of SNPs with most degraded DNA samples (Dixon et al. 2006, Fondevilla et al. 2008). These reduced-size STR assays have an advantage over SNPs in that more alleles exist to produce a higher power of discrimination. More importantly miniSTR assays offer compatibility with current DNA databases housing millions of DNA profiles comprised of core STR loci (see Chapter 8).

Thanks in large measure to technology being fueled by worldwide genomic sequencing efforts, SNP analysis has become less expensive and easier to perform on a variety of detection platforms (Sobrino et al. 2005) . Many technologies, such as capillary array electrophoresis and mass spectrometry are capable of performing analysis on both STR and SNP markers. Although at the end of 2010—when this chapter was written—SNP typing is not widely performed in forensic laboratories. SNP typing has been used to supplement partial STR results on highly degraded specimens (Fondevilla et al. 2008).

For SNPs to become more widely used in future forensic DNA testing, it is important that the field settle on common loci. STR typing was propelled forward when the Second Generation Multiplex was introduced and used to launch the United Kingdom's National DNA Database (see Chapter 8). Likewise, the selection of 13 core loci for the Combined DNA Index System (CODIS) aided standardization of information in the United States and around the world (see Chapter 5).

To aid in cataloging SNP loci of forensic interest and collating features of the markers in a common format, the U.S. National Institute of Standards and Technology has set up a forensic SNP website: http://www.cstl.nist.gov/biotech/strbase/SNP.htm. This website is intended to provide a resource to the community as further markers, assays, and technologies are developed for SNP analysis. With this information many loci can be compared and examined for their forensic value to aid in the selection of a consistent set of SNP loci for the community to use as their standard.

In the spring of 2004, the DNA working group of the European Network of Forensic Science Institutes (ENFSI) and the U.S.-based Scientific Working Group on DNA Analysis Methods (SWGDAM) jointly issued an assessment of whether SNPs will replace STRs in national DNA databases (Gill et al. 2004). Their conclusion was that "it is unlikely that SNPs will replace STRs as the preferred method of testing of forensic samples and database samples in the near to medium future." The assessment goes on to praise the capabilities of SNPs for specific purposes including mass disaster and paternity analysis and comments on the need for standardization of SNP loci used for human identity testing applications. More than seven years later, the message of this paper holds true—SNPs may have a role for specific applications but will not replace STRs as the primary workhorse of forensic DNA typing any time soon.

READING LIST AND INTERNET RESOURCES

Butler, J. M. (2010). *Fundamentals of forensic DNA typing*. San Diego: Elsevier Academic Press.

General Information

Brookes, A. J. (1999). The essence of SNPs. *Gene, 234*, 177–186.

Ku, C. S., et al. (2010). The discovery of human genetic variations and their use as disease markers: Past, present and future. *Human Genetics, 55*, 403–415.

STRBase forensic SNP information (assays, markers, etc.). <http://www.cstl.nist.gov/biotech/strbase/SNP.htm>.

Syvanen, A. C. (2001). Accessing genetic variation: Genotyping single nucleotide polymorphisms. *Nature Reviews Genetics, 2*, 930–942.

Pros and Cons of SNPs

Amorim, A., & Pereira, L. (2005). Pros and cons in the use of SNPs in forensic kinship investigation: A comparative analysis with STRs. *Forensic Science International, 150*, 17–21.

Balding, D. J. (2006). A tutorial on statistical methods for population association studies. *Nature Reviews Genetics, 7*, 781–791.

Butler, J. M., et al. (2007). STRs vs SNPs: Thoughts on the future of forensic DNA testing. *Forensic Science, Medicine, and Pathology, 3*, 200–205.

Chakraborty, R., et al. (1999). The utility of short tandem repeat loci beyond human identification: Implications for development of new DNA typing systems. *Electrophoresis, 20*, 1682–1996.

Gill, P. (2001). An assessment of the utility of single nucleotide polymorphisms (SNPs) for forensic purposes. *International Journal of Legal Medicine, 114*, 204–210.

Gill, P., et al. (2004). An assessment of whether SNPs will replace STRs in national DNA databases–joint considerations of the DNA working group of the European Network of Forensic Science Institutes (ENFSI) and the Scientific Working Group on DNA Analysis Methods (SWGDAM). *Science and Justice, 44*, 51–53.

Krawczak, M. (1999). Informativity assessment for biallelic single nucleotide polymorphisms. *Electrophoresis, 20*, 1676–1681.

SNP Marker Categories and Applications

Budowle, B., & van Daal, A. (2008). Forensically relevant SNP classes. *Biotechniques, 44*, 603–610.

Butler, J. M., et al. (2008). Report on ISFG SNP panel discussion. *Forensic Science International: Genetics Supplement Series, 1*, 471–472.

Kiehne, N., & Kauferstein, S. (2007). Mutations in the SCN5A gene: Evidence for a link between long QT syndrome and sudden death? *Forensic Science International: Genetics, 1*, 170–174.

Markers and Multiplexes

Batzer, M. et al. (1993). *Alu* repeats as markers for human population genetics. *Proceedings of the fourth international symposium on human identification* (pp. 49–57). Madison, Wisconsin: Promega Corporation.

Cordaux, R., et al. (2007). In search of polymorphic Alu insertions with restricted geographic distributions. *Genomics, 90*, 154–158.

Giardina, E., et al. (2007). In silico and in vitro comparative analysis to select, validate and test SNPs for human identification. *BMC Genomics, 8*, 457.

Kidd, K. K., et al. (2006). Developing a SNP panel for forensic identification of individuals. *Forensic Science International, 164*, 20–32.

Nicklas, J. A., & Buel, E. (2008). A real-time multiplex SNP melting assay to discriminate individuals. *Journal of Forensic Sciences, 53*, 1316–1324.

Pakstis, A. J., et al. (2007). Candidate SNPs for a universal individual identification panel. *Human Genetics, 121*, 305–317.

Pakstis, A. J., et al. (2010). SNPs for a universal individual identification panel. *Human Genetics, 127*, 315–324.

Phillips, C., et al. (2007). Evaluation of the Genplex SNP typing system and a 49plex forensic marker panel. *Forensic Science International: Genetics, 1*, 180–185.

Sanchez, J. J., et al. (2006). A multiplex assay with 52 single nucleotide polymorphisms for human identification. *Electrophoresis, 27*, 1713–1724.

Sanchez, J. J., et al. (2008). Forensic typing of autosomal SNPs with a 29 SNP-multiplex—results of a collaborative EDNAP exercise. *Forensic Science International: Genetics, 2*, 176–183.

SNPforID project. <http://www.snpforid.org/>.

Tomas, C., et al. (2008). Typing of 48 autosomal SNPs and amelogenin with GenPlex SNP genotyping system in forensic genetics. *Forensic Science International: Genetics, 3*, 1–6.

SNP Information Databases

ALFRED. <http://alfred.med.yale.edu/>.

Amigo, J., et al. (2008). SPSmart: Adapting population based SNP genotype databases for fast and comprehensive web access. *BMC Bioinformatics, 9*, 428.

Amigo, J., et al. (2008). The SNPforID browser: An online tool for query and display of frequency data from the SNP*for*ID project. *International Journal of Legal Medicine, 122*, 435–440.

dbSNP. <http://www.ncbi.nlm.nih.gov/sites/entrez?db=snp>.

Park, J., et al. (2007). SNP@Ethnos: A database of ethnically variant single-nucleotide polymorphisms. *Nucleic Acids Research, 35*, D711–D715.

Smigielski, E. M., et al. (2000). dbSNP: A database of single nucleotide polymorphisms. *Nucleic Acids Research, 28*, 352–355.

SNPforID browser. <http://spsmart.cesga.es/snpforid.php>.

The SNP Consortium (TSC) and now International HapMap Data. <http://snp.cshl.org/>.

Thorisson, G. A., & Stein, L. D. (2003). The SNP Consortium website: Past, present and future. *Nucleic Acids Research, 31*, 124–127.

SNP Analysis Techniques

Ahmadian, A., et al. (2000). Single-nucleotide polymorphism analysis by pyrosequencing. *Analytical Biochemistry, 280*, 103–110.

Andréasson, H., et al. (2002). Mitochondrial sequence analysis for forensic identification using pyrosequencing technology. *Biotechniques, 32*, 124–133.

Armstrong, B., et al. (2000). Suspension arrays for high throughput, multiplexed single nucleotide polymorphism genotyping. *Cytometry, 40*, 102–108.

Bell, P. A., et al. (2002). SNPstream UHT: Ultra-high throughput SNP genotyping for pharmacogenomics and drug discovery. *Biotechniques, June Suppl*, 70–77.

Budowle, B. (2004). SNP typing strategies. *Forensic Science International, 146S*, S139–S142.

Budowle, B., et al. (2004). Single nucleotide polymorphisms and microarray technology in forensic genetics—development and application to mitochondrial DNA. *Forensic Science Review, 16*, 21–36.

Chen, X., et al. (1999). Fluorescence polarization in homogeneous nucleic acid analysis. *Genome Research, 9*, 492–498.

Chen, X., & Sullivan, P. F. (2003). Single nucleotide polymorphism genotyping: Biochemistry, protocol, cost and throughput. *Pharmacogenomics Journal, 3*, 77–96.

Delahunty, C., et al. (1996). Testing the feasibility of DNA typing for human identification by PCR and an oligonucleotide ligation assay. *American Journal of Human Genetics, 58*, 1239–1246.

Divne, A. M., & Allen, M. (2005). A DNA microarray system for forensic SNP analysis. *Forensic Science International, 154*, 111–121.

Fan, J. -B., et al. (2003). Highly parallel SNP genotyping. *Cold Spring Harbor Symposia on Quantitative Biology, 68*, 69–78.

Germer, S., & Higuchi, R. (1999). Single-tube genotyping without oligonucleotide probes. *Genome Research, 9*, 72–78.

Giesendorf, B. A. J., et al. (1998). Molecular beacons: A new approach for semi-automated mutation analysis. *Clinical Chemistry, 44*, 482–486.

Gilles, P. N., et al. (1999). Single nucleotide polymorphic discrimination by an electronic dot bot assay on semiconductor microchips. *Nature Biotechnology, 17*, 365–370.

Gut, I. G. (2001). Automation in genotyping of single nucleotide polymorphisms. *Human Mutation, 17*, 475–492.

Haff, L. A., & Smirnov, I. P. (1997). Single-nucleotide polymorphism identification assays using a thermostable DNA polymerase and delayed extraction MALDI-TOF mass spectrometry. *Genome Research, 7*, 378–388.

Hecker, K. H., et al. (1999). Mutation detection by denaturing DNA chromatography using fluorescently labeled polymerase chain reaction products. *Analytical Biochemistry, 272*, 156–164.

Heller, M. J., et al. (2000). Active microelectronic chip devices which utilize controlled electrophoretic fields for multiplex DNA hybridization and other genomic applications. *Electrophoresis, 21*, 157–164.

Homer, N., et al. (2008). Resolving individuals contributing trace amounts of DNA to highly complex mixtures using high-density SNP genotyping microarrays. *PLoS Genetics, 4*(8), e1000167.

Hiratsuka, M., et al. (2005). Forensic assessment of 16 single nucleotide polymorphisms analyzed by hybridization probe assay. *Tohoku Journal of Experimental Medicine, 207*, 255–261.

Illumina. <http://www.illumina.com/>.

Kwok, P.-Y., et al. (1994). Comparative analysis of human DNA variations by fluorescence-based sequencing of PCR products. *Genomics, 23*, 138–144.

Kwok, P.-Y. (2001). Methods for genotyping single nucleotide polymorphisms. *Annual Reviews of Genomics and Human Genetics, 2*, 235–258.

Li, J., et al. (1999). Single nucleotide polymorphism determination using primer extension and time-of-flight mass spectrometry. *Electrophoresis, 20*, 1258–1265.

Li, L., et al. (2006). SNP genotyping by multiplex amplification and microarrays assay for forensic application. *Forensic Science International, 162*, 74–79.

Livak, K. J. (1999). Allelic discrimination using fluorogenic probes and the 5′ nuclease assay. *Genetic Analysis, 14*, 143–149.

McKeown, B., et al. (2006). Intramolecular controls for the generation of clinical-quality SNP genotypes and the assessment of normal heterozygote imbalance. *Electrophoresis, 27*, 1725–1731.

Nakahara, H., et al. (2010). Criterion values for multiplex SNP genotyping by the Invader assay. *Forensic Science International: Genetics, 4*, 130–136.

Nikiforov, T. T., et al. (1994). Genetic Bit Analysis: A solid phase method for typing single nucleotide polymorphisms. *Nucleic Acids Research, 22*, 4167–4175.

Perkel, J. (2008). SNP genotyping: Six technologies that keyed a revolution. *Nature Methods, 5*, 447–453.

Reynolds, R., et al. (2000). Detection of sequence variation in the HVII region of the human mitochondrial genome in 689 individuals using immobilized sequence-specific oligonucleotide probes. *Journal of Forensic Sciences, 45*, 1210–1231.

Saiki, R. K., et al. (1989). Genetic analysis of amplified DNA with immobilized sequence-specific oligonucleotide probes. *Proceedings of the National Academy of the United States of America, 86*, 6230–6234.

Sapolsky, R. J., et al. (1999). High-throughput polymorphism screening and genotyping with high-density oligonucleotide arrays. *Genetic Analysis, 14*, 187–192.

Sobrino, B., et al. (2005). SNPs in forensic genetics: A review on SNP typing methodologies. *Forensic Science International, 154*, 181–194.

Sosnowski, R. G., et al. (1997). Rapid determination of single base mismatch mutations in DNA hybrids by direct electric field control. *Proceedings of the National Academy of the United States of America, 94*, 1119–1123.

Tully, G., et al. (1996). Rapid detection of mitochondrial sequence polymorphisms using multiplex solid-phase fluorescent minisequencing. *Genomics, 34*, 107–113.

Wang, D. G., et al. (1998). Large-scale identification, mapping, and genotyping of single-nucleotide polymorphisms in the human genome. *Science, 280*, 1077–1082.

Ye, J., et al. (2002). Melting curve SNP (McSNP) genotyping: A useful approach for diallelic genotyping in forensic science. *Journal of Forensic Sciences, 47*, 593–600.

SNP Applications

Frudakis, T. N. (2008). *Molecular photofitting: Predicting ancestry and phenotype using DNA*. San Diego: Elsevier Academic Press.

Identity SNPs

Børsting, C., et al. (2008). Performance of the SNPforID 52 SNP-plex assay in paternity testing. *Forensic Science International: Genetics, 2*, 292–300.

Børsting, C., et al. (2009). Validation of a single nucleotide polymorphism (SNP) typing assay with 49 SNPs for forensic genetic testing in a laboratory accredited according to the ISO 17025 standard. *Forensic Science International: Genetics, 4*, 34–42.

Børsting, C., & Morling, N. (2011). Mutations and/or close relatives? Six case work examples where 49 autosomal SNPs were used as supplementary markers. *Forensic Science International: Genetics, 5*, 236–241.

Børsting, C., et al. (2011). SNP typing of the reference materials SRM 2391b 1-10, K562, XY1, XX74, and 007 with the SNPforID multiplex. *Forensic Science International: Genetics, 5*, e81–e82.

Dixon, L. A., et al. (2005). Validation of a 21-locus autosomal SNP multiplex for forensic identification purposes. *Forensic Science International, 154*, 62–77.

Drobnič, K., et al. (2010). Typing of 49 autosomal SNPs by SNaPshot in the Slovenian population. *Forensic Science International: Genetics, 4*, e125–e127.

Fang, R., et al. (2009). Multiplexed SNP detection panels for human identification. *Forensic Science International: Genetics Supplement Series, 2*, 538–539.

Fondevila, M., et al. (2008). Case report: Identification of skeletal remains using short-amplicon marker analysis of severely degraded DNA extracted from a decomposed and charred femur. *Forensic Science International: Genetics, 2*, 212–218.

Hinds, D. A., et al. (2005). Whole-genome patterns of common DNA variation in three human populations. *Science, 307*, 1072–1079.

Krjutskov, K., et al. (2009). Evaluation of the 124-plex SNP typing microarray for forensic testing. *Forensic Science International: Genetics, 4*, 43–48.

Lee, H. Y., et al. (2005). Selection of twenty-four highly informative SNP markers for human identification and paternity analysis in Koreans. *Forensic Science International, 148*, 107–112.

Musgrave-Brown, E., et al. (2007). Forensic validation of the SNP*for*ID 52-plex assay. *Forensic Science International: Genetics, 1*, 186–190.

Nakahara, H., et al. (2009). Automated SNPs typing system based on the Invader assay. *Legal Medicine, 11*(Suppl. 1), S111–S114.

Pakstis, A. J., et al. (2008). SNPs for individual identification. *Forensic Science International: Genetics Supplement Series, 1*, 479–481.

Phillips, C., et al. (2008). Resolving relationship tests that show ambiguous STR results using autosomal SNPs as supplementary markers. *Forensic Science International: Genetics, 2*, 198–204.

Pietrangeli, I., et al. (2010). Frequency assessment of 25 SNPs in five different populations. *Forensic Science International: Genetics, 4*, e131–e133.

Sanchez, J. J., et al. (2006). A multiplex assay with 52 single nucleotide polymorphisms for human identification. *Electrophoresis, 27*, 1713–1724.

Tomas, C., et al. (2010). Autosomal SNP typing of forensic samples with the GenPlex HID System: Results of a collaborative study. *Forensic Science International: Genetics* (in press) (doi:10.1016/j.fsigen.2010.06.007).

Vallone, P. M., et al. (2005). Allele frequencies for 70 autosomal SNP loci with U.S. Caucasian, African-American, and Hispanic samples. *Forensic Science International, 149*, 279–286.

Westen, A. A., et al. (2009). Tri-allelic SNP markers enable analysis of mixed and degraded DNA samples. *Forensic Science International: Genetics, 3*, 233–241.

Lineage SNPs

Bouakaze, C., et al. (2007). First successful assay of Y-SNP typing by SNaPshot minisequencing on ancient DNA. *International Journal of Legal Medicine, 121*, 493–499.

Brion, M., et al. (2005). Introduction of an single nucleotide polymorphism-based "major Y-chromosome haplogroup typing kit" suitable for predicting the geographical origin of male lineages. *Electrophoresis, 26*, 4411–4420.

Coble, M. D., et al. (2004). Single nucleotide polymorphisms over the entire mtDNA genome that increase the power of forensic testing in Caucasians. *International Journal of Legal Medicine, 118*, 137–146.

Ge, J., et al. (2010). Haplotype block: A new type of forensic DNA markers. *International Journal of Legal Medicine, 124*, 353–361.

Kline, M. C., et al. (2005). Mitochondrial DNA typing screens with control region and coding region SNPs. *Journal of Forensic Sciences, 50*, 377–385.

Mizuno, N., et al. (2010). A forensic method for the simultaneous analysis of biallelic markers identifying Y chromosome haplogroups inferred as having originated in Asia and the Japanese archipelago. *Forensic Science International: Genetics, 4*, 73–79.

Nelson, T. M., et al. (2007). Development of a multiplex single base extension assay for mitochondrial DNA haplogroup typing. *Croatian Medical Journal, 48*, 460–472.

Sanchez, J. J., et al. (2003). Multiplex PCR and minisequencing of SNPs—a model with 35 Y chromosome SNPs. *Forensic Science International, 137*, 74–84.
Tomas, C., et al. (2010). Forensic usefulness of a 25 X-chromosome single-nucleotide polymorphism marker set. *Transfusion, 50*, 2258–2265.
Vallone, P. M., et al. (2004). A multiplex allele-specific primer extension assay for forensically informative SNPs distributed throughout the mitochondrial genome. *International Journal of Legal Medicine, 118*, 147–157.
Vallone, P. M., & Butler, J. M. (2004). Y-SNP typing of U.S. African American and Caucasian samples using allele-specific hybridization and primer extension. *Journal of Forensic Sciences, 49*, 723–732.

Ancestry SNPs

Barnholtz-Sloan, J. S., et al. (2005). Informativeness of the CODIS STR loci for admixture analysis. *Journal of Forensic Sciences, 50*, 1322–1326.
Corach, D., et al. (2010). Inferring continental ancestry of Argentineans from autosomal, Y-chromosomal and mitochondrial DNA. *Annuals of Human Genetics, 74*, 65–76.
Frudakis, T., et al. (2003). A classifier for the SNP-based inference of ancestry. *Journal of Forensic Sciences, 48*, 771–782.
Halder, I., et al. (2008). A panel of ancestry informative markers for estimating individual biogeographical ancestry and admixture from four continents: Utility and applications. *Human Mutation, 29*, 648–658.
Halder, I., et al. (2009). Measurement of admixture proportions and description of admixture structure in different U.S. populations. *Human Mutation, 30*, 1299–1309.
Kersbergen, P., et al. (2009). Developing a set of ancestry-sensitive DNA markers reflecting continental origins of humans. *BMC Genetics, 10*, 69.
Kosoy, R., et al. (2009). Ancestry informative marker sets for determining continental origin and admixture proportions in common populations in America. *Human Mutation, 30*, 69–78.
Lao, O., et al. (2006). Proportioning whole-genome single-nucleotide–polymorphism diversity for the identification of geographic population structure and genetic ancestry. *American Journal of Human Genetics, 78*, 680–690.
Lao, O., et al. (2008). Correlation between genetic and geographic structure in Europe. *Current Biology, 18*, 1241–1248.
Lao, O., et al. (2010). Evaluating self-declared ancestry of U.S. Americans using autosomal, Y-chromosomal and mitochondrial DNA. *Human Mutation, 31*, E1875–E1893.
Myles, S., et al. (2009). An assessment of the portability of ancestry informative markers between human populations. *BMC Medical Genomics*, 2(45), 1–10.
Novembre, J., et al. (2008). Genes mirror geography within Europe. *Nature, 456*, 98–101.
Phillips, C., et al. (2007). Inferring ancestral origin using a single multiplex assay of ancestry-informative marker SNPs. *Forensic Science International: Genetics, 1*, 273–280.
Phillips, C., et al. (2009). Ancestry analysis in the 11-M Madrid bomb attack investigation. *PLoS ONE*, 4(8), e6583.
Pfaff, C. L., et al. (2004). Information on ancestry from genetic markers. *Genetic Epidemiology, 26*, 305–315.
Price, A. L., et al. (2008). Discerning the ancesty of European Americans in genetic association studies. *PLoS Genetics*, 4(1), e236.
Schlecht, J., et al. (2008). Machine-learning approaches for classifying haplogroup from Y chromosome STR data. *PLoS Computational Biology*, 4(6), e1000093.
Shriver, M. D., & Kittles, R. A. (2004). Genetic ancestry and the search for personalized genetic histories. *Nature Reviews Genetics, 5*, 611–618.
Wetton, J. H., et al. (2005). Inferring the population of origin of DNA evidence within the UK by allele-specific hybridization of Y-SNPs. *Forensic Science International, 152*, 45–53.

Phenotype SNPs

Axenovich, T. I., et al. (2009). Linkage analysis of adult height in a large pedigree from a Dutch genetically isolated population. *Human Genetics, 126*, 457–471.
Bastiaens, M., et al. (2001). The melanocortin-1 receptor gene is the major freckle gene. *Human Molecular Genetics, 10*, 1701–1708.
Bouakaze, C., et al. (2009). Pigment phenotype and biogeographical ancestry from ancient skeletal remains: Inferences from multiplexed autosomal SNP analysis. *International Journal of Legal Medicine, 123*, 315–325.

Branicki, W., et al. (2007). Determination of phenotype associated SNPs in the MC1R gene. *Journal of Forensic Sciences, 52*, 349–354.

Duffy, D. L., et al. (2007). A three-single-nucleotide polymorphism haplotype in intron 1 of OCA2 explains most human eye-color variation. *American Journal of Human Genetics, 80*, 241–252.

Frudakis, T., et al. (2003). Sequences associated with human iris pigmentation. *Genetics, 165*, 2071–2083.

Graham, E. A. M. (2008). DNA reviews: Predicting phenotype. *Forensic Science, Medicine, and Pathology, 4*, 196–199.

Grimes, E. A., et al. (2001). Sequence polymorphism in the human melanocortin 1 receptor gene as an indicator of the red hair phenotype. *Forensic Science International, 122*, 124–129.

Kayser, M., et al. (2008). Three genome-wide association studies and a linkage analysis identify *HERC2* as a human iris color gene. *American Journal of Human Genetics, 82*, 411–423.

Lalueza-Foc, C., et al. (2007). A melanocortin 1 receptor allele suggests varying pigmentation among Neanderthals. *Science, 318*, 1453–1455.

Lamason, R. L., et al. (2005). SLC24A5, a putative cation exchanger, affects pigmentation in zebrafish and humans. *Science, 310*, 1782–1786.

Lao, O., et al. (2007). Signatures of positive selection in genes associated with human skin pigmentation as revealed from analyses of single nucleotide polymorphisms. *Annuals of Human Genetics, 71*, 354–369.

Liu, F., et al. (2009). Eye color and the prediction of complex phenotypes from genotypes. *Current Biology, 19*, R192–R193.

Liu, F., et al. (2010). Digital quantification of human eye color highlights genetic association of three new loci. *PLoS Genetics, 6*(5), e1000934. Available at <http://www.plosgenetics.org>.

Meissner, C., & Ritz-Timme, S. (2010). Molecular pathology and age estimation. *Forensic Science International: Genetics, 203*, 34–43.

Mengel-From, J., et al. (2010). Human eye colour and *HERC2, OCA2,* and *MATP*. *Forensic Science International: Genetics, 4*, 323–328.

Pulker, H., et al. (2007). Finding genes that underlie physical traits of forensic interest using genetic tools. *Forensic Science International: Genetics, 1*, 100–104.

Schmeling, A., et al. (2007). Age estimation. *Forensic Science International, 165*, 178–181.

Soares, C. (2010). Portrait in DNA: Can forensic analysis yield police-style sketches of suspects? How your genes could reveal what you look like. *Scientific American*(May 11, 2010 news). Available at <http://www.scientific-american.com/article.cfm?id=portrait-in-dna>.

Sturm, R. A., et al. (2008). A single SNP in an evolutionary conserved region within intron 86 of the *HERC2* gene determines human blue-brown eye color. *American Journal of Human Genetics, 82*, 424–431.

Sturm, R. A. (2009). Molecular genetics of human pigmentation diversity. *Human Molecular Genetics, 18*, R9–R17.

Sulem, P., et al. (2007). Genetic determinants of hair, eye and skin pigmentation in Europeans. *Nature Genetics, 39*, 1443–1452.

Sundquist, T. (2010). Forensic phenotyping: What DNA can (and cannot) tell us about a criminal's appearance. *Promega Connections* (research blog April 26, 2010). Available at <http://promega.wordpress.com/>.

Tully, G. (2007). Genotype versus phenotype: Human pigmentation. *Forensic Science International: Genetics, 1*, 105–110.

Valenzuela, R., et al. (2010). Predicting phenotype from genotype: Normal pigmentation. *Journal of Forensic Sciences, 55*(2), 315–322.

Valverde, P., et al. (1995). Variants of the melanocyte-stimulating hormone receptor gene are associated with red hair and fair skin in humans. *Nature Genetics, 11*, 328–330.

Walsh, S., et al. (2010). IrisPlex: A sensitive DNA tool for accurate prediction of blue and brown eye colour in the absence of ancestry information. *Forensic Science International: Genetics, 5*, 170–180.

Walsh, S., et al. (2010). Developmental validation of the IrisPlex system: Determination of blue and brown iris colour for forensic intelligence. *Forensic Science International: Genetics* (in press). doi:10.1016/j/fsigen.2010.09.008

Zubakov, D., et al. (2010). Estimating human age from T-cell DNA rearrangements. *Current Biology, 20*, R970–R971.

Ethical Considerations with Phenotype and Ethnicity Prediction

Forensic DNA ethics. <http://forensicdnaethics.org/>.

Kayser, M., & Schneider, P. M. (2009). DNA-based prediction of human externally visible characteristics in forensics: Motivations, scientific challenges, and ethical considerations. *Forensic Science International: Genetics, 3*, 154–161.

Koops, B.-J., & Schellekens, M. (2008). Forensic DNA phenotyping: Regulatory issues. *The Columbia Science and Technology Law Review*, *9*, 158–202. Available at <http://www.stlr.org/html/volume9/koops.pdf>.

Insertion/Deletion Polymorphisms

Pereira, R., et al. (2009). A new multiplex for human identification using insertion/deletion polymorphisms. *Electrophoresis*, *30*, 3682–3690.

Pereira, R., et al. (2009). Insertion/deletion polymorphisms: A multiplex assay and forensic applications. *Forensic Science International: Genetics Supplement Series*, *2*, 513–515.

Santos, N. P. C., et al. (2010). Assessing individual interethnic admixture and population substructure using a 48-insertion-deletion (INDEL) ancestry-informative marker (AIM) panel. *Human Mutation*, *31*, 184–190.

Weber, J. L., et al. (2002). Human diallelic insertion/deletion polymorphisms. *American Journal of Human Genetics*, *71*, 854–862.

CHAPTER

13

Y-Chromosome DNA Testing

LINEAGE MARKERS

Autosomal DNA markers, such as the short tandem repeat (STR) loci discussed in Chapter 5 or the single-nucleotide polymorphisms (SNPs) covered in Chapter 12, are shuffled with each generation because half of an individual's genetic information comes from his/her father and half from his/her mother. However, the Y-chromosome (ChrY) and mitochondrial DNA (mtDNA) markers that will be discussed in this chapter and Chapter 14 represent "lineage markers." They are passed down from generation to generation without changing (except for mutational events). Maternal lineages can be traced with mitochondrial DNA sequence information while paternal lineages can be followed with Y-chromosome markers (Figure 13.1).

With lineage markers, the genetic information from each marker is referred to as a haplotype rather than a genotype because there is usually only a single allele per individual. Because Y-chromosome markers are linked on the same chromosome and are not shuffled with each generation, the statistical calculations for a random match probability cannot involve the product rule. Therefore, haplotypes obtained from lineage markers can never be as effective in differentiating between two individuals as genotypes from autosomal markers that are unlinked and segregate separately from generation to generation. However, Y-chromosome (this chapter), mitochondrial DNA (Chapter 14), and X-chromosome (Chapter 15) markers can play an important role in forensic investigations as well as other human identification applications.

APPLICATIONS OF ChrY TESTING

Y-chromosome DNA testing is important for a number of different applications of human genetics including forensic evidence examination, paternity testing, historical investigations, studying human migration patterns throughout history, and genealogical research. In terms of forensic applications, there are both advantages and limitations to Y-chromosome testing (Table 13.1).

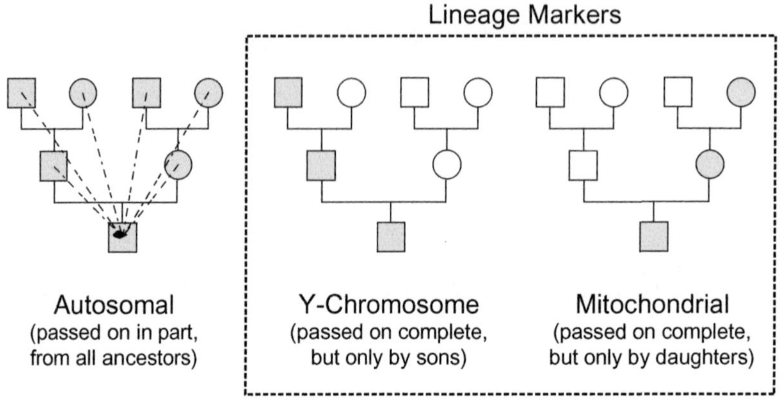

FIGURE 13.1 Illustration of inheritance patterns from recombining autosomal genetic markers and the lineage markers from the Y-chromosome and mitochondrial DNA.

TABLE 13.1 Advantages and Limitations of Y-Chromosome DNA Testing.

Advantages	Limitations
1. Male-specific amplification can enable examination of a male perpetrator's profile even in mixtures with high levels of female DNA in sexual assault cases. 2. Additional mixtures may possibly be analyzed (e.g., fingernail scrapings, saliva on skin, etc.) 3. Paternal transmission from a father to all of his sons extends possible reference sample providers and enables tracing family lineages.	1. Since paternal relatives are identical, Y-STR typing cannot be used to distinguish among brothers or even distant paternal relatives. 2. Without recombination between loci, the product rule cannot be used and thus the discrimination power of Y-STRs is limited by the size of the population database used. 3. Duplications and deletions can complicate the analysis.

The primary value of the Y-chromosome in forensic DNA testing is that it is found only in males. The SRY (sex-determining region of the Y) gene determines maleness. Since a vast majority of crimes where DNA evidence is helpful, particularly sexual assaults, involve males as the perpetrators, DNA tests designed to only examine the male portion can be valuable.

With ChrY tests, interpretable results can be obtained in some cases where autosomal tests are limited by the evidence, such as high levels of female DNA in the presence of minor amounts of male DNA (Figure 13.2). These situations include sexual assault evidence from azospermic or vasectomized males and blood–blood or saliva–blood mixtures where the absence of sperm prevents a successful differential extraction for isolation of male DNA (Prinz & Sansone 2001). In addition, the number of individuals involved in a "gang rape" may be easier to decipher with Y-chromosome results than with highly complicated autosomal STR mixtures. Using ChrY-specific PCR primers can improve the chances of detecting low levels of the perpetrator's DNA in a high background of a female victim's DNA (Hall & Ballantyne 2003). Y-chromosome tests have also been used to verify amelogenin Y-deficient males (Thangaraj et al. 2002).

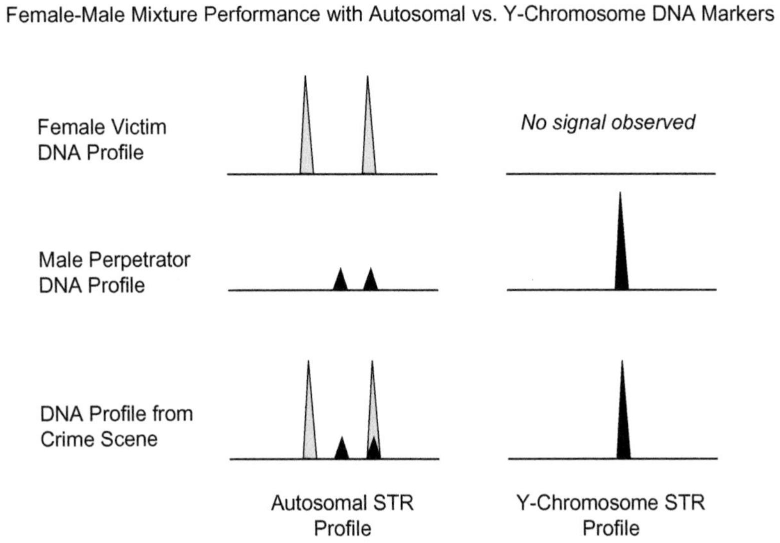

FIGURE 13.2 Schematic illustrating the types of autosomal or Y-STR profiles that might be observed with sexual assault evidence where mixtures of high amounts of female DNA may mask the STR profile of the perpetrator. In some cases, Y-STR testing permits isolation of the male component without having to perform a differential lysis.

The same feature of the Y-chromosome that gives it an advantage in forensic testing, namely maleness, is also its biggest limitation. A majority of the Y-chromosome is transferred directly from father to son without recombination to shuffle its genes and provide greater genetic variety to future generations. Random mutations are the only mechanisms for variation over time between paternally related males. Thus, while exclusions in Y-chromosome DNA testing results can aid forensic investigations, a match between a suspect and evidence only means that the individual in question could have contributed the forensic stain—as could a brother, father, son, uncle, paternal cousin, or even a distant cousin from his paternal lineage (Figure 13.3)! Needless to say, inclusions with Y-chromosome testing are not as meaningful as autosomal STR matches from a random match probability point-of-view (de Knjiff 2003).

On the other hand, the presence of relatives having the same ChrY (Figure 13.3) expands the number of possible reference samples in missing persons investigations and mass disaster victim identification efforts. ChrY testing also aids familial searching (Dettlaff-Kakol & Pawlowski 2002, Sims et al. 2008). Deficient paternity tests where the father is dead or unavailable for testing are benefited if ChrY markers are used (Santos et al. 1993). However, an autosomal DNA test is always preferred when possible since it provides a higher power of discrimination.

The Y-chromosome has also become a popular tool for tracing historical human migration patterns through male lineages (Jobling & Tyler-Smith 1995, 2003). Anthropological, historical, and genealogical questions can be answered through ChrY results. For example, ChrY results in 1998 linked modern-day descendants of Thomas Jefferson and Eston Hemings leading to the controversial conclusion that Jefferson fathered the slave (Foster et al. 1998).

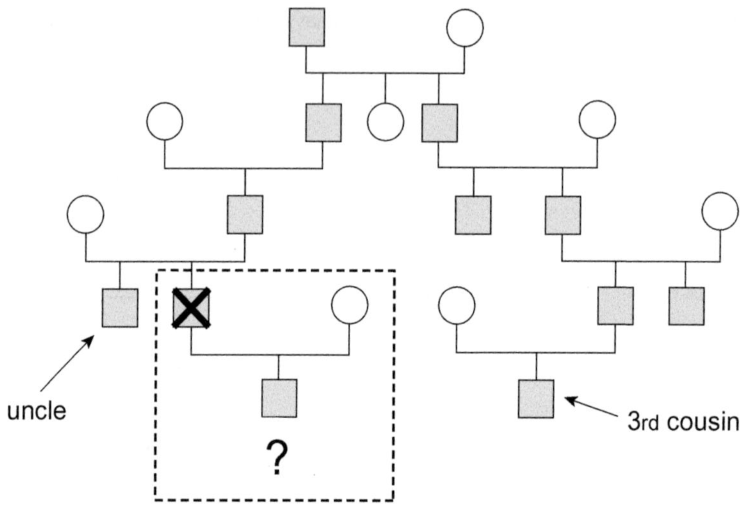

FIGURE 13.3 An example pedigree showing patrilineal inheritance where all shaded males have the same Y-chromosome barring any mutations. To help identify the person in question, any of the other males with the same patrilineage could provide a reference sample to assist in a missing persons investigation, mass disaster victim identification, or deficient paternity test (boxed region) where the father is deceased or not available for testing.

ChrY STRUCTURE

A detailed analysis of the "finished" reference Y-chromosome sequence was described in the June 19, 2003 issue of *Nature* by researchers from the Whitehead Institute and Washington University. Although it is stated as being a "finished" sequence, Skaletsky et al. (2003) report on only 23 Mb of the roughly 50 Mb present in a typical human ChrY.

The unreported and as yet unsequenced ≈30 Mb portion is a heterochromatin region located on the long arm of the Y-chromosome (Figure 13.4) that is not transcribed and is composed of highly repetitive sequences, which are impossible to sequence reliably with current technology. At 50 Mb, the Y-chromosome is the third smallest human chromosome—only slightly larger than chromosome 21 (47 Mb) and chromosome 22 (49 Mb).

The tips of the Y-chromosome, which are called the *pseudoautosomal regions* (PAR), recombine with their sister sex X-chromosome homologous regions. PAR1 located at the tip of the short arm (Yp) of the Y-chromosome is approximately 2.5 Mb in length while PAR2 at the tip of the long arm (Yq) is less than 1 Mb in size (Graves et al. 1998). The remainder of the Y-chromosome (≈95%) is known as the *non-recombining portion of the Y-chromosome*, or NRY (Figure 13.4a). The NRY remains the same from father to son unless a mutation occurs.

Some authors term the NRY the male-specific region (MSY) because of evidence of frequent gene conversion or intrachromosomal recombination (Skaletsky et al. 2003). A total of 156 known transcription units including 78 protein-coding genes are present on MSY.

Many sequences in the ChrY are highly duplicated either with themselves or with the X-chromosome. Three classes of sequences have been characterized in the Y-chromosome: X-transposed, X-degenerate, and ampliconic (Skaletsky et al. 2003). Two blocks on the short

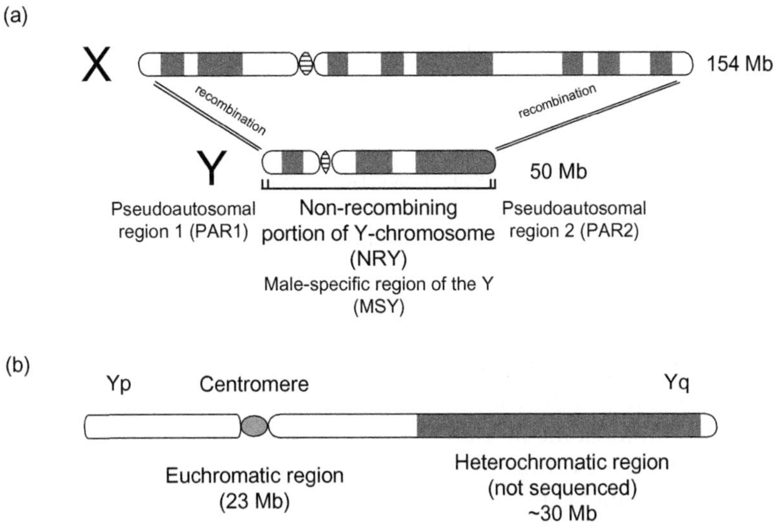

FIGURE 13.4 (a) Schematic of X and Y sex chromosomes. The two tips of the Y-chromosome known as pseudoautosomal region 1 (PAR1) and 2 (PAR2) recombine with the tips of the X-chromosome. The remaining 95% of the Y-chromosome is referred to as the non-recombining portion of the Y-chromosome (NRY) or male-specific region of the Y (MSY). (b) The Y-chromosome is composed of both euchromatic and heterochromatic regions of which only the 23 Mb of euchromatin has been sequenced.

arm of ChrY with a combined length of 3.4 Mb make up the X-transposed sequences. These sequences are 99% identical to sequences found in Xq21, contain two coding genes, and do not participate in X–Y crossing over during male meiosis.

X-degenerate segments of MSY occur in eight blocks on both the short arm and the long arm of the Y-chromosome with an aggregate length of 8.6 Mb. These X-degenerate segments possess up to 96% nucleotide sequence identity to their X-linked homologues. These X-homologous regions can make it challenging to design Y-chromosome assays that generate male-specific DNA results. If portions of an X-homologous region of the Y-chromosome are examined inadvertently, then female DNA, which possesses two X-chromosomes, will be detected. Thus, when testing Y-chromosome-specific assays it is important to examine them in the presence of female DNA (high levels) to verify that there is little-to-no cross talk with X-homologous regions of the Y-chromosome (Butler et al. 2002, Hall and Ballantyne 2003).

The ampliconic segments are composed of seven large blocks scattered across both the short arm and the long arm and covering about 10.2 Mb of the Y-chromosome (Skaletsky et al. 2003). Some 60% of these ampliconic sequences have intrachromosomal identities of 99.9% or greater. In other words, it is very difficult to tell these sequences apart from one another. Another interesting feature of these ampliconic segments is that many of them are palindromes—that is, the almost exact duplicate sequences are inverted with respect to each other's sequence essentially as mirror images. Eight large palindromes collectively comprise 5.7 Mb of Yq with at least six of these palindromes containing testis genes. Genetic markers within these palindromic regions will exist as multi-copy PCR products from single primer sets. For example, the DAZ (deleted in azospermic) gene occurs in four copies at ≈24 Mb along the reference sequence (Saxena et al. 1996, Skaletsky et al. 2003).

Different Classes of ChrY Genetic Markers

Two broad categories of DNA markers have been used to examine Y-chromosome diversity: bi-allelic loci, which exhibit two possible alleles, and multi-allelic loci. Results from typing the lower resolution bi-allelic markers are classified into haplogroups while multi-allelic results are characterized as haplotypes (de Knijff 2000).

Bi-allelic markers include single nucleotide polymorphisms (Y-SNPs) and an *Alu* element insertion. The Y-Alu polymorphism (YAP) was the first discovered Y-chromosome bi-allelic marker (Hammer 1994). Bi-allelic markers are sometimes referred to as unique event polymorphisms (UEPs) because of their low mutation rates ($\approx 10^{-8}$ to 10^{-9} per generation). More than 600 bi-allelic Y-chromosome markers have now been characterized into defined haplogroups (Y Chromosome Consortium 2002, Butler 2003, Karafet et al. 2008).

Y-chromosome multi-allelic markers include two minisatellites and several hundred short tandem repeat (Y-STR) markers (Kayser et al. 2004). These multi-allelic loci can be used to differentiate Y-chromosome haplotypes with fairly high resolution due to their higher mutation rates. Minisatellite loci have mutation rates as high as 6% to 11% per generation (Jobling et al. 1999) while the average mutation rate for Y-STRs is ≈0.2% per generation (Kayer et al. 2000, Dupuy et al. 2004).

Y-STR MARKERS

Y-chromosome DNA analysis can be performed with either Y-STRs or Y-SNPs. Since Y-STRs change more rapidly (mutation rate ≈ 1 in 10^3) compared to Y-SNPs (mutation rate ≈ 1 in 10^9), Y-STR results exhibit more variability and thus have greater use in forensic applications. Typically Y-STRs are described as defining haplotypes while Y-SNPs define haplogroups. As will be discussed at the end of the chapter, Y-SNPs can be useful in DNA ancestry studies.

Single Copy vs. Multi-Copy Markers

Due to the duplicated, palindromic regions of the Y-chromosome mentioned above, some Y-STR loci occur more than once and, when amplified with a locus-specific set of primers, produce more than one PCR product. This duplication can lead to some confusion in terms of counting the number of loci present in a haplotype. A single set of primers can produce two amplicons, which may be thought of as "two loci" for a Y-chromosome haplotype.

For example, the Y-STR locus DYS385 is present in two regions along the long arm of the Y-chromosome. These duplicated regions are located about 40,000 bp apart and can generate two different alleles when amplified with a single set of primers. The two alleles are typically labeled "a" and "b" with the "a" designation going to the smaller-sized allele. It is also possible to have both "a" and "b" alleles be the same size in which case only a single peak would appear in an electropherogram (Figure 13.5a). Due to the presence of two

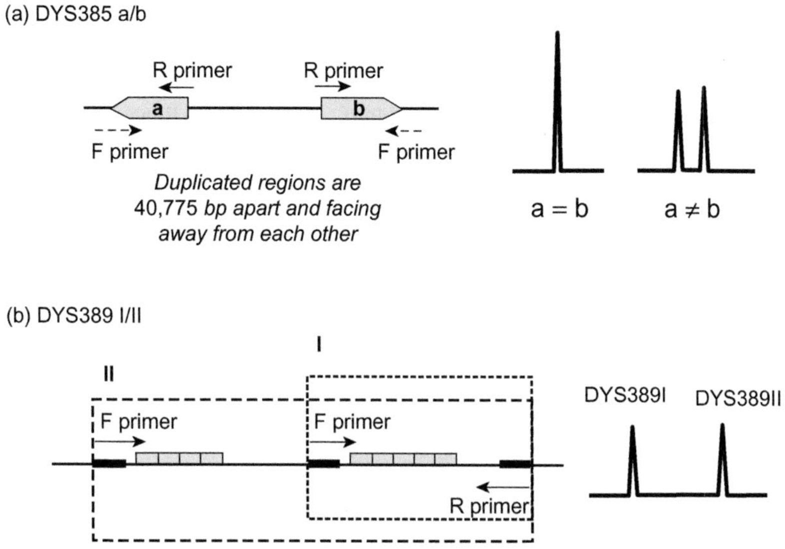

FIGURE 13.5 Schematic illustration of how multiple PCR primer binding sites give rise to multi-copy PCR products for (a) DYS385a/b and (b) DYS389I/II. Arrows represent either forward "F" or reverse "R" primers. In the case of DYS385a/b, the entire region around the STR repeat is duplicated and spaced about 40,775 bp apart on the long arm of the Y-chromosome. Thus, amplification with a single set of primers gives rise to one peak if the "a" repeat region is equal in size to the "b" repeat region or separate peaks if "a" and "b" differ in length. DYS389 possesses two primary repeat regions that are flanked on one side by a similar sequence. Widely used forward primers bind adjacent to both repeats generating amplicons that differ in size by ≈120 bp. Note that DYS389II is inclusive of the DYS389I repeat region and therefore some analyses subtract DYS389II–DYS389I repeats.

alleles, this duplicated locus is usually referred to as DYS385 a/b. It has been demonstrated that with a nested PCR approach, the "a" and "b" alleles for DYS385 can be amplified separately (Kittler et al. 2003, Seo et al. 2003). Other multi-copy Y-STRs besides DYS385 a/b that have been used in human identity testing include YCAII a/b and DYS464 a/b/c/d (Redd et al. 2002, Butler 2003, Schoske et al. 2004).

Two PCR products can also be generated at the DYS389 locus with a single set of primers. However in this case the DYS389I PCR product is a subset of the DYS389II amplicon because the forward PCR primer binds to the flanking region of two different repeat regions that are approximately 120bp apart (Figure 13.5b). Some analyses with DYS389I/II treat the larger PCR product as DYS389II–DYS389I to get a handle on the variation occurring in the two regions independent of each another (e.g., Redd et al. 2002).

Minimal Haplotype Loci

The number of Y-STR loci available for use in human identity testing has increased dramatically since the turn of the century and the availability of the human genome sequence. In the 1990s only a handful of Y-STR markers were characterized and available for use. At the beginning of 2002, only about 30 Y-STRs were available for researchers (Butler 2003).

TABLE 13.2 Characteristics of Commonly Used Y-Chromosome STR Loci. Adapted from Butler (2006) and Decker et al. (2007). Mutation Rates Are from as Many as 15000 Meioses Described in a YHRD Summary of 23 Publications as of January 2011 (See http://www.yhrd.org/Research/Loci/).

STR Marker	Position (Mb)	Repeat Motif	Allele Range	Mutation Rate
DYS393	3.19	AGAT	8–17	0.10%
DYS456	4.33	AGAT	13–18	0.42%
DYS458	7.93	GAAA	14–20	0.64%
DYS19	10.13	TAGA	10–19	0.23%
DYS391	12.61	TCTA	6–14	0.26%
DYS635	12.89	TSTA	17–27	0.35%
DYS437	12.98	TCTR	13–17	0.12%
DYS439	13.03	AGAT	8–15	0.52%
DYS389 I/II	13.12	TCTR	9–17/24–34	0.25%/0.36%
DYS438	13.38	TTTTC	6–14	0.03%
DYS390	15.78	TCTR	17–28	0.21%
GATA-H4	17.25	TAGA	8–13	0.24%
DYS385 a/b	19.26	GAAA	7–28	0.21%
DYS392	21.04	TAT	6–20	0.04%
DYS448	22.78	AGAGAT	17–24	0.16%

Since that time more than 400 new Y-STRs (Kayser et al. 2004, Leat et al. 2007) have been discovered and deposited in the Genome Database (GDB). These Y-STRs have been cataloged and mapped to their ChrY positions (Hanson & Ballantyne 2006). Unfortunately, operations with the GDB were halted in 2008 and thus this repository of DNA marker information is no longer available online.

Yet even with a limited number of loci available at the time, a core set was selected in 1997 that continue to serve as "minimal haplotype" loci (Kayser et al. 1997, Pascali et al. 1998). The minimal haplotype is defined by the single copy Y-STR loci DYS19, DYS389I, DYS389II, DYS390, DYS391, DYS392, DYS393, and the highly polymorphic multi-copy locus DYS385 a/b (Schneider et al. 1998). By means of a multicenter study, more than 4000 male DNA samples from 48 different subpopulation groups were studied with the single copy loci in the minimal haplotype set (de Knijff et al. 1997). This work formed the basis for what is now the online Y-STR Haplotype Reference Database (http://www.yhrd.org) that will be described in more detail below.

In January 2003, the U.S. Scientific Working Group on DNA Analysis Methods (SWGDAM) recommended use of the minimal haplotype loci plus two additional single-copy Y-STRs: DYS438 and DYS439 (Ayub et al. 2000). Information regarding these core loci and other loci present in commercial Y-STR kits may be found in Table 13.2. Their position along ChrY is illustrated in Figure 13.6. Although other Y-STRs may be added to databases

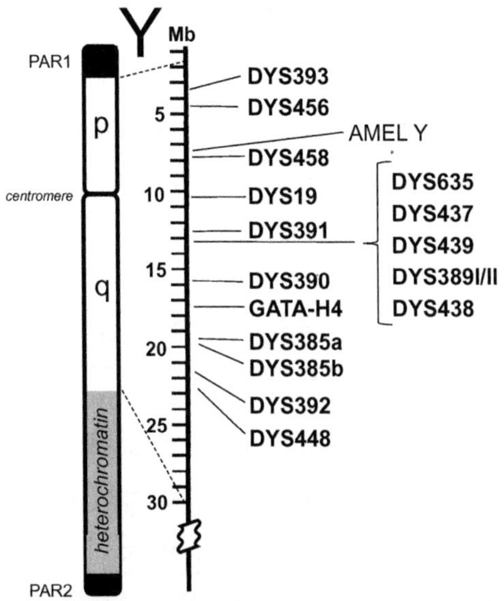

FIGURE 13.6 Relative positions of 17 Y-STR loci commonly used in ChrY testing. DYS458 is closest to amelogenin (AMEL Y) and thus may be lost with AMEL Y null alleles due to deletion of that portion of ChrY.

as their value is demonstrated and they become part of commercially available kits, the original minimal haplotype loci and SWGDAM recommended Y-STRs are likely to dominate human identity applications in the coming years.

Y-STR Kits

As noted in Chapter 5, forensic scientists rely heavily on commercially available kits to perform DNA testing. Thus, many laboratories especially in the U.S. were reluctant to move into Y-STR typing until Y-STR kits were offered. Table 13.2 lists the loci present in the two most widely used Y-STR kits (Figure 13.7): PowerPlex Y (Promega Corporation) and Yfiler (Applied Biosystems). Note that all of the European and U.S. core Y-STR loci are included in both kits. PowerPlex Y contains one additional locus (DYS437) and Yfiler has six additional loci (DYS437, DYS448, DYS456, DYS458, DYS635, and GATA-H4). Yfiler kit allelic ladders are shown in Figure 13.8.

Until 2005, ReliaGene Technologies (formerly of New Orleans, LA) sold the Y-PLEX 12 kit, which amplified the SWGDAM recommended loci plus the amelogenin marker (see Chapter 5). Reliagene had also supplied Y-PLEX 6 and Y-PLEX 5 kits (Sinha et al. 2004), which were precursors to the Y-PLEX 12 kit. Inclusion of amelogenin enables confirmation that the PCR reaction has not failed on female DNA samples since a single X amplicon will result. In addition, mixture levels of male and female DNA can be confirmed in many situations with the amelogenin X and Y peak height ratios. While the amelogenin primers provide a measure of quality control on PCR amplifications, they have the disadvantage of possibly tying up and consuming PCR reagents when high levels of female DNA are present in a mixture.

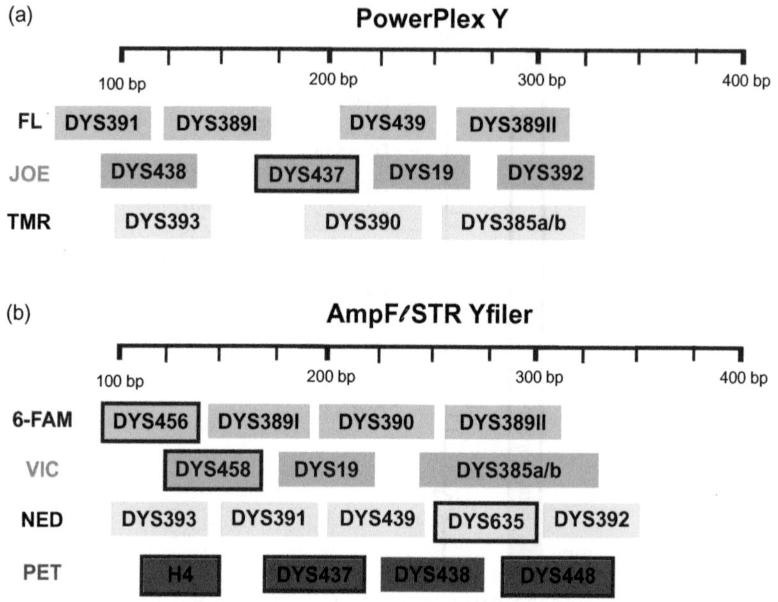

FIGURE 13.7 Comparison of relative size ranges and fluorescent dye labels for Y-STR loci present in (a) PowerPlex Y from Promega Corporation and (b) Yfiler from Applied Biosystems. The highlighted locus boxes are those additional loci included in the multiplex beyond the SWGDAM-recommended set.

Y-STR Allele Nomenclature

The DNA Commission of the International Society of Forensic Genetics (ISFG) has made a series of recommendations on the use of Y-STR markers (Gill et al. 2001, Gusmão et al. 2006). Their recommendations address allele nomenclature, use of allelic ladders, population genetics, and reporting methods.

The ISFG recommendations for Y-STR allelic ladders include the following: (a) the alleles should span the distance of known allelic variants for a particular locus, (b) the rungs of the ladder should be one repeat unit apart wherever possible, (c) the alleles present in the ladder should be sequenced, and (d) the ladders should be widely available to enable reliable interlaboratory comparisons. The existence of commercially available Y-STR kits has now facilitated the widespread use of consistent allelic ladders (e.g., Figure 13.8).

Prior to commercially available Y-STR kits and consistent allelic ladders, various researchers in the field took different approaches to naming alleles. For some loci there were instances of multiple published designations for the same allele. An example of this phenomenon that illustrates the importance of standardization is DYS439, which has been designated three different ways in the literature (Figure 13.9).

In an effort to provide a unified nomenclature for STR loci, a comparative analysis of the repeat and sequence structure of Y-chromosome markers in humans and chimpanzees has been proposed and 11 human Y-STRs have been studied (Gusmão et al. 2002). Since the chimpanzees examined in their study did not vary in the other regions outside of the variable core GATA repeat for DYS439, Gusmão and co-workers (2002) proposed a $[GATA]_n$

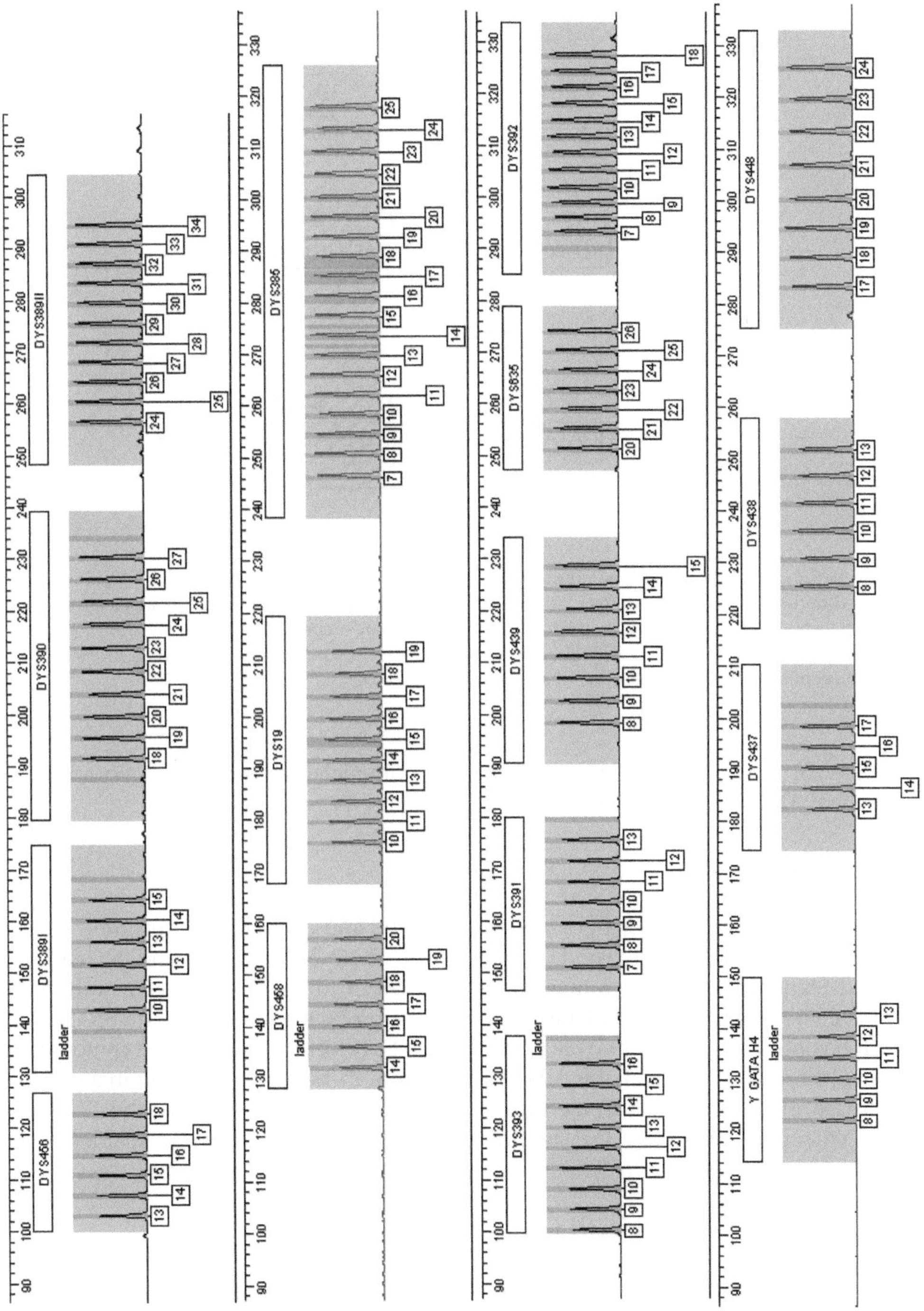

FIGURE 13.8 Yfiler kit allelic ladders.

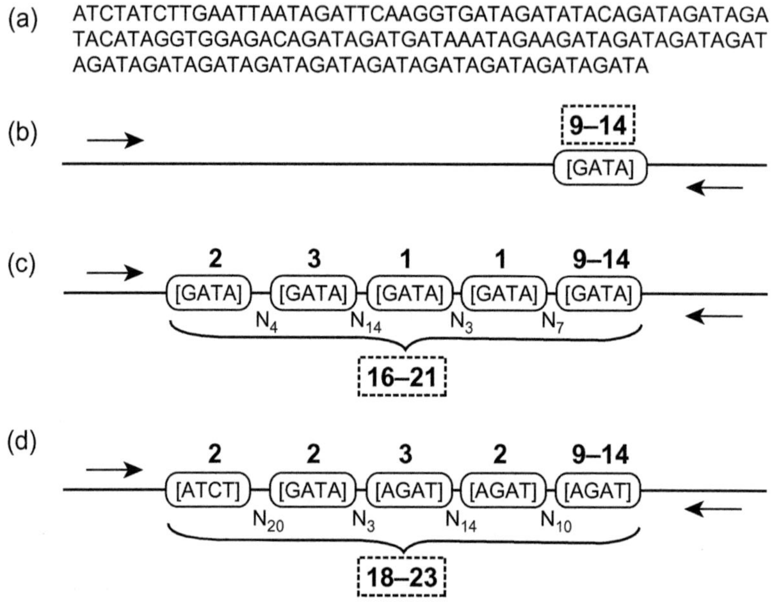

FIGURE 13.9 Various published allele nomenclatures for DYS439. (a) Sequence from DYS439 spanning the repeat regions used in the various nomenclatures; (b) Schematic of allele designation by Ayub et al. (2000)—repeat range is 9–14; (c) Schematic of allele designation by Grignani et al. (2000)—repeat range is 16-21; (d) Schematic of allele designation by Gonzalez-Neira et al. (2001)—repeat range is 18–23. The most widely accepted designation and what is used in commercial Y-STR kits is (b)—that of Ayub et al. (2000).

repeat structure for humans (see Figure 13.9b). This nomenclature has now been adopted for all commercial STR kits typing DYS439.

NIST SRM 2395

The use of reference samples aids in obtaining calibrated and consistent results among laboratories performing Y-STR testing. The U.S. National Institute of Standards and Technology (NIST) released Standard Reference Material (SRM®) 2395 in July 2003 to serve as a human Y-chromosome DNA profiling standard. Five male DNA samples are provided with SRM 2395, each of which has been sequenced at over 20 different Y-STR loci including the common core loci present in all commercially available kits. An additional 21 loci are sequenced in a revised certificate released in October 2008. In the future, SRM 2391c will be certified at the 17 Y-STR loci present in Yfiler (as well as other loci should additional Y-STR kits become available).

Y-STR HAPLOTYPE DATABASES

A number of online Y-STR databases exist (Table 13.3). The forensic databases contain collections of anonymous individuals and can be used to estimate the frequency of specified

TABLE 13.3 Summary of Available Online Y-STR Databases (as of January 2011). For Updated Information, See http://www.cstl.nist.gov/biotech/strbase/y_strs.htm.

Database	Number of Samples (Population Groups)	Number of Y-STR Markers Tested	Website
Y-STR Haplotype Reference Database (YHRD)	91,601 (710 groups)	7 to 17	http://www.yhrd.org
US Y-STR Database (US Y-STR)	18,547 (5 groups)	11 to 17	http://www.usystrdatabase.org
Yfiler Haplotype Database	11,393 (13 groups)	17	http://www6.appliedbiosystems.com/yfilerdatabase/
Ysearch (for genealogists)	93,194	Up to 100	http://www.ysearch.org
Ybase (for genealogists)	16,059	Up to 49	http://www.ybase.org
Sorenson Molecular Genealogy (for genealogists)	37,588	7 to 37	http://www.smgf.org

Y-STR haplotypes. The genetic genealogy databases, such as Ysearch and Ybase, contain Y-STR haplotype information gathered by genetic genealogy companies with different sets of loci from males trying to make genealogical connections. Thus, the haplotypes in these genealogy databases are associated with specific individuals and family names.

YHRD

The largest and most widely used forensic and general population genetics Y-STR database, known as the Y-STR Haplotype Reference Database (YHRD), was created by Lutz Roewer and colleagues at Humbolt University in Berlin, Germany, and has been available online since 2000 (Roewer 2003, Willuweit & Roewer 2007). YHRD is internet-accessible at http://www.yhrd.org. As of January 2011, YHRD contains results from more than 89,000 samples with minimal haplotype loci results representing 710 different groups of sample submissions from various populations and countries around the world. Searches on YHRD may be conducted by population group or geographic location.

US Y-STR Database

A U.S. population-specific Y-STR Database (US Y-STR) was launched in December 2007 to enable haplotype frequency estimates on five different U.S. groups using the 11 SWGDAM recommended loci. The original version of US Y-STR contained 4796 African American profiles, 820 Asian, 5047 Caucasians, 2260 Hispanics, and 983 Native Americans. In some cases, further subdivision of these five primary groups can be examined if desired. An analysis of a version of the US Y-STR Database containing 7812 samples with full 17-locus Yfiler results found that 93.7% were distinct and 92.9% of these haplotypes were population-specific (Ge et al. 2010).

As of January 2011, US Y-STR had expanded to 18,547 SWGDAM profiles of which 8376 contained information at the 17 Yfiler loci. Where possible, US Y-STR has attempted to

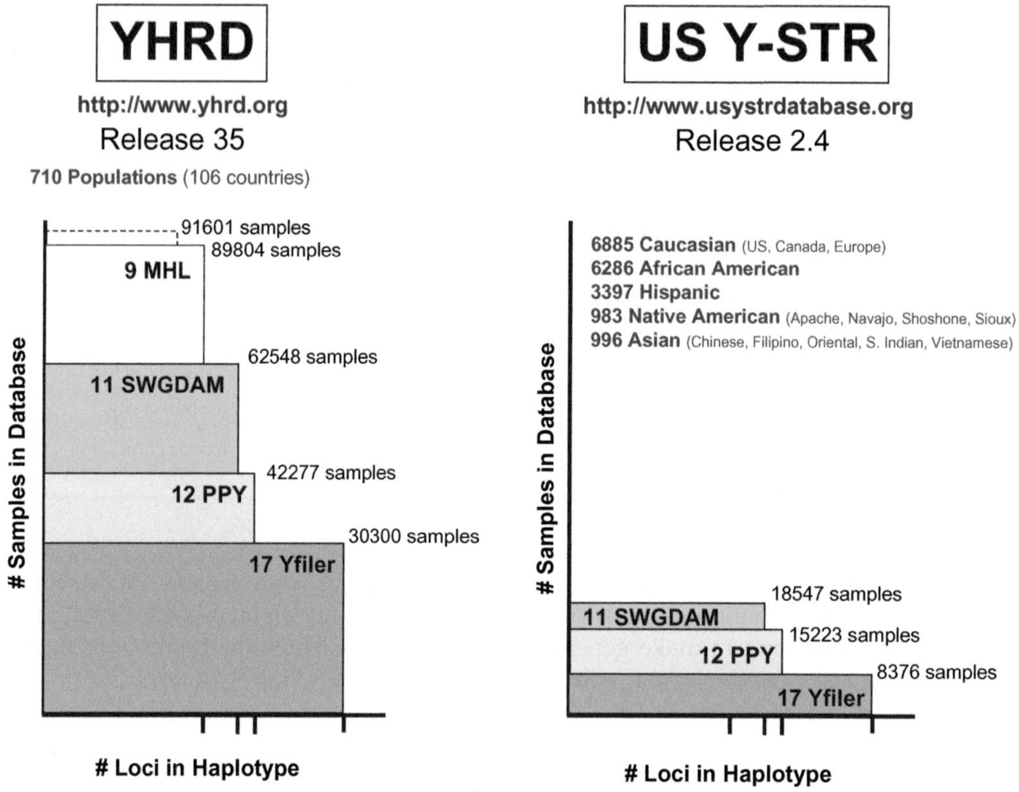

FIGURE 13.10 Comparison of YHRD and US YSTR database sample sizes and data content.

ensure that no duplicates are present through examining autosomal STR typing results on any samples possessing the same Y-STR profile. Having both autosomal and Y-STR data can be helpful in trying to sort out cases of common Y-STR haplotypes.

Figure 13.10 compares the numbers of samples containing various numbers of loci in YHRD and US Y-STR as of January 2011. When performing a search it is important to keep in mind that the denominator will change based on the loci selected in the search (see D.N.A. Box 13.1).

Genetic Genealogy Databases

Several genetic genealogy Y-STR haplotype databases are also available online (Table 13.3). These databases are typically not used for Y-STR forensic haplotype frequency estimates, but could be helpful in trying to associate a family surname with a particular haplotype if this information was desired in an investigation. These genetic genealogy databases contain information from the minimal haplotype loci, a subset of the minimal haplotype loci, or additional Y-STRs, and therefore cannot always be searched across all loci of interest.

D.N.A. BOX 13.1

A Y-STR PROFILE SEARCHED AGAINST SEVERAL HAPLOTYPE FREQUENCY DATABASES

The following profile was searched on January 15, 2011 against several databases (see Table 13.3): DYS19 (14), DYS389I (13), DYS398II (29), DYS390 (24), DYS391 (11), DYS392 (13), DYS393 (13), DYS385 a/b (11,15), DYS438 (12), DYS439 (13), DYS437 (15), DYS448 (19), DYS456 (17), DYS458 (18), DYS635 (23), and GATA-H4 (12).

The count and frequency of each of these searches is listed below.

The results shown here represent the counting method. Note that by adding additional loci the numerator goes down as the haplotype becomes more rare. Depending on the database and the type of haplotypes present (see Figure 13.10), the denominator can also become smaller as fewer profiles containing the requested information are being searched. As can be seen in the Yfiler column, there were no observations of the searched profile in the databases. The frequencies listed in this column are based on <1 observation in the size of the database.

The final column illustrates an upper bound 95% confidence interval for the frequency estimate when no observations are observed, which can be approximated by 3/N where N is the size of the database. The application of a 95% upper bound confidence interval on those results with at least one observation is covered in D.N.A. Box 13.2.

Database	Minimal Haplotype (9 loci)	SWGDAM (11 loci)	PowerPlex Y (12 loci)	Yfiler (17 loci)	3/N for Zero Observations
YHRD	403/89804 = 0.45%	29/62548 = 0.046%	14/42277 = 0.033%	0/30300 = <0.0033%	3/30300 = 0.0099%
US Y-STR	6/18547 = 0.032%	1/18547 = 0.0054%	1/15223 = 0.0066%	0/8376 = <0.012%	3/8376 = 0.036%
Yfiler database	64/11393 = 0.56%	4/11393 = 0.035%	4/11393 = 0.035%	0/11393 = <0.0088%	3/11393 = 0.026%

INTERPRETATION OF Y-STR RESULTS

Since the Y-chromosome is passed down unchanged (except for mutations) from father to son, the observation of a match with Y-STRs does not carry the same power of discrimination and weight in court as an autosomal STR match would. The lack of recombination between Y chromosome markers means that Y-STR results have to be combined into a haplotype for searching available databases as well as estimating the rarity of a particular haplotype.

Determining the Rarity of a Y-STR Profile

Generally speaking there are three possible interpretations resulting from comparing Y-STR haplotypes produced from question (Q) and known (K) samples: (1) *exclusion* because the Y-STR profiles are different and could not have originated from the same source, (2) *inconclusive* where there is insufficient data to render an interpretation or ambiguous results were obtained, or (3) *failure to exclude* (or *inclusion*) as the Y-STR haplotype results from the Q-K comparison are the same and could have originated from the same source.

When the Q and K samples (e.g., evidence and suspect haplotypes) do not match, then Y-STR typing is helpful in demonstrating the exclusion. However, estimating the strength of a match when a suspect's Y-STR haplotype cannot be excluded is more problematic because barring any mutations, paternal relatives (e.g., all brothers, male children, father, uncles, paternal grandfather, and paternal cousins) would be expected to have the same Y-STR profile (de Knijff 2003, see Figure 13.3).

Since it is common practice to place some significance on the likelihood of a random match with unrelated individuals, statistics derived from population data can be applied. Estimates for a random match with Y-STR haplotypes (and mtDNA sequence information) are done by the *counting method*, where the number of times the haplotype of interest is observed is divided by the total number of haplotypes in the database used. The size of the database used for the counting method makes a difference when trying to estimate the rarity of a Y-STR profile. The larger the number of unrelated individuals in the database (i.e., the denominator in the counting method calculation), the better the statistics will be for a random match frequency estimate.

D.N.A. Box 13.1 works through some example calculations with searches using subsets of the 17 Yfiler loci. This example explores the ability of different marker sets to resolve the Y-STR profile from unrelated lineages. When the full 17-locus profile was searched, it was not found in 30,300 17-locus haplotypes found in YHRD or in 8376 17-locus haplotypes located in US Y-STR.

An examination of 10,454 Yfiler profiles from 29 different population studies and the Yfiler haplotype database in 2006 found that approximately 95% of full 17-locus Yfiler profiles had never been observed before (Butler et al. 2007). In other words, these profiles were singletons in the population study or database. Frequency estimates calculated with the counting method, while not as powerful as those produced with unlinked autosomal STRs, may nevertheless be informative in many forensic casework scenarios and provide another piece of evidence in the overall framework of a case.

Charles Brenner, a forensic mathematician, has proposed the use of a probability estimate rather than a frequency estimate to judge the evidentiary value of a rare haplotype (Brenner 2010). Under the Brenner model, the fraction of singletons, or once-observed-haplotypes, in a data set become important to predict the rarity of future haplotypes that might be observed. For example, if 95% of 17-locus Y-STR profiles have never been observed before in a data set (see Butler et al. 2007), then a new 17-locus Y-STR profile being compared against this data set would likely not be observed 95% of the time. While this approach is not yet widely used, it has potential to help provide greater strength to rare haplotypes that are not present in current databases, such as the example shown in D.N.A. Box 13.1 with 17 loci.

SWGDAM Y-STR Interpretation Guidelines

The Scientific Working Group on DNA Analysis Methods (SWGDAM) approved Y-STR interpretation guidelines in July 2008 that were subsequently published in the January 2009 issue of *Forensic Science Communications* (SWGDAM 2009). These guidelines recommend that the loci on NRY should be considered linked as a single locus and that the source of the population database used in frequency estimation should be documented. Furthermore, searches of Y-STR haplotype frequency databases should be conducted using all loci for which results were obtained from the evidentiary sample. If there is less information on the known sample, then only those loci for which results were obtained from both the known and evidentiary sample should be used in the population database search.

SWGDAM endorsed the counting method with application of a confidence interval to correct for database size and sampling variation. The confidence interval equation commonly used for both Y-STR and mitochondrial DNA frequencies over the past decade assumes a normal distribution (Holland & Parsons 1999, Tully et al. 2000, SWGDAM 2009). At the January 2011 SWGDAM meeting, the Clopper-Pearson binomial model (Clopper & Pearson 1934) for calculating confidence intervals was discussed and advocated as being slightly more conservative than the normal distribution used previously (D.N.A. Box 13.2; see also D.N.A. Box 14.1).

Without providing a lot of guidance, the SWGDAM Y-STR Interpretation Guidelines also briefly address Y-STR mixtures, subpopulation (theta) corrections, and advocate joint match probabilities between Y-STRs and autosomal STR results (SWGDAM 2009).

Combining Y-STR Information and Autosomal DNA Results

In some cases, such as a fingernail scraping, a missing persons investigation, or a mass disaster reconstruction scenario, results from both Y-STR loci and a limited number of autosomal loci may be obtained. The question might then be asked can this information be combined to increase the rarity of a match since the autosomal data by itself may not be satisfactory? While this is a relatively new area and has not been investigated in detail yet, Sinha et al. (2004) reason that multiplication of the autosomal STR locus profile frequency obtained following the NRC II recommendations and the Y-STR haplotype frequency obtained with a minimal frequency threshold and correction for sampling (as demonstrated in the previous example) is still conservative based on lack of dependence between Y-STR loci and biological independence of chromosomes.

Bruce Walsh and colleagues at the University of Arizona have published an article expressing support for combining autosomal and Y-STR data (Walsh et al. 2008). This article was followed by a reminder that the approach should not be used with relatives (Amorim 2008).

Mutation Rates with Y-STR Markers

Several studies have examined mutation rates among the commonly used Y-STR loci. Most studies have focused on the minimal haplotype loci. Two different approaches

D.N.A. BOX 13.2

95% UPPER BOUND CONFIDENCE INTERVALS USING NORMAL AND CLOPPER-PEARSON APPROACHES

Confidence intervals may be used to reflect the reliability of a statistical estimate and are based on observed data. Provided that the statistical model is correct, confidence intervals are intended to offer assurance that all data obtained with a procedure, or that might be obtained in the future, should include the true value of the parameter the proportion of time set by the confidence level. A 95% confidence interval is most commonly calculated.

When a Y-STR haplotype (or mtDNA sequence) has not been observed in a database of size N, the 95% confidence interval is

$$1 - (0.05)^{1/N}$$

This value is very close to 3/N, which was used in the D.N.A. Box 13.1 example calculations.

An upper bound 95% confidence interval can be placed on a profile's frequency using

$$p + 1.96\sqrt{\frac{(p)(1-p)}{N}}$$

where the frequency (p) is determined from the number of observations (x) in a database containing N profiles. This "normal" approximation interval is the simplest formula to calculate and has been widely used (see Holland & Parsons 1999, Tully et al. 2001) but is known to be problematic in situations with small sample sizes or very few observations.

The Clopper-Pearson formula, named after the authors of the paper describing it in 1934, provides a more conservative value for confidence intervals when very low counts are observed from a haplotype database. The formula for the upper 95 percent confidence limit using Clopper-Pearson is

$$\sum_{k=0}^{x}\binom{N}{k}p_0^k(1-p_0)^{N-k} = 0.05$$

where N = the database size, x = the number of observations of the haplotype in the database, $k = 0, 1, 2, 3 \ldots x$ observations, and p = the haplotype frequency at which x or fewer observations are expected to occur 5% of the time. This cumulative binomial distribution formula is solved for p through serial iterations and therefore requires the use of a computer program. In the examples below, an Excel spreadsheet from Steven

Count Values (see D.N.A. Box 13.1)	Frequency p = x/N	Normal 95% Confidence Interval	Clopper-Pearson 95% Confidence Interval
YHRD 9 loci: **403**/89804	0.449%	0.485%	0.487%
YHRD 12 loci: **14**/42277	0.0331%	0.0477%	0.0518%
US Y-STR 12 loci: **1**/15223	0.0657%	0.0174%	0.0317%

D.N.A. BOX 13.2 *(cont'd)*

Myers (California Department of Justice) was utilized.

Note that with a large number of observations, such as 403 out of a database of 89,804, there is almost no difference between the normal and Clopper-Pearson approaches. However, the normal method is less conservative (i.e., provides a more rare frequency) when the haplotype frequency is low, such as 1 out of 15,223 or even 14 out of 42,277. Although there are differences in these calculations, re-evaluation by the Clopper-Pearson method will not suddenly change a reported result by orders of magnitude or likely change the outcome of a report significantly.

In March 2010 the US Y-STR database changed its 95% confidence interval calculations to the Clopper-Pearson method.

Sources:

Clopper, C.J., & Pearson, E.S. (1934). The use of confidence or fiducial limits illustrated in the case of the binomial. Biometrika, *26, 404–413.*

HaploCALc_1.0 Excel spreadsheet kindly provided by Steven P. Myers, California Department of Justice.

Holland, M.M., & Parsons, T.J. (1999). Mitochondrial DNA sequence analysis – validation and use for forensic casework. Forensic Science Review, *11, 21–50.*

Tully, G., et al. (2001). Considerations by the European DNA profiling (EDNAP) group on the working practices, nomenclature and interpretation of mitochondrial DNA profiles. Forensic Science International, *124, 83–91.*

http://en.wikipedia.org/wiki/Binomial_proportion_confidence_interval and http://en.wikipedia.org/wiki/Confidence_interval.

have been used: deep-rooted pedigrees (Heyer et al. 1997, Bonne-Tamir et al. 2003) and male germ-line transmissions from confirmed father/son pairs (Bianchi et al. 1998, Kayser et al. 2000, Dupuy et al. 2001, Dupuy et al. 2004, Kurihara et al. 2004, Gusmão et al. 2005, Budowle et al. 2005, Decker et al. 2008, Ge et al. 2009).

The pedigree approach has the advantage of not having to run as many samples but when differences are seen it can be hard to attribute the mutation to the proper generation (see Bonne-Tamir et al. 2003) or to potential illegitimacy (Heyer et al. 1997). Heyer et al. (1997) tested only 42 males but were able to infer information from 213 generations or meioses (once three illegitimate lines had been removed) while Bonne-Tamir et al. (2003) examined 74 male samples that spanned 139 generations. Of course the pedigree approach requires detailed genealogical records and no breakdown in the paternal lineages through illegitimacy.

The mutation rates for Y-STRs are in the same range as autosomal STRs, namely around one to four per thousand generational events (0.1% to 0.4%) (see Table 13.2). Only DYS458 and DYS439 mutate faster than 0.4% based on current data. A compilation of the various studies reveals that compound repeat locus DYS458 is the most likely to mutate with DYS438 being the least likely to change. As with autosomal STRs, single-repeat changes are favored over multiple-repeat jumps. Allele gains are more common than allele losses as the mutations occur with not only locus-specific but also allele-specific differences in mutation rate (Dupuy et al. 2004). Mutations typically only occur when 11 or more homogeneous repeats are immediately adjacent to one another (Kayser et al. 2000).

Kayser and Sajantila (2001) discuss the implications of mutations for paternity testing and forensic analysis. They observed mutations at two Y-STRs within the same father/son pair suggesting that differences at three or more Y-STRs are needed before an "exclusion" can be declared with paternity testing or kinship analysis, which is typically the same criteria used for paternity testing with autosomal loci. However, a recent study found a single instance of three mutations out of 17 Y-STRs tested in a confirmed father-son pair (Goedbloed et al. 2009).

Occasionally duplications or even triplications of a Y-STR locus have been reported, particularly for DYS19 (Butler et al. 2005). It is important to keep this fact in mind so that two peaks at the DYS19 locus are not automatically interpreted as coming from a mixture of two males. Both of these issues, namely mutations impacting paternity analysis and duplications of loci potentially confusing mixture interpretation, suggest that analysis of additional Y-STR loci can be helpful in these situations.

Y-STR USE IN FORENSIC CASEWORK

Y-STR assays have been used for several years on a limited basis to aid forensic casework. Their use has been much more widespread in Europe than the United States although a greater number of U.S. labs are now embracing Y-STR testing. Early work in the U.S. with Y-STRs was performed in the late 1990s by the New York City Office of the Chief Medical Examiner (OCME). ReliaGene Technologies, Inc. (New Orleans, LA) developed the first Y-STR kit, Y-PLEX 6, and started doing Y-chromosome testing in late 2000.

The New York City Office of the Chief Medical Examiner primarily uses Y-STR testing when any one of the four scenarios is met (Prinz 2003): (1) evidence is positive for semen but no DNA foreign to the victim can be detected, or potential male alleles are below the detection threshold with autosomal STR tests; (2) the evidence in question is amylase positive and a male/female mixture is expected; (3) a large number of semen stains need to be screened; and (4) the number of semen donors needs to be determined (e.g., suspected gang rape).

Determining the amount of male DNA present rather than the total amount of male and female DNA is important for getting on-scale results with Y-STR testing. One approach is to estimate the general level of male DNA present by assessing the strength of the p30 antibody signal (see Chapter 1) (Prinz 2003). The recent availability of real-time PCR assays specific to the male DNA component of a forensic mixture (e.g., Quantifiler Y kit) provides a more high-tech approach.

There have been several published reports describing the use and value of Y-STR testing in forensic casework. Some of these published results are summarized in Table 13.4. ReliaGene reported use of Y-STRs on 188 forensic samples from 2000 to 2003 with their Y-PLEX 6 and Y-PLEX 5 kits (Sinha et al. 2004). Samples were from epithelial cells including azospermic seminal fluid, sweat or saliva, sperm, fingernails, blood, and other tissues. Y-STR testing has been accepted in several jurisdictions throughout the United States (Sinha et al. 2004). Since Y-STR kits became more available in 2003 (PowerPlex Y) and 2004 (Yfiler), this information has been used in a growing number of cases to aid forensic investigations.

TABLE 13.4 Some Published Reports Describing Use of Y-STRs in Forensic Casework.

Kit/Loci Used	Reference	Comments
In-house assay with DYS19, DYS390, DYS389I/II	Prinz et al. (2001)	In one year at the New York City Office of the Chief Medical Examiner, Y-STR testing was performed in more than 500 cases with over 1000 evidence and reference samples examined. A full or partial profile was obtained on 81% of all tested evidence samples (740 worked/915 samples tested). Mixtures of at least two males were observed in 97 instances. In male/female mixtures of up to 1:4000, the male component could be cleanly detected.
In-house assay with 9 Y-STR loci amplified in 3 PCR reactions	Dekairelle & Hoste (2001)	Y-STR typing was attempted on 166 semen traces from 89 cases that failed to yield a detectable male autosomal profile following differential extraction. About half of the cases had sufficient DNA to produce a Y-STR profile.
In-house assay with DYS393, DYS389I/II	Sibille et al. (2002)	Y-STR results could still be obtained more than 48 hours after the sexual assault in 30% of the cases examined. In 104 swabs collected with no evidence of sperm, Y-STRs could be detected in ~29% of the samples tested.
In-house assay with DYS19, DYS390, DYS389I/II	Prinz (2003)	Six case studies are reviewed along with advantages and disadvantages of Y-STR testing in each case: (1) different semen donors on vaginal swab and underwear; (2) possible oligospermic perpetrator gave a nice Y-STR profile but failed to have a "male" fraction with differential extraction; (3) oral intercourse with no autosomal results—not possible to enrich male cell fraction with differential extraction in cases involving saliva; (4) presence of multiple semen donors created a complex autosomal mixture that could be sorted out with Y-STR results; (5) sperm cell fraction lacked amelogenin Y-specific peak due to known deletion—Y-STR results confirmed that the sperm cell fraction DNA was of male origin; and (6) Y-STR testing was used to rapidly screen 18 semen stains for comparison to 5 suspects and thus save the time of performing the differential extraction.
Y-PLEX 6 and Y-PLEX 5 kits	Sinha (2003)	Five cases are reviewed: (1) criminal paternity case with a male fetus where the alleged father could not be excluded as the biological father; (2) autosomal STR test resulted in an uninterpretable mixture—suspect was excluded at 3 of the 7 Y-STR loci tested; (3) Y-PLEX 6 STR profile matched suspect with sweat stains on cloth found at crime scene; (4) fingernail cuttings from a victim matched a suspect at 11 Y-STR loci while another suspect was excluded at 2 loci; (5) semen positive stain with no sperm cells produced a Y-PLEX 6 profile consistent with the male suspect.
Y-PLEX 6 and Y-PLEX 5 kits	Sinha et al. (2004)	Seven cases are reviewed (some are the same as Sinha 2003) and a list of cases where Y-STR results have been accepted in U.S. courts is provided.

ChrY Locus Duplications or Triplications

Due to the palindromic sequences often found on ChrY, Y-STR loci can sometimes exhibit as duplications or even triplications. These multi-allelic patterns may be inherited or passed on across generations as has been observed when studying father-son sample pairs (Decker et al. 2008). ChrY duplications, which occur in single-source samples, can confuse or complicate mixture interpretation if scientists are not aware of this phenomenon (Butler et al. 2005). Sequence regions flanking STR regions may also be duplicated elsewhere in the Y-chromosome and may create artifacts when PCR primers are moved during multiplex assay design (Butler & Schoske 2004).

Duplications or triplications of several Y-STRs have been reported for DYS19, DYS390, and DYS391. For example, one study found nine duplications for DYS19 in 7772 individuals (Kayser et al. 2000). Triplicated DYS385 alleles have also been reported (Kayser et al. 2000, Butler et al. 2002, Kurihara et al. 2004). These possible multi-allelic patterns need to be kept in mind so that a mixture is not expected when encountering multiple alleles at a single locus that could legitimately come from a single-source sample.

ChrY Deletions

Just as ChrY duplications may occur, deletions also exist in some individuals. An examination of father and son sample pairs found that these deletions may be inherited (Decker et al. 2008). Sometimes the deletions from the Y-chromsome can be greater than one megabase in size (Takayama et al. 2009). Deletions of the amelogenin Y region (see Chapter 5) can result in DYS458, the closest Y-STR locus (see Figure 13.6), being missing from a Yfiler profile.

Studies with Additional Y-STR Markers

Within the last several years, a number of new Y chromosome STR markers have been characterized and new multiplex assays developed (Prinz et al. 1997, Butler et al. 2002, Redd et al. 2002, Schoske et al. 2003, Hanson & Ballantyne 2007). Information on additional Y-STR loci and assays is available on the NIST STRBase website at http://www.cstl.nist.gov/biotech/strbase/y_str.htm.

A few population studies have been conducted that go beyond the minimal haplotype loci in order to assess the power of additional markers in resolving most common types. For example, Berger et al. (2003) found that addition of the multi-copy marker DYS464 to the minimal haplotype loci increased the number of different haplotypes in a set of 135 Austrian males from 110 to 122. Schoske and co-workers (2004) demonstrated that 25 samples, which possessed an indistinguishable most common minimal haplotype could be subdivided into 24 different groups (only one pair could not be resolved) with the addition of DYS438, DYS439, DYS464, DYS458, DYS460, and DYS437. Studies have been performed to compare various combinations of Y-STR loci to the minimal haplotype in order to determine the best order in which to apply the markers (Alves et al. 2003). Thus, other loci beyond the core minimal haplotype or SWGDAM-recommended loci are likely to play a valuable role with future forensic DNA analysis involving the Y-chromosome.

Table 13.5 demonstrates that additional loci can be helpful in subdividing shared common haplotypes. The minimal haplotype 9 loci, the SWGDAM 11 loci, the PowerPlex Y 12

TABLE 13.5 Numbers of Unique (Blue Font) and Shared Haplotypes Observed with Various Combinations of YSTR Loci across 656 U.S. Population Samples That Are Part of the Yfiler Haplotype Database (Butler et al. 2007). The Shared Haplotypes with Yfiler and ALL 37 are Highlighted in Red Font. Data Used for This Analysis Is Available at http://www.cstl.nist.gov/biotech/strbase/NISTpop.htm.

# Times Haplotype Observed	MHL	SWGDAM	PPY	Yfiler	ALL 37
1	429	486	505	626	652
2	34	33	34	12	2
3	13	10	14	2	.
4	4	6	3	.	.
5	3	1	2	.	.
6	1	1	.	.	.
7	1	2	1	.	.
8	1	.	.	.	.
9	2	.	.	.	.
10	.	1	.	.	.
11	1	.	.	.	.
12	.	.	1	.	.
13	1	.	.	.	.
14	.	.	.	.	.
15	.	1	.	.	.
16	.	.	.	.	.
17	.	.	.	.	.
18	.	.	.	.	.
19	.	.	.	.	.
20	.	.	.	.	.
21	.	.	.	.	.
22	.	.	.	.	.
23	.	.	.	.	.
24	.	.	.	.	.
25	.	.	.	.	.
26	1	.	.	.	.
Haplotype Diversity	0.997	0.998	0.999	0.999	0.999
Discrimination Capacity	0.748	0.825	0.854	0.976	0.997
Total Number of Haplotypes	491	541	560	640	654

loci, and the Yfiler 17 loci as well as an additional 20 Y-STRs (for a total of 37) (Butler et al. 2006, Decker et al. 2007) were examined to look for the number of unique and shared haplotypes (Table 13.5). The first column shows that 26 of the 656 samples examined possess a "most common type" 9-locus haplotype that is subdivided with additional loci. It is evident that the number of unique haplotypes increases as additional loci are used and that the number of samples sharing haplotypes is also reduced.

With the PowerPlex Y 12 loci, there are 505 unique haplotypes and the most common type is only shared in 12 individuals. The five additional loci present in Yfiler give rise to 626 unique types, 12 haplotypes that are shared twice, and two haplotypes that were observed three times (Table 13.5). At the 17-locus Yfiler level, 95% of this data set are resolved from one another (i.e., are singletons). Using Yfiler, the most common type that was shared in 12 individuals with the 12 PowerPlex Y loci is subdivided into 9 unique types and one shared by the remaining three individuals.

In the data set shown in Table 13.5, there is some information gained by going beyond the Yfiler loci but still two sample pairs could not be subdivided. These individuals could very well be paternal relatives (the samples are anonymous). These results also illustrate that there can be diminishing returns when examining additional loci.

Looking across multiple studies, the best additional Y-STRs for resolving common 9-locus, 12-locus, or 17-locus haplotypes appear to include DYS449, DYS481, DYS570, and DYS576 (Decker et al. 2007; Hanson & Ballantyne 2007; Rodig et al. 2007). One recent study utilized 14 additional Y-STRs in a single multiplex to subdivide all 8 remaining shared haplotypes found following analysis of 17-locus Yfiler types from 572 U.S. Caucasians and African Americans (Hanson & Ballantyne 2007). The 14 Y-STRs used were DYS444, DYS446, DYS449, DYS459a/b, DYS481, DYS508, DYS522, DYS527a/b, DYS549, DYS552, DYS570, DYS576, DYS607, and DYS627.

A group of scientists lead by Manfred Kayser from Erasmus University in The Netherlands examined 186 Y-STR markers in nearly 2000 DNA-confirmed father-son pairs (Ballantyne et al. 2010). They found that by using a set of 13 of the most mutable Y-STRs it was possible to distinguish distantly and even closely related males. The potential may exist in the future to individualize males rather than just male lineages using a battery of Y-STRs possessing high mutation rates.

Y-SNPS AND HAPLOGROUPS

Single nucleotide polymorphisms, *Alu* insertions, and insertion/deletion markers exist on the Y-chromosome just as they do throughout the rest of the human genome (see Chapter 12). Most of the focus to date in forensic DNA typing applications has been on Y-STRs rather than Y-SNPs due to the higher power of discrimination with the multi-allelic Y-STRs. However, Y-SNPs play an important role in human migration studies because they enable effective evaluation of major differences between population groups.

Y-SNP alleles are typically designated as either "ancestral" or "derived" and can be recorded in a simple binary format of 0 or 1 for ancestral and derived, respectively. The ancestral state of a Y-SNP marker is usually determined by comparison to a chimpanzee DNA sequence for the same marker (Underhill et al. 2000).

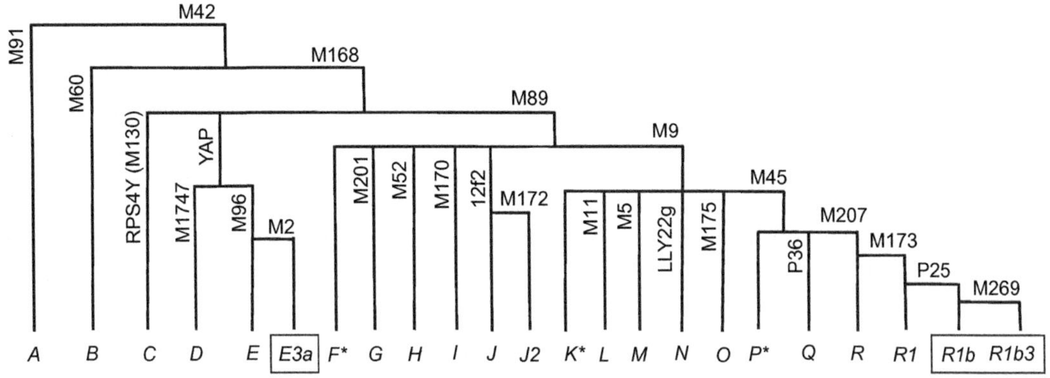

FIGURE 13.11 The original 2002 Y Chromosome Consortium Tree with 18 major haplogroups (A-R). Representative Y-SNP markers that define each haplogroup are listed next to the branch point. The most common African American haplogroup is E3a. The most common Caucasian (European) haplogroup is R1b/R1b3. Examination of additional samples and markers since 2002 has expanded the branches on this tree. For an up-to-date version, see http://www.isogg.org/tree/.

The Y Chromosome Consortium Haplogroup Tree

The Rosetta Stone for interpreting the plethora of Y-chromosome haplogroups listed in the literature was published by the Y Chromosome Consortium (YCC) in the February 2002 issue of *Genome Research* (YCC 2002) and updated in 2008 (Karafet et al. 2008). The YCC is an international group of scientists lead by Michael Hammer from the University of Arizona, Peter Underhill from Stanford University, Mark Jobling from Leicester University, and Chris Tyler-Smith who at that time was at Oxford University. Their paper entitled "A nomenclature system for the tree of human Y chromosomal binary haplogroups" opened the way for an easier understanding of seven previously published methods for describing information from the same SNP markers. The "YCC tree" as it is commonly called describes the position of almost 250 bi-allelic markers in differentiating 153 different haplogroups (YCC 2002).

A slightly modified and updated YCC tree was published in August 2003 (Jobling and Tyler-Smith 2003) and is regularly updated by a group of avid genetic genealogists who are part of the International Society of Genetic Genealogy (ISOGG). The YCC published an updated tree in the May 2008 issue of Genome Research (Karafet et al. 2008). With more than 600 Y-SNPs available on worldwide population data sets, the YCC tree expanded.

Figure 13.11 highlights the major branches of the 2002 YCC tree along with some of the Y-SNP markers that help define the various branches. For example, observation of the derived allele for M2 in a sample classifies it into the 2002 E3a haplogroup. Y-chromosome haplogroup designation and characterization has greatly benefited from the YCC tree.

Before 2002, if a "G" (derived state) was observed in a sample when typing the M2 (sY81 or DYS271) marker, then the sample could be reported as belonging to haplogroup (Hg) 8 by Jobling's nomenclature (Jobling & Tyler-Smith 2000), Hg III by Underhill's naming procedure (Underhill et al. 2000), or Hg 5 by Hammer's description (Hammer et al. 2001). On the YCC tree, M2 derived alleles define the Hg E3a. Needless to say, the unified and universal nomenclature is much easier to understand and permits comparisons of results across laboratories.

A number of the SNP typing technologies reviewed in Table 12.3 have also been used for Y-SNP typing (Butler 2003). Two of the more popular SNP typing methodologies have been allele-specific primer extension (ASPE) and allele-specific hybridization (ASH). Vallone and Butler (2004) observed complete concordance comparing ASPE and ASH in almost 4000 Y-SNP allele calls.

Y-SNPs have been useful in demonstrating some admixture in U.S. populations (Hammer et al. 2006) and have helped confirm self-declared ethnicities (Lao et al. 2010). Next-generation sequencing technology has been used to identify Y-SNPs between ancestral lineages (Xue & Tyler-Smith 2010).

ChrY HISTORICAL AND GENEALOGICAL STUDIES

Genealogists in large numbers are beginning to turn to Y-chromosome DNA testing to extend their research efforts (Brown 2002). Hundreds of thousands of genetic genealogy tests have been performed in the past few years. Family Tree DNA (Houston, TX) is probably the most progressive genetic genealogy company and offers routine tests for 67 Y-STRs with options to obtain further information from ChrY if desired.

Y-chromosome testing has played a role in addressing some interesting historical questions, such as the Thomas Jefferson-Sally Hemings affair (Foster et al. 1998), the genetic legacy of the Mongols (Zerjal et al. 2003), and the Romanov children identification (Coble et al. 2009). In addition, dozens of Y-chromosome markers are used to aid efforts in genealogical family history research. DNA information is only part of the evidence available in most investigations and should be considered carefully in the context of the "case" without overstepping the bounds of conclusions that can be drawn.

Genetic genealogy using Y-chromosome STR markers in conjunction with surname studies originated with a study published by Bryan Sykes in 2000 (Sykes & Irven 2000). Using four Y-STRs, DYS19, DYS390, DYS391, and DYS393, Sykes tested 48 men bearing the surname "Sykes" sampled from several regions of England. Of the 48 tested, 21 of them exhibited the core Sykes haplotype and several others were only one mutational step away from the core haplotype. Sykes interpreted these results to reflect a common origin coming from an ancestor that lived about 700 years ago. While some interesting connections are being made with DNA to aid genealogical research, results should be interpreted with caution.

SUMMARY

The field of Y-chromosome analysis and its application to human identity testing has undergone rapid improvements in recent years. New markers and population groups have been characterized. Commercial kits are now available and beginning to be used in greater numbers to aid forensic cases. Y-STR haplogroup databases are growing in size enabling greater statistical power with the counting method. In addition to benefiting forensic casework, ChrY testing is also aiding familial searching efforts in helping to screen out adventitious matches due to autosomal allele sharing (see Appendix 2). The future may involve more interaction between the application of genetic genealogy and forensic science to help bring cases to closure without prior suspects.

READING LIST AND INTERNET RESOURCES

General Information

Butler, J. M. (2003). Recent developments in Y-short tandem repeat and Y-single nucleotide polymorphism analysis. *Forensic Science Review, 15*, 91–111.

Gusmão, L., et al. (1999). Y chromosome specific polymorphisms in forensic analysis. *Legal Medicine, 1*, 55–60.

Jobling, M. A., & Tyler-Smith, C. (2003). The human Y chromosome: An evolutionary marker comes of age. *Nature Reviews Genetics, 4*, 598–612.

Applications

Bieber, F. R., et al. (2006). Finding criminals through DNA of their relatives. *Science, 312*, 1315–1316.

Brown, K. (2002). Tangled roots? Genetics meets genealogy. *Science, 295*, 1634–1635.

Cerri, N., et al. (2003). Mixed stains from sexual assault cases: autosomal or Y-chromosome short tandem repeats? *Croatian Medical Journal, 44*, 289–292.

de Knijff, P. (2003). Son, give up your gun: Presenting Y-STR results in court. *Profiles in DNA, 6*(2), 3–5. Available at <http://www.promega.com/profiles/602/ProfilesinDNA_602_03.pdf>.

Dekairelle, A. F., & Hoste, B. (2001). Application of a Y-STR-pentaplex PCR (DYS19, DYS389I and II, DYS390 and DYS393) to sexual assault cases. *Forensic Science International, 118*, 122–125.

Dettlaff-Kakol, A., & Pawlowski, R. (2002). First Polish DNA "manhunt"—an application of Y-chromosome STRs. *International Journal of Legal Medicine, 116*, 289–291.

Honda, K., et al. (1999). Male DNA typing from 25-year-old vaginal swabs using Y-chromosomal STR polymorphisms in a retrial request case. *Journal of Forensic Sciences, 44*, 868–872.

Jobling, M. A., et al. (1997). The Y chromosome in forensic analysis and paternity testing. *International Journal of Legal Medicine, 110*, 118–124.

Johnson, C. L., et al. (2005). Analysis of non-suspect samples lacking visually identifiable sperm using a Y-STR 10-plex. *Journal of Forensic Sciences, 50*, 1116–1118.

Mayntz-Press, K. A., et al. (2008). Y-STR profiling in extended interval (> or = 3 days) postcoital cervicovaginal samples. *Journal of Forensic Sciences, 53*, 342–348.

Parson, W., et al. (2003). Improved specificity of Y-STR typing in DNA mixture samples. *International Journal of Legal Medicine, 117*, 109–114.

Prinz, M., et al. (1997). Multiplexing of Y chromosome specific STRs and performance for mixed samples. *Forensic Science International, 85*, 209–218.

Prinz, M., et al. (2001). Validation and casework application of a Y chromosome specific STR multiplex. *Forensic Science International, 120*, 177–188.

Prinz, M., & Sansone, M. (2001). Y chromosome-specific short tandem repeats in forensic casework. *Croatian Medical Journal, 42*, 288–291.

Prinz, M. (2003). Advantages and disadvantages of Y-short tandem repeat testing in forensic casework. *Forensic Science Review, 15*, 189–196.

Roewer, L. (2009). Y chromosome STR typing in crime casework. *Forensic Science, Medicine, & Pathology, 5*, 77–84.

Santos, F. R., et al. (1993). Testing deficiency paternity cases with a Y-linked tetranucleotide repeat polymorphism. *EXS, 67*, 261–265.

Shewale, J. G., et al. (2003). DNA profiling of azoospermic semen samples from vasectomized males by using Y-PLEX 6 amplification kit. *Journal of Forensic Sciences, 48*, 127–129.

Sibille, I., et al. (2002). Y-STR DNA amplification as biological evidence in sexually assaulted female victims with no cytological detection of spermatozoa. *Forensic Science International, 125*, 212–216.

Sims, G., et al. (2008). The DNA partial match and familial search policy of the California Department of Justice. *Proceedings of the nineteenth international symposium on human identification*. Available at <http://www.promega.com/geneticidproc/>.

Sinha, S. K. (2003). Forensic casework applications using Y-PLEX 6 and Y-PLEX 5 systems. *Forensic Science Review, 15*, 197–201.

Sinha, S. K., et al. (2004). Utility of the Y-STR typing systems Y-PLEX 6 and Y-PLEX 5 in forensic casework and 11 Y-STR haplotype database for three major population groups in the United States. *Journal of Forensic Sciences, 49*, 691–700.

Thangaraj, K., et al. (2002). Is the amelogenin gene reliable for gender identification in forensic casework and prenatal diagnosis? *International Journal of Legal Medicine, 116*(2), 121–123.

ChrY Structure

Graves, J. A., et al. (1998). The origin and evolution of the pseudoautosomal regions of human sex chromosomes. *Human Molecular Genetics, 7*, 1991–1996.

Hall, A., & Ballantyne, J. (2003). Strategies for the design and assessment of Y-short tandem repeat multiplexes for forensic use. *Forensic Science Review, 15*, 137–149.

Saxena, R., et al. (1996). The DAZ gene cluster on the human Y chromosome arose from an autosomal gene that was transposed, repeatedly amplified and pruned. *Nature Genetics, 14*, 292–299.

Skaletsky, H., et al. (2003). The male-specific region of the human Y chromosome is a mosaic of discrete sequence classes. *Nature, 423*, 825–837.

Different Classes of ChrY Markers

de Knijff, P. (2000). Messages through bottlenecks: on the combined use of slow and fast evolving polymorphic markers on the human Y chromosome. *American Journal of Human Genetics, 67*, 1055–1061.

Hammer, M. F. (1994). A recent insertion of an Alu element on the Y chromosome is a useful marker for human population studies. *Molecular Biology and Evolution, 11*, 749–761.

Jobling, M. A., et al. (1999). Y-chromosome-specific microsatellite mutation rates re-examined using a minisatellite MSY1. *Human Molecular Genetics, 8*, 2117–2120.

Y-STR Markers

Ayub, Q., et al. (2000). Identification and characterisation of novel human Y-chromosomal microsatellites from sequence database information. *Nucleic Acids Research, 28*, e8.

Ballantyne, K. N., et al. (2010). Mutability of Y-chromosomal microsatellites: rates, characteristics, molecular bases, and forensic implications. *American Journal of Human Genetics, 87*, 341–353.

Berger, B., et al. (2003). Molecular characterization and Austrian Caucasian population data of the multi-copy Y-chromosomal STR DYS464. *Forensic Science International, 137*, 221–230.

Butler, J. M., & Schoske, R. (2005). U.S. population data for the multi-copy Y-STR locus DYS464. *Journal of Forensic Sciences, 50*, 975–977.

Butler, J. M. (2006). Genetics and genomics of core short tandem repeat loci used in human identity testing. *Journal of Forensic Sciences, 51*, 253–265.

Butler, J. M., et al. (2006). Allele frequencies for 27 Y-STR loci with U.S. Caucasian, African American, and Hispanic samples. *Forensic Science International, 156*, 250–260.

de Knijff, P., et al. (1997). Chromosome Y microsatellites: population genetic and evolutionary aspects. *International Journal of Legal Medicine, 110*, 134–149.

Gusmao, L., et al. (2002). Point mutations in the flanking regions of the Y-chromosome specific STRs DYS391, DYS437 and DYS438. *International Journal of Legal Medicine, 116*, 322–326.

Hanson, E. K., & Ballantyne, J. (2006). Comprehensive annotated STR physical map of the human Y chromosome: Forensic implications. *Legal Medicine, 8*, 110–120.

Kayser, M., et al. (1997). Evaluation of Y-chromosomal STRs: A multicenter study. *International Journal of Legal Medicine, 110* 125–133, 141–149

Kayser, M., et al. (2004). A comprehensive survey of human Y-chromosomal microsatellites. *American Journal of Human Genetics, 74*, 1183–1197.

Kittler, R., et al. (2003). Apparent intrachromosomal exchange on the human Y chromosome explained by population history. *European Journal of Human Genetics, 11*, 304–314.

Lim, S.-K., et al. (2007). Variation of 52 new Y-STR loci in the Y Chromosome Consortium worldwide panel of 76 diverse individuals. *International Journal of Legal Medicine, 121*, 124–127.

Pascali, V. L., et al. (1998). Coordinating Y-chromosomal STR research for the Courts. *International Journal of Legal Medicine, 112*, 1.

Redd, A. J., et al. (2002). Forensic value of 14 novel STRs on the human Y chromosome. *Forensic Science International, 130*, 97–111.

Schneider, P. M., et al. (1998). Tandem repeat structure of the duplicated Y-chromosomal STR locus DYS385 and frequency studies in the German and three Asian populations. *Forensic Science International, 97*, 61–70.

Seo, Y., et al. (2003). A method for genotyping Y chromosome-linked DYS385a and DYS385b loci. *Legal Medicine, 5*, 228–232.

SWGDAM (2004). Report on the current activities of the Scientific Working Group on DNA Analysis Methods Y-STR Subcommittee. *Forensic Science Communications*, 6(3). Available at <http://www.fbi.gov/hq/lab/fsc/backissu/july2004/standards/2004_03_standards03.htm>.

Y-STR Kits and Assays

Butler, J. M., et al. (2002). A novel multiplex for simultaneous amplification of 20 Y chromosome STR markers. *Forensic Science International, 129*, 10–24.

Gross, A. M., et al. (2006). Y-STR concordance study between Y-PLEX 5, Y-PLEX 6, Y-PLEX 12, PowerPlex Y, Y-Filer, MPI, and MPII. *Journal of Forensic Sciences, 51*, 1423–1428.

Gross, A. M., et al. (2008). Internal validation of the AmpFlSTR Yfiler Amplification Kit for use in forensic casework. *Journal of Forensic Sciences, 53*, 125–134.

Hanson, E. K., & Ballantyne, J. (2007). An ultra-high discrimination Y chromosome short tandem repeat multiplex DNA typing system. *PLoS ONE, 2*, e688.

Johnson, C. L., et al. (2003). Validation and uses of a Y-chromosome STR 10-plex for forensic and paternity laboratories. *Journal of Forensic Sciences, 48*, 1260–1268.

Krenke, B. E., et al. (2005). Validation of male-specific, 12-locus fluorescent short tandem repeat (STR) multiplex. *Forensic Science International, 151*, 111–124.

Mayntz-Press, K. A., & Ballantyne, J. (2007). Performance characteristics of commercial Y-STR multiplex systems. *Journal of Forensic Sciences, 52*, 1025–1034.

Mulero, J. J., et al. (2006). Development and validation of the AmpFlSTR Yfiler PCR Amplification Kit: a male specific, single amplification 17 Y-STR multiplex system. *Journal of Forensic Sciences, 51*, 64–75.

Park, M. J., et al. (2007). Y-STR analysis of degraded DNA using reduced-size amplicons. *International Journal of Legal Medicine, 121*, 152–157.

Parkin, E. J., et al. (2006). 26-locus Y-STR typing in a Bhutanese population sample. *Forensic Science International, 161*, 1–7.

Parkin, E. J., et al. (2007). Diversity of 26-locus Y-STR haployes in a Nepalese population sample: isolation and drift in the Himalayas. *Forensic Science International, 166*, 176–181.

Parson, W., et al. (2008). Y-STR analysis on DNA mixture samples—results of a collaborative project of the ENFSI DNA Working Group. *Forensic Science International: Genetics, 2*, 238–242.

Schoske, R. (2003). The design, optimization and testing of Y chromosome short tandem repeat megaplexes. PhD dissertation (American University). Available at <http://www.cstl.nist.gov/biotech/strbase/pub_pres/Schoske2003dis.pdf>.

Schoske, R., et al. (2003). Multiplex PCR design strategy used for the simultaneous amplification of 10 Y chromosome short tandem repeat (STR) loci. *Analytical and Bioanalytical Chemistry, 375*, 333–343.

Schoske, R., et al. (2004). High-throughput Y-STR typing of U.S. populations with 27 regions of the Y chromosome using two multiplex PCR assays. *Forensic Science International, 139*, 107–121.

Shewale, J. G., et al. (2004). Y-chromosome STR system, Y-PLEX 12, for forensic casework: development and validation. *Journal of Forensic Sciences, 49*, 1278–1290.

Y-STR Nomenclature

Butler, J. M., et al. (2008). Y-chromosome short tandem repeat (Y-STR) allele nomenclature. *Journal of Genetic Genealogy*, 4(2), 125–148.

Gill, P., et al. (2001). DNA Commission of the International Society of Forensic Genetics (ISFG): recommendations on forensic analysis using Y-chromosome STRs. *Forensic Science International, 124*, 5–10.

González-Neira, A., et al. (2001). Sequence structure of 12 novel Y chromosome microsatellites and PCR amplification strategies. *Forensic Science International, 122*, 19–26.

Grignani, P., et al. (2000). Highly informative Y-chromosomal haplotypes by the addition of three new STRs DYS437, DYS438 and DYS439. *International Journal of Legal Medicine, 114*, 125–129.

Gusmão, L., et al. (2002). Chimpanzee homologous of human Y specific STRs: A comparative study and a proposal for nomenclature. *Forensic Science International, 126*, 129–136.

Gusmão, L., et al. (2006). DNA Commission of the International Society of Forensic Genetics (ISFG): An update of the recommendations on the use of Y-STRs in forensic analysis. *Forensic Science International, 157*, 187–197.
Mulero, J. J., et al. (2006). Letter to the editor—nomenclature and allele repeat structure update for the Y-STR locus GATA H4. *Journal of Forensic Sciences, 51*, 694.
NIST SRM 2395 Human Y-Chromosome DNA Profiling Standard. <http://www.nist.gov/srm>.

Y-STR Haplotype Databases

Ballantyne, J., et al. (2006). Creating and managing effective Y-STR databases. *Profiles in DNA, 9*(2), 10–13.
Egeland, T., & Salas, A. (2008). Estimating haplotype frequency and coverage of databases. *PLoS ONE, 3*(12), e3988.
Fatolitis, L., & Ballantyne, J. (2008). The US Y-STR database. *Profiles in DNA, 11*(1), 13–14.
Ge, J., et al. (2010). US forensic Y-chromosome short tandem repeats database. *Legal Medicine, 12*, 289–295.
Kayser, M., et al. (2002). Online Y-chromosomal short tandem repeat haplotype reference database (YHRD) for U.S. populations. *Journal of Forensic Sciences, 47*, 513–519.
Lessig, R., et al. (2003). Asian online Y-STR haplotype reference database. *Legal Medicine, 5*(Suppl 1), S160–S163.
Roewer, L., et al. (2001). Online reference database of European Y-chromosomal short tandem repeat (STR) haplotypes. *Forensic Science International, 118*, 106–113.
Roewer, L. (2003). The Y-short tandem repeat haplotype reference database (YHRD) and male population stratification in Europe—impact on forensic genetics. *Forensic Science Review, 15*, 163–170.
STRBase Listing of Y-STR Databases. <http://www.cstl.nist.gov/biotech/strbase/y_strs.htm>.
US Y-STR Database. <http://www.usystrdatabase.org/>.
Willuweit, S., & Roewer, L. (2007). Y chromosome haplotype reference database (YHRD): Update. *Forensic Science International: Genetics, 1*, 83–87.
Ybase (Genetic Genealogy). <http://www.ybase.org/>.
Y-Chromosome Haplotype Reference Database (YHRD). <http://www.yhrd.org>.
Yfiler Haplotype Database. <http://www6.appliedbiosystems.com/yfilerdatabase/>.
Ysearch (Genetic Genealogy). <http://www.ysearch.org/>.

Interpretation

Brenner, C. H. (2010). Fundamental problem of forensic mathematics—the evidential value of a rare haplotype. *Forensic Science International: Genetics, 4*, 281–291.
Budowle, B., et al. (2005). Twelve short tandem repeat loci Y chromosome haplotypes: Genetic analysis on populations residing in North America. *Forensic Science International, 150*, 1–15.
Budowle, B., et al. (2009). Texas population substructure and its impact on estimating the rarity of Y STR haplotypes from DNA evidence. *Journal of Forensic Sciences, 54*, 1016–1021.
Kayser, M., et al. (2003). Y chromosome STR haplotypes and the genetic structure of U.S. populations of African, European, and Hispanic ancestry. *Genome Research, 13*, 624–634.
Krawczak, M. (2001). Forensic evaluation of Y-STR haplotype matches: a comment. *Forensic Science International, 118*, 114–115.
Redd, A. J., et al. (2006). Genetic structure among 38 populations from the United States based on 11 U.S. core Y chromosome STRs. *Journal of Forensic Sciences, 51*, 580–585.
SWGDAM. Y-STR interpretation guidelines. *Forensic Science Communications, 11*(1). Available at <http://www2.fbi.gov/hq/lab/fsc/backissu/jan2009/standards/2009_01_standards01.htm>.
Willuweit, S., et al. (2011). Y-STR frequency surveying method: a critical reappraisal. *Forensic Science International: Genetics, 5*, 84–90.

Insertions/Deletions

Balaresque, P., et al. (2009). Genomic complexity of the Y-STR DYS19: inversions, deletions and founder lineages carrying duplications. *International Journal of Legal Medicine, 123*, 15–23.
Budowle, B., et al. (2008). Null allele sequence structure at the DYS448 locus and implications for profile interpretation. *International Journal of Legal Medicine, 122*, 421–427.
Butler, J. M., & Schoske, R. (2004). Duplication of DYS19 flanking regions in other parts of the Y chromosome. *International Journal of Legal Medicine, 118*, 178–183.

Butler, J. M., et al. (2005). Chromosomal duplications along the Y-chromosome and their potential impact on Y-STR interpretation. *Journal of Forensic Sciences, 50*, 853–859.

Chang, Y. M., et al. (2007). A distinct Y-STR haplotype for Amelogenin negative males characterized by a large Yp11.2 (DYS458-MSY1-AMEL-Y) deletion. *Forensic Science International, 166*, 115–120.

Diederiche, M., et al. (2005). A case of double alleles at three Y-STR loci: Forensic implications. *International Journal of Legal Medicine, 119*, 223–225.

Takayama, T., et al. (2009). Determination of deletion regions from Yp11.2 of an amelogenin negative male. *Legal Medicine, 11*, S578–S580.

Y-STR Mixtures

Fukshansky, N., & Bär, W. (2005). DNA mixtures: Biostatistics for mixed stains with haplotypic genetic markers. *International Journal of Legal Medicine, 119*, 285–290.

Ge, J., et al. (2010). Interpreting Y chromosome STR haplotype mixture. *Legal Medicine, 12*, 137–143.

Wolf, A., et al. (2005). Forensic interpretation of Y-chromosomal DNA mixtures. *Forensic Science International, 152*, 209–213.

Joint Match Probabilities

Amorim, A. (2008). A cautionary note on the evaluation of genetic evidence from uniparentally transmitted markers. *Forensic Science International: Genetics, 2*(4), 376–378.

Ayadi, I., et al. (2007). Combining autosomal and Y-chromosomal short tandem repeat data in paternity testing with male child: Methods and application. *Journal of Forensic Sciences, 52*, 1068–1072.

Walsh, B., et al. (2008). Joint match probabilities for Y chromosomal and autosomal markers. *Forensic Science International, 174*, 234–238.

Mutation Rates

Ballard, D. J., et al. (2005). A study of mutation rates and the characterisation of intermediate, null and duplicated alleles for 13 Y chromosome STRs. *Forensic Science International, 155*, 65–70.

Bonne-Tamir, B., et al. (2003). Maternal and paternal lineages of the Samaritan isolate: Mutation rates and time to most recent common male ancestor. *Annals of Human Genetics, 67*, 153–164.

Decker, A. E., et al. (2008). Analysis of mutations in father-son pairs with 17 Y-STR loci. *Forensic Science International: Genetics, 2*, e31–e35.

Donbak, L., et al. (2006). Y-STR haplotypes in populations from the Eastern Mediterranean region of Turkey. *International Journal of Legal Medicine, 120*, 395–396.

Dupuy, B. M., et al. (2004). Y-chromosomal microsatellite mutation rates: differences in mutation rate between and within loci. *Human Mutation, 23*, 117–124.

Ge, J., et al. (2009). Mutation rates at Y chromosome short tandem repeats in Texas populations. *Forensic Science International: Genetics, 3*, 179–184.

Goedbloed, M., et al. (2009). Comprehensive mutation analysis of 17 Y-chromosomal short tandem repeat polymorphisms included in the AmpFlSTR Yfiler PCR amplification kit. *International Journal of Legal Medicine, 123*, 471–482.

Gusmão, L., et al. (2005). Mutation rates at Y chromosome specific microsatellites. *Human Mutation, 26*, 520–528.

Heyer, E., et al. (1997). Estimating Y chromosome specific microsatellite mutation frequencies using deep rooting pedigrees. *Human Molecular Genetics, 6*, 799–803.

Hohoff, C., et al. (2007). Y-chromosomal microsatellite mutation rates in a population sample from northwestern Germany. *International Journal of Legal Medicine, 121*, 359–363.

Kayser, M., et al. (2000). Characteristics and frequency of germline mutations at microsatellite loci from the human Y chromosome, as revealed by direct observation in father/son pairs. *American Journal of Human Genetics, 66*, 1580–1588.

Kayser, M., & Sajantila, A. (2001). Mutations at Y-STR loci: Implications for paternity testing and forensic analysis. *Forensic Science International, 118*, 116–121.

Lee, H. Y., et al. (2007). Haplotypes and mutation analysis of 22 Y-chromosomal STRs in Korean father-son pairs. *International Journal of Legal Medicine, 121*, 128–135.

Pollin, T. I., et al. (2008). Investigations of the Y chromosome male founder structure and YSTR mutation rates in the Old Order Amish. *Human Heredity, 65*, 91–104.

Sánchez-Diz, P., et al. (2008). Population and segregation data on 17 Y-STRs: Results of a GEP-ISFG collaborative study. *International Journal of Legal Medicine, 122*, 529–533.

Toscanini, U., et al. (2008). Y chromosome microsatellite genetic variation in two Native American populations from Argentina: Population stratification and mutation data. *Forensic Science International: Genetics, 2*, 274–280.

Turrina, S., et al. (2006). Y-chromosomal STR haplotypes in a Northeast Italian population sample using 17plex loci PCR assay. *International Journal of Legal Medicine, 120*, 56–59.

Yoshida, Y., et al. (2005). Population study of Y-chromosome STR haplotypes in Japanese from the Tokushima. *International Journal of Legal Medicine, 119*, 172–176.

Zhivotovsky, L. A., et al. (2004). The effective mutation rate at Y chromosome short tandem repeats, with application to human population-divergence time. *American Journal of Human Genetics, 74*, 50–61.

Impact of Additional Y-STR Loci

Alves, C., et al. (2003). Evaluating the informative power of Y-STRs: A comparative study using European and new African haplotype data. *Forensic Science International, 134*, 126–133.

Beleza, S., et al. (2003). Extending STR markers in Y chromosome haplotypes. *International Journal of Legal Medicine, 117*, 27–33.

Butler, J. M., et al. (2007). New autosomal and Y-chromosome STR loci: Characterization and potential uses. *Proceedings of the eighteenth international symposium on human identification*. Available at <http://www.promega.com/geneticidproc/>.

D'Amato, M. E., et al. (2010). Characterization of highly discriminatory loci DYS449, DS481, DYS518, DYS612, DYS626, DYS644, and DYS710. *Forensic Science International: Genetics, 4*, 104–110.

Decker, A. E., et al. (2007). The impact of additional Y-STR loci on resolving common haplotypes and closely related individuals. *Forensic Science International: Genetics, 1*, 215–217.

Leat, N., et al. (2007). Properties of novel and widely studies Y-STR loci in three South African populations. *Forensic Science International, 168*, 154–161.

Maybruck, J. L., et al. (2009). A comparative analysis of two different sets of Y-chromosome short tandem repeats (Y-STRs) on a common population panel. *Forensic Science International: Genetics, 4*, 11–20.

Redd, A. J., et al. (2002). Forensic value of 14 novel STRs on the human Y chromosome. *Forensic Science International, 130*, 97–111.

Rodig, H., et al. (2007). Population study and evaluation of 20 Y-chromosome STR loci in Germans. *International Journal of Legal Medicine, 121*, 24–27.

Rodig, H., et al. (2008). Evaluation of haplotype discrimination capacity of 35 Y-chromosomal short tandem repeat loci. *Forensic Science International, 174*, 182–188.

Vermeulen, M., et al. (2009). Improving global and regional resolution of male lineage differentiation by simple single-copy Y-chromosomal short tandem repeat polymorphisms. *Forensic Science International: Genetics, 3*, 205–213.

Y-SNPs and Haplogroups

Athey, T. W. (2006). Haplogroup prediction from Y-STR values using a Bayesian-allele-frequency approach. *Journal of Genetic Genealogy, 2*, 34–39.

Brión, M., et al. (2004). Hierarchical analysis of 30 Y-chromosome SNPs in European populations. *International Journal of Legal Medicine, 119*, 10–15.

Brión, M., et al. (2005). Introduction of an single nucleotide polymorphism-based "Major Y-chromosome haplogroup typing kit" suitable for predicting the geographical origin of male lineages. *Electrophoresis, 26*, 4411–4420.

Brión, M., et al. (2005). A collaborative study of the EDNAP group regarding Y-chromosome binary polymorphism analysis. *Forensic Science International, 153*, 103–108.

Hammer, M. F., et al. (2001). Hierarchical patterns of global human Y-chromosome diversity. *Molecular Biology and Evolution, 18*, 1189–1203.

Hammer, M. F., et al. (2006). Population structure of Y chromosome SNP haplogroups in the United States and forensic implications for constructing Y chromosome STR databases. *Forensic Science International, 164*, 45–55.

International Society of Genetic Genealogy (ISOGG) Y Haplogroup Tree. <http://www.isogg.org/tree/>.

Jobling, M. A., & Tyler-Smith, C. (2000). New uses for new haplotypes: the human Y chromosome, disease and selection. *Trends in Genetics, 16*, 356–362.

Karafet, T. M., et al. (2008). New binary polymorphisms reshape and increase the resolution of the human Y chromosome haplogroup tree. *Genome Research, 18*, 830–838.

Lao, O., et al. (2010). Evaluating self-declared ancestry of U.S. Americans using autosomal, Y-chromosomal and mitochondrial DNA. *Human Mutation, 31*, E1875–93.

Lessig, R., et al. (2005). Y-SNP genotyping—a new approach in forensic analysis. *Forensic Science International, 154*, 128–136.

Onofri, V., et al. (2006). Development of multiplex PCRs for evolutionary and forensic applications of 37 human Y chromosome SNPs. *Forensic Science International, 157*, 23–35.

Underhill, P. A., et al. (2000). Y chromosome sequence variation and the history of human populations. *Nature Genetics, 26*, 358–361.

Vallone, P. M., & Butler, J. M. (2004). Y-SNP typing of U.S. African American and Caucasian samples using allele-specific hybridization and primer extension. *Journal of Forensic Sciences, 49*, 723–732.

Xue, Y., & Tyler-Smith, C. (2010). The hare and the tortoise: one small step for four SNPs, one giant leap for SNP-kind. *Forensic Science International: Genetics, 4*, 59–61.

Y Chromosome Consortium (YCC). A nomenclature system for the tree of human Y-chromosomal binary haplogroups. *Genome Research, 12*, 339–348.

Y Haplogroup Predictor. <http://www.hprg.com/hapest5/index.html>.

Historical and Genetic Genealogy Studies

23 and Me. <https://www.23andme.com/>.

African Ancestry. <http://www.africanancestry.com/>.

Coble, M. D., et al. (2009). Mystery solved: the identification of the two missing Romanov children using DNA analysis. *PLoS ONE, 4*(3), e4838.

deCODEme. <http://www.decodeme.com/>.

DNA Ancestry. <http://dna.ancestry.com/>.

DNA Heritage. <http://www.dnaheritage.com/>.

EthnoAncestry. <http://www.ethnoancestry.com/>.

Family Tree DNA. <http://www.familytreedna.com/>.

Foster, E. A., et al. (1998). Jefferson fathered slave's last child. *Nature, 396*, 27–28.

GeneTree. <http://www.genetree.com/>.

International Society of Genetic Genealogy (ISOGG). <http://www.isogg.org/>.

ISOGG Y-DNA Comparison Chart. <http://www.isogg.org/ydnachart.htm>.

Journal of Genetic Genealogy (JoGG). <http://www.jogg.info/>.

Oxford Ancestors. <http://www.oxfordancestors.com/>.

Sorenson Molecular Genealogy Foundation. <http://www.smgf.org/>.

Sykes, B., & Irven, C. (2000). Surnames and the Y chromosome. *American Journal of Human Genetics, 66*, 1417–1419.

Wolinsky, H. (2006). Genetic genealogy goes global. *EMBO Reports, 7*, 1072–1074.

Zerjal, T., et al. (2003). The genetic legacy of the Mongols. *American Journal of Human Genetics, 72*, 717–721.

CHAPTER

14

Mitochondrial DNA Analysis

Conventional STR typing systems do not work in every instance—even with the development of miniSTR assays mentioned in Chapter 10. Ancient DNA specimens or samples that have been highly degraded often fail to produce results with nuclear DNA typing systems. However, recovery of DNA information from damaged DNA is sometimes possible with mitochondrial DNA (mtDNA). While a nuclear DNA test is usually more valuable, a mtDNA result is better than no result at all.

Because there are hundreds if not thousands of copies of mtDNA in each cell, the probability of obtaining a DNA typing result from mtDNA is higher than that of polymorphic markers found in nuclear DNA, particularly in cases where the amount of extracted DNA is very small, as in tissues such as bone, teeth, and hair. When remains are quite old or badly degraded, often bone, teeth, and hair are the only biological sources left from which to draw a sample.

This chapter will review the characteristics of mitochondrial DNA, the steps involved in obtaining results in forensic casework, and issues important to interpreting mtDNA results.

CHARACTERISTICS OF mtDNA

The primary characteristic that permits mitochondrial DNA (mtDNA) recovery from degraded samples is the higher copy number of mtDNA in cells relative to the nuclear DNA from which STRs are amplified. In short, though nuclear DNA contains much more information, there are only two copies of it in each cell (one maternal and one paternal) while mtDNA provides a bit of useful genetic information hundreds of times per cell. Because of their higher numbers, some mtDNA molecules are more likely to survive than nuclear DNA. Table 14.1 contains a comparison of some basic characteristics of nuclear DNA and mitochondrial DNA.

Location and Structure of mtDNA

The vast majority of the human genome is located within the nucleus of each cell (see Table 14.1). However, there is a small, circular genome found within the mitochondria, the

TABLE 14.1 Comparison of Human Nuclear DNA and Mitochondrial DNA Markers.

Characteristics	Nuclear DNA	Mitochondrial DNA (mtDNA)
Size of genome	≈3.2 billion bp	≈16,569 bp
Copies per cell	2 (1 allele from each parent)	Can be >1000
Percent of total DNA	99.75%	0.25% content per cell
Structure	Linear; packaged in chromosomes	Circular
Inherited from	Father and mother	Mother
Chromosomal pairing	Diploid	Haploid
Generational recombination	Yes	No
Replication repair	Yes	No
Unique	Unique to individual (except identical twins)	Not unique to individual (same as maternal relatives)
Mutation rate	Low	At least 5–10 times nuclear DNA
Reference sequence	Described in 2001 by the Human Genome Project	Described in 1981 by Anderson and co-workers

energy-producing cellular organelle residing in the cytoplasm. The number of mtDNA molecules within a cell can range from hundreds to thousands. On average there are 4 to 5 copies of mtDNA molecules per mitochondrion with a measured range of 1 to 15 (Satoh & Kuroiwa 1991). Because each cell can contain hundreds of mitochondria (Robin & Wong 1988), there can be up to several thousand mtDNA molecules in each cell as in the case of ovum or egg cells. However, the average has been estimated at about 500 in most cells (Satoh & Kuroiwa 1991). It is this large number of mtDNA molecules in each cell that enables greater success (relative to nuclear DNA markers) with biological samples that may have been damaged with heat or humidity.

Mitochondrial DNA has approximately 16,569 base pairs with the total number of nucleotides in a specific mtDNA genome (mtGenome) varying due to small insertions or deletions. For example, there is a dinucleotide repeat at positions 514 to 524, which in most individuals is ACACACACAC or $(AC)_5$ but has been observed to vary from $(AC)_3$ to $(AC)_7$ (Bodenteich et al. 1992, Szibor et al. 1997). Note that with two copies of nuclear DNA (3.2 billion bp from each parent) and even assuming that there are 1000 copies of mtDNA (16,569 bp per mtDNA) in a cell, mtDNA makes up only about 0.25% of the total DNA content of a cell.

Most of the mtGenome codes for 37 gene products used in the oxidative phosphorylation process or cellular energy production (Figure 14.1). The 37 transcribed "genes" of mtDNA found in the "coding region" include 13 proteins, 2 ribosomal RNAs (rRNA), and 22 transfer RNAs (tRNA). There is also a 1122bp "control" region that contains the origin of replication for one of the mtDNA strands but does not code for any gene products and is therefore referred to sometimes as the "non-coding" region.

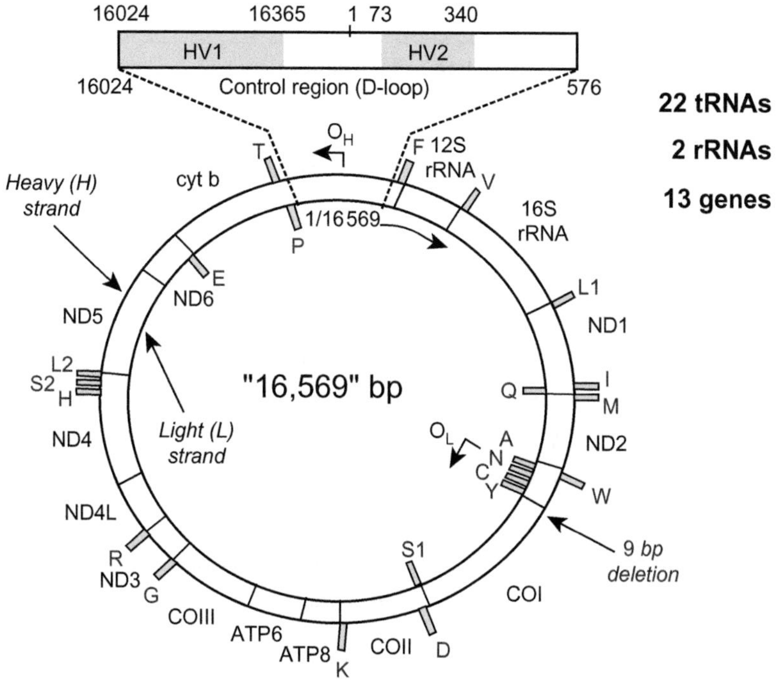

FIGURE 14.1 Illustration of the circular mitochondrial DNA genome (mtGenome). The heavy (H) strand is represented by the outside line and contains a higher number of C-G residues than the light (L) strand. The 37 RNA and protein coding gene regions are abbreviated around the mtGenome next to the strand from which they are synthesized (see Table 14.2). Most forensic mtDNA analyses presently examine only HV1 and HV2 (and occasionally HV3) in the non-coding control region or displacement loop (D-loop) shown at the top of the figure. Due to insertions and deletions that exist around the mtGenome in different individuals, it is not always 16,569 bp in length.

The nucleotide positions for each coding and non-coding segment of the mtGenome are indicated in Table 14.2. Note that the genes are very tightly packed with only 55 nucleotides in the 15,447 bp of the coding region *not* being used to transcribe a protein, rRNA, or tRNA molecule. Thus, the genes within mtDNA are economically packaged with no introns and none or only a few non-coding nucleotides between the coding regions.

An asymmetric distribution of nucleotides in the mtGenome gives rise to a "light" and "heavy" strand when mtDNA molecules are separated in alkaline CsCl gradients (Scheffler 1999). The "heavy" or H-strand contains a greater number of guanine nucleotides, which have the largest relative molecular mass of the four nucleotides (A, T, C, and G), than the "light" or L-strand. Replication of mtDNA begins with the H-strand in the non-coding "control region," also known as the displacement loop or D-loop (Figure 14.1). A total of 28 gene products are encoded from the H-strand while the L-strand transcribes eight tRNAs and an enzyme called ND6 (Table 14.2).

Since the D-loop does not code for gene products, the constraints are fewer for nucleotide variability, and polymorphisms between individuals are more abundant than in

TABLE 14.2 Mitochondrial DNA Information and Genes.

Nucleotide Position	Strand Transcribed	Abbreviation	Description	Size (bp)	Number of Non-coding Nucleotides
16024–16569, 1–576		D-loop	Control region	1122	1122
16104–16569, 1–191		OH	Replication origin (H-strand)	658	
16158–16172			D-loop termination signal	15	
531–568			H-strand transcription promoter	38	
577–647	H	F	tRNA phenylalanine	71	
648–1601	H	12S	12S rRNA	954	
1602–1670	H	V	tRNA valine	69	
1671–3229	H	16S	16S rRNA	1559	
3230–3304	H	L1	tRNA leucine 1	75	
3305–4263	H	ND1	NADH dehydrogenase 1	959	
4263–4331	H	I	tRNA isoleucine	69	
4329–4400	L	Q	tRNA glutamine	72	
4401		—	Non-coding	1	1
4402–4469	H	M	tRNA methionine	68	
4470–5511	H	ND2	NADH dehydrogenase 2	1042	
5512–5579	H	W	tRNA tryptophan	68	
5580–5586		—	Non-coding	7	7
5587–5655	L	A	tRNA alanine	69	
5656		—	Non-coding	1	1
5657–5729	L	N	tRNA asparagine	73	
5730–5760		OL	L-strand origin	31	31
5761–5826	L	C	tRNA cysteine	66	
5826–5891	L	Y	tRNA tyrosine	66	
5892–5900		—	Non-coding	9	9
5901–7445	H	COI	Cytochrome c oxidase I	1545	
7445–7516	L	S1	tRNA serine 1	72	
7517		—	Non-coding	1	1
7518–7585	H	D	tRNA aspartic acid	68	
7586–8294	H	COII	Cytochrome c oxidase II	709	
8295–8364	H	K	tRNA lysine	70	

(Continued)

TABLE 14.2 Mitochondrial DNA Information and Genes. (*Continued*)

Nucleotide Position	Strand Transcribed	Abbreviation	Description	Size (bp)	Number of Non-coding Nucleotides
8365–8572	H	ATP8	ATP synthase 8	208	
8527–9207	H	ATP6	ATP synthase 6	681	
9207–9990	H	COIII	Cytochrome c (oxidase III)	784	
9991–10058	H	G	tRNA glycine	68	
10059–10404	H	ND3	NADH (dehydrogenase 3)	346	
10405–10469	H	R	tRNA arginine	65	
10470–10766	H	ND4L	NADH (dehydrogenase 4L)	297	
10760–12137	H	ND4	NADH (dehydrogenase 4)	1378	
12138–12206	H	H	tRNA histidine	69	
12207–12265	H	S2	tRNA serine 2	59	
12266–12336	H	L2	tRNA leucine 2	71	
12337–14148	H	ND5	NADH (dehydrogenase 5)	1812	
14149–14673	L	ND6	NADH (dehydrogenase 6)	525	
14674–14742	L	E	tRNA glutamic acid	69	
14743–14746		—	Non-coding	4	4
14747–15887	H	cyt b	Cytochrome b	1141	
15888–15953	H	T	tRNA threonine	66	
15954		—	Non-coding	1	1
15955–16023	L	P	tRNA proline	69	

similarly sized portions of the coding region. More simply, there can be differences in the D-loop region because the sequences do not code for any substances necessary for the cell's function.

Most of the focus in forensic DNA studies to date has involved two hypervariable regions within the control region commonly referred to as HVI (HV1) and HVII (HV2). Occasionally a third portion of the control region, known as HV3, is examined to provide more information regarding a tested sample.

The numbering system for human mtDNA nucleotide positions is arbitrarily based on the L-strand from an *MboI* restriction enzyme site within the control region as defined in the original paper describing the mtGenome sequence (Anderson et al. 1981). Thus, position 1 is not the origin of replication. As can be seen in Figure 14.1, position 1 falls between hypervariable region 1 (HV1) and hypervariable region 2 (HV2).

Human mtDNA Reference Sequence(s)

Human mtDNA was first sequenced in 1981 in the laboratory of Frederick Sanger in Cambridge, England (Anderson et al. 1981). For many years, the original "Anderson" sequence (named after the first author listed in alphabetical order from the Sanger research group) was the reference sequence (GenBank accession: M63933) to which new sequences were compared. The Anderson sequence is also referred to as the Cambridge Reference Sequence (CRS). In 1999, the original placental material used by Anderson and co-workers to generate the CRS was re-sequenced (Andrews et al. 1999).

The 1981 sequence was derived primarily from a single individual of European descent; however, it also contained some HeLa and bovine sequences to fill in gaps resulting from early rudimentary DNA sequencing procedures (Anderson et al. 1981). With improvements in DNA sequencing technology over the intervening two decades, it was felt that any original errors should be rectified to enable robust use of this reference sequence in the future.

The reanalysis effort confirmed all but 11 of the original nucleotides identified in the original published sequence (Table 14.3). One of these differences was the loss of a single cytosine residue at position 3107. An additional seven nucleotide positions were demonstrated to be accurate but represent rare polymorphisms. These sites were 263A, 311–315CCCCC, 750A, 1438A, 4769A, 8860A, and 15326A. Fortunately, no errors were observed in the widely used control region. Thus, the original Anderson sequence (Anderson et al. 1981) was found to be

TABLE 14.3 Comparison of Nucleotide Differences Observed Between the Original Cambridge Reference Sequence (Anderson et al. 1981) and the Revised Cambridge Reference Sequence (Andrews et al. 1999) Based on Re-sequencing of the Original Placenta Material. The True Sequence at Position 3106–3107 Is Only a Single C Making the Entire mtGenome 16,568 bp Rather than the Originally Reported 16,569 bp. However, to Maintain the Historical Numbering, a Deletion at Position 3107 Is Used to Serve as a Placeholder (Andrews et al. 1999). Note That No Differences Exist Between These Sequences for the Two Hypervariable Regions Most Commonly Used in Forensic Applications That Span Positions 16024 to 16365 and 73 to 340. See MITOMAP for a Fully Annotated Version of the rCRS: http://www.mitomap.org/bin/view.pl/MITOMAP/HumanMitoSeq.

Nucleotide Position	Region of mtGenome	Original CRS	Revised CRS (rCRS)	Remarks
3106–3107	16S rRNA	CC	C	Error
3423	ND1	G	T	Error
4985	ND2	G	A	Error
9559	COIII	G	C	Error
11335	ND4	T	C	Error
13702	ND5	G	C	Error
14199	ND6	G	T	Error
14272	ND6	G	C	Error (bovine sequence inserted)
14365	ND6	G	C	Error (bovine sequence inserted)
14368	ND6	G	C	Error
14766	cyt b	T	C	Error (HeLa sequence inserted)

identical to the revised Cambridge reference sequence (Andrews et al. 1999) across the HV1 and HV2 regions that are widely used in forensic applications.

This revised Cambridge reference sequence (rCRS) is now the accepted standard for comparison and is available in GenBank using NCBI reference sequence NC_012920.1. While the loss of a single C nucleotide at position 3107 means that the reference mtGenome is 16,568 bp rather than the traditionally accepted value of 16,569 bp, historical numbering has been maintained by including an "N" in place of the 3107 deletion. Not including this extra space would have created an unacceptable amount of confusion and inability to easily correlate previous work. Therefore, Andrews and co-workers (1999) recommended that the original numbering be retained in the rCRS with a deletion in the sequence at position 3107 to serve as a place holder. The "16,569 bp" rCRS is available at the MITOMAP website: http://www.mitomap.org/mitoseq.htm.

Maternal Inheritance of mtDNA

Human mitochondrial DNA is considered to be inherited strictly from our mothers. At conception only the sperm's nucleus enters the egg and joins directly with the egg's nucleus. The fertilizing sperm is not believed to contribute other cellular components. When the zygote cell divides and a blastocyst develops, the cytoplasm and other cell parts save the nucleus are consistent with the mother's original egg cell. Mitochondria with their mtDNA molecules are passed directly to all offspring independent of any male influence. Thus, barring mutation, a mother passes along her mtDNA type to her children, and therefore siblings and maternal relatives have an identical mtDNA sequence. Hence, an individual's mtDNA type is not unique to him or her.

An example family pedigree is shown in Figure 14.2 to demonstrate the inheritance pattern of mtDNA. In this example, unique mtDNA types exist solely for individuals 1, 5, 7,

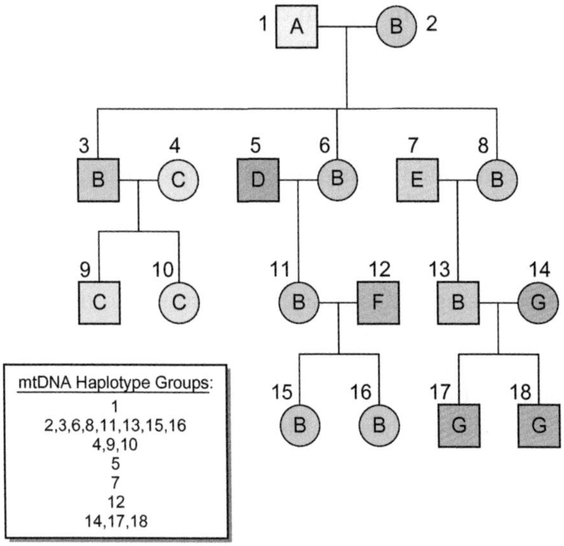

FIGURE 14.2 Illustration of maternal mitochondrial DNA inheritance for 18 individuals in a hypothetical pedigree. Squares represent males and circles females. Each unique mtDNA type is represented by a different letter.

and 12. Note that individual 16 will possess the same mtDNA type as seven of the other represented individuals (i.e., 2, 3, 6, 8, 11, 13, and 15). This can be helpful in solving missing persons or mass disaster investigations but will likely reduce the significance of a match in forensic cases. Since even distantly related maternal relatives should possess the same mtDNA type, this extends the number of useful reference samples that may be used to confirm the identity of a missing person.

Other Interesting Differences Between mtDNA and Nuclear DNA

Mitochondrial DNA uses a different genetic code than nuclear DNA (Scheffler 1999). For example, the codon for mitochondrial-transcribed amino acid tryptophan is UGA while the universal (nuclear) genetic code for UGA is a stop codon. In the mtDNA genetic code, AUA codes for methionine instead of isoleucine and AGA and AGG both code for stops rather than arginine.

Fewer DNA repair mechanisms exist in mitochondria thereby leading to higher mutation rates compared to nuclear DNA. In addition, lack of proofreading capabilities in the mtDNA polymerase increases mutations during replication. The 10-fold higher mutation rate (relative to nuclear DNA) helps introduce more variability in samples from identical maternal lineages that otherwise would not vary. This increased variability is a good thing for most applications in human identity testing although mutations can sometimes be a hindrance when trying to definitely establish familial relationships (e.g., when comparing remains to reference samples from distant maternal relatives).

The circular nature of mtDNA makes it less susceptible than genomic DNA to exonucleases that break down DNA molecules. The encapsulation of mtDNA in a two-walled organelle also enhances the mtDNA survival rate.

Various Applications for mtDNA Testing

Mitochondrial DNA variation is extensively studied in several disciplines besides forensic science. Medical scientists have linked a number of diseases to mutations in mtDNA (see Wallace et al. 1999). Evolutionary biologists examine human mtDNA sequence variation relative to other species in an effort to determine relationships. A good example of this application is the determination that Neanderthals are not the direct ancestors of modern humans based on control region sequences determined from ancient bones (Krings et al. 1997). Molecular anthropologists study differences in mtDNA sequences from various global population groups to examine questions of ancestry and migration of peoples throughout history (Relethford 2003). Hundreds of papers have been published in these fields over the past few decades. Genetic genealogists are now using mtDNA and Y-chromosome markers in an attempt to trace ancestry where paper trails run cold (Brown 2002).

In the past few years a number of interesting historical identifications have been performed with the aid of mtDNA testing. Remains from the Tomb of the Unknown Soldier associated with the Vietnam War have been identified as those of Michael Blassie (Holland & Parsons 1999). Bones discovered in Russia in 1991 were demonstrated to be those of the Tsar Nicholas II (Gill et al. 1994, Ivanov et al. 1996, Coble et al. 2009). The claims of Anna Anderson Manahan as the Russian princess Anastasia were proven false (Gill et al. 1995). The remains of the outlaw Jesse James were linked to living relatives putting to rest a myth that he had somehow escaped death at the hands of Robert Ford (Stone et al. 2001).

Different Methods for Measuring mtDNA Variation

Over the past three decades, methods for measuring mtDNA variation have progressed in their ability to separate unrelated and closely related maternal lineages. The first studies with mtDNA in the 1980s involved low-resolution restriction fragment length polymorphism (RFLP) analysis using five or six restriction enzymes (see Richards and Macaulay 2001). Higher-resolution restriction analysis involved polymerase chain reaction (PCR) amplification of typically nine overlapping fragments followed by digestion with 12 or 14 restriction enzymes. These restriction endonucleases included *Alu*I, *Ava*II, *BamH*I, *Dde*I, *Hae*II, *Hae*III, *Hha*I, *Hinc*II, *Hinf*I, *Hpa*I, *Msp*I, *Mbo*I, *Rsa*I, and *Taq*I (Torroni et al. 1996).

Genetically different population types or haplotypes have been defined in the literature based on site losses or site gains with the various restriction enzymes. For example, haplogroup A, which is found in Asians and Native Americans, is defined by a site gain at position 663 with *Hae*III (listed as + 663 *Hae*III). Haplogroup B was initially defined as a 9bp deletion in the intergenic region between the COII and $tRNA^{LYS}$ genes (see Table 14.2). Individuals belonging to haplogroup A may also be defined by control region polymorphisms 16223T, 16290T, and 16319A while haplogroup B individuals differ from the Anderson reference sequence at 16189C and 16217C.

In the early 1990s, DNA sequence analysis from portions of the control region came into wide acceptance. Most population data outside of the forensic community continues to be collected for only hypervariable segment I (HVS-I) spanning approximately mtDNA nucleotide positions 16024 to 16365. As will be seen below, the forensic DNA typing community has standardized on specific portions of the control region for most of the data that currently exists.

December 2000 marked the beginning of the mtDNA population genomics era with the publication of 53 entire mtGenomes from a diverse set of individuals representing populations from around the world (Ingman et al. 2000). As of December 2010 over eight thousand complete mtGenomes exist in public DNA databases (Ruiz-Pesini et al. 2004, Irwin et al. 2011).

MITOCHONDRIAL DNA SEQUENCING IN FORENSIC CASEWORK

The following section describes the methodologies used for determining the sequence contained in mitochondrial DNA. Several nice overviews of forensic mtDNA analysis have been published and may be consulted for further information on this topic (Holland & Parsons 1999, Budowle et al. 2003, Isenberg 2004, Edson et al. 2004).

Steps Involved in Obtaining mtDNA Results

The steps involved in performing mitochondrial DNA sequence comparisons are illustrated in Figure 14.3. Extraction of the mtDNA needs to be performed in a very clean

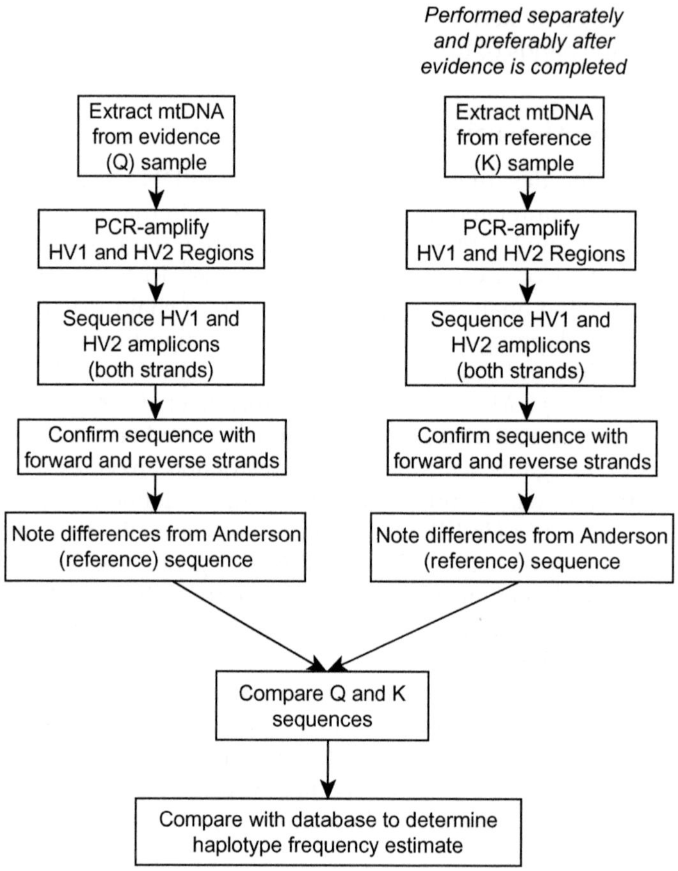

FIGURE 14.3 Process for evaluation of mtDNA samples. The evidence or question (Q) sample may come from a crime scene or a mass disaster. The reference or known (K) sample may be a maternal relative or the suspect in a criminal investigation. In a criminal investigation, the victim may also be tested and compared to the Q and K results.

laboratory environment because the high copy number per cell makes mtDNA more sensitive to contamination than nuclear DNA. Thus, it is preferable to analyze the reference samples after the evidence samples have been completely processed to avoid any potential contamination.

Mitochondrial DNA analysis is commonly performed using the Sanger sequencing chemistry (Sanger et al. 1977, Wilson et al. 1995). This DNA sequencing is performed in both the forward and reverse directions so that the complementary strands can be compared to one another for quality control purposes.

Typically laboratories report results in terms of variation compared to the rCRS. Thus, the observation of a C nucleotide at position 16126, which contains a T in the reference sequence, would be reported as 16126C. If no other nucleotide variants are reported, then it is assumed that the remaining sequence contains the same sequence as the rCRS.

Importance of a Clean Laboratory

The use of higher PCR cycle numbers (e.g., 36 or 42) and the high copy number of mtDNA per cell necessitate great care to avoid contamination. The DNA templates under investigation are often damaged so they may not be as readily amplified as even low amounts of high-quality DNA from laboratory personnel or reference samples. Reference samples from the victim, the suspect, and maternal relatives are typically available as blood stains or buccal swabs and generally contain large amounts of high-quality DNA.

Practices to reduce or minimize contamination often employed by forensic laboratories performing mtDNA testing include use of protective clothing such as disposable lab coats, frequent cleaning procedures with bleach and UV irradiation of hoods and lab bench surfaces, processing the question samples prior to the known samples, multiple glove changes during sample handling, using dedicated equipment for the mtDNA testing, and physically separating the pre- and post-amplification spaces. During an analytical procedure only one item of evidence from a case is opened at a time (Isenberg & Moore 1999).

Some laboratories even control movement of laboratory personnel between spaces. For example, a technician may not be permitted on the same day to return to a pre-amplification area after having entered a post-amplification area. Vigilance on the part of all laboratory personnel is important to keep a forensic mtDNA laboratory clean. Reagent blanks and negative controls are also run to monitor levels of exogenous DNA in reagents, laboratory environment, or instruments.

Sample Extraction for mtDNA Analysis

Mitochondrial DNA analysis typically involves materials where little DNA is present to begin with. Teeth, hair, and bones such as ribs and long bones (e.g., femur and humerus) are often materials used for mtDNA analysis in forensic cases. The mtDNA must be carefully extracted from these materials and often purified away from PCR inhibitors that can be co-extracted (Yoshii et al. 1992).

Because anthropological examination of a bone is often performed in addition to mtDNA testing, care must be taken to remove a section of the bone that will not destroy the physical features of the bone. Thus, an analyst might remove a small section from the middle of the bone without cutting all the way through the bone so that the overall length of the bone is not impacted. The same idea applies for teeth where odontological examinations are performed to aid an investigation. A tabulation of success rates for obtaining reportable mtDNA sequencing results across different skeletal materials found that ribs and femurs work best (Edson et al. 2004). A demineralization extraction protocol has dramatically improved success rates with mtDNA analysis (Loreille et al. 2007). In fact, improved DNA recoveries with new extraction protocols have enabled laboratories to obtain results with STRs or miniSTRs on bone samples where just a few years ago only mtDNA results were possible.

Special Considerations for Hair Evidence

Hair and fiber examiners can perform microscopic comparisons of hairs much more quickly than mtDNA can be analyzed. These comparisons therefore can be used as an effective screening tool to reduce the amount of evidence processed through the steps of mtDNA sequencing. A correlation of microscopic and mitochondrial DNA hair comparisons found that the techniques can be complementary (Houck & Budowle 2002).

With hair evidence, the physical examination by a hair examiner must be performed prior to the mtDNA testing as the hair is destroyed during the extraction process. Typically for analysis of hair shafts, a tissue grinder is used to break down the keratin structure of the hair and release the mtDNA molecules (Wilson et al. 1995a). Usually 1 cm to 2 cm of hair shaft is ground up after carefully cleaning the outside of the hair (Jehaes et al. 1998). A hair digestion protocol has also been used successfully to release nuclear DNA and mtDNA for analysis (Hellman et al. 2001).

Comparisons of head, pubic, and axillary hair shafts found the highest success rate with head hair shafts (Pfeiffer et al. 1999). The addition of bovine serum albumin (BSA) (Giambernardi et al. 1998) helped reduce the PCR inhibitory effects of melanin previously noted by Yoshii et al. (1992) and Wilson et al. (1995a). A nested PCR amplification approach has successfully recovered mtDNA sequence information from as little as 33 femtograms to 330 femtograms (10 to 100 copies) of mtDNA (Allen et al. 1998).

Estimating mtDNA Quantity

Many laboratories perform a nuclear DNA quantitation assay and then estimate the amount of mtDNA present assuming a fixed ratio between nuclear and mtDNA. For example, in some of the early work 50 pg or 500 pg of DNA template would be used in an mtDNA amplification based on a nuclear quantification result from Quantiblot (Wilson et al. 1995b). Newer approaches involving real-time PCR have been published (Meissner et al. 2000, Andreasson et al. 2002, von Wurmb-Schwark et al. 2002, Alonso et al. 2004) that enable direct characterization of the number of mtDNA molecules in a cell.

By incorporating a dual real-time nuclear and mtDNA quantitation assay into their workflow, the University of Innsbruck mtDNA group were able to reduce their re-amplifications from 18% down to 7% over a two-year period of examining some 12,000 casework samples (Niederstätter et al. 2007).

PCR Amplification

PCR amplification of mtDNA is usually done with 34 to 38 cycles. Protocols for highly degraded DNA specimens even call for 42 cycles (Gabriel et al. 2001a). Sometimes excess Taq is added to overcome PCR inhibitors such as melanin (Wilson et al. 1995a). It is important to keep in mind that sensitivity is maximized with mtDNA testing because it is usually only turned to as a last resort in efforts to obtain DNA results from a sample. The higher the sensitivity of any assay, the greater the chance for contamination and thus greater care is usually required with mtDNA work than with conventional STR typing.

The most extensive mtDNA variations between individuals in the human population are found within the control region, or displacement loop (D-loop). Two regions within the D-loop known as hypervariable region I (HV1, HVI, or HVS-I) and hypervariable region II (HV2, HVII, or HVS-II) are normally examined by PCR amplification followed by sequence analysis. Approximately 610 bp are commonly evaluated—342bp from HV1 (Figure 14.4a) and 268 bp from HV2 (Figure 14.4b).

The DNA sequence for each sample between nucleotide positions 16024 and 16365 in HV1 and 73 and 340 in HV2 is determined and then compared to the Anderson or the revised Cambridge Reference Sequence (as mentioned earlier, these reference sequences are equivalent for the control region). Differences are noted and reported with the nucleotide position and the altered base. Sometimes a third hypervariable region (HVIII) is examined that is 137bp long and spans nucleotide positions 438 to 574. Additional polymorphic sites within HVIII can sometimes help resolve indistinguishable HVI/HVII samples (Lutz et al. 2000, Bini et al. 2003).

A number of different PCR and sequencing primers have been used to generate the DNA sequence data for HV1 and HV2. Some of these primer combinations will be discussed later in the chapter. The mtDNA control region has been estimated to vary only about 1% to 2% (7 to 14 nucleotides out of the 610 bases examined are different) between unrelated individuals (Budowle et al. 1999). This variation is scattered throughout the HV1 and HV2 regions and is therefore best measured with DNA sequence analysis.

However, there are "hotspots" or hypervariable sites and regions where most of the variation is clustered (Stoneking 2000). Several methods for rapidly screening mtDNA variation have been developed that may be used for excluding samples that do not match. These methods often focus on measuring variation at the hypervariable hotspots and include using sequence-specific oligonucleotide probes (Stoneking et al. 1991), mini-sequencing (Tully et al. 1996), and denaturing gradient gel electrophoresis (Steighner et al. 1999) as well as a restriction digest assay for HV1 amplicons (Butler et al. 1998a) and a reverse dot blot or linear array assay approach (Comas et al. 1999, Gabriel et al. 2003).

In order to track work with a specific mtDNA sequence, results are commonly reported in comparison to the rCRS reference sequence. Nucleotide positions within the mtDNA molecule are numbered from 1 to 16569 using the L-strand sequence with position 1 arbitrarily coming from a restriction enzyme site found in the control region (Anderson et al. 1981). The HV1 region commonly used in forensic labs spans positions 16024 to 16365, or 342bp, while HV2 covers positions 73 to 340, or 268bp. Thus, use of both HV1 and HV2 provides examination of 610bp of mtDNA sequence.

DNA Sequencing

The Sanger method for DNA sequencing was first described over 30 years ago (Sanger et al. 1977). This Nobel Prize winning sequencing technique is still widely used. The process involves the polymerase incorporation of dideoxyribonucleotide triphosphates (ddNTPs) as chain terminators followed by a separation step capable of single nucleotide resolution. There is no hydroxyl group at the 3′-end of the DNA nucleotide with a ddNTP and therefore chain growth terminates when the polymerase incorporates a ddNTP into the synthesized strand. Extendable dNTPs and ddNTP terminators are both present in the reaction mix so that some portions of the DNA molecules are extended. At the end of the sequencing reaction, a series of molecules are present that differ by one base from one another.

In the Sanger sequencing process, each DNA strand is sequenced in separate reactions with a single primer. Often either the forward or reverse PCR primers are used for this purpose. Four different colored fluorescent dyes are attached to the four different ddNTPs. Thus, ddTTP (thymine) is labeled with a red dye, ddCTP (cytosine) is labeled with a blue

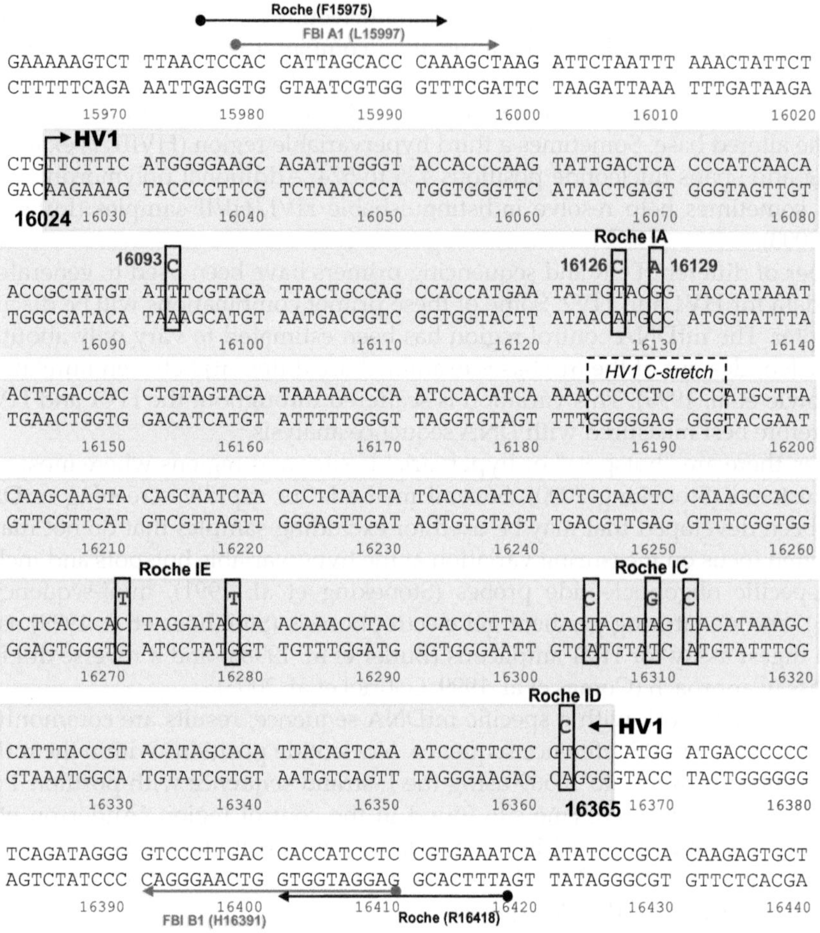

FIGURE 14.4a Annotation of the revised Cambridge Reference Sequence for the HV1 portion of the mtDNA control region with primer positions and common sequence polymorphisms examined in screening assays (see Figure 14.9).

dye, ddATP (adenine) is labeled with a green dye, and ddGTP (guanine) is labeled with a yellow dye although it is typically displayed in black for easier visualization. These are similar dyes to those used for STR detection as described in Chapter 6. Fluorescent dye labels have simplified DNA sequencing as have the widespread use of automated detection systems and capillary electrophoresis. The Human Genome Project was completed with these sequencing technologies.

The performance of DNA sequencing chemistries has progressed over the past decade from use of a simple Taq polymerase, which often had high backgrounds and poor incorporation rates for many nucleotide combinations, to the well-balanced Big Dye chemistries used today. Signal-to-noise ratios have improved with brighter dyes (Lee et al. 1997), which in turn now permit results to be obtained from less material. As little as 1 ng of mtDNA PCR product can now be used for each DNA sequencing reaction (Stewart et al. 2003).

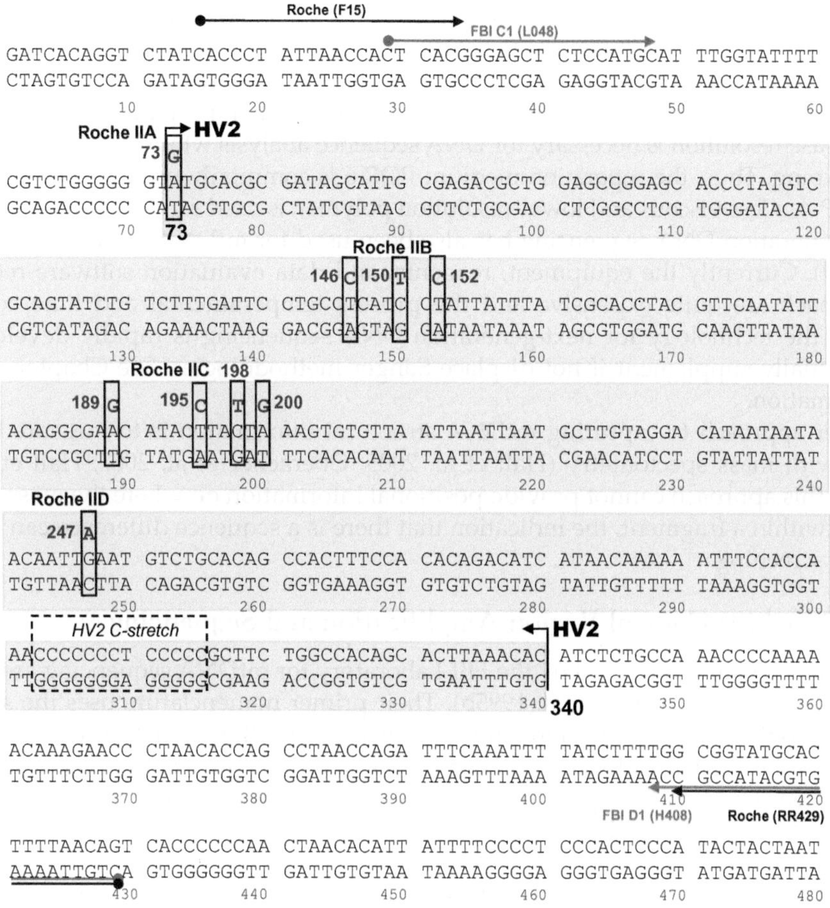

FIGURE 14.4b Annotation of the revised Cambridge Reference Sequence for the HV2 portion of the mtDNA control region with primer positions and common sequence polymorphisms examined in screening assays (see Figure 14.9).

DNA sequencing of mtDNA is usually performed with the following steps: (1) PCR amplification of the entire control region or a portion of it with various primer sets as will be explained below; (2) removal of remaining dNTPs and primers from PCR through spin filtration using a Microcon 100 filter or enzymatic digestion with shrimp alkaline phosphatase and exonuclease I (Dugan et al. 2002); (3) determination of PCR product quantity (Wilson et al. 1995a, 1995b); (4) performance of DNA sequencing reaction to incorporate fluorescent ddNTPs as described above with each reaction containing a different primer to dictate which strand is sequenced; (5) removal of unincorporated fluorescent dye terminators from the completed sequencing reaction usually through spin column filtration; (6) dilution of purified sequencing reaction products in formamide, (7) separation through a capillary electrophoresis instrument (see Chapter 6); and (8) sequence analysis of each reaction performed and interpretation of compiled sequence information as will be described below.

DNA sequencing has been reliably performed on a variety of platforms including the ABI 310, ABI 377, and ABI 3100 (Stewart et al. 2003). The multi-capillary ABI 3500 and 3730 instruments also work well. The primary difference between STR analysis and mtDNA sequencing on these multi-color fluorescence detection instruments is that a separation medium capable of single base resolution is necessary for DNA sequence analysis while it is not always needed for STR typing. Thus, the separation medium POP-6 is commonly used for DNA sequencing while POP-4, a less viscous and lower-resolution polymer, is used for STR typing.

Next-generation DNA sequencing has also been used for mtDNA sequencing (Mikkelsen et al. 2009). Currently the equipment, reagents, and data evaluation software required for this approach are quite expensive and the process temperamental and time consuming. However, the technology for next-generation DNA sequencing is rapidly developing and may eventually supplement if not displace Sanger methodologies. See Chapter 17 for further information.

Another approach to capturing mtDNA structural information is to measure base composition with mass spectometry (Hall et al. 2005, Oberacher et al. 2007, Hall et al. 2009). Although this approach cannot provide positional information on where the mass difference is located within a fragment, the indication that there is a sequence difference can be helpful in sample screening.

Primers Used for Control Region Amplification and Sequencing

PCR primers commonly used by the FBI Laboratory for mtDNA sequencing are shown as arrows in Figure 14.4 (Wilson et al. 1995b). Their primer nomenclature uses the strand corresponding to the primer (L for light and H for heavy) and the 3′ nucleotide position. Thus, primer A1 is designated as L15997 and corresponds to the light strand of the Anderson reference sequence and ends at position 15997. Note that this nomenclature system does not indicate the 5′-end of the primer and therefore can make it more difficult to determine the overall PCR product size.

Another approach to mtDNA primer nomenclature is used by the Armed Forces DNA Identification Laboratory (AFDIL). The primer positions for their primer sets (PS) I-IV are indicated in Figure 14.5. Strand designation in this case is by forward (F) and reverse (R) rather than light (L) and heavy (H). Also the 5′ nucleotide position is noted rather than the 3′ nucleotide as done by the FBI Laboratory. The AFDIL approach permits an easier determination of the overall PCR product size defined by a primer pair. It is worth noting that two of the primers in the FBI and AFDIL sets are identical even though their names are different: FBI B1 (H16391) is the same primer as AFDIL R16410 used in PSII.

Small Amplicons to Improve Amplification Success

As noted in Chapter 10 when encountering highly degraded DNA samples where the molecules have been fragmented to small sizes, the use of smaller-sized PCR products improves recovery of information from the original DNA template. This is also the case with mitochondrial DNA, and "mini-mito primer sets" have been developed to amplify smaller portions of HV1 and HV2 (Gabriel et al. 2001a, Edson et al. 2004).

The bottom portion of Figure 14.5 shows the relative position and PCR product sizes for eight mini-products ranging in size from 126bp to 170bp. Additional mini-mito primer

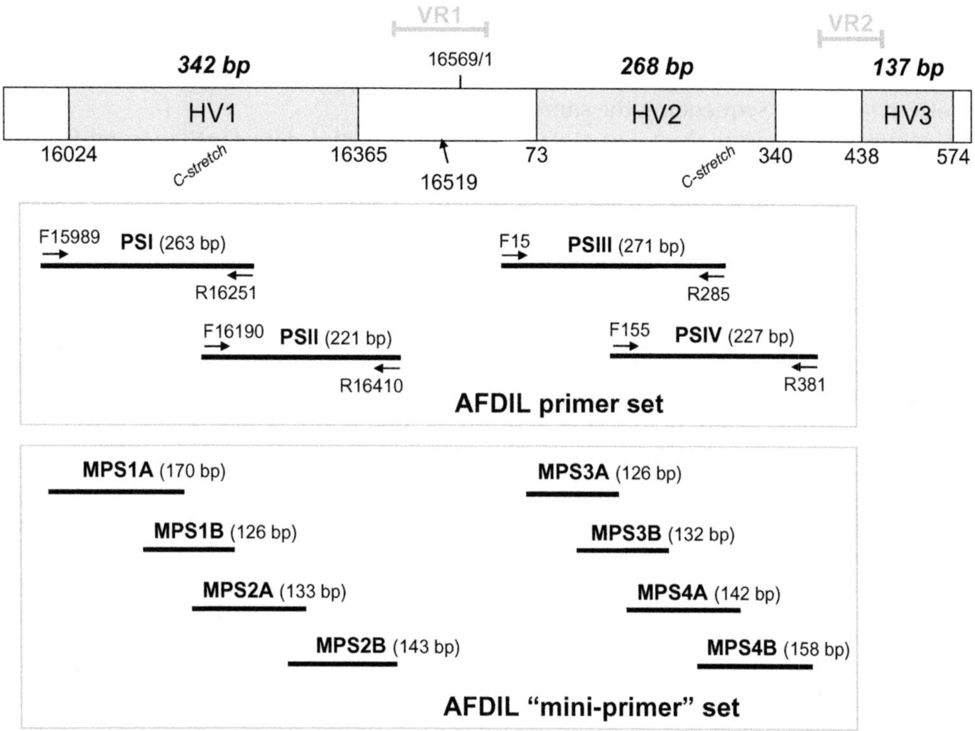

FIGURE 14.5 The three hypervariable (HV) regions of the mtDNA control region. HV1 spans nucleotide positions 16024–16365 (342bp), HV2 spans positions 73–340 (268bp), and HV3, which is rarely examined in forensic testing, spans positions 438–574 (137bp). The general positions for variable regions VR1 and VR2 are noted although these are rarely used. PCR primer sets (PS) commonly used by the Armed Forces DNA Identification Laboratory (AFDIL) are illustrated. Primer nomenclature designates the 5′-nucleotide for each primer. PCR product sizes for each set of primers are noted in parentheses. The bottom section shows "mini-primer" PCR product sizes that are used with highly degraded DNA samples to enable greater recovery of sequence information (see Gabriel et al. 2001a).

sets have been developed to aid work with highly degraded DNA specimens by a group at Innsbruck, Austria (Eichmann & Parson 2008, Berger & Parson 2009) and a team in South Korea (Lee et al. 2008).

The use of mini-amplicons that overlap one another is sometimes referred to as an "ancient DNA" approach and is capable of recovering abundant DNA in a sample that might otherwise fail to produce results with a standard protocol (Gabriel et al. 2001a, Melton and Nelson 2001). This approach has been used to successfully recover information from Neanderthal bones that are thousands of years old (Krings et al. 1997, 1999).

Data Review and Editing

DNA sequencing is performed in both the forward and reverse directions so that the complementary strands can be compared to one another for quality control purposes. If it is not possible to get a sequence from both strands, for example following a C-stretch (see below), then the same strand can be sequenced twice in separate reactions. The goal is to have at least double coverage of every nucleotide being assessed either through sequencing the top and bottom strand or sequencing the same strand twice.

The sequencing process does not always lead to beautiful data that is unambiguous for each base. Some regions, such as the C-stretches, are challenging to decipher and may not even be included in the final interpretation (Stewart et al. 2001). Further, as is discussed later in this chapter, the large copy number and relatively high mutation rate of mtDNA can lead to intra-individual sequence variability.

Sequencing chemistries and instruments have improved in recent years leading to more even peaks, better sensitivity, and less noise. However, experienced analysts must still manually review and potentially edit the software-provided base calls for each nucleotide. At present there is no publicly available software that can robustly evaluate mtDNA sequence data in a reliable and automated fashion without manual intervention.

The sequence editing process is aided by alignments from the multiple sequences generated over a region for the same sample. Computer programs such as Sequencer (GeneCodes, Ann Arbor, MI) align the forward and reverse sequencing reactions and allow the sequencing electropherograms for each reaction to be evaluated side-by-side. For casework samples that utilize smaller PCR products, the overlap between products (see Figure 14.5) permits a further measure of quality assurance in the final compiled sequence. In addition, two forensic analysts must independently examine, interpret, and edit sequence matching results as a final quality assurance measure (Isenberg 2004).

Challenges with Sequencing Beyond Polymeric C-Stretches

Note that a dotted box is found around a stretch of cytosine nucleotides in both the HV1 (Figure 14.4a) and HV2 (Figure 14.4b) regions. These regions are commonly referred to as "C-stretches." On the revised Cambridge Reference Sequence, the HV1 C-stretch spans nucleotides 16184 to 16193 with a T at position 16189. In some samples, position 16189 is a C giving rise to a stretch of 10 or more cytosines in a row (Figure 14.6). The HV2 C-stretch region spans positions 303 to 315 on the reference sequence with a T at position 310 (Figure 14.4b). This T can become a C in some samples leading to a homopolymeric C-stretch.

Unfortunately, this homopolymeric stretch of cytosines creates problems for polymerases as they synthesize a complementary strand to the mtDNA template present in the reaction. Length heteroplasmy in HV1 between positions 16184 and 16193 can result in C-stretch lengths ranging from 8 to 14 cytosine residues (Bendall & Sykes 1995). Length heteroplasmy likely results from replication slippage after a T to C transition has occurred at position 16189. The mixture of length variants may already be present in the original DNA or generated in the sequencing reaction itself. Regardless of the source of the length variants, the impact of a 16189 T-to-C transition on sequencing results downstream of the C-stretch region can be seen in Figure 14.6b.

A similar situation occurs with the HV2 C-stretch region when insertions of cytosines occur in the 303 to 310 area or a transition of T-to-C occurs at position 310 (Stewart et al. 2001). The presence of intra-individual variation in the number of cytosines observed when multiple hairs were tested from the same individual has led to the decision to not call an

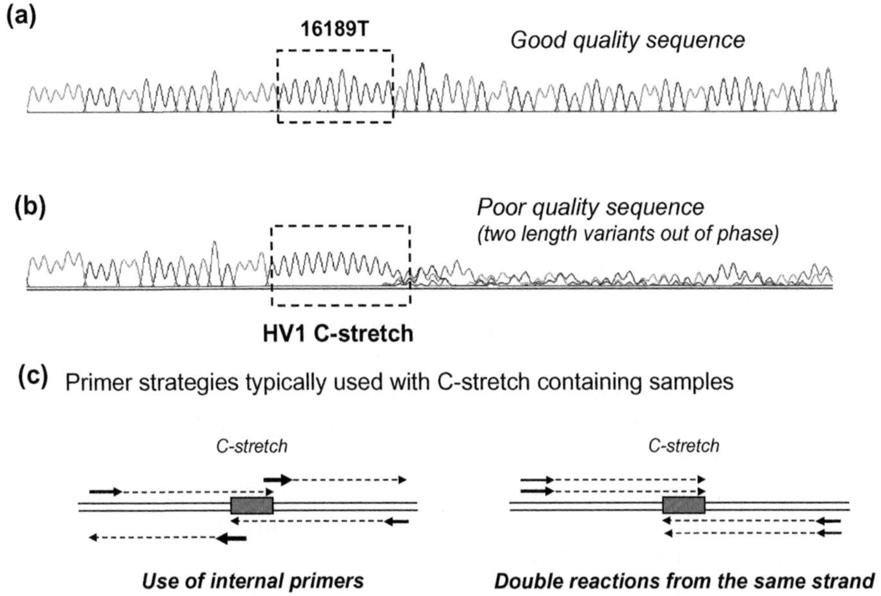

FIGURE 14.6 Comparison of a sample with (a) 16189T (no HV1 C-stretch) to (b) one with the C-stretch. Notice how the sequence quality quickly drops after the string of cytosine residues due to the presence of two or more length variants that creates a situation where the extension products are out of phase or register with one another. Different primer combinations are typically used on samples containing a C-stretch as illustrated in (c) to recover sequence information from both strands or to provide a double read of the same strand.

exclusion based solely on differences in the HV2 C-stretch region (Stewart et al. 2001). The issue of heteroplasmy and intra-individual variation will be discussed in more detail later in this chapter.

The ability to rapidly screen for the C-stretch prior to sequencing is advantageous and can be performed by noting the presence of extra heteroduplex peaks in quality control analyses of HV1 PCR products (Butler et al. 1998a). In the event that the C-stretch is present in a sample, different sequencing primers may be used to obtain reliable mtDNA sequence information downstream of the homopolymeric stretches (Rasmussen et al. 2002). For example, the FBI A4/B4 primer set (L16209 and H16164) shown in Figure 14.4a can be used on individuals possessing the HV1 C-stretch in order to recover sequence information from both sides of the homopolymeric stretch of cytosines (Wilson 1997). Alternatively the same strand may be examined twice in separate sequencing reactions to provide double coverage of all nucleotides (Figure 14.6c).

Use of Positive and Negative Controls

As noted by Melton and Nelson (2001) the two primary goals in mtDNA testing are (1) to protect the integrity of the evidence by preventing contamination at any stage in the testing and (2) to collect the maximum amount of available mtDNA data inherent to any sample.

Control samples that are processed in parallel with evidentiary samples through each step of the process serve to monitor performance and assess one's success with the two goals noted above.

Contamination assessment is performed with reagent blanks and negative controls. Reagent blanks monitor contamination from extraction to final sequence analysis while negative controls monitor contamination from amplification to final sequence analysis (SWGDAM 2003). All of the procedures performed on a sample are also performed on the reagent or extraction blank with the exception of adding DNA. Negative controls or amplification blanks are introduced at the PCR amplification step and use the same reagents as the sample with sterile water in place of the DNA template. If the reagent blank and/or the negative control associated with a particular amplification results in a sequence that is the same as that of the sample, all data for the sample must be rejected (Isenberg 2004). The analysis must then be repeated beginning with the re-amplification of the sample in question.

Reagent blank contamination is sometimes observed in spite of great efforts to keep the laboratory environment clean. Since mtDNA analysis is a very sensitive technique, the presence of low-level contamination is not uncommon (Isenberg 2004). For example, Mitotyping Technologies reported that reagent blanks resulted in amplification products in 29 of 1218 (2.4%) of PCR reactions performed in casework over a two-year period of time (Melton & Nelson 2001). These contaminants did not match a staff member's type or the type of the recently handled sample. This suggests sporadic contamination of disposable tips or PCR tubes during manufacture or packaging. This type of contamination is not uncommon when working with low-copy-number DNA as noted in Chapter 11.

If contamination is observed with either the reagent blank or the negative control, results from the unknown sample being run in parallel do not always have to be disregarded. Research with artificial sample mixtures has demonstrated that a threshold of background contamination can be set for still obtaining reliable sequence data. For example, the FBI Laboratory has established a 10:1 rule where any contamination seen in a reagent blank or negative control during post-PCR analysis must be less than one-tenth the amount of the sample being processed (Wilson et al. 1995a, 1995b). This sample-to-contamination ratio determination is possible due to the PCR product quantification analysis performed in their procedure (Butler et al. 1994). A more recent study demonstrated that the 10:1 rule is conservative and reliable (Stewart et al. 2003).

A positive control is a sample of known mtDNA sequence that serves to demonstrate that amplification and sequencing reaction components are working properly. This positive control is typically an extracted DNA sample that is processed through the steps of amplification, sequencing, and data analysis. For example, the FBI Laboratory uses the HL-60 cell line as a positive control (Levin et al. 2003).

Interlaboratory Studies

Interlaboratory studies in which laboratories perform testing on the same sample are valuable for demonstrating that a technique is reliable (see Chapter 7). As of 2010, no manufacturers supply commercially available kits for the entire process of mtDNA sequencing, such as are available for STR typing. Thus, a number of different methods exist for mtDNA testing without a single universal protocol.

A number of interlaboratory studies involving mtDNA sequencing have been conducted and have demonstrated that the same results can be successfully obtained in multiple laboratories using different protocols (Carracedo et al. 1998, Alonso et al. 2002, Prieto et al. 2003, Parsons et al. 2004, Tully et al. 2004).

Certified Reference Materials for mtDNA Sequence Analysis

Certified reference materials along with positive controls serve to demonstrate that mtDNA sequence analysis is being performed appropriately (Szibor et al. 2003a). The U.S. National Institute of Standards and Technology (NIST) has developed two Standard Reference Materials (SRMs) to aid in confirming sequencing results with mtDNA (Levin et al. 1999, Levin et al. 2003). Information is available for the entire mtGenome on the cell line HL-60 (SRM 2392-I) and on three samples (SRM 2392). The certificates for these reference materials were updated in 2007 and 2009, respectively.

The FBI Revised Quality Assurance Standards require that U.S. laboratories run a NIST SRM or material traceable to a NIST SRM at least once a year or whenever a protocol is changed to help verify that DNA sequencing and interpretation are being performed accurately (see Appendix 4, Standard 9.5.5).

INTERPRETATION OF mtDNA RESULTS

Following completion of mtDNA sequence analysis, as outlined in Figure 14.3, results from the edited and reviewed sequences for a question (Q) and a known (K) sample are compared as illustrated in Figure 14.7 for a portion of HV1. All 610 nucleotides (positions 16024–16365 and 73–340) are normally evaluated between samples being compared.

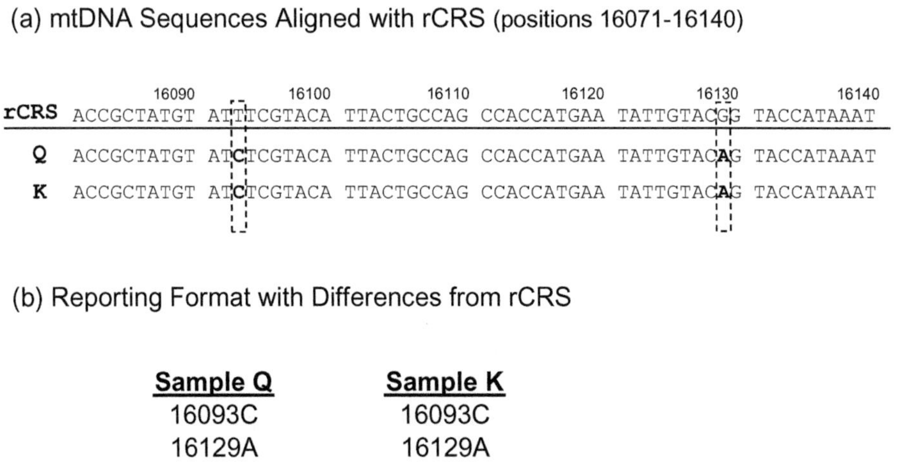

FIGURE 14.7 (a) Comparison of sequence alignments for hypothetical Q and K samples with (b) conversion to the revised Cambridge Reference Sequence (rCRS) differences for reporting purposes.

Based on the Q-K comparison, mtDNA sequence results can generally be grouped into three categories: exclusion, inconclusive, or failure to exclude. The SWGDAM guidelines for mtDNA interpretation makes the following recommendations (SWGDAM 2003):

- *Exclusion* – if there are two or more nucleotide differences between the questioned and known samples, the samples can be excluded as originating from the same person or maternal lineage.
- *Inconclusive* – if there is one nucleotide difference between the questioned and known samples, the result will be inconclusive.
- *Cannot Exclude (Failure to Exclude)* – if the sequences from questioned and known samples under comparison have a common base at each position or a common length variant in the HV2 C-stretch, the samples cannot be excluded as originating from the same person or maternal lineage.

A common base is defined as a shared base in the case of ambiguity (e.g., heteroplasmy) in the sequence (Isenberg 2004). For example, if one sequence possesses heteroplasmy at a site and another does not (see Figure 14.8), then they cannot be excluded from one another. A length variant alone especially in the HV2 homopolymeric C-stretch cannot be used to support an interpretation of exclusion (Stewart et al. 2001, SWGDAM 2003). Several examples are provided in Table 14.4 with their respective interpretations based on the SWGDAM guidelines.

The reason that a single base difference is classified in terms of an "inconclusive result" is that mutations have been observed between mother and children (Parsons et al. 1997). For example, if a maternal relative is used for a reference sample, the possibility of a single base

TABLE 14.4 Example mtDNA Sequences and Interpretations for Known (K) and Question (Q) Sample Pairs (Adapted from Isenberg 2004).

Sequence Results	Observations	Interpretation
Q TATTGTACGG **K** TATTGTACGG	Sequences are fully concordant with common bases at every position	Cannot Exclude
Q TATTGCACAG **K** TATTGTACGG	Sequences differ at two positions	Exclusion
Q TATTNTACGG **K** TATTGTACGG	A single unspecified base in one of the sequences; common base at every position	Cannot Exclude
Q TATTNTACGG **K** TATTGTACNG	Ambiguous bases in both sequences at different positions; common base at every position	Cannot Exclude
Q TATTGTACA/GG **K** TATTGTAC G G	Heteroplasmic mixture at a position in one sample that is not present in the other; common base at every position (G in both Q and K)	Cannot Exclude
Q TATTGTACA/GG **K** TATTGTACA/GG	Heteroplasmic mixture at the same site in both sequences; common base at every position	Cannot Exclude
Q TATTGCACGG **K** TATTGTACGG	Sequences identical at every position except one; no indication of heteroplasmy	Inconclusive

difference may exist between two samples that are in fact maternally related. Often additional samples, usually more reference samples, are run if an inconclusive result is obtained in an attempt to clarify the interpretation (Wilson et al. 1997). Hairs from an individual might be pooled in an attempt to detect heteroplasmy (Isenberg 2004).

More recently, Parson and Bandelt (2007) have offered some extended guidelines for mtDNA analysis and interpretation.

Reporting Statistics

When "failure to exclude" is the interpretation for reference and evidence samples, then a statistical estimate of the significance of a match is needed. Mitochondrial DNA is inherited in its entirety from our mother without recombination (discussed later in the chapter). Therefore individual nucleotide positions are inherited in a block and must be treated as a single locus haplotype, the same as with Y-chromosome information discussed in Chapter 13. The product rule applied to independently segregating STR loci found on separate chromosomes cannot be used with mtDNA polymorphisms.

As was previously noted with Y-STR interpretation, the current practice of conveying the rarity of a mtDNA type among unrelated individuals involves counting the number of times a particular haplotype (sequence) is seen in a database (Wilson et al. 1993, Budowle et al. 1999). This approach is commonly referred to as the "counting method" and depends entirely on the number of samples present in the database that is searched. Thus, the larger the number of unrelated individuals in the database, the better the statistics will be for a random-match frequency estimate.

The true population frequencies for around 60% of mtDNA sequences are not presently known because they occur only a single time in a database (Isenberg 2004). Based on available population information, confidence intervals can be used to estimate the upper and lower bounds of a frequency calculation (Holland & Parsons 1999, Tully et al. 2001). An example is worked in D.N.A. Box 14.1.

One of the challenges with rare mtDNA haplotypes is how to express the weight of evidence when a particular type has not been seen before in the database. Charles Brenner has developed an approach for handling this situation (Brenner 2010). Although other methods, such as likelihood ratios, may be used for estimating the weight of evidence, it is important to keep in mind that mtDNA can never have the power of discrimination that an autosomal STR marker can since its inheritance is uniparental.

Reporting Differences to the Revised Cambridge Reference Sequence

For reporting purposes, sequences are listed in a minimum data format as differences relative to the rCRS. When differences are observed, the nucleotide position is cited followed by the base present at that site. For example in Figure 14.7a, differences are observed at positions 16093 and 16129 and are noted in Figure 14.7b in their minimum data format at 16093C and 16129A. In this format, all other nucleotides are assumed to be identical to the revised Cambridge Reference Sequence. Bases that cannot be unambiguously determined are usually coded N. At confirmed positions of ambiguity (e.g., sequence heteroplasmy), the

D.N.A. BOX 14.1

CALCULATION OF mtDNA PROFILE FREQUENCY ESTIMATES USING THE COUNTING METHOD

In cases where an mtDNA profile is observed a particular number of times (X) in a database containing N profiles, its frequency (p) can be calculated as follows:

$$p = X/N$$

A 95% upper bound confidence interval can be placed on the profile's frequency using:

$$p + 1.96\sqrt{\frac{(p)(1-p)}{N}}$$

In cases where the profile has not been observed in a database, the 95% upper bound on the confidence interval is

$$1 - \alpha^{1/N} = 1 - (0.05)^{1/N}$$

where $\alpha = 0.05$ is the confidence coefficient and N is the number of individuals in the database.

For example, the mtDNA type 16129A, 263G, 309d, 315.1C occurs twice in 1148 African-American profiles, twice in 1655 Caucasian profiles, and not at all in 686 Hispanic profiles when searched against the mtDNA Population Database (Monson et al. 2002). Using the equations above, calculations for the rarity of this profile in the respective sample sets are as follows:

For African-Americans: $p = 2/1148 + 1.96\ [(2/1148)(1 - (2/1148))/1148]^{1/2} = 0.0017 + 0.002 = 0.004 = 0.40\%$

For Caucasians: $p = 2/1655 + 1.96\ [(2/1655)(1 - (2/1655))/1655]^{1/2} = 0.0012 + 0.0017 = 0.0029 = 0.29\%$

For Hispanics: $1 - (0.05)^{1/686} = 1 - 0.9956 = 0.0044 = 0.44\%$

These calculations demonstrate that the statistical weight can be similar whether or not a match is found to a few previously observed samples in a database.

As shown in D.N.A. Box 13.2, the Clopper-Pearson method (Clopper & Pearson 1934) may also be used to provide a conservative estimate for the upper 95% confidence interval.

Sources:

Clopper, C.J., & Pearson, E.S. (1934). The use of confidence or fiducial limits illustrated in the case of the binomial. Biometrika, *26, 404–413.*

Evett, I.W., & Weir, B.S. (1998). Interpreting DNA Evidence. *Sunderland, MA: Sinauer Associates, Inc., p. 142.*

Monson, K.L., et al. (2002). The mtDNA population database: an integrated software and database resource. Forensic Science Communications, *4(2). Available at <http://www2.fbi.gov/hq/lab/fsc/backissu/april2002/miller1.htm>.*

Tully, G., et al. (2001). Considerations by the European DNA profiling (EDNAP) group on the working practices, nomenclature and interpretation of mitochondrial DNA profiles. Forensic Science International, *124, 83–91.*

International Union of Pure and Applied Chemistry (IUPAC) codes should be used, such as A/G = R and C/T = Y (SWGDAM 2003).

Insertions in a DNA sequence relative to the rCRS are described by noting the site immediately 5′ to the insertion as compared to the rCRS followed by a point and a "1" (for the first insertion), a "2" (if there is a second insertion), and so on, and then by the nucleotide that is inserted (Isenberg 2004). For example, 315.1C is a common observation where six Cs are observed following the T at position 310 in the rCRS. The rCRS contains five Cs in positions 311 through 315 (Andrews et al. 1999). Therefore, the notation 315.1C describes the presence of an extra C as an insertion (".1C") prior to position 316.

Deletions are noted by a dash ("−") or a "D," "d" or "del" following the nucleotide position where the deletion was observed relative to the rCRS (e.g., 309D, 309-, or 309del). Some insertion and deletion combinations can lead to multiple possibilities for reporting a result in terms of differences from the reference sequence. Therefore, recommendations have been made for consistent treatment of length variants as will be described in the next section.

Nomenclature Issues

Ambiguities with respect to mtDNA nomenclature can result in different analysts describing the same sample differently although they agree on the nucleotide sequence. Likewise population databases could have multiple entries for the same mtDNA haplotype preventing an accurate estimate for the frequency of a particular type. Thus, standardization in designation of mtDNA sequences is important to generate comparable data that can easily be shared among laboratories.

Length variants present a challenge when alignments are made between a sample of interest and the Cambridge Reference Sequence. Treatments of insertions and deletions (gaps) can vary between laboratories causing some laboratories to code the same sequence differently. Mark Wilson and colleagues at the FBI Laboratory have made a number of recommendations to enable consistent treatment of length variants (Wilson et al. 2002a, 2002b). Three primary recommendations were made: (1) characterize profiles using the least number of differences from the reference sequence; (2) if there is more than one way to maintain the same number of differences with respect to the reference sequence, differences should be prioritized in the following manner: (a) insertions/deletions (indels), (b) transitions, and (c) transversions; (3) insertions and deletions should be placed 3′ with respect to the light strand. Insertions and deletions should be combined in situations where the same number of differences to the reference sequence is maintained. These recommendations are hierarchical; that is recommendation (1) should take precedence over recommendations (2) and (3). A total of 41 specific examples are provided to demonstrate the need for consistent treatment of length variants in mtDNA sequence analysis and reporting (Wilson et al. 2002a, 2002b).

Some groups prefer to use a phylogenetic approach to expressing the nomenclature of a mtDNA sequence (Brandstätter et al. 2004, 2007). In the future, string searches that utilize the full mtDNA sequence (Irwin et al. 2007, Röck et al. 2011) will remove the ambiguity and potential mismatches that can occur when reducing sequences to differences from a reference sequence using either hierarchical rules or phylogenetic approaches.

ISSUES IMPACTING INTERPRETATION

In this section, several issues that can arise when considering mtDNA evidence particularly in courts of law are further elaborated upon (see Walker 2003). A National Institute of Justice-funded study also found that there can be confusion and misperceptions by jurors in terms of the strength of the evidence when mtDNA data is presented in court (Dann et al. 2004).

Heteroplasmy

Heteroplasmy is the presence of more than one mtDNA type in an individual (Melton 2004). Two or more mtDNA populations may occur between cells in an individual, within a single cell, or within a single mitochondrion. It is now thought that all individuals are heteroplasmic at some level—many below the limits of detection in DNA sequence analysis (Comas et al. 1995, Bendall et al. 1996, Steighner et al. 1999, Tully et al. 2000). It is highly unlikely that millions of mtDNA molecules scattered throughout an individual's cells are completely identical given that regions of the mtGenome have been reported to evolve at 6 to 17 times the rate of single-copy nuclear genes (see Brown et al. 1979, Wallace et al. 1987, Tully 1999). Consider that whereas only a single copy of each nuclear chromosome is present in an egg, there are approximately 100,000 copies of the mtDNA genome present (Chen et al. 1995). Thus, for the transmission of a mtDNA mutation to become detectable it must spread to an appreciable frequency among a cell's mtDNA molecules.

Heteroplasmy may be observed in several ways: (1) individuals may have more than one mtDNA type in a single tissue; (2) individuals may exhibit one mtDNA type in one tissue and a different type in another tissue; and/or (3) individuals may be heteroplasmic in one tissue sample and homoplasmic in another tissue sample (Carracedo et al. 2000). In fact, heteroplasmy has been reported inside a single mitochondrion isolated with optical tweezers (Pfugradt et al. 2010, Reiner et al. 2010). Given that heteroplasmy happens, interpretation guidelines must take into account how to handle differences between known and questioned samples.

Both sequence and length heteroplasmy have been reported in the literature (Bendall & Sykes 1995, Bendall et al. 1996, Melton 2004). Length heteroplasmies often occur around the homopolymeric C-stretches in HV1 at positions 16184 to 16193 and HV2 at positions 303 to 310 (Stewart et al. 2001, Parson & Bandelt 2007) (see Figure 14.4). Sequence heteroplasmy is typically detected by the presence of two nucleotides at a single site, which show up as overlapping peaks in a sequence electropherogram (Figure 14.8).

Heteroplasmy at two sites in the same individual, a condition known as "triplasmy," has been reported (Tully et al. 2000), but occurs at lower frequencies than single-site heteroplasmy. Since it is rare to find more than one heteroplasmic position in the 610 nucleotides sequenced for HV1 and HV2, a report of as many as six heteroplasmic sites in an individual mtDNA sequence (Grzybowski 2000) raised suspicions about the sequencing strategy used. The Grybowski study has been criticized as possibly containing contamination due to the excessive number of amplification cycles used (Budowle et al. 2002a, Brandstätter & Parson 2003). A reanalysis of the same samples used in the original Grybowski study with a direct rather than a nested PCR approach resulted in a reduction in the reported number of samples with heteroplasmic positions (Grzybowski et al. 2003).

One of the major challenges of heteroplasmic samples is that the ratio of bases may not stay the same across different tissues, such as blood and hair or between multiple hairs (Sullivan et al. 1997, Wilson et al. 1997, Sekiguchi et al. 2003). Some mtDNA protocols now recommend sequencing multiple hairs from an individual in order to confirm heteroplasmy.

Hotspots for heteroplasmy include the following positions in HV1: 16093, 16129, 16153, 16189, 16192, 16293, 16309, and 16337 (Stoneking 2000, Tully et al. 2000, Brandstätter & Parson 2003) and 72, 152, 189, 207, and 279 in HV2 (Calloway et al. 2000, Melton & Nelson

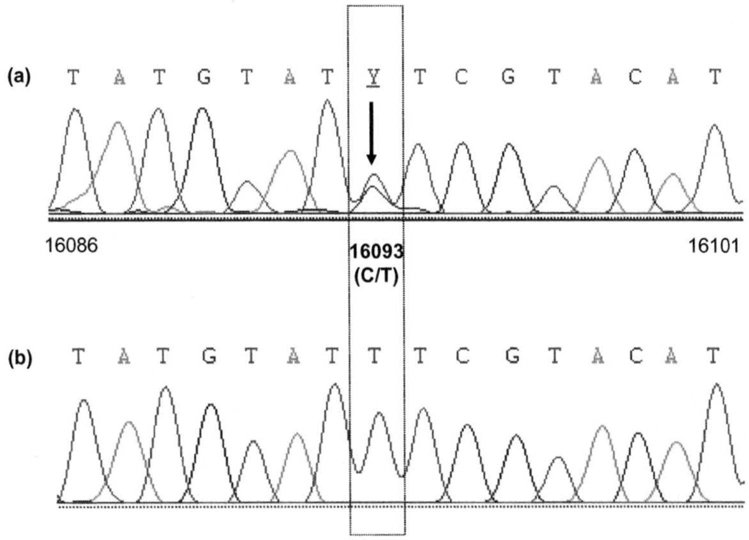

FIGURE 14.8 (a) Sequence heteroplasmy at position 16093 possessing both C and T nucleotides compared to (b) the same region (positions 16086–16101) on a different sample containing only a T at position 16093.

2001). One study found that the frequency of heteroplasmy can differ across tissue types, with muscle tissue being the highest, and was statistically significant across different age groups suggesting that heteroplasmy increases with age (Calloway et al. 2000). Heteroplasmy has also been reported to remain stable over time in the same individuals and thus be inherited rather than age related (Lagerström-Fermér et al. 2001). While heteroplasmy can sometimes complicate the interpretation of mtDNA results, the presence of heteroplasmy at identical sites can improve the probability of a match, such as seen in the Romanov study (Ivanov et al. 1996).

Sample Mixtures

A major advantage of mtDNA in terms of sequencing is that it is haploid and therefore only a single type exists (barring detectable heteroplasmy) for analysis. However, mixed samples from more than one biological source are commonly encountered in forensic settings. Generally speaking attempts are not made to decipher samples containing a mixture due to the complexity of the sequencing signals that could arise. Peak height ratios for two different bases cannot be used for reliable quantification of the two components because incorporation rates are not always even. Thus, the ratio of an A:G mixed base might be 50:50 at a particular position but when the complementary strand is sequenced a 70:30 or 80:20 ratio for the T:C bases might be observed because the polymerase incorporates the fluorescently-labeled ddTTP and ddCTP with different efficiencies than the A and G dideoxynucleotides.

If three or more sites within the 610 bases evaluated across HV1 and HV2 are found to possess multiple nucleotides at a position (i.e., sequence heteroplasmy), then the sample can usually be considered a mixture—either by contamination or from the original source material. Presently mixture interpretation is not attempted in forensic laboratories performing routine casework.

Some researchers are pursuing efforts to resolve mtDNA mixtures through cloning and sequencing the resulting HV1/HV2 regions from individual colonies (Bever et al. 2003, Walker et al. 2004). Theoretically, each individual colony produced during the process of cloning corresponds to the control region from a single individual or a single component of heteroplasmy. Interpretation of mixtures is being attempted with statistical analysis from multiple clones. A number of pitfalls exist with this approach including the possibility of overestimating the number of contributors due to the occurrence of heteroplasmic mitochondria. The number of contributors will be underestimated if individuals are closely related and members of the same mtDNA haplogroup (Walker et al. 2004). Denaturing HPLC has also been used for separating mtDNA amplicon mixtures (Danielson et al. 2007) as has a mismatch primer-induced restriction site analysis method (Szibor et al. 2003b).

Nuclear Pseudogenes

Segments of the mtGenome are present in the human nuclear genome (Collura & Stewart 1995, Zischler et al. 1995, Wallace et al. 1997). These "molecular fossils" or pseudogenes are rare events caused by migration and integration of a portion of the mtGenome into nuclear DNA and are sometimes referred to as "*numts*" (Lopez et al. 1994). Zischler et al. (1995) reported that human chromosome 11 carries a portion of the mtDNA control region that reflects an ancient genetic transposition from the mitochondrion to the nuclear genome. This element differs from typical modern mtDNA sequences by approximately 7.5% and has not created problems with regular forensic casework (Morgan et al. 1998).

Molecular fossils potentially complicate mtDNA human identity testing if they rather than the intended mtDNA target are amplified when a high number of PCR cycles are used to try to tease out mtDNA sequence information from a particularly difficult sample (Morgan et al. 1998). Under unique circumstances, nuclear pseudogenes could contaminate the true mtDNA sequence. Such was likely the case with the high degree of heteroplasmy reported on some hair samples amplified with a nested PCR approach involving a cumulative number of 60 cycles (Grzybowski 2000, Budowle et al. 2002a, Brandstätter & Parson 2003). However, with primer sets commonly used in forensic mtDNA testing and a direct PCR with fewer than 40 cycles, nuclear DNA sequences that are similar to mtDNA rarely cause a problem because their initial copy number is so much lower than that of mtDNA.

Possibilities of Recombination or Paternal Leakage

Several years ago three papers were published suggesting the possibility of recombination in mtDNA or inheritance from the paternal rather than the maternal line (Hagelberg et al. 1999, Eyre-Walker et al. 1999, Awadalla et al. 1999). Paternal inheritance of mtDNA has been reported in mice (Gyllensten et al. 1991). The Hagelberg and Eyre-Walker papers created quite a stir in the mtDNA forensic and population genetic circles (Macaulay et al. 1999, Parsons & Irwin 2000, Kivisild & Villems 2000, Jorde & Bamshad 2000, Kumar et al. 2000). Hagelberg and co-workers later retracted their paper due to problems with the data (Hagelberg et al. 2000). Since there really appears to be no direct evidence to support either recombination within or between mtGenomes, this issue has been laid to rest for most scientists in the field (see Ingman et al. 2000, Elson et al. 2001, Wiuf 2001, Herrnstadt et al. 2002).

However, there has been a single report published of the transmission of a paternal human mtDNA type in skeletal muscle (Schwartz & Vissing 2002). This paternal haplotype was not found in any other tissues though. Several additional studies with individuals having a similar muscle disease failed to find any evidence of paternal transmission of mtDNA (Johns 2003, Filosto et al. 2003, Taylor et al. 2003). With tens of thousands of mtDNA samples confirming the maternal inheritance pattern established over three decades ago (Giles et al. 1980), it is safe to conclude that the central dogma of maternal inheritance for mtDNA is sound.

Size of mtDNA Population Database and the Quality of Information

There are now population databases with thousands of mtDNA profiles in them. The availability of population data for the HV1/HV2 regions that are sequenced in forensic mtDNA analysis will be discussed in more detail later in the chapter.

Most Common Types

One of the biggest weaknesses of mtDNA analysis is that some haplotypes are rather common in various population groups. For example, in the FBI mtDNA Population Database of 1655 Caucasians there are 131 individuals who match at 263G, 315.1C and 264 additional profiles that have only a single difference. Thus, 395 out of 1655 (23.9%) of the Caucasian database would not be able to be excluded if a sample was observed with this common mtDNA type!

However, additional sequence information from polymorphic sites around the entire mtGenome have been characterized to help better resolve many of these most common types (Parsons & Coble 2001, Coble et al. 2004). Using this information, assays have been developed to help subdivide several of the most common Caucasian, African American, and Hispanic mtDNA types (Parsons 2006).

LABORATORIES PERFORMING mtDNA TESTING

The first efforts in mtDNA sequence analysis with a forensic applications focus were performed by the Forensic Science Service in England (Sullivan et al. 1991, Hopgood et al. 1992, Sullivan et al. 1992) although the FBI Laboratory had thought about its use in the late 1980s (Budowle et al. 1990). Today there are a number of laboratories internationally that perform mtDNA testing. One of the most widely respected is Walther Parson's lab at the University of Innsbruck in Austria. The EMPOP database described later in this chapter was created and is maintained by this group (Parson & Dür 2007). Within the United States, the Armed Forces DNA Identification Laboratory and the FBI Laboratory have led the efforts in mtDNA analysis but in slightly different arenas.

The Armed Forces DNA Identification Laboratory (AFDIL) is located in Rockville, Maryland and is charged with identifying the remains of military personnel (Holland et al. 1993). Bones recovered from Vietnam, Korea, and World War II operations have been successfully analyzed with mtDNA (Holland et al. 1995, Holland & Parsons 1999). AFDIL also aids mass disaster victim identification programs including those necessitated by U.S. airline crashes (see Chapter 9) and has helped solve historical puzzles such as identifying remains from the Tomb of the Unknown Soldier (Holland & Parsons 1999) and the Romanov family (Ivanov et al. 1996, Coble et al. 2009).

The FBI Laboratory focuses on the use of forensic evidence including mtDNA in criminal investigations. Until they were further subdivided in 2009, two DNA units existed within the FBI Laboratory: DNA Unit I, which focused exclusively on nuclear DNA, and DNA Unit II, which performed mtDNA analysis and aided missing persons investigations.

The FBI Laboratory first explored the feasibility of using mtDNA in human identity applications in the late 1980s (Budowle et al. 1990) and aggressively began researching analysis methods in 1992. The FBI Laboratory DNA Unit II, now called the Mitochondrial DNA Unit, has conducted mitochondrial DNA casework since June 1996. Their first case involving court testimony came in August 1996 with the State of Tennessee versus Paul William Ware, which involved mtDNA analysis of a single pubic hair found in the throat of a young victim that matched the defendant who was subsequently convicted (Marchi & Pasacreta 1997). Much of the mtDNA evidence processed by the FBI involves shed hairs to aid criminal and counterterrorism investigations.

In 2005, four regional FBI-funded mtDNA laboratories became operational to conduct mtDNA casework as an extension of the FBI's own operations. The four original regional mtDNA labs were the Arizona Department of Public Safety (Phoenix, Arizona), the Connecticut State Police (Meriden, Connecticut), the Minnesota Bureau of Criminal Apprehension (St. Paul, Minnesota), and the New Jersey State Police (Trenton, New Jersey). As of early 2011, Arizona, Minnesota, and New Jersey are the regional FBI mtDNA labs. Each of these satellite laboratories was originally designed to be able to analyze approximately 120 cases per year. Taken collectively, the goal of creating these regional mtDNA laboratories was to double the FBI's capacity to provide mtDNA analysis for the criminal justice system.

Several private laboratories in the United States have validated mtDNA procedures and offer mtDNA testing for a fee. These laboratories include Mitotyping Technologies, LLC (State College, Pennsylvania), Bode Technology Group (Lorton, Virginia), Orchid Cellmark (Dallas, Texas), and Laboratory Corporation of America (Research Triangle Park, North Carolina). These laboratories typically charge around $2000 per sample for mtDNA testing in order to sequence the 610 nucleotides in HV1 and HV2. The University of North Texas Center for Human Identification (Ft. Worth, Texas) is funded by the National Institute of Justice to perform mtDNA sequence analysis in aiding missing persons work (see Chapter 9).

Mitotyping Technologies reported processing 105 cases between February 1999 and February 2001 (Melton & Nelson 2001). These cases involved 199 questioned items of which 130 were hairs. A total of 137 known reference samples were also processed including 111 that were in the form of blood. Only 17 of their 199 questioned samples failed to yield any mtDNA amplification products. Length heteroplasmy was observed 15 times in the HV1 C-stretch region and 77 times in the HV2 C-stretch region with 17 samples having both HV1 and HV2 length heteroplasmy. Sequence site heteroplasmy was reported 19 times mostly at positions 16093 but also at nucleotide positions 16166, 16286, 72, 152, 189, 207, and 279. In 57 out of 105 cases (54.3%), the known reference sample could not be excluded as donor of a biological sample.

Mitotyping has also published an evaluation of their success with 691 casework hair samples (Melton et al. 2005) and 116 casework skeletal remains (Nelson & Melton 2007).

SCREENING ASSAYS FOR mtDNA TYPING

Due to the effort both in terms of time and labor required to obtain full sequence information from mtDNA sequencing, screening approaches and rapid low-resolution typing assays can and have been used to eliminate the need for full analysis of samples that can be easily excluded from one another. Many times physical screening methods can put samples into context without having to indiscriminately perform mtDNA sequencing on all samples. For example, microscopic examinations of hair can help eliminate as many questioned hairs as possible leaving the mtDNA laboratory to concentrate their efforts on only key hairs (Houck & Budowle 2002). Likewise anthropological evaluations of bones or teeth can be important first screens prior to making the effort to analyze the mtDNA sequence (see Edson et al. 2004).

With the expense and effort required to obtain full mtDNA sequences across HV1 and HV2, the ability to rapidly screen out samples that do not match can be advantageous to overworked, understaffed, and poorly funded crime laboratories. Several assays have been developed and even validated for use in screening forensic casework (Table 14.5).

SSO Probes and Linear Array Typing Assays

One of the most widely used screening assays for assessing mtDNA variation used to date are the sequence-specific oligonucleotide (SSO) probes originally designed by Mark Stoneking and colleagues in 1991. Rather than sequencing the entire HV1 and HV2 regions, the most polymorphic sites are examined through hybridization of PCR products to oligonucleotide probes designed to anneal to different variants. The original paper describes 23 probes across 9 regions that permit evaluation of variation at 14 different nucleotide positions (Stoneking et al. 1991). The sites that are probed include 16126, 16129, 16217, 16223, 16304, 16311, 16362, 73, 146, 152, 195, 199, 247, and 309.1. A number of population studies have been conducted with these SSO probes including an examination of 2282 individuals from North America (Melton et al. 2001).

The original SSO probe assay required that the PCR products be attached through UV cross-linking to a nylon membrane. Then each radioactively labeled probe was individually hybridized at different temperatures and finally exposed to autoradiographic film for several hours (Stoneking et al. 1991). Roche Molecular Systems (Alameda, CA) has converted the SSO probe assay into a more convenient format involving colorimetric detection (e.g., Gabriel et al. 2001b). In a "reverse dot blot" format, the SSO probes are attached to the nylon membrane in a linear array of spatially resolved lines of probes. Biotin-labeled PCR

TABLE 14.5 Methods for Screening mtDNA Variation (See Butler & Levin 1998; Budowle et al. 2004).

Technique	Description	Reference
Sequence-specific oligonucleotide (SSO) dot blot assay	23 SSO probes testing 14 sites within nine regions from HV1 and HV2; 274 mtDNA types observed among 525 individuals from five ethnic groups.	Stoneking et al. (1991); Melton et al. (2001)
Mini-sequencing	Single base primer extension with fluorescent ddNTPs and poly(T)-tailed primers to yield different electrophoretic mobilities; 10 substitution and two length polymorphisms measured in the control region; 65 haplotypes observed from 152 British Caucasian samples.	Tully et al. (1996); Morley et al. (1999)
Single-strand conformational (SSCP)	Differences in DNA secondary structure are detected on a native polyacrylamide gel; 25 mtDNA types observed polymorphism among 45 Spanish individuals tested.	Alonso et al. (1996)
Low-stringency single- specific-primer PCR (LSSP-PCR)	Following regular PCR, a single primer and a low annealing temperature are used to generate a "signature" pattern; for 30 unrelated individuals, all signature patterns were different across the control region (1024 bp).	Barreto et al. (1996)
PCR-restriction fragment length polymorphism (PCR-RFLP)	A 199 bp region of HV1 is digested with RsaI; 19 unrelated mother-child pairs were examined with an 8% probability of a random match.	Pushnova et al. (1994); Butler et al. (1998a)
Denaturing gradient gel electrophoresis (DGGE)	Two DNA samples are mixed and run on a denaturing gradient gel; heteroduplexes, which travel more slowly through the gel, may be separated from the homoduplexes; samples that differ at a single location have been resolved.	Steighner et al. (1999); Tully et al. (2000)
Affymetrix high-density DNA chip hybridization array	135,000 probes complementary to the entire mtGenome are contained on a microchip for parallel processing through hybridization.	Chee et al. (1996)
Pyrosequencing	Sequencing by synthesis over ~50 nucleotides per reaction through an enzyme cascade that produces visible light; a total of 4 HV1, 4 HV2, and 11 coding region reactions were run.	Andreasson et al. (2002)
SNaPshot (mini-sequencing)	Allele-specific primer extension with 11 coding region SNPs combined into a single multiplex amplification and detection assay.	Vallone et al. (2004)
Denaturing HPLC	HV1 and HV2 PCR products for a known and an unknown sample source are generated and then mixed together; samples that differ from one another by at least one nucleotide will form a heteroduplex on the HPLC.	LaBerge et al. (2003)
Luminex 100 liquid bead array	30 SNPs within HV1 and HV2 are examined by allele-specific hybridization with SSO probes attached to different colored beads that are separated using flow cytometry.	Budowle et al. (2004)
LINEAR ARRAYs	Reverse dot blot hybridization with lines instead of dots using 18 SNPs in the same general probe regions as Stoneking et al. (1991).	Gabriel et al. (2003)

products are washed over nylon membrane strips containing immobilized SSO probes in the linear array and hybridized under uniform conditions. A streptavidin-horseradish peroxidase enzyme conjugate coupled with 3,3′,5,5′-tetramethyl-benzidine creates a light-blue precipitate using the same chemistry described for HLA-DQα reverse dot blot SSO probes (Saiki et al. 1989).

Figure 14.9 illustrates the probe layout for the LINEAR ARRAY Mitochondrial DNA HVI/HVII Region-Sequence Typing Kit now available from Roche Applied Sciences (Indianapolis, IN). The final linear array format examines 18 SNPs with 33 SSO probes present on 31 different lines. The Roche SSO probe sites are shown in Figure 14.4.

Two hypothetical results are illustrated in Figure 14.9 for non-matching K and Q samples. The K sample reported type of 1-1-1-1-1-1-1-1-1-1 is equivalent to the Cambridge Reference Sequence (see Figure 14.4). The Q sample possesses a different pattern and therefore can be excluded from the K sample. Notice that probe IE within HVI did not produce a signal from any of the three possible probes. This result is referred to as a "blank" and occurs due to additional polymorphisms that are present in close proximity to the polymorphic sites designed for detection in the assay. These additional polymorphisms disrupt hybridization of the PCR product and therefore no signal is seen for any of the probes in HVIE. Likewise weak (w) signals such as the "w1" type are caused by mismatches between the PCR products and the SSO probes attached on the nylon strip.

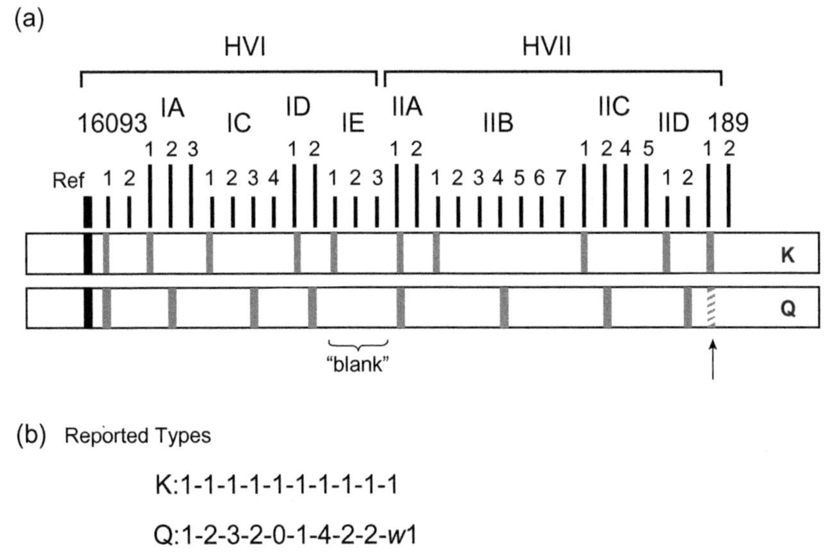

FIGURE 14.9 (a) Results schematically displayed of a known (K) reference and a question (Q) sample that do not match one another using the Roche LINEAR ARRAY mtDNA HVI/HVII Region-Sequence Typing Strips. (b) Types are reported as a string of numbers representing the LINEAR ARRAY probe results. Failure of the PCR product to bind to a probe region (e.g., HVIE in sample Q) is referred to as a "blank," is reported as a zero in the string of numbers, and is due to polymorphisms in the sample near the probe site that disrupt hybridization. Weak signals such as indicated by the arrow for 189 in sample Q are also due to a closely spaced polymorphism that disrupts full hybridization of the PCR product to the sequence-specific probe present on the LINEAR ARRAY.

Results from screening assays, such as the LINEAR ARRAY system described above, can be considered presumptive tests. They are useful in eliminating samples that can be excluded from one another. However, full HV1/HV2 sequencing would normally be performed to confirm any matches to see if differences outside of the SSO probe regions exist.

POPULATION DATABASES

Population databases play an important role in estimating the expected frequency of mtDNA haplotypes that are observed in casework when a suspect's mtDNA sequence matches that of an evidentiary sample. A great deal of effort has been expended to gather information from thousands of maternally unrelated individuals in various population groups around the world. Having high-quality information in the database is also important in order to make a reliable estimate of the frequency for a random match.

mtDNA typing results on samples from unknown sources are most useful if they are evaluated in comparison to a known sample or a database. Databases of more than 1000 unrelated individuals now exist and have been compiled from multiple population groups (Handt et al. 1998, Budowle et al. 1999, Attimonelli et al. 2000, Wittig et al. 2000, Röhl et al. 2001, Monson et al. 2002). The size of the database is important because without recombination between mtDNA molecules, an mtDNA sequence is treated as a single locus (i.e., haplotype instead of genotype).

The largest compiled database described to date contains HV1 and HV2 sequences from 14,138 individuals (Röhl et al. 2001). This information was collated from 103 mtDNA publications prior to January 2000, 13 data sets published in 2000 and 2001, and two unpublished data sets. Authors of the original publications were contacted in an effort to confirm and correct sequence errors, eliminate duplications, and harmonize nomenclatures, but not every query was answered. Of the 116 publications, 90 required some kind of change to correct errors or adjust nomenclature illustrating the challenge of compiling accurate mtDNA sequence databases. The authors conclude that their annotated database probably still contains errors and that while it can be used for qualitative identification of relevant reference populations for a given mtDNA type, the determination of a "legally defensible" frequency estimate of an mtDNA type within a population should be performed with higher-quality data yet to be produced (Röhl et al. 2001).

FBI mtDNA Database

The FBI has compiled the mtDNA Population Database also known as CODIS^{mt} (Monson et al. 2002) for the purpose of being able to determine a legally defensible frequency estimate. The CODIS^{mt} database has a forensic and a published literature component to it (Miller & Budowle 2001) in order to separate data obtained from laboratories following validated forensic protocols and academic research laboratories where data quality is not reviewed as carefully prior to publication.

The forensic database contains 4839 mtDNA profiles from 14 different populations (Table 14.6). These samples have been sequenced and the electropherograms carefully reviewed across positions 16024 to 16365 for HV1 and positions 73 to 340 for HV2.

TABLE 14.6 Summary of High Quality Forensic Profiles Present in the FBI Laboratory's mtDNA Population Database When It Was Released to the Public in April 2002 (Monson et al. 2002).

Population Name	Number of Profiles	Data Analysis on Group
African-American	1148	Budowle et al. (1999)
Apache	180	Budowle et al. (2002b)
Caucasian	1655	Budowle et al. (1999), Allard et al. (2002)
China/Taiwan	356	Allard et al. (2004)
Egypt	48	
Guam	87	Allard et al. (2004)
Hispanic	686	Budowle et al. (1999)
India	19	
Japan	163	Budowle et al. (1999)
Korea	182	Allard et al. (2004)
Navajo	146	Budowle et al. (2002b)
Pakistan	8	
Sierra Leone	109	Budowle et al. (1999)
Thailand	52	Allard et al. (2004)
Total	**4839**	

An additional 6106 published profiles have been compiled from the literature with annotated population information (Miller et al. 1996, Miller & Budowle 2001). For classification of mtDNA profiles, a standard 14-character nucleotide sequence identifier was assigned to each profile where the first three characters represent the country of origin, the second three characters the group or ethnic affiliation, and the final six characters are sequential acquisition numbers (Miller & Budowle 2001, Monson et al. 2002).

Both of these databases were publicly released in April 2002 in a Microsoft Access format and can be downloaded from the FBI website along with the "MitoSearch" analysis tool (Monson et al. 2002). MitoSearch can examine the population data sets listed in Table 14.6 for specific mtDNA sequences, which are entered based on differences from the Cambridge Reference Sequence. The software returns the number of times that the specified profile appears in each population group. For example, the mtDNA type 16129A, 263G, 309del, 315.1C occurs twice in 1148 African-American profiles, twice in 1655 Caucasian profiles, and not at all in 686 Hispanic profiles.

EMPOP

The European forensic mtDNA sequencing community has been actively engaged for a number of years in developing new high-quality population databases for forensic and human identity testing applications. A European DNA Profiling Group mitochondrial DNA population database project (EMPOP) has gathered thousands of mtDNA sequences and constructed a high-quality mtDNA database that can be accessed at http://www.empop.org (Parson & Dür 2007). As of December 2010, there were 12,247 "forensic" (high-quality) data that could be searched online. A majority of the current samples are classified as West Eurasian (Caucasian).

mtDNAmanager

A Korean group from Yonsei University (Seoul, Korea) has created an online mtDNA searchable population database called mtDNAmanager (Lee et al. 2008). As of December 2010, this database contains 9294 mtDNA control region sequences grouped into five subsets: African (1496), West Eurasian (3673), East Asian (2326), Oceanian (114), and Admixed (1685). Many of these sequences are shared among the FBI and EMPOP databases and thus are not from "unique" haplotypes from unrelated individuals. mtDNAmanager can be accessed at http://mtmanager.yonsei.ac.kr/.

Issues with Sequence Quality

Concerns with mtDNA database sequence quality and the impact that it might have on accurately estimating frequency estimates for random matches have been raised by Peter Forster and Hans Bandelt (Röhl et al. 2001, Bandelt et al. 2001, Bandelt et al. 2002, Forster 2003, Salas et al. 2005). Using a statistical analysis clustering approach called phylogenetics, the similarities and differences between multiple and closely related DNA sequences (i.e., from the same region) can be compared systematically (see Wilson & Allard 2004). Sequence alignments are created and compared to identify samples that are extremely different. Extreme or unusual differences may be an indication that the sample was contaminated or the sequence data was incorrectly recorded. For example, a laboratory may put HV1 data for a sample with another sample's HV2 sequence and thereby create an artificial recombinant or accidental composite sequence. Thus phylogenetic analyses can play a role in verifying sequence quality (Bandelt et al. 2001, Wilson & Allard 2004).

Errors that creep into mitochondrial DNA population databases can be segregated into four different classes (Parson et al. 2004): (1) mistakes in the course of transcription of the results (i.e., clerical errors); (2) sample mix-up (e.g., putting data from HV1 on one sample together with data from HV2 on another sample); (3) contamination; and (4) use of different nomenclatures.

From a pilot collaborative study of 21 laboratories, 14 non-concordant haplotypes (16 individual errors) were observed out of a total of 150 submitted samples/haplotypes representing the examination of approximately 150,000 nucleotides (Parson et al. 2004). Measures are being put into place for complete electronic transfer of data and base calling to avoid the primary problem of clerical errors when transferring information from raw sequence data to final report. In the future, mtDNA databases may require retention of raw data for population samples in order to more easily verify authenticity of results should an inquiry into the origin of sequence results be needed at a later date (Parson et al. 2004). Search strategies using the complete query sequence will also likely be implemented (Röck et al. 2011).

Whole Mitochondrial Genome Sequencing

The first description of a methodology for sequencing the entire mtGenome was by Deborah Nickerson's group at the University of Washington (Rieder et al. 1998). They used 24 pairs of primers to amplify PCR products ranging in size from 765bp to 1162bp. These primer pairs provide on average almost 200 bases of overlap between the various PCR products spanning the mtGenome. Ingman et al. (2000) used the Nickerson laboratory sequencing strategy to launch the era of mitochondrial population genomics when they sequenced 53 mtGenomes from diverse world population groups. Max Ingman maintains an mtGenome polymorphism database at http://www.genpat.uu.se/mtDB/.

In the past few years, a number of other methodologies have appeared in the literature for sequencing entire mtGenomes (Table 14.7). Regardless of the sequencing strategy used, the biggest challenge in conducting this work remains efforts to reduce and eliminate errors in sequence review (see Herrnstadt et al. 2003). Fortunately, the reference sequence (rCRS) was updated prior to the explosion of mtGenome information that began with Ingman et al. (2000).

Resolving "Most Common Types"

One of the major challenges of mtDNA typing lies in the fact that many sequences fall into common groupings termed "most common types." For example, a review of the HV1/HV2 type distribution in 1655 Caucasians of U.S. and European descent (Monson et al. 2002)

TABLE 14.7 Summary of Published mtGenome DNA Sequencing Efforts from December 2000 to February 2004 Representing Almost 1000 Complete mtGenomes. As of December 2010, over 8000 mtGenomes Are Available on GenBank (See http://mitomap.org/bin/view.pl/MITOMAP/MitoSeqs). See Also http://www.phylotree.org/mtDNA_seqs.htm.

Population	Number Sequenced	Reference (GenBank Accessions)	Approach Taken
Samples of diverse worldwide origin	53	Ingman et al. (2000) AF346963–AF347015	24 PCR reactions, 48 sequencing reactions
Samples of diverse worldwide origin	33	Maca-Meyer et al. (2001) AF381981–AF382013	32 PCR reactions, 64 sequencing reactions
African, Asian, European origin	560 (coding region only)	Herrnstadt et al. (2002) Sequences available at www.mitokor.com	68 PCR reactions, 136 sequencing reactions
East Asian lineages	48	Kong et al. (2003) AY255133–AY255180	15 PCR reactions, 47 sequencing reactions
Australian and New Guinean Aborigines and Polynesians	52	Ingman & Gyllensten (2003) AY289051–AY289102	24 PCR reactions, 48 sequencing reactions
Most common Caucasian types	241	Coble et al. (2004) AY495090–AY495330	12 PCR reactions, 95 sequencing reactions

found that the most common mtDNA type, which matches the rCRS, occurred 7.1% of the time (Coble et al. 2004). Furthermore, it was observed that only 18 mtDNA types account for 20.8% of the total Caucasian data set (Coble et al. 2004). The presence of these most common types suggests that one out of every five times a mtDNA sequence analysis is performed on a Caucasian individual, the result would be expected to match numerous other individuals in a population database. While the same analysis revealed that approximately 50% of the 1655 individuals present in the European Caucasian population are "unique in the databasem," having a sample that falls into one of these most common types can present a disappointing statistic after all of the hard work taken to generate the full mtDNA HV1/HV2 sequence.

There has been an extensive search for distinguishing single nucleotide polymorphisms in samples possessing the most common Caucasian types (Parsons & Coble 2001). A total of 241 complete mtGenomes were sequenced from the 18 common European Caucasian HV1/HV2 types mentioned above (Coble 2004, Coble et al. 2004). The samples typed come from mtDNA haplogroups H, J, T, V, and K (see the next section for more discussion on haplogroups).

Examination of whole mtGenome sequence information expanded the 18 most common Caucasian HV1/HV2 types to 209 resolvable haplotypes (Coble et al. 2004). This almost 12-fold improvement in resolving power for these common HV1/HV2 types required about 27 times the amount of DNA sequencing—from 610 bases for just HV1/HV2 alone to ≈16,569 for the entire mtGenome. Obviously, this approach is not a cost effective one. Furthermore, even with the expansion in sequence information, 32 of the 241 individuals matched one or more individuals across the entire mtGenome.

From their extensive sequencing information, Coble et al. (2004) selected a battery of SNP markers to aid in resolving the most common Caucasian mtDNA HV1/HV2 types without the costly and time-consuming venture of having to sequence the entire mtGenome. A total of 59 informative SNPs were placed into eight multiplex panels (Coble et al. 2004). The first panel provides maximum resolution of the most common Caucasian HV1/HV2 mtDNA type (i.e., that matching rCRS) and examines the following nucleotides spanning the mtGenome: 477, 3010, 4580, 4793, 5004, 7028, 7202, 10211, 12858, 14470, and 16519. Vallone et al. (2004) combined these 11 SNP sites into a multiplex allele-specific primer extension or "SNaPshot" assay (see Chapter 12) that can reliably type a sample that contains only a few hundred copies of mtDNA.

Defining mtDNA Haplogroups

Over the course of typing mtDNA samples from various populations, researchers have observed that individuals often cluster into haplogroups that can be defined by particular polymorphic nucleotides (see Wallace et al. 1999, Ruiz-Pesini et al. 2004). These haplogroups were originally defined in the late 1980s and 1990s by grouping samples possessing the same or similar patterns when subjected to a series of restriction enzymes that were used to separate various mtDNA types from diverse populations around the world (Table 14.8). Mitochondrial DNA haplogroups have now been correlated to HV1/HV2 polymorphisms as well as the entire mtGenome variation. Haplogroups A, B, C, D, E, F, G, and M

TABLE 14.8 Major Mitochondrial Haplogroups and the Specific Polymorphisms in the Coding Region or Control Region That Define Them (See Finnila et al. 2001, Herrnstadt et al. 2002, Brandstatter et al. 2003, Kong et al. 2003, Allard et al. 2004, Quintans et al. 2004). Note That Not All Haplogroups, which Have Been Defined in the Literature, Are Listed Here. For Updated Haplogroup Information, See van Oven & Kayser (2009) and http://mitomap.org/bin/view.pl/MITOMAP/HaplogroupMarkers.

Haplogroup (Population)	Coding Region Polymorphisms	Control Region Polymorphisms (*not including 263G, 315.1C)
A (Asian)	663G	16233T, 16290T, 16319A, 235G
B (Asian)	9bp deletion, 16159C	16217C, 16189C
C (Asian)	13263G	16233T, 16298C, 16327T
D (Asian)	2092T, 5178A, 8414T	16362C
H (Caucasian)	7028C, 14766C	73A and lack of CRS differences*
H1 (Caucasian)	3010A	73A and lack of CRS differences*
H2 (Caucasian)	1438A, 4769A	73A and lack of CRS differences*
H3 (Caucasian)	6776C	73A and lack of CRS differences*
H4 (Caucasian)	3992T	73A and lack of CRS differences*
H5 (Caucasian)	4336C	73A and lack of CRS differences*
H6 (Caucasian)	3915A	73A and lack of CRS differences*
H7 (Caucasian)	4793G	73A and lack of CRS differences*
I (Caucasian)	1719A, 8251A, 10238C	16223T, 199C, 204C, 250C
J (Caucasian)	4216C, 12612G, 13708A	16069T, 16126C, 295T
J1 (Caucasian)	3010A	462T
J2 (Caucasian)	7476T, 15257A	195C
K (Caucasian)	12372A, 14798C	16224C, 16311C
L1 (African)	2758A, 3594T, 10810C	16187T, 16189C, 16223T, 16278T, 16311C
L2 (African)	3594T	16223T, 16278T
L3 (African)	3594C	16223T
M (Asian)	10400T, 10873C	16223T, 16298C
T (Caucasian)	709A, 1888A, 4917G, 10463C, 13368A, 14905A, 15607G, 15928A, 8697A	16126C, 16294T
U5 (Caucasian)	3197C	16270T
V (Caucasian)	4580A, 15904T	16298C, 72C
W (Caucasian)	709A, 1243C, 8251A, 8697G, 8994A	16223T, 189G, 195C, 204C, 207A
X (Caucasian)	1719A, 6221C, 8251G, 14470C	16189C, 16223T, 16278T, 195C

are typically associated with Asians while most Native Americans fall into haplogroups A, B, C, and D. Haplogroups L0, L1, L2, and L3 are African, and haplogroups H, I, J, K, T, U, V, W, and X are typically associated with European populations (Wallace et al. 1999).

Along the same lines as the multiplex SNP detection assay described above for resolving samples containing the most common HV1/HV2 types, Brandstätter et al. (2003) described a multiplex SNP system for categorizing European Caucasian haplogroups. This approach involves the analysis of 16 coding region SNPs to aid assignment of individual samples into one of the nine major European Caucasian mtDNA haplogroups listed above. For example, the presence of a cytosine at position 7028 indicates that the sample can be grouped into haplogroup H as opposed to the other groups whose individuals possess a thymine at 7028.

Another SNP typing assay was recently reported to examine 17 coding region SNPs in a single multiplexed detection assay (Quintans et al. 2004). A SNaPshot reaction is used to probe the following mtDNA nucleotide positions: 3010, 3915, 3992, 4216, 4336, 4529, 4580, 4769, 4793, 6776, 7028, 10398, 10400, 10873, 12308, 12705, and 14766. This assay was capable of breaking 266 samples into 20 different mtDNA haplogroup designations and aided in resolving some of the most common type (i.e., 263G, 315.1C) haplogroup H samples from one another.

Forensic population databases have been analyzed in terms of haplogroup information to aid in quality control of samples contained within a population group (Allard et al. 2002, Budowle et al. 2003, Allard et al. 2004).

Genetic Genealogy with mtDNA

Scientists have been using DNA for several decades to try to understand human migration patterns (Relethford 2001, Relethford 2003). Samples have been gathered from a number of individuals around the world often from isolated populations such as the Australian aborigines. The uniparental inheritance of mtDNA and Y-chromosome markers (see Chapter 13) makes it easier to trace ancestral lineages through multiple generations since the shuffling effects of recombination that promotes the diversity of autosomal DNA profiles are not present in haploid systems. The ability to successfully obtain mtDNA results from ancient bones is also useful, as has been demonstrated with the recovery of HV1 and HV2 sequences from Neanderthal remains that are thousands of years old (Krings et al. 1997).

While the same DNA markers are being used in these types of studies as in forensic DNA typing, the sample groups are often analyzed differently since direct comparisons cannot usually be made. Rather the DNA information obtained is extrapolated over many generations between the various populations tested. There is not a one-to-one unique match being made between a "suspect" and "evidence." Instead scientists are often guessing at what genetic signatures existed in the past based on various assumptions—with a bit of "storytelling" mixed in (see Goldstein & Chikhi 2002). However, large amounts of data are being collected in an attempt to better understand our heritage and travels as a human species (e.g., Helgason et al. 2003). Forensic DNA testing, disease diagnostics and anthropological and genealogical research efforts will all continue to benefit from the growth and developments in mitochondrial DNA analysis.

READING LIST AND INTERNET RESOURCES

General Information

Bandelt, H.-J., Richards, M., & Macaulay, V. (Eds.), (2006). *Human mitochondrial DNA and the evolution of homo sapiens.* Berlin-Heidelberg: Springer-Verlag Press.

Butler, J. M., & Levin, B. C. (1998). Forensic applications of mitochondrial DNA. *Trends in Biotechnology, 16,* 158–162.

Butler, J. M., & Coble, M. D. (2006). *Y-Chromosome and mitochondrial DNA workshop.* Available at <http://www.cstl.nist.gov/biotech/strbase/YmtDNAworkshop.htm>.

Fisher, C. L. (2000). Mitochondrial DNA: Today and tomorrow. In *Proceedings of the 11th international symposium on human identification.* Available at <http://www.promega.com/geneticidproc/ussymp11proc/content/fisher.pdf>.

Fourney, R. M. (1998). Mitochondrial DNA and forensic analysis: A primer for law enforcement. *Canadian Society of Forensic Sciences Journal, 31,* 45–53.

Legros, F., et al. (2004). Organization and dynamics of human mitochondrial DNA. *Journal of Cell Science, 117,* 2653–2662.

Wong, L. J., & Boles, R. G. (2005). Mitochondrial DNA analysis in clinical laboratory diagnostics. *Clinica Chimica Acta, 354,* 1–20.

Characteristics of mtDNA

Anderson, S., et al. (1981). Sequence and organization of the human mitochondrial genome. *Nature, 290,* 457–465.

Andrews, R. M., et al. (1999). Reanalysis and revision of the Cambridge Reference Sequence for human mitochondrial DNA. *Nature Genetics, 23,* 147.

Bodenteich, A., et al. (1992). Dinucleotide repeat in the human mitochondrial D-loop. *Human Molecular Genetics, 1,* 140.

Brown, W. M., et al. (1979). Rapid evolution of animal mitochondrial DNA. *Proceedings of the National Academy of Science of the United States of America, 76,* 1967–1971.

Chen, X. J., & Butow, R. A. (2005). The organization and inheritance of the mitochondrial genome. *Nature Reviews Genetics, 6,* 815–825.

Foran, D. R. (2006). Relative degradation of nuclear and mitochondrial DNA: An experimental approach. *Journal of Forensic Sciences, 51,* 766–770.

Robin, E. D., & Wong, R. (1988). Mitochondrial DNA molecules and virtual number of mitochondria per cell in mammalian cells. *Journal of Cellular Physiology, 136,* 507–513.

Satoh, M., & Kuroiwa, T. (1991). Organization of multiple nucleoids and DNA molecules in mitochondria of a human cell. *Experimental Cell Research, 196,* 137–140.

Scheffler, I. E. (1999). *Mitochondria.* New York: Wiley-Liss.

Szibor, R., et al. (1997). Mitochondrial D-loop 3′ (CA)n repeat polymorphism: Optimization of analysis and population data. *Electrophoresis, 18,* 2857–2860.

Applications

Coble, M. D., et al. (2009). Mystery solved: The identification of the two missing Romanov children using DNA analysis. *PLoS ONE, 4,* e4838.

Gill, P., et al. (1994). Identification of the remains of the Romano family by DNA analysis. *Nature Genetics, 6,* 130–135.

Gill, P., et al. (1995). Establishing the identity of Anna Anderson Manahan. *Nature Genetics, 9,* 9–10. (Erratum in: *Nature Genetics, 9,* 218)

Ivanov, P. L., et al. (1996). Mitochondrial DNA sequence heteroplasmy in the Grand Duke of Russia Georgij Romanov establishes the authenticity of the remains of Tsar Nicholas II. *Nature Genetics, 12,* 417–420.

Just, R. S., et al. (2011). Titanic's unknown child: the critical role of the mitochondrial DNA coding region in a re-identification effort. *Forensic Science International: Genetics, 5,* 231–235.

Krings, M., et al. (1997). Neandertal DNA sequences and the origin of modern humans. *Cell, 90,* 19–30.

Stone, A. C., et al. (2001). Mitochondrial DNA analysis of the presumptive remains of Jesse James. *Journal of Forensic Sciences, 46,* 173–176.

Wallace, D. C., et al. (1999). Mitochondrial DNA variation in human evolution and disease. *Gene, 238,* 211–230.

Measuring mtDNA Variation

Ingman, M., et al. (2000). Mitochondrial genome variation and the origin of modern humans. *Nature, 408*, 708–713.

Richards, M., & Macaulay, V. (2001). The mitochondrial gene tree comes of age. *American Journal of Human Genetics, 68*, 1315–1320.

Ruiz-Pesini, E., et al. (2004). Effects of purifying and adaptive selection on regional variation in human mtDNA. *Science, 303*, 223–226.

Torroni, A., et al. (1996). Classification of European mtDNAs from an analysis of three European populations. *Genetics, 144*, 1835–1850.

Mitochondrial DNA Sequencing in Forensic Casework

Forensic Casework

Budowle, B., et al. (1990). Mitochondrial DNA: a possible genetic material suitable for forensic analysis. In H. C. Lee & R. E. Gaensslen (Eds.), *Advances in Forensic Sciences* (pp. 76–97). Chicago: Year Book Medical Publishers.

Holland, M. M., et al. (1993). Mitochondrial DNA sequence analysis of human skeletal remains: Identification of remains from the Vietnam War. *Journal of Forensic Sciences, 38*, 542–553.

Jarman, P. G., et al. (2009). Mitochondrial DNA validation in a state laboratory. *Journal of Forensic Sciences, 54*, 95–102.

Marchi, E., & Pasacreta, R. J. (1997). Capillary electrophoresis in court: The landmark decision of the People of Tennessee versus Ware. *Journal of Capillary Electrophoresis, 4*, 145–156.

Melton, T., & Nelson, K. (2001). Forensic mitochondrial DNA analysis: Two years of commercial casework experience in the United States. *Croatian Medical Journal, 42*, 298–303.

Mosquera-Miguel, A., et al. (2009). Testing the performance of mtSNP minisequencing in forensic samples. *Forensic Science International: Genetics, 3*, 261–264.

Reynolds, A. M., et al. (2005). Forensic casework analysis using the HVI/HVII mtDNA linear array assay. *Journal of Forensic Sciences, 50*, 548–554.

Sullivan, K. M., et al. (1992). Identification of human remains by amplification and automated sequencing of mitochondrial DNA. *International Journal of Legal Medicine, 105*, 83–86.

Steps Involved

Budowle, B., et al. (2003). Forensics and mitochondrial DNA: Applications, debates, and foundations. *Annual Reviews in Genomics and Human Genetics, 4*, 119–141.

Chong, M. D., et al. (2005). Optimization of a duplex amplification and sequencing strategy for the HVI/HVII regions of human mitochondrial DNA for forensic casework. *Forensic Science International, 154*, 137–148.

Hopgood, R., et al. (1992). Strategies for automated sequencing of human mitochondrial DNA directly from PCR products. *Biotechniques, 13*, 82–92.

Isenberg, A. R. (2004). Forensic mitochondrial DNA analysis. In R. Saferstein (Ed.), *Forensic science handbook* (Vol. II, pp. 297–327). Upper Saddle River, New Jersey: Pearson Prentice Hall.

Isenberg, A. R., & Moore, J. M. (1999). Mitochondrial DNA analysis at the FBI Laboratory. *Forensic Science Communications, 1*(2). Available at <http://www2.fbi.gov/hq/lab/fsc/backissu/july1999/dnalist.htm>.

Mabuchi, T., et al. (2007). Typing the 1.1 kb control region of human mitochondrial DNA in Japanese individuals. *Journal of Forensic Sciences, 52*, 355–363.

Sanger, F., et al. (1977). DNA sequencing with chain-terminating inhibitors. *Proceedings of the National Academy of Sciences of the United States of America, 74*, 5463–5467.

Sullivan, K. M., et al. (1991). Automated amplification and sequencing of human mitochondrial DNA. *Electrophoresis, 12*, 17–21.

Wilson, M. R., et al. (1995). Validation of mitochondrial DNA sequencing for forensic casework analysis. *International Journal of Legal Medicine, 108*, 68–74.

Bones & Hair

Allen, M., et al. (1998). Mitochondrial DNA sequencing of shed hairs and saliva on robbery caps: sensitivity and matching probabilities. *Journal of Forensic Sciences, 43*, 453–464.

Edson, S. M., et al. (2004). Naming the dead—confronting the realities of rapid identification of degraded skeletal remains. *Forensic Science Review, 16*, 63–90.
Giambernardi, T. A., et al. (1998). Bovine serum albumin reverses inhibition of RT-PCR by melanin. *Biotechniques, 25*, 564–566.
Hellmann, A., et al. (2001). STR typing of human telogen hairs—a new approach. *International Journal of Legal Medicine, 114*, 269–273.
Houck, M. M., & Budowle, B. (2002). Correlation of microscopic and mitochondrial DNA hair comparisons. *Journal of Forensic Sciences, 47*, 964–967.
Jehaes, E., et al. (1998). Evaluation of a decontamination protocol for hair shafts before mtDNA sequencing. *Forensic Science International, 94*, 65–71.
Lee, H. Y., et al. (2006). Differential distribution of human mitochondrial DNA in somatic tissues and hairs. *Annals of Human Genetics, 70*, 59–65.
Linch, C. A., et al. (2001). Human hair histogenesis for the mitochondrial DNA forensic scientist. *Journal of Forensic Sciences, 46*, 844–853.
Loreille, O., et al. (2007). High efficiency DNA extraction from bone by total demineralization. *Forensic Science International: Genetics, 1*, 191–195.
Melton, T., et al. (2005). Forensic mitochondrial DNA analysis of 691 casework hairs. *Journal of Forensic Sciences, 50*, 73–80.
Nelson, K., & Melton, T. (2007). Forensic mitochondrial DNA analysis of 116 casework skeletal samples. *Journal of Forensic Sciences, 52*, 557–561.
Pfeiffer, H., et al. (1999). Mitochondrial DNA in human hair shafts—existence of intra-individual differences? *International Journal of Legal Medicine, 112*, 172–175.
Pfeiffer, H., et al. (1999). Mitochondrial DNA typing from human axillary, pubic and head hair shafts – success rates and sequence comparisons. *International Journal of Legal Medicine, 112*, 287–290.
Wilson, M. R., et al. (1995). Extraction, PCR amplification and sequencing of mitochondrial DNA from human hair shafts. *Biotechniques, 18*, 662–669.
Yoshii, T., et al. (1992). Presence of a PCR-inhibitor in hairs. *Nihon Hoigaku Zasshi, 46*, 313–316.

mtDNA Quantitation

Alonso, A., et al. (2004). Real-time PCR designs to estimate nuclear and mitochondrial DNA copy number in forensic and ancient DNA studies. *Forensic Science International, 139*, 141–149.
Andréasson, H., et al. (2002). Real-time DNA quantification of nuclear and mitochondrial DNA in forensic analysis. *BioTechniques, 33*, 402–411.
Andréasson, H., et al. (2006). Nuclear and mitochondrial DNA quantification of various forensic materials. *Forensic Science International, 164*, 56–64.
Meissner, C., et al. (2000). Quantification of mitochondrial DNA in human blood cells using an automated detection system. *Forensic Science International, 113*, 109–112.
Niederstätter, H., et al. (2007). A modular real-time PCR concept for determining the quantity and quality of human nuclear and mitochondrial DNA. *Forensic Science International: Genetics, 1*, 29–34.
von Wurmb-Schwark, N., et al. (2002). Quantification of human mitochondrial DNA in a real time PCR. *Forensic Science International, 126*, 34–39.

PCR Amplification & Sequencing

Bini, C., et al. (2003). Different informativeness of the three hypervariable mitochondrial DNA regions in the population of Bologna (Italy). *Forensic Science International, 135*, 48–52.
Butler, J. M., et al. (1998). Rapid mitochondrial DNA typing using restriction enzyme digestion of polymerase chain reaction amplicons followed by capillary electrophoresis separation with laser-induced fluorescence detection. *Electrophoresis, 19*, 119–124.
Butler, J. M., et al. (1994). Quantitation of polymerase chain reaction products by capillary electrophoresis using laser fluorescence. *Journal of Chromatography B Biomedical Applications, 658*, 271–280.
Comas, D., et al. (1999). Analysis of mtDNA HVRII in several human populations using an immobilised SSO probe hybridization assay. *European Journal of Human Genetics, 7*, 459–468.

Dugan, K. A., et al. (2002). An improved method for post-PCR purification for mtDNA sequence analysis. *Journal of Forensic Sciences, 47*, 811–818.

Gabriel, M. N., et al. (2001). Improved mtDNA sequence analysis of forensic remains using a "mini-primer set" amplification strategy. *Journal of Forensic Sciences, 46*, 247–253.

Gabriel, M. N., et al. (2001). Population variation of human mitochondrial DNA hypervariable regions I and II in 105 Croatian individuals demonstrated by immobilized sequence-specific oligonucleotide probe analysis. *Croatian Medical Journal, 42*, 328–335.

Gabriel, M. N., et al. (2003). Identification of human remains by immobilized sequence-specific oligonucleotide probe analysis of mtDNA hypervariable regions I and II. *Croatian Medical Journal, 44*, 293–298.

Lee, L. G., et al. (1997). New energy transfer dyes for DNA sequencing. *Nucleic Acids Research, 25*, 2816–2822.

Lutz, S., et al. (2000). Is it possible to differentiate mtDNA by means of HVIII in samples that cannot be distinguished by sequencing the HVI and HVII regions? *Forensic Science International, 113*, 97–101.

Rasmussen, E. M., et al. (2002). Sequencing strategy of mitochondrial HV1 and HV2 DNA with length heteroplasmy. *Forensic Science International, 129*, 209–213.

Stewart, J. E., et al. (2003). Evaluation of a multicapillary electrophoresis instrument for mitochondrial DNA typing. *Journal of Forensic Sciences, 48*, 571–580.

Tully, G., et al. (1996). Rapid detection of mitochondrial sequence polymorphisms using multiplex solid-phase fluorescent minisequencing. *Genomics, 34*, 107–113.

Wilson, M. R. (1997). Update to: Extraction, PCR amplification and sequencing of mitochondrial DNA from human hair shafts. In U. Gyllensten & J. Ellingboe (Eds.), *The PCR technique: DNA sequencing II* (pp. 322–328). Natick, Massachusetts: Eaton Publishing.

Smaller Amplicons

Berger, C., & Parson, W. (2009). Mini-midi-mito: Adapting the amplification and sequencing strategy of mtDNA to the degradation state of crime scene samples. *Forensic Science International: Genetics, 3*, 149–153.

Eichmann, C., & Parson, W. (2008). "Mitominis" Multiplex PCR analysis of reduced size amplicons for compound sequence analysis of the entire mtDNA control region in highly degraded samples. *International Journal of Legal Medicine, 122*, 385–388.

Lee, H. Y., et al. (2008). A modified mini-primer set for analyzing mitochondrial DNA control region sequences from highly degraded forensic samples. *Biotechniques, 44*, 555–558.

von Wurmb-Schwark, N., et al. (2009). A new multiplex-PCR comprising autosomal and y-specific STRs and mitochondrial DNA to analyze highly degraded material. *Forensic Science International: Genetics, 3*, 96–103.

New Technologies

Hall, T. A., et al. (2005). Base composition analysis of human mitochondrial DNA using electrospray ionization mass spectrometry: A novel tool for the identification and differentiation of humans. *Analytical Biochemistry, 344*, 53–69.

Hall, T. A., et al. (2009). Base composition profiling of human mitochondrial DNA using polymerase chain reaction and direct automated electrospray ionization mass spectrometry. *Analytical Chemistry, 81*, 7515–7526.

Mikkelsen, M., et al. (2009). Application of full mitochondrial genome sequencing using 454 GS FLX pyrosequencing. *Forensic Science International: Genetics, 2*, 518–519.

Oberacher, H., et al. (2006). Profiling 627 mitochondrial nucleotides via the analysis of a 23-plex polymerase chain reaction by liquid chromatography-electrospray ionization time-of-flight mass spectrometry. *Analytical Chemistry, 78*, 7816–7827.

Oberacher, H., et al. (2007). Liquid chromatography-electrospray ionization mass spectrometry for simultaneous detection of mtDNA length and nucleotide polymorphisms. *International Journal of Legal Medicine, 121*, 57–67.

Collaborative and Interlab Studies

Alonso, A., et al. (2002). Results of the 1999-2000 collaborative exercise and proficiency testing program on mitochondrial DNA of the GEP-ISFG: an inter-laboratory study of the observed variability in the heteroplasmy level of hair from the same donor. *Forensic Science International, 125*, 1–7.

Carracedo, A., et al. (1998). Reproducibility of mtDNA analysis between laboratories: A report of the European DNA Profiling group (EDNAP). *Forensic Science International, 97*, 155–164.

Crespillo, M., et al. (2006). Results of the 2003-2004 GEP-ISFG collaborative study on mitochondrial DNA: Focus on the mtDNA profile of a mixed semen-saliva stain. *Forensic Science International, 160*, 157–167.

Montesino, M., et al. (2007). Analysis of body fluid mixtures by mtDNA sequencing: An inter-laboratory study of the GEP-ISFG working group. *Forensic Science International, 168*, 42–56.

Parson, W., et al. (2004). The EDNAP mitochondrial DNA population database (EMPOP) collaborative exercises: organization, results and perspectives. *Forensic Science International, 139*, 215–226.

Prieto, L., et al. (2003). The 2000-2001 GEP-ISFG Collaborative Exercise on mtDNA: Assessing the cause of unsuccessful mtDNA PCR amplification of hair shaft samples. *Forensic Science International, 134*, 46–53.

Prieto, L., et al. (2008). 2006 GEP-ISFG collaborative exercise on mtDNA: Reflections about interpretation, artifacts, and DNA mixtures. *Forensic Science International: Genetics, 2*, 126–133.

Salas, A., et al. (2005). Mitochondrial DNA error prophylaxis: assessing the causes of errors in the GEP'02-03 proficiency testing trial. *Forensic Science International, 148*, 191–198.

Tully, G., et al. (2004). Results of a collaborative study of the EDNAP group regarding mitochondrial DNA heteroplasmy and segregation in hair shafts. *Forensic Science International, 140*, 1–11.

Turchi, C., et al. (2008). Italian mitochondrial DNA database: results of a collaborative exercise and proficiency testing. *International Journal of Legal Medicine, 122*, 199–204.

Reference Materials

Levin, B. C., et al. (1999). A human mitochondrial DNA standard reference material for quality control in forensic identification, medical diagnosis, and mutation detection. *Genomics, 55*, 135–146.

Levin, B. C., et al. (2001). A review of the DNA standard reference materials developed by the National Institute of Standards and Technology. *Fresenius Journal of Analytical Chemistry, 370*, 213–219.

Levin, B. C., et al. (2003). Comparison of the complete mtDNA genome sequences of human cell lines—HL-60 and GM10742A—from individuals with pro-myelocytic leukemia and Leber hereditary optic neuropathy, respectively, and the inclusion of HL-60 in the NIST Human Mitochondrial DNA Standard Reference Material - SRM 2392-I. *Mitochondrion, 2*, 387–400.

Szibor, R., et al. (2003). Cell line DNA typing in forensic genetics—the necessity of reliable standards. *Forensic Science International, 138*, 37–43.

Interpretation of mtDNA Results

Brenner, C. H. (2010). Fundamental problem of forensic mathematics—the evidential value of a rare haplotype. *Forensic Science International: Genetics, 4*, 281–291.

Budowle, B., et al. (2010). Automated alignment and nomenclature for consistent treatment of polymorphisms in the human mitochondrial DNA control region. *Journal of Forensic Sciences, 55*, 1190–1195.

Carracedo, A., et al. (2000). DNA Commission of the International Society for Forensic Genetics: Guidelines for mitochondrial DNA typing. *Forensic Science International, 110*, 79–85.

Dann, B. M., et al. (2004). Testing the effects of selected jury trial innovations on juror comprehension of contested mtDNA evidence. Final Technical Report, National Institute of Justice, Grant No. 2002-IJ-CX-0026. Available at <http://www.ncjrs.gov/pdffiles1/nij/grants/211000.pdf>.

Holland, M. M., & Parsons, T. J. (1999). Mitochondrial DNA sequence analysis – validation and use for forensic casework. *Forensic Science Review, 11*, 21–50.

Parson, W., & Bandelt, H. -J. (2007). Extended guidelines for mtDNA typing of population data in forensic science. *Forensic Science International: Genetics, 1*, 13–19.

Parsons, T. J., et al. (1997). A high observed substitution rate in the human mitochondrial DNA control region. *Nature Genetics, 15*, 363–368.

Polanskey, D., et al. (2010). Comparison of Mitotyper rules and phylogenetic-based mtDNA nomenclature systems. *Journal of Forensic Sciences, 55*, 1184–1189.

Stewart, J. E., et al. (2001). Length variation in HV2 of the human mitochondrial DNA control region. *Journal of Forensic Sciences, 46*, 862–870.

SWGDAM (2003). Guidelines for mitochondrial DNA (mtDNA) nucleotide sequence interpretation. *Forensic Science Communications, 5*(2) Available at <http://www2.fbi.gov/hq/lab/fsc/backissu/april2003/swgdammitodna.htm>.

Tully, G., et al. (2001). Considerations by the European DNA profiling (EDNAP) group on the working practices, nomenclature and interpretation of mitochondrial DNA profiles. *Forensic Science International, 124*, 83–91.

Wilson, M. R., et al. (1993). Guidelines for the use of mitochondrial DNA sequencing in forensic science. *Crime Laboratory Digest, 20*, 68–77.

Wilson, M. R., et al. (2002). Recommendations for consistent treatment of length variants in the human mitochondrial DNA control region. *Forensic Science International, 129*, 35–42.

Wilson, M. R., et al. (2002). Further discussion of the consistent treatment of length variants in the human mitochondrial DNA control region. *Forensic Science Communications*, 4(4) Available at <http://www2.fbi.gov/hq/lab/fsc/backissu/oct2002/wilson.htm>.

Heteroplasmy

Bendall, K. E., & Sykes, B. C. (1995). Length heteroplasmy in the first hypervariable segment of the human mtDNA control region. *American Journal of Human Genetics, 57*, 248–256.

Bendall, K. E., et al. (1996). Heteroplasmic point mutations in the human mtDNA control region. *American Journal of Human Genetics, 59*, 1276–1287.

Bandelt, H. J., & Parson, W. (2008). Consistent treatment of length variants in the human mtDNA control region: a reappraisal. *International Journal of Legal Medicine, 122*, 11–21.

Berger, C., et al. (2011). Evaluating sequence-derived mtDNA length heteroplasmy by amplicon size analysis. *Forensic Science International: Genetics, 5*, 142–145.

Brandstätter, A., & Parson, W. (2003). Mitochondrial DNA heteroplasmy or artefacts—a matter of the amplification strategy? *International Journal of Legal Medicine, 117*, 180–184.

Brandstätter, A., et al. (2004). Monitoring the inheritance of heteroplasmy by computer-assisted detection of mixed basecalls in the entire human mitochondrial DNA control region. *International Journal of Legal Medicine, 118*, 47–54.

Budowle, B., et al. (2002). Critique of interpretation of high levels of heteroplasmy in the human mitochondrial DNA hypervariable region I from hair. *Forensic Science International, 126*, 30–33.

Calloway, C. D., et al. (2000). The frequency of heteroplasmy in the HVII region of mtDNA differs across tissue types and increases with age. *American Journal of Human Genetics, 66*, 1384–1397.

Chen, X., et al. (1995). Rearranged mitochondrial genomes are present in human oocytes. *American Journal of Human Genetics, 57*, 239–247.

Comas, D., et al. (1995). Heteroplasmy in the control region of human mitochondrial DNA. *Genome Research, 5*, 89–90.

Forster, L., et al. (2010). Evaluating length heteroplasmy in the human mitochondrial DNA control region. *International Journal of Legal Medicine, 124*, 133–142.

Grzybowski, T. (2000). Extremely high levels of human mitochondrial DNA heteroplasmy in single hair roots. *Electrophoresis, 21*, 548–553.

Grzybowski, T., et al. (2003). High levels of mitochondrial DNA heteroplasmy in single hair roots: reanalysis and revision. *Electrophoresis, 24*, 1159–1165.

He, Y., et al. (2010). Heteroplasmic mitochondrial DNA mutations in normal and tumour cells. *Nature, 464*, 610–614.

Irwin, J. A., et al. (2009). Investigation of heteroplasmy in the human mitochondrial DNA control region: A synthesis of observations from more than 5000 global population samples. *Journal of Molecular Evolution, 68*, 516–527.

Lagerström-Fermér, M., et al. (2001). Heteroplasmy of the human mtDNA control region remains constant during life. *American Journal of Human Genetics, 68*, 1299–1301.

Melton, T. (2004). Mitochondrial DNA heteroplasmy. *Forensic Science Reviews, 16*, 1–20.

Paneto, G. G., et al. (2010). Heteroplasmy in hair: study of mitochondrial DNA third hypervariable region in hair and blood samples. *Journal of Forensic Sciences, 55*, 715–718.

Pflugradt, R., et al. (2011). A novel and effective separation method for single mitochondria analysis. *Mitochondrion, 11*, 308–314.

Reiner, J. E., et al. (2010). Detection of heteroplasmic mitochondrial DNA in single mitochondria. *PLoS ONE, 5*, e14359.

Roberts, K. A., & Calloway, C. (2011). Characterization of mitochondrial DNA sequence heteroplasmy in blood tissue and hair as a function of hair morphology. *Journal of Forensic Sciences, 56*, 46–60.

Santos, C., et al. (2008). Frequency and pattern of heteroplasmy in the control region of human mitochondrial DNA. *Journal of Molecular Evolution, 67*, 191–200.

Sekiguchi, K., et al. (2003). Inter- and intragenerational transmission of a human mitochondrial DNA heteroplasmy among 13 maternally-related individuals and differences between and within tissues in two family members. *Mitochondrion, 2*, 401–414.

Sekiguchi, K., et al. (2004). Mitochondrial DNA heteroplasmy among hairs from single individuals. *Journal of Forensic Sciences, 49*, 986–991.

Stoneking, M. (2000). Hypervariable sites in the mtDNA control region are mutational hotspots. *American Journal of Human Genetics, 67*, 1029–1032.

Sullivan, K. M., et al. (1997). A single difference in mtDNA control region sequence observed between hair shaft and reference samples from a single donor: *Proceedings of the seventh international symposium on human identification-1996*. Madison, Wisconsin: Promega Corporation. pp. 126–130. Available at <http://www.promega.com/geneticidproc/ussymp7proc/0721.html>.

Steighner, R. J., et al. (1999). Comparative identity and homogeneity testing of the mtDNA HV1 region using denaturing gradient gel electrophoresis. *Journal of Forensic Sciences, 44*, 1186–1198.

Tully, G. (1999). Mitochondrial DNA: A small but valuable genome. In *First international conference on forensic human identification*. Forensic Science Service.

Tully, L. A., et al. (2000). A sensitive denaturing gradient-gel electrophoresis assay reveals a high frequency of heteroplasmy in hypervariable region 1 of the human mtDNA control region. *American Journal of Human Genetics, 67*, 432–443.

Wallace, D. C., et al. (1987). Sequence analysis of cDNAs for the human and bovine ATP synthase beta subunit: Mitochondrial DNA genes sustain seventeen times more mutations. *Current Genetics, 12*, 81–90.

White, H. E., et al. (2005). Accurate detection and quantitation of heteroplasmic mitochondrial point mutations by pyrosequencing. *Genetic Testing, 9*, 190–199.

Wilson, M. R., et al. (1997). A family exhibiting heteroplasmy in the human mitochondrial DNA control region reveals both somatic mosaicism and pronounced segregation of mitotypes. *Human Genetics, 100*, 167–171.

Mixtures

Andréasson, H., et al. (2006). Quantification of mtDNA mixtures in forensic evidence material using pyrosequencing. *International Journal of Legal Medicine, 120*, 383–390.

Bever, R. A., et al. (2003). Resolution of mixtures by cloning of the mitochondrial DNA control region. In *Proceedings of the 14th international symposium on human identification*. Available at <http://www.promega.com/geneticidproc/>.

Danielson, P. B., et al. (2007). Resolving mtDNA mixtures by denaturing high-performance liquid chromatography and linkage phase determination. *Forensic Science International: Genetics, 1*, 148–153.

Hatsch, D., et al. (2007). A rape case solved by mitochondrial DNA mixture analysis. *Journal of Forensic Sciences, 52*, 891–894.

Szibor, R., et al. (2003). Identification of the minor component of a mixed stain by using mismatch primer-induced restriction sites in amplified mtDNA. *International Journal of Legal Medicine, 117*, 160–164.

Walker, J. A., et al. (2004). Resolution of mixed human DNA samples using mitochondrial DNA sequence variants. *Analytical Biochemistry, 325*, 171–173.

Nuclear DNA Pseudogenes

Collura, R. V., & Stewart, C. B. (1995). Insertions and duplications of mtDNA in the nuclear genomes of Old World monkeys and hominoids. *Nature, 378*, 485–489.

Lopez, J. V., et al. (1994). Numt, a recent transfer and tandem amplification of mitochondrial DNA in the nuclear genome of the domestic cat. *Journal of Molecular Evolution, 39*, 171–190.

Morgan, M. A., et al. (1998). Amplification of human nuclear pseudogenes derived from mitochondrial DNA: A problem for mitochondrial DNA identity testing? *Proceedings of the eighth international symposium on human identification*. Madison, Wisconsin: Promega Corporation. Available at <http://www.promega.com/geneticidproc/ussymp8proc/34.html>.

Ramos, A., et al. (2009). Human mitochondrial DNA complete amplification and sequencing: a new validated primer set that prevents nuclear DNA sequences of mitochondrial origin co-amplification. *Electrophoresis, 30*, 1587–1593.

Wallace, D. C., et al. (1997). Ancient mtDNA sequences in the human nuclear genome: a potential source of errors in identifying pathogenic mutations. *Proceedings of the National Academy of Sciences of the United States of America, 94*, 14900–14905.

Zischler, H., et al. (1995). A nuclear "fossil" of the mitochondrial D-loop and the origin of modern humans. *Nature, 378*, 489–492.

Recombination/Paternal Leakage

Awadalla, P., et al. (1999). Linkage disequilibrium and recombination in hominid mitochondrial DNA. *Science, 286*, 2524–2525.

Elson, J. L., et al. (2001). Analysis of European mtDNAs for recombination. *American Journal of Human Genetics, 68*, 145–153.

Eyre-Walker, A., et al. (1999). How clonal are human mitochondria? *Proceedings of the Royal Society of London B Biological Sciences, 266*, 477–483.

Eyre-Walker, A. (2000). Do mitochondria recombine in humans? *Philosophical Transactions of the Royal Society of London B Biological Sciences, 355*, 1573–1580.

Filosto, M., et al. (2003). Lack of paternal inheritance of muscle mitochondrial DNA in sporadic mitochondrial myopathies. *Annals of Neurology, 54*, 524–526.

Giles, R. E., et al. (1980). Maternal inheritance of human mitochondrial DNA. *Proceedings of the National Academy of Sciences of the United States of America, 77*, 6715–6719.

Gyllensten, U., et al. (1991). Paternal inheritance of mitochondrial DNA in mice. *Nature, 352*, 255–257.

Hagelberg, E., et al. (1999). Evidence for mitochondrial DNA recombination in a human population of island Melanesia. *Proceedings of the Royal Society of London B Biological Sciences, 266*, 485–492.

Hagelberg, E., et al. (2000). Erratum: Evidence for mitochondrial DNA recombination in a human population of island Melanesia. *Proceedings of the Royal Society of London B Biological Sciences, 267*, 1595–1596.

Johns, D. R. (2003). Paternal transmission of mitochondrial DNA is (fortunately) rare. *Annals of Neurology, 54*, 422–424.

Jorde, L. B., & Bamshad, M. (2000). Questioning evidence for recombination in human mitochondrial DNA. *Science, 288*, 1931.

Kivisild, T., et al. (2000). Questioning evidence for recombination in human mitochondrial DNA. *Science, 288*, 1931.

Kumar, S., et al. (2000). Questioning evidence for recombination in human mitochondrial DNA. *Science, 288*, 1931.

Macaulay, V., et al. (1999). Mitochondrial DNA recombination—no need to panic. *Proceedings of the Royal Society of London B Biological Sciences, 266*, 2037–2039.

Parsons, T. J., & Irwin, J. A. (2000). Questioning evidence for recombination in human mitochondrial DNA. *Science, 288*, 1931.

Schwartz, M., & Vissing, J. (2002). Paternal inheritance of mitochondrial DNA. *New England Journal of Medicine, 347*, 576–580.

Taylor, R. W., et al. (2003). Genotypes from patients indicate no paternal mitochondrial DNA contribution. *Annals of Neurology, 54*, 521–524.

Wiuf, C. (2001). Recombination in human mitochondrial DNA? *Genetics, 159*, 749–756.

Population Data & Databases

Allard, M. W., et al. (2002). Characterization of the Caucasian haplogroups present in the SWGDAM forensic mtDNA dataset for 1771 human control region sequences. Scientific Working Group on DNA Analysis Methods. Journal of Forensic Sciences, 47, 1215–1223.

Allard, M. W., et al. (2004). Control region sequences for East Asian individuals in the Scientific Working Group on DNA Analysis Methods forensic mtDNA data set. *Legal Medicine, 6*, 11–24.

Allard, M. W., et al. (2005). Characterization of human control region sequences of the African American SWGDAM forensic mtDNA data set. *Forensic Science International, 148*, 169–179.

Allard, M. W., et al. (2006). Evaluation of variation in control region sequences for Hispanic individuals in the SWGDAM mtDNA data set. *Journal of Forensic Sciences, 51*, 566–573.

Behar, D. M., et al. (2007). The Genographic Project public participation mitochondrial DNA database. *PloS Genetics, 3*, e104.

Brandon, M. C., et al. (2009). MITOMASTER: A bioinformatics tool for the analysis of mitochondrial DNA sequences. *Human Mutation, 30,* 1–6. Available at <http://mammag.web.uci.edu/twiki/bin/view/Mitomaster>.

Brandstätter, A., et al. (2004). Mitochondrial DNA control region sequences from Nairobi (Kenya): Inferring phylogenetic parameters for the establishment of a forensic database. *International Journal of Legal Medicine, 118,* 294–306.

Brandstätter, A., et al. (2007). Generating population data for the EMPOP database – an overview of the mtDNA sequencing and data evaluation processes considering 273 Austrian control region sequences as example. *Forensic Science International, 166,* 164–175.

Budowle, B., et al. (1999). Mitochondrial DNA regions HVI and HVII population data. *Forensic Science International, 103,* 23–35.

Budowle, B., et al. (2002). HVI and HVII mitochondrial DNA data in Apaches and Navajos. *International Journal of Legal Medicine, 116,* 212–215.

EMPOP-Mitochondrial DNA control region database. <http://www.empop.org>.

Ingman, M., & Gyllensten, U. (2006). mtDB: Human Mitochondrial Genome Database, a resource for population genetics and medical sciences. *Nucleic Acids Research, 34,* D749–D751.

Irwin, J. A., et al. (2007). Development and expansion of high-quality control region databases to improve forensic mtDNA evidence interpretation. *Forensic Science International: Genetics, 1,* 154–157.

Irwin, J. A., et al. (2011). mtGenome reference population databases and the future of forensic mtDNA analysis. *Forensic Science International: Genetics, 5,* 222–225.

Lee, H. Y., et al. (2008). mtDNAmanager: a web-based tool for the management and quality analysis of mitochondrial DNA control-region sequences. *BMC Bioinformatics, 9,* 483. Available at <http://www.biomedcentral.com>.

Lee, Y. S., et al. (2009). MitoVariome: A variome database of human mitochondrial DNA. *BMC Genomics, 10,* S12.

Miller, K. W., & Budowle, B. (2001). A compendium of human mitochondrial DNA control region: Development of an international standard forensic database. *Croatian Medical Journal, 42,* 315–327.

MITOMAP: A human mitochondrial genome database. <http://www.mitomap.org/>.

Monson, K. L., et al. (2002). The mtDNA population database: An integrated software and database resource. *Forensic Science Communications,* 4(2) Available at: <http://www2.fbi.gov/hq/lab/fsc/backissu/april2002/miller1.htm>.

mtDB – Human mitochondrial genome database. <http://www.genpat.uu.se/mtDB/>.

mtDNAmanager. <http://mtmanager.yonsei.ac.kr/>.

Parson, W., et al. (2004). The EDNAP mitochondrial DNA population database (EMPOP) collaborative exercises: Organization, results and perspectives. *Forensic Science International, 139,* 215–226.

Parson, W., & Dür, A. (2007). EMPOP – a forensic mtDNA database. *Forensic Science International: Genetics, 1,* 88–92.

Pfeiffer, H., et al. (1999). Expanding the forensic German mitochondrial DNA control region database: Genetic diversity as a function of sample size and microgeography. *International Journal of Legal Medicine, 112,* 291–298.

Röck, A., et al. (2011). SAM: String-based sequence search algorithm for mitochondrial DNA database queries. *Forensic Science International: Genetics, 5,* 126–132.

Röhl, A., et al. (2001). An annotated mtDNA database. *International Journal of Legal Medicine, 115,* 29–39.

Weissensteiner, H., et al. (2010). eCOMPAGT integrates mtDNA: Import, validation and export of mitochondrial DNA profiles for population genetics, tumour dynamics and genotype-phenotype association studies. *BMC Bioinformatics, 11,* 122. Available at <http://dbis-informatik.uibk.ac.at/ecompagt>.

Quality Concerns with mtDNA Data

Bandelt, H. J., et al. (2001). Detecting errors in mtDNA data by phylogenetic analysis. *International Journal of Legal Medicine, 115,* 64–69.

Bandelt, H. J., et al. (2002). The fingerprint of phantom mutations in mitochondrial DNA data. *American Journal of Human Genetics, 71,* 1150–1160.

Bandelt, H. J., et al. (2004). Artificial recombination in forensic mtDNA population databases. *International Journal of Legal Medicine, 118,* 267–273.

Brandstätter, A., et al. (2005). Phantom mutation hotspots in human mitochondrial DNA. *Electrophoresis, 26,* 3414–3429.

Budowle, B., et al. (2004). Addressing the use of phylogenetics for identification of sequences in error in the SWGDAM mitochondrial DNA database. *Journal of Forensic Sciences, 49*, 1256–1261.

Budowle, B., & Polanskey, D. (2005). FBI mtDNA database: a cogent perspective. *Science, 307*, 845–847.

Forster, P. (2003). To err is human. *Annals of Human Genetics, 67*, 2–4.

Parson, W. (2007). The art of reading sequence electropherograms. *Annals of Human Genetics, 71*, 276–278.

Salas, A., et al. (2005). A practical guide to mitochondrial DNA error prevention in clinical, forensic, and population genetics. *Biochemical and Biophysical Research Communications, 335*, 891–899.

Salas, A., et al. (2007). Phylogeographic investigations: The role of trees in forensic genetics. *Forensic Science International, 168*, 1–13.

U.S. mtDNA Laboratories

Armed Forces DNA Identification Laboratory. <http://www.afip.org/consultation/AFMES/AFDIL/>.

Bode Technology Group. <http://www.bodetech.com>.

FBI Laboratory DNA Unit II. <http://www.fbi.gov/about-us/lab/mtdna>.

LabCorp. <http://www.labcorp.com>.

Mitotyping. <http://www.mitotyping.com>.

Orchid Cellmark. <http://www.orchidcellmark.com/forensicdna/>.

University of North Texas Center for Human Identification. <http://www.unthumanid.org/>.

Screening Assays

Brandstätter, A., et al. (2003). Rapid screening of mtDNA coding region SNPs for the identification of west European Caucasian haplogroups. *International Journal of Legal Medicine, 117*, 291–298.

Dario, P., et al. (2009). mtSNP typing before mtDNA sequencing: why do it? *Forensic Science International: Genetics Supplement Series, 2*, 187–188.

Kline, M. C., et al. (2005). Mitochondrial DNA typing screens with control region and coding region SNPs. *Journal of Forensic Sciences, 50*, 377–385.

Kristinsson, R., et al. (2009). Comparative analysis of the HV1 and HV2 regions of human mitochondrial DNA by denaturing high-performance liquid chromatography. *Journal of Forensic Sciences, 54*, 28–36.

Melton, T., et al. (2001). Diversity and heterogeneity in mitochondrial DNA of North American populations. *Journal of Forensic Sciences, 46*, 46–52.

Nelson, T. M., et al. (2007). Development of a multiplex single base extension assay for mitochondrial DNA haplogroup typing. *Croatian Medical Journal, 48*, 460–472.

Reynolds, R., et al. (2000). Detection of sequence variation in the HVII region of the human mitochondrial genome in 689 individuals using immobilized sequence-specific oligonucleotide probes. *Journal of Forensic Sciences, 45*, 1210–1231.

Stoneking, M., et al. (1991). Population variation of human mtDNA control region sequences detected by enzymatic amplification and sequence-specific oligonucleotide probes. *American Journal of Human Genetics, 48*, 370–382.

Whole mtGenome Sequencing

Coble, M. D. (2004). The identification of single nucleotide polymorphisms in the entire mitochondrial genome to increase the forensic discrimination of common HV1/HV2 types in the Caucasian population. PhD dissertation. Washington, DC: The George Washington University. Available at <http://www.cstl.nist.gov/biotech/strbase/pub_pres/Coble2004dis.pdf>.

Fendt, L., et al. (2009). Sequencing strategy for the whole mitochondrial genome resulting in high quality sequences. *BMC Genomics, 10*, 139.

Herrnstadt, C., et al. (2002). Reduced-median-network analysis of complete mitochondrial DNA coding-region sequences for the major African, Asian, and European haplogroups. *American Journal of Human Genetics, 70*, 1152–1171.

Herrnstadt, C., et al. (2003). Errors, phantoms and otherwise, in human mtDNA sequences. *American Journal of Human Genetics, 72*, 1585–1586.

Ingman, M., & Gyllensten, U. (2003). Mitochondrial genome variation and evolutionary history of Australian and New Guinean aborigines. *Genome Research, 13*, 1600–1606.

Kong, Q. P., et al. (2003). Phylogeny of east Asian mitochondrial DNA lineages inferred from complete sequences. *American Journal of Human Genetics, 73*, 671–676.

Maca-Meyer, N., et al. (2001). Major genomic mitochondrial lineages delineate early human expansions. *BMC Genetics, 2*, 13.

Rieder, M. J., et al. (1998). Automating the identification of DNA variations using quality-based fluorescence re-sequencing: analysis of the human mitochondrial genome. *Nucleic Acids Research, 26*, 967–973.

Most Common Types and Coding Region Assays

Brandstätter, A., et al. (2006). Dissection of mitochondrial superhaplogroup H using coding region SNPs. *Electrophoresis, 27*, 2541–2550.

Budowle, B., et al. (2005). Forensic analysis of the mitochondrial coding region and association to disease. *International Journal of Legal Medicine, 119*, 314–315.

Coble, M. D., et al. (2004). Single nucleotide polymorphisms over the entire mtDNA genome that increase the power of forensic testing in Caucasians. *International Journal of Legal Medicine, 118*, 137–146.

Coble, M. D., et al. (2006). Effective strategies for forensic analysis in the mitochondrial DNA coding region. *International Journal of Legal Medicine, 120*, 27–32.

Köhnemann, S., et al. (2008). A rapid mtDNA assay of 22 SNPs in one multiplex reaction increases the power of forensic testing in European Caucasians. *International Journal of Legal Medicine, 122*, 517–523.

Köhnemann, S., et al. (2009). An economical mtDNA SNP assay detecting different mitochondrial haplogroups in identical HVR 1 samples of Caucasian ancestry. *Mitochondrion, 9*, 370–375.

Nilsson, M., et al. (2008). Evaluation of mitochondrial DNA coding region assays for increased discrimination in forensic analysis. *Forensic Science International: Genetics, 2*, 1–8.

Parsons, T. J., & Coble, M. D. (2001). Increasing the forensic discrimination of mitochondrial DNA testing through analysis of the entire mitochondrial DNA genome. *Croatian Medical Journal, 42*, 304–309.

Parsons, T. J. (2006). Mitochondrial DNA genome sequencing and SNP assay development for increased power of discrimination. In *Final report on NIJ grant 2000-IJ-CX-K010*. Available at <http://www.ncjrs.gov/pdffiles1/nij/grants/213502.pdf>.

Quintáns, B., et al. (2004). Typing of mitochondrial DNA coding region SNPs of forensic and anthropological interest using SNaPshot minisequencing. *Forensic Science International, 140*, 251–257.

Vallone, P. M., et al. (2004). A multiplex allele-specific primer extension assay for forensically informative SNPs distributed throughout the mitochondrial genome. *International Journal of Legal Medicine, 118*, 147–157.

mtDNA Haplogroups and Phylogenetics

Phylotree. <http://www.phylotree.org/>.

van Oven, M., & Kayser, M. (2009). Updated comprehensive phylogenetic tree of global human mitochondrial DNA variation. *Human Mutation, 30*, E386–E394.

Wilson, M. R., & Allard, M. W. (2004). Phylogenetics and mitochondrial DNA. *Forensic Science Review, 16*, 37–62.

Genetic Genealogy and Human Migration Studies

Behar, D. M., et al. (2007). The Genographic Project public participation mitochondrial DNA database. *PLoS Genetics, 3*, e104.

Bolnick, D. A., et al. (2007). Genetics: The science and business of genetic ancestry testing. *Science, 318*, 399–400.

Brown, K. (2002). Tangled roots? Genetics meets genealogy. *Science, 295*, 1634–1635.

DNA Ancestry. <http://dna.ancestry.com>.

FamilyTree DNA. <http://www.familytreedna.com/>.

Genographic project website. <https://genographic.nationalgeographic.com/genographic/>.

Goldstein, D. B., & Chikhi, L. (2002). Human migrations and population structure: What we know and why it matters. *Annual Review of Genomics and Human Genetics, 3*, 129–152.

Helgason, A., et al. (2003). A populationwide coalescent analysis of Icelandic matrilineal and patrilineal genealogies: Evidence for a faster evolutionary rate of mtDNA lineages than Y chromosomes. *American Journal of Human Genetics, 72*, 1370–1388.

International Society of Genetic Genealogy. <http://www.isogg.org/>.

Jobling, M. A., Hurles, M. E., & Tyler-Smith, C. (2004). *Human evolutionary genetics: Origins, peoples, and diseases*. New York: Garland Science.

Journal of Genetic Genealogy. <http://www.jogg.info/>.

Olson, S. (2002). *Mapping human history*. New York: Houghton Mifflin.

Relethford, J. H. (2001). *Genetics and the search for modern human origins*. New York: Wiley-Liss.

Relethford, J. H. (2003). *Reflections of our past: How human history is revealed in our genes*. Boulder, Colorado: Westview Press.

Smolenyak, M. S., & Turner, A. (2004). *Trace your roots with DNA: Using genetic tests to explore your family tree*. New York: Rodale.

Sorenson Molecular Genealogy Foundation. <http://www.smgf.org/>.

Stix, G. (2008, July). Traces of a distant past. *Scientific American*, 56–63.

Underhill, P. A., & Kivisild, T. (2007). Use of Y chromosome and mitochondrial DNA population structure in tracing human migrations. *Annual Review of Genetics*, *41*, 539–564.

Wells, S. (2007). *Deep ancestry: Inside the genographic project*. Washington, DC: National Geographic.

CHAPTER

15

X-Chromosome Analysis

The X-chromosome (ChrX) has potential forensic and human identity testing applications due to its inheritance pattern compared to other genetic markers (Szibor et al. 2003, Table 15.1). Normal males possess one X-chromosome and one Y-chromosome while females possess two X-chromosomes although there are occasionally some irregular karyotypes, such as XXY (Klinefelter syndrome; Giltay & Maiburg 2010), XXX, and XYY. More than 40 STR markers have been characterized from the X-chromosome, and population studies have been performed with many of these X-chromosome STRs (X-STRs). Literature on the use of X-chromosome analysis is growing and is briefly reviewed in this chapter. The reading list and internet resources at the back of the chapter provide over 145 references to additional information so that interested readers can dig deeper into ChrX population studies and applications.

TABLE 15.1 Specific Relationships and the Probability of Transmitting Genetic Information (Barring Mutation). Some of the ChrY Information is Not Applicable (N/A) as Women Do Not Have a Y-Chromosome.

Inheritance	Autosomal Markers	ChrY Markers	mtDNA	ChrX Markers
Mother → Son	50%	N/A	100%	100%
Mother → Daughter	50%	N/A	100%	50%
Father → Son	50%	100%	0%	0%
Father → Daughter	50%	0%	0%	100%
Paternal Grandmother → Granddaughter	25%	N/A	0%	100%
Maternal Grandmother → Granddaughter	25%	N/A	100%	25%
Paternal Grandfather → Grandson	25%	100%	0%	0%

ChrX INHERITANCE AND APPLICATION

X-Chromosome Structure and Function

The X-chromosome was originally named X for "unknown" as early geneticists were puzzled how it remained apart from other chromosomal pairs (Gunter 2005). (Apparently when its smaller counterpart sex-chromosome was finally discovered, it received the next letter in the alphabet—Y.) With the completion of the Human Genome Project, a full sequence of human ChrX has been released and includes more than 99% coverage of the euchromatic sequence (Ross et al. 2005). The X-chromosome is 153 Mb in length and includes almost 1100 genes. ChrX represents almost 5% of the total genetic material in females but only about 2.5% in males, which only possess a single copy.

In males, the tips of the X-chromosome combine with the pseudoautosomal regions of the Y-chromosome to maintain proper segregation in cell division. In addition, there is a great deal of homology (similar or the same DNA sequence) between portions of ChrX and ChrY.

In the early embryonic development of females, one of their two X-chromosomes is inactivated or "silenced" to ensure that they only have one functional ChrX copy in each somatic cell. Either the paternal or maternal ChrX can become the active one. The inactivated X-chromosome is referred to as a Barr body after its 1949 discoverer Murray Barr (Barr & Bertram 1949). Recent research suggests that the Barr body may be more biologically active than was previously supposed (Carrel & Willard 2005). While genes are inactivated and not typically expressed from the Barr body, DNA testing results still reflect the genetic information present in both female X-chromosomes. In addition, the two female X-chromosomes can recombine during meiosis.

APPLICATIONS OF ChrX TESTING

X-chromosome STR typing can be helpful in some kinship analysis situations particularly with deficient paternity cases where a DNA sample from one of the parents is not available for testing. For example, if a father/daughter parentage relationship is in question, X-STRs may be helpful due to the 100% transmission of the father's X-chromosome to his daughter (Table 15.1). On the other hand, in a father/son parentage question, Y-chromosome results would be helpful (see Chapter 13). Table 15.2 lists several applications for X-chromosome DNA testing. ChrX testing can be especially helpful in some missing persons or disaster victim identification situations (see Chapter 9) where direct reference samples are not available and biological relatives must be sought to aid human identification.

TABLE 15.2 Applications of X-Chromosome Analysis (See Figure 15.1 for Illustration of Example Pedigrees).

- Complex kinship cases involving at least one female
- Disputed paternity to a daughter (especially in motherless cases)
- Half-sister testing where the father is the common relative
- Grandparent—grandchild comparisons
- Paternity testing in incest cases (see Figure 15.2)

X-chromosome markers can help infer parent-offspring relationships that involve at least one female, such as mother-daughter, mother-son, and father-daughter duos (illustrated in Figure 15.1). In complicated kinship scenarios, such as incest (Figure 15.2), ChrX markers may aid sorting out difficult relationship questions.

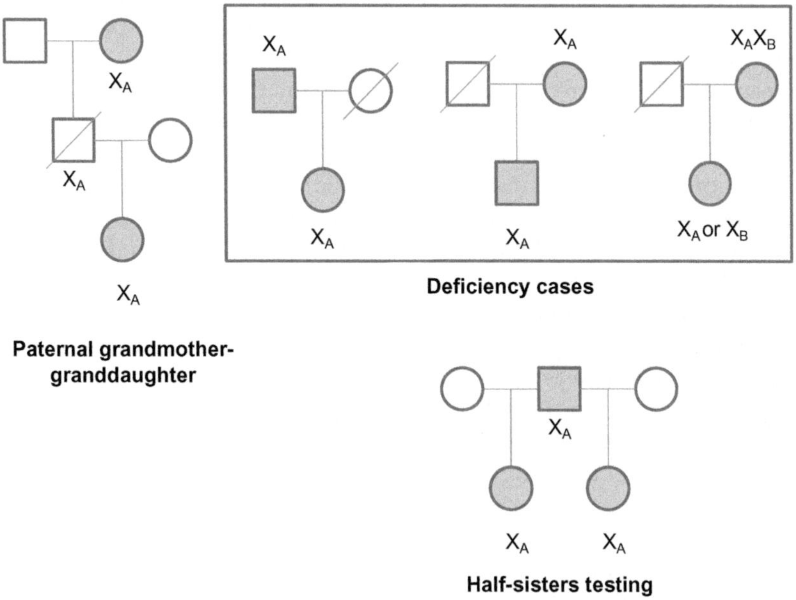

FIGURE 15.1 Some example pedigrees where ChrX testing can be helpful.

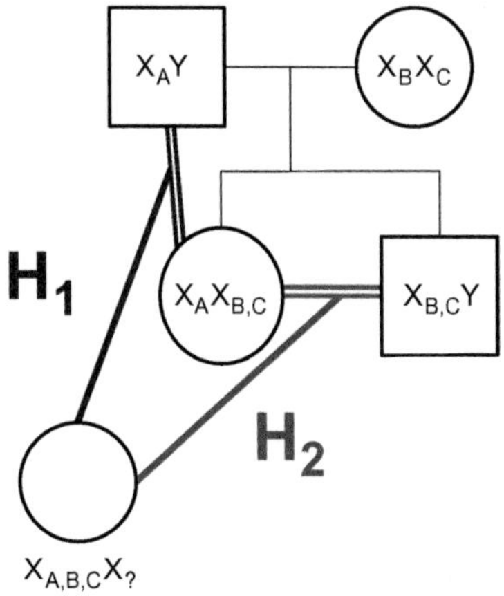

FIGURE 15.2 Use of ChrX testing in an incest case to help distinguish whether the victim's father (H_1) or brother (H_2) fathered the victim's daughter. The mother passes a combination of her X-chromosomes (X_B, X_C) on to her son ($X_{B,C}$). If either X_B or X_C is more abundant in the victim's daughter, then H_2 is more likely (her brother is the father). If X_A is more abundant in the victim's daughter, then H_1 is more likely (her father is the father). Autosomal genetic markers would probably not be very helpful in this situation due to the high degree of allele sharing expected among close relatives.

X-STR MARKERS COMMONLY USED

As with the rest of the human genome, STR markers are prevalent along the X-chromosome with comparable density to autosomal STRs (Subramanian et al. 2003). However, an enrichment of $[GATA]_n$ tetranucleotide repeats has been shown to occur in a 10Mb portion of the short arm of ChrX (McNeil et al. 2006). Over the past decade, a number of X-STRs have been studied.

When autosomal STRs were being characterized in the early 1990s by Tom Caskey's group at Baylor, two X-STRs named HPRTB and ARA were among them (Edwards et al. 1992). However, it would be almost another decade before much was attempted with these loci in the context of X-STR typing (Szibor et al. 2003a).

Reinhard Szibor at the Institute for Legal Medicine in Magdeburg, Germany and his colleagues including Jeanett Edelmann (Leipzig, Germany) and Sandra Hering (Dresden, Germany) brought X-STR typing into use within the forensic DNA community (Szibor 2007). Professors Szibor, Edelmann, and Hering have formed a forensic ChrX research website (http://www.chrx-str.org/) with information on X-STR markers. For his efforts in this area, in 2007 Dr. Szibor was awarded the prestigious biannual Scientific Prize by the International Society of Forensic Genetics.

Table 15.3 describes 33 X-STR loci that have been used within the forensic community. As with autosomal STR loci used in forensic analysis, tetranucleotide repeats are most commonly selected due to lower stutter product formation compared to dinucleotide or trinucleotide repeats (see Chapter 5). In Table 15.3, the chromosomal position for each locus is noted as is its physical location and its genetic distance based on a linkage/recombination map created at Rutgers University (Matise et al. 2007).

TABLE 15.3 Characteristics of 33 X-Chromosome STR Loci.

Position	ChrX Marker	Repeat Motif	Allele Range	Location (Mb)	Genetic Distance (cM)	Kit/Assay (see Table 15.4)
p22.33	**DXS6807**	GATA	11–17	4.753	14.76	F
p22.32	**DXS9895**	AGAT	11–18	7.387	17.09	G
p22.31	**DXS10148**	AAGA	13.3–38.1	9.198	19.84	A
p22.31	**DXS10135**	GAAA	13–39.2	9.266	20.03	B
p22.31	**DXS8378**	CTAT	7–17	9.330	20.21	A,B,C,D,E,F,H2
p22.2	**DXS9902**	GATA	7–16	15.234	32.32	E,H1,H2
p22.11	**DXS6795**	ATT/ATC	9–16	23.254	44.24	H2
Centromere	**DXS7132**	TCTA	6–20	64.572	90.75	A,B,C,D,E,F,G,H2
q12	**DXS10079**	AGAR	14–25	66.633	90.82	A,B
q12	HumARA	CAG	14–31	66.682	90.81	*No longer used!*
q12	**DXS10074**	AAGA	4–21	66.894	90.83	A,B

(Continued)

TABLE 15.3 Characteristics of 33 X-Chromosome STR Loci. (*Continued*)

Position	ChrX Marker	Repeat Motif	Allele Range	Location (Mb)	Genetic Distance (cM)	Kit/Assay (see Table 15.4)
q13.1	**DXS981(STRX1)**	TATC	9.3–17	68.114	92.81	–
q13.3	**DXS6800**	TAGA	15–23	78.567	97.49	G
q21.2	**DXS6803**	TCTA	8–15	86.318	99.40	H2
q21.31	**DXS9898**	TATC	7–16	87.683	101.29	D,E,G
q21.33	**DXS6809**	ATCT	27–40	94.825	108.12	D,E,F
q21.33	**DXS6789**	TATS	10–26	95.336	108.47	D,E,F,G,H1
q22.1	**DXS7424**	TAA	7–20	100.505	115.25	F,H1
q22.1	**DXS101**	CTT/ATT	14–32	101.300	116.15	D,F,H1
q22.3	**DXS7133**	ATAG	6–14	108.928	118.18	E,F,G
q23	**GATA172D05**	TAGA	5–17	113.061	124.36	D,E,F,H2
q24	**DXS7130**	TATC	10–18.3	118.084	130.28	G,H1
q25	**GATA165B12**	AGAT	8–13	120.706	136.18	H1
q26.2	**DXS10103**	YAGA	15–21	133.246	149.37	A
q26.2	**HPRTB**	AGAT	6–19	133.443	149.66	A,B,C,D,F,G,H2
q26.3	**DXS10101**	AAAG	24–38	133.482	149.75	A,B
q27.1	**GATA31E08**	AGGG/AGAT	7–16	140.062	160.54	E,F,G,H1
q28	**DXS8377**	AGA	33–60	149.317	183.66	D
q28	**DXS10146**	TTCC/CTTT	24–46.2	149.335	183.72	A
q28	**DXS10134**	GAAA	28–46.1	149.401	183.96	A,B
q28	**DXS10147**	AAAC	6–11	149.414	184.01	H2
q28	**DXS7423**	TCCA	8–19	149.462	184.19	A,B,C,D,E,F,G,H2
q28	**DXS10011**	GRAA	18–50	150.939	188.70	G

Adapted from Machado & Medina-Acosta (2009) and http://www.chrx-str.org. Genetic distance from Rutgers map v.2 of the human genome (http://compgen.rutgers.edu/old/map-interpolator/; see Matise et al. 2007). The four linkage groups are gray-shaded. Kit/assay configurations are shown in Table 15.4. Argus X12 encompasses all Argus X8 markers. The X-STR locus HumARA is shown in red font because it is associated with disease and no longer used (Szibor et al. 2005).

When loci are physically close together on a chromosome, they are considered linked and thus not inherited independently of one another. Genetic linkage is a function of the physical distance of DNA sequences along a chromosome. As discussed with Y-chromosome markers (see Chapter 13), information from linked loci are typically treated as a haplotype rather than using the product rule to multiply allele frequencies together.

Linkage Groups and Haplotype Blocks

Four linkage groups are typically associated with the X-chromosome (see Table 15.3). When information from loci in the same linkage group is included in a set of data, it needs to be combined into a haplotype. Within a linkage group, the haplotype frequencies rather than allele frequencies are collected during population studies. With closely linked loci, the product rule cannot be used to estimate the rarity of a DNA profile by multiplying results between loci within a linkage group. However, information between linkage groups is considered independent and can be multiplied together.

Thus, alleles observed in a sample with the three X-STRs located in linkage group 1 (DXS10148, DXS10135, and DXS8378) would be combined to form a haplotype DXS10148-DXS10135-DXS8378. Frequency information from this haplotype could then be combined (multiplied) with haplotype frequency information from linkage group 2 loci (DXS7132, DXS10079, and DXS10074) to estimate the rarity of the sample profile. Some statistical formulas for use with ChrX analysis are described in D.N.A. Box 15.1 (Krawczak 2007).

X-STR LOCUS HUMARA NO LONGER USED

HumARA was an early adopted X-STR marker (Desmarais et al. 1998) and was used for a number of years until it was directly linked to genetic disease and ethical concerns led to it being dropped from active use (Szibor et al. 2005). The HumARA trinucleotide repeat is found in exon 1 of the androgen receptor gene. The CAG repeat at this locus directly codes for a polyglutamine tract. Mutations at HumARA can result in spinal and bulbar muscular atrophy when the trinucleotide repeat expands (Szibor et al. 2005).

X-STR KITS AND MULTIPLEX ASSAYS

Several X-STR assays have been developed and reported in the literature (Table 15.4). A number of population studies have been performed using these various assays.

The first commercial X-STR kit came from Biotype (Dresden, Germany) and was called the Argus X-UL (UL for unlinked). This kit contains one X-STR from each of the four linkage groups. A few years later Biotype released the Argus X-8 that added one additional X-STR to each of the four linkage groups. In 2010, QIAGEN (Hilden, Germany) partnered with Biotype and began marketing the Investigator Argus X-12 with three X-STRs in each of the four linkage groups. Figure 15.3 displays the dye-label and X-STR locus size ranges for the Argus X-12 kit.

Other Markers

As with autosomal and Y-chromosome systems, single nucleotide polymorphisms (SNPs) and insertion-deletion (INDELs) exist on the X-chromosome and assays can be designed to utilize them. A 25plex X-SNP assay has been developed and shown to have forensic

D.N.A. BOX 15.1

STATISTICAL TREATMENT OF RESULTS FROM ChrX MARKERS

Using autosomal markers, the mean exclusion chance (MEC) for an unrelated male when paternity of a daughter is disputed may be calculated using (Szibor et al. 2003).

$$\sum_i p_i^3(1-p_i)^2 + \sum_i p_i(1-p_i)^3 + \sum_{i<j} p_i p_j(p_i+p_j)(1-p_i-p_j)^2$$

where p_i refers to the frequency of the ith allele for the genetic marker being evaluated. Alternatively with X-chromosome markers, the MEC equation for paternity trios involving daughters is.

$$\sum_i p_i^3(1-p_i) + \sum_i p_i(1-p_i)^2 + \sum_{i<j} p_i p_j(p_i+p_j)(1-p_i-p_j)$$

Krawczak (2007) notes that the two formulas differ by the exponent of the last factor in each summation. With the factor always smaller in the ChrX equation, the MEC of an X-chromosome marker will be larger than an autosomal marker possessing the same allele frequencies.

Further statistical calculations involving ChrX results include (Szibor et al. 2003):

MEC for ChrX markers in trios involving daughters:

$$1 - \sum_i p_i^2 + \sum_i p_i^4 - \left(\sum_{i<j} p_i^2\right)^2$$

MEC for ChrX markers in father/daughter duos:

$$1 - 2\sum_i p_i^2 + \sum_i p_i^3$$

Power of discrimination (PD) in females:

$$1 - 2\left(\sum_i p_i^2\right)^2 + \sum_i p_i^4$$

PD in males:

$$1 - \sum_i p_i^2$$

Sources:

Krawczak, M. (2007). Kinship testing with X-chromosomal markers: mathematical and statistical issues. Forensic Science International: Genetics, *1*, 111–114.

Szibor, R., et al. (2003). Use of X-linked markers for forensic purposes. International Journal of Legal Medicine, *117*, 67–74.

usefulness (Tomas et al. 2010). Results from a set of 33 X-linked insertion/deletion polymorphisms have also been reported (Freitas et al. 2010).

POPULATION DATA COLLECTION AND OTHER STUDIES

The reference list at the end of this chapter includes 66 published population studies using a variety of X-STR markers. Data has been collected on African, Amerindian, Bosnian,

TABLE 15.4 Configuration of Several X-STR Assay and Kits Reported in the Literature Showing Dye Color Labels and Relative Sizes of PCR Products. The Arbitrary Assay/Kit Designation (A, B, C, etc.) Is Used in Table 15.3.

A	**ARGUS X-12 KIT (QIAGEN/BIOTYPE)**					
	Blue:	Amel	DXS10103	DXS8378	DXS7132	DXS10134
	Green:	DXS10074	DXS10101	DXS10135		
	Yellow:	DXS7423	DXS10146	DXS10079		
	Red:	HPRTB	DXS10148			
B	**ARGUS X-8 KIT (BIOTYPE)**					
	Blue:	Amel	DXS8378	DXS7132	DXS10134	
	Green:	DXS10074	DXS10101	DXS10135		
	Yellow:	DXS7423	DXS10079	HPRTB		
C	**ARGUS X-UL KIT (BIOTYPE)**					
	Blue:	DXS7132	DXS7423	DXS8378	HPRTB	
	Green:	Amel				
D	**PORTUGUESE 10PLEX ASSAY A (GOMES et al. 2007)**					
	Blue:	DXS8378	DXS9898	DXS8377	HPRTB	
	Green:	GATA172D05		DXS7423	DXS6809	
	Yellow:	DXS7132	DXS101	DXS6789		
E	**PORTUGUESE 10PLEX ASSAY B (GUSMÃO et al. 2009)**					
	Blue:	DXS8378	DXS9898	DXS7133	GATA31E08	
	Green:	GATA172D05		DXS7423	DXS6809	
	Yellow:	DXS7132	DXS9902	DXS6789		
F	**ITALIAN 12PLEX ASSAY (TURRINA et al. 2007)**					
	Blue:	DXS7132	DXS8378	DXS6809		
	Green:	DXS7133	DXS6789	DXS7424		
	Yellow:	GATA172D05		HPRTB	DXS7423	DXS6807
	Red:	Amel	GATA31E08	DXS101		
G	**BRAZILIAN 11PLEX ASSAY (RIBEIRO RODRIGUES et al. 2008)**					
	Blue:	DXS7132	DXS7423	DXS7133	DXS10011	
	Green:	DXS7130	DXS6800	GATA31E08	HPRTB	
	Yellow:	DXS6789	DXS9898	DXS9895		

(Continued)

TABLE 15.4 Configuration of Several X-STR Assay and Kits Reported in the Literature Showing Dye Color Labels and Relative Sizes of PCR Products. The Arbitrary Assay/Kit Designation (A, B, C, etc.) Is Used in Table 15.3. (*Continued*)

AFDIL MINIX-STR ASSAYS (DIEGOLI & COBLE 2011)				
H1	*Blue:*	DXS6789		
	Green:	DXS7130	DXS9902	
	Yellow:	SRY	GATA31E08	DXS7424
	Red:	GATA165B12		DXS101
H2	*Blue:*	DXS6795	GATA172D05	DXS10147
	Green:	DXS8378	DXS7132	
	Yellow:	SRY	DXS6803	HPRTB
	Red:	DXS7423	DXS9902	

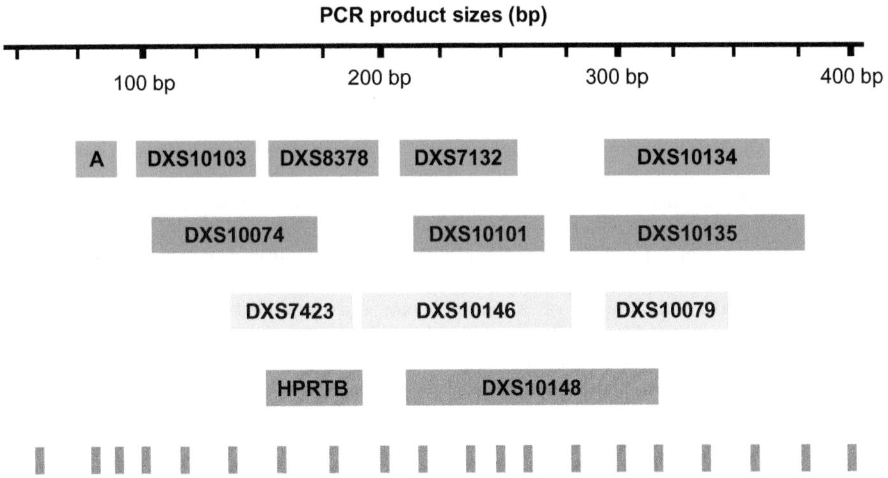

FIGURE 15.3 Investigator Argus X-12 kit (QIAGEN, Hilden, Germany) PCR product size ranges and dye color labels used for 12 X-STR loci and amelogenin (A).

Brazilian, Chinese, Finnish, German, Irish, Italian, Korean, Latin American, Latvian, Mongolian, Pakistani, Polish, Portuguese, Spanish, Taiwanese, Tibetan, UK, and U.S. populations.

Family inheritance studies have been performed (Hering et al. 2010, Tillmar et al. 2010) and even other species studied in terms of their ChrX variation (van Asch et al. 2010). While

X-chromosome analysis is still a niche application in forensic DNA typing, research efforts are ongoing to ensure its utility when it is needed.

READING LIST AND INTERNET RESOURCES

General Information

Forensic X-STR Research Website. <http://www.chrx-str.org/>.

Giltay, J. C., & Maiburg, M. C. (2010). Klinefelter syndrome: Clinical and molecular aspects. *Expert Review of Molecular Diagnostics, 10*, 765–776.

Santos-Lopes, S. S., et al. (2007). A worldwide phylogeography for the human X chromosome. *PLoS ONE, 2*(6), e557.

Schaffner, S. F. (2004). The X chromosome in population genetics. *Nature Reviews Genetics, 5*, 43–51.

Szibor, R., et al. (2006). A new Web site compiling forensic chromosome X research is now online. *International Journal of Legal Medicine, 120*, 252–254.

Szibor, R. (2007). X-chromosomal markers: Past, present and future. *Forensic Science International: Genetics, 1*, 93–99.

ChrX Structure & Function

Barr, M. L., & Bertram, E. G. (1949). A morphological distinction between neurones of the male and female, and the behavior of the nucleolar satellite during accelerated nucleoprotein synthesis. *Nature, 163*, 676–677.

Carrel, L., & Willard, H. F. (2005). X-inactivation profile reveals extensive variability in X-linked gene expression in females. *Nature, 434*, 400–404.

Gunter, C. (2005). She moves in mysterious ways. *Nature, 434*, 279–280.

Ross, M. T., et al. (2005). The DNA sequence of the human X chromosome. *Nature, 434*, 325–337.

Applications

Barbaro, A., et al. (2006). X-STR typing for an identification casework. *Progress in Forensic Genetics 11, ICS 1288*, 513–515.

Branicki, W., et al. (2008). Application of the Mentype Argus X-8 kit to forensic casework. *Problems of Forensic Sciences, 73*, 53–64.

Chen, D.-P., et al. (2009). Use of X-linked short tandem repeats loci to confirm mutations in parentage caseworks. *Clinica Chimica Acta, 408* 29–33.

Edelmann, J., et al. (2004). Advantages of X-chromosomal microsatellites in deficiency paternity testing: Presentation of cases. *Progress in Forensic Genetics 10, ICS 1261*, 257–259.

Esteve, C. A., et al. (2009). "GenderPlex" a PCR multiplex for reliable gender determination of degraded human DNA samples and complex gender constellations. *International Journal of Legal Medicine, 123*, 459–464.

Honda, K., et al. (2001). DNA testing of Klinefelter's syndrome in a criminal case using XY chromosomal STR multiplex-PCR. *Journal of Forensic Sciences, 46*, 1235–1238.

Pinto, N., et al. (2011). X-chromosome markers in kinship testing: A generalisation of the IBD approach identifying situations where their contribution is crucial. *Forensic Science International: Genetics, 5*, 27–32.

Szibor, R., et al. (2003a). Use of X-linked markers for forensic purposes. *International Journal of Legal Medicine, 117*, 67–74.

Szibor, R., et al. (2003b). Cell line DNA typing in forensic genetics–the necessity of reliable standards. *Forensic Science International, 138*, 37–43.

Szibor, R., et al. (2005). Haplotyping of STR cluster DXS6801-DXS6809-DXS6789 on Xq21 provides a powerful tool for kinship testing. *International Journal of Legal Medicine, 119*, 363–369.

Szibor, R. (2007). The X chromosome in forensic science: Past, present and future. Chapter 7. In R. Rapley & D. Whitehouse (Eds.), *Molecular Forensics* (pp. 103–126). Hoboken, New Jersey: Wiley.

Toni, C., et al. (2003). Population data of four X-chromosome markers in Tuscany, and their use in a deficiency paternity case. *Forensic Science International, 137*, 215–216.

Toni, C., et al. (2006). Usefulness of X-chromosome markers in resolving relationships: Report of a court case involving presumed half sisters. *Progress in Forensic Genetics 11, ICS 1288*, 301–303.

Tun, Z., et al. (1999). Simultaneous detection of multiple STR loci on sex chromosomes for forensic testing of sex and identity. *Journal of Forensic Sciences, 44*, 772–777.

Vauhkonen, H., et al. (2004). Correlation between the allelic distribution of STRs in a Finnish population and phenotypically different gastrointestinal tumours: A study using four X-chromosomal markers (DXS7423, DXS8377, ARA, DXS101). *Annuals of Human Genetics, 68*, 555–562.

Vecchione, G., et al. (2008). Fetal sex identification in maternal plasma by means of short tandem repeats on chromosome X. *Annals of the New York Academy of Sciences, 1137*, 148–156.

X-STR Markers

Augustin, C., et al. (2006). Forensic evaluation of three closely linked STR markers in a 13kb region at Xp11.23. *Progress in Forensic Genetics 11, ICS 1288*, 277–279.

Desmarais, D., et al. (1998). Development of a highly polymorphic STR marker for identity testing purposes at the human androgen receptor gene (HUMARA). *Journal of Forensic Sciences, 43*, 1046–1049.

Edelmann, J., & Szibor, R. (1999). Validation of the HumDXS6807 short tandem repeat polymorphism for forensic application. *Electrophoresis, 20*, 2844–2846.

Edelmann, J., & Szibor, R. (2001). DXS101: A highly polymorphic X-linked STR. *International Journal of Legal Medicine, 114*, 301–304.

Edelmann, J., et al. (2002). Sequence variation and allele nomenclature for the X-linked STRs DXS9895, DXS8378, DXS7132, DXS6800, DXS7133, GATA172D05, DXS7423 and DXS8377. *Forensic Science International, 129*, 99–103.

Edelmann, J., et al. (2002). Validation of the STR DXS7424 and the linkage situation on the X-chromosome. *Forensic Science International, 125*, 217–222.

Edelmann, J., et al. (2003). Validation of the X-chromosomal STR DXS6809. *International Journal of Legal Medicine, 117*, 241–244.

Edelmann, J., & Szibor, R. (2003). The X-linked STRs DXS7130 and DXS6803. *Forensic Science International, 136*, 73–75.

Edelmann, J., & Szibor, R. (2005). Validation of the X-linked STR DXS6801. *Forensic Science International, 148*, 219–220.

Edelmann, J., et al. (2008). Characterisation of the STR markers DXS10146, DXS10134 and DXS10147 located within a 79.1 kb region at Xq28. *Forensic Science International: Genetics, 2*, 41–46.

Edelmann, J., et al. (2010). Validation of six closely linked STRs located in the chromosome X centromere region. *International Journal of Legal Medicine, 124*, 83–87.

Gomes, I., et al. (2009). X-chromosome STR sequence variation, repeat structure, and nomenclature in humans and chimpanzees. *International Journal of Legal Medicine, 123*, 143–149.

Hearne, C. M., & Todd, J. A. (1991). Tetranucleotide repeat polymorphism at the HPRT locus. *Nucleic Acids Research, 19*, 5450.

Hering, S., & Szibor, R. (2000). Development of the X-linked tetrameric microsatellite marker DXS9898 for forensic purposes. *Journal of Forensic Sciences, 45*, 929–931.

Hering, S., et al. (2001). Development of the X-linked tetrameric microsatellite marker HumDXS6789 for forensic purposes. *Forensic Science International, 119*, 42–46.

Hering, S., et al. (2004). DXS10011: Studies on structure, allele distribution in three populations and genetic linkage to further q-telomeric chromosome X markers. *International Journal of Legal Medicine, 118*, 313–319.

Hering, S., et al. (2006). A cluster of six closely linked STR-markers: Recombination analysis in a 3.6Mb region at Xq12-13.1. *Progress in Forensic Genetics 11, ICS 1288*, 289–291.

Hering, S., et al. (2006). DXS10079, DXS10074 and DXS10075 are STRs located within a 280-kb region of Xq12 and provide stable haplotypes useful for complex kinship cases. *International Journal of Legal Medicine, 120*, 337–345.

Huang, D., et al. (2003). Development of the X-linked tetrameric microsatellite markers HumDXS6803 and HumDXS9895 for forensic purpose. *Forensic Science International, 133*, 246–249.

Hundertmark, T., et al. (2008). The STR cluster DXS10148-DXS8378-DXS10135 provides a powerful tool for X-chromosomal haplotyping at Xp22. *International Journal of Legal Medicine, 122*, 489–492.

Machado, F. B., & Medina-Acosta, E. (2009). Genetic map of human X-linked microsatellites used in forensic practice. *Forensic Science International: Genetics, 3*, 202–204.

Mahtani, M. M., & Willard, H. F. (1993). A polymorphic X-linked tetranucleotide repeat locus displaying a high rate of new mutation: Implications for mechanisms of mutation at short tandem repeat loci. *Human Molecular Genetics, 2*, 431–437.

Matise, T. C., et al. (2007). A second-generation combined linkage physical map of the human genome. *Genome Research, 17*, 1783–1786.

McNeil, J. A., et al. (2006). Word frequency analysis reveals enrichment of dinucleotide repeats on the human X chromosome and $[GATA]_n$ in the X escape region. *Genome Research, 16*, 477–484.

Mertens, G., et al. (1999). Mutation of the repeat number of the HPRTB locus and structure of rare intermediate alleles. *International Journal of Legal Medicine, 112*, 192–194.

Poetsch, M., et al. (2006). DXS6797 contains two STRs which can be easily haplotyped in both sexes. *International Journal of Legal Medicine, 120*, 61–66.

Rodig, H., et al. (2010). Evaluation of seven X-chromosomal short tandem repeat loci located within the Xq26 region. *Forensic Science International: Genetics, 4*, 194–199.

Subramanian, S., et al. (2003). Genome-wide analysis of microsatellite repeats in humans: Their abundance and density in specific genomic regions. *Genome Biology, 4*, R13. Available at <http://genomebiology.com/2003/4/2/R13>.

Szibor, R., et al. (2003). Sequence structure and population data of the X-linked markers DXS7423 and DXS8377–clarification of conflicting statements published by two working groups. *Forensic Science International, 134*, 72–73.

Szibor, R., et al. (2005). The HumARA genotype is linked to spinal and bulbar muscular dystrophy and some further disease risks and should no longer be used as a DNA marker for forensic purposes. *International Journal of Legal Medicine, 119*, 179–180.

Szibor, R., et al. (2009). Nomenclature discrepancies in the HPRTB short tandem repeat. *International Journal of Legal Medicine, 123*, 185–186.

Tamura, A., et al. (2004). Analysis of two types of novel alleles in the DXS10011 locus. *Legal Medicine, 6*, 52–54.

Watanabe, G., et al. (2000). DXS10011: A hypervariable tetranucleotide STR polymorphism on the X chromosome. *International Journal of Legal Medicine, 113*, 249–250.

Zarrabeitia, M. T., et al. (2002). Sequence structure and population data of two X-linked markers: DXS7423 and DXS8377. *International Journal of Legal Medicine, 116*, 368–371.

X-STR Kits and Assays

Asamura, H., et al. (2006). MiniX-STR multiplex system population study in Japan and application to degraded DNA analysis. *International Journal of Legal Medicine, 120*, 174–181.

Athanasiadou, D., et al. (2003). Development of a quadruplex PCR system for the genetic analysis of X-chromosomal STR loci. *Progress in Forensic Genetics 10, ICS 1239*, 311–314.

Bini, C., et al. (2005). Development of a heptaplex PCR system to analyse X-chromosome STR loci from five Italian population samples: A collaborative study. *Forensic Science International, 153*, 231–236.

Biotype's kit Argus X-8.<http://www.biotype.de/en/products/forensics/mentyper-argus-x-8.html>.

Biotype's kit Argus X-12. <http://www.biotype.de/en/products/forensics/mentyper-argus-x-12.html> and <http://www.qiagen.com/products/bylabfocus/forensics/default.aspx>.

Castella, V., et al. (2006). In-house validation of the PCR amplification kit Mentype Argus X-UL. *Progress in Forensic Genetics 11, ICS 1288*, 310–312.

Diegoli, T. M., & Coble, M. D. (2011). Development and characterization of two mini-X chromosomal short tandem repeat multiplexes: *Forensic Science International: Genetics* (in press). (doi: 10.1016/j.fsigen.2010.08.019).

Gehrig, C., & Teyssier, A. (2006). Validation of the Mentype Argus X-UL kit. *Progress in Forensic Genetics 11, ICS 1288*, 325–327.

Gomes, I., et al. (2006). A multiplex PCR design for simultaneous genotyping of X chromosome short tandem repeat markers. *Progress in Forensic Genetics 11, ICS 1288*, 313–315.

Henke, L., et al. (2004). A pentaplex PCR assay for the genetic analysis of ChrX short tandem repeat (STR) loci. *Progress in Forensic Genetics 10, ICS 1261*, 266–268.

Poetsch, M., et al. (2005). Development of two pentaplex systems with X-chromosomal STR loci and their allele frequencies in a northeast German population. *Forensic Science International, 155*, 71–76.

Ribeiro Rodrigues, E. M., et al. (2008). A multiplex PCR for 11 X chromosome STR markers and population data from a Brazilian Amazon Region. *Forensic Science International: Genetics, 2*, 154–158.

Turrina, S., et al. (2007). Development and forensic validation of a new multiplex PCR assay with 12 X-chromosomal short tandem repeats. *Forensic Science International: Genetics, 1*, 201–204.

Zarrabeitia, M. T., et al. (2002). A new pentaplex system to study short tandem repeat markers of forensic interest on X chromosome. *Forensic Science International, 129,* 85–89.

X-INDEL Assays

Freitas, N. S. C., et al. (2010). X-linked insertion/deletion polymorphisms: Forensic applications of a 33-markers panel. *International Journal of Legal Medicine, 124,* 589–593.

Rodrigues, E. M., et al. (2009). An INDEL polymorphism at the X-STR GATA172D05 flanking region. *International Journal of Legal Medicine, 123,* 89–94.

X-SNP Assays

Li, L., et al. (2010). Analysis of 14 highly informative SNP markers on X chromosome by TaqMan SNP genotyping assay. *Forensic Science International: Genetics, 4,* e145–e148.

Tomas, C., et al. (2010). Forensic usefulness of a 25 X-chromosome single-nucleotide polymorphism marker set. *Transfusion, 50,* 2258–2265.

Population Studies

Aler, M., et al. (2007). Genetic data of 10 X-STRs in a Spanish population sample. *Forensic Science International, 173,* 193–196.

Asamura, H., et al. (2006). Japanese population data for eight X-STR loci using two new quadruplex systems. *International Journal of Legal Medicine, 120,* 303–309.

Asmundo, A., et al. (2006). Allele distribution of two X-chromosomal STR loci in a population from Sicily (Southern Italy). *Progress in Forensic Genetics 11, ICS 1288,* 346–348.

Becker, D., et al. (2008). Population genetic evaluation of eight X-chromosomal short tandem repeat loci using Mentype Argus X-8 PCR amplification kit. *Forensic Science International: Genetics, 2,* 69–74.

Ca*i*né, L. M., et al. (2010). Genetic data of a Brazilian population sample (Santa Catarina) using an X-STR decaplex. *Journal of Forensic and Legal Medicine, 17,* 272–274.

Cerri, N., et al. (2006). Population data for four X-chromosomal STR loci in a population sample from Brescia (northern Italy). *Progress in Forensic Genetics 11, ICS 1288,* 286–288.

Chen, M. Y., et al. (2002). Population data on X chromosome short tandem repeat loci HPRTB and AR in Taiwan. *Forensic Science International, 126,* 171–172.

Chen, M. Y., & Pu, C. E. (2004). Population data on the X chromosome short tandem repeat loci DXS10011, DXS101, DXS6789, DXS7132, DXS8377, and DXS9895 in Taiwan. *Forensic Science International, 146,* 65–67.

Deng, J. Q., et al. (2003). Two X-chromosome STR loci DXS6804 and DXS9896 frequency data in Chinese population. *Journal of Forensic Sciences, 48* 886–886.

Deng, J. Q., et al. (2004). Population data of two X-chromosome STR loci GATA186D06 and GATA198A10 in China. *Journal of Forensic Sciences, 49,* 173.

Diegoli, T. M., et al. (2011). Population study of fourteen X chromosomal short tandem repeat loci in a population from Bosnia and Herzegovina. *Forensic Science International: Genetics* (in press). (doi: 10.1016/j.fsigen.2010.01.007).

Edelmann, J., et al. (2001). 16 X-chromosome STR loci frequency data from a German population. *Forensic Science International, 124,* 215–218.

Edelmann, J., et al. (2004). Allele frequencies for X-chromosomal microsatellites in different populations. *Progress in Forensic Genetics 10, ICS 1261,* 263–265.

Edwards, A., et al. (1992). Genetic variation at five trimeric and tetrameric tandem repeat loci in four human population groups. *Genomics, 12,* 241–253.

Ferreira da Silva, I. H., et al. (2010). An X-chromosome pentaplex in two linkage groups: haplotype data in Alagoas and Rio de Janeiro populations from Brazil. *Forensic Science International: Genetics, 4,* e95–e100.

Gao, S., et al. (2007). Allele frequencies for 10 X-STR loci in Nu population of Yunnan, China. *Legal Medicine, 9,* 284–286.

Gomes, I., et al. (2007). Genetic analysis of 3 US population groups using an X-chromosomal STR decaplex. *International Journal of Legal Medicine, 121,* 198–203.

Gomes, I., et al. (2007). Analysis of 10 X-STRs in three African populations. *Forensic Science International: Genetics, 1*, 208–211.

Gomes, I., et al. (2009). The Karimojong from Uganda: Genetic characterization using an X-STR decaplex system. *Forensic Science International: Genetics, 3*, e127–e128.

Gusmao, L., et al. (2009). A GEP-ISFG collaborative study on the optimization of an X-STR decaplex: Data on 15 Iberian and Latin American populations. *International Journal of Legal Medicine, 123*, 227–234.

Gu, S., & Li, S. (2006). X-chromosome STRs analysis of Ewenke ethnic population. *Forensic Science International, 158*, 72–75.

Hedman, M., et al. (2009). X-STR diversity patterns in the Finnish and the Somali population. *Forensic Science International: Genetics, 3*, 173–178.

Hou, Q. F., et al. (2007). Genetic polymorphisms of nine X-STR loci in four population groups from Inner Mongolia, China. *Genomics Proteomics. Bioinformatics, 5*, 59–65.

Hwa, H. L., et al. (2009). Thirteen X-chromosomal short tandem repeat loci multiplex data from Taiwanese. *International Journal of Legal Medicine, 123*, 263–269.

Jedrzejczyk, M., et al. (2008). Polymorphism of X-chromosome STR loci: DXS8378, DXS7132, HPRTB, DXS7423 in a population of Central Poland. *Problems of Forensic Sciences, 73*, 65–69.

Jia, Y., et al. (2004). Two X-chromosome STR loci DXS6803 and XS6793 frequency data in Chinese population. *Journal of Forensic Sciences, 49*, 845–846.

Kang, L., & Li, S. (2006). X-chromosome STR polymorphism of Luoba Ethnic Group living in Tibet (SW China). *Forensic Science International, 156*, 88–90.

Koyama, H., et al. (2002). Y-STR haplotype data and allele frequency of the DXS10011 locus in a Japanese population sample. *Forensic Science International, 125*, 273–276.

Lee, H. Y., et al. (2004). Genetic characteristics and population study of 4 X-chromosomal STRs in Koreans: Evidence for a null allele at DXS9898. *International Journal of Legal Medicine, 118*, 355–360.

Lee, S., et al. (2003). X-chromosome polymorphism in Koreans on DXS7132 and DXS6800. *Forensic Science International, 126*, 88–89.

Leite, F. P., et al. (2009). Linkage disequilibrium patterns and genetic structure of Amerindian and non-Amerindian Brazilian populations revealed by long-range X-STR markers. *American Journal of Physical Anthropology, 139*, 404–412.

Li, H., et al. (2009). A multiplex PCR for 4 X chromosome STR markers and population data from Beijing Han ethnic group. *Legal Medicine, 11*, 248–250.

Lim, E. J., et al. (2009). Genetic polymorphism and haplotype analysis of 4 tightly linked X-STR duos in Koreans. *Croatian Medical Journal, 50*, 305–312.

Liu, Q., & Li, S. (2006). Patterns of genetic polymorphism at the 10 X-chromosome STR loci in Mongol population. *Forensic Science International, 158*, 76–79.

Luo, H. B., et al. (2011). Characteristics of eight X-STR loci for forensic purposes in the Chinese population. *International Journal of Legal Medicine, 125*, 127–131.

Lv, M., et al. (2004). Allele frequency distribution of two X-chromosomal STR loci in Han population in China. *Journal of Forensic Sciences, 49*, 418–419.

Martins, J. A., et al. (2010). X-chromosome genetic variation in São Paulo State (Brazil) population. *Annals of Human Biology, 37*, 598–603.

Martins, J. A., et al. (2010). Genetic profile characterization of 10 X-STRs in four populations of the southeastern region of Brazil. *International Journal of Legal Medicine, 124*, 427–432.

Nadeem, A., et al. (2009). Development of pentaplex PCR and genetic analysis of X chromosomal STRs in Punjabi population of Pakistan. *Molecular Biology Reports, 36*, 1671–1675.

Oguzturun, C., et al. (2006). Population study of four X-chromosomal STR loci in the UK and Irish population. *Progress in Forensic Genetics 11, ICS 1288*, 283–285.

Peloso, G., et al. (2004). Allele distribution of five X-chromosome STR loci in an Italian population sample. *Progress in Forensic Genetics 10, ICS 1261*, 260–262.

Pepinski, W., et al. (2005). Polymorphism of four X-chromosomal STRs in a Polish population sample. *Forensic Science International, 151*, 93–95.

Pepinski, W., et al. (2007). X-chromosomal polymorphism data for the ethnic minority of Polish Tatars and the religious minority of Old Believers residing in northeastern Poland. *Forensic Science International: Genetics, 1*, 212–214.

Pereira, R., et al. (2007). Genetic diversity of 10 X-chromosome STRs in northern Portugal. *International Journal of Legal Medicine, 121*, 192–197.

Pico, A., et al. (2008). Genetic profile characterization and segregation analysis of 10 X-STRs in a sample from Santander, Columbia. *International Journal of Legal Medicine, 122*, 347–351.

Poetsch, M., et al. (2006). Population data of 10 X-chromosomal loci in Latvia. *Forensic Science International, 157*, 206–209.

Poetsch, M., et al. (2009). Allele frequencies of 11 X-chromosomal loci in a population sample from Ghana. *International Journal of Legal Medicine, 123*, 81–83.

Robino, C., et al. (2006). Development of two multiplex PCR systems for the analysis of 12 X-chromosomal STR loci in a northwestern Italian population sample. *International Journal of Legal Medicine, 120*, 315–318.

Shi, M. S., et al. (2003). Two X-chromosome STR loci DXS6807 and DXS7133 frequency data in Chinese population. *Journal of Forensic Sciences, 48* 689–689.

Shin, K. J., et al. (2004). Five highly informative X-chromosomal STRs in Koreans. *International Journal of Legal Medicine, 118*, 37–40.

Shin, S. H., et al. (2005). Genetic analysis of 18 X-linked short tandem repeat markers in Korean population. *Forensic Science International, 147*, 35–41.

Silva, F., et al. (2010). Genetic profiling of the Azores Islands (Portugal): Data from 10 X-chromosome STRs. *American Journal of Human Biology, 22*, 221–223.

Sim, J. E., et al. (2010). Population genetic study of four closely-linked X-STR trios in Koreans. *Molecular Biology Reports, 37*, 333–337.

Son, J. Y., et al. (2002). Polymorphism of nine X chromosomal STR loci in Koreans. *International Journal of Legal Medicine, 116*, 317–321.

Szibor, R., et al. (2000). Population data on the X chromosome short tandem repeat locus HumHPRTB in two regions of Germany. *Journal of Forensic Sciences, 45*, 231–233.

Tabbada, K. A., et al. (2005). Development of a pentaplex X-chromosomal short tandem repeat typing system and population genetic studies. *Forensic Science International, 154*, 173–180.

Tariq, M. A., et al. (2008). Allele frequency distribution of 13 X-chromosomal STR loci in Pakistani population. *International Journal of Legal Medicine, 122*, 525–528.

Tie, J., et al. (2010). Genetic polymorphisms of eight X-chromosomal STR loci in the population of Japanese. *Forensic Science International: Genetics, 4*, e105–e108.

Turrina, S., & De Leo, D. (2003). Population data of three X-chromosomal STRs: DXS7132, DXS7133 and GATA172D05 in North Italy. *Journal of Forensic Sciences, 48*, 1428–1429.

Wiegand, P., et al. (2003). Population genetic comparisons of three X-chromosomal STRs. *International Journal of Legal Medicine, 117*, 62–65.

Ying, B. W., et al. (2003). Chinese population data on DXS6797 and GATA144D04 loci. *Journal of Forensic Sciences, 48*, 1184.

Yu, B., et al. (2005). X-chromosome STRs polymorphisms of Han ethnic group from Northwest China. *Forensic Science International, 153*, 269–271.

Zarrabeitia, M. T., et al. (2004). X-linked microsatellites in two Northern Spain populations. *Forensic Science International, 145*, 57–59.

Zarrabeitia, M. T., et al. (2006). Study of six X-linked tetranucleotide microsatellites: Population data from five Spanish regions. *International Journal of Legal Medicine, 120*, 147–150.

Zarrabeitia, M. T., et al. (2009). Analysis of 10 X-linked tetranucleotide markers in mixed and isolated populations. *Forensic Science International: Genetics, 3*, 63–66.

Inheritance Studies, Mutation Rates, & Statistical Interpretation

Ayres, K. L., & Powley, W. M. (2005). Calculating the exclusion probability and paternity index for X-chromosomal loci in the presence of substructure. *Forensic Science International, 149*, 201–203.

Brenner, C. H. (2008). Counter example to a kinship conjecture of Krawczak. *Forensic Science International: Genetics, 2*, 75.

Fracasso, T., et al. (2008). An X-STR meiosis study in Kurds and Germans: Allele frequencies and mutation rates. *International Journal of Legal Medicine, 122*, 353–356.

Hering, S., et al. (2010). X chromosomal recombination – a family study analysing 39 STR markers in German three-generation pedigrees. *International Journal of Legal Medicine, 124*, 483–491.

Krawczak, M. (2007). Kinship testing with X-chromosomal markers: Mathematical and statistical issues. *Forensic Science International: Genetics, 1*, 111–114.

Tamura, A., et al. (2003). Sequence analysis of two de novo mutation alleles at the DXS10011 locus. *Legal Medicine, 5*, 161–164.

Tillmar, A. O., et al. (2008). Analysis of linkage and linkage disequilibrium for eight X-STR markers. *Forensic Science International: Genetics, 3*, 37–41.

Tillmar, A. O., et al. (2010). Using X-chromosomal markers in relationship testing: Calculation of likelihood ratios taking both linkage and linkage disequilibrium into account. *Forensic Science International: Genetics* (in press). doi:10.1016/j.fsigen.2010.11.004.

ChrX Work with Other Species

van Asch, B., et al. (2010). A framework for the development of STR genotyping in domestic animal species: Characterization and population study of 12 canine X-chromosome loci. *Electrophoresis, 31*, 303–308.

CHAPTER

16

Non-human DNA

While the vast majority of forensic DNA typing performed for criminal investigations involves human DNA, it is not the only source of DNA that may be useful in demonstrating the guilt or innocence of an individual suspected of a crime (Sensabaugh & Kaye 1998). Recent books have reviewed efforts with non-human DNA (Coyle 2008), wildlife DNA testing (Linacre 2009), and microbial forensics (Budowle et al. 2011).

Domestic animals such as cats and dogs live in human habitats and deposit hair that may be used to place a suspect at the crime scene (D'Andrea et al. 1998). DNA testing can benefit wildlife law enforcement efforts to eliminate poaching or sale of products from endangered species. Demonstration that a botanical specimen came from a particular plant can aid the linkage of a crime to a suspect or help demonstrate that the body of a deceased victim may have been moved from the murder site. DNA testing can be used to link sources of marijuana. A large area of future application for forensic DNA typing involves identification of bioterrorism materials such as anthrax. This chapter will briefly discuss each of these topics and the value of non-human DNA testing in forensic casework. The reference list at the back of the chapter will lead interested readers to additional sources of information on various topics relating to non-human DNA.

As most forensic DNA laboratories will not have the capability or in-house expertise to handle non-human DNA cases when they occasionally occur, samples are often outsourced to specialist laboratories with the appropriate expertise in species identification and animal or plant DNA testing (Ogden 2010). These laboratories may be academic research groups rather than forensic laboratories with established quality assurance measures.

A DNA Commission of the International Society of Forensic Genetics (ISFG) has provided 13 recommendations regarding the use of non-human (animal) DNA in forensic genetic investigations (Linacre et al. 2011; D.N.A. Box 16.1). Recommendations for animal DNA forensic and identity testing have also been made by a group of scientists from the United States, Italy, Germany, Austria, The Netherlands, and Australia who met at the September 2004 International Society for Animal Genetics (ISAG) meeting (Budowle et al. 2005). These recommendations review the importance of using established standard operating procotols (SOPs) along with positive and negative controls. Standardized nomenclatures for loci and alleles are advocated in order to facilitate interlaboratory comparisons and use of

D.N.A. BOX 16.1

ISFG RECOMMENDATIONS FOR USE OF NON-HUMAN (ANIMAL) DNA

Based on discussions held at the 23rd Congress of the International Society for Forensic Genetics (ISFG) in Buenos Aires, Argentina (September 2009), an ISFG DNA Commission has outlined 13 recommendations for animal DNA testing (Linacre et al. 2011):

1. The same procedures to ensure integrity and traceability of the items should be employed in the collection and examination of animal samples as undertaken for any other forensic investigation.
2. Validation studies from non-domesticated species should use voucher specimens where possible. If this is not possible, then a justification needs to be made for the sample type used.
3. The choice of locus/loci used in species identification, such as, but not restricted to, the mitochondrial genes cyt b, COI, and the D-loop region, needs to be justified based on the ability to identify the unknown species among those that are close genetic relatives.
4. The nucleotide sequence and map showing the location of the primers used in species testing needs to be provided or referenced to a previously published article.
5. Intraspecies and interspecies studies should be provided for any novel primer set used in species identification. The process undertaken to validate the test should be provided, including, but not exclusively, studies on sensitivity, specificity, reproducibility and mixed samples.
6. Primers used to amplify polymorphic DNA should be tested to ensure specificity and reproducibility and should be published in the public domain.
7. If repeat-based polymorphic loci are used for individualization, tetrameric short tandem repeat systems should be used preferentially.
8. Sequenced allelic ladders are essential for the accurate designation of alleles and should be used in all STR typing. The number of repeats should be the basis of reporting of results rather than using only the size based on the number of base pairs of any samples tested.
9. In relationship testing, the mutation probabilities of the STR alleles should be estimated if encountered, or at least the probability of a mutational event occurring should be considered when there is genetic inconsistency at a single or few loci while all other loci show genetic consistency.
10. Relevant population and forensic genetic parameters including allele frequencies should be estimated.
11. A kinship factor should be determined and applied in any calculation. The type of kinship factor applied should be stated clearly and justification should be made for the factor incorporated.
12. A comprehensive casefile should be maintained. A likelihood ratio approach is the recommended way to evaluate the weight of the evidence, considering more than one proposition.
13. Accreditation should be sought if DNA testing of non-human animal DNA for a particular purpose is to become routine.

Source:

Linacre, A., et al. (2011). ISFG: Recommendations regarding the use of non-human (animal) DNA in forensic genetic investigations. Forensic Science International: Genetics (in press). *doi:10.1016/j.fsigen.2010.10.017.*

well-characterized cell lines or reference DNA samples is encouraged to enable compatibility between testing laboratories. Population data should be collected in order to assess allele frequencies and data behind the reference database made available for review so that assumptions involved in the statistical estimate are transparent.

SOPs need to be based on laboratory validation that has defined the operational limits of the technique involved. Scientists using these protocols should successfully complete a qualifying test before performing casework and participate in regular proficiency testing. Casework files should be maintained for each case and should undergo technical and administrative review. Laboratories that do not meet these best practices should disclose to their customer what part of these recommended quality assurance practices are not being met (Budowle et al. 2005).

DOMESTIC ANIMAL DNA TESTING

Budowle et al. (2005) note that genetic analysis with animal DNA samples can help resolve criminal and civil cases as well as aiding kinship analysis with applications such as determining the sire of an offspring when a female has been exposed to multiple males. This chapter will first discuss DNA testing done with domestic animals and then review work with wildlife testing and species identification.

The American Pet Products Association reported in their 2007 and 2008 national pet owners survey that over 71 million U.S. households own a pet (see http://www.appma.org). Their survey found 88 million cats and 75 million dogs in these households, which make up almost two-thirds of all U.S. residences. Since many of these domestic animals shed hair, these hairs could be picked up or left behind at the scene of a crime by a perpetrator. An assailant may unknowingly carry clinging cat hairs from a victim's cat away from the scene of a crime, or hair from the perpetrator's cat may be left at the scene.

The Veterinary Genetics Laboratory (VGL) at the University of California-Davis (see http://www.vgl.ucdavis.edu/forensics) has been performing forensic animal DNA analyses since 1996. The VGL website notes that there are three types of animal DNA evidence: (1) the animal as victim, (2) the animal as perpetrator, and (3) the animal as witness.

Animal abuse cases or the theft of an animal can sometimes be benefited by the power of DNA testing. The remains of a lost pet can be positively identified through genetic analysis. Typically genetic markers like short tandem repeats (STRs) and mitochondrial DNA (mtDNA) are examined in much the same way as with human DNA.

When animals are involved in an attack on a person, DNA typing may be used to identify the animal perpetrator (e.g., a Pit Bull). If the victim is deceased, then DNA evidence may be the only witness that an animal in custody committed the crime. Animal DNA testing can "exonerate" innocent animals so that they are not needlessly destroyed.

Animal DNA has been used successfully to link suspects to crime scenes. A study on the transfer of animal hair during simulated criminal behavior found that hundreds of cat hairs or dog hairs could be transferred from the homes of victims to a burglar or an aggressor (D'Andrea et al. 1998). In fact, the number of hairs found was so high that the authors of this study felt that it is almost impossible to enter a house where a domestic animal lives without being "contaminated" by cat and/or dog hairs even when the owner describes his or her animal as a poor source of hair (D'Andrea et al. 1998). Due to the fact that shed hairs often do not contain roots, nuclear DNA may not be present in sufficient quantities for STR typing. Mitochondrial DNA may be a more viable alternative for many of these types of shed hair transfers.

Cat DNA

Cats have 18 pairs of autosomes and the sex chromosomes X and Y. Genetic markers have been developed on each of the *Felis catus* chromosomes (Menotti-Raymond et al. 1999). Menotti-Raymond et al. (2005) examined 49 candidate tri- and tetranucleotide STR loci and selected 11 of these as a forensic panel for genetic individualization of domestic cat samples. A multiplex PCR assay utilizing these 11 STRs, which are on nine different chromosomes, has been dubbed the "MeowPlex" (Butler et al. 2002). The power of discrimination with this 11plex feline STR multiplex ranged from 5.5×10^7 to 3.3×10^{13} across the various breeds (Menotti-Raymond et al. 2005).

A gender identification marker was also included in this assay through the addition of PCR primers that are specific for the SRY gene on the cat Y-chromosome. The PCR products for this 12plex amplification fall in the size range of 100bp to 400bp and use three dye colors (Figure 16.1). In another version of this assay, two of the loci were moved into a fourth dye color to avoid overlaps in PCR product sizes with the discovery of new alleles (Menotti-Raymond et al. 2005).

Feline STR allele frequencies from domestic cats have been published (Menotti-Raymond et al. 1997a) for the purpose of demonstrating uniqueness of DNA profiles in forensic investigations, such as used in the Beamish case with his cat "Snowball" (Menotti-Raymond et al. 1997b; see also Butler 2010, *Fundamentals*, D.N.A. Box 15.3). The International Cat Association (TICA; see http://www.tica.org/) recognizes 55 breeds of cat.

Population studies on over 1200 cats from 37 different breeds have been conducted by the Laboratory of Genomic Diversity at the National Cancer Institute-Frederick Cancer Research and Development Center in Frederick, Maryland (Menotti-Raymond et al. 2005). In an initial

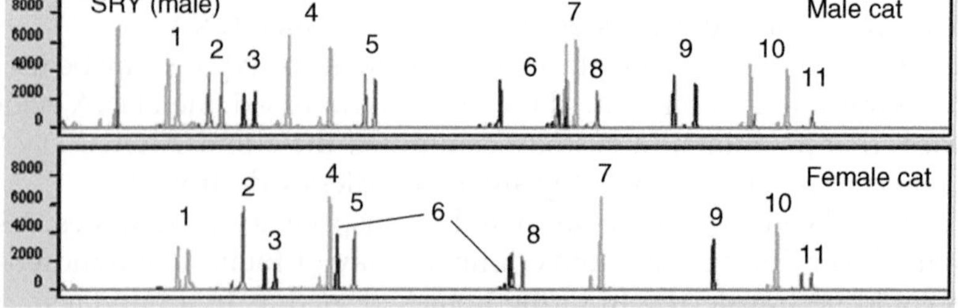

FIGURE 16.1 DNA profiles produced from male (top panel) and female (bottom panel) cat DNA using a multiplex STR typing assay dubbed the "MeowPlex" (Butler et al. 2002). This test examines 11 autosomal STRs and a region of the SRY gene contained on the Y-chromosome that can be used for sex determination.

study of 223 cats from 28 different breeds, the MeowPlex exhibited an average composite locus heterozygosity of 0.73 across the breeds (Menotti-Raymond et al. 2003).

The commonly used cat STR loci are described in Table 16.1. A section of the NIST STRBase website also includes information on cat STRs: http://www.cstl.nist.gov/biotech/strbase/catSTRs.htm.

A real-time quantitative polymerase chain reaction (qPCR) assay (see Chapter 3) for estimating the DNA yield extracted from domestic cat specimens has been developed (Menotti-Raymond et al. 2003). This assay is capable of detecting down to 10 femtograms of feline genomic DNA and uses high-copy number short interspersed nuclear elements (SINEs) similar to the *Alu* repeats described in Chapter 12.

TABLE 16.1 Commonly Used Cat STR Loci. The 11 Loci Shaded in Gray Are Part of a Proposed Forensic Typing System (Menotti-Raymond et al. 2005) Co-Amplified as the "MeowPlex" (Butler et al. 2002). The Additional Dinucleotide Loci and FCA 441 Make up a Core Panel for Cat Identification and Parentage Testing Proposed by the International Society for Animal Genetics (Lipinski et al. 2007).

Locus	Cat Chromosome	Repeat Motif	Size Range	Reference
FCA 733	B2	GATA	128–226 bp	Menotti-Raymond et al. (2005)
FCA 723	A1	$(GGAA)_nG(GAAA)_m$	243–317 bp	Menotti-Raymond et al. (2005)
FCA 731	B1	CCAT	337–401 bp	Menotti-Raymond et al. (2005)
FCA 736	B4	$(ATAC)_n$ $(CA)_3$ $(ATAG)_m$	164–222 bp	Menotti-Raymond et al. (2005)
F 124	E1	GAAA	225–367 bp	Menotti-Raymond et al. (2005)
FCA 742	D4	CTTT	122–175 bp	Menotti-Raymond et al. (2005)
F85	B1	$(CTTT)_n$ $(CT)_{10}$ $(T)_4$ $(CTTT)_m$	183–301 bp	Menotti-Raymond et al. (2005)
FCA 740	C1	GATA	308–336 bp	Menotti-Raymond et al. (2005)
F 53	A1	GAAA	115–272 bp	Menotti-Raymond et al. (2005)
FCA 749	F2	GATA	276–416 bp	Menotti-Raymond et al. (2005)
FCA 441	D3	TAGA	113–137 bp	Menotti-Raymond et al. (2005)
			133–173 bp	Lipinski et al. (2007)
FCA 069	B4	AC	88–116 bp	Lipinski et al. (2007)
FCA 075	E2	TG	112–146 bp	Lipinski et al. (2007)
FCA 105	A2	TG	173–207 bp	Lipinski et al. (2007)
FCA 149	B1	TG	120–136 bp	Lipinski et al. (2007)
FCA 220	F2	CA	208–224 bp	Lipinski et al. (2007)
FCA 229	A1	GT	150–174 bp	Lipinski et al. (2007)
FCA 310	C2	$(CA)_n$ TA $(CA)_m$ TA $(CA)_p$	112–138 bp	Lipinski et al. (2007)
FCA 678	A1	AC	222–236 bp	Lipinski et al. (2007)

Dog DNA

While cat DNA testing may be involved in situations where the animal hair acts as a silent witness to connecting a perpetrator to a crime scene, evidence from dogs is more frequently linked to situations where the animal is the perpetrator. Rottweilers, German Shepherds, Doberman Pinschers, and Pit Bulls can be trained as security animals and may attack, injure, or even kill people. For example, with a canine population in Australia of around 4 million, there are an estimated 100,000 dog attacks each year—and many of them go unsolved (Clarke & Vandenberg 2010).

Canine STR Loci and Assays

A number of STR markers have been mapped and characterized on the 38 pairs of autosomes and the X-chromosome of *Canis familiaris*, the domestic dog (Neff et al. 1999). Early dog STR assays included many dinucleotide repeat loci but tetranucleotide loci with lower stutter have been the focus of more recent efforts. However, different groups have targeted different sets of loci with almost no overlap between them (Halverson & Basten 2005, Berger et al. 2008, van Asch et al. 2009, Tom et al. 2010). There is a need for standardization on the loci and allele nomenclatures used (Berger et al. 2009). In an early effort, 15 canine STR loci were characterized with sequenced alleles (Eichmann et al. 2004).

The commonly used canine STR loci are described in Table 16.2. A section of the NIST STRBase website also includes information on dog STRs: http://www.cstl.nist.gov/biotech/strbase/dogSTRs.htm. The PEZ locus names come from Perklin-Elmer Zoogen, a company that developed the StockMark kits for Applied Biosystems back in the mid-to-late 1990s. The FH locus names came from the Fred Hutchinson Cancer Research Center (Seattle, Washington).

Finnzymes (Espoo, Finland) has also released a commercial kit with 18 STR loci and amelogenin for sex-typing that utilizes dinucleotide markers (see http://diagnostics.finnzymes.fi/canine_genotypes.html).

A set of 10 dinucleotide repeat STRs has been used to aid investigations in illegal animal deaths (Padar et al. 2001) and a dog attack that resulted in the death of a seven-year-old boy (Padar et al. 2002). In addition, it was demonstrated that DNA profiling of human blood recovered from a dog's fur can associate or exonerate the animal from connection to an attack (Brauner et al. 2001).

Canine mtDNA Testing

Canine mitochondrial DNA possesses two hypervariable regions (HV1 and HV2) similar to the human mtDNA described in Chapter 14. Savolainen et al. (1997) found 19 sequence variants across a 257bp segment of the hypervariable region 1 of the mtDNA control region in 102 domestic dogs of 52 different breeds. They concluded that on average 88 out of 100 tested animals could be excluded with this mtDNA sequence analysis. By way of comparison in 100 British white Caucasians an exclusion capacity of 0.97 was observed (Piercy et al. 1993). While domesticated dog mtDNA is not as variable as human mtDNA, it can still provide helpful clues in forensic cases (Savolainen and Lundeberg 1999, Schneider et al. 1999).

TABLE 16.2 Information on Some Commonly Used Dog STR Loci.

Locus	Canine Chromosome	Repeat Motif	Size Range	Reference
PEZ01	7	TACA	95–136bp	StockMarks kit
PEZ02	17	GGAA	104–144bp	Tom et al. (2010)
PEZ03	19	GAA	95–154bp	StockMarks kit
PEZ05	12	TTTA	92–116bp	Tom et al. (2010); StockMarks kit
PEZ15	16	AGAA	183–249bp	Berger et al. (2008)
PEZ16	27	GAAA	281–332bp	Tom et al. (2010)
PEZ17	4	GAAA	191–225bp	Tom et al. (2010)
PEZ20	22	AAAT	152–202bp	StockMarks kit
PEZ21	2	AAAT	83–103bp	Tom et al. (2010)
FH2001	23	GATA	119–160bp	Tom et al. (2010)
FH2004	11	AAAG	233–325bp	Tom et al. (2010)
			161–257bp	van Asch et al. (2008)
FH2010	24	ATGA TTCA	222–243bp	Tom et al. (2010)
			154–170bp	van Asch et al. (2008); StockMarks kit;
FH2017	15	AGGT/AGAT/GATA	257–276bp	Tom et al. (2010)
FH2054	12	GATA	139–177bp	Tom et al. (2010); Finnzymes kit StockMarks kit
FH2088	15	TTTA/TTCA	94–138bp	Tom et al. (2010)
FH2107	3	GAAA	292–426bp	Tom et al. (2010)
FH2309	1	GAAA	340–428bp	Tom et al. (2010)
FH2328	33	GAAA	171–213bp	Tom et al. (2010)
FH2361	29	GAAA TTTC	323–439	Tom et al. (2010)
			231–347bp	van Asch et al. (2008)
FH2079	24	GGAT	263–299	Berger et al. (2008); StockMarks kit
FH3313	19	GAAA	341–446bp	Tom et al. (2010)
FH3377	3	GAAAA	183–305bp	Tom et al. (2010)
FH2658	14	GAAA	106–138bp	van Asch et al. (2008)
FH3210	2	AAGA	230–315bp	van Asch et al. (2008)
FH3241	8	TTCT	250–270bp	van Asch et al. (2008)
FH4012	15	TTTC	119–143bp	van Asch et al. (2008)
REN214L11	16	GAAT	154–162bp	van Asch et al. (2008)
C38	38	TTCT	132–217bp	van Asch et al. (2008)
VWF.X	27	AGGAAT	151–187bp	Tom et al. (2010)

Efforts have been made to standardize the nomenclature for the canine mtDNA control region (Pereira et al. 2004) and informative sequence variants outside of the control region have also been identified (Webb & Allard 2009a, 2009b).

Other Domesticated Animals

While DNA testing of household animals like dogs and cats can help solve crimes, other domesticated animals—particularly animals used for recreation or sources of food—may be DNA tested for identification purposes. DNA tests have been developed for horses (Dimsoski 2003, van de Goor et al. 2010, Chen 2010), cattle (van de Goor et al. 2009), pigs (Robino et al. 2008), and sheep (Heaton et al. 2010). These genetic identification tests can be used to track the source of tainted meat products such as those obtained from cattle suffering from "mad cow disease." Horse DNA testing can be important for confirming genetic pedigrees and is required for registering some breeds including American Quarterhorses and many racehorses (Bowling et al. 1997, Tozaki et al. 2001).

Sources for Performing Non-Human DNA Testing

Testing of non-human DNA samples is not routinely performed in public forensic laboratories and thus these types of studies have to be outsourced to academic labs or speciality laboratories that focus on testing specific species (see Ogden 2010). As noted earlier, the Veterinary Genetics Laboratory (VGL) at the University of California-Davis has been performing forensic animal DNA analyses since 1996. As of October 2010, the VGL offers genetic analyses for parentage verfication, genetic disease screening, and diagnostic testing on alpaca, beefalo, bison, cat, cattle, deer, dog, elk, goat, horse, llama, pig, sheep, water buffalo, and yak samples.

The U.S. Fish and Wildlife Service Forensic Laboratory (http://www.lab.fws.gov/) in Ashland, Oregon conducts species identification as well as other DNA testing to aid fish and wildlife forensic investigations. Feline STRs and mtDNA testing is performed by QuestGen Forensics (http://www.questgen.biz/), which also does canine STR and mtDNA testing to aid forensic investigations.

SPECIES IDENTIFICATION

There is value in species identification particularly when bones or bone fragments are being uncovered from a gravesite. Are they human remains or those of an animal? Because mtDNA with its higher copy number survives better than nuclear DNA in highly processed or degraded bone or tissue, it has value in species identification. Several informative segments of mtDNA are conserved enough that universal primers can be employed to amplify a target region with subsequent sequence analysis to differentiate between species (Linacre & Tobe 2009).

Typical steps in species identification involve: (1) sequence analysis of a selected variable region of DNA with conserved primers and (2) comparison of these sequence results to a database of sequences such as GenBank usually through phylogenetic analysis to place the seqeuence obtained in context of other previously reported DNA sequences for the same region.

mtDNA Cytochrome b Gene

Sequence analysis of the mtDNA cytochrome b gene is effective at identifying the species of origin for a biological sample (Parson et al. 2000, Hsieh et al. 2001, Branicki et al. 2003, Linacre et al. 2004). Some tests have even been developed to simultaneously amplify both the human mtDNA control and the cytochrome b gene to enable simultaneous human and species identification (Bataille et al. 1999).

mtDNA 12S rRNA Gene

Another mtDNA region examined for species identification is the 12S ribosomal RNA gene (Balitzki-Korte et al. 2005, Melton & Holland 2007). In one study, DNA sequence analysis of an ≈150bp fragment of the 12S rRNA mtDNA successfully identified dog, feral pig, raccoon, cat, goat, sheep, rat, and yak DNA samples in 12 different forensic cases (Melton & Holland 2007).

mtDNA COI Gene

An international effort, known as the Barcode of Life Project (Ratnasingham & Hebert 2007), is working to catalog different species through utilizing a 648bp region from the mitochondrial cytochrome c oxidase 1 (COI) gene. The COI gene has proved effective for animals but the mutation rate is too slow to be useful in resolving various plant species from one another. The barcoding gene COI has been explored for use in a forensic context (Dawnay et al. 2007, Wilson-Wilde et al. 2010).

Application for Body Fluid Identification

Species identification techniques can also help with identification of body fluids. Researchers from New Zealand (Fleming & Harbison 2010) used the 16S-23S rRNA intergenic spacer region to help identify vaginal specific bacteria—*Lactobacillus crispatus* and *Lactobacillus gasseri*. They then incorporated their *Lactobacilli* markers into an 11plex mRNA multiplex system to enable identification of circulatory blood, menstrual blood, saliva, semen, and vaginal secretions.

Detection of Streptococcus bacteria, which are only found in the human mouth and saliva, has been used for saliva identification (Nakanishi et al. 2009) and distinguishing bloodspatter originating from an individual's oral cavity (i.e., mouth or nose) from other types of bloodstains (Donaldson et al. 2010).

WILDLIFE DNA TESTING

Interpol estimates that illegal trade of wildlife takes place in a growing global black market at a pace of approximately $20 billion per year (Wilson-Wilde 2010, Alacs 2010). The remains of stolen animals or illegally procured meat (e.g., endangered species or poaching) can be identified through DNA testing (Giovambattista et al. 2001, Poetsch et al. 2001). Genetic testing can be used to help prosecute individuals who exploit exotic or endangered animals. The U.S. Fish and Wildlife Service's forensic laboratory in Ashland, Oregon does some species identification using DNA (see http://www.lab.fws.gov). Other laboratories performing similar wildlife DNA testing are located in Canada and the UK.

As with any DNA testing method applied to forensic investigations, validation experiments are important to defining assay performance (Dawnay et al. 2008). Allele frequencies are measured to help underpin statistical calculations on the rarity of DNA profiles (Jobin et al. 2008). The small sample sizes collected in some wildlife studies can impact the minimum allele frequencies used.

Techniques for Assessing Genetic Differences

Several techniques may be utilized for assessing genetic differences between organisms being tested. Which technique is best to use will generally depend on the amount of prior information available. Advantages and disadvantages of each approach are compared in Table 16.3.

DNA Sequencing

DNA sequence analysis of specific genes, such as mtDNA cytochrome b, is beneficial in that complete details down to the molecular level are available for the tested specimen. However, sequence analysis is relatively expensive and time-consuming with mostly redundant information. Sample mixtures and multi-ploidy genomes are also more difficult to decipher from sequence information.

TABLE 16.3 Table of Advantages and Disadvantages of Each Approach (See Linacre & Tobe 2009, pp. 68–69).

Approach	Advantages	Disadvantages
Sequence Analysis (universal primers)	Can analyze a wide range of species if using universal primers A database can be built	Cannot separate mixtures
STR or SNP Typing (species-specific primers)	Able to separate mixtures May be possible to add new species to a multiplex assay	Prior sequence knowledge is needed to design primers
RAPD	Inexpensive	Difficult to reproduce within and between laboratories Cannot produce a database
AFLP/T-RFLP	Fairly inexpensive A database can be built	May not have the individual resolving power of STR typing

STR Typing

If a specific locus with many alleles can be determined, PCR primers can be designed and allele sizes differentiated. However, the genome sequences for many organisms of interest (plant and animal) are not yet available and STR loci have not been characterized. For this reason, other techniques are sometimes used to help screen for sample genetic differences and similarities.

RAPD

Randomly amplified polymorphic DNA, or RAPD, marker analysis utilizes short PCR primers consisting of random sequences usually in the size range of 8 to 15 nucleotides in length. Complex patterns of PCR products are generated as these random sequence primers anneal to various regions in an organism's genome. RAPD suffers from poor reproducibility between laboratories largely because of the requirement of consistent PCR amplification conditions including thermal cycler ramp speeds. The complex patterns of RAPD also prevent mixture interpretation and provide challenges in consistent scoring of electrophoretic images even in single-source samples.

AFLP

Patterns from amplified fragment length polymorphism markers can be generated with greater reproducibility compared to RAPDs. AFLPs are generated by first cutting a double-stranded DNA sample with one or more restriction enzymes (Vos et al. 1995, Ranamukhaarachchi et al. 2000). Specific "adaptor" sequences are then ligated to the restriction cut sites. PCR primers that recognize these ligated adaptor sequences are used to amplify different sized DNA fragments that can then be separated using electrophoresis. The final result is a complex series of peaks usually in the 50bp to 400bp size range that can be scored with computer software and compared with other AFLP patterns.

T-RFLP

In terminal restriction fragment length polymorphism (T-RFLP), PCR is used to amplify a region of bacterial DNA that contains conserved primer binding sites. One primer has a 5′-fluorescent tag to enable detection. Following PCR, the amplicons are digested with a restriction enzyme. Based on sequence differences within the amplified target sequence, different-sized products will be generated. Capillary electrophoresis separation and detection of the different fragments results in a bacterial T-RFLP profile. Profile patterns can be compared with multi-dimensional scaling (MDS) plots (Lenz & Foran 2010).

PLANT & POLLEN DNA TESTING

In the area of plant DNA testing, there are primarily two areas currently being investigated. The first is the linking of plant material to suspects or victims in order to make an association with a particular area where a crime was committed. The second is in linking marijuana to aid in forensic drug investigations. Some of the applications of forensic botany have been reviewed by Heather Miller-Coyle (Miller-Coyle et al. 2001, Coyle 2008).

Linking Plant Materials to Suspects

Crimes often occur in localized areas containing a unique combination of botanical growth. If these plants, algae, or grass are sufficiently rare, then recovery of trace evidence from the clothing of a victim or the personal property of a suspect may be helpful in making an association that can link them to a crime scene (Szibor et al. 1998, Norris and Bock 2000, Horrocks and Walsh 2001).

Although plant DNA testing is not yet used routinely (Bock and Norris 1997), it has helped link suspects to crime scenes and aided important investigations. In the first use of forensic botanical evidence, two small seedpods from an Arizona Palo Verde tree found in the back of a pick-up truck were used to place an accused murderer at the crime scene (Yoon 1993). Genetic testing on the seeds showed that in a "lineup" of 12 Palo Verde trees near the crime scene, DNA from the seeds matched only the tree under which the victim's body had been found. In *State v. Bogan*, the jury found the accused guilty based in large measure on the plant DNA evidence.

Marijuana DNA

Several DNA tests have been developed for *Cannabis sativa* (marijuana) because it is an illegal substance associated with many crime scenes. Marijuana is one of the most commonly identified drugs tested by U.S. forensic laboratories (see http://www.deadiversion.usdoj.gov/nflis).

Marijuana DNA testing can link an individual to a sample, link growers, and help track distribution networks (Miller-Coyle et al. 2001). However, it is important to keep in mind that if the marijuana plants were propagated clonally rather than by seed, then they will have identical DNA profiles. Clonal propagation in marijuana is performed by taking cuttings from a "mother" plant and rooting them directly in the soil to create large numbers of plants having identical DNA (Miller-Coyle et al. 2001).

Efficient extraction protocols have been developed that yield 125 ng to 500 ng of DNA per 100 mg of fresh plant tissue (Miller-Coyle et al. 2003a). DNA testing of marijuana as with other plants has traditionally been performed with one of three methodologies: randomly amplified polymorphic DNA markers (RAPDs), amplified fragment length polymorphisms (AFLPs), or short tandem repeats (STRs). These techniques and their specific application to marijuana DNA typing have been reviewed (Miller-Coyle et al. 2003b). Even highly inbred individual plants can be distinguished by their AFLP patterns (Miller-Coyle et al. 2003b).

A few STR markers have been characterized in *Cannabis sativa* and developed into effective DNA tests (Hsieh et al. 2003, Gilmore et al. 2003, Alghanim & Almirall 2003). As with human STRs, marijuana STR markers are highly polymorphic, specific to unique sites in the genome, and capable of deciphering mixtures. A hexanucleotide repeat marker showed repeat units ranging from 3 to 40 in 108 tested marijuana samples, and primers amplifying this locus produced no cross-reactive amplicons from 20 other species of plants tested (Hsieh et al. 2003).

Efforts have been made to improve molecular techniques for identifying marijuana plants and to develop comparative databases to serve as effective tools for law enforcement purposes. In order to determine the possibility of a random match with marijuana seizure samples, it is important to have a database of seizure samples so their DNA profiles can be used for comparison (Miller-Coyle et al. 2003).

Bacterial DNA in Soil

Soil is filled with a variety of microscopic organisms including bacteria and fungi. It has been shown that different combinations of bacteria in soil samples from different locations can be differentiated with DNA testing (Horswell et al. 2002, Heath & Saunders 2008, Lenz & Foran 2010).

The use of these DNA signatures from soil microbes are being explored to see if this information can be used to link individuals to a specific location based on soil found on their shoes or clothing. This type of forensic soil evaluation could then potentially link a suspect to a crime scene or identify where a victim was killed and whether the body was moved to a different location. Appropriate sampling still remains a challenge as well as overcoming PCR inhibitors present in soil, but this is an area that could bear fruit in the future.

IDENTIFICATION THROUGH HUMAN PARASITES

Research has demonstrated that it is possible to differentiate between individuals based on DNA sequence differences found within parasites, such as viruses found within the individuals. Japanese researchers have focused on various methods of typing the JC human polyomavirus as a means for tracing geographic origins of unidentified cadavers (Ikegaya et al. 2002, Ikegaya et al. 2008, Ikegaya 2008).

MICROBIAL FORENSICS

Unfortunately microbial forensics will likely become a larger part of DNA testing in the future with the threat of terrorism and the use of biological warfare agents. Microbial evidence can be obtained from either real terrorist events or hoaxes. The efforts in this area will likely require forensic laboratories to build strong collaborations with academia, private sector, and national laboratories. Important requirements of bio-threat detection assays are high sensitivity, high specificity in complex samples, fast measurement, compact design for portability and field use, and internal calibration and reference to ensure reliable results (Ivnitski et al. 2003).

In October 2001 a bioterrorism attack impacted the United States as government offices and media outlets received anthrax-laden letters sent anonymously through the postal service. This attack resulted in 22 anthrax cases and five deaths. In addition, many people were afraid to open their mail for months afterwards. In the two years following this attack, more than 125,000 samples were processed as part of this case (Popovic & Glass 2003). In August 2008, almost seven years after the anthrax attack, the FBI Laboratory announced a breakthrough in the "Amerithrax" investigation with plans to charge Dr. Bruce Ivins, a scientist at the U.S. Army Medical Research Institute for Infectious Diseases (USAMRIID) in Frederick, Maryland. Dr. Ivins committed suicide before the charges could be filed.

Several challenges arise when trying to gather evidence, identify the bio-crime organism(s), and trace the source of the organism(s). First responders to crime scenes where biological weapons have been dispersed have to be concerned about their own safety and the safety of others while maintaining chain of custody of any evidence collected from the crime scene, all the while trying to prevent contamination of the evidence and the environment. Databases need to be established for intrinsic background species and bio-threat strains. Reliable reference material is needed for comparison purposes. Proficiency and validation testing are necessary to estimate false-positive and false-negative rates (Kiem 2003).

The U.S. efforts in building a response to bioterrorism have been announced in a policy paper (Budowle et al. 2003). Shortly after the attacks of September 11, 2001, the FBI initiated a Scientific Working Group on Microbial Genetics and Forensics (SWGMGF) that helped develop guidelines related to the operation of microbial forensics (SWGMGF 2003). Currently there are an insufficient number of validated analytical tools to characterize and identify biological agents that might be used in a terrorist attack (Budowle 2003). Research efforts will continue in this area.

Comparative genome sequencing promises to be a powerful tool for investigating infectious disease outbreaks as was performed with the whole-genome sequencing of *Bacillus anthracis* (anthrax) (Read et al. 2002a, 2002b). Phylogenetic analyses of viral strains of human immunodeficiency virus (HIV) have been admitted and used as evidence in court (Metzker et al. 2002, Scaduto et al. 2010). However, since bacteria and viruses reproduce asexually, clones are prevalent. A perfect match between evidence collected and a reference sample is much less definitive than with human identity testing where sexual reproduction shuffles genetic material each generation.

For more information on microbial forensics, a reference book is now in its second edition and should be consulted by those interested in this topic (Budowle et al. 2011).

CHALLENGES WITH PRESENTING NON-HUMAN DNA IN COURT

In a 1998 article, George Sensabaugh and David Kaye considered several issues regarding whether a given application with non-human DNA is ready for court use (Sensabaugh & Kaye 1998). These issues include the novelty of the application, the validity of the underlying scientific theory, the validity of any statistical interpretations, and the existence of a relevant scientific community to consult in assessing the application.

Many times new methods are applied for the first time in microbial forensics or animal or plant DNA testing that have not yet undergone the scrutiny of regular forensic DNA testing techniques. Reference DNA databases for comparison purposes and use in calculating the probability of a chance match take time to develop and may not be in place prior to an investigation. Finding appropriate experts to review the scientific soundness of a novel application can also be challenging. Issues surrounding outsourcing of sample testing and appropriate validation will always be a challenge in this area. Nevertheless, the power and influence of forensic DNA testing will continue to grow as it is used in more and more diverse applications to solve crimes that were previously inaccessible.

READING LIST AND INTERNET RESOURCES

General Information

Budowle, B., et al. (2005). Recommendations for animal DNA forensic and identity testing. *International Journal of Legal Medicine, 119*, 295–302.

Budowle, B., et al. (Ed.). (2011). *Microbial forensics* (2nd ed.). San Diego: Elsevier Academic Press.

Coyle, H. M., et al. (Ed.). (2008). *Nonhuman DNA typing: Theory and casework applications*. Boca Raton: CRC Press.

D'Andrea, F., et al. (1998). Preliminary experiments on the transfer of animal hair during simulated criminal behavior. *Journal of Forensic Sciences, 43*, 1257–1258.

Halverson, J. L., et al. (2005). Forensic DNA identification of animal-derived trace evidence: tools for linking victims and suspects. *Croatian Medical Journal, 46*, 598–605.

International Society of Animal Genetics (ISAG). <http://www.isag.org.uk/>.

Linacre, A. (Ed.). (2009). *Forensic science in wildlife investigations*. Boca Raton: CRC Press.

Linacre, A., et al. (2011). ISFG: Recommendations regarding the use of non-human (animal) DNA in forensic genetic investigations. *Forensic Science International: Genetics* (in press). doi:10.1016/j.fsigen.2010.10.017.

Ogden, R. (2010). Forensic science, genetics and wildlife biology: getting the right mix for a wildlife DNA forensics lab. *Forensic Science, Medicine, and Pathology, 6*, 172–179.

Sensabaugh, G., & Kaye, D. H. (1998). Non-human DNA evidence. *Jurimetrics Journal, 38*, 1–16.

Domestic Animal DNA Testing

Fridez, F., et al. (1999). Individual identification of cats and dogs using mitochondrial DNA tandem repeats? *Science and Justice, 39*, 167–171.

Jeffreys, A. J., & Morton, D. B. (1987). DNA fingerprinting of dogs and cats. *Animal Genetics, 18*, 1–15.

Cats

Butler, J. M., et al. (2002). The MeowPlex: a new DNA test using tetranucleotide STR markers for the domestic cat. *Profiles in DNA*, 5(2), 7–10. Available at < http://www.promega.com/profiles/502/ProfilesInDNA_502_07.pdf/>.

Coomber, N., et al. (2007). Validation of a short tandem repeat multiplex typing system for genetic individualization of domestic cat samples. *Croatian Medical Journal, 48*, 547–555.

Lipinski, M. J., et al. (2007). An international parentage and identification panel for the domestic cat (*Felis catus*). *Animal Genetics, 38*, 371–377.

Lopez, J. V., et al. (1996). Complete nucleotide sequences of the domestic cat (Felis catus) mitochondrial genome and a transposed mtDNA tandem repeat (Numt) in the nuclear genome. *Genomics, 33*, 229–246.

Menotti-Raymond, M., et al. (1997a). Genetic individualization of domestic cats using feline STR loci for forensic applications. *Journal of Forensic Sciences, 42*, 1039–1051.

Menotti-Raymond, M., et al. (1997b). Pet cat hair implicates murder suspect. *Nature, 386*, 774.

Menotti-Raymond, M., et al. (1999). A genetic linkage map of microsatellites in the domestic cat (*Felis catus*). *Genomics, 57*, 9–23.

Menotti-Raymond, M., et al. (2003). Quantitative polymerase chain reaction-based assay for estimating DNA yield extracted from domestic cat specimens. *Croatian Medical Journal, 44*, 327–331.

Menotti-Raymond, M., et al. (2005). An STR forensic typing system for genetic individualization of domestic cat (*Felis catus*) samples. *Journal of Forensic Sciences, 50*, 1061–1070.

Menotti-Raymond, M., et al. (2008). Patterns of molecular genetic variation among cat breeds. *Genomics, 91*, 1–11.

Menotti-Raymond, M., et al. (2008). STR-based forensic analysis of felid samples from domestic and exotic cats. In H. M. Coyle (Ed.), *Nonhuman DNA typing: Theory and casework applications* (Chapter 5, pp. 69–91). Boca Raton: CRC Press.

Murphy, W. J., et al. (2007). A 1.5-Mb-resolution radiation hybrid map of the cat genome and comparative analysis with the canine and human genomes. *Genomics, 89*, 189–196.

O'Brien, S. J., et al. (2002). The fenine genome project. *Annual Review of Genetics, 36*, 657–686.

Pontius, J. U., et al. (2007). Initial sequence and comparative analysis of the cat genome. *Genome Research, 17*, 1675–1689.

QuestGen Forensics. <http://www.questgen.biz/> and <http://www.questgen.biz/cv.htm#casework/>.

The Pet Food Institute. <http://petfoodinstitute.org/>.

STRBase Cat STRs information. <http://www.cstl.nist.gov/biotech/strbase/catSTRs.htm/>.

Dogs

Allard, M. W. (2009). Building a genetic reference database for dog mtDNA sequences and SNPs. Final report for NIJ Grant 2004-DN-BX-K004. Available at <http://www.ncjrs.gov/pdffiles1/nij/grants/226936.pdf/>.

Angleby, H., & Savolainen, P. (2005). Forensic informativity of domestic dog mtDNA control region sequences. *Forensic Science International, 154*, 99–110.

Baute, D. T., et al. (2008). Analysis of forensic SNPs in the canine mtDNA HV1 mutational hotspot region. *Journal of Forensic Sciences, 53*, 1325–1333.

Berger, B., et al. (2008). Forensic canine STR analysis. In H. M. Coyle (Ed.), *Nonhuman DNA typing: Theory and casework applications* (Chapter 4, pp. 45–68). Boca Raton: CRC Press.

Berger, C., et al. (2009). Canine DNA profiling in forensic casework: the tail wagging the dog. *Forensic Science Review, 21*, 1–14.

Brauner, P., et al. (2001). DNA profiling of trace evidence—mitigating evidence in a dog biting case. *Journal of Forensic Sciences, 46*, 1232–1234.

Clarke, M., & Vandenberg, N. (2010). Dog attack: the application of canine DNA profiling in forensic casework. *Forensic Science, Medicine, and Pathology, 6*, 151–157.

Dayton, M., et al. (2009). Developmental validation of short tandem repeat reagent kit for forensic DNA profiling of canine biological material. *Croatian Medical Journal, 50*, 268–285.

De Munnynck, K., & Van de Voorde, W. (2002). Forensic approach to fatal dog attacks: a case report and literature review. *International Journal of Legal Medicine, 116*, 295–300.

DeNise, S., et al. (2004). Power of exclusion for parentage verification and probability of match for identity in American Kennel Club breeds using 17 canine microsatellite markers. *Animal Genetics, 35*, 14–17.

Eichmann, C., et al. (2004). A proposed nomenclature for 15 canine-specific polymorphic STR loci for forensic purposes. *International Journal of Legal Medicine, 118*, 249–266.

Eichmann, C., et al. (2004). Canine-specific STR typing of saliva traces on dog bite wounds. *International Journal of Legal Medicine, 118*, 337–342.

Eichmann, C., et al. (2005). Estimating the probability of identity in a random dog population using 15 highly polymorphic canine STR markers. *Forensic Science International, 151*, 37–44.

Eichmann, C., et al. (2007). Molecular characterization of the canine mitochondrial DNA control region for forensic applications. *International Journal of Legal Medicine, 121*, 411–416.

Gundry, R. L., et al. (2007). Mitochondrial DNA analysis of the domestic dog: control region variation within and among breeds. *Journal of Forensic Sciences, 52*, 562–572.

Halverson, J., et al. (1999). Microsatellite sequences for canine genotyping. U.S. Patent 5,874,217.

Halverson, J., & Basten, C. (2005). A PCR multiplex and database for forensic DNA identification of dogs. *Journal of Forensic Sciences, 50*, 352–363.

Hellmann, A. P., et al. (2006). A proposal for standardization in forensic canine DNA typing: allele nomenclature of six canine-specific STR loci. *Journal of Forensic Sciences, 51*, 274–281.

Himmelberger, A. L., et al. (2008). Forensic utility of the mitochondrial hypervariable region 1 of domestic dogs, in conjunction with breed and geographic information. *Journal of Forensic Sciences, 53*, 81–89.

Ichikawa, Y., et al. (2001). Canine parentage testing based on microsatellite polymorphisms. *Journal of Veterinary Medicine and Science, 63*, 1209–1213.

ISAG Canine Marker Panels. <http://www.isag.org.uk/ISAG/all/2005ISAGPanelDOG.pdf/>.

Kanthaswamy, S. (2009). Development and validation of a standardized canine STR panel for use in forensic casework. Final report for NIJ Grant 2004-DN-BX-K007. Available at <http://www.ncjrs.gov/pdffiles1/nij/grants/226639.pdf/>.

Kanthaswamy, S., et al. (2009). Canine population data generated from a multiplex STR kit for use in forensic casework. *Journal of Forensic Sciences, 54*, 829–840.

Kim, K. S., et al. (1998). The complete nucleotide sequence of the domestic dog (*Canis familiaris*) mitochondrial genome. *Molecular and Phylogenetic Evolution, 10*, 210–220.

Koskinen, M. T., & Bredbacka, P. (1999). A convenient and efficient microsatellite-based assay for resolving parentages in dogs. *Animal Genetics, 30*, 148–149.

Muller, S., et al. (1999). Use of canine microsatellite polymorphisms in forensic examinations. *Journal of Heredity, 90*, 55–56.

Neff, M. W., et al. (1999). A second generation genetic linkage map of the domestic dog, *Canis familiaris. Genetics, 151*, 803–820.

NHGRI Dog Genome Project. <http://research.nhgri.nih.gov/dog_genome/>.

Ostrander, E. A., & Wayne, R. K. (2005). The canine genome. *Genome Research, 15*, 1706–1716.

Pádár, Z., et al. (2001). Canine microsatellite polymorphisms as the resolution of an illegal animal death case in a Hungarian zoological gardens. *International Journal of Legal Medicine, 115*, 79–81.

Pádár, Z., et al. (2002). Canine STR analyses in forensic practice: observation of a possible mutation in a dog hair. *International Journal of Legal Medicine, 116*, 286–288.

Pereira, L., et al. (2004). Standardisation of nomenclature for dog mtDNA D-loop: a prerequisite for launching a *Canis familiaris* database. *Forensic Science International, 141*, 99–108.

Piercy, R., et al. (1993). The application of mitochondrial DNA typing to the study of white Caucasian genetic identification. *International Journal of Legal Medicine, 106*, 85–90.

Savolainen, P., et al. (1997). Sequence analysis of domestic dog mitochondrial DNA for forensic use. *Journal of Forensic Sciences, 42*, 593–600.

Savolainen, P., & Lundeberg, J. (1999). Forensic evidence based on mtDNA from dog and wolf hairs. *Journal of Forensic Sciences, 44*, 77–81.

Savolainen, P., et al. (2000). A novel method for forensic DNA investigations: repeat-type sequence analysis of tandemly repeated mtDNA in domestic dogs. *Journal of Forensic Sciences, 45*, 990–999.

Schneider, P. M., et al. (1999). Forensic mtDNA hair analysis excludes a dog from having caused a traffic accident. *International Journal of Legal Medicine, 112*, 315–316.

Shutler, G. G., et al. (1999). Removal of a PCR inhibitor and resolution of DNA STR types in mixed human-canine stains from a five year old case. *Journal of Forensic Sciences, 44*, 623–626.

STRBase Dog STRs information. <http://www.cstl.nist.gov/biotech/strbase/dogSTRs.htm/>.

Sundqvist, A.-K., et al. (2008). Wolf or dog? Genetic identification of predators from saliva collected around bite wounds on prey. *Conservation Genetics, 9*, 1275–1279.

Sutter, N. B., & Ostrander, E. A. (2004). Dog star rising: the canine genetic system. *Nature Reviews Genetics, 5*, 900–910.

Tom, B. K., et al. (2010). Development of a nomenclature system for a canine STR multiplex reagent kit. *Journal of Forensic Sciences, 55*, 597–604.

van Asch, B., et al. (2009). A new autosomal STR nineplex for canine identification and parentage testing. *Electrophoresis, 30*, 417–423.

van Asch, B., et al. (2009). Forensic analysis of dog (*Canis lupus familiaris*) mitochondrial DNA sequences: an inter-laboratory study of the GEP-ISFG working group. *Forensic Science International: Genetics, 4*, 49–54.

van Asch, B., et al. (2010). A framework for the development of STR genotyping in domestic animal species: characterization and population study of 12 canine X-chromosome loci. *Electrophoresis, 31*, 303–308.

van Asch, B., et al. (2010). Genetic profiles and sex identification of found-dead wolves determined by the use of an 11-loci PCR multiplex. *Forensic Science International: Genetics, 4*, 68–72.

Wetton, J. H., et al. (2003). Mitochondrial profiling of dog hairs. *Forensic Science International, 133*, 235–241.

Webb, K. M., & Allard, M. W. (2009a). Mitochondrial genome DNA analysis of the domestic dog: identifying informative SNPs outside of the control region. *Journal of Forensic Sciences, 54*(2), 275–288.

Webb, K. M., & Allard, M. W. (2009b). Identification of forensically informative SNPs in the domestic dog mitochondrial control region. *Journal of Forensic Sciences, 54*(2), 289–304.

Webb, K., & Allard, M. (2010). Assessment of minimum sample sizes required to adequately represent diversity reveals inadequacies in datasets of domestic dog mitochondrial DNA. *Mitochondrial DNA, 21*, 19–31.

Zenke, P., et al. (2011). Population genetic study in Hungarian canine populations using forensically informative STR loci. *Forensic Science International: Genetics, 5*, e31–e36.

Horses

Binns, M. M., et al. (1995). The identification of polymorphic microsatellite loci in the horse and their use in thoroughbred parentage testing. *The British Veterinary Journal, 151*, 9–15.

Bowling, A. T., et al. (1997). Validation of microsatellite markers for routine horse parentage testing. *Animal Genetics, 28*, 247–252.

Chen, J. W., et al. (2010). Identification of racehorse and sample contamination by novel 24-plex STR system. *Forensic Science International: Genetics, 4*, 158–167.

Choi, S. K., et al. (2008). Genetic characterization and polymorphisms for parentage testing of the Jeju horse using 20 microsatellite loci. *Journal of Veterinary Medical Science, 70*, 1111–1115.

Dimsoski, P. (2003). Development of a 17-plex microsatellite polymerase chain reaction kit for genotyping horses. *Croatian Medical Journal, 44*, 332–335.

Gurney, S. M. R., et al. (2010). Developing equine mtDNA profiling for forensic application. *International Journal of Legal Medicine, 124*, 617–622.

Marklund, S., et al. (1994). Parentage testing and linkage analysis in the horse using a set of highly polymorphic microsatellites. *Animal Genetics, 25*, 19–23.

Tozaki, T., et al. (2001). Population study and validation of paternity testing for Thoroughbred horses by 15 microsatellite loci. *Journal of Veterinary Medicine and Science, 63*, 1191–1197.

van de Goor, L. H. P., et al. (2010). A proposal for standardization in forensic equine DNA typing: allele nomenclature for 17 equine-specific STR loci. *Animal Genetics, 41*, 122–127.

Cows

Giovambattista, G., et al. (2001). DNA typing in a cattle stealing case. *Journal of Forensic Sciences, 46*, 1484–1486.

Kemp, S. J., et al. (1995). A panel of polymorphic bovine, ovine and caprine microsatellite markers. *Animal Genetics, 26*, 299–306.

van de Goor, L. H. P., et al. (2009). A proposal for standardization in forensic bovine DNA typing: allele nomenclature of 16 cattle-specific short tandem repeat loci. *Animal Genetics, 40*, 630–636.

Pigs

Nechtelberger, D., et al. (2001). DNA microsatellite analysis for parentage control in Austrian pigs. *Animal Biotechnology, 12*, 141–144.

Robino, C., et al. (2008). Forensic application of a multiplex PCR system for the typing of pig STRs. *Forensic Science International: Genetics Supplement Series, 1*, 614–615.

Sheep

Heaton, M. P., et al. (2010). Ovine reference materials and assays for prion genetic testing. *BMC Veterinary Research, 6*, 23.

Species Identification

Balitzki-Korte, B., et al. (2005). Species identification by means of pyrosequencing the mitochondrial 12S rRNA gene. *International Journal of Legal Medicine, 119*, 291–294.

Barcode of Life Project. <http://www.barcodinglife.org/> and <http://www.ncbi.nlm.nih.gov/genbank/barcode.html/>.

Bartlett, S. E., & Davidson, W. S. (1992). FINS (forensically informative nucleotide sequencing): a procedure for identifying the animal origin of biological specimens. *BioTechniques, 12*, 408–411.

Bataille, M., et al. (1999). Multiplex amplification of mitochondrial DNA for human and species identification in forensic evaluation. *Forensic Science International, 99*, 165–170.

Bellis, C., et al. (2003). A molecular genetic approach for forensic animal species identification. *Forensic Science International, 134*, 99–108.

Branicki, W., Kupiec, T., & Pawlowski, R. (2003). Validation of cytochrome b sequence analysis as a method of species identification. *Journal of Forensic Sciences, 48*, 83–87.

Bravi, C. M., et al. (2004). A simple method for domestic animal identification in Argentina using PCR-RFLP analysis of cytochrome b gene. *Legal Medicine, 6*, 246–251.

Dawnay, N., et al. (2007). Validation of the barcoding gene COI for use in forensic genetic species identification. *Forensic Science International, 173*, 1–6.

Donaldson, A. E., et al. (2010). Using oral microbial DNA analysis to identify expirated bloodspatter. *International Journal of Legal Medicine, 124*, 569–576.

El-Sayed, Y. S., et al. (2010). Using species-specific repeat and PCR-RFLP in typing of DNA derived from blood of human and animal species. *Forensic Science, Medicine, and Pathology, 6*, 158–164.

Fleming, R. I., & Harbison, S. (2010). The use of bacteria for the identification of vaginal secretions. *Forensic Science International: Genetics, 4*, 311–315.

Hsieh, H. M., et al. (2001). Cytochrome b gene for species identification of the conservation animals. *Forensic Science International, 122*, 7–18.

Kitano, T., et al. (2007). Two universal primer sets for species identification among vertebrates. *International Journal of Legal Medicine, 121*, 423–427.

Linacre, A., et al. (2004). Species determination: the role and use of the cytochrome B gene. *Methods in Molecular Biology, 297*, 45–52.

Linacre, A. (2006). Application of mitochondrial DNA technologies in wildlife investigations—species identification. *Forensic Science Review, 18*, 1–8.

Linacre, A., & Tobe, S. S. (2009). Species identification using DNA loci. In A. Linacre (Ed.), *Forensic science in wildlife investigations* (Chapter 4, pp. 61–94). Boca Raton: CRC Press.

Linacre, A., & Tobe, S. S. (2011). An overview to the investigative approach to species testing in wildlife forensic science. *Investigative Genetics, 2*, 2.

Melton, T., & Holland, C. (2007). Routine forensic use of the mitochondrial 12S ribosomal RNA gene for species identification. *Journal of Forensic Sciences, 52*, 1305–1307.

Nakanishi, H., et al. (2009). A novel method for the identification of saliva by detecting oral streptococci using PCR. *Forensic Science International, 183*, 20–23.

Parson, W., et al. (2000). Species identification by means of the cytochrome b gene. *International Journal of Legal Medicine, 114*, 23–28.

Ratnasingham, S., & Hebert, P. D. (2007). BOLD: the Barcode of Life Data System. *Molecular Ecology Notes, 7*, 355–364. <http://www.barcodinglife.org/>.

Ron, M., et al. (1996). Amplification of the conserved cytochrome b locus as a versatile internal control for PCR analysis in animals. *BioTechniques, 20*, 604–608.

Schulz, I., et al. (2006). Examination of postmortem animal interference to human remains using cross-species multiplex PCR. *Forensic Science, Medicine, and Pathology, 2*, 95–101.

Spears, T. F., & Binkley, S. A. (1994). The HemeSelect test: a simple and sensitive forensic species test. *Journal of Forensic Science Society, 34*, 41–46.

Teletchea, F., et al. (2005). Food and forensic molecular identification: update and challenges. *Trends in Biotechnology, 23*, 359–366.

Tobe, S. S., & Linacre, A. (2010). DNA typing in wildlife crime: recent developments in species identification. *Forensic Science, Medicine, and Pathology, 6*, 195–206.

Unseld, M., et al. (1995). Identification of the species origin of highly processed meat products by mitochondrial DNA sequences. *PCR Methods and Applications, 4*, 241–243.

Verma, S. K., & Singh, L. (2003). Novel universal primers establish identity of an enormous number of animal species for forensic application. *Molecular Ecology Notes, 3*, 28–31.

Wilson-Wilde, L., et al. (2010). Current issues in species identification for forensic science and the validity of using the cytochrome oxidase I (COI) gene. *Forensic Science, Medicine, and Pathology, 6*, 223–241.

Wong, K.-L., et al. (2004). Application of *cytochrome b* DNA sequences for the authentication of endangered snake species. *Forensic Science International, 139*, 49–55.

Wildlife Testing

Caniglia, R., et al. (2010). Forensic DNA against wildlife poaching: identification of a serial wolf killing in Italy. *Forensic Science International: Genetics, 4*, 334–338.

Caratti, S., et al. (2010). Analysis of 11 tetrameric STRs in wild boars for forensic purposes. *Forensic Science International: Genetics, 4*, 339–342.

Cassidy, B. G., & Gonzales, R. A. (2005). DNA testing in animal forensics. *Journal of Wildlife Management, 69*, 1454–1462.

Convention on International Trade in Endangered Species of Wild Fauna and Flora. <http://www.cites.org/>.

Dawnay, N., et al. (2008). A forensic STR profiling system for the Eurasian badger: a framework for developing profiling systems for wildlife species. *Forensic Science International: Genetics, 2*, 47–53.

Guglich, E. A., et al. (1993). Application of DNA fingerprinting to enforcement of hunting regulations in Ontario. *Journal of Forensic Sciences, 38*, 48–59.

Interpol Wildlife Crime (2007). <http://www.interpol.int/Public/EnvironmentalCrime/Wildlife/Default.asp/>.

Jobin, R. M., et al. (2008). DNA typing in populations of mule deer for forensic use in the Province of Alberta. *Forensic Science International: Genetics, 2*, 190–197.

Jobin, R. M. (2008). Use of forensic DNA typing in wildlife investigations. In H. M. Coyle (Ed.), *Nonhuman DNA typing: Theory and casework applications* (Chapter 7, pp. 99–116). Boca Raton: CRC Press.

Johnson, R. N. (2010). The use of DNA identification in prosecuting wildlife-traffickers in Australia: do the penalties fit the crimes? *Forensic Science, Medicine, and Pathology, 6*, 211–216.

Lee, J. C., et al. (2007). Racing pigeon identification using STR and chromo-helicase DNA binding gene markers. *Electrophoresis, 28*, 4274–4281.

Linacre, A. (2009). Nature of wildlife crimes, their investigations and scientific processes. In A. Linacre (Ed.), *Forensic science in wildlife investigations* (Chapter 1, pp. 1–9). Boca Raton: CRC Press.

Lorenzini, R. (2005). DNA forensics and the poaching of wildlife in Italy: A case study. *Forensic Science International, 153*, 218–221.

NOAA Marine Forensics Program. <http://www.chbr.noaa.gov/habar/marine_forensics.aspx/>.

Neme, L. A. (2010). INTERPOL's wildlife crime working group meeting. *Forensic Science, Medicine, and Pathology, 6*, 223–224.

Ogden, R., et al. (2009). Wildlife DNA forensics – bridging the gap between conservation genetics and law enforcement. *Endangered Species Research, 9*, 179–195.

Ogden, R. (2009). DNA profiling markers in wildlife forensic science. In A. Linacre (Ed.), *Forensic science in wildlife investigations* (Chapter 5, pp. 95–125). Boca Raton: CRC Press.

Poetsch, M., et al. (2001). Analysis of microsatellite polymorphism in red deer, roe deer, and fallow deer - possible employment in forensic applications. *Forensic Science International, 116*, 1–8.

Sellar, J. M. (2009). Illegal trade and the convention on international trade in endangered species of wild fauna and flora (CITES). In A. Linacre (Ed.), *Forensic science in wildlife investigations* (Chapter 2, pp. 11–18). Boca Raton: CRC Press.

Smith, L. M., et al. (2004). Collecting, archiving and processing DNA from wildlife samples using FTA databasing paper. *BMC Ecology, 4*, 4.

Smith, P. F., et al. (2002). Allele frequencies for three STR loci RT24, RT09, and BM1225 in northern New England white-tailed deer. *Journal of Forensic Sciences, 47*, 673–675.

Society of Wildlife Forensic Science. <http://www.wildlifeforensicscience.org/>.

Spencer, P. B. S., et al. (2010). Identification of historical specimens and wildlife seizures originating from highly degraded sources of kangaroos and other macropods. *Forensic Science, Medicine, and Pathology, 6*, 225–232.

Tepnel Wildlife DNA Forensics. <http://www.tepnel.com/ls-wildlife-forensic-applications.asp/>.

Tobe, S. S. (2009). Determining the geographic origin of animal samples. In A. Linacre (Ed.), *Forensic science in wildlife investigations* (Chapter 6, pp. 127–156). Boca Raton: CRC Press.

Trent University Wildlife Forensic DNA Laboratory. <http://www.forensicdna.ca/>.

U.S. Fish and Wildlife Service Forensics Laboratory. <http://www.lab.fws.gov/>.

Verma, S. K., et al. (2003). Was elusive carnivore a panther? DNA typing of faeces reveals the mystery. *Forensic Science International, 137*, 16–20.

Wilson-Wilde, L. (2010). Wildlife crime: a global problem. *Forensic Science, Medicine, and Pathology, 6*, 221–222.

Wong, K. L., et al. (2004). Application of cytochrome b DNA sequences for the authentication of endangered snake species. *Forensic Science International, 139*, 49–55.

Techniques

Alacs, E. A., et al. (2010). DNA detective: a review of molecular approaches to wildlife forensics. *Forensic Science, Medicine, and Pathology, 6*, 180–194.

Ranamukhaarachchi, D. G., et al. (2000). Modified AFLP technique for rapid genetic characterization in plants. *Biotechniques, 29*, 858–866.

Schienman, J. (2008). Techniques of DNA fingerprinting. In H. M. Coyle (Ed.), *Nonhuman DNA typing: Theory and casework applications* (Chapter 3, pp. 23–44). Boca Raton: CRC Press.

Vos, P., et al. (1995). AFLP: A new technique for DNA fingerprinting. *Nucleic Acids Research, 23*, 4407–4414.

Plant & Pollen DNA Testing

Bock, J. H., & Norris, D. O. (1997). Forensic botany: an under-utilized resource. *Journal of Forensic Sciences, 42*, 364–367.

Bruni, I., et al. (2010). Identification of poisonous plants by DNA barcoding approach. *International Journal of Legal Medicine, 124*, 595–603.

Bryant, V. M., & Jones, G. D. (2006). Forensic palynology: current status of a rarely used technique in the United States of America. *Forensic Science International, 163*, 183–197.

Coyle, H. M. (2009). Forensic botany: evidence and analysis. *Forensic Science Review, 21*, 15–24.

Craft, K. J., et al. (2007). Application of plant DNA markers in forensic botany: genetic comparison of Quercus evidence leaves to crime scene trees using microsatellites. *Forensic Science International, 165*, 64–70.

Horrocks, M., & Walsh, K. A. (2001). Pollen on grass clippings: putting the suspect at the scene of the crime. *Journal of Forensic Sciences, 46*, 947–949.

Mildenhall, D. C., et al. (2006). Forensic palynology: why do it and how it works. *Forensic Science International, 163*, 163–172.

Miller-Coyle, H., et al. (2001). The Green Revolution: botanical contributions to forensics and drug enforcement. *Croatian Medical Journal, 42*, 340–345.

Miller-Coyle, H., et al. (2005). Forensic botany: using plant evidence to aid in forensic death investigation. *Croatian Medical Journal, 46*, 606–612.

Norris, D. O., & Bock, J. H. (2000). Use of fecal material to associate a suspect with a crime scene: report of two cases. *Journal of Forensic Sciences, 45*, 184–187.

Stambuk, S., et al. (2007). Forensic botany: potential usefulness of microsatellite-based genotyping of Croatian olive (*Olea europaea L.*) in forensic casework. *Croatian Medical Journal, 48*, 556–562.

Szibor, R., et al. (1998). Pollen analysis reveals murder season. *Nature, 395*, 449–450.

Tsai, L.-C., et al. (2008). Bidens identification using the noncoding regions of chloroplast genome and nuclear ribosomal DNA. *Forensic Science International: Genetics, 2*, 35–40.

Virtanen, V., et al. (2007). Forensic botany: usability of bryophyte material in forensic studies. *Forensic Science International, 172*, 161–163.

Walsh, K. A., & Horrocks, M. (2008). Palynology: its position in the field of forensic science. *Journal of Forensic Sciences, 53*, 1053–1060.

Ward, J., et al. (2005). A molecular identification system for grasses: a novel technology for forensic botany. *Forensic Science International, 152*, 121–131.

Yoon, C. K. (1993). Forensic science: botanical witness for the prosecution. *Science, 260*, 894–895.

Marijuana DNA Testing

Alghanim, H. J., & Almirall, J. R. (2003). Development of microsatellite markers in Cannabis sativa for DNA typing and genetic relatedness analyses. *Analytical and Bioanalytical Chemistry, 376*, 1225–1233.

Gilmore, S., et al. (2003). Short tandem repeat (STR) DNA markers are hypervariable and informative in Cannabis sativa: implications for forensic investigations. *Forensic Science International, 131*, 65–74.

Gilmore, S., et al. (2007). Organelle DNA haplotypes reflect crop-use characteristics and geographic origins of Cannabis sativa. *Forensic Science International, 172*, 179–190.

Howard, C., et al. (2008). Developmental validation of a *Cannabis sativa* STR multiplex system for forensic analysis. *Journal of Forensic Sciences, 53*, 1061–1067.

Hsieh, H. M., et al. (2003). A highly polymorphic STR locus in Cannabis sativa. *Forensic Science International, 131*, 53–58.

Hsieh, H. M., et al. (2005). Characterization of the polymorphic repeat sequence within the rDNA IGS of Cannabis sativa. *Forensic Science International, 152*, 23–28.

Miller-Coyle, H., et al. (2003). A simple DNA extraction method for marijuana samples used in amplified fragment length polymorphism (AFLP) analysis. *Journal of Forensic Sciences, 48*, 343–347.

Miller-Coyle, H., et al. (2003). An overview of DNA methods for the identification and individualization of marijuana. *Croatian Medical Journal, 44*, 315–321.

Bacterial DNA in Soil

Heath, L. E., & Saunders, V. A. (2006). Assessing the potential of bacterial DNA profiling for forensic soil comparisons. *Journal of Forensic Sciences, 51*, 1062–1068.
Heath, L. E., & Saunders, V. A. (2008). Spatial variation in bacterial DNA profiles for forensic soil comparisons. *Canadian Society of Forensic Sciences Journal, 41*, 29–37.
Horswell, J., et al. (2002). Forensic comparisons of soils by bacterial community DNA profiling. *Journal of Forensic Sciences, 47*, 350–353.
Kang, S., & Mills, A. L. (2006). The effect of sample size in studies of soil microbial community structure. *Journal of Microbiological Methods, 66*, 242–250.
LaMontagne, M. G., et al. (2002). Evaluation of extraction and purification methods for obtaining PCR-amplifiable DNA from compost for microbial community analysis. *Journal of Microbiological Methods, 49*, 255–264.
Lenz, E. J., & Foran, D. R. (2010). Bacterial profiling of soil using genus-specific markers and multidimensional scaling. *Journal of Forensic Sciences, 55*(6), 1437–1442.
Lerner, A., et al. (2006). Can denaturing gradient gel electrophoresis (DGGE) analysis of amplified 16s rDNA of soil bacterial populations be used in forensic investigations? *Soil Biology and Biochemistry, 38*, 1188–1192.
Schwarzenbach, K., et al. (2007). Objective criteria to assess representativity of soil fungal community profiles. *Journal of Microbiological Methods, 68*, 358–366.

Identification through Human Parasites

Falush, D., et al. (2003). Traces of human migrations in *Helicobacter pylori* populations. *Science, 299*, 1582–1585.
Ikegaya, H., et al. (2002). JC virus genotyping offers a new means of tracing the origins of unidentified cadavers. *International Journal of Legal Medicine, 116*, 242–245.
Ikegaya, H., & Iwase, H. (2004). Trial for the geographical identification using JC viral genotyping in Japan. *Forensic Science International, 139*, 169–172.
Ikegaya, H., et al. (2008). JC viral DNA chip allows geographical localization of unidentified cadavers for rapid identification. *Forensic Science International: Genetics, 2*, 54–60.
Ikegaya, H. (2008). Geographical identification of cadavers by human parasites. *Forensic Science International: Genetics, 2*, 83–90.
Ikegaya, H., et al. (2008). Forensic application of Epstein-Barr genotype: correlation between viral genotype and geographic area. *Journal of Virology Methods, 147*, 78–85.

Microbial Forensics

Beeching, N. J., et al. (2002). Biological warfare and bioterrorism. *British Medical Journal, 324*, 336–339.
Breeze, R. G., Budowle, B., & Schutzer, S. E. (Eds.), (2005). *Microbial forensics*. San Diego: Elsevier Academic Press.
Budowle, B., Schutzer, S. E., Breeze, R. G., Keim, P. S., & Morse, S. A. (Eds.), (2011). *Microbial forensics* (2nd ed.). San Diego: Elsevier Academic Press.
Budowle, B. (2003). Defining a new forensic discipline: microbial forensics. *Profiles in DNA, 6*(1), 7–10.
Budowle, B., et al. (2003). Public health. Building microbial forensics as a response to bioterrorism. *Science, 301*, 1852–1853.
Budowle, B. (2004). Genetics and attribution issues that confront the microbial forensics field. *Forensic Science International, 146S*, S185–S188.
Budowle, B., et al. (2005). Genetic analysis and attribution of microbial forensics evidence. *Critical Reviews in Microbiology, 31*, 233–254.
Budowle, B., & Harmon, R. (2005). HIV legal precedent useful for microbial forensics. *Croatian Medical Journal, 46*, 514–521.
Budowle, B., et al. (2005). Toward a system of microbial forensics: from sample collection to interpretation of evidence. *Applied and Environmental Microbiology, 71*, 2209–2213.
Budowle, B., et al. (2005). Microbial forensics: the next forensic challenge. *International Journal of Legal Medicine, 119*, 317–330.

Budowle, B., et al. (2006). Quality sample collection, handling, and preservation for an effective microbial forensics program. *Applied and Environmental Microbiology, 72*, 6431–6438.
Budowle, B., et al. (2007). Role of law enforcement response and microbial forensics in investigation of bioterrorism. *Croatian Medical Journal, 48*, 437–449.
Budowle, B., et al. (2008). Criteria for validation of methods in microbial forensics. *Applied and Environmental Microbiology, 74*, 5599–5607.
Centers for Disease Control (CDC) Agent List. <http://emergency.cdc.gov/agent/agentlist.asp/>.
Enserink, M., & Ferber, D. (2003). Microbial forensics. Report spells out how to fight biocrimes. *Science, 299*, 1164–1165.
FBI Amerithrax Investigation. <http://www.fbi.gov/anthrax/amerithraxlinks.htm/>.
Ivnitski, D., et al. (2003). Nucleic acid approaches for detection and identification of biological warfare and infectious disease agents. *Biotechniques, 35*, 862–869.
Jarman, K. H., et al. (2008). Bayesian-integrated microbial forensics. *Applied and Environmental Microbiology, 74*, 3573–3582.
Keim, P., et al. (2001). Molecular investigation of the Aum Shinrikyo anthrax release in Kameido, Japan. *Journal of Clinical Microbiology, 39*, 4566–4567.
Keim, P. (2003). *Microbial forensics: a scientific assessment*. Washington, DC: American Academy of Microbiology. Available at <http://academy.asm.org/images/stories/documents/microbialforensics.pdf/>.
Keim, P., et al. (2008). Microbial forensics: DNA fingerprinting of *Bacillus Anthracis* (Anthrax). *Analytical Chemistry, 80*, 4791–4799.
Kenefic, L. J., et al. (2008). High resolution genotyping of Bacillus anthracis outbreak strains using four highly mutable single nucleotide repeat markers. *Letters in Applied Microbiology, 46*, 600–603.
Kenefic, L. J., et al. (2008). A high resolution four-locus multiplex single nucleotide repeat (SNR) genotyping system in Bacillus anthracis. *Journal of Microbiological Methods, 73*, 269–272.
Larkin, M. (2003). Microbial forensics aims to link pathogen, crime, and perpetrator. *Lancet Infectious Disease, 3*, 180.
McEwen, S. A., et al. (2006). Microbial forensics for natural and intentional incidents of infectious disease involving animals. *Reviews in Science and Technology, 25*, 329–339.
Metzker, M. L., et al. (2002). Molecular evidence of HIV-1 transmission in a criminal case. *Proceedings of the National Academy of Sciences of the United States of America, 99*, 14292–14297.
Morse, S. A., & Budowle, B. (2006). Microbial forensics: application to bioterrorism preparedness and response. *Infectious Disease Clinical North America, 20*, 455–473, xi.
Murch, R. S. (2003). Microbial forensics: building a national capacity to investigate bioterrorism. *Biosecurity & Bioterrorism, 1*, 117–122.
Popovic, T., & Glass, M. (2003). Laboratory aspects of bioterrorism-related anthrax--from identification to molecular subtyping to microbial forensics. *Croatian Medical Journal, 44*, 336–341.
Purcell, B. K., et al. (2007). Anthrax. In Z. F. Dembek (Ed.), *Medical aspects of biological warfare* (pp. 69–90) (rev ed). Falls Church, VA: Office of the Surgeon General United States Army and Washington, DC: Borden Institute, Walter Reed Medical Center. Available at <http://www.bordeninstitute.army.mil/published_volumes/biological_warfare/BW-ch04.pdf/>.
Read, T. D., et al. (2002). Comparative genome sequencing for discovery of novel polymorphisms in *Bacillus anthracis*. *Science, 296*, 2028–2033.
Read, T. D., et al. (2003). The genome sequence of *Bacillus anthracis Ames* and comparison to closely related bacteria. *Nature, 423*, 81–86.
Scaduto, D. I., et al. (2010). Inagural article: Source identification in two criminal cases using phylogenetic analysis of HIV-1 DNA sequences. *Proceedings of the National Academy of Sciences of the United States of America, 107*, 21242–21247.
Schutzer, S. E., et al. (2005). Biocrimes, microbial forensics, and the physician. *PLoS. Medicine, 2*, e337.
Scientific Working Group on Microbial Genetics and Forensics (SWGMGF), Quality Assurance Guidelines for Laboratories Performing Microbial Forensic Work. *Forensic Science Communications, 5*(4). Available at <http://www.fbi.gov/hq/lab/fsc/backissu/oct2003/2003_10_guide01.htm/>.
U.S. Army Medical Research Institute of Infectious Diseases (USAMRIID). <http://www.usamriid.army.mil/>.

CHAPTER

17

New Technologies and Automation

We live in an age of rapid discovery in biotechnology, and new technologies and instruments are continually being developed. Any attempt to predict in detail where the field of forensic DNA typing will be in five or ten years would be futile given the rate of technology change. Because of parallel efforts in biotechnology development (e.g., genome sequencing), there is growing set of tools for forensic DNA analysts to use, many of which are described in this book.

The forensic DNA field has advanced quickly over the past several decades but has now stabilized on short tandem repeat (STR) typing with capillary electrophoresis detection. However, a comparison of the new information found in this book with previous editions of *Forensic DNA Typing* illustrates that innovations are being made with almost every step along the process of producing a DNA profile. The goal of this chapter is to briefly discuss some technologies with potential impact on future forensic DNA analysis and the value of automation to increase sample throughput.

Similar to the Olympic motto of "faster, higher, stronger," there is a desire for faster DNA analysis, higher sensitivity in detection, and stronger powers of discrimination especially with related individuals. Rapid DNA analysis efforts, improved allelic resolution with mass spectrometry, and the capabilities and challenges of next-generation sequencing technology are discussed below as are some ongoing efforts with automation involving robotic liquid handling, laboratory information management systems, and expert systems for data review.

RAPID DNA ANALYSIS

The DNA testing process outlined in Chapter 1 to Chapter 6 can be performed in as little as 8 to 10 hours with the longest part of the process being the 3-hour PCR amplification step. As mentioned in Chapter 4, rapid PCR efforts using specialized DNA polymerases and faster temperature ramp rates have brought multiplex PCR amplification times down to around 30 minutes or less (Vallone et al. 2008, Giese et al. 2009).

TABLE 17.1 Groups Involved in Rapid DNA Analysis Efforts. For Additional Information (Provided as of Sept 2010), See Presentations from Special Rapid DNA Session at http://www.biometrics.org/bc2010/program.pdf.

Company or Group	Website/Reference
Forensic Science Service/ University of Arizona	Hopwood et al. (2010)
IntegenX	www.integenx.com
Lockheed Martin/ZyGEM/ MicroLab Diagnostics	www.lockheedmartin.com www.zygem.com Bienvenue et al. (2010)
Network Biosystems	www.netbio.com Giese et al. (2009)

Efforts are underway to integrate the various steps involved in DNA extraction, amplification, and STR allele detection. The primary players (as of early 2011) in the effort to develop rapid DNA analysis devices are listed in Table 17.1. Routine STR typing in less than an hour is a strong possiblity in the near future. Rapid analysis of DNA could open up a whole new set of DNA biometric applications such as analysis of individuals at a point of interest like an airport or a country border. Only time will tell to what extent technology will enable new applications.

The desire to take DNA testing capabilities out of the laboratory to a crime scene or close to a battlefield is propelling efforts into development of portable DNA testing devices. For example, some have claimed that a rapid DNA device might aid elimination of innocent suspects early in an investigation. Much of the work so far has been focused on miniaturizing the DNA separation steps.

Microfabrication techniques revolutionized the integrated circuit industry 20 years ago and have brought the world ever-faster and more powerful computers. These same microfabrication methods are now being applied to develop miniature, microchip-based laboratories, or so-called "labs-on-a-chip" (Paegel et al. 2003). Miniaturizing the sample preparation and analysis steps in forensic DNA typing could lead to devices that permit investigation of biological evidence at a crime scene or more rapid and less expensive DNA analysis in a conventional laboratory setting.

The primary advantage of analyzing DNA in a miniature capillary electrophoresis (CE) device is that shorter channels, or capillaries, lead to faster DNA separations. Separation speeds that are 10 to 100 times faster than conventional electrophoresis may be obtained with this approach (Figure 17.1). Over a decade ago, tetranucleotide STR alleles were separated in as little as 30 seconds (Schmalzing et al. 1997) using a 2-cm separation distance (compared to 36-cm for an ABI 310 capillary). However, routine and robust analyses of DNA with appropriate resolution of STR alleles have not yet been achieved at these speeds even though several groups are working extensively in this area.

Research is ongoing to improve separation speeds and ease of use with the hope that in the near future microchip CE devices will be used routinely for rapid DNA analyses. A report of DNA analysis performed in a mobile van in less than six hours at a mock crime scene was published in September 2008 (Liu et al. 2008). When portable devices become

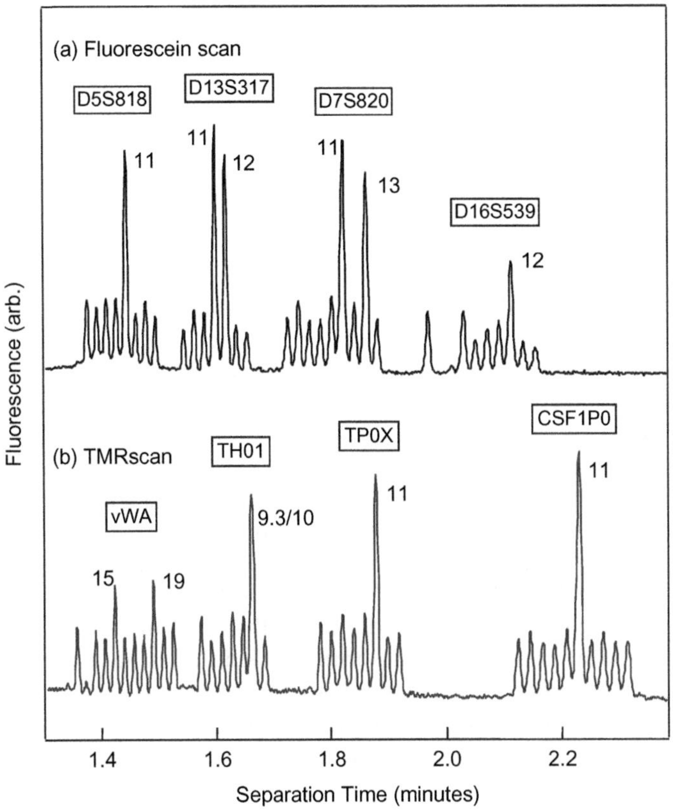

FIGURE 17.1 Rapid microchip CE separation of the 8 STR loci from PowerPlex 1.1 (Schmalzing et al. 1999). The electropherograms from scanning each color of a simultaneous two-color analysis are divided by color. The PCR-amplified sample is mixed with the allelic ladders prior to injection to provide a frame of reference for genotyping the sample. The allele calls for each locus are listed next to the corresponding peak. Figure courtesy of Dr. Daniel Ehrlich, Whitehead Institute.

available, there will be a need for sensitivity and resolution standards to make sure that DNA separation and detection devices at different locations have performance similar to one another.

A major challenge is the integration of DNA processing steps so that a "swab-to-profile" result can be obtained without any user intervention. The Forensic Science Service and the University of Arizona Center for Applied NanoBioscience and Medicine reported such an integrated device in August 2010 (Hopwood et al. 2010). Results were achieved in less than four hours with a DNA processing cartridge with wax seals that delivered sample and reagents to the necessary reaction chambers to permit DNA purification, PCR amplification, and collection of the amplified product. An accompanying CE chip connected by Telfon tubing performed the DNA separation (Hopwood et al. 2010, Hurth et al. 2010).

Richard Mathies' group at the University of California-Berkeley has been working on integration of PCR and microchip CE systems for years (Woolley et al. 1996) and has demonstrated a three hour integrated swab-to-profile result (Liu et al. 2011). Lockheed Martin and ZyGEM Microlab are also showing promising results towards full sample process integration with their RapI.D. system (Bienvenue et al. 2010, Reedy et al. 2011).

MASS SPECTROMETRY

Mass spectrometry is a versatile analytical technique that involves the detection of ions and the measurement of their mass-to-charge ratio. Because these ions are separated in a vacuum environment, the analysis times can be extremely rapid, on the order of seconds. Combined with robotic sample preparation, mass spectrometry offers the potential for processing vast numbers of DNA samples in an automated fashion.

With mass spectrometry, the actual mass of the DNA molecule is being measured, making it a more accurate technique than a relative-size measurement as is obtained in electrophoresis. In order to get the DNA molecules into the gas phase for analysis in the mass spectrometer, two different ionization techniques have been used: matrix-assisted laser desorption-ionization (MALDI) or electrospray ionization (ESI).

Over a decade ago, STR markers were successfully analyzed via MALDI time-of-flight mass spectrometry by redesigning the PCR primers to bind closer to the repeat region, and thereby reducing the size of the amplified alleles (Butler et al. 1998). While MALDI had a size limitation of ≈100 bp, recent ESI time-of-flight techniques have extended the size range for accurate mass spectrometry measurements to ≈250 bp.

Two ESI mass spectrometry approaches are in use: (1) ion-pair reversed-phase liquid chromatography coupled with an ESI quadrupole time-of-flight (qTOF) mass analyzer

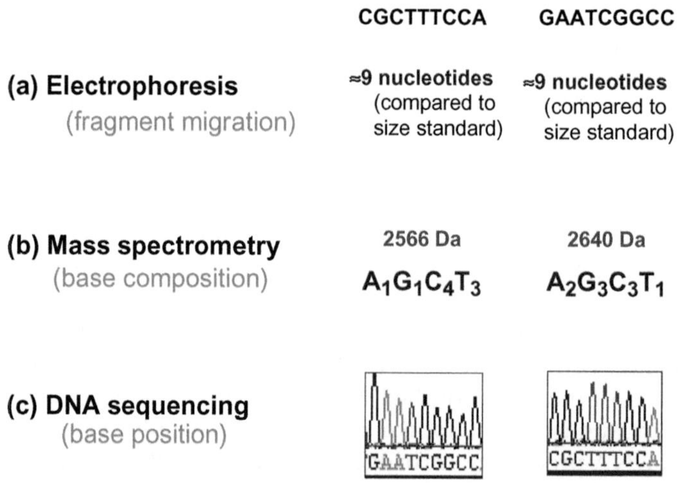

FIGURE 17.2 Comparison of measurement techniques with the ability to resolve two 9-base sequences. (a) Electrophoresis measures DNA fragment migration relative to a size standard. (b) Mass spectrometry measures the DNA fragment mass and can determine base composition using mass measurement conversion to numbers of individual nucleotides, which have different individual masses. (c) DNA sequencing measures the exact position of bases within a DNA fragment.

(Oberacher & Parson 2007) and (2) sample desalting prior to an ESI-Fourier transform ion cyclotron resonance (FT-ICR) (Hall et al. 2005, Jiang et al. 2007) or an ESI-time-of-flight (Hall et al. 2009) mass analyzer.

By analyzing the overall mass of an STR allele or a section of mtDNA, base composition of the measured DNA molecule can be deciphered and internal sequence differences ascertained (Hall et al. 2005, Oberacher & Parson 2007). STR alleles that are apparently homozygous by electrophoretic techiques have been subdivided into separate/unique alleles when internal sequence polymorphisms exist (Oberacher et al. 2008). However, the exact position of a sequence difference cannot be assessed with mass spectrometry (Figure 17.2).

The expense of mass spectrometers, the expertise required to keep them running, and the previous wide-scale acceptance of electrophoretic separation and fluorescence detection methodologies will likely keep mass spectrometry from becoming a major player in forensic DNA analysis of STR markers. However, capabilities for mitochondrial DNA base composition analysis and single nucleotide polymorphism (SNP) typing may enable mass spectrometry to play a useful role in the future of forensic DNA analysis.

PYROSEQUENCING

Pyrosequencing is based on detection of pyrophosphate released when a deoxynucleotide triphosphate (dNTP) is incorporated into a growing DNA strand (Ronaghi et al. 1998). In this sequencing-by-synthesis approach, dNTPs are added in a stepwise fashion through a directed dispensation (i.e., the user controls which nucleotide—A, T, C, or G—is added). If the nucleotide is incorporated (due to being a match to the complementary target DNA strand), pyrophosphate is released. Through an enzymatic reaction cascade involving the formation of ATP and luciferin being converted to oxyluciferin, light is emitted. Excess dNTP is degraded by apyrase prior to the addition of the next nucleotide. The light emitted is detected in a pyrogram where peak heights are proportional to the number of incorporated nucleotides (Figure 17.3).

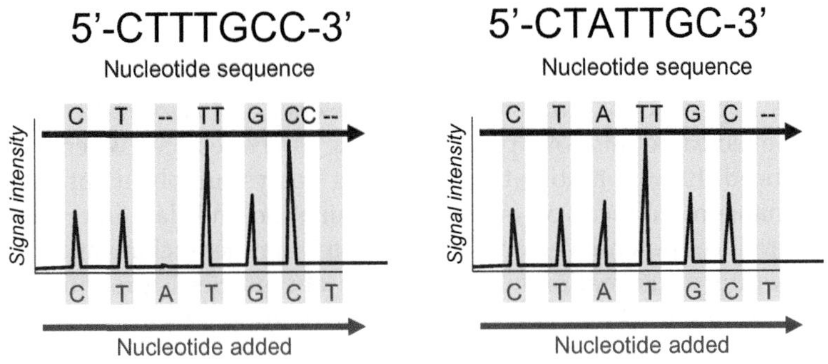

FIGURE 17.3 Schematic illustration of Pyrosequencing (sequencing-by-synthesis) results. These pyrograms are based on light produced and detected during nucleotide incorporation following a directed dispensation of nucleotides.

Pyrosequencing has been used for mitochondrial DNA sequence analysis (Andreasson et al. 2002, Allen & Andreason 2005), Y-STR typing (Edlund & Allen 2009), amelogenin sex typing (Tschentscher et al. 2008), autosomal STR typing (Divne et al. 2010), and SNP analysis (Zeng et al. 2010).

NEXT-GENERATION DNA SEQUENCING

Next-generation DNA sequencing involves rapid, high-throughput collection of short sections of DNA. This approach was first introduced in 2003 by the 454 Company. The desire for more genomic information is improving technology and reducing costs. A motivating goal for this new technology is to obtain a full human genome sequence for $1000 or less. Because these next-generation sequencing approaches generate short sequence reads of typically 25 to 250 bases in a massively parallel fashion, it has been possible to successfully obtain sequence information from ancient DNA samples, which are normally too fragmented to sequence by traditional techniques. A complete Neandertal mitochondrial genome sequence has been obtained (Green et al. 2008) as has DNA sequence information from the extinct woolly mammoth (Miller et al. 2008, Poinar et al. 2006).

It is unclear whether or not next-generation sequencing techniques will help traditional forensic testing as they are helping ancient DNA sample sequencing (Blow et al. 2008). Current methods have a difficult time with repetitive sequences and thus unless future improvements are made, STR regions would probably not be reliably analyzed with next-generation DNA sequencing (Hert et al. 2008). In addition, the amount of data produced by these next-generation systems with millions of short reads makes bioinformatics support crucial and would require a significant change in the way that forensic DNA laboratories do business as well as a switch of genetic markers from STRs to SNPs.

LABORATORY AUTOMATION

Laboratory automation is an important topic, especially because the demand for forensic DNA testing is increasing. Laboratories will take on more cases and have much larger numbers of samples to type because of expanding DNA database laws and more extensive use of DNA in casework applications. Automation aids efficiency and error reduction. Often sample throughput can be increased and total processing time can be reduced when a more consistent process is introduced through automation. Reducing analyst involvement in routine sample processing can enable more focus on evidence examination and data interpretation. In addition, automation reduces potential errors through better sample tracking and handling.

The use of laboratory automation in DNA typing laboratories is growing in several areas: liquid handling, sample tracking, and data analysis. Through adding automation, particularly in the area of expert systems data review, the FBI Laboratory's Federal DNA Database Unit (FDDU) was able to process 408,000 DNA samples in a single year (October 2009 to September 2010) in order to eliminate their backlog (Richard Guerrieri, FBI FDDU Unit Chief, personal communication).

Liquid Sample Handling Robots

Robotic liquid-handling platforms for aiding sample preparation enables higher throughput, increases laboratory efficiency, and aids quality assurance efforts. Robotic systems can reduce hands-on time for DNA analysts enabling them to focus on other aspects of the process such as data interpretation. Potential sample contamination or mix-ups by human operators can be reduced because instruments will perform mundane tasks of sample transfers and deliver precise volumes of liquids more quickly and reliably.

There are a number of liquid handling tasks performed in DNA typing laboratories during the DNA extraction, PCR setup, and PCR amplification analysis steps. These liquid handling tasks are typically performed with manual pipettes by a DNA technician or analyst. Small volumes of liquids are repeatedly moved from one tube to another. These repetitive tasks can lead to mistakes as laboratory personnel become fatigued or careless.

By introducing automated liquid handling with robotics, the level of human error can be greatly reduced. Computers and robotics do the same task the same way time after time without tiring. The challenge though lies in setting up the automation and maintaining it (Hale 1999). Sample-handling automation is being used regularly with the high-volume sample processing of convicted offender samples for computer DNA databases (see Chapter 8).

As of early 2011, a variety of small-scale and large-scale liquid-handling robotic platforms are available with new ones in development. Some of the robotic systems in use by forensic DNA laboratories include: the Maxwell 16 (Promega Corporation), the EZ1 and QIAcube (QIAGEN), the Janus Automated Workstation (Perkin-Elmer), the Tecan Freedom EVO (Tecan) (Figure 17.4), and the Biomek 2000 and Biomek FX (Beckman Coulter). New sample

FIGURE 17.4 Tecan Freedom EVO 150 robotic workstation used for preparation of capillary electrophoresis sample plates. Photo courtesy of FBI Laboratory Federal DNA Database Unit.

preparation chemistries for improved DNA extraction will likely be incorporated into these and future robotic sample workstations.

Each robotic system has different capabilities and should be carefully assessed in order to meet the needs and goals of one's own laboratory environment (see Crouse & Conover 2003).

The Beckman Biomek 2000 robot has been used in conjunction with DNA IQ chemistry from the Promega Corporation to enable automated isolation and quantification of DNA samples (Tereba et al. 2003). Sexual assault (mixed stain) samples, cigarette butts, blood stains, buccal swabs, and various tissue samples were successfully extracted with the Biomek 2000 and the DNA IQ system without any evidence of contamination throughout extensive validation studies (Greenspoon et al. 2004). Robotic liquid handling for the steps of DNA extraction, quantification, PCR amplification setup, and preparation of sample plates for STR typing will likely become more prevalent in forensic laboratories particularly as the need for higher-volume work increases.

Laboratory Information Management Systems (LIMS)

Managing large amounts of data becomes a problem for many laboratories as they scale up their efforts. Computer databases are often developed to aid in tracking samples and results obtained. Sample tubes can be bar-coded and tracked through the analysis process. An example of efforts in this area is the Overlord System developed at the Forensic Science Service (FSS; Hopwood et al. 1997). The FSS Overlord program is a laboratory information management system (LIMS) and aids sample tracking as well as overall control of the different robotic stations. LIMS systems are rather expensive and are typically used only by laboratories with very high sample volumes.

Commercial LIMS systems, such as the Crime Fighter B.E.A.S.T. (computerized Bar-coded Evidence Analysis, Statistics, and Tracking LIMS) from Porter Lee Corporation (Schaumburg, IL), are being used in a growing number of forensic laboratories to provide electronic case files and automated sample tracking capabilities. A LIMS manufacturer typically sets up their software and customizes it to accommodate protocols and processes within each customer laboratory.

The Armed Forces DNA Identification Laboratory (AFDIL, Rockville, MD) has worked in conjunction with Future Technologies Inc. (Fairfax, VA) to develop LISA, which stands for Laboratory Information Systems Applications. LISA contains a number of sub-systems that permit case accessioning and the ability to electronically track the life cycle of each evidence and reference sample. There are additional modules such as MFIMS (Mass Fatality Incident Management System) and ASAP (AFDIL Statistical Application Program) that manage victim and family reference data as well as easing the tedious process of reporting results.

STaCS (Sample Tracking and Control System) is a system co-developed by forensic DNA scientists at the Royal Canadian Mounted Police (RCMP) and Anjura Technology Corporation (Ottawa, Ontario) that integrates robotic sample processing with custom LIMS software. STaCS monitors instrument performance and can provide a variety of operational information reports to help make the process of DNA typing more efficient. This system has been set up in several DNA databasing laboratories including the Florida Department of Law Enforcement (Tallahassee, FL) and the FBI Laboratory (Quantico, VA).

Fully integrated systems with robotic liquid handling are especially useful for DNA databasing of convicted offender samples, which are usually more uniform in nature (i.e., are all bloodstains or buccal swabs), single-source samples, and relatively concentrated in amount. In one laboratory, over 17,000 DNA samples were processed in a 20-month period using robotics and LIMS with an overall typing success rate of 99.99 % (Parson & Steinlechner 2001).

While automation is being developed and implemented to robotically process and track samples through the steps of DNA extraction, quantitation, PCR amplification, and sample setup prior to electrophoretic separation, separate computer programs commonly referred to as "expert systems" are being constructed to enable automatic interpretation of STR alleles from the resulting electropherograms.

EXPERT SYSTEMS FOR STR DATA INTERPRETATION

One of the most laborious efforts in the process of typing STRs is the data interpretation stage. For many high-throughput laboratories, data assessment and interpretation of STRs represents approximately 50 % or more of the resource requirement to deliver final results for samples. In many cases, more time is actually spent evaluating the STR profiles than preparing and processing the sample. In order to reduce this resource requirement, software has been designed and implemented to aid or replace the traditional manual assessment.

Two of the first expert systems used operationally include FSS-i^3 developed by the Forensic Science Service in England (and sold by Promega Corporation in the U.S.) and TrueAllele developed by Mark Perlin of Cybergenetics (Pittsburgh, PA). Applied Biosystems (Foster City, CA) has also developed GeneMapper*ID-X*, a program that includes quality flags on data collected with the ABI 310 or 3130*xl*, or 3500 Genetic Analyzers. Following validation of the software performance, DNA profiles from samples given a "green light" are generally considered fine and therefore further manual review is not required. As noted in Table 8.4, specific versions of these three expert systems have been approved by the National DNA Index System for use in uploading data to the U.S. national DNA database.

These expert systems are designed to translate the electropherogram signal into a genotype compatible with a database. As these expert systems are developed and implemented, bottlenecks will shift to other areas in the DNA typing process and thus permit development of expert systems that can solve ever more complex and diverse problems. Several years ago the National Institute of Justice established an NIJ-Expert System Testbed (NEST) project at Marshall University (Huntington, WV) that has evaluated the various expert system platforms for both single-source and mixture interpretation. For more information on the NEST project, see http://forensics.marshall.edu/NEST/default.html.

STR Expert System Suite (STRess) and FSS i-cubed Software

In 1998, the Forensic Science Service (FSS) developed a data interpretation program called STRess (STR Expert System Suite) to aid their STR profile processing. Interpretation guidelines drawn from approximately 100,000 samples processed by the FSS and used by experienced operators were incorporated into the programming of STRess (Gill et al. 1996, Dunbar et al. 1998). FSS genotyping guidelines require that all samples are genotyped by two independent operators to ensure accuracy of DNA typing results followed by a third operator to review allele calls and confirm that they are concordant. The aim of STRess was to reduce the amount of manual effort needed to evaluate the STR data by replacing one of the genotype analysts. The FSS has estimated that incorporating the STRess program into routine analysis has resulted in a 10% to 20% time savings at the interpretation stage with improved standardization and quality of interpretation (Martin Bill, Forensic Science Service, personal communication).

The success of the original STRess program spawned the development of a number of systems that automate interpretation and interact as a suite configurable to any multiplex. The FSS-i^3 expert system has three modules: i-STRress for single-source sample review, i-STRream for interpreting two-person mixtures, and i-ntegrity for quality control data review (Bill & Knox 2005, Huston 2007).

Introduction of the suite of expert systems described above has resulted in a significant increase in efficiency and quality at the FSS with a large reduction in unit cost. Based largely on issues discovered during the development of the FSS-i^3 software, Martin Bill of the Forensic Science Service offers the following seven recommendations for expert system development:

1. **Integration** – Ensure that the information technology (IT) infrastructure, support, and storage issues are considered when designing and developing expert systems rather than concentrating solely on the interpretation aspects. Solutions that are selected without considering these IT issues may result in most of the financial benefits of the expert systems being lost in future IT expenditure.
2. **External influences** – Consider potential changes to the supply chain and ensure the system will still be able to perform as required. On occasion external influences may require a change to interpretation. Any expert system solution must be flexible enough to work around such changes without causing significant problems.
3. **Process design** – Implement a new process that encompasses the expert system; do not simply implement an expert system using existing protocols. Process re-engineering is invariably required to maximize benefits when implementing the expert system. If this is not considered, the benefits of the software may disappear and it can be difficult to undo the damage.
4. **Benefits measurement** – There is a trite statement "What gets measured gets done." Decide how the benefits of an expert system can be measured and ensure the measurement process takes place. Make sure the correct units of measurement are used. Remember you are trying to measure the actual benefits realized not just the potential of the software. Unit costs are invariably better indicators than timing exercises.
5. **People and culture** – Expect cultural issues until the scientists gain confidence in the expert system and include this aspect of the implementation in the project plan. Do not be surprised or disappointed if people need time to become accustomed to the idea of automated interpretation.
6. **Success rate** – This factor is often overlooked yet it is one of the most critical areas to consider. As a DNA unit moves from manual to automated interpretation, the success rate of the process will change. Expert systems will probably never have total concordance with manual interpretation because the computer is following a rigid set of rules. The change in success rate should be closely monitored during the initial phase of deployment.

7. **Target setting** – Set realistic targets for the project. Analysts do not spend all of their time analyzing data and therefore it is impossible to realize 100% analyst reduction irrespective of how good the expert system is. This aspect closely links with the process re-engineering. The same problem exists with projected error rates. Many laboratories refuse to acknowledge that an error rate exists. We should recognize that there are many opportunities for error to occur, some within and some outside the control of the DNA unit. It is better to openly acknowledge that error can occur as it is easier to look for solutions. *No expert system will ever be designed that has an error rate of zero* and therefore setting a target of zero is self-defeating. The real benefit of expert systems is that they behave predictably. It is this predictability and standardization that improves quality. As a starting point the objective should be to improve on the manual error rate (therefore making forward progress). When using expert systems, error rate and success rates are closely linked, one effectively determines the other. This level of control is extremely useful when attempting to optimize the output from a DNA unit.

TrueAllele

TrueAllele is a commercially available allele-calling program from Cybergenetics (Pittsburgh, PA) that uses quantitation and deconvolution algorithms to improve STR allele calls based upon quality measures (Pálsson et al. 1999, Perlin 2000). TrueAllele is written in Matlab and runs with Macintosh, Windows, or UNIX-based systems. The quality value assigned by TrueAllele ranges between 0.0 and 1.0 and reflects a peak's height, shape, and stutter pattern (Pálsson et al. 1999). The selection criteria used by the program are empirically derived through review of many STR profiles.

The first two forensic DNA laboratories to utilize TrueAllele as an expert system for STR analysis are the Forensic Science Service and the New York State Police in Albany, New York. In a comparison of allele calls from 2048 STR profiles between manual review with Genotyper and automated review with TrueAllele, only one significant difference was observed when the analyst using Genotyper interpreted a spike as a DNA peak at D8S1179 but TrueAllele correctly designated it as a spike (Kadash et al. 2004). Newer versions of TrueAllele are also capable of DNA mixture interpretation (Perlin et al. 2011).

GeneMapper*ID* and GeneMapper*ID-X*

Applied Biosystems (Foster City, CA) released a computer program in November 2003 named GeneMapper*ID* v3.1 (and later v3.2 and v3.2.1) that designates peaks in electropherograms and calls alleles through size comparisons to allelic ladders (Applied Biosystems 2003). GeneMapper*ID* still requires manual review of the data but process quality values (PQVs) provide confidence in allele calls and aid troubleshooting efforts. More recently, GeneMapper*ID-X* v1.1 and v1.2 software enables expert system processing of single-source samples and expert assistance support for DNA mixture interpretation.

Other DNA Interpretation Software Programs

The National Center for Biotechnology Information (NCBI) at the U.S. National Institutes of Health has developed a STR data interpretation software program called OSIRIS, which stands for Open Source Independent Review and Interpretation System. It is freely available for download in Mac or Windows formats at http://www.ncbi.nlm.nih.gov/projects/SNP/osiris/.

GenoProof 2 and GenoProof Mixture are STR data interpretation programs developed by Qualitype AG (Dresden, Germany) that enable information processing from raw data to biostatistical calculations. The GenoProof Mixture program was especially designed to handle complex DNA mixtures. For more information, see http://www.qualitype.de.

Soft Genetics, LLC (State College, PA) has developed STR typing software for human identity applications that can perform mixture analysis and database searches as well as paternity and kinship analysis (Holland & Parson 2011). More information is available at http://www.softgenetics.com/GeneMarkerHID.html.

SUMMARY AND FINAL THOUGHTS

The adoption of new technology by the forensic DNA community takes time (e.g., several years) for multiple reasons. First and foremost, methods need to be carefully validated to ensure that results with a new technology are accurate and reproducible (see Chapter 7). Second, methods should yield comparable results to current technologies so that genotype information can be compared over time. The development of large DNA databases make it necessary to have a constant currency so that convicted offender samples have been analyzed with the same DNA markers as crime scene samples (see Chapter 8).

A new set of markers or a new form of sample analysis, unless it gives an equivalent result to current technology, must have clear advantages and be very inexpensive to overcome legacy data in large DNA databases. Now that millions of DNA profiles are present

TABLE 17.2 Benefits and Limitations of Several Technologies for DNA Testing.

Technology	Benefits	Limitations
Rapid DNA analysis	Potentially portable system; faster results that could enable new applications of DNA testing	Some compromises in DNA result quality may be required
Mass spectrometry base composition	Enables measurement of both length and nucleotide variability with compatibility to existing STR databases; less expensive than sequencing for mtDNA	Higher instrument cost and more difficult to maintain than a CE system; unable to determine the location of a sequence change; cannot multiplex to a high-level (would likely require more DNA)
Pyrosequencing	Enables rapid sequence-based analysis of STRs or other PCR products	Cannot multiplex (would likely require more DNA); cannot cope with complex and long repeats
Next-generation DNA sequencing	Enables recovery of sequence information from highly degraded DNA (e.g., ancient DNA samples)	Significant increase in cost compared to current methods; short read lengths limit ability to capture STR repeat variation
Automation	Improved efficiency and speed in processing samples (particularly with expert systems data interpretation)	Initial cost for equipment and software

in national DNA databases it is highly unlikely that the field will abandon the current STR loci in the near-to-medium future. Yet as noted throughout this book, the continued progress being made in biotechnology around the world has led and will continue to lead to improved methods for DNA typing. Improvements in expert systems and data interpretation computer programs—particularly with the ability to handle DNA mixtures and low-level samples—are an important area for the future.

A brief review of the benefits and limitations of each technology discussed in this chapter is contained in Table 17.2. Each potential new method has advantages and disadvantages. Faster DNA analysis, higher levels of sensitivity, and stronger powers of discrimination are possible as new technology is embraced and adopted following validation by the forensic DNA typing community. Automation is also a key to the future—particularly in terms of data interpretation.

READING LIST AND INTERNET RESOURCES

Rapid DNA Analysis with Microchip CE Systems

Bienvenue, J. M., et al. (2010). An integrated microfluidic device for DNA purification and PCR amplification of STR fragments. *Forensic Science International: Genetics, 4*(3), 178–186.

Bienvenue, J. M., et al. (2006). Microchip-based cell lysis and DNA extraction from sperm cells for application to forensic analysis. *Journal of Forensic Sciences, 51*(2), 266–273.

Choi, J. Y., & Seo, T. S. (2009). An integrated microdevice for high-performance short tandem repeat genotyping. *Biotechnology Journal, 4*, 1530–1541.

Crouse, C. A., et al. (2005). Improving efficiency of a small forensic DNA laboratory: Validation of robotic assays and evaluation of microcapillary array device. *Croatian Medical Journal, 46*(4), 563–577.

Ehrlich, D. J., & Matsudaira, P. (1999). Microfluidic devices for DNA analysis. *Trends in Biotechnology, 17*, 315–319.

Forensic Science Service. <http://www.forensic.gov.uk/>.

Giese, H., et al. (2009). Fast multiplexed polymerase chain reaction for conventional and microfluidic short tandem repeat analysis. *Journal of Forensic Sciences, 54*, 1287–1296.

Goedecke, N., et al. (2004). A high-performance multilane microdevice system designed for the DNA forensics laboratory. *Electrophoresis, 25*, 1678–1686.

Greenspoon, S. A., et al. (2008). A forensic laboratory tests the Berkeley microfabricated capillary array electrophoresis device. *Journal of Forensic Sciences, 53*, 828–837.

Hopwood, A. J., et al. (2010). Integrated microfluidic system for rapid forensic DNA analysis: Sample collection to DNA profile. *Analytical Chemistry, 82*, 6991–6999.

Horsman, K. M., et al. (2005). Separation of sperm and epithelial cells in a microfabricated device: Potential application to forensic analysis of sexual assault evidence. *Analytical Chemistry, 77*(3), 742–749.

Horsman, K. M., et al. (2007). Forensic DNA analysis on microfluidic devices: A review. *Journal of Forensic Sciences, 52*(4), 784–799.

Hurth, C., et al. (2010). An automated instrument for human STR identification: Design, characterization, and experimental validation. *Electrophoresis, 31*, 3510–3517.

IntegenX. <http://www.integenx.com>.

Liu, P., et al. (2007). Integrated portable polymerase chain reaction-capillary electrophoresis microsystem for rapid forensic short tandem repeat typing. *Analytical Chemistry, 79*(5), 1881–1889.

Liu, P., et al. (2008). Real-time forensic DNA analysis at a crime scene using a portable microchip analyzer. *Forensic Science International: Genetics, 2*, 301–309.

Liu, P., & Mathies, R. A. (2009). Integrated microfluidic systems for high-performance genetic analysis. *Trends in Biotechnology, 27*, 572–581.

Liu, P., et al. (2011). Integrated DNA purification, PCR, sample cleanup, and capillary electrophoresis microchip for forensic human identification. *Lab-on-a-Chip, 11*, 1041–1048.

Mitnik, L., et al. (2002). High-speed analysis of multiplexed short tandem repeats with an electrophoretic microdevice. *Electrophoresis, 23,* 719–726.

Network Biosystems. <http://www.netbio.com>.

Paegel, B. M., et al. (2003). Microfluidic devices for DNA sequencing: Sample preparation and electrophoretic analysis. *Current Opinions in Biotechnology, 14,* 42–50.

Reedy, C. R., et al. (2010). Volume reduction solid-phase extraction of DNA from dilute, large-volume biological samples. *Forensic Science International: Genetics, 4,* 206–212.

Reedy, C. R., et al. (2010). Dual-domain microchip-based process for volume reduction solid phase extraction of nucleic acids from dilute, large volume biological samples. *Analytical Chemistry, 82,* 5669–5678.

Reedy, C. R., et al. (2011). A modular microfluidic system for deoxyribonucleic acid identification by short tandem repeat analysis. *Analytica Chimica Acta, 687,* 150–158.

Schmalzing, D., et al. (1997). DNA typing in thirty seconds with a microfabricated device. *Proceedings of the National Academy of Sciences of the United States of America, 94,* 10273–10278.

Schmalzing, D., et al. (1999). Two-color multiplexed analysis of eight short tandem repeat loci with an electrophoretic microdevice. *Analytical Biochemistry, 270,* 148–152.

Vallone, P. M., et al. (2008). Demonstration of rapid multiplex PCR amplification involving 16 genetic loci. *Forensic Science International: Genetics, 3,* 42–45.

Woolley, A. T., & Mathies, R. A. (1994). Ultra-high-speed DNA fragment separations using microfabricated capillary array electrophoresis chips. *Proceedings of the National Academy of Sciences of the United States of America, 91,* 11348–11352.

Woolley, A. T., et al. (1996). Functional integration of PCR amplification and capillary electrophoresis in a microfabricated DNA analysis device. *Analytical Chemistry, 68,* 4081–4086.

Yeung, S. H., et al. (2009). Integrated sample cleanup-capillary electrophoresis microchip for high-performance short tandem repeat genetic analysis. *Analytical Chemistry, 81*(1), 210–217.

Yeung, S. H., et al. (2006). Rapid and high-throughput forensic short tandem repeat typing using a 96-lane microfabricated capillary array electrophoresis microdevice. *Journal of Forensic Sciences, 51*(4), 740–747.

Yeung, S. H., et al. (2008). Rapid determination of monozygous twinning with a microfabricated capillary array electrophoresis genetic-analysis device. *Clinical Chemistry, 54*(6), 1080–1084.

Yeung, S. H., et al. (2008). Fluorescence energy transfer-labeled primers for high-performance forensic DNA profiling. *Electrophoresis, 29,* 2251–2259.

Zhang, Y., & Ozdemir, P. (2009). Microfluidic DNA amplification—a review. *Analytical Chimica Acta, 638,* 115–125.

ZyGEM. <http://www.zygem.com>.

Other Rapid Approaches to DNA Testing

French, D. J., et al. (2008). Interrogation of short tandem repeats using fluorescent probes and melting curve analysis: A step towards rapid DNA identity screening. *Forensic Science International: Genetics, 2,* 333–339.

Halpern, M. D., & Ballantyne, J. (2009). A single nucleotide polymorphism melt curve assay employing an intercalating dye probe fluorescence resonance energy transfer for forensic analysis. *Analytical Biochemistry, 391,* 1–10.

Halpern, M. D., & Ballantyne, J. (2011). An STR melt curve genotyping assay for forensic analysis employing an intercalating dye probe FRET. *Journal of Forensic Sciences, 56,* 36–45.

Nogami, H., et al. (2008). Rapid and simple sex determination method from dental pulp by loop-mediated isothermal amplification. *Forensic Science International: Genetics, 2,* 349–353.

Villablanca, A., et al. (2008). Suspension bead array branch migration displacement assay for rapid STR analysis. *Electrophoresis, 29,* 4109–4114.

Mass Spectrometry

Butler, J. M., et al. (1998). Reliable genotyping of short tandem repeat loci without an allelic ladder using time-of-flight mass spectrometry. *International Journal of Legal Medicine, 112,* 45–49.

Butler, J. M., et al. (2000). DNA typing by mass spectrometry with polymorphic DNA repeat markers. U.S. Patent 6,090,558.

Butler, J. M., & Becker, C. H. (2001). Improved analysis of DNA short tandem repeats with time-of-flight mass spectrometry. Final Report for NIJ Grant 97-LB-VX-0003, Office of Justice Programs, National Institute of Justice (75 published pages); http://www.ojp.usdoj.gov/nij/pubs-sum/188292.htm.

Hall, T. A., et al. (2005). Base composition analysis of human mitochondrial DNA using electrospray ionization mass spectrometry: A novel tool for the identification and differentiation of humans. *Analytical Biochemistry, 344*, 53–69.

Hofstadler, S. A., et al. (2009). Analysis of DNA forensic markers using high throughput mass spectrometry. *Forensic Science International: Genetics Supplement Series 2*, 524–526.

IBIS Biosciences. <http://www.ibisbiosciences.com/>.

Jiang, Y., & Hofstadler, S. A. (2003). A highly efficient and automated method of purifying and desalting PCR products for analysis by electrospray ionization mass spectrometry. *Analytical Biochemistry, 316*, 50–57.

Jiang, Y., et al. (2007). Mitochondrial DNA mutation detection by electrospray mass spectrometry. *Clinical Chemistry, 53*, 195–203.

Manduzio, H., et al. (2010). Comparison of approaches for purifying and desalting polymerase chain reaction products prior to electrospray ionization mass spectrometry. *Analytical Biochemistry, 398*, 272–274.

Oberacher, H., et al. (2005). Detection of DNA sequence variations in homo- and heterozygous samples via molecular mass measurements by electrospray ionization time-of-flight mass spectrometry. *Analytical Chemistry, 77*, 4999–5008.

Oberacher, H., et al. (2006). Some guidelines for the analysis of genomic DNA by PCR-LC-ESI-MS. *Journal of American Society of Mass Spectrometry, 17*, 124–129.

Oberacher, H., & Parson, W. (2007). Forensic DNA fingerprinting by liquid chromatography-electrospray ionization mass spectrometry. *Biotechniques, 43*(4), vii–xiii.

Oberacher, H., et al. (2007). Liquid chromatography-electrospray ionization mass spectrometry for simultaneous detection of mtDNA length and nucleotide polymorphisms. *International Journal of Legal Medicine, 121*, 57–67.

Oberacher, H., et al. (2008). Increased forensic efficiency of DNA fingerprints through simultaneous resolution of length and nucleotide variability by high-performance mass spectrometry. *Human Mutation, 29*, 427–432.

Oberacher, H. (2008). On the use of different mass spectrometric techniques for characterization of sequence variability in genomic DNA. *Analytical and Bioanalytical Chemistry, 391*, 135–149.

Pitterl, F., et al. (2008). The next generation of DNA profiling—STR typing by multiplexed PCR-ion-pair RP LC-ESI time-of-flight MS. *Electrophoresis, 29*, 4739–4750.

Pitterl, F., et al. (2010). Increasing the discrimination power of forensic STR testing by employing high-performance mass spectrometry, as illustrated in indigenous South African and Central Asian populations. *International Journal of Legal Medicine, 124*, 551–558.

Planz, J. V., et al. (2009). Enhancing resolution and statistical power by utilizing mass spectrometry for detection of SNPs within the short tandem repeats. *Forensic Science International: Genetics Supplement Series 2*, 529–531.

PLEX-ID system (Abbott). <http://us.plex-id.com/index.html>.

Pyrosequencing

Andreasson, H., et al. (2002). Mitochondrial sequence analysis for forensic identification using pyrosequencing technology. *Biotechniques, 32*, 124–133.

Allen, M., & Andreasson, H. (2005). Mitochondrial D-loop and coding sequence analysis using pyrosequencing. *Methods in Molecular Biology, 297*, 179–196.

Andreasson, H., et al. (2006). Quantification of mtDNA mixtures in forensic evidence material using pyrosequencing. *International Journal of Legal Medicine, 120*, 383–390.

Andreasson, H., et al. (2007). Forensic mitochondrial coding region analysis for increased discrimination using pyrosequencing technology. *Forensic Science International: Genetics, 1*, 35–43.

Balitzki-Korte, B., et al. (2005). Species identification by means of pyrosequencing the mitochondrial 12S rRNA gene. *International Journal of Legal Medicine, 119*, 291–294.

Brenig, B., et al. (2010). Shotgun metagenomics of biological stains using ultra-deep DNA sequencing. *Forensic Science International: Genetics, 4*, 228–231.

Divne, A. M., et al. (2010). Forensic analysis of autosomal STR markers using Pyrosequencing. *Forensic Science International: Genetics, 4*, 122–129.

Edlund, H., & Allen, M. (2009). Y chromosomal STR analysis using Pyrosequencing technology. *Forensic Science International: Genetics, 3*, 119–124.

Fierer, N., et al. (2010). Forensic identification using skin bacterial communities. *Proceedings of the National Academy of Sciences of the United States of America, 107*, 6477–6481.

Karlsson, A. O., & Holmlund, G. (2007). Identification of mammal species using species-specific DNA pyrosequencing. *Forensic Science International, 173*, 16–20.

Ronaghi, M., et al. (1998). A sequencing method based on real-time pyrophosphate. *Science, 281*, 363–365.

Tschentscher, F., et al. (2008). Amelogenin sex determination by pyrosequencing of short PCR products. *International Journal of Legal Medicine, 122*, 333–335.

Zeng, Z., et al. (2010). Genome-wide screen for individual identification SNPs (IISNPs) and the confirmation of six of them in Han Chinese with pyrosequencing technology. *Journal of Forensic Sciences, 55*, 901–907.

Next-Generation DNA Sequencing

454 Life Sciences (Roche). <http://www.454.com/>.

Ansorge, W. J. (2009). Next-generation DNA sequencing techniques. *New Biotechnology, 25*, 195–203.

Droege, M., & Hill, B. (2008). The Genome Sequencer FLX System--longer reads, more applications, straight forward bioinformatics and more complete data sets. *Journal of Biotechnology, 136*, 3–10.

Duncan, S., et al. (2010). DraGnET: Software for storing, managing and analyzing annotated draft genome sequence data. *BMC Bioinformatics, 11*, 100.

Hert, D. G., et al. (2008). Advantages and limitations of next-generation sequencing technologies: A comparison of electrophoresis and non-electrophoresis methods. *Electrophoresis, 29*, 4618–4626.

Illumina, Inc. <http://www.illumina.com/>.

Mardis, E. R. (2008). Next-generation DNA sequencing methods. *Annual Review of Genomics & Human Genetics, 9*, 387–402.

Misra, S., et al. (2011). Anatomy of a hash-based long read sequence mapping algorithm for next generation DNA sequencing. *Bioinformatics, 27*, 189–195.

Pacific Bbiosciences. <http://www.pacificbiosciences.com/>.

Shendure, J., & Ji, H. (2008). Next-generation DNA sequencing. *Nature Biotechnology, 26*, 1135–1145.

SOLiD. <http://www.appliedbiosystems.com/absite/us/en/home/applications-technologies/solid-next-generation-sequencing.html>.

Szelinger, S., et al. (2011). Bar-coded, multiplexed sequencing of targeted DNA regions using the Illumina Genome Analyzer. *Methods in Molecular Biology, 700*, 89–104.

White, R. A., et al. (2009). Digital PCR provides sensitive and absolute calibration for high throughput sequencing. *BMC Genomics, 10*, 116.

Ancient DNA Sequencing

Allentoft, M., et al. (2009). Identification of microsatellites from an extinct moa species using high-throughput (454) sequence data. *Biotechniques, 46*, 195–200.

Blow, M. J., et al. (2008). Identification of ancient remains through genomic sequencing. *Genome Research, 18*, 1347–1353.

Green, R. E., et al. (2008). A complete Neandertal mitochondrial genome sequence determined by high-throughput sequencing. *Cell, 134*, 416–426.

Miller, W., et al. (2008). Sequencing the nuclear genome of the extinct woolly mammoth. *Nature, 456*, 387–390.

Poinar, H. N., et al. (2006). Metagenomics to paleogenomics: Large-scale sequencing of mammoth DNA. *Science, 311*, 392–394.

Automation

Cowan, C., & Schwandt, M. (2008). A discussion of automation for the forensic DNA laboratory. *Forensic Magazine, 5*(5), 12–21.

Crouse, C. A., & Conover, J. (2003). Successful validation and implementation of (semi)-automation in a small case working laboratory. *Proceedings of the fourteenth international symposium on human identification*. Available at http://www.promega.com/geneticidproc/ussymp14proc/oralpresentations/Crouse.pdf.

Dunbar, H. N., et al. (1998). Latest developments in forensic DNA profiling – the UK National DNA Database. *Proceedings of the second european symposium on human identification*. Available at http://www.promega.com/geneticidproc/eusymp2proc/14.pdf.

Hale, A. N. (1999). Building realistic automated production lines for genetic analysis, Chapter 5. In A. G. Craig & J. D. Hoheisel (Eds.), *Methods in Microbiology*, *28*, 93–129. San Diego: Academic Press.

Hedman, J., et al. (2008). A fast analysis system for forensic DNA reference samples. *Forensic Science International: Genetics*, *2*, 184–189.

Robotic Sample Preparation

AutoMate Express Forensic DNA Extraction System (Applied Biosystems). <http://marketing.appliedbiosystems.com/mk/get/AUTOMATE_MS_MLANDING>.

Frégeau, C., et al. (2007). Optimized configuration of fixed-tip robotic liquid-handling stations for the elimination of biological sample cross-contamination. *Journal of the Association for Laboratory Automation*, *12*, 339–354.

Frégeau, C., et al. (2008). Automated processing of forensic casework samples using robotic workstations equipped with nondisposable tips: Contamination prevention. *Journal of Forensic Sciences*, *53*, 632–651.

Frégeau, C., et al. (2010). Validation of a DNA IQ™-based extraction method for TECAN robotic liquid handling workstations for processing casework. *Forensic Science International: Genetics*, *4*, 292–304.

Greenspoon, S. A., et al. (2004). Application of the BioMek 2000 Laboratory Automation Workstation and the DNA IQ System to the extraction of forensic casework samples. *Journal of Forensic Sciences*, *49*, 29–39.

Hopwood, A., et al. (1997). A fully integrated robotic system for high sample throughput within a DNA databasing unit. *Proceedings of the eighth international symposium on human identification*. Available at http://www.promega.com/geneticidproc/ussymp8proc/09.html.

Maxwell 16. <http://www.promega.com/maxwell16/>.

Parson, W., & Steinlechner, M. (2001). Efficient DNA database strategy for high-throughput STR typing of reference samples. *Forensic Science International*, *122*, 1–6.

Pizzamiglio, M., et al. (2006). Robotic DNA extraction system as a new way to process sweat traces rapidly and efficiently. *Progress in Forensic Genetics 11, ICS 1288*, 598–600.

QIAGEN EZ1 and other robotic systems. <http://www.qiagen.com/products/automation/default.aspx>.

Tecan Freedom EVO. <http://www.tecan.com/freedomevo>.

Tereba, A., et al. (2003). Advances in developing an automated "black box" for casework sample preparation. *Proceedings of the fourteenth international symposium on human identification*. Available at http://www.promega.com/geneticidproc/ussymp14proc/oralpresentations/Tereba.pdf.

Laboratory Information Management Systems (LIMS)

Future Technologies Inc. <http://www.ftechi.com/dna_biometric.shtml>.

Hansen, A. J., et al. (2006). Semi-automatic preparation of biological database samples for STR typing. *Progress in Forensic Genetics 11, ICS 1288*, 663–665.

JusticeTrak Inc. <http://www.justicetrax.com/>.

Parson, W., & Steinlechner, M. (2001). Efficient DNA database laboratory strategy for high throughput STR typing of reference samples. *Forensic Science International*, *122*, 1–6.

Porter Lee Corporation (the crime fighting B.E.A.S.T. LIMS). <http://www.porterlee.com/lims.html>.

Process Analysis & Automation Ltd (Overlord3). <http://www.paa.co.uk/>.

Qualitype AG. <http://www.qualitype.de/company/index.jsp>.

STaCS DNA. <http://www.stacsdna.com/>.

Starfruit DNA LIMS. <http://www.duii.com/lims.htm>.

STARLIMS. <http://www.starlims.com/LIMS_For_DNA_Forensic.htm>.

Steinlechner, M., & Parson, W. (2001). Automation and high throughput for a DNA database laboratory: Development of a laboratory information management system. *Croatian Medical Journal*, *43*, 252–255.

Expert Systems

Applied Biosystems. (2003). GeneMapper ID Software Version 3.1 Human Identification Analysis User Guide. Foster City, California.

Bill, M., & Knox, C. (2005). FSS-i3 expert system. *Profiles in DNA*, *8*(2), 8–10.

Frappier, R., et al. (2008). Improving forensic DNA laboratory throughput: Enhanced data analysis and expert systems capability. *Forensic Magazine*, *5*(1), 25–31.

FSS-i3 software (from FSS and Promega). <http://www.promega.com/applications/hmnid/productprofiles/fssi3/default.htm>.

GeneMapperID-X (from Applied Biosystems). <http://idx.appliedbiosystems.com>.

GeneMarker HID (from SoftGenetics). <http://www.softgenetics.com/GeneMarkerHID.html>.

Gill, P., et al. (1996). A new method of STR interpretation using inferential logic – development of a criminal intelligence database. *International Journal of Legal Medicine, 109*, 14–22.

Holland, M. M., & Parson, W. (2011). GeneMarker HID: A reliable software tool for the analysis of forensic STR data. *Journal of Forensic Sciences, 56*, 29–35.

Huston, K. (2007). FSS-i^3 expert systems software. *Profiles in DNA, 10*(1), 11–13.

Kadash, K., et al. (2004). Validation study of the TrueAllele automated data review system. *Journal of Forensic Sciences, 49*, 660–667.

NIJ-Expert System Testbed (NEST) Project. <http://forensics.marshall.edu/NEST/default.html>.

Oldroyd, N., & Schade, L. L. (2008). Expert assistant software enables forensic DNA analysts to confidently process more samples. *Forensic Magazine, 5*(6), 25–28.

OSIRIS. <http://www.ncbi.nlm.nih.gov/projects/SNP/osiris/>.

Pálsson, B., et al. (1999). Using quality measures to facilitate allele calling in high-throughput genotyping. *Genome Research, 9*, 1002–1012.

Perlin, M. (2000). An expert system for scoring DNA database profiles. *Proceedings of the eleventh international symposium on human identification*. Available at <http://www.promega.com/geneticidproc/ussymp11proc/>.

Perlin, M. W., et al. (2011). Validating TrueAllele DNA mixture interpretation. *Journal of Forensic Sciences* (in press).

Power, T., et al. (2008). FaSTR DNA: A new expert system for forensic DNA analysis. *Forensic Science International: Genetics, 2*, 159–165.

Roby, R. K., & Christen, A. D. (2007). Validating expert systems: Examples with the FSS-i3™ expert systems software. *Profiles in DNA, 10*(2), 13–15.

TrueAllele (from Cybergenetics). <http://www.cybgen.com/>.

CHAPTER

18

Legal Aspects of DNA Testing and the Scientific Expert in Court

INCLUDING INPUT FROM INTERVIEWS WITH DR. ROBIN COTTON, TED HUNT, BRAD BANNON, THE ORANGE COUNTY (CA) DISTRICT ATTORNEY'S DNA UNIT, AND DR. CHARLOTTE WORD

There are important differences between the quest for truth in the courtroom and the quest for truth in the laboratory. Scientific conclusions are subject to perpetual revision. Law, on the other hand, must resolve disputes finally and quickly (U.S. Supreme Court Justice Harry Blackmun in the 1993 decision of Daubert v. Merrell Dow Pharmaceuticals, Inc.*).*

As noted on the American Academy of Forensic Sciences website (http://www.aafs.org), forensic science is the application of science to the just resolution of legal issues. Thus, forensic DNA scientists produce results that directly impact the criminal justice system. These results and their subsequent conclusions are usually presented in the form of a case report. DNA analysts are sometimes called upon to testify in court regarding the conclusions derived from the test results produced during the course of their examination of the evidence provided to them and recorded in their case reports. The Southwestern Association of Forensic Scientists' Code of Professional Conduct reminds their members that. "Forensic scientists…have an obligation to provide opinions and facts to a court of law that are truthful, honorable, and of sound judgment… The work product of the forensic scientist is culminated in the conclusions stated in their report and during testimony." (see http://www.swafs.us/pdf/2009/2008bylaws.pdf). The purpose of this chapter is to discuss the roles and responsibilities of expert witnesses in the framework of the U.S. legal system to aid DNA analysts preparing to testify in court. Lawyers and judges need to understand some science to do their jobs well. Likewise, scientists should comprehend and appreciate some law to serve effectively in court.

Although I am not permitted to testify as an expert witness because of my current position as a federal government employee at the National Institute of Standards and Technology, I have been asked to do so many times. I have taken courtroom testimony training and given a lot of thought to the issues involved from my perspective on the sidelines of courtroom drama. Over the past few years, I have also had the privilege of talking to and teaching numerous lawyers (both prosecuting and defense attorneys) about DNA testing. Based in large part on these discussions, I feel a need to add this chapter to Advanced Topics in Forensic DNA Typing: Methodology *to help bridge the divide between science and law that can and does exist for many people. As a disclaimer, the material provided herein is not intended to be complete in its coverage of legal issues. Remember that I am a scientist and not a lawyer! I welcome feedback from members of the legal community and forensic DNA scientists in order to improve and expand the content in future editions.*

In addition to what I have gleaned from studying the resources listed at the back of this chapter, I have interviewed several individuals who have extensive experience as expert witnesses or other roles in the courtroom. In covering various topics, I will include direct quotes from these interviews (citing the individual contributions through their initials). Complete responses to interview questions are available in Appendix 4 at the back of this book. Prior to submission of this text, all those interviewed reviewed what I have written in order to confirm that I have quoted them correctly and placed their words in an appropriate context.

(RWC) Robin W. Cotton, Ph.D., is associate professor and director of the biomedical forensic sciences program at Boston University. She has over 20 years experience with forensic DNA analysis and served as the Laboratory Director for Cellmark Diagnostics from 1994 to 2006. Robin has served as an expert witness and testified in over 200 trials regarding DNA evidence including the O.J. Simpson trial in 1995. For more information, see http://www.bumc.bu.edu/biomedforensic/faculty-and-staff/faculty/robin-cotton/.

(CJW) Charlotte J. Word, Ph.D., is currently a private consultant with over 20 years of experience in forensic DNA analysis. She spent 15 years at Cellmark Diagnostics, in Germantown, Maryland, and was one of the Laboratory Directors there. She has testified in numerous admissibility hearings and in over 200 trials regarding DNA evidence. Charlotte also serves on the editorial board for the *Journal of Forensic Sciences* and was a member of the Postconviction Issues Working Group of the National Commission on the Future of DNA Evidence.

(TRH) Ted R. Hunt, J.D., is Chief Trial Attorney at the Jackson County Prosecutor's Office in Kansas City, Missouri. He has been a prosecuting attorney for 20 years and tried over 100 felony cases, most of which involved the presentation of DNA evidence. He is also actively involved in training attorneys and law enforcement officials in forensic DNA-related litigation for a number of state and federal organizations.

(OCDA) Orange County (California) District Attorney's DNA Unit is comprised of experienced deputy district attorneys who possess expertise regarding the utilization of forensic DNA evidence to solve crime. The OCDA DNA Unit provides assistance and training to all of the county's law enforcement agencies. Members of the OCDA DNA Unit, which include attorneys Bruce Moore, Camille Hill, Scott Scoville, Jennifer Contini, Terry Cleaveland, and Tammy Spurgeon, work closely with local law enforcement investigators, prosecutors, crime lab forensic scientists and OCDA local DNA database forensic scientists to effectively use forensic DNA technology and resources.

(BB) Bradley Bannon, J.D., is a criminal trial defense attorney for the law firm of Cheshire, Parker, Schneider, Bryan, and Vitale in Raleigh, North Carolina. He has been practicing law for 13 years and has helped draft legislation to strengthen the right of the accused to pretrial discovery in criminal cases in North Carolina. He was instrumental in using DNA evidence to help exonerate the Duke lacrosse players of false accusations of rape in 2006 and 2007. For more information, see http://www.cheshirepark.com/bbannon.html.

The 2001 Scientific Working Group on DNA Analysis Methods (SWGDAM) Training Guidelines emphasize in section 7 on legal issues that a DNA analyst trainee should be instructed on the legal system of his/her own jurisdiction (SWGDAM 2001). Furthermore, these guidelines suggest that a trainee should receive instruction on the following topics: (1) courtroom procedures and rules of evidence, (2) examiner/analyst qualifications, (3) technical testimony, (4) courtroom demeanor and attire, (5) testimony practice, (6) moot court(s), (7) discovery and admissibility rules, (8) ethical responsibility of an expert witness, (9) court system structure, and (10) evidence presentation. In addition, the examiner/analyst is encouraged to prepare a curriculum vitae and observe expert testimony, read relevant and appropriate transcripts or pertinent case law, and successfully complete at least one moot court (SWGDAM 2001). This chapter and the accompanying interview transcripts in Appendix 4 are intended to benefit this instruction for DNA analysts operating in U.S. courts of law.

SCIENCE AND LAW: DIFFERENT PERSPECTIVES

Several years ago I was asked by the American Prosecutor's Research Institute (APRI) to help prepare a DNA training course for lawyers. I and one other scientist were in a room with four prosecutors and an educational consultant for two days. I recall hearing terms like "Brady," "Frye," and "admissibility" being used regularly without any explanation. To these lawyers, a mere mention of "Brady" brought a concept of the requirement for disclosure of case information to opposing counsel based on the 1963 case of Brady v Maryland (373 US 83, 1963).

This experience helped me appreciate what terms like "stutter," "capillary electrophoresis," "allele dropout," and "pull-up" must seem like to lawyers and the general public. Likewise, when a scientist enters the legal arena, there are basic terminology and processes that must be understood in order to function in this environment. While not intended to be comprehensive in coverage, some important legal terms and concepts will be introduced in this chapter that should benefit DNA scientists going to court.

Terms and concepts that are second nature to forensic DNA scientists must be conveyed correctly in reports of analysis and in a court of law. Communication is a key factor. Thus, a discussion of jury comprehension is included in this chapter because in U.S. courts of law the expert testimony delivered by a DNA analyst needs to be understood by (typically) a dozen fellow citizens who have little-to-no science background. If this chapter and book can open the dialogue and help as a beginning translation between the different languages of science and the law, then I will have been successful.

Cultural Differences

As the majority decision in the landmark 1993 *Daubert* ruling notes (see opening quote for the chapter): "There are important differences between the quest for truth in the

TABLE 18.1 Differences in Culture between Science and the Law (Adapted from Bowen 2010, p. 33).

Issue	Science	Law
Truth	Serves the interest of itself	Serves the interest of the client
Communication	Open	Privileged
Process	Unbiased and systematic	Adversarial; defending a specific position
Goals	Provide socially valued goods and services; advance human knowledge; eliminate false beliefs; document knowledge through publication so that others can benefit	Serve the client; produce a better argument to the trier-of-fact than the opposing counsel

courtroom and the quest for truth in the laboratory." Table 18.1 contrasts some of these differences in culture between science and the law. Thus, when a scientist enters the culture of the courtroom to serve as an expert witness, he or she will probably feel out of place. As Clay Strange, a prosecutor in Travis County, Texas, has shared, "No amount of 'moot court' conducted by forensic scientists pretending to be judge, jury, prosecutor, and defense lawyer will fully prepare the expert for entry into the world of the criminal court. It has to be experienced to be believed" (Strange 2002).

As highlighted in Table 18.1, scientists are typically used to operating in an environment where information is shared in an open and hopefully unbiased fashion with a goal to advance human knowledge. Lawyers, particularly in a U.S. court environment, are adversarial meaning that they are arguing a particular position on behalf of a client.

For a criminal trial, the prosecution typically represents the government's position on behalf of a victim (or complainant) while the defense attorney represents a defendant who is being accused of having committed a crime against the alleged victim. Thus, neither side necessarily has the goal to find out "the truth;" however, all parties have an obligation to not permit a truly innocent person to be convicted.

Forensic science, on the other hand, is supposed to assist in finding out "the truth" through the collection and analysis of impartial data. However, because an individual's perspective, training, and experience can influence the interpretation of results, in some cases, conclusions may not always be impartial. The reality is that the ideal of finding "the truth" may not be reached by either science or the law. Nevertheless, hopefully everyone is doing their best in whatever role they have within the criminal justice system.

As Robin Bowen in her book *Ethics and the Practice of Forensic Science* has succinctly put it, "Attorneys are advocates, whereas experts [DNA scientists] are educators" (Bowen 2010, p. 36). Dr. Charlotte Word, an experienced expert witness, adds that. "It is the role of the expert witness to educate the trier-of-fact, who is either the jury in a jury trial or the judge in a hearing or a bench trial. It is often the role of the expert witness in pretrial meetings to educate the attorney asking questions on direct examination and to assist in the preparation of questions to be asked in the direct examination so that the qualifications, science, and evidence can be presented in a logical and coherent manner to the trier-of-fact. It is not the role of the expert witness to take sides or be an advocate for the victim, the state or government, or the defendant. The expert witness is simply an advocate for good science" (CJW).

Right to Defense

Within the United States of America, defendants in criminal trials have a number of rights that are primarily declared by the Sixth and Fourteenth Amendments to the United States Constitution.

The Sixth Amendment, which was added with the original Bill of Rights in 1789, states:

> "In all criminal prosecutions, the accused shall enjoy the right to a speedy and public trial, by an impartial jury of the State and district wherein the crime shall have been committed, which district shall have been previously ascertained by law, and to be informed of the nature and cause of the accusation; to be confronted with the witnesses against him; to have compulsory process for obtaining witnesses in his favor, and to have the Assistance of Counsel for his defence" (see http://www.usconstitution.net/).

The Fourteenth Amendment, which was adopted in July 1868, states (in part):

> "All persons born or naturalized in the United States, and subject to the jurisdiction thereof, are citizens of the United States and of the State wherein they reside. No State shall make or enforce any law which shall abridge the privileges or immunities of citizens of the United States; nor shall any State deprive any person of life, liberty, or property, without **due process of law**; nor deny to any person within its jurisdiction the equal protection of the laws" (see http://www.usconstitution.net/; emphasis added).

In the context used here, the term "due process of law" refers to how and why laws are enforced for the protection of individual rights. As noted on the website USConsitution.net, due process generally guarantees (among other things): the right to a fair and public trial conducted in a competent manner, right to be present at the trial, right to an impartial jury, and right to be heard in one's own defense. A defendant is also permitted to know what evidence is being brought against him or her—a process known as *discovery*.

Discovery

Discovery is the legal process whereby information and materials relating to the prosecution of a defendant in an upcoming trial are shared between the prosecution team (e.g., law enforcement, crime laboratory, prosecuting attorney) and the defense counsel. The specific requirements of discovery are regulated by federal and state laws and, in some cases, the judge in a particular case may rule on the materials that must be provided during the discovery process. It is the obligation of the prosecution team to "turn over" to the defense attorney(s) all information and materials that relate to the prosecution of the defendant as well as any evidence or information that may be viewed as exculpatory (i.e., clearing of guilt) or that impeach (i.e., to dispute, disparage, or contradict) a prosecution witness. The defense generally has the responsibility to provide to the prosecution all reports and opinions from any experts expected to testify during the defense portion of the case. Additional information may also be provided by the defense, however the requirements tend to vary based on the jurisdiction and the type of proceeding.

Crime laboratory personnel are usually asked to provide the laboratory reports stating the opinions and conclusions from testing in a particular case as well as the basis for those opinions, which generally entails the complete laboratory case file with all supporting data. It is helpful if these materials are provided in a manner suitable for review by both sets of attorneys and other experts assisting either of the attorneys. Additional materials may also be requested from the crime laboratory depending on the jurisdiction and the challenges to the case. These materials may include laboratory standard operating procedures (SOPs), quality control manuals and/or records, training files, proficiency test records and files, audit documents including findings and corrective actions taken, validation studies, and publications from the laboratory.

LEGAL TERMS, CONCEPTS, AND IMPORTANT COURT CASES

Reviewing some legal terms, concepts, and court cases may help readers understand other aspects of this chapter.

Legal Terms and Concepts

***Voir dire*:** a French word for "to speak the truth" this term refers to the process of qualifying a juror or an expert witness to serve in court.

Trier-of-fact: the individual(s) who makes a ruling in court based on the evidence presented; for a jury trial, the jury is the trier-of-fact while for a bench trial or admissibility hearing the judge is the trier-of-fact.

Admissibility hearing: before specific evidence for a case can be heard by the trier-of-fact, the evidence must be deemed sufficiently reliable to be of value for presentation in court; the judge may decide the evidence is generally accepted (because it has been used in previous court cases) or may require a separate hearing with arguments for and against the evidence being admitted into court.

Custodian of records: Under the Federal Laws of Evidence (see below), a "custodian of records," who is, for example, a DNA analyst from a laboratory with knowledge of the lab's records and the specific case report and its preparation, is permitted to testify to records prepared in the routine course of business. An individual who meets the requirements of custodian of records may be permitted to testify to the records and findings in a case once the appropriate legal foundation for the testimony under these rules are established and meet the requirements of the court. A DNA laboratory report and case file are typically considered the "business records." However, after the recent case of *Melendez-Diaz v. Massachusetts* (see below), lab reports may no longer qualify as "business records."

Care in discussing original source of reference sample in a cold database hit: Connecting an individual to a crime through a DNA database cold hit can complicate things in the courtroom. Attorneys have to be very careful not to mention that the defendant's DNA profile was on a "convicted offender" index within a DNA database as this could be prejudicial to the defendant in the jurors' minds to know that the defendant has a prior criminal record. A mistrial could result from mentioning that a prior criminal record is the reason the individual's DNA profile was in the database that led to connecting him or her to the crime under consideration. Sometimes testimony may be given though to matching on "a database" with no mention of the "convicted offender" portion of the database.

Important U.S. Court Cases

Below are a few of the more prominent cases that impact scientific evidence and expert witnesses. Several of these cases will be covered in more detail later in the chapter.

Frye v. United States: a 1923 Court of Appeals case establishing the initial legal precedence for admissibility of scientific evidence

Brady v. State of Maryland: a 1963 Supreme Court case requiring that the prosecution must disclose any exculpatory evidence to the defense

Gideon v. Wainwright: a 1963 Supreme Court case that established the right to defense counsel (public defender) in state court proceedings for indigents accused of serious crimes

Daubert v. Merrell-Dow Pharmaceuticals: a 1993 Supreme Court case making the trial judge a gatekeeper to scientific evidence admissibility

Crawford v. Washington: a 2004 Supreme Court case strengthening defendants' rights to confront and cross-examine witnesses against them

Melendez-Diaz v. Massachusetts: a 2009 Supreme Court case requiring that submission of a forensic laboratory report in court requires the testimony of the person who performed the test

THE COURTROOM SCENE

While different state-specific laws mean that some aspects of trials vary between states and legal jurisdictions, the courtroom scene is generally the same throughout the United States and other countries formerly under British rule. An effort was made to keep the material presented here as general as possible while providing specific details where deemed appropriate.

The actions of a court of law are somewhat analogous to a scripted play conducted in a theater. Just as in a major theatrical production, in courts there are actors with scripts to be followed who take specific actions at specific times, extensive preparation before the actual performance, events that play out behind the "curtains," drama for the defendant who has a major stake in the outcome, and oversight by a director. The following sections will discuss the personnel or "actors" involved in a trial along with their individual responsibilities, the actions taken as the courtroom proceedings unfold, and the preparation that precedes the actual trial.

Although this analogy to a theatrical production may help to provide better understanding towards the actions of a court of law, it is important to keep in mind that court proceedings are very serious and can have a major impact on the lives of defendants, victims, and their families.

Courtroom Proceedings

For a jury trial involving a criminal case in the United States, a jury, composed of a sufficient number of members of the general public (typically 12) and often including alternate members of the jury, is first selected. While a judge presides over the trial, the selected jury will be responsible for coming to a conclusion regarding the individual(s) on trial—either "guilty" or "not guilty"—based on the evidence presented.

Opening statements are made by both the prosecution and the defense outlining the issues in the trial. After opening statements have been made, the prosecution, representing the government's position on behalf of the victim(s), presents its case by putting witnesses before the jury and entering items of evidence. The prosecution has the burden of proof to establish beyond a reasonable doubt the guilt of the defendant(s).

After the prosecution has made its case, the defense team may, but is not required to, introduce additional witnesses to try to cast doubt on the prosecution's case. Closing arguments are offered by both sides at the conclusion of the trial. The jury then considers the evidence presented and testimony heard and renders a verdict of "guilty" or "not guilty." In a criminal trial, for a defendant to be convicted, the jury must unanimously reach a "guilty" verdict based on "proof beyond a reasonable doubt." In a civil trial, although the jury's verdict must typically also be unanimous in favor of one party, the "burden of proof" is somewhat lessened requiring only a "preponderance of evidence."

For each expert witness who is part of a trial, there are five parts to the testimony after being called to the witness stand and sworn in: (1) establishing the witness's qualifications or *voir dire*, (2) direct examination, (3) cross-examination, (4) re-direct and re-cross-examination, and (5) the judge retaining or excusing the witness. Expert witnesses may also be called to testify during a preliminary hearing.

Courtroom Personnel

Like a set in a play or movie, there are a number of actors who each have a specific role in the production of a trial. These include the judge, the court reporter, the plaintiff(s), the defendant(s), the prosecuting attorney(s), the defense attorney(s), the jury, and the expert witnesses or other witnesses called to testify in the witness box/stand.

The **judge** oversees the proceedings of the trial. He or she makes decisions about admissibility of evidence and decides on objections raised by lawyers during the course of the trial. The judge's aim is to ensure that both sides receive a fair trial and that only legally admissible evidence is presented to the trier-of-fact. The judge is always mindful that a conviction may be followed by an appeal, and that the appellate court will scrutinize the evidence to determine if the defendant received a fair trial. For that reason, the judge will pay close attention to the "record," including whether the court reporter can produce an accurate transcript of the expert witness testimony.

The **court reporter** creates a transcript of the court proceedings. Every word is recorded so that this information may be reviewed if necessary. What the court reporter writes becomes the facts of the case so it is important for witnesses to speak clearly.

The **prosecutor** seeks justice on behalf of the plantiff or complainant. Ted Hunt, a prosecutor from Kansas City, Missouri, remarks: "The prosecutor's role in the criminal justice system is to seek justice in each case rather than to merely convict. In many instances, seeking justice equates with the aggressive prosecution of a criminal defendant. In other cases, however, seeking justice might mean dismissing a case because the evidence of guilt is in doubt. It may also mean reducing a charge when the evidence reveals that a defendant's degree of culpability is less than previously believed" (TRH).

The Orange County (California) District Attorney's DNA Unit adds: "A prosecuting attorney has an obligation and duty to see that 'justice is done." This obligation extends well beyond merely convicting the guilty. It includes ensuring that no one is unfairly convicted and that the innocent are exonerated:

> [The prosecutor] is the representative not of an ordinary party to a controversy, but of a sovereignty whose obligation to govern impartially is as compelling as its obligation to govern at all; and whose interest, therefore, in a criminal prosecution is not that it shall win a case, but that justice shall be done. As such, he is in a peculiar and very definite sense the servant of the law, the twofold aim of which is that guilt shall not escape or innocence suffer. He may prosecute with earnestness and vigor — indeed, he should do so. But, while he may strike hard blows, he is not at liberty to strike foul ones. It is as much his duty to refrain from improper methods calculated to produce a wrongful conviction as it is to use every legitimate means to bring about a just one (*Berger v. United States* (1935) 295 U.S. 78, 88)." (OCDA).

The **defense attorney** plays a key role in the criminal justice system on behalf of a defendant. Brad Bannon, a defense attorney in Raleigh, North Carolina, shares: "The role of a defense attorney is to provide independent and zealous representation to people accused of crimes, and to give as much meaning as possible to the presumption of innocence and the burden of proof that the government must meet before it may limit or deprive a person of freedom. First, you review the prosecution's evidence and independently pursue as much evidence as you can and should in each case. After evaluating all of that evidence in light of your practical and legal knowledge and experience, you provide your best advice to the accused about what he or she should do, whether that involves going to trial or exploring resolutions outside of trial, such as a plea agreement. Finally, if the case ends up in a contested forum, you do your absolute best to make sure the prosecution is put to its constitutional burdens in that forum" (BB).

An **expert witness** (e.g., a DNA analyst) is called to testify in court regarding data collected and conclusions drawn based on that data. Law professor K. A. Philipps once wrote: "Just as the lawyer has a job to do in the courtroom, so does the scientist. The job of the forensic expert is only half done after the scientific tests have been done and the written reports have been prepared. The other half is to present the results of the tests in a form that is legally admissible and in a manner that is understandable to the judge and jury" (Philipps 1977).

Most experts presenting testimony regarding DNA test results and conclusions will be called to court by the prosecution to provide some link of the evidence from a crime to a victim or to the defendant. Most crime laboratory personnel never have the opportunity to be called by the defense since generally inconclusive results and/or results that excluded other suspects are not presented in court and are generally of no or limited value to the defense. In some cases, experts may be called by the defense to provide differing opinions or challenges to the DNA testing. The processes described below are the same regardless of whether the expert witness is being called to testify in a case by the prosecution or the defense.

Preparation of the Expert Witness

As with any performance, prior preparation is vital for success. Additional thoughts on details of this preparation will be covered later in the chapter.

Ted Hunt offers a prosecutor's perspective: "Perhaps the most vital aspect of testimonial preparation is [the witness] meeting with the prosecutor for a pretrial conference. If at all possible, this conference should be done in person, rather than over the phone. At this meeting, the prosecutor should ask the expert what issues or anomalies are present in the evidence, case data, or test results. The prosecutor should also review his or her anticipated questions and areas of inquiry with the expert and receive his or her feedback. It's also helpful for the expert to suggest issues or topics to highlight, de-emphasize, or exclude. In addition, the prosecutor and the expert witness should collaborate to determine what, if any, visual aids may help enhance the jury's comprehension and retention of the evidence. Finally, an informal 'dry-run' of the expert's direct examination or anticipated cross-examination during the pretrial conference may also help the prosecutor and the expert enhance their courtroom presentations" (TRH).

Charlotte Word shares her opinion as a frequent expert witness: "It is important for the expert witness and the attorney to meet prior to testifying. This provides an excellent opportunity to discuss if all discovery has been supplied, ensure that the attorney understands your limitations and the limitations of the testing, and to draft and/or discuss the series of questions that will be asked in court. Having a pretrial meeting helps ensure that the attorney covers all of the relevant qualifications of the witness, scientific parameters of the test and of the specific test results and conclusions. Neither the attorney nor witness should be 'blind-sided' with surprise questions or answers at the trial. Remember that it is the responsibility of the expert witness to educate the jury by providing them with sufficient information to understand the meaning of the test results obtained in the laboratory as well as have a good sense of the quality of the work performed and the credibility of the witness and the crime laboratory. This can best be achieved by pretrial preparation. If the attorney has never been to the laboratory, it may be helpful to invite the attorney to the laboratory for a tour and more detailed explanations" (CJW).

Courtroom Performance of the Expert Witness

Swearing in and Offering Testimony

Raymond Davis in his Courtroom Skills training course on expert testimony offers: "Pay attention to the little details. For example, if you carry your file or briefcase in your left hand, then you will be able to easily raise your right hand to be sworn in as you enter the witness stand." Remember that anything you take to the stand can be examined by both sides, including any personal notes used to assist with testimony.

A transcript is prepared by court reporters who attempt to capture every word stated by the lawyers and the witnesses as part of the court proceedings. In a sense, the "script" for the courtroom "stage performance" is produced after the performance is over. This transcript provides a written record of every word and can be reviewed to confirm previous aspects of the trial during the trial or used following the trial as a complete record of the events that transpired.

Speak slowly and simply. If there is a difficult word, define the word in lay terms for the jury and spell it out to make life easier for the court reporter. The judge is the "director of the performance" and is in charge. The witness is a member of the "performance cast" and may not leave the witness stand or the courtroom until excused by the judge.

Qualification (Voir dire)

Before an expert is allowed to offer testimony in court, he or she must be qualified by the court to speak on the topic at hand in what is known as *voir dire*, which as stated earlier is French for "to speak the truth." To demonstrate the qualifications of the expert witness, the attorney who called the witness to testify asks questions detailing the expert's education, training, and experience. Some example questions are included in Table 18.2. This testimony lays the foundation for allowing the expert to testify to the analysis performed in the laboratory and to the results and conclusions derived.

A copy of the expert's *curriculum vitae* or CV is generally provided to opposing counsel, and may also be entered into the court's record during testimony. The CV contains educational background, experience in current and previous positions, training, and a listing of any professional societies of which the witness is a member along with any scientific articles published. According to Dr. Robin Cotton, who has testified in more than 200 trials: "Your CV should be only the organizations you are a member of, your publications, your job title, your job description, and your education. Testimony is not a qualification, neither is your volunteer work or anything else" (RWC). Some attorneys will use the expert's CV to help craft questions covered as part of the *voir dire* process.

The opposing counsel has the opportunity to ask additional questions regarding the witness's qualifications either during the *voir dire* or during cross-examination. In some jurisdictions, the judge makes a formal acceptance of the witness as an expert in a particular scientific field (e.g., expert in forensic DNA testing).

Direct Examination

As noted in the court proceedings section above, following *voir dire* and the witness being qualified to provide expert testimony, direct examination will begin. Some common questions asked during a direct examination are listed in Table 18.3.

There is not likely to be an ideal direct examination because details to a particular case will be case specific. However, as noted by Robin Cotton: "Lawyers like it when you have a list of prepared questions for your direct examination. However, you need to go through the

TABLE 18.2 Some Potential Questions during Qualifying the Expert (*Voir Dire*) Courtesy of Bruce Heidebrecht (DNA Technical Leader, Maryland State Police Crime Laboratory).

1) Please state your name and spell it for the court.
2) Where are you currently employed?
3) How long have you been employed at the Crime Laboratory?
4) What is your current job position?
5) What are your current job duties?
6) Prior to working at the Crime Laboratory, what was your previous work experience?
7) What is your educational background?
8) What type of training have you had in the field of forensic DNA analysis?
9) Have you previously been qualified as an expert in the field of forensic DNA analysis? How many times and in which courts?

TABLE 18.3 Some Potential Questions during a Direct Examination Courtesy of Bruce Heidebrecht (DNA Technical Leader, Maryland State Police Crime Laboratory).

1) What is DNA?
2) Where is DNA found in humans?
3) Will two different people have the same DNA?
4) What type of DNA testing was performed in this case?
5) Can you briefly explain what steps are involved in STR analysis?
6) Is STR analysis a new technology?
7) Why has the forensic community adopted the use of STR analysis?
8) Is the field of forensic science the only area where STR analysis is utilized?
9) Are all of the procedures used at the Crime Laboratory generally accepted in the scientific community?
10) Have STR analysis results been accepted in the courts in this state, and in other states?
11) What safeguards and controls are in place at the Crime Laboratory to ensure the integrity of the testing procedures and the integrity of the DNA results?
12) If any of these controls do not work properly, what conclusions will be made?
13) Did there come a time when the Crime Laboratory was requested to conduct STR analysis in the investigation of ___________?
14) What evidence was submitted to the DNA unit for analysis?
15) Which of these samples were then subjected to STR analysis?
16) Were results obtained from all of the evidence tested?
17) Were you able to reach a conclusion based on the STR analysis of this evidence? And if yes, what are the conclusions?
18) Were you able to reach a conclusion as to the frequency of this DNA profile occurring in the general population? And if yes, what are those conclusions?
19) After analysis is completed, are your case files subject to peer review?

questions with them because some of the questions may not fit a particular case or your role in the expert testimony you are offering" (RWC).

Ted Hunt shares his perspective as a seasoned prosecutor: "I have an outline of the facts I need to establish or the topics I need to cover, but I don't write out my questions. I believe that writing down questions verbatim locks you into a script that takes away the flexibility needed during witness examinations. Glancing down at a topic or an anticipated answer rather than a question gives me the flexibility needed to formulate a question that will elicit the desired information. If you get out of sync with an expert in court based on a prepared script, both prosecutor and expert are going to get lost and will look unprepared to the jury"(TRH).

Explaining DNA Results to a Jury

The concepts of DNA can be challenging for lay jurors to comprehend. Brad Bannon advises expert witnesses: "Understand that you are not lecturing to your professional colleagues. You are speaking to people who will likely have little or no experience in your area of expertise, but you must effectively share that expertise with them without their eyes glazing over. Speak in language that is accessible but not condescending" (BB).

Charlotte Word recommends: "Just show a final table of results and conclusions rather than raw data. However, some attorneys may want to present the actual electropherograms. This may be necessary to lay appropriate background to expected opposing counsel challenges (e.g., is the allele major or minor, is the peak a stutter product or an allele, etc.)" (CJW).

When Ted Hunt was asked how much detail should be shared with the jury, he replied: "I think Albert Einstein summed it up best when he said, "Everything should be made as simple as possible, but not simpler.' The jury needs just enough information to accomplish its assigned task—to determine whether or not the DNA test results in question are relevant, reliable, and persuasive in the context of a given case" (TRH).

Cross Examination

Cross examination, where the opposing counsel is trying to discredit the testimony of the witness, can be particularly grueling and challenging for the witness. When asked what she enjoyed least about being an expert witness, Robin Cotton said, "Very aggressive, very loud, very unpleasant cross-examination tactics. I don't personally care to be shouted at." She astutely observes: "When somebody is attacking your testimony, there are two bad things that happen. One is that you get mad. The other thing is you get tired so you tend to start giving in or you just shut down or you glare at everybody and you look uncomfortable. It can take some practice at home, such as rehearsing how you might respond to challenging questions" (RWC).

In spite of how a witness is treated by the opposing counsel, Dr. Cotton continues: "You should not treat the prosecution and defense attorneys any different in how you respond to them. However you talk to one attorney, you need to talk to the other attorney the exact same way. You don't want to change your body language. You don't want to change your tone or the speed in which you answer questions or your demeanor to the jury" (RWC).

She goes on: "It is very hard not to take a tough cross-examination personally. Anytime you feel like you are being attacked then your anxiety goes up, your adrenalin goes up, and you feel like you have to defend yourself. I think that is just part of the tactic. You are not being attacked really. You are there just to say, "This is the data." And the defense attorneys are there to say, "Are you sure, did you do it right?" That is their job. If you didn't do your work right, then they need to know! It is their job to discuss anything that may be incorrect in what you did. They want and need to point it out" (RWC).

Being cross-examined can be exhausting and emotionally taxing. Dr. Cotton shares, "I learned how to fix my feelings of frustration after participating in the courtroom drama by remembering that it was a show. *As an expert witness, I have a very important role in this show—and the show has very important consequences—but the show isn't my permanent world.* I have strengths and other things outside of this arena. Whatever happens in the courtroom, I don't have to carry it out with me."

We have briefly covered courtroom proceedings and personnel and explored the preparation and performance expected of an expert witness in a court of law. The next section examines the role of a scientific expert in more detail.

THE SCIENTIFIC EXPERT WITNESS

In 1901, a future federal judge named Learned Hand from Albany, NY, published an oft-quoted treatise in the *Harvard Law Review* on expert witnesses. He begins his article: "No one will deny that the law should in some way effectively use expert knowledge wherever it will aid in settling disputes. The only question is as to how it can do so best..." Judge Hand expressed concern over use of expert witnesses because (1) they are typically "a hired champion of one side" in a case and thus can lose objectivity and (2) dueling experts are permitted in the court proceedings that may contradict one another and thus confuse the jury (Hand 1901, p.53). He feared that the exchange of technical arguments would not make sense to the jury and the more charismatic of the experts could influence a jury's decision rather than appropriate scientific issues.

An expert is someone who has specialized knowledge on a particular topic based on education, training, experience, or skill. Based on this education, training, experience, and/or skill, the expert knows more than a lay person on a particular subject. Thus, the expert is called upon to use this specialized knowledge to enlighten the court of law.

Role of the Expert Witness

Robin Bowen notes that "expert witnesses are held in high esteem by the jury, so it is important to provide information accurately and authoritatively" (Bowen 2010, p. 64). In addressing the role of an expert witness, Robin Cotton states: "Your job is to represent your data. I think people forget that usually just one person signs the report. I think that it is important that many people in the lab would have the same opinion about that report. When you are sitting there on the witness stand, you are the lab! For purposes of that jury, you are the laboratory. Whatever they think about the laboratory comes from what they think about you... Doing a poor job with courtroom testimony, can cause serious problems for a laboratory and the analyst. If laboratory personnel are testifying all of the time, then every one of those people has to be good <u>every time</u>" (RWC).

Responsibilities of the Expert Witness

Robin Cotton notes: "You have to be really focused in the courtroom. You cannot mentally be somewhere else. You need to listen to those questions. The longer you are listening to questions, the harder it is to stay focused. Just like anything, you get tired. The attorneys get to take a little rest, they trade off, etc., but you cannot get tired. You have to be very focused. You cannot be paying attention to everything in the courtroom. It will distract you. I just look to the attorney and I just look to the jury and that's it" (RWC).

Some suggestions and informal rules (distilled from Bowen 2010, p. 63):

- Do not discuss the case with anyone outside of court including other witnesses. "In some jurisdictions, the expert is not permitted to discuss the case or testimony with either attorney once the testimony has begun" (CJW).
- Avoid advocating one position or another.
- Do not be defensive or argumentative in responses to questions.
- Stop talking if interrupted by the judge or an attorney (respect courtroom protocol).
- Request permission to answer in greater detail if something beyond a "yes/no" answer is needed to clarify a response.
- Do not avoid a question if you believe your answer will support the opposing side (credibility will be negatively impacted if a bias is shown or there is hesitation in providing an objective answer).

- Do not volunteer information without being asked.
- Do not guess.
- Do not generalize answers.
- It is acceptable to answer with "I do not know – but if I looked at my case notes, it would refresh my memory" (RWC).
- Make sure that you fully understand the question before answering.
- Present opinions truthfully after all information is collected and examinations are completed.
- "If you make or find a mistake, correct it. Do not let errors remain uncorrected for the jury or the court record" (CJW).

Think before you speak. You may be asked challenging hypothetical questions regarding the conclusions made. Pay close attention to the question asked and only answer the question.

Robin Cotton advocates that as an expert witness you should have "unconditional positive regard" for everyone in the courtroom. She emphasizes: "in that arena of the courtroom, they all get my equal respect genuinely. I think that is where the creditability comes from that you should have as an expert witness" (RWC).

Trial Preparation with Attorneys

Prior preparation prevents poor performance (the 5 P's). The expert witness and attorney must work closely together to obtain optimal performance in the courtroom. The expert should have carefully reviewed the entire case file and report especially if the work was performed several years before. Refresh your memory of the details. Work through the calculations to make sure you understand all of them. Re-review the results and conclusions to be sure everything was reported correctly.

In a pretrial conference find out if the attorney assigned to the case has handled DNA evidence previously. If not, then invite the attorney for a lab visit to help familiarize him/her with the steps involved in DNA analysis. This can improve communication. Offer a prepared list of questions that can be used for *voir dire* (see Table 18.2) and direct examination (see Table 18.3).

When an expert witness cannot appear in person, an affidavit can be provided. An *affidavit* is a written declaration or statement of facts made voluntarily and confirmed by oath. Ted Hunt comments: "After the *Melendez-Diaz* decision, affidavits can no longer be provided in lieu of live testimony at trial. However, most courts have held that the sixth Amendment right to confrontation does not apply at pretrial or preliminary hearings. The U.S. Supreme Court has not yet definitively spoken on this issue" (TRH).

Some jurisdictions utilize a *deposition* where opposing counsel formally asks an expert witness questions prior to trial. This approach is generally only used for civil proceedings. While the proceedings are done without a judge being present, it is part of the court record and a transcript is made of all questions and responses. Charlotte Word emphasizes: "Preparation for the deposition should be as thorough as for the trial. If the deposition transcript is available, the witness should read it prior to testifying in the trial taking special note of any discrepancies between what was said versus what was recorded and noting any information that might have changed since the time of the deposition. The attorney and the expert witness should be prepared to address any differences between what is present in the transcript and what will be said at the trial as this should be an obvious expected challenge from opposing counsel" (CJW).

Communication in Court

An expert witness is a teacher, an educator. The purpose of being present in a court of law is to explain scientific results under direct examination and to defend them when cross-examined by the opposing counsel. In a jury trial, the expert witness should face the jury and address them as they are the decision makers (the "triers-of-fact") needing the expert's input.

Simple visuals in a "show and tell" format can be effective in many circumstances. However, Charlotte Word reminds experts: "Be sure any presentations are coordinated between the attorney and the witness. Be sure to preview and carefully check for accuracy any exhibits related to your testimony that the attorney has prepared" (CJW).

Most modern courtrooms have PowerPoint projection capability. Keep in mind though that everything you present should have a specific purpose. You are not in court to give a genetics lecture—nor would the judge and opposing counsel likely permit you to pontificate endlessly without addressing a specific question!

Ted Hunt states: "The best advice I have for any speaker, expert DNA witnesses included, is to know your audience and speak to them in their native tongue. A brilliant analyst can make a lousy expert witness when he or she fails to connect with the jury. *Many times, this failure to connect stems from the fact that the expert testifies as if he or she is delivering a scientific dissertation to a room full of colleagues rather than teaching a classroom full of novices.* Given the time and procedural constraints of the courtroom, the use of scientific jargon, industry acronyms, and excessively complicated explanations creates cognitive barriers for jurors that are difficult to overcome" (TRH).

Several years ago, two Los Angeles County prosecutors asked the question, "How do you prepare to testify in front of twelve average citizens?" They answered their own question with: "One way to assess your ability is to practice on friends who have no scientific background. Explain DNA testing to them simply and see how they respond. This will give you a sense of whether you are reaching your audience. It is also helpful to be familiar with the basic content of most expert testimony and to review these areas in advance each time you testify" (Kahn & Feldstern 1998). Robin Cotton agrees: "Go explain [DNA] to your mother until she understands or father or brother or whatever. It does take a lot of practice to say it without using your normal language, your normal scientific terms" (RWC).

Credibility

Your actions both on and off the stand impact the perceptions that others will have of you. Be professional. Act confident but not condescending. Your credibility as an expert witness can be impacted by your attitude and demeanor. Robin Cotton explains: "The minute you walk into the courthouse you need to be aware that anyone around you could be a juror, an attorney, or someone else involved in the trial. Your professional behavior starts when you walk in the door and you don't change that until you are far away from that courtroom" (RWC).

Gil Sapir offers 12 points to help maintain credibility during court testimony: (1) be nervous, (2) always tell the truth, (3) listen to the question, (4) pause, then answer, (5) admit mistakes and problems, (6) admit limitations, (7) admit inability to remember, (8) do not hedge or obfuscate, (9) speak to the jury, (10) maintain a consistent attitude, (11) never argue with counsel, and (12) answer just the question (Sapir 2002). Concerning the above recommendation to be nervous, Charlotte Word shares: "This is an excellent set of recommendations, although I question the need to be nervous. Being well prepared should alleviate most nerves. However, as before any presentation, it is always helpful to be alert and perhaps have a small jolt of adrenaline" (CJW).

Having read a number of trial court transcripts involving DNA testimony, not all expert witnesses follow these recommendations in many cases so there is room for improvement by even experienced experts! One last point under credibility: keep your CV up-to-date if you testify regularly as you should continually have attendance at meetings or training workshops to include.

Dress and Appearance

How you dress will impact what others think of you and either add or detract from your credibility. When you look your best you will also act more professionally. A suit and tie are appropriate for men and a business suit or dress and jacket fitting for women. Speaking on how she dresses for court, Robin Cotton states: "I wear dark clothes. I wear jewelry but I don't wear anything big. I don't wear a red suit. I don't look like I am going to a party. Nobody in that courtroom is there because something good happened, and so you have to respect that things have happened and you have to have respect for the proceeding and you have to have respect for the individuals who are there" (RWC).

In terms of what she takes into the courtroom, Dr. Cotton relates: "I take whatever I think I am going to need to the witness box. If there were a *Frye* hearing, I might bring in scientific articles. For a case, I might bring some notes along with my copy of the case folder. I don't have things with me that I'm not willing to give over. Some people take a book if they think they might be waiting—and that is fine. I usually take some scientific journal articles just because *People* magazine doesn't seem to be the right thing to have in a courtroom" (RWC).

Charlotte Word adds: "The case file may be carried into court for reference, but if you are taking additional materials (e.g., references, SOPs, etc.) a small business folder or briefcase is appropriate to use. Ladies may carry small professional handbags, as needed, but if possible, all coats, umbrellas, large handbags, luggage, and any other accessories not needed to enhance the testimony should be left in the car, the attorney's office, or any other appropriate place. Care should be taken to stay professional and in professional attire anywhere near the court where the jury has a chance of seeing you; changing into work or travel clothes should take place away from the courthouse" (CJW).

Ethics

Ethics is commonly defined as a set of moral values or precepts that govern rules of conduct followed by an individual. Expert witnesses need to be ethical in their scientific work and in their court presentation. An expert witness must be impartial and not have a professional interest in the outcome of the trial. You should be true to the evidence and the science NOT to either the prosecution's or the defense's position. The advice, attributed to President Harry S Truman, to "Always tell the truth; that way you never have to remember what you said" applies to forensic scientists in their role as expert witnesses.

Charlotte Word comments: "Providing unbiased and neutral testimony is the best and easiest position for an expert witness to take. If an expert can answer the question, 'Would my answer be the same if it were asked by the other attorney in this case?' with a resounding 'Yes!,' then the testimony is likely to be impartial. The expert has no obligation to answer a question the way one of the attorneys requests particularly if the answer is disingenuous in any manner" (CJW).

Robin Bowen in her book *Ethics and the Practice of Forensic Science* provides several challenges expert witnesses may face including:

- Resisting attorneys who want testimony that supports their client's position
- Producing evaluations that prove disadvantageous to the side that has retained them
- Being asked by an attorney to not write a report which would then be discoverable and possibly help the opposing attorney
- Having opinions distorted and their reputation impugned (Bowen 2010, pp. 38–89).

The various professional associations of forensic scientists have codes of ethics and conduct. For example, the American Academy of Forensic Sciences Bylaws Article II, section 1(c) states: "No member or affiliate of the Academy shall materially misrepresent data or scientific principles upon which his or her conclusion or professional opinion is based" (http://www.aafs.org/aafs-bylaws). The American Society of Crime Laboratory Directors Laboratory Accreditation Board (ASCLD/LAB) has developed guiding principles for forensic scientists and their management. They are available at http://www.ascld-lab.org/about_us/guidingprinciples.html and cover ethics and professionalism, competency and proficiency, and the importance of clear communication in court testimony.

ADMISSIBILITY OF EVIDENCE

Standard DNA tests are widely used and deemed admissible by courts around the world. However, as new tests are developed and implemented, their results must be deemed admissible in court. Charlotte Word comments: "I think it is still important to understand what an admissibility hearing is all about so that one can be prepared if challenges to the testing procedures are raised" (CJW). In this section, several important court cases regarding admissibility of scientific evidence and testimony are reviewed.

The *Frye* General Acceptance Standard

A landmark court case in 1923 established the initial legal precedence for admissibility of scientific evidence in a U.S. court of law. *Frye v. United States* was a Court of Appeals of the District of Columbia decision rendered December 3, 1923. It was based on an appeal from a lower court's refusal to admit test results from a systolic blood pressure device (a polygraph or "lie detector"). James Alphonzo Frye, convicted for second degree murder and trying to use his passing of a lie detector test to show he did not commit the crime, has achieved a level of legal immortality through lending his last name to criteria for accepting scientific evidence in court. In the end, the lie detector results were deemed inadmissible and Mr. Frye's conviction was upheld.

In its now famous ruling, the court crafted a "general acceptance" standard to determine whether scientific evidence was sufficiently reliable to warrant consideration by a trier-of-fact:

> "Just when a scientific principle or discovery crosses the line between the experimental and demonstrable stages is difficult to define. Somewhere in this twilight zone the evidential forces of the principle must be recognized, and while courts will go a long way in admitting expert testimony deduced from a well-recognized scientific principle of discovery, the thing from which the deduction is made must be sufficiently established to have gained general acceptance in the particular field in which it belongs" (*Frye v. United States*, 54 App. D.C. 46, 293 F. 1013 [1923]; emphasis added).

The general acceptance criterion has often been interpreted to mean the science of the underlying principle has been published in a peer-reviewed scientific journal and is used and accepted by other scientists in general, as well as scientists in the "relevant" field. It must also show that the general technology has been correctly applied to forensic evidence. In jurisdictions following the Frye general acceptance standard, a "Frye hearing" may be held prior to the trial in order for the judge to assess whether or not the scientific evidence should be admitted into court. These hearings can sometimes be quite contentious and involve experts brought in to represent both sides to the argument.

Although most jurisdictions in the United States have moved to a more recent standard for assessing scientific evidence (the following section on the *Daubert* ruling), states still following the *Frye* standard include California, Florida, Illinois, Kansas, Maryland, Michigan, Minnesota, Missouri, New Jersey, New York, Pennsylvania, and Washington (http://en.wikipedia.org/wiki/Frye_standard).

Federal Rules of Evidence

In the United States, whether or not evidence may be admitted to a court of law is controlled by federal or state rules of evidence (depending on the court). The Federal Rules of Evidence (FRE) were originally enacted in 1975 by Public Law 93–595 and have been amended periodically by Congress or the U.S. Supreme Court over the years (for an up-to-date version, see http://www.federalevidence.com).

There are 11 articles in the FRE making it similar in format to the U.S. Constitution. Article VII deals with opinions and expert testimony and contains six rules (Rule 701 through Rule 706). FRE Rule 702 governs "Testimony by Experts" and is the primary rule pertinent to expert witnesses:

> If scientific, technical, or other specialized knowledge will assist the trier-of-fact to understand the evidence or to determine a fact in issue, a witness qualified as an expert by knowledge, skill, experience, training, or education, may testify thereto in the form of an opinion or otherwise, if (1) the testimony is based upon sufficient facts or data, (2) the testimony is the product of reliable principles and methods, and (3) the witness has applied the principles and methods reliably to the facts of the case. (As amended Apr. 17, 2000, eff. Dec. 1, 2000.)

FRE Rule 702 opens the door for judges to permit expert testimony if it assists the trier-of-fact (e.g., the jury in a jury trial) in understanding evidence. Several other Federal Rules of Evidence also pertain to witnesses and evidence including Rule 104(a) which gives the trial judge the power to determine the admissibility of the evidence and expert witnesses; Rule 401, which defines "relevant evidence"; Rule 402, which allows all relevant evidence to be admissible; Rule 403, which permits relevant evidence to be excluded from the trial if it is deemed to be a waste of time or to be misleading to the jury; and Rule 615, which gives the trial judge the authority to exclude a witness so that he or she cannot hear the testimony of other witnesses in the trial.

States have similar rules of evidence that typically adopt the FRE in regards to the "testimony by experts" section. Links to state rules of evidence can be found on the National Clearing House for Science, Technology, and the Law website: http://www.ncstl.org/resources/702.

California's Kelly/Frye General Acceptance

A California Supreme Court case in 1976 of *People v. Kelly* (549 P.2d 1240 [Cal 1976]) has shaped California's legal landscape for admissibility and builds upon the *Frye* general acceptance. Kelly/Frye requires a preliminary showing of general acceptance of the new technique in the relevant scientific community followed by establishment of method reliability based on testimony from a qualified expert. California still applies its *Kelly/Frye* standard for admissibility of expert testimony despite the 1993 U.S. Supreme Court *Daubert* decision.

The *Daubert* Ruling

In 1993, 70 years after the *Frye* standard was set, the U.S. Supreme Court ruled that the Federal Rules of Evidence, which had been enacted in 1975, should supersede *Frye* in their *Daubert v. Merrell-Dow Pharmaceuticals* case (509 U.S. 579 [1993]). This case involved the parents of two children, Jason Daubert and Eric Schuller, born with birth defects that they claimed came from taking a morning sickness drug named Bendectin produced by Merrell-Dow Pharmaceuticals. The plaintiffs in this civil trial offered eight different experts with animal studies, chemical structure analysis, and other studies generated for specific use in this court case that had not previously been peer-reviewed and published in the scientific literature. The original trial court had barred this expert testimony and Daubert's lawyers appealed the case to the U.S. Supreme Court.

In a 7-2 decision, the Supreme Court ruled against the plantiffs (agreeing with the original court ruling) and offered a new standard for admissibility of expert witness testimony during federal legal proceedings where the trial judge is permitted to act as a "gatekeeper" to scientific evidence admissibility. *Daubert* thus provided greater flexibility over the "general acceptance" criteria of *Frye*.

The U.S. Supreme Court sent the *Daubert* case back to the Ninth Circuit Court of Appeal, which two years later sustained the original trial court ruling barring the plantiff's experts' opinions (*Daubert v. Merrell Dow Pharmaceuticals* 43 F. 3d 1311 9th Cir. 1995]). This court ruling concluded: "...in determining whether proposed expert testimony amounts to good science, we may not ignore the fact that a scientist's normal workplace is the lab or the field, not the courtroom or the lawyer's office" (p. 1317).

There are two "prongs" or portions to the *Daubert* decision—namely is the scientific evidence and testimony offered by the expert witness both (1) *reliable* and (2) *relevant* to the case at hand. Five factors are described in this decision in helping the judge determine whether there is a scientifically valid and reliable foundation for the evidence. These include: (1) the theory or technique must be falsifiable, refutable, and testable, or in other words involve the scientific method, (2) the theory or technique has been subjected to peer review and publication, or in other words submitted "to the scrutiny of the scientific community," (3) the court should consider the known or potential rate of error with the theory or technique, (4) standards or controls for the theory or technique exist and are maintained, and (5) the theory or technique is generally accepted in the relevant scientific community. Thus, the *Frye* standard is actually included within the *Daubert* ruling albeit with further details.

With the second *Daubert* prong of "relevance," the trial court must decide if the methodology can be properly applied to the facts under consideration. In other words, is the method appropriate or "fit for purpose" in the case at hand? The Supreme Court decision in *Daubert* emphasizes scientific validity with a focus "on principles and methodology, not on the conclusions that they generate."

Two other U.S. Supreme Court cases—*General Electric Company v. Joiner* (118 S.Ct 512 [1997]) and *Kumho Tire Company v. Carmichael* (119 S.Ct 1167 [1999])—build on the *Daubert* ruling to form a so-called "*Daubert* trilogy." These cases emphasize that the test of reliability is flexible and that the *Daubert* list of specific factors does not necessarily apply to all experts or in every case (see Harmon 2005).

The laboratory error rate issue raised in the *Daubert* decision's third factor is a difficult point to address (see Michaelis et al. 2008, p. 225). Proficiency tests, which test an individual analyst's ability to get the correct answer on a specific test using the laboratory's standard procedures, will not provide a reliable estimate of the probability of a laboratory error. Most courts consider the issue of possible laboratory error to influence the weight of the evidence rather than the admissibility (Michaelis et al. 2008, p. 227).

Charlotte Word comments: "Many types of errors can occur in a laboratory, but these are mostly human error. There are few errors in the technology with the exception of maybe stochastic effects and allele drop-in under low copy number conditions (see Chapter 11). Most laboratory standard operating procedures (SOPs) and quality control measures are designed to decrease the possibility of error and/or alert analysts to possible problems or errors. In the end, as recommended by the 1996 NRC II report, re-testing remains the best option if there is any reason to think an error was made. Thus, *it is best to save a portion of sample whenever possible for independent re-testing*. However, although the possibility of re-testing is an option, the burden is not on the defense to perform re-testing just because a sample remains. The burden is on the prosecution to "prove" their case in court" (CJW).

Summary of Admissibility Rulings

In summary, we have (1) *Frye* admissibility standards that emphasize general acceptance of theory and practice, (2) the Federal Rules of Evidence (FRE 702) that focuses on "helpful, relevant, and reliable" evidence, and (3) *Daubert* that makes the judge the gatekeeper for admitting evidence.

A study conducted 10 years after the June 28, 1993 *Daubert* ruling found a division in its application across the United States (Keierlber & Bohan 2005). This study classified the 50 states into (1) *Frye* states of which there were 15 (and 10 with codified evidence rules patterned after the FRE); (2) *Daubert* states of which there were 26 states (and 24 with FRE-based rules), and (3) non-*Frye*/non-*Daubert* states of which there were 9 (and 7 with FRE-based rules).

In commenting on what kinds of challenges are seen in admissibility hearings, Charlotte Word states: "In most situations, the challenges are the same seen routinely during trials, but with more emphasis on the unreliability of the technique or the limitations of the test system for forensic samples in general. The "newness" of the technique to the analyst and/or to the particular laboratory is often discussed with the focus being that something new must not be trustworthy and that the lack of extensive prior experience must lead to a higher risk of mistakes. As in trials, often hypothetical situations and "what if" questions are brought up. The specific challenges introduced will largely reflect the scientific background and knowledge of the expert testifying for opposing counsel. Reading any reports, affidavits, declarations, and/or prior testimony from the expert testifying for opposing counsel can be very helpful for understanding in advance what types of challenges to prepare for" (CJW).

TYPES OF DNA CASES AND OPPOSING COUNSEL TACTICS

Most forensic DNA scientists will be testifying for the prosecution particularly since the result of their DNA test can be a major or corroborating reason that a defendant is being prosecuted. If the DNA test result did not match a suspect, they would in most cases be exonerated and there would not be a trial. However, it has been noted that there are different types of cases where the DNA evidence might just be confirmatory or DNA may be the primary reason that a trial is being held at all. In addition, there will be varying degrees of defense challenges depending on the type of case and the defense lawyers and experts involved.

Categories of Cases Involving DNA

In explaining the approaches to presenting DNA evidence, one prosecutor has grouped the situations where DNA evidence is presented into three basic types of trials (Strange 2002):

> **Type #1:** The victim can identify the defendant or there is other equally compelling evidence establishing guilt. The DNA evidence is just confirming the other evidence.
>
> **Type #2:** The DNA evidence consists of a 9 or 13 [locus] STR match and is straight forward. The statistical power of discrimination in the match is trillion fold. However, without the DNA evidence, there is no case.
>
> **Type #3:** The DNA evidence may be a mixture (and there's little other evidence of guilt), mitochondrial DNA, "Y" chromosome, or SNP's. It's unlikely any of these will be used unless the DNA evidence is crucial.

He goes on to emphasize: "Quite clearly in Type 1 cases the DNA direct examination should consist of no more than the following: (a) Who are you and how employed? [name and job title, entity you are with], (b) What type of work do you do? [the very basics of your job description], (c) How did you become qualified to do that? [education, training, and experience], (d) How do you do what you do? [Explain DNA typing and how you perform it in 5 minutes or less. Do not mention capillary electrophoresis by name.], (e) What did you do in this case? [explain what samples were tested and compared], and (f) What was the result? [same DNA profile, etc.]. The principle difference in the presentation of a Type 2 case is that more time needs to be spent on the credentials, particularly how often the examiner has performed this work" (Strange 2002).

These categories represent the opinion of a single prosecutor almost a decade ago and are probably too simplistic in today's world. However, the approach of categorizing cases can be helpful in spite of the fact that DNA evidence is often more complex now with improvements in technology and sensitivity.

Discovery Requests

As mentioned earlier in the chapter, discovery involves a request made (most often) by the defense counsel for copies of records used by the prosecution in their case against a defendant. Right to information against an accused individual goes back to the Sixth and Fourteenth Amendments to the U.S. Constitution (see earlier in chapter).

A 1963 Supreme Court case known as *Brady v. Maryland* (373 U.S. 83, 10 L.Ed.2d 215, 83 S.Ct. 1194 [1963]) mandates that prosecutors provide the defendant with copies of any exculpatory evidence in a timely manner (for some interesting background on the *Brady* case, see Klinkosum & Bannon 2006). The *Brady* ruling states that "the suppression by the prosecution of evidence favorable to an accused upon request violates due process where the evidence is material either to guilt or punishment." Michaelis and colleagues in their book *A Litigator's Guide to DNA* note that "if exculpatory evidence comes to the states' attention after conviction, the prosecutor has a responsibility to provide this evidence to the defense" (Michaelis et al. 2008, pp. 228-229).

In terms of DNA results, this request is typically for copies of the case report as well as the underlying data and case notes for all samples tested as part of the case—even those deemed to be inconclusive. Laboratory protocols and quality assurance measurements are often included in a discovery request. In many cases, information from validation studies or proficiency test results may also be requested. Discovery requests from the defense should be made through the prosecutor rather than directly to the laboratory. Although in some cases there may be pushback in terms of delivery of all requested material, the court expects responses to discovery requests to be complete and timely—that is delivery to the requesting party in a reasonable time period.

Prosecutors from the Orange County DA's DNA Unit remark: "Generally speaking, the defense is entitled to receive all discovery materials that would help them prepare their case. So, if the items requested are relevant, they should be provided. The law in California includes provisions that state that the defense must first approach the prosecutor for discovery materials. Upon occasion, discovery requests are improperly sent directly to the crime lab by the defense and are responded to by crime lab personnel without prosecutorial input. Without a thorough understanding of the law and a complete review of entire prosecution and investigation case files, a forensic scientist is not in the best position to make decisions regarding the release of discovery materials" (OCDA).

While turning over your results and underlying validation studies may seem disconcerting, discovery should not be feared. It is part of the due process of law guaranteed under the Fourteenth Amendment of the U.S. Constitution and emphasized in the 1963 U.S. Supreme Court case *Brady v. Maryland*. If you are confident in your work product and protocols as a DNA analyst, sharing your data should not be a problem. As noted by the NRC II report, "there are no strictly scientific justifications for withholding information in the discovery process" (NRC II 1996, p. 167).

Robin Cotton shares: "I think the most important question for a lab (in fact, any discipline in the lab), is if you were to hand this information—the information you are going to give over to the defense—to a respected colleague, would you have given them everything they need to evaluate your work? If the answer is "yes", then that's about what you should be giving on discovery. For DNA that might be your case folder, your procedures, and your electronic data. I know that the defense often asks for lots of other documents: validation studies, proficiency test results, etc. Different states have different rules and different prosecutor's offices have different attitudes about giving over that extra material.... In any case, you should give over, *without question and happily*, the things that you would need from another competent DNA person to perform the review. *Do not worry about who might look at the information as a defense expert!*" (RWC).

With the advent of computer collection of DNA typing data (see Chapter 6), electronic data files, rather than just copies of DNA results, are requested by some defense experts for the purpose of reanalyzing the data to see if the same conclusions can be drawn. Charlotte Word notes: "Electronic data should be turned over if the profiles are not present in the case file or if they are not in a format that an independent expert can sufficiently review the data obtained to assess how the laboratory came to the decisions made" (CJW).

Sample Retesting

If any untested sample remains after the initial evidence examination, the defense has a right to go through the court to get access to the evidence for re-testing and perform its own independent testing provided sufficient sample is available to do so. The NRC II committee in its 1996 report stated, "A wrongly accused person's best insurance against the possibility of being falsely incriminated is the opportunity to have the testing repeated. Such an opportunity should be provided whenever possible" (NRC II 1996, p. 87). NRC II recommendation 3.3 states: "Whenever feasible, forensic samples should be divided into two or more parts at the earliest practicable stage and the unused parts retained to permit additional tests. The used and saved portions should be stored and handled separately. Any additional tests should be performed independently of the first by personnel not involved in the first test and preferably in a different laboratory" (NRC II 1996, p. 88). The committee concludes that: "A defendant who believes that the match is spurious should welcome the opportunity for an independent repeat test" (NRC II 1996, p. 87).

Charlotte Word summarizes: "Although the possibility of re-testing is an option for the defendant, the burden of proof is on the state to "prove" their case beyond a reasonable doubt. The defense attorney is not required to prove the defendant's innocence since that is already presumed for the defendant under the U.S. Constitution. Therefore, the defense attorney has no responsibility or obligation to perform re-testing just because a sample remains. In many jurisdictions and cases, if the defense attorney requests re-testing and decides to call the expert who tested the evidence as a witness at trial, those results must also be provided to the prosecution. The attorney would therefore not be acting in the best interest of his/her client to request re-testing since it cannot be known prior to re-testing that different results would be obtained" (CJW).

Common Opposing Counsel Tactics

Table 18.4 lists several common lines of attack on forensic DNA testing results and testimony offered in court including chain-of-custody, qualifications of the expert, reliability of the technique for testing evidence, reliability of the analyst(s) performing the work, and reliability of the laboratory in which testing was performed including the standard operating procedures developed therein. Potential contamination of evidence and/or test results may be raised as a concern. The statistical calculations performed may also be questioned including whether or not appropriate equations or data were used or appropriate population(s) allele frequencies for the perpetrator versus the defendant.

Some other common challenges to DNA results and testimony include mishandling of evidence, human error during testing, bias in testing (getting "the answer" that is wanted by the client requesting the testing), lack of information regarding when and how the DNA was deposited on an item, and lack of control over the handling of the evidence prior to receipt in the laboratory.

Ted Hunt notes: "Defense challenges come in a variety of forms depending on the nature of the case and the significance of the DNA evidence. If the DNA results are clean and fairly unassailable, a popular defense tactic is to concede that the detected profile belongs to the defendant but that its presence at the scene was the innocuous result of a secondary or tertiary transfer... When the evidentiary context of the DNA leaves little room for innocuous explanations, the attacks turn to evidence handling, the testing process, and the interpretation of the results..." (TRH).

This seasoned prosecutor concludes: "By and large I would say that these tactics are ultimately not successful. I have yet to lose a case involving DNA evidence. Juries may have

TABLE 18.4 Common Challenges to DNA Results and Testimony.

- Chain-of-custody
- Qualifications of the expert
- Reliability of the technique for testing evidence
- Reliability of the analyst(s) performing work
- Reliability of the laboratory in which testing was performed, SOPs
- Contamination of evidence and/or test results
- Mishandling of evidence
- Human error during testing
- Bias in testing (getting "the answer" that is wanted by the client requesting testing)
- Statistical calculations, appropriate population(s) for the perpetrator vs. defendant, appropriate equations used, appropriate data used
- Lack of information regarding when and how the DNA was deposited on an item, and lack of control over the handling of the evidence prior to receipt in the laboratory

more information to sort through at the end of a case when a defense DNA expert is called, but a well-prepared state's expert will usually win the day in court" (TRH).

Brad Bannon offers his perspective as a defense attorney: "When the evidence supports challenging a DNA expert's conclusion, you must demystify the process and demonstrate to the jury that DNA analysis is a subjective human exercise. Contamination and chain-of-custody arguments are only the tip of the iceberg. It's important to portray the entire process for what it is: one that involves human beings at all levels, from sample handling, to sample processing, to sample interpretation, to final reporting. Each level is vulnerable to human error or bias, and so is the analyst's courtroom testimony" (BB).

He continues: "If there were steps along the way when the analyst deviated from scientific standards, lab protocols, or the analyst's own customary practice, or if the analyst made an interpretation or judgment call that could have gone either way but ended up favoring the prosecution, the lawyer should be prepared to highlight the importance of those things for the jury and, if necessary, confront the analyst about them in the courtroom. While it's never my intent to get into a "contest" with a DNA expert about who knows more about DNA, my goal is to have a meaningful dialogue with the expert about the case-specific DNA issues and to make the points I set out to make—or even a few new ones, should the opportunity present itself—without being intimidated by the knowledge gap" (BB).

Forensic scientists facing defense attorneys in court may become frustrated during cross-examination and not fully understand the important role they play in the criminal justice system. More than three decades ago, some wise advice was published in the *Journal of Forensic Sciences*: "The forensic scientist should see the defense lawyer not as his enemy but as an officer of the court sworn to do the best job possible for his client, regardless of whether the client has retained the lawyer or whether the defense lawyer has been appointed by the court or is a public defender" (Phillips 1977).

As the next section describes, one important lesson we can learn from the recent post-conviction exonerations enabled by DNA testing is that not everyone who was prosecuted and convicted in the past was "guilty." It is hoped that as we go forward with better science in the future, this tragedy of justice can be avoided. The expert witness has an important role to be vigilant in efforts to support the data accurately, without overstatement, and not be biased towards either the prosecution or the defense.

Post-Conviction Testing

DNA testing has played an important role in post-conviction exonerations. Ted Hunt states: "To the extent that DNA evidence has been able to help exonerate the truly innocent, everyone has reason to celebrate" (TRH). Brad Bannon adds: "I'm not sure anything has had a greater impact on the criminal justice system since I've been practicing law. Though skepticism of criminal accusation has long been embodied in the presumption of innocence and the requirement of proof beyond a reasonable doubt for conviction, collecting all of the most eloquent speeches in the world about *why that skepticism is right* does not add up to the power of one, let alone dozens, let alone hundreds, of stories about people who served 5, 10, 15, sometimes up to 30 years for crimes they did not commit" (BB).

Brad Bannon continues: "Because many of the original convictions in the DNA exoneration cases were based on mistaken eyewitness identification, it has also given stakeholders in the criminal justice system—judges, prosecutors, defense attorneys, law enforcement—a healthy concern about such evidence and has led to reforms in many eyewitness identification procedures across the country. As importantly, in addition to exonerating the innocent, post-conviction DNA analysis has also resulted in the identification, apprehension, and conviction of the actual perpetrators of the crimes. After all, forensic science is not just about making sure that the wrong guy does not get convicted; it's about making sure the right one does" (BB).

It is important for the integrity of evidence to be maintained for it to be useful in these old cases. Old samples, which were frequently handled without gloves in the laboratory or by attorneys, witnesses, etc., in court, can lead to contamination. In these old cases, elimination samples from legitimate people who may have come in contact with these samples may not be possible to obtain. Issues can arise if the DNA results exclude the convicted defendant. Is the post-conviction DNA evidence result from the profile of the true perpetrator, thus proving the innocence of the individual in prison? Or can the DNA results be explained by other means such as another individual with access to evidence but not associated with the crime (e.g., consensual partner, contamination during evidence handling, testing, or storage)?

Contamination might only rarely impact a careful forensic DNA laboratory. However, it can have potential significance in old cases under review including those that are part of the Innocence Project. For example, if biological evidence from a 20-year-old case was handled by ungloved police officers or evidence custodians (prior to knowledge regarding the sensitivity of modern DNA testing), then the true perpetrator's DNA might be masked by contamination from the collecting officer. Thus, when a DNA test is performed, the police officer's or evidence custodian's DNA would be detected rather than the true perpetrator. In the absence of other evidence, the individual in prison might then be falsely declared "innocent" because his DNA profile was not found on the original crime scene evidence. This scenario emphasizes the importance of considering DNA evidence as an investigative tool within the context of a case rather than the sole absolute proof of guilt or innocence.

JURY COMPREHENSION OF DNA EVIDENCE

Over 30 years ago, a serologist from Palm Beach Sheriff's Crime Laboratory wrote (Tanton 1979): "When the forensic scientist testifies in court, both he and his testimony are usually evaluated by a group of people that has never seen him before and has little or no scientific background. These people, the jury, are exposed to the forensic scientist for only a relatively short time, during which they are privy to a strictly regulated question-and-answer conversation carried on between the scientist and the attorneys in the case. As a result of this exposure, the jurors must answer several important questions:

1. What did the expert say?
2. What is the significance of the expert's testimony?
3. Is the expert competent?
4. Is the expert honest?

Once they have answered these questions, and they always do, either directly or indirectly, they must decide what weight to give his evidence in their total deliberation" (Tanton 1979).

Testimony from forensic DNA analysts can be overwhelming to jury members—who often have limited exposure to the concepts of biology, genetics, and the technology used to generate DNA profiles. Lisa Kahn and David Feldstern from the Los Angeles County District Attorney's Office note that "When DNA testimony is properly presented, most jurors feel empowered by their newly found understanding of this important forensic evidence" (Kahn & Feldstern 1998).

When asked how you know whether or not you are connecting with the jury, Robin Cotton responded: "You can just forget it. You don't know" (RWC). Remember that it takes effort to select appropriate, understandable words to describe the DNA testing process in lay terms rather than scientific jargon. Take time to carefully consider the best words to use to describe your results. How you communicate will benefit juror comprehension.

The National Research Council's 1996 publication entitled *The Evaluation of Forensic DNA Evidence* (NRC II) recommended that research be conducted on juror comprehension of DNA evidence. NRC II recommendation 6.1 states: "Behavioral research should be carried out to identify any conditions that might cause a trier-of-fact [judge or jury] to misinterpret evidence on DNA profiling and to assess how well various ways of presenting expert testimony on DNA can reduce any such misunderstandings" (NRC 1996).

A 2004 study in Australia found that juries were 23 times more likely to vote guilty in homicide cases and 33 times more likely to vote guilty in sexual assault cases when DNA evidence was admitted in the trial (Briody 2004). Several such studies have been performed including one aimed at seeing if jurors comprehended that a mitochondrial DNA (mtDNA) match had less strength than a nuclear DNA result (Dann et al. 2004).

Expert witnesses need to connect with the jury and teach them at a level that they can comprehend the information shared. Results should be confidently conveyed but not overstated. New Zealand scientists John Buckleton and James Curran have written: "There is a considerable aura to DNA evidence. Because of this aura it is vital that weak evidence is correctly represented as weak or not presented at all" (Buckleton & Curran 2008). Where there is uncertainty in the data (e.g., with complex DNA mixtures, partial profiles from degradation, or low level DNA results), this should be emphasized so that the jurors (and attorneys for both sides) may appropriately evaluate the weight of the evidence presented.

As recommended in SWGDAM Interpretation Guideline 4.1 (SWGDAM 2010): "The laboratory must perform statistical analysis in support of any inclusion that is determined to be relevant in the context of a case, irrespective of the number of alleles detected and the quantitative value of the statistical analysis." Clearly a "1 in 300" statistic does not have the same weight as "1 in 300 billion." Make sure that the court—and especially the jury who will be making a decision based on your information and other aspects of the case presented to them—understands what your data says and what it does not say.

FACING THE "CSI EFFECT"

The so-called "CSI effect" is prevalent in juries today because of the popularity of crime solving TV shows (Houck 2006, Durnal 2010, Holmgrem & Fordham 2011). CBS's "CSI: Crime Scene Investigation" has been a top-rated show on television for many years. CSI and other crime shows have made forensic science seem easy and rapid. These television dramas influence the general public to a point where they expect all cases to be solved with forensic evidence—and especially DNA results—when they serve on a jury. This false expectation can make life challenging for prosecutors trying to prove their cases. Equally important is that jurors may have a false perception of what forensic scientists outside of Hollywood can and cannot accomplish.

FINAL THOUGHTS

When I asked Dr. Robin Cotton what was the single most important thing to remember when serving as an expert witness, she replied: ***"You are the voice of the data!*** You are not a voice for the victim, which is what some prosecutor's describe their role as. People will talk about the 'prosecution team.' I really don't think you are on somebody's team, but that isn't to say you wouldn't assist them in understanding or assist them in answering questions so that the data is clear to the jury. Just because you help in appropriate ways, it doesn't mean you are on 'their side.' If you want to feel like you are on someone's side, then you are welcome to feel so. You just cannot behave like you are on their side. You cannot let that feeling influence how you behave, how you speak, and most importantly, how you look at the data. I think it is a hard issue because you want to please the people you are working with, right? It is the prosecutor who is supposed to worry about the consequences of the trial. If you represent the data accurately in a scientific sense, then it is hard to go wrong" (RWC).

In their *Profiles in DNA* article, Lisa Kahn and David Feldstern conclude: "In many ways, the expert witness has the easiest job in the courtroom. If you are qualified and prepared, testifying should be an enjoyable and rewarding experience. An outstanding expert witness is one whose demeanor does not change from direct to cross-examination. If a person walks into the courtroom while you are testifying, they should find it difficult to tell whether you are still under direct examination, or are under cross-examination" (Kahn & Feldstern 1998).

Good luck with your experience in court as an expert witness! I hope that the material provided in this chapter has been helpful. Please see Appendix 4 for additional information from those interviewed in preparing this chapter.

READING LIST AND INTERNET RESOURCES

General Information

Billings, P. R. (Ed.). (1992). *DNA on Trial: Genetic identification and criminal justice.* Plainville, NY: Cold Spring Harbor Laboratory Press.

Clarke, G. W. (2007). *Justice and science: Trials and triumphs of DNA evidence.* New Brunswick, New Jersey: Rutgers University Press.

Denver DA DNA Resource. <http://www.denverda.org/DNA/DNA_INDEX.htm>.

DNA: A prosecutor's practice notebook. <http://dna.gov/training/prosecutors-notebook/>.

DNA Resource.com. <http://www.dnaresource.com>.

The Innocence Project. <http://www.innocenceproject.org>.

Kaye, D. H. (2010). *The double helix and the law of evidence.* Cambridge, MA: Harvard University Press.

David H. Kaye's articles. <http://www.personal.psu.edu/dhk3/activities-archive.htm>.

Kolilinsky, L., Liotti, T., & Oeser-Sweat, J. (2005). *DNA: Forensic and legal applications*. Hoboken, NJ: Wiley-Interscience.

Kreeger, L. R., & Weiss, D. M. (2003). *Forensic DNA fundamentals for the prosecutor: Be not afraid*. Alexandria, Virginia: American Prosecutors Research Institute. Available at <http://www.ndaa.org/apri/programs/dna/dna_home.html>.

Lazer, D. (Ed.). (2004). *DNA and the criminal justice system: The technology of justice*. Cambridge, Massachusetts: The MIT Press (see also <http://www.dnapolicy.net/>.

Michaelis, R. C., Flanders, R. G., & Wulff, P. H. (2008). *A litigator's guide to DNA: From the laboratory to the courtroom*. New York: Elsevier Academic Press.

National Institute of Justice. <http://www.ojp.usdoj.gov/nij>.

Palmer, L. J. (2004). *Encyclopedia of DNA and the United States criminal justice system*. Jefferson, North Carolina: McFarland & Co.. (Topics: Admissibility of DNA Test Results)

Principles of forensic DNA for officers of the court. <http://www.dna.gov/training/otc/>.

Sapir, G. I. (2002). Legal aspects of forensic science (2nd ed.). In R. Saferstein (Ed.), *Forensic science handbook* (Vol. I). Upper Saddle River, New Jersey: Prentice Hall.

Science and law blog. <http://lawprofessors.typepad.com/science_law/>.

SWGDAM (2001). Training guidelines. *Forensic Science Communications*, *3*(4). Available at <http://www2.fbi.gov/hq/lab/fsc/backissu/oct2001/kzinski.htm>.

Different Perspectives of Science and Law

Pollack, S. (1973). Observations on the adversary system and the role of the forensic scientist: "scientific truth" vs. "legal truth." *Journal of Forensic Sciences*, *18*, 173–177.

Taroni, F., & Aitken, C. G. G. (1998). Probabilistic reasoning in the law. Part 1: Assessment of probabilities and explanation of the value of DNA evidence. *Science & Justice*, *38*, 165–177.

Walsh, S. (2005). Legal perceptions of forensic DNA profiling. Part I: A review of the legal literature. *Forensic Science International*, *155*, 51–60.

Expert Witness

Bode Technology Group website on "Testimony Questions." <http://www.bodetech.com/services/training_testimony.html>.

Brodsky, S. (1999). *The expert expert witness: More maxims and guidelines for testifying in court*. Washington, DC: American Psychological Association.

Bronstein, D. A. (2007). *Law for the expert witness* (3rd ed.). Boca Raton, Florida: CRC Press.

Cooper, J., & Neuhaus, I. M. (2000). The "hired gun" effect: Assessing the effect of pay, frequency of testifying, and credentials on the perceptions of expert testimony. *Law and Human Behaviour*, *24*, 149–171.

Davis, R. J. (2007). Surviving and thriving in the courtroom. In W. J. Chisum & B. E. Turvey (Eds.), *Crime reconstruction* (Chapter 13, pp. 483–506). San Diego: Elsevier Academic Press.

Davis, R. J. (2010). Friendly persuasion: Review of Feder's succeeding as an expert witness. *The CAC News*, *2nd quarter*, 10–11.

Feder, H. A., & Houck, M. M. (2008). *Feder's succeeding as an expert witness* (4th ed.). Boca Raton, Florida: CRC Press.

Froede, R. C. (1997). *The scientific expert in court: Principles and guidelines*. Washington, DC: AACC Press.

Hand, L. (1901). Historical and practical considerations regarding expert testimony. *Harvard Law Review*, *15*, 40–58.

Hiss, J. (2007). The forensic expert witness—an issue of competency. *Forensic Science International*, *168*, 89–94.

Kahn, L., & Feldstern, D. (1998). How to succeed as an expert witness. *Profiles in DNA*, 2(2), 9–11. Available at <http://www.promega.com/profiles/202/ProfilesinDNA_202_09.pdf>.

Marne, B. A. (2007). *Presentation on "expert witness testimony" at the sixth annual advanced DNA technical workshop (Bode East Meeting)*. (See <http://www.bodetech.com/documents/Captiva_Program.pdf>.

Murphy, C. F. (1993). Experts, liars, and guns for hire: A different perspective on the qualification of technical expert witnesses. *Indiana Law Journal*, *69*, 637–649.

Philipps, K. A. (1977). The "nuts and bolts" of testifying as a forensic scientist. *Journal of Forensic Sciences*, *22*, 457–463.

Starrs, J. E. (1985). In the land of Agog: An allegory for the expert witness. *Journal of Forensic Sciences*, *30*, 289–308.

Strange, C. (1995). Confronting the culture of the courtroom: What to do when it's your turn to testify. In *Proceedings of the sixth international symposium on human identification*. (Available at <http://www.promega.com/geneticidproc/ussymp6proc/strange.htm>).

Stufflebean, D. G. (2008). The expert witness: Knowledge and communication (the deadly or dynamic duo). *The CAC News, 2nd Quarter*, 8–13. Available at <http://www.cacnews.org/news/2ndq08.pdf>; previously published in 1991 in the *Journal of Forensic Economics*, *4*(3), 317–327.

Wooley, J. R. (1997). Presenting DNA evidence at trial: The "K.I.S.S. principle." *Profiles in DNA*, *1*(1), 3–4. Available at <http://www.promega.com/profiles/>.

Ethics

Barnett, P. D. (2001). *Ethics in forensic science: Professional standards for the practice of criminalistics*. Boca Raton, Florida: CRC Press.

Bowen, R. T. (2010). *Ethics and the practice of forensic science*. Boca Raton, Florida: CRC Press.

Fanelli, D. (2009). How many scientists fabricate and falsify research? A systematic review and meta-analysis of survey data. *PLoS ONE*, *4*(5), e5738.

Frankell, M. (1989). Ethics and the forensic sciences: Professional automony in the criminal justice system. *Journal of Forensic Sciences*, *34*(3), 763–771.

Hollien, H. (1990). The expert witness: Ethics and responsibilities. *Journal of Forensic Sciences*, *35*, 1414–1423.

Kates, J., & Guttenplan, H. (1983). Ethical considerations in forensic science services. *Journal of Forensic Sciences*, *28*(4), 972–976.

Lucas, D. (1989). The ethical responsibilities of the forensic scientist: Exploring the limits. *Journal of Forensic Sciences*, *34*(3), 719–729.

National Research Council (2009). *Strengthening forensic science in the United States: A path forward*. Washington, DC: National Academies Press. Available at <http://www.nap.edu> or <http://www.ncjrs.gov/pdffiles1/nij/grants/228091.pdf>.

Peterson, J. (1988). Teaching ethics in a forensic science curriculum. *Journal of Forensic Sciences*, *33*(4), 1081–1085.

Peterson, J., & Murdock, J. (1989). Forensic science ethics: Developing an integrated system of support and enforcement. *Journal of Forensic Sciences*, *34*(3), 749–762.

Rogers, T. (2004). Crime scene ethics: Souvenirs, teaching materials, and artifacts. *Journal of Forensic Sciences*, *49*(2), 307–311.

Saks, M. (1989). Prevalence and impact of ethical problems in forensic science. *Journal of Forensic Sciences*, *34*(3), 772–793.

Saviers, K. (2002). Ethics in forensic science: A review of the literature on expert testimony. *Journal of Forensic Identification*, *52*(4), 449–462.

Schroeder, O. (1984). Ethical and moral dilemmas confronting forensic scientists. *Journal of Forensic Sciences*, *29*(4), 966–986.

Admissibility of Evidence

Berger, M. A. (2005). What has a decade of Daubert wrought? *American Journal of Public Health*, *95*, S59–S65.

Cotton, R. W. (2000). From the scientist's point of view: What constitutes general acceptance? In *Proceedings of the 11th international symposium on human identification*. Available at http://www.promega.com/geneticidproc/ussymp11proc/content/cotton.pdf>.

Daubert v. Merrell Dow Pharmaceuticals, Inc., 509 U.S. 579 (1993).

Frye v. United States, 54 App. D.C. 46, 47, 293 F. 1013, 1014 (1923). Full text available at <http://www.daubertontheweb.com/frye_opinion.htm>.

Federal Rules of Evidence (FRE) 702. <http://www.law.cornell.edu/rules/fre/rules.htm#Rule702>.

Harmon, R. (2005). Admissibility standards for scientific evidence. In R. G. Breeze, B. Budowle & S. E. Schutzer (Eds.), *Microbial forensics* (Chapter 18, pp. 381–392). New York: Elsevier Academic Press.

Keierlber, J. A., & Bohan, T. L. (2005). Ten years after Daubert: The status of the states. *Journal of Forensic Sciences*, *50*, 1154–1163.

Redding, S. (2000). STR DNA admissibility hearings and the Minnesota legislative response to the statute of limitations for sexual assaults. In *Proceedings of the 11th international symposium on human identification*. (Available at <http://www.promega.com/geneticidproc/ussymp11proc/content/redding.pdf>).

Rules of evidence on expert testimony. <http://www.ncstl.org/resources/702>.

Tomsic, A. B. (2000). DNA admissibility in Colorado: *People v. Shreck*. In *Proceedings of the 11th international symposium on human identification*. Available at <http://www.promega.com/geneticidproc/ussymp11proc/content/tomsic.pdf>.

Types of DNA Cases, Discovery Issues, and Opposing Counsel Tactics

Giannelli, P. C. (1999). Defense tactics for DNA litigation. *Profiles in DNA, 2*(3), 10–11. Available at <http://www.promega.com/profiles/>.

Haesler, A. (2006). Dealing with DNA in court: Its use and misuse. *Judicial Review, 8*(1), 121–144. Available at <http://www.lawlink.nsw.gov.au/lawlink/pdo/ll_pdo.nsf/pages/PDO_dnadealingwithincourt>.

Hunt, J. (2006). Disclosure under *Brady v. Maryland* – a prosecutor's view. *The North Carolina State Bar Journal, 11*(4), 22–23. Available at <http://www.ncbar.gov/journal/archive/journal_11,4.pdf>.

Klinkosum, M., & Bannon, B. (2006). *Brady v. Maryland* and its legacy—forging a path for disclosure. *The North Carolina State Bar Journal, 11*(2), 8–11. Available at <http://www.ncbar.gov/journal/archive/journal%2011,2.pdf>.

Strange, C. (2002). Testifying in the 2000's: Still confronting the culture of the courtroom. In *Proceedings of the 13th international symposium on human identification*. Available at <http://www.promega.com/geneticidproc/ussymp13proc/contents/strange.pdf>.

Thompson, W. C., et al. (2003). Evaluating forensic DNA evidence: Elements of a competent defense review. *The Champion, 27*, 16–25. Available at <http://www.nacdl.org/public.nsf/$$searchChampion>.

Post-Conviction DNA Testing

Postconviction Issues Working Group of the National Commission on the Future of DNA Evidence (1999). *Postconviction DNA testing: Recommendations for handling requests*. Washington, DC: National Institute of Justice. Available at <http://www.ncjrs.gov/pdffiles1/nij/177626.pdf>.

Jury Comprehension

Adams, J. (2005). Nuclear and mitochondrial DNA in the courtroom. *Journal of Law and Policy, 13*, 69–97.

Briody, M. (2004). The effects of DNA evidence on homicide cases in court. *The Australian and New Zealand Journal of Criminology, 37*, 231–252.

Buckleton, J., & Curran, J. (2008). A discussion of the merits of random man not excluded and likelihood ratios. *Forensic Science International: Genetics, 2*, 343–348.

Cecil, J. S., et al. (1991). Citizen comprehension of difficult issues: Lessons from civil jury trials. *American University Law Review, 40*, 727–774.

Dann, B. M., et al. (2004). Testing the effects of selected jury trial innovations on juror comprehension of contested mtDNA evidence. Final Technical Report, National Institute of Justice, Grant No. 2002-IJ-CX-0026. (Available at <http://www.ncjrs.gov/pdffiles1/nij/grants/211000.pdf>).

Dann, B. M., et al. (2006). Can jury trial innovations improve juror understanding of DNA evidence?. *National Institute of Justice Journal, 255*, 2–6. Available at <http://www.ojp.usdoj.gov/nij/journals/255/trial_innovations.html>.

Dann, B. M., et al. (2007). Can jury trial innovations improve jury understanding of DNA evidence?. *Judicature, 90*, 152–156.

Dartnall, S., & Goodman-Delahunty, J. (2006). Enhancing juror understanding of probabilistic DNA evidence. *Australian Journal of Forensic Sciences, 38*(2), 85–96.

Durnal, E. W. (2010). Crime scene investigation (as seen on TV). *Forensic Science International, 199*, 1–5.

Findlay, M., & Grix, J. (2003). Challenging forensic evidence? Observations on the use of DNA in certain criminal trials. *Current Issues in Criminal Justice, 14*, 283–298.

Findlay, M. (2008). Juror comprehension and the hard case: Making forensic evidence simpler. *International Journal of Law, Crime, and Justice, 36*, 15–53.

Goodman-Delahunty, J., & Tait, D. (2006). DNA and the changing face of justice. *Australian Journal of Forensic Sciences, 38*, 97–106.

Goodman-Delahunty, J., & Hewson, L. (2010, March). Enhancing fairness in DNA jury trials. *Trends & Issues in Crime and Criminal Justice*(392). Available at <http://www.aic.gov.au>.

Goodman-Delahunty, J., & Hewson, L. (2010). *Improving jury understanding and use of expert DNA evidence.* Australian Institute of Criminology. Available at <http://www.aic.gov.au>.

Hans, V. (2007). Judges, juries, and scientific evidence. *Journal of Law and Policy, 16,* 19–46.

Hans, V. P., et al. (2011). Science in the jury box: Jurors' comprehension of mitochondrial DNA evidence. *Law and Human Behavior, 35,* 60–71.

Hewson, L., & Goodman-Delahunty, J. (2008). Using multimedia to support jury understanding of DNA profiling evidence. *Australian Journal of Forensic Sciences, 40*(1), 55–64.

Holmgren, J. (2005). DNA evidence and jury comprehension. *Canadian Society of Forensic Sciences Journal, 38,* 123–142.

Holmgren, J. A., & Fordham, J. (2011). The CSI effect and the Canadian and the Australian jury. *Journal of Forensic Sciences, 56 (Supple.1),* S63–S71.

Houck, M. M. (2006). CSI: Reality. *Scientific American, 295,* 85–89.

Koehler, J. J. (1993). Error and exaggeration in the presentation of DNA evidence at trial. *Jurimetrics Journal, 34,* 21–39.

Koehler, J. J. (2001). When are people persuaded by DNA match statistics?. *Law and Human Behavior, 25,* 493–513.

Levett, L. M., & Kovera, M. B. (2008). The effectiveness of opposing expert witnesses for educating jurors about unreliable expert evidence. *Law and Human Behavior, 32,* 363–374.

Lieberman, J., et al. (2008). Gold vs platinum: Do jurors recognize the superiority and limitations of DNA evidence compared to other types of forensic evidence?. *Psychology, Public Policy, & Law, 14,* 27–62.

Lindsey, S., et al. (2003). Communicating statistical DNA evidence. *Jurimetrics, 43,* 147–163.

Myers, R. D., et al. (1999). Complex scientific evidence and the jury. *Judicature, 83,* 150–156.

Nance, D. A., & Morris, S. B. (2005). Jury understanding of DNA evidence: An empirical assessment of presentation formats for trace evidence with relatively small probability. *Journal of Legal Studies, 34,* 395–444.

Schklar, J., & Diamond, S. S. (1999). Juror reactions to DNA evidence: Errors and expectancies. *Law and Human Behavior, 23,* 159–184.

Schweitzer, N. J., & Saks, M. J. (2007). The CSI effect: Popular fiction about forensic science affects the public's expectations about real forensic science. *Jurimetrics, 47,* 357–364.

Tanton, R. L. (1979). Jury preconceptions and their effect on expert scientific testimony. *Journal of Forensic Sciences, 24,* 681–691.

Thompson, W. C., & Schumann, E. L. (1987). Interpretation of statistical evidence in criminal trials: The prosecutor's fallacy and the defense attorney's fallacy. *Law and Human Behavior, 11,* 167–187.

Vidmar, N. (2005). Expert evidence, the adversary system, and the jury. *American Journal of Public Health, 95,* S137–S143.

Visher, C. A. (1987). Jury decision making: The importance of evidence. *Law and Human Behavior, 11,* 1–17.

APPENDIX

1

Reported Sizes and Sequences of STR Alleles

Explanation of information included in the following tables:

This appendix material describes the reported alleles for the 23 short tandem repeat (STR) loci most commonly used in the United States and around the world. Note that the number of alleles present for a particular locus is an indication of the polymorphic nature of that marker and its value for use in human identity testing. The STR locus FGA is more variable than TPOX because it possesses more alleles and thus there is a greater chance that two individuals selected at random would have different genotypes at FGA than at TPOX. Of course, the frequency at which alleles occur in a population plays an important role in the effectiveness of STR loci to distinguish between individuals. Allele frequency information for these 23 STR loci will be included in the forthcoming volume *Advanced Topics in Forensic DNA Typing: Interpretation.*

As described in Chapter 5, STR alleles are named based on the number of full repeat units that they contain while partial repeats (i.e., microvariants) are designated by the number of full repeats, a decimal, and the number of nucleotides present in the partial repeat in accordance with International Society of Forensic Genetics (ISFG) recommendations (1994). Some of the alternative allele nomenclatures that were present in previous editions of *Forensic DNA Typing* have been removed. Alleles that are the same overall length but possess a different known internal sequence structure are sub-labeled below as "(a)," "(b)," etc. (e.g., FGA 27(a) and FGA 27(b)). Adjacent rows containing same-size, different-sequence alleles are shaded in gray.

Known flanking sequence differences that alter the DNA sequence length or electrophoretic migration of a PCR product are designated according to the 2006 ISFG recommendations with additional information after the number of complete STR repeat units (Gusmão et al. 2006, Butler et al. 2008). For example, a TPOX allele with 8 repeats and a single deletion of an adenine ("A" nucleotide) 48bp downstream of the repeat is designated 7.3 due to its migration (Allor et al. 2005) or 8(D48Adel) to describe its flanking sequence information, where 8 stands for the number of complete repeats, D48 indicates the direction and position of the mutation relative to the STR repeat block (i.e., the mutation is located 48 bases downstream of the repeat), and "Adel" indicates that an A nucleotide has been deleted.

The polymerase chain reaction (PCR) product size for each of the possible alleles is listed based on the commercial STR kit used to amplify the particular locus. Commercially available STR kits can produce different DNA fragment sizes because their primers hybridize to different positions in the flanking regions of the STR sequence. The expected DNA fragment sizes (based on their actual sequence) for all reported alleles are calculated for the designated Promega PowerPlex kit or the Applied Biosystems AmpFlSTR kit. These PCR product sizes are listed without any nontemplate addition, i.e., they are in the "−A" rather than the "+A" form. *STR allele sizes measured in a laboratory may also vary from the actual sequence-based size listed here due to the internal sizing standard used and the particular electrophoretic conditions.* In addition, some of the Applied Biosystems loci have mobility modifiers to alter the relative size of the PCR products during electrophoretic measurement.

The common repeat sequence motif for each STR locus is listed according to the 1997 ISFG recommendations (Bär et al. 1997). In most cases, the sequence changes in the repeat region are the only variation occurring and the flanking sequences remain constant. However, variation in the flanking sequence is also a possibility as has been shown with base composition mass spectrometry studies (Oberacher et al. 2008). Finally, the reference is listed where each new allele (and its sequence if published) has been described.

New (rare) alleles will be discovered as more samples are analyzed using these STR loci. As this listing becomes outdated, readers are encouraged to consult the STRBase variant allele listing (http://www.cstl.nist.gov/biotech/strbase/var_tab.htm) and to contribute newly discovered alleles so that they may be categorized for fellow workers in this field. The complete sequence for one of the alleles listed for each locus may be found by using the GenBank accession number listed for that locus or by checking the reference sequence in STRBase (http://www.cstl.nist.gov/biotech/strbase/seq_info.htm).

CSF1PO

GenBank Accession: X14720 (allele 12). PCR product sizes of observed alleles

Allele (Repeat #)	Promega PowerPlex 16	ABI Identifiler	Repeat Structure $[AGAT]_n$	Reference
5	317bp	301bp	$[AGAT]_5$	Kline et al. (2010)
6	321bp	305bp	$[AGAT]_6$	Lazaruk et al. (1998)
6.3	324bp	308bp	Not published	STRBase
7	325bp	309bp	$[AGAT]_7$	Huang et al. (1995)
7.3	328bp	312bp	Not published	STRBase
8	329bp	313bp	$[AGAT]_8$	Puers et al. (1993)
8.3	332bp	316bp	Not published	STRBase
9	333bp	317bp	$[AGAT]_9$	Puers et al. (1993)
9.1	334bp	318bp	Not published	STRBase
9.3	336bp	320bp	Not published	STRBase
10	337bp	321bp	$[AGAT]_{10}$	Puers et al. (1993)
10.1	338bp	322bp	Not published	Huel et al. (2007)
10.2	339bp	323bp	Not published	Allor et al. (2005)
10.3	340bp	324bp	Not published	Lazaruk et al. (1998)
11	341bp	325bp	$[AGAT]_{11}$	Puers et al. (1993)
11.1	342bp	326bp	Not published	Scherczinger et al. (2000)
11.3	344bp	328bp	Not published	STRBase
12	345bp	329bp	$[AGAT]_{12}$	Puers et al. (1993)
12.1	346bp	330bp	Not published	Budowle & Moretti (1998)
12.2	347bp	331bp	Not published	STRBase
12.3	348bp	332bp	Not published	STRBase
13	349bp	333bp	$[AGAT]_{13}$	Puers et al. (1993)
13.1	350bp	334bp	Not published	STRBase
14	353bp	337bp	$[AGAT]_{14}$	Puers et al. (1993)
14.1	354bp	338bp	Not published	STRBase
15	357bp	341bp	$[AGAT]_{15}$	Lazaruk et al. (1998)
15.1	358bp	342bp	Not published	STRBase
16	361bp	345bp	$[AGAT]_{16}$	Margolis-Nunno et al. (2001)
17	365bp	349bp	Not published	Huel et al. (2007)

29 observed alleles

FGA

GenBank Accession: M64982 (allele 21). PCR product sizes of observed alleles

Allele (Repeat #)	Promega PP16	ABI Identifiler	Repeat Structure $[TTTC]_3$ TTTT TTCT$[CTTT]_n$ CTCC $[TTCC]_2$	Reference
12.2	308bp	196bp	Not published	STRBase
13	310bp	198bp	$[TTTC]_3$TTTT TTCT$[CTTT]_5$CTCC$[TTCC]_2$	Jiang et al. (2011)
13.2	312bp	200bp	Not published	STRBase
14	314bp	202bp	Not published	STRBase
14.3	317bp	205bp	Not published	STRBase
15	318bp	206bp	$[TTTC]_3$TTTT TTCT$[CTTT]_7$CTCC$[TTCC]_2$	Barber et al. (1996)
15.3	321bp	209bp	Not published	STRBase
16	322bp	210bp	Not published	STRBase
16.1	323bp	211bp	$[TTTC]_3$TTTT TTCT$[CTTT]_5$T$[CTTT]_3$ [CTCC$[TTCC]_2$	Griffiths et al. (1998)
16.2	324bp	212bp	Not published	STRBase
17	326bp	214bp	$[TTTC]_3$TTTT TTCT$[CTTT]_9$CTCC$[TTCC]_2$	Barber et al. (1996)
17.2	328bp	216bp	Not published	STRBase
18	330bp	218bp	$[TTTC]_3$TTTT TTCT$[CTTT]_{10}$CTCC$[TTCC]_2$	Barber et al. (1996)
18.2	332bp	220bp	$[TTTC]_3$TTTT TT$[CTTT]_{11}$CTCC$[TTCC]_2$	Barber et al. (1996)
19	334bp	222bp	$[TTTC]_3$TTTT TTCT$[CTTT]_{11}$CTCC$[TTCC]_2$	Barber et al. (1996)
19.1	335bp	223bp	Not published	STRBase
19.2	336bp	224bp	$[TTTC]_3$TTTT TT $[CTTT]_{12}$CTCC$[TTCC]_2$	STRBase
19.3	337bp	225bp	Not published	STRBase
20	338bp	226bp	$[TTTC]_3$TTTT TTCT$[CTTT]_{12}$CTCC$[TTCC]_2$	Barber et al. (1996)
20.1	339bp	227bp	Not published	Huel et al. (2007)
20.2	340bp	228bp	$[TTTC]_3$TTTT TT $[CTTT]_{13}$CTCC$[TTCC]_2$	Barber et al. (1996)
20.3	341bp	229bp	Not published	STRBase
21	342bp	230bp	$[TTTC]_3$TTTT TTCT$[CTTT]_{13}$CTCC$[TTCC]_2$	Barber et al. (1996)
21.1	343bp	231bp	$[TTTC]_3$TTTT [TTCT$[CTTT]_{10}$**T**$[CTTT]_3$ CTCC$[TTCC]_2$	Allor et al. (2005)
21.2	344bp	232bp	$[TTTC]_3$TTTT TT $[CTTT]_{14}$CTCC$[TTCC]_2$	STRBase
21.3	345bp	233bp	Not published	STRBase
22	346bp	234bp	$[TTTC]_3$TTTT TTCT$[CTTT]_{14}$CTCC$[TTCC]_2$	Barber et al. (1996)
22.1	347bp	235bp	Not published	STRBase

(Continued)

FGA (*Continued*)

Allele (Repeat #)	Promega PP16	ABI Identifiler	Repeat Structure [TTTC]$_3$ TTTT TTCT[CTTT]$_n$ CTCC [TTCC]$_2$	Reference
22.2	348 bp	236 bp	[TTTC]$_3$TTTT TT [CTTT]$_{15}$CTCC[TTCC]$_2$	Barber et al. (1996)
22.3	349 bp	237 bp	Not published	Gill et al. (1996)
23	350 bp	238 bp	[TTTC]$_3$TTTT TTCT[CTTT]$_{15}$CTCC[TTCC]$_2$	Barber et al. (1996)
23.1	351 bp	239 bp	Not published	STRBase
23.2	352 bp	240 bp	[TTTC]$_3$TTTT TT [CTTT]$_{16}$CTCC[TTCC]$_2$	Barber et al. (1996)
23.3	353 bp	241 bp	Not published	STRBase
24	354 bp	242 bp	[TTTC]$_3$TTTT TTCT[CTTT]$_{16}$CTCC[TTCC]$_2$	Barber et al. (1996)
24.1	355 bp	243 bp	Not published	STRBase
24.2	356 bp	244 bp	[TTTC]$_3$TTTT TT [CTTT]$_{17}$CTCC[TTCC]$_2$	Barber et al. (1996)
24.3	357 bp	245 bp	Not published	STRBase
25	358 bp	246 bp	[TTTC]$_3$TTTT TTCT[CTTT]$_{17}$CTCC[TTCC]$_2$	Barber et al. (1996)
25.1	359 bp	247 bp	Not published	STRBase
25.2	360 bp	248 bp	[TTTC]$_3$TTTT TT [CTTT]$_{18}$CTCC[TTCC]$_2$	STRBase
25.3	361 bp	249 bp	Not published	STRBase
26	362 bp	250 bp	[TTTC]$_3$TTTT TTCT[CTTT]$_{18}$CTCC[TTCC]$_2$	Barber et al. (1996)
26.1	363 bp	251 bp	Not published	STRBase
26.2	364 bp	252 bp	Not published	Huel et al. (2007)
26.3	365 bp	253 bp	Not published	STRBase
27 (a)	366 bp	254 bp	[TTTC]$_3$TTTT TTCT[CTTT]$_{19}$CTCC[TTCC]$_2$	Barber et al. (1996)
27 (b)	366 bp	254 bp	[TTTC]$_3$TTTT TTCT[CTTT]$_{13}$CCTT[CTTT]$_5$CTCC [TTCC]$_2$	Griffiths et al. (1998)
27.1	367 bp	255 bp	Not published	STRBase
27.2	368 bp	256 bp	Not published	Huel et al. (2007)
27.3	369 bp	257 bp	Not published	STRBase
28	370 bp	258 bp	[TTTC]$_3$TTTT TTCT[CTTT]$_{20}$CTCC[TTCC]$_2$	Barber et al. (1996)
28.2	372 bp	260 bp	[TTTC]$_3$TTTT TT [CTTT]$_{21}$CTCC[TTCC]$_2$	STRBase
29	374 bp	262 bp	[TTTC]$_3$TTTT TTCT[CTTT]$_{15}$CCTT[CTTT]$_5$CTCC [TTCC]$_2$	Barber et al. (1996)
29.1	375 bp	263 bp	Not published	STRBase
29.2	376 bp	264 bp	Not published	STRBase
30	378 bp	266 bp	[TTTC]$_3$TTTT TTCT[CTTT]$_{16}$CCTT[CTTT]$_5$CTCC [TTCC]$_2$	Griffiths et al. (1998)

(Continued)

FGA (*Continued*)

Allele (Repeat #)	Promega PP16	ABI Identifiler	Repeat Structure $[TTTC]_3$ TTTT TTCT$[CTTT]_n$ CTCC $[TTCC]_2$	Reference
30.2	380 bp	268 bp	$[TTTC]_4$TTTT TT $[CTTT]_{14}[CTTC]_3[CTTT]_3$CTCC $[TTCC]_4$	Barber et al. (1996)
31	382 bp	270 bp	Not published	STRBase
31.2	384 bp	272 bp	$[TTTC]_4$TTTT TT $[CTTT]_{15}[CTTC]_3[CTTT]_3$CTCC $[TTCC]_4$	Griffiths et al. (1998)
32	386 bp	274 bp	Not published	SGM Plus
32.1	387 bp	275 bp	Not published	STRBase
32.2	388 bp	276 bp	$[TTTC]_4$TTTT TT $[CTTT]_{16}[CTTC]_3[CTTT]_3$CTCC $[TTCC]_4$	Griffiths et al. (1998)
33.1	391 bp	279 bp	$[TTTC]_3$TTTTTTCT$[CTTT]_{13}$TTTCT$[CTTT]_{11}$CTC C$[TTCC]_2$	Allor et al. (2005)
33.2	392 bp	280 bp	$[TTTC]_4$TTTT TT $[CTTT]_{17}[CTTC]_3[CTTT]_3$CTCC $[TTCC]_4$	Griffiths et al. (1998)
34.1	395 bp	283 bp	$[TTTC]_3$TTTTTTCT$[CTTT]_{13}$TTTCT$[CTTT]_{12}$CTC C$[TTCC]_2$	Allor et al. (2005)
34.2	396 bp	284 bp	$[TTTC]_4$TTTT TT $[CTTT]_{18}[CTTC]_3[CTTT]_3$CTCC $[TTCC]_4$	Barber et al. (1996)
35.2	400 bp	288 bp	Not published	STRBase
41.1	423 bp	311 bp	Not published	STRBase
41.2	424 bp	312 bp	$[TTTC]_4$TTTT TT $[CTTT]_{11}[CTGT]_3[CTTT]_{11}$ $[CTTC]_3$ $[CTTT]_3$CTCC$[TTCC]_4$	Allor et al. (2005)
42	426 bp	314 bp	Not published	STRBase
42.1	427 bp	315 bp	Not published	STRBase
42.2	428 bp	316 bp	$[TTTC]_4$TTTT TT $[CTTT]_8$ $[CTGT]_4[CTTT]_{13}$ $[CTTC]_3[CTTT]_3$CTCC$[TTCC]_4$	Griffiths et al. (1998)
43.1	431 bp	319 bp	Not published	STRBase
43.2	432 bp	320 bp	$[TTTC]_4$TTTT TT $[CTTT]_8$ $[CTGT]_5[CTTT]_{13}$ $[CTTC]_4[CTTT]_3$CTCC$[TTCC]_4$	Griffiths et al. (1998)
44	434 bp	322 bp	Not published	Steinlechner et al. (2002)
44.2	436 bp	324 bp	$[TTTC]_4$TTTT TT $[CTTT]_{11}[CTGT]_3[CTTT]_{14}$ $[CTTC]_3[CTTT]_3$CTCC$[TTCC]_4$	Griffiths et al. (1998)
44.3	437 bp	325 bp	Not published	STRBase
45	438 bp	326 bp	Not published	STRBase
45.1	439 bp	327 bp	Not published	STRBase

(*Continued*)

FGA (*Continued*)

Allele (Repeat #)	Promega PP16	ABI Identifiler	Repeat Structure $[TTTC]_3$ TTTT TTCT$[CTTT]_n$ CTCC $[TTCC]_2$	Reference
45.2	440bp	328bp	$[TTTC]_4$TTTT TT $[CTTT]_{10}[CTGT]_5[CTTT]_{13}$ $[CTTC]_4[CTTT]_3$CTCC$[TTCC]_4$	Griffiths et al. (1998)
46	442bp	330bp	Not published	STRBase
46.1	443bp	331bp	Not published	STRBase
46.2	444bp	332bp	$[TTTC]_4$TTTT TT $[CTTT]_{12}[CTGT]_5[CTTT]_{13}$ $[CTTC]_3[CTTT]_3$CTCC$[TTCC]_4$	Barber et al. (1996)
47	446bp	334bp	Not published	STRBase
47.2	448bp	336bp	$[TTTC]_4$TTTT TT $[CTTT]_{12}[CTGT]_5[CTTT]_{14}$ $[CTTC]_3[CTTT]_3$CTCC$[TTCC]_4$	Griffiths et al. (1998)
48	450bp	338bp	Not published	STRBase
48.2	452bp	340bp	$[TTTC]_4$TTTT TT $[CTTT]_{14}[CTGT]_3[CTTT]_{14}$ $[CTTC]_4[CTTT]_3$CTCC$[TTCC]_4$	Griffiths et al. (1998)
49	454bp	342bp	Not published	STRBase
49.1	455bp	343bp	Not published	STRBase
49.2	456bp	344bp	Not published	SGM Plus
50.2	460bp	344bp	$[TTTC]_4$TTTT TT $[CTTT]_{14}[CTGT]_4[CTTT]_{15}$ $[CTTC]_4[CTTT]_3$CTCC$[TTCC]_4$	Griffiths et al. (1998)
50.3	461bp	345bp	Not published	STRBase
51	462bp	346bp	Not published	STRBase
51.2	464bp	348bp	Not published	SGM Plus

95 observed alleles

TH01

GenBank Accession: D00269 (allele 9). PCR product sizes of observed alleles

Allele (Repeat #)	Promega PowerPlex 16	ABI Identifiler	Repeat Structure $[AATG]_n$ *or other strand* $[TCAT]_n$	Reference
3	152 bp	160 bp	$[AATG]_3$	Espinheira et al. (1996)
4	156 bp	164 bp	$[AATG]_4$	Griffiths et al. (1998)
5	160 bp	168 bp	$[AATG]_5$	Brinkmann et al. (1996b)
5.3	163 bp	171 bp	Not published	SGM Plus manual
6	164 bp	172 bp	$[AATG]_6$	Brinkmann et al. (1996b)
6.1	165 bp	173 bp	Not published	STRBase
6.3	167 bp	175 bp	$[AATG]_3ATG[AATG]_3$	Klintschar et al. (1998)
7	168 bp	176 bp	$[AATG]_7$	Brinkmann et al. (1996b)
7.1	169 bp	177 bp	Not published	STRBase
7.3	171 bp	179 bp	Not published	STRBase
8	172 bp	180 bp	$[AATG]_8$	Brinkmann et al. (1996b)
8.1	173 bp	181 bp	Not published	STRBase
8.3	175 bp	183 bp	$[AATG]_5ATG[AATG]_3$	Brinkmann et al. (1996b)
9	176 bp	184 bp	$[AATG]_9$	Brinkmann et al. (1996b)
9.1	177 bp	185 bp	Not published	STRBase
9.2	178 bp	186 bp	Not published	STRBase
9.3	179 bp	187 bp	$[AATG]_6ATG[AATG]_3$	Brinkmann et al. (1996b)
10	180 bp	188 bp	$[AATG]_{10}$	Brinkmann et al. (1996b)
10.3	183 bp	191 bp	$[AATG]_6ATG[AATG]_4$	Brinkmann et al. (1996b)
11	184 bp	192 bp	$[AATG]_{11}$	Brinkmann et al. (1996b)
12	188 bp	196 bp	$[AATG]_{12}$	van Oorschot et al. (1994)
13	192 bp	200 bp	Not published	STRBase
13.3	195 bp	203 bp	$[AATG][AACG][AATG]_8$ $ATG[AATG]_3$	Gene et al. (1996); Griffiths et al. (1998)
14	196 bp	204 bp	Not published	SGM Plus manual

24 observed alleles

TPOX

GenBank Accession: M68651 (allele 11). PCR product sizes of observed alleles

Allele (Repeat #)	**Promega PP 16**	**ABI Identifiler**	**Repeat Structure $[AATG]_n$**	**Reference**
4	254 bp	209 bp	$[AATG]_4$	STRBase
5	258 bp	213 bp	$[AATG]_5$	STRBase
6	262 bp	217 bp	$[AATG]_6$	Lazaruk et al. (1998)
7	266 bp	221 bp	$[AATG]_7$	Amorim et al. (1996)
7.1	267 bp	222 bp	Not published	STRBase
7.2	268 bp	223 bp	Not published	STRBase
7.3 or **8(D48Adel)**	269 bp	224 bp	$[AATG]_8$ with A deletion 48 bp downstream	Allor et al. (2005)
8	270 bp	225 bp	$[AATG]_8$	Puers et al. (1993)
9	274 bp	229 bp	$[AATG]_9$	Puers et al. (1993)
10	278 bp	233 bp	$[AATG]_{10}$	Puers et al. (1993)
10.1	279 bp	234 bp	Not published	STRBase
10.3 or **11(D157Gdel)**	281 bp	236 bp	$[AATG]_{11}$ with G deletion 157 bp downstream	Kline et al. (2010)
11	282 bp	237 bp	$[AATG]_{11}$	Puers et al. (1993)
12	286 bp	241 bp	$[AATG]_{12}$	Puers et al. (1993)
13	290 bp	245 bp	$[AATG]_{13}$	Amorim et al. (1996)
13.1	291 bp	246 bp	Not published	STRBase
14	294 bp	249 bp	$[AATG]_{14}$	Huang et al. (1995)
15	298 bp	253 bp	Not published	STRBase
16	302 bp	257 bp	Not published	STRBase

19 observed alleles

VWA

GenBank Accession: M25858 (allele 18). PCR product sizes of observed alleles

Allele (Repeat #)	Promega PP 16	ABI Identifiler	Repeat Structure TCTA[TCTG]$_{3-4}$[TCTA]$_n$	Reference
10	123 bp	152 bp	TCTA TCTG TCTA [TCTG]$_4$[TCTA]$_3$	Griffiths et al. (1998)
11	127 bp	156 bp	TCTA[TCTG]$_3$[TCTA]$_7$	Brinkmann et al. (1996b)
12	131 bp	160 bp	TCTA[TCTG]$_4$[TCTA]$_7$	Griffiths et al. (1998)
13 (a)	135 bp	164 bp	[TCTA]$_2$[TCTG]$_4$[TCTA]$_3$TCCA [TCTA]$_3$	Griffiths et al. (1998)
13 (b)	135 bp	164 bp	TCTA[TCTA]$_4$[TCTA]$_8$TC**C**ATCTA	Brinkmann et al. (1996b)
13 (c)	135 bp	164 bp	TCTA[TCTA]$_4$[TCTA]$_8$TC**T**ATCTA	Brinkmann et al. (1996b)
13 (d)	135 bp	164 bp	TCTA[TCTA]$_3$[TCTA]$_9$	Cruz et al. (2004)
14 (a)	139 bp	168 bp	TCTA[TCTG]$_4$[TCTA]$_9$	Brinkmann et al. (1996b)
14 (b)	139 bp	168 bp	TCTA TCTG TCTA[TCTG]$_4$[TCTA]$_3$ TCCA[TCTA]$_3$	Brinkmann et al. (1996b)
14 (c)	139 bp	168 bp	TCTA [TCTG]$_5$[TCTA]$_3$TCCA[TCTA]$_3$	Lins et al. (1998)
14 (d)	139 bp	168 bp	TCTA[TCTA]$_3$[TCTA]$_{10}$	Cruz et al. (2004)
15 (a)	143 bp	172 bp	TCTA[TCTG]$_4$[TCTA]$_{10}$	Brinkmann et al. (1996b)
15 (b)	143 bp	172 bp	TCTA[TCTG]$_3$[TCTA]$_{11}$	Brinkmann et al. (1996b)
15.2	145 bp	174 bp	[TCTA]$_2$[TCTG]$_4$[TCTA]$_5$T–A[TCTA]$_4$	Gill et al. (1995)
16 (a)	147 bp	176 bp	TCTA[TCTG]$_4$[TCTA]$_{11}$	Brinkmann et al. (1996b)
16 (b)	147 bp	176 bp	TCTA[TCTG]$_3$[TCTA]$_{12}$	Brinkmann et al. (1996b)
16.1	148 bp	177 bp	Not published	STRBase
17	151 bp	180 bp	TCTA[TCTG]$_4$[TCTA]$_{12}$	Brinkmann et al. (1996b)
18 (a)	155 bp	184 bp	TCTA[TCTG]$_4$[TCTA]$_{13}$	Brinkmann et al. (1996b)
18 (b)	155 bp	184 bp	TCTA[TCTG]$_5$[TCTA]$_{12}$	Brinkmann et al. (1996b)
18.1	156 bp	185 bp	TCTA[TCTG]$_4$[TCTA]$_{12}$A(TCTA)	Kido et al. (2003)
18.2	157 bp	186 bp	Not published	SGM Plus
18.3	158 bp	187 bp	TCTA[TCTG]$_4$[TCTA]$_{11}$TCA[TCTA]$_2$	Dauber et al. (2008)
19 (a)	159 bp	188 bp	TCTA[TCTG]$_4$[TCTA]$_{14}$	Brinkmann et al. (1996b)
19 (b)	159 bp	188 bp	TCTA[TCTG]$_5$[TCTA]$_{13}$	Cruz et al. (2004)
19.2	161 bp	190 bp	Not published	SGM Plus
20 (a)	163 bp	192 bp	TCTA[TCTG]$_4$[TCTA]$_{15}$	Brinkmann et al. (1996b)
20 (b)	163 bp	192 bp	TCTA[TCTG]$_3$[TCTA]$_{16}$	Cruz et al. (2004)

(Continued)

VWA (*Continued*)

Allele (Repeat #)	Promega PP 16	ABI Identifiler	Repeat Structure $TCTA[TCTG]_{3–4}[TCTA]_n$	Reference
21 (a)	167bp	196bp	$TCTA[TCTG]_4[TCTA]_{16}$	Brinkmann et al. (1996b)
21 (b)	167bp	196bp	$TCTA[TCTG]_5[TCTA]_{15}$	Cruz et al. (2004)
21 (c)	167bp	196bp	$TCTA[TCTG]_6[TCTA]_{14}$	Cruz et al. (2004)
22 (a)	171bp	200bp	$TCTA[TCTG]_4[TCTA]_{17}$	Brinkmann et al. (1996b)
22 (b)	171bp	200bp	$TCTA[TCTG]_5[TCTA]_{16}$	Cruz et al. (2004)
23	175bp	204bp	Not published	SGM Plus
24	179bp	208bp	Not published	STRBase
25	183bp	212bp	Not published	STRBase

36 observed alleles

D3S1358

GenBank Accession: AC099539 (allele 16). PCR product sizes of observed alleles

Allele (Repeat #)	Promega PowerPlex 16	ABI Identifiler	Repeat Structure TCTA[TCTG]$_{2-3}$[TCTA]$_n$	Reference
6	91bp	89bp	Not published	Phillips et al. (2011)
8	99bp	97bp	Not published	STRBase
8.3	102bp	100bp	Not published	STRBase
9	103bp	101bp	Not published	Allor et al. (2005)
10	107bp	105bp	Not published	STRBase
11 (a)	111bp	109bp	TCTA[TCTG]$_3$[TCTA]$_7$	Heinrich et al. (2005)
11 (b)	111bp	109bp	TCTA[TCTG]$_2$[TCTA]$_8$	Dauber et al. (2009)
12	115bp	113bp	TCTA[TCTG]$_3$[TCTA]$_8$	Heinrich et al. (2005)
13	119bp	117bp	TCTA[TCTG]$_2$[TCTA]$_{10}$	Mornhinweg et al. (1998)
13.3	122bp	120bp	Not published	STRBase
14	123bp	121bp	TCTA[TCTG]$_2$[TCTA]$_{11}$	Szibor et al. (1998)
14.2	125bp	123bp	Not published	STRBase
14.3	126bp	124bp	Not published	STRBase
15 (a)	127bp	125bp	TCTA[TCTG]$_3$[TCTA]$_{11}$	Szibor et al. (1998)
15 (b)	127bp	125bp	TCTA[TCTG]$_2$[TCTA]$_{12}$	Szibor et al. (1998)
15 (c)	127bp	125bp	TCTA[TCTG]$_1$[TCTA]$_{13}$	Heinrich et al. (2005)
15.1	128bp	126bp	TCTA[TCTG]A[TCTA]$_{13}$	Allor et al. (2005)
15.2	129bp	127bp	TCTA[TCTG]$_3$TC [TCTA]$_{11}$	Heinrich et al. (2005)
15.3	130bp	128bp	Not published	STRBase
16 (a)	131bp	129bp	TCTA[TCTG]$_3$[TCTA]$_{12}$	Szibor et al. (1998)
16 (b)	131bp	129bp	TCTA[TCTG]$_2$[TCTA]$_{13}$	Mornhinweg et al. (1998)
16 (c)	131bp	129bp	TCTA[TCTG]$_1$[TCTA]$_{14}$	Heinrich et al. (2005)
16.2	133bp	131bp	Not published	Budowle et al. (1997)
17 (a)	135bp	133bp	TCTA[TCTG]$_3$[TCTA]$_{13}$	Szibor et al. (1998)
17 (b)	135bp	133bp	TCTA[TCTG]$_2$[TCTA]$_{14}$	Mornhinweg et al. (1998)
17 (c)	135bp	133bp	TCTA[TCTG]$_1$[TCTA]$_{15}$	Heinrich et al. (2005)
17.1	136bp	134bp	Not published	Allor et al. (2005)
17.2	137bp	135bp	Not published	STRBase

(Continued)

D3S1358 (*Continued*)

Allele (Repeat #)	**Promega PowerPlex 16**	**ABI Identifiler**	**Repeat Structure TCTA[TCTG]$_{2-3}$[TCTA]$_n$**	**Reference**
18 (a)	139bp	137bp	TCTA[TCTG]$_4$[TCTA]$_{13}$	Heinrich et al. (2005)
18 (b)	139bp	137bp	TCTA[TCTG]$_3$[TCTA]$_{14}$	Szibor et al. (1998)
18 (c)	139bp	137bp	TCTA[TCTG]$_2$[TCTA]$_{15}$	Heinrich et al. (2005)
18.1	140bp	138bp	Not published	STRBase
18.2	141bp	139bp	Not published	STRBase
18.3	142bp	140bp	Not published	STRBase
19 (a)	143bp	141bp	TCTA[TCTG]$_3$[TCTA]$_{15}$	Mornhinweg et al. (1998)
19 (b)	143bp	141bp	TCTA[TCTG]$_2$[TCTA]$_{16}$	Heinrich et al. (2005)
20 (a)	147bp	145bp	TCTA[TCTG]$_3$[TCTA]$_{16}$	Mornhinweg et al. (1998)
20 (b)	147bp	145bp	TCTA[TCTG]$_2$[TCTA]$_{17}$	Heinrich et al. (2005)
20.1	148bp	146bp	Not published	Allor et al. (2005)
21	151bp	149bp	TCTA[TCTG]$_3$[TCTA]$_{17}$	Heinrich et al. (2005)
21.1	152bp	150bp	Not published	STRBase
22	155bp	153bp	TCTA[TCTG]$_3$[TCTA]$_4$TCTG [TCTA]$_{13}$	A. Raziel (unpublished)
23	159bp	157bp	TCTA[TCTG]$_3$[TCTA]$_{19}$	Kline et al. (2010)
26	171bp	169bp	TCTA[TCTG]$_3$[TCTA]$_9$ [TCTG]$_2$[TCTA]$_{11}$	Grubwieser et al. (2005)

44 observed alleles

D5S818

GenBank Accession: AC008512 (allele 11). PCR product sizes of observed alleles

Allele (Repeat #)	Promega PowerPlex 16	ABI Identifiler	Repeat Structure $[AGAT]_n$	Reference
4	107bp	122bp	Not published	STRBase; Cho et al. (2010)
5	111bp	126bp	Not published	STRBase
6	115bp	130bp	Not published	STRBase; Cho et al. (2010)
7	119bp	134bp	$[AGAT]_7$	Lins et al. (1998)
8	123bp	138bp	$[AGAT]_8$	Lins et al. (1998)
9	127bp	142bp	$[AGAT]_9$	Lins et al. (1998)
10	131bp	146bp	$[AGAT]_{10}$	Lins et al. (1998)
10.1	132bp	147bp	A $[AGAT]_{10}$	Kline et al. (2010)
11	135bp	150bp	$[AGAT]_{11}$	Lins et al. (1998)
11 (D55G→T)	135bp	150bp	$[AGAT]_{11}$ with G→T 55bp downstream	Jiang et al. (2011)
11.1	136bp	151bp	Not published	STRBase
11.3	138bp	153bp	Not published	STRBase
12	139bp	154bp	$[AGAT]_{12}$	Lins et al. (1998)
12.1	140bp	155bp	Not published	STRBase
12.3	142bp	157bp	$[AGAT]_3$ GAT $[AGAT]_9$	Allor et al. (2005)
13	143bp	158bp	$[AGAT]_{13}$	Lins et al. (1998)
13.3	146bp	161bp	Not published	STRBase
14	147bp	162bp	$[AGAT]_{14}$	Lins et al. (1998)
15	151bp	166bp	$[AGAT]_{15}$	Lins et al. (1998)
16	155bp	170bp	$[AGAT]_{16}$	Profiler Plus
17	159bp	174bp	Not published	STRBase
18	163bp	178bp	$[AGAT]_{14}$ ACAT $[AGAT]_3$	Allor et al. (2005)
20	171bp	186bp	Not published	STRBase
29	207bp	222bp	$[AGAT]_{12}$ {48bp} $[AGAT]_5$	Kline et al. (2010)

24 observed alleles

D7S820

GenBank Accession: AC004848 (allele 13). PCR product sizes of observed alleles

Allele (Repeat #)	Promega PowerPlex 16	ABI Identifiler	Repeat Structure $[GATA]_n$	Reference
5	211 bp	253 bp	Not published	STRBase; Cho et al. (2010)
5.2 or **9(D41-14 bp-del)**	213 bp	255 bp	$[GATA]_9$ with 14 bp deletion 41 bp downstream	Allor et al. (2005)
6	215 bp	257 bp	$[GATA]_6$	Lins et al. (1998)
6.2	217 bp	259 bp	Not published	STRBase
6.3 or 7(D14Tdel)	218 bp	260 bp	$[GATA]_7$ with T deletion 14 bp downstream	Kline et al. (2010)
7	219 bp	261 bp	$[GATA]_7$	Lins et al. (1998)
7.1	220 bp	262 bp	Not published	STRBase
7.3	222 bp	264 bp	Not published	Ayres et al. (2002)
8	223 bp	265 bp	$[GATA]_8$	Lins et al. (1998)
8.1	224 bp	266 bp	Not published	Balamurugan et al. (2000)
8.2	225 bp	267 bp	Not published	STRBase
8.3	226 bp	268 bp	$[GATA]_9$ with A deletion 22 bp downstream	Kline et al. (2010)
9	227 bp	269 bp	$[GATA]_9$	Lins et al. (1998)
9.1	228 bp	270 bp	Not published	Ayres et al. (2002)
9.2	229 bp	271 bp	Not published	STRBase
9.3	230 bp	272 bp	Not published	Huel et al. (2007)
10	231 bp	273 bp	$[GATA]_{10}$	Lins et al. (1998)
10.1 or **10(U1Ains)**	232 bp	274 bp	A $[GATA]_{10}$	Kline et al. (2010)
10.3	234 bp	276 bp	Not published	Allor et al. (2005)
11	235 bp	277 bp	$[GATA]_{11}$	Lins et al. (1998)
11.1	236 bp	278 bp	Not published	Huel et al. (2007)
11.2	237 bp	279 bp	Not published	STRBase
11.3	238 bp	280 bp	Not published	Allor et al. (2005)
12	239 bp	281 bp	$[GATA]_{12}$	Lins et al. (1998)
12.1	240 bp	282 bp	Not published	Allor et al. (2005)
12.2	241 bp	283 bp	Not published	STRBase
12.3	242 bp	284 bp	Not published	STRBase

(Continued)

D7S820 (*Continued*)

Allele (Repeat #)	**Promega PowerPlex 16**	**ABI Identifiler**	**Repeat Structure $[GATA]_n$**	**Reference**
13	243bp	285bp	$[GATA]_{13}$	Lins et al. (1998)
13.1	244bp	286bp	Not published	Allor et al. (2005)
14	247bp	289bp	$[GATA]_{14}$	Lins et al. (1998)
14.1	248bp	290bp	Not published	STRBase
15	251bp	293bp	Not published	Huel et al. (2007)
16	255bp	297bp	Not published	Ayres et al. (2002)

33 observed alleles

D8S1179 (listed as D6S502 in early papers)
GenBank Accession: AF216671 (allele 13). PCR product sizes of observed alleles

Allele (Repeat #)	Promega PowerPlex 16	ABI Identifiler	Repeat Structure $[TCTR]_n$	Reference
6	199bp	119bp	Not published	STRBase
7	203bp	123bp	$[TCTA]_7$	Griffiths et al. (1998)
8	207bp	127bp	$[TCTA]_8$	Barber & Parkin (1996)
9	211bp	131bp	$[TCTA]_9$	Barber & Parkin (1996)
10	215bp	135bp	$[TCTA]_{10}$	Barber & Parkin (1996)
10.1	216bp	136bp	Not published	STRBase
10.2	217bp	137bp	Not published	STRBase
11	219bp	139bp	$[TCTA]_{11}$	Barber & Parkin (1996)
12	223bp	143bp	$[TCTA]_{12}$	Barber & Parkin (1996)
12.1	224bp	144bp	Not published	STRBase
12.2	225bp	145bp	Not published	STRBase
12.3	226bp	146bp	Not published	STRBase
13 (a)	227bp	147bp	$[TCTA]_1[TCTG]_1[TCTA]_{11}$	Barber & Parkin (1996)
13 (b)	227bp	147bp	$[TCTA]_2[TCTG]_1[TCTA]_{10}$	Kline et al. (2010)
13 (c)	227bp	147bp	$[TCTA]_1[TCTG]_1$TGTA $[TCTA]_{10}$	Kline et al. (2010)
13 (d)	227bp	147bp	$[TCTA]_{13}$	Kline et al. (2010)
13.1	228bp	148bp	Not published	STRBase
13.2	229bp	149bp	Not published	STRBase
13.3	230bp	150bp	Not published	STRBase
14	231bp	151bp	$[TCTA]_2[TCTG]_1[TCTA]_{11}$	Barber & Parkin (1996)
14.1	232bp	152bp	Not published	STRBase
14.2	233bp	153bp	Not published	STRBase
15	235bp	155bp	$[TCTA]_2[TCTG]_1[TCTA]_{12}$	Barber & Parkin (1996)
15.1	236bp	156bp	Not published	STRBase
15.2	237bp	157bp	Not published	STRBase
15.3	238bp	158bp	Not published	STRBase
16	239bp	159bp	$[TCTA]_2[TCTG]_1[TCTA]_{13}$	Barber & Parkin (1996)
16.1	240bp	160bp	Not published	STRBase
17	243bp	163bp	$[TCTA]_2[TCTG]_2[TCTA]_{13}$	Barber & Parkin (1996)

(Continued)

D8S1179 (*Continued*)

Allele (Repeat #)	Promega PowerPlex 16	ABI Identifiler	Repeat Structure $[TCTR]_n$	Reference
17.1	244 bp	164 bp	Not published	STRBase
17.2	245 bp	165 bp	Not published	STRBase
18	247 bp	167 bp	$[TCTA]_2[TCTG]_1[TCTA]_{15}$	Barber & Parkin (1996)
19	251 bp	171 bp	$[TCTA]_2[TCTG]_2[TCTA]_{15}$	Griffiths et al. (1998)
20	255 bp	175 bp	Not published	STRBase

34 observed alleles

D13S317

GenBank Accession: AL353628 (allele 11). PCR product sizes of observed alleles

Allele (Repeat #)	Promega PowerPlex 16	ABI Identifiler*	Repeat Structure $[TATC]_n$	Reference
5	157bp	193bp	Not published	Allor et al. (2005)
6	161bp	197bp	Not published	Allor et al. (2005)
7	165bp	201bp	$[TATC]_7$	Lins et al. (1998)
7.1	166bp	202bp	Not published	Allor et al. (2005)
8	169bp	205bp	$[TATC]_8$	Lins et al. (1998)
8.1	170bp	206bp	Not published	STRBase
9	173bp	209bp	$[TATC]_9$	Lins et al. (1998)
9.1	174bp	210bp	Not published	STRBase
10 (a)	177bp	213bp	$[TATC]_{10}$	Lins et al. (1998)
10 (b)	177bp	213bp	$[TATC]_{10}$ AATC	Lins et al. (1998)
10.3	180bp	216bp	Not published	STRBase
11	181bp	217bp	$[TATC]_{11}$	Lins et al. (1998)
11.1	182bp	218bp	Not published	STRBase
11.3	184bp	220bp	Not published	STRBase
12	185bp	221bp	$[TATC]_{12}$	Lins et al. (1998)
13	189bp	225bp	$[TATC]_{13}$	Lins et al. (1998)
13.3	192bp	228bp	Not published	STRBase
14	193bp	229bp	$[TATC]_{14}$	Lins et al. (1998)
14.3	196bp	232bp	Not published	STRBase
15	197bp	233bp	$[TATC]_{15}$	Lins et al. (1998)
16	201bp	237bp	Not published	Huel et al. (2007)
17	205bp	241bp	Not published	Huel et al. (2007)

22 observed alleles

**Mobility modified PCR products so observed size will not equal expected DNA sequence size*

D16S539

GenBank Accession: AC024591 (allele 11). PCR product sizes of observed alleles

Allele (Repeat #)	Promega PowerPlex 16	ABI Identifiler*	Repeat Structure $[GATA]_n$	Reference
4	260bp	248bp	Not published	STRBase
5	264bp	252bp	$[GATA]_5$	Lins et al. (1998)
6	268bp	256bp	$[GATA]_6$	STRBase
7	272bp	260bp	$[GATA]_7$	STRBase
8	276bp	264bp	$[GATA]_8$	Lins et al. (1998)
8.3	279bp	267bp	Not published	STRBase
9	280bp	268bp	$[GATA]_9$	Lins et al. (1998)
9.3	283bp	271bp	Not published	STRBase
10	284bp	272bp	$[GATA]_{10}$	Lins et al. (1998)
10.1	285bp	273bp	Not published	STRBase
10.3	287bp	275bp	Not published	STRBase
11	288bp	276bp	$[GATA]_{11}$	Lins et al. (1998)
11.1	289bp	277bp	Not published	STRBase
11.3	291bp	279bp	Not published	STRBase
12	292bp	280bp	$[GATA]_{12}$	Lins et al. (1998)
12.1	293bp	281bp	Not published	Huel et al. (2007)
12.2	294bp	282bp	Not published	STRBase
12.3	295bp	283bp	Not published	STRBase
13	296bp	284bp	$[GATA]_{13}$	Lins et al. (1998)
13.1	297bp	285bp	Not published	STRBase
13.2	298bp	286bp	Not published	STRBase
13.3	299bp	287bp	Not published	STRBase
14	300bp	288bp	$[GATA]_{14}$	Lins et al. (1998)
14.1	301bp	289bp	Not published	STRBase
14.2	302bp	290bp	Not published	STRBase
14.3	303bp	291bp	Not published	STRBase
15	304bp	292bp	$[GATA]_{15}$	Lins et al. (1998)
16	308bp	296bp	Not published	Huel et al. (2007)
17	312bp	300bp	Not published	STRBase

29 observed alleles

**Mobility modified PCR products so observed size will not equal expected DNA sequence size*

D18S51

GenBank Accession: AP001534 (allele 18). PCR product sizes of observed alleles

Allele (Repeat #)	Promega PP 16	ABI Identifiler	Repeat Structure $[AGAA]_n$ 3′ flanking region	Reference
5.3 or **8(D1–9 bp-del)**	281 bp	259 bp	$[AGAA]_8$ immediate downstream deletion of (AAAGAGAGA)	Kline et al. (2010)
6	282 bp	260 bp	Not published	STRBase
7	286 bp	264 bp	Not published	Allor et al. (2005)
8	290 bp	268 bp	$[AGAA]_8$	Griffiths et al. (1998)
9	294 bp	272 bp	$[AGAA]_9$	Barber & Parkin (1996)
9.2*	296 bp	274 bp	Not published	STRBase
10	298 bp	276 bp	$[AGAA]_{10}$	Barber & Parkin (1996)
10.2	300 bp	278 bp	Not published	SGM Plus
11	302 bp	280 bp	$[AGAA]_{11}$	Barber & Parkin (1996)
11.1**	303 bp	281 bp	Not published	STRBase
11.2	304 bp	282 bp	$[AGAA]_{12}$ with AG deletion in 3′ flanking region	Dauber et al. (2008)
11.3	305 bp	283 bp	Not published	STRBase
12	306 bp	284 bp	$[AGAA]_{12}$	Barber & Parkin (1996)
12.2	308 bp	286 bp	Not published	Allor et al. (2005)
12.3	309 bp	287 bp	Not published	STRBase
13	310 bp	288 bp	$[AGAA]_{13}$	Barber & Parkin (1996)
13.1	311 bp	289 bp	Not published	STRBase; Phillips et al. (2011)
13.2	312 bp	290 bp	$[AGAA]_{13}$ [AGAG]AG	Barber & Parkin (1996)
13.3 or **14(D76Adel)**	313 bp	291 bp	$[AGAA]_{14}$ with A deletion 76 bp downstream	Allor et al. (2005)
14	314 bp	292 bp	$[AGAA]_{14}$	Barber & Parkin (1996)
14.1	315 bp	293 bp	Not published	STRBase
14.2	316 bp	294 bp	$[AGAA]_{14}$ [AGAG]AG	Barber & Parkin (1996)
15	318 bp	296 bp	$[AGAA]_{15}$	Barber & Parkin (1996)
15.1	319 bp	297 bp	Not published	STRBase
15.2	320 bp	298 bp	$[AGAA]_{15}$ [AGAG]AG	Barber & Parkin (1996)
15.3	321 bp	299 bp	Not published	STRBase
16	322 bp	300 bp	$[AGAA]_{16}$	Barber & Parkin (1996)
16.1	323 bp	301 bp	$[AGAA]_3$**A**$[AGAA]_{13}$	Allor et al. (2005)

(Continued)

D18S51 (*Continued*)

Allele (Repeat #)	**Promega PP 16**	**ABI Identifiler**	**Repeat Structure [AGAA]$_n$ 3′ flanking region**	**Reference**
16.2	324bp	302bp	$[AGAA]_{16}$ [AGAG]AG	Dauber et al. (2009)
16.3	325bp	303bp	Not published	STRBase
17	326bp	304bp	$[AGAA]_{17}$	Barber & Parkin (1996)
17.1	327bp	305bp	Not published	SGM Plus
17.2	328bp	306bp	$[AGAA]_{17}$ [AGAG]AG	Gill et al. (1996)
17.3	329bp	307bp	Not published	Allor et al. (2005)
18	330bp	308bp	$[AGAA]_{18}$	Barber & Parkin (1996)
18.1	331bp	309bp	Not published	Allor et al. (2005)
18.2	332bp	310bp	Not published	STRBase
18.3	333bp	311bp	Not published	STRBase
19	334bp	312bp	$[AGAA]_{19}$	Barber & Parkin (1996)
19.1	335bp	313bp	Not published	STRBase
19.2	336bp	314bp	$[AGAA]_{19}$ [AGAG]AG	Gill et al. (1996)
20	338bp	316bp	$[AGAA]_{20}$	Barber & Parkin (1996)
20.1	339bp	317bp	$[AGAA]_{20}$ AAAAG	Dauber et al. (2009)
20.2	340bp	318bp	Not published	Allor et al. (2005)
21	342bp	320bp	$[AGAA]_{21}$	Barber & Parkin (1996)
21.1	343bp	321bp	Not published	STRBase
21.2	344bp	322bp	Not published	Allor et al. (2005)
22	346bp	324bp	$[AGAA]_{22}$	Barber & Parkin (1996)
22.1	347bp	325bp	Not published	STRBase
22.2	348bp	327bp	Not published	STRBase
23	350bp	328bp	$[AGAA]_{23}$	Barber & Parkin (1996)
23.1	351bp	329bp	Not published	SGM Plus
23.2	352bp	330bp	Not published	STRBase
24	354bp	332bp	$[AGAA]_{24}$	Barber & Parkin (1996)
24.2	356bp	334bp	Not published	STRBase
25	358bp	336bp	$[AGAA]_{25}$	Barber & Parkin (1996)
26	362bp	340bp	$[AGAA]_{26}$	Barber & Parkin (1996)
27	366bp	344bp	$[AGAA]_{27}$	Barber & Parkin (1996)
28	370bp	348bp	$[AGAA]_{28}$	Morales-Valverde et al. (2009)

(*Continued*)

D18S51 (*Continued*)

Allele (Repeat #)	**Promega PP 16**	**ABI Identifiler**	**Repeat Structure $[AGAA]_n$ 3′ flanking region**	**Reference**
28.1	371 bp	349 bp	Not published	Allor et al. (2005)
28.3	373 bp	351 bp	Not published	STRBase
29	374 bp	352 bp	$[AGAA]_{29}$	Morales-Valverde et al. (2009)
29.3	377 bp	355 bp	Not published	STRBase
30	378 bp	356 bp	$[AGAA]_{30}$	Morales-Valverde et al. (2009)
31	382 bp	360 bp	$[AGAA]_{31}$	Morales-Valverde et al. (2009)
32	386 bp	364 bp	$[AGAA]_{32}$	Morales-Valverde et al. (2009)
33	390 bp	368 bp	$[AGAA]_{33}$	Morales-Valverde et al. (2009)
34	394 bp	372 bp	$[AGAA]_{34}$	Morales-Valverde et al. (2009)
35	398 bp	376 bp	$[AGAA]_{35}$	Morales-Valverde et al. (2009)
36	402 bp	380 bp	$[AGAA]_{36}$	Morales-Valverde et al. (2009)
37	406 bp	384 bp	$[AGAA]_{37}$	Morales-Valverde et al. (2009)
38	410 bp	388 bp	$[AGAA]_{38}$	Morales-Valverde et al. (2009)
40	418 bp	396 bp	$[AGAA]_{40}$	Morales-Valverde et al. (2009)

73 observed alleles

**x.2 alleles involve a replacement of the 3′ flanking sequence AAAG with [AGAG]AG (see Dauber et al. 2009)*

***x.1 alleles involve a replacement of the 3′ flanking sequence AAAG with AAAAG (see Dauber et al. 2009)*

D21S11

GenBank Accession: AP000433 (allele 29.1). PCR product sizes of observed alleles

Allele (Repeat #)	Promega PP16	ABI Identifiler	Repeat Structure [TCTA]$_n$[TCTG]$_n${[TCTA]$_3$TA[TCTA]$_3$TCA [TCTA]$_2$TCCATA} [TCTA]$_n$ TA TCTA	Reference
12	155bp	138bp	Not published	Ayres et al. (2002)
24	203bp	186bp	[TCTA]$_4$[TCTG]$_6${43bp}[TCTA]$_6$	Griffiths et al. (1998)
24.2	205bp	188bp	[TCTA]$_5$[TCTG]$_6$ {[TCTA]$_3$ TCA [TCTA]$_2$ TCCA TA}[TCTA]$_9$	Griffiths et al. (1998)
24.3 or **28(D11–13bp-del)**	206bp	189bp	[TCTA]$_5$[TCTG]$_6${43bp}[TCTA]$_9$ with 13bp deletion 11bp downstream	Dauber et al. (2009)
25	207bp	190bp	[TCTA]$_4$[TCTG]$_3${43bp}[TCTA]$_{10}$	Schwartz et al. (1996)
25.2	209bp	192bp	[TCTA]$_5$[TCTG]$_6$ {[TCTA]$_3$ TCA [TCTA]$_2$ TCCA TA}[TCTA]$_{10}$	Griffiths et al. (1998)
25.3	210bp	193bp	Not published	Allor et al. (2005)
26	211bp	194bp	[TCTA]$_4$[TCTG]$_6${43bp}[TCTA]$_8$	Möller et al. (1994)
26.1	212bp	195bp	Not published	SGM Plus
26.2	213bp	196bp	Not published	STRBase
27 (a)	215bp	198bp	[TCTA]$_4$[TCTG]$_6${43bp}[TCTA]$_9$	Möller et al. (1994)
27 (b)	215bp	198bp	[TCTA]$_6$[TCTG]$_5${43bp}[TCTA]$_8$	Schwartz et al. (1996)
27 (c)	215bp	198bp	[TCTA]$_5$[TCTG]$_5${43bp}[TCTA]$_9$	Griffiths et al. (1998)
27.1	216bp	199bp	Not published	Allor et al. (2005)
27.2	217bp	200bp	Not published	STRBase
27.3	218bp	201bp	Not published	SGM Plus
28 (a)	219bp	202bp	[TCTA]$_4$[TCTG]$_6${43bp}[TCTA]$_{10}$	Möller et al. (1994)
28 (b)	219bp	202bp	[TCTA]$_5$[TCTG]$_6${43bp}[TCTA]$_9$	Zhou et al. (1997)
28.2 (a)	221bp	204bp	[TCTA]$_4$[TCTG]$_6${43bp}[TCTA]$_{10}$	Griffiths et al. (1998)
28.2 (b)	221bp	204bp	[TCTA]$_5$[TCTG]$_6${43bp}[TCTA]$_8$ TA TCTA	Zhou et al. (1997)
28.3	222bp	205bp	Not published	SGM Plus
29 (a)	223bp	206bp	[TCTA]$_4$[TCTG]$_6${43bp}[TCTA]$_{11}$	Griffiths et al. (1998)
29 (b)	223bp	206bp	[TCTA]$_6$[TCTG]$_5${43bp}[TCTA]$_{10}$	Zhou et al. (1997)
29.1	224bp	207bp	Not published	Allor et al. (2005)
29.2	225bp	208bp	[TCTA]$_5$[TCTG]$_5${43bp}[TCTA]$_{10}$ TA TCTA	Zhou et al. (1997)
29.3	226bp	209bp	Not published	Amorim et al. (2001)

(Continued)

D21S11 (*Continued*)

Allele (Repeat #)	Promega PP16	ABI Identifiler	Repeat Structure $[TCTA]_n[TCTG]_n\{[TCTA]_3TA[TCTA]_3TCA$ $[TCTA]_2TCCATA\}$ $[TCTA]_n$ TA TCTA	Reference
30 (a)	227bp	210bp	$[TCTA]_4[TCTG]_6\{43bp\}[TCTA]_{12}$	Schwartz et al. (1996)
30 (b)	227bp	210bp	$[TCTA]_5[TCTG]_6\{43bp\}[TCTA]_{11}$	Zhou et al. (1997)
30 (c)	227bp	210bp	$[TCTA]_6[TCTG]_5\{43bp\}[TCTA]_{11}$	Griffiths et al. (1998)
30 (d)	227bp	210bp	$[TCTA]_6[TCTG]_6\{43bp\}[TCTA]_{10}$	Brinkmann et al. (1996a)
30.1	228bp	211bp	Not published	SGM Plus
30.2 (a)	229bp	212bp	$[TCTA]_5[TCTG]_6\{43bp\}[TCTA]_{10}$ TA TCTA	Griffiths et al. (1998)
30.2 (b)	229bp	212bp	$[TCTA]_5[TCTG]_5\{43bp\}[TCTA]_{11}$ TA TCTA	Schwartz et al. (1996)
30.3	230bp	213bp	$[TCTA]_6[TCTG]_5\{43bp\}[TCTA]_5$ TCA $[TCTA]_6$	Tsuji et al. (2006)
31 (a)	231bp	214bp	$[TCTA]_5[TCTG]_6\{43bp\}[TCTA]_{12}$	Griffiths et al. (1998)
31 (b)	231bp	214bp	$[TCTA]_6[TCTG]_5\{43bp\}[TCTA]_{12}$	Möller et al. (1994)
31 (c)	231bp	214bp	$[TCTA]_6[TCTG]_6\{43bp\}[TCTA]_{11}$	Zhou et al. (1997)
31 (d)	231bp	214bp	$[TCTA]_7[TCTG]_5\{43bp\}[TCTA]_{11}$	Schwartz et al. (1996)
31.1	232bp	215bp	Not published	Allor et al. (2005)
31.2	233bp	216bp	$[TCTA]_5[TCTG]_6\{43bp\}[TCTA]_{11}$ TA TCTA	Griffiths et al. (1998)
31.3	234bp	217bp	Not published	SGM Plus
32 (a)	235bp	218bp	$[TCTA]_6[TCTG]_5\{43bp\}[TCTA]_{13}$	Griffiths et al. (1998)
32 (b)	235bp	218bp	$[TCTA]_5[TCTG]_6\{43bp\}[TCTA]_{13}$	Zhou et al. (1997)
32.1	236bp	219bp	Not published	Steinlechner et al. (2002)
32.2 (a)	237bp	220bp	$[TCTA]_5[TCTG]_6\{43bp\}[TCTA]_{12}$ TA TCTA	Griffiths et al. (1998)
32.2 (b)	237bp	220bp	$[TCTA]_4[TCTG]_6\{43bp\}[TCTA]_{13}$ TA TCTA	Brinkmann et al. (1996a)
32.2 (c)	237bp	220bp	$[TCTA]_5[TCTG]_6\{[TCTA]_2TA[TCTA]_3TCA$ $[TCTA]_2TCCATA\}$ $[TCTA]_{13}$ TATCTA	Brinkmann et al. (1996a)
32.3	238bp	221bp	Not published	SGM Plus
33	239bp	222bp	$[TCTA]_5[TCTG]_6\{43bp\}[TCTA]_{14}$	Zhou et al. (1997)
33.1	240bp	223bp	Not published	Steinlechner et al. (2002)
33.2 (a)	241bp	224bp	$[TCTA]_5[TCTG]_6\{43bp\}[TCTA]_{13}$ TA TCTA	Griffiths et al. (1998)
33.2 (b)	241bp	224bp	$[TCTA]_6[TCTG]_5\{43bp\}[TCTA]_{13}$ TA TCTA	Brinkmann et al. (1996a)
33.2 (c)	241bp	224bp	$[TCTA]_6[TCTG]_6\{43bp\}[TCTA]_{12}$ TA TCTA	Brinkmann et al. (1996a)

(Continued)

D21S11 (*Continued*)

Allele (Repeat #)	**Promega PP16**	**ABI Identifiler**	**Repeat Structure $[TCTA]_n[TCTG]_n\{[TCTA]_3TA[TCTA]_3TCA$ $[TCTA]_2TCCATA\}$ $[TCTA]_n$ TA TCTA**	**Reference**
33.3	242 bp	225 bp	$[TCTA]_5[TCTG]_6$\{43 bp\} $[TCTA]_8TCA[TCTA]_3TCA[TCTA]_2TA$ TCTA	Brinkmann et al. (1996a)
34 (a)	243 bp	226 bp	$[TCTA]_5[TCTG]_6$\{43 bp\}$[TCTA]_{15}$	Zhou et al. (1997)
34 (b)	243 bp	226 bp	$[TCTA]_{10}[TCTG]_5$\{43 bp\}$[TCTA]_{11}$	Brinkmann et al. (1996a)
34.1	244 bp	227 bp	Not published	Ayres et al. (2002)
34.2	245 bp	228 bp	$[TCTA]_5[TCTG]_6$\{43 bp\}$[TCTA]_{14}TATCTA$	Griffiths et al. (1998)
34.3	246 bp	229 bp	$[TCTA]_5[TCTG]_6$\{43 bp\} $[TCTA]_{10}TCA[TCTA]_4TATCTA$	Brinkmann et al. (1996a)
35 (a)	247 bp	230 bp	$[TCTA]_{10}[TCTG]_5$\{43 bp\}$[TCTA]_{12}$	Griffiths et al. (1998)
35 (b)	247 bp	230 bp	$[TCTA]_{11}[TCTG]_5$\{43 bp\}$[TCTA]_{11}$	Brinkmann et al. (1996a)
35.1	248 bp	231 bp	Not published	Steinlechner et al. (2002)
35.2	249 bp	232 bp	$[TCTA]_5[TCTG]_6$\{43 bp\}$[TCTA]_{15}$ TA TCTA	Zhou et al. (1997)
35.3	250 bp	233 bp	Not published	SGM Plus
36 (a)	251 bp	234 bp	$[TCTA]_{11}[TCTG]_5$\{43 bp\}$[TCTA]_{12}$	Griffiths et al. (1998)
36 (b)	251 bp	234 bp	$[TCTA]_{10}[TCTG]_5$\{43 bp\}$[TCTA]_{13}$	Brinkmann et al. (1996a)
36 (c)	251 bp	234 bp	$[TCTA]_{10}[TCTG]_6$\{43 bp\}$[TCTA]_{12}$	Brinkmann et al. (1996a)
36.1	252 bp	235 bp	Not published	Allor et al. (2005)
36.2	253 bp	236 bp	$[TCTA]_5[TCTG]_6$\{43 bp\}$[TCTA]_{16}$ TA TCTA	Zhou et al. (1997)
36.3	254 bp	237 bp	Not published	SGM Plus
37 (a)	255 bp	238 bp	$[TCTA]_{11}[TCTG]_5$\{43 bp\}$[TCTA]_{13}$	Griffiths et al. (1998)
37 (b)	255 bp	238 bp	$[TCTA]_9[TCTG]_{11}$\{43 bp\}$[TCTA]_{12}$	Brinkmann et al. (1996a)
37.2 (a)	257 bp	240 bp	$[TCTA]_7[TCTG]_{14}\{[TCTA]_3$ TCA $[TCTA]_2$ TCCA TA\}$[TCTA]_{12}$	Walsh et al. (2003)
37.2 (b)	257 bp	240 bp	$[TCTA]_9[TCTG]_{12}\{[TCTA]_3$ TCA $[TCTA]_2$ TCCA TA\}$[TCTA]_{12}$	Walsh et al. (2003)
37.2 (c)	257 bp	240 bp	$[TCTA]_9[TCTG]_{13}\{[TCTA]_3$ TCA $[TCTA]_2$ TCCA TA\}$[TCTA]_{11}$	Walsh et al. (2003)
37.2 (d)	257 bp	240 bp	$[TCTA]_{10}[TCTG]_{11}\{[TCTA]_3$ TCA $[TCTA]_2$ TCCA TA\}$[TCTA]_{12}$	Walsh et al. (2003)
37.2 (e)	257 bp	240 bp	$[TCTA]_{11}[TCTG]_{11}\{[TCTA]_3$ TCA $[TCTA]_2$ TCCA TA\}$[TCTA]_{11}$	Walsh et al. (2003)
38 (a)	259 bp	242 bp	$[TCTA]_{13}[TCTG]_5$\{43 bp\}$[TCTA]_{12}$	Griffiths et al. (1998)
38 (b)	259 bp	242 bp	$[TCTA]_9[TCTG]_{11}$\{43 bp\}$[TCTA]_{12}$	Brinkmann et al. (1996a)

(Continued)

D21S11 (*Continued*)

Allele (Repeat #)	Promega PP16	ABI Identifiler	Repeat Structure $[TCTA]_n[TCTG]_n\{[TCTA]_3TA[TCTA]_3TCA$ $[TCTA]_2TCCATA\}$ $[TCTA]_n$ TA TCTA	Reference
38 (c)	259 bp	242 bp	$[TCTA]_{10}[TCTG]_{11}\{43\,bp\}[TCTA]_{13}$	Brinkmann et al. (1996a)
38 (d)	259 bp	242 bp	$[TCTA]_{11}[TCTG]_{11}\{43\,bp\}[TCTA]_{11}$	Brinkmann et al. (1996a)
38.2 (a)	261 bp	244 bp	$[TCTA]_9[TCTG]_{12}\{[TCTA]_3$ TCA $[TCTA]_2$ TCCA TA$\}[TCTA]_{13}$	Walsh et al. (2003)
38.2 (b)	261 bp	244 bp	$[TCTA]_9[TCTG]_{13}\{[TCTA]_3$ TCA $[TCTA]_2$ TCCA TA$\}[TCTA]_{12}$	Walsh et al. (2003)
38.2 (c)	261 bp	244 bp	$[TCTA]_{10}[TCTG]_{11}\{[TCTA]_3$ TCA $[TCTA]_2$ TCCA TA$\}[TCTA]_{13}$	Walsh et al. (2003)
39	263 bp	246 bp	Not published	STRBase
39.2 (a)	265 bp	248 bp	$[TCTA]_{10}[TCTG]_{13}\{[TCTA]_3$ TCA $[TCTA]_2$ TCCA TA$\}[TCTA]_{12}$	Bagdonavicius et al. (2002); Walsh et al. (2003)
39.2 (b)	265 bp	248 bp	$[TCTA]_{11}[TCTG]_{12}\{[TCTA]_3$ TCA $[TCTA]_2$ TCCA TA$\}[TCTA]_{12}$	Bagdonavicius et al. (2002); Walsh et al. (2003)
40.2	269 bp	252 bp	Not published	Ayres et al. (2002)
41.2	273 bp	256 bp	$[TCTA]_{10}[TCTG]_{15}\{[TCTA]_3$ TCA $[TCTA]_2$ TCCA TA$\}[TCTA]_{12}$	Bagdonavicius et al. (2002); Walsh et al. (2003)
43.2	281 bp	264 bp	$[TCTA]_5[TCTG]_6\{[TCTA]_3$ TA $[TCTA]_3$ TCA $[TCTA]_2$ TCCA TA$\}[TCTA]_8$ TCA $[TCTA]_2$ TCCA TA$[TCTA]_{13}$ TA TCTA	Grubwieser et al. (2005)

90 observed alleles

D2S1338

GenBank Accession: AC010136 (allele 23). PCR product sizes of observed alleles

Allele (Repeat #)	Promega ESX 17	Promega ESI 17	ABI Identifiler*	Repeat Structure $[TGCC]_m[TTCC]_n$	Reference
10	197bp	223bp	287bp	$[TGCC]_4[TTCC]_6$	Heinrich et al. (2005)
11	201bp	227bp	291bp	Not published	STRBase
12 (a)	205bp	231bp	295bp	$[TGCC]_4[TTCC]_8$	Kline et al. (2010)
12 (b)	205bp	231bp	295bp	$[TGCC]_6[TTCC]_6$	Kline et al. (2010)
12.3	208bp	234bp	298bp	Not published	STRBase
13	209bp	235bp	299bp	$[TGCC]_6[TTCC]_7$	Kline et al. (2010)
14	213bp	239bp	303bp	Not published	STRBase
15	217bp	243bp	307bp	Not published	SGM Plus
16	221bp	247bp	311bp	Not published	SGM Plus
17	225bp	251bp	315bp	$[TGCC]_6[TTCC]_{11}$	Heinrich et al. (2005)
18	229bp	255bp	319bp	$[TGCC]_6[TTCC]_{12}$	Heinrich et al. (2005)
18.3	232bp	258bp	322bp	Not published	STRBase
19 (a)	233bp	259bp	323bp	$[TGCC]_8[TTCC]_{11}$	Heinrich et al. (2005)
19 (b)	233bp	259bp	323bp	$[TGCC]_7[TTCC]_{12}$	Heinrich et al. (2005)
19.1	234bp	260bp	324bp	Not published	STRBase
19.3	236bp	262bp	326bp	Not published	STRBase
20 (a)	237bp	263bp	327bp	$[TGCC]_7TCCC[TTCC]_{12}$	Heinrich et al. (2005)
20 (b)	237bp	263bp	327bp	$[TGCC]_7[TTCC]_{10}GTCC[TTCC]_2$	Heinrich et al. (2005)
20.1	238bp	264bp	328bp	Not published	STRBase
21	241bp	267bp	331bp	$[TGCC]_7[TTCC]_{11}GTCC[TTCC]_2$	Heinrich et al. (2005)
21.2	243bp	269bp	333bp	Not published	Montelius et al. (2008)
22	245bp	271bp	335bp	$[TGCC]_7[TTCC]_{12}GTCC[TTCC]_2$	Heinrich et al. (2005)
22.2	247bp	273bp	337bp	Not published	STRBase
22.3	248bp	274bp	338bp	Not published	STRBase
23 (a)	249bp	275bp	339bp	$[TGCC]_7[TTCC]_{13}GTCC[TTCC]_2$	Heinrich et al. (2005)
23 (b)	249bp	275bp	339bp	$[TGCC]_7[TTCC]_{13}GTCC\ [TTCC]_2$	GenBank allele
23.2	251bp	277bp	341bp	Not published	STRBase
23.3	252bp	278bp	342bp	$[TGCC]_7[TTCC]_4TTC[TTCC]_9GTCC[TTCC]_2$	Kline et al. (2010)
24	253bp	279bp	343bp	$[TGCC]_7[TTCC]_{14}GTCC[TTCC]_2$	Heinrich et al. (2005)
24.2	255bp	281bp	345bp	Not published	STRBase

(Continued)

D2S1338 (*Continued*)

Allele (Repeat #)	Promega ESX 17	Promega ESI 17	ABI Identifiler*	Repeat Structure $[TGCC]_m[TTCC]_n$	Reference
25	257bp	283bp	347bp	$[TGCC]_7[TTCC]_{15}GTCC[TTCC]_2$	Heinrich et al. (2005)
25.2	259bp	285bp	349bp	Not published	STRBase
25.3	260bp	286bp	350bp	Not published	STRBase
26 (a)	261bp	287bp	351bp	$[TGCC]_7[TTCC]_{16}GTCC[TTCC]_2$	Heinrich et al. (2005)
26 (b)	261bp	287bp	351bp	$[TGCC]_7[TTCC]_{19}$	Kline et al. (2010)
27	265bp	291bp	355bp	$[TGCC]_7[TTCC]_{17}GTCC[TTCC]_2$	Heinrich et al. (2005)
28	269bp	295bp	359bp	Not published	SGM Plus
29.3	276bp	302bp	366bp	Not published	STRBase
30.3	280bp	306bp	370bp	Not published	STRBase
31	281bp	307bp	371bp	$[TGCC]_7[TTCC]_6TTAC[TTCC]_{14}GTCC[TTCC]_2$	Kline et al. (2010)

40 observed alleles

**Mobility modified PCR products so observed size will not equal expected DNA sequence size*

D19S433

GenBank Accession: AC008507 (allele 14). PCR product sizes of observed alleles

Allele (Repeat #)	Promega ESX 17	Promega ESI 17	ABI Identifiler	Repeat Structure (AAGG)AAAG(AAGG) TAGG[AAGG]$_n$	Reference
5.2	193bp	163bp	92bp	Not published	STRBase
6.2	197bp	167bp	96bp	(AAGG)AA–(AAGG) TAGG[AAGG]$_5$	Heinrich et al. (2005)
7	199bp	169bp	98bp	Not published	STRBase
8	203bp	173bp	102bp	Not published	STRBase
8.1	204bp	174bp	103bp	Not published	STRBase
9	207bp	177bp	106bp	(AAGG)AAAG(AAGG) TAGG(AAGA)[AAGG]$_6$	Heinrich et al. (2005)
9.1	208bp	178bp	107bp	Not published	STRBase
10	211bp	181bp	110bp	(AAGG)AAAG(AAGG) TAGG[AAGG]$_8$	Heinrich et al. (2005)
10.1	212bp	182bp	111bp	Not published	STRBase
10.2	213bp	183bp	112bp	Not published	STRBase
11	215bp	185bp	114bp	(AAGG)AAAG(AAGG) TAGG[AAGG]$_9$	Heinrich et al. (2005)
11.1	216bp	186bp	115bp	(AAGG)AAAG(AAGG) TAGG(AAGG)A[AAGG]$_8$	Heinrich et al. (2005)
11.2	217bp	187bp	116bp	Not published	STRBase
12	219bp	189bp	118bp	(AAGG)AAAG(AAGG) TAGG[AAGG]$_{10}$	Heinrich et al. (2005)
12.1	220bp	190bp	119bp	(AAGG)AAAG(AAGG) TAGG[AAGG]$_5$A[AAGG]$_5$	Heinrich et al. (2005)
12.2	221bp	191bp	120bp	Not published	STRBase
13	223bp	193bp	122bp	(AAGG)AAAG(AAGG) TAGG[AAGG]$_{11}$	Heinrich et al. (2005)
13.1	224bp	194bp	123bp	Not published	STRBase
13.2	225bp	195bp	124bp	(AAGG)AA–(AAGG) TAGG[AAGG]$_{12}$	Heinrich et al. (2005)
13.3	226bp	196bp	125bp	Not published	STRBase
14	227bp	197bp	126bp	(AAGG)AAAG(AAGG) TAGG[AAGG]$_{12}$	Heinrich et al. (2005)
14.1	228bp	198bp	127bp	Not published	STRBase
14.2	229bp	199bp	128bp	Not published	STRBase
14.3	230bp	200bp	129bp	Not published	STRBase

(Continued)

D19S433 (*Continued*)

Allele (Repeat #)	Promega ESX 17	Promega ESI 17	ABI Identifiler	Repeat Structure (AAGG)AAAG(AAGG) TAGG[AAGG]$_n$	Reference
15	231 bp	201 bp	130 bp	(AAGG)AAAG(AAGG) TAGG[AAGG]$_{13}$	Heinrich et al. (2005)
15.2	233 bp	203 bp	132 bp	(AAGG)AA–(AAGG) TAGG[AAGG]$_{14}$	Heinrich et al. (2005)
16	235 bp	205 bp	134 bp	(AAGG)AAAG(AAGG) TAGG[AAGG]$_{14}$	Heinrich et al. (2005)
16.2	237 bp	207 bp	136 bp	(AAGG)AA–(AAGG) TAGG[AAGG]$_{15}$	Heinrich et al. (2005)
17	239 bp	209 bp	138 bp	(AAGG)AAAG(AAGG) TAGG[AAGG]$_{15}$	Heinrich et al. (2005)
17.2	241 bp	211 bp	140 bp	(AAGG)AA–(AAGG) TAGG[AAGG]$_{16}$	Heinrich et al. (2005)
18	243 bp	213 bp	142 bp	(AAGG)AAAG(AAGG) TAGG[AAGG]$_{16}$	Heinrich et al. (2005)
18.1	244 bp	214 bp	143 bp	Not published	STRBase
18.2	245 bp	215 bp	144 bp	Not published	STRBase
19	247 bp	217 bp	146 bp	Not published	STRBase
19.2	249 bp	219 bp	148 bp	AA–(AAGG)TAGG[AAGG]$_{18}$	M. Kline (unpublished)
20	251 bp	221 bp	150 bp	Not published	STRBase

36 observed alleles

Penta D

GenBank Accession: AP001752 (allele 13). PCR product sizes of observed alleles

Allele (Repeat #)	Promega PP16	Repeat Structure $[AAAGA]_n$	Reference
1.1	370 bp	Not published	STRBase
1.2	371 bp	Not published	STRBase
2.2	376 bp	$[AAAGA]_5$ (U13-13 bp-del)	Bacher et al. (1998)
3	379 bp	Not published	STRBase
3.2	381 bp	$[AAAGA]_5$ (U8-8 bp-del)	Bacher et al. (1998)
4	384 bp	Not published	STRBase
4.1	385 bp	Not published	STRBase
5	389 bp	$[AAAGA]_5$	Krenke et al. (2002)
5.4	393 bp	Not published	STRBase
6	394 bp	$[AAAGA]_6$	Kline et al. (2010)
6.4	398 bp	Not published	STRBase
7	399 bp	$[AAAGA]_7$	Krenke et al. (2002)
7.1	400 bp	Not published	STRBase
7.4	403 bp	$[AAAGA]_8$ (U1A-del)	Kline et al. (2010)
8	404 bp	$[AAAGA]_8$	Krenke et al. (2002)
8.1	405 bp	Not published	STRBase
8.2	406 bp	$[AAAGA]_{11}$ (U13-13 bp-del)	Kline et al. (2010)
8.4	408 bp	Not published	STRBase
9	409 bp	$[AAAGA]_9$	Kline et al. (2010)
9.1	410 bp	Not published	STRBase
9.2	411 bp	$[AAAGA]_{10}$ (D128TAA-del)	Miozzo et al. (2007)
9.4	413 bp	Not published	STRBase
10	414 bp	$[AAAGA]_{10}$	Kline et al. (2010)
10.1	415 bp	Not published	STRBase
10.2	416 bp	Not published	STRBase
10.3	417 bp	Not published	STRBase
11	419 bp	$[AAAGA]_{11}$	Kline et al. (2010)
11.1	420 bp	Not published	STRBase
11.2	421 bp	Not published	Huel et al. (2007)

(Continued)

Penta D (*Continued*)

Allele (Repeat #)	**Promega PP16**	**Repeat Structure** $[AAAGA]_n$	**Reference**
11.3	422 bp	Not published	STRBase
11.4	423 bp	Not published	STRBase
12	424 bp	$[AAAGA]_{12}$	Krenke et al. (2002)
12.1	425 bp	Not published	Huel et al. (2007)
12.2	426 bp	Not published	Huel et al. (2007)
12.3	427 bp	Not published	STRBase
12.4	428 bp	Not published	STRBase
13	429 bp	$[AAAGA]_{13}$	Krenke et al. (2002)
13.2	431 bp	Not published	STRBase
13.3	432 bp	Not published	Bacher et al. (1998)
13.4	433 bp	Not published	STRBase
14	434 bp	$[AAAGA]_{14}$	Krenke et al. (2002)
14.1	435 bp	Not published	Huel et al. (2007)
14.4	438 bp	Not published	STRBase
15	439 bp	$[AAAGA]_{15}$	Krenke et al. (2002)
15.1	440 bp	Not published	STRBase
15.4	443 bp	Not published	STRBase
16	444 bp	$[AAAGA]_{16}$	Krenke et al. (2002)
17	449 bp	$[AAAGA]_{17}$	Krenke et al. (2002)
18	454 bp	$[AAAGA]_{18}$	Kline et al. (2010)
19	459 bp	$[AAAGA]_{19}$	Kline et al. (2010)

50 observed alleles

Penta E

GenBank Accession: AC027004 (allele 5). PCR product sizes of observed alleles

Allele (Repeat #)	Promega PP16	Repeat Structure $[AAAGA]_n$	Reference
5	379 bp	$[AAAGA]_5$	Krenke et al. (2002)
5.1	380 bp	Not published	STRBase
6	384 bp	$[AAAGA]_6$	Krenke et al. (2002)
7	389 bp	$[AAAGA]_7$	Krenke et al. (2002)
8	394 bp	$[AAAGA]_8$	Krenke et al. (2002)
9	399 bp	$[AAAGA]_9$	Krenke et al. (2002)
9.1	400 bp	Not published	STRBase
9.2	401 bp	Not published	STRBase
9.4	403 bp	Not published	STRBase
10	404 bp	$[AAAGA]_{10}$	Krenke et al. (2002)
10.1	405 bp	Not published	STRBase
10.2	406 bp	Not published	STRBase
11	409 bp	$[AAAGA]_{11}$	Krenke et al. (2002)
11.4	413 bp	Not published	STRBase
12	414 bp	$[AAAGA]_{12}$	Krenke et al. (2002)
12.1	415 bp	Not published	STRBase
12.2	416 bp	Not published	STRBase
12.3	417 bp	Not published	STRBase
13	419 bp	$[AAAGA]_{13}$	Krenke et al. (2002)
13.2	421 bp	Not published	STRBase
13.4	423 bp	Not published	STRBase
14	424 bp	$[AAAGA]_{14}$	Krenke et al. (2002)
14.2	426 bp	Not published	STRBase
14.4	428 bp	Not published	STRBase
15	429 bp	$[AAAGA]_{15}$	Krenke et al. (2002)
15.2	431 bp	Not published	STRBase
15.4	433 bp	Not published	STRBase
16	434 bp	$[AAAGA]_{16}$	Krenke et al. (2002)
16.2	436 bp	Not published	STRBase
16.4	438 bp	Not published	Huel et al. (2007)

(Continued)

Penta E (*Continued*)

Allele (Repeat #)	**Promega PP16**	**Repeat Structure $[AAAGA]_n$**	**Reference**
17	439bp	$[AAAGA]_{17}$	Krenke et al. (2002)
17.2	441bp	Not published	STRBase
17.4	443bp	Not published	Huel et al. (2007)
18	444bp	$[AAAGA]_{18}$	Krenke et al. (2002)
18.2	446bp	Not published	Huel et al. (2007)
18.4	448bp	$[AAAGA]_6AAAA[AAAGA]_{12}$	Mizuno et al. (2003)
19	449bp	$[AAAGA]_{19}$	Krenke et al. (2002)
19.2	451bp	Not published	STRBase
19.4	453bp	$[AAAGA]_6AAAA[AAAGA]_{13}$	Mizuno et al. (2003)
20	454bp	$[AAAGA]_{20}$	Krenke et al. (2002)
20.2	456bp	Not published	STRBase
21	459bp	$[AAAGA]_{21}$	Krenke et al. (2002)
22	464bp	$[AAAGA]_{22}$	Krenke et al. (2002)
23	469bp	$[AAAGA]_{23}$	Krenke et al. (2002)
23.4	473bp	Not published	STRBase
24	474bp	$[AAAGA]_{24}$	Krenke et al. (2002)
26	484bp	Not published	STRBase
26.2	486bp	Not published	STRBase
27	489bp	$[AAAGA]_{27}$	Kline et al. (2010)
29	499bp	$[AAAGA]_{29}$	Kline et al. (2010)
30	504bp	$[AAAGA]_{30}$	Kline et al. (2010)
31	509bp	$[AAAGA]_{31}$	Kline et al. (2010)
32	514bp	$[AAAGA]_{32}$	Kline et al. (2010)

53 observed alleles

D1S1656

GenBank Accession: G07820 (allele 15.3). PCR product sizes of observed alleles

Allele (Repeat #)	Promega ESX 17	Promega ESI 17	ABI NGM	Repeat Structure [TAGA]$_4$[TGA]$_{0-1}$ [TAGA]$_n$TAGG[TG]$_5$	Reference
8	133bp	222bp	171bp	[TAGA]$_8$[TG]$_5$	Phillips et al. (2011)
9	137bp	226bp	175bp	[TAGA]$_9$[TG]$_5$	Phillips et al. (2011)
10 (a)	141bp	230bp	179bp	[TAGA]$_{10}$[TG]$_5$	Lareu et al. (1998)
10 (b)	141bp	230bp	179bp	[TAGA]$_{10}$TAGG[TG]$_5$	Phillips et al. (2011)
11	145bp	234bp	183bp	[TAGA]$_{11}$[TG]$_5$	Lareu et al. (1998)
12 (a)	149bp	238bp	187bp	[TAGA]$_{12}$[TG]$_5$	Lareu et al. (1998)
12 (b)	149bp	238bp	187bp	[TAGA]$_{11}$TAGG[TG]$_5$	Lareu et al. (1998)
13 (a)	153bp	242bp	191bp	[TAGA]$_{12}$TAGG[TG]$_5$	Lareu et al. (1998)
13 (b)	153bp	242bp	191bp	[TAGA]$_{13}$[TG]$_5$	Phillips et al. (2011)
13.3	156bp	245bp	194bp	[TAGA]$_1$TGA[TAGA]$_{11}$TAGG[TG]$_5$	Phillips et al. (2011)
14 (a)	157bp	246bp	195bp	[TAGA]$_{13}$TAGG[TG]$_5$	Lareu et al. (1998)
14 (b)	157bp	246bp	195bp	[TAGA]$_{14}$[TG]$_5$	Phillips et al. (2011)
14.3	160bp	249bp	198bp	[TAGA]$_4$TGA[TAGA]$_9$TAGG[TG]$_5$	Phillips et al. (2011)
15	161bp	250bp	199bp	[TAGA]$_{14}$TAGG[TG]$_5$	Lareu et al. (1998)
15.3	164bp	253bp	202bp	[TAGA]$_4$TGA[TAGA]$_{10}$TAGG[TG]$_5$	Lareu et al. (1998)
16	165bp	254bp	203bp	[TAGA]$_{15}$TAGG[TG]$_5$	Lareu et al. (1998)
16.3	168bp	257bp	206bp	[TAGA]$_4$TGA[TAGA]$_{11}$TAGG[TG]$_5$	Lareu et al. (1998)
17	169bp	258bp	207bp	[TAGA]$_{16}$TAGG[TG]$_5$	Lareu et al. (1998)
17.1	170bp	259bp	208bp	Not published	Schröer et al. (2000)
17.3	172bp	261bp	210bp	[TAGA]$_4$TGA[TAGA]$_{12}$TAGG[TG]$_5$	Lareu et al. (1998)
18	173bp	262bp	211bp	[TAGA]$_{17}$TAGG[TG]$_5$	Phillips et al. (2011)
18.3	176bp	265bp	214bp	[TAGA]$_4$TGA[TAGA]$_{13}$TAGG[TG]$_5$	Lareu et al. (1998)
19	177bp	266bp	215bp	Not published	Asamura et al. (2008)
19.3	180bp	269bp	218bp	[TAGA]$_4$TGA[TAGA]$_{14}$TAGG[TG]$_5$	Lareu et al. (1998)
20.3	184bp	273bp	222bp	Not published	Gamero et al. (2000)

25 observed alleles

D2S441

GenBank Accession: AC079112 (allele 12). PCR product sizes of observed alleles

Allele (Repeat #)	Promega ESX 17	Promega ESI 17	ABI NGM	Repeat Structure $[TCTA]_4(TCA)_{0-1}[TCTA]_n [TTTA]_{0-1}[TCTA]_2$	Reference
8	88bp	347bp	76bp	$[TCTA]_8$	Coble & Butler (2005)
9	92bp	351bp	80bp	$[TCTA]_9$	Coble & Butler (2005)
9.1	93bp	352bp	81bp	$A[TCTA]_9$	Hill et al. (2010)
10 (a)	96bp	355bp	84bp	$[TCTA]_{10}$	Coble & Butler (2005)
10 (b)	96bp	355bp	84bp	$[TCTA]_5TCAA[TCTA]_4$	Phillips et al. (2011)
10 (c)	96bp	355bp	84bp	$[TCTA]_5TCAA[TCTA]_2$ TCTGTCTA	Phillips et al. (2011)
10 (d)	96bp	355bp	84bp	$[TCTA]_8$TCTGTCTA	Phillips et al. (2011)
11 (a)	100bp	359bp	88bp	$[TCTA]_{11}$	Coble & Butler (2005)
11 (b)	100bp	359bp	88bp	$[TCTA]_2TCAA[TCTA]_8$	Phillips et al. (2011)
11.3	103bp	362bp	91bp	$[TCTA]_4TCA[TCTA]_7$	Phillips et al. (2011)
12 (a)	104bp	363bp	92bp	$[TCTA]_{12}$	Coble & Butler (2005)
12 (b)	104bp	363bp	92bp	$[TCTA]_5TCAA[TCTA]_6$	Phillips et al. (2011)
12.3	107bp	366bp	95bp	$[TCTA]_4TCATCCA[TCTA]_7$	Phillips et al. (2011)
13	108bp	367bp	96bp	Not published	Coble & Butler (2005)
13.3	111bp	370bp	99bp	Not published	Coble & Butler (2005)
14 (a)	112bp	371bp	100bp	$[TCTA]_{11}TTTA[TCTA]_2$	Phillips et al. (2011)
14 (b)	112bp	371bp	100bp	$[TCTA]_5TCAA[TCTA]_5TTTA$ $[TCTA]_2$	Phillips et al. (2011)
14.3	115bp	374bp	103bp	Not published	Coble & Butler (2005)
15	116bp	375bp	104bp	Not published	Coble & Butler (2005)
16 (a)	120bp	379bp	108bp	$[TCTA]_{13}TTTA[TCTA]_2$	Phillips et al. (2011)
16 (b)	120bp	379bp	108bp	$[TCTA]_5TCAA[TCTA]_7TTTA$ $[TCTA]_2$	Phillips et al. (2011)
17	124bp	383bp	112bp	$[TCTA]_{14}TTTA[TCTA]_2$	Phillips et al. (2011)

22 observed alleles

D10S1248

GenBank Accession: AL391869 (allele 13). PCR product sizes of observed alleles

Allele (Repeat #)	Promega ESX 17	Promega ESI 17	ABI NGM	Repeat Structure $[GGAA]_n$	Reference
7	79bp	282bp	73bp	$[GGAA]_7$	Phillips et al. (2011)
8	83bp	286bp	77bp	$[GGAA]_8$	Coble & Butler (2005)
9	87bp	290bp	81bp	$[GGAA]_9$	Coble & Butler (2005)
10	91bp	294bp	85bp	$[GGAA]_{10}$	Coble & Butler (2005)
11	95bp	298bp	89bp	$[GGAA]_{11}$	Coble & Butler (2005)
12	99bp	302bp	93bp	$[GGAA]_{12}$	Coble & Butler (2005)
13	103bp	306bp	97bp	$[GGAA]_{13}$	Coble & Butler (2005)
14	107bp	310bp	101bp	$[GGAA]_{14}$	Coble & Butler (2005)
15	111bp	314bp	105bp	$[GGAA]_{15}$	Coble & Butler (2005)
16	115bp	318bp	109bp	$[GGAA]_{16}$	Coble & Butler (2005)
17	119bp	322bp	113bp	$[GGAA]_{17}$	Coble & Butler (2005)
18	123bp	326bp	117bp	$[GGAA]_{18}$	Coble & Butler (2005)
19	127bp	330bp	121bp	$[GGAA]_{19}$	Coble & Butler (2005)

13 observed alleles

D12S391

GenBank Accession: G08921 (allele 20). PCR product sizes of observed alleles

Allele (Repeat #)	Promega ESX 17	Promega ESI 17	ABI NGM	Repeat Structure $[AGAT]_n\{GAT\}_{0-1}(AGAC)_m[AGAT]_{0-1}$	Reference
13	126bp	287bp	226bp	Not published	Poetsch et al. (2011)
14	130bp	291bp	230bp	$[AGAT]_8(AGAC)_5$AGAT	Phillips et al. (2011)
15	134bp	295bp	234bp	$[AGAT]_8(AGAC)_6$AGAT	Lareu et al. (1996)
16	138bp	299bp	238bp	$[AGAT]_9(AGAC)_6$AGAT	Lareu et al. (1996)
17 (a)	142bp	303bp	242bp	$[AGAT]_{10}(AGAC)_6$AGAT	Lareu et al. (1996)
17 (b)	142bp	303bp	242bp	$[AGAT]_{11}(AGAC)_5$AGAT	Phillips et al. (2011)
17.1	143bp	304bp	243bp	Not published	Hill et al. (2010)
17.3	145bp	306bp	245bp	[AGAT]GAT$[AGAT]_8(AGAC)_7$AGAT	Phillips et al. (1998)
18	146bp	307bp	246bp	$[AGAT]_{11}(AGAC)_6$AGAT	Lareu et al. (1996)
18.1	147bp	308bp	247bp	Not published	Hill et al. (2010)
18.3	149bp	310bp	249bp	[AGAT]GAT$[AGAT]_9(AGAC)_7$AGAT	Phillips et al. (1998)
19	150bp	311bp	250bp	$[AGAT]_{12}(AGAC)_6$AGAT	Lareu et al. (1996)
19.1	151bp	312bp	251bp	Not published	Hill et al. (2010)
19.2	152bp	313bp	252bp	Not published	Berti et al. (2010)
19.3 (a)	153bp	314bp	253bp	[AGAT]GAT$[AGAT]_{10}(AGAC)_7$AGAT	Phillips et al. (1998)
19.3 (b)	153bp	314bp	253bp	$[AGAT]_5$GAT$[AGAT]_7(AGAC)_7$	Phillips et al. (1998)
19.3 (c)	153bp	314bp	253bp	$[AGAT]_5$GAT$[AGAT]_7(AGAC)_6$AGAT	Phillips et al. (2011)
20 (a)	154bp	315bp	254bp	$[AGAT]_{13}(AGAC)_6$AGAT	Lareu et al. (1996)
20 (b)	154bp	315bp	254bp	$[AGAT]_{11}(AGAC)_9$	Lareu et al. (1996)
20 (c)	154bp	315bp	254bp	$[AGAT]_{10}(AGAC)_9$AGAT	M. Kline (unpublished)
20 (d)	154bp	315bp	254bp	$[AGAT]_{12}(AGAC)_7$AGAT	M. Kline (unpublished)
20.1	155bp	316bp	255bp	Not published	Hill et al. (2010)
20.3	157bp	318bp	257bp	Not published	Phillips et al. (1998)
21 (a)	158bp	319bp	258bp	$[AGAT]_{14}(AGAC)_6$AGAT	Lareu et al. (1996)
21 (b)	158bp	319bp	258bp	$[AGAT]_{12}(AGAC)_9$	Lareu et al. (1996)
21 (c)	158bp	319bp	258bp	$[AGAT]_{12}(AGAC)_8$AGAT	Phillips et al. (2011)
21 (d)	158bp	319bp	258bp	$[AGAT]_{13}(AGAC)_7$AGAT	Phillips et al. (2011)
21 (e)	158bp	319bp	258bp	$[AGAT]_{11}(AGAC)_{10}$	M. Kline (unpublished)

(Continued)

D12S391 (*Continued*)

Allele (Repeat #)	Promega ESX 17	Promega ESI 17	ABI NGM	Repeat Structure $[AGAT]_n\{GAT\}_{0-1}(AGAC)_m[AGAT]_{0-1}$	Reference
22 (a)	162bp	323bp	262bp	$[AGAT]_{15}(AGAC)_6AGAT$	Lareu et al. (1996)
22 (b)	162bp	323bp	262bp	$[AGAT]_{12}(AGAC)_{10}$	Lareu et al. (1996)
22 (c)	162bp	323bp	262bp	$[AGAT]_{11}(AGAC)_{11}$	Phillips et al. (2011)
22 (d)	162bp	323bp	262bp	$[AGAT]_{13}(AGAC)_9$	M. Kline (unpublished)
22.2	164bp	325bp	264bp	Not published	Hill et al. (2010)
22.3	165bp	326bp	265bp	$[AGAT]_3GAT[AGAT]_{10}(AGAC)_9$	Phillips et al. (2011)
23 (a)	166bp	327bp	266bp	$[AGAT]_{14}(AGAC)_8AGAT$	Lareu et al. (1996)
23 (b)	166bp	327bp	266bp	$[AGAT]_{14}(AGAC)_9$	Lareu et al. (1996)
24 (a)	170bp	331bp	270bp	$[AGAT]_{15}(AGAC)_8AGAT$	Lareu et al. (1996)
24 (b)	170bp	331bp	270bp	$[AGAT]_{14}(AGAC)_9AGAT$	Lareu et al. (1996)
24 (c)	170bp	331bp	270bp	$[AGAT]_{15}(AGAC)_9$	Lareu et al. (1996)
24 (d)	170bp	331bp	270bp	$[AGAT]_{14}(AGAC)_{10}$	Phillips et al. (2011)
24 (e)	170bp	331bp	270bp	$[AGAT]_{18}(AGAC)_6$	M. Kline (unpublished)
24.2	172bp	333bp	272bp	$[AGAT]_{12}AT[AGAT]_6(AGAC)_6$	Phillips et al. (2011)
24.3	173bp	334bp	273bp	Not published	Hill et al. (2010)
25 (a)	174bp	335bp	274bp	$[AGAT]_{16}(AGAC)_8AGAT$	Lareu et al. (1996)
25 (b)	174bp	335bp	274bp	$[AGAT]_{16}(AGAC)_9$	Lareu et al. (1996)
25.2	176bp	337bp	276bp	$[AGAT]_{12}AT[AGAT]_7(AGAC)_5AGAT$	Phillips et al. (2011)
26 (a)	178bp	339bp	278bp	$[AGAT]_{17}(AGAC)_8AGAT$	Lareu et al. (1996)
26 (b)	178bp	339bp	278bp	$[AGAT]_{17}(AGAC)_9$	Lareu et al. (1996)
26.2 (a)	180bp	341bp	280bp	$[AGAT]_{12}AT[AGAT]_8(AGAC)_5AGAT$	Phillips et al. (2011)
26.2 (b)	180bp	341bp	280bp	$[AGAT]_{14}AT[AGAT]_6(AGAC)_5AGAT$	Phillips et al. (2011)
27	182bp	343bp	282bp	$[AGAT]_{18}(AGAC)_8AGAT$	Phillips et al. (2011)
27.2	184bp	345bp	284bp	$[AGAT]_{15}AT[AGAT]_6(AGAC)_5AGAT$	Phillips et al. (2011)

52 observed alleles

D22S1045

GenBank Accession: AL022314 (allele 17). PCR product sizes of observed alleles

Allele (Repeat #)	**Promega ESX 17**	**Promega ESI 17**	**ABI NGM**	**Repeat Structure $[ATT]_n$ ACT $[ATT]_2$**	**Reference**
7	79bp	306bp	77bp	Not published	Promega allelic ladders
8	82bp	309bp	80bp	$[ATT]_5$ ACT $[ATT]_2$	Coble & Butler (2005)
9	85bp	312bp	83bp	$[ATT]_6$ ACT $[ATT]_2$	Coble & Butler (2005)
10	88bp	315bp	86bp	$[ATT]_7$ ACT $[ATT]_2$	Coble & Butler (2005)
11	91bp	318bp	89bp	$[ATT]_8$ ACT $[ATT]_2$	Coble & Butler (2005)
12	94bp	321bp	92bp	$[ATT]_9$ ACT $[ATT]_2$	Coble & Butler (2005)
13	97bp	324bp	95bp	$[ATT]_{10}$ ACT $[ATT]_2$	Coble & Butler (2005)
14	100bp	327bp	98bp	$[ATT]_{11}$ ACT $[ATT]_2$	Coble & Butler (2005)
15	103bp	330bp	101bp	$[ATT]_{12}$ ACT $[ATT]_2$	Coble & Butler (2005)
16	106bp	333bp	104bp	$[ATT]_{13}$ ACT $[ATT]_2$	Coble & Butler (2005)
17	109bp	336bp	107bp	$[ATT]_{14}$ ACT $[ATT]_2$	Coble & Butler (2005)
18	112bp	339bp	110bp	$[ATT]_{15}$ ACT $[ATT]_2$	Coble & Butler (2005)
19	115bp	342bp	113bp	$[ATT]_{16}$ ACT $[ATT]_2$	Coble & Butler (2005)
20	118bp	345bp	116bp	$[ATT]_{17}$ ACT $[ATT]_2$	Coble & Butler (2005)

14 observed alleles

SE33

GenBank Accession: V00481 (allele 26.2). PCR product sizes of observed alleles. As the SE33 repeat motif pattern is more complex than other STR loci and would take too much space to write out in full, the short-hand method of Rolf et al. (1997) has been adopted with the repeat motif pattern included across the top of the table and the number of repeats for each pattern indicated in the table. Thus, for allele 6.3, 2-1-3-1-7-3-1 means the flanking and central repeat sequence is [AAAG]2 AG [AAAG]3 AG [AAAG]7 [AAAG]3 AG. The light blue shaded AAAG repeat is the primary source of variation with the light yellow shaded AAAG repeat playing a role with larger alleles. PCR product sizes of observed alleles

Allele (Repeat #)	ABI SEfiler	Promega ESX 17	Promega ESI 17	Repeat Motif Patterns															Reference
				AAAG	AG	AAAG	AG	AAAG	AAAAAG	AG	AGAAAG	**AAAG**	AAAAAG	AAAG	G	**AAGG**	AAAG/ANAG	AG	
				5′ flanking					**central repeat**					3′ flanking					
3	197 bp	258 bp	300 bp	Not published															STRBase
4.2	203 bp	264 bp	306 bp	Not published															PowerPlex ESI allelic ladder
6.3	212 bp	273 bp	315 bp	2	1	3	1	7	0	0	0	0	0	0	0	0	3	1	Rolf et al. (1997)
7	213 bp	274 bp	316 bp	Not published															Lászik et al. (2001)
7.3	216 bp	277 bp	319 bp	2	1	3	1	8	0	0	0	0	0	0	0	0	3	1	Dauber et al. (2004)
8	217 bp	278 bp	320 bp	Not published															Poetsch et al. (2010)
8.1	218 bp	279 bp	321 bp	Not published															Lászik et al. (2001)
9 (a)	221 bp	282 bp	324 bp	2	1	3	1	9	0	0	0	0	0	0	1	0	3	1	Dauber et al. (2009)
9 (b)	221 bp	282 bp	324 bp	2	1	3	1	9	0	0	0	0	0	0	1	1	2	1	Kline et al. (2010)
9.2	223 bp	284 bp	326 bp	Not published															Lászik et al. (2001)
10	225 bp	286 bp	328 bp	Not published															Poetsch et al. (2011)
10.2	227 bp	288 bp	330 bp	2	1	0	0	18	0	0	0	0	0	0	1	0	3	1	Dauber et al. (2009)
10.3	228 bp	289 bp	331 bp	2	1	3	1	11	0	0	0	0	0	0	1	1	2	1	Urquhart et al. (1993)
11	229 bp	290 bp	332 bp	Not published															Poetsch et al. (2010)
11.1	230 bp	291 bp	333 bp	0	1	3	1	18	0	0	0	0	0	0	0	0	0	1	Urquhart et al. (1993)
11.2	231 bp	292 bp	334 bp	2	1	0	0	15	0	0	0	0	0	0	1	0	3	1	Dauber et al. (2004)

12	233 bp	294 bp	336 bp	2	1	3	1	12	0	0	0	0	0	0	1	0	3	1	Rolf et al. (1997)
12.2 (a)	235 bp	296 bp	338 bp	2	1	3	0	13	0	0	0	0	0	0	1	0	3	1	Rolf et al. (1997)
12.2 (b)	235 bp	296 bp	338 bp	0	1	3	1	16	0	0	0	0	0	0	1	0	3	1	Urquhart et al. (1993)
13	237 bp	298 bp	340 bp	2	1	3	1	13	0	0	0	0	0	0	1	0	3	1	Delghandi et al. (2001)
13.2	239 bp	300 bp	342 bp	2	1	3	0	14	0	0	0	0	0	0	1	0	3	1	Rolf et al. (1997); Kline et al. (2010)
13.3	240 bp	301 bp	343 bp	Not published															Poetsch et al. (2010)
14 (a)	241 bp	302 bp	344 bp	2	1	3	1	14	0	0	0	0	0	0	1	0	3	1	Rolf et al. (1997)
14 (b)	241 bp	302 bp	344 bp	2	1	3	1	14	0	0	0	0	0	0	1	1	2	1	Kline et al. (2010)
14.1	242 bp	303 bp	345 bp	Not published															Poetsch et al. (2010)
14.2	243 bp	304 bp	346 bp	2	1	3	0	15	0	0	0	0	0	0	1	0	3	1	Kline et al. (2010)
15	245 bp	306 bp	348 bp	2	1	3	1	15	0	0	0	0	0	0	1	0	3	1	Rolf et al. (1997)
15.2	247 bp	308 bp	350 bp	Not published															Lászik et al. (2001)
16 (a)	249 bp	310 bp	352 bp	2	1	3	1	16	0	0	0	0	0	0	1	0	3	1	Rolf et al. (1997)
16 (b)	249 bp	310 bp	352 bp	2	1	3	1	16	0	0	0	0	0	0	1	1	2	1	Kline et al. (2010)
16.1	250 bp	311 bp	353 bp	Not published															Berti et al. (2010)
16.2	251 bp	312 bp	354 bp	Not published															Lászik et al. (2001)
16.3	252 bp	313 bp	355 bp	Not published															Egyed et al. (2005)
17	253 bp	314 bp	356 bp	2	1	3	1	17	0	0	0	0	0	0	1	0	3	1	Rolf et al. (1997)
17.2	255 bp	316 bp	358 bp	Not published															Lászik et al. (2001)
17.3	256 bp	317 bp	359 bp	Not published															Lászik et al. (2001)
18	257 bp	318 bp	360 bp	2	1	3	1	18	0	0	0	0	0	0	1	0	3	1	Rolf et al. (1997)
18.2	259 bp	320 bp	362 bp	2	1	3	1	9	1	0	0	8	0	0	1	1	2	1	Dauber et al. (2009)
18.3	260 bp	321 bp	363 bp	2	1	0	0	19	0	0	0	0	+G	3	1	0	3	1	Urquhart et al. (1993)
19 (a)	261 bp	322 bp	364 bp	2	1	3	1	19	0	0	0	0	0	0	1	0	3	1	Rolf et al. (1997)

(Continued)

SE33 (*Continued*)

Allele (Repeat #)	ABI SEfiler	Promega ESX 17	Promega ESI 17	Repeat Motif Patterns															Reference
				AAAG	AG	AAAG	AG	AAAG	AAAAAG	AG	AGAAAG	**AAAG**	AAAAAG	AAAG	G	**AAGG**	AAAG/ANAG	AG	
19 (b)	261 bp	322 bp	364 bp	2	1	3	1	19	0	0	0	0	0	0	1	1	2	1	Kline et al. (2010)
19.2	263 bp	324 bp	366 bp	2	1	3	1	10	1	0	0	8	0	0	1	1	2	1	Rolf et al. (1997)
19.3	264 bp	325 bp	367 bp	Not published															Berti et al. (2010)
20 (a)	265 bp	326 bp	368 bp	2	1	3	1	20	0	0	0	0	0	0	1	0	3	1	Rolf et al. (1997)
20 (b)	265 bp	326 bp	368 bp	2	1	3	1	20	0	0	0	0	0	0	1	1	2	1	Kline et al. (2010)
20.2	267 bp	328 bp	370 bp	2	1	3	1	11	1	0	0	8	0	0	1	1	2	1	Rolf et al. (1997)
21	269 bp	330 bp	372 bp	2	1	3	1	21	0	0	0	0	0	0	1	0	3	1	Rolf et al. (1997)
21.2 (a)	271 bp	332 bp	374 bp	2	1	3	1	9	1	0	0	11	0	0	1	1	2	1	Rolf et al. (1997)
21.2 (b)	271 bp	332 bp	374 bp	2	1	3	1	11	1	0	0	9	0	0	1	1	2	1	Rolf et al. (1997)
21.2 (c)	271 bp	332 bp	374 bp	2	1	3	1	7	0	7	0	11	0	0	1	1	2	1	Kline et al. (2010)
22 (a)	273 bp	334 bp	376 bp	2	1	3	1	22	0	0	0	0	0	0	1	0	3	1	Rolf et al. (1997)
22 (b)	273 bp	334 bp	376 bp	2	1	3	1	21	0	0	0	0	0	0	1	1	3	1	Kline et al. (2010)
22.2 (a)	275 bp	336 bp	378 bp	2	1	3	1	7	1	0	0	14	0	0	1	1	2	1	Rolf et al. (1997)
22.2 (b)	275 bp	336 bp	378 bp	2	1	3	1	8	0	5	0	12	0	0	1	1	2	1	Rolf et al. (1997)
22.2 (c)	275 bp	336 bp	378 bp	2	1	3	1	9	1	0	0	12	0	0	1	1	2	1	Rolf et al. (1997)
22.2 (d)	275 bp	336 bp	378 bp	2	1	3	1	10	1	0	0	11	0	0	1	1	2	1	Rolf et al. (1997)
22.2 (e)	275 bp	336 bp	378 bp	2	1	3	1	11	1	0	0	10	0	0	1	1	2	1	Rolf et al. (1997)
22.2 (f)	275 bp	336 bp	378 bp	2	1	3	1	12	1	0	0	9	0	0	1	1	2	1	Rolf et al. (1997)
22.3	276 bp	337 bp	379 bp	Not published															Poetsch et al. (2010)
23	277 bp	338 bp	380 bp	Not published															Lászik et al. (2001)

23.2 (a)	279 bp	340 bp	382 bp	2	1	3	1	7	1	0	0	15	0	0	1	1	2	1	Rolf et al. (1997)
23.2 (b)	279 bp	340 bp	382 bp	2	1	3	1	8	1	0	0	14	0	0	1	1	2	1	Rolf et al. (1997)
23.2 (c)	279 bp	340 bp	382 bp	2	1	3	1	9	1	0	0	13	0	0	1	1	2	1	Rolf et al. (1997)
23.2 (d)	279 bp	340 bp	382 bp	2	1	3	1	10	0	3	0	12	0	0	1	1	2	1	Rolf et al. (1997)
23.2 (e)	279 bp	340 bp	382 bp	2	1	3	1	10	1	0	0	12	0	0	1	1	2	1	Rolf et al. (1997)
23.2 (f)	279 bp	340 bp	382 bp	2	1	3	1	11	1	0	0	11	0	0	1	1	2	1	Rolf et al. (1997)
23.2 (g)	279 bp	340 bp	382 bp	2	1	3	1	12	1	0	0	10	0	0	1	1	2	1	Rolf et al. (1997)
24	281 bp	342 bp	384 bp	Not published															Lászik et al. (2001)
24.2 (a)	283 bp	344 bp	386 bp	2	1	3	1	5	1	0	0	18	0	0	1	1	2	1	Rolf et al. (1997)
24.2 (b)	283 bp	344 bp	386 bp	2	1	3	1	7	1	0	0	16	0	0	1	1	2	1	Rolf et al. (1997)
24.2 (c)	283 bp	344 bp	386 bp	2	1	3	1	8	1	0	0	15	0	0	1	1	2	1	Rolf et al. (1997)
24.2 (d)	283 bp	344 bp	386 bp	2	1	3	1	9	1	0	0	14	0	0	1	1	2	1	Dauber et al. (2008)
24.2 (e)	283 bp	344 bp	386 bp	2	1	3	1	10	1	0	0	13	0	0	1	1	2	1	Rolf et al. (1997)
24.2 (f)	283 bp	344 bp	386 bp	2	1	3	1	11	1	0	0	12	0	0	1	1	2	1	Rolf et al. (1997)
24.2 (g)	283 bp	344 bp	386 bp	2	1	3	1	12	1	0	0	11	0	0	1	1	2	1	Rolf et al. (1997)
24.2 (h)	283 bp	344 bp	386 bp	2	1	3	1	6	1	0	0	16	0	0	1	1	3	1	U134C→T – Kline et al. (2010)
25	285 bp	346 bp	388 bp	Not published															Lászik et al. (2001)
25.2 (a)	287 bp	348 bp	390 bp	2	1	3	1	8	1	0	0	16	0	0	1	1	2	1	Delghandi et al. (2001)
25.2 (b)	287 bp	348 bp	390 bp	2	1	3	1	9	1	0	0	15	0	0	1	1	2	1	Rolf et al. (1997)
25.2 (c)	287 bp	348 bp	390 bp	2	1	3	1	10	0	0	1	14	0	0	1	1	2	1	Rolf et al. (1997)
25.2 (d)	287 bp	348 bp	390 bp	2	1	3	1	10	1	0	0	14	0	0	1	1	2	1	Rolf et al. (1997)
25.2 (e)	287 bp	348 bp	390 bp	2	1	3	1	11	1	0	0	13	0	0	1	1	2	1	Rolf et al. (1997)
25.2 (f)	287 bp	348 bp	390 bp	2	1	3	1	12	1	0	0	12	0	0	1	1	2	1	Rolf et al. (1997)
25.2 (g)	287 bp	348 bp	390 bp	2	1	3	1	14	1	0	0	10	0	0	1	1	2	1	Rolf et al. (1997)
25.2 (h)	287 bp	348 bp	390 bp	2	1	3	1	9	1	0	0	15	0	0	1	1	2	1	D75C→T – Kline et al. (2010)

(Continued)

SE33 (*Continued*)

Allele (Repeat #)	ABI SEfiler	Promega ESX 17	Promega ESI 17	Repeat Motif Patterns															Reference
				AAAG	AG	AAAG	AG	AAAG	AAAAAG	AG	AGAAAG	**AAAG**	AAAAAG	AAAG	G	**AAGG**	AAAG/ANAG	AG	
25.2 (i)	287 bp	348 bp	390 bp	2	1	3	1	6	1	0	0	17	0	0	1	2	2	1	U134C→T – Kline et al. (2010)
25.3	288 bp	349 bp	391 bp	Not published															Berti et al. (2010)
26	289 bp	350 bp	392 bp	Not published															Lászik et al. (2001)
26.2 (a)	291 bp	352 bp	394 bp	2	1	3	1	8	1	0	0	17	0	0	1	1	2	1	Rolf et al. (1997)
26.2 (b)	291 bp	352 bp	394 bp	2	1	3	1	9	1	0	0	16	0	0	1	1	2	1	Rolf et al. (1997)
26.2 (c)	291 bp	352 bp	394 bp	2	1	3	1	10	1	0	0	15	0	0	1	1	2	1	Rolf et al. (1997)
26.2 (d)	291 bp	352 bp	394 bp	2	1	3	1	11	0	0	1	14	0	0	1	1	2	1	Rolf et al. (1997)
26.2 (e)	291 bp	352 bp	394 bp	2	1	3	1	11	1	0	0	14	0	0	1	1	2	1	Rolf et al. (1997)
26.2 (f)	291 bp	352 bp	394 bp	2	1	3	1	14	1	0	0	11	0	0	1	1	2	1	Rolf et al. (1997)
26.2 (g)	291 bp	352 bp	394 bp	2	1	3	1	6	1	0	0	18	0	0	1	1	3	1	U134C→T – Kline et al. (2010)
27	293 bp	354 bp	396 bp	Not published															Lászik et al. (2001)
27.2 (a)	295 bp	356 bp	398 bp	2	1	3	1	8	0	0	1	18	0	0	1	1	2	1	Rolf et al. (1997)
27.2 (b)	295 bp	356 bp	398 bp	2	1	3	1	8	1	0	0	18	0	0	1	1	2	1	Rolf et al. (1997)
27.2 (c)	295 bp	356 bp	398 bp	2	1	3	1	9	0	0	1	17	0	0	1	3	0	1	Rolf et al. (1997)
27.2 (d)	295 bp	356 bp	398 bp	2	1	3	1	10	1	0	0	16	0	0	1	1	2	1	Rolf et al. (1997)
27.2 (e)	295 bp	356 bp	398 bp	2	1	3	1	11	1	0	0	15	0	0	1	1	2	1	Rolf et al. (1997)
27.2 (f)	295 bp	356 bp	398 bp	2	1	3	1	12	1	0	0	14	0	0	1	1	2	1	Rolf et al. (1997)
27.2 (g)	295 bp	356 bp	398 bp	2	1	3	1	12	1	0	0	15	0	0	1	1	2	1	Rolf et al. (1997)
27.2 (h)	295 bp	356 bp	398 bp	2	1	3	1	13	0	0	1	13	0	0	1	3	0	1	Rolf et al. (1997)
27.2 (i)	295 bp	356 bp	398 bp	2	1	3	1	13	1	0	0	13	0	0	1	1	2	1	Rolf et al. (1997)
27.2 (j)	295 bp	356 bp	398 bp	2	1	3	1	15	1	0	0	11	0	0	1	1	2	1	Rolf et al. (1997)

27.2 (h)	295bp	356bp	398bp	2	1	3	1	7	0	9	0	15	0	0	1	1	3	1	U134C→T – Kline et al. (2010)
27.3	296bp	357bp	399bp	Not published															Hill et al. (2010)
28	297bp	358bp	400bp	2	1	0	0	14	1	0	0	16	0	0	1	1	2	1	Dauber et al. (2009)
28.2 (a)	299bp	360bp	402bp	2	1	3	1	8	1	0	0	19	0	0	1	1	2	1	Rolf et al. (1997)
28.2 (b)	299bp	360bp	402bp	2	1	3	1	9	0	0	0	18	0	0	1	1	2	1	Rolf et al. (1997)
28.2 (c)	299bp	360bp	402bp	2	1	3	1	9	0	0	0	15	0	0	1	1	2	1	Rolf et al. (1997)
28.2 (d)	299bp	360bp	402bp	2	1	3	1	9	1	0	0	18	0	0	1	1	2	1	Rolf et al. (1997)
28.2 (e)	299bp	360bp	402bp	2	1	3	1	10	1	0	0	17	0	0	1	1	2	1	Rolf et al. (1997)
28.2 (f)	299bp	360bp	402bp	2	1	3	1	11	1	0	0	16	0	0	1	1	2	1	Rolf et al. (1997)
28.2 (g)	299bp	360bp	402bp	2	1	3	1	12	1	0	0	15	0	0	1	1	2	1	Rolf et al. (1997)
28.2 (h)	299bp	360bp	402bp	2	1	3	1	13	1	0	0	14	0	0	1	1	2	1	Rolf et al. (1997)
28.2 (i)	299bp	360bp	402bp	2	1	3	1	14	1	0	0	13	0	0	1	1	2	1	Rolf et al. (1997)
28.2 (j)	299bp	360bp	402bp	2	1	3	1	14	1	0	0	13	0	0	1	3	0	1	Rolf et al. (1997)
28.2 (k)	299bp	360bp	402bp	2	1	3	1	16	1	0	0	11	0	0	1	1	2	1	Rolf et al. (1997)
28.3	300bp	361bp	403bp	2	1	3	1	10	1	0	0	12	+A	4	1	1	2	1	Dauber et al. (2009)
29	301bp	362bp	404bp	2	1	0	0	15	1	0	0	16	0	0	1	1	2	1	Dauber et al. (2009)
29.2 (a)	303bp	364bp	406bp	2	1	3	1	8	1	0	0	20	0	0	1	1	2	1	Rolf et al. (1997)
29.2 (b)	303bp	364bp	406bp	2	1	3	1	9	0	0	1	19	0	0	1	1	2	1	Rolf et al. (1997)
29.2 (c)	303bp	364bp	406bp	2	1	3	1	9	1	0	0	19	0	0	1	1	2	1	Rolf et al. (1997)
29.2 (d)	303bp	364bp	406bp	1	1	3	1	10	1	0	0	19	0	0	1	1	2	1	Rolf et al. (1997)
29.2 (e)	303bp	364bp	406bp	2	1	3	1	11	0	5	0	16	0	0	1	1	2	1	Rolf et al. (1997)
29.2 (f)	303bp	364bp	406bp	1	1	3	1	11	1	0	0	18	0	0	1	1	2	1	Rolf et al. (1997)
29.2 (g)	303bp	364bp	406bp	1	1	3	1	11	0	0	1	18	0	0	1	1	2	1	Urquhart et al. (1993)
29.2 (h)	303bp	364bp	406bp	2	1	3	1	11	1	0	0	17	0	0	1	1	2	1	Rolf et al. (1997)
29.2 (i)	303bp	364bp	406bp	2	1	3	1	12	1	0	0	16	0	0	1	1	2	1	Rolf et al. (1997)

(Continued)

SE33 (*Continued*)

Allele (Repeat #)	ABI SEfiler	Promega ESX 17	Promega ESI 17	Repeat Motif Patterns															Reference
				AAAG	AG	AAAG	AG	AAAG	AAAAAG	AG	AGAAAG	**AAAG**	AAAAAG	AAAG	G	**AAGG**	AAAG/ANAG	AG	
29.2 (j)	303bp	364bp	406bp	2	1	3	1	13	0	0	1	15	0	0	1	3	0	1	Rolf et al. (1997)
29.2 (k)	303bp	364bp	406bp	2	1	3	1	13	1	0	0	15	0	0	1	1	2	1	Rolf et al. (1997)
29.2 (l)	303bp	364bp	406bp	2	1	3	1	14	1	0	0	14	0	0	1	1	2	1	Rolf et al. (1997)
29.2 (m)	303bp	364bp	406bp	2	1	3	1	15	1	0	0	13	0	0	1	1	2	1	Delghandi et al. (2001)
29.2 (n)	303bp	364bp	406bp	2	1	3	1	16	1	0	0	12	0	0	1	1	2	1	Rolf et al. (1997)
29.2 (o)	303bp	364bp	406bp	2	1	3	1	11	1	0	0	17	0	0	1	1	2	1	D41-TTG-deletion – Kline et al. (2010)
29.3	304bp	365bp	407bp	Not published															Hill et al. (2010)
30	305bp	366bp	408bp	Not published															Lászik et al. (2001)
30.2 (a)	307bp	368bp	410bp	2	1	3	1	11	1	0	0	18	0	0	1	1	2	1	Rolf et al. (1997)
30.2 (b)	307bp	368bp	410bp	2	1	3	1	12	1	0	0	17	0	0	1	1	2	1	Rolf et al. (1997)
30.2 (c)	307bp	368bp	410bp	1	1	3	1	12	1	0	0	18	0	0	1	1	2	1	Rolf et al. (1997)
30.2 (d)	307bp	368bp	410bp	2	1	3	1	13	1	0	0	16	0	0	1	1	2	1	Rolf et al. (1997)
30.2 (e)	307bp	368bp	410bp	2	1	3	1	14	1	0	0	15	0	0	1	1	2	1	Rolf et al. (1997)
30.2 (f)	307bp	368bp	410bp	2	1	3	1	15	1	0	0	14	0	0	1	1	2	1	Rolf et al. (1997)
31	309bp	370bp	412bp	Not published															Lászik et al. (2001)
31.2 (a)	311bp	372bp	414bp	1	1	3	1	9	1	0	0	22	0	0	1	1	2	1	Rolf et al. (1997)
31.2 (b)	311bp	372bp	414bp	1	1	3	1	10	1	0	0	21	0	0	1	1	2	1	Rolf et al. (1997)
31.2 (c)	311bp	372bp	414bp	2	1	3	1	12	1	0	0	18	0	0	1	1	2	1	Rolf et al. (1997)

31.2 (d)	311 bp	372 bp	414 bp	2	1	3	1	13	1	0	0	17	0	0	1	1	2	1	Rolf et al. (1997)
31.2 (e)	311 bp	372 bp	414 bp	2	1	3	1	14	1	0	0	16	0	0	1	1	2	1	Rolf et al. (1997)
32	313 bp	374 bp	416 bp	2	1	3	1	11	1	0	0	9	1	9	1	1	2	1	Dauber et al. (2008)
32.2 (a)	315 bp	376 bp	418 bp	2	1	3	1	13	1	0	0	18	0	0	1	1	2	1	Rolf et al. (1997)
32.2 (b)	315 bp	376 bp	418 bp	2	1	3	1	14	1	0	0	17	0	0	1	1	2	1	Rolf et al. (1997)
33 (a)	317 bp	378 bp	420 bp	2	1	2	1	10	1	0	0	12	1	9	1	1	2	1	Rolf et al. (1997)
33 (b)	317 bp	378 bp	420 bp	2	1	3	1	10	1	0	0	11	1	9	1	1	2	1	Rolf et al. (1997)
33.2 (a)	319 bp	380 bp	422 bp	1	1	3	1	10	1	0	0	23	0	0	1	1	2	1	Rolf et al. (1997)
33.2 (b)	319 bp	380 bp	422 bp	2	1	3	1	12	1	0	0	20	0	0	1	1	2	1	Dauber et al. (2004)
33.2 (c)	319 bp	380 bp	422 bp	2	1	3	1	14	1	0	0	18	0	0	1	1	2	1	Delghandi et al. (2001)
34 (a)	321 bp	382 bp	424 bp	2	1	3	1	9	1	0	0	13	1	9	1	1	2	1	Rolf et al. (1997)
34 (b)	321 bp	382 bp	424 bp	2	1	3	1	10	1	0	0	12	1	9	1	1	2	1	Delghandi et al. (2001)
34 (c)	321 bp	382 bp	424 bp	2	1	3	1	11	1	0	0	11	1	9	1	1	2	1	Dauber et al. (2008)
34 (d)	321 bp	382 bp	424 bp	2	1	3	1	13	1	0	0	9	1	9	1	1	2	1	Delghandi et al. (2001)
34.2	323 bp	384 bp	426 bp	2	1	3	1	13	1	0	0	20	0	0	1	1	2	1	Dauber et al. (2004)
35	325 bp	386 bp	428 bp	Not published															Poetsch et al. (2010)
35.2 (a)	327 bp	388 bp	430 bp	1	1	3	1	13	1	0	0	22	0	0	1	1	2	1	Rolf et al. (1997)
35.2 (b)	327 bp	388 bp	430 bp	2	1	3	1	13	0	5	0	20	0	0	1	1	1	3	Urquhart et al. (1993)
36 (a)	329 bp	390 bp	432 bp	2	1	3	1	10	1	0	0	14	1	9	1	1	2	1	Rolf et al. (1997)
36 (b)	329 bp	390 bp	432 bp	2	1	3	1	11	1	0	0	5	1	17	1	1	2	1	Delghandi et al. (2001)
36 (c)	329 bp	390 bp	432 bp	2	1	3	1	12	1	0	0	10	1	11	1	1	2	1	Dauber et al. (2009)
36.2	331 bp	392 bp	434 bp	Not published															Lászik et al. (2001)
37 (a)	333 bp	394 bp	436 bp	2	1	3	1	9	1	0	0	16	1	9	1	1	2	1	Rolf et al. (1997)
37 (b)	333 bp	394 bp	436 bp	2	1	3	1	12	1	0	0	11	1	11	1	1	2	1	Dauber et al. (2008)
39	341 bp	402 bp	444 bp	Not published															PowerPlex ESI allelic ladder

(Continued)

SE33 (*Continued*)

Allele (Repeat #)	ABI SEfiler	Promega ESX 17	Promega ESI 17	Repeat Motif Patterns															Reference
				AAAG	AG	AAAG	AG	AAAG	AAAAAG	AG	AGAAAG	**AAAG**	AAAAAG	AAAG	G	**AAGG**	AAAG/ANAG	AG	
39.2	343 bp	404 bp	446 bp	Not published															Lászik et al. (2001)
41	349 bp	410 bp	452 bp	2	1	3	1	12	1	0	0	12	1	14	1	1	2	1	Lederer et al. (2008)
42	353 bp	414 bp	456 bp	Not published															PowerPlex ESI allelic ladder
49	381 bp	442 bp	484 bp	2	1	3	1	14	1	0	0	16	1	16	1	1	2	1	Klein et al. (2003)

178 observed alleles

References

Allor, C., et al. (2005). Identification and characterization of variant alleles at CODIS STR loci. *Journal of Forensic Sciences*, *50*, 1128–1133.

Amorim, A., et al. (1996). Population and formal genetics of the STRs TPO, TH01 and VWFA31/A in North Portugal. *Advances in Forensic Haemogenetics*, *6*, 486–488.

Amorim, A., et al. (2001). STR data (AmpFlSTR Profiler Plus) from North Portugal. *Forensic Science International*, *115*, 119–121.

Applied Biosystems (1998), *AmpFlSTR COfiler PCR amplification kit user's bulletin*. Foster City, California: Applied Biosystems.

Applied Biosystems (1998), *AmpFlSTR Profiler Plus PCR amplification kit user's manual*. Foster City, California: Applied Biosystems.

Applied Biosystems (1999), *AmpFlSTR SGM Plus PCR amplification kit user's manual*. Foster City, California: Applied Biosystems.

Asamura, H., et al. (2008). Population data on 10 non-CODIS STR loci in Japanese population using a newly developed multiplex PCR system. *Journal of Forensic and Legal Medicine*, *15*, 519–523.

Ayres, K. L., et al. (2002). Implications for DNA identification arising from an analysis of Australian forensic databases. *Forensic Science International*, *129*, 90–98.

Bacher, J. W., et al. (1998). Pentanucleotide repeats: Highly polymorphic genetic markers displaying minimal stutter artifact. *Proceedings of the ninth international symposium on human identification* (pp. 24–37). Available at <http://www.promega.com/geneticidproc/ussymp9proc/content/08.pdf>.

Bagdonavicius, A., et al. (2002). Western Australian sub-population data for the thirteen AMPFISTR Profiler Plus and COfiler STR loci. *Journal of Forensic Sciences*, *47*, 1149–1153.

Balamurugan, K., et al. (2000). Allele frequencies for nine STR loci in African American and Caucasian populations from Marion County, Indiana, U.S.A. *Journal of Forensic Sciences*, *45*, 744–746.

Bär, W., et al. (1994). DNA recommendations – 1994 report concerning further recommendations of the DNA Commission of the ISFH regarding PCR-based polymorphisms in STR (short tandem repeat) systems. *International Journal of Legal Medicine*, *107*, 159–160.

Bär, W., et al. (1997). DNA recommendations – further report of the DNA Commission of the ISFH regarding the use of short tandem repeat systems. *International Journal of Legal Medicine*, *110*, 175–176.

Barber, M. D., et al. (1996). Structural variation in the alleles of a short tandem repeat system at the human alpha fibrinogen locus. *International Journal of Legal Medicine*, *108*, 180–185.

Barber, M. D., & Parkin, B. H. (1996). Sequence analysis and allelic designation of the two short tandem repeat loci D18S51 and D8S1179. *International Journal of Legal Medicine*, *109*, 62–65.

Berti, A., et al. (2010). Allele frequencies of the new European Standard Set (ESS) loci in the Italian population. *Forensic Science International: Genetics* (in press). doi:10.1016/j.fsigen.2010.01.006.

Brinkmann, B., et al. (1996). Complex mutational events at the HumD21S11 locus. *Human Genetics*, *98*, 60–64.

Brinkmann, B., et al. (1996). Population genetic comparisons among eight populations using allele frequency and sequence data from three microsatellite loci. *European Journal of Human Genetics*, *4*, 175–182.

Budowle, B., et al. (1997). Zimbabwe black population data on the six short tandem repeat loci - CSF1PO, TPOX, TH01, D3S1358, VWA, and FGA. *Forensic Science International*, *90*, 215–221.

Budowle, B., & Moretti, T. R. (1998). Examples of STR population databases for CODIS and for casework. *Proceedings from the ninth international symposium on human identification* (pp. 64–73). Madison, Wisconsin: Promega Corporation.

Butler, J. M., et al. (2008). Addressing Y-chromosome short tandem repeat (Y-STR) allele nomenclature. *Journal of Genetic Genealogy*, *4*(2), 125–148.

Cho, E. H., et al. (2010). Variant alleles detected in a large Korean population using AmpFlSTR Profiler Plus. *Forensic Science International: Genetics* (in press). doi:10.1016/j.fsigen.2010.06.001.

Coble, M. D., & Butler, J. M. (2005). Characterization of new miniSTR loci to aid analysis of degraded DNA. *Journal of Forensic Sciences*, *50*, 43–53.

Cruz, C., et al. (2004). vWA STR locus structure and variability. *Progress in Forensic Genetics 10, ICS 1261*, 248–250.

Dauber, E. M., et al. (2000). Further sequence and length variation at the STR loci HumFES/FPS, HumVWA, HumFGA and D12S391. *International Journal of Legal Medicine*, *113*, 76–80.

Dauber, E. M., et al. (2004). New sequence data of allelic variants at the STR loci ACTBP2 (SE33), D21S11, FGA, vWA, CSF1PO, D2S1338, D16S539, D18S51 and D19S433 in Caucasoids. *Progress in Forensic Genetics 10, ICS 1261*, 191–193.

Dauber, E. M., et al. (2008). Unusual FGA and D19S433 off-ladder alleles and other allelic variants at the STR loci D8S1132, vWA, D18S51 and ACTBP2 (SE33). *Forensic Science International: Genetics Supplement Series, 1*, 109–111.

Dauber, E. M., et al. (2009). Further allelic variation at the STR-loci ACTBP2 (SE33), D3S1358, D8S1132, D18S51 and D21S11. *Forensic Science International: Genetics Supplement Series, 2*, 41–42.

Delghandi, M., et al. (2001). Evaluation of a quadruplex short tandem repeat system (HUMVWA31/A, HUMD11S554, HUMAPOAI1, and HUMACTBP2 loci) for forensic identity testing, confident typing of complex alleles, and population databases. *Croatian Medical Journal, 42*, 33–44.

Egyed, B., et al. (2005). Population genetic data on the STR loci D2S1338, D19S433 and SE33 in Hungary. *Journal of Forensic Sciences, 50*, 720–721.

Espinheira, R., et al. (1996). STR analysis–HUMTH01 and HUMFES/FPS for forensic application. *Advances in Forensic Haemogenetics, 6* 528–528.

Gamero, J. J., et al. (2000). A study on ten short tandem repeat systems: African immigrant and Spanish population data. *Forensic Science International, 110*, 167–177.

Gene, M., et al. (1996). Population study of the STRs HUMTH01 (including a new variant) and HUMVWA31A in Catalonia (northeast Spain). *International Journal of Legal Medicine, 108*, 318–320.

Gill, P., et al. (1995). Automated short tandem repeat (STR) analysis in forensic casework–a strategy for the future. *Electrophoresis, 16*, 1543–1552.

Gill, P., et al. (1996). A new method of STR interpretation using inferential logic–development of a criminal intelligence database. *International Journal of Legal Medicine, 109*, 14–22.

Griffiths, R. A. L., et al. (1998). New reference allelic ladders to improve allelic designation in a multiplex STR system. *International Journal of Legal Medicine, 111*, 267–272.

Grubwieser, P., et al. (2005). Unusual variant allele in commonly used short tandem repeat loci. *International Journal of Legal Medicine, 119*, 164–166.

Gusmão, L., et al. (2006). DNA Commission of the International Society of Forensic Genetics (ISFG): An update of the recommendations on the use of Y-STRs in forensic analysis. *Forensic Science International, 157*, 187–197.

Heinrich, M., et al. (2004). Allelic drop-out in the STR system ACTBP2 (SE33) as a result of mutations in the primer binding region. *International Journal of Legal Medicine, 118*, 361–363.

Heinrich, M., et al. (2005). Characterisation of variant alleles in the STR systems D2S1338, D3S1358 and D19S433. *International Journal of Legal Medicine, 119*, 310–313.

Hering, S., et al. (2002). Sequence variations in the primer binding regions of the highly polymorphic STR system SE33. *International Journal of Legal Medicine, 116*, 365–367.

Hill, C. R., et al. (2010). Concordance and population studies along with stutter and peak height ratio analysis for the PowerPlex ESX 17 and ESI 17 Systems. *Forensic Science International: Genetics* (in press). doi:10.1016/j.fsigen.2010.03.014.

Hsieh, H.-M., et al. (2002). Sequence analysis of STR polymorphisms at locus ACTBP2 in the Taiwanese population. *Forensic Science International, 130*, 112–121.

Huang, N. E., et al. (1995). Chinese population data on three tetrameric short tandem repeat loci–HUMTH01, TPOX, and CSF1PO–derived using multiplex PCR and manual typing. *Forensic Science International, 71*, 131–136.

Huel, R., et al. (2007). Variant alleles, triallelic patterns, and point mutations observed in nuclear short tandem repeat typing of populations in Bosnia and Serbia. *Croatian Medical Journal, 48*(4), 494–502.

Jiang, W., et al. (2011). Identification of dual false indirect exclusions on the D5S818 and FGA loci. *Legal Medicine, 13*, 30–34.

Kido, A., et al. (2003). Nine short tandem repeat loci analysis in aged semen stains using the AmpFLSTR Profiler Kit and description of a new vWA variant allele. *Legal Medicine (Tokyo), 5*, 93–96.

Klein, R., et al. (2003). A very long ACTBP2 (SE33) allele. *International Journal of Legal Medicine, 117*, 235–236.

Kline, M. C., et al. (2010). STR sequence analysis for characterizing normal, variant, and null alleles. *Forensic Science International: Genetics* (in press). doi:10.1016/j.fsigen.2010.09.005.

Klintschar, M., et al. (1998). A study on the short tandem repeat systems HumCD4, HumTH01, and HumFIBRA in population samples from Yemen and Egypt. *International Journal of Legal Medicine, 111*, 107–109.

Krenke, B. E., et al. (2002). Validation of a 16-locus fluorescent multiplex system. *Journal of Forensic Sciences, 47*, 773–785.

Lareu, M. V., et al. (1996). Sequence variation of a hypervariable short tandem repeat at the D12S391 locus. *Gene, 182*, 151–153.

Lareu, M. V., et al. (1998). Sequence variation of a hypervariable short tandem repeat at the D1S1656 locus. *International Journal of Legal Medicine, 111*, 244–247.

Lazaruk, K., et al. (1998). Genotyping of forensic short tandem repeat (STR) systems based on sizing precision in a capillary electrophoresis instrument. *Electrophoresis, 19*, 86–93.

Lászik, A., et al. (2001). Frequency data for the STR locus ACTBP2 (SE33) in eight populations. *International Journal of Legal Medicine, 115*, 94–96.

Lederer, T., et al. (2008). Characterization of two unusual allele variants at the STR locus ACTBP2 (SE33). *Forensic Science, Medicine, and Pathology, 4*, 164–166.

Lins, A. M., et al. (1998). Development and population study of an eight-locus short tandem repeat (STR) multiplex system. *Journal of Forensic Sciences, 43*, 1168–1180.

Luis, J., et al. (1994). Improved conditions for genotype diagnosis of a STR of the hTPO locus. *Advances in Forensic Haemogenetics, 5*, 366–368.

Margolis-Nunno, H., et al. (2001). A new allele of the short tandem repeat (STR) locus, CSF1PO. *Journal of Forensic Sciences, 46*, 1480–1483.

Miozzo, M. C., et al. (2007). Characterization of the variant allele 9.2 of Penta D locus. *Journal of Forensic Sciences, 52*, 1073–1076.

Mizuno, N., et al. (2003). Variant alleles on the Penta E locus in the PowerPlex 16 kit. *Journal of Forensic Sciences, 48*, 358–361.

Möller, A., & Brinkmann, B. (1994). Locus ACTBP2 (SE33): Sequencing data reveal considerable polymorphism. *International Journal of Legal Medicine, 106*, 262–267.

Möller, A., et al. (1994). Different types of structural variation in STRs: HumFES/FPS, HumVWA, and HumD21S11. *International Journal of Legal Medicine, 106*, 319–323.

Montelius, K., et al. (2008). STR data for the AmpFlSTR Identifiler loci from Swedish population in comparison to European, as well as with non-European population. *Forensic Science International: Genetics, 2*, e49–e52.

Morales-Valverde, A., et al. (2009). Characterisation of 12 new alleles in the STR system D18S51. *Forensic Science International: Genetics Supplement Series, 2*, 43–44.

Mornhinweg, E., et al. (1998). D3S1358: Sequence analysis and gene frequency in a German population. *Forensic Science International, 95*, 173–178.

Oberacher, H., et al. (2008). Increased forensic efficiency of DNA fingerprints through simultaneous resolution of length and nucleotide variability by high-performance mass spectrometry. *Human Mutation, 29*(3), 427–432.

Phillips, C. P., et al. (1998). Band shift analysis of three base-pair repeat alleles in the short tandem repeat locus D12S391. *Forensic Science International, 93*, 79–88.

Phillips, C., et al. (2011). Analysis of global variability in 15 established and 5 new European Standard Set (ESS) STRs using the CEPH human genome diversity panel. *Forensic Science International: Genetics, 5*, 155–169.

Pitterl, F., et al. (2010). Increasing the discrimination power of forensic STR testing by employing high-performance mass spectrometry, as illustrated in indigenous South African and Central Asian populations. *International Journal of Legal Medicine, 124*, 551–558.

Poetsch, M., et al. (2010). First experiences using the new PowerPlex ESX17 and ESI17 kits in casework analysis and allele frequencies for two different regions in Germany. *International Journal of Legal Medicine* (in press). doi: 10.1007/s00414-010-0480-2.

Poetsch, M., et al. (2011). The new PowerPlex ESX17 and ESI17 kits in paternity and maternity analyses involving people from Africa—including allele frequencies for three African populations. *International Journal of Legal Medicine, 125*, 149–154.

Puers, C., et al. (1993). Analysis of polymorphic short tandem repeat loci using well-characterized allelic ladders. *Proceedings from the fourth international symposium on human identification* (pp. 161–172). Madison, Wisconsin: Promega Corporation.

Rolf, B., et al. (1997). Sequence polymorphism at the tetranucleotide repeat of the human beta-actin related pseudogene H-beta-Ac-psi-2 (ACTBP2) locus. *International Journal of Legal Medicine, 110*, 69–72.

Scherczinger, C. A., et al. (2000). Allele frequencies for the CODIS core STR loci in Connecticut populations. *Journal of Forensic Sciences, 45*, 938–940.

Schröer, K., et al. (2000). Analysis of the co-amplified STR loci D1S1656, D12S391 and D18S51: Population data and validation study for a highly discriminating triplex-PCR. *Forensic Science International, 113*, 17–20.

Schwartz, D. W. M., et al. (1996). AMPFLP-typing of the D21S11 microsatellite polymorphism: Allele frequencies and sequencing data in the Austrian population. *Advances in Forensic Haemogenetics, 5*, 622–625.

Steinlechner, M., et al. (2002). Gabon black population data on the ten short tandem repeat loci D3S1358, VWA, D16S539, D2S1338, D8S1179, D21S11, D18S51, D19S433, TH01 and FGA. *International Journal of Legal Medicine, 116*, 176–178.

STRBase variant allele reports. <http://www.cstl.nist.gov/biotech/strbase/var_tab.htm>.

Szibor, R., et al. (1998). Population genetic data of the STR HUMD3S1358 in two regions of Germany. *International Journal of Legal Medicine, 111*, 160–161.

Tsuji, A., et al. (2006). The structure of a variant allele which is considered to be 30.3 in the STR locus D21S11. *Legal Medicine, 8*, 182–183.

Urquhart, A., et al. (1993). Sequence variability of the tetranucleotide repeat of the human beta-actin related pseudogene H-beta-Ac-psi-2 (ACTBP2) locus. *Human Genetics, 92*, 637–638.

Urquhart, A., et al. (1994). Variation in short tandem repeat sequences–a survey of twelve microsatellite loci for use as forensic identification markers. *International Journal of Legal Medicine, 107*, 13–20.

van Oorschot, R. A. H., et al. (1994). HUMTH01: Amplification, species specificity, population genetics and forensic applications. *International Journal of Legal Medicine, 107*, 121–126.

Walsh, S. J., et al. (2003). Characterisation of variant alleles at the HumD21S11 locus implies unique Australasian genotypes and re-classification of nomenclature guidelines. *Forensic Science International, 135*, 35–41.

Zhou, H. G., et al. (1997). The HumD21S11 system of short tandem repeat DNA polymorphisms in Japanese and Chinese. *Forensic Science International, 86*, 109–188. 77

APPENDIX

2

Familial DNA Searches: Potential, Pitfalls, and Privacy Concerns

Privacy rights groups feel that familial searching is going too far. In March 2008, the FBI Laboratory organized a meeting held in Washington, D.C. to discuss the advantages and concerns with familial searching. Scientists, lawyers, and legal scholars presented their points of view (see Rozen 2009). Although no formal proceedings were published from this meeting, the forum permitted a vigorous discussion of the issues by proponents and opponents of familial searching.

Since a successful California familial search was announced in July 2010 (D.N.A. Box 8.5, Miller 2010), a number of laboratories and lawmakers are considering the potential of familial searching. However, the technique has technical pitfalls and privacy concerns that will be discussed below.

As of 2010, two states within the U.S. permit active familial searching (California and Colorado), two ban familial searching (Maryland and the District of Columbia), and several others are exploring the possibility of this extended searching (Virginia) or to allow follow up on partial matches (New York).

An examination of the differences between a direct match, a partial match, and no match is helpful to begin our discussion of familial searching, how it works, and its limitations. In Figure A2.1, three different suspect profiles are compared against an evidentiary DNA profile. Suspect 1 matches at all 10 alleles shown—and is therefore a complete or direct match. Suspect 3 does not match the evidence (is excluded) as the profiles fail to share any alleles at two of the loci and only has a single allele in common at the remaining three loci. However, Suspect 2 is a partial match or what may be termed a "near miss" because only 7 out of 10 possible alleles are in common between the compared samples. Note that some of the loci, such as D8S1179 and D13S1358, share two alleles while the remaining three loci only have a single allele in common at each locus. In terms of the CODIS software match stringency discussed in Chapter 8, these single allele-sharing loci exhibit low stringency (L) rather than

(a)

	D8S1179		D21S11		D7S820		CSF1PO		D3S1358		
Evidence	13	14	31	31.2	9	11	12	13	15*	15	
Suspect 1	13	14	31	31.2	9	11	12	13	15*	15	Direct Match
Alleles shared	*2*		*2*		*2*		*2*		*2*		*10 alleles shared*
Match stringency	H		H		H		H		H		

(b)

	D8S1179		D21S11		D7S820		CSF1PO		D3S1358		
Evidence	13	14	31	31.2	9	11	12	13	15	15	
Suspect 2	**13**	**14**	30	**31.2**	**9**	10	9	**12**	**15**	**15**	**Partial Match**
Alleles shared	*2*		*1*		*1*		*1*		*2*		*7 alleles shared*
Match stringency	H		L		L		L		H		

(c)

	D8S1179		D21S11		D7S820		CSF1PO		D3S1358		
Evidence	13	14	31	31.2	9	11	12	13	15	15	
Suspect 3	12	**13**	29	30	10	**11**	**12**	12	14	14	**No Match**
Alleles shared	*1*		*0*		*1*		*1*		*0*		*3 alleles shared*
Match stringency	L		--		L		L		--		**Excluded at 2 loci**

*Although shown as two alleles ("15,15") in this example, homozygous genotypes are recorded as only a single allele within the CODIS software (i.e., "15" instead of "15,15").

FIGURE A2.1 Three different suspect profiles are compared against an evidentiary DNA profile (only 5 of 15 tested STR loci are shown here for space purposes). (a) Suspect 1 matches at all 10 alleles. (b) Suspect 2 is a partial match or a "near miss" with 7 out of 10 possible alleles being shared. Note that at least one allele is shared with the evidentiary profile at every locus suggesting that there is a possible parent-child relationship. (c) Suspect 3 does not match the evidence because he is excluded at 2 loci and only shares 3 out of 10 possible alleles.

high stringency (H) where both alleles match between the compared samples. (Note that routine CODIS searches are done at moderate stringency, and low stringency searching is only used in missing persons cases when a parent is looking for a missing child or vice versa.)

Alleles can be shared between samples due to common ancestry (identical by descent, IBD) or have the same characteristics (e.g., repeat number) by chance (identical by state, IBS). Alleles that are more common (i.e., have a higher frequency) will have a greater chance of being IBS. When rare alleles are present in a DNA profile, there is a greater chance of them being IBD with a matching profile and thus useful in familial searching.

There are two primary methods of expressing the strength of a match between samples. The first is allele sharing, which simply tabulates the number of alleles in common. The second is the likelihood ratio (LR), which compares the hypothesis that the samples being compared are related versus the hypothesis that they are unrelated. LRs will be discussed in greater detail in the forthcoming volume *Advanced Topics in Forensic DNA Typing: Interpretation*.

For a father-child comparison, the LR is known as the paternity index (PI). For sibling comparisons, the LR is referred to as the sibship index (SI). When multiple loci are considered, a combined paternity index (CPI) or combined sibship index (CSI) is calculated by multiplying the individual PI or SI values for each locus. More generally, either the PI or SI can be called a kinship index (KI). The LR calculation is more informative than simply counting the number of alleles shared because it incorporates the frequencies for those alleles observed in a profile. Sharing rare alleles is less likely with unrelated individuals and therefore will create a higher LR value.

Even though relatives share more DNA than unrelated individuals, there will be partial matches with unrelated individuals especially if the crime scene sample contains common alleles. These common alleles can give rise to false positives in a familial search.

Pitfalls of False Positives and False Negatives

The SWGDAM recommendations on partial matches note that current CODIS searching rules and algorithms, which use allele sharing (and thus cannot incorporate information from rare alleles) have a very low efficiency for locating true relatives in offender databases (SWGDAM 2009). These recommendations further comment that true siblings very rarely share alleles at all 13 CODIS loci and the number of unrelated individuals who do share at least one allele at all loci increases as offender DNA databases get larger. Thus, LR methods that enable allele frequency as well as allele sharing information are typically preferred for familial searching.

Tom Reid and colleagues at DNA Diagnostics Center, a paternity testing laboratory near Cincinnati, Ohio, studied the ability of different search strategies to locate true siblings within a simulated offender database (Reid et al. 2008). One of each pair from 109 sibling pairs with CSI values ranging from four to greater than one billion were added to a simulated offender database containing 12,292 profiles. The remaining sibling from each pair was used to probe the database to see if its partner (familial) profile could be located within the first 100 best matches in the database. An allele sharing method detected 62 of the 109 known sibling pairs (57%) while a likelihood ratio (kinship matching) approach detected 90 of the sib pairs (83%).

Another study using a different set of STR loci found a 72% chance of the true sibling being in the top 100 profiles using allele sharing and a 78% chance using a likelihood ratio approach that takes into account the rarity of the alleles being shared (Curran & Buckleton 2008). It is worth noting that these simulated databases of a few thousand DNA profiles are much smaller than a state DNA database that contains hundreds of thousands or even greater than a million profiles like California. It is likely that these published approximately 70% to 80% chances will dramatically decrease with increased database size.

Not surprisingly, the Reid et al. study found that the efficiency of a search (how high up the ranked list the true sibling was) was inversely correlated with the CSI value. The presence of rarer alleles in the profile being shared between siblings increases the CSI value and hence the probability of matching.

Of the sibling pairs having a CSI value greater than 10,000, all but one pair matched on the first hit (i.e., were first on the rank-ordered database match list). Sibling pairs with CSIs between 1000 and 10,000 averaged approximately three false hits to obtain a correct match. However, sibling pairs with CSIs between 10 and 100 required an average of 52 false hits before a true match was found (Reid et al. 2008).

The DNA Diagnostics Center study demonstrates that sibling searches will not always work because not all loci share alleles as with parent-child matches (barring mutations). The authors conclude that without further data filtering using geography or other factors, "familial searching using DNA profile data may not consistently produce enough usable leads to make it meaningful" (Reid et al. 2008).

CSI values can vary within a single family due to allele inheritance. For example, I have four brothers whose 13-locus CSI values (relative to being my brother) are 2300, 490, 1.5, and 0.83. While my first two brothers with likelihood ratios of 490 and 2300 might be identified in a familial search, it is highly unlikely that my lower-CSI-value brothers would. Many other non-related individuals would likely share alleles with me by chance and be higher on a ranked list than my true brothers. If my DNA profile was the crime scene profile being searched and if my brothers with low CSI values of 1.5 and 0.83 were in the database, our true familial connection would be missed and result in false negatives for that search. They are my brothers, they are in the database, but due to allele inheritance patterns where we inherited different non-overlapping alleles from our parents, a familial search based on the CODIS 13 autosomal STR loci would not identify them.

To filter out false positives or adventitious matches due to chance allele sharing (D.N.A. Box 8.3) following a familial search, further information is needed to narrow possibilities. Metadata, such as geographic information or possible ages of individuals if available, can be effective and has been used in the UK. Alternatively, additional loci, such as Y-STRs (Bieber et al. 2006, Myers et al. 2010), that are run on the crime scene sample and the list of potential familial offenders can eliminate male individuals with different paternal lineages.

Barring mutations, true fathers, sons, and full brothers will have the same Y-STR haplotype (see Chapter 13). If additional loci are typed on the putative familial offender profiles after the familial search, as long as the profiles of the potential relatives are in the ranked list for comparison purposes, the Y-STR testing should filter out most if not all of the non-relatives as occurred in the Grim Sleeper case (D.N.A. Box 8.5).

Low Success Rates

The UK, which has the most experience so far with attempting familial searches, has reported a success rate of anywhere between 11% and 27%. Chris Maguire, representing the Forensic Science Service at the 21st International Symposium on Human Identification meeting held in October 2010, reported 35 successful uses of familial searches on 131 cases

(≈27%) where the approach was attempted. However, an *LA Times* article on the topic published in November 2008 claimed that "British authorities" reported 158 familial searching attempts with only 18 successful leads (≈11%) (Dolan & Felch 2008). Regardless of the actual percentage, the success rate is low, particularly when only 10 STRs are being used (with the SGM Plus kit). This low success rate is due to the many false positives and false negatives that can arise when attempting to make kinship comparisons with 10 STRs or to the lack of a close relative on the database.

The Grim Sleeper case described in D.N.A. Box 8.5 was the tenth familial search attempted by California—and so far is the only successful familial search in this state (Myers et al. 2010). Thus, at this early stage in the California program the success rate is about 10%. Low success rates result from a lack of close relatives of the perpetrator in the database or from false negatives where true relatives in the database are missed due to the search strategy used and that only 13 or 15 autosomal STR loci are typically available in the initial search. More autosomal loci can increase the power to perform familial searches (O'Connor et al. 2010), but would have to be run on both the offender samples and the crime scene stain being used for the familial search.

Lineage Markers to Improve Success Rates

In order to reduce the number of false positives (because of sharing common alleles) and false negatives (because of genetic inheritance patterns in the family members), lineage markers are necessary to increase success rates. The use of Y-STRs and mtDNA in combination with autosomal results improves the success of familial searching (Lewis 2009). However, using these additional markers requires that both the evidentiary profile and the searched database samples have the same loci. False positives can be reduced by using Y-STR testing on male samples identified in a ranked list (Myers et al. 2010). Unfortunately, as noted above, false negatives will be missed unless the additional loci are tested on all or a significant portion of the database samples.

Supposed "Genetic Surveillance" of Families

In their coverage of the familial searching issue, reporters and law professors often raise the specter of so-called "genetic surveillance"—that families will come under some kind of oppressive suspicion because they are related to an offender whose DNA profile resides on a DNA database (NY Times 2010, Rosen 2009, Suter 2010, Murphy 2010). Loosening the search parameters does not in and of itself produce associations to family members. There is greater uncertainty in the results returned following a familial search because a direct match is not involved (Figure A2.2). The most significant problem with familial searching is the production of false positives due to the crime profile having common alleles that are shared by unrelated individuals, potentially producing likelihood ratio values indicative of a putative relationship. Even with relatively low LRs for individual loci, the combination of LRs across 13 to 15 STR loci can produce fairly large LRs that appear high in a ranked list.

As was done in the Grim Sleeper case, additional screening using Y-STR typing needs to be performed prior to sharing any information with investigators so that false leads are minimized or eliminated. Perhaps even more importantly, the California familial search policy states that no potential candidate names can be shared with the requesting agency

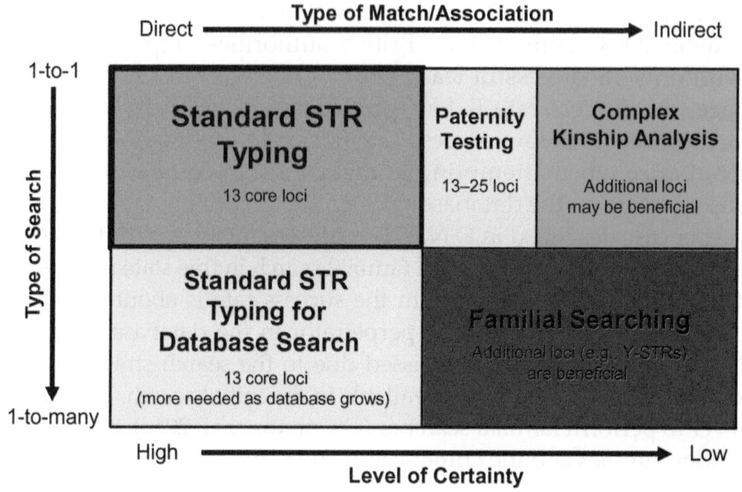

FIGURE A2.2 Illustration of the relationship between the types of matches being attempted, the types of searches being conducted, and the numbers of markers used. Familial searching attempts to identify a parent-offspring or full sibling relationship by comparing an evidence profile to the entire database of offender profiles. This one-to-many search will result in fortuitous matches due to chance allele sharing, and not allele sharing due to a common ancestor. Figure courtesy of Kristen Lewis O'Connor, NIST.

(i.e., Los Angeles Police Department in the Grim Sleeper case) until further investigation is performed using public records. If a candidate familial association is identified, investigative footwork through public records searches is performed. Within the California Department of Justice, investigators are careful not to talk to people (e.g., potential family members) and the requesting agency until the candidate familial association has cleared the investigative and scientific hurdles (Steinberger & Sims 2008). Thus, if everything is done right, no one (outside of the investigative team) knows when a candidate familial association does not pan out as a true relative of the perpetrator.

It is important to keep in mind that familial searches, as presently conducted, can produce many false negative results with true siblings and work best with father-son situations, where alleles are shared across an entire profile as in the Grim Sleeper case (D.N.A. Box 8.5). However, the majority of convicted offenders with DNA profiles in the database do not have children old enough to be committing crimes (see Table 8.10).

As of 2010, national databases have been in operation for about 15 years. As their time of use expands, the number of relatives in DNA databases is likely to increase as children of previous offenders could start to be included. In the Grim Sleeper case (D.N.A. Box 8.5), the son's newly added profile helped catch a father who was not in the database. Conversely with aging DNA databases and familial searching capabilities, a father's profile could lead to a son's apprehension as the younger man begins a life of crime.

The data in Table 8.10 illustrate that the largest numbers of individuals in prison are 20 to 45 years of age. This range is roughly the span of a generation or 25 years. Hence, where family members may be in prison (and therefore have their DNA profiles in databases enabling present-day familial searching), we might infer that siblings are more likely than parent-offspring to be present. Siblings are less likely to share alleles with one another than parent-offspring. However, as databases are used for longer periods of time, they may begin to include the offspring of former offenders. If this occurs, then there will begin to be a higher number of relatives on the database with a greater chance of allele sharing. More genetic markers will be needed in DNA databases of the future to help discriminate between familial and random matches.

READING LIST AND INTERNET RESOURCES

Familial Searching

Bieber, F. R., et al. (2006). Finding criminals through DNA of their relatives. *Science, 312*, 1315–1316.

Bieber, F. R. (2006). Turning base hits into earned runs: Improving the effectiveness of forensic DNA data bank programs. *Journal of Law, Medicine & Ethics, 34*, 222–233.

Budowle, B. (2010). Familial searching: Extending the investigative lead potential of DNA typing. *Profiles in DNA, 13*(2). Available at <http://www.promega.com/profiles/1302/1302_07.html>.

Chung, Y.-K., et al. (2010). Familial database search on two-person mixture. *Computational Statistics and Data Analysis, 54*, 2046–2051.

Cowen, S., & Thompson, J. (2008). A likelihood ratio approach to familial searching of large DNA databases. *Forensic Science International: Genetics Supplement Series, 1*, 643–645.

Curran, J. M., & Buckleton, J. S. (2008). Effectiveness of familial searches. *Science & Justice, 48*, 164–167.

Epstein, J. (2009). "Genetic surveillance" – the bogeyman response to familial DNA investigations. *University of Illinois Journal of Law, Technology, and Policy, 1*, 141–173.

Flimmers, R., et al. (2008). STR-profiling for the differentiation between related and unrelated individuals in cases of citizen rights. *Forensic Science International: Genetics Supplement Series, 1*, 510–513.

Forensic Science Service. (2008). Craig Harman – family DNA link offers crime breakthrough. Available at <http://www.forensic.gov.uk/html/media/case-studies/f-39.html>.

Fu, J., et al. (2007). Considerations for the interpretation of STR results in cases of questioned half-sibship. *Transfusion, 47*, 515–519.

Gabel, J. D. (2010). Probable cause from probable bonds: A genetic tattle tale based on familial DNA. *Hastings Women's Law Journal, 21*, 3–57.

Ge, J., et al. (2010). Comparing DNA based familial searching policies. *Proceedings of the twenty first international symposium on human identification*. Available at <http://www.promega.com/geneticidproc/ussymp21proc/oralpresentations/Ge.pdf>.

Gershaw, C. J., et al. (2011). Forensic utilization of familial searches in DNA databases. *Forensic Science International: Genetics, 5*, 16–20.

Greely, H. T., et al. (2006). Family ties: The use of DNA offender databases to catch offenders' kin. *Journal of Law, Medicine & Ethics, 34*, 248–252.

Grimm, D. J. (2007). The demographics of genetic surveillance: Familial DNA testing and the Hispanic community. *Columbia Law Review, 107*, 1164–1194.

Hicks, T., et al. (2010). Use of DNA profiles for investigation using a simulated national DNA database: Part II. Statistical and ethical considerations on familial searching. *Forensic Science International: Genetics, 4*, 316–322.

Kaye, D. H. (2010). "Familial searching": Ten questions and answers. Available at <http://www.personal.psu.edu/dhk3/blogs/DoubleHelixLaw/blog/>.

Lewis, K. E. (2009). Genomic approaches to forensic DNA analysis. PhD dissertation. University of Washington, Department of Genome Sciences.

Liu, H.-M., et al. (2007). Y-chromosome short tandem repeats analysis to complement paternal lineage study: A single institutional experience in Taiwan. *Transfusion, 47*, 918–926.

Miller, G. (2010). Familial DNA testing scores a win in serial killer case. *Science, 329*, 262.

Myers, S. P., et al. (2010). Searching for first-degree familial relationships in California's offender DNA database: Validation of a likelihood ratio-based approach. *Forensic Science International: Genetics* (in press). doi:10.1016/j.fsigen.2010.10.010.

Murphy, E. (2010). Relative doubt: Familial searches of DNA databases. *Michigan Law Review, 109*, 291–348.

O'Connor, K. L., et al. (2010). Evaluating the effect of additional forensic loci on likelihood ratio values for complex kinship analysis. *Proceedings of the twenty first international symposium on human identification*. Available at <http://www.promega.com/geneticidproc/ussymp21proc/oralpresentations/OConnor.pdf>.

Presciuttini, S., et al. (2003). Allele sharing in first-degree and unrelated pairs of individuals in the GeFI AmpFlSTR Profiler Plus database. *Forensic Science International, 131*, 85–89.

Reid, T. M., et al. (2004). Specificity of sibship determination using the ABI Identifiler multiplex system. *Journal of Forensic Sciences, 49*, 1262–1264.

Reid, T. M., et al. (2008). Use of sibling pairs to determine the familial searching efficiency of forensic databases. *Forensic Science International: Genetics, 2*(4), 340–342.

Rozen, J. (2009, March 17). Genetic surveillance for all. *Slate Magazine*. Available at <http://www.slate.com/id/2213958/>.

Sjerps, M., & Kloostermann, A. D. (1999). On the consequences of DNA profile mismatches for close relatives of an excluded suspect. *International Journal of Legal Medicine, 112*, 176–180.

Steinberger, E., & Sims, G. (2008). Finding criminals through the DNA of their relatives—familial searching of the California offender DNA database. *Prosecutor's Brief, 31*, 28–32.

Suter, S. M. (2010). All in the family: Privacy and DNA familial searching. *Harvard Journal of Law & Technology, 23*, 309–399.

SWGDAM (2009). SWGDAM recommendations to the FBI Director on the "Interim plan for the release of information in the event of a 'partial match' at NDIS". *Forensic Science Communications, 11*(4). Available at <http://www2.fbi.gov/hq/lab/fsc/backissu/oct2009/standard_guidlines/swgdam.html>.

Willing, R. (2005, June 8). Suspects get snared by a relative's DNA. *USA Today*. Available at <http://www.usatoday.com/news/nation/2005-06-07-dna-cover_x.htm>.

Grim Sleeper Case and California Familial Search Policy

ACLU (2010). "Grim Sleeper" case doesn't justify expanding the reach of DNA databases. <http://www.aclu-sc.org/news_stories/view/102863/>.

Dolan, M., & Felch, J. (2008, November 25). Tracing a suspect through a relative. *Los Angeles Times*. Available at <http://articles.latimes.com/2008/nov/25/local/me-familial25>.

Dolan, M., et al. (2010, July 8). DNA leads to arrest in Grim Sleeper killings. *Los Angeles Times*. Available at <http://articles.latimes.com/2010/jul/08/local/la-me-grim-sleeper-20100708>.

Editorial (2010, July 13). A yellow light to DNA searches. *New York Times*. Available at <http://www.nytimes.com/2010/07/13/opinion/13tue1.html>.

Miller, G. (2010). Familial DNA testing scores a win in serial killer case. *Science, 329*, 262.

Myers, S. P., et al. (2010). Searching for first-degree familial relationships in California's offender DNA database: Validation of a likelihood ratio-based approach. *Forensic Science International: Genetics* (in press). doi:10.1016/j.fsigen.2010.10.010.

Pelisek, C. (2008, August 28). Grim Sleeper returns: He's murdering Angelenos, as cops hunt his DNA. *LA Weekly*. Available at <http://www.laweekly.com/2008-08-28/news/grim-sleeper/>.

Pelisek, C. (2008, August 28). Grim Sleeper's victims. *LA Weekly*. Available at <http://www.laweekly.com/2008-08-28/news/eleven-lives-stolen-and-one-lucky-survivor/>.

Sims, G., et al. (2008). The DNA partial match and familial search policy of the California Department of Justice. *Proceedings of the nineteenth international symposium on human identification*. Available at <http://www.promega.com/geneticidproc/ussymp19proc/oralpresentations/Sims.pdf>.

Steinhauer, J. (2010, July 8). "Grim Sleeper" arrest fans debate on DNA use. *New York Times*. Available at <http://www.nytimes.com/2010/07/09/us/09sleeper.html>.

APPENDIX

3

List of Suppliers for DNA Instruments, Reagents, Services

Contact information for a variety of organizations that supply DNA testing instrumentation, reagents, and services are included in this appendix. Every attempt has been made to be comprehensive in this listing as of late 2010. As new information becomes available, it will be added to the website links section of the NIST STRBase website: http://www.cstl.nist.gov/biotech/strbase/weblink.htm.

Certain commercial equipment, instruments, and materials are identified in order to specify experimental procedures as completely as possible. In no case does such identification imply a recommendation or endorsement by the National Institute of Standards and Technology nor does it imply that any of the materials, instruments, or equipment identified are necessarily the best available for the purpose.

Company Name	Street Address	Contact Information	Products/Services
Abacus Diagnostics	P.O. Box 4040 West Hills, CA 91308	818-716-4735 www.abacusdiagnostics.com	ABAcard® HemaTrace®, PSA ABAcard® Tests
Affiliated Genetics	P.O. Box 58535 Salt Lake City, UT 84158	800-362-5559 Fax: 801-582-8460 www.affiliatedgenetics.com	Paternity testing, DNA banking
Affymetrix	3380 Central Expressway Santa Clara, CA 95051	888-362-2447 Fax: 408-731-5441 www.affymetrix.com	GeneChip DNA hybridization products
African Ancestry	5505 Connecticut Ave # 297 Washington, DC 20015	202-439-0641 Fax: 202-318-0742 www.africanancestry.com	Genetic genealogy with mtDNA and Y-STRs
Agilent	395 Page Mill Rd. Palo Alto, CA 94303	650-752-5000 www.agilent.com	Analysis instrumentation; BioAnalyzer 2100
AMRESCO Inc.	30175 Solon Industrial Pkwy Solon, OH 44139	800-366-1313 www.amresco-inc.com	Formamide, capillary electrophoresis buffers
American Type Culture Collection (ATCC)	10801 University Boulevard Manassas, VA 20110-2209	703-365-2700 Fax: 703-365-2750 www.atcc.org	Genomic DNA and cell cultures for research purposes
Andergene Labs	3618 Ocean Ranch Blvd Oceanside, CA 92056 U.S.A.	www.andergene.com	DNA tests, parentage tests, family history, immigration and DNA storage
Applied Biosystems by Life Technologies	850 Lincoln Centre Drive Foster City, CA 94404	800-345-5224 Fax: 650-638-5884 www.appliedbiosystems.com	STR typing kits; thermal cyclers; analysis instrumentation; genotyping software; ABI 310, 3130, 3500, and 3730 instruments
ARTEL	25 Bradley Drive Westbrook, ME 04092	888-406-3463 www.artel-usa.com	Pipet calibration
ASCLD/LAB	139 J Technology Drive Garner, NC 27529	919-773-2600 Fax: 919-773-2602 www.ascld-lab.org	Crime laboratory accreditation and audits
Beckman Coulter, Inc.	250 South Kraemer Blvd Brea, CA 92821-6232	800-742-2345 Fax: 800-232-3828 www.beckmancoulter.com	Analysis instrumentation and robotics for liquid handling
Bio-Rad Laboratories	2000 Alfred Nobel Drive Hercules, CA 94547	800-424-6723 Fax: 800-879-2289 www.biorad.com	Chelex beads for DNA extraction

Biosynthesis Inc.	612 East Main St. Lewisville, TX 75057	800-227-0627 Fax: 972-420-0442 www.biosyn.com	Oligo synthesis, molecular biology products, paternity testing
Biotage LLC	10430 Harris Oak Blvd Suite C Charlotte, NC 28269	800-446-4752 Fax: 704-654-4917 www.biotage.com	Pyrosequencing information & materials
Biotype Diagnostic Gmbh	Moritzburger Weg 67 D-01109 Dresden GERMANY	+ 49 351 8838 400 Fax: + 49 351 8838 403 www.biotype.de	Autosomal and Y-STR typing kits
BioVentures, Inc.	1435 Kensington Square Ct. Murfreesboro, TN 37130	877-852-7846 Fax: 877-286-0330 www.bioventures.com	DNA size standards
Bode Technology Group	10430 Furnace Rd., Suite 107 Lorton, VA 22079	866-263-3443 Fax: 703-646-9741 www.bodetech.com	Contract forensic DNA testing and research
Cambrex Corporation	One Meadowlands Plaza East Rutherford, NJ 07073	201-804-3000 Fax: 201-804-9852 www.cambrex.com	LongRanger gels; agarose gel materials
Copan Diagnostics Inc	26055 Jefferson Avenue Murrieta, CA 92562	800-216-4016 www.copanusa.com	Nylon flocked swabs
Coriell Institute for Medical Research	403 Haddon Avenue Camden, NJ 08103	856-966-7377 Fax: 856-964-0254 www.coriell.org	Genomic DNA samples and cell cultures for genetic research reagents; CEPH family samples
Cybergenetics, Inc.	160 N. Craig St., Suite 210 Pittsburgh, PA 15213	888-FAST-MAP Fax: 412-683-3005 www.cybgen.com	Software for automated genotyping
DNA Diagnostics Center Paternity Testing	205-C Corporate Ct. Fairfield, OH 45014	412-683-3004 Fax: 412-683-3005 www.dnacenter.com	Paternity testing
DNA Heritage	P.O. Box 160 Carmine, TX 78932-0160	866-736-2362 www.dnaheritage.com	Genetic genealogy with Y-STRs

(Continued)

Company Name	Street Address	Contact Information	Products/Services
DNA Reference Laboratory	7271 Wurback Rd., Suite 125 San Antonio, TX 78240	877-362-0362 Fax: 210-615-0100 www.dnareferencelab.com	Forensic and paternity testing, mtDNA testing
Fairfax Identity Laboratories	601 Biotech Drive Richmond, VA 23235	800-735-9224 www.fairfaxidlab.com	Paternity testing; DNA databanking services
Family Tree DNA	1445 North Loop West Suite 820 Houston, TX 77008	713-868-1438 Fax: 832-201-7147 www.familytreedna.com	Genetic genealogy; Y-chromosome and mtDNA testing
Fitzco	4300 Shoreline Drive Spring Park, MN 55384	800-367-8760 Fax: 952-224-2717 www.fitzcoinc.com	FTA paper for DNA storage and extraction
Forensic Science Associates	3053 Research Drive Richmond, CA 94806	510-222-8883 Fax: 510-222-8887 www.fsalab.com	Consulting services for case review
Forensic Source	13386 International Parkway Jacksonville, FL 32218	800-852-0300 www.forensicsource.com	DNA extraction, thermal cyclers, safety, evidence storage
Future Technologies Inc.	3877 Fairfax Ridge Rd Suie 110N Fairfax, VA 22030	Tel.: 703-278-0199 Fax: 703-385-0886 www.ftechi.com	Develops information management systems such as AFDIL's LISA suite of software programs
The Gel Company	665 Third Street, Suite 240 San Francisco, CA 94107	415-247-8760 www.gelcompany.com	Reagents for gels and capillary electrophoresis
Gene Codes Corporation	775 Technology Drive Suite 100A Ann Arbor, MI 84108	800-497-4939 Fax: 734-769-7074 www.genecodes.com	Sequencher software for DNA sequencing
Gene Code Forensics	775 Technology Drive Suite 100A Ann Arbor, MI 48108	800-497-4939 Fax: 734-769-7249 www.genecodesforensics.com	M-FISys mass disaster reconstruction software (used in WTC victim identification)
Genelex Corporation	3000 First Ave., Suite One Seattle, WA 98121	800-523-3080 Fax: 206-382-6277 www.healthanddna.com	Forensic and paternity testing, genetic genealogy
Genetica DNA Laboratories, Inc.	8740 Montgomery Road Cincinnati, OH 45236	800-433-6848 Fax: 513-985-9777 www.genetica.com	Paternity testing

Genetic Profiles Corporation	10675 Treena St., Suite 103 San Diego, CA 92121	800-551-7763 Fax: 858-348-0048 www.geneticprofiles.com	Paternity testing
GeneTree DNA Testing Center	2480 South Main St., Suite 200 Salt Lake City, UT 84115	866-740-6362 Fax: 801-820-3081 www.genetree.com	Genetic genealogy, paternity testing
GKT Inc. (South Korea)	Cheonan Institute, Lab of Genetics, Department of Biological Science, Dankook University, Cheonan, Choong-Nam 330-714, Korea	82-41-550-3447 Fax:82-41-553-3447 www.genekotech.com	Y-STR silver stain kits
Hamilton Company	4970 Energy Way Reno, NV 89502	800-648-5950 Fax: 775-856-7259 www.hamiltoncomp.com	Robotic pipetting stations
Identigene, Inc.	2495 S. West Temple Salt Lake City, UT 84115	801-462-1401 Fax: 801-462-1403 www.identigene.com	Forensic and paternity testing
Identity Genetics, Inc.	801 32nd Avenue Brookings, SD 57006	800-861-1054 Fax: 605-697-5306 www.identitygenetics.com	Forensic and paternity testing
Interstate Blood Bank, Inc.	5700 Pleasant View Road Memphis, TN 38134	901-384-6200 Fax: 901-384-6255 www.interstatebloodbank.com	Liquid blood samples that may be used for population databasing
Invitrogen by Life Technologies	5791 Van Allen Way P.O. Box 6482 Carlsbad, CA 92008	888-584-8929 Fax: 888-584-8930 www.invitrogen.com	Nucleic acid purification reagents
Laboratory Corporation of America	1912 Alexander Drive Research Triangle Park, NC 27709	800-742-3944 (forensics) 800-742-3944 (paternity) www.labcorp.com	Forensic and paternity testing, immigration testing, HLA testing
Maven Analytical	P.O. Box 52, Milton WV 25541	888-986-2836 www.mavenanalytical.com	MavenQST quant assay

(Continued)

Company Name	Street Address	Contact Information	Products/Services
Micronic Europe BV Micronic North America	3901 Washington Rd., Suite 302 McMurray, PA 15317	724-941-6411 Fax: 724-941-8662 www.micronic.com	Storage tubes certified to be DNA free
Millipore Corporation	290 Concord Road Billerica, MA 01821	800-645-5476 www.millipore.com	DNA separation/purification products, Microcon filters
Misonix Inc.	1938 New Highway Farmingdale, NY 11735	800-694-9612 Fax: 631-694-9412 www.misonix.com	PCR laminar flow hoods
Mitotyping Technologies, LLC	2565 Park Center Blvd, #200 State College, PA 16801	814-861-0676 Fax: 814-861-0576 www.mitotyping.com	Mitochondrial DNA & STR testing
MWG Biotech Eurofins Operon	2211 Seminole Drive Huntsville, AL 35805	256-704-8200 Fax: 251-252-7794 www.mwgbiotech.com	Oligo synthesis; genetic analysis equipment; thermal cyclers; robotics for liquid handling
Myriad Genetics	320 Wakara Way Salt Lake City, UT 84108	801-584-3600 801-584-3640 www.myriad.com	High volume genetic and clinical testing
National Medical Services	3701 Welch Road Willow Grove, PA 19090	800-522-6671 Fax: 215-657-2972 www.nmslab.com	Forensic testing
National Forensic Science Technology Center (NFSTC)	7881 114th Avenue North Largo, FL 33773	727-549-6067 Fax: 727-549-6070 www.nfstc.org	Forensic laboratory accreditation and training programs
National Institute of Standards and Technology (NIST)	100 Bureau Drive Gaithersburg, MD 20899	301-975-2200 Fax: 301-948-3730 www.nist.gov/srm	Standard Reference Materials for confirming DNA testing methodologies
Orchid Cellmark-Dallas	2600 Stemmons Freeway #133 Dallas, TX 75207	800-752-2774 Fax: 214-634-2898 www.orchidcellmark.com	Forensic and paternity testing; DNA databanking services
Orchid Cellmark-UK	P.O. Box 265, Abingdon, Oxfordshire, OX14 1YX, UK	01235 528000 www.cellmark.co.uk	Forensic and paternity testing
Orchid Gene Screen	5698 Springboro Pike Dayton, OH 45449	800-443-2383 www.genescreen.com	Paternity testing

Oxford Ancestors Ltd.	P.O. Box 288, Kidlington, Oxfordshire, OX5 1WG UK	www.oxfordancestors.com	Genetic genealogy with mtDNA and Y-STR testing
P.A.L.M. Microlaser Technologies AG	Am Neuland 9 + 12 82347 Bernried, Germany	+ 49(0)8158-9971-0 www.palm-microlaser.com	Laser microdissection equipment
Paternity Testing Corporation	300 Portland Street Columbia, MO 65201	888-837-8323 Fax: 573-442-9870 www.ptclabs.com	Paternity testing
Porter Lee Corporation	1072 South Roselle Rd. Schaumburg, IL 60193	847-985-2060 www.porterlee.com	Crime Fighter B.E.A.S.T. LIMS system
PRO-DNA Diagnostic Inc.	5345 de I'Assumption #125 Montreal, Quebec HIT4B3	877-236-6444 Fax: 514-899-9669 www.proadn.com	Paternity testing
Promega Corporation	2800 Woods Hollow Road Madison, WI 53711	800-356-9526 Fax: 608-277-2516 www.promega.com	STR typing kits; DNA extraction kits; Plexor HY; FSS-i3 software
QIAGEN, Inc.	28159 Stanford Avenue Valencia, CA 91355	800-426-8157 Fax: 800-718-2056 www.qiagen.com	DNA isolation products; sample preparation robotics; STR kits in Europe
Rainin Instrument Company, Inc.	7500 Edgewater Drive Oakland, CA 94621	800-472-4646 www.rainin.com	Pipetting products and services
Roche Applied Science	9115 Hague Road Indianapolis, IN 46250-0414	800-262-1640 www.biochem.roche.com	Molecular biology supplies, mtDNA LINEAR ARRAYs
Savillex Corporation	10321 West 70th Street Eden Prairie, MN 55344	952-935-4100 www.savillex.com	PFA (Teflon) tubes
Seratec	Ernst-Ruhstrat-Str. 5, 37079 Goettingen, Germany	+ 49 551 50480-0 www.seratec.com	PSA kit for presumptive test of semen
Serological Research Institute (SERI)	3053 Research Drive Richmond, CA 94806-5206	510- 223-7374 Fax: 510-222-8887 www.serological.com	Proficiency test provider, training services, casework consultation
Sigma-Aldrich	3050 Spruce Street St. Louis, MO 63103	800-325-3010 www.sigmaaldrich.com	Molecular biology supplies, Genosys custom oligos
Soft Genetics LLC	100 Oakwood Ave., Suite 350 State College, PA 16803	888-791-1270 www.softgenetics.com	GeneMarker HID software for genotyping, mixtures, and kinship

(Continued)

Company Name	Street Address	Contact Information	Products/Services
STaCS DNA Inc.	2255 St-Laurent Blvd. Suite 206 Ottawa, Ontario K1H 8P5, Canada	703-825-2941 Fax: 703-825-2942 www.stacsdna.com	STaCS (sample tracking and control system) LIMS
Tecan U.S., Inc.	4022 Stirrup Creek Dr., #310 Durham, NC 27703	800-352-5128 www.tecan.com	Robotics for liquid handling
Transgenomic, Inc.	12325 Emmet Street Omaha, NE 68164	888-233-9283 www.transgenomic.com	Denaturing HPLC instruments for genetic analysis
University of North Texas Center for Human Identification	3500 Camp Bowie Blvd. Ft. Worth, TX 76107	800-687-5301 www.unthumanid.org	Missing persons testing; paternity testing
Whatman, Inc.	9 Bridewell Place Clifton, NJ 07014	800-942-8626 www.whatman.com	FTA paper, GeneSpin DNA purification kit

APPENDIX

4

Interviews Supporting Legal Aspects of DNA Testing

As part of completing my research on legal aspects of DNA testing for Chapter 18, I was privileged to interview several scientists and lawyers. What they had to say was informative and insightful—and so their full responses to my interview questions are included here with their permission. Portions of these responses have been used to create content for Chapter 18.

INTERVIEW WITH DR. ROBIN COTTON ON BEING AN EXPERT WITNESS

Dr. Cotton is associate professor and director of the biomedical forensic sciences program at Boston University. She has over 20 years experience with forensic DNA analysis and served as the Laboratory Director for Cellmark Diagnostics from 1994 to 2006. She has served as an expert witness and testified in over 200 trials regarding DNA evidence including the O.J. Simpson trial in 1995.

How many times have you testified in court?

At least 220 times in 35 different states. I know that you are supposed to have an exact count, but I don't have it. I stopped counting when I left Orchid Cellmark in 2006 but have probably testified 20 times since then.

Have all of your expert witness testimonies been for the prosecution? If not, what is the breakdown of prosecution vs. defense?

Almost all of my testimonies have been for the prosecution. I have testified 2 or 3 times for the defense. Cellmark used to do defense consulting but for the most part with DNA results, you do not get called to testify for the defense—unless you are willing to go beyond what you really think or there is an important mistake in the testing.

The best thing you can do to help a defense attorney, if the lab has done a competent job in testing, is to tell the defense attorney what he should be hearing from the expert. I have seen transcripts where the testing was fine but what the witness said about the testing isn't so fine or more likely it is very imprecise and therefore it could be misleading.

Would your preparation and performance in court be any different if you were testifying for the defense rather than the prosecution? How?

No. You need to know what you are talking about in either case. Remember that you are there to explain the data. As an expert witness, you are not there to take a side. Some attorneys would like you to take sides. If it is a defense attorney, they may tell you all the things about the case that make it seem like the defendant is getting beaten up by the prosecutor. The prosecutor may tell you all of the bad things that the person did in this case.

There is no question that some of these defendants have big issues and have hurt people. Our role as expert witnesses isn't to participate in that discussion. If you are in a law enforcement lab, you are at serious risk especially if you have no process by which you can tell somebody that you are being leaned on by an attorney—because it can happen. It happened to me—and I was from a private lab.

What do you enjoy most about being an expert witness?

I am going to use the word "contest." I don't really like the win/lose ambiance that you experience in the courtroom. But sometimes the defense attorney or whoever is on the other side—but in my case it was mostly the defense attorney—really knows what they are doing. It is almost like you are having a really tough discussion. They are doing things that are a little bit hard to contend with—and if you can manage that well (so that you are managing to make your points well) that feels good.

It can be really boring. If you have said the same thing 200 times, sometimes it can be really boring—and you can't be bored! You cannot allow yourself to be bored. It is sometimes hard if it is a very routine case. If everything sounds so practiced, that you are not being spontaneous, then I would be concerned that the jurors would notice that. Remember that this is their only case. The jury will not see you again.

What is your role as an expert witness?

Your job is to represent the data. I think people forget that usually just one person signs the report. I think that it is important that many people in the lab would have the same opinion about that report. When you are sitting there on the witness stand, you are the lab! For purposes of that jury, you are the laboratory. Whatever they think about the laboratory comes from what they think about you.

Have you have ever taken one of those classes regarding risk management, where they talk about what you do not often do but if it fails, it is a catastrophe? Courtroom testimony is one of those things. Doing a poor job with courtroom testimony can cause serious problems for a laboratory and the analyst. If laboratory personnel are testifying all of the time, then every one of those people has to be good every time.

How do you make sure that testimony is consistent across your laboratory?

At Cellmark, we had two people signing every report so either one of them would go to court and testify to the results. The technical reviewer was also signing along with the analyst who did the initial interpretation. Thus, we had two people available to go to court because we were testifying all over the country. It also allowed us when there were *Frye* hearings to send the person with the more academic background. This approach gave us versatility. But we were not paired up. A case from any analyst could be picked up by any technical reviewer. This approach helped to have consistency across the lab. If we had something where they were not agreeing, we would bring in a number of people to look at it.

The thing that worries me the most is that a brand new person is being technically reviewed by another brand new person. They could reach an interpretation that others in the lab would not agree with and off goes the report. This would be a problem!

What did you least enjoy about being an expert witness?

Very aggressive, very loud, very unpleasant cross-examination tactics. I don't personally care to be shouted at.

How did you handle being shouted at during cross-examination?

Well, I had a big advantage when I started testifying. When I was a postdoc in Iowa, I did volunteer work for three years at a crisis intervention center. The experience taught me a lot about talking to people. You were talking to people that were very upset, very depressed, and very angry—and sometimes verging on out-of-control. We learned that if someone is shouting at you then keeping your voice down will bring their voice down. Keeping your speaking tempo slow will get their tempo to slow. I used those approaches in the courtroom to slow my pace. And I always remain attentive. If you are being attentive to the defense attorney who is yelling at you, it makes him or her look poorly if they are shouting at you. If I am sitting here being quiet, listening intently, answering slowly, and he is shouting at me, then he will not look good!

Have prosecutors ever tried to push you to say things that were beyond what you thought were appropriate?

Yes, there have been times that I was leaned on. I learned that a lot of prosecutors will say "can you make a stronger statement?" I think that is an okay question. But once I say "No!" then I do not think they should ask again. When giving court testimony, people need to know the limits of their data and stick to them.

How do you know what your limits are?

You need a thorough understanding of the literature and your protocols. If you cannot go directly to the source, you shouldn't be saying it. Unfortunately some analysts today don't read very much and therefore do not know the source information very well. So when they say it is "this" and you lean on them, they won't know!

The reason that it was so easy to do *Frye* hearings was coming from an academic background. You are used to understanding that there is literature to back this up, how do I find it, and what does it say.

How has being an expert witness evolved over the years?

After the Simpson case everyone decided it was a disaster to give a lot of explanation so now they give almost no explanation. I am not sure that that is not going a little far over the edge but it is hard to give a lot of explanation. For example—"capillary electrophoresis"—that is a little tricky!

Do you ever show electropherograms to the jury?

I don't, but I do show them the allele results table. The table isn't that hard to figure out. People should be showing the jury the table, it's not that hard. Here are the names of the loci and here are the samples and here is the data. If you have taken the time to explain something simple, like paternity, for one person each locus has two alleles—you get one from mom and one from dad. Then the jury sees the two alleles or more than two. You can say to them that the instrument data is more quantitative than the data in the table. So I can tell you if I go back to the instrument data, and determine whether there is more DNA represented in this "10" or this "11" and then you have made that connection. You can even draw it.

Do you use PowerPoint slides to emphasize a point or to teach a concept?

Never! I never do, but this is personal to me. I think that when you go to be an expert witness you have to think about how do you best explain things. If you love PowerPoint slides, then use them.

I had an important insight early on in my court testimony experience. When you are sitting in the witness chair, you only have your hands. An attorney in Seattle said to me: "Why don't you come down and diagram it?" It was like night and day. As soon as I stepped down and starting drawing, I was no longer confined to the rigid position of the witness chair. I was me. I was teaching! I was connecting with the audience. I could draw and if I didn't like it, I could undo it.

Is it a challenge that juries cannot ask questions and therefore you don't really know what they are thinking?

There are courtrooms in certain states where the juries are allowed to ask questions. They do it by writing the questions during the testimony and then when you are done, they pass the questions to the judge. The judge reads them and if he thinks they are okay, he will read them to you so that you can respond.

I don't think courts should be on TV. I think it is fine to have plenty of people in there but I think that having things on TV is not a good idea. I think that everywhere jurors should be allowed to ask questions. I know they can in grand jury. You can figure out immediately from the question asked how well they understood what you have said. Sometimes judges will ask questions, but that is more often in an admissibility hearing because they are the ones having to make the decisions. You can have two or three questions from a jury and realize that you didn't make something clear and you have another opportunity. It makes a huge difference!

Normally you only get one pass. I have been in the witness chair listening to what I am saying and thinking. "Are you out of your mind? The jury could not have possibly understood that statement. That's gibberish!" Sometimes it comes out well and sometimes not.

Do you ever read your transcripts to see what you said in a trial?

I prefer not to read my transcripts. I know that is bad on one account. Sometimes when you have to do a retrial they want you to read your transcript. But my feeling is that if I answered it the best I could the first time, I am going to answer it the same. If I read the transcript, then I am worried about whether I am remembering what I said previously. If I don't read the transcript, I have taken that concern off the plate. If the attorneys say, "Well, that is not what you said the first time," then I am allowed to ask to look at what I said the first time. Then I can say but that question was slightly different or I was answering that question about a different locus or whatever. As long as you tell the truth, you don't have to remember exactly what you said.

How do you prepare for trial?

I prefer to prepare the day before testimony. Now that does not mean that I might not look at the case a couple of weeks before, go over it and see if there are any issues: Are there typos? Is there anything I need to amend? Is there any problem that I need to be aware of? But the details, I don't do until the day before and then I outline the results. I just take the case folder apart as if I were doing that technical review all over again. I go through absolutely everything—from the evidence log-in sheet through every piece of paper so I know actually what's where. I may have the original case folder with me, but I have a copy of the whole case folder or the pieces of paper that are most important to me so that I can mark them up. Whenever you mark up paperwork and you carry something extra into court, you do have to be aware that you may have to turn that over. So I make my markings neat. I might highlight something if there are a lot of samples and you are trying to keep track of them, I will highlight the name of the sample. I want something that will draw my eyes to exactly where I need to look. I will put an arrow over certain peaks or I will use stickies. Whatever I do, I do it neatly. I work such that if I have to give it over...I am not going to be embarrassed by what I have written or marked up. When I study this way, the information that I need in preparing for trial stays with me better. I also know that I will not be fumbling around with the case folder.

We used to compile our case folder with the first thing being the bottom page and new information just got piled on top. For court, I would disassemble the case folder and I would put all of the pages for one sample together if there were many samples. If there were not many samples, I would organize the pages by the step: here are the extractions, here is the next thing, and so forth. So I would reassemble them in an order that made sense to me—at least in my copy so that I could work from it easily in the witness stand.

I talked to Gary Sims [from the California Department of Justice DNA Laboratory] after the Simpson trial. He did his whole testimony from memory. I can't do that. It is a big risk if you try it and are not good at it. The risk is that you will say something wrong. I use the paperwork when I need to. I look down at my notes while I am talking if needed. You sometimes have to ask permission to do that or the attorney will say, "Do you need to look at your casework to refresh your memory?" and then you are good to go. I would much rather see the jury see me rely on the paperwork than say something and go "Oh, my! I misspoke. It wasn't that piece of evidence, it was this piece."

There are a couple of things that I think the juries aren't going to worry about. Number one, who in their daily routine doesn't write lists or have to look at pieces of paper. The other thing is that expert witnesses get worried a lot when there is a mistake. A lot of times the mistakes are little, but occasionally the mistakes are big. But if you have to say you made a mistake, I don't think that it wrecks your credibility or your testimony because everyone sitting in that jury—whether they have a high school education or a Ph.D.—makes mistakes. And to think that you would not make a mistake is unrealistic. It's embarrassing, it's hard. I had to testify to early mistakes in proficiency tests at Cellmark for 15 years—and every time it was hard. It doesn't get easier to say it, but you have to say it. There is nothing else to do so you might as well get comfortable with the idea that it happened and get comfortable with the idea that they are not going to hold it against you.

What was the most challenging trial you were involved in and why was it so challenging?

There were several. One was the O.J. Simpson trial. There was another one in Colorado where the defense attorney was just the most aggressive, most angry, most mean, that I have ever experienced. He raised his voice all the time, he insinuated that I was a liar, that I was unethical, and untruthful. And it is very hard. It is hard not to get angry, it is hard to keep your cool, and it is hard not to give in when you are being badgered. The Colorado case was not the length of the Simpson trial but still difficult especially since the prosecutor wasn't terribly helpful. He didn't object and the judge just let it happen. It is difficult when a judge is not trying to exercise any control.

How do you prepare yourself for testifying in court?

You have to be really focused in the courtroom. You cannot mentally be somewhere else. You need to listen to the questions. The longer you are listening to questions, the harder it is to stay focused. Just like anything, you get tired. The attorneys get to take a little rest, they trade off, etc., but you cannot get tired. You have to be very focused. You cannot be paying attention to everything in the courtroom. It will distract you. I just look to the attorney and I just look to the jury and that's it.

How do you dress when you go to court?

I wear dark clothes. I wouldn't choose a red suit. I don't want to look like I am going to a party. Nobody in that courtroom is there because something good happened. You have to respect that things have happened and you have to have respect for the proceeding and for the individuals that are there.

Do you have a routine you follow as you enter a courtroom?

The minute you walk into the courthouse you need to be aware that anyone around you could be a juror, an attorney, or someone else involved in the trial. Your professional behavior starts when you walk in the door and you don't change that until you are far away from that courtroom. You are not pals with the police officer. You are not pals with the attorney. You are not there to be somebody's friend.

Are there any specific things that you bring with you or do when you sit in the witness box?

I take whatever I think I am going to need to the witness box. If there were a *Frye* hearing, I might bring in scientific articles. For a case, I might bring some notes along with my copy of the case folder. I don't have things with me that I'm not willing to turn over. Some people take a book if they think they might be waiting—and that is fine. I usually take some scientific journal articles just because *People* magazine doesn't seem to be the right thing to have in a courtroom.

How much time do you normally spend talking to the lawyer who has called you to testify before your appearance in court?

It really depends on how much the lawyer knows. Sometimes you have to force the lawyer to talk to you, and that can be very hard for analysts from crime labs. At Cellmark, as a private laboratory, we had a way to get the lawyer's attention. We would say, "I am not getting on the plane until I know we are going to have time to sit down and talk!" An analyst in a public crime lab may not have that option but if there are issues, your lab director should meet with the district attorney and work on improving relations between the lawyers and the lab.

Do you have a list of prepared questions that you share with your lawyer before and encourage him/her to use while you are on the stand?

Lawyers like it when you have a list of prepared questions for your direct examination. However, you need to go through the questions with them because some of the questions may not fit a particular case or your role in the expert testimony you are offering.

What is the most important thing for the jury to know about you when you are explaining your qualifications?

I don't know. It's the worst part of the testimony. I have never been comfortable with it. I actually feel embarrassed when I have to say my qualifications because I know the people in the jury may not have had as many educational opportunities. So I just say my qualifications and hope to move on quickly.

What should be included in a CV (*curriculum vitae*) that is submitted to court as part of being qualified to be an expert?

Your CV should be only the organizations you are a member of, your publications, your job title, your job description, and your education. Testimony is not a qualification, neither is your volunteer work or anything else. I am careful about what I am qualified in. For example, I never allow the attorneys to qualify me as an expert in statistics, but they may qualify me as an expert in the calculations of frequencies as it relates to the DNA testing because I know how the frequencies are calculated.

How do you know whether or not you are connecting with the jury?

You can just forget it. You don't know. Of course it's important to connect with the jury. I want them to understand. I'm choosing words carefully. When we changed from doing RFLP testing to PCR testing, the first time I went to court I realized that I hadn't figured out what to say yet. So I sat down and wrote out the absolute basic pieces of information that a person has to understand in order to understand what I am saying. Those are the things you want to talk about in plain language.

Do you use analogies to help explain DNA results to the jury?

I am not an analogy person, but some people are. An analogy that I almost always use is that the variation in DNA repeats, which gives size differences in the DNA between people, is similar to the number of boxcars on a train. More boxcars lead to a longer length train. It can be hard for people to envision DNA so another analogy that I have used in the past is to say, "Suppose I line up on the table here in front of me 46 spools of thread, two blue, two orange, two green, and so on. Then we unroll the thread from the spool and that's the DNA."

Some people are very fluid with analogies. Their analogies are simple and they use them well. Other people think they are very fluid with analogies, and the analogy is so complicated that nobody can figure it out! You have to be careful about using analogies because you don't want to talk down to the jury too much or too often. If you use an analogy for everything, the jury may get tired of it. In addition, they won't know which analogy went with what, which is even more dangerous.

What do you want jury members to come away with after your testimony?

If you are going to talk about DNA, you have to know something about the fact that people have chromosomes, and each one of those chromosomes is a piece of DNA. For each chromosome pair, you get one from your mother and one from your father. You can work out what is the most simple thing they have to know and then how to say that using the simplest possible language. You quickly find out that there are a few scientific terms you can't do without. You can't do without "allele." You can call it a "type" or you can call it whatever, but you have to have a word for it that you have defined. Make sure you have as-plain-as-day explanations for the scientific words you use.

It used to be a lot more fun when you could make a good joke about Southern blots—because you are sitting there talking about DNA and it is supposed to be really high-tech. Then you talk about having this gel that is sort of like Jello and you are putting a big stack of paper-towels on it like a big weight on top and the jury is thinking, "How high-tech is this?" There are places you could have fun. The CE (capillary electrophoresis) doesn't quite do as well.

Were there ever times when you felt like the jury did not understand what you were trying to explain?

Oh, absolutely! After listening to your explanation of a topic and seeing the blank look on the jurors' faces, you may need to say, "I don't think I got that out right. Can I try it again?"

What do you find to be the most difficult thing to explain to a jury?

It is hard to explain a differential extraction to a jury. I think it is easier to draw something as a diagram than to sit in the chair and explain it with your hands waving in the air. A PowerPoint slide can do the same thing for you. However, the jury does not see you create the slide. If I stand up in front of them and diagram the concept I am trying to teach, they are seeing that I am making this out of my head. I think you connect better with them, plus they know that you know what you are saying if you are drawing the concept in front of them. I can put a lot of information on a PowerPoint slide and not really own it, but if I am drawing it for them I have to own it.

Sometimes if I have been given a difficult question, I will say, "I can explain this to you, but I can't do it without a diagram." As part of preparing for my testimony, I try to remember to tell the attorney to bring an easel and paper to the courtroom so that I can be prepared to diagram an explanation.

Are there any props or handouts that you regularly use to help explain DNA to the jury?

Some attorneys like props and others don't. I had one really bad experience where I went to a trial, and the attorneys had made a lot of posters—and had not just taken the table from the report. They had made posters with pictures of the evidence, which was kind of gruesome. I was very uncomfortable with that.

Is there an ideal direct examination in your opinion?

No, because that's just so case-specific. It could make sense though to have questions prepared to help you logically flow through the information being presented.

What are your thoughts about how to handle discovery requests? Do you push back if you feel like too much information is being requested by the opposing counsel and experts?

I think the most important question for a lab (in fact, any discipline in the lab), is if you were to hand this information—the information you are going to give over to the defense—to a respected colleague, would you have given them everything they need to evaluate your work? If the answer is yes, then that's about what you should be giving on discovery. For DNA that might be your case folder, your procedures, and your electronic data. I know that the defense often asks for lots of other documents: validation studies, proficiency test results, etc. Different states have different rules and different prosecutor's offices have different attitudes about giving over that extra material.

I don't see anything wrong with asking people to pay for getting a copy of the discovery information. At Cellmark, we used to get huge requests. We found out that the nicer, neater, tidier, and more organized the paperwork was that we gave to them, the less we ever heard about it again. It was almost as if they looked at it and said, "Oh my! This information is organized. It must be good."

In any case, you should give over, *without question and happily*, the things that you would need from another competent DNA person to perform the review. *Do not worry about who might look at the information as a defense expert!*

The defense attorney can take it to any defense expert. The defense attorney isn't necessarily going to control what this expert does with your data, but hopefully the defense attorney would try to recognize whether or not their expert was making a legitimate argument with your data. If the reviewing expert does not make a legitimate argument with your data, then that is their problem—not yours. Unfortunately, I find a discovery request can become the start of an "us" against "them" mentality.

You know what you did and you know what your standard operating procedures are. You know hopefully why you did not choose to look at peaks below a particular RFU [relative fluorescence unit] level. If their review of your data makes you have to study why you are doing what you are doing, then that's part of your job, too. You wrote a scientific report. Your data should be outlined in the report. The table should be in the report.

The stats should be in the report. That is the basis of your scientific opinion. However, it is the case folder that holds the entirety of what you did; and it is the SOP that says how you did it. So let the defense attorney have all of this information! If I were reviewing results from a case, I would ask for all of this information.

Have you ever done an affidavit instead of testifying in court?

I have done affidavits, but I have never done them as a replacement for testifying. I know that sometimes the prosecutor and the defense have stipulated to our report and just put it into the court record. Maybe the DNA testing wasn't particularly probative, but they just wanted to show that they did it. However, this is different than writing an affidavit.

Are depositions more challenging relative to testifying in court?

Depositions are more challenging because there is no judge, so the defense attorney can ask you something really obnoxious, such as, "How much do you make?" They can ask personal questions and there is nobody there as an arbitrator. While that doesn't happen very often, I have had it happen—and I've been forced to answer. The prosecutor will say "I object" and that goes on the record.

What are the lawyers like whom you have met in your court experience?

You learn that some lawyers are fabulous and some lawyers are awful—like a regular bell curve. You can learn so much from a good lawyer. A really good lawyer will (a) not press your testimony, and (b) can give you coaching that you are not going to get anywhere else. I don't mean coaching in what to say. I mean coaching in how to deal with a difficult or badgering defense attorney.

What was the best coaching you ever received from an attorney?

The best coaching I ever received was from an attorney in Montana years ago. He was one of two attorneys on the case in a *Frye* hearing and I was one of several witnesses. We were watching other experts and he was commenting on them. He taught me that you can say too much when trying to answer a question. I had not previously realized this because in my efforts to be helpful, I was giving people a lot of information. The defense attorney in that case was very good with his questions and every time a witness would go beyond the question with additional information, the defense attorney took the information the witness had told him and dreamed up another question on the spot. It was miraculous. The person I was with was from the Attorney General's office, and had many years of trial experience. For example, he taught me that if you would just say in response to a question from the defense attorney, "No, capillary electrophoresis (or whatever the question relates to) does work very well. There is scientific literature to back that up!", the defense attorney does not know what the scientific literature is and so you are not giving him something to ask about next—except maybe "Have you read the scientific literature?"

When I got up on the witness stand, I tried this approach—and it was helpful! As soon as I started providing short responses without the elaboration which he had not requested, the defense attorney had less to say. He was remarkable at thinking of the next thing to ask from a witness's previous answer. But when I just said, "No, that is not correct" without any further explanation, he didn't have anything to build on. The best thing I ever learned was to say less and just answer the question—and only the question! I am not withholding information. I am just not giving explanations that were not requested.

How do you handle situations where the opposing attorney is attacking your testimony?

When somebody is attacking your testimony, there are two bad things that happen. One is that you get mad. The other thing is you get tired so you tend to start giving in or you just shut down or you glare at everybody and you look uncomfortable. It can take some practice at home, such as rehearsing how you might respond to challenging questions.

If the opposing attorney is just attacking you, and it is a really small point and they are correct, just say "You're right!" Sometimes they're making a point and they are correct. However, our natural tendency is to think "I'm not giving in or giving up on anything." You have to let go of that.

If the opposing attorney finds a typo in my report or case folder, I just acknowledge the point. I do it in as easy a manner as possible. Sometimes they are trying to make a point that's kind of partially right and that's the hardest thing, because they want to make it simple but you know scientifically that where they are going is not correct.

Do you try to think about where they are going with a particular line of questioning while you are answering questions?

You have got to be careful with trying to think about where they are going to go. Because (a) you can get very distracted by that and, (b) you don't really know. It is very easy to think "Oh! I see where this is going." Most of the time you may be able to see where a particular line of questioning is going but sometimes you will not. My advice to people is to just focus on the question at hand. If your mind is five questions away, you will not be paying attention to the question that is in front of you.

Sometimes questions get very hard and you can't always just manage the situation by saying that it is more complicated than the way they have described something. You may be faced with agreeing with something that you don't totally agree with or saying it is wrong when it is not totally wrong. That to me is the hardest thing to deal with because you have to weave your way through a series of questions while trying not to be an obstructionist or giving in. Sometimes you just have to say "It's more complicated than that but under this assumption it would be true…"

Do you ever restate a question to try and help the attorney?

It depends—most of the time you are just correcting their question. For example, they may have just said to you, "The RFLP technology used in this DNA typing procedure is new or novel, isn't it?" So you go, "No, this isn't RFLP, this is PCR?" Their verbiage is all wrong, sometimes just out of kindness or not to be totally obnoxious you are fixing the question and answering it.

Be respectful of the attorneys. They know a lot of law that you don't know. It is just that they don't know the DNA information as well as you. Sometimes they have pre-prepared questions that came from years ago so the vocabulary is incorrect. Attorneys for some reason cannot capture the word "locus." You don't want to correct them too much—but you can help them a little bit. If it is a cross examination, and they are being not very friendly, then I'm careful about what I add.

If the attorneys on both sides are allowing you to answer the question and you are not taking advantage of that and talking for 10 minutes, then you can usually say "Well under this circumstance that's true, but sometimes under other circumstances it is not..." But if there are a lot of objections, and there has been antagonism between the two attorneys during the trial and you know that the defense attorney is going to say "Non-responsive!," then you can feel pretty stuck and you just have to figure it out as you go.

Have you ever felt that the side you are testifying for is not supporting you—that you have been abandoned?

It's not so much that. It's all about the lawyer's skill. I have walked into a courtroom with a lawyer who was so good—and we did not do very much pretrial work—but he was so in charge and so careful to listen. I felt completely safe even when it was somewhat adversarial. I have also felt completely like neither the judge nor the attorneys were going to be helpful. It may be they don't know what to do. It may be that they are out of their league. It could be any number of things. Then you just do the best you can.

What is the worst thing that you can do on the witness stand?

I actually think that there is only one mistake you can really make—other than telling a lie, of course. You should not treat the prosecution and defense attorneys any different in how you respond to them. However you talk to one attorney, you need to talk to the other attorney the exact same way. You don't want to change your body language. You don't want to change your tone or the speed in which you answer questions or your demeanor to the jury.

What is your attitude toward defendants in a trial?

Respect for everyone in the courtroom is important. I always refer to the defendant as Mr. Smith—never as "the subject" or "the suspect." As far as I am concerned until that verdict comes down that person is innocent.

Early on in my career a prosecutor taught me that in her view individuals were being prosecuted for an event, which did not necessarily define them as a person. Defendants are human beings. This important lesson from this prosecutor gave me a much better perspective.

What is your attitude toward defense attorneys having faced more than 200 of them?

Some defense attorneys completely understand their role and they are able, like a good prosecutor, to pull it off without avarice. They can be hard. They can be tough, which is not the same as being mean and angry. You can really tell the difference between the two. Defense attorneys have their role. Often, the first thing that new people think, which I thought too, is "Oh my! How can you defend this person who serially raped 25 women?" Well, those defendants have a right to their day in court and deserve the protections that the law provides.

What is the best advice you have received from an attorney?

I had a couple of very good attorneys to work with early in my career of testifying. They spent the time to teach me because the DNA data was so important to their case. I received lots of on-the-job training from some very skilled people—both defense attorneys and prosecutors—because the early DNA cases were all admissibility issues, and people weren't spending the money unless it was an important case. With an important case, you generally have very good lawyers on both sides so I was privileged to have worked with these very good lawyers early on, a bunch of them.

In one of my early *Frye* hearings, I was stressed about whether or not the judge would find the DNA results admissible. The defense attorney was difficult, and I could feel that things were not going well. Sensing my anxiety and feeling my sense of responsibility for the outcome, the prosecutor looked at me and said, "I win or lose this case – not you!"

How do you act around the lawyers and other participants in the courtroom?

I may be friendly with the lawyers in their office but not inside the courthouse. I would never be unfriendly to a victim or a victim's family, but I also don't want to have a conversation with them in the courthouse. If they say something to me, I will answer the question quietly, but I won't engage in a big conversation with them. I'll just be polite—just like I would if the defense attorney asked me a question. *Equal respect to everyone...*

At the crisis intervention center where I worked while a postdoc, they had a phrase for this behavior: "unconditional positive regard." That should be your attitude to anyone in the courtroom. If I have a private thought about some player, then I can articulate it when I come home. I can articulate it with the attorney I am working with in his office. I can go back to the lab and talk to a colleague, but in that arena of the courtroom, they all get my equal respect genuinely. I think that is where the creditability comes from that you should have as an expert witness.

What do you say when you are not certain of an appropriate response or not certain you have the right answer?

Depending on how uncertain I am, either I say "I cannot answer the question because I'm not sure" or if I am reasonably sure but not positive, then I will say "I think the answer is such in such, but I'm not sure. However, I could find out where to get the answer."

Have you ever made a mistake in your testimony and then realized it afterwards? How do you handle this situation?

I have made mistakes in testimony. I usually realize it during the testimony and simply say, "I realize I just misspoke." If you make some real mistake, then you have got to tell somebody. Don't try to cover it up.

What do you say to defense experts who seem to exaggerate claims or concerns about the data?

I don't think that a defense expert should make statements that are not scientifically appropriate. I don't think that a defense expert should insinuate that people aren't ethical when they have no history of that. I don't ever try to use that kind of heavy language. This type of behavior brings drama into the courtroom when there really should not be drama. The prosecutor or defense attorney may want the trial to turn into drama—but the science is better without it.

How do you deal with what can sometimes be harsh cross-examination tactics?

No one can really protect you except you. The minute angry or sarcastic words come out of your mouth then you have lost control. It is hard to get it back. It is almost like you have to hear the question minus the tone, minus the face, and minus the waving of hands. You have to train yourself to hear it like that. You have to not let the opposing counsel's behavior bother you. You have to be able to let go of the anger or not have it.

It is very hard not to take a tough cross-examination personally. Anytime you feel like you are being attacked then your anxiety goes up, your adrenalin goes up, and you feel like you have to defend yourself. I think that is just part of the tactic. You are not being attacked really. You are there just to say, "This is the data." And the defense attorneys are there to say, "Are you sure, did you do it right?" That is their job. If you didn't do your work right, then they need to know! It is their job to discuss anything that may be incorrect in what you did. They want and need to point it out.

How do you feel after having your testimony challenged in court?

Lots of people don't like to talk about how they feel, but if you don't talk about how you feel, then it is hard to change. You may talk about what the defense expert said or didn't say—and how they said it or didn't say it. You may begin to think that how other people treated you is the problem rather than "I'm my problem!" My feelings are my problem. Defenses attorneys can say anything in challenging your testimony. You cannot change this or fix this; it is part of the trial experience.

I learned how to fix my feelings of frustration after participating in the courtroom drama by remembering that it was a show. *As an expert witness, I have a very important role in this show—and the show has very important consequences—but the show isn't my permanent world.* I have strengths and other things outside of this arena. Whatever happens in the courtroom, I don't have to carry it out with me.

Having this perspective doesn't always keep you from feeling upset—but I don't have to carry those feelings of anger or frustration out of the courtroom with me, and I don't have to lay that anger on somebody else. I can just say, "You know, that was hard!" I can say, "I think that attorney, that argument was ridiculous!" But I don't have to get all riled up.

How do you handle questions outside of your expertise?

You just tell them it is outside your expertise and you can't answer them.

What advice do you have for DNA analysts who have never testified in court before?

Go explain it to your mother or father or brother until they understand. It does take a lot of practice to say it without using your normal scientific terms. Sometimes if you get tired on the witness stand, then you find that you are drifting back into the scientific language because it is easier.

Have you ever taken a court testimony workshop? If so, what were some valuable things that you learned from such training?

Yes, I have taken testimony workshops, but not very many. It is like other workshops that I have taken—you get small bits of information. Even now, when I sit in on a moot court class I learn things or I get reminded of things. So you can always get better.

Could the U.S. court system be better? Would better training lead to better treatment of expert witnesses?

You can't change the defense attorney's role. That's not going to work. Prosecutors should not lean on people to provide testimony that they would like to hear. That would help.

There is a lot of talk about ethics today. What are you opinions on the importance of ethics in courtroom testimony?

Well, it is obviously important because you are under oath. You are giving people information that is important and may have an impact on other people's lives.

What advice do you have for DNA experts in terms of being impartial as a witness?

You state what the data says or what it means. Then you are impartial because you haven't spoken outside of what your scientific testing has told you. If you think you know what your role is, then you had better make sure that is what your role really is. You are really there to explain and speak to what that data says. If you keep thinking about that, then you realize you are not there to assist the prosecutor or the defense attorney. The data is what it is—maybe messy, maybe not. This is science.

What is the single most important thing to remember when serving as an expert witness?

You are the voice of the data! You are not a voice for the victim, which is what some prosecutor's describe their role as. People will talk about the "prosecution team." I really don't think you are on somebody's team, but that isn't to say you wouldn't assist them in understanding or assist them in answering questions so that the data is clear to the jury. Just because you help in appropriate ways, it doesn't mean you are on "their side." If you want to feel like you are on someone's side, then you are welcome to feel so. You just cannot behave like you are on their side. You cannot let that feeling influence how you behave, how you speak, and most importantly, how you look at the data. I think it is a hard issue because you want to please the people you are working with, right? It is the prosecutor who is supposed to worry about the consequences of the trial. If you represent the data accurately in a scientific sense, then it is hard to go wrong.

INTERVIEW WITH DR. CHARLOTTE WORD ON ADMISSIBILITY HEARINGS

Dr. Word is currently a private consultant after working for more than 20 years with Cellmark Diagnostics. She has testified in numerous admissibility hearings and in over 200 trials regarding DNA evidence. She also serves on the editorial board for the Journal of Forensic Sciences.

How many times have you testified in court?

I have testified about 300 times in about 25 states from 1990 to 2010. A large number of the testimonies were in admissibility hearings (RFLP, DQα/DQA1/PM, CTTA silver stain, D1S80) with most of the remainder in trials. I do not believe that I testified in an admissibility hearing for fluorescent STRs using capillary electrophoresis as our lab

[Cellmark Diagnostics] only had a few cases, maybe two, requiring admissibility hearings since we performed CTT for many years prior to using the newer technology.

Is there a difference in preparation for an admissibility hearing vs. preparation for trial testimony?

Yes and no.

Yes, because just as in preparation for a trial testimony, the expert witness and attorney in an admissibility hearing must work closely together to prepare and present a series of coordinated and organized questions and answers to educate the judge about the issues and the case. And yes, just as in a trial, the expert witness is still a neutral witness in an admissibility hearing. He or she is an advocate for good science and good procedures only, not an advocate for the prosecution or defense.

No, because unlike in trials, the expert witness will often need to take a very active and involved role in the preparation for an admissibility hearing. First, it is important that the expert witness and the attorney have a good grasp on the legal issues of general acceptability controlling the hearing so that the appropriate supporting documents can be provided and foundation laid to assist the judge in the final ruling. Most states in the US are bound by either the *Frye* or *Daubert* cases, and some states have additional cases which further define the requirements for admissibility in that particular state, for example, *Kelly* in California and *Davis* in Maryland. Since admissibility hearings are rare these days, the attorneys often need to research the relevant cases, and the witness and attorney may need to network to get guidance from other attorneys and/or experts more experienced in these types of hearings.

Second, unlike trials where only the final report and/or evidence may be admitted during the proceedings and the attorney generally decides what should be admitted in a particular case, in admissibility hearings the expert witness will often have a big responsibility to assist the attorney in deciding what documents should be provided to the judge in the hearing as well as procuring and copying the necessary documents. Some of the documents that may be needed in addition to the case file include: primary research scientific literature underlying the techniques being used as well as literature showing the application to the forensic sciences, developmental and internal validation studies, reference lists, training manuals, publications and presentations from the laboratory, laboratory SOPs, glossary, list of court cases where the test results were previously admitted, and rulings from other cases. The expert witness may also have to help the attorney find other experts to testify regarding the general acceptance of a technique.

Last, unlike many trials, there is always at least one opposing witness testifying in admissibility hearings. The expert witness will often need to help educate the attorney seeking admissibility regarding the opposing witness' issues and opinions so that the attorney can prepare cross-examination questions to ask the opposing witness.

Is there a difference in the actual testimony in a hearing vs. in a trial?

Yes, definitely. Science, science, science, is what it is all about in an admissibility hearing. Sometimes the specifics of the case are not even discussed, or very minimally, in these proceedings. My briefcase is often packed full of papers and other documents that I may need to refer to in a hearing—far more than what I routinely take to a trial. I especially like the well prepared, logical, and practical manner in which the questions are laid out to best educate the judge in the scientific issues. Since no jury is present, the testimony often proceeds with fewer interruptions and less drama.

Testimony is given while looking at the judge, which can be quite difficult sometimes if the judge is seated above and behind you. Finding a comfortable position to look at the attorney asking the questions, see the judge and have the court reporter hear you can be challenging. And sometimes the judge is so busy taking notes that you end up testifying to the back of his or her head and never make eye contact! Admissibility hearings also offer a great chance to see and hear other experts testify. This is a terrific opportunity to learn different approaches to presenting the science and how to be a better witness. You can also learn first-hand about the challenges of opposing experts.

Do you prefer testifying in a hearing vs. testifying in a trial?

I like both for different reasons. In an admissibility hearing, the testimony is all about the science. I get a chance to really describe the literature and techniques in detail, maybe even draw pictures. Since the judge often asks questions to clarify anything, it is possible to have a good handle on what the judge "is getting" and what areas still need more explanation and testimony. It is very rewarding to know, based on the questions asked, that the judge has a good grasp on the science and the relevant issues. I also enjoy working closely with the attorney during preparation and testimony.

During trials, the testimony is mostly about the laboratory work done in a case, the test results, and the conclusions. It is always fun to present the nice work from your laboratory. Often the jury is quite engaged, and it is possible to tell that they understand the testimony when they nod, smile, or grimace while silently answering the questions on cross-examination before I get a chance to answer them aloud!

What advice do you have to offer experts regarding testifying?

Be prepared! The more prepared you are, the more information is readily available to you and thus you will be more confident. A well-prepared witness who has carefully thought about the science, the case, opposing challenges, and possible issues will generally be able to handle any question asked by either attorney or the judge and can comfortably avoid answering a question outside of his/her expertise.

How do the questions asked in hearings vs. trials differ?

The questions qualifying the witnesses are largely the same from hearings to trials. And the general preliminary questions of: "What is DNA?" "Does DNA differ amongst individuals?" "What samples can be used for DNA testing?" etc., are also basically the same. Then the differences start. In the admissibility hearing, since the legal burden is to demonstrate to the judge that the scientific technique being used is a generally accepted and reliable technique in the scientific community and also that the technique works appropriately when applied to the forensic science arena, the line of questioning introduces the basic techniques, the necessary and critical steps of the procedure, and how this technique is routinely used in the general scientific community, for example, in clinical laboratories, research studies, biomedical applications, environmental or industrial applications, etc. Particular examples may be introduced; for instance, in admissibility hearings for the introduction of DNA testing, it was common to discuss the use of DNA testing in human cancer diagnostics, organ transplantation, paternity testing, identification of war dead, identification of microorganisms in the environment, and so on. Primary research publications are often provided to the judge to demonstrate the use of the technique in a few of these "basic science" and non-forensic applications.

The next line of questioning introduces the foundational studies for the application of the technique to evidence analysis and verification that the technique works on samples traditionally analyzed by forensic scientists in crime labs. During these questions and testimony, the initial presentations at meetings and publications of the techniques and developmental validation studies are discussed and copies are generally given to the judge. Additional information regarding the validation studies performed in the testing laboratory and the development of the laboratory SOPs is often presented, and sometimes a copy of the lab's SOPs is provided to the judge. Publications and/or presentations from other laboratories using the technique may also be introduced. The reliability of the testing and any limitations of the technique would also be discussed during this part of the testimony. This is a good place to introduce safeguards in the testing procedures, quality control measures used by the laboratory, and to discuss other areas such as training, corroboration of results with other laboratories, proficiency testing, etc. The attorney may also ask you to identify other court cases where the technique has been admitted and discuss any cases where the technique was not admitted and your understanding of the reasons the judge did not admit the technique. Having knowledge regarding what other laboratories in the US and around the world are doing and in what jurisdictions the testing has been admitted can be very helpful here. Some judges will ask questions to clarify points and enhance their understanding. As I said earlier, this is an excellent way to gauge whether your testimony has been clear and educational or completely confusing!

Depending on the scope of the hearing, the discussion regarding the actual testing and results in a particular case may follow. In some hearings, this phase is omitted, while in others it is the primary focus of the hearing. This testimony is generally very similar to what is routinely presented to a jury during a trial; however, the answers may be more in depth to demonstrate the uses of the technique and the reliability of the testing.

What kinds of challenges are seen in admissibility hearings?

In most situations, the challenges are the same seen routinely during trials, but with more emphasis on the unreliability of the technique or the limitations of the test system for forensic samples in general. The "newness" of the technique to the analyst and/or to the particular laboratory is often discussed with the focus being that something new must not be trustworthy and that the lack of extensive prior experience must lead to a higher risk of mistakes. As in trials, often hypothetical situations and "what if" questions are brought up. The specific challenges introduced will largely reflect the scientific background and knowledge of the expert testifying for opposing counsel. Reading any reports, affidavits, declarations, and/or prior testimony from the expert testifying for opposing counsel can be very helpful for understanding in advance what types of challenges to prepare for.

We do not hear much about admissibility hearings for DNA testing these days. Why is it important for DNA analysts and attorneys to know about how to do an admissibility hearing now?

That is true. Although there were huge challenges to RFLP (restriction fragment length polymorphism) testing in the late 1980s and early-to-mid 1990s and to PCR testing using DQA1/PM and silver-stained STRs in the 1990s, by the time fluorescent STR testing with capillary electrophoresis became the predominant DNA testing technique worldwide, many of the basic issues of forensic DNA testing and interpretation had already been addressed by the courts at the trial and appellate levels. In the past decade, there have been very few significant challenges to the introduction of fluorescent STR DNA or mtDNA testing in the courts, so most analysts and attorneys have no or limited experience with these types of hearings.

However, I think it is still important to understand what an admissibility hearing is all about so that one can be prepared if challenges to the testing procedures are raised. What I see most often happening today is what we can call "pre-admissibility hearings" that are being held to determine whether there is a need for a true admissibility hearing. The underlying question at these hearings is whether there has been a significant enough modification to the basic and current generally accepted forensic DNA techniques to make it necessary to have an admissibility hearing on the modification(s). I think this brings up a very interesting scientific and legal question—when is a modification to the generally accepted procedures different enough to warrant a new admissibility hearing? Adding a new STR kit, capillary electrophoresis instrumentation, or software has not usually required a hearing. A few recent proceedings that I am aware of have focused on the testing, analysis, and interpretation of samples having, or allegedly having, small amounts of DNA (low-template DNA, or LT-DNA) that have been tested with or without modifications to increase sensitivity. And as is always possible for a variety of reasons, there can be hearings to rule on the admissibility of the test results of certain items of evidence in a specific case.

INTERVIEW WITH TED HUNT, J.D., ON A PROSECUTOR'S PERSPECTIVE

Mr. Hunt is the Chief Trial Attorney at the Jackson County Prosecutor's Office in Kansas City, Missouri. He has been a prosecuting attorney for 20 years and tried over 100 felony cases, most of which involved the presentation of DNA evidence. He is also actively involved in training attorneys and law enforcement officials in forensic DNA-related litigation for a number of state and federal organizations.

What is your role in the criminal justice process?

The prosecutor's role in the criminal justice system is to seek justice in each case rather than to merely convict. In many instances, seeking justice equates with the aggressive prosecution of a criminal defendant. In other cases, however, seeking justice might mean dismissing a case because the evidence of guilt is in doubt. It may also mean reducing a charge when the evidence reveals that a defendant's degree of culpability is less than previously believed.

As a lawyer, how much do you want or need to know about the details of DNA testing?

As a prosecutor, I want to have a solid working knowledge of all aspects of forensic DNA testing. However, that doesn't mean that I want to orchestrate a courtroom class on forensic genetics or analytical techniques. I believe that the true value of being literate in the field of DNA analysis is to provide myself with the opportunity to make an informed choice about what topics and questions should be included, and perhaps more importantly, *excluded* from my courtroom examinations of both prosecution and defense experts.

Aside from a strong working knowledge of the biological, technological, genetic, and statistical aspects of forensic DNA analysis, I believe it is also important that prosecutors have a firm understanding of the quality standards and guidelines in the field. It's very difficult to follow the "game" without knowing the "rules." These criteria provide a benchmark against which the overall work product in each case is judged. Confidence in DNA test results can be enhanced by prosecutors who familiarize jurors with the rigorous quality processes and procedures to which the analyst's work was subjected. Alternatively, jurors can rightly be made skeptical of a system or an expert who failed to follow community-wide quality standards and guidelines.

What resources have been helpful to you in understanding DNA?

The resource that has most helped me understand forensic DNA testing over the years has been my local lab analysts. There's simply no substitute for regular access to and asking questions of helpful and knowledgeable experts in the field of forensic DNA analysis. In addition, I'm fortunate to have had the opportunity to teach with and learn from some of the best forensic DNA experts in the nation at various meetings and conferences I've attended over the years. Aside from my interaction with experts, reading each edition of *Forensic DNA Typing* as well as other texts, journals, and web-based forensic DNA resources (such as STRBase) have greatly enhanced my understanding of DNA typing.

How much detail do you think that the jury needs regarding DNA testing?

I think Albert Einstein summed it up best when he said "Everything should be made as simple as possible, but not simpler." The jury needs just enough information to accomplish its assigned task—to determine whether or not the DNA test results in question are relevant, reliable, and persuasive in the context of a given case. In most cases this can be accomplished by the following: 1) demonstrate that the analyst is qualified and competent; 2) show that he or she works in a lab that follows established quality standards; 3) present a brief, basic explanation of DNA and the common biological materials in which it is found; 4) define essential terms to be used by the expert during his or her testimony; 5) provide an explanation of the evidence examined, including the results of any preliminary serological or trace testing; 6) offer a basic and brief explanation of the testing process, including the use of relevant controls; 7) explain that one or more genetic profiles were detected from the evidence and interpreted; 8) compare the profile(s) to the known standards and announce the testing outcome (i.e. match, partial match, inconclusive, exclusion); 9) provide the statistical frequency of the profile(s) developed; and 10) give a source attribution statement, if applicable and utilized by the testing laboratory.

What advice do you have to expert witnesses testifying on DNA evidence?

The best advice I have for any speaker, expert DNA witnesses included, is to know your audience and speak to them in their native tongue. A brilliant analyst can make a lousy expert witness when he or she fails to connect with the jury. Many times, this failure to connect stems from the fact that the expert testifies as if he or she is delivering a scientific dissertation to a room full of colleagues rather than teaching a classroom full of novices. Given the time and procedural constraints of the courtroom, the use of scientific jargon, industry acronyms, and excessively complicated explanations creates cognitive barriers for jurors that are difficult to overcome.

Expert witnesses should strive to testify in a user-friendly and ampliative *[enlarging a concept by adding to what is already known]* manner, only employing essential scientific terms after they have been properly defined. Additionally, more advanced concepts should be addressed only after their basic logical and factual predicates have been established.

How should expert witnesses prepare for their role in a trial?

Reviewing a case record before trial and preparing for trial testimony are not synonymous activities. A thorough review of the record is a necessary first step. However, being truly prepared for court requires additional preparation. This includes self-reflection on how to best equate, translate, and communicate scientific terms or concepts to the jury, mentally self-editing unnecessary terminology or redundant information, and anticipating the possible issues that may arise on both direct and cross-examination given the history of the evidence examined, the case data, and the test results.

Perhaps the most vital aspect of testimonial preparation is meeting with the prosecutor for a pretrial conference. If at all possible, this conference should be done in person, rather than over the phone. At this meeting, the prosecutor should ask the expert what issues or anomalies are present in the evidence, case data, or test results. The prosecutor should also review his or her anticipated questions and areas of inquiry with the expert and receive his or her feedback. It's also helpful for the expert to suggest issues or topics to highlight, de-emphasize, or exclude. In addition, the prosecutor and the expert witness should collaborate to determine what, if any, visual aids may help enhance the jury's comprehension and retention of the evidence. Finally, an informal "dry-run" of the expert's direct examination or anticipated cross-examination during the pretrial conference may also help the prosecutor and the expert enhance their courtroom presentations.

How much time do you take with a DNA expert prior to court to prepare them for the courtroom?

To avoid wasting everyone's time, I make sure that I have done my homework before meeting with the expert witness. This means that I will have already reviewed the relevant documents and have isolated the issues, questions, and anomalies that are not explained by these materials. This allows me to focus on the unknown and the unclear rather than a time-wasting review of the test documentation that could have been done well ahead of the meeting. Ideally, by the time I meet in person with the expert, I will have a rough draft of his or her direct examination and a fairly good idea of the issues and questions that will be the subject of cross-examination. After the pretrial conference, I will typically revise and extend my outline based on the information learned during the meeting. If done efficiently, preparation of the DNA expert can be done in about an hour in most cases. However, if the DNA results are *the* issue being litigated in the case, preparation may take multiple hours and a number of meetings.

Do you have a list of prepared questions that you use for your direct examination?

I have an outline of the facts I need to establish or the topics I need to cover, but I don't write out my questions. I believe that writing down questions verbatim locks you into a script that takes away the flexibility needed during witness examinations. Glancing down at a topic or an anticipated answer rather than a question gives me the flexibility needed to formulate a question that will elicit the desired information. If you get out of sync with an expert in court based on a prepared script, both prosecutor and expert are going to get lost and will look unprepared to the jury.

From your experience, is there anything unreasonable that the defense requests during discovery?

At times, some defense attorneys manipulate the discovery rules and make oppressive, burdensome, and unreasonable requests for the purpose of harassing the prosecution. One example of this is a request for all raw data generated incident to a lab's internal validation of a particular instrument or commercial DNA testing kit. Other examples include asking for all raw data generated from the profiles included in the lab's population database, and a request that all the electropherograms (which we provide on a CD) be printed rather than provided electronically—ostensibly because the defense expert does not own the necessary software. Another burdensome request is asking the government to produce the lab's procedures, protocols, audits, and analyst proficiency tests in each case, despite the fact that the same materials have been provided to the same attorney numerous times in the past on other cases. A popular request in the early 2000s was to ask for primer sequence information for the Profiler Plus and COfiler kits. The danger in not aggressively responding to these and similar requests is that judges who are not familiar with the subject matter may automatically order the state to produce the requested materials. In so doing, they wrongly assume the request is made in good faith and necessary to defend against the charges.

What are some of the common tactics that you have seen used by the defense attorneys and experts in challenging DNA evidence?

Defense challenges come in a variety of forms depending on the nature of the case and the significance of the DNA evidence. If the DNA results are clean and fairly unassailable, a popular defense tactic is to concede that the detected profile belongs to the defendant but that its presence at the scene was the innocuous result of a secondary or tertiary transfer. Along these same lines, when preliminary testing was not attempted or cannot determine the nature of the biological substance from which the profile was developed, the defense may concede that the profile belongs to the defendant, while asserting that it came from biological material whose presence at the scene or on the victim is easily and innocently explainable.

When the evidentiary context of the DNA leaves little room for innocuous explanations, the attacks turn to evidence handling, the testing process, and the interpretation of the results. Depending on the jurisdiction, evidentiary chain of custody can be quite complex and involve many different people and locations, both inside and outside the lab. Attacking gaps in various links in the chain is an attack that is often available. Another popular defense tactic is to allege that the questioned DNA profile was the result of contamination from either inside or outside the lab (or both). This includes exploring prior instances of laboratory contamination on tests not related to the case being litigated. The failure of an analyst to strictly follow applicable standards, procedures, protocols, and internally validated methods is another topic that is a favorite of defense experts. (This is highly ironic because many such experts follow no written protocols at all in their own labs.) Also, a laboratory's past audit performances and an analyst's previous competency and proficiency test results make popular fodder for defense challenges.

An alternative interpretation of the analytical results produced by the state's lab is another routine defense challenge. Re-examining the raw data with computer software at a level beneath the lab's internally validated RFU threshold is a tactic routinely utilized by some DNA experts in the defense community. The purpose is to call into question the interpretation of the data by the government's analyst.

In addition, a defense expert's alternative interpretation of a DNA mixture is a fairly common occurrence. Such interpretations will frequently be used to argue that the defendant should be excluded from the profile(s) generated. Alternatively, it may be used to argue that alleles at certain loci should not be utilized in determining the population frequency of the genetic profile.

In cases involving cold hits, some defense experts argue that the only valid method of calculating the population frequency of the match is to use the database match probability rather than the random match probability.

Have these tactics been successful? Do you have any examples from specific cases that you would like to share where the defense successfully challenged DNA evidence?

By and large I would say that these tactics are ultimately not successful. I have yet to lose a case involving DNA evidence. Juries may have more information to sort through at the end of a case when a defense DNA expert is called, but a well-prepared state's expert will usually win the day in court. The danger for a defendant who calls a DNA expert is that such an expert will usually be obliged under cross-examination to concede a number of facts about the state's DNA evidence that are not helpful to his or her defense. Typically, I find it to be a net gain for my case if a defense DNA expert testifies at trial.

How has post-conviction DNA testing and the Innocence Project impacted the legal system and specifically your perspective on the criminal justice system?

To the extent that DNA evidence has been able to help exonerate the truly innocent, everyone has reason to celebrate. Although, at first blush, it may seem counterintuitive that finding and exposing past instances of injustice would enhance overall confidence in the criminal justice system, I think that will be the ultimate effect. Public perception of a fair and just process for correcting judicial mistakes will ultimately overshadow the tragedy of individual cases that resulted in wrongful convictions.

The cold case projects currently being operated by police departments, prosecutors, and crime labs across the country are an inverse but complimentary enterprise to that of the

Innocence Project. These projects take aim at delivering long-awaited justice from a different direction—providing closure for victims by cracking unsolved cold cases. These projects (including the one I oversee in Kansas City, which has resulted in over 100 cold case convictions with DNA to date) have disproven the old adage that justice delayed is justice denied.

My perspective on the system has changed to the extent that I have personally seen cold cases solved and justice achieved when police, prosecutors, and victims had abandoned all hope decades ago. To date, we have not had a DNA exoneration in Kansas City but have worked with the Innocence Project and other advocates on a number of cases that we found appropriate for post-conviction DNA testing.

What are some of the challenges faced by prosecutors with the new era of post-conviction DNA testing?

The most basic challenge faced by prosecutors is making an informed choice about when to agree with or object to a request for post-conviction DNA testing. This decision must take into account the nature and contextual significance of the evidence, its history since recovery, its suitability for particular testing methods, and the collateral facts and issues in the case. This can be a very difficult decision to make given the amount of information that must be located, reassembled, and carefully analyzed many years after a conviction.

Most of the disagreements I've had with the Innocence Project have stemmed from our differing opinions on the contextual significance of the evidence they want to test. An exclusionary DNA result is not synonymous with an exculpatory result. Due to the sensitivity of modern DNA technology, the number of items and samples typically collected at crime scenes, their unknown or equivocal history, and the nature of the sample, developing a genetic profile that does not match a convicted defendant in an old case may not be all that surprising. In short, depending on the context of the evidence, detecting an exclusionary profile may be much less probative than detecting an inculpatory one. Additionally, it only takes a single trial judge to determine that post-conviction DNA results are "exculpatory," whereas it takes a jury of 12 to unanimously agree that inculpatory DNA evidence should result in a guilty verdict. Thus, before stipulating to post-conviction DNA testing, prosecutors must fully realize the potential implications of this decision.

Other challenges in this new era include complying with new laws in some states that mandate the permanent post-conviction retention of evidence in certain cases; attempting to locate and determine the history and chain of custody of evidence that is the subject of a post-conviction testing request; finding old case files and transcripts; and searching for individuals from whom elimination samples are needed to compare against DNA profiles detected during post-conviction testing.

In many of my interactions with DNA analysts, I have found that they sometimes view the defense attorney and expert(s) as their enemies in a courtroom battle. What advice do you have to share in order to help DNA analysts appreciate the important role that a defense attorney has?

Science is a dynamic discipline. One of the hallmarks of good science is openness to criticism and revision. I believe this is also the hallmark of a good scientist. It's a rare fact that can only support a single rational inference. It's the defense attorney's job to question, challenge, and attempt to refute inferences that support the state's case—including incriminating DNA evidence. Any analyst should take pride in the ability to withstand a well-prepared defense attack on his or her bench work and interpretive findings. It might even make them a better scientist by causing them to see old practices from new perspectives. To put it more bluntly, I'd remind analysts of the old adage, "What doesn't kill you makes you stronger."

DNA protocols, particularly with mixture interpretation, can change over time as the science improves and the laboratory embraces new techniques. How can these changes impact previous cases? Can you briefly explain *Brady* issues that may arise and why it is important for DNA analysts to understand the potential impact of protocol changes?

The *Brady* line of decisions requires the prosecution, as an aspect of due process and without a defense request, to disclose any information, either in its possession or in the possession of other governmental personnel, which is material to guilt or punishment. This includes information that is either exculpatory or has impeachment value. "Materiality" has been ruled to mean information that, had it been known at the time of trial, would have made a different result reasonably probable. The prosecution's good or bad faith in having knowledge of and disclosing such evidence is irrelevant.

Government laboratories, or those that contract with law enforcement agencies, should be aware that they are considered to be "state actors" for constitutional purposes when conducting tests used by the prosecution. This means that, irrespective of their good or bad faith, a lab's knowledge, actions, or inactions relative to *Brady* information in their possession is attributable to the prosecution. If a new interpretive protocol would cause a result-altering outcome on a DNA test in a pending case, the prosecutor must provide this information to the defense and the court. Prosecutors should make analysts with whom they work familiar with these obligations.

The United States Supreme Court, in *District Attorney's Office for Third Judicial Dist. vs. Osborne*, 129 S.Ct. 2308, 2320 (2009), recently made it clear that the prosecutor's constitutional duty of disclosure pursuant to *Brady* is a *trial right* enjoyed by the defendant. Thus, *Brady does not* control in the post-conviction context. Convicted defendants must now seek access to *Brady*-type information through the post-conviction procedures and legal precedents provided by the jurisdiction in which they were convicted. *Osborne* also held that the federal right to due process is only violated if a jurisdiction's post-conviction procedures offend a fundamental principle of justice or are fundamentally inadequate to vindicate a convicted defendant's substantive rights. Accordingly, prosecutors should make lab analysts with whom they work familiar with the post-conviction duties and obligations of disclosure imposed by the relevant jurisdiction.

Despite the *Osborne* decision, I would recommend that whenever interpretive protocol changes cast doubt on a convicted defendant's inclusion in a sample (mixture or not), or when a new protocol reduces the number of loci or alleles attributable to the defendant, thus increasing the frequency of his profile, the testing laboratory should immediately notify the prosecutor of the relevant facts. This will allow the prosecutor to make the appropriate decisions consistent with the legal and ethical dictates of the relevant jurisdiction and his or her responsibilities as an officer of the court.

INTERVIEW WITH THE ORANGE COUNTY (CALIFORNIA) DISTRICT ATTORNEY'S DNA UNIT

The Orange County (California) District Attorney's (OCDA) DNA Unit is comprised of experienced deputy district attorneys who possess expertise regarding the utilization of forensic DNA evidence to solve crime. They provide assistance and training to all of the county's law enforcement agencies. Members of the OCDA DNA Unit, which include attorneys Bruce Moore, Camille Hill, Scott Scoville, Jennifer Contini, Terry Cleaveland, and Tammy Spurgeon, work closely with local law enforcement investigators, prosecutors, crime lab forensic scientists, and OCDA local DNA database forensic scientists to effectively use forensic DNA technology and resources.

What is your role in the criminal justice process?

A prosecuting attorney has an obligation and duty to see that "justice is done." This obligation extends well beyond merely convicting the guilty. It includes ensuring that no one is unfairly convicted and that the innocent are exonerated:

> [The prosecutor] is the representative not of an ordinary party to a controversy, but of a sovereignty whose obligation to govern impartially is as compelling as its obligation to govern at all; and whose interest, therefore, in a criminal prosecution is not that it shall win a case, but that justice shall be done. As such, he is in a peculiar and very definite sense the servant of the law, the twofold aim of which is that guilt shall not escape or innocence suffer. He may prosecute with earnestness and vigor – indeed, he should do so. But, while he may strike hard blows, he is not at liberty to strike foul ones. It is as much his duty to refrain from improper methods calculated to produce a wrongful conviction as it is to use every legitimate means to bring about a just one (*Berger v. United States* (1935) 295 U.S. 78, 88).

As a lawyer how much do you want or need to know about the details of DNA testing?

As prosecutors, it is necessary for us to have at least a basic understanding of forensic DNA analysis so that we can spot potential issues and defenses. As the proponents who are seeking to introduce DNA evidence into trial, our level of understanding should include the ability to determine the probative quality of the DNA evidence, to explain the DNA evidence to a jury, and to determine the soundness and reliability of the DNA testing that was performed in any given case. We feel that a good understanding of forensic DNA evidence can empower a courtroom advocate. The jury intuitively grasps that you understand the science and are attempting to present reliable DNA evidence in a straightforward manner.

Of course, there is obviously a limit to the amount of forensic DNA knowledge an attorney can really possess, particularly those who present DNA evidence in a criminal case only occasionally. We have found it extremely helpful to have a core group of attorneys specially trained regarding the science and presentation of DNA evidence. These "DNA Unit Attorneys" possess more than basic knowledge regarding forensic DNA analysis, are well informed regarding DNA-related case law, and can assist other attorneys, forensic scientists, and local law enforcement investigators with complex legal forensic issues. Our DNA Unit Attorneys often act as liaisons between forensic scientists and non-DNA Unit prosecutors. They also help forensic scientists triage or screen cases prior to DNA analysis.

What resources have been most effective for you to learn the things you needed to learn regarding DNA?

In addition to reading scientific literature such as peer-reviewed journal articles and books, attending DNA conferences and seminars has been particularly helpful. Forensic scientists and academicians from all over the world have been generous with their time and knowledge. Joining scientific professional organizations has also been beneficial. Lawyers who present forensic DNA evidence in a courtroom setting should definitely be part of this human identification network.

How important is communication between forensic scientists and lawyers?

Forensic scientists, police investigators, and lawyers need to learn to effectively communicate with one another. One of the biggest issues is the lack of teamwork that exists between scientists, prosecutors, and investigators. A common refrain frequently heard from forensic scientists to lawyers is "You are not scientists!" As lawyers, we do understand and agree that our ability to understand complex DNA matters is limited. But, by the same token, scientists need to understand that they are not lawyers and cannot determine what is and is not relevant in a particular case.

Our worlds are colliding. We need expert witnesses. Many forensic scientists do not understand that a prosecutor's dual obligation is to be a zealous advocate and, at the same time, ensure fairness at every stage of the criminal proceedings. It is our duty, as prosecuting attorneys, to present the results of valid, correctly performed scientific analysis. Each time we intend to present DNA evidence to a judge or jury, we need to determine, among other things, if a problem occurred during the analysis of a sample; if the methodology is flawed; or if the analyst violated lab protocols. We cannot simply accept a DNA forensic conclusion expressed in a short paragraph of a one-page report at face value. Our exploration of these important issues as we prepare for trial should be welcomed by forensic scientists. A forensic scientist should be able and willing to explain and defend their scientific results leaving aside personal bias, ego, rancor, and defensiveness.

How much detail do you think that the jury needs regarding DNA testing? Are there things you can do during the trial to make sure the jury understands?

Generally it is wise to keep it simple, particularly if the evidence is not really being challenged. However, if it is anticipated that the challenges by the defense will be extensive, it will sometimes be necessary to educate the jury with more detail. We are finding, more and more because of the whole CSI effect, that jurors expect DNA evidence to be presented or they expect an explanation as to why there is not DNA. The jury does not need to know and understand as much DNA technology as a forensic scientist or attorney. The expert witness, however, should be prepared to respond to any issues the defense might raise in an articulate and straightforward manner. Our goal is for jurors to understand and believe that the DNA results presented at trial are reliable and reproducible.

With reference to DNA evidence, we find it helpful to train our attorneys to walk into court with a "can do" attitude. By this we mean to present your case as simply as possible, firm in the belief that the jury can and will understand what you are about to present. Even if you have the battle of the experts occurring, both attorney and forensic scientist should, at all times, maintain a poised and confident demeanor. What prosecutors and forensic scientists often do not realize is that juries tend to stop listening after the first 20 to 30 minutes of technical DNA testimony. Jurors primarily make their decisions regarding DNA evidence both on the science presented and on the behaviors and attitudes of the expert witnesses and attorneys.

There is a group in Australia examining juror comprehension. They advocate discussing the basics of DNA and the non-contested parts of a case upfront before the trial actually starts. The jurors would then be in a better situation to handle the complexities that may arise later in the trial. Do you think something like that would work in the U.S. court system?

This is the equivalent of having the defense and the prosecution agreeing to a stipulation regarding forensic testing that would be read to the jury at an appropriate time. We are finding more and more that the defense attorney is willing to stipulate to DNA evidence, particularly in the cases where identity is not an issue or the evidence does not have significant bearing to the defense of a case. When DNA evidence, however, goes to the heart of a matter, the defense will rarely agree to a stipulation.

What advice do you have to expert witnesses testifying on DNA evidence?

The expert should keep it simple even when there are extensive challenges by the defense. Explanations need to contain enough detail to establish the credibility of the expert and the reliability of the science. The expert should thoroughly review the lab case file well in advance of a prospective trial date and should inform the prosecutor of any problems or issues that occurred during the analysis of a case. If errors did occur, the forensic scientists should immediately provide to the prosecutor a supplemental report and any corrective action documentation that was generated.

Forensic scientists should always strongly insist on a conference with the attorney who has requested that they testify prior to taking the witness stand. In a perfect world, the lawyers would be contacting the forensic scientists to arrange such a conference. But if the lawyer fails to do so, the forensic scientist should take the initiative and insist that a meeting take place. A forensic scientist should make clear during that meeting the facts or inferences that he or she is willing to state based on the scientific evidence. It is also important for the forensic scientist to gauge how much the prosecutor knows about DNA evidence.

The primary job of the forensic scientist at this stage is to defend the science. A forensic scientist should never confuse his or her duty to defend the science with the belief that they need to defend themselves. Too often, forensic scientists view an attack on the science as a personal attack. Falling into this trap will result in errors in judgment, incorrect statements, and will ultimately undermine a forensic scientist's ability to effectively respond to attacks on the science.

Remember, a forensic scientist's personal biases have no place in the analysis and interpretation of forensic DNA evidence. Simply put, a forensic scientist is not entitled to the luxury of expressing his or her feelings while performing their duties as an impartial scientist.

Do you provide feedback to expert witnesses after they have provided testimony?

Yes, in Orange County the prosecutors fill out an evaluation and send it to the lab where it is reviewed by their laboratory director and the scientist involved in the trial. In lieu of the form, we often talk to the forensic scientists personally regarding their testimony. Most often, the advice and feedback that we provide is well received.

From your experience, is there anything unreasonable that the defense requests during discovery?

Sometimes defense attorneys use a boilerplate discovery request that asks for everything "including the kitchen sink." Our standard discovery packet includes the report, all bench notes, a disk that contains electronic data, corrective action reports, and proficiency test results of the analysts who performed the testing.

Generally speaking, the defense is entitled to receive all discovery materials that would help them prepare their case. So, if the items requested are relevant, they should be provided. The law in California includes provisions that state that the defense must first approach the prosecutor for discovery materials. Upon occasion, discovery requests are improperly sent directly to the crime lab by the defense and are responded to by crime lab personnel without prosecutorial input. Without a thorough understanding of the law and a complete review of entire prosecution and investigation case files, a forensic scientist is not in the best position to make decisions regarding the release of discovery materials.

The discovery decision is first and foremost a legal and ethical decision for prosecutors. It might be easy for a forensic scientist to look at a discovery request and say "I understand what the defense means when they ask for 'all proficiency test reports.'" But a simple request for "all proficiency test reports" can become quite complex: Should the response include all proficiency test reports since the beginning of the lab's DNA testing? Should the response include all proficiency test reports for the last 10 years? Should there be any limitation in time? Should just the reports for DNA analysts be included? Should the response be limited to just the reports for DNA analysts who worked on a particular case? Should the reports include all written documentation from the entity that provided the proficiency test kits? Should the reports include a comparison of how local DNA analysts compared to analysts throughout the nation? Should all reports related to failed proficiency tests along with any corrective action reports generated also be included?

Depending upon jurisdictional rules and as a safe practice tip, forensic scientists should avoid placing themselves in the position of independently determining the legal and ethical requirements of providing discovery to the defense. It is the prosecution's duty and obligation to maintain a complete and thorough record of all discovery materials provided to the defense. Likewise, it is critical that forensic scientists maintain a complete log of all discovery materials provided to both the defense and prosecution. There is a very famous murder case here in Orange County that was reversed because of a discovery error. In that case, the crime lab indicated that they had provided a single-page report to the defense that was not provided to the prosecution. The report contained exculpatory evidence. On appeal, the defense claimed that they did not receive the report. Since the report was not provided to the defense through the prosecutor's office, no documentation existed that proved that the defense did indeed receive the report.

Communication between the prosecutor and forensic scientist is essential during the discovery process. The prosecution can be charged with the failure of turning over discovery materials to the defense even though they were not aware that the materials existed in the control of a third party such as a police agency or a crime lab. Many cold cases, some decades old, are being solved with DNA technology. The prosecution may be unaware that additional records exist besides a recent DNA report. Forensic scientists must take care to provide all notes and reports related to such cases even those stored in musty warehouses or basements that were written before the advent of computers and modern laboratory information management systems. Some discovery requests can indeed be quite burdensome to the crime lab by requiring the production or copying of voluminous materials. Forensic scientists should communicate these concerns to the prosecution. Prosecutors can help place limitations on the items requested or can arrange for a monitored viewing of the items by a defense expert at the crime lab.

Is it a problem to share electronic data files with the defense?

We see no problem providing electronic data files to the defense since any changes to the inherent data would be detectable by the crime lab forensic scientist. We have seen instances of some defense experts manipulating the appearance of the data by changing various parameters. However, with the aid of the forensic scientist, a prosecutor will be able to immediately recognize what was done and cross-examine the witness regarding the motives for the changes.

What are some of the common tactics that you have seen used by the defense attorneys and experts in challenging DNA evidence?

Challenges to DNA evidence fall into the following categories: contamination of the evidence at the crime scene or lab; erroneous determination of allele peak calls; improper interpretation of data especially with low levels of DNA or mixtures; improper frequency calculations; improper methodology used to conduct validation studies, set stutter limits, set analytical thresholds, and set stochastic thresholds; forensic scientist bias both pro-prosecution and pro-defense; analyst errors such as failed proficiency tests or failure to follow lab protocols; failure to follow basic scientific method; and lack of transparency.

One of the latest tactics we have seen: the defense will call multiple experts to the stand but limit their area of testimony. For instance, the defense attorney will call an "on the fringe expert" to the stand who will make questionable calls by including spikes, stutter, and obvious noise as allele peak calls. Then they will call a human geneticist well versed in both the interpretation of DNA data and statistics to only testify regarding frequency calculations. This tactic is easy to defuse by having the geneticist recalculate frequencies using only valid allele calls while on the stand.

"Dueling Guidelines" is another tactic. Sections of the manufacturer's guidelines and validation studies are put up on a screen in the courtroom next to copies of the laboratory's interpretation guidelines to highlight the differences. Also, defense experts will sometimes change the lab's threshold values or narrowly evaluate data ignoring relevant sections of the lab's protocols.

The forensic scientists need to be strong enough to say that they did something a certain way because of their laboratory's validation studies. With these types of challenges, it is important that a forensic scientist feel comfortable and knowledgeable with the relevant laboratory protocols and validation studies. A forensic scientist exhibiting a lack of confidence or understanding of their own protocols and validation studies will undermine his or her credibility with the jury.

One of the challenges with forensic DNA analysis today is mixtures...

One major area where forensic scientists could benefit from additional study and training is the statistical interpretation of complex mixtures. Mixture interpretations are often difficult and many forensic DNA analysts do not yet have the skill set to properly interpret complex mixtures. In California, the presentation of DNA results during a courtroom proceeding must be accompanied by a statistical frequency. It is paramount that forensic laboratories provide additional statistical training for their DNA analysts. It would also be beneficial to have at least one person in a lab who is an expert in the field of statistics.

How are new mixture interpretation guidelines going to impact you in cases you are dealing with?

Forensic scientists may not realize that a revision of their lab's mixture interpretation protocols may also necessitate a review of all previous mixture interpretation results and conclusions. We agree with other prosecution experts that whenever interpretive protocol changes cast doubt on an individual's inclusion in a sample or when new DNA interpretation guidelines reduce the number of loci or alleles attributable to that person, thus increasing the frequency of the profile, the testing laboratory should immediately notify the prosecutor of the relevant facts. Timely notifications will allow the prosecutor to make the appropriate decisions consistent with the legal and ethical dictates of the relevant jurisdiction and his or her responsibilities as an officer of the court.

So how do you handle this balance then for the future? The challenge is that science is always going to improve and if the law doesn't want it to improve then that impedes the science.

Improvements in science are always welcome. There needs to be an understanding, however, that forensic scientists have a duty and obligation to notify prosecutors whenever scientific improvements occur that would change a previous scientific conclusion.

I just think that the forensic community is in a very precarious situation with how mixtures are being handled right now...

One suggestion for a forensic lab would be not to allow new DNA analysts to interpret complex mixtures. Perhaps a lab should have a core team of 3 or 4 highly experienced DNA analysts that work together to interpret each complex mixture and thoroughly document all of their assumptions and conclusions.

You will notice that the new SWGDAM guidelines are very clear that you need to document all of your assumptions. There is a reason that requirement was put in there.

It does not help if all findings and conclusions are not thoroughly detailed in a lab report or notes. When a forensic scientist interprets a complex mixture, care needs to be taken to document every aspect of that interpretation. Another scientist examining the notes should be able to see and understand the basis of all of the mixture interpretation decisions.

That comes down to a training issue then. Why is there that kind of disparity in knowledge between the new analyst and the experienced analyst? Why can't there be better training so the newer analyst can come up to speed faster on mixture interpretation?

Better training would indeed help, particularly the inclusion of more statistical training. Acquiring knowledge and experience takes time. Unfortunately, there is no substitute for the experience a forensic scientist will gain from analyzing thousands of cases and samples. Since we know that complex mixture interpretations are based, in large part, on the experience and training of the analysts performing the interpretations, the lab needs to ensure that all persons performing complex mixture interpretations have achieved an appropriate level of training and competence in this area.

How has post-conviction DNA testing and the Innocence Project impacted the legal system and specifically your perspective on the criminal justice system?

California law allows for post-conviction DNA testing pursuant to Penal Code section 1405. Moreover, Orange County District Attorney's Office has an Innocence Review Panel that reviews all cases where a defendant believes his/her case deserves another review when forensic evidence exists. With both of these vehicles in place, the criminal justice system is better equipped to ensure that justice is served.

On those types of cases where there is testing on someone who says they are innocent, do you keep any stats on how many times that DNA comes back matching?

We have tested three or four cases as part of our Innocence Review Panel and each time the DNA results inculpate the defendant. As prosecutors, we are advocating for a certain position. But we also have the dual responsibility to ensure that justice is served.

We had a recent case that involved the kidnap and sexual assault of two young girls from the 1980s. The case against the defendant was extremely compelling even without DNA evidence. Nevertheless, we agreed, as part of the Innocence Review Panel, to perform DNA testing. The DNA profile from the crime scene evidence matched the defendant.

INTERVIEW WITH BRADLEY BANNON, J.D., ON A DEFENSE ATTORNEY'S PERSPECTIVE

Mr. Bannon is a criminal trial defense attorney for the law firm of Cheshire, Parker, Schneider, Bryan, and Vitale in Raleigh, North Carolina. He has been practicing law for 13 years and has helped draft legislation to strengthen the right of the accused to pretrial discovery in criminal cases in North Carolina. He was instrumental in using DNA evidence to help exonerate the Duke lacrosse players of false accusations of rape in 2006 and 2007.

What is your role in the criminal justice process?

To provide independent and zealous representation to people accused of crimes, and to give as much meaning as possible to the presumption of innocence and the burden of proof that the government must meet before it may limit or deprive a person of freedom or the full rights and privileges of citizenship.

There are several phases of that representation. First, you review the prosecution's evidence and independently pursue as much evidence as you can and should under the particular circumstances of each case. After evaluating all of the evidence in light of your practical and legal knowledge and experience, you provide your best advice to the accused about what he or she should do, whether that involves going to trial or exploring resolutions outside of trial, such as a plea agreement. Finally, if the case ends up in a contested forum, whether a trial or sentencing hearing, you do your absolute best to make sure the prosecution is put to its constitutional burden in that forum.

You were defense counsel in the Duke rape case. What lessons were learned from this experience that you would like to share?

The biggest lesson was learning that you should never accept at face value what you see in a report that you receive from an expert. That does not mean the expert is necessarily lying or trying to pull the wool over anyone's eyes, though that certainly does happen. The reason for not accepting a forensic scientific report at face value is that, whatever science is being applied, it is being applied by human beings. The scientific standards and laboratory protocols are being followed—or *not*—by people, and *people* are the ones reporting the conclusions, not machines.

At a time when the need to confront forensic evidence issues effectively in the courtroom is directly proportionate to the explosion of the portrayal of such evidence in American media and pop culture, it is more important than ever for lawyers to know the fundamentals of the forensic sciences. You can't just put your head in the sand and approach cases as you would have in the 1980s or even in the 90s. Advocates for the accused must evolve with the evolving types of theories, themes, and evidence presented in prosecutions of serious crimes.

Partly because of advances in the forensic sciences, and partly because jurors increasingly expect to see "CSI" evidence in criminal trials, forensic evidence such as DNA analysis is increasingly prevalent in criminal courtrooms. To the extent it is being presented through "experts" associated with law enforcement, such as those who work in state and local crime labs, it carries a tremendous presumption of credibility with jurors. But because those experts are human beings who are just as prone to human frailty as the rest of us, defense lawyers have an increasing duty to understand the forensic sciences being used in the courtroom to try to convict their clients, and, when those sciences are not being used appropriately or accurately, to make that known to the court and jury.

For the most part, over my first decade of defense work, I never had occasion to question a DNA report. I treated DNA evidence like I treated any other type of evidence: if it was consistent with my understanding of the facts and theory of the defense, I saw no need to question or challenge it. But if the accused is adamantly telling you "I did not do this, I wasn"t there, it cannot possibly be me...," or if the DNA evidence is otherwise inconsistent with the theory of defense, then it is a defense lawyer's duty and responsibility to become familiar with the fundamental concepts of DNA analysis in order to review that evidence.

That first happened with me when the Duke case came along. I absolutely believed the accusations were false, and I had zero confidence in the prosecution's portrayal of the evidence. As a result of having the lives of innocent people in my hands, and anticipating that the prosecutor would try to use DNA evidence to convict them, I felt that I needed to learn something about DNA so that I could determine what that evidence in the case truly showed, whether the prosecution's portrayal of it was complete and accurate, and, if not, how we could make the truth be known.

There is a school of thought among some lawyers that you can just ship off the DNA data in a case to an expert and let her tell you what it means. The problem with that approach is that the expert doesn't usually know *all* of the facts of the case, what the applicable laws and rules of evidence are, and how *all* of the facts, law, and science interact in the particular case. Just as importantly, the expert is not responsible for presenting her own testimony in the courtroom or for cross-examining the opponent's experts. Only the lawyers can do that. So if there is a flaw in your opponent's portrayal or presentation of DNA evidence *in the courtroom*, but all you have done with DNA up to that point in the case is to rely on an expert to tell you about it, and you have not also learned the fundamentals of DNA analysis yourself—if, in effect, you have allowed yourself to be given a fish rather than taught how to fish—then when the time comes *in the courtroom* to effectively confront questionable DNA evidence, you won't know how to do it. For example, if you're dealing with a lab analyst who violated the lab's own protocols, or applied them selectively, to reach certain conclusions in a case, you won't be able to effectively engage the expert on those very serious credibility issues in the courtroom, because you won't know what protocols *are*, you won't know why they exist, and you won't know how they are applied.

But don't get me wrong: familiarizing oneself with basic concepts of the forensic sciences does not and should not replace meaningful consultation with independent experts in those sciences. The point here is that such consultation is no substitute for the lawyer knowing all of these concepts, because he or she is the only one who is going to know all of the law, all of the facts, and how they interact with the science in the case, and the lawyer is the only one who can do anything about it in a courtroom on behalf of the accused.

What resources have been helpful to you in understanding DNA?

I began learning fundamentals about DNA mostly through your book, *Forensic DNA Typing, Second Edition*, and a couple of very informative articles in *The Champion*, the magazine published by the National Association of Criminal Defense Lawyers. Though I did not have any kind of scientific background, the book and articles were accessible to me, which means they should be accessible to everyone.

As I was reading the materials, the first light that went off in my head was that, while DNA analysis is widely accepted as the gold standard of forensic science, its application is much more open to human error than I had ever known. When I started out, I thought you simply shoved samples into a machine, and it spit out a report—and that was it. In reality, DNA testing—especially regarding samples that are weak or degraded, or contain DNA mixtures, which many evidentiary samples do—involves a lot of subjective interpretation of the electropherograms and what an analyst identifies as a "true peak." That's one of the main reasons I learned why it is so important for analysts to have and consistently follow protocols.

How much do you want or need to know about the details of DNA testing?

I think the most important thing to know is that there are between 13 and 16 areas (loci) that are examined for the presence of genetic markers, or "alleles" or "peaks," and those peaks are portrayed in charts known as "electropherograms." It is important to be able to read electropherograms and to know the protocols of the lab that analyzed the samples, interpreted the charts, and produced the final report. It's also important to know concepts surrounding the difference between what is or might be a true DNA marker and what is or might be an "artifact," such as "pull-up." It's important to know that the strength of the marker, or the height of the peak, can mean a number of different things—that a sample is strong, or that more than one person's shared DNA characteristics may be in a mixture, etc.

Recognizing when a mixture is present in an evidentiary sample, or when the sample is weak or degraded, is also very important and raises all sorts of questions about how the DNA analyst chose to interpret and report (or not report) the sample. Again, there is no big DNA machine that intakes samples and outputs reports, so it's important to portray the entire process for what it is: one that involves human beings at all levels, from sample handling, to sample processing, to sample interpretation, to final reporting. Since reporting is driven by interpretation, and interpretation is necessarily subjective, that's why it's so important to know the lab's protocols.

Simply put, the protocols are the rules, and a core concept of scientific analysis is whether you apply the same rules and standards consistently in your work. If you choose to deviate from those rules on a case-by-case basis, and if you have no credible scientific explanation for doing so, that's not really science at all. Knowing whether an analyst followed established protocols to reach and report a conclusion is as important as knowing the conclusion itself. If there is not a credible scientific explanation for a deviation from protocols, it obviously calls into question the credibility of the conclusions. In the Duke case, we were able to effectively attack the credibility of a DNA lab's work based, among other things, on its violation of multiple protocols in reaching and reporting its conclusions.

Another lesson I learned in the Duke case is that language is very important, and the words an expert chooses to use in a final DNA report do not always accurately or completely reflect the underlying data. To determine the accuracy and appropriateness of the reporting language, the lawyer needs to learn some of these fundamental concepts about DNA analysis and reporting. The lawyer should also explore the lab's protocols (if any) and the expert's own customary practice regarding what analyses make it into the final report and what language she uses to characterize the analyses and conclusions. Is she always consistent? Does everyone in her lab apply the same rules and use the same language? Or do they sometimes report (or decline to report) certain things, or use different phrases to explain the same thing, or the same phrase to explain different things? If so, why would that be?

For example, I've seen reports from different DNA analysts in the same lab that use "match" versus "cannot be excluded" or "partial match" versus "cannot be excluded." The term "partial match" seems very compelling. What does it mean to say "cannot be excluded?" How many other people may also not be excluded? Does one profile truly "match," or even "partially match," another? If there is a "match" between a suspect's DNA sample and an evidentiary DNA sample at three or four of the 13 or 16 loci, should that be reported as any kind of a "match" at all? And how many other people could be a "match" to that sample in the lab's profile database? Or in the world? Should you even be able to introduce DNA evidence against a defendant if there was only a "match" at a single locus?

When talking to other defense attorneys, do you find that most of them just give up when they hear that a case involves DNA?

It can be daunting to face any new complex subject matter, particularly when it involves scientific analysis. DNA is scary to a lot of people. It was scary to me. When I had to learn about DNA for the Duke case, it's not like I was excited about it. I didn't think to myself, "Wow! This is a great opportunity for me to learn something new!" I was thinking, "Wow, I got an English degree in college and took no science classes." This is a subject matter that people go to school, and graduate school, and post-graduate school, for years and years to learn. If you're like me and have no real talent or educational background when it comes to math or science, then learning about DNA is a challenge. That said, I'm living proof that, with the right source materials and the commitment of time, you can learn the basics necessary to provide effective assistance of counsel to accused people in cases involving DNA.

What do you normally request for discovery when DNA evidence will be presented? Have you had any problems obtaining the case folder materials, the electronic data, or the Standard Operating Procedures for the DNA analysis?

In the Duke case, I asked for everything I could get, from underlying data to protocols to the DNA profiles of the lab technicians and analysts. One of the labs resisted a little bit, saying it would be costly, but the presiding judge ultimately issued an order requiring the lab to comply. In addition to receiving the underlying data with the exculpatory evidence that had not been mentioned in the final report, we got the lab's protocols, which allowed us to discover and highlight that the lab had violated them.

Here in North Carolina, in light of several very high-profile post-conviction exonerations of people who had been convicted and sent to prison (and even death row) because the defense had not been provided with information that the U.S. Constitution requires to be disclosed to defendants before trial, our legislature fundamentally changed the state discovery laws in 2004 to require state prosecutors to provide criminal defendants before trial with everything in the prosecution and law enforcement files, including the results and underlying data regarding any testing done in the case.

That said, defense lawyers here and all over America have historically faced resistance to discovery requests from labs, particularly when the requests seem aimed at probing the credibility of the lab's work and conclusions, and particularly when the lab is a creature of law enforcement. When the lab is essentially an arm of law enforcement, as are many crime labs throughout America, including ours in North Carolina, there is a real danger for development of a lab culture that subordinates scientific mentality to a team mentality, with the team being law enforcement and prosecution, not the scientific method. As long as that occurs in theory and practice, at best, the credibility of the lab's work and conclusions will always be in question. At worst, innocent people will be accused and convicted of crimes they did not commit, the real perpetrators of those crimes will not face justice, and the victims of crime will be further victimized.

Do you have sufficient access to experts to review the material when DNA evidence will be presented?

Yes, we have a solid and talented criminal defense bar in North Carolina and lawyers who are always willing to share their knowledge and experience with DNA in the courtroom. We also have a database of recommended experts and an active listserv where lawyers regularly post and respond to requests for recommendations for experts to help on a case. Some people may want a DNA expert who can sit down with them for a day or two and explain the basics of DNA analysis. Others may want someone to run independent sample analyses and testify about them in court. Others may want someone who can help interpret the data. I've been very satisfied with the experts who have agreed to work with me over the years.

What are some common tactics that you have used in challenging DNA evidence?

Contamination—and I'm including secondary and tertiary transfer arguments under this umbrella—is, of course, the most commonly known method of attacking DNA evidence. Contamination can happen at the scene of collection, or in the laboratory, or somewhere in between. Preservation of evidence and the chain of custody are important. It's important to make sure the evidence wasn't comingled with other evidence that might have impacted the credibility of the analysis and results.

But contamination and chain-of-custody arguments are only the tip of the iceberg of potential challenges to DNA evidence. Beneath the surface are all of the types of challenges that really require the lawyer to know the fundamentals of DNA analysis itself. Did the lab follow acceptable standards of DNA analysis? Did it follow its own protocols? Is the lab applying those standards and protocols consistently or selectively? For example, why do you call a peak below 150 RFU as a true allele for one purpose, or in one case, but not for another? If there are such internal inconsistencies, do they usually inure to the benefit of one side's theory of the case? If so, is that evidence of bias?

Other factors that impact the credibility of a DNA expert's work are the amount and quality of his training and experience. Lawyers should seek the expert's CV and review the training and experience sections. Obviously, not all experts are the same.

The goal is being able to identify, where it exists, the weakness or flaw in the expert's analysis, reporting, and conclusion. If there were steps along the way when the DNA analyst had to make a judgment call, and if that judgment call went consistently in favor of the prosecution—especially if those judgment calls were inconsistent with other work that expert had done, either within the same case or in other cases—that is important for the judge and jury to know when you're asking them to reject the analyst's conclusion or the prosecution's portrayal of it.

This all returns to the main point: when the evidence supports challenging a DNA expert's conclusion, you must demystify the process and demonstrate to the jury that DNA analysis is a subjective human exercise. It is not foolproof. It is subject to human nature, human error, and human bias. So is any conclusion reached and reported by a DNA expert, and so is the expert's courtroom testimony.

What advice do you have to expert witnesses testifying on DNA evidence?

Always remember that your sole allegiance on the witness stand is to the scientific method and to the facts. You are not an advocate. If you are a defense expert, you are not carrying the torch for the defense's theory. If you are the state's expert, you are not carrying the torch for the theory of prosecution. In the courtroom, you are first, foremost, and only a scientist, and your duty is to explain your analysis and conclusions truthfully, factually, and consistently with the scientific method, in language that is as basic and accessible to normal people like me as possible.

Which brings me to my second piece of advice: understand that you are not lecturing to your professional colleagues. You are speaking to people who will likely have little or no experience in your particular area of expertise, but you must effectively share that expertise with them without their eyes glazing over. Speak in language that is accessible but not condescending to them.

How has post-conviction DNA testing and the Innocence Project impacted the legal system and specifically your perspective on the criminal justice system?

I'm not sure anything has had a greater impact on the criminal justice system since I've been practicing. It seems like people are being released from prison on a weekly basis these days based on post-conviction DNA exoneration. Without question, the American public now knows that police and prosecutors, even in good faith, sometimes pick—and juries sometimes convict—the wrong people. Though skepticism of criminal accusation has long been embodied in the presumption of innocence and the requirement of proof beyond a reasonable doubt for conviction, collecting all of the most eloquent speeches in the world about *why that skepticism is right* does not add up to the power of one, let alone dozens, let alone hundreds, of stories about people who served 5, 10, 15, sometimes up to 30 years for crimes they did not commit. Because many of the original convictions in the DNA exoneration cases were based on mistaken eyewitness identification, it has also given stakeholders in the criminal justice system—judges, prosecutors, defense attorneys, law enforcement—a healthy concern about such evidence and has led to reforms in many eyewitness identification procedures across the country. As importantly, in addition to exonerating the innocent, post-conviction DNA analysis has also resulted in the identification, apprehension, and conviction of the actual perpetrators of the crimes. After all, forensic science is not just about making sure that the wrong guy does not get convicted: it's about making sure the right one does.

The sad thing to think about is this: how many other wrongful convictions—whether based on eyewitness testimony or other circumstantial evidence—did *not* involve the collection of physical evidence that can now be DNA-tested? Without question, many people are sitting in prison today based solely on such evidence, proclaiming their innocence as loudly as those who have been exonerated by DNA evidence, but without the ability to test their convictions in a similarly decisive fashion. I don't think anyone could intellectually honestly say that the only people who have been wrongfully convicted of serious crimes in America are just those people who have been exonerated through post-conviction DNA analysis.

How do you prepare for cross-examination of a DNA expert?

I suppose if I am in the position of cross-examining a DNA expert, I've already gone through the process of determining that there is a factual and legal need and basis for challenging the expert's conclusions and/or the prosecution's characterization of the DNA evidence. If that's the case, I brush up on the concepts of DNA analysis that I first learned while working on the Duke case, and I try to find out the extent to which they've changed. As important as it is to learn the fundamentals of DNA analysis in the first place, it is equally important to update that knowledge.

Then I basically apply the rest of the approach I've talked about in this interview. Depending on what kind of challenge I'm mounting, I focus on the part of the expert's process and conclusions that will support that challenge, and I design a cross-examination around those issues that is accessible to the jury. But no script is ever followed in a courtroom. That's why it's important for the lawyer to know the law, the facts, and the fundamentals of the science. Another reason is that some experts, consciously or subconsciously, become advocates for the prosecution, and you have to be able to recognize the difference between science and advocacy when an expert is testifying. If I suspect before trial that I am facing such an advocate-expert, or I have some other reason to doubt the expert's credibility or objectivity, I will seek input from other lawyers who have had cases involving that expert, and I will seek and review the expert's previous work and testimony.

While it's never my intent during cross-examination of a DNA expert to get into a "contest" of who knows more about DNA, my goal always is, as it is with any forensic science expert, to be able to have a meaningful dialogue with the expert about the case-specific issues in her area of expertise and to make the points I set out to make—or even a few new ones, should the opportunity present itself—without being intimidated by the knowledge gap.

Subject Index

Note: Page numbers followed by "*f*", "*t*", and "*b*" refer to figures, tables, and boxes, respectively.

D

E

F

G

M

Q

T

U

Z